Liberty, Equality, Power
A History of the American People, Volume I: to 1877

Liberty, Equality, Power
A History of the American People, Volume I: to 1877

John M. Murrin
Princeton University

Paul E. Johnson
University of Utah

James M. McPherson
Princeton University

Gary Gerstle
The Catholic University of America

Emily S. Rosenberg
Macalester College

Norman L. Rosenberg
Macalester College

HARCOURT
BRACE

Harcourt Brace College Publishers

Fort Worth   Philadelphia   San Diego   New York   Orlando   Austin
San Antonio   Toronto   Montreal   London   Sydney   Tokyo

Acquisitions Editor	Drake Bush
Developmental Editor	Sue A. Lister
Assistant Editor	Kristie Kelly
Production Manager	Tad Gaither
Manuscript Editors	Everett M. Sims, Ruth Steinberg
Fact Checker	Bernard Sinsheimer
Proofreaders	Charles Arensman, Stacy Simpson
Text Design	Jim Taylor
Cover Design and Illustration	David A. Day
Photo Editors	Lili Weiner, Cindy Robinson
Marketing Manager	Steven Drummond
Marketing Coordinator	Leanne Winkler
Maps	Geosystems
Production Services	Seaside Publishing Services
Compositor and Color Separator	ColorType
Printer and Binder	R. R. Donnelley & Sons
Cover Printer	Lehigh Press
Text Type	10.5/12 Bembo

Address for Editorial Correspondence
Harcourt Brace College Publishers, 301 Commerce Street, Suite 3700, Fort Worth, TX 76102

Address for Orders
Harcourt Brace College Publishers, 6277 Sea Harbor Drive, Orlando, FL 32887-6277
1-800-782-4479, or 1-800-433-0001 (in Florida)

ISBN: 0-15-500580-4
Library of Congress Catalog Number: 95-78531
Printed in the United States of America
5 4 3 4 5 6 7 8 9 0 1 2 048 9 8 7 6 5 4 3 2 1
Harcourt Brace College Publishers

ABOUT THE AUTHORS

John M. Murrin, Princeton University
John M. Murrin, specializing in American colonial history, is the author of the first section (Chapters 1–7) of *Liberty, Equality, Power*. He has edited one multi-volume series and five books, including *Colonial America: Essays in Politics and Social Development*, Fourth Edition (1993) and *Saints and Revolutionaries* (1984). His many essays on early American history show a diversity of interests, ranging from ethnic tensions, the early history of trial by jury, and the political culture of Revolutionary America, to the rise of professional baseball and college football.

Paul E. Johnson, University of Utah
Paul E. Johnson is the author of the second section of the text (Chapters 8–13). A specialist in early national social and religious history, he is the author of *A Shopkeeper's Millennium: Society and Revivals in Rochester, New York, 1815–1837* (1978); coauthor (with Sean Wilentz), of *The Kingdom of Matthias: Sex and Salvation in 19th-Century America* (1994); and editor of *African-American Christianity: Essays in History* (1994). He has been awarded the Merl Curti Prize of the Organization of American Historians (1980) and a John Simon Guggenheim Memorial Fellowship (1995).

James M. McPherson, Princeton University
James M. McPherson is the author of the third section of the text (Chapters 14–19). A distinguished Civil War historian, he won the 1989 Pulitzer Prize for his book *Battle Cry of Freedom: The Civil War Era*. His other publications include *Marching Toward Freedom: Blacks in the Civil War*, Second Edition (1991), *Ordeal by Fire: The Civil War and Reconstruction*, Second Edition (1992), and *Abraham Lincoln and the Second American Revolution* (1991). In addition, he is the editor of *The Atlas of the Civil War* (1994) and, along with Gary Gerstle 9author of the fourth section of *Liberty, Equality, Power)*, a consulting editor of *American Political Leaders: From Colonial Times to the Present* (1991) and *American Social Leaders: From Colonial Times to the Present* (1993).

Gary Gerstle, The Catholic University of America
Gary Gerstle is the author of the fourth section of the text (Chapters 20–25). A specialist in labor, immigration, and political history, he has published *Working-Class Americanism: The Politics of Labor in a Textile City, 1914–1960* (1989), *The Rise and Fall of the New Deal Order, 1930–1980* (1989) and artices in the *American Historical Review, Journal of American History, American Quarterly*, and many other journals. He is a consulting editor, along with James M. McPherson (author of the third section of *Liberty, Equality, Power)*, of *American Political Leaders: From Colonial Times to the Present* (1991) and *American Social Leaders: From Colonial Times to the Present* (1993). He has been awarded many fellowships, including a National Endowment for the Humanities Fellowship for University Teachers, an Institute for Advanced Study Membership, and a John Simon Guggenheim Memorial Fellowship.

Emily S. Rosenberg, Macalester College
Emily S. Rosenberg is the author, along with Norman L. Rosenberg, of the last section of the text (Chapters 26–31). She specializes in United States foreign relations in the twentieth century and is the author of the widely-used book *Spreading the American Dream: American Economic and Cultural Expansion, 1890–1945* (1982). Her other publications include (with Norman L. Rosenberg) *In Our Times: America Since 1945*, Fifth Edition (1995) and numerous articles on subjects such as international finance, gender issues, and foreign relations.

Norman L. Rosenberg, Macalester College
Norman L. Rosenberg is coauthor, along with Emily S. Rosenberg, of the final section of the text (Chapters 26–31). He specializes in legal history with a particular interest in legal culture and First Amendment issues. His books include *Protecting the "Best Men": An Interpretive History of the Law of Libel* (1990) and (with Emily S. Rosenberg) *In Our Times: America Since 1945*, Fifth Edition (1995). He has published articles in *Rutgers Law Review, Constitutional Commentary, Law & History Review*, and many other legal journals.

PREFACE

This survey hopes to capture the drama and excitement of America's past. The focus is global in the early and most recent chapters; in between, it is continental. We begin where the human story began, with the Indian settlement of the Americas. The typical United States history textbook opens with a snapshot of Indian cultures on the East coast around 1600. This type of presentation suggests that these societies were stagnant and unchanging; that they are of more interest as curiosities than as participants in history; that history is something that Europeans did for themselves and to others; and that only their arrival brings focus and purposeful change to the Americas. We have rejected this formula. Indians had their own long and highly complex history before 1492, and much of that story is now being recovered. We have tried to tell it. We have also tried to alert readers to parallel or contrasting Canadian events from the beginnings of New France through the adoption of Canadian Confederation in 1867. And, we have moved the Spanish borderlands much closer to the center of American history in the century and a half before the Mexican war.

This book attempts to integrate social and cultural history into a political story. We have tried not to ghettoize the concerns and achievements of women, Indians, African Americans, Hispanics, Asians, and other minorities. We believe that the larger story of what is now the United States simply will not make sense unless the potent influence of race and gender is made clear. To give a simple but important example, the rise of capitalism in the eighteenth and nineteenth centuries depended on specific assumptions about gender among European settlers. Women rarely owned property, but they lived in fixed households where goods could be accumulated, and an acquisitive ethic could take hold among both men and women. By contrast, most Indian women in the eastern woodlands had to move twice a year. They had no interest in acquiring any more goods than they could carry on their backs. For them, an ethic of accumulation made no sense, even though their husbands, as hunters and trappers, played an active role as producers for a global market.

Liberty, Equality, Power recognizes that power has often been the critical variable in determining which contending group got what. The Revolutionary generation conceived of liberty mostly as a negation of governmental power and embraced equality as a way of diffusing political liberty. Later eras discovered that without power, liberty and equality can become crippled ideals, appealing but ineffective. The Reconstruction era marked a tremendous shift in these sensibilities. Only if the federal government asserted new powers could the liberty and equality of former slaves have a chance to thrive.

Though Reconstruction was but a qualified success, the idea of the strong state as a guarantor of liberty and equality lived on in the social movements of farmers, workers, feminists, and minorities, and in the politics of liberal reform (Populism, Progressivism, the New Deal, the Great Society) from the 1890s through the 1960s. The building of a strong liberal state — and of opposition to it — becomes an ever more prominent theme of this survey as the history of the twentieth century unfolds. We conclude this story with a look at how conservatives of the 1970s and 1980s discredited strong-state liberalism and called for a return to the revolutionary generation's original notion: that liberty will thrive the most in circumstances where the state governs the least.

Politics always involves power, but for the authors of this survey, power implies much more than politics. All four of our photo essays explore themes of power. We see power operating at all levels of American society: between husbands and wives, parents and children, among racial and ethnic groups, between social classes, and, of course, in government and politics. Power has structured relations between men and women, immigrants and the native-born, the city and the country, whites and blacks, and between the United States and other countries. We have tried to analyze the role of power in shaping these relationships, how power was gained and lost, and what effect the rise of a strong state had on other prevailing relations of power.

This book reflects our strong interest in politics, but we have not returned to an older political history organized around presidents, political parties, and Congress. Ours is a new and expansive political history oriented toward understanding how power is gained, lost, and used in both public and private life.

Because of our interest in power, we take warfare and imperialism, the naked imposition of force, more seriously than most United States history textbooks have done. Recognizing that some wars are more significant than others, we have made no attempt to provide a comprehensive military narrative for every armed conflict in which the United States has been involved. But we do give considerable space to formative struggles, those that have helped to define the people we have become, from some of the earliest Indian wars through the Seven Years' War, the Revolution, the Civil War, and World War II.

Another distinctive feature of this survey is an effort to trace transformations of popular culture across the centuries, from the founding of the first newspapers in the early eighteenth century to the rise of movies, jazz, and the comics in the twentieth century, to the cable television revolution in recent years. The popular novel gets more attention than the classics of American literature in our nineteenth-century chapters. The structure of households, popular culture, and *changing* family values have always been linked throughout America's past. We have tried to trace these relationships.

We hope that we have done justice to political values, from the republicanism espoused by the Revolutionary generation, to the equality demanded by slaves, to the liberal reforms of the Progressive and New Deal eras, to the radical demands of the civil rights movement, and to the committed conservation that has become a powerful force in American politics since the 1960s. Political beliefs have often unfolded in complex ways that we have tried to unravel. Today, for example, liberals favor an activist government on economic and social questions, but they insist on making their own moral choices without government interference on such questions as abortion and sexual orientation. Conservatives try to minimize government's role on economic and social matters but urge the state to police morality, even when it involves highly intimate behavior. We hope that our survey will clarify how and why these particular values have clustered and cohered in this way.

Finally, as part of our effort to integrate social and cultural history with politics, we have also tried to construct a narrative of American history that is both coherent and absorbing. We hope that our text is more effective for that reason, and that students will find it lucid and readable.

Ancillary Package

Instructor's Resource Manual to accompany Liberty, Equality, Power
Peter Field, Larry Whitaker, Jeffrey Roberts
Tennessee Technological University
This comprehensive teaching tool includes an introductory section for each chapter that discusses the themes of *Liberty, Equality, Power* and its integration into the classroom. Other resources include lecture topics and notes, chapter outlines, classroom and group activities, discussion questions, paper topics, an audio-visual bibliography, and the instructor's guide to the student video package. Free to instructors.

Study Guide to accompany Liberty, Equality, Power
Volume I: To 1877
Mary Jane McDaniel   University of North Alabama
Volume II: Since 1863
Mary Jane McDaniel   University of North Alabama
This student resource provides not only chapter overviews, but also guidance for the students when considering the importance of liberty, equality, and power within each chapter. An in-depth chronological overview is featured along with a glossary of important terms. Completion exercises, multiple-choice questions, essay questions, and discussion and analysis questions allow students to test their comprehension of the text. Each chapter contains a crossword puzzle that will challenge the student in a very different manner.

Test Bank to accompany Liberty, Equality, Power
Thomas Wermuth   Marist College
The test bank provides a wide variety of question styles with graded levels of difficulty. In addition to learning objectives, the test bank offers multiple-choice questions, true-false questions, short and long essay questions, and others. Free to instructors.

Computerized Test Banks
Available in four formats
IBM® 5.25″   Macintosh®
IBM® 3.50″   MS Windows™

Overhead Transparency Package

100 four-color transparencies. Free to instructors.

American History Documents to accompany Liberty, Equality, Power
Volume I: To 1877
Marvin Schultz   Ouachita Technical College
Volume II: Since 1863
Marvin Schultz   Ouachita Technical College

One hundred primary source documents are interspersed with thirty-one political cartoons and advertisements. In-depth chapter openers and questions integrate both documents and the theme of liberty, equality, and power. Available for purchase by students and available free to instructors.

Mapping Workbook to accompany Liberty, Equality, Power
Volume I: To 1877
Charles A. Dranguet, Jr., Roman J. Heleniak
Southeastern Louisiana University
Volume II: Since 1863
Charles A. Dranguet, Jr., Roman J. Heleniak
Southeastern Louisiana University

The mapping workbook provides a variety of mapping exercises for students. It provides one to two map analyses per chapter from *Liberty, Equality, Power*, with one focusing on the textbook theme. Available for purchase by students.

Core Concept Video to accompany Liberty, Equality, Power
Volume I: To 1877
Lynn Wilson   Tarrant County Junior College Northeast
William D. Young   Johnson County Community College
Marilyn Rinehart North Harris Community College
Volume II: Since 1863
Marilyn Rinehart North Harris Community College
Chuck Chalberg   Normandale Community College
Joe Jaynes   Collin County Community College

This video package is uniquely designed for both students and instructors. Created by Films for Humanities exclusively for Harcourt Brace, each video contains eight segments consisting of an introduction by the respective author of each section of *Liberty, Equality, Power,* concept clues for viewing, running video segments of about ten minutes, and concluding questions that take the student from image to text. Video segments are arranged chronologically and relate to a topic of importance in *Liberty, Equality, Power.* A User's Manual accompanies each video. Available for purchase by students. Free to instructors.

U.S. History Videos / Films for the Humanities

Choose from a wide variety of videos from the extensive Films for the Humanities American history catalog. Contact your local Harcourt Brace sales representative for a complete listing of available videos. Adoption requirements apply.

A&E U.S. History Videos

Many outstanding selections are available from the Arts&Entertainment video library. Choose from: *American Revolution; Civil War Journal; The Real West; Mike Wallace's The Twentieth Century;* and selections from A&E's extensive biography collection. Adoption requirements apply.

American History Video Disk from Instructional Resources

A Level 1/III CAV double-sided disk featuring more than 2,400 images and 68 full-motion video sequences arranged in 10 distinct units spanning the entirety of U.S. history. The package (U.S.) includes a user's manual with captions and bar codes for easy presentation to students. Software is available for both Macintosh™ and IBM™. Adoption requirements apply.

Twentieth Century American History Video Disk

This one-hour video disk, produced expressly for Harcourt Brace by Fountain Communications, addresses the pressing issues Americans have faced in this century: immigration, the Great Depression, World War II, the Cold War, the United States in the 1950s, the civil rights movement, Vietnam, and the women's movement. Adoption requirements apply.

Acknowledgments

The authors have had the good fortune to work with an excellent staff at Harcourt Brace. Our editor, Drake Bush, has nurtured this project and us for almost ten years; he has been a source of great wisdom and support. He has also allowed us to write the kind of textbook we wanted to write. Sue Lister became the developmental editor at a perilous moment in the project's history and has guided the complex project to completion with the kind of skill, confidence, and calm that has amazed us all. Lynne Bush, the production manager, has matched Sue's efficiency, dedication, and cool; in the last year she has performed at least ten miracles to keep the book on what everyone knew to be an impossible schedule. We were fortunate to have two excellent manuscript editors, Everett Sims for the first draft and Ruth Steinberg for the final draft, each of whom made important contributions to the book's content and prose. Lili Weiner, the photo editor, was indefatigable and good-natured in her efforts to find the right photographs for a group of finicky authors. Bernard Sinsheimer, an extraordinarily knowledgable American historian, scrupulously checked the entire manuscript for errors of fact. And we received invaluable feedback from the many instructors who class-tested a sample chapter of the textbook. To the many editorial and production assistants with whom we did not work directly but who contributed significantly to this textbook, we express our hearty thanks.

We have also benefited greatly from the many historians who reviewed portions of the manuscript. We would like to thank each of them by name.

James Axtell	College of William and Mary
Charles Bolton	Mississippi Oral History Program
Betty Brandon	University of South Alabama
Vincent Clark	Johnson County Community College
Gregory E. Dowd	University of Notre Dame
George Forgie	University of Texas at Austin
Wendell Griffith	Okaloosa-Walton Community College
William H. Freehling	University of Kentucky
Van Beck Hall	University of Pittsburgh
Kenneth Hamilton	Southern Methodist University
Elizabeth Kessel	Anne Arundel Community College
Thomas J. Knock	Southern Methodist University
Gary L. Roberts	Abraham Baldwin Agricultural College
Roy Rosenzweig	George Mason University
Mike Ruddy	St. Louis University
William K. Scarborough	University of Southern Mississippi
Rebecca Seaman	Southern Union State Community College
John E. Selby	*William and Mary Quarterly,* Institute of Early American History and Culture
Irvin D. Solomon	Edison Community College
Donald Strasser	Mankato State University
Steve Whitfield	Brandeis University
Laura Matysek Wood	Tarrant County Junior College Northwest

Finally, each of us would like to offer particular thanks to those historians, friends, and family members who helped to bring this project to a successful conclusion.

John M. Murrin: Mary R. Murrin has read each chapter, offered numerous suggestions, and provided the kind of moral and personal support without which this project would never have been completed. James Axtell and Gregory Evans Dowd saved me from many mistakes about Indians. John E. Selby and Eugene R. Sheridan were particularly helpful on Chapters 5–7. At an early phase, William J. Jackson and Lorraine E. Williams offered some very useful suggestions. Several colleagues and graduate students have also contributed in various ways, especially Stephen Aron, Ignacio Gallup-Diaz, Evan P. Haefeli, Geoffrey Plank, and Nathaniel J. Sheidley.

Paul E. Johnson: My greatest debt is to the community of scholars who write about the United States between the Revolution and the Civil War. Closer to home, I owe thanks to the other writers of this book—particularly to John Murrin. The Tanner Humanities Center and the Department of History at the University of Utah provided time to work, while my wife, Kasey Grier, and a stray dog we named Lucy provided the right kinds of interruptions.

James M. McPherson: My family provided an environment of affection and stability that contributed immeasurably to the writing of my chapters, while undergraduate students at Princeton University who have taken my courses over the years provided feedback, questions, and insights that helped me to understand what students know and don't know and what they need to know.

Gary Gerstle: I would like to thank a number of people who provided me with invaluable assistance. My work benefited enormously from the input of Roy Rosenzweig and Tom Knock, who gave each of my chapters an exceptionally thorough, thoughtful, and insightful critique. Kathleen Trainor was a gifted research assistant: she researched subjects I knew too little about, contributed to the design of charts and maps, checked facts, and solved countless thorny problems. To all these tasks she brought imagination, efficiency, and good cheer. Jerald Podair helped me to compile chapter bibliographies, offered me excellent ideas for maps and tables, and, on numerous occasions (and at all hours of the day and night) allowed me to draw on his encyclopedic knowledge of American history. Christopher Gildemeister dropped his own work at short notice to help me out with a difficult map problem. And Elliott Shore graciously shared his time and expert librarian skills to help me locate obscure information for maps and illustrations. Our trip with Maria Sturm to locate a little-known Ben Shahn mural was a true adventure.

Emily and Norman Rosenberg: We would like to thank our children — Sarah, Molly, Ruth, and Joe — and other people who provided assistance: Paul Solon, Sonya Michlin, Lorenzo Nencioli, Katie Kelley, Justin Brandt, and Jessica Ford.

Although this textbook is the result of a team effort, we individually or jointly are primarily responsible for writing our own sections. John Murrin wrote Chapters 1–7, which begin with the prehistory of the Americas and conclude with the ratification of the Unied States Constitution. Paul Johnson did Chapters 8–13, which start with the organization of the new federal government in 1789 and carry the story into the 1840s. James McPherson wrote Chapters 14–19, which open with the crisis over Texas and the Mexican War and conclude with the crisis of the 1890s. In Chapters 20–25, Gary Gerstle covers the twentieth century up to 1940.

Emily and Norman Rosenberg coauthored Chapters 26–31, which begin with American entry into World War II and conclude with Newt Gingrich's Contract with America.

Finally, no team of authors can complete a project of this scope without making some errors. We welcome all corrections and suggestions for improvement. Please send them to Drake Bush, History Editor, Harcourt Brace College Publishers, 301 Commerce St., Suite 3700, Fort Worth, TX 76102.

John M. Murrin
Paul E. Johnson
James M. McPherson
Gary Gerstle
Emily S. Rosenberg
Norman L. Rosenberg

A NOTE ON THE PAPERBOUND EDITION

This volume is part of a variant printing of *Liberty, Equality, Power* in a two-volume paperbound format, which reproduces the text of the one-volume version. A two-volume paperbound version is useful because it enables instructors ro fit the text into the particular patterns of their teaching and scheduling. The first volume begins with the prehistory of the Americas and continues through Reconstruction. The second volume, repeating the chapter on Reconstruction (Chapter 18, Reconstruction, 1863–1867), carries this account forward to the present day. This variant printing is intended as a convenience to those instructors and students who have occasion to use either one part or the other of *Liberty, Equality, Power.* The pagination and index of the one-volume version, as well as the illustrations, maps, charts and photo essays, are retained in the variant printing. The difference between the one-volume version and two-volume versions of the book is a difference only in form.

CONTENTS

MAPS

CHARTS AND TABLES

Liberty, Equality, Power
A History of the American People, Volume I: to 1877

Chapter 1

When Old Worlds Collide: Contact, Conquest, Catastrophe

The Encounter of Cortés and Moctezuma, or the clash of one old world with another, a painting attributed to the seventeenth-century Mexican artist Juan Correa. It is painted on a *Biombo*, or folding screen, a device borrowed by Spain from Japan. Correa understood that the Spanish empire, for the first time in history, had brought Europe, Africa, Asia, and the Americas into sustained contact with each other.

When Christopher Columbus crossed the Atlantic, he did not know where he was going, and until his death he never figured out where he had been. Yet he changed history forever. In the forty years after 1492, European navigators mastered the oceans of the world, joining together societies that had lived in isolation for thousands of years. European invaders conquered the Americas, not just with sails, gunpowder, and steel, but also with their plants and livestock and, most of all, their diseases. They brought staple crops and slavery with them as well. By 1600 they had created the first global economy in the history of mankind and also inflicted upon the Indian peoples of the Americas—unintentionally, for the most part—the greatest known catastrophe that human societies have ever experienced.

Americans like to believe that their history is a story of progress. They are right about its European phase. After its tragic beginnings in conquest, depopulation, and enslavement, things had to improve.

PEOPLES IN MOTION

Like all other countries of North and South America, the United States is a nation of immigrants. Even the Indians were once explorers who became settlers in a strange land.

Long before Europeans discovered and explored the wide world around them, many different peoples had migrated thousands of miles over thousands of years across oceans and continents. Before Columbus sailed west from Spain in 1492, five distinct waves of immigrants had already swept over the Americas. Three came from Asia. The fourth, from the Pacific Islands, or Oceana, may have just brushed America.

The last of the pre-Columbian intruders, from northern Europe, decided not to stay.

From Beringia to the Americas

Before the most recent Ice Age ended about twelve thousand years ago, glaciers covered huge portions of the Americas, Europe, and Asia. The ice captured so much of the world's water that sea level fell drastically. Twice it dropped more than two hundred feet, enough to create a land bridge six hundred miles wide across the Bering Strait between Siberia and Alaska. For several thousand years around 50,000 B.C.E. (before the Common Era, which began in A.D. 1), and again for more than ten thousand years after 23,000 B.C.E., this exposed area — geographers call it Beringia — was dry land on which plants, animals, and humans could live. Probably without realizing that they were moving from one continent to another, people drifted in small bands from Asia to North America. No doubt many generations lived on Beringia itself, though the harsh environment of this land on the edge of the Arctic Circle required unusual skills just to survive. These first immigrants to the Americas hunted animals for meat and furs and built small fishing vessels that could weather the

Arctic storms. Faced by impassable glaciers to the north and east, they made snug homes to keep themselves warm through the fierce winters. Their numbers were, in all likelihood, quite small.

Just when they arrived remains a matter of some controversy. Many archaeologists believe that humans crossed Beringia and began spreading through the Americas during the first land bridge more than forty thousand years ago. Canadians digging at the Old Crow site in the Yukon claim that they have found evidence of human habitation that may be at least fifty thousand years old. A French team working in northeastern Brazil, thousands of miles from Beringia, is examining a site that may be 48,000 years old. It provides the strongest evidence yet found for such early settlement of the Americas. Other experts remain skeptical, however. Until the Brazilian find, which is still being evaluated, all very old sites have had something wrong with them, archaeologically speaking. Natural forces have disturbed the setting, for example, or have carried the artifacts away from their original environment. A bone that looks to one investigator as though it had been shaped into a tool strikes another as merely the product of some natural accident, perhaps of an animal falling and breaking its leg. Finally, the Yukon and Brazilian sites

An Indian Wall Painting   Found in northeastern Brazil, this painting may be 32,000 years old. If so, it is one of the oldest in the world.

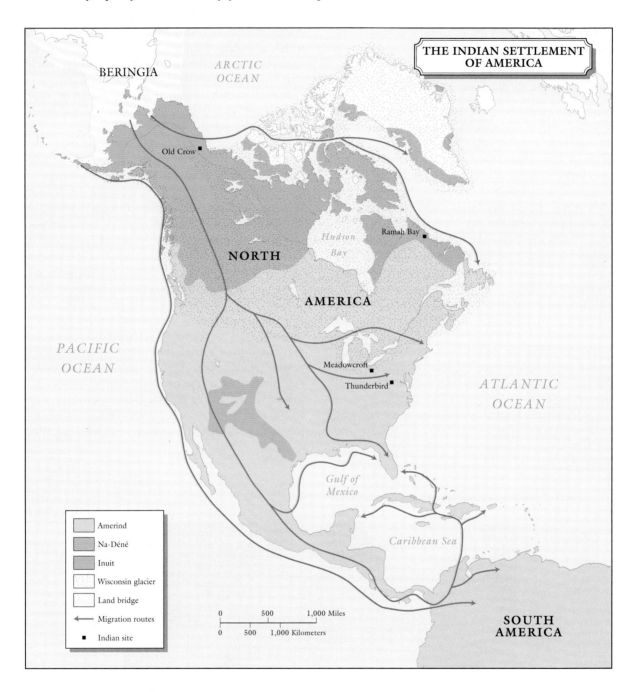

THE INDIAN SETTLEMENT OF AMERICA

BERINGIA

ARCTIC OCEAN

Old Crow

NORTH

Ramah Bay

Hudson Bay

AMERICA

PACIFIC OCEAN

Meadowcroft

Thunderbird

ATLANTIC OCEAN

Gulf of Mexico

Caribbean Sea

SOUTH AMERICA

Amerind

Na-Déné

Inuit

Wisconsin glacier

Land bridge

Migration routes

Indian site

0   500   1,000 Miles
0   500   1,000 Kilometers

notwithstanding, no conclusive evidence has yet been found that humans were living in eastern Siberia as far back as thirty thousand years ago. Even if some people did make it to the Americas in that era, they did not multiply very rapidly.

Dissatisfaction with this evidence has prompted speculation about very early direct crossings of the Pacific from Asia to South America, where many sites of human habitation are at least as old as those found in Alaska. One weakness of this theory is that any such adventurers should have left traces of their presence on the Pacific islands along the way. Such evidence has never been found. A more plausible explanation for the almost simultaneous settlement of North and South America is that small groups of migrants, moving south from Beringia by sea, entered the American continents at many different points up and down the Pacific coast and then spread eastward. Scholars, drawing upon evidence from tooth structure and the distribution of blood types, agree that the Americas were first settled by Asians, some or all of whom came by way of Beringia. Whether a few others came by different routes remains possible but seems unlikely.

The record becomes clearer toward the end of the last Ice Age, about twelve thousand years ago. By then, humans definitely were living in eastern Siberia, western Alaska, and Beringia. (Because Beringia is once again under water, it cannot easily be investigated, though fossils of mammoths have been found on the ocean floor.) As the glaciers receded for the last time, these people spread throughout the Americas. By 8000 B.C.E. they had reached all the way to Tierra del Fuego off the southern tip of South America. Near the eastern coast of North America, the Meadowcroft site in Pennsylvania may be sixteen thousand years old, and the Thunderbird dig in Virginia's Shenandoah Valley shows signs of continuous human occupation from before 9000 B.C.E. until the arrival of Europeans.

These Asians probably came in three waves. Those in the first wave, which began more than fourteen thousand years ago, spread over most of the two continents and spoke "Amerind," the forerunner of the vast majority of Indian languages on both continents. The Algonquian, Iroquoian, Muskogean, Siouan, Nahuatl (Aztec), Mayan, and all South American tongues derive from this source. Those in the middle wave, which came a few thousand years later, spoke what linguists call "Na-Déné," which eventually gave rise to the various Athapaskan languages of the Canadian Northwest as well as the Apache, Navajo, and related tongues in the American Southwest. The last to arrive, the ancestors of the Inuits (called Eskimos by other Indians), crossed after 7000 B.C.E., when Beringia was again under water. About four thousand years ago, these people began to migrate from the Aleutian Islands and Alaska to roughly their present sites in the Americas. Unlike their predecessors, they found the Arctic environment to their liking and migrated across the northern rim of North America and then across the North Atlantic to Greenland, where they encountered the first Europeans migrating westward — the Norsemen. Some-

how, the Inuits maintained at least limited contact with one another across six thousand miles of bleak Arctic tundra. The Thule, or final pre-Columbia phase of Inuit culture, which lasted from A.D. 1000 to 1700, somehow managed to maintain similar folkways all the way from Siberia to Greenland.

The Great Extinction and the Rise of Agriculture

As the glaciers receded and the climate warmed, the people who had wandered south and east found an attractive environment teeming with game. Imperial mammoths, huge mastodons, woolly rhinoceroses, a species of enormous bison, and giant ground sloths roamed the plains and forests, along with camels and herds of small horses. These animals had no instinctive fear of the two-legged intruders, who became ever more skillful at hunting them. A superior spear point, the Clovis tip, appeared in the New Mexico–Texas area some time before 9000 B.C.E. and within a thousand years was in use nearly everywhere in North and South America. As its use spread, the big game died off along with horses, which were not large enough to ride and were valued only as food. Overhunting cannot explain the entire extinction, but it was a major factor, along with climatic change. Mammoths, for example, survived until 2000 B.C.E. on uninhabited Wrangell Island near Alaska. Except for buffalo, whose instinct told them to herd together and run for their lives when hunters approached, most large animals of the Americas disappeared nine or ten thousand years ago.

Their passing left the hemisphere with a severely depleted number of animal species. Nothing as big as the elephant survived. The largest beasts left were bears, buffalo, and moose; the biggest cat was the jaguar. So long as the giant species lasted, the human population had multiplied and spread with ease. Their extinction probably led to a sharp population contraction as people scrambled for new sources of food. Some Indians raised guinea pigs, turkeys, or ducks. But apart from dogs on both continents, Indians domesticated no large animals except for llamas (useful for hauling light loads in mountainous terrain) and alpacas (valued for their wool) in South America.

One Indian culture adapted to these demands with an energy that archaeologists are only now beginning to recognize. About 5000 B.C.E., along the northeast coast of North America, a gifted maritime people emerged who ventured out onto the North Atlantic to catch swordfish and, probably, whales. They carried on a vigorous trade from Labrador to Maine and perhaps as far south as New Jersey, spanning a coastline of over fifteen hundred miles. They are sometimes called the Red Paint People (a more technical term is Maritime Archaic) because of their use of red ocher in funeral ceremonies. Their burial mounds are the oldest yet found in America, several thousand years older than the earliest ones in the Mississippi Valley. They lived in multiroom houses up to one hundred yards long. Most remarkable of all, their religious monuments—mounds and stone markers—bear a close artistic resemblance to others found in Brittany and Norway, but these monuments are several hundred years older than the most ancient ones yet found in Europe. It is just possible that these Indian seafarers followed the Gulf Stream across the Atlantic to Europe thousands of years before Europeans voyaged to America. The culture of the Red Paint People vanished four thousand years ago. No one knows why.

Some Indians settled comfortably into their local environments without becoming farmers. The peoples of the Pacific Northwest, who developed strong hierarchical traditions and complex art forms that continue to fascinate modern collectors, sustained themselves through fishing, hunting, and the gathering of nuts, berries, and other edible plants. Men fished and hunted; women gathered. California Indians achieved some of the densest populations north of Mexico by collecting acorns and processing them into meal, which was then baked into cakes. In the rain forests of Brazil and the cold woodlands of northern New England, other hunter-gatherers also got along nicely without agriculture.

But most Indians could not depend solely on hunting and gathering food. In a few places some Indians, probably the women, began to learn how to plant and harvest crops, not just gather and eat them. In Asia and Africa, this practice was closely linked to the domestication of animals and happened quickly enough to be called the neolithic (late Stone Age) revolution. In the Americas, however, the turn toward farming had little to do with animals, occurred more gradually, and might better be termed the neolithic *evolution*. For its first 3,500 years, farming supplemented a diet that still depended mostly on fishing and hunting, though now of smaller animals.

Somewhere between 4000 and 1500 B.C.E., permanent farm villages began to dominate parts of Peru, south-central Mexico, northeast Mexico, and the southwestern United States. Their crops were distinct from those of Europe, the Middle East, or East Asia, which provides a strong argument for the independent invention of agriculture in the Americas. The first American farmers grew amaranth (a cereal), manioc (also known as cassava and familiar to modern Americans as tapioca), chili peppers, pumpkins, sweet potatoes, several varieties of beans, and, above all, maize, or Indian corn, which became a staple throughout most of the two continents. Some Indians also raised white potatoes and tomatoes. The spread of these crops launched another population surge, which in parts of the Americas eventually supported cities of great size.

The Polynesians and Hawaii

Asians migrating across Beringia were not the only people on the move in prehistoric times. Polynesians, from their original home near the coast of Southeast Asia, moved out into the Pacific around 1600 B.C.E. and over the next two thousand years settled hundreds of islands scattered across more than 30 million square miles of ocean. Their ability to bring families and plants safely across thousands of miles of open sea in what were essentially large dugout canoes with sails and attached outriggers was the most remarkable maritime feat of the era. Nearly all of their settlements were in the tropics. By the first century A.D., with Fiji as a kind of cultural and linguistic center, they had reached as far as Hawaii, nearly 2,500 miles to the northeast, and by A.D. 300 they had colonized Easter Island, over 4,000 miles to the east and only 200 miles off the coast of South America. Before A.D. 1000 they also settled New Zealand, far to the south of Fiji. Hawaii's population, organized into stratified societies and multiple chiefdoms, grew to 800,000 before the first Europeans arrived in the 1770s. This threat finally compelled Hawaiians to recognize a common emperor, Kamehameha I, in 1810.

Did Polynesians ever reach the American mainland in prehistoric times? It seems hard to believe that such daring mariners would not have sailed on beyond Hawaii and Easter Island, despite the dangerous ocean currents they would have encountered. And yet, if some of them did reach the Ameri-

The Canoes of Polynesia   These double-hulled canoes were painted in the 1770s by the first Europeans to reach Hawaii. Polynesians conquered the Pacific with this technology.

cas, they left no discernible influence on the Indian societies already there. Someone—either an Indian or a Polynesian—must have brought the sweet potato from South America to Easter Island, and from there it may have been carried westward toward Asia. Yet the culture of Easter Island was Polynesian, while that of South America remained thoroughly Indian.

The Norsemen

About the time that Polynesians were settling Easter Island, Europeans also began trekking long distances. Pushed by fierce invaders from central Asia, various Germanic tribes overran the western provinces of the Roman Empire. The pattern of their infiltration and assimilation pretty much defined the linguistic map of Europe between A.D. 500 and 1100. The Norse, a Germanic people who had occupied Scandinavia, were among the most innovative of these invaders. For centuries their Viking warriors raided the coasts of the British Isles and France. Their sleek longboats, propelled by both sails and oars, gave them great flexibility in challenging the contrary currents of the north Atlantic. Some of them began to gaze westward across the ocean.

Beginning in A.D. 874, Vikings occupied Iceland, dislodging the island's only inhabitants, a community of perhaps one thousand Irish monks who had fled west around the year 800. In 982–983 Erik the Red, accused of manslaughter in Norway and then outlawed for committing more mayhem in Iceland, led his Norse followers farther west to Greenland. There the Norse made Europe's first contact with Inuits and established permanent settlements.

Leif, Erik's son, sailed west from Greenland in 1001 and began to explore the coast of North America. Leif made three more voyages, the last one in 1014, and started a colony that he called "Vinland" on the northern coast of Newfoundland at a place now named L'Anse aux Meadows. The local Indians (called "Skrellings" by the Norse, which means "barbarians" or "weaklings") resisted vigorously. In one engagement, just as the Norse were about to be routed, Freydis, the bastard daughter of old Erik and the first European woman known to North American history, saved the day by baring her breasts, slapping them with a sword, and screaming ferociously. Awed, the Skrellings fled. But the Norse soon quarreled among themselves and destroyed the colony. During the 1014 voyage, Freydis and her husband murdered one of her brothers and seized his ship. When Leif found out, he cursed Freydis's offspring, who, Norse poets assure us, never amounted to anything after that. The Norse abandoned Vinland, but they continued to visit North America for another century, probably to get wood. A twelfth-century Norse coin, recovered from an Indian site in Maine, gives proof of their continuing contact with the mainland.

Norsemen   An Inuit carving, in ivory, of a Norse settler on Greenland.

Five hundred years after Erik the Red's settlement, the Norse also lost Greenland. There, not long before Columbus sailed in 1492, the last Norse settler died a lonely death. In the chaos that followed the Black Death in mid-fourteenth-century Europe and Greenland, the colony had suffered a severe population decline and had gradually lost regular contact with the homeland. Then it slowly withered away. Though the exploits of some Vikings were spectacular, they had no impact on the subsequent course of American history. They were a dead end.

EUROPE AND THE WORLD IN THE FIFTEENTH CENTURY

The Norse failure is suggestive. Had E.T., Hollywood's famous extra-terrestrial, decided to visit Earth's most complex cultures in 1400, he would not have landed anywhere near Europe, nor would he have been likely to predict the course of European expansion that was about to begin. In 1400, Europe stood at the edge, not the center, of world commerce.

China: The Rejection of Overseas Expansion

By just about every standard, China under the Ming dynasty was the world's most complex culture. In

the fifteenth century the government of China, staffed by well-educated bureaucrats, ruled 100 million people, a total half again as large as the combined populations of all European states west of Russia. The Chinese had invented the compass, gunpowder, and early forms of printing and paper money. Foreigners coveted the silks, teas, and other fine products available in China, but they had little to offer in exchange. Most of what Europe knew about China came from *The Travels* of Marco Polo, a merchant from the Italian city-state of Venice, who reached the Chinese court in 1271 and served the emperor, Kublai Khan, for the next twenty years. This "Great Khan is the mightiest man, whether in respect of subjects or of territory or of treasure, who is in the world today or who ever has been, from Adam our first parent down to the present moment," Marco assured Europe. The Khan's capital city (today's Beijing) was the world's largest and grandest, Marco insisted, and received a thousand cartloads of silk a day. The Khan's palace was "so immense and so well constructed that no man in the world . . . could imagine any improvement in design or execution." In brief, China outshone Europe and every other culture.

The Chinese agreed. Between 1405 and 1434 a royal eunuch, Cheng Ho, led six large fleets from China to the East Indies and the coast of East Africa, trading and exploring along the way. His largest ships, four hundred feet long, displaced fifteen hundred tons and were certainly large enough to sail around the southern tip of Africa and "discover" Europe. Had China wanted to throw its resources and talents into overseas expansion, the later history of the world would be vastly different. But most of what the Chinese learned about the outside world merely confirmed their belief that other cultures had little to offer the Celestial Kingdom. Cheng Ho's energy and curiosity about the wider world were unique. No one followed his lead after he died. Instead, the emperor banned the further construction of ocean-going ships and later forbade anyone to own a vessel with more than two masts. China, a self-contained economic and political system, turned inward. It did not need the rest of the world.

Europe versus Islam in the Fifteenth Century

Western Europe was a rather backward place in 1400. Compared with China or the Islamic world, it faced severe disadvantages. Its location on the Atlantic rim of the Eurasian continent had always made access to Asian trade difficult and costly. Its military situation had become precarious. Mounted knights in heavy armor could not stop the Ottoman Turks, who took Constantinople in 1453, then overran the Balkans by the 1520s, and threatened Vienna. The Islamic world, not Christian Europe, controlled overland trade to Asia and the existing seaborne route through the Persian Gulf. Europeans desired the fine silks of China and the East Indian spices that could enliven the taste of their food and help preserve it through the long winters. But because Europeans made nothing that Asians wished to buy, Europe had to pay for these imports with silver or gold, and the supply of both was limited. Moreover, most of what little profit was to be made from trade with Asia ended up in the hands of Islamic middlemen.

In fact, while Europe's sphere of influence appeared to be shrinking and China seemed content with what it already had, Islam was well embarked on another great phase of expansion. Conquering Turks kept Christian Europe in terror, and the Safavid Empire in Iran (Persia) rose to a new splendor. Other Moslems carried the Koran to Indonesia and northern India, where the powerful Mogul empire they created eventually formed the basis for the twentieth-century states of Pakistan and Bangladesh. As of 1400, Arab mariners were the most skillful in the world. Had E.T. decided to land on Earth around 1460, he might well have chosen to visit an Islamic commercial center, such as Constantinople or Baghdad, rather than Europe.

Yet Europe had advantages, too, although not all of them were obvious. The European economy had made impressive gains in the Middle Ages, primarily

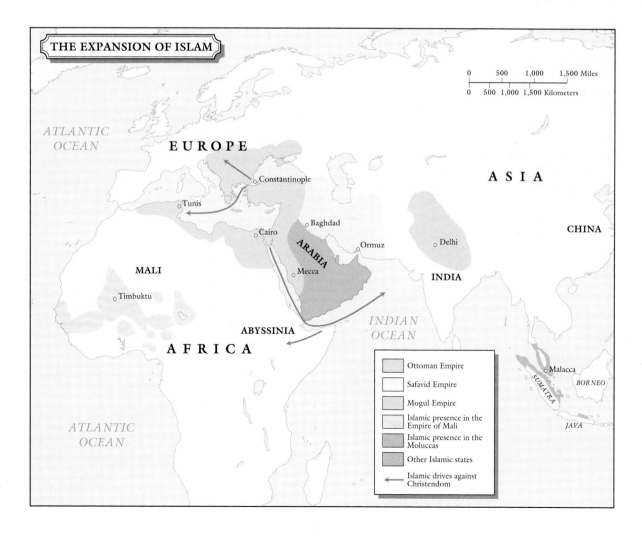

owing to agricultural advances that also fostered rapid population growth. More than 100 million people inhabited Europe by the year 1300. After 1300, however, Europe's farms could not sustain further growth. Lean years and famine years ensued, leaving people undernourished, and then the Black Death (bubonic plague) of 1348 devastated the population, reducing it by more than a third. Recurring bouts of plague kept population low until about 1500, when vigorous growth resumed. But the long decline of the fifteenth century also brought unexpected benefits. Overworked soil regained its fertility, and per capita income rose considerably among a population that had also acquired stronger immunities to disease.

Agriculture was not Europe's only asset. By the fifteenth century, metallurgy and architecture were as sophisticated in Europe as anywhere on the globe. The Renaissance, which revived interest in the literature of ancient Greece and Rome, also gave a new impetus to European culture, especially after Johann Gutenberg invented the printing press and movable type in the 1430s. By the end of the century, information circulated more rapidly and efficiently throughout Europe than anywhere else in the world. This revolution in communications permitted improvements in ship design and navigational techniques to build on each other and become a self-reinforcing process. The Arabs, by contrast, had borrowed a form of printing from China in the tenth century, only to give it up by 1400.

Unlike China, none of Europe's kingdoms was a self-contained economy. All of them needed to trade with one another and with the non-Christian world. In 1400 this contrast worked to Europe's disadvantage, but this drawback slowly became an asset. No one state had a monopoly on the manufacture of firearms or controlled the flow of capital, a situation that proved advantageous to Europe in the long run. During the fifteenth century, European societies began to compete with each other in acquiring access to these resources and in mastering new maritime and military techniques. European armies were far more formidable in 1520 then they had been in 1453, and European navies could outsail and outfight anyone else on the globe. Had E.T. chosen to visit in 1520, he might well have selected Europe, even if it still could not make anything that Asians wished to buy.

The Legacy of the Crusades

Quite apart from the Norse explorers, Europe had its own heritage of expansion, derived from the efforts of the crusaders to conquer the Holy Land from Islam. Crusaders had established their own Kingdom of Jerusalem, which survived less than a century before the city was retaken in 1187. Thereafter, while a new wave of Islamic expansion seemed about to engulf much of the world, Christian Europe gained only a few Mediterranean and Atlantic islands before 1492. But this overseas venture taught the Europeans several important lessons. To make Jerusalem profitable, the crusaders had taken over sugar plantations already there and worked them with slave labor. After they were driven from the Holy Land, they retreated to the Mediterranean islands of Cyprus, Malta, Crete, and Rhodes, where they continued to use slaves to grow sugar cane or to raise grapes for wine.

Long before the time of Columbus, these planters had put together the main economic ingredients of sustained overseas expansion. They assumed that colonies should produce a staple crop, probably through slave labor, for sale within Europe. The first slaves were Moslem captives. In the fourteenth and fifteenth centuries, planters turned to pagan Slavs (hence the word "slave") from the Black Sea area. Some black Africans had also been enslaved, probably acquired from Arab merchants who controlled the caravan trade across the Sahara Desert.

The crusades also left a cultural legacy in the legend of Prester John. For centuries after the loss of Jerusalem, many Europeans still cherished the hope of linking up somewhere deep in the African interior with this mythical Christian king, whose legend reflected the garbled information that Europe had acquired about the Coptic Christian kingdom of Ethiopia. As late as the fifteenth century, Europeans still hoped to inflict a mortal blow upon Islam by uniting with that powerful prince.

The Unlikely Pioneer: Portugal

That Europe stood on the verge of a dramatic expansion seemed highly improbable in 1400. That the kingdom of Portugal would lead the way seemed even less likely. Portugal was a small country of fewer than a million people and had been united for less than a century. Lisbon, with a population of forty thousand, was the only city with more than eight thousand inhabitants. Portugal's maritime traditions lagged well behind those of the Italian states, western France, and England. Its merchant class was tiny, it had accumulated little capital, and its educational institutions were so inadequate that the pope refused to recognize theology degrees from the University of Lisbon.

Yet Portugal also had some advantages. It enjoyed internal peace and a reasonably efficient government at a time when its neighbors were beset by war and internal upheaval. Moreover, Portugal's location at the intersection of the Mediterranean and Atlantic worlds led its mariners to ask how the Atlantic might be transformed from a barrier into a highway. At first, most of them were merely interested in short-term gains. The search for an all-water route to Asia would come later. The Portuguese knew that Arab caravans crossed the Sahara to bring gold, slaves, and ivory from black Africa to Europe. Arab traders spoke of how the Mandingo King *(Mansa)* Musa (d. 1332) of the empire of Mali controlled more gold than any other ruler in the world and of how he could field an army of one hundred thousand men. Musa's fame reached all the way to Europe, where he was described as "the richest and most noble lord of all this region on account of the abundance of gold which is gathered in his kingdom." The Portuguese believed that an Atlantic voyage to coastal points south of the Sahara Desert would undercut the Arabs and bring large profits. The greatest problem the Portuguese faced in this quest was Cape Bojador, with its treacherous shallows, awesome waves, and strong northerly winds. Several captains had sailed boldly around the cape. None had returned.

Mastering the African Coast   A crusading member of the Portuguese royal family, Prince Henry, decided to conquer this barrier. In 1420 he became head of the Order of Christ and used its revenues to sponsor fifteen voyages along the African coast. One of his captains, Gil Eannes, finally succeeded in 1434. After passing the cape and exploring the coastline, Eannes sailed west into the Atlantic beyond the sight of land until he met favorable winds and currents that carried him back to Europe.

Henry had launched Portugal's era of expansion, but he soon lost interest in the process. While the prince indulged in costly and futile crusades against

Morocco, less exalted men continued to push farther south along the African coast. But only after they made it beyond the Sahara did these efforts begin to pay off.

Such an achievement required innovations. During the fifteenth century Portugal vaulted past all rivals in two major areas—the ability to navigate the high seas beyond sight of land, and the capacity to defeat any non-European fleet on the world's oceans. These successes were the result of careful and systematic inquiry. The Portuguese collected geographical information from classical sources, foreigners, and modern navigators until the learning

Astronomers in the Shahinhahnama Observatory, Ottoman Empire, 1581   Well into the fifteenth century, Arabs and other Moslems knew more than Europeans about astronomy and geography.

process became self-reinforcing. They studied the superior designs of Arab vessels, copied them, and then made improvements. They increased the ratio of length to beam (width at the broadest point of the hull) from 2:1 to 3:1, borrowed the lateen (triangular) sail from the Arabs, and combined it with square rigging in the right proportion to produce a superb, new ocean-going vessel, the caravel. A caravel could make from 3 to 12 knots and could beat closer to a head wind than any other sailing ship.

The Portuguese also learned how to mount heavy cannon on the decks of their ships, a formidable advantage in an age when naval battles were fought by grappling and boarding enemy ships. Portuguese ships were able to stand farther off and literally blow their opponents out of the water. Portuguese captains also made full use of the compass and adopted the astrolabe from the Arabs, a device that permitted accurate calculation of latitude, or distances north and south. (The calculation of longitude — distances east and west — is much more difficult and was not satisfactorily resolved until the eighteenth century.) As they skirted the African coast, they made precise charts and maps, which then became available to other skippers. Knowledge grew quickly, as Portugal institutionalized this learning process.

Colonization and the Slave Trade   As the fifteenth century advanced, Portuguese vessels explored ever farther along the African coast, looking for wealth, news of Prester John, and a direct, cheap route to Asia. Beyond the Sahara they found the wealth they had been seeking — gold, ivory, and slaves. These riches kept the enterprise alive. Unlike the Chinese after Cheng Ho's death, the Portuguese saw every advantage in continuing their explorations.

They also founded offshore colonies along the way. The Portuguese began to settle the uninhabited Madeira Islands in 1418, took possession of the Azores between 1427 and 1450, occupied the Cape Verde group in the 1450s, and took over São Tomé in 1470. Like exploration, colonization also turned a profit. Lacking investment capital and experience in overseas settlement, the Portuguese drew on Italian merchants for both. In this way, the plantation complex of staple crops and slavery migrated from the Mediterranean to the Atlantic. Beginning in the 1440s, Portuguese planters on the islands produced sugar or wine with slave labor imported from nearby Africa.

Caravel   A fifteenth-century caravel, in this case a modern reconstruction of the *Niña*, which crossed the Atlantic with Columbus in 1492.

The slave trade began crudely, with intruders landing on the African coast, attacking agricultural villages, and carrying off everyone they could catch. But these raids alienated coastal peoples, making other forms of trade more difficult. In the decades after 1450, the slave trade assumed its classic form. The Portuguese established small posts, or "factories," along the coast or, ideally, on small offshore islands, such as Arguin Island near Cape Blanco, where they built their first African fort in 1448. Operating out of these bases, traders would buy slaves from the local rulers, who usually acquired the slaves by waging war against neighboring peoples of the interior. During the long history of the Atlantic slave trade, nearly every African shipped overseas had first been enslaved by other Africans.

Slavery had long existed in Africa, but in a form less brutal than what the Europeans would impose. When the Atlantic slave trade began, no African middleman could have foreseen how the enslavement of Africans by Europeans would differ from the enslavement of Africans by Africans. But the differences were crucial. For example, in Africa slaves were not forced to toil endlessly to produce staple crops, and their descendants often became fully assimilated into the captors' society. Moreover, within Africa, slaves were not isolated as a separate caste. By the time that African middlemen learned about the conditions of slavery under European rule, the commerce had already become too lucrative to stop, although several African societies tried unsuccessfully to do so. African states

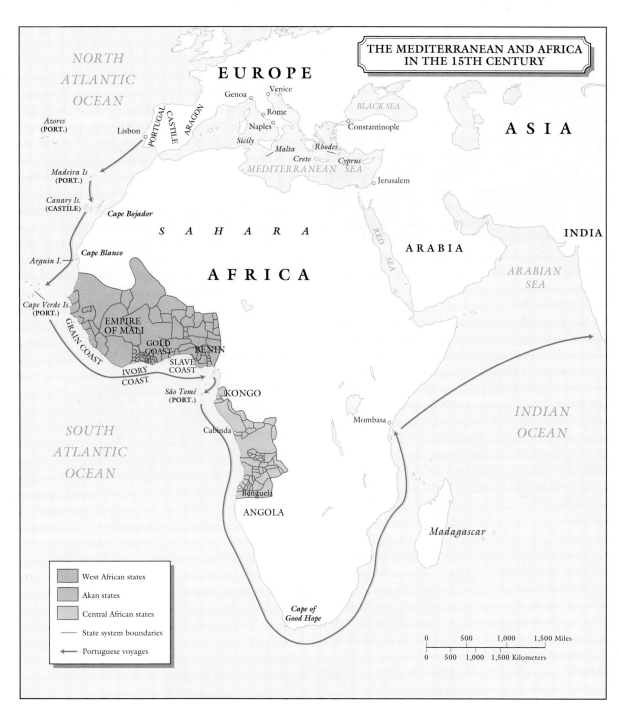

discovered, however, that those who refused to participate in the trade were likely to become its victims.
When the rulers of the Kingdom of the Kongo embraced Catholicism in the sixteenth century, they
protested eloquently against the Atlantic slave trade,

only to find that their moral protests left their own
people vulnerable to enslavement by others. The non-
Christian kingdom of Benin learned the same lesson.

In the fifteenth century, West Africa was inhabited
by a mostly agricultural population that also included

The Portuguese Slave-Trading Fortress of Elmina   Located on the Gold Coast of West Africa, the fortress was built in 1481.

The Portuguese were able to build a profitable slave trade by exploiting rivalries among the more than two hundred small states of West and Central Africa. This part of Africa was far removed from the historically powerful interior states that were tied to the northern caravan trade. Indeed, it was divided into more language groups and small states than Europeans would encounter anywhere else in the world. And despite many cultural similarities that crossed these linguistic and state barriers, West Africans had never thought of themselves as a single people. Nor did they share a common, universal religion that might have restrained them from selling strange and distant Africans into slavery. Europeans, though they were quite capable of waging destructive wars against one another, strongly believed that enslaving fellow Christians was immoral. Enslaving pagan or Moslem Africans was another matter. Some Europeans even persuaded themselves that they were doing Africans a favor by buying them and making their souls eligible for conversion and salvation.

skilled craftsmen. West Africans had probably learned how to use iron long before Europeans, and they had been supplying Europe with most of its gold for hundreds of years through indirect trade across the Sahara. West Africa's political history had been marked by the rise and subsequent decline of a series of large inland states. The most recent of these, the empire of Mali, was already in severe decay by the time the Portuguese got past the Sahara. As the Portuguese advanced steadily southward along the coast, their "factories" began to pull trade away from the Sahara caravans, which further weakened Mali and other interior states. The empire fell apart by 1550.

Portugal's Asian Empire   Thus, precisely because it paid for itself through trade in gold and slaves, Portuguese exploration continued through the fifteenth century. By the 1480s the Portuguese government was actively supporting the quest for an all-water route to Asia. In 1487 Bartolomeu Días succeeded in reaching the southernmost tip of Africa and headed east toward the Indian Ocean, but his crew rebelled in those dangerous waters and forced him

The City of Luanga   Located in the Kingdom of the Kongo, this seventeenth-century city is a good example of the urbanization of parts of West Africa.

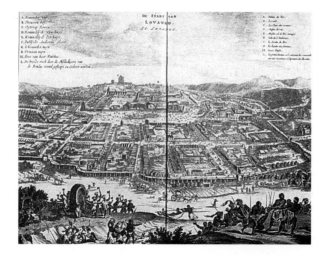

Bronze Portrait Head   This bronze head is of an Oni, or West African ruler, of thirteenth-century Ife (now Nigeria), two centuries before Europeans arrived.

to sail back to Portugal. Ten years later Vasco da Gama finally led a small fleet around the Cape of Good Hope and sailed on to the Malibar Coast of southwestern India. In a voyage that lasted more than two years (1497–1499), da Gama bargained and fought for spices that eventually brought profits of twenty to one over the voyage's initial investment.

Da Gama opened the way for Portugal's empire in the East. Under the leadership of Admiral Afonso de Albuquerque, the Portuguese established a chain of naval bases to secure their Asian trade. These posts extended from East Africa to the mouth of the Persian Gulf, then to Goa on the west coast of India, and from there to the Moluccas, or East Indies. The Moluccas became the Asian center of the Portuguese seaborne empire, with their spices providing most of the wealth that Portugal extracted from its eastern holdings. Content to protect its vital sea lanes, Portugal chose not to challenge the military power of India or China directly.

As Portuguese traders and missionaries spread more widely throughout the East, their persistence baffled many Asians. "Why do you expose yourself to such hardships?" asked one ruler. Unsatisfied with the explanation, he reflected, "The fact that these people journey so far from home to conquer territory indicates clearly that there must be very little

justice and a great deal of greed among them." Portuguese missionaries even ventured as far as Japan. Their success there prompted a government massacre of most Japanese converts. By 1639 Japan had closed all but the port of Nagasaki to Europeans.

Beyond assuring its continued access to spices, Portugal did not try very hard to govern its holdings. The conversion of Indonesia to Islam took place at precisely the time when Portugal was taking over the spice trade and asserting at least nominal control over those islands. In fact, Portugal's eastern empire did not rest on colonies of settlement. In all of their Asian holdings, the Portuguese remained heavily outnumbered by native peoples. Only in the other hemisphere—in Brazil, discovered accidentally by Pedro Álvares Cabral in 1500 when he was blown off course while trying to round the Cape of Good Hope—did settlement become a major goal by the late sixteenth century.

The contrast between Norse failure and Portuguese success can be instructive. The ability to navigate the high seas, while an impressive feat in its own right, nevertheless gave no guarantee of lasting success. Only with continuous support from the homeland were overseas ventures likely to survive, as the ultimate failure of Greenland, even after five centuries of occupation, demonstrates. On the other hand, having mastered oceanic travel, the ability to reach foreign shores was more important than the distance traveled.

Successful European expansion overseas required the support of a stable government and also made use of the experience and resources of other states. Experience acquired in nearby Rhodes or Cyprus could be passed on to the Portuguese by Italian merchants and applied in the Atlantic islands of Madeira or the Azores. What was learned there could be extended to distant Brazil. The Portuguese also drew on Italian capital and maritime skills, as well as Arab learning and technology, in launching their ventures. Spaniards, in turn, would learn much from the Portuguese, and the French, Dutch, and English would borrow from all of their predecessors. All except the Dutch employed Italians in the early phases of expansion.

The economic impulse behind colonization was thus in place long before Columbus. The desire for precious metals provided the initial stimulus, but staple crops and slavery generated the continuing impetus for European settlement of the Americas.

Before the nineteenth century, most people who crossed the Atlantic were not free Europeans but slaves, brought to America to grow sugar or other staples.

Indeed, the Europeans who crossed the ocean seldom expected to work. Early modern Europe was a hierarchical society in which men with prestige and wealth did virtually no physical labor. Upward social mobility in European society meant advancing toward the goal of "living nobly," without the need to labor. Moreover, in both Portugal and Spain, the social barriers between aristocrats and commoners were flexible. Professional men, famous soldiers, and rich merchants could acquire titles and begin to "live nobly." The opening of the Americas offered even greater possibilities. Once in America, even Iberian peasants could aspire to higher social status and a life without labor, though not to a formal title. The ability to coerce the labor of others, then, became a central thrust of the whole overseas enterprise. Again the contrast between the Norse and later European expansion is instructive. The Norse had colonized Greenland and Vinland in quest of a place to live and till their own soil. And they had failed. No one would return to that pattern until the English Puritan migration after 1630, and even the Puritans would long remain an exception to the rule.

Spain, Columbus, and the Americas

While the Portuguese surged to the east, Spaniards began to move more sluggishly to the west. Just as Portugal gained valuable experience by colonizing Madeira and the Azores, so did the Spanish kingdom of Castile learn similar lessons while taking over the Canary Islands, beginning shortly after 1400. The invaders then spent the rest of the century conquering the islands' inhabitants, the Guanches, a Berber people who had left North Africa before the rise of Islam and had been almost completely cut off from Africa and Europe for over a thousand years. By the 1490s the Spanish had all but exterminated them, the first people to face extinction in the wake of European expansion.

But apart from the Canary Islands, the Spaniards devoted little attention to exploration or colonization. Instead, for most of the fifteenth century the Iberian kingdoms of Aragon and Castile warred with other powers, quarreled with each other, or dealt with internal unrest. But in 1469 Prince Ferdi-

nand of Aragon married Princess Isabella of Castile, and they soon inherited their respective thrones to form the modern kingdom of Spain with a population of about 4.9 million by 1500. Aragon, a Mediterranean society, had made good an old claim to the Kingdom of Naples and Sicily and thus already possessed a small imperial bureaucracy with experience in administering overseas possessions. Castile, landlocked on three sides, was larger than Aragon but in many ways more parochial. Its people, though suspicious of foreigners, had turned much of their small overseas trade over to merchants and mariners from Genoa in northern Italy who had settled in the port of Seville. Crusading Castilians, not traders, had taken the lead in expelling the Moors from the Iberian peninsula. Castilians, then, were more likely than the Portuguese to identify expansion with conquest, rather than with the opportunity to trade, and they would lead Spain across the Atlantic.

In January 1492 Isabella and Ferdinand completed the reconquest of Spain by taking Granada, the last outpost of Islam on the Iberian peninsula. Still flush with their victory, they then gave unconverted Jews six months to become Christians or be expelled from Spain. Just over half of Spain's eighty thousand Jews fled, mostly to nearby Christian lands that were more tolerant than Spain. A decade later Ferdinand and Isabella also evicted all unconverted Moors. Spain entered the sixteenth century as Europe's most fiercely Catholic society, and this attitude would accompany its soldiers and settlers across the Atlantic.

Columbus   A talented navigator from Genoa named Cristoforo Columbo (or Christopher Columbus in Latin) witnessed the victory at Granada and promptly sought to benefit from it. He had served the Portuguese Crown for several years, had engaged in the growing slave trade between Africa and the Atlantic islands, had married the daughter of a very prominent Madeira planter, and may even have sailed to Iceland. By 1492 he had been pleading for years with the courts of Portugal, England, France, and Spain to give him the ships and men to attempt an unprecedented feat. He was convinced that he could reach East Asia by sailing west across the Atlantic. Columbus's proposed voyage was controversial, but not because he assumed the earth is round. Learned men had long agreed on that point. But they disagreed about the earth's circumference. Columbus cited the Bible as evidence that there must be far more land than water on the surface of the globe. By underestimating the expanse of the oceans, he put the earth's circumference at only 16,000 miles. This arithmetic convinced him that he could reach Japan or China by sailing west a mere three thousand miles. The Portuguese scoffed at his reasoning. They estimated the planet's circumference at about 26,000 miles, and they warned Columbus that he would perish on the vast ocean if he tried his mad scheme.

The Portuguese calculations were, of course, far more accurate than those of Columbus; the earth is about 25,000 miles in circumference at the equator. But the fall of Granada gave Columbus another chance to plead his case. Isabella, who now had men and resources to spare, became more receptive to his request. She appointed him "Admiral of the Ocean Sea" in charge of a fleet of two caravels, the *Niña* and the *Pinta,* together with a larger, square-rigged vessel, the *Santa María,* which Columbus made his flagship.

Columbus's motives were both religious and practical. He believed that the world was going to end around the year 1648 but that God would make the Gospel available to all mankind before the last days. As the Christ-bearer (the literal meaning of his first name), Columbus was convinced that he had a role to play in bringing on the millennium, the period at the end of history when Christ is expected to return and rule with His saints for a thousand years.

However devout, Columbus was not at all averse to acquiring a little wealth and glory along the way to the millennium. Embarking from the Spanish port of Palos in August 1492, he headed south to the Canaries and added provisions. Then he sailed due west across the uncharted Atlantic. He kept two ship's logs, one to show his men, in which he deliberately underestimated the distance they had traveled, and the other for his eyes only. (Ironically, the false log turned out to be more accurate than the official one.) After several weeks at sea, he promised a prize to the first sailor to sight land. Despite his assurances that they had not sailed very far, the crews had grown restless by early October. Columbus pushed on. When land was spotted, on October 12, he claimed the prize for himself, on the grounds that he had seen a light in the distance the previous night.

The Spaniards splashed ashore on San Salvador, now Watling's Island in the Bahamas (a few histori-

ans argue for Samana Cay, sixty miles south of San Salvador, as the site of the first landfall). Convinced that he was somewhere in the East Indies, near Japan or China, Columbus called the local inhabitants "Indians," a word that meant nothing to them but one that has endured. When the peaceful Tainos (or Arawaks) claimed that the Carib Indians on nearby islands were cannibals, Columbus interpreted their word for "Carib" to mean the great "Khan" or emperor of China, known to him through Marco Polo's *Travels.* Columbus set out to track them down. For several months he poked about the Caribbean, mostly along the coasts of Cuba and Hispaniola. Then, on Christmas, the *Santa María* ran upon rocks and had to be abandoned. A few weeks later Columbus sailed for Spain on the *Niña.* Some speculate that he arranged the Christmas disaster as a way of forcing some of the crew to stay behind as a garrison on Hispaniola. But even the gentle Tainos had seen enough. By the time Columbus returned on his second voyage in late 1493, they had killed every man he left behind.

Columbus's first voyage had immediate consequences. The crews of the *Niña* and *Pinta* probably carried syphilis back to Spain with them. This disease, unknown in Europe before then, spread anguish and death with terrifying speed. At the level of high politics, the voyage also had major results. In 1493 Pope Alexander VI (a Spaniard) issued a bull, *Inter Caeteras,* which divided all non-Christian lands between Spain and Portugal. A year later, in the Treaty of Tordesillas, the two countries adjusted the dividing line, with Spain claiming most of the western hemisphere, and Portugal most of the eastern.

Columbus made three more voyages in quest of China and also served as governor of the Spanish Indies. But Castilians never really trusted this Genoese opportunist, who spoke their language with a Portuguese accent and was a poor administrator to boot. The colonists often defied him, and after his third voyage they shipped him back to Spain in chains in 1500. He died in 1506, a bitter, disappointed man.

Spain and the Caribbean   By then overseas settlement had acquired a momentum of its own as thousands of ex-soldiers, bored minor nobles *(hidalgos)* with little wealth, and assorted adventurers drifted across the Atlantic. They carried with them Europe's cereal crops and livestock, including horses, cows,

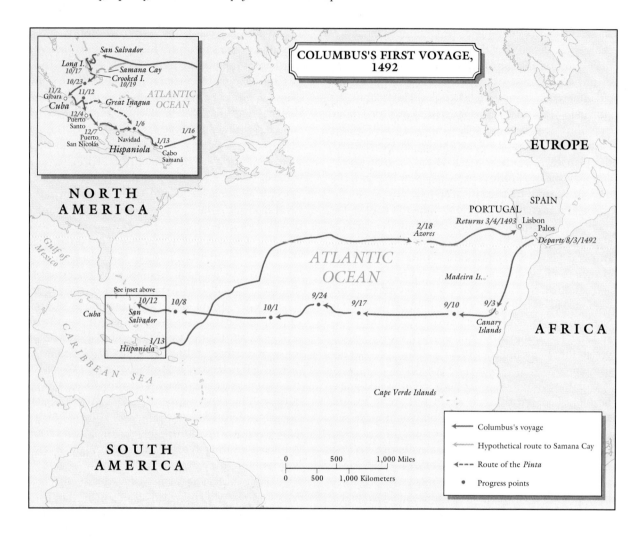

sheep, goats, and pigs. On islands without fences, these beasts roamed freely, eating everything in sight, and soon threatened the Tainos' food supply. Unconcerned, the Spaniards forced the increasingly malnourished Indians to work for them, mostly panning for gold. Under these pressures, even before the onset of major infectious diseases, the Indian population declined catastrophically throughout the Caribbean. By 1514 only 22,000 able-bodied adults remained on Hispaniola, out of an initial population of perhaps one million. The Indians disappeared even more rapidly than the meager supply of placer gold. This story was soon repeated on Cuba, Jamaica, and other islands. A whole way of life all but vanished from the earth to be replaced by sugar, slaves, and livestock as the Spaniards despaired of finding other forms of wealth. The first African slaves soon arrived to replace dead Indians as a labor force.

The Spaniards continued their explorations, however. Juan Ponce de León tramped through Florida in quest of a legendary fountain of youth, shrewdly calculating that such an elixir would certainly bring a handsome price in Europe. Vasco Núñez de Balboa became the first European to reach the Pacific Ocean, after crossing the Isthmus of Panama in 1513. But as late as 1519—a full generation after Columbus's first voyage—it seemed highly doubtful that Spain would ever find much wealth in these new possessions, whatever and wherever they turned out to be. One geographer concluded that Spain had found a whole new continent, which he named "America" in honor of his informant, the explorer Amerigo Vespucci. For those who doubted, Ferdinand Magellan, a Portuguese captain serving the king of Spain, settled the issue when his fleet sailed around the world between 1519 and 1522. Magellan himself never completed the voyage. He was killed in the Philippines.

But during the same three years, Hernán Cortés sailed from Cuba, conquered Mexico, and found the treasure trove that Spaniards had been hunting for. In 1519 he landed at a place he named Vera Cruz ("The True Cross") and over the next several months succeeded in tracking down the fabulous empire of the Aztecs, high in the Valley of Mexico. When his small army of four hundred men first laid eyes on the Aztec capital of Tenochtitlán (a metropolis of 200,000, much larger than any city in Western Europe), they wondered if they were dreaming. But they marched on. Moctezuma, the Aztec "speaker," or ruler, sent rich presents to persuade the Spaniards to leave, but the gesture had the opposite effect. "They picked up the gold and fingered it like monkeys," an Aztec later recalled. "They longed and lusted for gold. Their bodies swelled with greed, and their hunger was ravenous. . . . They snatched at the golden ensigns, waved them from side to side and examined every inch of them." Cortés had stumbled upon a wholly different world in the Americas, one with its own long and varied past.

THE EMERGENCE OF COMPLEX SOCIETIES IN THE AMERICAS

In 1500 the Americas were in some ways a more ancient world than Western Europe. For example, the Portuguese, Spanish, French, and English languages were only beginning to assume their modern forms during the century or two on either side of Columbus's voyage. But centuries earlier, at a time when Rome was falling into ruins and Paris and London were still little more than hamlets, there were large, thriving cities in the Andes and Mesoamerica (the area embracing Central America and southern and central Mexico). Which world was old and which was new is a matter of perspective.

The Rise of Sedentary Cultures

After 4000 B.C.E., agriculture transformed Indian life in most parts of North and South America. As farming slowly became the principal source of food in the Americas, settled villages in a few locations grew into large cities. Most of them appeared in the Valley of Mexico, Central America, or the Andes, but for

centuries, dense settlements also thrived in Chaco Canyon in present-day New Mexico and in the lower Mississippi Valley. Meanwhile, farming continued to spread. By the time Columbus sailed, the great majority of Indians were raising crops.

Indians differed in how completely sedentary (locally rooted or nonmigratory) they became. Most of those north of Mexico lived a semisedentary life; that is, they were migratory for part of each year. After a tribe had selected a suitable location, the men chopped down some of the trees, girded others, burned away the underbrush, and often planted tobacco, a mood-altering sacred crop grown exclusively by men. Burning the underbrush fertilized the soil with ash and gave the community several years of high productivity. Indian women usually erected the dwellings (longhouse, wigwam, tepee) and planted and harvested food crops, especially corn. Planting beans among the corn helped to maintain good crop yields. In the fall, either the men alone or entire family groups went off hunting or fishing.

Under this "slash and burn" system of agriculture, farming became women's work, beneath the dignity of men, whose role was to hunt and make war. Because the "slash and burn" method eventually depleted the soil, the whole tribe had to move to new fields after several years. Given this semisedentary way of life, few Indians cared to acquire more personal property than the women could lug from one place to another, either during the annual hunt or when the whole community had to move. This limited interest in consumption would profoundly condition their response to capitalism after contact with Europeans.

Indians who became fully sedentary usually developed strong attachments to particular places, but individuals did not own land. Clans or families zealously guarded their "use rights" to land that had been allocated to them by their chiefs. In sedentary societies both men and women worked in the fields, and families accumulated surpluses for trade. Not all sedentary peoples developed monumental architecture and elaborate state forms. The Tainos of the Greater Antilles in the Caribbean were fully sedentary, for example, but they never erected massive temples or created powerful states. But, with a few striking exceptions, such manifestations of cultural complexity emerged only among sedentary populations. In Mesoamerica and the Andes, intensive farming, cities, states, and monumental architecture

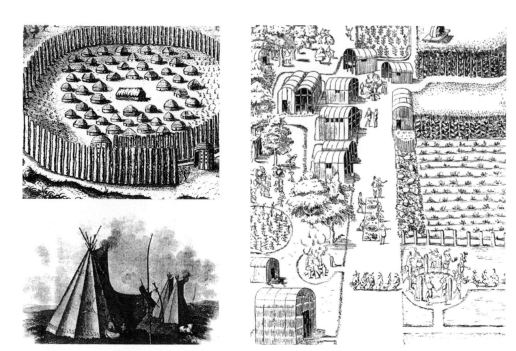

Longhouse, Wigwam, and Tepee   The longhouse (right), made from bark or mats stretched over a wooden frame, was the standard, communal dwelling of the Iroquois and Huron peoples. Most Algonquian peoples of the eastern woodlands lived in wigwams (top left), which were smaller than longhouses and made by bending the boughs of trees and covering this frame with animal skins. West of the Mississippi most Plains Indians lived in small but strong tepees (bottom left), which were usually made from buffalo hides. All of these dwellings were made by women.

came together at several different times to produce distinctive high cultures.

The spread of farming produced another population surge among both sedentary and semi sedentary peoples. Estimates vary greatly, but according to the more moderate ones, there were at least 50 million people living in the western hemisphere by 1492, and there probably were about 70 million, which was one-seventh of the world's population. High estimates exceed 100 million. The Valley of Mexico in 1500 was one of the most densely inhabited regions on earth.

Despite their large populations, even the most complex societies in the Americas remained Stone Age cultures in their basic technology. Indeed, the urban societies of Mesoamerica and the Andes became the largest and most complex Stone Age cultures in the history of the world. The Indians made some use of metals, though more for decorative than practical purposes. This skill originated in South America and spread to Mesoamerica a few centuries before Columbus. By 1520 Indians had amassed enough gold and silver to provide dozens of

plundering Europeans with princely fortunes. As far north as the Great Lakes copper had been mined and fashioned into fishing tools and art objects since the first millennium B.C.E. It was traded over large areas of North America. But Indians had not found a way to make bronze (a compound of copper and tin), nor discovered any use for iron. Nearly all of their tools were made of stone or bone, and their sharpest weapons were crafted from obsidian, a dark, hard, glassy volcanic rock. Nor did they use the wheel or devices based on the wheel, such as pulleys or gears. They knew how to make a wheel, for they had a number of wheeled toys. But they never found a practical purpose for this invention, probably because North America had no draft animals, and in South America llamas were used mostly in steep mountainous areas where wheeled vehicles would have made no sense.

The Andes: Cycles of Complex Cultures

Within these technological limitations, Indians accomplished a great deal. During the second millen-

Indian Women as Farmers   A French depiction of sixteenth-century Indian women in southeastern North America.

nium B.C.E., elaborate urban societies began to take shape both in the Andes and along the Mexican coast. Because no Andean culture had developed a written language before the Europeans arrived, we know much less about what happened there than we do about Mesoamerica. But we do know that ancient Andean societies devised extremely productive agricultural systems at forbidding altitudes as high as 12,000 feet, far higher than anyone else has ever been able to raise crops. In the 1980s, when archaeologists rebuilt part of the prehistoric Andean irrigation system according to ancient specifications, they discovered that it was far more productive on the same land than a system based on modern machinery and fertilizers. The Andean system could produce ten metric tons of potatoes per hectare (about 2.4 acres), as against one to four tons on nearby modern fields—and lands using the Andean irrigation system never had to lie fallow. This type of irrigation originally took hold around Lake Titicaca about 1000 B.C.E. and spread throughout Andean societies. It was abandoned around A.D. 1000, apparently in response to a monstrous drought that endured, with only brief intermissions, for two centuries.

Monumental architecture and urbanization began in the Andes even before the canal system at Lake Titicaca. Between 3000 and 2100 B.C.E., organized communities appeared both along the Peruvian coast and in the interior. These communities usually emerged around a U-shaped temple about three stories high. Some of the earliest temples were pyramids, the oldest of which are as ancient as those of Egypt. In later centuries, as more people moved into the mountains, more temples became pyramids, some of them immense, such as the one at Sechin Alto near Lima, over ten stories high, which was built between 1800 and 1500 B.C.E. Eventually these accomplishments merged into what archaeologists called the "Pre-Classic" Chavin culture, which was well established by 1000 B.C.E., only to collapse suddenly around 300 B.C.E. Water has always been a scarce resource in the Andes, and this culture maintained huge irrigation works. It was probably never dominated by any single state.

Chavin culture had two offshoots, one on the coast, one in the mountains. Together they constitute the "Classic" phase of pre-Columbian history in South America. The Mochica culture, which emerged around A.D. 300 on the northwest coast of Peru, produced finely detailed pottery, much of it erotic, and built pyramids as centers of worship, particularly of the moon but also of the sun. At about the same time, another Classic culture arose in the mountains around the city of Tiwanaku, 12,000 feet

Table 1-1

Complex Cultures of Pre-Columbian America

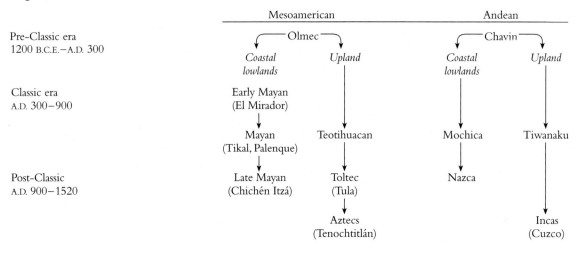

	Mesoamerican		Andean	
Pre-Classic era 1200 B.C.E.–A.D. 300	Olmec		Chavin	
	Coastal lowlands	*Upland*	*Coastal lowlands*	*Upland*
Classic era A.D. 300–900	Early Mayan (El Mirador)			
	Mayan (Tikal, Palenque)	Teotihuacan	Mochica	Tiwanaku
Post-Classic A.D. 900–1520	Late Mayan (Chichén Itzá)	Toltec (Tula)	Nazca	
		Aztecs (Tenochtitlán)		Incas (Cuzco)

above sea level. The people of this society grew a great variety of food plants, both tropical and temperate. Terraces, laid out at various altitudes on the mountainside, permitted the community to raise crops from different climatic zones, all within a few hours distance from each other. At the lowest levels, Tiwanakans could plant cotton in the hot, humid air. Farther up the mountain, they could raise maize (corn) and other crops suitable to a temperate zone. At still higher elevations, they could grow potatoes and graze their alpacas and llamas. They even learned to freeze-dry some food by carrying it far up the mountains to take advantage of the frost that fell most nights of the year. The Tiwanaku empire, with its capital on the southern shores of Lake Titicaca, flourished during these centuries, until even its sophisticated irrigation system could not survive the horrendous drought that began at the end of the tenth century A.D. The Classic Andean cultures collapsed between the sixth and eleventh centuries A.D., possibly after a conquest of the Mochica region by the people of Tiwanaku, who controlled the water supply for coastal peoples until they themselves were overwhelmed by the drought.

The disruption that followed this decline was not permanent, for complex Post-Classic cultures soon thrived both north and west of Tiwanaku. The coastal culture of the Nazca people has long fascinated both scholars and tourists because of their exquisite textiles, many examples of which survive, and above all because of a unique network of lines that they etched in the desert. Some lines form the outlines of birds or animals, but others simply run straight ahead for miles until they disappear at the horizon. Only from the air are these patterns fully visible.

Around A.D. 1400 the Incas (the word applied to both the ruler and to the empire's dominant nation) emerged as the new imperial power in the Andes. They built their capital at Cuzco, high in the mountains. From that upland center, the Incas controlled an empire that eventually extended more than two thousand miles from south to north, and they bound it together with an efficient network of roads and suspension bridges. Along these roads the Incas maintained numerous storehouses for grain. High-altitude runners, who memorized the Inca's oral messages with perfect accuracy, raced along the roads to deliver these commands over vast distances. The Incas also invented a decimal system and used it to keep accounts on a device they called a *quipu*. By 1500 the Inca empire ruled perhaps 8 to 12 million people. No other nonliterate culture has come close to matching that feat.

Terraced Agriculture of the Andes   This example is from the Incas, but the technology is much older than the Inca civilization.

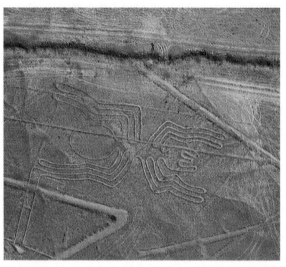

Nazca Lines   The Nazca lines, patterns in the desert of Peru, can be fully seen only from the air.

Inca Quipu   This accounting device is based on the decimal system.

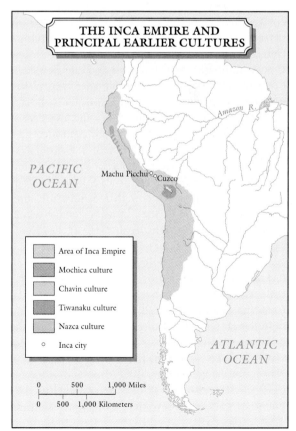

THE INCA EMPIRE AND PRINCIPAL EARLIER CULTURES

PACIFIC OCEAN

Amazon R.

Machu Picchu   Cuzco

ATLANTIC OCEAN

Area of Inca Empire

Mochica culture

Chavin culture

Tiwanaku culture

Nazca culture

○   Inca city

0   500   1,000 Miles

0   500   1,000 Kilometers

Mesoamerica: Cycles of Complex Cultures

Mesoamerica experienced a similar cycle of change, but over a somewhat shorter period of time. It had its own Pre-Classic, Classic, and Post-Classic cultures comprising both upland and lowland societies. The parent culture for the region was that of the Olmecs, who appeared along the Gulf Coast around 1200 B.C.E. The culture centered on three cities. The oldest, San Lorenzo (names are modern, as is "Olmec," which means "people of rubber," for the rubber trees that thrive in this tropical region) flourished from 1200 to 900 B.C.E., when it was conquered by invaders. Olmec influence reached its zenith during the domination of La Venta, which became an urban center around 1100 B.C.E., reached its peak three hundred years later, and then declined. After La Venta was demolished between 500 and 400 B.C.E., leadership passed to the city of Tres Zapotes, which thrived for another four centuries.

These three Olmec centers were small, with permanent populations of only about a thousand, not enough to sustain large armies. Yet Olmec commerce and culture spread broadly across Mesoamerica. The colossal stone heads that are the most distinctive artifacts of Olmec culture appeared only in the homeland, but other aspects became widely diffused. The Olmecs built the first pyramids and the first ballparks in Mesoamerica. In a game that they played with a heavy rubber ball and that spread into what is now the southwestern United States, the losers were, at least on certain religious occasions, beheaded. The Olmecs also had the beginnings of a written language and developed a dual calendar system that endured through the Aztec era. It took fifty-two years for the two calendars to complete a full cycle, after which the first day of the "short" calendar would once again coincide with the first day of the "long" calendar. The Olmecs faced the closing days of each cycle with dread, lest the gods allow the sun and all life on earth to be destroyed—something, Olmecs believed, that had already happened several times. Only the sacrifice of a god had started the sun, and only the blood of human sacrifice could placate the gods and keep it going.

With much variation, these beliefs endured in Mesoamerica for perhaps three thousand years, regardless of the rise and fall of empires and cities. The essentials may even be older than Olmec culture. The creation myths of both Mesoamerican and An-

Olmec Stone Head   This giant head of stone is nine feet, four inches tall.

dean peoples are similar, for example, which may suggest a common origin in the distant past. Though modified by time, Olmec beliefs retained immense power. The arrival of Spanish invaders in 1519 became a religious as well as a political crisis because the year 1519 marked the end of a fifty-two-year cycle.

The Olmecs were succeeded by two Classic cultures, both of which created great cities and studied the heavens. The city and empire of Teotihuacan emerged in the mountains not far from modern Mexico City. Mayan culture took shape mostly in the southern lowlands of Yucatán. Teotihuacan, a city of forty thousand by A.D. 1, grew to five times that size over the next three centuries. Its temples included large pyramids, but its most impressive art form was its brightly painted murals, of which only a few survive. Teotihuacan was able to extend its influence throughout Mesoamerica and remained a powerful force until its sudden collapse around A.D. 750, when its shrines were toppled, possibly by priests who believed that their gods had abandoned them. In all likelihood, Teotihuacan's growth had so depleted the resources of the area that the city could no longer sustain itself. Popular beliefs to the contrary, Indians enjoyed no mystical protection from ecological disasters. They created several gigantic ones.

In the lowlands, Classic Mayan culture went through a similar cycle from expansion to ecological

El Caracol, a Late Mayan Observatory, at Chichén Itzá Astronomy was highly developed in all of the pre-Columbian high
cultures of Mesoamerica. If the Mayans used any specialized instruments to study the heavens, we do not know what they
were.

crisis. It was also urban but less centralized than that
of Teotihuacan, although some Mayan temples were
just as monumental. For more than a thousand years,
Mayan culture rested upon a network of competing
city-states which, as in ancient Greece, shared similar
values. The Mayan city of Komchen in the northwest corner of the Yucatán peninsula already existed
in 500 B.C.E. Because of poor soil, Komchen and
neighboring cities exported salt and imported food
to survive. The salt was shipped along the Caribbean
coast to a plateau that became the portage to rivers
flowing into the Gulf of Mexico. One of the largest
Mayan cities, Tikal, emerged at this site and controlled commerce with Teotihuacan. Tikal housed
one hundred thousand at its peak before A.D. 800.
An additional twenty cities, most about one-fourth
the size of Tikal, flourished throughout the region.
Mayan engineers built a labyrinth of canals to provide the crops needed to support this growing urban
system, which was well established by the first century B.C.E. The Danta pyramid at the Pre-Classic
city of El Mirador, which has only recently been ex-
cavated, was probably the most massive architectural
structure in pre-Columbian Mesoamerica and was
completed more than a century before the birth of
Christ. By the beginning of the Classic era, it had already declined.

The earliest Mayan writings date to 50 B.C.E., but
few survive from the next three hundred years.
Around A.D. 300, Mayans began to record their history in considerable detail. Since 1960 scholars have
been able to decipher most Mayan inscriptions,
which means that the Classic phase of Mayan culture is completing a shift from a prehistoric to a historic (or written) past. Mayan texts can now be
studied much like Europe's. Mayan art and writings
reveal the religious sensibilities of these people, including the place of human sacrifice in their cosmos
and the role of ritual self-mutilation, particularly
among the elite, in their worship. Scholars can also
read, for example, inscriptions describing the long
reign of Pacal the Great, the king, or "Great Sun," of
the elegant city of Palenque, who was born on
March 26, 603 and died on August 31, 683. On his
sarcophagus is a list of his ancestors going back six
generations. Other monuments tell us something of
the Great Suns of other cities whom Pacal vanquished and sacrificed to the gods.

Classic Mayan culture began to collapse about fifty
years after the desertion of Teotihuacan, which disrupted trade with the Valley of Mexico. Once the fall
began, it spread rapidly. Palenque and a half-dozen
other cities were abandoned between 800 and 820.
The last date recorded at Tikal was in 869; the last
throughout the southern lowlands came forty years
later. The Mayan aristocracy had probably grown
faster than the ability of commoners to support it,
until population outstripped local resources and generated irreversible ecological decay. Frequent wars
also hastened the decline. Trade with the Valley of
Mexico, to the extent that it continued, shifted
northward to other cities. With the disintegration of
the southern cities, the population of the region fell
drastically, partly through out-migration northward.

After A.D. 900, the Post-Classic era saw a kind of
Mayan renaissance in the northern lowlands of the
Yucatán, where many refugees from the south had
fled. Chichén Itzá, a city that had existed for centuries, preserved many distinctive Mayan traits, but
now merged them with new influences from the
Valley of Mexico, where the Toltecs had become
dominant in the high country and may even have
conquered Chichén Itzá. The Toltecs were a fierce,
warrior people with a capital at Tula, which at forty
thousand people was one-fifth as large as Teotihuacan at its peak. They prospered on the cocoa trade
with tropical lowlands but otherwise did nothing to

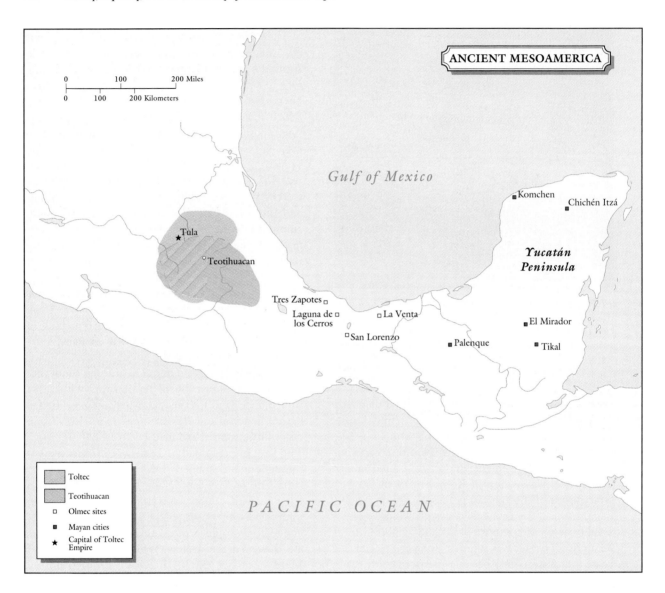

expand the region's food supply. They controlled the Valley for almost three centuries before they too declined by A.D. 1200. They left a legacy of conquest to later rulers in the Valley, all of whom claimed descent from Toltec kings.

The Aztecs and Tenochtitlán

By the fifteenth century, power in the Valley of Mexico was passing to the Aztecs, a warrior people who had migrated from the north one or two centuries earlier and had settled, with the bare sufferance of their neighbors, on a forbidding stretch of the shore of Lake Texcoco. They then proceeded to erect a great city, Tenochtitlán, out on the lake itself. Its only connection with the mainland was by several broad causeways. The Aztecs raised their agricultural productivity by building highly productive *chinampas*, or floating gardens, right on the lake. Yet their mounting population pressed against the food supply, and for several years in the 1450s the threat of famine was severe.

The Temple of the Sun at Teotihuacan   The giant, stepped pyramid is one of pre-Columbian America's most elegant pyramids.

Wall Paintings at Bonampak   The wall paintings at Bonampak from the Teotihuacan era are a spectacular example of pre-Columbian art.

Mayan Sacrificial Victim   Human sacrifice played a major role in Mesoamerican religion. The artist who crafted this disembowelled man recognized the agony of the victim.

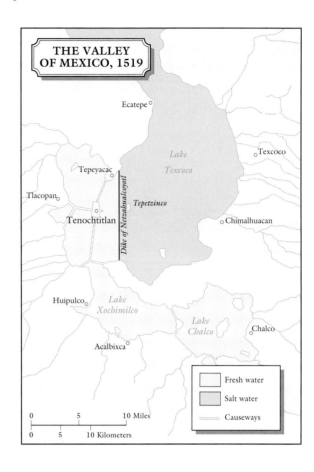

THE VALLEY OF MEXICO, 1519

The Chacmool   The Chacmool, or glowering statue, at Tula was a huge receptacle for the hearts of sacrificial victims. It became the most distinctive contribution of the Toltecs to Mesoamerican art. The Mayans copied it at Chichén Itzá, as did the Aztecs at Tenochtitlán.

Tenochtitlán, with a population of something over two hundred thousand, had forged an alliance with Texcoco and Tlacopan, two smaller lakeside cities. Together they dominated the area, but by the second quarter of the fifteenth century, leadership was clearly passing to the Aztecs. As newcomers to the region, the Aztecs felt a need to prove themselves worthy heirs to Teotihuacan, Tula, and the ancient culture of the Valley. They adopted the old religion but practiced it with a terrifying intensity. They waged perpetual war, usually with neighboring cities, to gain captives for their ceremonies. They built and constantly rebuilt and enlarged their Great Pyramid of the Sun. At its dedication in 1487, they sacrificed—if we can believe later accounts—about fourteen thousand people in a ceremony that went on for four days until the priests dropped from exhaustion. Each captive climbed the steep steps of the pyramid and was held by his wrists and ankles over the sacrificial slab while a priest cut open his breast, ripped out his heart, held it up to the sun, placed it inside the statue of a god, and then rolled the carcass down the steps so that parts of the body could later be eaten, mostly by members of the captor's family, but never by the captor himself. He fasted instead, and mourned the death of a worthy foe.

Human sacrifice was an ancient ritual in Mesoamerica, familiar to everyone. But the Aztecs practiced it on a scale that had no parallel anywhere else in the world. The need for thousands of victims each year created potential enemies everywhere. Though neighboring peoples shared the value system of the Aztecs, they nevertheless hated these conquerors from the north. After 1519, many of them would help the Spaniards bring down the Aztecs. By contrast, Spanish invaders found only a few allies in the Andes, where resistance in the name of the Inca would persist for most of the sixteenth century and would even revive in the late eighteenth century, 250 years after the conquest. No one in the Valley of Mexico demanded the restoration of Aztec rule.

Urban Cultures North of Mexico

North of Mexico, from 1500 B.C.E. to about A.D. 1700, three distinct "moundbuilding" societies succeeded each other and exerted a cultural influence over broad areas. Named for the distinctive earthen mounds that they constructed, these cultures arose near the Ohio and Mississippi Rivers, or their tributaries. The earliest moundbuilders became semisedentary even before learning to grow crops. Fish, game, and the lush vegetation of the river valleys sustained them for most of the year and enabled them to erect permanent dwellings.

Apart from the Red Paint People, the oldest moundbuilding culture flourished in northeastern Louisiana from 1500 to 700 B.C.E. Its chief city, Poverty Point (named for a nineteenth-century plantation), contained perhaps five thousand inhabitants at its peak around 1000 B.C.E. During the second, or Adena-Hopewell phase from 500 B.C.E. to A.D. 400, another distinctive moundbuilding society emerged in the Ohio Valley. Its mounds were increasingly elaborate burial sites, which indicate belief in an afterlife. Moundbuilding communities participated in a commerce that spanned most of the continent between the Appalachians and the Rockies, the Great Lakes and the Gulf of Mexico. Obsidian from the Yellowstone Valley in the Far West, copper

from the Great Lakes Basin, and shells from the Gulf are all buried in the Adena-Hopewell mounds. Both the moundbuilding and the long-distance trade largely ceased after A.D. 400, for reasons that remain unclear. The people even stopped growing corn for a few centuries.

Moundbuilding revived in a final Mississippian phase between A.D. 1000 and 1700. This culture dominated the Mississippi River valley from St. Louis to Natchez, with the largest center at Cahokia, near modern St. Louis, and another important one at Moundville in Alabama. Ordinary people became "Stinkards" in this culture, while some families had elite status, and the Great Sun ruled with authority and was transported by litter from place to place. When he died, some of his wives, relatives, and retainers even volunteered to be sacrificed at his funeral and join him in the afterlife. Burial mounds thus became much grander in Mississippian communities. The Indians interred their leaders within the mounds but also topped them with elaborate places of worship and residences for the priests and the "Great Suns" who ruled these highly stratified societies.

The city of Cahokia flourished from A.D. 900 to 1250 and may have had over thirty thousand inhabitants at its peak, making it the largest city north of Mexico and almost as populous as the contemporary Toltec capital at Tula. Cahokia's enormous central mound, one hundred feet high, is the world's largest earthen work and the fourth largest structure built in pre-Columbian America. Similarities with Mesoamerican practices and artifacts have led many scholars to look for direct links between the two cultures. But although it was possible to travel between the Mississippi and Mesoamerica, by land or water, no Mesoamerican artifacts have yet been found in the southeastern United States.

Other complex societies emerged in the semiarid Southwest, among them the Hohokam, the Anasazi, and the Pueblo. The Hohokam Indians settled in what is now central Arizona somewhere between 300 B.C.E. and A.D. 300. Their irrigation system, consisting of several hundred miles of canals, produced two harvests a year. They also wove cotton cloth and made pottery with a distinctive red color. They traded with places as distant as California and Mesoamerica and even imported a version of the Mesoamerican ball game. Perhaps because unceasing irrigation had increased the salinity of the soil, this

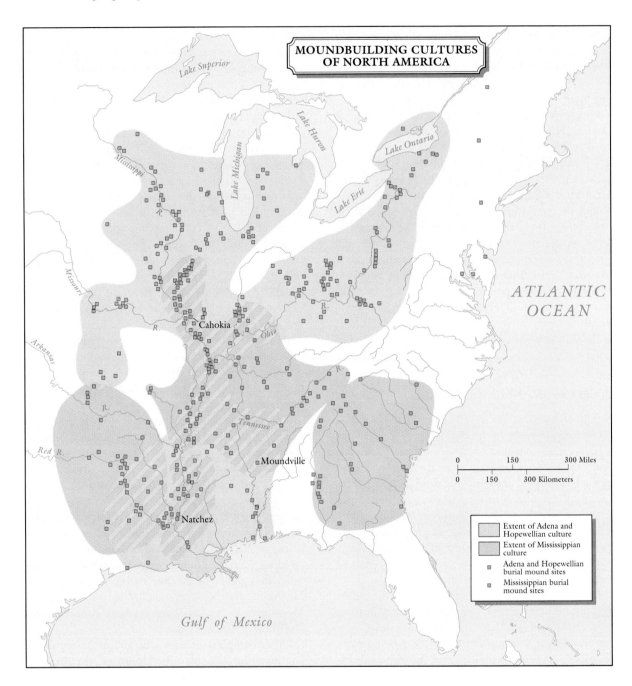

culture, after enduring for more than a thousand years, went into irreversible decline by 1450.

Even more tantalizing and mysterious is the brief flowering of the Anasazi (a Navajo word meaning "the ancient ones"), a cliff-dwelling people who have left behind some remarkable artifacts at Chaco Canyon in New Mexico, at Mesa Verde in Colorado, and at other sites. In their caves and cliffs they constructed apartment dwellings five stories high with as many as five hundred rooms and elegant and spacious kivas, or meeting rooms for religious functions. The Anasazi were superb astronomers. Through an arrangement of rock slabs, open to the sun and moon at the mouth of a cave, and of spirals on the interior wall that plotted the movement of the sun and moon, they created a calendar with

Woodcut of a Queen, or the Wife of a "Great Sun" of the Mississippian Moundbuilders, Being Carried on a Litter The engraving is by Theodore de Bry, and was executed in the sixteenth century.

Cahokia Lloyd Kennett Townsend's modern depiction of Cahokia at the height of its power, in the twelfth or thirteenth century.

which they could track the summer and winter solstices and even the nineteen-year cycles of the moon, an astronomical refinement Europeans had not yet achieved. To get to their fields and to bring in lumber and other distant supplies, they built a network of roads that ran for scores of miles in several directions. They achieved most of these feats over a period of about two centuries, though Anasazi pottery has been found that dates from much earlier times. In the last quarter of the thirteenth century, apparently overwhelmed by a prolonged drought and hostile invaders, they abandoned their principal sites. The Pueblo Indians claim descent from these people. Pueblo architecture most closely resembles that of the Anasazi.

Contact and Cultural Misunderstandings

After the voyage of Columbus, the peoples of Europe and America, both with pasts of great antiquity, confronted each other. Mutual understanding was unlikely except on the most superficial level. Nothing in the histories of Europeans or Indians had prepared either of them for the encounter. The scholars of Renaissance Europe, busily engaged in recovering the wonders of ancient Greece and Rome, were becoming increasingly aware of the differences between these classical or pagan cultures and the Christian values of the Middle Ages. They were developing a strong sense of their own history, an awareness that their past had been quite different from their present.

They were also used to dealing with Moslem "infidels," whom they regarded as terribly alien but whose monotheistic beliefs were in fact not all that different from their own. And they understood that East Asia was neither classical nor Christian, not Islamic or "barbaric." But none of this experience prepared them for what they found in America.

When Christians encountered American Indians, they had trouble understanding how such people could exist at all. The Bible, they were certain, had recorded the creation of all mankind, but it never mentioned these people. From which of the sons of Noah had they descended? Were they perhaps the "lost ten tribes" of Israel? This idea was first suggested by Spanish missionaries and would later become a favorite hypothesis among British Protestants. Some theologians, such as the Spaniard Juan Ginés de Sepúlveda, tried to resolve this dilemma by arguing that Indians were animals without souls, not human beings at all. The pope and the royal courts of Portugal and Spain listened instead to a Dominican missionary, Fray Bartholomé de Las Casas, who passionately defended the Indians' humanity. But, asked Europeans, if Indians (and Asians) did possess immortal souls, would a compassionate God have left them in utter darkness for centuries without making the Gospel known to them? Rejecting that possibility, some early Catholic missionaries concluded that

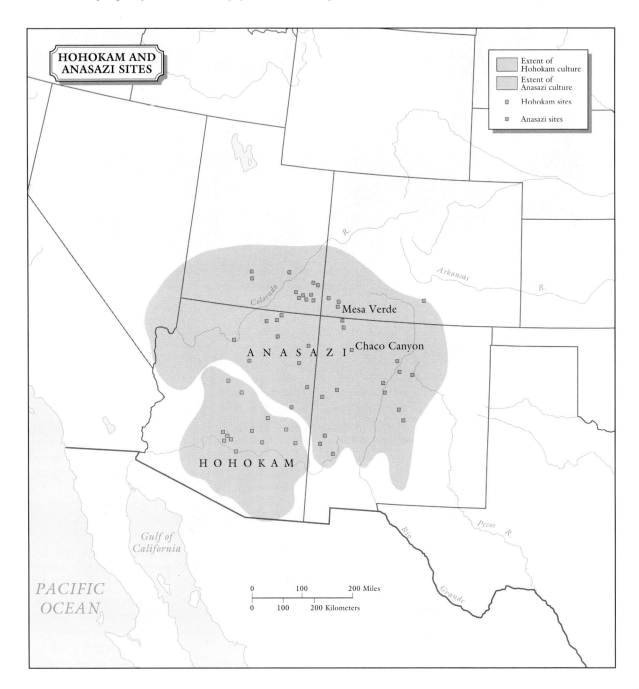

one of the apostles must have visited America (and India) and that the Indians must have rejected his message. The Portuguese claimed in the 1520s that they had discovered the tomb of St. Thomas the Doubter in India, and then in 1549 a Jesuit claimed to have found Thomas's footprint in Brazil. If only to satisfy the spiritual yearnings of Europeans overseas, St. Thomas got around!

To European Christians who encountered the sacrificial temples, skull racks, and snake motifs of Mesoamerica, one conclusion seemed inevitable. These Indians wallowed hopelessly in the overt worship of Satan. Their statues and even their writings had to be destroyed.

Human sacrifice and ritual cannibalism were indeed widespread throughout the Americas, although

Pueblo Bonito A modern imagining of Pueblo Bonito at its height in the thirteenth century. The circular structures are the tops of kivas.

Modern Restoration of an Anasazi Kiva This kiva, or meeting room, is underground and is usually accessed by ladder through a hole in its ceiling.

Aztec Skull Rack Altar   This rack held the skulls of hundreds of sacrificial victims and shocked the invading Spaniards.

nowhere else on the two continents did the scale approach that practiced by the Aztecs. The Incas, whose creation myth resembled that of Mesoamerica, offered an occasional victim to the sun or to some other god. The Indians of eastern North America frequently tortured to death their adult male captives, and every Indian warrior was taught from boyhood how to endure such torments. Christians were shocked by human sacrifice and found cannibalism revolting, but some of their own practices seemed similar to the Indians. In the sixteenth and seventeenth centuries, for example, Europeans burned or hanged hundreds of thousands of people, usually grandmothers, for conversing with the wrong spirits — that is, for witchcraft. The Spanish Inquisition burned thousands of heretics. To outsiders these executions awkwardly resembled human sacrifice.

The dilemma that Indians posed for Europeans emerged almost at once. On his second voyage, Columbus brought the first missionaries to the Americas. After one of them preached to a group of Tainos and presented them with some holy images, the Indians "left the chapel, . . . flung the images to the ground, covered them with a heap of earth, and pissed upon it." The governor, a brother of Colum-

bus, had them burned alive. The Indians probably saw this punishment as a form of human sacrifice to a vengeful god. They had no way of grasping the Christian distinction between human sacrifice and punishment for desecration.

The moral message conveyed by Christians was also ambiguous. Missionaries were eager to bring news of the Christ, how He had died to save mankind from sin. Catholic worship, then as now, centered on the Mass, the Eucharist, in which a priest turns bread and wine into the literal body and blood of Christ. "Except ye eat the flesh of the Son of man, and drink his blood," Jesus told his disciples (John 6:53), "ye have no life in you." Most Protestants also accepted this sacrament but interpreted it symbolically, not literally. To the Indians, however, the Christians seemed to be a people who ate their own god but grew outraged at the lesser matter of sacrificing a human being or consuming human flesh to please an Indian god.

When Europeans offered salvation to Indians who converted, the Indians concluded that the converts would spend the afterlife with the souls of Europeans, separated forever from their own ancestors, whose memory they revered. Neither side fully recognized these obstacles to mutual understanding. Although early Christian missionaries converted thousands of Indians, the results were, at best, mixed. Some Indians willingly abandoned their previous beliefs, while others strongly resisted Christian doctrines. Most converts found ways to accommodate Christian practices while continuing many of their old religious rituals, often in secret.

Such misunderstandings multiplied as Indians and Europeans came into closer contact. Both waged war, but with different objectives. Europeans tried to settle matters on a battlefield and expected to kill many enemies. Indians fought mostly to obtain captives, whether for sacrifice (as with the Aztecs) or to replace tribal losses through adoption (as with the Iroquois). To them, massive deaths on the battlefield were almost a blasphemy, an appalling waste of life that could in no way appease the gods. Europeans and Indians also differed profoundly on what kinds of acts constituted atrocities. The torture and ritual sacrifice of captives horrified Europeans; the execution of heretics appalled Indians.

Indian social organization also differed fundamentally from that of Europeans. European men owned almost all property, set the rules of inheritance, farmed the land, and performed nearly all public functions. Among many Indian peoples, especially those first encountered by Europeans north of Mexico, descent was matrilineal and women owned nearly all movable property. In semisedentary cultures, women also did the farming, and they often could demand a war or try to prevent one, although the final decision rested with men. When Europeans tried to transform warriors into farmers, Indian males resisted bitterly, protesting that they were being turned into women. Only over fully sedentary peoples were Europeans able to impose direct rule because there they could build upon the social hierarchy, division of labor, and system of tribute already in place.

CONQUEST AND CATASTROPHE

Spanish *conquistadores,* or conquerors, led small armies that rarely exceeded a thousand men. Yet they subdued two empires much larger than Spain itself and then looked around for more worlds to vanquish. There, beyond the great empires, Indians had greater success in resisting them.

Cortés, Pizarro, and Their Imitators

When Cortés entered Tenochtitlán in 1519, he seized Moctezuma, the Aztec ruler, as prisoner and hostage. Though overwhelmingly outnumbered, Cortés and his men began to destroy Aztec religious objects, replacing them with images of the Virgin Mary or other Catholic saints. In response, the Aztecs rose against the intruders, Moctezuma was killed, and the Spaniards were driven out with heavy losses. But the smallpox they left behind was soon killing Aztecs by the thousands. Cortés found refuge with the nearby Tlaxcalans, a proudly independent people who had never submitted to Aztec rule. With thousands of their warriors, he returned the next year, built several warships armed with cannon to dominate Lake Texcoco, and systematically destroyed Tenochtitlán. That was something he had not wanted to do. Cortés had intended to leave the great city intact, not wreck it, but he and his enemies found no common understanding that would allow them to stop fighting before Tenochtitlán lay in ruins. A literate people, the Aztecs expressed their grief in a poem:

> We have pounded our hands in despair
> against the adobe walls,
> for our inheritance, our city, is lost and dead.
> The shields of our warriors were its defense,
> but they could not save it.
>
> We have chewed dry twigs and salt grasses;
> we have filled our mouths with dust and bits of adobe;
> we have eaten lizards, rats and worms. . . .

With royal support from Spain, the *conquistadores* established themselves as a new imperial government in Mesoamerica, looted all the precious metals they could find, and built Mexico City on the ruins of Tenochtitlán.

Rumors abounded about an even richer empire far to the south, and in 1531–1532 Francisco Pizarro finally located the Inca Empire high in the Andes. Smallpox had preceded him and had killed the reigning Inca. In the civil war that followed, Atahualpa had defeated his brother to become the new Inca. Pizarro captured Atahualpa, held him hostage, and managed to win a few allies from among the Inca's recent enemies. Atahualpa filled his throne room with precious metals as a truly royal ransom, but Pizarro had him strangled anyway. Tens of thousands of angry Indians besieged the Spaniards for months in Cuzco, the Inca capital, but Pizarro, though vastly outnumbered, just managed to hold out and finally

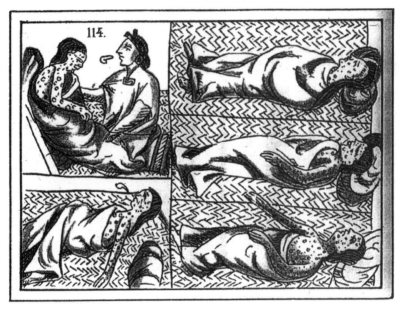

The Ravages of Smallpox   The impact of smallpox on the Aztecs, as depicted in the Aztec Codex.

Mita (or Tribute) Labor in the Silver Mines   The silver mines of Potosí, in the Andes, are about two miles above sea level. The work, as depicted in Theodore de Bry's 1603 engraving, was extremely onerous and often dangerous.

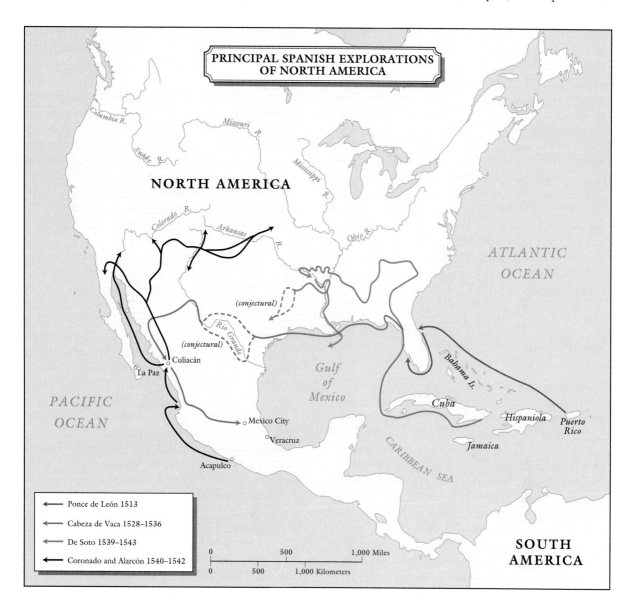

PRINCIPAL SPANISH EXPLORATIONS
OF NORTH AMERICA

prevailed. After subduing the insurgents, the Spanish established a new capital at Lima on the coast.

In a little more than ten years, some hundreds of Spanish soldiers with thousands of Indian allies had conquered two enormous empires with a combined population perhaps five times greater than that of all Spain. But only in the 1540s did the Spanish finally locate the bonanza they had been seeking. The fabulous silver mines at Potosí in present-day Bolivia and other smaller lodes in Mexico became the source of Spain's wealth and power for the next hundred years. So wondrous did the exploits of the *conquistadores* seem by then that anything became believable,

including rumors that cities of pure gold lay somewhere in the interior of North America.

The epic journey of Alvar Núñez Cabeza de Vaca is a case in point. One of four survivors of Pánfilo de Narváez's disastrous 1528 expedition to Florida, Cabeza de Vaca made his way back to Mexico City in 1536 after an overland journey that took him from Florida through Texas and northern Mexico. In a published report of his adventures, he made a single, intriguing reference to Indian tales of great and populous cities to the north, and this claim soon became magnified into stories about "golden cities." Hernando de Soto landed in Florida in 1539 and marched through much of the southeastern United States in quest of these treasures. He crossed the Mississippi in 1541, wandered through the Ozarks and eastern Oklahoma, and then marched back to the great river. He died there in 1542. His companions continued to explore for another year before returning to Spanish territory. Farther west, an armor-clad Francisco Vasquez de Coronado clanked into New Mexico and Arizona, where he encountered several Pueblo towns but no golden cities. The expedition "discovered" the Grand Canyon, then headed east into Texas and as far north as Kansas before returning to Mexico in 1542. North of Mexico, Indians menaced and sometimes even defeated Spanish soldiers, who finally gave up, but left their diseases behind. There were no cities of gold and no new empires to match those of the Aztecs and Incas.

The Spanish Empire and Demographic Catastrophe

By the late sixteenth century, the Spanish empire had emerged as a system of direct colonial rule in Mexico and Peru, protected by a strong defensive perimeter in the Caribbean, and surrounded by a series of frontier missions, extending in the north into Florida, New Mexico, and eventually California. In 1570 the Jesuits even established a mission as far north as Virginia. When an expedition of Spaniards reconnoitered Chesapeake Bay at mid-century, they took the young son of a local chief back to Spain, where he was baptized as Don Luis and given a European education. Then he went back to his people to help the Jesuits with their mission. When Don Luis celebrated his homecoming in 1571 by taking several wives, the Jesuits reproached him for his sin. He retaliated by wiping out the mission. Historian Carl Bridenbaugh has argued that his Indian name then became Opechancanough (which means "he whose soul is white"), the war chief who later attacked the English at Jamestown (see Chapter 2). More likely, Don Luis was an uncle or cousin of that famous warrior.

The Spaniards brought new systems of labor and new religious institutions to their overseas colonies, although both were altered by local conditions. The first Spanish rulers in Mexico and Peru relied on the same system of labor tribute that had helped to depopulate the Greater Antilles. Called the *encomienda,*

this system permitted the holder, or *encomendero,* to claim labor from a particular Indian district for a stated period of time. *Encomienda* worked because it resembled the way the Aztecs and the Incas had routinely levied labor for their own massive public buildings and irrigation projects. In time, the Spanish Crown intervened to correct abuses and to limit labor tribute to projects it had itself initiated, such as mining and the construction of churches or other public buildings. Spanish settlers resisted the reforms at first but then shifted from demanding labor to claiming land. In the countryside the *hacienda,* a large estate with its own crops and herds, became a familiar institution.

Although the Church never had enough clergy to meet its needs, it also became a massive presence during the sixteenth century. But America changed it, too. As missionaries acquired land and labor, they began to exhibit less concern for Indian souls. The Franciscans, the gentlest of Catholic religious orders in Europe, brutally and systematically tortured their Mayan converts in the 1560s whenever they were caught worshipping their old gods. To the Franciscans, the slightest lapse could mark a reversion to Satan-worship, with human sacrifice a likely consequence. They did not dare to be kind.

Most important of all, the Spaniards brought deadly microbes with them. Smallpox, which could be fatal but which most Europeans survived in childhood, devastated the Indians, who had almost no immunity to it. Even measles were often fatal, and common colds turned into pneumonia. When Cortés arrived in 1519, the Indian population of Mexico probably exceeded 15 million. By the 1620s, following wave after wave of killing epidemics, it finally bottomed at 700,000. It would not regain its pre-Spanish level until the 1950s. Peru suffered nearly as horribly. Its population fell from about 10 million in 1525 to 600,000 a century later. For the hemisphere as a whole, any given region probably lost 90 or 95 percent of its population within a century of sustained contact with Europeans. Lowland tropical areas suffered the heaviest casualties; in some of these places, all Indians died. Highland areas and sparsely settled regions fared somewhat better.

The Spanish monarchy spent much of the sixteenth century trying to keep abreast of these changes, but eventually it imposed administrative order on the unruly *conquistadores.* At the center of the imperial bureaucracy, in Seville, stood the Council of the Indies. It administered the three American viceroyalties of New Spain, Peru, and eventually New Granada, which were further subdivided into smaller *audiencias,* executive and judicial jurisdictions supervised by the viceroys. The Council appointed the viceroys and other major officials, who ruled from the new cities the Spaniards built with Indian labor at Havana, Mexico City, Lima, and elsewhere. Although rigidly centralized and autocratic in theory, the Spanish imperial system permitted a fair degree of initiative by local officials, if only because months or even years could elapse in trying to communicate across the empire's immense distances. "If death came from Spain," mused one official, "we should all live long lives."

Brazil

Portuguese Brazil was theoretically autocratic too, but it was divided into fourteen "captaincies," or provinces, and thus was far less centralized. The Portuguese invasion meant, not the direct rule of Indian peoples, but their displacement or enslavement. As the colonists on the northeast coast specialized in sugar production during the seventeenth century, Brazilian frontiersmen, or *bandeirantes,* foraged deep into the continent to enslave more Indians. Sometimes they even raided remote Spanish missions, rounded up the converts, and dragged them thousands of miles across mountains and through the jungle to be worked to death on the sugar plantations. On several occasions, while Brazil was ruled by Spain (see below), outraged missionaries persuaded the king to abolish slavery altogether. The aftermath revealed the limits of absolutism. Slavery continued without pause.

Global Colossus, Global Economy

American silver made the king of Spain the most powerful monarch in Christendom. Philip II (1556–1598) commanded by far the largest army in Europe, held the Ottoman Turks in check in the Mediterranean, and tried to suppress the Protestant Reformation that was spreading into the Netherlands and France (see Chapter 2). Philip had other ambitions as well. When the king of Portugal died without a direct heir, Philip claimed his throne in 1580,

The Martyrdom of San Felipe de Jesús (St. Philip of Jesus)
This event, which occurred in Nagasaki, Japan in 1597, is here depicted by an unknown Mexican sculptor in the seventeenth century. The art of the Spanish empire had a global reach. An event that happened in Japan is here commemorated in Spanish style by a Mexico City artist.

thereby uniting the entire Iberian Peninsula under one Christian prince for the first time since the fall of Rome. He thus brought together under his rule Portugal's Asian empire, Brazil, and Spain's American possessions. This colossus, the greatest empire the world had ever seen, also provided the framework for the first truly global economy. The Portuguese could continue importing spices and silks from Asia only by paying for them with the silver that Spain extracted from America. The union of Spain and Portugal lasted until the 1640s, when Portugal revolted and regained its independence.

The Spanish colossus became part of an even broader economic phenomenon. Serfdom had been Europe's predominant labor system in the early Middle Ages. It tied peasants to their lords and to the land. Although peasants were not free to move, neither could they be sold, and thus they were not slaves. Serfdom had been decaying in Western Europe since the twelfth century and was nearly gone by 1500. A system of free labor arose in its place,

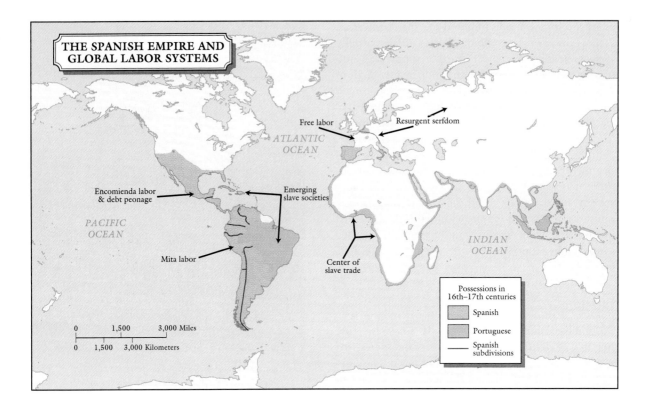

THE SPANISH EMPIRE AND GLOBAL LABOR SYSTEMS

and overseas expansion strengthened that trend in Western Europe. While free labor prevailed in the West European homeland, however, unfree labor systems took deep root all around Europe's periphery, and the two were structurally linked. In general, free labor reigned where populations were large and continued to grow. Large pools of labor kept wages low. But around the periphery of Western Europe, where land was cheap and labor expensive, coercive systems became the only efficient way for Europeans to extract from those areas the goods that they desired.

The forms of unfree labor varied greatly across space and time, from slavery to less brutal systems. In New Spain, as the Indian population dwindled, the practice of *encomienda* slowly yielded to debt peonage. Debts that could not be paid kept Indians tied to the emerging *haciendas* of the countryside. The mining of precious metals, on the other hand, was so dangerous and unpleasant that it almost always required a large degree of physical coercion. Similarly, any colonial region that devoted itself to the production of staple crops for sale in Europe also turned to unfree labor and eventually overt slavery. The pro-

duction of sugar first reduced Indians to bondage in the Caribbean and Brazil and then, as they died off, led to the importation of African slaves by the millions. Other staples—tobacco, rice, cotton, coffee—later followed roughly similar patterns. At first these crops were considered luxuries and commanded high prices. But as they became widely available on the world market, their prices fell steeply, profit margins contracted, and planters turned overwhelmingly to coerced labor. Even in Eastern Europe, which increasingly specialized in the production of cereal crops for sale in the more diversified West, serfdom vigorously revived. In Russia the condition of a serf became not all that different from that of a slave in one of the Atlantic empires. Serfs were even bought and sold.

Spain's rise had been spectacular, but the empire was also vulnerable. Silver from the Americas vastly expanded the Crown's ability to wage war, but the costs of continuous conflict, the inflation generated by a steady influx of silver, and the need to defend a much greater perimeter absorbed Spain's new resources and a great deal more. Between 1492 and

Arizona Indian Wall Painting of a Passing Spanish Expedition, Sixteenth Century   The horses may have been the first that these Indians ever saw.

1580 Spain's population grew from 4.9 million to 8 million. But over the course of the next century, it fell by 20 percent, mostly because of the escalating costs, both financial and human, of Spain's wars. As the population declined, taxes rose. Castile grew poorer, not richer, in its century and a half of imperial glory. Most of the wealth of the Indies went elsewhere — to merchants in Genoa, to manufacturers in Lombardy and the Low Countries, and to bankers in Augsburg.

EXPLANATIONS: PATTERNS OF CONQUEST, SUBMISSION, AND RESISTANCE

By the middle of the eighteenth century, those Europeans who gave serious consideration to the discovery of America and its global implications generally agreed that the whole process had been a moral disaster, possibly the worst in history. Conquest and settlement had killed millions of Indians, enslaved millions of Africans, and degraded Europeans. The benefits seemed small by comparison, even though economic gains were undeniably large by 1750. Had the cruelest of the conquerors been able to foresee the results of this process, asked the Abbé Raynal, would he have proceeded? "Is it to be imagined that there exists a being infernal enough," he responded, "to answer this question in the affirmative!" The success of the American Revolution, with its message of freedom and human rights, quieted this way of thinking for a time, but the critique has revived in recent years.

Modern historians, less moralistic than Raynal, also realize that he considerably *under*estimated the death toll. But they are more interested in finding explanations for what happened. Did "civilization" triumph over "savagery"? Did a superior social system vanquish an inferior one? If so, why was it easier for Europeans to conquer the most complex and hierarchical Indian cultures? And why were less complex societies, such as those that had frustrated de Soto and Coronado, able to resist more successfully?

The most compelling explanation for European success involves the prolonged isolation of the Americas from the rest of the world, although the Americas were not unique in this respect. Australia, New Zealand, and the Pacific islands (including

Hawaii) would later undergo the same process with just about the same results. Isolation explains Europe's technological advantages. If two peoples of equal ability are kept apart, those with the larger and more varied population will invent more things and learn more rapidly from one another. For example, the use of iron spread gradually through nearly all of Asia, Africa, and Europe. And even though Europeans knew little about China, they slowly acquired such Chinese inventions as the compass and gunpowder. But more than any other technological factor, far more than muskets or cannon or even horses, steel made military conquest possible. European armor stopped Indian spears and arrows, and European swords killed enemies rapidly without any need to reload.

Even more momentous were the biological consequences of isolation. European plants, once introduced into the Americas, thrived at the expense of native vegetation. For example, when British settlers first crossed the Appalachian mountains, they marveled at the lush quality of Kentucky bluegrass. They did not realize that they were looking at an accidental European import that had conquered the landscape even faster than they had. European animals also prevailed over potential American rivals. Horses multiplied at an astonishing rate in America, and wild herds moved north from Mexico faster than the Spaniards, to transform the way of life of the Apaches and the Sioux. Likewise, the lowly sparrow never had it so good until someone turned a few loose in North America. The same thing later happened to rabbits in Australia.

Among humans, the spread of European microbes had catastrophic effects. Their devastation of the Indian population remains the greatest tragedy yet uncovered in the history of mankind. The Indians' genetic makeup was more uniform than that of Europeans, Africans, or Asians. That is, the Indians were descended from a rather small sample of the total gene pool of Eurasia. Centuries spent in Beringia's forbidding climate had weeded out weaker people and killed the microbes that produce most diseases, although tuberculosis survived the crossing. The Indians first encountered by Europeans were bigger, stronger, and—at the very outset—healthier than the newcomers. But they died in appalling numbers because they had almost no resistance to the diseases the invaders brought with them. Apparently Indians did give syphilis, which was not nearly as deadly, to

the Europeans. Other American exports, such as corn, potatoes, and tomatoes, have greatly enriched the diet of the rest of the world. Historian Alfred W. Crosby has called this larger process the Columbian exchange. It ranks as one of the most important events of all time.

For thousands of years the Americas had been cut off from the rest of the globe. In Eurasia and Africa, the major cultures had existed in relative isolation, maintaining direct contacts only with their immediate neighbors. Islam, which shared borders with India, the East Indies, black Africa, and Europe, had been the principal mediator among these cultures and, in that era, was more tolerant than most Christians. Then suddenly, in just over one generation, daring European navigators supported by the crowns of Portugal and Spain joined the world together and challenged Islam's mediating role. Between 1492 and 1532 Europe, Africa, Asia, the Spice Islands, the Philippines, the Caribbean, Aztec Mexico, Inca Peru, and other parts of the Americas came into intense and often violent contact with one another. A few individuals gained much, and Spain acquired a military advantage within Europe that would last for the next hundred years. Nearly everybody else suffered, millions horribly, especially in the Americas and Africa. And Spain spent the rest of the sixteenth century trying to erect an imperial system that had a chance of imposing order on this turbulent reality.

But Spain had many enemies. The lure of wealth and land overseas would be just as attractive to them.

SUGGESTED READING

Brian M. Fagan, *The Great Journey: The Peopling of Ancient America* (1987); Stuart J. Fiedel, *Prehistory of the Americas,* 2nd ed. (1992); Alfred M. Josephy, ed., *America in 1492: The World of the Indian Peoples before the Arrival of Columbus* (1993); and Francis Jennings, *The Founders of America: How Indians Discovered the Land, Pioneered in It, and Created Great Classical Civilizations . . .* (1993) offer general discussions of pre-Columbian America. Joseph H. Greenberg, *Language in the Americas* (1987) and William M. Denevan, ed., *The Native Population of the Americas in 1492* (1976) are standard. Philip Kopper, *The Smithsonian Book of North American Indians before the Coming of the Europeans* (1986) is accurate, accessible, and wonderfully illustrated. Michael Coe, Dean Snow, and Elizabeth Benson, *Atlas of Ancient America* (1986) provides a narrative and maps for the major cultures of North and South America. Lynda Norene Shaffer, *Native Americans before 1492:*

The Moundbuilding Centers of the Eastern Woodlands (1992) provides a brief survey that covers thousands of years, while Thomas E. Emerson and R. Barry Lewis, eds., *Cahokia and the Hinterlands: Middle Mississippian Cultures of the Midwest* (1991) gives a series of detailed studies of the last cycle of moundbuilding. Frederich Katz, *The Ancient American Civilizations* (1972) remains an excellent introduction. Norman Hammond, *Ancient Maya Civilization* (1982); Michael D. Coe, *The Maya,* 3rd ed. (1984); Linda Schele and Mary Ellen Miller, *The Blood of Kings: Dynasty and Ritual in Maya Art* (1986); Linda Schele and David Freidel, *A Forest of Kings: The Untold Story of the Ancient Maya* (1990); and Inga Clendinnen, *Aztecs: An Interpretation* (1991) cover the complex cultures of the Americas. For the prehistory of the Pacific and Hawaii, see Peter Bellwood, *The Polynesians: Prehistory of an Island People,* rev. ed. (1987); and David E. Stannard, *Before the Horror: The Population of Hawaii on the Eve of Western Contact* (1989).

G. V. Scammell, *The First Imperial Age: European Overseas Expansion c. 1400–1715* (1989); Carlo M. Cipolla, *Guns, Sails, and Empire: Technological Innovation and the Early Phases of European Expansion 1400–1700* (1965); Charles Verlinden, *The Beginnings of Modern Colonization: Eleven Essays with an Introduction* (1970); Samuel Eliot Morison, *The European Discovery of America: The Northern Voyages, A.D. 500–1600* (1971) and Morison's *The European Discovery of America: The Southern Voyages, A.D. 1492–1616* (1974) trace the early expansion of Europe. P. E. Russell's elegant lecture, *Prince Henry the Navigator* (1960), greatly reduces Henry's importance. William D. Phillips, Jr., and Carla Rahn Phillips, *The Worlds of Christopher Columbus* (1992) is a strong, recent biography. Pauline Moffitt Watts, "Prophecy and Discovery: On the Spiritual Origins of Christopher Columbus's 'Enterprise of the Indies,'" *American Historical Review* 90 (1985): 73–102 explores the religious motives of Columbus, while Arthur Davies, "The Loss of the *Santa Maria,* Christmas Day, 1492," *American Historical Review* 58 (1952–53): 854–865 argues that Columbus scuttled his flagship. Alfred W. Crosby analyzes the long-term consequences of expansion in *The Columbian Exchange: Biological and Cultural Consequences of 1492* (1972) and in *Ecological Imperialism: The Biological Expansion of Europe, 900–1900* (1986).

J. D. Fage, *A History of West Africa: An Introductory Survey,* 4th ed. (1969), though aging, is still useful. John Thornton, *Africa and Africans in the Making of the Modern World, 1400–1680* (1992) insists that Africans retained control of their affairs, including the slave trade, before 1700. Patrick Manning, *Slavery and African Life: Occidental, Oriental, and African Slave Trades* (1990) emphasizes the devastating impact of the slave trade in the eighteenth and nineteenth centuries. Philip D. Curtin, *The Atlantic Slave Trade: A Census* (1969) is a classic, though modified by Paul E. Lovejoy, "The Volume of the Atlantic Slave Trade: A Synthesis," *Journal of African History* 23 (1982): 473–501. Lovejoy, "The Impact of the African Slave Trade on Africa: A Review of the Literature," *Journal of African History* 30 (1989): 365–94 is a strong introduction. David Brion Davis, *Slavery and Human Progress* (1984) is a meditation on the changing significance of slavery between the onset of European expansion and the abolition of the institution.

James Lockhart and Stuart B. Schwartz, *Early Latin America: A History of Colonial Spanish America and Brazil* (1983) is a superb survey. Charles R. Boxer, *The Portuguese Seaborne Empire: 1415–1825* (1969) is excellent. David E. Stannard, *American Holocaust: Columbus and the Conquest of the New World* (1992) is an angry account of the European conquest. Major studies of the early Spanish empire include J. H. Parry, *The Spanish Seaborne Empire* (1966); Carl O. Sauer, *The Early Spanish Main* (1966); Tzvetan Todorov, *The Conquest of America* (1984); Charles Gibson, *The Aztecs under Spanish Rule: A History of the Indians of the Valley of Mexico, 1519–1810* (1964); John Hemming, *The Conquest of the Incas* (1970); James Lockhart, *Spanish Peru, 1532–1560: A Colonial Society* (1968); David Noble Cook, *Demographic Collapse: Indian Peru, 1520–1620* (1981); and James Lockhart, "Encomienda and Hacienda: The Evolution of the Great Estate in the Spanish Indies," *Hispanic American Historical Review* 49 (1969): 411–29. John Hemming, *Red Gold: The Conquest of the Brazilian Indians, 1500–1760* (1978) is careful and sobering.

Immanuel Wallerstein, *The Modern World System: Capitalist Agriculture and the Origins of the European World Economy in the Sixteenth Century* (1974) and Fernand Braudel, *Capitalism and Material Life, 1400–1800* (1967) both explore the emergence of a global economy. Charles A. Levinson, ed., *Circa 1492: Art in the Age of Exploration* (1991) provides a global view of art in the same era.

Videos: The Nova series on PBS has produced two outstanding documentaries on pre-Columbian America. *Search for the First Americans* (1992) assembles evidence for very early occupancy of the Americas. *Secrets of the Lost Red Paint People* (1987) is a fascinating example of how archaeologists reconstruct the distant past and the surprises that this process creates. Another challenging program is *The Sun Dagger* (1982), narrated by Robert Redford, on Anasazi astronomy, available through Pacific Arts Publishing.

Chapter 2

The Challenge to Spain and the Spectrum of European Settlement

The crude housing shown in this modern reconstruction of Jamestown remained typical of Virginia and Maryland for the rest of the seventeenth century.

After 1600 the Spanish empire made few efforts to expand north of Mexico. The Spanish established missions in Florida and New Mexico, while their European rivals planted settlements along the North American coast. The French, the Dutch, and the English all contested Spanish control of the continent, a process that involved continuous challenges to the Indians who possessed the land. The French and the Dutch brought Indian hunters into the world market by trading European goods to them in exchange for furs. The English also engaged in the fur trade, but increasingly they coveted the land itself.

The societies that Europeans created in America differed as much from one another as they did from their parent cultures in Europe. Europeans, Indians, and Africans interacted in contrasting ways in this strange "new world." In Mexico and Peru, the Spaniards set themselves up as a European ruling class over a much larger Indian population of farmers, ar-

tisans, and miners. Spain's rivals created different kinds of colonies, though many colonies, including Virginia, eventually followed the precedent Spain set in the Caribbean by growing staple crops with imported African slaves. New France and New Netherland developed a thriving trade with semisedentary and even nomadic Indians without depriving them of their autonomy. In New England the Puritans relied upon free labor provided by hard-working family members.

CATHOLIC SPAIN, THE PROTESTANT CHALLENGE, AND AMERICA

Spain, the most militantly Catholic society in Europe, also exported much of this zeal to North America, where Florida and New Mexico became examples of the "soft" or idealistic side of Spanish

Spaniards Torturing Indians, as Depicted by Theodore de Bry, Late Sixteenth Century   Among Protestants in northern Europe, such images merged into a "black legend" of Spanish cruelty, which in turn helped to justify their own challenge to Spanish power overseas. But in practice their own behavior toward Indians was often as harsh as anything the Spaniards had done.

imperialism. Many of Spain's European enemies became Protestants in the sixteenth century. They had strong religious motives for exposing Spanish "cruelties" in the Americas, but most Protestants proved no more humane than the Spaniards once they began to deal directly with Indians.

The Spiritual Frontier of Spain in North America

After the failure of the Jesuits' Chesapeake mission in 1571 (see Chapter 1), Spain decided to treat the Indians of Florida and New Mexico with decency and fairness, partly so that they, in turn, could provide a wall of defense against the English and French. The Jesuits withdrew and Franciscans took their place. In 1573 Philip II issued the Royal Orders for New Discoveries, which made it illegal to enslave Indians or even attack them. Instead, unarmed priests would bring them together in missions and convert them into peaceful Catholic subjects of Spain. The Franciscans quickly discovered that, without military support, they were more likely to win martyrdom than converts. They reluctantly accepted military protection, but they were careful not to let the few soldiers who accompanied them behave like *conquistadores*.

Missionary work demanded commitment and faith, and the Franciscans had both. A belief in miracles also sustained them. In 1631 a mystical nun in Castile, María de Jesús de Agreda, claimed that angels had carried her across the Atlantic several times and that she preached to Indians in their own languages. When Pueblo Indians reported that a "Lady in Blue" once preached to them, the Franciscans put the two accounts together into a miraculous event that enchanted thousands for a century, even though the nun retracted most of her story in 1650.

At first Indian women willingly supplied the labor needed to build and sustain the missions of New Mexico and Florida. By 1630 about 86,000 Pueblo, Apache, and Navajo Indians of New Mexico had accepted baptism (as against two thousand in the major New England missions by 1675). They lived in a chain of missions north and south of Santa Fe, 1,500 arduous and dusty miles from the colonial capital at Mexico City. By mid-century there were thirty missions in Florida containing about 26,000 baptized Indians and covering an area extending some 250 miles from the Atlantic coast of what is now Georgia westward into the Florida panhandle. The Franciscans also tried, with limited success, to get their converts to wear European clothing. In 1671 the bishop of Havana counted 4,081 newly converted women in Florida who went about topless with their lower legs exposed. He ordered them to cover up.

In the second half of the seventeenth century, the zeal of the Franciscans began to slacken. Fewer priests took the trouble to master Indian languages, insisting instead that the Indians learn Spanish. For all of their good intentions, the missionaries regarded Indians as children and often whipped or shackled them for minor infractions. Disease also took a heavy toll. A declining Indian population made labor demands by the missionaries more onerous over time, and despite strong prohibitions, some Spaniards enslaved some Indians in both Florida and New Mexico. The spiritual possibilities of the early seventeenth century seemed far less promising by the 1670s. By then Florida also faced new encroachments from English Protestants.

The Protestant Reformation

By the time other powers felt strong enough to challenge Spain overseas, the Protestant Reformation had shattered the religious unity of Europe. In November 1517, a little more than one year before

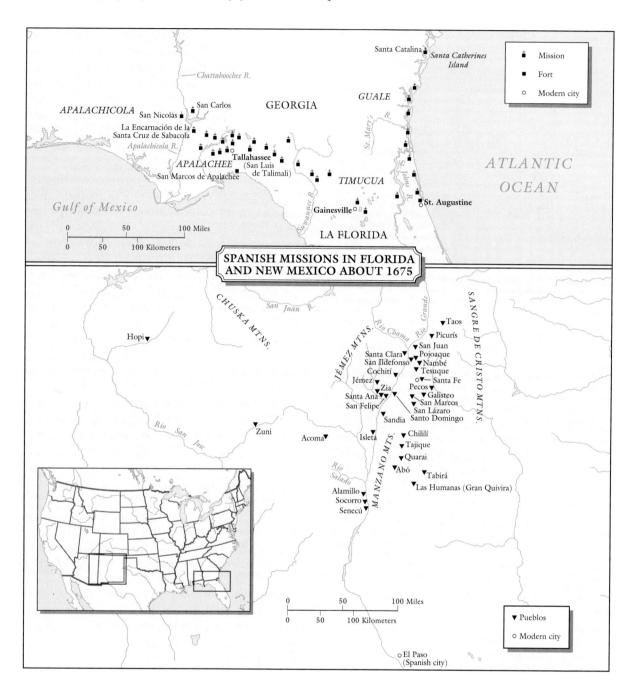

Cortés landed at Vera Cruz, Martin Luther nailed his Ninety-Five Theses to the cathedral door at Wittenberg in the German duchy of Saxony and launched the Reformation. No human act, or "good work," can ever be meritorious in the sight of God, Luther insisted. "Work righteousness" must lead to damnation. Salvation comes through faith alone, and God grants saving faith only to those who hear His Word preached to them, struggle to understand it, and admit that they are worthless without God's grace. Within a generation, the states of northern Germany and Scandinavia had embraced Lutheranism, but the Lutheran Church never played a major role in founding colonies overseas. Calvinism did.

John Calvin, a French Protestant who published *The Institutes of the Christian Religion* in 1536, put his principles into practice in the Swiss canton of Geneva, which became a center of militant Protestantism after 1541. The Huguenot movement in France, the Dutch Reformed Church in the Netherlands, and the Presbyterian Kirk (or Church) of Scotland all tried to implement Calvin's principles. In England the formal doctrine, but not the liturgy, of the Church of England also became Calvinist, prompting a reform movement, Puritanism, to challenge the established church as insufficiently Calvinist. Calvinists won highly significant victories against Catholic opponents within Europe in the last half of the sixteenth century, and eventually Puritans carried their religious vision across the Atlantic to New England.

Calvinists rejected papal supremacy, the seven sacraments (most Protestants kept only baptism and the Lord's Supper), clerical celibacy, veneration of the saints, and the acts of charity and the penitential rituals by which Catholics tried to earn grace and store up merits. Protestants denounced these rites as work righteousness. Calvin seized on Luther's principle of predestination and gave it central importance. According to that doctrine, God has decreed, even before He created the world, who will be saved and who will be damned. Christ died, Calvin insisted, not for *all* humankind, but only for God's elect. Calvinists retained the Lord's Supper, but in denying that Christ is physically present in the bread and wine, they broke with Luther as well as Rome. Because salvation and damnation were beyond human power to alter, Calvinists—especially English Puritans—felt a compelling inner need to find out whether or not they were saved. They struggled to recognize in themselves a true conversion experience, the process by which God's elect discovered that they had been chosen.

THE CHALLENGE TO SPAIN

In the wake of the Protestant Reformation, Spain faced challenges in Europe and abroad from France, the Netherlands, and England. Until 1559 France was the main threat, with Italy as the battleground, but Spain won that phase. In the 1560s, with France embroiled in its own civil wars between Catholics

and Huguenots, a new challenge came from the seventeen provinces of the Netherlands, which Spain ruled. The Dutch rebelled against the heavy taxes, bureaucratic reorganization, and severe Catholic orthodoxy imposed by Philip II. As Spanish armies put down the rebellion in the ten southern provinces (modern Belgium), Protestants and merchants fled north. Many went to Amsterdam, which replaced Spanish-controlled Antwerp as the leading economic center of northern Europe. The seven northern provinces gradually took shape as the Dutch republic, or the United Provinces of the Netherlands. The Dutch turned their resistance into a war for independence from Catholic Spain. The conflict went on for eighty years until 1648. It drained Spanish resources, and it spread to Asia, Africa, and America. By contrast, England long remained on the periphery of this triangular struggle among Spain, France, and the Netherlands, but in the long run the English became the biggest winners overseas.

The French Challenge

About 16 million people lived in France in 1500, more than three times the population of Spain. The French made a few stabs at overseas expansion in the sixteenth century, but with little success. "The sun shines for me as for the others," growled King Francis I of France when reminded that the pope had divided all non-Christian lands between Spain and Portugal. "I should like to see the clause of Adam's will which excludes me from a share of the world." Anticipating the position of Spain's other challengers, he insisted that only by occupying a distant land could one acquire a valid claim to it.

Early French Explorers   In 1524 Francis dispatched Giovanni da Verrazzano, an Italian, to America in search of a northwest passage to Asia after Magellan's voyage revealed how difficult it was to sail around South America and across the vast Pacific. Verrazzano explored the North American coast from the Carolinas to Nova Scotia and noted that Manhattan Island had superb potential as a harbor. Between 1534 and 1543 Jacques Cartier made three voyages to North America. He sailed up the St. Lawrence River in search of a wealthy kingdom, Saguenay, rumored to be in the interior. Instead he discovered the severity of a Canadian winter and gave up. The French ignored Canada for the rest of the century, except

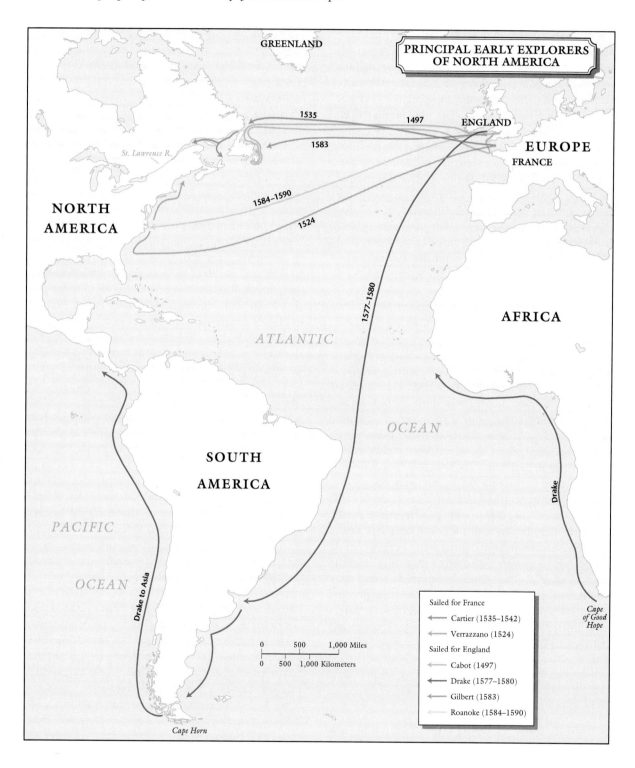

GREENLAND

PRINCIPAL EARLY EXPLORERS OF NORTH AMERICA

1535   1497   ENGLAND

EUROPE

FRANCE

1583

St. Lawrence R.

NORTH AMERICA

1584–1590

1524

AFRICA

ATLANTIC

1577–1580

OCEAN

SOUTH AMERICA

Drake

PACIFIC

OCEAN

Drake to Asia

Cape of Good Hope

Sailed for France
← Cartier (1535–1542)
← Verrazzano (1524)
Sailed for England
← Cabot (1497)
← Drake (1577–1580)
← Gilbert (1583)
← Roanoke (1584–1590)

| 0 | 500 | 1,000 Miles |
| 0 | 500 | 1,000 Kilometers |

Cape Horn

for fishermen, who were already descending on Newfoundland each year, and for the occasional maritime fur trader after 1580.

By the 1550s the French concentrated on warmer climates. Some Huguenots tried unsuccessfully to dislodge the Portuguese from Brazil. French corsairs sacked Havana, prompting Spain to turn it into a fortified, year-round naval base under the able command of Admiral Pedro Menéndez de Avilés. In 1565, after Huguenots planted a settlement on the Carolina coast (they called it Florida), Menéndez attacked them, talked them into surrendering, and then executed every man who refused to swear loyalty to the Catholic faith.

In France the wars of religion between Catholics and Huguenots blocked further efforts at expansion for the rest of the century. In 1598 King Henry IV, a Protestant, converted to Catholicism and granted limited toleration to Huguenots through the Edict of Nantes, thus ending the civil wars. Henry was a *politique*, a man who insisted that the survival of the state must take precedence over religious differences. Moreover, he believed in toleration for its own sake. Another *politique* and admirer of Henry was the Catholic soldier and explorer, Samuel de Champlain, who with aristocratic support revived French colonization efforts after 1600.

The Beginnings of New France   Champlain, who may have been born a Huguenot, believed that Catholics and Huguenots could work together, Europeanize the Indians, convert them, and even marry them. Before his death in 1635, he made eleven voyages to Canada. During his second trip (1604–1606), he planted a predominantly Huguenot settlement in Acadia (Nova Scotia). On his next voyage in 1608 he sailed up the St. Lawrence, established friendly relations with the Montagnais, Algonquin, and Huron Indians, and founded Quebec. "Our sons shall wed your daughters," he told one group of Algonquians, "and we shall be one people." Although many Frenchmen cohabited with Indian women, only fifteen formal marriages took place between them in the seventeenth century. But Champlain's friendship toward the Indians of the St. Lawrence Valley also had some dangerous and unpleasant consequences. It soon drew him into their wars against the Iroquois Five Nations farther south. At times, Iroquois hostility very nearly destroyed New France.

Champlain failed in his effort to bring Catholics and Protestants together in harmony. The Acadian colony had a Catholic priest and a Huguenot minister who exasperated the settlers with their endless wrangling over theology. When both died of scurvy, the settlers buried them in a common grave to see whether they could get along better dead than alive.

Although Huguenot merchants in France were eager to trade with Canada, few Protestants settled in Quebec. Huguenot ministers showed no interest in converting the Indians, whereas Catholics were committed to missionary work. Their efforts won the support of French aristocrats at home. To end the bickering, France declared in 1625 that only the Catholic faith could be practiced in New France. So ended Champlain's dream of a colony more tolerant than the parent society. Acadia soon became Catholic as well.

The early history of New France is a tale of missionaries and furs, of attempts to convert the Indians and of efforts to trade with them. These goals were often incompatible, as is illustrated by the career of Etienne Brûlé, the first French *coureur de bois* (roamer of the woods). Champlain left this teenage lad with the Indians in the winter of 1610 to learn their languages and customs. Brûlé absorbed much more than that. He enjoyed hunting, the sexual permissiveness of Indian culture, and the chance to go where no European had ever been. He soon forgot most of his religious training. Once when he was about to be tortured to death by hostile Indians, he tried to cry out to God, but, ominously, the only prayer he could remember was grace before meals. In desperation he flashed a religious medal, and when a thunder clap signaled divine approval, the Indians let him go. But he learned little from that experience. In 1632 he was caught robbing an Indian grave and was executed and eaten by the injured tribe. *Coureurs de bois*, such as Brûlé, did much for the fur trade but made life difficult for the missionaries.

The Jesuit Missions   With the arrival of the Jesuits in force by 1630, French missionaries made heroic efforts to bring Christ to the wilderness. The Society of Jesus, or Jesuits, emerged in the sixteenth century as the best educated and most militant religious order in the Catholic church. Uncompromising in their opposition to Protestants, Jesuits proved remarkably flexible in dealing with non-Christian peoples, from China to North America. Other missionaries insisted that Indians must be Europeanized before they could be converted, but the Jesuits disagreed. They saw nothing contradictory about a nation of Christians retaining Indian customs, provided these practices could be brought into conformity with Catholic morality. Many Jesuits tried to protect their converts from contamination by the *coureurs de bois*.

Samuel de Champlain's Drawing of an Early Battle with the Iroquois

After mastering several Algonquian and Iroquoian dialects, the Jesuits concentrated on converting the five confederated Huron nations. The Jesuits baptized several thousand Hurons, but their success antagonized Indians still attached to their own rituals. Then in the mid-1640s, smallpox devastated the Hurons. When Jesuits baptized hundreds of dying victims, other Indians noted that death usually followed this mysterious rite. Resistance grew stronger. A second disaster occurred when the Iroquois attacked the Hurons, defeated and scattered them, and even threatened the very survival of New France.

Although Jesuit efforts produced some famous martyrs, such as Isaac Jogues and Jean de Brebeuf, the missionary effort slowly lost ground to the fur trade and other economic pursuits in the St. Lawrence Valley, especially after the French Crown assumed direct control of the colony in 1663. Despite these setbacks, French Jesuits mastered Indian languages, lived in Indian villages, accepted most Indian customs, and converted ten thousand Indians in forty years, far more than all English missionaries throughout the entire colonial era.

New France under Louis XIV   The fur trade and the missions characterized New France throughout its history, but royal intervention transformed Canada after 1663, when Louis XIV and his minister, Jean-Baptiste Colbert, took direct charge of the colony. The two men tried to turn New France into a model absolutist society — peaceful, orderly, and deferential. Government centered upon two appointive officials, a governor general responsible for military and diplomatic affairs, and an *intendant* who administered the system of justice (which was made affordable to everyone, partly by banning lawyers). Apart from a few import duties, there were no taxes, and the church tithe was set at half its rate in France.

The governor appointed all militia officers, who earned promotions through merit. Unlike France, offices were not for sale in the colony. When the Crown sent professional soldiers to New France beginning in the 1660s, the governor put experienced Canadian officers, who knew the woodlands, in charge of these men, a decision that had no parallel in the English colonies. To increase the population, Colbert shipped 774 young women to the St. Lawrence to provide brides for settlers and soldiers. He offered bonuses to couples who produced large families, and he threatened to fine fathers whose children failed to marry in their teens. Yet when Louis XIV began to persecute Huguenots and in 1685

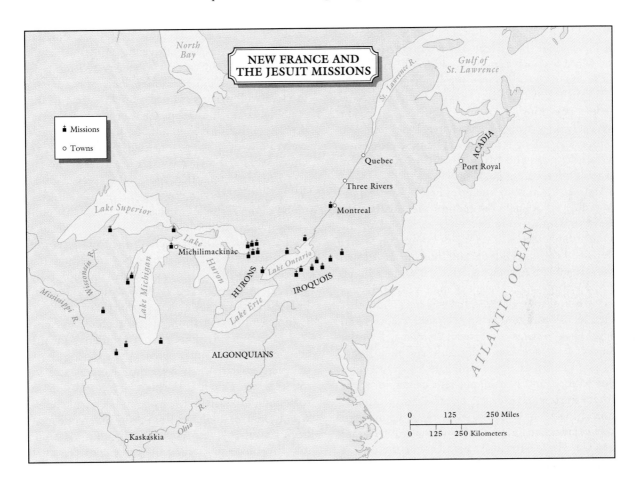

even revoked the Edict of Nantes which had given them toleration, the government refused to let the victims emigrate to New France. Between 1663 and 1700 the population of New France increased anyway, from three thousand to about fourteen thousand, although close to 70 percent of the ten thousand people who came to the colony from France went back to the mother country, usually to claim a tiny inheritance. About one-fourth of the population concentrated in three cities—Quebec, Three Rivers, and Montreal, the largest and the center of the fur trade.

Colbert encouraged the development of agriculture in the St. Lawrence Valley, and by the 1690s Canada produced enough wheat to feed itself and to maintain its *habitants*, or settlers, at a level of comfort about equal to that in New England at the same time. A new class of *seigneurs*, or landed gentry,

claimed most of the land between Quebec and Montreal, but their feudal privileges were few, and they never exercised the kind of political power proper to aristocrats in France. Few of them, for example, became militia captains, an office open to ordinary *habitants*. Yet when the church was also the *seigneur*, as often happened in the countryside near Quebec and Montreal, the obligations imposed on farmers could be considerable.

The French Court was less successful in challenging the *coureurs de bois*, although over time a stint in the forests became something that a man did once or twice in his youth before settling down. Colbert even tried to forbid Frenchmen from entering Indian territory at all by confining the fur trade to annual fairs at Montreal and Quebec. The Indians would then have to come to the settlers, not the settlers to the Indians. This policy failed and even led, by 1700, to a quiet rebellion in the west. Hundreds of Frenchmen simply settled down on the banks of the Mississippi between the missions of Cahokia and Kaskaskia in what became the Illinois country. By 1750 these communities contained three thousand people, one-third of whom were African slaves. The settlers rejected *seigneurs*, feudal dues, tithes, and even compulsory militia service. Most became prosperous wheat farmers, and many took Christian Indian brides from the missions.

Canada was not the center of French overseas activity for very long. In the century after 1660 its entire population never exceeded one-third of the population of the single English colony of Massachusetts. Like other Europeans, most of the French who crossed the Atlantic preferred the warmer climes of the Caribbean. For much of the seventeenth century the French in the West Indies joined with other enemies of Spain to prey upon Spanish colonies and ships. They even gave the word "buccaneer" to the English language. Gradually, however, they transformed the islands of St. Domingue (modern Haiti), Guadeloupe, and Martinique into centers of sugar production, where a small planter class prospered from the labor of thousands of slaves. In the imperial scale of things, the sugar islands were worth far more than Canada. St. Domingue soon became the world's richest colony.

The Dutch and Swedish Challenge

For most of the seventeenth century, the Dutch did more overseas than the French. In alliance with France during Europe's Thirty Years' War (1618–1648), the Dutch wore down and finally destroyed Spain's bid for "universal monarchy" within Europe. The Netherlands, the most densely populated part of Europe, surpassed northern Italy in manufacturing and moved ahead of all competitors in finance, shipping and trade. As the Dutch republic took shape as an independent state with a population of 2 million by 1600, its constitutional and commercial practices presented an ideological challenge to the absolutism of imperial Spain.

Republicans versus Orangists   Dutch republicanism emphasized local liberties, commercial prosperity, and religious toleration, ideals that would later have an indirect impact on the United States, mediated mostly through seventeenth-century England. While Spain represented Catholic orthodoxy and the centralizing tendencies of Europe's "new monarchies," the United Provinces marked a last flowering of the medieval commune, independent or nearly independent cities that thrived within the gaps of feudal society. Political power remained decentralized in Dutch cities and their merchant oligarchies, who favored religious toleration and tried to keep trade as free as possible, while resisting the monarchical instincts of the House of Orange, the dynasty that provided military leadership for the republic. William I commanded the Dutch forces in the early phases of the war with Spain. Maurice of Nassau became the most famous Protestant commander in Europe by 1600. Both were chosen *stadholder* (captain-general) of Holland, the richest Dutch province.

Merchant republicanism, which centered in Amsterdam, competed with Calvinist orthodoxy for the allegiance of the Dutch people. Only during times of severe military crisis were the Orangists able to mobilize the Dutch Reformed clergy and impose something like Calvinist orthodoxy. The Republic — with Protestant dissenters from many different countries, a sizable Jewish community, and a Catholic minority that approached 40 percent of the total population — was actually a polyglot confederation. Its weak central government was embodied in the States General, to which each province sent representatives. The broader public did not vote or participate actively in public life. The tension between tolerant merchant republicanism and Calvinist orthodoxy carried over into the Dutch settlements in North America.

Profit provided the most important motive for Dutch expansion overseas. By 1600 Dutch commercial assets were already enormous. The Bank of Amsterdam, founded in 1609, became the most important financial institution in Europe for the next century. As early as 1620 the volume of Dutch overseas commerce probably exceeded that of the rest of Europe combined. Even during the long war for independence from Spain, the Dutch traded regularly with Lisbon and Seville for products from the East Indies and America. This effrontery so annoyed Spain's Philip II that he committed a grave blunder and exposed his empire to mortal peril. Twice in the 1590s he waited until Dutch ships crowded his ports

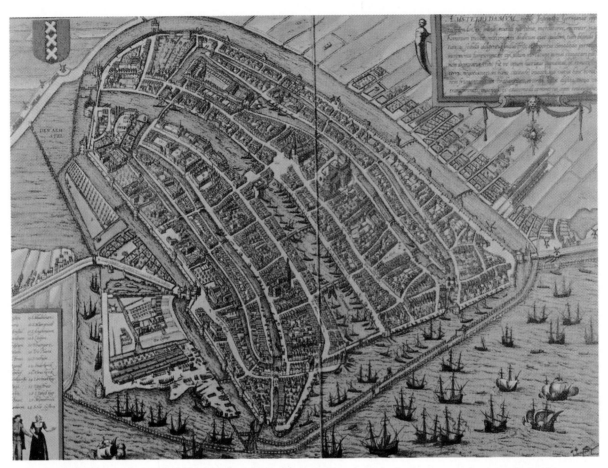

The City of Amsterdam   The capital of the wealthy province of Holland in the Netherlands, seventeenth-century Amsterdam was a center of world commerce and a bastion of merchant republicanism in Dutch politics.

and then confiscated them. The Dutch retaliated, not by attacking Spain directly, but by sailing into the Atlantic and Indian oceans to get Spanish and Portuguese colonial goods at the source.

The East India Company versus the Portuguese Empire
In 1602 the States General chartered the Dutch East India Company, the wealthiest corporation the world had yet seen. Its directors pressured Spain where it was weakest, in its Portuguese possessions in the East Indies (see Chapter 1). Going beyond Portuguese practice, the Dutch tried to monopolize the production of spices, not just their export. By massacring farmers and destroying crops, they reduced the supply and raised the price of nutmegs and cloves. El-

bowing the Portuguese out of the East Indies and even Nagasaki in Japan, the Dutch set up their own capital at Batavia (now Jakarta) on the island of Java. In Africa they took over the slave-trading posts on the Gold Coast and for a while even dominated Portuguese Angola. In South America they seized the richest sugar-producing region of Brazil for two decades until the Portuguese took it back in the 1640s. The constant Dutch threat also forced Spain to use expensive convoys to protect the annual silver fleet as it crossed the Atlantic.

Overwhelmed by these pressures, Spanish power crumbled. Spain's supply of precious metals, after peaking in the 1590s, fell sharply in the 1630s, as the population decline among the Indians reduced the labor supply for the silver mines. In the 1640s Portugal won its independence from Spain and retook Brazil and Angola from the Dutch.

The West India Company, the Atlantic, and New Netherland   North America also attracted the Dutch, though never as ardently as the East Indies. In 1609, during a twelve-year truce between Spain and the Netherlands, Henry Hudson, an Englishman in Dutch service, sailed up what the Dutch called the North River (the English renamed it the Hudson) and claimed the whole area for the Netherlands. In 1614 an expedition dispatched by Lutheran refugees in Amsterdam built a fort near modern Albany and traded with the Mahicans and Iroquois for furs. They did not occupy the site on a year-round basis.

In 1621, with the renewal of war between the Netherlands and Spain, interest in the Americas picked up significantly. The States General chartered the Dutch West India Company and gave it jurisdiction over the African slave trade, Brazil, the Caribbean, and North America. To Dutch investors, the East India Company was always more important than the West India Company. Within the West India Company, all other activities—such as Piet Heyns's dramatic capture of the entire Spanish treasure fleet in 1627—were more attractive than opportunities in what became New Netherland. While the East India Company was a secular enterprise with almost no interest in converting anyone, the West India Company retained strong Orangist sympathies and harbored a certain Calvinist fervor, sustained by refugees from the depredations of the Spanish army. Some of this ardor took hold in the Hudson Valley.

The Dutch claimed three major river systems—the Delaware, the Hudson, and the Connecticut. After some uncertainty they put most of their energy into the Hudson Valley. The first permanent settlers arrived in 1624. Two years later, Deacon Pierre (Peter) Minuit, leading about thirty Walloon (French-speaking) Protestant refugee families, bought Manhattan Island from the Indians and began to build the port town of New Amsterdam. The Dutch established Fort Orange 150 miles upriver to conduct trade with the Iroquois. Much like New France, early New Netherland depended for survival on the good will of nearby Indians. It too acquired a distinctly urban flavor through the fur trade, though its cities remained small. Unlike the settlers of New

France, the Dutch seldom ventured into the deep woods themselves. There were no *coureurs de bois*, and no missionary efforts among the Indians. Instead the Dutch waited for the Indians to bring their furs to Fort Orange in exchange for the metal pots, firearms, textiles, and alcohol that the Dutch could supply more cheaply than anyone else.

Other parallels existed between New Netherland and New France. In the 1630s, a generation before the French tried to create *seigneuries* in the St. Lawrence Valley, the Dutch granted patents, mostly along the Hudson, for what they called "patroonships," vast estates under a single landlord. But Dutch settlers, like the French, had no interest in becoming peasants, and the system never thrived. The one exception was Rensselaerswyck, a gigantic estate on both banks of the Hudson above and below Fort Orange. Its patroon was less interested in agriculture than in stealing the Indian trade of Fort Orange from the West India Company. He never achieved this goal. Instead he exported wheat and flour to the Caribbean, eventually in large quantities.

New Netherland as a Pluralistic Society   New Netherland became North America's first experiment in ethnic and religious pluralism. The results were not always happy. The Dutch were themselves a mixed people with a Flemish majority and a Walloon minority. Both came to the colony. So did Scots, Germans, Danes, Norwegians, Swedes, and Finns. All were swept into the Dutch republic through its network of commerce around the Baltic and North seas. One observer in the 1640s counted eighteen languages among the 450 inhabitants of New Amsterdam.

The government of the colony tried to keep peace amid all this diversity by drawing upon two conflicting precedents from the Netherlands. It appealed to religious refugees by emphasizing the province's Protestant unity against Catholic Spain. This policy, roughly speaking, reflected the Orangist position in the Netherlands. On the other hand, a frank acceptance of religious diversity might stimulate trade. The pursuit of prosperity through toleration was the normal role of the city of Amsterdam in Dutch politics. Minuit and Pieter Stuyvesant represented the religious formula for unity, other governors the commercial alternative. Neither choice worked satisfactorily. This tension carried over past the English conquest of New Netherland in 1664 (see Chapter 3).

After Minuit returned to Europe in 1631, the emphasis shifted rapidly from piety to trade. The Dutch sold muskets to the Iroquois to expand their own access to the fur trade. They began to export grain to the Caribbean, a more elusive goal in which the patroonships were supposed to give the colony a strong agricultural base. But Willem Kieft, a particularly stupid and quarrelsome governor, slaughtered the men, women, and children of a tribe of Indian refugees to whom he had granted asylum from other Indians. This so-called Pavonia Massacre of 1643, which took place across the Hudson from Manhattan, set off a war with neighboring Algonquian tribes that nearly destroyed the colony.

Johan Printz   Johan Printz (1592–1663) was governor of New Sweden for most of its existence. He served in that capacity from 1643 to 1653, then returned to Sweden to become governor of Jönköping County. New Sweden was overtaken by New Netherland in 1655.

By the time Stuyvesant replaced Kieft in 1647, the population of the colony had fallen to about seven hundred people. An autocrat, Stuyvesant made peace and then strengthened town governments and the Dutch Reformed Church. During his administration, the population rose to six thousand by 1664, twice that of New France. Most newcomers arrived as members of healthy families and reproduced easily. With few immigrants after 1664, the population doubled each generation anyway.

New Sweden   Stuyvesant faced competition from two Protestant rivals, the Swedes and the English. When Minuit returned to Europe, he organized another refugee project, this one for Flemings uprooted by the war with Spain. When Dutch authorities refused to back him, he turned for support to the aggressively Protestant Court of Sweden. Financed by private Dutch capital, he returned to America in 1638 with Flemish and Swedish settlers to found New Sweden, with its capital at Fort Christina (modern Wilmington) near the mouth of the Delaware River, well within boundaries claimed by New Netherland. After Minuit died on the return trip to Europe, the colony became less Flemish and Calvinist and more Swedish and Lutheran, at a time when Stuyvesant was trying to make New Netherland an orthodox Calvinist society.

The Swedes and Dutch lost another common bond in 1648 when their long war with Spain finally ended. In 1654 the Swedes subdued Fort Casimir, a Dutch post that controlled access to the Delaware. Stuyvesant took over all of New Sweden the next year, and the city of Amsterdam began shipping in settlers to guarantee Dutch control. Stuyvesant actively persecuted the Lutherans of New Amsterdam. Orthodoxy and harmony were not easily reconciled.

English Encroachments on New Netherland   The English, already entrenched around Chesapeake Bay to the south and New England to the east (see below), created a serious threat as they moved from New England onto Long Island and into what is now Westchester County, New York. Kieft welcomed them and gave them local privileges greater than those enjoyed by the Dutch, probably in the hope that their farms and herds would give the colony an agricultural surplus for export to the

Caribbean. Stuyvesant regarded these "Yankees" (a Dutch word that meant something like "land pirates") as orthodox Calvinists, the English-speaking equivalent of his Dutch Reformed Church. They agitated for a more active role in government, and their loyalty was questionable. If England attacked the colony, would these Puritans side with the Dutch Calvinists or the Anglican invaders? Which ran deeper, their religious or their ethnic loyalties? Stuyvesant learned the unpleasant answer when England invaded in 1664.

The Challenge from Elizabethan England

England's interest in America emerged slowly, even though ships from the West Country port of Bristol may have reached North America several years before Columbus's first voyage. If so, the English did nothing about it. Then in 1497 Henry VII sent Giovanni Cabato (John Cabot), an Italian mariner who had moved to Bristol, to search for a northwest passage to Asia. Cabot probably reached Newfoundland, which he took to be part of Asia. He sailed again in 1498 with five ships but was lost at sea. Only one vessel returned, but Cabot's voyages gave England a vague claim to portions of the North American coast.

The English Reformation   By the time interest in America revived during the reign of Elizabeth I (1558–1603), England was rapidly becoming a Protestant nation. Henry VIII (1509–1547), desperate for a male heir, had broken with the pope to divorce his queen and remarry. He proclaimed himself the "Only Supreme Head" of the Church of England, confiscated all monastic lands, and unintentionally gave strong encouragement to Protestant reformers. Under Edward VI (1547–1553), Elizabeth's younger brother, England went dramatically Protestant, but Mary I (1553–1558), her older sister, reimposed Catholicism, burned hundreds of Protestants at the stake, and drove thousands into exile, where many of them became committed Calvinists. Elizabeth accepted Protestantism, and the exiles returned.

The Church of England, as reconstituted under Elizabeth, became an odd compromise—Calvinist in doctrine and theology, still largely Catholic in structure, liturgy, and ritual. By the time of her death, England's Catholics would be a tiny minority, often persecuted. Yet they still had powerful allies abroad, especially in Spain.

Some Protestants demanded a fuller reformation—the eradication of Catholic vestiges and the replacement of the Anglican *Book of Common Prayer* with sermons and psalms as the dominant mode of worship. These Puritans resisted any relaxation of Calvinist rigor and played a major role in English expansion overseas. More extreme Protestants, called Separatists, denied that the Church of England was a true church and began to set up independent congregations of their own. They played a smaller role overseas, but some of them founded Plymouth Colony.

John Hawkins and Francis Drake   In 1560 England was a rather backward country of 3 million people. Its chief export was woolen cloth, most of which was shipped to the Netherlands where the Dutch turned it into finished textiles. During the sixteenth century the numbers of people and sheep grew rapidly, with the two sometimes competing for the same land. Whenever farm land was enclosed and converted to sheep pasture, farm laborers were set adrift and created a widespread sense that England was overpopulated. Quite apart from the pressures of enclosure, internal migration was becoming a routine part of the life cycle for many, perhaps most people. Thousands headed for London. Although deaths greatly outnumbered births in London, new arrivals lifted the city's population from about 50,000 in 1500 to 200,000 in 1600 and, including the suburbs, 575,000 by 1700. By then London was the largest metropolis in western Europe, with over 10 percent of England's population of 5 million. After 1600 England's internal migration fueled overseas settlement. But in the sixteenth century interest in America was centered, not in London, but in the smaller ports of southwestern England that were already involved in the Newfoundland fisheries.

Taking advantage of the friendly relations that still prevailed between England and Spain, John Hawkins of Plymouth made three voyages to New Spain between 1562 and 1569. On his first trip he forced the Portuguese along the African coast to sell him slaves. He sold the slaves to the Spaniards in Hispaniola where, by paying all legal duties, he tried to set himself up as a legitimate trader. Spanish authorities disapproved, and on his second voyage the only way he could trade in New Spain was at gunpoint. On his third trip his six vessels were caught in a Mexican port by the Spanish viceroy, who commanded a much larger fleet. After promising Hawkins quarter, the viceroy sank four ships. Hawkins and his young kinsman Francis Drake escaped, both vowing vengeance against Spain.

Drake even began talking of bringing liberty to America by freeing Spanish slaves. His most dramatic exploit came between 1577 and 1580 when he rounded Cape Horn and plundered Spanish possessions along the undefended Pacific coast of Peru. Knowing that the Spaniards would be waiting for him if he returned by the same route, he sailed north, explored San Francisco Bay, and continued west around the world to England—the first circumnavigation since Magellan's.

Ireland as the Model for American Colonization   All the talk of travel and plunder kept England buzzing and planted the idea of permanent colonization in several enterprising minds. England had a model close at hand in Ireland, which the English Crown had claimed for centuries. As of 1560, however, England had achieved little direct control over Ireland, except in the Dublin Pale. After 1560 the English tried to impose their agriculture, language, local government, legal system, aristocracy, and religion upon a clan-based, mostly pastoral and Gaelic-speaking people. The Irish responded by becoming more fiercely Roman Catholic than they had ever been before.

Most of the ideas about Indians that the English brought to America derived from their experience with the Irish who, according to one Elizabethan, "live like beasts, void of law and all good order" and are "more uncivil, more uncleanly, more barbarous and more brutish in their customs and demeanors, than in any part of the world that is known." The English tried to conquer the most Gaelic provinces of Ireland, Ulster in the northeast and Munster in the southwest. In Ulster the Protestant invaders drove out most of the people and claimed the land for themselves. In the south they ejected the Catholic leaders and tried to turn the Catholic Irish into tenant farmers under Protestant landlords. Terror became an acceptable way to subdue the Irish, as when the English slaughtered two hundred of them at a Christmas feast in 1574.

Sir Humphrey Gilbert, a well-educated humanist, was one of the most brutal of Elizabeth's captains in the Irish wars of the 1560s. "He thought his dogs' ears too good to hear the speech of the greatest nobleman amongst them," reported an admirer. In subduing Munster in 1569, Gilbert killed nearly every-

one in his path and destroyed all the crops, a strategy that was later employed against American Indians. Massacring women and children "was the way to kill the men of war by famine," explained an apologist. Gilbert once decapitated numerous victims, staked their severed heads to form a corridor, and forced his prisoners to march down that path and beg for mercy. For eighty years after 1560, Ireland attracted more English settlers than all American and Caribbean colonies combined. Only after 1641, when the Irish retaliated by killing thousands of settlers, did the West Indies and North America replace Ireland as preferred sites for colonization.

Fresh from his Irish exploits, Gilbert began to think about exporting his experience across the Atlantic. In "A Discourse How Her Majesty May Annoy the King of Spain" (1577), he proposed that England grab control of the Newfoundland fisheries, a nursery of seamen and naval power. He urged the founding of settlements close enough to New Spain to provide bases for plundering. He obtained a royal patent in 1578 and sent out a fleet, but after getting into a fight somewhere short of America, his ships limped back to England. He tried again in 1583. This time his fleet sailed north to claim Newfoundland. The crews of twenty-two Spanish and Portuguese ships and eighteen French and English vessels listened in astonishment as he divided up the land among them, assigned them rents, established the Church of England among this mostly Catholic group, and then sailed away to explore more of the American coast. His ship went under during a storm.

Sir Walter Ralegh and Roanoke   Gilbert's half-brother, Sir Walter Ralegh, obtained his own patent from Elizabeth and tried twice to plant a colony in North America. A 1584 exploratory voyage brought two Indians back to England to learn English and act as interpreters. In 1585 a larger expedition landed on Roanoke Island in Pamlico Sound, but the settlers planted no crops and exasperated the Indians with demands for food. In June 1586 the English killed the local chief, Wingina, whose main offense was apparently a threat to resettle his people on the mainland and leave the colonists to starve. Days later, when the expected supply vessels did not arrive on schedule, the colonists sailed back to England on the ships of Sir Francis Drake, who had just burned the Spanish city of St. Augustine with the support of Florida

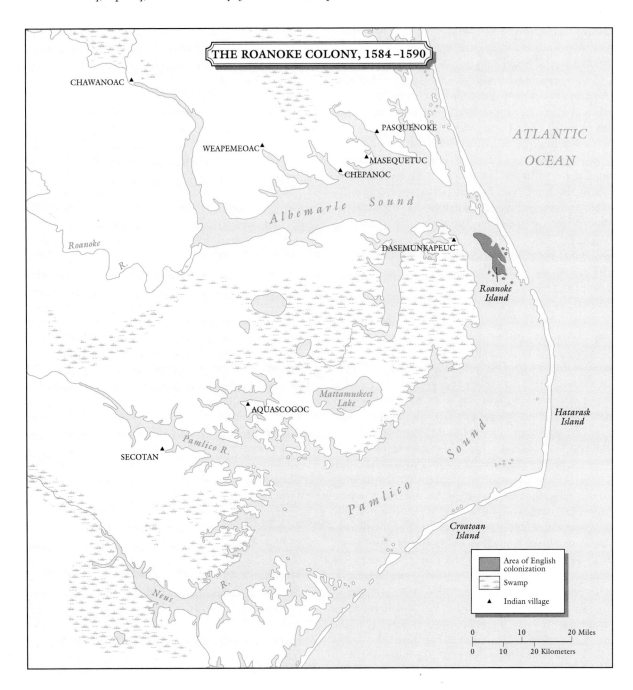

THE ROANOKE COLONY, 1584–1590

CHAWANOAC

PASQUENOKE

WEAPEMEOAC

MASEQUETUC

CHEPANOC

ATLANTIC

OCEAN

Albemarle   Sound

Roanoke

R.

DASEMUNKAPEUC

*Roanoke
Island*

*Mattamuskeet
Lake*

AQUASCOGOC

Pamlico R.

SECOTAN

Pamlico   Sound

*Hatarask
Island*

Pamlico   Sound

*Croatoan
Island*

Neus

R.

Area of English
colonization

Swamp

▲   Indian village

0   10   20 Miles

0   10   20 Kilometers

Indians, whom he freed. The supply squadron reached Roanoke a few weeks later, only to find the site abandoned. It left behind a small garrison before sailing off in quest of Spanish plunder. The garrison was never heard from again.

Ralegh sent a second expedition to Roanoke in 1587. This time women came along, an indication that Ralegh envisioned a permanent colony, not just an outpost for raiding the Spaniards. When Governor John White went back to England to arrange for more supplies, his return to Roanoke was delayed by the assault of the Spanish Armada in 1588. By the time he reached Roanoke in 1590, the settlers had vanished, leaving a mysterious message — "CROA-

TOAN"—carved on a tree. The colonists may have moved north to settle among the Chesapeake nation of Indians in lower Chesapeake Bay. Sketchy evidence suggests that the Powhatan chiefdom, the most powerful Indians in the area, wiped out the Chesapeakes, and any English living with them, in the spring of 1607, just as another English fleet arrived in the bay.

In 1588 the launching of Spain's Armada against Protestant England touched off a war that lasted until 1604. The exploits of Hawkins, Drake, and Ralegh helped provoke this conflict, as did Elizabeth's intervention in the Dutch war for independence from Spain. The loss of the Armada, first to nimbler English ships in the English Channel and then to fierce storms off the Irish coast, was a heavy blow to Spain, but the war strained English resources as well.

By 1600 neither the French, the Dutch, nor the English had yet managed to plant a permanent settlement in North America or the Caribbean. But England possessed two strong advocates of colonization, Richard Hakluyt the elder and younger (they were cousins). They systematically collected accounts of English exploits overseas and offered advice on how to make future colonization efforts more successful. During the 1590s the English conquest of Ireland also proceeded at its grim pace, killing possibly half of the native Irish. And for the first time London became intensely involved in American affairs by launching privateering fleets to harass Spain.

Hawkins, Drake, Gilbert, and Ralegh were all West Country men with large ambitions and limited financial resources. Their plundering expeditions continued to pay, but they could not afford to sustain a colony like Roanoke until it could return profits. Even though London merchants remained far more interested in trade with India, the Mediterranean, and Muscovy than in North American projects, the city's growing involvement with the Atlantic marked a significant shift. The marriage of London capital to West Country experience permitted Virginia to succeed where Gilbert and Ralegh had failed.

THE SWARMING OF THE ENGLISH

Before 1700 more than 700,000 people sailed from Europe or Africa to the English colonies in North America and the Caribbean. Most of the European migrants were unmarried younger sons. With no inheritance in England, they hoped to improve their material conditions in a warmer climate. Instead they spent much of their time trying to stay alive under the threat of malaria, yellow fever, and other lethal maladies. Most Europeans, men and women, arrived as servants. At first even many Africans were considered servants, not lifelong slaves. Most of the men, whether European or African, never fathered children.

Only a few of the European migrants shared a religious vision of building a better society in America. Those who settled in New England or in the Hudson and Delaware valleys were the most fortunate. Because Puritans and Quakers migrated as families into wholesome and healthy regions, their population expanded at a rate far beyond anything known in Europe. By 1700 the descendants of this small, idealistic minority had become a much larger percentage of the surviving population. What initially seemed an insignificant part of the migration stream multiplied to play a disproportionately large role in American history ever since. As Table 2-1 shows, the New England and Middle Atlantic colonies attracted only 5.4 percent of the total migration stream, but in 1700 they contained over a third of the total population of the English colonies and just over half of the European settlers.

From Opportunity to Caste: The Chesapeake and the West Indies

In 1606 King James I of England (1603-1625) chartered the Virginia Company, granting it authority to colonize North America between the 34th and 45th parallels. The company had two headquarters. One, in the English city of Plymouth, raised only a small amount of capital but won jurisdiction over the northern portion of the grant. This branch carried on the West Country expansionist traditions of Gilbert and Ralegh and was known as the Plymouth Company. In 1607 it planted a colony at Sagadahoc on the coast of Maine. But the colonists found the cold winter and the Abenaki Indians unpleasant and abandoned the site in September 1608. The Plymouth Company ran out of money and gave up.

The other branch had its offices in London and decided to colonize the Chesapeake Bay area. In 1607 the London Company sent out three ships carrying

Table 2-1

The Pattern of Settlement in the English Colonies up to 1700

Region	Who Came (in thousands)		Population in 1700 (in thousands)	
	Europeans	*Africans*	*Europeans*	*Africans*
West Indies	220 (29.8%)	316 (42.8%)	33 (07.8%)	115 (27.3%)
South	135 (18.3%)	25 (03.4%)	104 (24.7%)	22 (05.2%)
Mid-Atlantic	20 (02.7%)	2 (00.3%)	51 (12.1%)	3 (00.7%)
New England	20 (02.7%)	1 (00.1%)	91 (21.6%)	2 (00.5%)
Total	395 (53.4%)	344 (46.6%)	279 (66.3%)	142 (33.7%)

104 settlers. They sailed up the Powhatan River (which they renamed the James), landed at a defensible peninsula, built a fort and other crude buildings, and called the place Jamestown. The investors hoped to find gold or silver, a northwest passage to Asia, a plant to cure syphilis, or other valuable products that could be sold in Europe. They expected the settlers to get the local Indians to work for them, much as the Spanish had done. If the Indians proved hostile, the settlers were told to imitate Cortés, form alliances with more distant Indians, and subdue those who resisted. Company officials did not realize that a *werowance* (or war chief) named Powhatan had organized virtually all of the Indians of the area below the fall line.[1] He had no serious rival within striking distance. The company's other expectations proved equally skewed.

The Jamestown Disaster   Jamestown became a death-trap. Only thirty-eight settlers survived the first year. Of a total of 325 who came before 1609, fewer than a hundred were still alive in the spring of that year. Every summer the James River became badly contaminated around the settlement and sent out killing waves of dysentery and typhoid fever. Before long malaria set in as well.

Those who survived owed most of their good fortune to the energy and initiative of Captain John Smith, a soldier and adventurer who outmaneuvered other members of the colony's ruling council and took charge. When his explorations uncovered no gold or silver nor any quick route through the continent to Asia, he concentrated on survival. He tried to awe Powhatan, buy corn, and maintain friendly relations. Through the help of Pocahontas, Powhatan's twelve-year-old daughter, he avoided war. Smith gave conflicting versions of the story later on, but he clearly believed that Pocahontas saved his life in late 1607.

Food remained scarce. The colony was top-heavy with gentlemen and specialized craftsmen (including a perfumer), who considered farming beneath their dignity. Despite their protests, Smith made everyone work in the fields raising grain for four hours a day. The colony still produced nothing to offset the cost of settlement.

In 1609 the Virginia Company sent out six hundred more settlers under Lt. Governor Thomas Gates, but his ship ran aground on Bermuda, and the crew spent a year building another vessel. Four hundred of the new settlers reached Virginia before Gates. Smith, after suffering a severe injury in an explosion, was shipped back to England, and the colony lacked firm leadership for a year. Wearying Powhatan with their endless demands for corn, they provoked the Indian war that Smith had avoided. The settlers almost starved during the winter of 1610. One settler was executed for cannibalizing his spouse, a delicacy Smith called "powdered wife."

---

[1] The fall line, defined by the first waterfall encountered on each river by a vessel sailing inland from the Atlantic, marked a significant barrier to penetration of the North American continent. On the southern coastal shelf, the area between the ocean and the falls is called the Tidewater. The land above the falls but below the Appalachian Mountains is called the Piedmont.

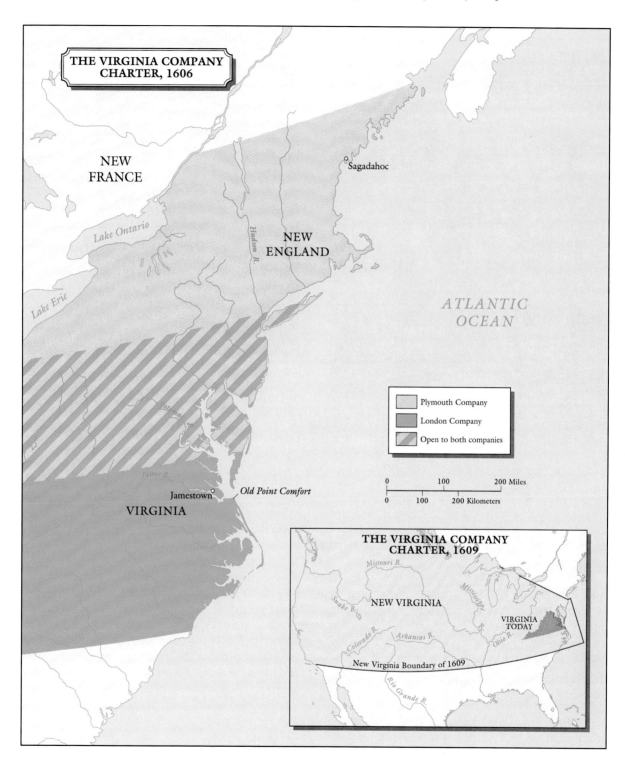

THE VIRGINIA COMPANY
CHARTER, 1606

NEW
FRANCE

Lake Ontario

Lake Erie

Sagadahoc

Hudson R.

NEW
ENGLAND

ATLANTIC
OCEAN

Potomac R.

James R.

Jamestown

Old Point Comfort

VIRGINIA

Plymouth Company

London Company

Open to both companies

0		100		200 Miles
0	100		200 Kilometers	

THE VIRGINIA COMPANY
CHARTER, 1609

Missouri R.

Snake R.

NEW VIRGINIA

Mississippi R.

VIRGINIA
TODAY

Colorado R.

Arkansas R.

Ohio R.

New Virginia Boundary of 1609

Rio Grande R.

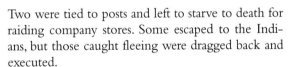

Captain John Smith Subduing Opechancanough, the Warrior Chief of the Pamunkey Indians, 1608 Note how much taller Opechancanough was, even to a European artist.

English Portrait of Pocahontas (Matoaka), 1616, at Age Twenty-Two When baptized, she took the name Rebecca. The Latin inscription reads: "Matoaka, alias Rebecca, Daughter of the Mighty Prince Powhatan, Emperor of Virginia."

Two were tied to posts and left to starve to death for raiding company stores. Some escaped to the Indians, but those caught fleeing were dragged back and executed.

When Gates finally reached Jamestown with 175 colonists in June 1610, he found only sixty settlers alive (plus a garrison at Point Comfort) and the food supply nearly exhausted. Gates decided the situation was hopeless, packed everyone aboard ship, and started down river. Virginia was going the way of Roanoke and Sagadahoc, despite its greater resources. Instead, the small fleet came abreast of the new governor, Thomas West, baron de la Warr, sailing up the James with three hundred newcomers. They all went back to Jamestown, and the colony endured. Virginia's survival involved more than a little luck.

De la Warr and Gates found themselves in the middle of the colony's first Indian war, which began in 1609 and lasted until 1614. Powhatan's warriors picked off any settlers who strayed far from Jamestown. The English retaliated by slaughtering whole villages and destroying crops, as they had in Ireland, even though the settlers were still dependent upon some Indians for their food supply. In August 1610, for example, Commander George Percy led an expedition against the Paspahegh Indians, who had refused to give the colonists more corn and had sheltered some runaways. He burned their crops, massacred most of them, captured the ruler and her children, and started back to Jamestown by boat. When the soldiers murmured "because the queen and her children were spared," Percy had the children thrown overboard and allowed his men to shoot "out their brains in the water." At Jamestown, a settler suggested burning the queen alive. But Percy merely put her to the sword instead.

Like the English atrocities in Ireland, Percy had resorted to overt terrorism. Annihilating one tribe might intimidate the others. The war finally ended after the English captured Pocahontas and used her as a hostage to negotiate peace. She converted to

Christianity and in 1614 married John Rolfe, a widower ten years older than she.

Despite the Indian war, prospects improved for the settlers after 1610. Autocratic governors used martial law to impose discipline on the settlers and sent some of them to healthier locations, such as Henrico, fifty miles upstream. Through the efforts of John Rolfe, the colony not only made peace with Powhatan but also began to produce a cash crop. In 1613 Rolfe imported from the Spanish West Indies a species of tobacco milder than the local variety. The new crop brought such an attractive price in England that the king, who had complained that no one could build a colony upon smoke, was proved wrong. By 1617 the settlers were even growing tobacco in the streets of Jamestown.

Reorganization, Reform, and Crisis   In 1609 a new royal charter extended Virginia's boundaries to the Pacific. A third charter in 1612 made the London Company a joint-stock company. It resembled a modern corporation except that a stockholder had only one vote regardless of how many shares he owned. The "adventurers," as the stockholders were called, met quarterly in the company's General Court but entrusted everyday management to the company's treasurer, who until 1618 was Sir Thomas Smyth, a wealthy London merchant. The company had two other factions besides Smyth's merchants. Some aristocrats, led by Robert Rich, earl of Warwick, wanted to use Virginia as a base for piratical raids against New Spain in the tradition of Drake and Ralegh, even though the two countries were at peace and the king had recently ordered Ralegh beheaded for plundering the Spanish. The third faction was a group of gentry and small investors led by Sir Edwin Sandys, Puritan son of the archbishop of York. They saw Virginia as a patriotic venture, a projection of English power overseas. Within the company, Smyth and Warwick controlled most of the capital; Sandys had a majority of shareholders.

In 1618 the company approved an ambitious set of reforms for Virginia. It encouraged economic diversification, such as glass blowing, raising silkworms, and planting grape vines. English common law replaced martial law. The settlers were allowed to elect their own assembly, the House of Burgesses, to meet with the governor and his council and make local laws. Finally—the most popular reform in Virginia—settlers were permitted to own land. Under the so-called headright system, a colonist received fifty acres for everyone whose passage to America he financed. Warwick and Sandys then joined forces to dislodge Smyth, elect Sandys treasurer, and implement the reforms.

Between 1618 and 1623 four thousand settlers poured into Virginia, but the diversification program was a fiasco. The only product that found a market was tobacco. Corn provided most of the food. Instead of growing silkworms and grapes, Virginia still raised Indian crops with Indian farming methods, which meant using hoes instead of plows.

The flood of newcomers strained the food supply and soured relations with the Indians, especially after Powhatan died and was succeeded by his militant brother, Opechancanough. On Good Friday in March 1622, the new chief launched an attack intended to wipe out the whole colony. Without a last-minute warning from a friendly Indian, Jamestown might not have survived. As it turned out, 347 settlers were killed that day, and most of the outlying settlements were destroyed. Newcomers who arrived in subsequent months had nowhere to go and, with food again scarce, hundreds died over the winter.

Back in London Smyth and Warwick turned against Sandys, withdrew their capital, and asked the king to intervene. A royal commission visited the colony and found only 1,200 settlers alive out of 6,000 sent over. In 1624 the king declared the London Company bankrupt and assumed direct control of Virginia, making it the first royal colony, with a governor and council appointed by the Crown. The London Company had invested some £200,000 in the enterprise, equal to £1,400 or £1,500 for every surviving settler at a time when skilled English craftsmen were lucky to earn £50 a year. Such extravagance guaranteed that future colonies would be organized and financed in different ways.

Tobacco, Servants, and Survival   Between Opechancanough's 1622 attack and the 1640s, Virginia proved that it could survive even when the price of tobacco fell drastically in the 1630s. Despite an appalling death rate, about a thousand settlers arrived each year, and population grew slowly, to 5,200 by 1634 and 8,100 by 1640. For ten years the settlers warred against Opechancanough. In 1623 they poisoned two hundred Indians they had invited to a peace conference. In most years they attacked the Indians just before harvest time, destroying their crops and villages. By the time both sides made peace in 1632, all Indians had been expelled from the peninsula between the James and York Rivers below Jamestown.

This area became secure for tobacco, and the export of tobacco financed the importation of indentured servants. Most servants were younger sons who agreed to work for their masters for a term of years in exchange for the cost of passage, for bed and board during their years of service, and for modest freedom dues when their term was up. Those signing indentures in England usually possessed valuable skills and negotiated terms of four or five years. Those arriving in Virginia without an indenture were sold by the ship captain to a planter. Most of them were younger and less skilled. Those over nineteen years old served five years. Those under nineteen served until age twenty-four. The system gradually turned servants into freemen who hoped to prosper on their own account. Most former servants became tenants for several years while they tried to save enough to buy their own land. In the 1640s and 1650s, good tobacco prices enabled many to succeed. But those who imported the servants were always in a stronger economic position, collecting the headright of fifty acres for each one. Because deaths outnumbered births for most of the century, the colony needed a steady flow of newcomers to survive.

Virginia also acquired a more complex institutional structure. The colony was divided into counties in 1634, each with its own justices of the peace, who sat together as the county court and, by filling their own vacancies, soon became a self-perpetuating oligarchy. Most counties also became Anglican parishes, with a church and a vestry of prominent laymen, usually the justices. The vestry managed temporal affairs for the church, including the choice of the minister. Though the king did not recognize the House of Burgesses until 1639, it met almost every year after 1619 and by 1640 was well-established. Before long, only a justice could hope for election to the House.

Until 1660 many former servants managed to acquire land. Some even served on the county courts and in the House of Burgesses. But as tobacco prices fell after 1660, upward mobility became more difficult. Political offices usually went to the richest 15 percent of the settlers, those able to pay their own way across the Atlantic. They, and eventually their descendants, monopolized the posts of justice of the peace and vestryman, the pool from which burgesses and councilors were normally chosen. Virginia was becoming an oligarchy.

The Founding of Maryland   Early Maryland had different origins but became much the same kind of society as Virginia. It grew out of the social and religious vision of Sir George Calvert and his son Cecilius, both of whom became Catholics and looked to America as a refuge for persecuted English and Irish Catholics. Sir George, a prominent officeholder, had invested in the London Company. When he resigned his post because of his Catholicism, a grateful King James I made him baron Baltimore in the Irish peerage. Both James and Charles I (1625-1649) encouraged his colonial projects.

The Maryland charter of 1632 made Baltimore "lord proprietor" of the colony with all the powers of a medieval palatine lord, a noble who received vast discretionary powers to defend against Welsh or Scottish raids. It was the most sweeping delegation of power that English law allowed the king to give. It came close to making Baltimore king within Maryland. The London Company had been an expensive failure. After 1630 most English colonies began as proprietary projects, often with the Maryland charter as a model. Many of these projects embodied the distinctive social vision of their founders.

George Calvert died as the Maryland patent was being issued, and Cecilius inherited Maryland and the peerage. Like Champlain, he believed that Catholics and Protestants could live together in peace in the same colony. But he expected the servants, most of whom were Protestants, to continue to serve the Catholic gentlemen of the colony after their indentures expired. Baltimore made the gentlemen manor lords, complete for a time with the power to preside over courts leet and courts baron, feudal tribunals that were obsolete in England.

Maryland never fulfilled these plans. The condition of Catholics in England improved under Charles I and his queen, Henrietta Maria, a French Catholic for whom the province was named. Few Catholics were willing to emigrate, and from the outset most settlers were Protestants. Lord Baltimore even encouraged a band of Puritans, driven from Virginia by its Anglican governor, to settle in northern Maryland.

The civil war that erupted in England between king and Parliament in 1642 (see Chapter 3) soon

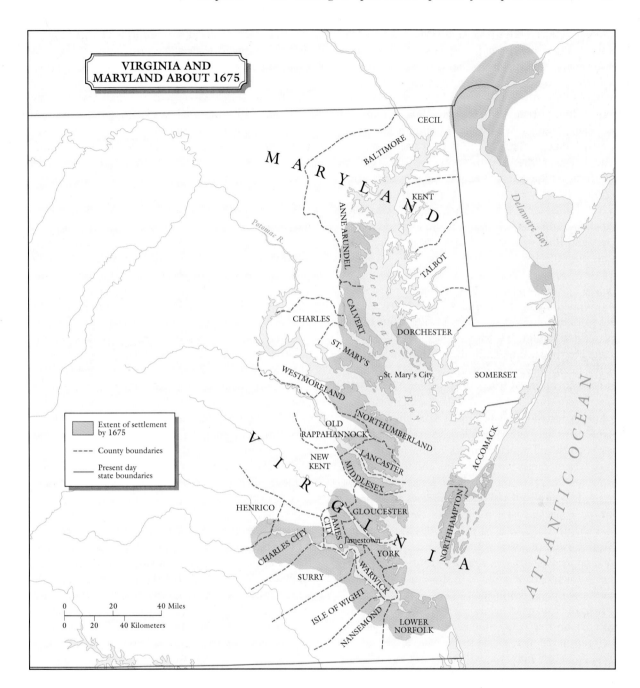

had its counterpart in Maryland. On several occasions in the 1640s and 1650s the Protestant majority overthrew Lord Baltimore's rule, but the English government always sided with him, even when the Puritans were in power there. During these struggles, Baltimore conceded a bicameral legislature to the colony, with the expectation that Protestants would dominate the elective assembly and Catholics the appointive council. He also approved the Toleration Act of 1649, which granted freedom of religion to Christians but not to the tiny Jewish minority in the province.

The manorial system did not survive these upheavals. Protestant servants, after their indentures expired, acquired their own land rather than remain as tenants to Catholic landlords, most of whom died or returned to England. When Maryland's unrest ended around 1660, the colony was raising tobacco, corn, and livestock and was governed by county courts similar to those in Virginia. If anything, the proprietary family's Catholicism and its claims to special privileges made the Maryland assembly more articulate than the Virginia House of Burgesses in demanding the rights of Englishmen. Otherwise religion provided the biggest difference between the two colonies. Virginia was Anglican, but Maryland had no established church and no vestries. Most Maryland Protestants had to make do without ministers until the 1690s.

Family Life in the Chesapeake Colonies   At first, men outnumbered women in Virginia and Maryland by five to one. Among new settlers as late as the 1690s, the ratio was still five to two. Population did not become self-sustaining until about 1680, when live births finally began to outnumber deaths. Among adults this transition was felt only after 1700. Until then, most prominent people were immigrants.

Life expectancy slowly improved as the colonists planted orchards to provide wholesome cider to drink, but it still remained much lower than in England, where those who survived childhood could expect to live into their fifties. Chesapeake immigrants had survived childhood diseases in Europe, but life expectancy for men at age twenty hovered around forty-five, with 70 percent dead by age fifty. Women died at even younger ages, especially in areas ravaged by malaria, a disease that is highly dangerous for pregnant women. In those places women rarely lived past their thirties.

England's patriarchal households were hard to maintain in this environment. About 70 percent of the men never married or, if they did, produced no children. Most men waited years after completing their service before they could marry. And since women could not marry until they had fulfilled their indentures, most spent a significant percentage of their childbearing years unwed. About one-fifth had illegitimate children, despite severe legal penalties, and roughly one-third were pregnant on their wedding day. Virtually all women married, most as soon as they could.

In a typical Chesapeake marriage, the groom was in his thirties and the bride eight or ten years younger.

Though men outlived women, this age gap meant that the husband usually died before his wife, who then quickly remarried. In one Virginia county, one-fourth of the children lost at least one parent by age five; by age thirteen, half had lost one. About three-fourths of all children lost a parent before adulthood, and fully one-third lost both. Native-born settlers married at a much earlier age than immigrants; women were often in their mid to late teens when they wed. Orphans were a major community problem. Stepparents were common, because surviving spouses with property usually remarried, but very few people lived long enough to become grandparents. By the time the oldest child in a household was twenty, the husband and wife heading the family might not even be its blood relatives. Younger children might be stepbrothers or stepsisters of the eldest, but the youngest might have altogether different parents.

Under these circumstances, family loyalties tended to focus on other kin — on uncles, aunts, cousins, older stepbrothers or stepsisters — probably contributing to the high value that Virginia and Maryland placed upon hospitality. Patriarchalism remained weak. Because fathers died young, at first even members of the officeholding elite that took shape around midcentury rarely passed their status on to their sons. Only toward the end of the century were the men holding office likely to be the sons of fathers of comparable distinction.

England's Transition to Slavery: The West Indies   Far more Englishmen went to the West Indies than to the Chesapeake in the seventeenth century. Between 1624 and 1640 they settled the Leeward Islands (St. Christopher, Nevis, Montserrat, and Antigua) and Barbados, tiny possessions covering just over four hundred square miles. In the 1650s England conquered Jamaica from the Spanish, increasing this total by a factor of ten. At first English planters grew tobacco with labor supplied by indentured servants. Then, beginning around 1645 in Barbados, sugar replaced tobacco, with dramatic social consequences. The Dutch, who were then being driven from Brazil by the Portuguese, provided some of the capital for this transition, showed the English how to raise sugar, introduced them to slave labor on a massive scale, and for a time dominated the exportation and marketing of the crop. Sugar became so valuable that planters imported most of their food from North

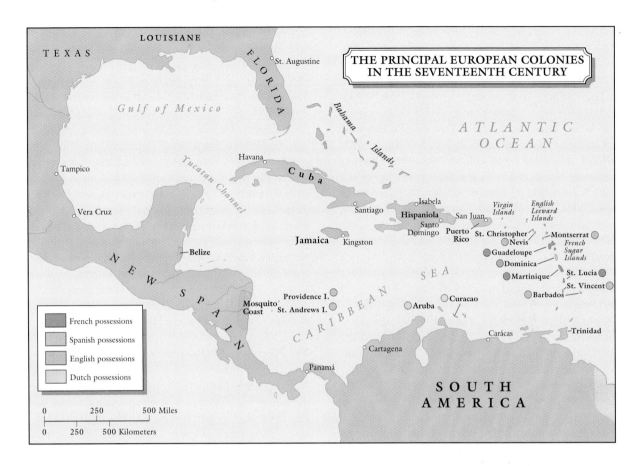

America rather than divert land and labor from the cash crop.

Sugar required a heavy investment in slaves, mills, and other equipment. Large planters with many slaves soon dominated the islands. Since they had little use for ex-servants, most former bondsmen left after their terms expired. Many joined the buccaneers or moved to the mainland. Their exodus hastened the transition to slavery. In 1660 Europeans outnumbered slaves in the islands by 33,000 to 22,000. For the rest of the century, the European population stagnated while the slave population increased sixfold. By 1775 it tripled again.

Observers were depressed by the moral climate on the islands, where underworked and overfed planters arrogantly dominated their overworked and underfed slaves. Some of the islands were "of no advantage," remarked one governor, who thought they were "better under water than above." In 1671 another governor canvassed forty parishes in the Leeward Islands and found just "one drunken orthodox [Anglican] priest, one drunken sectary priest, and one drunken [unordained] parson." Barbados "is the Dunghill whereon England doth cast forth its rubbish," claimed Henry Whistler in the 1650s. "Rogues and whores . . . are those which are generally brought here. A Rogue in England will hardly make a cheater here; a Bawd brought over puts on a demure comportment; a whore if handsome makes a wife for some rich planter."

The Rise of Slavery in North America   Africans reached Virginia as early as 1619 when, John Rolfe reported, a Dutch ship "sold us twenty Negars." Their status in early Virginia and Maryland remained ambiguous for decades, even after slavery had been sharply defined in the West Indies. In the Chesapeake some Africans were treated as servants and won their freedom after several years. In Northampton County, one "Anthony Johnson Negro" even became the master of other Africans, one of whom complained that Johnson held him beyond the term of his indenture. (The court backed Johnson.) But other Africans almost from the beginning were held to lifetime bondage, a pattern that gradually prevailed. This uncertainty about status is not surprising. The English had no experience with slavery at home.

The rigidity typical of a society organized into racial castes also took time to crystallize. When Hugh Davis was whipped in 1630 "for abusing himself to the dishonor of God and shame of Christians, by defiling his body in lying with a negro," his offense may have been sodomy rather than miscegenation. The record is unclear. Fifty years later when Katherine Watkins, a white woman, accused John Long, a mulatto, of raping her, the neighbors (both men and women) blamed her, not him, for engaging in seductive behavior, which they described in lurid detail. Similar ambiguity is evident in the case of Elizabeth Key, a mulatto, a Christian, and the bastard daughter of Thomas Key. In 1655 when she claimed her freedom, her new owner fought to keep her enslaved. William Grimstead, a lawyer who had already fathered two children by her, sued on her behalf, won, and then married her. One planter had no qualms about keeping her in bondage because she was darker than he, despite the known wishes of her deceased father. Another—Grimstead—fell in love with her.

In the generation after 1680, the caste structure of the Chesapeake colonies became firmly set. Fewer indentured servants reached the Chesapeake from England, as the Delaware Valley and the expanding English army and navy competed more successfully for the same young men. Slaves took their place. They cost more to buy but also served for life. Planters who could afford them acquired an economic edge over other settlers. In 1705 the Virginia legislature forbade the whipping of a white servant without a court's permission, a restriction that did not apply to the punishment of slaves. Virginia also promised every ex-servant fifty acres of land. The message was obvious. Every white was now superior to any black. Racial caste was replacing opportunity as the organizing principle of Chesapeake society.

The New England Colonies

Captain John Smith coined the term New England years before the first Puritans left for America. It became an apt phrase. Other Europeans founded colonies to engage in economic activities they could not pursue at home. But the settlers of New England reproduced the mixed economy of old England, with minor variations. Their family farms raised livestock and European grains, as well as corn. Their artisans specialized in a broad range of crafts, from printing to carpentry and shipbuilding. Their quarrel with England was over religion, not economic issues. They came to America, they insisted, to worship as God commanded, not as the Church of England required. That imperative made them critical of other English practices as well. Driven by a radical communitarian vision, the first generation of settlers created towns, congregations, and law courts that suited Puritan purposes very well but differed significantly from the English models on which they drew. Subsequent generations were less certain of their place in the world, less eager to quarrel with English demands, and more inclined to drift back toward English models abandoned by the founders. They were increasingly content to preserve what had already been accomplished. They became conservative communitarians.

The Pilgrims and Plymouth   The Pilgrims were Separatists (see above, p. 56) who left England for the Netherlands between 1607 and 1609, convinced that the Church of England was no true daughter of the Reformation. They hoped to worship freely in Holland. After several years in the city of Leiden, they realized that their children were growing up Dutch, not English. That dilemma prompted a minority of the congregation to move to America. After negotiating rather harsh terms with a London merchant and the London Company, they sailed for Virginia on the *Mayflower*. But the ship got blown off course late in 1620, landing first on Cape Cod, and then on the mainland well north of the 1609 charter boundaries of Virginia, at a place they called Plymouth. Two-thirds of the settlers were not Pilgrims at all; they had been added to the passenger list by the London investors. Before landing, the passengers, who numbered about one hundred, signed a document called the Mayflower Compact. It bound them all to obey the decisions of the majority, an essential precaution. No one really knew what authority they were acting under.

Short on supplies, the colonists suffered keenly during the first winter. Half of them died, including the governor. He was succeeded by William Bradford, who would be reelected annually for all but five years until his death in 1656. The settlers fared much better when spring came. The Patuxet Indians of the area had been wiped out by disease in 1617, but they had left their fields ready for planting. Squanto, the only Patuxet to survive, had been kidnapped in 1614 and carried to England. He had just made his way home and showed up at Plymouth one day in March 1621. He taught the settlers Indian methods of fishing and growing corn. He also introduced them to Massasoit, the powerful Wampanoag sachem (or chief), whose people celebrated the first thanksgiving feast with the settlers after the 1621 harvest. After a decade the settlers numbered about three hundred. By paying off their London creditors, they gained political autonomy and private ownership of their flourishing farms. During the 1630s they founded several new towns, mainly to generate surplus crops that could be sold to the colonists now flooding into the Massachusetts Bay area.

Covenant Theology and the Puritan Quarrel with England

A much larger Puritan exodus settled Massachusetts Bay between 1630 and 1641. The best-educated group that had yet crossed the Atlantic, the settlers included 130 men who had attended a university, most often Cambridge, a Puritan center.

Puritans deeply distrusted Charles I and his courtiers, especially William Laud, archbishop of Canterbury, whom they accused of Catholic sympathies and of "Arminianism," a heresy named for Jacobus Arminius, a Dutch theologian who had challenged the strict Calvinist position on predestination a generation earlier. To Puritans the stakes were high indeed by the late 1620s. During that early phase of Europe's Thirty Years' War (1618-1648), Catholic armies seemed about to crush the German Reformation. Charles I blundered into a brief war against both Spain and France (potentially Spain's most dangerous enemy), raised money for the war by dubious methods, and sent Parliament packing when it protested. Laud's church courts punished Puritans, they complained, but allowed sinners to go their way. God would not be mocked, they warned. His wrath would descend on England.

These matters were of genuine urgency to Puritans, who embraced what they called covenant theology. According to this system, God had made two personal covenants with humans, the covenant of works and the covenant of grace. Under the covenant of works God promised Adam that if he kept God's law he would never die, but Adam ate of the

The Oldest Meetinghouse in America   Built in 1681, this Massachusetts meetinghouse is still standing in the town of Hingham. Puritans modelled their meetinghouses on what they knew of Jewish synagogues in Central Europe. Consciously rejecting the architecture of the Catholic past, they hoped to build something that more closely resembled the earliest Christian churches.

forbidden fruit, was expelled from the Garden of Eden, and died. All of Adam's descendants remain under the same covenant, but because of his Fall none will ever be capable of keeping the law. Thus all humans deserve damnation. But God is merciful, and He answered sin with the covenant of grace, first announced to Noah and then Abraham and the prophets. God will save those He has chosen: "I will be their God, and they shall be my people" (Jer. 31: 34). Everyone else is damned: "Saith the Lord: yet I loved Jacob, and I hated Esau" (Malachi 1: 3).

At this level, covenant theology merely restated Calvinist orthodoxy. Puritans gave it a novel social dimension by pairing each personal covenant with a communal counterpart. The social equivalent of the covenant of grace was the church covenant, by which every Puritan congregation in New England organized itself into a church, a community of the elect. The founders, or "pillars," of each church, after satisfying one another that they had had true conversions, agreed that within their church the Gospel would be properly preached and discipline would be strictly maintained. God, in turn, promised to bestow saving grace within that church — not to everyone, of course, but presumably to most of the children of the elect.

The communal counterpart of the covenant of works was the key to secular history. Puritans called it the "national" covenant. It determined, not who was saved or damned, but the rise and fall of nations or peoples. As a people, New England Puritans agreed to obey the law, and God promised to prosper them. They, in turn, covenanted with their magistrates to punish sinners. If magistrates enforced God's law and the people did not stubbornly resist these efforts, God would not punish the whole community for the misdeeds of individuals. But if sinners were not called to public account, God's anger would be terrible, especially among his chosen people of New England. God gave them much and expected much in return.

Thus, even though the covenant of works no longer brought eternal life, it always remained in force. It established the strict moral standards that every Christian must strive to follow, before and after conversion. A Christian's inability to keep the law usually triggered the conversion experience by demonstrating that only faith could save.

For New Englanders the idea of the covenant became a powerful social metaphor, explaining everything from crop failures and untimely deaths to Indian wars and political contention. Towns and militia companies used covenants to organize themselves. If only because a minister could always think of something that had not been properly corrected, the covenant generated almost an automatic sense of moral crisis. It had a built-in dynamic of moral reform which was becoming obvious even before the migrants crossed the ocean.

In England the government refused to assume its proper role. The Puritans who fled to America hoped to escape the coming wrath that was about to overwhelm England and to create in America the kind of churches that God demanded. A few hoped to erect a model "city upon a hill" to inspire all humankind. Although Governor John Winthrop developed this idea in a famous sermon of 1630, this theme seldom appeared in the writings of other founders. It became more common a generation later when, ironically, any neutral observer could see that the rest of the world no longer cared what New Englanders were doing.

The Founding of Massachusetts Bay   In 1629 several English Puritans obtained a royal charter for the Massachusetts Bay Company, a joint-stock corporation like the Virginia Company of London. But there was one major difference. The charter did not specify where the company was to be located. Puritan stockholders going to New England bought out the other investors. Led by Winthrop, they carried the charter to America, beyond the gaze of Charles I. They used it, not to organize a joint-stock company, but as the constitution for the colony. In the 1630s the Great and General Court created by the charter became instead the colony's legislature.

The settlers came from the broad middle range of English society. Few were rich, few very poor. Most had owned property in England. When they sold it to go to America, they probably liquidated far more capital than the London Company had invested in Virginia. A godly haven was very expensive to build.

An advance party that sailed in 1629 took over a fishing village on the coast and renamed it Salem. The Winthrop fleet brought another thousand settlers in 1630. In small groups they scattered around the bay, founding Dorchester, Roxbury, Boston, Charlestown, and Cambridge. Most of these towns coalesced around a minister and a magistrate. The local congregation was the first institution to take shape. From it evolved the town meeting, as the settlers began to distinguish more sharply between religious and secular affairs. Soon the colonists were raising European livestock and growing English wheat and other grains, along with corn. Yet during the severe first winter, perhaps 30 percent of the settlers perished. A few hundred others grew discouraged and returned to England in the spring.

Conditions rapidly got better, as they had at Plymouth a decade earlier. About 13,000 settlers came to New England by 1641, most as families — virtually a unique event in the history of Atlantic empires to that time. Once the settlers formed a typical farming town, they grew reluctant to admit "strangers" to their communities. New England largely avoided slavery, but not out of sympathy for Africans or abhorrence for the institution. (In 1630 other Puritans founded a colony on Providence Island in the Caribbean which adopted slavery even earlier than Barbados, but Spain destroyed the settlement in 1641.) New Englanders kept slaves out of most of their towns to preserve their religion uncontaminated by outsiders.

In Massachusetts those on the ground did a brisk business selling surplus crops to the newcomers arriving each year. When the flow of migrants ceased in 1641, that market collapsed, creating a crisis that ended only after Boston merchants opened up West Indian markets for New England grain, lumber, and fish. New Englanders possessed this flexibility because, as early as 1631, they began to build their own ships, and shipbuilding soon became a major industry. The economic viability of the region depended on its ability to export food and lumber products to other colonies that grew staple crops.

In this sense the New England settlements were secondary colonies. The very existence of colonies committed to free labor was an oddity. To prosper, they had to trade with primary colonies, the more typical unfree labor societies elsewhere in the hemisphere that sent tobacco and sugar to Europe. New England legislatures encouraged trade and simple manufacturing and eradicated feudal restraints on commerce, some of which were still powerful in England.

The region's economy imperiled Puritan orthodoxy. Most Boston merchants and nearly all fisherman could not meet the religious standards of a Puritan society. Few of them became church members in the first generation. But the colony needed their services and had to put up with them. Life among the fishermen on the Isle of Shoals off the New Hampshire coast became so raucous that Massachusetts forbade women from going there. The fishing towns of Marblehead and Gloucester made almost no effort to implement Puritan values or even to found churches in the early decades, while Boston merchants pressed for toleration of Protestant dissenters because it would be good for business. Although these contrasts softened as the decades passed, Puritan orthodoxy was mostly a rural phenomenon.

Puritan Family Life   In rural areas, settlers soon observed a remarkable fact. After the first winter, deaths were rare. Mariners plying their trade between the Chesapeake and New England noted the contrast between the pale and sickly Virginians and the ruddy and robust New Englanders. "The air of the country is sharp, the rocks many, the trees innumerable, the grass little, the winter cold, the summer hot, the gnats [mosquitoes] in summer biting, the wolves at midnight howling," complained one woman. But

the place was undeniably healthy, and families grew rapidly as six or even ten children reached maturity. The settlers left most European diseases behind and encountered no new ones in New England's bracing climate. For the founders and their children, life expectancy far exceeded the European norm. More than one-fifth of the men who founded Andover lived past eighty. Fathers usually refused to grant land titles to their sons until their own deaths. Because they lived so long, New England became intensely patriarchal. Infant mortality also fell, and few mothers died in childbirth.

Settlers moved often at first, looking for the richest soil, the most congenial neighbors, and the most inspiring minister. By about 1645 most of them had found what they were looking for. Migration into or out of country towns became much lower than in England, and the New England town settled into a tightly knit community that slowly became an intricate web of cousins.

Conversion, Dissent, and the Expansion of New England   Migration within New England had major effects. It occurred so rapidly that within a decade Massachusetts Bay had spawned several new colonies. Competing visions of the godly society energized much of this activity. The vital force behind New England Puritanism was the quest for conversion. Probably because of John Cotton's stirring sermons in Boston, the settlers crossed an invisible boundary in the mid-1630s. As they listened to Cotton's converts offer passionate descriptions of their religious experiences, they turned from analyzing the legitimacy of their own conversions to assessing the validity of their neighbors'. Churches began to test for regeneracy, and the standards of acceptability escalated rapidly. "These times have lately shown . . . more false hearts than ever we saw before," noted one minister as early as 1636. Too many people "expected to believe by some power of their own, and not only and wholly from Christ."

The conversion experience was always ambiguous to a Puritan. Anyone who found no inner trace of saving grace was damned. Anyone absolutely certain of salvation had to be relying on personal merit and was also damned. Conversion took months, even years to achieve. It began with the discovery that one was utterly incapable of keeping God's commands and that one *deserved* damnation, not for an occasional misdeed, but for what one was at one's best—a wretched sinner. It progressed through despair to hope, which always rested on appropriate passages of Scripture that spoke to that person's condition. A true Christian at last found reason to believe that God had saved him or her. The whole process involved a painful balance between assurance and doubt. A saint was sure of salvation, but never too sure.

The quest for conversion also generated dissent and new colonies. The founders of Connecticut feared that Massachusetts had become too strict in certifying church members. The founders of New Haven Colony worried that the Bay Colony was much too lenient. The first Rhode Islanders disagreed with all of them.

In the mid-1630s, Rev. Thomas Hooker, fearing spiritual anarchy in Cotton's preaching in Boston, led his people west to the Connecticut River where they founded Hartford and other towns just south of the charter boundary of Massachusetts. John Winthrop, Jr., built Saybrook Fort at the mouth of the river, and it soon merged with the upriver towns into the colony of Connecticut. In 1639 an affluent group planted New Haven Colony farther west, on Long Island Sound. Their leaders were Theophilus Eaton, a wealthy London merchant with a considerable reputation, and John Davenport, the most severe and uncompromising Puritan minister to come to America. In northern New England, New Hampshire and Maine had independent origins under their own proprietary charters, but when England dissolved into civil war after 1642, Massachusetts extended its authority over these small settlements and ruled them for most of the seventeenth century.

The residents of most towns agreed on the kind of worship they preferred. Everywhere, the sermon replaced the Anglican liturgy as the central ritual of the community. But some settlers, especially Roger Williams and Anne Hutchinson, made even greater demands. Williams, who served briefly as Salem's minister, was a Separatist who refused to worship with anyone who did not explicitly repudiate the Church of England. Nearly all Massachusetts Puritans were Nonseparatists who claimed only to be reforming the Anglican Church. In 1636, after Williams also challenged the king's right as a Christian to grant Indian lands to anyone at all, Massachusetts banished him. He fled to Narragansett Bay with a

few disciples and founded Providence. He developed an eloquent argument for toleration and for the separation of church and state, principles that Rhode Islanders warmly embraced.

Anne Hutchinson, a merchant's wife and a fervent admirer of John Cotton, announced that virtually all other ministers were preaching only the covenant of works rather than the covenant of grace. She thought that they were leading people to hell. She attracted a large following in Boston. At her trial in the General Court, she claimed to have received direct messages from God (the "Antinomian" heresy). Banished in 1638, she and her followers also fled to Narragansett Bay, where they founded Portsmouth and Newport. These towns united with Providence to form the colony of Rhode Island.

By 1640 Massachusetts, Plymouth, Rhode Island, Connecticut, New Haven, New Hampshire, and Maine were all organizing as distinct colonies, even though only Massachusetts, New Hampshire, and Maine could claim legal authority from England. Puritans who moved to Long Island or to the upper Connecticut Valley also showed signs of going their own way.

Much of this activity reflected, not just religious idealism, but a quest for the best land in New England. Expansion threatened the Indians. Connecticut and Massachusetts waged a war of annihilation against the Pequot Indians, who controlled the mouth of the fertile Thames River valley in southeastern Connecticut. In May 1637 New England soldiers debated with their chaplain which of two Pequot forts to attack, the one occupied by warriors or the one holding women, children, and the elderly. He probably told them to remember Saul and the Amalekites because, with horrified Narragansett Indians looking on as nominal allies of the settlers, the Puritan army chose the second fort, set fire to the wigwams of the noncombatants, and shot everyone who tried to flee. The godly had their own uses for terror.

Other Indians—Wampanoags, Narragansetts, Nipmucks, Mohegans—grew cautious and wary in dealing with these dangerous intruders. Like Opechancanough in Virginia, Miantonomo, sachem of the Narragansetts, called for a war of extermination against the settlers, to be launched by a surprise attack in 1642. He abandoned the idea when settlers discovered the plan. The colonists created their own defensive, military alliance in 1643, the New England

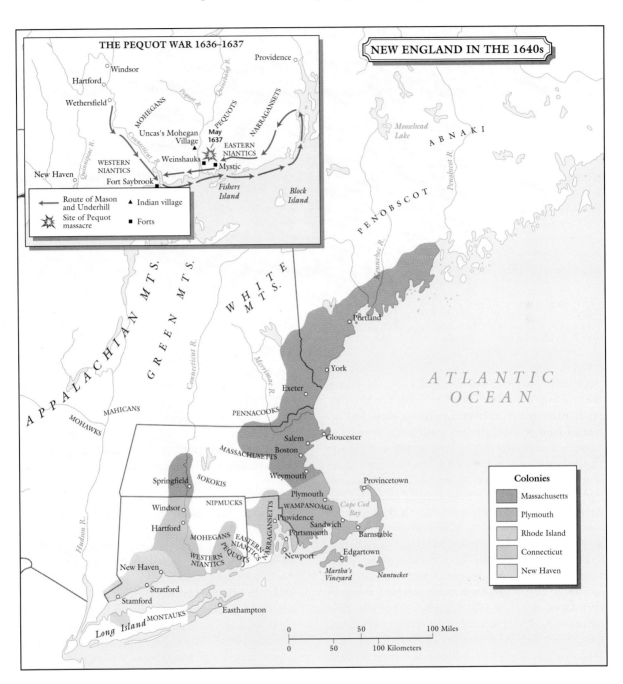

THE PEQUOT WAR 1636–1637

Windsor
Hartford
Wethersfield
MOHEGANS
Uncas's Mohegan Village
WESTERN NIANTICS
New Haven
Fort Saybrook
Weinshauks
Mystic
EASTERN NIANTICS
PEQUOTS
NARRAGANSETS
Providence
May 1637
Fishers Island
Block Island

Pequot R.
Quinnipiac R.
Connecticut R.
Quinebaug R.

→ Route of Mason and Underhill
✴ Site of Pequot massacre
▲ Indian village
■ Forts

NEW ENGLAND IN THE 1640s

Moosehead Lake
ABNAKI
PENOBSCOT
Penobscot R.
Kennebec R.
Portland
York
WHITE MTS.
Exeter
PENNACOOKS
Merrimac R.
Salem
Gloucester
MASSACHUSETTS
Boston
Weymouth
Provincetown
Springfield
SOKOKIS
Plymouth
WAMPANOAGS
Cape Cod Bay
Windsor
NIPMUCKS
Providence
Sandwich
Hartford
MOHEGANS
EASTERN NIANTICS
NARRAGANSETTS
Portsmouth
Barnstable
WESTERN NIANTICS
PEQUOTS
Newport
Edgartown
New Haven
Stratford
Stamford
MONTAUKS
Easthampton
Martha's Vineyard
Nantucket
Long Island

APPALACHIAN MTS.
GREEN MTS.
MAHICANS
MOHAWKS
Connecticut R.
Hudson R.

ATLANTIC OCEAN

Colonies
- Massachusetts
- Plymouth
- Rhode Island
- Connecticut
- New Haven

0   50   100 Miles
0   50   100 Kilometers

Confederation, which united the four orthodox colonies of Massachusetts, Plymouth, Connecticut, and New Haven. Plymouth was acceptable to the other three because, with the Church of England in utter disarray during the civil war at home, the differences between Separatists and Nonseparatists no longer seemed vital. Rhode Island was not invited to participate. The Confederation soon persuaded the Mohegans to kill Miantonomo.

Congregations, Towns, and Colony Governments
New England's institutions took shape in the midst of these internal and external struggles. Congregations abolished the distinctive rites of Anglicanism—

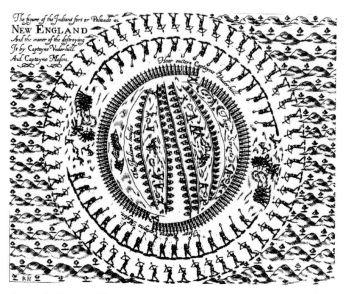

The Puritan Massacre of the Pequot Indians, 1637   The massacre took place at what is now Mystic, Connecticut. Most of the victims were women and children. The Indians in the outer circle were Narragansett allies of the settlers and were appalled by the carnage.

vestments, incense, *The Book of Common Prayer*, church courts, bishops. The sermon became the center of worship, and each congregation chose and ordained its own minister. No singing was permitted, except of psalms, with each worshiper warbling in his or her own key. Individual churches sometimes sent ministers and laymen to a synod, but its decisions were advisory, not authoritative. In 1648 a synod issued the Cambridge Platform, which defined what was coming to be called "Congregationalist" worship and church organization.

By then the town had become a secular entity distinct from the congregation. Towns showed more structural variety. Although some adopted independent farms from the outset, many chose open-field agriculture. Under this medieval system, which appeared nowhere else in colonial America, farmers owned scattered strips of land within a common field, and the town as a whole decided what crops to grow. The emphasis on communal cooperation may have appealed to the founding generation, who were also short of oxen and plows at first and had to share them. But open fields did not survive the first generation.

Town meetings also decided who got how much land. It was distributed broadly but never equally. In Springfield, at one extreme, the Pynchon family controlled most of the land and most labor as well. In many other towns, such as Dedham, differences were small. In some villages, town meetings occurred often, made most of the decisions, and left only the details to a board of elected "selectmen." In others the selectmen did most of the actual governing. All adult males usually participated in local decisions, but Massachusetts and New Haven restricted the vote at the colony level to men who were full church members, a decision that greatly narrowed the electorate by the 1660s.

Massachusetts had a bicameral legislature by the 1640s. Lawful voters elected representatives from their towns who met as a Chamber of Deputies, or lower house. In colonywide elections, voters chose the governor and the magistrates, or upper house (the Council or, in its judicial capacity, the Court of Assistants). The magistrates also staffed the county courts. Final appeals rested with the General Court, with the two houses sitting together on judicial questions.

Massachusetts defined its legal system in the "Body of Liberties" of 1641, which has a strong claim to be regarded as history's first bill of rights. A more comprehensive law code of 1648 was widely imitated in other provinces. The colony sharply reduced the number of capital offenses, which were listed in the order of the Ten Commandments. Unlike England, Massachusetts seldom executed anyone for a crime against property. Other distinctive features of the legal system included the explicit recognition of the liberties of women, children, servants, foreigners, and even "the Bruite Creature," or animals; a serious effort to ban professional lawyers; the swift punishment of crime; and major alterations in the use of juries.

New Haven abolished juries altogether because they were not mentioned in the Bible. In civil (noncriminal) cases in other New England colonies, juries decided appeals as well as the initial suits, and often law as well as fact—a dramatic expansion of their role in England, where juries determined facts and judges applied the law, but appeals were decided by judges. Except in capital trials, the criminal jury, a fixture of English justice, almost disappeared in New England. The punishment of sin involved fidelity to the covenant. It was too important to leave to twelve ordinary men. This system worked well in the orthodox colonies because even sinners shared its values. Most offenders appeared in court and accepted their punishments. Acquittals were rare, almost unheard of in New Haven. Yet hardly anyone ran away.

Infant Baptism, New Dissent, and the Half-Way Covenant   Although most of the founders became church members during the fervor of the 1630s, their children had trouble achieving conversion. They had never lived as part of a beleaguered minority in England, nor had they experienced the joy of joining with other holy refugees in founding their own church. They had to find God on their own and then persuade their elders—on guard because leniency had let Williams, Hutchinson, and other deviants through—that their conversions were authentic. Most could not do it. They grew up, married, and requested baptism for their children. The Cambridge Platform declared that only "saints" (the converted) and their children could be baptized. Other children could not be. But what about the grandchildren of the saints if their parents had failed to experience conversion? No one was sure. By 1660 this problem was becoming a major dilemma.

Dissenters offered two answers, the ministers a third. In the 1640s some New Englanders went frankly Baptist. Noting that Scripture contains no mandate to baptize infants, Baptists believed that only converted adults should receive that rite. Their position seemed to undermine the whole logic of a community in special covenant with the Lord. It implied that New England was no different from old England or Europe. It was a mass of sinners from whom God would randomly choose a few saints. Samuel Gorton, a Baptist expelled from Massachusetts and Plymouth (he denounced the magistrates as "just asses"), founded Warwick, Rhode Island, in the 1640s. When Massachusetts arrested him anyway, accused him of blasphemy, and put him on trial for his life, Gorton appealed to Parliament, and Massachusetts backed down. Baptist principles also attracted Henry Dunster, the able president of Harvard College, which had been founded in 1636 to educate ministers and magistrates for a Puritan society. When the courts began to harass Baptists, Dunster left Massachusetts for more tolerant Plymouth.

Even more alarming were the Quakers, or Society of Friends, who invaded the region from England in the 1650s (see Chapter 3). Quakers rejected Calvinism. They found salvation within themselves—through God, the Inner Light present in all people if they will only let it shine forth. They even abolished baptism and the Lord's Supper. To Puritans the Quaker answer to the conversion dilemma seemed self-delusive, unscriptural, blasphemous, and Antinomian. Between 1659 and 1661, Massachusetts hanged four Quakers who refused to stop preaching, including Mary Dyer, once a disciple of Anne Hutchinson.

The clergy's answer to the lack of conversions, worked out at a synod in 1662, eventually became known as the Half-Way Covenant. Parents who had been baptized but had not yet experienced conversion could bring their children before the church, "own the covenant" (that is, subject themselves and their offspring to the doctrine and discipline of the church), and have their children baptized. In practice women often experienced conversion before age thirty, men closer to forty. But many never did. In most churches women also began to outnumber men as full members. For fifteen or twenty years after 1662, most churches were still dominated by the lay members of the founding generation. Despite the urging of the clergy (by then most ministers were young Harvard graduates, not venerable saints), aging church members resisted implementation of the Half-Way Covenant. As the founders died off in the 1670s and 1680s, the Half-Way Covenant took hold and soon led to something like universal baptism. Virtually every child had some ancestor who had been a full church member.

But dissent persisted. The orthodox colonies were divided over whether to persecute or simply ignore their Baptist and Quaker minorities. Ministers issued shrill warnings against any backsliding from the standards of the founding generation, but many lay people disliked the persecution of conscientious Protestants. By the 1670s, innovation seemed dangerous and divisive, but the past was also becoming a burden that no one could shoulder. As towns buried the founders, they began to move their cemeteries from outlying fields to meetinghouse hill. The city on a hill was becoming a city of the dead.

THE ATLANTIC PRISM AND THE SPECTRUM OF SETTLEMENT

Over thousands of years, the Indians of the Americas, a fairly homogeneous people, had become diversified into hundreds of distinct cultures and languages. The colonists of seventeenth-century North America and the Caribbean were following much the same course. America divided them. The Atlantic gave them what unity they could sustain.

Some observers predicted the rise of new nations in the wilderness. "Will not you believe that a Nation can be borne in a day?" asked Edward Johnson in 1654. New England, he suggested, "is a worke come very neare to it." "By Concord and Union a small Collony may growe into a great and renouned Nation," Lord Baltimore told his quarrelsome people in 1649. It was easy to imagine that New England or the Chesapeake colonies might emerge as distinct nations. But no one yet thought that all of the English mainland colonies would one day be able to unite into a single political system distinct from England's. The colonies seemed much too diverse.

As long as their populations remained small, no colony could duplicate the complexity of England. All of them had to make choices about what to bring with them and what to leave behind, about what they could do for themselves and what they would have to import. These choices were determined both by the settlers' motives for crossing the ocean and by what the new environment would permit. The colonists sorted themselves out along a vast arc from the cold north to the sub-tropical Caribbean. If we can imagine England as a source of white light and the Atlantic as a prism refracting that light, seventeenth-century America becomes a spectrum of settlement, with each color fading imperceptibly into the shade next to it.

Each province had much in common with its near neighbors, but shared few traits with more distant colonies. At the extremes, the sugar colony of Barbados had almost nothing in common with Massachusetts, organized around intense, family-centered piety. Similar contrasts appeared between Canada and the French West Indies.

Demographic Differences

The most pronounced differences involved life expectancy, the sex ratio (the ratio of men to women in any society), and family structure. At one extreme were the all-male, multiethnic buccaneering societies in the Caribbean that lived only for plunder. In the sugar colonies, European men were usually dead by age forty, and slaves a good bit sooner. Because women settlers were scarce for much of the century, the family itself seemed an endangered institution. Even when the sex ratio evened out and families developed, they had few children. In the Chesapeake Bay area, life expectancy for men rose to about forty-five years during the last half of the century, higher than in the islands but still lower than in England, where it exceeded fifty. As natural increase replaced immigration as the main source of population growth in Virginia and Maryland, women became more numerous, married much earlier, and raised larger families.

The northern colonies were much healthier. In New Netherland life expectancy and family size exceeded Europe's by 1660, and men outnumbered women among the newcomers by only two to one. On Long Island in the 1680s, one woman claimed that she had more than 300 living descendants. New England was one of the healthiest places in the world. Because the sex ratio rapidly approached equality and because the thriving economy permitted couples to marry perhaps two years earlier than in England, population grew at an explosive rate. Canada followed a similar pattern. Once the French government began to ship over boatloads of women in the 1660s, the birth rate in New France equaled New England's, and population grew at a comparable pace.

These demographic differences had significant consequences. For example, the Caribbean and Chesapeake colonies were youthful societies in which men with good connections could expect to reach high office while still in their thirties, or even their twenties. By contrast, the New England colonies gradually became dominated by grandfathers. A man was not likely to be elected as a selectman before his forties. Magistrates were even older. Simon Bradstreet was ninety when he completed his last term as governor of Massachusetts in 1692. Despite the appalling death rate in the sugar and tobacco colonies, young men remained optimistic and upbeat, as they looked forward to challenging the world and making their fortunes. But in New England, people grew ever more despondent as the century progressed, even though they lived much longer. The typical sermon was a gloomy jeremiad in which the beleaguered clergy deplored the failings of the rising generation.

Race, Ethnicity, and Economy

The degree of racial and ethnic mixture also varied from region to region, along with economic priorities. The West Indies already had a large slave majority by 1700 and were well on their way to becoming a New Africa, except that the European minority had a firm grip on wealth and power. In 1700 English settlers were still a clear majority in the Chesapeake colonies, but African slaves were increasing rapidly and would become 40 percent of Virginia's population by the 1730s. Africans were less numerous in the Delaware and Hudson Valleys, although slavery became deeply entrenched in New York City and parts of New Jersey. But in the Middle Atlantic region settlers from all over northwestern Europe were creating a new ethnic mosaic, especially in New Jersey and Pennsylvania (see Chapter 3). English colonists were probably always a minority throughout the Mid-Atlantic region, outnumbered at first by the Dutch, and later by Germans, Scots, and Irish. But New England was in every sense the most English of the colonies. In ethnic composition, it may have been more English than England, which by 1700 had sizable Dutch Reformed, French Huguenot, and Scottish Presbyterian minorities. New France was as French as New England was English. The farther south one went on the spectrum, the more diverse the population; the farther north, the more uniform.

Slavery and staple crops went together. The slave societies raised sugar or tobacco for sale in Europe. At the outset, the Dutch and French acquired furs from the Indians for sale abroad, but by 1700 New France raised its own food, and the Middle Atlantic was the wheat belt of North America. The New Englanders caught fish and raised wheat for sale in the West Indies, until a blight in the 1660s forced them to switch to corn. General farming and family labor also went together.

Religion

With the exception of Spanish Florida, the intensity of religious observance varied immensely across the spectrum of settlement, ranging from irreverence and indifference in the islands to intense piety in New England and New France. Because formal education nearly always had a religious base in the seventeenth century, literacy followed a similar pattern. Colonists everywhere tried to prevent slaves from learning to read, and low literacy prevailed wherever slavery predominated. Chesapeake settlers provided almost no formal schooling for their children prior to the founding of the College of William and Mary in 1693 and a Latin grammar school in Annapolis at about the same time. Even some of the justices of the peace in Maryland and Virginia were unable to write. By contrast, the Dutch maintained several good schools in New Netherland. Massachusetts founded Harvard College in 1636 and in 1642 required every town to have a writing school, and larger towns to support a Latin grammar school, in order to frustrate "ye old deluder Satan," as a 1647 school law put it. The Jesuits founded a college (closer to a secondary school) in Quebec a few years before Harvard opened. France sent a bishop to Quebec in 1659, and he established a seminary (now Laval University) in the 1660s. Along the spectrum, literacy and education both increased from south to north.

Public support for the clergy also followed the same pattern. By 1700 the established church of the mother country was the legally established church in the West Indies, Virginia, and (after 1692) Maryland. Establishment and dissent fought each other to a standstill in the Middle Atlantic, with toleration claiming the real victory. In New England, Old World dissent became New World establishment. Public support for the clergy was much greater in the north than the south. The sugar islands possessed the greatest wealth, but they maintained only one clergyman for every three thousand to nine thousand people, depending on the island. In the Chesapeake the

Table 2-2

The Spectrum of Settlement: Demography, Ethnicity, Economy, 1650–1700

Category	West Indies	Lower South*	Chesapeake	Mid-Atlantic	New England	New France
Life expectancy for men, age 20	40	42	45	60+	late 60s	60s
Family Size	Below replacement rate	About two children	Rising after 1680	Very large	Very large	Very large
Race and Ethnicity	Black majority by ca. 1670s	Black majority by ca. 1710	Growing black minority	Ethnic mix, N.W. Europe, English a minority	Almost all English	Almost all French
Economy	Sugar	Rice, 1690s ff	Tobacco	Furs, farms	Farms, fishing, shipbuilding	Furs, farms

*For a discussion of the Lower South, see Chapter 3.

comparable ratio was about one for every fifteen hundred people by 1700. It was perhaps one for every thousand in the Hudson Valley and one for every six hundred in New England. It was lower still in New France.

Contemporaries expected moral standards to rise from south to north. New Englanders, gloomy though they were among themselves, boasted that they were far more godly than all other colonists. The Puritans "give out that they are Israelites," reported a Dutch visitor to Connecticut, "and that we in our colony are Egyptians, and that the English in the Virginias are also Egyptians." As early as 1638 one Marylander said roughly the same thing when he quipped that a neighbor deserved to be "whippt at virginea" or "hanged in new England."

Local and Provincial Governments

Governmental forms varied considerably along the spectrum. Drawing on their English experience, the settlers could choose from among parishes, boroughs (towns), counties, and other local institutions. Their choices followed the gradations of the spectrum of settlement.

The only important local institution in the islands was the parish. The Chesapeake colonies relied primarily on the county but also made increasing use of the parish. Few parishes were ever organized in the Middle Atlantic colonies, but counties arrived with the English conquest of New Netherland in 1664 and became powerful institutions. Townships also appeared. New England's most basic local institution was the town, although Massachusetts adopted counties in the 1640s, followed twenty years later by Connecticut and in the 1680s by Plymouth. Rhode Island and New Hampshire waited until the eighteenth century before creating counties. After 1700 New England towns large enough to support more than one church also adopted the parish system. In local government as in other activities, New England's use of the full range of parishes, towns and counties made the region more completely English than other colonies.

At the provincial level, the West Indian colonies all had royal governments by the 1660s. Proprietary forms dominated the mainland south of New England, except for royal Virginia. Until the 1680s New England relied upon corporate forms of government in which all officials, even governors, were elected. This system survived in Connecticut and Rhode Island until independence and beyond.

Some Unifying Trends: Language, War, Law, and Inheritance

Despite all this diversity, a few trends toward greater homogeneity developed in the seventeenth century.

Table 2-3

The Spectrum of Settlement: Religion and Government, ca. 1675–1700

Category	West Indies	Lower South*	Chesapeake	Mid-Atlantic	New England	New France
Formal religion	Anglican Church establishment	Anglican Church establishment by ca. 1700	Anglican Church establishment (after 1692 in Md.)	Competing sects, no established church	Congregational Church established	Catholic Church established
Religious tone	Irreverent	Contentious	Low-church Anglican	Family-based piety, sectarian competition	Family-based piety, intensity declining	Intensely Catholic
Local	Parish	Parish and phantom counties (i.e., no court)	County and parish	County and township	Towns and counties; parishes after 1700	Cities
Provincial	Royal	Proprietary	Royal (Va.), proprietary (Md.)	From proprietary to royal	Corporate, with Mass. becoming royal	Royal absolutism

*For a discussion of the Lower South, see Chapter 3.

Language became more uniform in America than it was in England. True, the New England twang derived mostly from East Anglia, the southern accent from southern and western England, and Middle Atlantic speech from north-central England. But Londoners went to all of the colonies (in England, other people went to London), and London English affected every American province and softened the differences among these emerging regional dialects.

The settlers waged war in their own way, not with the professional armies that were becoming the European norm, but through short-term volunteers for whom terror against Indian women and children was often the tactic of choice. Europe was moving toward limited wars; the colonists demanded total victory through annihilation.

Everywhere in America law became a much simplified version of England's complex legal system. Justice was local and uncomplicated, mostly because an organized legal profession did not emerge before the eighteenth century. Most settlers applauded the absence of lawyers.

Finally, no mainland American colony rigidly followed English patterns of inheritance. Women had a better chance of acquiring property, particularly in the Chesapeake colonies during the long period when men greatly outnumbered them. The single women who came as servants to the Chesapeake settlements were desperate people who had hit bottom in England. If women managed to stay alive, Virginia and Maryland offered them a fantastic chance at upward mobility. Many achieved a respectability never available to them in England. In every colony younger sons also found their situation improved. They played a disproportionate role in settling the colonies, particularly among the Chesapeake elite, and they showed little inclination to perpetuate institutions that offered them no inheritance in England. Most families made no distinction between the eldest and other sons, except in New England. The Puritan colonies honored a biblical mandate to give the eldest son a double share. That practice strengthened patriarchy in the region, but it was much less discriminatory than the English custom of primogeniture, which gave all land to the eldest son.

The American continent was turning European intruders into quite distinct peoples. After 1700, the colonies grew more alike by reaffirming their shared English heritage. They had to become more English before they would even think of becoming American.

SUGGESTED READING

David J. Weber, *The Spanish Frontier in North America* (1992) is excellent on the Franciscan missions in Florida and New Mexico. W. J. Eccles, *France in America* (1972) is a concise and authoritative survey. Peter N. Moogk, "Reluctant Exiles: The Problem of Colonization in French North America," *William and Mary Quarterly*, 3d ser., 46 (1989), 463–505; Morris Altman, "Economic Growth in Canada: Estimates and Analysis," *William and Mary Quarterly*, 3d ser., 45 (1988), 684–711; and Winstanley Briggs, "Le Pays des Illinois," *William and Mary Quarterly*, 3d ser., 47 (1990), 30–56 are very helpful. Simon Schama, *The Embarrassment of Riches: An Interpretation of Dutch Culture in the Golden Age* (1987), and Charles R. Boxer, *The Dutch Seaborne Empire: 1600–1800* (1965) provide superb overviews. George Masselman, *The Cradle of Colonialism* (1963); and Jonathan I. Israel, *Dutch Primacy in World Trade, 1585–1740* (1989) are more specialized. Oliver A. Rink, *Holland on the Hudson: An Economic and Social History of Dutch New York* (1986), and S. G. Nissenson, *The Patroon's Domain* (1937) cover New Netherland. On Elizabethan expansion, David B. Quinn, *England and the Discovery of America, 1481–1620* (1974), and Kenneth R. Andrews, *Trade, Plunder, and Settlement: Maritime Enterprise and the Genesis of the British Empire, 1480–1630* (1984) offer fine narratives. Karen O. Kupperman, *Roanoke: The Abandoned Colony* (1984) is briefer than David B. Quinn, *Set Fair for Roanoke: Voyages and Colonies, 1584–1606* (1985). Both are masterful. Nicholas P. Canny, *The Elizabethan Conquest of Ireland: A Pattern Established, 1565–1576* (1976), and his *Kingdom and Colony: Ireland in the Atlantic World, 1560–1800* (1988) place the conquest of Ireland in a broad, Atlantic context.

Jack P. Greene, *Pursuits of Happiness: The Social Development of Early Modern British Colonies and the Formation of American Culture* (1988) surveys all thirteen colonies within the context of Britain's other Atlantic provinces, including Ireland and the West Indies. David Hackett Fischer, *Albion's Seed: Four British Folkways in America* (1989) traces the regional identities of New England, the upper South, the Mid-Atlantic, and the early backcountry to specific subcultures within the British Isles. Bernard Bailyn, *The Peopling of British North America: An Introduction* (1985) is a broadly conceived overview of the settlement process. Stanley N. Katz, John M. Murrin, and Douglas Greenberg, eds., *Colonial America: Essays in Politics and Social Development*, 4th ed. (1993), and Jack P. Greene and J. R. Pole, eds., *Colonial British America: Essays in the New History of the Early Modern Era* (1984) contain major interpretative essays.

Edmund S. Morgan, *American Slavery, American Freedom: The Ordeal of Colonial Virginia* (1975) remains the best history of any American colony. J. Frederick Fausz, "An Abundance of Blood Shed on Both Sides': England's First Indian War, 1609–1614," *Virginia Magazine of History and Biography*, 98 (1990), 3–56 is sobering. Thad W. Tate and David L. Ammerman, eds., *The Chesapeake in the Seventeenth Century: Essays on Anglo-American Society* (1979); Lois Green Carr, Philip D. Morgan, and Jean B. Russo, eds., *Colonial Chesapeake Society* (1988); and Aubrey Land, Lois Green Carr, and Edward C. Papenfuse, eds., *Law, Society, and Politics in Early Maryland* (1977) provide recent perspectives on the social history of the Chesapeake colonies. Darrett and Anita Rutman, *A Place in Time* (1984) is a community study of Middlesex County, Virginia. Martin H. Quitt, "Immigrant Origins of the Virginia Gentry: A Study of Cultural Transmission and Innovation," *William and Mary Quarterly*, 3d ser., 45 (1988), 629–655 explores the role of younger sons in shaping cultural values. Strong studies of Maryland include Gloria L. Main, *Tobacco Colony: Life in Early Maryland, 1650–1720* (1982); Russell R. Menard, *Economy and Society in Early Colonial Maryland* (1985); and David W. Jordan, *Foundations of Representative Government in Maryland, 1632–1715* (1987). On the West Indies, see Carl and Roberta Bridenbaugh, *No Peace beyond the Line: The English in the Caribbean, 1624–1690* (1972), and Richard S. Dunn, *Sugar and Slaves: The Rise of the Planter Class in the English West Indies, 1624–1713* (1972). Winthrop Jordan, *White over Black: American Attitudes toward the Negro, 1550–1812* (1968), and Orlando Patterson, *Slavery and Social Death: A Comparative Study* (1982) are classics.

Perry Miller, *The New England Mind: The Seventeenth Century* (1939); Edmund S. Morgan, *Visible Saints: The History of a Puritan Idea* (1963); and David D. Hall, *Worlds of Wonder, Days of Judgment: Popular Religious Belief in Early New England* (1989) are indispensable studies of New England Puritanism. Other major contributions include Sacvan Bercovitch, *The Puritan Origins of the American Self* (1975), Charles L. Cohen, *God's Caress: The Psychology of Puritan Religious Experience* (1986); Harry S. Stout, *The New England Soul: Preaching and Religious Culture in Colonial New England* (1986); and Andrew Delbanco, *The Puritan Ordeal* (1989). William Bradford, *Of Plymouth Plantation, 1620–1647*, ed. Samuel Eliot Morison (1959) is the best edition of an American classic.

David Hall, John M. Murrin, and Thad W. Tate, eds., *Saints and Revolutionaries: Essays on Early American History* (1984) contains several important contributions on early New England. Virginia D. Anderson, *New England's Generation: The Great Migration and the Formation of Society and Culture in the Seventeenth Century* (1991) is the best study of the migration process. Major community and demographic studies include Darrett B. Rutman, *Winthrop's Boston: A Portrait of a Puritan Town, 1630–1649* (1965); John Demos, *A Little Commonwealth: Family Life in Plymouth Colony* (1970); Philip J. Greven, Jr., *Four Generations: Population, Land, and Family in*

Colonial Andover, Massachusetts (1970); Kenneth A. Lockridge, *A New England Town, the First Hundred Years: Dedham, Massachusetts, 1636–1736*, rev. ed. (1985); and Stephen Innes, *Labor in a New Land: Economy and Society in Seventeenth-Century Springfield* (1983). Laurel T. Ulrich, *Good Wives: Images and Reality in the Lives of Women in Northern New England, 1650–1750* (1982) has been pathbreaking. Major studies of the New England economy include Bernard Bailyn, *The New England Merchants in the Seventeenth Century* (1955); Stephen Innes, *Creating the Commonwealth: The Economic Culture of Puritan New England* (1995); and Daniel Vickers, *Farmers and Fishermen: Two Centuries of Work in Essex County, Massachusetts, 1630–1850* (1994). Karen O. Kupperman, *Providence Island, 1630–1641: The Other Puritan Colony* (1993) tells the very different story of Puritan colonization in the tropics. Studies of dissent in New England include Edmund S. Morgan, *Roger Williams: The Church and the State* (1967); Emery Battis, *Saints and Sectaries: Anne Hutchinson and the Antinomian Controversy in the Massachusetts Bay Colony* (1962); and Carla G. Pestana,

Quakers and Baptists in Colonial Massachusetts (1991). Robert E. Wall shows how the political and legal systems of Massachusetts took shape in response to dissent and controversy in *Massachusetts Bay: The Crucial Decade, 1640–1650* (1972). Robert G. Pope, *The Half-Way Covenant: Church Membership in Puritan New England* (1969) is insightful and thorough. For Indian relations in early New England, see William Cronon, *Changes in the Land: Indians, Colonists, and the Ecology of New England* (1983); Richard Slotkin, *Regeneration through Violence: The Mythology of the American Frontier* (1973); and Francis Jennings, *The Invasion of America: Indians, Colonialism, and the Cant of Conquest* (1975). Both Slotkin and Jennings carefully analyze the massacre of the Pequots.

Videos: *Black Robe*, a 1991 Canadian film based on Brian Manning's novel of the same name, is a powerful evocation of the early Jesuit missions in New France. The PBS miniseries, *Roanoak* explores tensions between settlers and Indians in England's first sustained attempt to colonize North America.

Chapter 3

England Discovers Its Colonies: Upheaval, War, Trade, and Empire

The first coffeehouses, such as this London one, dated from the 1650s. By the eighteenth century, merchants routinely met in them to transact their colonial business, and specialized establishments emerged to accommodate them, such as the Virginia Coffeehouse and the New England Coffeehouse. England's rapidly growing consumption of coffee, tea, and chocolate stimulated most of the demand for sugar, which in turn sustained the Atlantic slave trade.

In 1603, when James VI of Scotland ascended the throne of England as King James I, England was still a weak power on the fringes of Europe with no colonies overseas, except in Ireland. By 1700 England was a global giant, capable of tipping the balance of power within Europe. It possessed about twenty colonies in North America and the West Indies, had acquired direct control of much of the African slave trade, and had muscled its way even into distant India. Everyone agreed that commerce and colonies had immensely strengthened England's influence within Europe.

This transformation occurred during a century of political and religious upheaval at home. King and Parliament fought a long struggle over their respective powers, a contest that led to civil war and the execution of one king in the 1640s and to the over-

throw of another in 1688. The result was a distinctive form of constitutionalism that rested upon parliamentary supremacy and responsible government. Ministers of the Crown became answerable for their actions.

Within England, this upheaval generated competing visions of politics and the good society. At one extreme the ruling Stuart dynasty often seemed to be trying to create an absolute monarchy, similar to that of Spain or France. Opponents of absolutism groped for ways to guarantee government by consent without undermining public order.

England's American colonies shared in the turmoil. Those founded after 1660 reflected the distinctive hopes and beliefs of their founders, many of whom expressed profound dissatisfaction with existing English ways. The founders of Carolina tried to create an ideal aristocratic society. New York, the domain of the duke of York (later James II), actively experimented with absolute government. In the Delaware Valley, Quakers founded societies of brotherly love that respected liberty and property while granting full religious toleration and wide participation in public life. Yet by 1700 all of the colonies, new and old, had begun to converge around the newly defined principles of English constitutionalism. All of them adopted representative government at some point in the century. All of them affirmed the values of liberty and property under the English Crown.

UPHEAVAL IN ENGLAND AND THE COLONIES

The 1640s were a critical decade in England and across the spectrum of settlement, affecting even New France and New Netherland. From 1629 to 1640 King Charles I governed without Parliament. But when he tried to impose the Anglican *Book of Common Prayer* upon the Presbyterian Kirk (Church), his Scottish subjects rebelled and even invaded England. Needing revenue, Charles summoned a new Parliament in 1640 only to find that many of its members, especially the Puritans, sympathized with the Scots. Civil war erupted in the aftermath of a massive revolt of Irish Catholics in 1641 against the Protestant colonizers of their land. King and Parliament agreed that the Irish must be crushed, but neither dared trust the other with the men and resources to do the job. Fighting soon broke out between them.

The English Civil Wars

In 1642 King and Parliament raised their own armies and went to war. As Parliament gradually won the military struggle, it had to govern most of England without a king. In January 1649, after its moderate members had been purged by its own "New Model" army, Parliament beheaded Charles, abolished the House of Lords, and proclaimed England a commonwealth (or republic). The royal heir, Charles II, fled to the continent. Within a few years Oliver Cromwell, Parliament's most successful general, dismissed Parliament, and the army then proclaimed

him Lord Protector of England. He convened several of his own Parliaments, including one that consisted entirely of godly men, but these experiments failed. The army, even when it drafted a written constitution for England, could not win legitimacy for a government that ruled without the ancient trinity of king, Lords, and Commons.

Most of the republican ideas later associated with the American Revolution were passionately debated in England during the 1640s and 1650s. In 1640 even the parliamentary opposition still spoke of the divine right of kings and declared that God's vice-regent could not be guilty of the wicked things that were happening in England. Instead, the King's advisers must be responsible for those evils, and the House of Commons impeached most of them. The pressures of civil war shattered the consensus about divine right and inspired new ideas about the sovereignty of the people. The king's opponents increasingly said that they spoke for "the people," but they could not agree on who best expressed that voice — the complete Parliament, or only its most godly members; the New Model army, or only its officers; or perhaps ordinary people themselves, whom the so-called "levelers," "diggers," and "ranters" claimed to represent as they demanded sweeping social reforms.

Many republicans insisted that if power now resided in Parliament, it must be limited, perhaps by a written constitution. But who had the right to draft a constitution? Who could amend it? For a time, the inability of republicans to resolve these dilemmas discredited the idea that the people must be sovereign, especially after the restoration of Charles II in 1660. Anglican ministers preached the divine right of kings after 1660, but it had lost most of its power to persuade. The notion of popular sovereignty never died, and it emerged again with new force in the colonies in the eighteenth century.

Upheaval in America

England's civil wars rocked the rest of the emerging empire, politically and economically. Cromwell conquered Scotland and then Ireland. As royal power collapsed in the 1640s, England's West Indian colonies demanded and received elective assemblies, just before the introduction of sugar transformed the social structure of the islands. The Dutch, taking advantage of the chaos in England, helped finance the sugar revolution in Barbados, and seized control of trade in and out of the West Indian and Chesapeake colonies. By 1650 most sugar and tobacco was going to Amsterdam, not London.

During the civil war, nobody in England exercised effective control over the colonies. The king had declared that their trade was to remain in English hands, but no agency existed to enforce that claim. The newly created representative assemblies of Barbados and the Leeward Islands preferred to trade with the Dutch, even after the Crown took over those colonies in 1660. The mainland colonies had been organized by joint-stock companies or proprietary lords under charters from the Crown, but these colonists also governed themselves. As the New England settlements expanded, the new colonies of Connecticut, Rhode Island, and New Haven did not even bother to obtain royal charters. The king appointed a governor only in Virginia.

Although the Indians of the eastern woodlands never combined into an effective league or adopted a uniform policy, many of them began to entertain thoughts of driving the Europeans out altogether. "So must we be one as [the English] are, otherwise we shall all be gone shortly," declared Miantonomo, a Narragansett sachem. "For you know our fathers had plenty of deer and skins, our plains were full of deer, as also our woods, and of turkeys, and our coves full of fish and fowl. But these English have gotten our land, they with scythes cut down the grass, and with axes fell the trees; their cows and horses eat the grass, and their cows spoil our clam banks." Unless Indians united to thrown out the invaders, he warned, "we shall be starved." And the 1640s seemed to give them a unique opportunity. The disruption of trade with England during the civil wars also threatened to cut the settlements off from regular supplies of muskets and gunpowder, giving the Indians a powerful advantage. That danger seemed so ominous that Rhode Island ordered young men to learn how to use bows and arrows.

Indians greatly outnumbered settlers, except in eastern New England and the Virginia tidewater. Between 1643 and 1647, the Iroquois nearly wiped out New France, and the Hudson Valley Algonquians almost destroyed New Netherland. Maryland, beset by conflicts with Susquehannock Indians and by civil war among its colonists, nearly ceased to exist. Its settler population may have fallen to a mere three hundred by 1648. In Virginia the aging warrior Opechancanough staged another massacre, killing five hundred settlers without warning on a holy day in 1644. This time the settlers recovered more quickly, took Opechancanough prisoner in 1646, and murdered him in captivity. They then broke up his chiefdom and reduced its member tribes to a state of dependency.

Only New England avoided war with the Indians —but just barely. The Narragansetts planned a war of extermination against the settlers in 1642 but abandoned the idea after the colonists heard rumors about it (see Chapter 2). These Indians controlled some of the finest land in New England. Massachusetts, Plymouth, and Connecticut all wanted it. But the Narragansett people were still too powerful to inti-midate. When threatened, they withdrew into swampy places, knowing that the settlers were terrified by the wilderness and would not pursue them. The Indians made it clear that they would fight if they had to, and the Puritans backed down. Nevertheless, recurring military alarms occupied much of the settlers' attention into the 1650s.

The English Restoration

After Cromwell died in September 1658, his regime collapsed. Part of the army then invited Charles II (1660–1685) back from exile to claim his throne. This "Restoration" government by king, Lords, and Commons made surprisingly few constitutional changes after twenty years of turmoil. The Church of England was reestablished under its episcopal form of government. The English state, denying any right of dissent, persecuted both Catholics and Protestant dissenters—Presbyterians, Independents (Congregationalists), Baptists, and Quakers. Renewed persecution drove a small but important band of Puritan clergymen to New England in the 1660s, and much larger numbers of Quaker families to the Delaware Valley after 1675. Actually, both Charles II and his brother James II (1685–1688) favored much broader toleration of Catholics and dissenters than the strongly Anglican Parliament was willing to grant.

Events in the colonies seemed remote from the urgent concerns of the English people in the turbulent 1640s. But as the debris of civil war was cleared away and the commercial ascendancy of the Dutch became ever more obvious, the English turned their eyes westward once again. In a sense, England discovered its colonies and their importance around 1650.

MERCANTILISM, THE ANGLO-DUTCH WARS, AND THE NAVIGATION ACTS

During the seventeenth century, most of the European powers followed a set of policies loosely described as "mercantilistic." The decline of the Spanish Empire persuaded many observers that the power of a state depended more on the underlying economy than on armies alone or even the silver that paid for them. Mercantilists agreed that power derived ultimately from the wealth of a country, that the creation of wealth required vigorous trade, and that colonies had become essential to that process. Clearly, a state had to control the commerce of its colonies. Mercantilists disagreed over other ways to promote the growth of a country's wealth. The Dutch favored virtual free trade within Europe. Others, including England, preferred some kind of state intervention in the economy.

Mercantilism as a Moral Revolution

After a century of bitter warfare, neither Catholics nor Protestants had been able to win a decisive victory in Europe. To European statesmen of the time, the seemingly endless conflicts of the previous century merely confirmed their belief that governments rested upon the passions of men. Philosophers agreed that the major passions are, in descending order, glory, love, and greed. Glory was nobler than carnal love, and love more inspiring than greed, which in any case was beneath the dignity of a gentleman. But a century of religious wars, motivated by glory and the love of particular causes, had crippled Spain and killed one-third of the German people.

Statesmen began to look more favorably upon greed. In that passion they found interesting properties. The pursuit of glory and love inspired intense, but unpredictable activity, followed by relaxation or even exhaustion. But because it can never be satiated, greed could foster *predictable* behavior, since individuals nearly always pursue their self-interest. By providing economic incentives, then, a state could induce its people to engage in activities that would increase not just their own wealth and power but that of the country as well. And through the imposition of import duties and other disincentives, the state could discourage actions detrimental to its power.

At first these ideas were as gloomy as the world in which they arose. Early mercantilists assumed that the world contained a fixed supply of wealth. A state, to augment its own power, would have to expropriate the wealth of a rival. Trade wars would replace religious wars, but presumably these conflicts would be less destructive, which they usually were. Gradually a more radical idea took hold. The growth of trade might multiply the wealth of the whole world, with all nations benefiting and becoming so interdependent that war between them would be recognized as suicidal. That vision of peace and unending growth has never been realized, but it still inspires people today.

In two respects, mercantilism marked a major breakthrough toward modernity. Over time it became closely associated with the emerging idea of

A Pictish Man Holding a Human Head, by John White, Late Sixteenth Century   In the ancient world, the Picts were among the ancestors of the English and the Scots. White, who painted many Indian scenes on Roanoke Island in the 1580s, believed that the English had been "savages" not all that long ago and that American Indians, like the English, could progress to "civility." America made him think of "progress."

indefinite progress, and it also made statesmen re-think the role of legislation in their societies.

Europeans were already familiar with two kinds of progress, one associated with Christianity, the other more secular and humanist. The opening of the Americas had already reinforced both visions. Humanists knew that the distant ancestors of Europeans had all been "barbarians," who had advanced over the centuries toward "civility." Their own encounters with the peoples of Africa, Ireland, and America underscored this dualistic view by revealing new "savages" who seemed morally and culturally inferior to "civilized" colonists. Most Christians shared these convictions, but they also believed with varying degrees of urgency that human society was progressing toward a future millennium in which Christ will return to earth and reign with His saints in perfect harmony for a thousand years. To missionaries, both Catholic and Protestant, the discovery of millions of "heathens" in the Americas gave a strong boost to millennial thinking. God had chosen this moment to open a new hemisphere to Christians, they explained, because the millennium was near. The common thread in humanist and Christian thinking about progress is that both were static ideas. Humanity would advance to a certain level, and then change would cease. Mercantilism, by contrast, marked a revolution of the human imagination precisely because it aroused visions of unending progress.

Mercantilism also promoted a much more modern concept of law. In the past, most jurists believed that legislation merely reduced natural laws or immemorial customs to written form. They did not see new laws as agents of change. Mercantilists did. They intended to modify behavior, perhaps even transform society. They had no illusions about achieving perfection, however. At first, they probably considered anything a triumph that made their exhausted world less terrible. But as the decades passed, mercantilists became more confident of their ability to improve society.

The Navigation Acts

English merchants began debating trade policy during a severe depression in the 1620s and soon reached a consensus of sorts. They agreed that a nation's wealth depended on its balance of trade, that a healthy nation ought to export more than it imports, and that

the difference—or balance—could be converted into military strength. They also believed that a state needed colonies to produce essential commodities unavailable at home. Finally, they argued that a society ought to export, not import luxuries. As English merchants observed, the commercial success of the Dutch seemed to rest on a mastery of these principles. For England to catch up, Parliament would have to intervene.

England began to address these problems of regulation during the decades of upheaval. With the close of the Thirty Years' War in Europe in 1648, the three major Protestant powers—Sweden, the Netherlands, and England—no longer had reason to avoid fighting one another. England reacted quickly after the execution of Charles I. London merchants clamored for measures to stifle Dutch competition, and Parliament listened to them, not to Cromwell and other Puritans who thought that war between the two Protestant republics would be a scandal and an abomination. The merchants got their Navigation Acts—and their war.

In 1650 Parliament banned foreign ships from English colonies. One year later, it passed the first comprehensive Navigation Act, aimed at Dutch competition. Asian and African goods could be imported into the British Isles or the colonies only in English-owned ships, and the master and at least half of each crew also had to be Englishmen. European goods could be imported into Britain or the colonies in either English ships or the vessels of the producing country, but trade between one English port and another was forbidden to foreigners. At a time when thousands of English sailors were serving in the vast Dutch merchant marine, and a smaller number of Dutch seamen served on English ships, Parliament was determined to gain control of English trade and to compel English seamen to sail aboard English ships.

This new attention from the English government angered the colonists in the West Indies and North America. Mercantilists assumed that the colonies existed only to enrich the mother country. Why else had England permitted them to be founded? But the young men growing sugar in Barbados or tobacco in Virginia intended to prosper on their own. Selling their crops to the Dutch, who offered the lowest freight rates, added to their profits. Although New England produced no staple desired in Europe except fish, Yankee skippers cheerfully swapped their fish or forest products in the Chesapeake for tobacco, which they then carried directly to Europe, usually to Amsterdam.

Barbados greeted the Navigation Act by proclaiming virtual independence. "But we declare, that we will never be so unthankful to the Netherlanders for their former help and assistance, as to deny or forbid them, or any other nation, the freedom of our harbours, and the protection of our Laws, by which they may continue, if they please, all freedom of commerce and traffic with us," the islanders announced. They had founded their settlement at their own expense, not England's, they insisted. "We cannot think, that there are any amongst us, who are soe simple, and so unworthily minded, that they would not rather chuse a noble death, than forsake their ould liberties and privileges." The Chesapeake colonies also continued to welcome Dutch and Yankee traders. In 1651–1652, England dispatched a naval force to America. It compelled Barbados to submit to Parliament and then sailed to the Chesapeake, where Virginia capitulated in 1652. In return, the Virginians received the right to elect their own governor, a privilege that the Crown revoked in 1660. But in the absence of resident officials to enforce English policy, trade with the Dutch continued.

By 1652 England and the Netherlands were at war. For two years the English navy, trim and efficient after a decade of struggle against the king's forces, dealt heavy blows to the Dutch. Finally, in 1654, Cromwell sent Parliament home and made peace. A militant Protestant, he preferred to fight Catholic Spain rather than the Netherlands. In the tradition of Drake, Gilbert, Ralegh, and Warwick, he sent a fleet to conquer Hispaniola. It failed, but it did take Jamaica in 1655.

By the Restoration era after 1660, mercantilist thinking had become widespread. Although the new royalist Parliament invalidated all legislation passed during the Commonwealth period, these "Cavaliers" (supporters of the Stuart dynasty during the civil wars) promptly reenacted and extended the original Navigation Act in a series of new measures. The Navigation Act of 1660 required that all colonial trade be carried on English ships (a category that included colonial vessels but now excluded the Scots), but the master and *three-fourths* of the crew had to be English. The act also created a category of "enumerated commodities," of which sugar and tobacco were the most important. These products had to be shipped from the colony of origin only to England or to another English colony, the intent being to give England a monopoly over the export of major staples from every English colony to Europe and the rest of the world. The colonists could still export unenumerated commodities elsewhere. New Englanders could send fish to a French sugar island, for example, and Virginians could export wheat to Cuba, provided the French and the Spanish would let them.

In a second measure, the Staple Act of 1663, Parliament regulated goods going to the colonies. With few exceptions, products from Europe, Asia, or Africa could not be delivered to the settlements unless they had first been landed in England.

A third measure, the Plantation Duty Act of 1673, required captains of colonial ships to post bond in the colonies that they would deliver all enumerated commodities to England, or else pay on the spot the duties that would be owed in England (the "plantation duty"). This measure, England hoped, would eliminate all incentives to smuggle. To make it effective, England for the first time sent customs officers to the colonies to collect the duty and prosecute all violators. Because the only income these officials received came from the fees they imposed and from their share of condemned vessels, their livings remained precarious. At first colonial governments regarded customs collectors as parasites. Maryland officials even murdered one of them in the 1680s.

Parliament intended nothing less than a revolution in Atlantic commerce. Properly enforced, these measures would dislodge the Dutch and establish English hegemony over this trade. That is precisely what happened over the next generation. In 1600, 90 percent of England's exports consisted of woolen cloth. By 1700 colonial and Asian commerce accounted for 30 to 40 percent of England's overseas trade, and London had become the largest city in western Europe. Its population nearly tripled during the seventeenth century.

Enforcement long remained uneven, but in the 1670s a war between France and the Netherlands diverted critical Dutch resources from trade to defense, thus helping England to catch up with the Dutch. By 1710 the British Navy had become the most powerful fleet in the world. By then virtually all British colonial trade was carried on British ships. Sugar, tobacco, and other staple crops all passed through

Britain on their way to their ultimate destination. Nearly all of the manufactured goods consumed in the colonies were made in Britain. Most products from Europe or Asia destined for the colonies passed through Britain first, though some smuggling of these goods continued.

Few government policies have ever been as successful as England's basic Navigation Acts, but England achieved these results without pursuing a steady course. For example, in granting royal charters to Rhode Island in 1662 and to Connecticut in 1663, Charles II approved elective governors and legislatures in both colonies. (The Connecticut charter also absorbed the New Haven Colony into the Hartford government.) These elective officials could not be dismissed or punished for failure to enforce the Navigation Acts. Moreover, the Crown also authorized the creation of several new colonies in which the organizers received broad powers but had little incentive to observe English mercantilist policies.

THE RESTORATION COLONIES

England had founded six of the original thirteen colonies before 1640. Six others were founded or came under English rule during the Restoration Era (1660–1688). The last, Georgia, was settled in the 1730s (see Chapter 4).

Most of the Restoration colonies shared certain common features and also differed in some respects from earlier settlements. All were proprietary in form. As with Maryland earlier, a proprietary charter empowered one man or a group of men to pursue daring social experiments. All of the Restoration colonies except Pennsylvania were founded by men with big ideas and small purses. The proprietors tried to attract settlers from the older colonies because importing them from Europe was too expensive, especially after England's population finally stopped growing.

The most available prospects were the young men completing their indentures in the West Indies and being driven out by the sugar revolution. The most prized settlers were New Englanders. Although the proprietors disliked their piety and distrusted their politics, New Englanders had built the most successful colonies in North America. Cromwell tried but failed to attract New Haven settlers to Jamaica. The Carolina proprietors did lure one group of Yankees

to the Cape Fear region in the 1660s, but they departed after a year, leaving behind a sign that proclaimed the place to be unfit for human habitation. Few New Englanders were willing to go farther south than New York and New Jersey. Instead, settlers from the West Indies populated the southern mainland, especially South Carolina.

The Restoration colonies made it easy to acquire land, and they competed with one another for settlers by offering strong guarantees of civil and political liberties. They all promised religious toleration, at least for Christians. Whereas Virginia and the orthodox colonies of New England were still homogeneous societies, all Restoration settlements attracted a mix of religious and ethnic groups. None of them found it easy to translate this human diversity into political stability.

Most of the new proprietors were cavaliers who had depleted their fortunes supporting Charles I. Charles II owed them something, and a colonial charter cost nothing to grant. Nearly all of the proprietors were close associates of the king's brother, James, duke of York, and many of them took part in more than one project. The eight proprietors who obtained charters for Carolina in 1663 and 1665, for example, were also prominent in settling the Bahamas and in organizing the Royal African Company, which soon made England a major participant in the African slave trade. Two of the Carolina proprietors obtained a charter from the duke of York for New Jersey as well. William Penn, the son of a Commonwealth admiral, nevertheless became a friend of James and invested in New Jersey before acquiring his own charter for Pennsylvania. James was clearly at the center of things.

Far more than New England or Virginia, the Restoration Colonies foreshadowed what the United States became in later centuries. In the 1790s South Carolina became the first home of the cotton kingdom. The Middle Atlantic provinces eventually stamped their character on the Midwest. At the same time, the new colonies did not much alter the spectrum of settlement that was already in place. They filled in gaps and confirmed the most prominent features (see Chapter 2).

Carolina and the Aristocratic Ideal

In 1663 eight courtiers obtained a charter which made them the board of proprietors for a colony to be founded on the mainland south of Virginia. Calling their province Carolina in honor of Charles II, the proprietors made several efforts to colonize the region in the 1660s but achieved little success until the following decade. Most settlers came from two directions. Former servants from Virginia and Maryland, many hopelessly in debt, sensed that they might be left alone if they claimed land around Albemarle Sound in what would eventually be called North Carolina. Another wave of former servants and younger sons came from Barbados. Hoping to export grain and meat to the sugar islands, they settled the area that became South Carolina, 300 miles south of Albemarle.

To the proprietors in England, these scattered settlements made up a single colony called Carolina. Led by Anthony Ashley-Cooper, later the first earl of Shaftesbury and the principal organizer of England's Whig Party, the proprietors drafted the Fundamental Constitutions of Carolina in 1669, an incredibly complex plan for organizing the new colony. The philosopher John Locke, Shaftesbury's young secretary, helped write the document.

The Fundamental Constitutions drew upon the work of Commonwealth England's most prominent republican thinker, James Harrington, author of *Oceana* (1656). This book asked how to design an enduring republic. The Greek city states, Rome, and all of the medieval Italian communes except Venice had decayed into despotisms or empires. Harrington argued that the distribution of land ought to be the key factor in deciding whether government should be entrusted to one man (monarchy), a few men (aristocracy), or many (a republic). Where land was widely owned, he insisted, absolute government could not survive. He also proposed several devices for preserving the vitality of a republic, such as frequent rotation of officeholders (called "term limits" today), the secret ballot, and a bicameral legislature in which the smaller house would propose legislation and the larger approve or reject it. Harrington had a stronger impact on American governments than any other political thinker of his century.

Shaftesbury believed that Harrington had uncovered the laws of history. By emphasizing the vast downward redistribution of land that followed Henry VIII's confiscation of monastic properties and their sale to an emerging gentry, Harrington seemed to have a persuasive explanation for the civil wars and the execution of Charles I—an explanation that

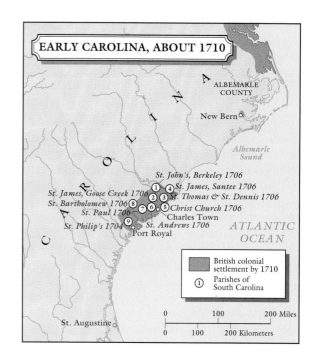

EARLY CAROLINA, ABOUT 1710

ALBEMARLE COUNTY

New Bern

Albemarle Sound

St. John's, Berkeley 1706
St. James, Goose Creek 1706
St. James, Santee 1706
St. Bartholomew 1706
St. Thomas & St. Dennis 1706
St. Paul 1706
Christ Church 1706
Charles Town
St. Philip's 1704
St. Andrews 1706
Port Royal

ATLANTIC OCEAN

British colonial settlement by 1710

Parishes of South Carolina

0   100   200 Miles
0   100   200 Kilometers

St. Augustine

was anathema to the king because, if Harrington was correct, the dynasty was still in trouble. English writers did not dare to discuss Harrington's ideas in the 1660s. But by applying Harrington's rules at a safe distance of three thousand miles, the Carolina proprietors could choose the kind of society they desired and then devise institutions to ensure its success. Well aware that the House of Lords had been abolished between 1649 and 1660, they were not yet certain of the ability of the English aristocracy to survive at home. They chose Carolina as their laboratory for a properly designed aristocratic society.

The Fundamental Constitutions proposed a complex government, one suitable only for a very large society. England had three supreme courts; Carolina would have eight, along with lower tribunals in every county, precinct, and barony. A Grand Council of eight proprietors and forty-two councilors would exercise executive power and propose all legislation. All bills would be submitted for approval to a Parliament of commoners and nobles, whose titles included "landgrave" and "casique." Below them in the social hierarchy would be a larger group, the manor lords. On ordinary matters the Parliament would sit as a unicameral body, but on constitutional questions it would split into four distinct chambers. The aristocracy would always control 40 percent of the land.

According to a later revision of the Fundamental Constitutions, a noble who lost his land or became an absentee would forfeit his title, an intriguing application of Harringtonian principles. The document guaranteed religious toleration to all who believed in God, but everyone had to join some church or lose his citizenship. It also took slavery for granted. "Every Freeman of Carolina shall have absolute Power and Authority over his Negro Slaves, of what Opinion or Religion soever," declared Article 110. And it envisioned a class of lowly whites, "leetmen," who would live on ten-acre tracts and serve the manor lords.

Conditions looked unfavorable on Barbados for ex-servants, but they were not dismal enough to make the Fundamental Constitutions attractive to most potential Carolina settlers. Between 1670 and 1700, the proprietors tried several times, without success, to win their approval. In the 1680s, weary of resistance from the predominantly Anglican Barbadians, the proprietors brought one thousand dissenters from England and Scotland to South Carolina. These newcomers formed the nucleus of a proprietary party in South Carolina politics and made religious diversity a social fact. But they never provided a base large enough to win approval for the Fundamental Constitutions. The Barbadians retained political control.

Barbadian resistance was not the only reason for the failure of this aristocratic experiment. Carolina presented obstacles its organizers had never anticipated. The proprietors assumed that land ownership would be the key to everything else, including wealth and status. But settlers found that they could acquire wealth in other ways. Some of them, especially in Albemarle, exploited the virgin forests all around them to produce masts, turpentine, tar, and pitch for sale to English shipbuilders. Other settlers raised cattle and hogs by letting them run free on open land. Some of South Carolina's early slaves may well have been America's first cowboys. The settlers also traded with the Indians, mostly for deerskins acquired far in the interior, often west of the Appalachian Mountains. As in New France and New Netherland, the Indian trade sustained a genuine city, Charleston, the first in the American South, founded in 1680 at the confluence of the Ashley and Cooper rivers. As in Brazil (see Chapter 1), the Indian trade also became something more dangerous than hunting or trapping animals. Carolina traders allied themselves with some Indians to attack others and drag the captives, mostly women and children, to Charleston for sale as slaves.

In the early eighteenth century, South Carolina and North Carolina became separate colonies, and South Carolina's economy had moved in a new direction. For two decades until 1720, a parliamentary subsidy sustained a boom in South Carolina's naval stores industry, which in turn stimulated a large demand for slaves. But Charleston merchants increasingly invested their capital, acquired in the Indian trade, in rice plantations. In the 1690s planters learned how to grow this lucrative crop from slaves who had cultivated it in Africa. Rice quickly became the staple export of South Carolina and triggered a massive growth of slavery. In 1700 over 40 percent of the colony's population of 5,700 were African or Indian slaves engaged in a wide variety of activities. By 1730 two-thirds of the colony's thirty thousand people were African slaves toiling on rice plantations.

Early New York: An Experiment in Absolutism

In 1664 James, duke of York, obtained a charter from his royal brother for a colony between the Delaware and Connecticut rivers. Charles II claimed that the territory of New Netherland was rightfully England's because it was included in the Virginia charter of 1606. James ordered his agents to foment an uprising against the Dutch among the English settlers on Long Island, and he dispatched a fleet to Manhattan. Reluctantly, Pieter Stuyvesant surrendered the colony without resistance. The English renamed the province New York and took over all of Long Island. The Dutch town of New Amsterdam became New York City, and Fort Orange became Albany.

This conquest, along with clashes along the African coast, provoked the second Anglo-Dutch War (1665-1667), in which England fared poorly. One Dutch squadron actually sailed up the Thames River and sank much of London's merchant fleet. Another entered Chesapeake Bay and destroyed or captured many ships loaded with the year's tobacco crop. But when the struggle ended, the Dutch ceded New Netherland to England with few regrets. The colony had never been profitable anyway.

Richard Nicolls, the first English governor of New York, planned to lure Yankees to the Jersey coast as a way of offsetting the preponderance of Dutch settlers in the Hudson Valley. Although English soldiers abused many civilians in New York City, Esopus (modern Kingston), and Albany, official policy toward the Dutch was generally conciliatory. Those who chose to leave could take their property with them. Those who stayed retained their property and were assured of religious toleration. Most stayed. Except in New York City and the small Dutch portion of Long Island, Dutch settlers still lived under Dutch law. Dutch inheritance practices, which were far more generous to women and younger sons than English law, survived in New York well into the next century. Although England expected prompt implementation of the Navigation Acts, New York's early governors realized that a total ban on commerce with Amsterdam would be a disaster for the colony. Under various legal subterfuges, they allowed this trade to continue.

The duke of York boldly tried to do in New York what he and his brother Charles II did not dare attempt in England, that is, to govern without an elective assembly. This decision irritated English settlers on Long Island far more than it upset the Dutch, who had never adopted representative government. Governor Nicolls compiled a code of laws ("the Duke's Laws"), culled mostly from New England statutes. In 1665 he presented them to an assembly of delegates from the English towns at Hempstead on Long Island. With difficulty, he secured their consent to the code. Thereafter, he taxed and governed on his own, seeking only the advice and consent of his appointed council and of a somewhat larger court of assize, also appointive, that dispensed justice to English settlers.

This policy made it difficult to attract English colonists to New York, especially after the duke of York made New Jersey a separate colony in 1665 under two proprietors—Sir George Carteret, and John, baron Berkeley. The two proprietors granted settlers the right to elect an assembly, which made New Jersey far more attractive to English settlers than New York. The creation of New Jersey also slowed the flow of Dutch settlers across the Hudson and helped to keep New York Dutch.

Although some English newcomers accompanied the duke's conquering fleet, most of those who settled in New York married Dutch women and raised their children in the Dutch Reformed Church be-

cause very few single English women came to the colony. No Anglican parish was created in New York City before the 1690s.

The transition of New York from a Dutch to an English colony did not go smoothly. Although the duke expected his English invaders to supplant and assimilate the conquered Dutch, the reverse was more common for two or three decades. Through intermarriage, the Dutch majority assimilated individual Englishmen. Nor did the Dutch give up their loyalty to the Netherlands. In the third Anglo-Dutch war (1672-1674), a Dutch naval force again mauled the Chesapeake tobacco fleet and then headed north toward Manhattan in 1673. The Dutch burghers did not even try to assist the English garrison of Fort James at the southern tip of Manhattan. Eastern Long Island showed more interest in reuniting with Connecticut than in fighting the Dutch. Much as Stuyvesant had done nine years earlier, the English garrison gave up without resistance. New York City now became New Orange and Fort James was renamed Fort William, both in honor of young William III of Nassau, Prince of Orange, the new military leader of the Dutch republic in its struggle with France. Thus James and William became antagonists in New York fifteen years before William drove James from the English throne.

New Orange survived for fifteen months. But once again, the Dutch republic concluded that the colony was not worth what it cost and gave it back to England at the end of the war. The duke's new governor, Major Edmund Andros, thereupon arrested seven prominent Dutch merchants after they refused to swear an oath of loyalty to England that might oblige them to fight other Dutchmen. Andros tried them as aliens. Threatened with the confiscation of all their property, they finally gave in. Andros also helped to secure bilingual ministers for Dutch Reformed pulpits. These preachers made a great show of their loyalty to the duke, a delicate matter now that James, back in England, had openly proclaimed himself a Roman Catholic. These efforts to transform Dutchmen into Englishmen aroused considerable resentment among ordinary Dutch settlers, who looked with suspicion on the wealthier Dutch families who socialized with the governor or sent their sons to schools in New England.

For their part, the English merchants of New York City resented the continuing Amsterdam trade and

the staying power of the Dutch elite. When Andros forgot to renew the colony's basic revenue act before returning to England in 1680, the merchants refused to pay any import duties that had not been voted by an elective assembly. The court of assize, supposedly a bastion of absolutist sentiment, supported the tax strike, arrested the duke's customs collector, con-

victed him of usurping authority, and sent him to England for punishment where, of course, the duke exonerated him. The justices also fined several Dutch officeholders for failing to respect English liberties. The English (but not Dutch) towns on Long Island joined in the demand for an elective assembly, an urgent matter now that William Penn's much freer colony on the Delaware threatened to drain away the small English population of New York. Several prominent merchants did indeed move to Philadelphia.

The duke finally relented and conceded an assembly. When it met in 1683, it adopted a Charter of Liberties that proclaimed government by consent and other basic rights. It also imposed English law on the Dutch parts of the province. Although the drain of English settlers to Pennsylvania probably declined, few newcomers came to New York at a time when thousands were landing in Philadelphia. Philadelphia's thriving trade also cut into New York City's profits. The colony of New York remained a Dutch society with a Yankee enclave and a government run by English conquerors. In 1689, when James and William fought for nothing less than the English throne, the colony fell apart.

Brotherly Love: The Society of Friends in the Delaware Valley

The most fascinating social experiment of the period took place in the Delaware Valley where Quakers led another family-based, religiously motivated migration of more than ten thousand settlers between 1675 and 1690. Founded by George Fox during England's civil wars, the Society of Friends expanded dramatically in the 1650s as it went through a heroic phase of missionaries and martyrs, including four who were executed in Massachusetts (see Chapter 2). After the Restoration Quakers faced harsh persecution in England and began to think of America as a place of refuge.

Quaker Religious Beliefs   Quakers infuriated other Christians. They insisted that God, in the form of the Inner Light, is present in all people, who can become good—even perfect—if only they will let It shine forth. They took quite literally Jesus' advice to "Turn the other cheek." They became pacifists. This attitude enraged Catholics and most other Protestants, all of whom had found ways to justify warfare and other forms of violence. Quakers also obeyed Jesus's command to "Swear not." They denounced all oaths as sinful. Again other Christians reacted with horror because their judicial systems rested on oaths.

Though an orderly and peaceful people, Quakers struck others as dangerous radicals whose beliefs would bring anarchy. They opposed war, and slavery

made them uncomfortable, although the Society did not embrace abolitionism until a century later (see Chapter 6). In what they called "the Lamb's war" against human pride, Quakers refused to doff their hats to social superiors. More than any other simple device, hats symbolized the social hierarchy of Europe. Everyone knew his place so long as he understood whom to doff to, and who should doff to him. Quakers also refused to accept or to confer titles. Instead they addressed everyone as "Thee" or Thou," familiar terms used by superiors when addressing inferiors, especially servants.

Although Quakers were not much given to theological speculation, the implications of their beliefs appalled other denominations. Without the bother of a formal refutation, the Inner Light seemed to obliterate original sin, predestination, and even the Trinity. Quakers abandoned all of the sacraments and even an organized clergy. They denounced Protestant ministers as "hireling priests," no better than the "papists." Other Protestants retorted that the Quakers were conspiring to return the world to "popish darkness" by abolishing a learned ministry. (The terms "papists" and "popery" were abusive labels applied to Catholics by English Protestants.) Quakers also held distinctive views about revelation. They believed that God speaks directly to His saints in the present. His word to them now could be every bit as inspired as anything in the Bible. Thus Quakers compiled and published books of their "sufferings," which they thought were fully comparable to the New Testament's Acts of the Apostles, a claim that seemed a hideous blasphemy to other Christians.

Contemporaries expected the Society to fall apart, as each Friend followed his or her own Light in some unique direction. It did nothing of the kind. In the 1660s Quakers developed effective institutions for containing discord. The heart of Quaker worship was the "weekly meeting" of the local congregation. There was no formal religious service. People spoke only when the Spirit moved them. But because a few men and women spoke often and with great effect, they became recognized as "public friends," the closest that Quakers came to having a clergy. The public friends occupied special, elevated seats in the meetinghouse and sometimes went on missionary tours in Europe or America. All of the weekly meetings within a given region sent representatives to a "monthly meeting," where questions of policy and discipline were resolved. The monthly

Hexagonal Quaker Meetinghouse, Delaware Valley   This architecture emphasized spiritual equality rather than social hierarchy.

meetings sent representatives to the "yearly meeting" in London. At every level, all decisions had to be unanimous because there is only one Inner Light, and It must convey the same meaning to every believer. This insistence on unanimity provided a powerful safeguard against schism.

Quaker Families   Quakers transformed the structure of the family as well. Women enjoyed almost complete equality, and some of them, such as Mary Dyer in Massachusetts, became extremely effective preachers, even martyrs. Women held their own formal meetings and made important community decisions, mostly about marriage proposals.

Quakers were equally innovative in their dealings with children. Puritans saw children as tiny sinners whose wills had to be broken by severe discipline. Anglican and Catholic views on children were not all that different. But once Quakers stopped worrying about original sin, they were able to see their children as innocents in whom the Light would surely shine if only the little ones could be protected from worldly corruption.

In America, Quakers created warm and affectionate families, built larger houses than non-Quaker neighbors with equivalent resources, and worked hard to acquire land for all of their children. Earlier than other Christians, Quakers began to limit family size to give more love to the children they did have. After the missionary impulse declined among them, they seldom associated with non-Quakers, and the needs of their own children became paramount. To marry an outsider meant "disownment," or expulsion, from the Society, a fate much more likely to afflict poor Friends than wealthy ones. Poor Quakers had difficulty finding spouses precisely because their children were not likely to receive the advantages that Friends had come to expect. Persecution in England helped to drive Quakers across the ocean, but the need to provide ample resources for their children was certainly an equally powerful motive. Before 1700, one-half of all Quakers in England and Wales had moved to America.

The Colony of West New Jersey   The Quakers founded two colonies in America: West New Jersey and Pennsylvania. In the 1680s, when they bought out the lord proprietor of East New Jersey and also gained power in what is now Delaware, it looked as though they might dominate the entire region between Maryland and New York, although their hold on East Jersey and Delaware was weak. Accordingly, their yearly meeting met alternately in Philadelphia and Burlington, the capital of West New Jersey.

In 1674 the New Jersey proprietors split their holding into two colonies. Sir George Carteret claimed what he now called East New Jersey, a province near New York City with half a dozen towns populated by Baptist, Quaker, Puritan, and Dutch Reformed settlers. Lord Berkeley claimed West New Jersey and promptly sold it in 1674 to two Quakers who, along with other investors, divided their proprietary into one hundred shares. Two of the proprietors were Edward Byllinge, a "leveler" or social radical from Commonwealth England, and William Penn. Both were influenced by Harrington and other republicans. They revived in West Jersey many of the rejected ideals of the 1650s.

In 1676 Byllinge drafted a document, the West Jersey Concessions and Agreements, which was approved by more than one hundred settlers in 1677. The Concessions divided the colony into one hundred "properties" (units of local government), each entitled to elect by secret ballot a representative to the colony's unicameral assembly. Voters could bind their representative with explicit instructions. Voting, but not debate, was open to public scrutiny. Ten "properties" constituted a "tribe" or a "tenth." Each tenth chose a "commissioner" to sit on a board that would serve as a weak plural executive for the colony. In the court system, juries would decide both fact and law. Judges would merely preside over the court and, if asked by a juror, offer advice.

The West Jersey Quakers believed that godly men could live together in love — without war, lawyers, or internal conflict. They meant to keep government close to the people. They made land easy to acquire and tolerated all religions. For various reasons, they never had a chance to implement their entire program, but in the 1680s lawsuits often ended with one litigant forgiving the other, and criminal trials sometimes closed with the victim embracing the perpetrator. But as social and religious diversity increased, the system broke down. Non-Quakers increasingly refused to cooperate. After 1690 the courts became impotent, and Quaker rule collapsed years before the Crown took over the colony in 1702.

William Penn and Pennsylvania

By 1681 Quaker attention was already shifting to the west bank of the Delaware River. There William Penn launched a much larger, if rather more cautious, "Holy Experiment" in brotherly love. The son of Admiral Sir William Penn, young William grew up surrounded by privilege. He knew well both Charles II and the duke of York, attended Oxford and the Inns of Court (England's law schools), went on the grand tour of Europe, and began to manage his father's extensive Irish estates. Then something terrible happened that left his family hideously embarrassed. "Mr. William Pen," reported a neighbor in December 1667, ". . . is a Quaker again, or some very melancholy thing." Penn often traveled to the continent on behalf of the Society of Friends, winning converts and eventually recruiting settlers in the Netherlands and Germany. In England he was jailed several times for his beliefs, and in the so-called Penn–Meade trial of 1670 he challenged a judge's right to compel a jury to reconsider its verdict. In a landmark decision, a higher court vindicated his position.

A gentleman and a Quaker, Penn was no ordinary colonizer. Using his contacts at court, he converted an old debt, owed to his father by the king, into a charter for a proprietary colony that Charles named "Pennsylvania" in honor of the deceased admiral. The emerging imperial bureaucracy disliked the whole project and, after failing to block it entirely, inserted several restrictions into the charter. Penn agreed to enforce the Navigation Acts, to let the Crown approve his choice of governor, to submit all legislation to the English Privy Council for approval, and to allow appeals from Pennsylvania courts to the king's Privy Council in England.

Contemporaries said little about the most striking innovation attempted by these colonists. The Quakers entered America unarmed. The Pennsylvania government did not even organize a militia until the 1750s. Friendly relations with Indians were essential to the project's success, and Penn was careful to deal fairly with the Lenni Lenape, or Delaware Indians. They liked him and called him "Miquon," an Algonquian word for "quill" and thus a pun on Penn's name.

More thought went into the launching of Pennsylvania than into the organization of any other colony. Twenty drafts survive of Penn's First Frame of Government, his 1682 constitution for the province. He too was fascinated with Harrington's republican ideas. His plan evolved from roughly a larger version of the West Jersey Concessions and Agreements into something rather more restrained but still quite liberating. The settlers would elect a council of

Penn and the Indians, by Benjamin West (1771)   This painting celebrates William Penn's efforts, nearly a century before, to establish peaceful relations with the Delaware Indians.

seventy-two men to staggered three-year terms. The council would draft all legislation and submit copies to the voters. In the early years the voters would meet to approve or reject these bills. But as the province expanded, these meetings would become impractical. Voters, Penn expected, would then elect an assembly of two hundred, which would gradually increase to five hundred, about the size of the House of Commons, though for a much smaller population. Government would still remain close to the people. Penn gave up the power to veto bills but retained control of the distribution of land. Capital punishment for crimes against property and most other offenses, except murder, was abolished. Toleration, trial by jury, Magna Carta, and habeas corpus all received strong affirmation.

Settlers had been arriving in Pennsylvania for more than a year when Penn landed in 1682 with his First Frame of Government. Some colonists lived in caves along the river. Others, imitating the nearby Swedes, built log cabins. The colonists persuaded

Penn that the Frame was too cumbersome for a small colony, and the first legislature worked with him to devise a simpler government. In what became known as the Second Frame, or the Pennsylvania Charter of Liberties of 1683, the council was reduced to eighteen men and the assembly to thirty-six. In this smaller government, the assembly's inability to initiate legislation quickly became a major grievance.

Penn laid out the city of Philadelphia as "a green country town" and organized other settlements. Then he returned to England in 1684 to answer Lord Baltimore's complaint that Philadelphia fell within the charter boundaries of Maryland, a claim that was soon verified. This dispute troubled the Penn family until the eve of independence, when the Mason-Dixon line finally established the boundary.

In England, persecution had kept Quaker anti-authoritarian attitudes in check, at least in relations with other Friends. In Pennsylvania these resentments soon became public. Penn expected his settlers to defer to the leaders among them, but many of the people that he put in responsible positions did not prosper. For example, Penn chartered the Free Society of Traders to control commerce with England and gave high offices to its members. But from the start, wealth in Pennsylvania rested on trade with other colonies, not with England. That trade was dominated by Quakers from Barbados, Jamaica, New York, and Boston. These men owed little to Penn and began to organize an anti-proprietary faction in the colony. They and others demanded more land, especially in Philadelphia. They claimed that they could not afford the quitrents[1] attached to their deeds, and quarreled more often than was seemly for men of brotherly love.

In exasperation, Penn finally appointed a friend and old Cromwellian soldier, John Blackwell, as governor in 1688, ordering him to end the quarrels and collect quitrents but to rule "tenderly." Nobody greeted the soldier-governor on his arrival, and boys jeered him as he tried to enter Penn's Philadelphia house. The leader of the council refused to let him use the colony's great seal. Debate in the legislature became angrier than ever. After six months, Blackwell resigned. Each Quaker, he claimed, "prayed for the rest on the First Day [of the week], and preyed on them the other six." He told Penn "that the wild beasts that fill his forests can better govern than the witless zealots who make a monkey-house of his assembly." Philadelphia's mosquitoes, he added, "were worse than armed men but not nearly so nettlesome as the men without Armes." The Pennsylvania government changed several more times before 1701, when Penn and the assembly finally agreed on the Fourth Frame, or Charter of Privileges, which gave the colony a unicameral legislature. Yet the colony's politics remained turbulent and unstable into the 1720s.

Despite these controversies, Pennsylvania quickly became an economic success, well established in the Caribbean trade as an exporter of wheat and flour. Quaker families were thriving, and the colony's policy of toleration attracted thousands of outsiders. Some were German pacifists who shared the social goals of the Society of Friends. Others were Anglicans and Presbyterians who warned London that Quakers were unfit to rule — anywhere.

---

[1] A feudal relic, a quitrent was an annual fee, usually small, required by the patent that gave title to a piece of land. It differed from ordinary rents in that non-payment led to a suit for debt, not ejection from the property.

Filling in the Spectrum of Settlement

Pennsylvania and South Carolina already fit snugly into their respective bands along the spectrum of settlement. Pennsylvania confirmed what the Middle Atlantic colonies had already become, much as New York largely extended the social patterns established earlier in New Netherland. Except in Philadelphia, whose thousands of immigrants brought many diseases with them, both life expectancy and family size exceeded English norms, though not by quite as much as in New England. Pennsylvania's ethnic mix was already complex, with considerable numbers of German and Welsh pacifists coming in the early waves. They were followed after 1720 by tens of thousands of Ulster Scot Presbyterians and German Lutherans and Calvinists. By about 1750 the English had become a minority of only one-fourth or one-third. Although Penn set up townships, this institution did not thrive. The New England town never got farther south than New Jersey. Most Pennsylvanians lived on scattered farms. The county court, however, became an important institution, as Quaker magistrates and a disproportionate number of Quaker jurors tried to resolve disputes between Quakers and outsiders, or simply between outsiders. Problems among Quakers were usually settled in less public ways.

South Carolina also fitted into its niche on the spectrum. There the percentage of slaves was much higher than in Virginia but lower than in the West Indies. Despite the colony's religious diversity, the Church of England became established by law shortly after 1700. Mostly because of malaria, life expectancy was about two or three years lower than in the Chesapeake but a few years longer than in the West Indies. The only local institution of any consequence was the parish. Counties were laid out, but

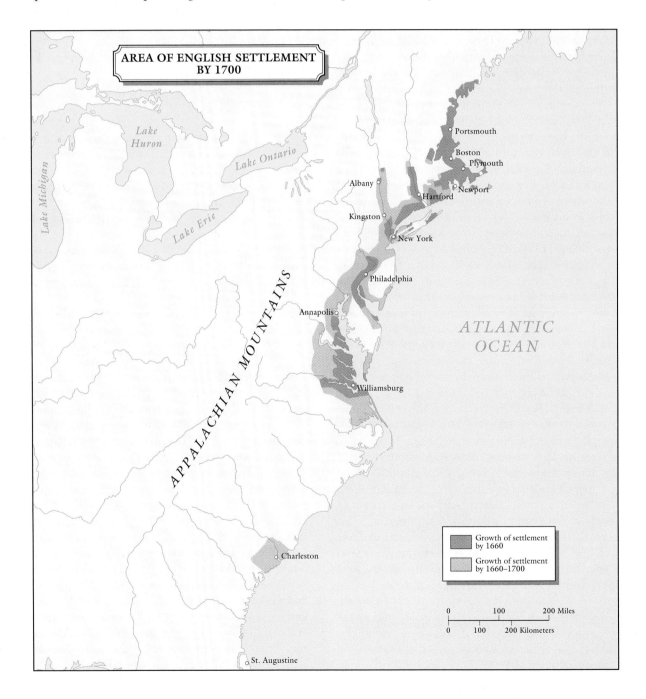

AREA OF ENGLISH SETTLEMENT BY 1700

Lake Huron

Lake Ontario

Lake Michigan

Lake Erie

APPALACHIAN MOUNTAINS

Portsmouth

Boston

Plymouth

Albany

Newport

Hartford

Kingston

New York

Philadelphia

Annapolis

ATLANTIC OCEAN

Williamsburg

Charleston

St. Augustine

	Growth of settlement by 1660
	Growth of settlement by 1660–1700

0   100   200 Miles

0   100   200 Kilometers

there were no county courts. Justice was dispensed from Charleston.

Thus even new settlements launched for quite distinct purposes after 1660 merely confirmed the broad pattern of the spectrum of settlement already in place.

INDIANS, SETTLERS, UPHEAVAL

As of about 1670, there were still no sharp boundaries between Indian lands and colonial settlements. Even Boston, the largest city north of Mexico, was only about fifteen miles from an Indian village. The towns in the Connecticut Valley were surrounded by Indians. The outposts on the Delaware River were islands in a sea of Indians. In the event of war, nearly every European settlement was vulnerable to attack.

As time passed, the commercial possibilities and limitations of the continent were becoming much clearer, however. The French and Dutch had mastered the fur trade because they controlled the two all-water routes to the interior, via the St. Lawrence system and the Hudson and Mohawk valleys. South Carolinians gained access to the interior because they could go around the southern extreme of the Appalachians. Other colonies remained blocked, both by Indians and by the mountain barrier.

Indian Strategies of Survival

By the 1670s most of the coastal tribes in regular contact with Europeans had already been devastated by disease or soon would be. European diseases, by magnifying the need for captives, also increased the number and intensity of wars among Indian peoples. The Iroquois, for example, though hard hit by smallpox and other ailments, acquired muskets from the Dutch and used these arms, first to attack other Iroquoian peoples and then Algonquians. These "mourning wars," were often initiated by the widow or bereaved mother or sister of a deceased loved one. She insisted that her male relatives repair the loss. Her warrior relatives then launched a raid and brought back captives. Although adult male prisoners were usually tortured to death, most women and children were adopted and assimilated. Adoption worked because the captives shared the cultural values of their captors. They became Iroquois. As early as the 1660s, a majority of the Indians in the Five Nations were

adoptees, not native-born Iroquois. In this way the Confederacy remained strong while other nations declined or disappeared.

In the southern Piedmont, the warlike, Sioux-speaking Catawba Indians also assimilated thousands from other tribes. Further in the southern interior, the numerous Cherokees (an Iroquoian-speaking people) and the Muskogean-speaking Creeks, Choctaws, Chickasaws, and Natchez Indians had more time to adapt. The Creeks became adept at assimilating adoptees from a wide variety of ethnic backgrounds. These southern nations soon learned how to play the Spaniards off against the English (and later the French).

In some ways, America became as much a new world for the Indians as it did for the colonists. European cloth, muskets, hatchets, knives, and pots were welcomed among the Indians, but they came at a price. Indians who learned to use them gradually abandoned traditional skills and became more and more dependent on trade with Europeans, a process not complete until the nineteenth century. Alcohol, the one item always in demand, was also dangerous. Indian men drank to alter their mood and achieve visions, not for sociability. A man who had no cultural experience with it sometimes drank himself into a homicidal rage.

Settlers who understood that their future depended on the fur trade, as in New France, tried to stay on good terms with the Indians. Pieter Stuyvesant put New Netherland on such a course, and the English governors of New York after 1664 followed his lead, particularly Edmund Andros, governor from 1674 to 1680. He cultivated the friendship of the Iroquois League, in which the five member nations had promised not to wage war against one another. In 1677 Andros and the Five Nations agreed to make New York the easternmost link in what the English called this "covenant chain" of peace, a huge defensive advantage for a lightly populated colony. While New England and Virginia fought bitter Indian wars in the 1670s, New York avoided conflict. The covenant chain later proved flexible enough to incorporate other Indians and colonies as well.

Where the Indian trade was slight, war became far more likely, and it erupted in both New England and the Chesapeake in 1675. Virginia had reduced the member nations of the Powhatan Chiefdom to dependent status in the 1640s. The colony negotiated treaties with them and other nearby Indians, in the hope of keeping them loyal in the event of war with other Indians. The New England colonies had similar understandings with the larger non-Christian nations of the region. But the Puritan governments placed increasing reliance on a growing number of Christianized Indians.

Puritan Indian Missions

Serious efforts to convert Indians to Protestantism began in Plymouth Colony under Thomas Mayhew, Senior and Junior, and in Massachusetts under John Eliot, pastor of the Roxbury church. Eliot tried to make his nearby Indian town of Natick into a model mission community.

The Mayhews were more successful than Eliot, though he got most of the publicity. They worked with local sachems and challenged only the tribal powwows (prophets or medicine men). The Mayhews encouraged Indian men to teach the settlers of Martha's Vineyard and Nantucket how to catch whales, an activity that made them a vital part of the settlers' economy without challenging their identity as males. Eliot, by contrast, attacked the authority of the sachems as well as the powwows, challenged the traditional tribal structure, and insisted on turning Indian men into farmers, a female role in Indian society. Yet he did translate the entire Bible and several other religious works into the Wampanoag language.

By the early 1670s more than one thousand Indians, nearly all of them survivors of coastal tribes that had been decimated by disease, lived in a string of seven "praying towns," and Eliot was busy organizing five more, mostly among the Nipmucks of the interior. About 2,300 Indians in Massachusetts and Plymouth, perhaps one-quarter of all those living in southeastern New England, were in various stages of conversion to Christianity by 1675. But only 160 of them had achieved the kind of conversion experience that Puritans required for full membership in a church. Indians did not share the Puritan sense of sin. They could not easily grasp why their best deeds should stink in the nostrils of the Lord. Resistance to Christianity was one cause of war by 1675, as the more powerful tribes felt threatened by this pressure to convert. Other causes of conflict were the settlers' lust for Indian lands and the fear, especially among younger warriors, that their whole way of life was in danger of extinction.

Metacom (whom the English called King Philip) was one of those Indians. He was sachem of the Wampanoags and the son of Massassoit, who had celebrated the first thanksgiving with the Pilgrims. Metacom once remarked that if he became "a praying sachem, I shall be a poor and weak one, and easily be trod upon."

Metacom's (or King Philip's) War

War broke out not long after Plymouth executed three Wampanoags for the murder of John Sassamon, a Harvard-educated Indian preacher who may have been spying on Metacom. The fighting began in the frontier town of Swansea in June 1675, after settlers killed an Indian they found looting an abandoned house. When the Indians demanded satisfaction the next day, the settlers laughed in their faces. The Indians took their own revenge, and the conflict escalated into Metacom's War.

The settlers, remembering their easy triumph over the Pequots a generation earlier (see Chapter 2), were confident of victory. But, since the 1630s, the Indians had acquired firearms. They had built forges to make musket balls and repair their muskets. They had also become marksmen with the smoothbore musket by firing several smaller bullets with each charge. The settlers, who had usually paid Indians to do their hunting for them, were terrible shots. They discharged volleys without aiming. To the shock of the colonists, Metacom won several engagements against Plymouth militia, usually by ambushing the noisy invaders. He then escaped from Plymouth Colony and headed toward the upper Connecticut Valley, where he burned five towns in three months.

Massachusetts and Connecticut then joined the fray. But rather than attack Metacom's Wampanoags they went after the Narragansetts, who were trying hard to remain neutral. Many settlers dreamed of acquiring the fertile lands of the Narragansetts. In the Great Swamp Fight of December 1675, a Puritan army, with the aid of Indian guides, attacked an unfinished Narragansett fort and massacred hundreds of Indians, nearly all of them women and children. The surviving warriors joined Metacom and showed that they too could use terror. They torched more frontier settlements. Altogether about eight hundred settlers were killed and two dozen towns were destroyed or badly damaged in the war.

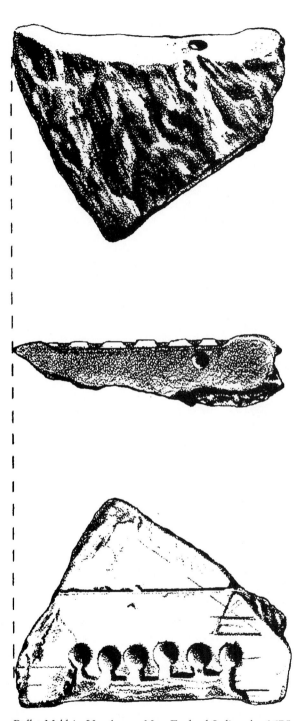

Bullet Mold in Use Among New England Indians by 1675
Indians could make bullets and repair muskets, but they remained dependent on Europeans for their supply of gun powder. In early 1676, Metacom ran out of powder after failing to acquire more from New France.

Atrocities became common on both sides. When a settler boasted that his Bible would save him from harm, the Indians disemboweled him and stuffed the book in his belly. When at least seventeen friendly Indians were murdered by settlers, some in cold blood before dozens of witnesses, New England juries refused to convict anyone. On one occasion, when some Maine Indians were brought to Marblehead as prisoners, the women of that fishing village literally tore them to pieces with their bare hands.

Frontier residents demanded the extermination of all neighboring Indians, including the Christian converts. The government of Massachusetts, shocked to realize that it could not win the war without Indian allies, resisted these demands and tried to protect the "praying" Indians. The magistrates had to evacuate the Christian Indians to a bleak island in Boston harbor, where they spent a miserable winter but still enlisted to fight against Metacom in the spring campaign. Some settlers may even have tried to assassinate Eliot by ramming his boat in Boston harbor. The accused men, who insisted that the collision was accidental, were acquitted.

The war nearly tore New England apart. It split the clergy. Increase Mather, a prominent Boston minister, saw the conflict as God's judgment on a sinful people and warned that no victory would come until New England repented and reformed. At first the Massachusetts General Court agreed. It blamed the war on young men who wore their hair too long, on boys and girls going on leisurely horse rides together, on people who dressed above their station in life, and on Quaker blasphemies. Another Boston minister, William Hubbard, insisted that the war was only a brief testing time, after which the Lord would lead His saints to victory over the heathen. To Daniel Gookin, a magistrate closely involved in Eliot's mission work, the war was an unspeakable tragedy for all parties, both settlers and Indians.

Despite their disagreements, the settlers won a decisive military victory in 1676. Governor Andros of New York persuaded the Mohawks to attack Metacom's winter encampment and disperse his people when he was short of gunpowder. The New Englanders, working closely with Mohegan and Christian Indian allies, then hunted down Metacom's war parties, killed hundreds of Indians including Metacom, and sold hundreds more into West Indian slavery. Some of those enslaved had not even been party to

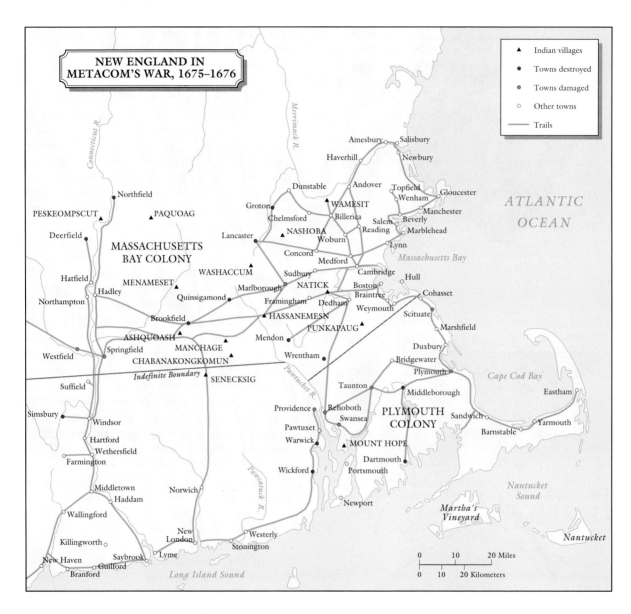

the conflict. As the tide turned, the Massachusetts government sided with Hubbard by ordering a day of thanksgiving, but Increase Mather made his church observe a fast day instead. The colony had not reformed adequately, he explained.

Bacon's Rebellion in Virginia

In Virginia, Governor Sir William Berkeley, who had led the colony to victory over Opechancanough by 1646, rejoiced in the New Englanders' woes. Metacom's War was the least they deserved for the way

the Puritans had ripped England apart and executed Charles I during the civil wars. Then Virginia began to have similar troubles of its own.

In 1675 the Doegs, a dependent Indian nation in the Potomac Valley, demanded payment of an old debt from a local planter. When he refused, they ran off some of his livestock. After his overseer killed one of them, the Indians fled but later returned to ambush and kill the man. The county militia mustered and followed the Doegs across the Potomac into Maryland. At a fork in the trail, they split into two parties. Each party found a body of Indians in a shack a few hundred yards up the path. Both fired at pointblank range, killing eleven at one cabin and fourteen at the other. One of the bands was indeed Doeg; the other was not. "Susquehannock friends," blurted an Indian as he dodged the fire.

The Susquehannocks were a formidable Iroquoian-speaking people with firearms who had defeated a Maryland force three decades earlier. They had moved south to escape Iroquois attacks, and, at the invitation of the Maryland government, had recently occupied land along the Potomac. Governor Berkeley, still hoping to avoid war with them, dispatched John Washington (ancestor of George) with a force of Virginia militia to investigate the killings and, if possible, to set things right.

Washington preferred more vengeance. After crossing the Potomac, his Virginia militia joined with a Maryland force, and together they besieged a formidable Susquehannock fort on the north bank of the river. With four stout walls, raised embankments against each wall, bastions at each corner to enfilade attackers, plus a surrounding ditch and a palisade outside the ditch, the place was too strong to take without artillery, even though the attackers greatly outnumbered the Indians. When the Indians sent out five or six sachems to negotiate, the militia murdered them. For the next six weeks, the militia laid siege to the fort, until the Indians, running short of provisions, broke out one night with all of their people, killing several militiamen. The Susquehannocks disappeared into the forest, hurling taunts of defiance and promises of vengeance. They apparently blamed Virginia more than Maryland. When they killed about three dozen Virginia settlers in January 1676, the colonists began to panic.

Berkeley favored a defensive strategy against the Indians; most settlers wanted to attack. In March 1676 the governor summoned a special session of the legislature to approve the creation of a string of forts above the fall line of the major rivers, with companies of rangers to patrol the stretches between them. Berkeley also hoped to maintain a distinction between the clearly hostile Susquehannocks and other Indians who might still be neutral or friendly. Frontier settlers demanded war against *all* neighboring Indians. Finally, to avoid further provocation, he restricted the fur trade to a few close associates. To men excluded from Berkeley's circle, his actions looked like gross favoritism. To former servants in frontier counties, whose access to land was blocked by neigh-

boring Indians, this defensive strategy appeared intolerable and needlessly expensive.

In both the Second and Third Anglo-Dutch wars, Berkeley had built costly forts to protect the colony from the Dutch navy, but Dutch warships had sailed around the forts and mauled the tobacco fleet anyway. Accordingly, colonists denounced the building of any more forts and demanded an offensive campaign waged by unpaid volunteers, who would take their rewards in the form of plunder and enslaved Indian captives. In April the frontier settlers found a reckless leader in Nathaniel Bacon, a young newcomer to the colony with a scandalous past and £1800 to invest. Using his political connections as the governor's cousin by marriage, he got himself appointed to the council soon after his arrival in the colony in 1674. Bacon, who owned a plantation and trading post in Henrico County at the falls of the James River (now Richmond), was one of the men excluded from the Indian trade under Berkeley's new rules.

Ignoring Berkeley's orders, Bacon marched his frontiersmen south in search of the elusive Susquehannocks. After several days his weary men reached a village of friendly Occaneechees, who offered them shelter, announced that they knew where to find one of the Susquehannocks' camps, and even offered to attack it. The Occaneechees surprised and defeated the Susquehannocks and returned with their captives to celebrate the victory with Bacon. But after the Indians fell asleep, Bacon's men massacred them and seized their furs and prisoners. On their return to Henrico in May, they boasted of their prowess as Indian killers.

By then, Berkeley had outlawed Bacon, dissolved the legislature, and called the first general election since 1661. He asked the newly elected burgesses to bring their grievances with them to Jamestown for redress at the June assembly. "How miserable that man is," he complained, "that Governes a People where six parts of seaven at least are Poore Endebted Discontented and Armed."

Henrico's voters elected Bacon to the House of Burgesses. Berkeley had him arrested when he reached Jamestown and made him go to his knees and apologize for his disobedience before the governor and council, after which Berkeley forgave him and restored him to his seat in the upper house. By then, even the governor had abandoned his effort to distinguish between hostile and friendly Indians, but he still favored a defensive war. While the burgesses

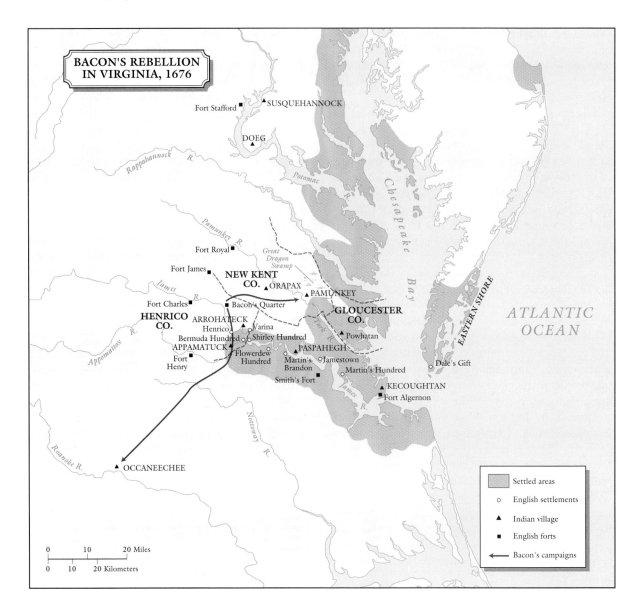

were passing laws to reform the county courts, the vestries, and the tax system, Bacon slipped away to Henrico, summoned his followers again, and marched on Jamestown. At gunpoint, he forced Berkeley to commission him as general of volunteers and compelled the legislature to authorize another expedition against the Indians.

Berkeley retreated down river to Gloucester County and mustered its militia but they refused to follow him against Bacon. They would fight only Indians. Mortified, Berkeley fled to the eastern shore, the only part of the colony that was safe from Indian at-

tack and thus still loyal to him. Bacon hastened to Jamestown, summoned a meeting of planters at the governor's Green Spring mansion, got them to swear an oath of loyalty to him, and ordered the confiscation of the estates of Berkeley's supporters. Meanwhile, Berkeley raised his own force on the eastern shore by promising the men an exemption from taxes for twenty-one years and the right to plunder the rebels.

Royal government collapsed. During the summer of 1676, hundreds of Virginians set out to make their fortunes by plundering Indians, other colonists, or

Modern Reconstruction of a Small Planter's Cabin at St. Mary's, Maryland, Seventeenth Century   Most of the ex-servants who followed Nathaniel Bacon in 1676 lived in this kind of house, or even smaller ones.

both. Bacon's Rebellion was the largest upheaval in the American colonies before 1775. Later legends to the contrary, it had little to do with liberty.

Bacon never did kill a hostile Indian. While Bacon was slaughtering and enslaving the unresisting Pamunkeys along the frontier, Berkeley assembled a small fleet and retook Jamestown in August. Bacon rushed east, exhibiting his Indian captives along the way, and laid siege to Jamestown. He also captured the wives of prominent Berkeley supporters and forced them to stand in the line of fire as he dug his trenches closer to the capital. After suffering only a few casualties, the governor's men grew discouraged, and in early September the whole force returned to the eastern shore. Bacon burned Jamestown to the ground. He also boasted to a neighbor that he thought he could hold off an English army, unite Virginia with Maryland and North Carolina, and win Dutch support for setting up an independent Chesapeake republic. Instead he died of dysentery in October.

Berkeley soon regained control of Virginia. He commandeered the ships of the London tobacco fleet as they entered Chesapeake Bay and used them to overpower all the plantations that Bacon had fortified. Then, in January 1677, an English army arrived one thousand strong, too late to help but in time to strain the colony's depleted resources. Ignoring royal orders to show clemency to the rebels, Berkeley hanged twenty-three of them. A new assembly repudiated the reforms of 1676, and in many counties the governor's men used their control of the courts to continue plundering the Baconians through confiscations and fines. By then Berkeley was also dead. Summoned to England to defend himself, he died in 1677 before he could present his case.

Henry Latrobe's Sketch of Green Spring, the Home of Governor Sir William Berkeley at the Time of Bacon's Rebellion   Green Spring was one of the first great houses to be built in Virginia. Latrobe's drawing was made in the 1790s.

CRISIS IN ENGLAND AND THE REDEFINITION OF EMPIRE

Bacon's Rebellion helped trigger a political crisis in England. Because Virginia produced little tobacco in 1676, English customs revenues fell sharply, and the king was obliged to ask Parliament for more money. Parliament's response was tempered by the much deeper problem of the royal succession. Charles II had fathered many bastards, but his royal marriage was childless. After the queen reached menopause in the mid-1670s, his brother James, duke of York, became his heir. By then James had become a Catholic, and he made no attempt to conceal his conversion. When Charles dissolved the Restoration Parliament that had sat from 1661 until 1678, he knew that he would have to deal with a new House of Commons terrified by the prospect of a Catholic king.

The Popish Plot, the Exclusion Crisis, and the Rise of Party

In this atmosphere of distrust, a cynical adventurer, Titus Oates, fabricated the sensational story that he had uncovered a sinister "Popish Plot" to assassinate Charles and bring James to the throne. The king's ministry disintegrated in the wake of these accusations, and the parliamentary opposition won majorities in three successive elections between 1678 and 1681. Organized by Lord Shaftesbury (Carolina's most important lord proprietor), the opposition demanded that James be excluded from the throne in favor of his Protestant daughters, Mary and Anne. It also called for a guarantee of frequent elections and for an independent electorate not under the influence of wealthy patrons. By 1681 the king's men were castigating Shaftesbury's followers as "Whigs," the name of an obscure sect of Scottish religious extremists who favored the assassination of both Charles and James. Whigs in turn denounced Charles's courtiers as "Tories," an inflammatory label for Irish Catholic peasants who murdered Protestant landlords. Like "Puritan," "Quaker," "Papist," and other terms of abuse, both words stuck.

England's party struggle reflected a deep rift between "Court" and "Country" forces. As of 1681 Tories were a Court party. They favored the legitimate succession, a standing army with adequate rev-

enues to maintain it, the Anglican Church without toleration for Protestant dissenters, and a powerful monarchy. The Whigs were a Country opposition that stood for the exclusion of James from the throne, a decentralized militia rather than a standing army, toleration for Protestant dissenters but not Catholics, and an active role in government for a reformed Parliament. During this struggle, James fled in virtual exile to Scotland. But Charles, after obtaining secret financial support from King Louis XIV of France, dissolved Parliament in 1681. While governing without a Parliament for the last four years of his reign, he restructured voting requirements in enough boroughs to guarantee a Tory majority in future elections.

The Lords of Trade and Imperial Reform

English politics of the 1670s and 1680s had a profound impact on the colonies. The duke of York emerged from the Third Anglo-Dutch War as the most powerful shaper of imperial policy. At his urging the government created a new agency in 1675, the Lords Committee of Trade and Plantations, or more simply, the Lords of Trade. This agency, a permanent committee of the Privy Council, enforced the Navigation Acts and administered the colonies. Although Virginia was the oldest royal colony, the West Indies became the object of most of these policies, simply because the Caribbean remained a much more important theater of international competition. The instruments of royal government first took shape in the islands and were then extended to the mainland.

In the 1660s the Crown took control of the governments of Barbados, Jamaica, and the Leeward Islands. The king appointed the governor and upper house of each colony; the settlers elected an assembly. The Privy Council in England reserved to itself the power to hear appeals from colonial courts and to disallow colonial legislation after the governor had approved it. The Privy Council also issued a formal commission and a lengthy set of instructions to each royal governor. In the two or three decades after 1660, these documents rapidly became standardized, especially after the Lords of Trade began to apply the lessons learned in one colony to problems anticipated in others.

The king's commission to the governor established and defined a governor's powers. From the

Popish Plot Playing Cards   This device became one way of popularizing the Protestant conviction that Catholics were conspiring to assassinate the king in 1678. The king of hearts depicts Titus Oates revealing the plot to the King and Council. The two of hearts shows Sir Edmund Berry Godfrey, a respected magistrate, taking depositions from Oates. The murder of Godfrey, which was never resolved, gave credibility to the plot.

Crown's point of view, the governor's commission *created* the constitutional structure of each colony, a claim that few settlers accepted. The colonists believed that they had an inherent right to constitutional rule even without the king's explicit warrant.

Each governor also received a set of royal instructions which told him how to use his broad powers. They laid out things he must do, such as command the militia, and things he must avoid, such as approve laws detrimental to English trade. Despite some confusion at first, Crown lawyers eventually agreed that royal instructions were binding only on the governor, not on the colony as a whole. In other words, instructions never acquired the force of law.

The Lords of Trade also insisted that every colony pay for the cost of its own government. This requirement, ironically, strengthened colonial claims to self-rule. After a long struggle in Jamaica, the Crown imposed a constitutional compromise in 1681 that had broad significance for all the colonies. The Lords of Trade threatened to make the Jamaica assembly as weak as the Irish Parliament, which could debate and approve only those bills that had first been adopted by the English Privy Council. Under the compromise, the Jamaica assembly retained its power to initiate and amend legislation, in return for agreeing to a permanent revenue act, a measure designed to free the governor from financial dependence on the assembly.

Metacom's War and Bacon's Rebellion lent a sense of urgency to these administrative reforms and accelerated their application to the mainland colonies. The Lords of Trade ordered soldiers to Virginia along with a royal commission to investigate grievances there. In 1676 they also sent an aggressive customs officer, Edward Randolph, to Massachusetts. His lengthy reports recommended that the colony's charter be revoked. The Lords of Trade viewed New England and all proprietary colonies with deep suspicion, but they could not prevent Charles and James from establishing Pennsylvania as a new proprietary venture. They had reason for concern. As late as 1678, Virginia remained the only royal colony on the mainland. The Lords of Trade might enforce compliance with the Navigation Acts elsewhere, but they possessed no effective instruments for punishing violators in North America. The king could demand and reprimand, but not command.

Still, the Lords of Trade did not pursue a monolithic policy towards all colonies. They experimented with several options. The Jamaica model assumed that each royal governor would summon an assembly on occasion, though not very often. In the 1680s the Crown compelled Virginia to accept a similar arrangement—an occasional assembly with full powers of legislation in exchange for a permanent revenue act. Though New York had been a running experiment in autocracy since the English conquest of 1664, James conceded an assembly to that colony too in exchange for a permanent revenue act in 1683.

The Jamaica model, it seemed, had become the norm. James's real preferences reemerged only when the English Court of Chancery finally revoked the Massachusetts Charter in 1684, a few months before Charles II died and the duke of York became King James II in early 1685. The possibility of a vigorous autocracy in America suddenly reappeared.

The Dominion of New England

Absolutist New York now became the king's model for reorganizing New England. James disallowed the New York Charter of Liberties of 1683 (see above,

p. 93) and abolished the colony's assembly but kept the permanent revenue act in force. In 1686 he sent Sir Edmund Andros, the autocratic governor of New York from 1674–1680, to Massachusetts to establish a new government called the Dominion of New England. By 1688 Andros had added New Hampshire, Plymouth, Rhode Island, Connecticut, New York and both Jerseys to the Dominion. He governed this vast domain through an appointive council and a superior court that rode circuit dispensing justice throughout the Dominion. There was no elective assembly. Andros also imposed religious toleration on the Puritans. He even forced one Boston church to let Anglicans use its meetinghouse for public worship for part of each Sunday.

At first, Andros won considerable support from merchants who had been excluded from politics by the Puritan requirement that they be full church members, but his rigorous enforcement of the Navigation Acts soon alienated them. When he tried to compel all New England farmers to take out new land titles that included annual quitrents, he antagonized the whole countryside. His suppression of a tax revolt in Essex County, Massachusetts, started many people thinking more highly of their ancient rights as Englishmen than of their peculiar privileges as Puritans. Government by consent probably seemed more valuable by 1688 than it ever had before.

THE GLORIOUS REVOLUTION

Events in England and France undercut the Dominion of New England. James II proclaimed toleration for Protestants and Catholics and began to name Catholics to high office, in violation of recent laws. In 1685 Louis XIV revoked the Edict of Nantes (see Chapter 2) and launched a vicious persecution of French Huguenots. About 160,000 fled the kingdom, the largest forced migration in the history of early modern Europe. Many went to England, and several thousand crossed the Atlantic to the English mainland colonies. James II tried to suppress the news of this persecution, which made his own professions of toleration seem hypocritical, even though his commitment was probably genuine. Then in 1688 the queen, Mary of Modena (his second wife and a Catholic), gave birth to a son who would clearly be raised Catholic, thus imposing a Catholic *dynasty* on England. Swallowing their mutual hatred, several

Whig and Tory leaders secretly invited William of Orange, the stadtholder of the Netherlands, to England. The husband of the king's older Protestant daughter Mary by James's first marriage, William had emerged in the 1670s as the most prominent Protestant soldier in Europe during a long war between the Netherlands and Catholic France.

William landed in England in November 1688. During the next few weeks most of the English army sided with him, and James fled to France in late December. Parliament declared that James had abdicated the throne and named William III (1689–1702) and Mary II (1689–1694) as joint sovereigns. It also passed a Toleration Act that gave Protestant dissenters (but not Catholics) the right to worship publicly, and a Bill of Rights that guaranteed a Protestant succession and declared illegal many of the acts of James II. This "Glorious Revolution" also brought England and the Netherlands into war against Louis XIV, who supported James.

The Glorious Revolution in America

The Boston militia overthrew Andros on April 18 and 19, 1689, even before they knew whether William had succeeded against James. Andros's attempt to suppress the news of William's landing convinced the Puritans that he was part of a global popish plot to undermine Protestant societies everywhere. With Andros gone, Rhode Island and Connecticut resumed their charter governments.

In May and June, the New York City militia took over Fort James at the southern tip of Manhattan and renamed it Fort William. To hostile observers, this rising seemed almost a replay of the events of 1673, when the Dutch had reconquered New York and renamed the fort for William (see above, p. 91). Francis Nicholson, lieutenant governor in New York under Andros, refused to proclaim William and Mary as sovereigns without direct orders from England and soon sailed for home. The active rebels in New York City were nearly all Dutch who had little experience with traditional English liberties. Few had held high office. Their leader, Captain Jacob Leisler, dreaded a French invasion that would subject the colony to popish domination.

Military defense became Leisler's highest priority, but his demands for supplies soon alienated even his Yankee supporters on Long Island. Although he summoned an elective assembly, he made no effort to revive the Charter of Liberties of 1683 while continuing to collect duties under the permanent revenue act of that year. He showed little respect for the legal rights of his opponents, most of whom were English or were Dutch merchants who had cheerfully served the Dominion of New England. He jailed several Anti-Leislerians for months without bringing them to trial, and when his own assembly raised questions about their legal rights, he sent it home. Leisler's opponents, in turn, told England that he was a nobody who deserved only scorn and contempt, even though he was descended from a very prominent Calvinist family of northern Europe and could speak French, German, Dutch, and English.

Maryland used the Glorious Revolution to overthrow Lord Baltimore's Catholic government. The governor of Maryland refused to proclaim William and Mary, even after all the other colonies had done so. To Lord Baltimore's dismay, the messenger he sent to Maryland with orders to accept the new monarchs died before leaving England. Had the man reached the colony, the Maryland government probably would have survived the crisis.

The English Response

England responded in different ways to each of these upheavals. The Maryland rebels won the royal government they requested from England and soon established the Anglican Church in the colony. Catholics could no longer worship in public, hold office, or even expect toleration. Most prominent Catholic families braced themselves against the Protestant storm and remained loyal to their faith.

New York's revolutionary leadership suffered a deadly defeat. Leisler and his Dutch followers, who had no significant contacts at the English Court, watched helplessly as their enemies, working through the imperial bureaucracy that William inherited from James, manipulated a Dutch king of England into undermining his loyal Dutch supporters in New York. The new governor, Henry Sloughter, named prominent Anti-Leislerians to his council, arrested Leisler and his son-in-law in 1691, tried both for treason, and had them hanged, drawn, and quartered. The assembly elected in 1691 was also controlled by Anti-Leislerians, most of whom were English. It passed a modified version of the Charter of Liberties of 1683 that denied toleration to Catholics. Like its predecessor, it was later disallowed. Bitter struggles between Leislerians and Anti-Leislerians would characterize New York politics until after 1700.

Another complex struggle involved Massachusetts. In 1689 Increase Mather, acting as the colony's agent in London, tried but failed to get Parliament to restore the charter of 1629. Over the next two years he negotiated a new charter which gave the Crown what it had been demanding since 1664 — the power to appoint governors, justices, and militia officers; and the power to veto laws and to hear judicial appeals. The 1691 charter also granted toleration to all Protestants and based voting rights on property qualifications, not church membership. In effect, liberty and property triumphed over godliness.

While insisting on these concessions, William also accepted much of the previous history of the colony, even if it did not augur well for the emerging model of royal government. The General Court, not the governor as in other royal colonies, retained control over the distribution of land. The council remained an elective body, though it was chosen annually by the full legislature, not directly by the voters. The governor could veto any choice. Finally, Massachusetts absorbed the colonies of Plymouth and Maine. New Hampshire regained its autonomy, but until 1741 it usually shared the same royal governor with Massachusetts. The charter governments of Rhode Island and Connecticut also survived the upheavals of 1689.

When Mather sailed into Boston harbor with the new charter in May 1692, he found the province besieged by witches. The accusations arose in Salem Village (modern Danvers) among a group of girls, most of whom had been orphaned during the Indian wars. They had been adopted into households more pious than their original families. Uncertain whether anyone had a responsibility to find husbands for them, they asked Tituba, a Carib Indian slave in the household of the Reverend Samuel Parris, to tell their fortunes. This occult activity imposed too heavy a burden of guilt on the girls and, beginning with the youngest, they broke under the strain. They howled, barked, and stretched themselves into frightful contortions. With adult encouragement, they accused many neighbors of witchcraft. Most of the accused were old women in families that had opposed the appointment of Parris as village minister.

The trials began in June. The court, composed mostly of judges who had compromised their Puritanism through willing service to the Dominion of

New York from Brooklyn Heights, 1679   This sketch, probably by Jasper Danckaerts or Peter Sluyter, two Dutch visitors, shows the fort at the southern tip of Manhattan Island. When the English conquered New Netherland in 1664, the fort was renamed for James. When the Dutch retook the fort in 1673, it was renamed Fort William for William of Orange. The English again renamed it Fort James in 1674, but when James II was overthrown in the Glorious Revolution of 1688–1689, the settlers named it for William once again. Thereafter, the fort took the name of the reigning British monarch.

New England, hanged nineteen people, pressed one man to death because he refused to plead, and allowed four other people to die while awaiting trial. Most of those hanged were grandmothers, several quite conspicuous for their piety. One victim was a former minister at Salem village who had become a Baptist.

The governor finally halted the prosecutions when the girls accused his wife. The witch trials provided a bitter finale to the era of political upheaval that had afflicted Massachusetts since the loss of the colony's charter in 1684. Along with the new charter, they brought the Puritan era to a close.

The Completion of Empire

In effect, the Glorious Revolution killed absolutism in English America and guaranteed representative government in the colonies. Both Crown and colonists took it for granted that any colony settled by the English would elect an assembly to vote on all taxes and consent to all local laws. Governors would be appointed by the Crown or a lord proprietor, except in Rhode Island and Connecticut. In short, royal government became the norm, especially after the New Jersey proprietors surrendered their powers of government in 1702, and the Carolina proprietors

followed suit after their last governor was deposed by the settlers in 1719. On the other hand, the Crown restored proprietary rule in Maryland in 1716, after the fifth Lord Baltimore converted to the Church of England. But by the 1720s Maryland and Pennsylvania (along with Delaware, which became a separate colony under the Penn proprietorship in 1704) were the only surviving proprietary provinces on the mainland, and their proprietors were usually careful to abide by the rules of imperial administration.

This transition to royal government seems smoother in retrospect than it did at the time. London almost lost control of the empire in the 1690s. Overwhelmed by the pressures of the French war, the Lords of Trade could not keep pace with events in the colonies. When French privateers disrupted the tobacco trade, Scottish smugglers stepped in and began to divert it to Glasgow in defiance of the Navigation Acts. New York became a haven for pirates. The northern colonies were still too dissimilar to cooperate effectively in the war against New France. Parliament grew so exasperated that it threatened to take control of the colonies away from the king, whom it suspected of favoring Dutch interests over English.

William III took action in 1696. With his approval Parliament passed a comprehensive Navigation Act that plugged several loopholes in earlier laws and extended to America the English system of vice-admiralty courts, which dispensed quick justice without juries. When the new courts settled routine maritime disputes or condemned enemy merchant ships captured by colonial privateers, their services were highly regarded. But when they tried to assume jurisdiction over the Navigation Acts, they aroused controversy.

William also replaced the Lords of Trade in 1696 with a new agency, the Board of Trade. Its powers were almost purely advisory. It corresponded with governors and other officials in the colonies, listened to lobbyists in England, and made policy recommendations to appropriate governmental bodies in England, whether Parliament, the Treasury, or a Secretary of State. The main purpose of the Board of Trade was to collect reliable information on complex questions and to offer helpful advice. It was, in short, an early attempt at government through experts. John Locke, England's foremost philosopher and an able economist, was one of the board's first members.

Another difficult problem was resolved in 1707 when England and Scotland agreed to merge their separate parliaments and become the single kingdom of Great Britain. At a stroke, the Act of Union placed Scotland inside the Navigation Act system, legalized Scottish participation in the tobacco trade, and opened numerous colonial offices to ambitious Scots. The economic effects were disappointing at first, but by the middle of the eighteenth century most of Scotland's rapidly expanding prosperity derived from its participation in colonial trade. In a very real sense, the tobacco trade built Glasgow.

Imperial Federalism

The transformations that took place between 1689 and 1707 defined the structure of the British Empire up to the time of the American Revolution. Although Parliament claimed full power over the colonies, in practice it seldom regulated anything colonial except Atlantic commerce. Even the Woolens Act of 1699, designed to protect the English woolens industry from Irish and colonial competition, did not prohibit the manufacture of woolen textiles in the colonies. It simply prohibited their export. The Hat Act of 1732 was similarly designed, except for a clause limiting the number of apprentices or slaves a

colonial hatter could maintain. Nobody enforced that provision.

When Parliament regulated oceanic trade, its measures were usually enforceable. But compliance was minimal to nonexistent when Parliament tried to regulate inland affairs through statutes protecting white pines (needed as masts for the navy) or through the Iron Act of 1750, which prohibited the erection of new plating and splitting mills. To get things done within the colonies, the Crown had to win the settlers' agreement through their lawful assemblies. In effect, the empire had stumbled into a system of de facto federalism, an arrangement that no one could quite explain or justify. The central government exercised only a limited number of powers, and the colonies controlled the rest. What seemed an arrangement of convenience in London eventually acquired overtones of right in America, the right to consent to all taxes and local laws.

The Mixed and Balanced Constitution and British Political Culture

The Glorious Revolution transformed British politics in a way that profoundly affected the colonies after 1700. Throughout the seventeenth century, England's government had seemed hopelessly unstable. The execution of Charles I shocked European opinion. When the Glorious Revolution ended the monarchy's bid for absolutism, most observers expected more instability. To the great surprise of Europe, Britain's limited government after 1689 quickly became a far more powerful state than the Stuart kings had been able to sustain. The British constitution, which made ministers legally responsible for their public actions, proved remarkably stable. Before long many Englishmen were celebrating this achievement as the wonder of the age. In the ancient world, as Harrington pointed out, free societies had degenerated into tyrannies. Liberty had always been fragile and was quite easily lost. Yet England had retained it and grown stronger. England had defied history.

The explanation, everyone agreed, lay in England's "mixed and balanced" constitution. This concept embraced Harrington's ideas about republican liberty but absorbed them into a monarchial framework. Government by King, Lords, and Commons mirrored society itself—the monarchy, aristocracy, and commonality—and literally embodied all three in its very structure. As long as each freely consented

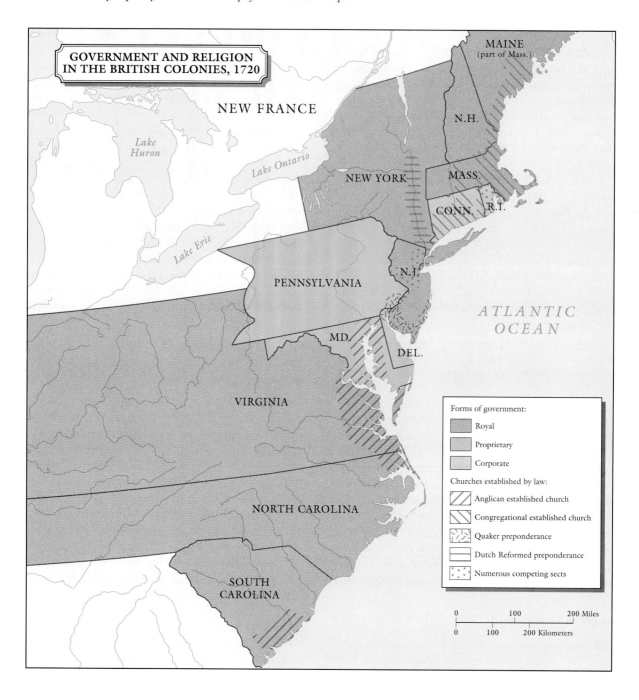

GOVERNMENT AND RELIGION
IN THE BRITISH COLONIES, 1720

NEW FRANCE

MAINE
(part of Mass.)

N.H.

Lake
Huron

Lake Ontario

NEW YORK

MASS.

CONN.   R.I.

Lake Erie

N.J.

PENNSYLVANIA

ATLANTIC
OCEAN

MD.

DEL.

VIRGINIA

Forms of government:

Royal

Proprietary

Corporate

Churches established by law:

Anglican established church

Congregational established church

Quaker preponderance

Dutch Reformed preponderance

Numerous competing sects

NORTH CAROLINA

SOUTH
CAROLINA

0   100   200 Miles

0   100   200 Kilometers

to government measures, English liberty would be secure because each had voluntarily placed the public good ahead of its own particular interests. But if one of the three acquired the power to dominate or manipulate the other two, English liberty would indeed be in peril. This danger fueled an unending dialogue in eighteenth-century Britain. The underlying drama was always the struggle of power against liberty, and liberty usually meant a negation or limitation of governmental power.

Power had to be controlled, or liberty would be lost. Nearly everyone agreed that a direct assault on Parliament through a military coup was highly unlikely. The real danger lay in corruption, in the abil-

The Reception of King George I at St. James Palace, September 20, 1714, An Engraving by A. Allard   This event marked the accession of the Protestant Hanoverian dynasty to the British throne and evokes the hierarchy and pageantry associated with the "Court" side of British politics.

ity of Crown ministers to undermine the independence and integrity of the House of Commons.

The wars with France made Britain one of Europe's great powers, but they also aroused acute constitutional anxieties. After 1689 England raised larger fleets and armies than the kingdom had ever mobilized before. To support them the government created for the first time a funded national debt, in which the state agreed to pay the interest due to its creditors ahead of all other obligations. This simple device gave Britain almost unlimited borrowing power. In 1694 the government chartered the Bank of England to facilitate its own finances, and the London Stock Exchange also emerged in the 1690s. Parliament levied a heavy land tax on the gentry and numerous excises on ordinary people to meet these expenses.

Together, debt, bank, stock market, and new sources of revenue added up to a financial revolution, which enabled England to outspend France, even though France had four times as many people. These resources and the dramatic expansion of offices during the wars vastly increased the government's patronage. By giving offices or war contracts to members of Parliament, the ministry was almost assured of majority support for its measures.

Public debate over these measures pitted the "Court" against the "Country." The Court favored policies that strengthened its war-making capacity. The Country stood for liberty. Each of the parties, Whig and Tory, had Court and Country wings. But between 1680 and 1720 they reversed their polarities. The Tories began as Charles II's Court party, but by 1720 most of them were a Country opposition. Whigs defended Country positions in 1680, but by 1720 most of them were strong advocates for the Court policies of George I (1714–1727). Court spokesmen defended the military buildup, the financial revolution, and the new patronage as essential to victory over France. Their Country opponents denounced standing armies, favored an early peace with France, called for more frequent elections, and tried to ban "placemen" (officeholders who also sat in Parliament) from the House of Commons.

Court Whigs emerged victorious with the establishment of the long ministry of Sir Robert Walpole (1721-1742), but their opponents were more eloquent and controlled more presses. By the 1720s, the opposition claimed many of the kingdom's best writers, especially the Tories Alexander Pope, Jonathan Swift, John Gay, and Henry St. John, viscount Bolingbroke. Their detestation of Walpole was also shared by

A Country Scene in Early Eighteenth-Century England   In British political culture, liberty was strongly associated with the "independence" of landed country gentlemen, who, in turn, stood near the top of a hierarchically ordered rural society. In England, men who worked with their hands could not vote and seldom played an active political role.

a smaller band of radical Whigs, such as John Trenchard and Thomas Gordon. The central theme of opposition writers was always "corruption"—the indirect and insidious means by which ministers threatened the independence of Parliament and English liberty. As these writers became popular in the colonies, the debate over liberty crossed the Atlantic.

THE CONVERGENCE: LIBERTY, PROPERTY, NO POPERY

After moving in wildly different directions for most of the seventeenth century, England and the colonies converged during the Glorious Revolution and its aftermath. They all affirmed liberty under law. Englishmen throughout the empire insisted that the right to property was sacred, that without it liberty could never be secure. And Protestants not only barred Catholics from succession to the throne but also loaded them with severe disabilities of other kinds. In an empire dedicated to liberty, property, and no popery, Catholics were big losers.

SUGGESTED READING

Derek Hirst, *Authority and Conflict: England, 1603–1658* (1986), and J. R. Jones, *Country and Court: England, 1658–1714* (1978) provide strong overviews of public events in England. Wesley F. Craven, *The Colonies in Transition,*

1660–1713 (1968) remains a strong survey of colonial developments. Edmund S. Morgan, *Inventing the People: The Rise of Popular Sovereignty in England and America* (1988) connects political thought in the English civil wars with the American Revolution more than a century later. J. G. A. Pocock, "Machiavelli, Harrington, and English Political Ideologies in the Eighteenth Century," *William and Mary Quarterly,* 3d ser., 22 (1965), 549–583 has had enormous influence. His *The Machiavellian Moment: Florentine Political Thought and the Atlantic Republican Tradition* (1975) is difficult but essential.

Albert O. Hirschman, *The Passions and the Interests: Political Arguments for Capitalism before its Triumph* (1977) is brief and brilliant. Important studies of trade wars and the Navigation Acts include Charles Wilson, *Profit and Power: A Study of England and the Dutch Wars* (1957); Charles M. Andrews, *The Colonial Period of American History,* vol. 4 (1938); Lawrence A. Harper, *The English Navigation Acts: A Seventeenth-Century Experiment in Social Engineering* (1939); and Michael Kammen's brief *Empire and Interest: The American Colonies and the Politics of Mercantilism* (1969).

Peter H. Wood, *Black Majority: Negroes in Colonial South Carolina from 1670 through the Stono Rebellion* (1974) remains the best book on early South Carolina. Charles Hudson, *The Southeastern Indians* (1976) and James H. Merrell, *The Indians' New World: Catawbas and Their Neighbors from European Contact through the Era of Removal* (1989) are superb studies of southern Indians. Other contributions on South Carolina include Richard Waterhouse, *A New World Gentry: The Making of a Merchant and Planter Class in South Carolina, 1670–1770* (1989); David C. Littlefield, *Rice and Slaves: Ethnicity and the Slave Trade in Colonial South Carolina* (1981); and M. Eugene Sirmans, *Colonial South Carolina: A Political History, 1663–1763* (1966).

Robert C. Ritchie, *The Duke's Province: A Study of New York Politics and Society, 1664–1691* (1977); Joyce D. Goodfriend, *Before the Melting Pot: Society and Culture in Colonial New York City, 1664–1730* (1992); and Donna Merwick, *Possessing Albany, 1630–1710: The Dutch and English Experiences* (1990) cover Restoration New York. John E. Pomfret, *The Province of East New Jersey, 1609–1702* (1962), and his *The Province of West New Jersey, 1609–1702* (1956) are still standard. Melvin B. Endy, *William Penn and Early Quakerism* (1973) and the essays in Richard S. Dunn and Mary Maples Dunn, eds., *The World of William Penn* (1986) are comprehensive. Barry J. Levy, *Quakers and the American Family: British Settlement in the Delaware Valley* (1988) is strong on family life, while Gary B. Nash, *Quakers and Politics: Pennsylvania, 1681–1726* (1968) is one of the best political histories of any American colony.

Daniel K. Richer, *The Ordeal of the Longhouse: The Peoples of the Iroquois League in the Era of European Colonization* (1992) and Francis Jennings, *The Ambiguous Iroquois Empire: The Covenant Chain Confederation of Indian Tribes with English Colonies from Its Beginnings to the Lancaster Treaty of 1744* (1984) are both essential. Harold W. Van Lonkhuyzen, "A Reappraisal of the Praying Indians: Acculturation, Conversion, and Identity at Natick, Massachusetts, 1646–1730," *New England Quarterly*, 63 (1990), 396–428 is brief and up to date. Patrick M. Malone, *The Skulking Way of War: Technology and Tactics among the New England Indians* (1991) and Richard I. Melvoin, *New England Outpost: War and Society in Colonial Deerfield* (1989) are transforming the way that historians approach Indian wars. Edmund S. Morgan, *American Slavery, American Freedom: The Ordeal of Colonial Virginia* (1975) has the strongest analysis of Bacon's Rebellion, but Wilcomb Washburn, *The Governor and the Rebel: A History of Bacon's Rebellion in Virginia* (1957) remains useful.

Stephen S. Webb analyzes the origins of royal government in *The Governors General: The English Army and the Definition of Empire, 1569–1681* (1979). Winfred T. Root, "The Lords of Trade, 1675–1696," *American Historical Review*, 23 (1917–1918), 20–41 remains impressive. David S. Lovejoy, *The Glorious Revolution in America* (1972) covers all of the colonies. For more specific studies of the Glorious Revolution in New England, New York, and Maryland, see Richard R. Johnson, *Adjustment to Empire: The New England Colonies, 1675–1715* (1981); John M. Murrin, "The Menacing Shadow of Louis XIV and the Rage of Jacob Leisler: The

Constitutional Ordeal of Seventeenth Century New York," in Stephen L. Schechter and Richard B. Bernstein, eds., *New York and the Union: Contributions to the American Constitutional Experience* (1990), 29-71; and Lois G. Carr and David W. Jordan, *Maryland's Revolution of Government, 1689–1692* (1974). Paul Boyer and Stephen Nissenbaum, *Salem Possessed: The Social Origins of Witchcraft* (1974); John P. Demos, *Entertaining Satan: Witchcraft and the Culture of Early New England* (1982); and Richard Weisman, *Witchcraft, Magic, and Religion in 17th Century Massachusetts* (1984) all provide imaginative and distinctive perspectives on the Salem witch trials, but Carol F. Karlsen, *The Devil in the Shape of a Woman: Witchcraft in Colonial New England* (1987) is a conceptual breakthrough.

John Miller, *Popery and Politics in England, 1660–1688* (1973); Robert Willman, "The Origins of 'Whig' and 'Tory' in English Political Language," *Historical Journal,* 17 (1974), 247-264; Clayton Roberts, *The Growth of Responsible Government in Stuart England* (1966); W. A. Speck, *Reluctant Revolutionaries: Englishmen and the Revolution of 1688* (1989); J. H. Plumb, *The Growth of Political Stability in England, 1675–1725* (1967); John Brewer, *The Sinews of Power: War, Money, and the English State, 1688–1783* (1989); P. G. M. Dickson, *The Financial Revolution in England: A Study in the Development of Public Credit, 1688–1756* (1967); Geoffrey Holmes, *The Electorate and the National Will in the First Age of Party* (1976); and Isaac Kramnick, *Bolingbroke and His Circle: The Politics of Nostalgia in the Age of Walpole* (1968) together lay out various aspects of the transformation of English politics between 1660 and 1720. Peter Laslett, "John Locke, the Great Recoinage, and the Origins of the Board of Trade: 1695–1698," *William and Mary Quarterly*, 3d ser., 14 (1957), 370–402 is an unusually thoughtful essay. Ian K. Steele, *The English Atlantic, 1675–1740: An Exploration of Communication and Community* (1986) is careful and original. John M. Murrin looks for similarities and differences in the English and American Revolutions in "The Great Inversion, or Court versus Country: A Comparison of the Revolution Settlements in England (1688–1721) and America (1776–1816)," in J. G. A. Pocock, ed., *Three British Revolutions: 1641, 1688, 1776* (1980), 368–453.

Videos: The PBS miniseries, *Three Sovereigns for Sarah* (1985), starring Vanessa Redgrave, is a superb dramatization of the Salem witch trials.

Chapter 4

Expansion, Diversity, and Anglicization in Provincial America

Front Page of the New-England Courant, April 16, 1722 Newspapers had an enormous impact on the British colonies. By contrast, none was founded in the French or Spanish colonies before the American Revolution. In this particular issue of the *Courant*, the printer, James Franklin, did not know that "Silence Dogood," author of the lead essay, was his sixteen-year-old brother and apprentice, Benjamin Franklin.

For most of the seventeenth century, the Spanish, French, and English empires in North America remained isolated from one another. Conflict occurred often in the Caribbean but was rare on the mainland, where the three empires developed in quite different ways. Spain sent unarmed missionaries to convert the Indians. France, once the heroic age of the early Jesuit missions had passed, emphasized trade with Indians of the Great Lakes region and the lower Mississippi Valley. The English, while also interested in trade and occasionally even in missions, put their energies into settlement and expansion. Toward the end of the century, the three powers entered a long period of intense warfare in Europe that engulfed their American possessions as well.

CONTRASTING EMPIRES: SPAIN AND FRANCE IN NORTH AMERICA

Spain and France, both Catholic countries, showed a zeal for converting Indians that exceeded anything displayed by English Protestants. Yet their North American empires had little else in common.

Crisis along Spain's Frontier: The Pueblo Revolt

Spain faced a major crisis on its North American frontier. The Florida missions were beginning to decline at just the time Spain faced a dangerous new enemy there: the English out of South Carolina, eager

Table 4-1

British Wars against France (and Usually Spain), 1689–1763

European Name	American Name	Years	Peace
War of the League of Augsburg	King William's War	1689–1697	Ryswick
War of the Spanish Succession	Queen Anne's War	1702–1713	Utrecht
War of Jenkins' Ear, merging with		1739–1748	
War of the Austrian Succession	King George's War	1744–1748	Aix-la-Chapelle
Seven Years' War	French and Indian War	1754–1763*	Paris

*The French and Indian War began in America in 1754 and then merged with the Seven Years' War in Europe, which began in 1756.

to enslave unarmed Indians. Disease also took a heavy toll. But the greatest challenge to the Catholic Church and Spanish rule arose in New Mexico, where the Pueblo population had fallen from 80,000 to 17,000 since 1598. A prolonged drought and Apache and Navajo attacks prompted many Pueblos to abandon the Christian God and resume their old forms of worship. The missionaries responded with severe whippings and even several executions in 1675.

Popé was a San Juan Pueblo medicine man who had been whipped for his beliefs. He then moved north to Taos Pueblo, where he organized the most successful Indian revolt in American history. In 1680, in an a carefully timed uprising, the Pueblos killed four hundred of the 2,300 Spaniards in New Mexico and destroyed or plundered every Spanish building in the province. They desecrated every church and killed twenty-one of New Mexico's thirty-three missionaries. "Now," they exulted, "the God of the Spaniards, who was their father, is dead," but the God [of the Pueblos], whom they obeyed, "[had] never died." Spaniards who survived fled from Santa Fe down the Rio Grande to El Paso (see map on p. 46).

Popé lost influence when the revival of traditional rites did not end the drought or stop attacks from hostile Indians. When the Spanish returned in the 1690s, this time as military conquerors, the Pueblos were badly divided. Most of the Pueblo villages yielded without much resistance, and Spain accepted their submission, but Santa Fe held out until December 1693. When it fell, the Spanish executed seventy warriors and distributed four hundred women and children as slaves among the returning settlers. The

Hopi Indians to the west, however, never again submitted to Spanish rule.

Before these crises, in both Florida and New Mexico, missionaries often resisted the demands of Spanish governors. By 1700 the state ruled, and missionaries obeyed. Spain's daring, idealistic attempt to create a demilitarized Christian frontier was becoming a tragic failure for both Indians and missionaries.

New France, Indians, and the Emergence of a Middle Ground

A different story unfolded along the western frontier of New France between the late seventeenth century and the British conquest of Canada in 1760. Here, the Iroquois menace made possible an unusual accommodation between the government of New France and the Indians of the Great Lakes region. The survival of the Iroquois Five Nations depended on their ability to assimilate captives, seized from other tribes through incessant warfare (see Chapter 3). Iroquois raiders, armed with muskets, terrorized western Indians, carried away thousands of captives, and left behind grisly trophies of their cruelty to discourage revenge. The Iroquois wars depopulated nearly all of what is now the state of Ohio and much of the Ontario peninsula. In the last half of the seventeenth century, the Indians around Lakes Erie and Huron either fled west to escape these horrors or were absorbed by the Iroquois. The refugees, mostly Algonquian-speaking peoples, founded new communities farther west. Most of these villages contained families from several different tribes, and village

Iroquois Warriors Leading an Indian Prisoner into Captivity, 1660s This is a French copy of an Iroquois pictograph.

loyalties gradually supplanted older tribal (or ethnic) loyalties, which often broke down under Iroquois pressure. But when the refugees disagreed with one another or came into conflict with the Sioux to their west, the absence of traditional tribal structures made it difficult to resolve these conflicts. Over time, French soldiers, trappers, and missionaries stepped in to act as mediators.

The Middle Ground of the Great Lakes Region   The French were not always welcome. In 1684, the only year for which we have a precise count, the Algonquians killed thirty-nine French traders. Yet the leaders of thinly populated New France were nevertheless eager to erect an Algonquian shield against the Iroquois and, in later decades, against the British. They began by easing tensions among the Algonquians and supplying them with firearms, brandy, and other European goods. In fact, to the exasperation of missionaries, brandy became the lubricant of the fur trade. It kept the warriors hunting for pelts and dependent on French traders. New France served, in turn, as a shield behind which the Algonquians could regroup and strike back against the Iroquois. By 1701 Iroquois losses became so heavy that the Five Nations negotiated a peace treaty with the French and the western Indians by which they agreed to remain neutral in any war between France and England. France's Indian allies, supported by a new French fort erected at Detroit in that year, began

returning to the fertile lands around Lakes Erie and Huron. That region became a Middle Ground over which New France exercised considerable influence, but only by respecting Indian customs and goals. Although France always ran a deficit supporting the fur trade, it kept it going mostly to block British expansion westward.

The survival of the French on the Middle Ground required uncommon skill and constant effort. The replacement of a seasoned negotiator by an inexperienced official from France could destroy decades of hard-won achievements overnight. Officials who gave orders instead of fostering negotiations merely alienated France's Indian allies. Blind obedience to commands, grumbled the warriors, was slavery. The Indians came to respect those Frenchmen who played by Indian rules and honored their ways. French missionaries were more successful than the English in winning converts because they accepted Indian cultures on their own terms. Many Indian women converted. Admirers of the Virgin Mary and of Catholic nuns, they became the first Indians to accept the Catholic insistence on sexual abstinence before marriage.

France's success in the interior rested more on intelligent negotiation than on force. Hugely outnumbered, the French knew that they could not impose their will on the Indians. From an Indian perspective, New France was not a centralized, authoritarian empire. The French conducted diplomacy according to

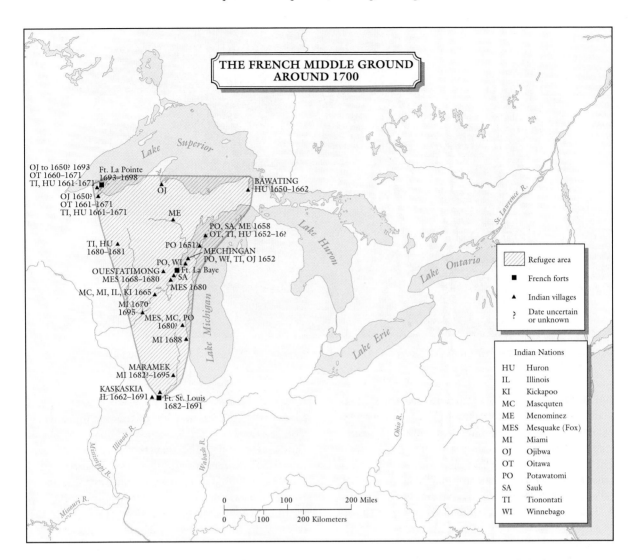

THE FRENCH MIDDLE GROUND AROUND 1700

OJ to 1650? 1693
OT 1660–1671
TI, HU 1661–1671

Ft. La Pointe
1693–1698

OJ

BAWATING
HU 1650–1662

OJ 1650?
OT 1661–1671
TI, HU 1661–1671

ME

PO, SA, ME 1658
OT, TI, HU 1652–16?

TI, HU
1680–1681

PO 1651

MECHINGAN
PO, WI, TI, OJ 1652

PO, WI

OUESTATIMONG
MES 1668–1680

Ft. La Baye
SA
MES 1680

MC, MI, IL, KI 1665

MI 1670
1695

MES, MC, PO
1680?

MI 1688

MARAMEK
MI 1682?–1695

KASKASKIA
IL 1662–1691

Ft. St. Louis
1682–1691

Lake Superior
Lake Huron
Lake Ontario
Lake Erie
Lake Michigan
St. Lawrence R.
Mississippi R.
Illinois R.
Wabash R.
Ohio R.
Missouri R.

	Refugee area
	French forts
	Indian villages
?	Date uncertain or unknown

Indian Nations

HU	Huron
IL	Illinois
KI	Kickapoo
MC	Mascquten
ME	Menominez
MES	Mesquake (Fox)
MI	Miami
OJ	Ojibwa
OT	Oitawa
PO	Potawatomi
SA	Sauk
TI	Tionontati
WI	Winnebago

0   100   200 Miles
0   100   200 Kilometers

Indian, not European rules. The governor of New France became a somewhat grander version of a traditional Indian chief. Algonquians called him *Onontio* ("Great Mountain"), the supreme alliance chief who won cooperation through persuasion and who quickly learned that, among the Indians, persuasion was always accompanied by presents. The respect accorded to peacetime chiefs was roughly proportionate to how much they gave away, not to how much they accumulated. The English, by contrast, tried to "buy" land from the Indians and regarded the sale of the land and of the right to use it as irrevocable. The French understood that this idea had no place in Indian culture. Agreements were not final contracts,

never to be altered. They represented a continuing process that required regular renewal, always with an exchange of gifts, in which the stronger party had to be more generous than anyone else.

French Louisiana and Spanish Texas   The pattern worked out by the French and the Indians on the Great Lakes Middle Ground also took hold, though somewhat more weakly, in the lower Mississippi Valley. In quest of a northwest passage to Asia, Father Jacques Marquette and trader Louis Joliet paddled down the Mississippi to its juncture with the Arkansas River in 1673. But once they became convinced that the Mississippi flowed into the Gulf of Mexico

La Salle and Father Hennepin on the Mississippi   This drawing by Father Louis Hennepin was done in around 1683.

and not the Pacific Ocean, they turned back. Then, in 1682, the sieur de la Salle traveled down the Mississippi to its mouth, claiming possession of the entire area for France and calling it Louisiana (for King Louis XIV). But when la Salle returned by way of the Gulf of Mexico to plant a small colony in 1684, he overshot the mouth of the Mississippi and landed in Texas, where he wandered about in search of the great river until his own men murdered him in 1687.

In 1699, during a brief lull in the wars between France and England, the French returned to the Gulf. Pierre le Moyne d'Iberville, a Canadian, landed with eighty men at Biloxi, built a fort, and set about establishing friendly relations with the Indians. In 1702 he moved his headquarters to Mobile to get closer to the more populous nations of the interior, especially the Choctaws, who were looking for allies against the English. The Choctaws could still field five thousand warriors but had already suffered terrible losses from slaving raids organized by South Carolinians and carried out mostly by that colony's Chickasaw and Creek allies. About 1,800 Choctaws were killed during the previous decade and five hundred enslaved. Using the Choctaws as the anchor of their trading system, the French created a weaker, southern version of the Great Lakes Middle Ground, acting as mediators and trading brandy,

firearms, and other European products for furs and food. Often, during the War of the Spanish Succession (1702–1713), the French were unable to obtain European supplies, and they remained heavily outnumbered by the Indians. Although European diseases had been ravaging the area since the 1540s, the Indian nations of the lower Mississippi Valley still numbered about 70,000. In 1708 the French had fewer than three hundred people, including eighty Indian slaves. The French had to be careful, and they barely survived.

Spain, alarmed at any challenge to its monopoly on the Gulf of Mexico, founded Pensacola in 1698, more to counter the English than the French. Competition from France prompted the Spanish to move into Texas in 1690, establishing missions near the modern Texas–Louisiana border. At first, the missionaries were cordially received by the Tejas (Texas) Indians, but they brought smallpox with them. Their explanation that the epidemic was God's "holy will" failed to mollify the Indians, who in 1693 told the missionaries to get out or be killed. They departed, leaving Texas to the Indians for another twenty years. Yet Europe's imperial rivalries were clearly becoming a part of daily life throughout the Gulf region. Even Texas Indians desired French trade goods.

AN EMPIRE OF SETTLEMENT: THE BRITISH COLONIES

In 1700, when only about 250,000 settlers and slaves were living in England's mainland colonies, the population was already growing at an explosive rate. England's five million subjects outnumbered them by 20 to 1, and Scotland's one million by 4 to 1. Although the Scottish population reached 1.5 million around 1760, the British colonies had already exceeded that total in the previous decade. By the outbreak of the Revolutionary War in 1775, close to 2.5 million people (excluding Indians) inhabited the thirteen colonies, surpassing Scotland by almost a million and rapidly closing the gap on England's 6.7 million. The population of the settlements had grown from 5 percent of England's total population to more than 37 percent in just seventy-five years. By 1750, Benjamin Franklin could foresee the time when a large majority of English-speaking people would be living on the western side of the Atlantic. He wondered whether the imperial capital, in the next century or so, might move from London to North America.

A Persistent Tension: Expansion versus Anglicization

This relentless growth had paradoxical results. On the one hand, British colonists tried to emulate the ways of their homeland as never before. From the professions to consumer goods, things left behind in the seventeenth century began to reappear in the eighteenth. Imports of British goods rose even faster than population after 1740. The colonial gentry dressed in the latest London fashions and embraced the city's standards of taste and elegance. Between 1720 and 1750 wealthy settlers built graceful mansions in the older portions of the colonies. Virginia planters erected their "big houses," such as Mount Vernon, built by Lawrence Washington and bequeathed to his half-brother George. In Boston, the merchant Thomas Hancock built a stylish residence on Beacon Hill, which later passed to his nephew John. Newspapers and the learned professions, also copied from English models, took hold in the same era, and the largest colonial seaports began to look like Bristol and other prosperous English provincial cities.

On the other hand, no institution could sustain its impact unless it continued to grow. The population of British North America doubled every twenty-five years, which meant that each generation required twice as many colleges, ministers, lawyers, physicians, craftsmen, printers, sailors, and unskilled laborers as its predecessor. Otherwise, colonial standards of "civility" would decline. Eighteenth-century America became the scene of a contest between the brutal, unrelenting pace of raw expansion and these newer, anglicizing tendencies — those forces that were trying to make American society, now more diverse than ever before, more like England, which itself was becoming quite diverse after its 1707 union with Scotland. While many Scots and Irish moved to North America, thousands of others achieved prominence in the economic, political, and cultural life of London and other English cities.

In 1700 Oxford and Cambridge universities in England could fill the colonies' needs for Anglican clergymen by sending over their surplus graduates. By 1750 that supply was inadequate, and the colonies were trying to entice Scottish and Irish clergymen.

It was still not enough. Colonial institutions that looked only to Europe to satisfy their needs for skilled talent could no longer get all they wanted. Colonies that anglicized at a deeper level were better able to maintain the pace. By building their own colleges and other systems of passing on formal skills, they began to *replicate* much of what gave Britain its preeminence within the empire.

Much of this change occurred during prolonged periods of warfare. War interrupted expansion, which then resumed at an even more frantic pace with the return of peace. By mid-century, these wars were becoming a titanic struggle for control of the North American continent. Indians began to realize that they would become the ultimate victims of any British victory. Unending expansion for British colonial households meant unending retreat for them.

The Engine of British Expansion: The Colonial Household

Virginia's Robert "King" Carter, who died in 1730, became the first settler to acquire a thousand slaves and several hundred thousand acres of land. His household was very different from that of an ordinary farmer in Pennsylvania or Connecticut. Yet both households had something in common that distinguished them from those in eighteenth-century

Sitting Room of the Verplanck Residence   The Verplanck residence, on Wall Street in New York City, was typical of the opulence of the homes of the urban rich in the 1760s. Everything depicted here was in the house at the time.

England. With few exceptions, colonial families did not adopt the English customs of entail and primogeniture. Entail prohibited a landowner, or his heir, from dividing up his landed estate (that is, selling part of it) during his lifetime. Primogeniture was a legal device that required him to leave all of his land to his eldest surviving son. Under this system, younger sons were clearly not equal to the oldest son, and daughters usually ranked behind all the sons.

Primogeniture and entail were used more frequently in the eighteenth-century colonies than they had been before, but they never acquired the same power to structure social relations in North America that they had in England. A prominent Virginia planter, for example, might entail his home plantation (the one on which he had erected his big house) and bequeath it to his oldest son, but he would also leave land and slaves, sometimes whole plantations, to his other sons. The primacy of the eldest son was far more sentimental than structural. The patriarchs of North American households remained distinctive because they shared the same ambition: to pass on their status to *all* their sons, and to provide dowries for *all* their daughters to enable them to marry men of equal status.

For younger sons, then, the colonies were a land of unique opportunity. Benjamin Franklin began his *Autobiography*, colonial America's greatest success story, by boasting that he was "the youngest Son of the youngest Son for 5 Generations back." Despite those odds, Franklin had become a gentleman with an international reputation. He made enough money to retire as a printer, commissioned a genteel portrait of himself, engaged in scientific experiments, and entered public life. He no longer worked with his hands.

English households became "Americanized" in the colonies, but this trend was not a cumulative process. It was something that happened in the earliest years of settlement, as soon as Virginia and Plymouth made land available to nearly all male settlers. By the eighteenth century, the big question was whether this system could survive the pressures of a rising population. Social change began to drive American households back toward European norms. Without continual expansion on to new lands, the colonial household had no chance of providing equal opportunity for all sons, much less all daughters.

The colonial household was patriarchal. Fathers expected to be loved and revered by their wives and children, but they insisted on being obeyed. Children also had to obey their mother. A man's standing in the community depended on his success as a master at home. A mature male was something less than a man until he became the master of others. Thus, while the colonial household usually accorded opportunity and dignity to younger sons, it gave nothing comparable

Robert Feke's Portrait of Benjamin Franklin as a Gentleman
This portrait was painted at about the time that Franklin retired as a printer in 1747. Note the wig and the ruffled cuffs, indicating that Franklin would no longer be working with his hands.

to wives and daughters, and this disparity between men and women continued to grow.

Anglicizing the Role of Women   The changing status of women marked an early and dramatic example of the anglicizing tendencies of the century. When they married, most women received a dowry from their fathers, usually in cash or goods, not land. Under the common law doctrine of coverture, women could not make a contract while married. The legal personality of the husband "covered" the wife, and he made all legally binding decisions. If he died first, his widow was entitled to dower rights, usually one-third of the estate, which was then passed on, after her death, to the couple's surviving children.

To sustain male opportunity in America, then, women had to become more English, thus reversing several seventeenth-century trends. Before 1700 many Chesapeake widows had inherited all of their husbands' property and administered their own estates. These arrangements became rare after 1700. In the

Hudson Valley, Dutch law, while it prevailed, was much more generous than English common law in bestowing property rights on women, but by the mid-eighteenth century, English law had replaced it. Even in New England, where Puritan intensity was on the wane, the trend was similar. There, seventeenth-century courts had routinely punished men for sexual offenses, such as fornication, and many men had pleaded guilty and accepted their sentences. After about 1700 almost no male would plead guilty to any sexual offense, except making love to his wife before their wedding day. To the acute humiliation of their wives, some husbands even denied that charge, merely to avoid a small fine, even after their pregnant wives had already pled guilty. Courts rarely convicted men of sex offenses, not even serious crimes such as rape. The European double standard of sexual behavior, which tolerated male infractions but punished women severely for their indiscretions, had been in some jeopardy under the Puritan regime. It now revived.

The Household and the Market   The male head of the household was not an individualist, although in New England and Pennsylvania he probably thought himself the rough equal of most other householders. Above all, he tried to perpetuate the household itself into the next generation and to preserve his own economic "independence," or autonomy. Of course, complete independence was impossible. Every household owed small debts or favors to its neighbors, and these transactions were often recorded in accounts, called book debts, that carried no interest. Once a year or so, a man would balance his accounts with his neighbor, and they would determine who owed whom how much. Cash might change hands, but if the net debt was small, it might be carried for another year.

Farmers rarely set out to maximize profits, but they did try to grow an agricultural surplus, if only as a hedge against drought, storms, and other unpredictable events. For rural Pennsylvanians this surplus averaged about 40 percent of the total crop. With the harvest in, farmers marketed their produce, often selling it for cash to merchants in Boston, New York, or Philadelphia for local consumption or for export to the West Indies or Europe. Farmers used cash to pay taxes or their ministers' salaries and to buy British imports. Though these arrangements sometimes placed families in short-term debt to merchants, most farmers and artisans successfully avoided long-term dependence on other people. Settlers accepted temporary forms of dependency among freemen — of sons on their parents, indentured servants on their masters, or journeymen on master craftsmen. Sons often worked for neighbors as farm laborers, sailors, or journeymen craftsmen, provided this dependence was a normal part of the life cycle and thus temporary. A man whose dependency became permanent lost the respect of his community.

Anglicization and the Threat to Householder Autonomy

Yet as population increased, some families acquired more prestige than others. Although the status of "gentleman" was less rigid in the colonies than in Europe, it usually implied a person who performed no manual labor, and these men began to dominate public life. Before 1700 ordinary farmers and small planters had often sat in colonial assemblies. In the eighteenth century these assemblies grew in size much more slowly than the overall population. In fact, in the five colonies from New York to Maryland, they remained almost unchanged despite the enormous rise of population. Those who participated in public life above the local level came increasingly from a higher social status. They had more wealth, a more impressive lineage, and a better education than ordinary farmers or craftsmen. But unlike their counterparts in England, few colonial gentlemen enjoyed a patron–client relationship with the voters. In England, a family or two dominated each of the "pocket boroughs" that elected most members of Parliament, but most colonial voters remained independent.

By mid-century, even as householders jealously protected their autonomy, patterns of dependency were indeed emerging. In one Maryland county, for example, 27 percent of the householders were tenants who worked small tracts of land with no slaves, or men who owned a slave or two but had no claim to land. These families could not satisfy the ambitions of all their children. In Pennsylvania's Chester County, a new social class of married couples arose who earned their living as farm laborers. Without granting them title or lease, their employer permitted them to use a small patch of his land, on which they built a cottage and raised some food. In England, such people were called cottagers. In Chester County records, they are listed as "inmates." By 1800 they made up 25 percent of the county population.

Tenants on New York manors had to accept higher rents and shorter leases after 1750. And in Chebacco Parish in Ipswich, Massachusetts, half of the farmers could not provide land for all of their sons by 1760.

Faced with these waning prospects, families reverted to English social norms. A father with insufficient resources for all his children favored his sons over his daughters, unless he could enhance the family's prestige by marrying a daughter to a wealthy suitor. In Connecticut, from the 1750s to the 1770s, the likelihood of sons inheriting land held at about 75 percent, but for daughters it fell from 44 to 34 percent. When an estate could not support all the sons, the eldest was favored at the expense of his younger brothers. They, in turn, took up a trade or headed for the frontier. Many New England families added a craft or two to the task of farming. The three hundred households of Haverhill, Massachusetts, supported forty-four workshops and nineteen mills by 1767. In Northampton more than one-third of all the farming families also practiced a craft. The town of Lynn specialized in making shoes, which found a market in several other colonies.

Most families added a craft in order to sustain household autonomy, not abandon it. In many, perhaps most, cases, women had to work harder — at the spinning wheel, for example — to maintain the household's status. The goal of independence continued to exercise great power, but it was also under siege. The fear of imperiled independence energized the whole westward movement.

The Voluntaristic Ethic and Public Life

The householder's quest for independence also affected the way that settlers conducted politics and waged war. In those spheres, householder autonomy took on the guise of voluntarism, a set of attitudes that limited the degree of anglicization that the colonies would accept. Few freemen could be coerced into doing something they disapproved of. They had to be persuaded or induced. "Obedience by compulsion is the Obedience of Vassals, who without compulsion would disobey," explained one essayist. "The Affection of the People is the only Source of a Cheerful and rational Obedience." Local officials served without pay and would not carry out orders that in their judgment did not serve their own interests or the welfare of their community.

Most young men accepted military service only if it made sense in terms of their own future plans. Most would serve only under officers they knew and then for only a single campaign. Few reenlisted. To the exasperation of professional British soldiers, provincials, like Indians, regarded blind obedience to commands as "slavery." They did not enlist to become soldiers in the European sense. After serving, they used their bonus and pay, and often the promise of a land grant, to hasten their progress toward becoming masters of their own households. Military service, for those who survived it, could lead to the ownership of land and an earlier marriage. For New England women, however, war reduced the supply of eligible males and raised the median age of marriage by about two years, which usually meant one fewer pregnancy per marriage. For the first time, lifelong spinsters were becoming a statistically significant phenomenon.

Three Warring Empires, 1689–1716

Smart diplomacy with the Indians protected the western flank of New France, but in the east the colony was vulnerable to an English invasion. The governors of New France knew that Indian attacks against English towns would keep the English colonies disorganized and force them to disperse their resources. Within a year of the outbreak of war between France and England in 1689, Indians had devastated most of coastal Maine and had attacked the Mohawk Valley town of Schenectady and forced most of its inhabitants into captivity.

In each of the four colonial wars between Britain and France, New Englanders called for the conquest of New France, usually through a naval expedition against Quebec, combined with an overland attack on Montreal. In King William's War (1689–1697), Sir William Phips of Massachusetts forced Acadia to surrender in 1690 (the French soon regained it) and then sailed up the St. Lawrence. At Quebec, he was bluffed into retreating by the French governor, the comte de Frontenac, who kept marching the same small band of soldiers around his ramparts until the attackers became intimidated and withdrew. The overland attack collapsed amidst intercolonial bickering. French attacks, with Indians providing most of the fighters, continued to ravage the frontier.

In 1704, during Queen Anne's War (1702–1713), the French and Indians destroyed Deerfield, Mass-

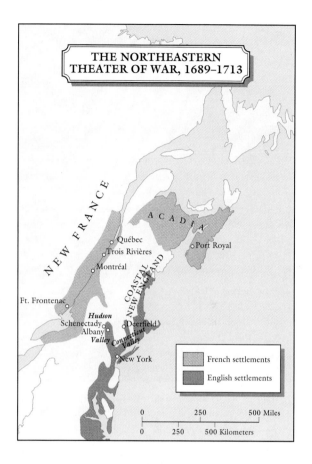

achusetts, in a winter attack and marched most of its people off to captivity in Canada. Hundreds of New Englanders spent months or even years as captives. One of them was Eunice Williams, the young daughter of John Williams, the pastor of Deerfield. Refusing to return to New England when the town's captives were released, she remained in Canada, became a Catholic, and married an Indian. Another New England woman who refused to return was Esther Wheelwright, daughter of a prominent Maine family. Captured by the Abenakis, she was taken to New France, where she also refused repatriation, converted to Catholicism, became a nun (Esther Marie Joseph de L'Enfant Jésus), and finally emerged as mother superior of the Ursuline Order in Canada—surely an unlikely career for a proper Puritan girl!

As the war dragged on, New Englanders twice failed to take Port Royal in Acadia, but a combined British and colonial force finally succeeded in 1710, renaming the colony Nova Scotia. An effort to subdue

Portrait of Esther Wheelwright   Esther Wheelwright (1696–1780) who became Sister Esther Marie Joseph de l'Enfant Jésus, was mother superior of the Ursuline nuns in New France.

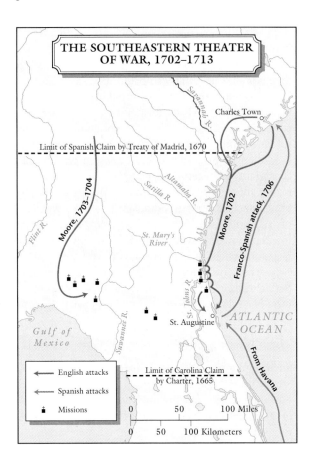

THE SOUTHEASTERN THEATER OF WAR, 1702–1713

Quebec the following year met with disaster when many of the British ships ran aground in a treacherous part of the St. Lawrence River.

Farther south the imperial struggle was grimmer and even more tragic. The Franciscan missions of Florida were already in decline, but their Indians still attracted Carolina slavers, who invaded Florida between 1702 and 1704 with a large force of Indian allies, dragged off four thousand women and children as slaves, drove nine thousand Indians from their homes, and wrecked the missions. Though they failed to take the Spanish fortress of St. Augustine, they wreaked havoc throughout the interior and spread devastation as far west as the land of the Choctaws. Spain and France retaliated with an attack on Charleston in 1706, but it failed.

The greed of Carolinians for Indian slaves finally alienated their strongest Indian allies, the Yamasees, who, fearing that they would be the next to be enslaved, attacked South Carolina in 1715 and almost destroyed it before being thrust back and nearly exterminated. Some of the Yamasees and a number of escaped African slaves fled as refugees to Spanish Florida.

The wars of 1689–1716 stopped and then reversed the movement of British settlers onto new lands in New England and the Carolinas. Only four Maine towns survived the wars; after half a century, South Carolina's white population was still only between five thousand and six thousand in 1720. But in Pennsylvania, Maryland, and Virginia—areas not under attack—the westward thrust continued.

EXPANSION, IMMIGRATION, AND REGIONAL DIFFERENTIATION

The return of peace once again encouraged expansion, with some colonies gaining more land than others. Over the century, the colonies became grouped into distinct regions, although only New England had acquired a strong sense of regional identity by the time of independence.

South Carolinians Enslaving an Indian Although the painting depicts incidents that took place around 1680, it was painted much later.

After Britain and France made peace at Utrecht in 1713, the settled portions of North America entered one of their longest periods of peace since the arrival of Europeans. Massachusetts waged a halfhearted war in Maine against the Abenaki Indians in 1722–1724, but most of North America east of the Appalachian Mountains remained at peace until the 1740s. By 1713 warfare had emptied the New England borderlands of most of their people, both Indians and settlers. In the Deep South, North Carolina's victory over the Tuscaroras in 1711–1713 (the losers moved north to become the sixth nation of the Iroquois League) and South Carolina's defeat of the Yamasees in 1715–1716 opened up the rest of the coastal shelf and much of the Piedmont Region to Carolina settlers.

For about a generation, people poured into these areas without antagonizing the strong Indian nations of the interior. Even in Pennsylvania, the only colony that never had an Indian war before the 1750s, disease depleted the Delaware Indians. When the proprietary government cheated the Delawares out of a huge tract of land through the nefarious Walking Purchase of 1737, many of them, instead of fighting, moved west to the upper Ohio Valley, where they joined the returning Shawnees. With their departure, most of southern Pennsylvania east of the mountains was opened to settlement. New York expanded into the Hudson Valley below Albany, where a century of contact and disease had decimated the original Algonquian inhabitants. The Iroquois Six Nations blocked New York's westward expansion up the Mohawk Valley. The Iroquois maintained their policy of neutrality between Britain and France, while trading primarily with the Dutch burghers of Albany. British officials preferred to regard the Iroquois as allies, despite the Five Nations' treaty of neutrality with the French in 1701. That fiction permitted Britain to claim all the land seized by the Iroquois during the previous century, including the Great Lakes region, even though the Algonquians and the French had reversed those losses in the 1690s.

Immigration: Free and Unfree

Between 1492 and 1810 about 12 million people crossed the Atlantic to the Americas. Fewer than one-third of them came from Europe. A huge majority were Africans dragged in chains from the continent of their birth. The African slave trade was not an unfortunate exception to the story of liberty in the Americas. It was the norm. Even the continental colonies that had few slaves were an integral part of an imperial and economic system that included the West Indies, where slaves outnumbered Europeans even in the seventeenth century and swamped them in the eighteenth. The economies of the free-labor colonies thrived because they found markets for their fish, grain, and lumber in the more typical slave societies.

Renewed immigration, both unfree and free, powered much of the expansion that followed the Treaty of Utrecht. During the first seven decades of the eighteenth century, the slave trade to North America reached its zenith. In all but two of those decades, the inflow of slaves exceeded that of all whites. In addition, Britain shipped thousands of convicts to North America, mostly to Maryland and Virginia, where they served long terms before receiving their freedom. Between 1700 and 1770, 260,000 slaves and 50,000 convicts reached the mainland, as against 210,000 voluntary migrants. Free migration finally dwarfed the slave and convict trades only in the twelve years after 1763.

Almost 90 percent of the slaves went to the southern colonies. Charleston took at least 84,000 slaves, Virginia at least 70,000, and Maryland 25,000 to 30,000. Smaller southern ports—the Cape Fear region in North Carolina, Georgetown and Beaufort in South Carolina, and Savannah in Georgia—bought thousands more. One-eighth of the slaves went to northern colonies. New England had 15,000 blacks by 1770, New York 19,000, and New Jersey, Pennsylvania, and Delaware 16,000. About 80 percent of the slaves arrived from Africa on British-owned vessels. Most of the rest came, a few at a time, from the West Indies on New England ships. Of the colonial seaports, only Newport, Rhode Island, became deeply involved in slave trading along the African coast. Newport never supplied a large percentage of North America's slaves, but that traffic became important to the city's growth.

Emergence of the Old South

The massive influx of slaves between 1700 and 1740 created the Old South—a society consisting of wealthy slaveholding planters, a much larger class of small planters, and thousands of slaves. By 1720 slaves made up 70 percent of South Carolina's population. They were 40 percent of Virginia's by 1740, when Maryland's total was approaching 30 percent. Slaves performed most of the manual labor in the southern colonies, especially the production of staple crops for sale in Britain and Europe.

Their arrival transformed the social structure of these colonies. In 1700 most members of Virginia's House of Burgesses were small planters who raised tobacco with a few indentured servants and perhaps a slave or two. By 1730 most burgesses were great planters, each owning more then twenty slaves. By 1750 the rice planters of South Carolina were richer than any other group in British North America. But tobacco and rice planters had few contacts with each other and did not yet think of themselves as "southerners."

Slavery: Gang Labor versus the Task System   The lives of slaves in the Chesapeake colonies (Maryland, Virginia, and the Albemarle region of North Carolina) differed considerably from those of slaves in the Lower South (from Cape Fear in North Carolina through South Carolina and Georgia). Tobacco planters organized their slaves into gangs, supervised them closely, and kept them in the fields all day, weather permitting. But in their efforts to make their plantations self-sufficient, Chesapeake planters trained perhaps 10 percent of their slaves as blacksmiths, carpenters, coopers, or as other skilled artisans. Planters justified their active supervision of slaves in paternalistic terms. They explained even brutal whippings as the fatherly correction of members of their own household.

South Carolina planters began with similar objectives, but rice swamps and swarms of mosquitoes defeated them. "Carolina is in the spring a paradise, in the summer a hell, and in the autumn a hospital," claimed one visitor. Europeans who tried to supervise slave gangs in the rice fields quickly caught malaria. Although the disease itself was seldom fatal, it left its victims vulnerable to other maladies that often did kill them. Rice planters gradually relocated their big houses on higher ground, out of sight of the rice fields.

This situation altered work patterns. Africans seemed to fare much better than Europeans in the marshy rice fields. (As modern medicine has explained, many of them possess a "sickle cell" that grants them a degree of protection against malaria but can also expose their children to a deadly form of inherited anemia.) As the ability of slaves to resist malaria became clearer, planters seldom ventured close to the rice fields, and they exerted far less paternalistic control than their Virginia counterparts. After midcentury, many of them chose to spend the summer months not on their plantations but in Charleston, where they also patronized a large group of white artisans. Others found summer homes on higher ground in the interior of the colony. A few ventured as far away as Newport, Rhode Island, to avoid the heat of July and August. To get their rice planted and harvested, they devised the task system, in which the slaves had to complete certain specific assignments each day, after which their time was their own.

Thus, while many Chesapeake slaves were acquiring new skills, Carolina slaves headed in the other direction. Before rice became the colony's chief export, these slaves had performed a wide variety of tasks. But the huge profits from rice now condemned nearly all of them to monotonous, unpleasant labor among the mosquitoes, even as it also freed them from the direct oversight of their masters. Slaves preferred the task system over gang labor because it gave them greater control over their own lives.

The Gold Coast of Africa at the Height of the Slave Trade   From this view of the Gold Coast in the eighteenth century, five European slaving posts were visible, including "Mina" or Elmina, the Portuguese fortress built in 1481 and captured by the Dutch in the seventeenth century. (See illustration on page 14 of Chapter 1.)

This freedom also meant slower assimilation. African customs and vocabulary survived longer in South Carolina than in the Chesapeake and later had a strong impact across the entire cotton belt. Newly imported slaves spoke Gullah, originally a pidgin language (that is, a simple, second language for everyone who spoke it). It began with a few phrases common to many West African languages, but it increasingly added English words, acquired its own complexities, and became the natural language of subsequent generations. Modern black English, which derives in large part from Gullah, was born in the rice fields and sea islands of Carolina.

In Maryland and Virginia the slave population began to grow by natural increase during the 1720s. The same pattern emerged in South Carolina perhaps fifty years later. There, even the planters had difficulty replacing themselves before 1760. But by the time of independence, the emerging South had become the world's most viable slave society, where the natural increase of the slave population allowed the planters to thrive without continuous slave imports from Africa. In the West Indies and Brazil they could not.

Southern Prosperity   The southern colonies prospered in the eighteenth century by exchanging their staple crops for British imports. This trade was still carried on English ships in 1700, but by mid-century much of it had been taken over by Scots. Glasgow became the leading tobacco port of the Atlantic. Although the profit on tobacco was slight through the 1720s, it improved in later decades, partly because Virginia guaranteed a high-quality leaf by passing an inspection law in 1730 (Maryland followed suit in 1747), and partly because a tobacco contract between Britain and France brought lucrative revenues to both governments and opened up a vast continental market for Chesapeake tobacco. By 1775, over 90 percent of it was reexported to Europe from Britain.

Other trades also contributed to rising prosperity. North Carolina, where the population increased fivefold between 1720 and 1760 and more than doubled again by 1775, sold naval stores (pitch, resin, turpentine, and lumber) to British shipbuilders. South Carolina continued to export provisions to the sugar islands and deerskins to Britain. Indigo, used as a dye by the British textile industry, received a bounty from Parliament and emerged at mid-century as a second staple crop, pioneered by a woman planter, Eliza Lucas Pinckney. As the century progressed, many Chesapeake planters turned to wheat as a second cash crop. Wheat required mills to grind it into flour, barrels in which to pack it, and ships to carry it away. It did for the Chesapeake what tobacco had failed to do. It created cities. Norfolk and Baltimore had nearly ten thousand people by 1775, and smaller

Carter's Grove Plantation   Located near Williamsburg, Virginia, Carter's Grove is an example of the great house and formal gardens favored by wealthy planters in the eighteenth century.

cities, such as Alexandria and Georgetown, were also emerging. Shipbuilding, closely tied to the export of wheat, became an important regional industry.

The Mid-Atlantic Colonies: The "Best Poor Man's Country"?

The Hudson and Delaware valleys had been pluralistic societies since they were founded. Eighteenth-century immigration confirmed that pattern and added to its complexity. The region contained the most prosperous family farms in North America and, by 1760, the two largest cities. Huge manors, granted by New York governors to political supporters, mostly in the 1680s and 1690s, dominated the Hudson Valley and discouraged immigration. As late as 1750, the small colony of New Jersey had as many settlers as New York, but fewer slaves. Thus Pennsylvania's growth, stimulated by both natural increase and an enormous surge of immigration, outpaced New York's. Pennsylvania was the twelfth colony to be founded out of the original thirteen. By 1770 it was the second most populous, surpassed only by Virginia.

Irish and German Immigration   In the seventeenth century, most European immigrants came from England. In the 1720s, Ireland and Germany became the major suppliers, although many settlers also came from Scotland and northern England, especially after 1760.

Ireland's northern province of Ulster provided about 70 percent of its emigrants. Nearly all of them were Presbyterians whose forebears came to Ireland from Scotland in the previous century. (Historians now call them the Scots-Irish, a term seldom used at the time.) Most of them left home to avoid an increase in rents and to enjoy greater trading privileges than the British Parliament allowed Ireland.

The first Ulsterites sailed for New England in 1718, expecting a friendly reception from fellow Calvinists. They were soon disabused of that notion. The Yankees treated them with suspicion and hostility. Those who stayed founded a few towns in New Hampshire and introduced linen manufacturing to the region, but after 1718 most Ulster emigrants headed for the Delaware Valley.

The rest of the Irish immigrants came from southern Ireland. Most were Roman Catholics, but perhaps a quarter were Anglicans. They too headed for the Middle Colonies. Altogether about 80,000 Irish made their way to the Delaware Valley by 1775. New York attracted fewer immigrants, from either Ireland or Germany, partly because its frontier was dangerously exposed during wartime, and partly because its large landlords offered less favorable terms.

Some 70,000 immigrants were Germans. Most of them arrived as families, often as "redemptioners," a new form of indentured servitude attractive to married couples because it allowed servants to find and bind themselves to their own masters. Families could stay together. Once they had completed their term of service, most of them streamed into the interior of Pennsylvania. By 1750 Germans outnumbered the original English and Welsh settlers, prompting an uncharacteristic outburst by Benjamin Franklin, who complained that German "boors" were taking over the colony. Other Germans moved to the southern backcountry with the Irish.

Middle Colony Prosperity   The Middle Colonies, which became North America's breadbasket, were favored by free immigrants because their expanding economies offered many opportunities to newcomers. These colonies grew excellent wheat and built their own ships to carry it abroad. Into the 1720s New York flour outsold Pennsylvania's, but then a carefully regulated system of inspection and quality control gave Pennsylvania the edge. After Europe's population began to surge around 1740, merchants in New York City and Philadelphia shipped flour across the Atlantic. Both cities grew rapidly and by 1760 had surpassed Boston's stagnant population of 15,000. Philadelphia's 32,000 people made it the largest city in British North America by 1775, but it remained much smaller than London at 700,000, Dublin at 170,000, or Bristol and Edinburgh with 60,000. Philadelphia and New York, unlike Boston, experienced no sharp increase of poverty before the 1760s.

The Backcountry

Many of the Scots-Irish, together with some of the Germans, pushed west into the mountains and then up the river valleys into the interior parts of Virginia and the Carolinas. In South Carolina, about a hundred miles of pine barrens stood between these backcountry settlements and the rice plantations along the coast. Most of the English-speaking colonists were

immigrants from Ulster, northern England, or lowland Scotland who brought their folkways with them and soon made the backcountry into a region with its own distinctive culture. Although most settlers farmed, many turned to hunting or raising cattle. Unlike the coastal settlements, the backcountry showed few signs of anglicizing. It had no newspapers, few clergymen or other professionals, and little elegance. Parts of it, especially in South Carolina, had almost no government. A visiting Anglican clergyman bemoaned "the abandon'd Morals and profligate Principles" of the settlers. In 1768 he preached to a gathering who had never heard a minister before, or even the Lord's Prayer. "After the Service," he wrote, "they went out to Revell[in]g, Drinking, Singing, Dancing and Whoring, and most of the Company were drunk before I quitted the Spott." To refined easterners, the backcountry seemed more than a little frightening.

Backcountry settlers were clannish, violent, and drank heavily. Most of them hated Indians. The situation became particularly tense in Pennsylvania after 1750. The Quaker legislature insisted on handling differences with the Indians through peaceful negotiation, even though few Quakers lived on the frontier. (The Moravian Brethren, a pacifist German sect, maintained Indian missions in Pennsylvania and North Carolina, but their impact on other colonists was small.) Once fighting broke out between settlers and Indians, most backcountry residents demanded the extermination of their foes. In less extreme form, Virginia and South Carolina faced the same problem.

New England

Eighteenth-century New England was a land of farmers, fishermen, lumberjacks, shipwrights, and merchants. It still considered itself more pious and respectable than the rest of the British empire. But the region faced serious new problems.

A Faltering Economy   Few immigrants, either slave or free, went to New England in the eighteenth century. In fact, since the mid-seventeenth century more people had been leaving the region, mostly for New York and New Jersey, than had been arriving. New England's relative isolation before 1700 began to have negative effects after 1700. Life expectancy declined as diseases from Europe, especially smallpox and diphtheria, invaded the area through the web of Atlantic commerce. The first settlers and their children had left these diseases behind in Europe, but lack of exposure in childhood made the third and fourth generations vulnerable.

In 1721 smallpox devastated Boston until a self-taught local doctor, Zabdiel Boylston—urged on by Cotton Mather, the city's most prominent minister—began inoculating people with it on the theory that healthy people would survive the injection and acquire immunity to the disease. Mather had no better authority than vague newspaper accounts of similar experiments in obscure corners of Europe, and Boston's leading physician, Dr. William Douglass, opposed the practice. Inoculation, Douglass warned, might give everyone a fatal dose of smallpox. Fortunately for Boston, Boylston and Mather proved correct. Some of those who were inoculated died, but at a much lower rate than those who simply caught the disease. Yankees found no comparable defense against diphtheria, which people called the "throat distemper," when it struck in the late 1730s. Sometimes it carried off all of the children of large families in a matter of days. New England's high military casualties also reduced the rate of population growth, which fell behind that of other regions.

New England's economy began to weaken after the Peace of Utrecht in 1713. The region had prospered in the seventeenth century, mostly by exporting cod, grain, and barrel staves to the West Indies. But after 1700 Yankees had trouble feeding themselves, much less others. A blight called the "wheat blast" first appeared in the 1660s and spread slowly until cultivation of wheat nearly ceased. Because Yankees preferred wheat bread to corn bread, they had to import flour from New York and Pennsylvania and, eventually, wheat from Chesapeake Bay. After grain exports declined, the once-profitable West Indian trade barely broke even. But its volume remained large, especially after enterprising Yankees opened up new markets in the lucrative French sugar islands. British West Indian planters, alarmed by the threat of cheap French molasses, urged the British government to stamp out trade with the French West Indies. Parliament responded with the Molasses Act of 1733, which placed a prohibitive duty of six pence per gallon on all foreign molasses imported into the colonies. Strictly enforced, the act could have strangled New England trade, but instead it generated bribery and smuggling, and the molasses continued to flow.

Within the West Indian market, competition from New York and Philadelphia grew almost too severe for New Englanders to meet because those cities had flour to export and shorter distances over which to ship it. Mostly, the New Englanders imported molasses from the islands, which they used as a sweetener (cheaper than sugar) or distilled into rum, which joined cod and lumber as a major export. Whale oil, used in lamps, stimulated a prosperous whaling industry on the island of Nantucket, where surviving Indians taught settlers how to use harpoons and actively participated in the trade until they were decimated by disease. New England ran unfavorable balances with nearly every trading partner, especially England. Yankees imported many British products but produced little that anybody in Britain wanted to buy. The grain trade with the Middle and Chesapeake colonies also was unfavorable, though less so. Settlers there eagerly bought rum and small numbers of slaves jammed aboard Yankee vessels that stopped on their way back from the West Indies. The heart of the New England economy was shipbuilding. Yankees made more ships than all the other colonies combined, although the Chesapeake colonies and the Delaware Valley were closing the gap by the 1760s. These ships earned enough from freight in most years to offset other disadvantages, but Boston merchants often had to scramble to pay for their British imports. Poverty became a huge social problem in Boston, where by the 1740s about one-third of all adult women were widows, mostly poor.

Paper Money Experiments   New England's experience with paper money illustrates these economic difficulties. In response to a military emergency in 1690, Massachusetts invented fiat money—that is, paper money backed only by the promise of the government to accept it in payment of taxes. Yet it worked well until serious depreciation set in after the Treaty of Utrecht. By then most other colonies had also adopted paper money.

The declining value of money touched off a fierce debate in 1714 that occupied Massachusetts for forty years. Creditors attacked paper money as fraudulent; only gold and silver had real value. Defenders retorted that, in most other colonies, paper held its value. The problem, they insisted, lay with the New England economy, which could not gener-

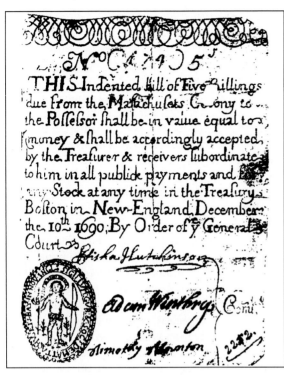

A Massachusetts Bill of Credit, 1690 This emission of paper money, the first of its kind in the history of the world, derived its value from the promise of the government to accept it in payment of taxes. After brief hesitation, Boston merchants also accepted it in their transactions. Other colonies gradually imitated Massachusetts because none of them had easy access to silver or gold.

ate enough exports to pay for the region's imports. The elimination of paper, they warned, would deepen New England's problems, not solve them.

Heavy military appropriations in the 1740s sent New England currency to a new low. But when Parliament agreed in 1749 to reimburse these expenditures at the 1745 exchange rate, Governor William Shirley and House Speaker Thomas Hutchinson, an outspoken opponent of paper money, just barely persuaded the legislature to use the grant to retire all paper and convert to silver money. This decision was a drastic example of anglicization. Fiat money was a unique American idea, invented in Massachusetts. By 1750 the province repudiated its own offspring in favor of orthodox methods of British public finance, only to prove their critics' point. Silver gravitated to Boston and back to London to pay for imports. New England's economy entered a deep depression

in the early 1750s and did not revive until the next French war.

ANGLICIZING PROVINCIAL AMERICA

What made these diverse regions more alike was what they retained or acquired from Britain. In the eighteenth century, printing and newspapers, the learned professions, and the intellectual movement known as the Enlightenment all made their impact on British North America. The new colony of Georgia was in many ways a byproduct of the English Enlightenment. A powerful transatlantic religious revival, the Great Awakening, also swept across the empire in the 1730s and 1740s.

Printing, the Professions, and the Enlightenment

Seventeenth-century America was almost a society without presses. Few settlers owned books, nor, except in early New England, did they expect to participate in the intellectual debates of the day. Only Massachusetts had printers, first in Cambridge to serve Harvard College, the clergy, and the government, and then in Boston beginning in 1674. For the next century, Boston was the print capital of North America. William Bradford became Philadelphia's first printer in the 1680s, but he moved to New York in 1693 in response to a religious schism among the Quakers. Philadelphia failed to find another printer until 1699. By 1740 Boston had eight printers; New York and Philadelphia each had two. No other community had more than one.

The Rise of Newspapers   Not surprisingly, Boston also led the way in newspaper publishing. John Campbell, the city's postmaster, established the *Boston News-Letter* in 1704. By the early 1720s two more papers had opened in Boston, and Philadelphia and New York City had each acquired one. Several German-language newspapers later appeared in Pennsylvania. In the South, the *South Carolina Gazette* was founded in Charleston in 1732 and the *Virginia Gazette* at Williamsburg in 1736. By then, Boston had added two or three more (depending on the year), Benjamin Franklin took charge of *The Pennsylvania Gazette* in 1729, and John Peter Zenger started the controversial *New York Weekly Journal* in 1733. In 1735, after vigorously attacking Governor William Cosby, Zenger won a major victory for freedom of the press when a jury acquitted him of "seditious libel," the crime of criticizing the government or its officials. Between the 1730s and 1775, Boston supported between four and six newspapers, more than the entire colonial South until the 1760s.

These papers were weeklies and devoted nearly all of their space to European affairs. Before mid-century, they rarely reported local news because they assumed their readers already knew it. At first, they merely reprinted items from *The London Gazette.* But beginning in the 1720s, the *New England Courant,* under James Franklin (and Benjamin, his brother and apprentice), also began to reprint Richard Steele's essays from *The Spectator,* Joseph Addison's literary pieces from *The Tatler,* and the angry, polemical writings, mostly against religious bigotry and political and financial corruption, of John Trenchard and Thomas Gordon, both of whom published under the name of "Cato." Essays from *Cato's Letters,* printed in several four-volume London editions, became immensely popular among colonial printers. In short, newspapers began to spread the English Enlightenment throughout the North American colonies.

The Enlightenment   The English Enlightenment rejected the idea of a vengeful God and exalted man's capacity for knowledge and social improvement. It grew out of the rational and benevolent piety favored by low church (latitudinarian) Anglicans in Restoration England. They disliked rigid doctrine, scoffed at personal conversion experiences, attacked superstition, and rejected all forms of "fanaticism," whether represented by the high-church Laudians, who had brought on the political and religious crisis of 1640–1642 or by the Puritans, who had retaliated by dismantling the monarchy. High-church men, a small group in the eighteenth century, stood for orthodoxy, ritual, and liturgy.

Enlightened writers greeted Sir Isaac Newton's laws of motion as one of the greatest intellectual achievements of all time, joined the philosopher John Locke in looking for ways to improve society, and began to suspect that moderns had surpassed the ancients in learning and wisdom. John Tillotson, archbishop of Canterbury until his death in 1694, embodied this "polite and Catholick [i.e., universal]

spirit." He preached morality rather than dogma and had a way of defending the doctrine of eternal damnation that left his listeners wondering how a merciful God could possibly have ordained such a cruel punishment.

Enlightened ideas won an elite constituency in the mainland colonies even before newspapers appeared to spread them around. Tillotson had an extraordinary impact on America. His sermons appeared in more southern libraries than did the writings of any other contemporary. His arguments made a deep impression at Harvard College, beginning in the 1680s with two young tutors, William Brattle and John Leverett, Jr. When Leverett succeeded Increase Mather as college president in 1707, Tillotson's ideas became entrenched in the curriculum. For the rest of the century most Harvard-trained ministers, although they still claimed to be Calvinists, warmly embraced Tillotson's latitudinarian piety. They stressed the similarities between Congregationalists and Anglicans, rather than the differences, and they favored broad religious toleration. By 1800 most Harvard-educated ministers were becoming Unitarians. They could no longer accept the divinity of Jesus or eternal damnation.

In 1701, largely in reaction to this trend at Harvard, the older clergy founded a new college in Connecticut. When it finally settled in New Haven, it was named Yale College in honor of a wealthy English benefactor, Elihu Yale, who donated his library to it. Those Anglican books did to the Yale faculty what Tillotson had done at Harvard—and more. At the commencement of 1722, the entire Yale faculty, except for a nineteen-year-old tutor, Jonathan Edwards, stunned everyone by announcing their conversion to the Church of England. They departed for England to be ordained by the bishop of London. Their leader, Timothy Cutler, became the principal Anglican spokesman in Boston. Samuel Johnson, another defector, served a new Anglican church in Connecticut until mid-century when he became the first president of King's College (now Columbia University) in New York City. There he earned a considerable reputation as a moral philosopher.

The Legal and Medical Professions   The rise of the legal profession encouraged the fascination with Enlightenment ideas. Most seventeenth-century colonists hated lawyers as men who seemed to profit only from the misery of others and who deliberately stirred up discord. Virginia and Massachusetts briefly abolished the legal profession. Only in Maryland did it take firm hold before 1700, and then it began to spread everywhere. In 1692 three English lawyers handled nearly all cases in the province of New York; by 1704 there were eight. In Boston, the practice of law remained disreputable as late as the 1730s. Before 1720 three British immigrants, all of them Anglicans, litigated most cases. And when a Congregational clergyman resigned his Connecticut pulpit and moved to Boston to practice law, he too joined Anglican King's Chapel. Benjamin Gridley, a Harvard graduate who won fame for his impiety, also took up law. He wrote enlightened essays for Boston newspapers in the 1730s, turned his office into an informal law school, and set up a debating society, the Sodalitas, in which students disputed legal questions within the broad context of eighteenth-century oratory and philosophy. By then, a college education was rapidly becoming a prerequisite to a legal career in New England.

Most Massachusetts lawyers before 1760 were either Anglicans or young men who had rejected the ministry as a career. Some were scoffers and skeptics, and most probably thought of themselves as a new cultural elite, as did John Adams in Boston and Thomas Jefferson in Virginia. When Mahlon Dickerson of New Jersey began studying for the bar in the 1790s, he browsed in the library of a profane lawyer friend. He spent little time on legal treatises and a lot reading Adam Smith (the founder of modern economics), the philosophers John Locke and David Hume, the French *philosophes* Montesquieu and Abbé Raynal, and various novels. By that time, lawyers were already beginning to regard themselves as the cultural vanguard of the new republic. Poet John Trumbull, playwright Royall Tyler, and novelist Hugh Henry Brackenridge all continued to practice law while writing on the side. Others turned from the law to full-time writing, including the poet William Cullen Bryant, the writer Washington Irving, and the novelist Charles Brockden Brown. Clearly, law and the Enlightenment rode together in eighteenth-century America.

Medicine also became an enlightened profession, with Philadelphia setting the pace. William Shippen earned degrees at Princeton and Edinburgh, the best medical school in the world at the time, before returning to Philadelphia in 1762, where he became the first American to lecture on medicine, publish a treatise on chemistry, and dissect human cadavers, a practice that scandalized the unenlightened. His student, John Morgan, became the first professor of medicine in North America when the College of Philadelphia established a medical faculty a few years later. These two were joined by Benjamin Rush, who also studied at Princeton and then Edinburgh. He brought the latest Scottish techniques to the Philadelphia Hospital. Like Jefferson and Adams, he saw himself as an enlightened reformer. He attacked slavery, favored the prohibition of alcohol, and supported the Revolution. Many other physicians embraced radical politics.

The Enlightenment Personified: Benjamin Franklin

Benjamin Franklin embodied most aspects of the American enlightenment. As a boy, though raised as a Congregationalist in Boston, he stayed home from church on Sundays to read Addison and Steele and to perfect his own prose style. As a young printer with the *New England Courant* in the 1720s, he helped to publish the writings of John Checkley, an Anglican whom Massachusetts prosecuted twice in a vain attempt to silence him. Franklin joined the Church of England after moving to Philadelphia. In 1729 he took over the *Pennsylvania Gazette* and made it the best-edited newspaper in America. It spread improvement everywhere along with the news and developed a circulation of about two thousand subscribers, four times that of a typical Boston weekly.

In 1727 Franklin and several friends founded the Junto, a debating society that met Friday evenings to discuss literary and philosophical questions. It later evolved into the American Philosophical Society, which still meets near Independence Hall. Franklin helped found North America's first Masonic lodge in 1730, the Library Company of Philadelphia a year later, the Union Fire Company in 1736, the Philadelphia Hospital in 1751, and an academy that became the College of Philadelphia (now the University of Pennsylvania) in the 1750s. But his greatest fame rested on his electrical experiments during the 1740s and 1750s, which brought him honorary M.A. degrees from Harvard, Yale, and William and Mary, and an honorary doctorate from St. Andrews University in Scotland. He invented the Franklin stove (much more efficient than a standard fireplace) and the lightning rod. By the 1760s he had become the most celebrated North American in the world and was thinking of retiring to England.

Georgia: The Failure of an Enlightenment Utopia

In the 1730s Anglican humanitarianism and the Enlightenment belief in the possibility of social improvement converged in Britain to provide support for the founding of the colony of Georgia, named for King George II (1727–1760). The sponsors of this project had several goals. They hoped to create a society that could make productive use of England's "deserving" poor, as against the lazy or criminal poor. Believing that South Carolina would be almost helpless if attacked by Spain, they also intended—with no sense of irony—to shield that colony's slave society from Spanish Florida by populating Georgia with armed and disciplined freemen. They hoped to strengthen the imperial economy by producing silk and wine, items that no other British colony had yet succeeded in making. Finally, they prohibited slavery and hard liquor. To permit slavery would make Georgia a simple extension of South Carolina, with all of its vulnerabilities. And, like many enlightened gentlemen of their age, the founders of Georgia were appalled by what cheap English gin was doing to the sobriety and industry of ordinary people.

The trustees set up their corporation on a nonprofit basis and announced that they would give land away, not sell it. Led by James Oglethorpe and John, viscount Percival (later earl of Egmont), a distinguished group of trustees (including members of both houses of Parliament) obtained a twenty-year charter from Parliament in 1732, used their Anglican charitable network to raise money, and then launched the colony. They recruited foreign Protestants, including some Germans from Salzburg who had just been driven out of that state by its Catholic bishop, a small number of Moravian Brethren (a German pacifist sect led by Count Nicholas von Zinzendorf), and French Huguenots. In England, they interviewed many prospective settlers to distinguish the worthy poor from the unworthy. They engaged silk and wine experts and recruited Scottish Highlanders as soldiers.

There was one thing the trustees failed to do: they never consulted the settlers about what might be good for them and for Georgia. The founders, as men of refinement, enlightenment, and rational piety,

already knew what Georgia needed. They created no elective assembly, nor did they give the British government much chance to supervise the colony. Because their charter required them to submit all laws to the British Privy Council for approval, the trustees passed only three laws during their twenty years of rule. One of these laid out the land system, and the others prohibited slavery and all alcoholic beverages stronger than wine or beer. Instead of drafting laws, the trustees governed by issuing "regulations." An elective assembly could come later, after the trustees had firmly established Georgia's character.

When the first settlers arrived in 1733, they laid out Savannah, a town with spacious streets. During the first ten years, 1,800 charity cases and just over one thousand self-supporting colonists reached Georgia. The most successful were the Germans from Salzburg, who agreed with the prohibitions on slavery and alcohol and built a thriving settlement at Ebenezer, farther up the Savannah River. The Moravian Brethren left for North Carolina after five years rather than bear arms. The most discontented settlers were some Lowland Scots who became known as the Malcontents. When everyone ignored their complaints, they left in disgust for South Carolina in 1740.

The land system never worked as planned. The trustees granted fifty acres to every male settler whose passage was paid for out of charitable funds. Those paying their own way could claim up to five hundred acres. Ordinary farmers did poorly because fifty acres of sandy soil around Savannah would not support a family farm. Because the military goals of the proprietors envisioned every landowner as a soldier, women could not inherit land, nor could any landowner sell his farm.

The settlers were unable to grow grapes or to persuade the sickly worms that had survived the Atlantic crossing to make silk out of mulberry leaves. The colonists clamored for rum, smuggled it into the colony when they could, and insisted that Georgia would never thrive until, like South Carolina, it permitted slavery. Enough people died or left to reduce the colony's population by more than half by the mid-1740s, and in 1752 it did not even equal the 2,800 people who had arrived by 1742.

Between 1750 and 1752 the trustees gave up. They dropped their ban on alcohol, allowed the importation of slaves, summoned an elective assembly (but only to consult, not legislate), and finally surrendered their charter to Parliament. Thus Georgia

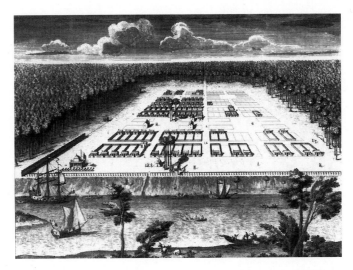

A View of Savannah on March 29, 1734   This painting by Peter Gordon emphasizes the wide streets and spacious atmosphere of this planned city.

became what it was never meant to be, a smaller version of South Carolina, producing rice and indigo with slave labor.

Only with the establishment of royal government after 1752 did Georgia finally get an elective assembly with the power to legislate. But by then, in one of the supreme ironies of the age, the colony had done more to spread religious revivalism than to demonstrate the viability of enlightened humanitarianism. Georgia helped to launch both John Wesley and George Whitefield upon their careers as the greatest revivalists of the century.

The Great Awakening

Between the mid-1730s and the early 1740s, an immense religious revival, the Great Awakening, swept across the Protestant world. Within the British empire, it affected some areas more intensely than others. England, Scotland, Ulster, New England, the Middle Colonies, and for a time South Carolina responded warmly to emotional calls for a spiritual rebirth. Southern Ireland, the West Indies, and the Chesapeake colonies remained on the margins, although Virginia and Maryland would be drawn into a later phase of revivalism in the 1760s and 1770s.

Origins of the Revivals   Some of the earliest revivals arose among the Dutch in New Jersey in the 1690s. Guiliam Bertholf, a farmer and cooper (or barrel-

maker), was a lay reader in New Jersey who got himself ordained in an obscure corner of the Netherlands in 1694 (Amsterdam did not approve) and returned to preach to his former neighbors in Hackensack and Passaic. His emotional piety attracted Dutch farmers who were disillusioned with the orthodox Dutch Reformed clergy because of their resistance to Jacob Leisler, the leader of New York's Glorious Revolution who had been hanged in 1691 (see Chapter 3). After 1720 Bertholf's mantle passed to another outsider, Theodorus Jacobus Frelinghuysen, who sparked several revivals in his Dutch congregation in New Brunswick, New Jersey. The local Presbyterian pastor, Gilbert Tennent, watched and learned.

Tennent was a younger son of William Tennent, Sr., who had once defected from the Presbyterian to the Anglican church in northern Ireland before becoming a Presbyterian minister and moving to Pennsylvania. In the 1730s he set up the Log College at Neshaminy, Pennsylvania, where he trained his sons and other young men as evangelical preachers. The Tennent family dominated the Presbytery of New Brunswick and used it to ordain ministers and send them off to any congregation that requested one, including some in other presbyteries. That practice triggered a conflict within the Philadelphia Synod, the highest governing body of the Presbyterian church in the colonies. Most of its ministers emphasized orthodoxy over the experience of personal conversion. In a 1740 sermon entitled *The Dangers of*

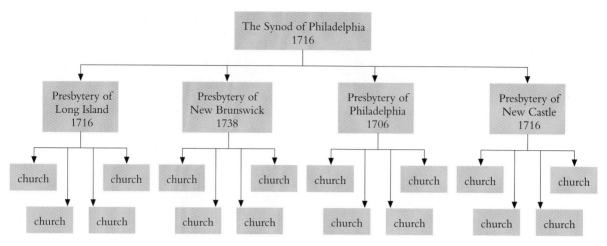

In actuality, some presbyteries had more churches than others.   Arrows indicate descending lines of authority

The Synod of Philadelphia by 1738

an Unconverted Ministry, Gilbert Tennent warned those lifeless preachers that they would only lead people to hell. His attack split the church. In 1741 the outnumbered revivalists withdrew to found the Synod of New York, although their main strength lay in northern New Jersey and Long Island, rather than New York City.

By the 1730s a similar pattern was emerging in New England, where Solomon Stoddard of Northampton presided over six revivals, what he called "harvests of souls," between the 1670s and his death in 1729. Jonathan Edwards, his grandson and successor—the only member of the Yale faculty who had not defected to the Anglicans in 1722—touched off a revival of unprecedented force that rocked dozens of Connecticut Valley towns in 1734–1735. It ended suddenly when a member of Edwards's congregation, overwhelmed by the burden of his sins, slit his own throat. Edwards' *A Faithful Narrative of the Surprising Work of God* (1737) explained what a revival was—an emotional earthquake in which scores of people experienced sudden conversions. He described these in acute detail and won admirers in Britain as well as New England.

In England, John Wesley and George Whitefield set the pace. At worldly Oxford University, Wesley and his brother founded the Holy Club, a high-church society whose members fasted until they could barely walk. One member of the Holy Club even lay prostrate for hours on the frigid earth, lost in prayer while his hands turned black. These me-

thodical practices prompted scoffers to call them "Methodists." Still dissatisfied with the state of his soul, Wesley went to Georgia as a missionary in 1735, an unhappy experience for him. He fell in love with a woman who did not return his affection, and the settlers did not welcome his ascetic piety. In 1737, on the return voyage to England, some Moravians convinced him that, for all his zeal, he had never grasped the central Protestant message, justification by faith alone. Some months later he was deeply moved by Edwards' *Faithful Narrative.* Soon, Wesley found his life's mission, the conversion of sinners, and he embarked on an extraordinary preaching career for the next fifty years.

Whitefield Launches the Transatlantic Revival
Younger than Wesley, George Whitefield had been a talented amateur actor in his youth and had joined the Holy Club at Oxford before being ordained an Anglican minister. He followed Wesley to Georgia, founded an orphanage, then returned to England and preached all over the kingdom to raise money for it. Whitefield had the power to move masses of people through a single sermon, and he too began to preach the "new birth," or necessity of a personal conversion experience. When Anglican ministers took offense and banned him from their pulpits, he responded with a daring innovation. He began preaching in open fields to anyone who would listen. Newspapers reported the controversy, and soon Whitefield's admirers began to notify the press where

he would be on any given day. Colonial newspapers, keenly sensitive to the English press, closely followed his movements.

In 1739 Whitefield made his second trip to America, ostensibly to raise funds for his orphanage at Bethesda, Georgia. Everyone knew who he was from newspaper accounts, and thousands flocked to hear him preach. After landing at Lewes, Delaware, he preached his way northward through Philadelphia, New Jersey, and New York City, then headed south through the Chesapeake colonies and into South Carolina. In September 1740 he took ship for Newport, Rhode Island, and for the next two months toured New England. During his travels he met Benjamin Franklin, Gilbert Tennent, and Jonathan Edwards. In the larger cities he sometimes attracted as many as thirty thousand people, or twice the population of Boston. His voice was so musical and so commanding, noted one observer, that he could seduce a crowd just by the way he said "Mesopotamia." Using his acting skills, he imitated Christ on the cross, shedding "pious tears" for poor sinners. Or, he became God at the Last Judgment, thundering: "Depart from me ye accursed into everlasting fire!" When he wept, his audience also sobbed. When he condemned them, they fell to the ground in agony.

Although Whitefield wore the surplice of an Anglican minister and carried the *Book of Common Prayer* when he preached, Anglicans treated him with reserve or hostility. In Charleston and New York City, he was denounced by the official spokesmen for the bishop of London. But Presbyterians, Congregationalists, and Baptists embraced him, at least until some of them began to fear that he was doing more harm than good. Most saw him as the embodiment of the old non-separatist ideal (see Chapter 2) that, despite denominational differences, all English Protestants were really members of the same church.

The Disruptive Aftermath: South Carolina
This unity dissipated as other preachers tried to sustain Whitefield's role after he moved on. In South Carolina Hugh Bryan, a Savannah River planter, began preaching the evangelical message to his slaves. He soon went further. In 1742, not long after a major slave revolt had rocked the colony (see Chapter 5), Bryan announced that slavery was a sin and that God would pour out his wrath on the planters unless they rejected it. Proclaiming himself an American Moses, he boldly attempted to part the waters of the

Savannah River and lead the slaves to freedom. Instead, he almost drowned. He apologized to the planters and confessed that he had been deluded. Though this fiasco discredited evangelical piety among the settlers of the Lower South for another generation, Bryan and his relatives continued to convert their own slaves. African-American evangelicalism, including some of the first black preachers, took root from these efforts.

The Disruptive Aftermath: New England
After Whitefield left New England, Gilbert Tennent arrived and created fierce divisions. Lacking Whitefield's musical voice and Oxford diction, Tennent spoke with a Scottish burr and specialized in "Holy Laughter," the scornful peals of a triumphant God as sinners tumble into hell. At about this time he abandoned the usual garb of a minister for a robe and sandals and let his hair grow long, symbolically proclaiming himself a new John the Baptist heralding the second coming of Christ. Many ecstatic followers believed that the Millennium was at hand.

After Tennent left, James Davenport arrived from Long Island. Denouncing unregenerate ministers by name, he liked to preach by eerie candlelight, roaring damnation at his hearers, even grabbing Satan and wrestling him back to hell. He advised his admirers to drink rat poison rather than listen to another lifeless sermon. In 1743 he established the "Shepherd's Tent" in New London to train awakened preachers. This outdoor school abandoned the classical curriculum of existing colleges and insisted only on a valid conversion experience. He organized a book-burning (including some titles by Increase Mather) and threw his britches on the fire, declaring them a mark of human vanity. A New England grand jury, asked to indict him, proclaimed him mad instead. Like Bryan in South Carolina, he suddenly repented and claimed that he had been deluded. The Shepherd's Tent collapsed.

Long-term Consequences of the Great Awakening

The revival movement had dramatic consequences. It feminized evangelical churches, though not right away. Amidst the high enthusiasm of Whitefield's tour, more men than usual experienced conversions and joined a church, but after another year or two, men became hard to convert. The number of women church members began to soar until, by 1800, they often had a majority of three or four to one. In some congregations they even acquired an informal veto over the choice of the minister.

Thousands of men became Freemasons, often *instead* of joining a church. The Masons took hold after 1730 among the merchants and professionals of Philadelphia and Boston, but during and after the Revolution they grew spectacularly. They appealed to men from all denominations, accepting even a few Catholics, Jews, and Indians. Artisans began to dominate city lodges, and the Masons also penetrated deeply into the countryside. Masons very nearly turned their order into a religion of manliness, complete with secret and mysterious rituals. They extolled sobriety, industry, brotherhood, benevolence, and responsible citizenship. At first most clergymen saw the Masons as a force for good. Only in the 1820s would the order finally draw angry criticism.

The revivals also shattered the unity of New England's Congregational Church. Evangelicals seceded from dozens of congregations to form their own "Separate" churches. Many of those that survived went Baptist by the 1760s, thereby gaining protection under the toleration statutes of the New England colonies. In the Middle Colonies, the revivals strengthened denominational loyalties and energized the clergy. In the 1730s most people in the region, particularly in New Jersey and Pennsylvania, did not even join a church. But the revivals obliged them to decide whether to become New Side (evangelical) Presbyterians, Old Side (anti-revival) Presbyterians, or unevangelical Anglicans. Similar cleavages ran through the German population. The southern colonies were less affected, though evangelical Presbyterians made modest gains in the Virginia backcountry after 1740. Finally, in the 1760s, the Baptists began to win thousands of converts, to be followed and overtaken by the Methodists a decade later.

The revivals also broke down localism by creating new cosmopolitan links with Britain and among the colonies. Whitefield ran the most efficient publicity machine in the Atlantic world. In London, Glasgow, and Boston, periodicals called *The Christian History* carried news of revivals occurring anywhere in the empire. For years, London evangelicals held regular "Letter Days," at which they read accounts of revivals in progress. Revivalists wrote often to one another. When fervor declined in New England, Jon-

athan Edwards organized a Concert of Prayer with his Scottish correspondents, setting regular times for them all to beseech the Lord to pour out His grace once more. As Anglicans split into Methodists and Latitudinarians, Congregationalists into New Lights (pro-revival) and Old Lights (anti-revival), and Presbyterians into comparable New Side and Old Side synods, evangelicals discovered that they had more in common with revivalists in other denominations than with anti-revivalists in their own. When New Side Presbyterians chose a new president of the College of New Jersey in 1757, they saw nothing strange in naming a Congregationalist, Jonathan Edwards.

Jonathan Edwards and the Theology of Revivals   Edwards was the ablest apologist for revivals in Britain or America and probably the most profound religious thinker that North America has ever produced. When Boston's Charles Chauncy (very much a man of the Enlightenment) attacked the revivals as frauds because of their emotional excesses, Edwards replied at great length in *A Treatise concerning Religious Affections* (1746), which displayed his own mastery of Enlightenment sources, including Newton and Locke. Though admitting that no emotional response, however intense, was proof by itself of the presence of God in a person's soul, he insisted that intense feeling must always accompany the reception of divine grace. That view upset people who believed that a rational God must have established a polite and genteel religion. For Edwards, an unemotional piety could never be the work of God. In effect, Edwards countered Chauncy's emotional defense of reason with his own rational defense of emotion.

New Colleges   New colleges also arose from the revivals. Each college was set up primarily by a single denomination, but all of them were willing to admit other Protestants. In 1740 North America had only three colleges: Harvard in Massachusetts, William and Mary in Virginia, and Yale in Connecticut. Although Yale eventually embraced the revivals, all three opposed them at first. In 1746 Middle Colony evangelicals, eager to insist on a classical education to demonstrate their own respectability after the fiasco of the Shepherd's Tent, persuaded a royal governor to charter the College of New Jersey. It graduated its first class in 1748 and moved to Princeton in 1756. Unlike the older colleges, it drew students from

A Revival in Late Eighteenth-Century Virginia   Note how many of the participants were women.

all thirteen colonies and sent its graduates throughout America, though primarily to the middle and southern colonies after the first two decades.

Evangelical Baptists founded the College of Rhode Island (now Brown University) in the 1760s. The revivalist wing of the Dutch Reformed Church established Queens College (now Rutgers University) in New Brunswick, New Jersey, mostly to train evangelical ministers who could preach in English. Eleazer Wheelock opened an evangelical school for Indians in Lebanon, Connecticut. His first graduate, Samson Occum, raised £12,000 in England for the school, but Wheelock moved to New Hampshire, where he used most of the money to found Dartmouth College. By the 1790s Dartmouth would be turning out more graduates, and far more ministers, than any other American college.

In the 1750s Anglicans countered with two new institutions of their own: the College of Philadelphia (now the University of Pennsylvania), which also had Old-Side Presbyterian support, and King's College in New York (now Columbia University). But their undergraduate programs remained small, and few of their students chose a ministerial career.

Evangelicals won the battle for the loyalties of students. When the Presbyterian Church healed its schism and reunited in 1758, the New Siders set the

terms. They had been outnumbered in 1741 but held a large majority of ministers by 1758. Through control of Princeton, their numbers increased rapidly. The Old Side still relied on the University of Glasgow in Scotland and could barely replace those who died.

The Denominational Realignment   By 1800 the revivals had transformed the religious life of America. A century earlier, the three strongest denominations had been the Congregationalists in New England, the Quakers in the Delaware Valley, and the Anglicans in the South. By 1800 they had all lost ground to newcomers: the Methodists, who grew at an astonishing rate as the Church of England collapsed during the Revolution; the Baptists, who leaped into second place; and the Presbyterians. Neither the Methodists nor the Baptists expected their preachers to attend college, and they recruited ministers from a much broader segment of the population than their rivals could tap. While they never organized their own Shepherd's Tent, they embraced the same principles, demanding only personal conversion, integrity, knowledge of the Bible, and a talent for preaching. Anti-revivalist denominations, especially the Anglicans and the Quakers, lost heavily. New Light Congregationalists made only slight gains because, when their people left behind the established churches of New England and moved west, they usually became Presbyterians. That church provided structure that isolated congregations did not have.

THE AWAKENING, THE ENLIGHTENMENT, AND THE REVOLUTION

Finally, the revivals affected the Revolution in complex, even contradictory ways. The revivals empowered many Protestants with a new readiness to resist authority, and evangelicals overwhelmingly supported independence. Anti-evangelicals, by contrast, ranged across the entire political spectrum. Thomas Jefferson and Thomas Paine, both political radicals, had no use for revivals. Many moderate to conservative men, such as George Washington and Alexander Hamilton, also opposed revivals. All prominent loyalists were also Old Lights. In effect, evangelicals gave indispensable support to a revolutionary political cause led by men who admired the Enlightenment far more than the Great Awakening. Only in New Jersey and Connecticut did evangelicals become major revolutionary leaders.

The antagonism between the Enlightenment and the Awakening was never absolute. To be sure, when Whitefield attacked Harvard College in 1741, he named the enlightened Archbishop Tillotson among the authors of the "bad books [that] are become fashionable." But to spread his own message Whitefield had to rely on non-evangelical printers, such as Benjamin Franklin, who published whatever Whitefield sent him, opened the columns of the *Pennsylvania Gazette* to both supporters and opponents of the revivals, and cheerfully collected the profits as his business doubled. When Chauncy tried to club the revivals to death with Enlightenment weapons, Edwards fought him off, clad in Enlightenment armor. For educated colonials on the eve of independence, the Enlightenment was beginning to provide a common ground that they could no longer find in organized religion.

John Witherspoon may provide the most interesting case. As a Scottish evangelical, he had made his reputation attacking the moderate Presbyterians who launched Scotland's own enlightenment before 1750 — such men as Francis Hutcheson and William Robertson, who preferred ethical and historical an-

swers to human questions and in the process seemed to ignore (but without repudiating) such basic Christian teachings as Original Sin. For this reason evangelical Presbyterians in America selected Witherspoon as president of the College of New Jersey in 1768. But when he reached Princeton and examined the curriculum, he changed it dramatically by introducing the Scottish enlightenment, precisely the people he had been attacking, including Hutcheson and the skeptic David Hume. To Witherspoon, not knowing the most challenging ideas of the day was far more dangerous than facing them with one's faith intact. He urged students to become learned *and* to embrace conversion. Forty miles away at the College of Philadelphia, an anti-revivalist Scot, Francis Alison, also urged his students to absorb the Scottish enlightenment and live moral (but not regenerate) lives. In a remarkably short period of time, Scottish common sense and moral sense philosophy reorganized the curriculum at most American colleges and established a dominance that would last about a century.

Religion divided Thomas Jefferson and John Witherspoon, president of the College of New Jersey and the only clergyman to sign the Declaration of Independence. But they agreed about politics because both men were deeply read in the Scottish Enlightenment. The Enlightenment helped bring together even those whom religion drove apart.

SUGGESTED READING

Ramón A. Gutiérrez, *When Jesus Came, the Corn Mothers Went Away: Marriage, Sexuality, and Power in New Mexico, 1500–1846* (1991) has a strong account of the Pueblo Revolt. David J. Weber, *The Spanish Frontier in North America* (1992) treats the Florida missions and Texas. Richard White, *The Middle Ground: Indians, Empires, and Republics in the Great Lakes Region, 1650–1815* (1991) is superb. Daniel H. Usner, *Indians, Settlers, and Slaves in a Frontier Exchange Economy: The Lower Mississippi Valley before 1783* (1992) imaginatively covers Louisiana.

Important studies of the eighteenth-century household are James A. Henretta, "Families and Farms: Mentalité in Pre-Industrial America," *William and Mary Quarterly*, 3d ser., 35 (1978), 3–32; Daniel Vickers, "Competency and Competition: Economic Culture in Early America," *William and Mary Quarterly*, 3d ser., 47 (1990), 3–27; Toby L. Ditz, "Ownership and Obligation: Inheritance and Patriarchal Households in Connecticut, 1750–1820," *William and Mary Quarterly*, 3d ser., 47 (1990), 235–65; Lucy Simler, "The Landless Worker: An

Index of Economic and Social Change in Chester County, Pennsylvania, 1750–1820," *Pennsylvania Magazine of History and Biography,* 94 (1990), 163–199; Mary M. Schweitzer, *Custom and Contract: Household, Government, and the Economy in Colonial Pennsylvania* (1987); and Laurel Thatcher Ulrich, *Good Wives: Images and Reality in the Lives of Women in Northern New England* (1982). Allan L. Kulikoff, *Tobacco and Slaves: The Development of Southern Culture in the Chesapeake, 1680–1800* (1986) and Rhys Isaac, *The Transformation of Virginia* (1982) are outstanding on Virginia and Maryland, while Joyce E. Chaplin, *An Anxious Pursuit: Agricultural Innovation and Modernity in the Lower South, 1730–1815* (1993) covers rice and the rise of cotton. John J. McCusker and Russell R. Menard, *The Economy of British America, 1607–1789* (1985) covers most economic patterns and questions.

The best studies of immigration are Bernard Bailyn, *Voyagers to the West: A Passage in the Peopling of America on the Eve of the Revolution* (1986); A. G. Roeber, *Palatines, Liberty, and Property: German Lutherans in Colonial British America* (1993); R. J. Dickson, *Ulster Emigration to Colonial America, 1718–1775* (1966); Alan L. Karras, *Sojourners in the Sun: Scottish Migrants in Jamaica and the Chesapeake, 1740–1800* (1992); and A. Roger Ekirch, *Bound for America: The Transportation of British Convicts to the Colonies, 1718–1775* (1987).

Ian K. Steele, *The English Atlantic, 1675–1740: An Exploration of Communication and Community* (1986) discusses the quickening pace of Atlantic commerce; and Richard L. Bushman, *The Refinement of America: Persons, Houses, Cities* (1992) explores the rise of elegance. Henry F. May, *The Enlightenment in America* (1976) needs to be supplemented by Norman Fiering, "The First American Enlightenment: Tillotson, Leverett, and Philosophical Anglicanism," *New England Quarterly,* 54 (1981), 307–344; and by Charles E. Clark, "Boston and the Nurturing of Newspapers: Dimensions of the Cradle, 1690–1741," *New England Quarterly,* 64 (1991), 243–271. Phinzey Spalding, *Oglethorpe in America* (1977); and Harold E. Davis, *The Fledgling Province: Social and Cultural Life in Colonial Georgia, 1733–1776* (1976) are standard.

John Walsh "Origins of the Evangelical Revival," in G. V. Bennett and J. D. Walsh, eds., *Essays in Modern English Church History in Honor of Norman Sykes* (1966), 132–162; W. R. Ward, *The Protestant Evangelical Awakening* (1992); Susan O'Brien, "A Transatlantic Community of Saints: The Great Awakening and the First Evangelical Network, 1735–1755," *American Historical Review,* 91 (1986), 811–832; and Frank J. Lambert, *"Pedlar in Divinity": George Whitefield and the Transatlantic Revivals* (1994) are indispensable. Perry Miller, *Jonathan Edwards* (1949) is brilliant and controversial. Richard Warch, "The Shephard's Tent: Education and Enthusiasm in the Great Awakening," *American Quarterly,* 30 (1978), 177–198; Martin E. Lodge, "The Crisis of the Churches in the Middle Colonies, 1720–1750," *Pennsylvania Magazine of History and Biography,* 95 (1971), 195–220; Milton J Coalter, *Gilbert Tennent, Son of Thunder* (1986); Leigh Eric Schmidt, "'The Grand Prophet,' Hugh Bryan: Early Evangelicalism's Challenge to the Establishment and Slavery in the Colonial South," *South Carolina Historical Magazine,* 87 (1986), 238–250; and Mark A. Noll, *Princeton and the Republic, 1768–1822* (1989) are important but more specialized. Harry S. Stout, "Religion, Communications, and the Ideological Origins of the American Revolution," *William and Mary Quarterly,* 3d ser., 34 (1977), 519–541; and Nathan O. Hatch, *The Sacred Cause of Liberty: Republican Thought and the Millennium in Revolutionary New England* (1977) explore links between revivalism and revolution.

Chapter 5

War, Victory,
and Imperial Reform

A Perspective View of the Battle Fought near Lake George, by Thomas Jeffreys (1755).

By the middle of the eighteenth century, the British colonists believed that they were the freest people on earth. They attributed this fortune to their widespread ownership of land and to the constitutional principles that they had inherited from Britain and incorporated into their own governments. They saw themselves as heirs and beneficiaries of the Glorious Revolution of 1688–1689, and they proudly proclaimed their loyalty to the Hanoverian dynasty that had guaranteed a Protestant succession to the British throne in 1714, when George I (1714–1727) had become king. In their minds, the British empire had become the world's last bastion of liberty. Everywhere else absolutism, or even naked tyranny, had triumphed. When the British again went to war against Spain and France after 1739, the settlers joined in these struggles and insisted that liberty itself was at stake in the contest. They grew alarmed to discover that less fortunate people among them did not share these values. Slaves in the southern colonies saw Spain, not Britain, as a beacon of liberty. Throughout

the eastern woodlands, most Indians identified France, not Britain, as the one ally genuinely committed to their continuing independence.

POLITICAL CULTURE IN BRITISH AMERICA

A quarter century of warfare after 1689 convinced the settlers that they needed the protection of the British state and increased their admiration for its parliamentary system. Most colonial voters and assemblymen were more "independent" than their British counterparts, who lived in a hierarchical world of patrons and clients. Despite these differences, provincial politics began to absorb many of the values and practices that had taken hold in Britain since the Glorious Revolution.

Before 1700 most of the people founding colonies believed that they could improve on England. The Puritan and Quaker commonwealths, Lord

Baltimore's vision of a harmonious feudal society, the modern aristocracy of the Carolina proprietors, and even the absolutist designs of the duke of York all reflected this belief. But by the eighteenth century, Britain had become a model to emulate, not a society in need of profound change.

Britain's astonishing rise to great-power status, the celebrated success of its mixed and balanced constitution (see Chapter 3), and the praise of French *philosophes* such as Montesquieu and Voltaire raised powerful echoes across the Atlantic. Colonists agreed that they were free because they were British, because they too had mixed constitutions that united monarchy, aristocracy, and democracy in almost a perfect balance.

The Rise of the Assembly

By the 1720s every colony except Connecticut and Rhode Island had an appointive governor, either royal or proprietary, plus a council and an elective assembly. The governor stood for monarchy and the council for aristocracy. In Massachusetts, Rhode Island, and Connecticut the council or upper house was elected (indirectly in Massachusetts). Under the Pennsylvania Charter of Privileges, agreed upon by Penn and the assembly in 1701, the assembly insisted that the appointive council existed only to give advice to the governor; it was not an upper house. Yet the governor occasionally converted it into an informal upper house simply by asking it whether he should approve or veto a bill, or demand amendments. In other colonies, an appointive council played an active legislative role. The office of councilor was not hereditary, but many councilors served for life, especially in Virginia, and some were succeeded by their sons.

In all thirteen colonies, once Georgia became royal, the settlers elected the assembly, which embodied a colony's "democratic" elements. The right to vote in the colonies, though narrowing as population rose, was more broadly distributed than in England, where two-thirds of adult males were disfranchised, a ratio that was still rising. By contrast, something like three-fourths of free adult white males could vote in the colonies, and a fair number of those ineligible at any given time could expect to win that right by acquiring property as they got older. The frequency of elections varied greatly—every year in Massachusetts, Rhode Island, Connecticut, Pennsylvania, and Delaware; every three years in New Hampshire, Mary-

land, and South Carolina; every seven in New York (beginning in the 1740s) and Virginia, as well as in Britain; unregulated but fairly frequent by mid-century in New Jersey, North Carolina and Georgia. As the century advanced, legislatures sat longer and passed more laws, and assemblymen usually took the initiative in drafting major bills. The rise of the assembly was a major political fact of the era.

The Rise of the Governor

Although every royal colony except New York and Georgia already had an assembly when the first royal governor arrived, the governors also grew more powerful. A colony's first governor faced an assembly that already had a strong sense of what it could do. Since the governor's instructions usually challenged this tradition on some matters, the result was often a clash in which the governor never got all of his demands. But he did win concessions, and as time passed, royal governors became much more effective. In almost every colony the most successful governors served between 1730 and 1765. By then most of them had learned that their success depended less on their prerogatives (specific royal powers embodied in their commissions) than on their ability to win over the assembly through persuasion or patronage.

Early in the century, when a typical conflict pitted the governor against an assembly majority, exchanges were legalistic. Technical precedents were invoked by the governor to defend his prerogatives or by the assembly to justify its privileges. Later on, when conflict spilled over into the newspapers, it often pitted an aggrieved minority (unable to win an assembly majority) against both governor and assembly. These confrontations were ideological. The opposition accused the governor of corruption. His defenders attacked the opposition's factional behavior. Everyone denounced factions or political parties as wicked, self-interested, and destructive. "Party is the madness of many for the gain of a few," declared the poet Alexander Pope. As a result, no one claimed to be a party leader. Everyone stood for the public good; only the other side was factional.

"Country" Constitutions: The Southern Colonies

Although all colonies were aware of the ideological currents in British politics, they reacted quite differently to them. In most southern colonies, the "Country" principles of the British opposition (see Chapter 3) became the common assumptions of public life, acceptable to both governor and assembly. In the 1720s and 1730s the planters of both Virginia and South Carolina concluded that their societies embodied almost exactly what British opposition writers were demanding at home. Factions disappeared, and both the governor and the assembly pursued the common good in an atmosphere remarkably free of corruption. Governors received permanent salaries, which the assemblies could not cut off. But whenever a governor, such as Virginia's Alexander Spotswood (1710–1722), used his patronage to create his own "placemen" in the assembly, the voters overwhelmed them at the next election.

The governor could not manipulate the assembly through patronage, and the assembly could not coerce the governor. Both colonies avoided an impasse by cultivating a "politics of harmony," a system of ritualized mutual flattery. Governors learned that they got more done through persuasion than through patronage or bullying. Georgia fell into the same pattern in the 1750s.

This system worked well because the planters were doing what Britain wanted them to do: ship staple crops to Britain. Both sides could agree on measures that would make this process more efficient, such as the Virginia Tobacco Inspection Act of 1730. Public controversy simply disappeared in Virginia. Between 1720 and 1765, particularly during the able administration of Sir William Gooch (1727–1749), the governor and House of Burgesses engaged in only one public quarrel, a remarkable record of political harmony. South Carolina's politics became almost as placid from the 1730s into the 1760s, but its harmony masked serious social problems that were beginning to emerge in the unrepresented backcountry. By contrast, the politics of harmony never took hold in Maryland, where the lord proprietor always tried to seduce assemblymen with his lavish patronage, nor in factional North Carolina where the tobacco and rice

The Governor's Palace at Williamsburg, Virginia   The governor's palace was built under Governor Alexander Spotswood (1710–1722) and restored in the twentieth century. For Spotswood, the palace was an extension of royal might and splendor across the ocean. He set a standard of elegance that many planters imitated when they built their own great houses in the second quarter of the century.

Table 5-1

The Spectrum of Colonial Politics

Constitutional Type	Successful	Unsuccessful
Northern "Court"	New York, ca. 1710–1728 New Hampshire after 1741 Massachusetts after 1741 New Jersey after 1750	New York after 1728 Pennsylvania (successful in peace, ineffective in war)
Southern "Country"	Virginia after 1720 South Carolina after 1730 Georgia after 1752	Maryland North Carolina

Connecticut and Rhode Island never really belonged to this system.

planters could not get along with each other and where the backcountry disliked both.

"Court" Constitutions: The Northern Colonies

Northern colonies had more diverse economic interests and ethnic groups to satisfy and were much more likely to give rise to political factions. Governors with a larger vision of the public welfare could win support by using their patronage to reward some groups and discipline others. William Shirley, governor of Massachusetts from 1741 to 1756, used judicial and militia appointments and wartime contracts to build a majority in the assembly. Like Sir Robert Walpole in Britain, he was a master of "Court" politics (see Chapter 3). Governor Benning Wentworth of New Hampshire created a powerful political machine that gave something to just about every assemblyman between 1741 and 1767. An ineffective opposition in both provinces accused the governor of corrupting the assembly, but each man could claim that what he did was essential to his colony's wartime needs. Both governors remained very much in command.

The opposition, though seldom able to implement its demands at the provincial level, was important nonetheless. It kept settlers alert to any infringements on their liberties. It dominated the town of Boston in most years from 1720 into the 1760s, and it reminded people that resistance to authority might be the only means to preserve liberty. Samuel

Adams, perhaps Boston's most ardent patriot during the Revolution, acquired his political education in the city's politics during the 1740s and 1750s. Boston artisans lustily engaged in ritualized mob activities, which also had a political edge. On Guy Fawkes' day (November 4) every year, a North End mob competed with a South End mob to be the first to carry effigies of the Pope, the Devil, and the Stuart pretender to the British throne to the top of Beacon Hill where they were consumed in flames. These clashes became a way for laborers to celebrate liberty, property, and no popery—or the British constitution as they had come to understand it. The violence made many wealthy merchants nervous. Some of them would become its targets by 1765.

New York's governors, particularly Robert Hunter (1710–1719), achieved spectacular success even earlier, mostly by playing off one faction against another in a colony that had been fiercely divided since Leisler's rebellion (see Chapter 3). Hunter's salary and perquisites became more lucrative than those attached to any other royal office in North America, and after 1716 he and his successor were so satisfied with their control of the assembly that they went ten years without calling a general election. Hunter's success turned into a weakness during the twenty-five years after 1730, mostly because London gave the governorship to a series of men, all eager to rebuild their tattered fortunes at New York's expense. This combination of greed and need gave new leverage to the assembly, which aggressively attacked royal prerogatives during the 1740s. In all the mainland

Portrait of William Shirley   Shirley, the royal governor of Massachusetts Bay (1741–1756), organized the Louisbourg expedition of 1745, strongly supported the Albany Congress of 1754, and was instrumental in greatly expanding the war against New France in 1755. This portrait is by Thomas Hudson.

colonies, only the governor of New York emerged from the period from 1730 to 1754 as manifestly weaker than he had been at the outset.

Pennsylvania, by contrast, kept its proprietary governor weak well into the 1750s. After three decades of intense factionalism, a unified Quaker party emerged to claim undisputed control of the assembly during the 1730s. The governor, who by this time was never a Quaker, had a lot of patronage to dispense. But it was of little use in disciplining a Quaker assembly, whose members had lost interest in becoming judges if that meant administering oaths, nor could they be won over with military contracts, no matter how lucrative. For as long as it could, the Quaker party maintained the colony's commitment to pacifism.

The colonists, both north and south, absorbed British opposition ideology, which warned that power was always trying to destroy liberty and that corruption was its most effective weapon. By 1776 these convictions would justify independence and the repudiation of a "corrupt" king and Parliament. But before the 1760s they served different purposes. They convinced the settlers that they were free in a way

that French and Spanish colonists were not. For example, only the British colonies had newspapers, which gave them a forum for the discussion of public events. The French and Spanish colonies had nothing comparable. In the southern colonies, moreover, British opposition ideology celebrated both the political success of Virginia and South Carolina and the strength of Anglo-American harmony. In the north, it replicated its role in Britain. It became the language of frustrated minorities unable to defeat the governor or control the assembly.

THE RENEWAL
OF IMPERIAL CONFLICT

A new era of imperial war began in 1739 and continued, with only a brief interruption, until 1763. The British colonies, New Spain, and New France all became involved, and eventually so did all Indians east of the Mississippi.

Challenges to French Power

In the decades of peace after 1713, the French tried, with mixed results, to strengthen their position throughout the continent. At great cost they erected the most formidable fortress in North America, Louisbourg on Cape Breton Island. A naval force stationed there, even a small one, could protect the French fishery and guard the approaches to the St. Lawrence River. The French also built Fort St. Frédéric, on what the British called Crown Point, to protect their hold on Lake Champlain, and they maintained their Great Lakes posts at Forts Frontenac, Michilimackinac, and Detroit.

To protect its weak hold on the Gulf of Mexico, France created the Company of the Indies, which shipped seven thousand settlers and two thousand slaves to Louisiana between 1717 and 1721 and then was unable to supply them. By 1726 half of them had starved to death or fled. Another five thousand slaves, but few settlers, reached the colony by 1730. The French founded the city of New Orleans, which became the capital of Louisiana in 1722. There, in 1725, Ursuline nuns opened a convent school for girls, which is still in operation. It admitted Africans and Indians as well as settlers. Other attempts to establish a school for boys failed.

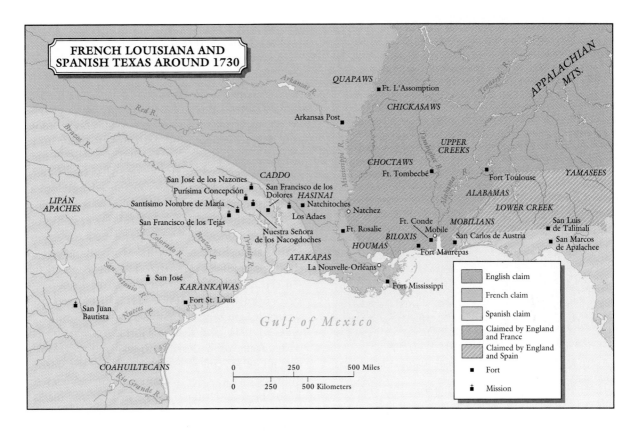

To counter the French effort, Spain sent missionaries and soldiers into Texas between 1716 and 1720, establishing a capital at Los Adaes, a few miles from the French trading post at Natchitoches. To prevent smuggling, Spain refused to open a seaport on the Gulf Coast. As a result, its tiny outposts had to depend on the French for trade goods, sometimes even for food. The Spanish missions in eighteenth-century Texas won few converts and suffered frequent depredations by Indians with firearms. In 1719 the refugees from one such attack abandoned their six missions in East Texas and fled west to San Antonio, founded in 1718. It finally became the capital in the 1770s.

Yet the French hold on the interior began to weaken, both north and south. From all points of the compass Indians returned to what is now Ohio, mostly to trade with the British, who built their own post, Fort Oswego, on Lake Ontario. Compared with French diplomacy, the British were often clumsy, but they had one advantage: their merchandise was cheaper than French trade goods, though not superior in quality. Many of the Indians founded what

the French disparagingly called "republics," independent villages that were willing to trade with the British and that remained outside the French alliance system. The chiefs at Venango, Logstown, and other "republics" welcomed newcomers from all tribes — Mingoes (Iroquois willing to leave the Six Nations) from the north, Delawares from the east, Shawnees from the south and east, and the various other Algonquian peoples of the Great Lakes region to the west. Because the inhabitants of each new village had blood relatives living among all the nearby nations, the chiefs hoped that none of their neighbors would attack them. To the annoyance of British officials, the French at Montreal encouraged an active contraband trade with Albany by which each side acquired the other's trade goods for distribution among the western Indians.

Occasionally the French system of mediation broke down. In the northwest from 1712 to 1737, the French and their Algonquian allies fought a long, intermittent war with the Fox nation. In the southwest an arrogant French officer decided to take over the lands of the Natchez Indians (the last of the

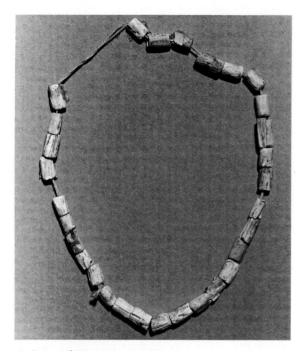

A String of Wampum Indians made wampum from conch and clam shells along the Atlantic coast. It served as the currency of the fur trade and as a mark of status. Wampum belts preserved communal memories and conveyed messages. Wampum necklaces were buried with prominent Indians in much the same manner that Europeans decorated the coffins of kings and nobles with gold, silver, and jewels. As Indians were driven from the Atlantic coast, Dutch settlers took over the manufacture of wampum in the eighteenth century.

Mississippian moundbuilders) and ordered them to move. While pretending to comply, the Natchez planned a counterstroke and on November 28, 1729, killed every French male in the vicinity. In the war that followed, the French and their Choctaw allies destroyed the Natchez as a distinct people, although some Natchez refugees found homes among the Chickasaws and the Creeks.

During the war, in 1730, the French barely averted a massive slave uprising in New Orleans. To stir up hatred between Indians and Africans, the French turned over some of the leaders of the revolt to the Choctaws to be burned alive. They also encouraged hostilities between the Choctaws and the Chickasaws, largely because they could not afford enough presents to hold an alliance with both nations. This policy did real damage to the French. Instead of weakening the pro-British Chickasaws, it touched off a civil war among the Choctaws. France lost power and prestige.

The War of Jenkins' Ear and the Danger of Slave Revolts

The British were having troubles of their own, especially in South Carolina. In the 1570s and 1580s, Francis Drake had proclaimed himself a liberator when he attacked the Spanish Main and promised freedom to Indians and Africans groaning under Spanish tyranny (see Chapter 2). By the 1730s these roles had been reversed. On several occasions after 1680, Spanish Florida had promised freedom to slaves escaping from Carolina who were willing to accept Catholicism. In 1738 the governor established, just north of St. Augustine, a new town, Gracia Real de Santa Teresa de Mose (or Mose for short, pronounced *Moe*-sha). He put a remarkable African in charge, a man who took the name Francisco Menéndez at baptism. He had escaped from slavery, fought with the Yamasees against South Carolina in 1715, and fled to Florida, only to be enslaved again. Yet he learned to read and write Spanish and, while still a Spanish slave, was appointed a militia captain. After winning his freedom in the 1730s, he took charge of Mose in 1738 and made it the first community of free blacks in what is now the United States. The very existence of Mose acted as a magnet for Carolina slaves, especially those who were Catholic.

The Stono Uprising Shortly before Britain declared war on Spain in 1739, the governor of Spanish Florida offered liberty to any slaves from the British colonies who could make their way to Florida. This manifesto, and rumors about Mose, touched off the Stono Rebellion in South Carolina, the largest slave revolt in the history of the thirteen colonies. Some of the rebellion's leaders were Catholics from the African Kingdom of the Kongo, which Portuguese missionaries had converted in the sixteenth century. These slaves thus had religious as well as personal reasons for identifying with Spain.

On Sunday morning, September 9, 1739, twenty slaves attacked a store at Stono (a settlement south of Charleston), killed the owner, seized weapons, and moved on to assault other houses. Heading toward Florida, they killed about twenty-five settlers that day and nearly captured Lieutenant Governor William Bull, who happened to be riding by and just managed to gallop away. When the rebels reached the Edisto River, they stopped, raised banners, and

Savages of Several Nations, New Orleans, 1735   This painting by Alexandre de Batz depicts a multi-ethnic Indian village near New Orleans. The woman at lower left was a Fox Indian who had been captured and enslaved. The African boy was an adoptee.

shouted "liberty," hoping that other slaves would join them and begin a general uprising. There, the militia caught them and killed about two-thirds of the growing force. In the weeks that followed, the settlers killed another sixty. Apparently none of the rebels made it to Florida, but as the founders of Georgia had foreseen, South Carolina was extremely vulnerable in time of war.

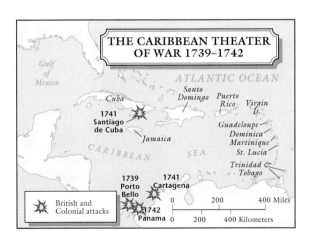

The War of Jenkins' Ear, derisively named for a ship captain who displayed his severed ear to Parliament as proof of Spanish cruelty, cost Britain dearly. Spanish defenses held everywhere. Eager for plunder, three thousand colonists from the mainland volunteered to join Caribbean expeditions in 1741–1742 against Cartegena on the South American coast, then against Cuba and Panama. All were disasters. Most of the men died of disease; only 10 percent got home again. But Lawrence Washington so admired the British naval commander, Edward Vernon, that he named his plantation after him upon returning to Virginia. About all that Britain got from the war was a surge of superpatriotism. Both *God Save the King* and *Rule Britannia* were written during the struggle. More medals were struck in honor of Admiral Vernon than for any other hero, British or American, before or since, simply because the Panamanian city of Porto Bello surrendered to him in 1739 after a short bombardment.

The New York Slave Conspiracy Trials   Georgia had been created to protect South Carolina. Its governor, General James Oglethorpe, retaliated against the Spanish by invading Florida in 1740. He dispersed the black residents of Mose and occupied the site, but the Spaniards mauled his garrison in a surprise counterattack. Oglethorpe retreated without taking St. Augustine and brought some disturbing reports back to Georgia. Spain, he said, was sending blacks into the British colonies to start slave uprisings. And Spanish priests in disguise were intermingled with the black conspirators. This news set off panics throughout the rice and tobacco colonies. But its biggest impact was felt in New York City.

Back in 1712 a bloody slave revolt had broken out there. Slaves had set fire to a barn one night and shot fifteen settlers as they rushed to put out the blaze, killing nine. Twenty-one slaves were executed, some after gruesome tortures. By 1741 New York City's two thousand slaves were the largest concentration of blacks in British North America outside of Charleston. On March 18 of that year, Fort George burned down in what was probably an accident, but then a series of suspicious fires broke out that made the settlers nervous. Some of the blazes probably provided cover for an interracial larceny ring that operated out of the tavern of John Hughson, a white. Public anxiety turned into a judicial massacre when the New York Supreme Court offered freedom to Mary Burton, a sixteen-year-old Irish-Catholic servant girl at the tavern, in exchange for her testimony. She swore that the tavern was the center of a monstrous popish plot to murder the city's whites, free the slaves, and make Hughson king of the Africans. Several free black Spanish sailors, who had been captured and enslaved by New York privateers, were also accused, though apparently their only crime was to insist that they were free. When Oglethorpe's warning reached New York in June, the number of the accused escalated, and John Uty, a high churchman and a Latin teacher who had just moved to New York, was hanged as the likely Spanish priest.

The New York conspiracy trials continued from May into August of 1741 and reminded one observer of the Salem witch frenzy of 1692, in which the testimony of several girls had led to nineteen hangings (see Chapter 3). The death toll in New York was worse. Four whites and eighteen slaves were hanged, thirteen slaves were burned alive, and seventy were banished to the West Indies. These sentences were accompanied by Judge Daniel Horsmanden's bombast about the inviolable liberties of Englishmen, once again in peril from popish conspirators, which to him somehow justified slavery.

Failed Liberators: The Spanish Invasion of Georgia   In 1742 King Philip V of Spain nearly accomplished what Oglethorpe and Horsmanden most dreaded. He sent thirty-six ships and two thousand soldiers from Cuba with instructions to devastate Georgia and South Carolina, "sacking and burning all the towns, posts, plantations, and settlements" along the way and freeing the slaves. Although the Spanish probably outnumbered the entire population of Georgia, Oglethorpe raised nine hundred men and met them on St. Simons Island in July. After he ambushed two patrols, Spanish morale collapsed. When a British soldier deserted to the Spanish with word of how weak Georgia actually was, Oglethorpe arranged to have the Spanish intercept a letter, indicating that the deserter was a spy sent to lure them to their death. Taking no chances, they departed, leaving British North America behind as a safe haven once again for liberty, property, no popery — and slavery.

France versus Britain: King George's War

In 1744 France joined Spain in the war against Britain, and the main struggle shifted northward. The French laid siege to Port Royal, the capital of Nova Scotia. Only the intervention of Governor William Shirley of Massachusetts saved the small garrison, and the French withdrew. Shirley then planned his own foolhardy offensive, an attack on awesome Fort Louisbourg on Cape Breton Island. With only a few lightly armed Yankee vessels at his disposal, he asked the commander of the British West Indian squadron, Sir Peter Warren, to come to his assistance. But Shirley's expedition, which carried something like one-sixth of all the adult males of Massachusetts, set out before Warren could respond. With no heavy artillery of his own, Shirley ordered the commander, William Pepperrell of Maine, to subdue the outer batteries of the fortress, capture their guns, and use them to batter down its walls. Had the expedition met a French fleet instead of the Royal Navy, which arrived in the nick of time, nearly every family in New England might have lost a close relative. The most amazing thing about this incredible plan is that it worked. The British navy drove off the French, and the untrained Massachusetts volunteers subdued the mightiest fortress in America with its own guns. Louisbourg fell on June 16, 1745.

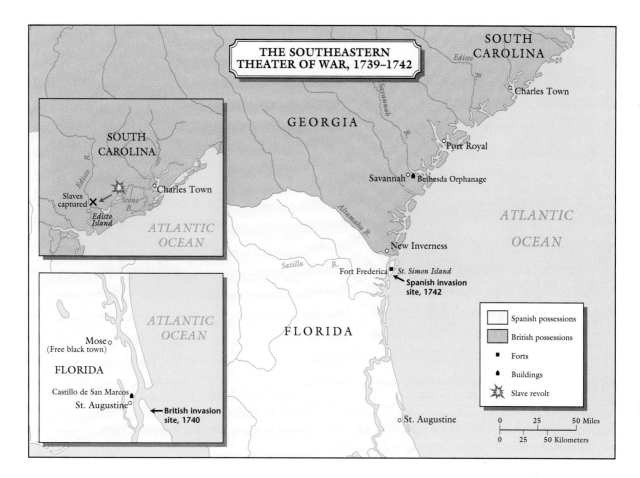

THE SOUTHEASTERN
THEATER OF WAR, 1739–1742

SOUTH CAROLINA

Charles Town

GEORGIA

Port Royal

Savannah○ ▪ Bethesda Orphanage

SOUTH CAROLINA

Edisto R.

Slaves captured ✕

Charles Town

Stono R.

Edisto Island

ATLANTIC OCEAN

New Inverness

Fort Frederica ▪ *St. Simon Island*
Spanish invasion site, 1742

ATLANTIC OCEAN

Satilla R.

Altamaha R.

FLORIDA

Mose ○
(Free black town)

FLORIDA

Castillo de San Marcos
St. Augustine○ ← **British invasion site, 1740**

○ St. Augustine

Spanish possessions
British possessions
▪ Forts
▲ Buildings
✳ Slave revolt

0   25   50 Miles
0   25   50 Kilometers

But after that, nothing went right. Hundreds of volunteers died of various afflictions before regular troops arrived to take over. Elaborate plans to attack Quebec by sea in 1746 and 1747 came to nothing because no British fleet appeared. French and Indian raiders devastated the frontier, weakly defended because Shirley was holding most of his force for the naval assault on Canada, which never took place. Farmers in Bristol County rioted against high taxes. When the Royal Navy finally got to Boston in late 1747, its commander sent gangs of sailors ashore to compel anyone they could grab into serving with the fleet. An angry crowd descended on the sailors, took several officers hostage, and controlled the streets of Boston for three days before the naval commander relented and released all of the Massachusetts men he had impressed. (The rioters let him keep outsiders.) Finally, Britain had to return Louisbourg to France in the Treaty of Aix-la-Chapelle, which ended the war in 1748. New England had suffered enormous losses and had gained nothing except pride. Yet well into 1747, public opinion had strongly supported the war. The clergy, in particular, saw it as an apocalyptic struggle of free British Protestants against popish tyranny.

Renewed Expansion and Preparations for War

Although King George's War drove back the frontiers of British settlement in North America, the colonies had promised to give land to many volunteers after the war. Thus, peace stimulated a frenzy of expansion that alarmed Indians and French alike. The British government, worried that its hold on Nova Scotia was feeble, recruited 2,500 Protestants from the continent of Europe to settle the colony, accompanied by four regiments of redcoats. In 1749 they founded the town of Halifax, which became the new capital. The governor also emphasized that his colony would be European, not Indian, by offering bounties

The Fortress of Louisbourg, 1745   Located on Cape Breton Island, now in the province of Nova Scotia, it has been restored to its 1745 condition by the Canadian government.

for Indian scalps even though the war was over. The Micmac Indians, who had lived in peace with French settlers for more than a century, turned to Acadian farmers for support, and the British relented. There were still too many Acadians to challenge.

A Frenzy of British Expansion   In the thirteen colonies, settlers pressed eagerly against the frontiers. New Englanders swarmed north into Maine and New Hampshire and west into New York and Pennsylvania, creating serious tensions in both colonies. By refusing to pay rent to the manor lords of the Hudson Valley, they sparked a major tenant revolt in 1753 that the wealthy Livingston family subdued with difficulty. A year later, Connecticut's delegation to the Albany Congress used bribes to acquire an Indian title to all of northern Pennsylvania, which Connecticut claimed on the basis of its sea-to-sea charter. The blatant encroachments of New York speculators and settlers on Mohawk lands west of Albany so infuriated Chief Hendrik that he bluntly told the governor of New York in 1753 that "the Covenant Chain is broken between you and us [the Iroquois Six Nations]. So brother you are not to hear of me any more, and Brother we desire to hear no more of you." New York, Pennsylvania, and Virginia competed with each other to control trade with the new Indian "republics" between Lake Erie and the Ohio River. The expansionist thrust was pitting colony against colony, as well as settler against Indian.

Virginians, whom the Indians called "long knives," were particularly aggressive. Citing their 1609 sea-to-sea charter (see map on p. 61), they claimed the Ohio country and in 1747 organized the Ohio Company of Virginia to settle the area, establishing their first outpost at the place where the Monongahela and Allegheny Rivers converge to form the Ohio River (modern Pittsburgh). The company hired George Washington as a surveyor and militia officer. Farther south, the settlement of the backcountry was finally beginning to antagonize the powerful Cherokee Nation, long an ally of South Carolina.

The Confrontation: New France versus Virginia   The French response to these intrusions, which verged on panic, came at a bad time for New France. The men who had long been conducting the colony's Indian diplomacy either died or left office in the late 1740s. They were replaced by authoritarian newcomers from France who gave orders to Indians rather than negotiate with them. The French made some obvious and constructive moves. They rebuilt Louisbourg and erected Fort Beauséjour to protect the overland approach from Canada to Nova Scotia. In 1755 they built Fort Carillon (the British called it Ticonderoga) at Lake Champlain south of Crown Point.

Far more controversial was the policy the French now implemented in the area between the Great

Portrait of Chief Hendrik of the Mohawks   Hendrik's ultimatum to New York in 1753 precipitated the summoning of the Albany Congress a year later.

Lakes and the Ohio. Without trying to explain themselves to the Indians, they launched two expeditions into the area. In 1749 Pierre-Joseph Céloron de Blainville led several hundred men down the Allegheny to the Ohio, then up the Miami and back to Canada. He ordered western Indians to join him, but most of them refused. To them, the French were acting like British settlers, intruding on their lands. Along the way Blainville posted plaques, claiming the area for France. Indians removed them. Marquis Duquesne then sent two thousand Canadians, with almost no Indian support, to erect a line of forts from what is now Erie, Pennsylvania (Fort Presque Isle) to Pittsburgh (Fort Duquesne).

The object of this activity was clear enough. The French intended to prevent British settlement west of the Alleghenies. To Duquesne, this policy was so obviously beneficial to the Indians that it needed no explanation. Yet the Mingoes warned him not to build a fort in their territory, and a delegation of Delawares and Shawnees asked the Virginians if they would be willing to expel the French from the Ohio country and then go home. The Indians did not like Virginia's response.

In 1753 Virginia sent Washington to the Ohio country to warn Duquesne to withdraw, and a small Virginia force began building a fort at the forks of the Ohio. Washington was not one to win over wavering Indians, who, he declared, had "nothing human except the shape." Duquesne ignored Washington, advanced toward the Ohio, expelled the Virginians, took over their fort, and finished building it. Virginia sent Washington back to the Ohio in 1754. On May 28, after discovering a French patrol nearby, he ordered an attack. That command started a world war.

THE WAR FOR NORTH AMERICA

Beginning in 1755, the modernizing British state with its disciplined professional army came into direct and sustained contact with North America's householder society and its voluntaristic principles. The encounter was often unpleasant, but the gap between the two sides got smaller as each became more familiar with the other. At first, the war with France generated fierce tensions between Britain and the colonies, but as time passed both sides learned to cooperate until they achieved victory together. After the war, relations again became hostile and, eventually, explosive.

Of the four wars fought between Britain and France from 1689 to 1763, only the last began in America. That conflict, popularly known as the French and Indian War, was also the biggest and produced the most sweeping results. Among all of America's wars from the eighteenth century to the present, according to unpublished calculations by Thomas L. Purvis, it achieved the fourth highest rate of mobilization and, measured by casualties per capita (excluding Indians), it was the third bloodiest contest we have ever fought. Only World War II, the Civil War, and the Revolution put a higher percentage of adult males under arms. And only the Civil War and the Revolution killed a higher percentage of those mobilized. In proportional terms, the French and Indian War killed far more North Americans than World War II or the conflicts in Korea and Vietnam.

The Albany Congress and the Onset of War

In the spring of 1754 both New France and Virginia were expecting to clash near the forks of the Ohio. But neither anticipated the titanic struggle that they would set off. Nor did their parent governments in Paris and London, which hoped to limit any confron-

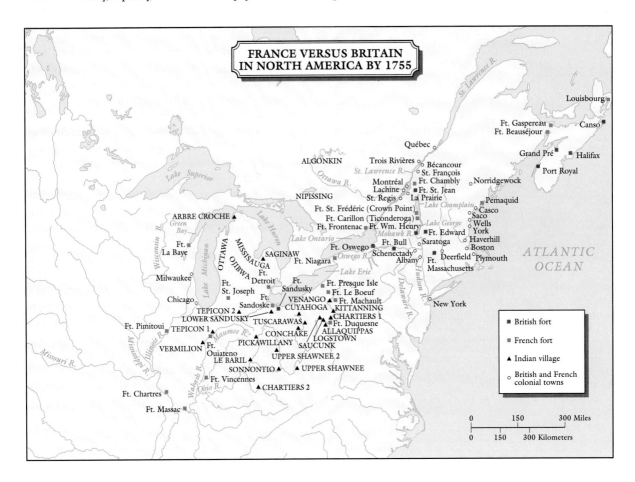

FRANCE VERSUS BRITAIN IN NORTH AMERICA BY 1755

tation to a few strategic points on their common North American frontier. New Englanders, however, sensed that an apocalyptic struggle was in the making between "Protestant freedom" and "popish slavery," with the North American continent as the battleground. What was the purpose of all the new French forts, Jonathan Mayhew, a Boston preacher, asked the Massachusetts General Court in May 1754, except to serve as bases for the conquest of the British colonies? "The slaves [i.e., the French] are content to starve at home in order to injure freemen abroad, and to extend their territories by violence and usurpation. The continent is not wide enough for us both, and they intend to have the whole."

Britain, fearful that the growing hostility of the Iroquois League might convince nearly all Indians to side with New France, ordered New York's governor to summon an intercolonial congress at Albany to meet with the Iroquois and redress their grievances. He invited every colony as far south as Virginia, except for the nearly autonomous charter colonies of Connecticut and Rhode Island. Virginia and New Jersey declined to attend. But Governor William Shirley of Massachusetts, on his own initiative, invited Connecticut and Rhode Island to participate, and he persuaded the Massachusetts General Court to instruct its commissioners to work for a plan of intercolonial union.

In Philadelphia, Benjamin Franklin was also thinking about colonial union. On May 9, 1754, his *Pennsylvania Gazette* printed the first political cartoon in American history, a snake cut into several pieces, each identified as a colony or a bloc of colonies. The caption said, "Unite, or die!" A month later he drafted his "Short hints towards a scheme for uniting the Northern Colonies," which he presented to the Albany Congress in June. His plan called for a "President general" to be appointed by the Crown as commander-in-chief and to administer the laws of the union, and for a "Grand Council," to be elected for three-year terms by the lower houses of each colony. Deputies would be apportioned according to

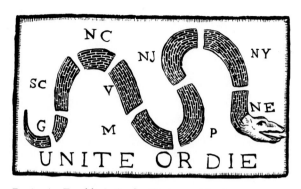

Benjamin Franklin's Snake Cartoon   The first newspaper cartoon in colonial America, this device appeared in the Pennsylvania Gazette in the spring of 1754. It was a call for colonial union on the eve of the Albany Congress. It drew on the folk legend that a snake could revive and live if it somehow joined its severed parts together before sundown.

tax receipts. The union would have power to raise soldiers, build forts, levy taxes, regulate the Indian trade when it touched the welfare of more than a single colony, purchase land from the Indians, and supervise western settlements until the Crown organized them as new colonies. To take effect, the plan would have to be approved by the Crown and by each colonial legislature and then be presented to Parliament for its consent. The Albany Congress adopted an amended version of Franklin's proposal.

Both Shirley and Franklin were far ahead of public opinion. Every colony rejected the Albany Plan, most with little debate, some unanimously. The voting was close only in Massachusetts, which had borne the heaviest burden in the three earlier wars with New France. As Franklin later explained, the colonies feared that the President General might become too powerful. But they also distrusted one another. Despite the French threat, they were not ready to patch up their differences and unite. They did not see themselves as "Americans." The only unity they possessed came from their shared status as British subjects.

London responded to the Albany Plan by ordering the Board of Trade to draft its own proposal. That plan resembled Franklin's, except that the Grand Council could only requisition instead of tax, and colonial union would not require Parliament's approval. Then, after news arrived that George Washington had surrendered his small Virginia force to the French at Great Meadows in July 1754, London decided that the colonies were incapable of uniting in their own defense. Even if they could, the prece-

dent would be dangerous. So the ministry sent redcoats to Virginia instead—two regiments, commanded by Edward Braddock. For the home government, colonial union and direct military aid from Britain were policy *alternatives*. Although soldiers were more expensive to the home government than the proposed union, they seemed the safer political risk. By the winter 1754–1755, colonial union was a dead issue on both sides of the ocean.

Yet the Albany Congress achieved one major objective. Sympathizing with Iroquois grievances against New York, it urged the Crown to assume direct charge of diplomatic relations with all western Indians. London responded by creating two Indian superintendencies—one for the nations south of the Ohio, which went to John Stuart; and one for those north of the Ohio, which went to William Johnson, an Irish immigrant to New York who had great influence with the Mohawks. The superintendencies would survive the war. So did Braddock's new office of commander-in-chief of the British Army in North America. He would be followed by others. But as of 1755, London hoped that a quick, decisive victory by Braddock at the forks of the Ohio would keep the war from spreading.

Britain's Years of Defeat

In early 1755 Braddock landed with his two regiments in Virginia, a signal that London probably intended to let Virginia, rather than Quaker Pennsylvania, control the upper Ohio Valley, including what is now Pittsburgh. When Braddock tried to requisition supplies from nearby colonies, North Carolina complied, but Maryland, Pennsylvania, and New Jersey refused. Only through the efforts of Franklin, who dealt directly with Pennsylvania farmers, did Braddock get the wagons and supplies he needed.

The Campaign of 1755   Braddock also called a council of high officials at Alexandria, Virginia. There, Governor Shirley persuaded him to accept New England's much broader war objectives. Instead of a single expedition aimed at one fort, to be followed by others if time permitted, the campaign of 1755 became four simultaneous offensives designed to crush the outer defenses of New France and leave it open to British invasion. Braddock was so impressed with Shirley that he named him second in command of the British Army in North America,

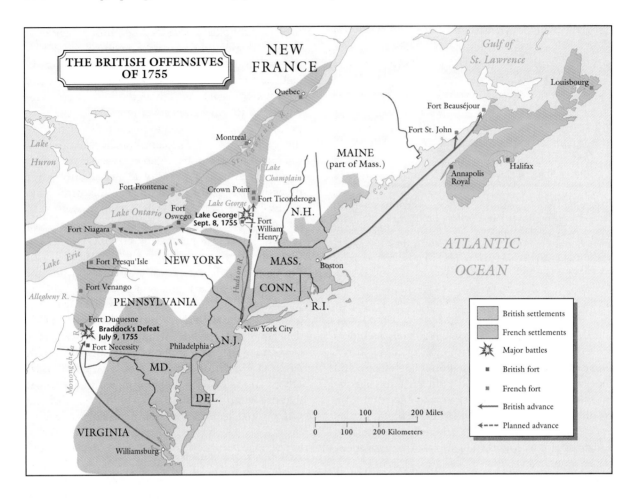

THE BRITISH OFFENSIVES OF 1755

NEW FRANCE

MAINE (part of Mass.)

NEW YORK

N.H.

MASS.

CONN.

R.I.

PENNSYLVANIA

N.J.

MD.

DEL.

VIRGINIA

ATLANTIC OCEAN

Gulf of St. Lawrence

Lake Huron

Lake Ontario

Lake Erie

Quebec

Montreal

Fort Frontenac

Fort Niagara

Fort Oswego

Fort Presqu'Isle

Fort Venango

Fort Duquesne

Braddock's Defeat July 9, 1755

Fort Necessity

Crown Point

Lake George

Fort Ticonderoga

Lake George Sept. 8, 1755

Fort William Henry

Boston

New York City

Philadelphia

Williamsburg

Louisbourg

Fort Beauséjour

Fort St. John

Annapolis Royal

Halifax

Allegheny R.

Monongahela R.

Hudson R.

Lake Champlain

British settlements
French settlements
Major battles
British fort
French fort
British advance
Planned advance

0   100   200 Miles
0   100   200 Kilometers

not bad for an English lawyer with no military training who had arrived in Boston almost without resources in 1730.

Braddock and Shirley tried to make maximum use of both redcoats and provincials. The redcoats were highly disciplined professional soldiers who served long terms and had been trained to fight other professional armies. Irregular war in the dense forests of North America made them uncomfortable. Provincial soldiers, by contrast, were recruited by individual colonies. They were volunteers, often quite young, who usually enlisted only for a single campaign. They knew little about military drill, expected to serve under the officers who had recruited them, and sometimes refused to obey orders that they disliked. Provincials admired the courage of the redcoats but were shocked by their irreverence and by the ferocious discipline imposed on them by their officers. Nevertheless, several thousand

colonists also enlisted in the British army, both during and after the war.

Under Shirley's enlarged plan for 1755, the regular garrison of Nova Scotia, accompanied by New England provincials, would assault Fort Beauséjour, on the narrow neck that connected the Acadian peninsula with the mainland. New England and New York provincials would attack Crown Point, while Shirley, who had also been commissioned as a colonel in the British army, would lead two regiments of redcoats (recently recruited in New England) to Niagara and cut off New France from the Great Lakes and the western Indians. Braddock, who had the strongest force, would take Fort Duquesne.

Instead, Braddock alienated the Indians and marched to disaster on the Monongahela. In April the western Delawares asked him whether their villages and hunting rights would be secure under British protection. He replied that "No Savage Should Inherit the Land." Shingas and the other chiefs retorted "that if they might not have Liberty To Live on the Land they would not Fight for it." Braddock responded "that he did not need their Help." Braddock took several months to hack a road through the wilderness wide enough for his artillery. As he approached the Monongahela he took care to prevent ambushes at two fords, but once he crossed the stream on July 9 his force seemed finally to have overcome all obstacles. He pushed confidently ahead.

At Fort Duquesne the French commander, Liénard, sieur de Beaujeu, could muster only 72 French, 146 Canadians, and 637 Indians against the 1,400 regulars under Braddock and the 450 Virginia provincials under Washington. Beaujeu had planned to attack the British at the fords of the Monongahela, but the Indians thought such an attack would be suicidal and refused. "Will you allow your father to act alone?" he finally asked melodramatically. "I am sure to defeat them." As Beaujeu marched out, the Indians followed reluctantly. Too late to attack at the fords, the French ran into the leading British troops a few miles southeast of the fort. They clashed along a narrow path with thick forest and brush on either side. Beaujeu was killed at once by British fire, and his force almost broke. But the French, Canadians, and Indians quickly rallied and took cover on the British flanks, and Braddock's rear elements rushed forward toward the sound of the guns. There, massed together, they formed a gigantic red bull's-eye. The Indians and the French poured round after round into them, while the British fired wild volleys at an invisible enemy. The British lost 977 killed or wounded, along with their artillery. Braddock was killed. Only thirty-nine French and Indians were killed or wounded. The redcoats finally broke and ran. They were so demoralized that on July 29 their new commander asked the governor of Pennsylvania if he could begin to set up his winter quarters in Philadelphia. Washington, who fought bravely as the commander of Virginia's provincials, agreed that any further offensive operations would be impossible for the rest of the year. Braddock's road through the wilderness now became a highway for the enemy. For the first time in the history of Quaker Pennsylvania, its settlers would have to endure the terrors of a frontier war.

The British offensive in Nova Scotia took Fort Beauséjour easily on June 17, 1755, but then the commanders did something to indicate that this war would not be a conventional, limited, European struggle. When the Acadians refused to take an oath that might have obliged them to bear arms against other Frenchmen, the victors responded with an eighteenth-century version of ethnic cleansing. They rounded up between six thousand and seven thousand Acadians, forced them aboard ships, and expelled them from the province, to be distributed unannounced among the thirteen colonies. A second roundup in 1759 caught most of the families who had evaded the first one. The British also resumed their relentless war against the Micmac Indians.

The British and New England officers who organized these expulsions insisted that they had found a humane way of turning French Catholics into loyal Protestant subjects by forcing them to assimilate with the majority. Reasoning also that the Acadians were not British subjects because they had not taken the oath, and that only British subjects could own land in a British colony, the government of Nova Scotia concluded that the land the Acadians had farmed for generations was not legally theirs, confiscated all of it, and redistributed it to Protestant settlers. The Acadian refugees, of course, never accepted these arguments. After spending miserable years as unwanted Catholic exiles in a Protestant world, some three thousand of them finally made it to French Louisiana, where their descendants became known as Cajuns. Others went to France, and some even made their way back to Nova Scotia or what later became New Brunswick. Very few assimilated into the Protestant population of the thirteen colonies.

In the principal northern theater of 1755, William Johnson led his provincials in the campaign against Crown Point. The French commander, Jean-Armand, baron Dieskau, hoping to repeat the French success against Braddock, attacked a column of provincials on September 8 and drove them back in panic to their base camp, the improvised Fort William Henry near Lake George. French regulars then tried to storm the fort but were driven off with heavy losses in a six-hour struggle. Colonial newspapers proclaimed the Battle of Lake George a great victory because the provincials had not only held the field but had also captured Dieskau, who had been wounded. Johnson probably could have taken poorly defended Crown Point, but he too had been wounded and was content to hold Fort William Henry and nearby Fort Edward at the headwaters of the Hudson. It probably required a more professional eye than his to distinguish the carnage of victory from the carnage of defeat. In the west, Shirley's Niagara cam-

General Johnson Saving a Wounded French Officer [Baron Dieskau] from the Tomahawk of a North American Indian, by Benjamin West, ca. 1762–1766   The setting is the Battle of Lake George, 1755. Obviously West intended to contrast the civility of Europeans, both British and French, with the savagery of Indians, including those allied with the British. In fact, this incident never happened. When the French retreated, according to Dieskau's own account, he had been shot in the thigh and the knee and was left on the battlefield, propped sitting against a tree. He tried to signal his surrender when a British colonist approached, only to be shot again in the hip. Only then was he carried before the wounded William Johnson, where he formally surrendered.

paign got no farther than Oswego on Lake Ontario and then stopped for the winter, held in check by the French at Fort Frontenac on the lake's northern shore. Oswego was soon cut off by heavy snows. Malnutrition and disease ravaged the garrison.

A World War   With the death of Braddock and the capture of Dieskau, military amateurs took over both armies: Shirley in the British colonies and Governor-General Pierre de Rigaud de Vaudreuil in New France. Vaudreuil was a Canadian who understood the Middle Ground and his colony's utter weakness without Indian support. The population of the thir-

teen colonies outnumbered that of New France by twenty to one. Virginia alone had over five times New France's population, and Massachusetts nearly three times. If the British colonies could concentrate their resources in a few places, they had a good chance of overwhelming New France. As horrible as it was, frontier war waged by New France primarily against ordinary settlers was the most effective way to force the British colonies to disperse their resources over a vast area.

As long as Vaudreuil made most of the decisions, in 1756 and 1757, New France kept winning. Oswego fell in the summer of 1756. When Fort William Henry surrendered the next year, the French promised to permit the garrison to march unmolested to Fort Edward. But France's Indian allies then killed or carried off 308 people out of the 2,300 prisoners, an event that colonial newspapers called the Fort William Massacre. Most of those killed were trying to save their property, which the Indians considered their rightful plunder. Under Vaudreuil, devastation along the Pennsylvania frontier became immense. But the French government decided that New France needed a professional general and in 1756 sent Louis-Joseph, marquis de Montcalm. Shocked and repelled by the brutalities of frontier warfare, Montcalm tried to turn the conflict into a traditional European struggle of sieges and battles in which, as Vaudreuil well understood, the advantage would pass to the British.

Braddock's defeat, combined with the British loss of Minorca in the Mediterranean, convinced the British government that the struggle with France could not be limited to a few outposts. Britain declared war on France in 1756, and the colonial contest merged into a general European struggle that pitted France, Austria, and Russia against Prussia, which was heavily subsidized by Britain. The Seven Years' War (1756–1763) created a sharper confrontation between Protestant and Catholic states than Europe had seen in more than a century. To many North American clergymen, the war took on apocalyptic significance. A Protestant victory might herald the onset of the Millennium. The conflict spread even to India, where British forces expelled the French from all but a toehold on the vast subcontinent.

Yet for most of the war, Spain remained neutral, a choice that had huge implications within North America. In the previous war, Spanish Florida had shown an ability to turn the slaves of South Carolina against their masters and to create enormous unrest as far north as New York. At a minimum, Spanish hostilities early in the war would have forced the British to fight in another large theater of conflict. Instead, Spanish neutrality permitted Britain to concentrate its resources against New France. By 1762, when Spain finally entered the war in a vain effort to prevent a total British victory, the French had already surrendered Canada, and Britain's seasoned army and navy easily rolled over Spain's less experienced forces.

Imperial Tensions   When the British government, to its dismay, suddenly realized in 1755 that Shirley, a lawyer, had taken command of the British army in North America, it dispatched an irascible Scot, John Campbell, earl of Loudoun, to replace him and began pouring in reinforcements. General Loudoun had a special talent for alienating provincials. Colonial units did not care to serve under his command and sometimes bluntly rejected his orders. Provincials were volunteers who believed they had a contractual relationship with *their* officers; they had never agreed to serve under Loudoun's professionals. They refused to serve beyond their term of enlistment, which usually expired on November 1 or December 1. If a British officer tried to hold them longer, they sometimes just marched off toward home.

Rank was another problem. British army captains, who were career officers, protested vehemently when a provincial field officer, such as the youthful and inexperienced Colonel Washington, presumed to give orders to them and their men. London responded by declaring that all provincial field officers (majors and above) were subordinate to any British captain. But this arrangement upset veteran New England officers, such as General John Winslow of Massachusetts and his six colonels, who resisted being placed under direct British command in the summer of 1756. As Winslow tried to explain to General Loudoun, "the privates universally hold it as one part of the terms on which they enlisted that they were to be commanded by their own officers; and this is a principle so strongly imbibed that it is not in the power of man to remove it." If Loudoun insisted on putting provincials under the direct command of British officers, Winslow warned, the men would desert, the army would disintegrate, and the assemblies would be unable to raise new regiments.

Discipline proved equally troublesome. The British army was a rigid hierarchy in which gentlemen officers gave orders and demanded obedience. Soldiers who deserted or struck an officer were shot. For lesser offenses they received from five hundred to one thousand lashes, which could also be fatal. In one respect this brutal code of discipline helped keep the men healthy. Because professional soldiers obeyed orders, British army camps were carefully laid out with latrines posted away from the tents and the fresh water supply. Colonial officers led more by example and persuasion than by direct command, but because nobody volunteered for latrine duty or to wash clothes, their men were filthy and relieved themselves anywhere they chose, thus contaminating the drinking water. New England men, it seems, literally preferred to die rather than perform menial tasks that women took care of at home. Provincial camps were so slovenly that a visitor approaching from downwind sometimes picked up the stench several miles away. Death from disease was far higher among provincials than among regulars and carried off far more men than were killed in combat. When provincial officers imposed punishments on their men in the early years of the war, the penalties were usually modest—twenty or thirty lashes, and never more than the biblical limit of thirty-nine. One provincial so disciplined in Nova Scotia in 1754 retaliated by "pulling up the whipping post and carrying it off." As punishment for this gesture he was dismissed from the service, hardly a deterrent to others.

Redcoats and provincials also had different ideas about combat. Regulars were trained to fire disciplined volleys at other armies and then charge with fixed bayonets. Provincials, like Indians, looked for cover and aimed at specific targets while setting their own rate of fire. They thought it mad to stand closely packed in an open field while the enemy discharged volley after volley at them. And they hated bayonet charges.

Most British officers serving in America disliked the provincials, especially their officers. "The Americans are in general the dirtiest most contemptible cowardly dogs that you can conceive," snarled General James Wolfe. "There is no depending on 'em in action. They fall down dead in their own dirt and desert by battalions, officers and all." General John Forbes was usually more positive, but after hearing that the provincials had fled in panic when the redcoats were decimated at Ticonderoga in 1758, he exploded: "There is no faith or trust to be put in them." He suggested "shooting dead a Dozen of their cowardly Officers at the Head of the Line."

Yet some British officers were more charitable. Horatio Gates, Richard Montgomery, Hugh Mercer, and Arthur St. Clair all chose to remain in America after the war and later became generals in the American army during the Revolution. Colonel Isaac Barré praised American courage in the House of Commons in 1765 in a speech in which he coined the phrase "Sons of Liberty," a label instantly adopted by radical colonists who strongly opposed Britain's postwar policies.

Another imperial tension arose from the presence of thousands of redcoats in the colonies, which created a huge housing, or "quartering," problem. On dubious legal grounds, General Loudoun insisted that the British Mutiny Act, which regulated quartering within Great Britain, applied to the colonies, and he proceeded to enforce it. When soldiers landed in a city, he demanded that the assembly provide adequate quarters, or else, he warned, he would take them by force. Massachusetts, New York, Pennsylvania, and South Carolina all went through angry crises over this question at various times between 1755 and 1758. The assemblies, insisting on their privileges, won the right to be consulted, but eventually they all found ways to quarter British troops.

To help fund the war effort, Braddock and Loudoun also tried to requisition revenue from the colonies. New England, New York, and Virginia responded generously, but at first Maryland, Pennsylvania, and New Jersey refused. North Carolina sat out the war after 1755. This situation prompted a flurry of petitions from governors, army officers, and other officials to Britain, usually calling for direct taxation of the colonies by Parliament.

Colonial smuggling also enraged the British, particularly the molasses trade between the French sugar islands and the northern colonies. Loudoun several times imposed embargoes on all shipping out of particular ports in an effort to stamp out the traffic. By cutting off the islands from their normal supply of foodstuffs, he hoped to force the planters to surrender—or else watch their slaves die of starvation. The Royal Navy vigorously pursued smugglers. But ingenious merchants managed to evade these obstacles. For example, by 1759 a lively trade in flags-of-truce had developed out of Philadelphia. Nominally used for the exchange of prisoners, the flags became a ruse for carrying on trade as usual.

What most British officers saw in North America before 1758 left them contemptuous of the settlers and their ability to fight. They underestimated the colonists' commitment to their liberties and their willingness to fight for what they believed in.

New Policies: William Pitt   A reorganization of the British government in 1757 brought William Pitt to power as war minister. He quickly found solutions to most of these difficulties. In virtually every case Loudoun and his supporters had favored authoritarian measures—the direct subordination of provincial units to regular officers, the imposition of British discipline on provincials, the forced quartering of soldiers in colonial cities, the imposition of direct parliamentary taxes, and the ruthless suppression of smuggling. Pitt sharply reversed this authoritarian emphasis by appealing to the very real patriotism of provincials and by opening voluntaristic ways for them to support the war effort.

Pitt won the cooperation of provincial officers by declaring that every provincial field officer would rank immediately behind the equivalent British rank but above all lesser officers, British or provincial. He then promoted every British lieutenant colonel to the rank of "colonel in America only." That decision left only about thirty British majors vulnerable to being ordered about by a provincial colonel. But since few majors held independent commands, that situation was unlikely to arise. Now that provincial units were controlled by their own officers, they could serve with British units without undermining their own command structure.

Ironically, perhaps, this effort to placate provincial officers also made them much more willing to impose British discipline on their own men. With their status formally recognized by Britain, provincial officers began to act like true gentlemen. During the last years of the war, they often sentenced provincial soldiers to hundreds of lashes for routine offenses. The quartering crisis also eased by 1758 as individual assemblies decided to build barracks for the king's troops whenever they passed through, so that they could be housed without being quartered upon civilians.

Pitt solved the revenue problem by drawing upon a precedent set after the Louisbourg expedition in the previous war, when Parliament had reimbursed Massachusetts. He adopted a policy of *partial* reimbursement for military expenses incurred by the colonies. Beginning in 1758 he set aside £200,000 sterling per year (later reduced to £133,000) and told the colonies that they could claim a share of it in direct proportion to their contribution to the war effort. In practice, the subsidies paid slightly less than half of the cost of fielding twenty thousand provincials each year from 1758 through 1760, and somewhat fewer in the next two years as the theater of operations shifted to the Caribbean. The influx of specie also tended to stabilize the value of colonial paper money and stimulated a boom in British exports to America, all of which had the unintended effect of persuading British visitors that the settlers were wallowing in luxury while paying very little in taxes. Actually, war taxes were quite heavy, especially in New England and New York. Smuggling angered Pitt as much as anyone else, but British conquests rapidly contained the problem. By 1762 French Canada, Martinique, and Guadeloupe, as well as Spanish Havana, were all in British hands. Few places remained worth smuggling to, except St. Domingue.

Pitt had little patience with military failure. When Loudoun's proposed attack on Louisbourg in 1757 turned into another fiasco, he replaced him with James Abercrombie. He also put Jeffrey Amherst in charge of a new Louisbourg expedition, with James Wolfe as one of his brigadiers. By 1758 the British empire had finally put together a military force capable of overwhelming New France and had learned how to use it. In the last years of the war, unlike the early ones, cooperation between redcoats and provincials became routine and devastatingly effective.

The Years of British Victory

By 1758 the Royal Navy had cut Canada off from reinforcements and even from routine supplies. Britain had sent more than thirty regiments to North America. Combined with twenty thousand provincials, thousands of bateau men rowing supplies into the interior, and swarms of privateers preying on French commerce, Britain had mustered perhaps sixty thousand men in North America or in nearby waters. Most of them now closed in on the seventy-five thousand people of New France. Montcalm, who in any case was running out of trade goods for use as Indian presents, refused to encourage more Indian attacks on the frontier. Instead, he prepared to defend the approaches to Canada at Forts Duquesne, Niagara, Frontenac, Ticonderoga, Crown Point, and Louisbourg.

Indian Withdrawal   Spurred on by Quaker intermediaries, the British and colonial governments came to terms with the western Indians in 1758,

promised not to seize their lands after the war, and arranged an uneasy peace. Few settlers or officials had yet noticed a new trend that was emerging during the conflict. Before the 1750s, Indian nations had often waged terrible wars with one another, but now few Indians in the northeastern woodlands were willing to attack others. In 1755, for example, some Senecas fought with New France and some Mohawks with the British, but they maneuvered carefully to avoid direct conflict with each other. This Iroquois sense of solidarity was beginning to spread. Iroquois and western Algonquians, once deadly enemies, saw real advantages in cooperation. A sense of pan-Indian identity began to take shape, encouraged by Indian prophets, mostly among the Delawares and Shawnees, who urged all Indians to return to their ancestral ways and to free themselves from European corruption. Though most Indians regarded the French as far less dangerous than the British and even fought with New France, they were never puppets of the French. Above all, they fought, negotiated, and made peace in 1758 to preserve their hold on the land.

The Campaign of 1758   Peace with the western Indians permitted the British in 1758 to revive the grand military plan of 1755, except that this time the overall goal was clear—the conquest of New France. In the east, Amherst and Wolfe, with nine thousand regulars and five hundred provincials, besieged Louisbourg for sixty days until it surrendered in September, thus adding Cape Breton Island to the British province of Nova Scotia. A force of three thousand provincials under Colonel John Bradstreet advanced to Lake Ontario, took Fort Frontenac, and began building a fleet. This victory cut off French garrisons in the Ohio Valley from their supply base. A powerful force of regulars under John Forbes and provincials under Washington marched west, this time through Pennsylvania, to attack Fort Duquesne, but the French blew up the fort and retreated north just before they arrived. The British erected Fort Pitt on the ruins.

The only British failure in 1758 occurred in northern New York when Abercrombie sent six thousand regulars and nine thousand provincials against Ticonderoga (Carillon), which was defended by Montcalm and 3,500 troops. Instead of waiting for his artillery to arrive or of trying to outflank the French, Abercrombie ordered a frontal assault against a heav-

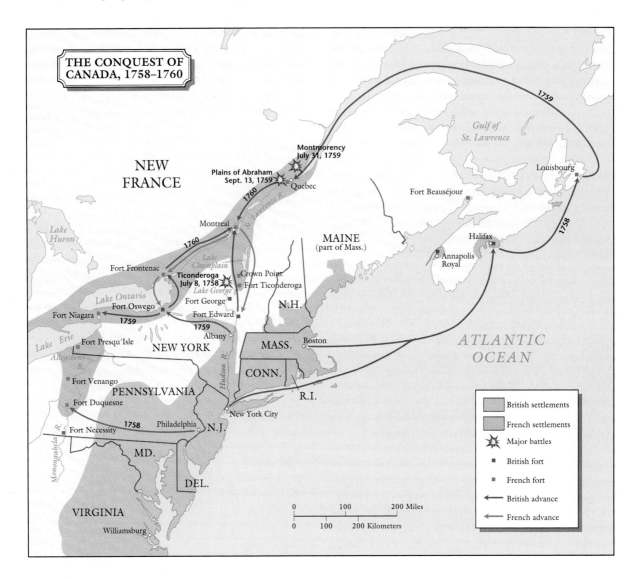

THE CONQUEST OF
CANADA, 1758–1760

ily fortified position, and his regulars were butchered by the withering fire. The provincials fled. Like the Indians, they regarded such an attack as sheer madness. When Pitt heard the news, he sacked Abercrombie, put Amherst in charge of the New York theater of war, and left Wolfe at Louisbourg to plan an attack on the St. Lawrence Valley and the fortress city of Quebec.

The Conquest of Canada

In 1759 while the provincials on Lake Ontario moved west to take Niagara, Amherst spent the summer cautiously taking Ticonderoga and Crown Point. (Pitt expected him to reach

Montreal.) The most dramatic American campaign occurred farther east. In June, Wolfe ascended the St. Lawrence with eight thousand redcoats and colonial rangers and laid siege to Quebec, defended by Montcalm with sixteen thousand regulars, Canadian militia, and Indians. "Montcalm is at the head of a great number of bad soldiers," said Wolfe, "and I am at the head of a small number of good ones, that wish for nothing so much as to fight him." When an attack below the city failed, Wolfe mounted howitzers on high ground across the river from Quebec and began reducing most of the city to rubble. Frustrated by the French refusal to surrender, he turned loose his American rangers ("the worst soldiers in the universe," he boasted), who ravaged and burned more than 1,400 farms. Anyone who resisted was shot and scalped. Still the French held out.

By September both Wolfe and Montcalm realized that the British fleet would soon have to depart or else risk being frozen in during the long winter. Wolfe made a last desperate effort, preferring to die rather than fail. His men silently sailed up the river, climbed a formidable cliff above the city in darkness, and on the morning of September 13, 1759, deployed on the Plains of Abraham behind Quebec. Montcalm panicked. Instead of using his artillery to defend the walls from inside (Wolfe's force had been able to drag only two guns with them), he marched out of Quebec onto the Plains. Both generals now had what they craved most, a set-piece European battle that lasted about fifteen minutes. Wolfe and Montcalm were both mortally wounded. But the British quickly drove the French from the field, and Quebec surrendered. When a French relief force failed to retake the city from its garrison, which shivered amidst the rubble through the long winter, the North American war was all but over. In 1760 armies converged from all sides on Montreal, and Canada finally surrendered.

The Cherokee War and Spanish Intervention   In January 1760, as the British triumph over France was becoming complete, the Cherokees, whose three thousand warriors had long been allies and trading partners of South Carolina, reacted to a long string of violent incidents by attacking the backcountry settlements. In one year, they drove the settlers back by nearly a hundred miles. South Carolina had to appeal to General Amherst for help, and he sent regular soldiers who laid waste the Cherokee Lower Towns in the Appalachian foothills. When that expedition failed to bring peace in 1760, another one the following year devastated the Middle Towns farther west, while Virginia threatened the Overhill Towns. The Cherokees made peace in December 1761, but the war left backcountry settlers brutalized and lawless. Their problems soon became severe political issues for the South Carolina government.

Only then, in January 1762, after both the French and the Cherokees had been defeated, did Spain finally enter the war. British forces quickly took Havana and even Manila in the distant Philippines. Both France and Spain finally sued for peace.

The Peace of Paris

In 1763 the Peace of Paris finally ended the war. France surrendered to Great Britain several minor West Indian islands and all of North America east of the Mississippi, except the port of New Orleans. In exchange for Havana, Spain ceded Florida to the British and also paid a large ransom for the return of Manila. To compensate its Spanish ally, France gave all of Louisiana west of the Mississippi and the city of New Orleans to Spain. Most of the Spanish and African occupants of Florida withdrew to other parts of the Spanish empire, but nearly all French settlers remained behind in Canada, the Illinois country, and what was now Spanish Louisiana.

The colonists were jubilant. The age of warfare and frontier carnage seemed over at last. Britain and the colonies could now develop their vast resources in a continuing imperial partnership and would share unprecedented prosperity. Instead, just twelve years after the Peace of Paris, Massachusetts militiamen clashed with British redcoats at Lexington and Concord, setting off a war even more destructive than the previous struggle, one that would end with American independence.

It is hard to find another example in world history of an empire falling apart so soon after reaching the peak of its success. Some contemporaries saw a causal connection between the two. Etienne-François, duc de Choiseul, the French foreign minister who had to swallow the humiliation of the peace treaty in 1763, preferred to think of France's cession of Canada to Britain as a master stroke of his diplomacy. In French hands, he told an Englishman, Canada "would always be of service, to keep our [Britain's] Colonies in that dependence which they would not fail to shake off the moment Canada should be ceded." By 1776 many British and colonial loyalist observers agreed that the British conquest of Canada had permitted the thirteen colonies to go their independent way. That argument seems rather weak, however. The cession of Canada prompted most colonists to fancy a rosier future for themselves, but the French Canadians hardly disappeared from the map in 1763. Most of them refused to support the American Revolution after 1775, and Canada again became a staging ground for attacks on the northern frontier of the thirteen colonies. Anglo-American settlers did not rebel because the danger of invasion from Canada no longer existed. They revolted even though they knew that this peril had revived.

Patriots saw a different connection between the French war and the Revolution. Many noted that the colonies that made the greatest sacrifices for the empire in the 1750s, such as Massachusetts and Virginia, later became the most ardent revolutionaries. Instead of rewarding and building upon their loyalty and patriotism, Britain drove them into rebellion, despite their sincere, even frantic efforts to preserve the empire. "I do seriously and positively affirm," wrote John Witherspoon, himself a recent immigrant from Scotland, to a fellow Scot, ". . . that congress itself, it if had . . . direct[ed] the measures of the British ministry, could not or would not have directed them to measures so effectual to forward and establish the independence of America, as those which they chose of their own accord." The American Revolution was a crisis of imperial *integration* that the British state could not handle. The colonists insisted that they wanted nothing more than their traditional rights as Englishmen. Britain's seeming determination to deprive them of those rights finally drove most of them out of the empire they had fought hard to save. In a word, a triumphant empire somehow destroyed itself.

Western Indians angrily rejected the peace settlement. No one had conquered them, they pointed out, and they denied the right or the power of France to surrender their lands to Great Britain. They began to plan their own war of Indian liberation.

IMPERIAL REFORM AND COLONIAL PROTEST

In 1760 George II died and was succeeded by his twenty-two-year-old grandson, George III (1760–1820). The new king's frequent and sincere pronouncements on behalf of religion and virtue at first won him many admirers in North America. But the political coalition that was leading Britain to victory soon fell apart.

The Bute and Grenville Ministries

The king, along with his tutor and principal adviser, John Stuart, earl of Bute, feared that the war with France was becoming so expensive that it would soon bankrupt Great Britain. While London jubilantly celebrated one victory after another from 1758 on, George and Bute grew ever more despondent. When

Pitt urged a preemptive assault on Spain before Spain could attack Britain, Bute forced him to resign in October 1761, even though Pitt had become the most popular public official of the century. But Bute soon learned that Pitt had been right. Spain declared war on Britain in January 1762 as soon as the annual treasure fleet from America had arrived safely.

Then, in May 1762, Bute forced Thomas Pelham-Holles, duke of Newcastle and the most powerful politician of the previous twenty-five years, to resign as first lord of the treasury in order to economize on subsidies to Prussia. So eager were the king and Bute to make peace with France that they agreed to return the wealthy, conquered West Indian islands of Guadeloupe and Martinique; they probably would have relinquished Canada as well, but France never asked for it.

By then, the British press, often subsidized by Pitt, Newcastle, and even Frederick the Great (the soldier-king of Prussia), was merciless in its crude denunciations of Bute. Once Parliament had approved of the Treaty of Paris, Bute dismayed the king by resigning. He had had enough.

In this odd way, in April 1763, George Grenville became prime minister (technically, first lord of the treasury and chancellor of the exchequer). The king and Bute, from whom the king still sought advice, did not trust Grenville, and Pitt (Grenville's brother-in-law) and Newcastle would have nothing to do with him. Both believed that Grenville had deserted them when Bute had forced them to resign.

The Wilkes Crisis Grenville spent most of his first year trying to survive a major domestic crisis that later dovetailed into colonial events. As Parliament adjourned in the spring, John Wilkes, a radical journalist, all but accused the king of lying, in an essay that Wilkes published in the 45th number of *The North Briton,* a newspaper founded to vilify Bute, a Scot, or "North Briton." The government used a general warrant (one that did not specify the person or place to be searched) to invade the paper's offices and arrest Wilkes, who was also a member of Parliament. He was charged with the publication of a seditious libel (see Chapter 4). But Chief Justice Charles Pratt, an admirer of Pitt, declared general warrants illegal and freed Wilkes. The government immediately arrested Wilkes on a special warrant, and Pratt again freed him, this time declaring that parliamentary privilege extended to the publication

John Wilkes, Esq., a satirical engraving by William Hogarth
Note the *North Briton* on the table.

than half of the kingdom's annual revenues went to pay interest on the debt, and Britain was already one of the most heavily taxed societies in the world. Despite the scale of Britain's victory over France and Spain, imperial expenses would be higher than they had been before the war because Britain's conquests had to be garrisoned. In 1762 and 1763 Bute and Grenville decided to leave twenty battalions with about ten thousand men in America, mostly in Canada and Florida, with smaller garrisons scattered throughout Indian territory. Somebody would have to pay for these new expenses. Because the colonists received the most obvious benefits from this protection, Grenville argued, they ought to be willing to pay for a reasonable portion of these costs, and eventually for all of them. He never asked the settlers to contribute anything to the national debt or to Britain's heavy domestic needs. But he did insist that they begin to pay something for their own defense.

In implementing this decision, instead of building on the voluntaristic measures that Pitt had employed to win the war, Grenville reverted to the authoritarian demands for imperial reform that had crisscrossed the Atlantic during Britain's years of defeat between 1755 and 1757. Grenville's subsequent policies—the army itself, the Proclamation of 1763, a vigorous crackdown on smuggling, the Sugar Act, the Stamp Act, the Currency Act, and the Quartering Act—together marked a concerted effort to give the home government effective centralized control over the colonies. To the settlers, victory would bring heavier burdens, not relief.

To Grenville, the voluntaristic cooperation of 1758–1762 was a sign of Britain's weakness, not of the empire's strength. To his mind, Britain had won the war, not through the cooperation of the colonies, but despite their obstruction. Because the colonies were doubling in population and wealth every twenty-five years, he believed that the British government had to act quickly and decisively to establish its authority before they slipped completely out of Britain's control. In effect, Grenville set in motion a self-fulfilling prophecy in which he and his successors brought about precisely what they were trying to prevent. Nearly every step they took served to alienate the colonies and to intensify their resistance. The alternative to a variety of voluntaristic colonial societies in British America, governed mostly through persuasion, was not a collection of dutiful and obedient provinces under an omnipotent Parlia-

of seditious libels. London artisans lustily embraced the cause of "Wilkes and liberty!" Opposition factions fully expected to overturn Grenville on general warrants and parliamentary privilege during the winter session of 1763–1764. Only a public reading of Wilkes's pornographic *Essay on Woman* in the House of Lords mustered enough votes for the Grenville ministry to win narrow victories on both questions. Wilkes fled to France for the next few years and was outlawed, but "45" became a symbol of liberty on both sides of the ocean. By 1768 Wilkes would have thousands of ardent admirers in the colonies.

Rethinking Colonial Policy   As the Wilkes affair subsided, Grenville turned his attention to the colonies. Britain's national debt had nearly doubled during the war and stood at more than £130 million. More

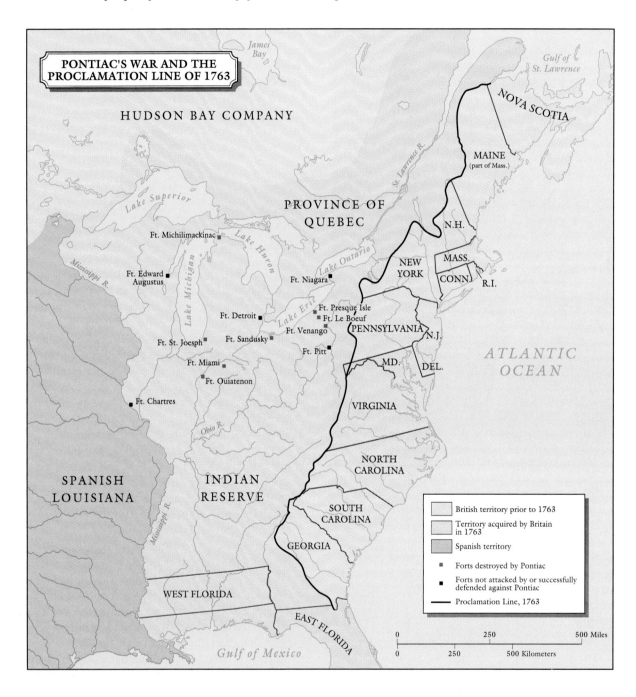

ment. It was, to the colonists' surprise, an independent America.

Indian Policy and Pontiac's War

The king honored wartime commitments to the western Indians by issuing the Proclamation of 1763. It set up governments in Canada, Florida, and other

conquered colonies, and it tried to regulate the pace of western settlement. It established the so-called Proclamation Line along the Appalachian watershed. No settlements could be planted west of that line unless, acting through the Indian superintendents, Britain first purchased the land by treaty from the Indians. Prospective settlers would be encouraged to move instead to Nova Scotia, northern New England, Georgia, or Florida. Because most of the lands of the Iroquois League lay east of the Proclamation Line, the Six Nations felt threatened by the new policy, even though Sir William Johnson, the northern superintendent, carefully protected their claims. Nor were Indians pleased by General Amherst's decision, after the fall of Montreal in 1760, to cut back sharply on traditional presents to Indians. That decision violated the customs of the Middle Ground and thus deprived British officials of most of their leverage with western Indians, at a time when both the Indians' discontents and their ability to organize had reached new peaks.

In 1761 a western Delaware named Neolin reported a vision in which God demanded that Indians return to their ancestral ways. Neolin called for an end to Indian dependence on the Anglo-Americans, but his visions also incorporated such Christian ideas as heaven and hell. European vices, especially rum, were blocking the path to heaven. "Can ye not live without them?" he asked. God was punishing Indians for accepting European ways. Deer were already scarce, and worse hardships would follow. "If you suffer the English among you, you are dead men. Sickness, smallpox, and their poison will destroy you entirely." Neolin's condemnation did *not* extend to those French who were still living in the Great Lakes region, however. Indeed, many of his followers hoped that by demonstrating their unity and power, they might induce King Louis XV of France to return to North America, restore the friendly relations typical of the old Middle Ground, and halt British expansion.

With a unity and determination never seen before, the Indians struck in the spring and summer of 1763 in a conflict that came to be known as "Pontiac's Rebellion," after a prominent Ottawa chief who did not regard himself as a British subject. Senecas, Mingos, Delawares, Shawnees, Wyandots, Miamis, Ottawas, and other nations attacked Britain's garrisons in the west. Sandusky, Michilimackinac, Fort St. Joseph, Fort Miami, Fort Ouiatenon, Fort Venango, Fort LeBoeuf, and Fort Presque Isle all fell between May 16 and June 20—every British garrison west of Niagara except Fort Pitt, Detroit, and a tiny outpost on Green Bay, the only one that the Indians did not bother to attack. For months the Indians kept Detroit and Fort Pitt under close siege, something Indians were supposed to be incapable of doing. Colonel Henry Bouquet, marching to the relief of Fort Pitt, suffered heavy casualties in a two-

day battle at Bushy Run in early August. The Indians' losses were light, but they broke off the engagement when they ran out of ammunition, allowing Bouquet to get through and proclaim the engagement a victory.

These Indian successes so enraged Amherst that he ordered the commander of Fort Pitt to distribute smallpox-infested blankets among the western tribes, touching off a severe epidemic in 1763–1764. "You will do well to try to Inoculate the Indians by means of Blankets," wrote Amherst to Bouquet, "as well as to Try Every other Method that can serve to Extirpate this Execrable Race." Only in 1764 did British and provincial forces bring resistance to an end and restore peace. In the aftermath, the British government ineptly and reluctantly embraced the role that the French had once played in the Great Lakes region by distributing presents and mediating differences.

But ten years of frontier conflict from 1755 through 1764 had brutalized the frontiersmen, especially in Pennsylvania. Perhaps sensing the growing revulsion that Indians felt about warring against one another, many settlers began to assume that all Indians must therefore be the enemies of all whites. Unable to strike back at the swift warriors threatening frontier settlements, the Scots-Irish of Paxton Township in Lancaster County, Pennsylvania, assaulted a small group of Christianized Susquehannock Indians at nearby Conestoga. On December 14, 1763, the "Paxton Boys" murdered six unarmed Indians—two old men, three women, and a child. Two weeks later, they massacred fourteen others who had been brought to the town of Lancaster for their own protection. One of the oldest victims had actually signed a treaty with William Penn back in 1701. When Governor John Penn removed 140 Moravian Mission Indians from the frontier to Philadelphia for safety, the Paxton Boys mustered several hundred men and marched on the capital to murder them all. "If I tho't that any of their Colour was to be admitted to the Heavenly World," explained one insurgent, "I would not desire to go there myself." Alarmed, even some Quakers began drilling in the streets of Philadelphia.

Benjamin Franklin denounced the Paxton Boys as "Christian white Savages," helped to organize Philadelphia's defenses against them, and led a delegation from the assembly which met the marchers en route at Germantown and persuaded them to go back home after receiving a list of their grievances. The Moravian Indians had been saved. But when all efforts to bring the murderers to justice failed, the frontiersmen of Pennsylvania and Virginia virtually declared an open season on Indians that continued through the next decade. Settlers in Augusta County, Virginia, slaughtered nine Shawnees in 1765. Frederick Stump, a German settler in backcountry Pennsylvania, murdered ten more in 1768 but could not be brought to justice because of the strong anti-Indian sentiment in the frontier counties. These and numerous individual homicides kept the western Indians smoldering on the verge of war for ten years after the collapse of Pontiac's coalition in 1764. In London, the British government hoped that its officials would bring an even-handed justice to the frontier that the settlers were incapable of achieving. Though the Indians derived real benefits from the Indian superintendents, such as protection from land speculators, they found little to choose between Amherst's smallpox blankets and the murderous rage of the Paxton Boys.

The Sugar Act

The Sugar Act of 1764 was the centerpiece of Grenville's war against smuggling. He had already ordered absentee customs officials to their posts and had commanded the navy to pursue illegal traders. The Sugar Act vastly increased the amount of paperwork required of merchants and ship captains and permitted seizures for what owners considered mere technicalities. In effect, Grenville tried to make it easier and much more profitable for British officials to hound colonial merchants than to accept bribes from them. The Sugar Act encouraged them to prosecute violators in vice-admiralty courts, which did not use juries, rather than in common law courts, which did. Moreover, under the act, British prosecutors were made virtually immune from any countersuit for damages, even when the merchant won an acquittal, provided the judge certified that there had been "probable cause" for the seizure.

In an innovation that most settlers found even more ominous, the Sugar Act proclaimed that "it is just and necessary, that a revenue be raised, in your Majesty's . . . dominions in *America,* for defraying the expenses of defending, protecting, and securing the same." The act put duties on Madeira wine, coffee, and certain other products, but Grenville expected the greatest revenue from the molasses duty of three pence per gallon. The Molasses Act of 1733, passed at the urging of British West Indian planters, had been designed to keep French molasses out of North America by imposing a prohibitive duty of six pence per gallon. Instead, through a bribe of about a penny a gallon, merchants were able to get French molasses certified as British. By 1760 over 90 percent of all molasses imported into New England came from the French islands. Planters in the British West Indies, with almost no North American market left to them, lost interest in New England, built their own stills, turned their molasses into high-quality rum, and sold it in Britain and Ireland. Nobody, in short, had any serious interest in wiping out the trade in French molasses. New England merchants said they were willing to pay a duty of one or perhaps even two pence, or roughly what bribes were costing them, but Grenville insisted on three. He hoped to generate a revenue of £100,000 per year from molasses, although in public he seldom put the figure above £40,000.

The Stamp Act

But the army in North America cost Britain about £225,000 a year. Other essential expenses, including the navy, transport, and Indian gifts, brought the annual total closer to £400,000. Grenville needed more revenue, and by 1764 he had decided that a stamp tax was the best way to raise it. Such a measure would almost be self-enforcing. By declaring that all contracts, licenses, commissions, and most other legal documents would be null and void unless they were executed on stamped paper, which had to be purchased from the government, a stamp act would require no other enforcement network once the system was in place. The courts would simply refuse to recognize any document that lacked the proper stamp. In the process, the colonists would quietly and voluntarily, even if grudgingly, accept the sovereign authority of Parliament in colonial affairs. A stamp duty would also have to be paid on all newspapers and pamphlets, a requirement likely to anger every printer on the continent. Playing cards and dice would also be taxed.

When Grenville pushed the Sugar Act through Parliament in early 1764, he announced that it might also be necessary to impose a stamp tax on America. No one in the House of Commons doubted that Parliament had the right to impose such a tax, he declared, and then announced the postponement of the measure until 1765. But because Parliament had never imposed a direct tax on the colonies, Grenville had to persuade the settlers that the Stamp Act was

The Deplorable State of America, or SC–H [i.e., Scotch] Government, March 22, 1765   This highly allegorical London cartoon was issued on the day that the Stamp Act became law. It blames Lord Bute (Scotch government) for the Stamp Act, portrays the Stamp Act as Pandora's box about to unloose its evils on Britain and the colonies, shows American liberty as a prostrate female about to die, and depicts Mercury (the god of trade) as about to flee. The king of France is bribing Bute (both a boot and the sun) to create more disturbances, while an ill wind shakes the Liberty Tree.

not really an innovation. His supporters insisted that the measure did not violate the principle of no taxation without representation. Each member of Parliament, they argued, represented the entire empire, not just a local constituency. The settlers were no different from the large non-voting majority of subjects within Great Britain. All were *virtually,* though not actually, represented in Parliament. Grenville also denied that there was any legal difference between *external* taxes (port duties, such as those imposed by the Sugar Act) and *internal* (or inland) taxes, such as those in the proposed Stamp Act.

Postponement, Protest, and Passage   At this point Grenville created great confusion, and, finally, a public relations disaster for the government. He favored postponement to collect fuller information about legal forms in the colonies, but he also indicated that, if the colonies could devise a plan more equitable and efficient than a stamp tax, he would be willing to listen. Without exception, all thirteen colonial assemblies at some point in 1764 or 1765 petitioned Parliament to object to a stamp act as a violation of

the principle of no taxation without representation. Some of the West Indian assemblies joined the protest. Most of the mainland colonies also attacked the revenue clauses of the Sugar Act. They too rejected the distinction between internal and external taxes by insisting that both violated the British constitution. While agreeing that they ought to contribute to their own defense, they urged the government to return to the traditional method of requisitions, in which the ministry asked a colony for a specific sum, and the assembly decided how (or whether) to raise it. Colonial spokesmen feared that direct parliamentary taxation might enable Britain to dispense with their assemblies altogether.

When the first round of these petitions reached London by early 1765, however, Parliament refused to receive them, citing a standing rule that forbade the acceptance of petitions against money bills and declaring that any petition that challenged the right of Parliament to pass such a tax was inadmissible on those grounds alone. To Grenville, the request for a return to requisitions was not a new idea. The system had often been tried, had never worked efficiently, and never would. He rejected the petitions with a clear conscience. But to the colonists, Grenville seemed to have acted in bad faith from the beginning. He had asked their advice and had then refused even to listen to it. Clearly, he had always meant to ram the tax down their throats, and nothing they could say mattered. By a margin of 245 to 49, the House of Commons approved the Stamp Act in February 1765, to go into effect on November 1.

The Currency Act and the Quartering Act   By then, Grenville had passed two other imperial measures. The Currency Act of 1764 was a response to the wartime protests of London merchants against Virginia's emissions of paper currency, which had been used for the colony's defense. (Virginia paper did depreciate somewhat after the war. In 1759, £140 of Virginia paper had been equivalent to £100 sterling; five years later, it took £160 of Virginia currency to acquire £100 sterling.) The Currency Act forbade the colonies to issue any paper money as a legal tender. The money question became all the more urgent because both the Sugar Act and the Stamp Act required that all duties be paid in specie, which usually meant silver, but also included gold. Supporters pointed out that both acts kept the specie in America to pay the armed forces, but the colonists responded that there was not enough specie to meet all of these demands, that the geographical distribution of this burden would not be equitable, and that the drain of specie from some colonies would put impossible constraints on trade. Boston and Newport, for instance, would pay quite disproportionate shares of the molasses tax, but the specie collected there would then follow the army to Quebec, New York, the Great Lakes, and Florida. Grenville saw "America" as a single region within which specie could circulate to the benefit of all. The colonists knew better. In 1765, America existed only in British minds, not yet in colonial hearts.

A final reform measure was the Quartering Act of 1765, which was requested by Sir Thomas Gage, General Amherst's successor as commander-in-chief. Gage requested parliamentary authority to quarter soldiers in private homes, if necessary, when on the road and away from their barracks. Grenville turned the problem over to Thomas Pownall, who had been governor of Massachusetts during its 1757 quartering crisis, which had been resolved by building the barracks that Gage now feared might not be adequate.

Pownall drafted a law that addressed the old situation, not the new one. It ordered the colonial assemblies to vote specific provisions, such as candles and beer, for the troops, which the assemblies were already doing voluntarily. But the act also required the army to quarter its soldiers only in public buildings, including taverns, which existed in large numbers only in cities. Pownall's Quartering Act became law. It solved no real problem, but as the government would soon discover, it created several new ones.

CONFRONTATION

The Stamp Act passed despite the protests of every colonial assembly and over the objections of most imperial officials within North America. After exhausting all legal means of preventing its passage, most colonial leaders resigned themselves to a situation beyond their power to change. Daniel Dulany, a Maryland lawyer who did more than any other colonist to expose the contradictions in Grenville's version of virtual representation, also drew a line short of overt resistance. "I am upon a Question of *Propriety,* not of Power," he explained. ". . . at the same Time that I invalidate the Claim upon which [the Stamp Act] is founded, I may very consistently recommend a Submission to the Law, whilst it endures." Some colonists, such as Jared Ingersoll in Connecticut and Richard Henry Lee in Virginia, even sought positions as stamp distributors. Ingersoll got one and earned the hatred of his neighbors. Lee changed his mind and emerged as a major patriot. But ordinary settlers were less fatalistic than their leaders. Some of them began to take direct action to accomplish what words alone could not do—prevent the implementation of the act.

British officials barely understood the householder economy of North America and its voluntaristic political values. The settlers were about to give them a painful education. Somehow, the British would manage to learn all the wrong lessons from the encounter.

SUGGESTED READING

Bernard Bailyn, *The Origins of American Politics* (1968) and Jack P. Greene, "Political Mimesis: A Consideration of the Historical and Cultural Roots of Legislative Behavior in the British Colonies in the Eighteenth Century," *American Histor-*

ical *Review,* 75 (1969), 337–367 clash sharply over provincial politics. Greene elaborates his position in *Peripheries and Center: Constitutional Development in the Extended Policies of the British Empire and the United States, 1607–1788* (1987). Alan Tully, *Forming American Politics: Ideas, Interests, and Institutions in Colonial New York and Pennsylvania* (1994), is a strong comparative study. More specialized studies include David Alan Williams, *Political Alignments in Colonial Virginia Politics* (1989); Robert M. Weir, " 'The Harmony We Were Famous For': An Interpretation of Pre-Revolutionary South Carolina Politics," *William and Mary Quarterly,* 3d ser., 26 (1969), 473–501; W. W. Abbot, *The Royal Governors of Georgia, 1754–1775* (1959); Alan Tully, *William Penn's Legacy: Politics and Social Structure in Provincial Pennsylvania, 1726–1755* (1977); Patricia U. Bonomi, *A Factious People: Politics and Society in Colonial New York* (1971); Stanley N. Katz, *Newcastle's New York: Anglo-American Politics, 1732–1753* (1968); William Pencak, *War, Politics, and Revolution in Provincial Massachusetts* (1981); Richard L. Bushman, *King and People in Provincial Massachusetts* (1985); and Jere R. Daniell, "Politics in New Hampshire under Governor Benning Wentworth," *William and Mary Quarterly,* 3d ser., 23 (1966), 76–105.

Richard Harding, *Amphibious Warfare in the Eighteenth Century: The British Expeditions to the West Indies* (1991) is the best account of the Caribbean theater during the War of Jenkins' Ear, while Carl E. Swanson, *Predators and Prizes: American Privateering and Imperial Warfare, 1739–1748* (1991) covers the privateering war against Spanish and French shipping. Jane Landers, "Gracia Real de Santa Teresa de Mose: A Free Black Town in Spanish Colonial Florida," *American Historical Review,* 95 (1990), 9–30; John Thornton, "African Dimensions of the Stono Rebellion," *American Historical Review,* 96 (1991), 1101–1113; and Larry E. Ivers, *British Drums on the Southern Frontier: The Military Colonization of Georgia, 1733–1749* (1974) provide important perspectives on the crisis in the Deep South, 1739–1742. T. J. Davis, *A Rumor of Revolt: The "Great Negro Plot" in Colonial New York* (1985) is standard. John A. Schutz, *William Shirley, King's Governor of Massachusetts* (1961) is a good introduction to King George's War. Strong specialized studies include Robert E. Wall, Jr., "Louisbourg, 1745," *New England Quarterly,* 37 (1964), 64–83; and John Lax and William Pencak, "The Knowles Riot and the Crisis of the 1740s in Massachusetts," *Perspectives in American History,* 10 (1976), 163–214.

Lawrence H. Gipson, *The British Empire before the American Revolution,* 15 vols. (1936–1972) is the most detailed narrative ever written for the period 1748–1776 and is ardently pro-empire. Volumes 4–5 cover the background to the fourth Anglo–French war, which Gipson calls "the Great War for the Empire." Volumes 6–7 cover the war in North America. Robert C. Newbold, *The Albany Congress and Plan of Union of 1754* (1955); Alison G. Olson, "The British Government and

Colonial Union in 1754," *William and Mary Quarterly,* 3d ser., 17 (1960), 22–34; and Paul E. Kopperman, *Braddock at the Monongahela* (1977) are standard. Francis Jennings, *Empire of Fortune: Crowns, Colonies, and Tribes in the Seven Years' War in America* (1988) tries to put Indians at the center of the conflict, not on the margins, as do other narratives. Guy Frégault, *Canada: The War of the Conquest* (1968) and D. Peter MacLeod, "The Canadians against the French: The Struggle for Control of the Expedition to Oswego in 1756," *Ontario History,* 80 (1988), 143–157 provide much-needed Canadian perspectives on the war and are both highly critical of Montcalm. Ian K. Steele, *Betrayals: Fort William Henry and the "Massacre"* (1990) is innovative and persuasive. Victor L. Johnson explores some of the dilemmas of smuggling in "Fair Traders and Smugglers in Philadelphia, 1754–1763," *Pennsylvania Magazine of History and Biography,* 83 (1959), 125–149. Fred Anderson, *A People's Army: Massachusetts Soldiers and Society in the Seven Years' War* (1984) emphasizes the contractual principles of colonial soldiers at the outset of the war. In *Empire and Liberty: American Resistance to British Authority, 1755–1763* (1974), Alan Rogers overstates the confrontation between colonists and imperial officials by failing to notice that it had largely been resolved by 1758. Harold E. Selesky, *War and Society in Colonial Connecticut* (1990) argues that the colonists became more soldierly as the war progressed. James Titus studies the impact of the war on Virginia society, in *The Old Dominion at War: Society, Politics, and Warfare in Late Colonial Virginia* (1991).

Tom Hatley, *The Dividing Paths: Cherokees and South Carolinians through the Era of Revolution* (1993) covers the Cherokee War. Howard H. Peckham, *Pontiac and the Indian Uprising* (1947), though aging badly, remains the standard narrative. Gregory E. Dowd, *A Spirited Resistance: The North American Indian Struggle for Unity, 1745–1815* (1992) explores the religious roots of pan-Indian identity; and his "The French King Wakes Up in Detroit: 'Pontiac's War' in Rumor and History," *Ethnohistory,* 37 (1990), 254–278 offers a fresh perspective on the goals of the rising. Bernhard Knollenberg, in "General Amherst and Germ Warfare," *Mississippi Valley Historical Review,* 41 (1954–1955), 489–494, 762–763, set out to refute the allegation of germ warfare and ended up affirming it. Alden T. Vaughan, "Frontier Banditti and the Indians: The Paxton Boys' Legacy, 1763–1775," *Pennsylvania History,* 51 (1984), 1–29 describes the murderous violence that followed the war.

Important recent studies of British politics and policy during and immediately after the war include Marie Peters, *Pitt and Popularity: The Patriot Minister and London Opinion during the Seven Years' War* (1981); Richard Middleton, *The Bells of Victory: The Pitt–Newcastle Ministry and the Conduct of the Seven Years' War, 1757–1762* (1985); John Brewer, *Party, Ideology, and Popular Politics at the Accession of George III* (1976); and John L. Bullion, *A Great and Necessary Measure: George Grenville and the Genesis of the Stamp Act, 1763–1765* (1982).

Chapter 6

Resistance, Revolution, and Independence

A View of the South Part of Lexington, April 19, 1775   This piece by Amos Doolittle, done in 1775, shows the retreat of the British toward Boston, under heavy fire, on the first day of the Revolutionary War.

Three successive crises destroyed the first British empire between 1765 and 1775. In the first, the Stamp Act crisis, the colonists began by petitioning for a redress of grievances, but when that effort failed, they nullified the Stamp Act and continued their resistance until Parliament repealed the tax in 1766. The colonists celebrated wildly. In the second, the Townshend crisis of 1767–1770, Parliament imposed several new taxes. The colonists petitioned and resisted simultaneously, mostly through an intercolonial non-importation movement. The British government responded by sending troops to Boston. After several violent confrontations, the British withdrew the soldiers and Parliament modified, rather than repeal, the Townshend Revenue Act, retaining only the duty on tea. Those gestures broke the back of the non-importation movement, but nobody celebrated the result. The third crisis began with the Tea Act of 1773 and quickly escalated. The colonists destroyed British tea without bothering to

petition first, Parliament responded with the Coercive Acts of 1774, and the settlers created a Continental Congress to organize further resistance. Because neither side dared to back down by 1775, the confrontation careened rapidly toward military violence. The war began in April 1775. Fifteen months later the colonies declared their independence.

Between 1765 and 1776 both sides found themselves trapped in a series of self-fulfilling prophecies. The British feared that without major imperial reforms the colonies would drift toward independence. Colonial resistance after 1765 increasingly convinced the British that an organized movement for independence was indeed under way, a fear that led to even sterner measures. The colonists denied that they desired independence, but they feared that the British government was deliberately planning to deprive them of their liberties. British taxes drove them toward a closer union with one another and finally provoked armed resistance. With the onset of war,

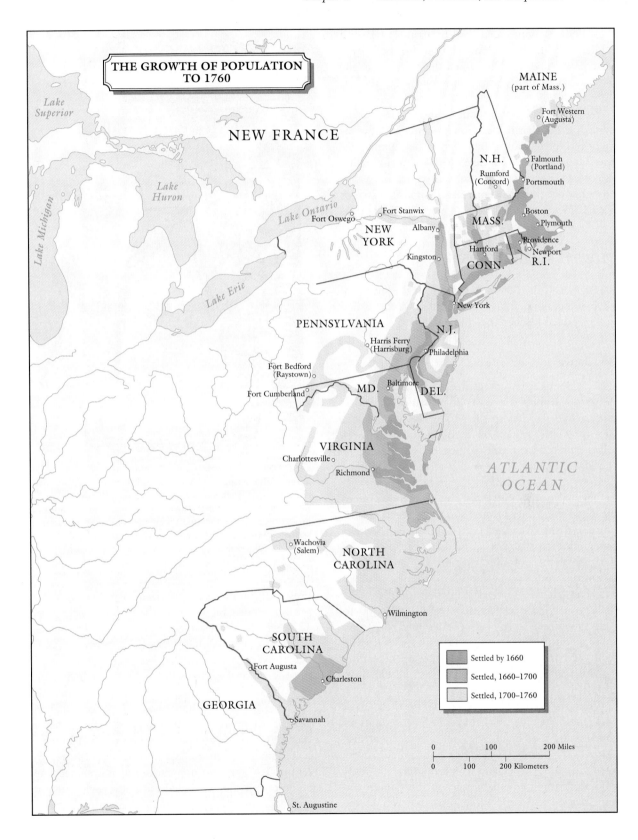

THE GROWTH OF POPULATION
TO 1760

Lake Superior

NEW FRANCE

Lake Michigan

Lake Huron

Lake Erie

Lake Ontario

MAINE
(part of Mass.)

Fort Western
(Augusta)

N.H.

Rumford
(Concord)

Falmouth
(Portland)

Portsmouth

Fort Oswego

Fort Stanwix

NEW
YORK

Albany

MASS.

Boston

Plymouth

Kingston

Hartford

Providence

Newport

CONN.

R.I.

New York

PENNSYLVANIA

N.J.

Harris Ferry
(Harrisburg)

Philadelphia

Fort Bedford
(Raystown)

Baltimore

Fort Cumberland

MD.

DEL.

VIRGINIA

Charlottesville

Richmond

ATLANTIC
OCEAN

Wachovia
(Salem)

NORTH
CAROLINA

Wilmington

SOUTH
CAROLINA

Fort Augusta

Charleston

GEORGIA

Savannah

	Settled by 1660
	Settled, 1660–1700
	Settled, 1700–1760

0   100   200 Miles

0   100   200 Kilometers

St. Augustine

both sides felt vindicated. The thousands of British soldiers heading toward America did not bode well for colonial liberties. And when the colonists finally did leave the empire, British ministers could also say, "I told you so."

Yet both sides were wrong. The British government had no plan to destroy representative government in North America, and almost no colonists favored independence before 1776. Only by following the three crises in some detail can we see how they brought about what no one had desired in 1765, or even 1774.

THE STAMP ACT CRISIS

Resistance to the Stamp Act began in the spring of 1765 and continued for a year until news that it had been repealed reached the colonies.

Resistance

Patrick Henry, a newcomer to the Virginia House of Burgesses, launched a wave of resistance by introducing five resolutions on May 30 and 31, 1765, after most of the members had gone home. His resolves passed by margins ranging between 22 to 17 and 20 to 19, and one was rescinded and expunged the next day. Henry had two more in his pocket that he decided not to introduce. But over the summer the *Newport Mercury* printed six of the seven resolutions, and the *Maryland Gazette* all seven. Neither paper reported that not all of them had passed. To the rest of the colonies, Virginia seemed to have taken a far more radical position than it actually had. The last two resolves printed in the *Maryland Gazette* claimed that Virginians "are not bound to yield Obedience to any Law ... designed to impose any Taxation upon them" except those passed by their own assembly, and that any person defending Parliament's right to tax Virginia "shall be Deemed, *an Enemy to this his Majesty's Colony.*"

When the colonial legislatures met for their fall or winter sessions, eight of them passed new resolutions condemning the Stamp Act. Nine colonies sent delegates to the Stamp Act Congress which met in New York City in October, and it passed a series of resolutions affirming colonial loyalty to the Crown and respect for Parliament while also condemning the Stamp Act and the Sugar Act. The Stamp Act Con-

Lord Bute and George Grenville Hung in Effigy, 1765 or 1766 This image, which shows both men (Bute is in kilts) chained to the devil, borrowed from the popular rites of Pope's Day (Guy Fawkes' Day), November 4. Especially in Boston, images of the pope, the Stuart pretender to the British throne, and the devil were destroyed each year on this day. Bute was especially vulnerable because his family name was Stuart.

gress, summoned to resist British policy, won far greater popular support than the Albany Congress of 1754, which had met to coordinate colonial resistance to French encroachments. By 1765 nearly all colonial spokesmen agreed that the Stamp Act was an unconstitutional measure, that colonial representation in Parliament (urged by a few writers) was impractical because of the distance and the huge expense, and that therefore the Stamp Act had to be repealed. North Americans accepted the idea of virtual representation, in which the assemblies claimed to represent both voters and nonvoters, *within* their separate colonies, but they ridiculed the notion when it was applied across the Atlantic. If a disfranchised Englishman acquired sufficient property, he became qualified to vote, pointed out Daniel Dulany of Maryland, whose pamphlet against the Stamp Act was widely admired, even in Britain. But, Dulany explained, no colonist, no matter how wealthy he became, could vote for a member of Parliament. Members of Parliament paid the taxes that they levied on others within Britain. But they paid none of the duties they imposed on the colonies.

Nullification

Resolutions and pamphlets alone, no matter how eloquent, could not defeat the Stamp Act. Street violence might, and Boston showed the way, led by angry men who called themselves "Sons of Liberty." On August 14 the town awoke to find an effigy of Andrew Oliver, the stamp distributor, hanging on what became the town's Liberty Tree (a symbol for the gallows on which enemies of the people deserved to be hanged). The sheriff admitted that he dared not remove the effigy, and after dark a crowd of men roamed the streets, shouted defiance at the governor and the council, demolished a new building Oliver was erecting that "they called the Stamp Office," beheaded Oliver's effigy and burned it on Fort Hill, and finally invaded Oliver's home "declaring they would kill Him," according to the governor's report. Oliver had already fled to a neighbor's home. Thoroughly intimidated, he resigned his office.

On August 26 an even angrier crowd all but demolished the elegant mansion of Lt. Governor Thomas Hutchinson, widely hated ever since he had led the fight to replace paper money with silver in 1749. Most Bostonians also believed, quite incorrectly, that Hutchinson had defended and even helped to draft the Stamp Act in letters to British friends. In fact he had opposed it, though quietly. Shocked by the destruction of property, the militia finally appeared to police the streets. But when Governor Sir Francis Bernard tried to arrest those responsible for the first riot, he got nowhere. Bostonians deplored the events of August 26 but approved those of August 14. No one was punished for either event even though the whole city knew that Ebenezer McIntosh, a poor shoemaker and a leader of the annual Pope's Day processions (see Chapter 5), had organized both riots.

Similar events took place in other colonies. Merchants adopted non-importation agreements to pressure the British into repeal. Everywhere except Georgia, the stamp master was forced to resign before the

law took effect on November 1. With no one to distribute the stamps, the act could not be implemented. Following Boston's lead, men calling themselves the Sons of Liberty took control of the streets and, after forcing the stamp master to resign, concentrated on reopening the ports and courts, all of which closed down on November 1 rather than operate without stamps. As winter gave way to spring, most of them resumed business. Only Newport matched Boston's level of violence, but in New York City a clash between the Sons of Liberty and the British garrison grew ugly and almost became an armed encounter. The violent resistance worked wonders. In twelve colonies, and eventually even in Georgia, the Stamp Act was nullified. Neither the courts nor the customs officers had any stamps to use because nobody dared to distribute them. Clearly, the next move was up to Britain.

Repeal

For reasons that had nothing to do with the colonies, the king dismissed George Grenville in the summer of 1765 and replaced his ministry with a narrow coalition organized primarily by William Augustus, duke of Cumberland, the king's uncle. Cumberland was known in some circles as "Billy the Butcher" for his ruthless suppression in 1746 of the Jacobite rebellion in Scotland, which had tried to restore the Stuart claimant, Charles III (or "Bonnie Prince Charlie"), to the British throne. An untested young nobleman, Charles Watson-Wentworth, marquess of Rockingham, took over the treasury. This "Old Whig" ministry had to deal with the riots in America, and Cumberland—the man who had dispatched Braddock to America in the winter 1754–1755—may have favored a similar use of force in late 1765. If so, he never had a chance to issue the order. Minutes before an emergency cabinet meeting summoned to consider the American crisis on October 31, he died of a heart attack, leaving young Rockingham in charge of the government. At first, Rockingham preferred simply to amend the Stamp Act, but by December he had decided on repeal. To persuade the other ministers, the king, and Parliament to agree would demand great skill. Rockingham encountered resistance to repeal from all of them.

To Rockingham, the only alternative to repeal seemed to be ruinous civil war in America. Only the massive use of force could reclaim the cities from the rioters. But as the king's chief minister, Rockingham could hardly admit to Parliament that mob action was forcing the world's greatest empire to back down. He needed a more persuasive reason for repeal. On December 6, even before the first American non-importation agreements were printed in London on December 12 (New York City's) and December 26 (Philadelphia's), he began to mobilize "public opinion," specifically, the major British merchants and manufacturers who traded with America. They cheerfully petitioned Parliament for repeal. They regarded the Grenville program as an economic disaster, and their arguments gave Rockingham the excuse he needed for repeal.

To win the concurrence of the other ministers, Rockingham had to promise his support for a Declaratory Act (modeled on an earlier one for Ireland, which had been passed but never really implemented), which would affirm the sovereignty of Parliament over the colonies. When William Pitt eloquently demanded repeal in the House of Commons on January 14, 1766, Rockingham gained a powerful though temporary ally. "I rejoice that America has resisted," Pitt declared. "Three millions of people, so dead to all the feelings of liberty, as voluntarily to submit to be slaves, would have been fit instruments to make slaves of the rest." Parliament "may bind [the colonists'] trade, confine their manufactures, and exercise every power whatsoever," he concluded, "except that of taking their money out of their pockets without their consent."

Rockingham also faced resistance from the king, who hinted to a member of Parliament that he favored "modification" rather than outright repeal. George III was apparently willing to repeal all of the stamp duties except those on dice and playing cards, the two items most difficult to enforce. But because only Grenville was ready to use the army to enforce even an amended Stamp Act, Rockingham brought the king around by threatening to resign, which would have forced the king to bring back Grenville, whom he hated. A long parade of pro-American witnesses appeared before Parliament to urge repeal, including Benjamin Franklin, who gave a masterful performance. Slowly, Rockingham put together his majority.

Three major pieces of legislation ended the crisis. The first repealed the Stamp Act because its "continuance . . . would be . . . greatly detrimental to the commercial interests" of the empire. The second, the Declaratory Act, affirmed that Parliament had "full power and authority to make laws and statutes of sufficient force and validity to bind the colonies and people of *America* . . . in all cases whatsoever." Rockingham successfully resisted pressure to insert the word "taxes" along with "laws and statutes." That omission permitted the colonists, who drew a sharp distinction between legislation (which, they conceded, Parliament had a right to pass) and taxation (which it could not), to interpret the act as an affirmation of their position, while nearly everyone in Britain read precisely the opposite meaning into the phrase "laws and statutes." Old Whigs hoped that Parliament would never again have to proclaim its sovereign power over America. Like the royal veto of an act of Parliament, that power existed, explained Edmund Burke; and like the veto, which had not been used for sixty years, it should never again be invoked. Colonists agreed with Burke, while fully conceding the power of Parliament to regulate their trade. They read the Declaratory Act as a face-saving gesture that made repeal of the Stamp Act possible. The Irish Declaratory Act had not led to parliamentary taxation of Ireland, and the settlers expected the same results for themselves in 1766.

The third measure was the Revenue Act of 1766, which amended the Sugar Act by reducing the duty on molasses from three pence per gallon to one penny. But the duty was imposed on all molasses, British or foreign, imported by the mainland colonies. Although the act was more favorable to colonial commerce than any other legislation affecting molasses yet passed by Parliament, it was hardly a simple regulation of trade. It was, beyond any doubt, a revenue measure, and it generated more income for the empire than did any other colonial tax. Burke justified it as a trade concession because, for the first time, it accepted the French molasses trade as legitimate. Colonial merchants welcomed it for precisely that reason, and few colonial spokesmen attacked it for violating the principle of no taxation without representation. On balance, the Rockingham ministry showed itself far more willing than the Grenville ministry to listen to colonial claims and to find mutually satisfactory solutions to problems.

Against the advice of their British friends, the colonists greeted repeal of the Stamp Act with wild celebrations, and over the next decade many communities publicly observed March 18 as the anniversary of the Stamp Act's repeal. Neither side grasped the misunderstandings that had made repeal possible and that would continue to perplex both of them over the coming decade.

In the course of the struggle, both sides, British and colonial, had rejected the distinction between "internal" taxes (the Stamp Act and other direct impositions) and "external" taxes (port duties). They could find no legal or philosophical basis for condemning the one while approving the other. Hardly anyone except Benjamin Franklin noticed in 1766 that the difference was quite real and that the crisis had in fact been resolved precisely according to that distinction. Parliament had tried to extend its authority over the internal affairs of the colonies and had lost. But it continued to collect duties on colonial trade, some for purposes of regulation, others explicitly for revenue. Though nobody knew how to justify this division of authority, the internal–external cleavage marked, even defined, the power axis of the empire, the boundary between what Parliament could do on its own and what the Crown could accomplish only with the consent of the colonial legislatures. Another misunderstanding was equally grave. Only the riots had created a crisis severe enough to push Parliament into repeal, but both sides preferred to believe that economic pressure had been decisive.

For the colonies, this conviction set the pattern of resistance for the second and third imperial crises. Powerful echoes resonated down through the nineteenth century, especially in Thomas Jefferson's embargo of 1807 and the Confederacy's cotton embargo of 1861. None of them really worked.

THE TOWNSHEND CRISIS

The atmosphere of peace and good will did not last long. In the summer of 1766 the king once more decided to replace his ministry, again for reasons that had nothing to do with the colonies. This time he persuaded William Pitt, the popular war minister in the struggle against France, to form a government (see Chapter 5). He and Pitt shared a contempt for the bloc of aristocratic families that had governed Britain most of the time since the Hanoverian Succession of 1714, most of whom were now Rockingham Whigs. Both considered political parties or factions immoral and put their faith in a government of "measures, not men." Pitt appealed to men of good will from all factions, but few responded. His ministry included many men who had supported the Grenville program, and it faced formidable opposition within Parliament. Pitt compounded his problems

The Repeal or the Funeral of Miss Americ-Stamp   This London cartoon of 1766 shows George Grenville carrying the coffin of the Stamp Act with Lord Bute behind him. Contemporaries would easily have identified the other personalities.

by accepting a peerage as earl of Chatham, a decision that removed his magnificent oratorical skills from the House of Commons to the House of Lords, and, after several months, left Charles Townshend as the government's chief spokesman in the Commons. A brilliant and witty extemporaneous speaker, Townshend had betrayed every leader he ever served under. The only point of real consistency in his political career of twenty years was his attitude toward the colonies. He always took hardline positions.

The Townshend Program

Chatham, who announced that he would solve Britain's revenue shortage by extracting millions from the East India Company, soon discovered that he could not control his government from the House of Lords without loyal spokesmen in the Commons. His East India bill got tied up in committee and had almost no chance of passage. During the Christmas recess in 1766–1767, Chatham apparently recognized his failure and began to slip into an acute depression that lasted more than two years. He refused to communicate with other ministers or even with the king. The colonists, who admired him more than any other Englishman of his day, expected sympathy and support from his administration. Instead they got Townshend, who began to take charge of colonial policy in the spring of 1767. The Stamp Act had taught Townshend, not that the measure was a bad idea and unenforceable, but that royal power was too weak in the colonies and had to be strengthened as a prelude to more substantial reforms.

But first, New York set off a small crisis by objecting to the Quartering Act of 1765 as a disguised form of taxation without consent. Under the old rules, when the army had asked for quarters and supplies and the assembly had voted them, consent had been an integral part of the process. Now one legislature, Parliament, was telling other legislatures, the colonial assemblies, precisely what they must do, and New York refused. The British government, after considering several draconian measures, passed the New York Restraining Act in 1767, which forbade the governor of the province from assenting to any legislation until the assembly had complied with the Quartering Act. The crisis fizzled out when the governor, by bending the rules a little, decided that the assembly had already complied with the essentials (but not all the specifics) of the Quartering Act even before the Restraining Act went into effect. The Quartering Act was supposed to help the army. Instead it weakened royal authority and colonial loyalties to Britain.

The Triumph of America (1766)   This London cartoon suggests that the pro-American attitudes of William Pitt, earl of Chatham, will drive Britain over a precipice. Chatham is the coachman, and America has taken over the British coach. Each horse is a different minister, some rushing eagerly to destruction, others more hesitant. Instead, Charles Townshend led the Chatham administration into renewed conflict with the colonies.

As chancellor of the exchequer, Townshend had to present the ministry's budget to the Commons. A central aspect of it was the Townshend Revenue Act of 1767, which imposed duties in colonial ports on certain imports that the colonies could legally get only from Britain: tea, paper, glass, red and white lead, and painter's colors. At the same time, Townshend removed more duties on tea within Britain than he could offset with the new revenue collected in the colonies. Revenue, clearly, was not his main object. His real goal was stated in the statute's preamble, which proposed that the new revenues be used to pay the salaries of governors and judges in the colonies, thereby freeing them from dependence on their assemblies. This rather devious strategy set off a wave of conspiratorial thinking in the colonies. Many otherwise sober provincials began to believe that, deep in the recesses of the British government, evil men were plotting to deprive them of their liberties.

Other measures gave appellate powers to the vice-admiralty courts in Boston, Philadelphia, and Charleston and established a separate American Board of Customs Commissioners to enforce the trade and revenue laws in the colonies. The Commissioners' headquarters was located in Boston, where resistance to the Stamp Act had been fiercest, rather than in centrally positioned Philadelphia, which would have been more convenient for administrative purposes and which had been rather quiet in 1765. Apparently, Townshend wanted a confrontation. At about this time the British army began to withdraw from nearly all the frontier posts and concentrate near the coast. Though the primary motive was to save money, the symbolic implications were striking. It was one thing to keep an army in America to guard new conquests and police the frontier and to ask the colonists to pay part of its cost. But an army far distant from the frontier presumably existed only to police the colonists themselves. Why should they pay any part of the army's expenses if its only role was to enforce policies that would deprive them of their traditional liberties? The Indians also felt threatened. Though the Proclamation Line of 1763 was still official policy, apparently the British government no longer intended to use force to protect Indian claims to their lands. When settlers provoked a frontier conflict in the Ohio Valley in 1774 (Lord Dunmore's War), the army was nowhere in sight. It was too busy with Boston.

Townshend justified his Revenue Act, first by ridiculing the distinction between internal and external taxes (which he attributed to Chatham and the colonists) and then by declaring that he would honor it anyway. Having won approval for his program, he died suddenly in September 1767, passing on to others the dilemmas he had created. Frederick, Lord North became chancellor of the exchequer.

Resistance and the Politics of Escalation

The internal–external distinction was troublesome for the settlers. Since 1765 they had been objecting to all taxes for revenue, but in 1766 they accepted the penny duty on molasses almost without complaint. Defeating the Revenue Act of 1767 proved tougher than nullifying the Stamp Act. Parliament had never managed to impose its will on the internal affairs of the colonies, as the Stamp Act fiasco had demonstrated, but it could control the ocean. Goods subject to duties might be aboard any of the hundreds of ships from Britain each year, but screening the cargo of every arriving vessel threatened to impose an enormous, perhaps impossible burden on the Sons of Liberty. A broader policy of general non-importation would be easier to implement, but British trade played a bigger role in the North American economy than North American trade did in the British economy. In order to hurt Britain a little, the colonies would have to harm themselves a lot.

Faced with these difficulties, the colonists divided over strategies of resistance. On August 31, 1767, the radical *Boston Gazette* proclaimed the death of liberty in America and called for complete non-importation of all British goods. The merchants' paper, the *Boston Evening Post,* disagreed. In October, even the Boston town meeting temporized by encouraging greater use of home manufactures, without explaining why women, who could not vote, should be willing to work harder to produce them (many of them were indeed willing). Boston also authorized the voluntary non-consumption of British goods. But no one was responsible for setting an agenda of resistance to the new measures, and for months nothing much happened.

Resistance emerged slowly. Whereas the Stamp Act had been nullified before it could go into effect, the Townshend duties became operative in November 1767 with little opposition. Beginning in December

1767 John Dickinson, a Philadelphia lawyer writing as "a Pennsylvania farmer," tried to rouse his fellow colonists to action through twelve urgent letters that were reprinted in nearly every colonial newspaper. Dickinson's *Letters of a Pennsylvania Farmer* denied the distinction between internal and external taxes, insisted that all parliamentary taxes for revenue violated the rights of the colonists, and wondered what Townshend's real motives may have been.

Once again, Boston set the pace of resistance. In February 1768 the Massachusetts assembly petitioned the king, but not Parliament, against the new measures. Without waiting for a reply, it also dispatched a Circular Letter to the other assemblies, urging all the colonies to pursue "constitutional measures" of resistance against the Quartering Act, the revenue acts, and the use of Townshend's revenue to pay the salaries of governors and judges. The implication was that, since Britain listened only to organized resistance, the colonies had better get together.

The British government got the point but did not like it. Wills Hill, earl of Hillsborough and secretary of state for the American colonies (an office that had just been created), responded so sharply that he turned tepid opposition into serious resistance. He ordered the Massachusetts assembly to rescind the Circular Letter and instructed all governors to dissolve any assembly that dared to accept it. The Massachusetts House voted 92 to 17 in June 1768 not to rescind, and the Sons of Liberty castigated the 17 dissenters as enemies of the people. Most of the other assemblies had shown little interest in the Townshend program, particularly in the southern colonies where all governors already had fixed salaries. But they bristled when told what they could or could not debate. All of them took up the Circular Letter or began to draft one of their own. One by one, the governors dissolved their assemblies until government by consent did indeed seem in peril.

The next escalation again came from Boston. On March 18, 1768, the town's celebration of the anniversary of the Stamp Act's repeal grew so raucous that the governor and the new American Board of Customs Commissioners asked Hillsborough for troops. Hillsborough ordered General Sir Thomas Gage, based in New York, to send two regiments to Boston. But on June 10, before Gage could do so, a big riot broke out in Boston when customs collectors seized John Hancock's sloop *Liberty* for having smuggled Madeira wine (taxed under the Sugar Act)

on its *previous* voyage. By waiting until the ship had a new cargo, informers and customs officials would have larger shares to split when the sloop was condemned. Terrified by the fury of the popular response, the customs commissioners fled to Castle William in Boston Harbor and again wrote Hillsborough for troops. This time, he dispatched two regiments from Ireland to Boston.

At about this time, non-importation at last began to take hold. Two dozen Massachusetts towns adopted pacts in which they agreed not to consume British goods. Boston merchants had drafted a non-importation agreement on March 1, 1768, conditional on its acceptance by New York and Philadelphia. New York agreed but Philadelphia balked, preferring to wait and see whether Parliament would make any effort to redress colonial grievances. There the matter rested until June, when the *Liberty* riot prompted most Boston merchants to agree to non-importation, effective January 1. New York again concurred, but Philadelphia held out until early 1769. By then it was obvious that Parliament would offer no concessions during the current session. Spurred on by the popular but mistaken belief that the non-importation agreements of 1765 had forced Parliament to repeal the Stamp Act, the colonists were again turning to a strategy of economic sanctions. Non-importation affected only exports from Britain. Tea, which was consumed mostly by women, was the most objectionable import of all. No one tried to block the importation of West Indian molasses, which was essential to the rum industry of Boston and Newport and which brought in about £30,000 a year under the Revenue Act of 1766. Rum was consumed mostly by men. On the other hand, the Sons of Liberty understood that virtually all molasses came from the French islands, and that non-importation could injure only French planters and American manufacturers and consumers, while putting no pressure on Parliament or British merchants. The only effective way to resist the penny duty was through smuggling, which continued at a reduced pace.

Believing that he now held a winning hand with the army on its way to intimidate the opposition, Massachusetts Governor Sir Francis Bernard leaked the news in late August that redcoats were approaching Boston. The public response left him flabbergasted. A delegation from the Boston town meeting asked him to call a special session of the legislature, which Bernard had dissolved in June after it stood by its Circular Letter. When Bernard refused, the Sons of Liberty asked the other towns to elect delegates to a "convention" in Boston. The convention became virtually the Massachusetts House of Representatives without its more conservative members. It had no legal connection to the institutions of royal government. Boston, professing to be alarmed by the possibility of a French invasion, also urged its citizens to arm themselves. When the convention met, it accepted Boston's definition of colonial grievances but refused to sanction violent resistance. The Boston radicals had no choice but to go along. They could not call the shots for the whole colony. Instead, the *Boston Gazette* portrayed the city as an orderly community (which it was most of the time) that had no need of British troops to keep the peace.

An Experiment in Military Coercion

The British fleet entered Boston Harbor in battle array by October 2, and landed about one thousand soldiers, sent by General Gage from Nova Scotia. They soon discovered that their most troublesome enemy was not the Sons of Liberty but the Quartering Act, which required that British soldiers be lodged in public barracks where available. Massachusetts had built such barracks—in Castle William, on an island miles away in Boston Harbor, where the soldiers

could hardly function as a police force. According to the act, any attempt to quarter soldiers on private property would expose the officer responsible to being cashiered from the service, after conviction by any two justices of the peace. And patriots controlled several justices, including John Hancock, James Bowdoin, Richard Dana, James Otis, Jr., and others. The soldiers pitched their tents on Boston Common (which was public property). Seventy men deserted in the first week, about 6 percent of the force. Eventually the soldiers took over a public building, the Manufactory House, which had once been used as a poorhouse. The two regiments from Ireland joined them later.

To warn the public against the dangers posed by a standing army in time of peace, the patriots compiled a "Journal of the Times" describing the ways in which British soldiers were undermining public order in Boston—clashing with the town watch, endangering the virtue of young women, disturbing church services, and starting fights. The Journal always appeared for the first time as a newspaper column in some other city, usually New York. Only later was it reprinted in Boston, after memories of any specific incident had probably grown hazy. Yet violence against customs officers ceased for many months. John Mein (pronounced "mean"), loyalist editor of the *Boston Chronicle,* caricatured leading patriots

Paul Revere's Engraving of the British Army Landing in Boston, 1768   The navy approached the city in battle array, a sight familiar to veterans of the French wars. To emphasize the peaceful, Christian character of Boston, Revere exaggerated the height of the church steeples.

(John Hancock, for example, became "the milch-cow of the disaffected") and began to publish customs documents that exposed merchants who were violating the non-importation agreement. This information was capable of destroying intercolonial resistance by discrediting leading Bostonians. Britain's experiment in military coercion seemed successful enough to justify withdrawal of half the soldiers in the summer of 1769.

Meanwhile, when news of the Massachusetts convention of towns reached Britain, Hillsborough angrily sent it on to the House of Lords. That body promptly escalated the crisis another notch by drafting a set of ominous resolutions that called for the deportation of colonial political offenders to England for trial. Instead of quashing dissent, this threat infuriated the southern colonies, which had not been deeply involved in resistance to the Townshend program. Virginia, Maryland, and South Carolina proceeded to adopt non-importation agreements. In the Chesapeake colonies, the movement had more support among planters than among the tobacco merchants, most of whom were Scots loyal to their parent firms. No enforcement mechanism was ever put in place. But Charleston took non-importation seriously. Up and down the continent, the feeble resistance of mid-1768 was becoming formidable in 1769. But its impact on Britain remained disappointing.

The Second Wilkes Crisis

In 1768, just as the Townshend Crisis was taking shape, George III dissolved Parliament and issued writs for the usual septennial elections. John Wilkes, an outlaw since 1765 (see Chapter 5), returned from France, ran for Parliament, and won a seat for the county of Middlesex. He then submitted to the law and received a sentence of one year in King's Bench Prison. Often, hundreds of supporters gathered on St. George's Field outside the prison to chant "Wilkes and Liberty!" or even "God save great Wilkes our king!" On May 10, 1768, the day that the new Parliament convened, his followers clashed with soldiers, who fired into the crowd, killing and wounding several. Wilkes denounced what he called "the massacre of St. George's Fields."

The House of Commons promptly expelled Wilkes and ordered a new election, but the voters again chose Wilkes. Two more expulsions and two more elections consumed the next year, until in April 1769,

after Wilkes had defeated his fourth opponent by 1,143 votes to 296, the exasperated Commons voted to seat the loser.

Wilkes had created a huge constitutional crisis. His adherents founded the Society of Gentlemen Supporters of the Bill of Rights, which raised money to pay off his very large debts and organized a national campaign on his behalf. About one-fourth of the voters of the entire kingdom signed petitions calling for the dissolution of Parliament and a new general election. Wilkites began to demand a reduction of royal patronage and sweeping reforms of the electoral system. In defiance of parliamentary privilege, they began the systematic publication of parliamentary debates. They also sympathized openly with North American protests, while in the colonies the Sons of Liberty began to identify their own cause with that of Wilkes.

If Wilkes lost, warned many colonists, their own liberties would be in jeopardy. The Wilkite number 45 (see Chapter 5), often combined with the number 92 (for those who refused to rescind the Massachusetts Circular Letter), became sacred in America. Two Virginians, Arthur and William Lee, became ardent Wilkites and quite active in London politics. Boston even printed a Wilkite parody of the Apostles' Creed. It began: "I believe in Wilkes, the firm patriot, maker of number 45. Who was born for our good. Suffered under arbitrary power. Was banished and imprisoned." And it ended by expressing faith in "the resurrection of liberty, and the life of universal freedom forever. Amen."

Wilkes's biggest impact was in South Carolina, where a newspaper hailed him as the "unshaken colossus of freedom; the patriot of England, the rightful and legal representative of Middlesex; the favourite of the people; the British Hercules, that has cleaned a stable fouler than the Augean." In 1769 the South Carolina assembly took a dramatic initiative by borrowing £1,500 sterling from the colony's treasurer and donating it to Wilkes's Bill of Rights Society. When the assembly included a £1,500 appropriation in the annual tax bill to cover the gift, the governor and council rejected the bill. Because neither side would back down, the assembly voted no taxes after 1769 and passed no laws after 1771. The colony's royal government came to a standstill over the Wilkes question.

The Townshend crisis and the Wilkite movement became an explosive combination in America. For

A Wilkite Cartoon, London, about 1774 John Wilkes, second from the right, finally gained a seat in Parliament in the general election of 1774. Here he points to Lord North, who is offering a bribe while North America burns in the background. Wilkes took strong, pro-American positions.

the first time, many colonists began to question the fundamental decency of the British government and its commitment to liberty. A ministerial conspiracy against liberty on both sides of the ocean began to seem quite credible.

The Boston Massacre and Partial Repeal

After the reduction of the Boston garrison, the Sons of Liberty resumed the tactics of direct confrontation, and the city again faced a serious crisis. The redcoats had intimidated Boston for nearly a year. Now Boston explored ways of intimidating them. The town watch often clashed with the army's guardposts because the watch, when challenged by the call "Who goes there?" refused to give the required answer: "Friends."

Under English common law, soldiers could not fire on civilians, without an order from a civil magistrate, except in self-defense when their lives were in jeopardy. By the fall of 1769 no magistrate dared to issue such a command. Clashes between soldiers and civilians grew more frequent, and justices of the peace singled out the soldiers for punishment. At one point, when town officials tried to arrest a British officer who was on duty commanding the guard at Boston Neck, Captain Ponsonby Molesworth intervened. He confronted a stone-throwing crowd by ordering the soldiers to bayonet anyone who got too close. A Boston justice later told him that common law did not regard a bayonet thrust as an act of self-defense against a stone, which was not a life-threatening weapon. Had the soldiers carried out the order, Molesworth could have been hanged for issuing the command.

By 1770 the power of the army had been sharply curtailed. When rioters drove editor John Mein out of town, the soldiers offered him no protection. "Go, Mein, to some dark corner of the world repair," mocked one poet, "And spend thy life in horror and despair." Once again the Sons of Liberty felt free to intimidate merchants who did not honor nonimportation. They nearly lynched Ebenezer Richardson, a customs informer who fired shots from his home into an angry stone-throwing crowd and killed an eleven-year-old boy, Christopher Seider (or Snider). Seider's funeral on February 26, 1770, was an enormous display of public mourning. Four or five hundred schoolboys marched ahead of the bier, which was carried by six youths and followed by thirty coaches and several thousand mourners. Richardson, though convicted of murder in April, was pardoned by George III.

A few days after the funeral, tensions between soldiers and citizens reached a fatal climax. Off-duty soldiers in Boston often tried to supplement their meager wages with part-time employment, a practice that angered hard-pressed artisans who resented the competition in the city's depressed economy. On Friday, March 2, 1770, three soldiers appeared at John Hancock's wharf looking for work. "Soldier, will you work?" asked Samuel Gray, a rope maker. "Yes," replied one. "Then go and clean my s——house," sneered Gray. The soldiers attacked but were beaten off. They returned with ten more soldiers but again had to retreat. Forty soldiers had no better luck. By then, Gray's employer, his brother John, had

The Life and Humble Confession of Richardson, the Informer (Philadelphia, 1770)   This shows Ebenezer Richardson firing from his window into a crowd of boys carrying his effigy. He killed Christopher Seider.

appealed to Colonel William Dalrymple to confine his men to barracks. Peace prevailed through the long Puritan sabbath that ran from sundown on Saturday to sunrise on Monday, but everyone expected trouble on Monday, March 5.

After dark, on Monday, firebells began ringing throughout the town, hundreds rushed into the streets, and civilians and soldiers clashed at several places. Finally, a crowd hurling snowballs and rocks closed in on the lone sentinel guarding the hated customs house, where the king's revenue was stored. The guard primed his musket and called for help. A corporal and seven soldiers, including two who had participated in the wharf brawl, rushed to his aid and loaded their weapons. Captain Thomas Preston then arrived, took command, and ordered the soldiers to drive the attackers slowly back with fixed bayonets. The crowd taunted the soldiers, daring them to fire. Apparently, one soldier slipped and discharged his musket into the air as he fell. The others then fired into the crowd, killing five civilians and wounding six. One of the victims was Samuel Gray; another was Crispus Attucks, a free black sailor.

With the whole town taking up arms, Governor Thomas Hutchinson averted civil war by ordering the soldiers to Castle William in Boston harbor, where the Sons of Liberty had insisted they belonged all along. Captain Preston and six of his men

stood trial for murder and were defended, brilliantly, by two radical patriot lawyers, John Adams and Josiah Quincy, Jr., who believed that every accused person ought to have a proper defense. Preston and four of the soldiers were acquitted, and the other two were convicted only of manslaughter, which permitted them to plead a legal technicality called "benefit of clergy." Through this device, they were branded on the thumb and released.

The Boston Massacre, as the Sons of Liberty called this encounter, instantly became the colonial counterpart to the Massacre of St. George's Fields in England. It marked the failure of Britain's first attempt at military coercion, as Benjamin Franklin had predicted four years earlier. When asked whether soldiers could impose the Stamp Act on unwilling settlers, he had told the House of Commons that the army "will not find a rebellion; they may indeed make one."

March 5, 1770, the day of the massacre, marked a turning point in Britain as well, for on that day Lord North asked Parliament to repeal the Townshend duties, except the one on tea. North regarded the duties as an anti-mercantile restriction on Britain's own exports and favored the repeal of all of them. But the cabinet had rejected complete repeal by a five-to-four vote back on May 1, 1769. As with the Stamp Act, Britain had three choices: enforcement, modification, or repeal. The ministry feared that Parliament would lose all credibility in North America if it again retreated completely, as it had in 1766. In effect, North chose the middle ground rejected in 1766 — modification rather than enforcement or total repeal. In his public pronouncements, he claimed to be retaining only a preamble without a statute, a vestige of the Townshend Revenue Act, while repealing the substance. In fact, he did the opposite. Tea provided nearly three-fourths of the revenue under the act. North retained the substance while surrendering the trivial.

This news reached the colonies just after the non-importation movement had achieved its most effective year in 1769. Although this effort had reduced imports by about one-third from what they had been in 1768, the impact on Britain was slight, partly because Britain found a lucrative new market for textiles when a clever British entrepreneur managed to sell new uniforms to Catherine II for the entire Russian army (see Table 6–1). North had hoped that partial repeal, though it might not placate all the colonists, would at least divide them. His reasoning proved correct. Most of the merchants faced depleted inventories and favored renewed importation of everything but tea, while the Sons of Liberty, most of whom were artisans, demanded the continuation of complete non-importation, a policy that would increase demand for their own manufactures.

Resistance collapsed first in Newport, where smuggling had long been the preferred method of challenging British authority. Then it spread to New York City, where the boycott on imports had been most effective. Soon Philadelphia caved in, followed by Boston in October 1770. By contrast, non-importation had hardly caused a ripple in the import trade of the Chesapeake colonies, where repeal in 1771 was only a formality. North's repeal was followed everywhere by an orgy of importation of British goods, setting record highs in all of the colonies.

Disaffection: The Aftermath of Repeal

Repeal in 1770 did not have the same impact as in 1766. There was no public rejoicing, not even when Lord North's government (he had become first lord of the treasury in January 1770) took further steps to reduce tension. The Quartering Act expired quietly in 1770, some of the more objectionable features of the vice-admiralty courts were softened, and the Currency Act of 1764 was repealed in stages between 1770 and 1773, as even London began to recognize that it was harming trade. Yet North failed to achieve reconciliation. Though he had turned some colonists against others, he had not restored confidence in the justice and decency of the British government. To a

Table 6-1

Exports in £000 Sterling from England and Scotland to the American Colonies, 1766–1775

Colony	1766	1767	1768	1769	1770	1771	1772	1773	1774	1775
New England	419	416	431	224	417	1,436*	844	543	577	85.0
New York	333	424	491	76	480	655*	349	296	460	1.5
Pennsylvania	334	383	442	205	140	747*	526	436	646	1.4
Chesapeake[†]	520	653	670	715	997*	1,224*	1,016	589	690	1.9
Lower South[‡]	376	292	357	385*	228	515*	575*	448	471	130.5
Totals	1,982	2,168	2,391	1,605	2,262	4,577*	3,310	2,312	2,844	220.3

Average total imports, 1766–1768 = £2,180
1769 = 73.6% of that average, or 67.1% of 1768 imports
1770 = 103.8% of that average, or 94.6% of 1768 imports

*These totals surpassed all previous highs

[†]Chesapeake = Maryland and Virginia

[‡]Lower South = Carolinas and Georgia

degree hard to appreciate today, the empire ran on trust, or what people at the time called "affection." Its opposite was *dis*affection, which meant something more literal and dangerous to them than it does now.

Many settlers blamed each other for failing to persevere until they had won complete repeal of the duties. A Philadelphia merchant attacked the "little dirty colony of Rhode Island" for having been the first to capitulate. Bostonians lamented the "immortal shame and infamy" of New Yorkers for abandoning resistance: "Let them . . . be despised, hated, detested, and handed down to all future ages as the betrayers of their country." One New Yorker retaliated by calling Boston "the common sewer of America into which every beast that brought with it the unclean thing has disburthened itself."

These recriminations, gratifying as they must have been to British officials, actually masked a vast erosion of trust in the imperial government. The colonists were angry with one another for failing to appreciate how menacing British policy still was. The tax on tea stood as a commitment to Parliament's unaltered sovereignty over the colonies. It symbolized a centralized imperial system, and—eventually, no doubt—it would bring higher taxes.

That underlying fear sometimes broke through the surface calm of the years 1770–1773. Rhode Islanders had often clashed with customs officials and had even fired on the king's ships on one or two occasions without arousing much interest in the other colonies. Then, in 1772, an unusually predatory customs vessel, the *Gaspée,* ran aground near Providence while pursuing some peaceful coastal ships. After dark, men with blackened faces boarded the ship, seriously wounded its commander, and burned the *Gaspée.* Britain responded by dispatching a panel of dignitaries to the colony with instructions to arrest the offenders and send them to England for trial. The inquiry failed, because no one would talk.

Twelve colonial assemblies considered this investigation so ominous that they created permanent committees of correspondence to keep in touch with one another and to *anticipate* the next assault on their liberties. Even colonial moderates now believed that the British government was conspiring to destroy freedom in America. When Governor Hutchinson announced in 1773 that, under the Townshend Act, the judges of the Massachusetts Superior Court would henceforth receive their salaries from the imperial treasury instead of from the General Court,

Boston established its own committee of correspondence and urged other towns to do the same. Hutchinson, amused at first, grew alarmed when most of the towns of any size created their own committees. That there was a plot to destroy their liberties seemed quite plausible to them. Boston's role as leader of the resistance movement had grown dramatically since the convention of 1768, and Boston lawyers, such as James Otis and John Adams, had become major spokesmen for the resistance movement.

The Boston Massacre trials and the *Gaspée* affair convinced London that it was pointless to prosecute individual patriots for breaking the law. Henceforth, whole communities would be punished. That choice brought the government to the edge of a precipice: Was the empire held together by law and consent, or only by force? The use of force against entire communities could easily lead to outright war, and war is not and cannot be a system of government. The spread of committees of correspondence within Massachusetts and throughout the colonies suggested that settlers who had been unable to unite against New France at Albany in 1754 now deemed unity against Britain essential to their liberties. By 1773 several New England newspapers were calling for a political union of the colonies.

In effect, the Townshend crisis had never ended. With the tea tax standing as a symbol of Parliament's right to tax the colonies without their consent, genuine imperial harmony was becoming impossible. North's decision to retain the tea tax in 1770 did not guarantee that armed resistance would break out five years later, but it severely narrowed the ground upon which any compromise could be built. The price of miscalculation had grown enormously.

INTERNAL CLEAVAGES: THE CONTAGION OF LIBERTY

For elite families in the colonies, any direct challenge to British authority carried high risks. They depended on the British Crown for their public offices, official honors, and government contracts, which in turn ratified their status in the social hierarchy and their claim to deference from lesser householders. Ever since the Stamp Act crisis, these families had faced a dilemma. Like the Hutchinsons of

Massachusetts, the DeLanceys of New York, or the Galloways of Pennsylvania, they could keep on good terms with Britain at the price of incurring the scorn and even hatred of many of their neighbors. Or they could champion the grievances of the community at the price of alienating British authorities. The Hancock and Bowdoin families in Massachusetts chose the second course, as did the Livingstons and Schuylers of New York, the Dickinsons of Pennsylvania, and most of the planter dynasties of Virginia. Within this process, the Townshend crisis became a far more accurate predictor of future behavior than response to the Stamp Act had been. Nearly everyone had denounced the Stamp Act, including such future loyalists as Daniel Dulany of Maryland and William Smith, Jr., of New York. By contrast, the merchants and lawyers who resisted non-importation in 1768 were likely to become loyalists by 1775. Artisans, merchants, and lawyers who supported the boycotts, especially those who favored continuing them past 1770, became patriots.

But even patriot leaders faced new challenges from within their own ranks. Artisans, who had mobilized to resist Britain in 1765 and 1769, began to demand more power, and tenant farmers in the Hudson Valley began to protest violently against their landlords. Discontent ran especially high in Boston, a city of fifteen thousand people, more than one thousand of whom were widows, most of them poor. Boston's economy had been faltering since the 1740s, but its taxes were still high. Britain's policies bore particularly hard on the town and gave an angry edge to its protests. From August 1765 until late 1774, Boston set the pace of resistance in every imperial crisis. In New York City, Philadelphia, and Charleston, artisans also began to play a much more assertive role in public affairs. Could the relatively new social hierarchy of the eighteenth century withstand these strains?

The Feudal Revival and Rural Discontent

Tensions increased in the countryside as well as in the cities. Three interrelated processes magnified social tensions in rural areas: a dramatic revival of long dormant proprietary charters, massive immigration, and the settlement of the backcountry from Pennsylvania to Georgia.

Between about 1730 and 1750, the men who had bought or inherited seventeenth-century proprietary or manorial charters began to see, for the first

time, the prospect of huge profits. These activities profoundly affected every colony from New York through North Carolina. The great estates of the Hudson Valley attracted few settlers before the middle decades of the eighteenth century, and those who arrived first received generous leases. A typical manor lord took in between £1,000 and £2,000 a year, while the Livingston and Van Rensselaer families did much better. But discontent increased as leases became more restrictive and as New Englanders moved into the area in the 1750s. The proprietor of Livingston Manor had difficulty putting down Yankee rioters in 1753. Dissatisfaction spread through much of the Hudson Valley over the next decade. In the summer of 1766 several thousand angry farmers, inspired by the Stamp Act riots, took to the fields and the roads, threatening to kill the lord of Livingston Manor or to pull down the New York City mansions of absentee landlords. The landlords had to bring in redcoats to suppress the rioters.

The proprietors of East New Jersey challenged many of the land titles of the descendants of the original settlers of Newark and Elizabethtown so that they could sell or lease the land, most of which had long been occupied by settlers who thought they owned their farms. The East Jersey proprietors, in firm control of the New Jersey courts, expelled several occupants and replaced them with their own tenants. A succession of land riots, in which farms were burned and jails broken open, rocked much of northern New Jersey for ten years after 1745. Even after the riots stopped, tensions remained high.

The Maryland and Pennsylvania colonies had brought few returns to the Calvert and Penn families before 1730, but in the last three or four decades before independence both families organized land sales much more carefully and began to collect quit-rents on a major scale. Frederick, seventh and last Lord Baltimore, milked Maryland for the princely income of £30,000 sterling per year until his death in 1771. His dissolute habits, which led to a notorious rape trial in which he was acquitted, brought him opprobrium on both sides of the Atlantic. Somewhat more slowly, the Penns made similar gains in their province. Their landed income rose to about £15,000 to £20,000 in the 1760s and then soared above £50,000 in 1772 and reached £67,000 in 1773, only to fall off sharply as the Pennsylvania government disintegrated over the next three years. With over half of their land still unsettled, they seemed well

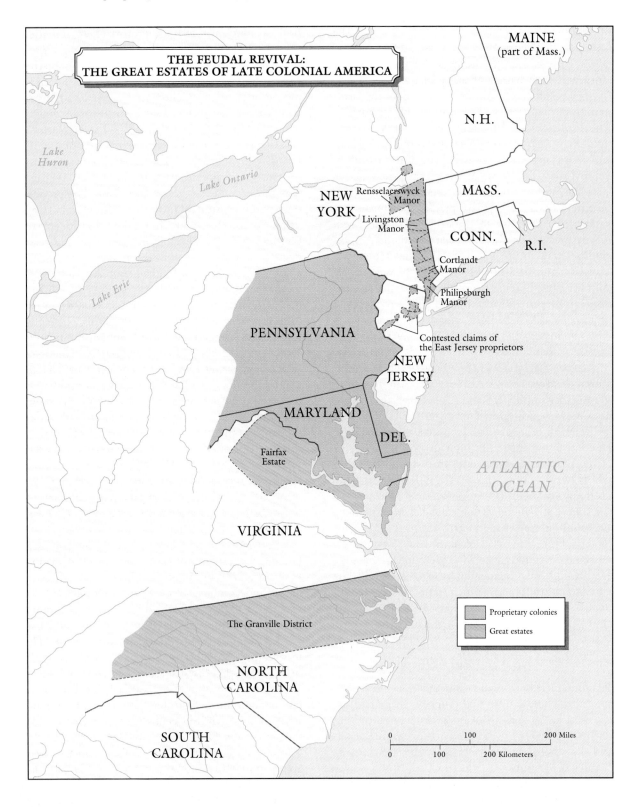

THE FEUDAL REVIVAL:
THE GREAT ESTATES OF LATE COLONIAL AMERICA

on their way to turning their colony into the most lucrative piece of real estate in the entire Atlantic world. But their reluctance to contribute to the war effort in the 1750s so angered Benjamin Franklin that, with the assembly's support, he went to London to urge the Crown to make Pennsylvania a royal colony. This campaign greatly weakened the province's resistance to the Stamp Act and the Townshend Revenue Act.

In Virginia, Thomas, sixth baron Fairfax acquired title to the entire northern neck of the colony (the land between the Potomac and the Rappahannock Rivers), which Charles II had granted to two courtiers in the mid-seventeenth century. The Fairfax estate contained five million acres and, by 1775, twenty-one counties. By then, he was drawing perhaps £5,000 a year from his holdings, but he managed to mute criticism by moving to the colony and setting himself up as a great planter (and the patron of young George Washington). Taken together, the New York manor lords, the New Jersey proprietors, and the Penn, Baltimore, and Fairfax claims blanketed the colonies from the Hudson Valley to the Rappahannock River. They became the biggest winners in the high stakes of America's "feudal revival," the reliance on old feudal charters for all of the profits that could be wrung from them.

In North Carolina, John Carteret, earl Granville—the only heir of the original Carolina proprietors to refuse to sell his share to the Crown in 1729 when both North and South Carolina formally became royal colonies—consolidated his claim as the Granville District after 1745, from which he received about £5,000 per year while living in England. This vast holding, which embraced over one-half of the colony's land and two-thirds of its population, deprived the North Carolina government of potential revenue from land sales and quitrents and forced it to resort to direct taxation. For several years after Granville's death in 1763, his land office remained closed, making it impossible for new settlers to acquire legal titles and touching off several riots.

For the most part, New England stood outside the feudal revival, except for Maine (then part of Massachusetts), where the effort to exploit old proprietary claims led to an explosion of rural discontent, most of it erupting after independence.

Massive immigration from Europe, mostly through the port of Philadelphia, and the settlement of the backcountry intensified social resentments. Most of the newcomers were Scottish or Scots-Irish Presbyterians, Lutherans, and German Reformed Protestants. They were dissenters from the prevailing faith in the colonies they entered, whether it was the Quaker religion in Pennsylvania or the Church of England from Maryland to Georgia. They antagonized Indians by squatting on their land and, quite often, by murdering those who seemed in the way—behavior that the Paxton Boys' march on Philadelphia in 1763 attempted to justify (see Chapter 5). In the Carolina backcountry, the newcomers provoked the devastating Cherokee War of 1760–1761, which left the region brutalized and demoralized.

The Regulator Movements in the Carolinas

In the aftermath of the Cherokee War, backcountry South Carolina faced an enormous crime problem. Great bands of outlaws, men who had been dislocated by the war, began roaming the countryside, plundering the more prosperous farmers and often raping their wives and daughters. As the violence reached a peak between 1765 and 1767, the more respectable settlers organized themselves as "regulators" (a later generation would call them vigilantes) to impose order in the absence of any organized government. Although South Carolina had long claimed jurisdiction over the backcountry, the colony's law courts were located in Charleston, over 100 miles to the east. The Anglican parish system, which provided what local government there was, had barely reached the backcountry. Even though a majority of the colony's white settlers now lived in the backcountry, it elected only two of the forty-eight members of the lower house of the legislature. In effect, it had no government.

The regulators, after obtaining commissions from Charleston as justices of the peace and militia officers, chased the outlaws out of the colony, many of them into North Carolina. They then returned home to impose order on what they called the "little people," poor settlers who often made a living through hunting, many of whom were suspected of having aided the outlaws. The discipline imposed by the regulators, typically whippings and forced labor, outraged its victims, who organized as "moderators" and petitioned the Charleston government to grant them legal recognition. With both sides claiming legality, about six hundred armed regulators confronted an equal force of moderators at the Saluda River in 1769. Civil war was avoided only by the arrival of an emissary from the governor bearing the striking message that South Carolina had finally decided to bring government to the backcountry by providing a circuit court system for the entire colony. Violence ebbed, but tensions remained. Eastern planters, by now a very wealthy group, continued to distrust the western settlers, at least until cotton brought plantations and slavery to the backcountry after independence and made the two regions more alike.

In North Carolina, the backcountry's problem was not the absence of government but its corruption. The settlers, mostly immigrant newcomers pushing south from Pennsylvania, found the county courts firmly under the control of men who had strong blood or business ties with powerful families in the eastern counties. As merchants, lawyers, and justices, these men seemed to regard local government as an engine for fleecing ordinary farmers through regressive poll taxes, fees, and court costs. North Carolina's own regulator movement took shape to reform these abuses. Although the backcountry counties contained over one-half of the colony's population, they elected only seventeen of the assembly's seventy-eight representatives by 1771. Since county officials were appointed by the governor, who got ahead depended on who had access to the governor's circle.

In 1768, inspired partly by South Carolina's example, North Carolina regulators refused to pay taxes in Orange County, which was part of the Granville District. Governor William Tryon responded by mustering 1,300 eastern militiamen, one-sixth of whom were officers, including over one-half of the assemblymen from the eastern counties. With eight generals and fourteen colonels, and led by an elite unit of Gentlemen Volunteer Light Dragoons, the force overawed the regulators for a time. But then, in a bid for a voice in the 1769 assembly, the regulators captured six seats, only to be consistently outvoted by the uncompromising eastern majority. Regulator assemblymen drafted some interesting petitions calling for the secret ballot, regular salaries (instead of fees) for justices and other officials, and a land tax rather than poll taxes. But when the regulators lost ground in the 1770 election, they stormed into the town of Hillsborough, closed the Orange County Court, and

whipped Edmund Fanning, a Yale graduate whose aggressive pursuit of fees had made him the most detested official in the backcountry. They also seized the court docket and scribbled unflattering comments next to many of the names of their creditors. Governor Tryon responded by marching one thousand militiamen westward. They engaged and scattered over two thousand regulators in early 1771 at the battle of Alamance Creek. Seven regulator leaders were hanged, while others fled the colony. North Carolina would enter the struggle for independence as a bitterly divided society. In that colony, the eastern elite defied British authority only to find their own legitimacy violently challenged.

An Alliance of the Powerless: Women and Slaves

In Charleston, South Carolina, in 1765, the Sons of Liberty paraded through the streets chanting "Liberty and No Stamps." Later, they were stunned to see slaves marching in a parade of their own shouting, "Liberty! Liberty!" Without much success, merchant Henry Laurens tried to reassure himself that Africans probably did not know the meaning of the word.

Around the middle of the century, slavery came under sustained fire for the first time. The antislavery movement arose on both sides of the Atlantic and attracted both advocates and opponents of the American Revolution. Some of them came from unlikely backgrounds. John Newton, for instance, had been the skipper of a slave ship until he experienced a mid-Atlantic conversion in the 1750s, returned to England, became an Anglican clergyman, and joined others in denouncing the slave trade. He wrote what may well be the best-loved hymn in the English language, and its first stanza probably does reflect what the slave trade had taught him:

> Amazing grace, how sweet the sound
> That saved a wretch like me.
> I once was lost, but now I'm found,
> Was blind, but now I see.

In the colonies, Quakers led the assault on slavery. In the 1740s and 1750s, Benjamin Lay, John Woolman, and Anthony Benezet urged fellow members of the Society of Friends to emancipate their slaves. Between 1754 and 1758 the Quaker Yearly Meeting prohibited any involvement in the slave trade and finally, in 1774, forbade slaveholding altogether. Any member who had not complied by 1779 was disowned. Britain's Methodist leader John Wesley, in almost every other respect a social conservative, also attacked slavery, as did several disciples of Jonathan Edwards. Two and three decades after the Great Awakening, many evangelicals began to agree with the position taken by Hugh Bryan in South Carolina in 1742 (see Chapter 4), that slavery was a sin.

By the 1760s and 1770s, for the first time, supporters of slavery had to defend the institution. Hardly anyone had bothered to justify it before 1750, probably because social hierarchy seemed both necessary and inevitable. Slavery was merely an extreme example of a pattern in which most people were dependent upon someone of higher social status. But as many people began speaking about equal rights, a few of them started to ask whether *all* people could claim the benefit of this principle. Thus slavery came under attack. In Scotland, Adam Smith, soon to become the leading economic thinker of the age, praised African slaves for their "magnanimity" which, he claimed, "the soul of the sordid master is scarce capable of conceiving." Arthur Lee, a wealthy Virginian, ably defended the character of his fellow planters against Smith's charge but discovered that he could not justify slavery, "always the deadly enemy to virtue and science." Patrick Henry agreed. Slavery, he wrote, "is as repugnant to humanity as it is inconsistent with the Bible and destructive of liberty." He himself kept slaves, but only because of "the general inconvenience of living without them. I will not, I cannot justify it." In England, Granville Sharp, an early abolitionist, brought the Somerset case before the Court of King's Bench in 1771 and compelled a very reluctant Chief Justice William Murray, baron Mansfield, to declare that slavery was incompatible with the "free air" of England. That decision gave the ten thousand to fifteen thousand slaves living in England a chance to claim their freedom. (The U.S. Supreme Court, ruling on the same question in the Dred Scott case of 1857, would reach the opposite conclusion.)

With the courts challenging slavery in Britain, with Quakers taking decisive steps against it in the Middle Colonies, and with even great planters expressing doubts about it, New Englanders began to move as well. Two women, Sarah Osborn and Phyllis Wheatley, played influential roles in the movement. Osborn, an English immigrant to Newport, Rhode Island, opened a school in 1744 to support her fam-

ily after having been widowed twice. A friend of the revivalist George Whitefield, she admitted women and blacks to her classes and began holding evening religious meetings, which turned into a big local revival. At one point in the 1760s, about one-sixth of Newport's Africans were attending her school, which made them the most literate African population in the colonies, though located in the most active slave-trading port on the continent. Her students strongly supported abolition of the slave trade and, later, slavery itself. Osborn sent two of her African pupils to Princeton to be tutored in classics by John Witherspoon. Had the Revolutionary War not broken out, they would have become the first black college students in American history.

Eight-year-old Phillis Wheatley arrived in Boston from Africa in 1761 and was bought by wealthy John Wheatley as a servant for his wife Susannah, who treated her more like a daughter than a slave, taught her to read and write, and emancipated her when she came of age. Phillis published her first poem in Boston in 1767, and in 1772 a volume of her poetry was printed in London, making her a transatlantic celebrity by age twenty. Her poems rejoiced in the Christianization of Africans while deploring slavery.

As time passed, many of the slaves in Boston began to sense an opportunity for emancipation. On several occasions in 1773–1774, they petitioned the legislature or the governor for freedom, pointing out that, though they had never forfeited their natural rights, they were being "held in slavery in the bowels of a free and Christian Country." When the legislature passed one bill on their behalf, Governor Hutchinson vetoed it. Boston slaves made it clear to General Gage, Hutchinson's successor, that they would even serve him as a loyal militia, provided he gave them their freedom. In short, they offered political allegiance to whichever side supported their emancipation. Many patriots began to rally to their cause. "If we would look for Liberty ourselves," the town of Medfield advised the Boston Committee of Correspondence in 1773, ". . . we ought not to continue to enslave others but immediately set about some effectual method to prevent it for the future."

As the colonies entered the final imperial crisis, they faced the possibility that any direct challenge to British power would set off enormous social changes among themselves. Freedom's ferment made a heady wine.

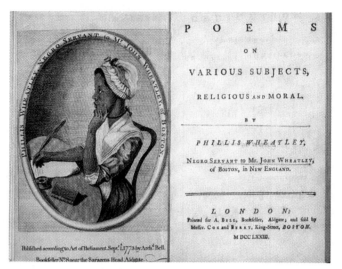

Phillis Wheatley   Engraving of Phillis Wheatley opposite the title page of her collected poems, published in 1773.

THE LAST IMPERIAL CRISIS

The surface calm between 1770 and 1773 ended when Lord North's government, reeling under a severe credit crisis since 1772, moved to bail out the East India Company, Britain's largest business corporation, which was hovering on the brink of bankruptcy. The company, undersold in populous southeastern England and the colonies by smuggled Dutch tea, had warehouses bulging with millions of pounds of tea and no place to sell it. North's response was aimed at saving the company. The colonies played only a secondary role in his thinking. His policy threw North America into a crisis too big for Britain to handle, without solving the East India Company's problems.

The Tea Crisis and the Boston Tea Party

North decided that the best way to restore the East India Company's health was to empower it to undersell its rivals, especially the smugglers of Dutch tea. Benjamin Franklin, still in London as the agent of several colonies, reminded the government that it could accomplish that objective in the colonies by repealing the Townshend duty. North rejected that idea. Instead, his Tea Act of 1773 repealed existing taxes on tea within England but retained the Townshend duty in the colonies. In both places, North calculated, the East India Company's tea would be cheaper than anyone else's. The company would be

saved, and the settlers, by voluntarily buying legal tea, would accept Parliament's right to tax them. Nobody, he reasoned, would tear a government apart for lowering the price of tea. He was wrong.

One other aspect of the Tea Act antagonized most merchants in the colonies. Formerly, the company had sold its tea to all comers at public auctions in London, but the Tea Act also gave it a monopoly on the shipping and distribution of tea in the colonies. Its own vessels would carry it, and a small group of consignees in each port would have the exclusive right to sell it. The combined dangers of taxation and monopoly again brought together the coalition of artisans and merchants that had defeated the stamp tax in 1765 and resisted the Townshend duties in 1769. The Sons of Liberty believed that the Tea Act was a Trojan horse that would undermine colonial liberty forever by prompting the settlers to accept Parliament's power to tax them. Merchants were enraged by the company's monopoly over the distribution of tea. Quite unintentionally, North gave a tremendous advantage to those determined to resist the Tea Act. He had devised an "external," or oceanic, measure that the colonists could nullify despite Britain's control of the seas. This time, no one had to police the entire waterfront looking for offenders. The Sons of Liberty had only to wait for the specially chartered tea ships and then prevent them from landing their cargoes.

Direct threats usually did the job. As Captain Ayres approached Philadelphia with the hated tea, the Sons of Liberty greeted him with a rude welcome: "What think you Captain, of a halter around your neck—ten gallons of liquid tar decanted on your pate—with the feathers of a dozen wild geese laid over that to enliven your appearance? Only think seriously of this—and fly to the place from whence you came—fly without hesitation—without the formality of a protest—and above all, Captain Ayres, let us advise you to fly without the wild geese feathers." Ayres quickly gathered his clearance papers and departed without trying to land the tea, a scene that was repeated in every port except Boston.

There, Governor Hutchinson, whose relatives were the local tea consignees, decided that someone had to face down the radicals. To force the issue, he refused to grant clearance papers to the three ships carrying the tea. Under the law, they had to pay the Townshend duty within twenty-one days of their arrival or face confiscation. Throughout the first half of December this timetable provided the opportunity for mass meetings and generated a growing sense of crisis. Finally convinced that there was no other way to block the landing of the tea, Boston radicals disguised themselves as Indians and threw 342 chests of tea, worth about £11,000 sterling (roughly $700,000 in 1995 dollars), into Boston harbor on the night of December 16, 1773.

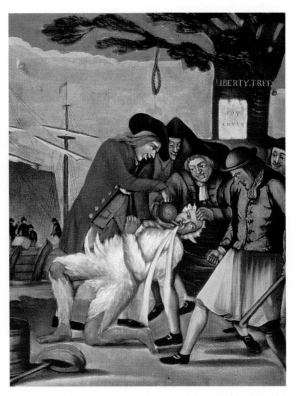

The Bostonians Paying the Excise-Man, or Tarring and Feathering   This London cartoon of 1774 satirized the Sons of Liberty.

Britain's Response: The Coercive Acts

This willful destruction of private property shocked many supporters of colonial resistance in both Britain and America. The news swiftly crossed the Atlantic and reached Parliament in January, early in its annual session. Convinced that severe punishment was essential to British credibility, North's government passed four Coercive Acts during the spring of 1774. The Boston Port Act, which became law in late March, closed the port of Boston. Until the tea had been paid for, only food could be imported. A new Quartering Act gave British officers the power to quarter soldiers on civilians if necessary. The Administration of Justice Act (a response to the Boston Massacre trials) permitted a British soldier or official who was charged with a crime while carrying out his duties to be tried either in another colony or in Great Britain. Most controversial of all was the Massachusetts Government Act, passed in late May, which amended the Massachusetts Charter of 1691 by making the council appointive and by sharply restricting

the power of town meetings. To enforce the new policies, the king made General Gage, already the commander-in-chief of the British Army in North America, the new governor of Massachusetts, with the clear implication that he could use military force against civilians whenever he thought it necessary.

Passed at the same time as the Coercive Acts was a fifth, unrelated measure. The Quebec Act established French civil law and the Roman Catholic Church in the Province of Quebec, provided for trial by jury in criminal but not in civil cases, gave legislative power (but *not* the power to tax) to an appointive governor and council, and extended the administrative boundaries of Quebec to the area between the Great Lakes and the Ohio River, saving only the legitimate charter claims of other colonies which presumably would have to be adjudicated later. Historians now regard the act as a farsighted measure that showed much greater toleration for French Catholics than the empire had been willing to accord the Acadians twenty years earlier. But settlers from New England to Georgia

The Able Doctor, or America Swallowing the Bitter Draught   This engraving by Paul Revere (1774) used *The Bostonians Paying the Excise-Man* as a model but turned it into a patriot statement. In Revere's version, the British are forcing tea down the throat of America (who also represents liberty), and they are imposing martial law on Boston.

disagreed. They saw not a new policy of conciliation and toleration but a deliberate revival of the power of New France and the Catholic Church on their northern boundary, this time bolstered by Britain's naval and military might. Like the Townshend program and the Tea Act, the Quebec Act gave credibility to the fear that wicked ministers in London were conspiring to destroy British and colonial liberties. Many British colonists suspected that the autocratic government of Quebec would eventually provide a model for restructuring their own provinces. The settlers lumped the Quebec Act together with the Coercive Acts and coined their own name for all of them. They called them the Intolerable Acts.

The Radical Explosion

The interval between the passage of the Boston Port Act in March 1774 and the Massachusetts Government Act in May of that year permits us to measure with some precision the response that each provoked. The Port Act, which was quite enforceable and could not be directly countered by the colonists, led to another round of non-importation and to the summoning of the First Continental Congress. The Massachusetts Government Act, by contrast, was nullified by the colonists. It led to war. The soldiers who marched to Concord on April 19, 1775, went

there to enforce that statute against settlers who had no intention of obeying it.

General Gage took over the governorship of Massachusetts in May 1774 (before the Massachusetts Government Act had been passed). In early June he closed the ports of Boston and Charlestown, just north of Boston. British naval support gave him more than enough power to do so. At first, the Bostonians split over the Port Act. Many merchants wanted to abolish the Boston Committee of Correspondence and pay for the tea in order to avoid an economic catastrophe. But they were badly outvoted in a huge town meeting. The committee then called for a colonial union and for immediate non-importation and non-consumption of British goods. But, by this time, many radicals were losing patience with non-importation as a tactic. After all, the Port Act, by closing Boston, already made it impossible to import or export. The radicals grew discouraged when a mass meeting in New York City rejected immediate non-importation in favor of an intercolonial congress. Philadelphia followed New York's lead. Cautious merchants hoped that a congress might postpone or prevent radical measures of resistance.

North assumed that his policy could isolate Boston from the rest of the province, Massachusetts from the rest of New England, and New England from the other colonies, a goal that Britain would pursue through 1777. Despite momentary success among New York and Philadelphia merchants, Gage quickly learned that none of these objectives was achievable. London kept hoping, however, despite the evidence.

Soon, contributions were pouring in from all the colonies to help Boston survive. The Stamp Act crisis and the Townshend crisis had been largely urban affairs. This one mobilized the countryside on a scale never seen before. When royal governors prorogued, or dissolved, their assemblies to prevent them from joining the resistance movement, the colonies did what Massachusetts had done in 1768. They elected conventions, usually called provincial congresses, to organize resistance. These bodies tended to be much larger than the legal assemblies that they displaced, and they played a major role in politicizing the countryside. As the congresses took hold in the summer of 1774, royal government began to collapse almost everywhere.

Demands for a continental congress increased so dramatically that by June the movement was irresistible. It was also becoming obvious, even to conservative New York and Philadelphia merchants, that any congress would have to adopt non-importation, and even they had already committed themselves to the results of such a congress. Except for some details, that issue was settled, even before the Congress met, by the mandates that the delegates brought with them.

Despite all this activity, Gage remained optimistic through most of the summer. Then, news of the Massachusetts Government Act arrived on August 6. Gage's authority disintegrated when he tried to enforce the act, which marked the most dramatic attempt yet made by Parliament to assert control over the internal affairs of the colonies. The so-called mandamus councilors, whom Gage appointed to the new upper house under the act, either resigned their seats or fled to Boston to seek the protection of the army. The Superior Court could not hold its sessions, even in Boston under the guns of the army, because jurors refused to take an oath under the new law. At the county level, the real center of royal power in Massachusetts, a series of unprecedented conventions closed the courts and took charge of local events in August and September.

Before this explosion of radical activity, Gage had called for a new General Court to meet in Salem in October. Many towns elected representatives. But others followed the lead of the Worcester County Convention, which in August called on all towns to elect delegates to a provincial congress that would meet in the town of Concord, seventeen miles inland, out of range of the British navy. Although Gage revoked his call for a new General Court, about ninety representatives met at Salem anyway. When Gage refused to recognize them, they adjourned to Concord in early October, where they joined two hundred delegates already gathered there as the Massachusetts Provincial Congress. This body promptly emerged as the de facto government of the colony and began to implement the radical demands of the Suffolk County Convention. The Suffolk Resolves called for a purge of unreliable militia officers, the creation of a special force of "minutemen" capable of rapid response to any emergency, and the payment of all provincial taxes to the congress in Concord, not to Governor Gage in Boston. To carry out its own executive functions, the Provincial Congress named some of its members as a Committee of Public Safety and began to collect arms and ammunition at Concord.

North had assumed that Gage's army would uphold his new government in Massachusetts. Instead, Gage's government survived only where the army could protect it around the clock. That did not include Salem, which was supposed to remain Gage's capital until the tea was paid for. The alternative to government by consent was becoming no British authority in Massachusetts. For example, in the pre-dawn hours of September 1, Gage sent an expedition to confiscate 250 half-barrels of gunpowder, the largest supply in New England, stored a few miles outside Boston. He got the powder, but the incursion prompted perhaps one-third of the militia of New England to march toward Boston, until they were turned back with the assurance that no one had been killed. In several later raids, the colonists always beat Gage's men to the gunpowder. By October, Gage's power was limited to the town of Boston, which his garrison and the fleet still controlled. Increasingly despondent and unable to put his three thousand soldiers to any constructive use, he tried on October 30 to explain to North that the commitment of "a small Force rather encourages Resistance than terrifys." He then stunned the British government by requesting twenty thousand redcoats, nearly as many as had been needed to conquer New France.

The First Continental Congress

From 1769 into 1774, colonial patriots had looked to John Wilkes in London for leadership. With the meeting of the First Continental Congress, they began relying on themselves. Twelve colonies (all but Georgia) sent delegates to the Congress, which gathered at Philadelphia's Carpenters' Hall, a center of artisan strength, in September 1774. The delegates scarcely even debated non-importation except for some details. Southern colonies insisted, for example, that non-importation finally be extended to molasses, which continued to generate taxes under the Revenue Act of 1766, and the New Englanders agreed. The delegates were almost unanimous in approving non-exportation as a second step to be taken by August 1775, if Britain had not redressed colonial grievances by then. Non-exportation was a much more radical tactic than non-importation because it contained the implicit threat of repudiating debts to British merchants, which were normally paid off with colonial exports. Joseph Galloway, already Pennsylvania's leading loyalist, submitted an imaginative plan of imperial union that would have required all legislation affecting the colonies to be passed by both Parliament and an intercolonial congress in America, but his proposal was tabled by a vote of six colonies to five.

The Congress spent three weeks debating how to define American rights. Everyone (even Galloway) agreed that the Coercive Acts, the Quebec Act, and all surviving revenue acts had to be repealed and that encroachments on trial by jury had to be rejected. Issues of specific interest to merchants — customs abuses, paper currency, the Tea Act — were listed as "Grievances" but were not included among the issues that had to be resolved to end the crisis. The delegates, in other words, generally agreed on what was needed to break the impasse, but they had difficulty finding the legal and ideological language in which to embody their demands.

The slogans of 1765 were no longer adequate in 1774. Neither "No taxation without representation" nor the distinction between taxation and legislation addressed the problem created by the Massachusetts Government Act, in which Parliament had changed the internal government of a colony against its obvious wishes. Following the lead of such pamphleteers as Thomas Jefferson of Virginia and James Wilson of Pennsylvania, Congress declared that any *legislation* affecting them but passed without their consent was a violation of their rights as Englishmen and as men. But this formulation raised a new dilemma. Few delegates wanted to challenge the empire's navigation and trade acts, passed as far back as 1650. And yet those acts were obvious examples of parliamentary legislation that directly affected the colonists. The delegates finally accepted John Adams' wording that "from the necessity of the case . . . , we cheerfully consent to the operation of such acts of the British parliament, as are bona fide, restrained to the regulation of our external commerce, . . . excluding every idea of taxation, internal or external, for raising a revenue upon the subjects in America, without their consent." The delegates believed that this article enabled them to uphold the trade laws. In Britain it looked like a prelude to repudiating them. If the acts now rested only on colonial consent, that consent could be withdrawn.

The Congress petitioned the king rather than Parliament because it no longer recognized Parliament as a legitimate legislature for the colonies. It sent addresses to the people of the thirteen colonies, the people of Quebec, and the people of Great Britain. It took two other radical steps. On October 20, it created the Association to enforce its trade sanctions against Britain, and it asked every local community to establish committees of observation to carry out non-importation. This call became a major step in the radicalization of the countryside. Most towns and counties heartily embraced the idea, and perhaps seven thousand settlers served on such committees during the winter of 1774–1775. In approving the Association, the Congress was beginning to act as a central government for the united colonies. In a second dramatic step, it agreed to meet again in May 1775 if the British response was not satisfactory.

Toward War

The news from Boston and Philadelphia shook the North ministry. "The New England Governments are in a State of Rebellion," George III told North; "blows must decide whether they are to be subject to this Country or independent." Although Benjamin Franklin kept assuring the British that Congress meant exactly what it said, both the government and the opposition assumed that conciliation could be achieved on lesser terms than those demanded by Congress. Edmund Burke, out of office since 1766, urged a return to pre-1763 understandings. "A great empire and little minds go ill together," he cautioned in a speech urging conciliation. Lord Chatham (William Pitt) introduced a plan of conciliation that would have prohibited Parliament from taxing the colonies, would have recognized the Congress, and would even have asked Congress to make provision for North American defense and to contribute to the national debt. When a government minister accused him of haste, he retorted that "any plan of reconciliation, however moderate, wise, and feasible, must fail in your hands." Who could wonder, he asked, that the ministry would try to defeat a proposal "which must annihilate your power, deprive you of your emoluments, and at once reduce you to that state of insignificance for which God and nature designed you?" Neither Burke's nor Chatham's proposals passed.

The initiative lay, of course, with Lord North. In a vague kind of way he still hoped for an amicable solution to the crisis, but in January 1775 he took a step that made peace impossible. He ordered Gage to send troops to Concord, destroy the arms stored

there, and arrest John Hancock and Samuel Adams. Only after sending this dispatch did he introduce his own Conciliatory Proposition, in which Parliament pledged that it would not tax any colony whose legislature met its share of the costs of imperial defense and paid adequate salaries to its royal officeholders. To reassure hardliners that he was not turning soft, he introduced the New England Restraining Act on the same day. It barred New Englanders from the vital North Atlantic fishery and banned all commerce between New England and any place except Britain and the British West Indies, precisely the trade routes that the Congress had resolved to block through non-importation. Both sides could play the sanction game, but Britain dominated the seas.

North's orders to Gage arrived before his Conciliatory Proposition reached America, and the general prepared to carry them out. He hoped to surprise the town of Concord with another predawn march, but Boston radicals knew about the expedition and its destination almost as soon as the orders were issued. They had already made careful preparations to alert

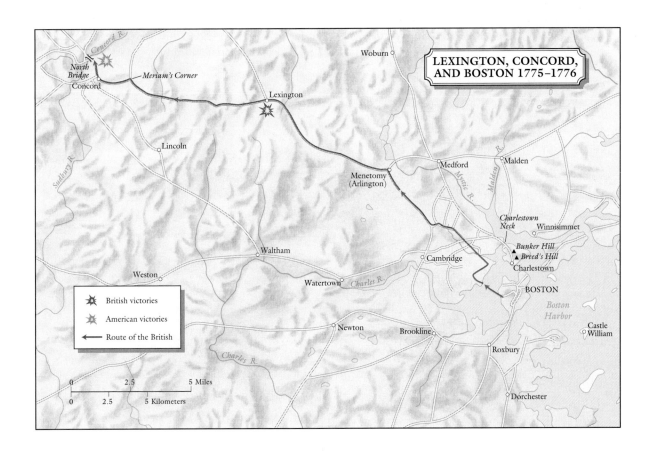

LEXINGTON, CONCORD, AND BOSTON 1775–1776

British victories
American victories
Route of the British

the whole countryside. Their informant, in all likelihood, was the general's wife, Margaret Kemble Gage, who had been born in New Jersey. On the night of April 18–19, about seven hundred grenadiers and light infantry were silently ferried from Boston past Charlestown and by 2 A.M. had begun the march toward Concord. Occasional flares on their flanks and the mysterious gallop of a horse or two suggested that they had been spotted. Paul Revere, an energetic Boston silversmith and engraver who had done as much as anyone to create the information network that he now set in motion, went dashing west with the news that "The redcoats are coming." When Revere was captured past Lexington by a small British patrol, Dr. Samuel Prescott, returning from a lady friend's house at the awkward hour of 3 A.M., managed to get the message through to Concord. As the British approached Lexington Green at dawn, they found sixty to seventy militiamen drawn up to face them. Hopelessly outnumbered, the militia began to withdraw when somebody—probably a colonial bystander and possibly also a British soldier—fired the first shots. Without orders, the British returned the fire and inflicted several casualties.

Secrecy had become pointless, and the British broke out their regimental fifes and drums. Cheered by the tunes, they marched on to Concord and into

another world war. Behind and ahead of them, like hives of angry bees, the whole countryside swarmed toward them.

THE IMPROVISED WAR

In April 1775 neither side had a grand strategy, a plan for winning a major war. Gage's soldiers were trying to enforce acts of Parliament, not fight battles. The militia who resisted them fought to preserve a political order Parliament was trying to change. The thousands who grabbed their muskets, drove the British from Concord Bridge, and then pursued them all the way back to Boston were, in a sense, participants in the largest crowd action of the era. While suffering only 95 casualties, they inflicted 273 on the British. Had a relief force of one thousand redcoats not met the battered British survivors east of Lexington, they might all have been lost.

The colonists, though they lacked an adequate command structure, put Boston under siege. After two months, Gage issued a proclamation declaring that all colonists bearing arms, and those who aided them, were rebels and traitors. He offered to pardon anyone who returned to his allegiance, except John Hancock and Samuel Adams. Instead of complying,

The Battle of Lexington, April 19, 1775 Amos Doolittle's work of 1775 portrays the opening shots of the Revolutionary War. The British are firing a volley into the Lexington militia, who are trying to leave the field without offering resistance. In fact, the first British soldiers who fired did so without orders, possibly in response to a shot from a colonial bystander. The militia were indeed trying to withdraw.

the besiegers escalated the struggle two days later. When they began to fortify the high ground on Breed's Hill (next to Bunker Hill) near Charlestown and overlooking Boston, the British sent 2,400 men, about one-fifth of the garrison, to take the hills on June 17. Merely by seizing Charlestown Neck, a smaller force could have cut off the Yankee militia at low risk to itself. But to demonstrate that mere civilians had no chance against a regular army, General William Howe launched three frontal attacks. Secure behind their defenses, the settlers shot more than one thousand of the attackers, including ninety-two officers (about one-sixth of those lost in the entire war), before the colonists ran out of ammunition and withdrew. The defenders suffered about 370 casualties, nearly all during the retreat.

This "defeat" persuaded some participants that sheer patriotism could make New England farmers and artisans a match for the rigorously trained British army. But as the war progressed, "Bunker Hillism" became one of the worst enemies of the American army. Time after time, Americans fortified a hill and then waited for the stupid frontal assault that never came. The British got the message at Bunker Hill. A few more such victories, reflected one of them, and no one would be left alive to carry the news to London.

Well into 1776 both sides fought an improvised war. In May 1775 Vermont and Massachusetts militia surprised the small garrison of Ticonderoga on Lake Champlain and seized the artillery and gunpowder that would be used months later in the siege of Boston. Crown Point also fell. With nearly all of their forces in Boston, the British were too weak to defend other positions. The widespread collapse of royal government meant that the insurgents, not the king's officials, controlled the militia and the royal powderhouses almost everywhere.

During the long war that now engulfed North America, the militia became the key to political allegiance. Compulsory service with the local militia politicized many waverers, who decided that they really were patriots after a redcoat shot at them or after they drove a loyalist into exile. The militia kept the countryside committed to the Revolution wherever the British army was too weak to overwhelm them.

The Second Continental Congress

When the Second Continental Congress met in May 1775, it found that it had inherited the war. Through most of 1775 it pursued the conflicting strategies of resistance and conciliation. It voted to

Death of General Warren at Bunker's Hill   Painted by John Trumbull in 1786, this work celebrated the heroism of Dr. Joseph Warren, the most prominent American fatality in the British attack on Breed's Hill in June 1775. Trumbull was a disciple of Benjamin West and was deeply influenced by West's *Death of General Wolfe* (see photo essay following Chapter 7).

turn the undisciplined men besieging Boston into a "Continental Army." As in earlier wars, the men who took up arms were volunteers who expected to serve for only a few months, or at most a single campaign. In the absence of royal authority, they began electing their officers, who in turn tried to win compliance through persuasion, not command. At first, no one was responsible for supplying the soldiers with food and munitions.

Though most of the soldiers were New Englanders who would have preferred to serve under their own officers, Congress realized that a successful war effort would have to engage the other colonies as well. On June 15, at the urging of John Adams of Massachusetts, it named George Washington of Virginia as commanding general. When Washington took charge of his army, he was appalled by the poor discipline among the soldiers and their casual familiarity with their officers. He thought he detected "an unaccountable kind of stupidity in the lower class of the people which, believe me, prevails too generally among the officers . . . who are nearly of the same kidney with the privates." He insisted that officers behave with a dignity that would instill obedience, and as the months passed, he grew to respect them. But as the year ended, most of the men went home, and he had to train a new army for 1776. Enthusiasm for the cause remained strong, however, and new volunteers soon filled his camp.

In late June 1775, Congress, fearing that the British in Canada might recruit a French force to attack New York, authorized a preemptive invasion of Canada, designed to win the French to the American cause before they could side with the British. Two forces of about one thousand men each moved northward. One under General Richard Montgomery took Montreal in November. The other, commanded by Colonel Benedict Arnold, advanced on Quebec through the Maine wilderness and laid siege to the city, where Montgomery joined Arnold in December. With enlistment terms due to expire at year's end, they decided to assault the city, partly to get the last bit of service out of their volunteers, partly to inspire some of them to reenlist. Their attack on December 31 was a disaster. Nearly one-half of their force of nine hundred was killed, wounded, or captured. Montgomery was killed and Arnold was wounded. Both were hailed as heroes.

The colonial objective in all of this fighting was still to restore government by consent under the Crown. After rejecting Lord North's Conciliatory Proposition out of hand (see above, p. 199), Congress agreed to send an "Olive Branch Petition" to George III on July 5 in the hope of ending the bloodshed. Moderates, led by John Dickinson of Pennsylvania, strongly favored the measure. The Olive Branch affirmed the colonists' loyalty to the crown, made no claim of right, and implored the king to take the initiative in devising "a happy and permanent reconciliation." An accompanying document written mostly by Thomas Jefferson, "The Declaration of the Causes and Necessities of Taking Up Arms," set forth the grievances of the colonies and justified their armed resistance. "We have counted the cost of this contest," Jefferson proclaimed, "and find nothing so dreadful as voluntary slavery." Like the Olive Branch, the Declaration assured the British people "that we mean not to dissolve that Union which has so long and so happily subsisted between us." The very moderation of the Olive Branch, which reached London along with the news of Bunker Hill, strengthened colonial radicals when the king refused even to receive the petition. Instead, George III issued a formal proclamation of rebellion on August 23.

The war made Congress act more and more like a government. But, with few exceptions, it assumed royal powers rather than parliamentary powers, which instead were taken over by the individual colonies. Congress did not tax or regulate trade. It did not assert the power to make law. It took command of the American army, printed paper money, opened diplomatic relations with Indian nations, took over the royal post office, and assumed the power to decide which government was legitimate in individual colonies—all functions that had been performed by the Crown. In short, it thought of itself not as a legislature but as a temporary plural executive for the continent.

War and Legitimacy, 1775–1776

Throughout 1775 the British reacted with fitful displays of violence and grim threats of racial warfare— of turning slaves and Indians against the settlers. When the weak British forces on the scene could neither restore order nor make good their threats, they conciliated no one, enraged thousands, and further undermined British claims to legitimacy. The British navy burnt Falmouth (now Portland), Maine,

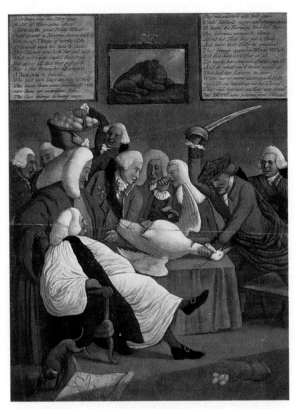

The Wise Men of Gotham and Their Goose This British opposition cartoon of February 1776 sees Britain's massive war effort as insane and suicidal. The government will kill the goose that laid the golden egg. It will destroy the prosperity that American trade had brought to the entire empire.

in October. On November 7, John Murray, earl of Dunmore and governor of Virginia, offered freedom to any slaves of rebel planters who joined his force of two hundred redcoats. About eight hundred slaves mustered under his banner only to suffer terrible losses from smallpox after the Virginia militia defeated them in a single engagement. Dunmore took revenge by bombarding Norfolk on January 1, which set several buildings ablaze. The patriot militia, whose members considered Norfolk a loyalist bastion, burned the rest of the city, but nearly all colonists blamed Dunmore for its destruction. Overall, his campaign undermined whatever loyalist sentiment survived among Virginia planters beyond Norfolk.

British efforts at intimidation in Boston and the Carolinas proved equally disastrous. The greatest achievement for American arms occurred at Boston, where most of the British army lay virtually impris-

oned. On March 17, 1776, after Washington fortified Dorchester Heights south of the city and brought heavy artillery (from Ticonderoga) to bear on it, the British pulled out and sailed for Halifax, Nova Scotia. A loyalist uprising by Highland Scots in North Carolina was crushed at Moore's Creek Bridge on February 27, and a British naval expedition sent to take Charleston was repulsed with serious losses in June. Cherokee attacks against Virginia in 1776 were easily defeated because they occurred after Dunmore had left and did not fit into any larger general strategy. Before spring turned to summer, patriot forces had won control of the territory of all thirteen colonies. Except in East and West Florida, Quebec, and Nova Scotia, the British had been driven from the continent.

Independence

Toward the end of 1775, Congress authorized an American navy, created the Marine Corps, and established a committee to begin corresponding with foreign powers. George III's dismissal of the Olive Branch Petition left moderates no option but either to yield or fight. By early 1776 the delegates from New England, Virginia, and Georgia already favored independence, but they knew that unless all thirteen colonies approved of such a step, the British would get the leverage they needed to divide the colonists. The failed British effort to take Charleston in June helped to swing the Carolinas toward independence.

Resistance to independence came mostly from the mid-Atlantic colonies, from New York through Maryland. Elsewhere, provincial congresses had supplanted the colonial assemblies in 1774–1775. In the Middle Colonies, however, both assemblies and congresses met and competed for the loyalties of the people. The New York and New Jersey assemblies even considered making a positive response to North's Conciliatory Proposition. Not one of the five legal assemblies in the mid-Atlantic region ever repudiated the Crown. All of them had to be overthrown along with royal (or proprietary) government itself. The last royal governor to be driven from his post was New Jersey's William Franklin, Benjamin's natural son, who was finally arrested on June 19, 1776, to prevent him from summoning a new session of the legally constituted assembly.

In the struggle for the minds and hearts of Middle Colony settlers, Thomas Paine's pamphlet, *Common*

Sense, became a sensational success. Paine, a recent immigrant from England who had waged his own contests with the British government, had none of the reverence for Britain's mixed and balanced constitution that still made an assault on monarchy unthinkable to most colonists. Published in Philadelphia in January 1776, *Common Sense* sold more than one hundred thousand copies within a few months and reached more people than any other tract printed in the colonies ever had. For Paine, George III was "the Pharaoh of England" and "the Royal Brute of Great Britain." Paine denounced monarchy and aristocracy as degenerate institutions and declared that Americans could do better under a simple republican government of their own. "Reconciliation and ruin are nearly related," he insisted. "There is something very absurd, in supposing a Continent to be perpetually governed by an island. In no instance hath nature made the satellite larger than its primary planet."

British policy continued to alienate more colonists. The king named Lord George Germain, a notorious hardliner, as Secretary of State for the American Colonies, and thus as war minister. The government tried to hire twenty thousand Russian mercenaries who, smirked one official, would make "charming visitors at New York and civilize that part of America wonderfully." When that effort failed, the British bought seventeen thousand soldiers from Hesse and other north German states, men who were called "Hessians" by the colonists. Jefferson described the decision to use mercenaries as "the last stab to [the] agonizing affection" that had once bound together the people of Britain and North America. Disturbing (though false) rumors also reached Philadelphia that Britain and France were about to sign a "partition treaty" dividing the eastern half of North America between them. Many congressmen concluded, some of them quite sadly, that only independence could counter these dangers by engaging Britain's European enemies on America's side. So long as conciliation remained the foremost goal of Congress, France would not enter the war, because an American victory would then mean restoring the British empire to its former glory. But Louis XVI might well strike to cripple Britain permanently by helping the colonies win their independence. In May 1776 he authorized covert aid to the American rebels.

As public opinion shifted away from Britain, Congress moved to break the mid-Atlantic stalemate. On May 15, 1776, when the delegates voted to suppress "every kind of authority" under the British Crown, they gave radicals an opportunity to seize power in Pennsylvania and New Jersey. Moderates remained in control in New York, Delaware, and Maryland, but they reluctantly accepted independence as inevitable. In early June, Congress postponed a vote on independence but named a committee of five, including Jefferson, John Adams, and Benjamin Franklin, to prepare a declaration that would justify American independence to the world.

With the necessary votes in place, Congress on July 2 passed Richard Henry Lee's resolution "that these United colonies are, and of right, ought to be, Free and Independent States; . . . and that all political connexion between them, and the state of Great Britain, is, and ought to be, totally dissolved." On that same day, the first ships of the largest armada yet sent across the Atlantic by any European state began landing British soldiers on Staten Island. Two days later, twelve colonies, with only New York abstaining, unanimously approved Jefferson's Declaration of Independence, as amended by Congress. Americans announced their independence at the very moment they faced a military challenge from Britain more enormous than any they had ever met before.

SUGGESTED READING

Good general histories of the American Revolution include Robert M. Calhoon's moderate *Revolutionary America: An Interpretive Overview* (1976), Edward Countryman's more radical *The American Revolution* (1985), and Colin Bonwick's recent British perspective in *The American Revolution* (1991). Major attempts to understand the broader significance of the Revolution include Robert R. Palmer, *The Age of the Democratic Revolution, 1760–1800,* 2 vols. (1959–1964), which sees a close affinity between the American and French Revolutions; Marc Egnal, *A Mighty Empire: The Origins of the American Revolution* (1988), which argues that westward expansion provided the underlying thrust for independence; and Gordon S. Wood, *The Radicalism of the American Revolution* (1992), which insists that the Revolution was the most important defining event in American history. Merrill Jensen's *The Founding of a Nation: A History of the American Revolution, 1763–1776* (1968) remains the best one-volume history of the coming of the Revolution. Robert W. Tucker and David C. Hendrickson, *The Fall of the First British Empire: Origins of the War of American Independence* (1982) is intelligent but argumentative. Bernard Bailyn's *The Ideological Origins of the Amer-*

ican Revolution (1967) has had an enormous impact on studies of the Revolution and the early republic.

The best studies of British politics in this period are John Brewer, *Party Ideology and Popular Politics at the Accession of George III* (1976); Peter D. G. Thomas, *British Politics and the Stamp Act Crisis: The First Phase of the American Revolution, 1763–1767* (1975); Paul Langford, *The First Rockingham Administration, 1765–1766* (1973); George F. E. Rudé, *Wilkes and Liberty: A Social Study of 1763 to 1774* (1962); Peter D. G. Thomas, *The Townshend Duties Crisis: The Second Phase of the American Revolution, 1767–1773* (1987); and Thomas, *Tea Party to Independence: The Third Phase of the American Revolution, 1773–1776* (1991).

Edmund S. and Helen M. Morgan, *The Stamp Act Crisis, Prologue to Revolution* (1953) has become a classic. Pauline Maier, *From Resistance to Revolution: Colonial Radicals and the Development of American Opposition to Britain, 1765–1776* (1972) emphasizes the links between the Sons of Liberty and the English Wilkite movement. The best studies of merchants and the resistance movement are John W. Tyler, *Smugglers and Patriots: Boston Merchants and the Advent of the American Revolution* (1986); and Thomas H. Doerflinger, *A Vigorous Spirit of Enterprise: Merchants and Economic Development in Revolutionary Philadelphia* (1986). Hiller Zobel's *The Boston Massacre* (1970) is the standard study, but Jesse Lemisch's review in *The Harvard Law Review,* 84 (1970–1971), 485–504 makes some telling criticisms. Richard D. Brown, *Revolutionary Politics in Massachusetts: The Boston Committee of Correspondence and the Towns* (1970) is a fine study of the growth of disaffection. John Shy's *Toward Lexington: The Role of the British Army in the Coming of the American Revolution* (1965) remains indispensable.

Gary B. Nash, *The Urban Crucible: Social Change, Political Consciousness, and the Origins of the American Revolution* (1979) is a superb study of social tensions in Boston, New York, and Philadelphia. Rowland Berthoff and John M. Murrin, "Feudalism, Communalism, and the Yeoman Freeholder: The American Revolution Considered as a Social Accident," in Stephen G. Kurtz and James H. Hutson, eds., *Essays on the American Revolution* (1973), 256–288 lays out the feudal revival. Conflicting views about the New York manor lords emerge from Sung Bok Kim's favorable portrait in *Landlord and Tenant in Colonial New York: Manorial Society, 1664–1775* (1978) and from Edward Countryman's more negative analysis in *A People in Revolution: The American Revolution and Political Society in New York, 1760–1790* (1981). Thomas L. Purvis, "Origins and Patterns of Agrarian Unrest in New Jersey," *William and Mary Quarterly,* 3d ser., 39 (1982), 600–627 is excellent on the New Jersey riots. James H. Hutson, *Pennsylvania Politics, 1746–1770: The Movement for Royal Government and Its Consequences* (1972) explores the assault on Pennsylvania's proprietary regime. Ronald Hoffman's *A Spirit of Dissen-*

sion: *Economics, Politics, and the Revolution in Maryland* (1973) is the best study of internal tensions in Revolutionary Maryland. Together, A. Roger Ekirch, *"Poor Carolina": Politics and Society in Colonial North Carolina, 1729–1776* (1981); James P. Whittenburg, "Planters, Merchants, and Lawyers: Social Change and the Origins of the North Carolina Regulation," *William and Mary Quarterly,* 3d ser., 34 (1977), 214–238; and E. Merton Coulter, "The Granville District," *James Sprunt Historical Studies,* 13 (1913), 33–56 cover North Carolina's internal tensions quite admirably. Richard M. Brown, *The South Carolina Regulators* (1963); Rachel N. Klein, *Unification of a Slave State: The Rise of the Planter Class in the South Carolina Backcountry, 1760–1808* (1990); and Jack P. Greene, "Bridge to Revolution: The Wilkes Fund Controversy in South Carolina, 1769–1775," *Journal of Southern History,* 29 (1963), 19–52 are excellent on South Carolina. Alan Taylor, *Liberty Men and Great Proprietors: The Revolutionary Settlement on the Frontier 1760–1820* (1990) finds strong backcountry resentments in Maine, although they peaked rather later. David Grimsted, "Anglo-American Racism and Phillis Wheatley's 'Sable Veil,' 'Length'ned Chain,' and 'Knitted Heart,'" in Ronald Hoffman and Peter J. Albert, eds., *Women in the Age of the American Revolution* (1989), 338–444 is a superb study of the emerging antislavery movement and the role of women in it.

Benjamin W. Labaree's *The Boston Tea Party* (1964) is the fullest study of that event. David Ammerman's *In the Common Cause: American Response to the Coercive Acts of 1774* (1974) carefully traces its aftermath. Philip Lawson, *The Imperial Challenge: Quebec and Britain in the Age of the American Revolution* (1989) ends with the Quebec Act. David Hackett Fischer, *Paul Revere's Ride* (1994) is a brilliant study of how the Revolutionary War began. Jerrilyn Greene Martson, *King and Congress: The Transfer of Political Legitimacy from the King to the Continental Congress, 1774–1776* (1987) is fresh and insightful. Together, Richard A. Ryerson's *The Revolution Is Now Begun: The Radical Committees of Philadelphia, 1765–1776* (1978) and Larry R. Gerlach's *Prologue to Revolution: New Jersey in the Coming of the American Revolution* (1976) analyze the radicalization of politics in two critical colonies. Eric Foner's *Tom Paine and Revolutionary America* (1976), Jack N. Rakove's *The Beginnings of National Politics: An Interpretive History of the Continental Congress* (1979), and James H. Hutson, "The Partition Treaty and the Declaration of American Independence," *Journal of American History,* 58 (1971–1972), 877–896 explore different aspects of the movement toward independence. Garry Wills, *Inventing America: Jefferson's Declaration of Independence* (1978) and Jay Fliegelman, *Declaring Independence: Jefferson, Natural Language, and the Culture of Performance* (1993) are imaginative studies by literary scholars.

Chapter 7

The Republican Experiment

Women Voting in Late Eighteenth-Century New Jersey   Alone among the thirteen states, the New Jersey constitution of 1776 permitted women to vote if they were the heads of their households, a category that included mostly widows. This privilege was revoked in 1807.

The Revolutionary War killed a higher percentage of the men it mobilized than any other American conflict except the Civil War. It was a civil war in its own right. Neighbors were far more likely to shoot at neighbors during the Revolution than they were between 1861 and 1865, when the geographical line separating the two sides was much cleaner than it ever was between 1775 and 1783. Twice, in 1776 and again in 1780, the British had at least a chance to win a decisive military victory, but in both years the Americans somehow rallied.

Even as the war raged around them and the economy disintegrated, Americans spoke eloquently of universal human rights while drafting state constitutions and bills of rights. Americans knew that they were attempting something truly daring, something that could easily fail, something that had *always* failed in the past—a republican experiment. In the Atlantic world of 1775, political stability seemed to require monarchical government. The English monarchy was about one thousand years old. No republic had ever survived that long. Educated people knew a great deal about the republics of classical Greece and Rome—how they had called forth the noblest sentiments of patriotism for a time and had then decayed into despotisms. Yet, once Americans broke with Britain, they embraced republicanism with enthusiasm and, after some initial hesitation, they never looked back from that decision. Americans were able to build viable republican governments because they grasped the voluntaristic dynamics of their society. They knew they had to persuade one another of the wisdom of every step they took. Once the loyalists had been banished, the use of force against armed fellow voters would be self-defeating.

More than ever before, Americans also began thinking in terms of race, and ideas about racial inferiority clashed sharply against claims of universal rights. As settlers and Indians, whites and blacks began defining their differences, they often embraced crude, hostile racial stereotypes. Indians achieved a higher level of unity during this struggle than at any other time, before or since. Most Indians and slaves hoped that Britain would win the war. The Americans triumphed only by bringing in France as an ally, and France brought in Spain.

The war and its aftermath also demonstrated how weak Congress really was, even after ratification of the Articles of Confederation in 1781. Unable to pay its debts, to expel the British from their posts on the Great Lakes, or to defeat the Indians of the Ohio country, the Congress nevertheless announced plans to create new states in that region and to admit them to the union on terms of complete equality with the original thirteen. The details of that policy were contained in the Northwest Ordinance of July 1787. During that same summer, the Philadelphia Convention drafted a new Constitution for the United States. After ratification by eleven states in 1787–1788, it went into effect in April 1789. The American federal system became the most distinctive achievement of the Revolutionary generation.

HEARTS AND MINDS: THE WAR IN THE NORTHERN STATES, 1776–1777

Many settlers hoped they would never have to face the decisions that the Revolutionary War forced upon them. The price of resistance escalated once independence became the goal because the men who governed Britain believed that the loss of the colonies would be a fatal blow to British power. Britain raised more soldiers and larger fleets than ever before and more than doubled its national debt in the process. Americans, confident of their patriotism and valor after their early successes, soon staggered under Britain's powerful blows.

The British Onslaught

The first setback came in Canada. Americans besieging Quebec were forced to retreat when British reinforcements sailed up the St. Lawrence in May 1776. Sir Guy Carleton's attack drove them back to Ticonderoga on Lake Champlain by July, and both sides set to work building ships to win control of

that strategic waterway. Largely through Benedict Arnold's leadership, the Americans held. Carleton withdrew to Canada for the winter of 1776–1777.

Farther south, Richard viscount Howe, admiral of the British fleet, and his brother General William Howe prepared an awesome striking force on Staten Island. Because both had pro-American reputations in British politics, the Howes had also been sent as peace commissioners, with power to restore whole colonies to the king's peace and to pardon rebels who submitted to the Crown. They hoped that they would not have to use the immense force that they brought with them, but when they sent a letter to Washington to open negotiations, he refused to accept it because they had failed to address him as "General." To do so would have implied that the British recognized the legitimacy of his appointment. Franklin, an old friend of the Howe brothers, wrote the admiral that "it must give your lordship pain to be sent so far on so hopeless a business." Unable to negotiate, the Howes had to fight.

Since spring, Washington had moved his army from Boston to New York City, where he mustered about nineteen thousand men to face more than thirty thousand redcoats and Hessians. Early successes had kept morale high in the American army and helped to sustain the *rage militaire* (enthusiasm for the cause) that had prompted thousands to volunteer for service in 1775 and 1776, including about four thousand veterans of 1775 who reenlisted for 1776. Although some volunteered for service in the Continental Army and others for the militia, the difference between the two was not yet large. Both served for short terms, and neither had formal military training.

Washington, well aware that morale could be the key to victory, was reluctant to abandon any large city to the invaders. In the face of a superior foe, against conventional military wisdom, he divided his inferior force and sent about one-half of his men from Manhattan to Long Island. Most of them dug in on Brooklyn Heights, just two miles from lower Manhattan, and waited for a frontal attack. The British invaded Long Island, a loyalist stronghold, and on August 27, 1776, sent a force around the American left flank through unguarded Jamaica Pass. While Hessians feinted a frontal assault, the flanking force crushed the American left and rear and sent the survivors reeling.

The Howes made no attempt to prevent the evacuation of the rest of the army to Manhattan, even though the navy could have cut them off. Instead, the British opened informal negotiations with John Adams, Benjamin Franklin, and other members of Congress on Staten Island on September 11, without acknowledging the legality of Congress. But when the Americans insisted at the outset that the British recognize their independence, no progress was possible. Washington evacuated lower Manhattan, while the Howes occupied New York City, much of which burned in an accidental fire on September 21. From New York City, the Howes appealed directly to the people to lay down their arms and return to British allegiance within sixty days in exchange for a full pardon. On Long Island, Manhattan, and in Westchester County, thousands complied.

In October, the Howes drove Washington out of Manhattan and Westchester and then turned on two garrisons that he had left behind. On November 16, at a cost of 460 casualties, the British compelled three thousand men to surrender at Fort Washington on the Manhattan side of the Hudson River. General Nathanael Greene, a lame Rhode Island Quaker who had given up pacifism for soldiering, saved his men by abandoning Fort Lee on the New Jersey side but lost a huge store of precious supplies.

The Howes have been criticized for not destroying Washington's army on Long Island or Manhattan, but the British commanders probably understood quite well what they were doing. The combination of British victories and the Americans' voluntaristic ethic was destroying Washington's army. British success seemed to prove that no American force could stand before a properly organized British army. But to capture Washington's entire army would have been a political embarrassment, leading to massive treason trials, executions, and great bitterness. Instead, Britain's impressive but limited victories encouraged American soldiers to go home, with or without their muskets. In September, there were twenty-seven thousand Americans fit for duty in the northern theater (including the Canadian border); by December, only six thousand remained. Most of them intended to go home when their enlistments expired on December 31.

The Howes' strategy nearly worked, in part because it exploited the sharp divisions in the Middle States over independence. As British forces swept across New Jersey as far south as Burlington by December, they captured Charles Lee, next in command after Washington, and Richard Stockton, a signer of the Declaration of Independence. Several thousand New Jersey residents, including Stockton, took the king's oath. To seal off Long Island Sound from both ends, the Howes also captured Newport, Rhode Island. Many observers thought the war was all but over as sad remnants of the Continental Army crossed the Delaware River into Pennsylvania, confiscating all private boats so that the British could not follow them. One general believed that the time had come to "bargain away the Bubble of Independency for British Liberty well secured." Charles Carroll, another signer of the Declaration of Independence, agreed. Even Thomas Jefferson began to speculate about the terms on which a restoration of the monarchy might be acceptable.

The Trenton–Princeton Campaign

Washington knew he had to do something dramatic to restore morale and encourage some of his men to reenlist. On the night of December 25, 1776, he crossed the ice-choked Delaware River and marched south, surprising the Trenton garrison at dawn. At almost no cost to the attackers, a thousand Hessians, not yet recovered from their Christmas hangovers, surrendered. The British reacted quickly, sending their most energetic general, Charles earl Cornwallis, south with eight thousand men to "bag the fox" — Washington and the five thousand Continentals and militia still with him. Cornwallis caught him at Trenton near sunset on January 2 but decided to wait until dawn before attacking. His patrols watched the Delaware River to prevent another escape into Pennsylvania, but Washington tried nothing of the kind. With campfires burning, he muffled the wheels of his wagons and guns and stole around the British left flank, heading north. At dawn, the Americans clashed with a British regiment that was just beginning its march from Princeton to Trenton. The Battle of Princeton was a series of sharp engagements in which the Americans, who had a five-to-one edge, mauled still another outpost.

Though Washington's two quick victories brought only about one thousand reenlistments, their impact on the war was enormous. The British, afraid that he might pick off their garrisons one at a time, now called in all their occupying forces and concentrated them along the Raritan River from New Brunswick to the sea, partly to protect a war chest of £75,000 at New Brunswick. As the British departed, the

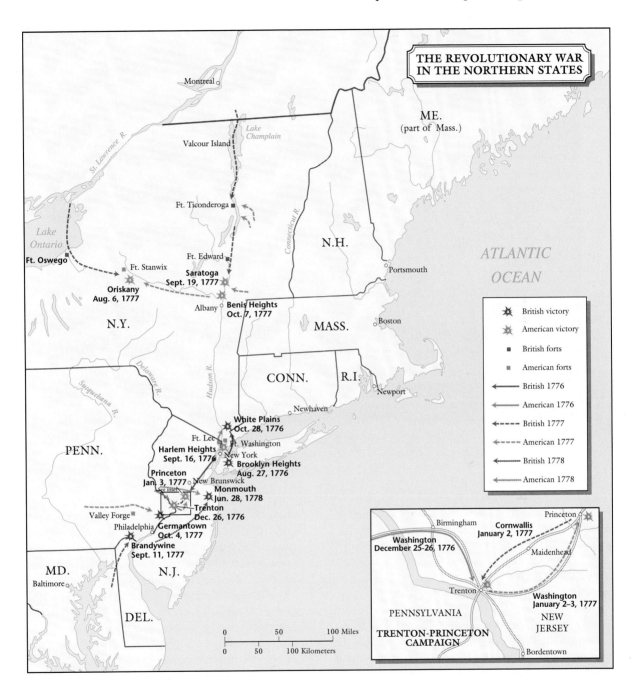

American militia returned, asking who had sworn oaths to the king. Those who had now groveled, as the price of acceptance, or fled to the British lines.

The Howes, who until January had shown remarkable understanding of the demands of a revolutionary war, made a fatal mistake in not hounding Washington's tiny army to its destruction after Prince-

ton. British forces, especially the German mercenaries, had already aroused ferocious hatred by looting and raping their way across New Jersey. But by encouraging loyalists to come forward, and then abandoning them to the king's enemies, the British lost the hearts and minds of the settlers. In 1777, very few would be willing to declare for the Crown. The

The Passage of the Delaware This painting by Thomas Sully, done in 1818, celebrates George Washington's daring attack on the Hessian garrison of Trenton, New Jersey, December 26, 1776, as a turning point of the Revolutionary War.

Howes had won all the large battles, but Washington took the 1776 campaign. The Revolution survived.

THE CAMPAIGNS OF 1777 AND FOREIGN INTERVENTION

Britain's thoughtful strategy of 1776 gave way to incoherence in 1777. The Howes again had a plan for winning the war, but it required twenty thousand reinforcements that London refused to raise. Instead, Lord George Germain, Britain's war minister, ordered the Howes to take Philadelphia. He also sent John Burgoyne, a poet and playwright as well as a general, with a few thousand reinforcements to Canada with orders to march south and link with the garrison of New York City, which was placed under the command of Sir Henry Clinton. A smaller force under Barry St. Leger was to march from Oswego down the Mohawk Valley and threaten Albany from the west.

When the Howes realized that they would not get many reinforcements, they rejected an overland march to Philadelphia as too risky and decided to invade by sea, a decision that allowed Washington to shift some of his men north to oppose Burgoyne.

The British campaign made little sense. If the point of Burgoyne's march was to get his army to New York City, he should have gone by sea. If the point was to force a battle with militant New Englanders, the invading army should have been much bigger. And if Howe's army—Britain's largest—did not care to challenge Washington's, how did the British propose to win the war?

The Loss of Philadelphia

Washington's victories at Trenton and Princeton helped him to recruit what was virtually a new army in 1777. He demanded stricter discipline and that the men be commited to serve for more than a single campaign. As a result, Congress raised the number of lashes a soldier could receive from thirty-nine to one hundred, and it promised a cash bonus to anyone enlisting for three years and a land bounty to anyone serving for the duration. Congress never came close to raising the 75,000 men it hoped for, but these new policies did create the basis for the Continental Line, or Army. Longer terms made military training a real possibility, which in turn made the Continentals much more professional than the militia. But this difference did not take hold until 1778 and later, after the first year of service. The men who volunteered for longer terms, as in Europe, were poor. For example, about half of those from New Jersey came from families not on the tax rolls. Some recruits were British or Hessian deserters. Short-term militiamen, by contrast, usually held a secure place in their local communities and often were more religious than the Continentals. As the 1777 recruits came in, the two northern armies, swelled by militia, grew to about twenty-eight thousand men fit for duty — seventeen thousand in northern New York by October, and eleven thousand in Pennsylvania under Washington.

The Howes' success in 1777 could not offset what Burgoyne lost. After failing to lure Washington from the Watchung Mountains of New Jersey in June, the Howes sailed south with thirteen thousand men. When river pilots were unable to guarantee a safe ascent of the Delaware River against American fire, the fleet continued south to Chesapeake Bay, sailed to its northern extreme, and landed the troops at Head of Elk, Maryland, on August 24. The British army marched on Philadelphia through southeastern Pennsylvania, a region thickly populated with loyalists and Quaker neutralists. Nevertheless, most residents, well aware of the atrocities the Hessians had committed in New Jersey, fled instead of greeting the army as liberators. The British burned many of their abandoned farms.

After his 1776 experience in New York, Washington was quite wary of again being trapped in a city, and he made no serious effort to garrison Philadelphia. But he took up strong positions at Brandywine Creek along the British line of march. Howe again outmaneuvered Washington on September 11, drove in his right flank, inflicted one thousand casualties while suffering half that many, and forced the Americans to retreat. As Congress fled to Lancaster, the British occupied Philadelphia on September 26.

Eight days later, Washington tried to repeat his successes at Trenton and Princeton in an attack on a British outpost at Germantown, but the defenders rallied from early losses and drove him off. The British had taken another city but not many hearts and minds.

Washington headed west to Valley Forge, where the army endured a miserable winter. There, baron von Steuben, a Prussian officer who had volunteered to serve with the Continental Army and would soon become a major general, devised a drill manual based on Prussian standards that he modified for American conditions. Through his efforts, the professionalism of the Continentals improved greatly. Washington received help from other European volunteers. From France came marquis de Lafayette and Johann, baron de Kalb. The Poles sent Thaddeus Kosciuszko (a

Congress Fleeing Philadelphia by Balloon, 1777   This British cartoon mocked Congress as it fled from the British army in the 1777 campaign. Hot air balloon flights were still in an experimental phase but were becoming a popular rage in France and Britain. The first flight across the English Channel would occur in 1783.

talented engineer) and Casimir, count Pulaski. De Kalb and Pulaski died in American service. By the last years of the war, more than one-fifth of all Continental officers were professional soldiers from Europe, and they helped give the American officer corps an aristocratic air that disturbed civilians.

Saratoga

In northern New York, little went right for the British after Ticonderoga fell to Burgoyne on June 2, 1777. Colonel St. Leger, with nine hundred soldiers and an equal number of Indians, advanced down the Mohawk Valley to besiege Fort Schuyler in August and ambushed a relief force of eight hundred militia at Oriskany. But when Benedict Arnold approached with an additional one thousand men, the Indians fled, and St. Leger had to withdraw to Oswego.

Burgoyne's army of 7,800, advancing from Ticonderoga toward Albany, was overwhelmed in the upper Hudson Valley. As his supply line to Canada grew longer, American militia swarmed to his rear and cut it. When he detached seven hundred Hessians to forage in the Green Mountains, they ran into 2,600 militia raised by John Stark of New Hampshire. At Bennington, Vermont, Stark killed or captured nearly all of them on August 16. A relief force of 650 Hessians was also badly mauled. By the time Burgoyne's surviving soldiers reached the Hudson and advanced toward Albany, the Americans under Horatio Gates outnumbered them three to one. The British got as far as Bemis Heights, thirty miles north of Albany, but failed to break through in two costly battles on September 19 and October 7, with Arnold again distinguishing himself. Burgoyne retreated ten miles to Saratoga, where he surrendered the entire army on October 17. The American victory at Saratoga helped bring France into the war and, eventually, Spain as well.

French Intervention

Colonial resistance delighted the French court, which was still trying to recover from its defeats in the previous war (see Chapter 5). In May 1776, France had authorized secret aid to the American rebels. A French dramatist, Pierre Augustin Caron de Beaumarchais, author of *The Barber of Seville* (1775) and later of *The Marriage of Figaro,* set up the firm of

Roderique Hortalez et Compagnie as a front for smuggling supplies past Britain's ineffective blockade of the American coast. (The British navy had deployed most of its ships to transport and supply the British army and had few left over for blockade duty.) Perhaps 90 percent of the gunpowder used by Americans from 1775 to 1777 came either from captured British supplies or from abroad. Hortalez et Compagnie's fourteen ships brought in most of what arrived from Europe. Without this aid, the Americans could not have continued the war.

In December 1776 Benjamin Franklin arrived in France as an agent of the American Congress. The French court could not officially receive him without risking a declaration of war by Britain, but the seventy-year-old Franklin took Paris society by storm by adapting simple clothes, replacing his wig with a fur cap, and playing to perfection the role of an innocent man of nature. Through Beaumarchais, he kept

Benjamin Franklin and his Grandsons in Paris Adding to his other accomplishments, Franklin became America's most skillful diplomat in Europe. His grandsons were sixteen-year-old William Temple Franklin, who served as Benjamin's secretary, and eighteen-year-old Benjamin Franklin Bache, who later became a radical Democratic–Republican newspaper editor. William Temple was the son of William Franklin, the last royal governor of New Jersey. Benjamin took the lad to Paris to rescue him from William's Tory principles.

A FAMOUS PENNSYLVANIAN IN PARIS.
Benjamin Franklin and his grandsons in the Paris streets.

the supplies flowing and organized privateering raids on British commerce, which the French government claimed it could not stop.

Reports of the fall of Philadelphia and the surrender of Burgoyne finally persuaded the French to intervene openly. The loss of Philadelphia alarmed Foreign Minister Charles Gravier, comte de Vergennes, who feared that Congress might surrender unless direct support from France was forthcoming. And Burgoyne's disaster convinced Louis XVI (1774–1793) that the Americans could win and that intervention was a good risk. Franklin and Vergennes signed two treaties in February 1778. One, a commercial agreement, granted Americans generous trading terms with France. In the other, France established a perpetual alliance with the United States, recognized American independence, agreed to fight until Britain conceded independence, and disavowed all territorial ambitions on the North American continent. Americans could not have hoped for more. Vergennes also brought Spain into the war a year later.

News of the Franco–American treaties stunned London. Lord North tried to resign, but the king would not hear of it. William Pitt, earl of Chatham warned that American independence would be a disaster for Britain, then collapsed on the floor of the House of Lords after finishing his speech, and died a month later. North put together a plan of conciliation that conceded virtually everything but independence to the Americans and dispatched a distinguished group of commissioners under Frederick Howard, earl of Carlisle, to present them to Congress and block the French alliance. In 1775 such terms would have resolved the imperial crisis. But, in June 1778, Congress recognized them as a sign of British desperation and scornfully rejected them. "We can find no safety but in [Britain's] ruin," wrote Patrick Henry, ". . . which cannot happen until she is deluged with blood, or . . . purged by a revolution."

Americans now expected a quick victory, while the British reevaluated their military strategy. North's government declared war on France, recalled the Howe brothers, and ordered General Clinton to abandon Philadelphia. Unwilling to risk being caught at sea by the French, Clinton marched overland toward New York in June 1778. Washington's newly

The Death of the Earl of Chatham   This painting by John Singleton Copley, completed between 1779 and 1781, shows William Pitt, earl of Chatham, collapsing on the floor of the House of Lords after finishing his last speech. In it he warned that American independence, achieved through French aid, would be fatal to Britain. Chatham was still widely respected by Americans. Copley, a disciple of Benjamin West, was strongly influenced by West's *Death of General Wolfe* (1771) (see photo essay following Chapter 7).

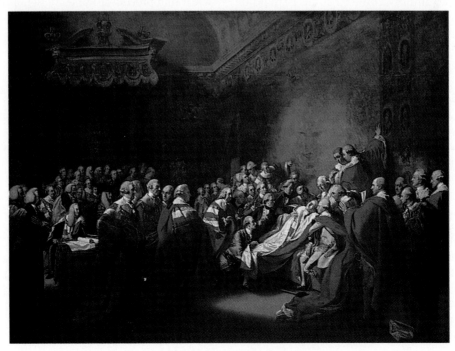

disciplined army attacked Clinton at Monmouth Court House and almost drove the British from the field, but they regrouped and won the day. The British, realizing that French intervention placed even the British Isles in danger of invasion, especially with most of the Royal Navy in American waters, now redeployed their forces on a global scale. They stood on the defensive in North America through most of 1778 and 1779 and even evacuated Newport, although American loyalists kept up continual raids of New Jersey and Connecticut from their base in New York City.

Spain's Opportunity: Expansion, Intervention, and Consolidation

Like France, Spain had old defeats to avenge against Britain. Charles III, king of Spain since 1759, had endured the loss of Florida shortly after ascending the throne but had received Louisiana from France in compensation. Spanish rule there did not begin smoothly. In 1769 Spain suppressed a small revolt against its restrictions on trade, but in later years, when trade policy became more favorable, Louisiana enjoyed a level of prosperity it had never known before. The province attracted two thousand immigrants from the Canary Islands, perhaps three thousand Acadian refugees (see Chapter 5), and other French settlers from the Illinois country, some of whom founded St. Louis in 1764. Louisiana remained heavily French throughout the period of Spanish rule.

During this time, Spaniards also moved into California, in part to counter a Russian migration into Alaska to hunt sea otters for sale in China. Spain founded a base at San Diego in 1769. In the next few years, Spain explored the Pacific coastline as far north as southern Alaska, set up an outpost at San Francisco Bay, and built a chain of Franciscan missions under Junípero Serra. Spain's California frontier duplicated many aspects of seventeenth-century Florida, though in a very different environment. Facing little danger from other Europeans, Spain sent relatively few soldiers to California. Instead, and for the last time in the history of North America, missionaries would set the tone for a whole province. As in Florida, the Indians of California began to die in appalling numbers from European diseases, and many objected to the severe discipline of the missions.

Charles III, who understood that it was dangerous for one imperial power to urge the subjects of an-

other to revolt, never made a direct alliance with the United States during the war. But in 1779 he joined with France in its war against Britain, hoping thereby to retake Gibraltar and to stabilize Spain's North American borders. Though Spain failed to get Gibraltar, it managed to overrun British West Florida, and at the end of the war Britain ceded East Florida as well. By 1783, for the first time in a century, Spain once again controlled the entire Gulf of Mexico.

THE RECONSTITUTION OF AUTHORITY

The approach of independence touched off an intense American debate on constitutionalism in 1776. The settlers knew that they would have to reconstitute their governments along more popular lines, now that the British Crown no longer provided the basis for legitimacy. With virtually no dissent, they decided that every state would need a written constitution that would limit the powers of government itself, something more explicit than the precedents, statutes, and customs that made up Britain's unwritten constitution. They now moved toward ever fuller expressions of popular sovereignty — the theory that all power must be derived from the people themselves. This process sparked lively debates and ignited a learning process of immense significance. By 1780 Americans had acquired a much sharper idea of what they meant when they affirmed that the people of a republic must be their own governors.

John Adams: Toward the Separation of Powers

No one reflected this learning process better than John Adams, who grew alarmed in 1776 when Thomas Paine advocated a simple, unicameral legislature to carry out the people's will. Adams replied in *Thoughts on Government,* a tract that strongly influenced the drafting of Virginia's constitution, which in turn was imitated by other states.

In 1776 Adams was already moving away from the British notion of a "mixed and balanced" constitution that could be stable only if the government embodied the distinct social orders of British society — the king, the lords, and the commons. He was groping toward a very different notion, the separation of powers, according to which the government should be divided into three branches — an executive armed

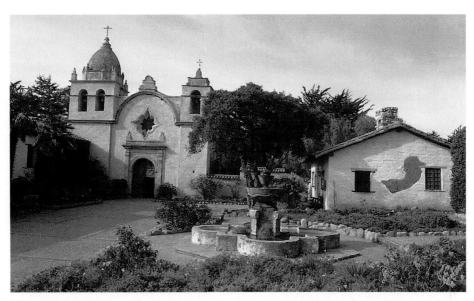

The Mission of San Carlos Borromeo   The Spanish mission at Carmel, California, was founded in 1770.

with a veto power, a legislature, and a judiciary independent of both. The legislature, he insisted, had to be bicameral, so that each house could expose the failings of the other. A government need not embody distinct social orders to be free and stable. It could uphold republican values by being properly balanced within itself.

Governments exist to promote the happiness of the people, Adams declared, and happiness must rest on "virtue," both public and private. "Public virtue" meant "patriotism," the willingness of free and independent householders to subordinate their interests to the common good and even to die for their country. The government that rests entirely on virtue, Adams argued, is a republic. Americans must elect legislatures that would, as nearly as possible, mirror the diversity of society. Britain had put the nobility in one house and the commoners in another. But in the colonies, everyone was a commoner. There were no "social orders." In what sense, then, could any government reflect American society? Adams came close to saying that the legislature should represent the "interests" of its citizens, but he did not face the implications of this claim. Should citizens enter politics to pursue their selfish interests? What then of selfless patriotism?

In 1776 Adams knew only that the legislature should somehow mirror society and that a republican

government should be more complex and balanced than what Paine advocated. Unicameral legislatures, which Georgia, Pennsylvania, and Vermont adopted in their first state constitutions, horrified him: "Because a single assembly, possessed of all the powers of government, would *make* arbitrary laws for their own interest, *execute* all laws arbitrarily for their own interest, and *adjudge* all controversies in their own favor."

Despite his belief in popular sovereignty, Adams found no way in 1776 to distinguish between ordinary legislation and the power to create a constitution. Nor did his admirers. While struggling to define what a virtuous republic ought to be, they could not escape from two assumptions of European politics—that government itself must be sovereign, and that it alone could define the rights of the people. A few ordinary settlers had already spotted the dangers of these claims. As the citizens of Concord, Massachusetts, warned in October 1776, "The Same Body that forms a Constitution have of Consequence a power to alter it," and "A Constitution alterable by the Supreme Legislative [Power] is no Security at all to the Subject against any Encroachment of the Governing part on any or all of their Rights and Privileges."

This concern would finally prompt Americans, including Adams, to invent something new, the constitutional convention, to embody popular sovereignty in its purest form. But in the constitutions of 1776–1777, no state quite made that connection. They all lodged sovereign power in the legislature and let it define the rights of citizens. In 1776 the American reply to Britain's sovereign Parliament was thirteen sovereign state parliaments—or fourteen, if Vermont is included. It took years of struggle to expose the inadequacy of this formulation.

Early State Constitutions

In June 1776 Virginia became the first state to adopt a permanent constitution, one that envisioned a republican future. The provincial congress (called a "convention" in Virginia), which had assumed all legislative powers of the colony, affirmed "that the legislative and executive powers of the State should be separate and distinct from the judiciary" but then wrote a constitution that made the legislature sovereign. The legislature chose the governor, his council, and all judges above the level of justice of the peace. The governor had no veto and hardly any patronage. The lower house faced annual elections, but members of the upper house served four-year terms.

George Mason, a highly respected planter, drafted a declaration of rights that the delegates passed before approving the constitution itself, on the theory that the people should define their rights before deciding what powers to give the government. Mason's text affirmed the right to life, liberty, property, and the pursuit of happiness. It condemned all forms of hereditary privilege, called for rotation (frequent turnover) in office, provided strong guarantees for trial by jury and other legal protections, and extolled religious toleration. Legally, Virginia's bill of rights was merely a statute, with no more authority than any other law. But because the planters accepted its terms, it was not very controversial and was copied by many other states.

Other states adopted variations of the Virginia model. Because America had no aristocracy, uncertainty about the upper house was widespread. Some states imposed higher property qualifications on "senators" than on "representatives." Three states permitted the lower house to elect the upper. Maryland chose its state senators through an electoral college, but most states created separate election districts for senators. Nearly every state sharply increased the size of the lower house. Inland counties,

formerly underrepresented, became better represented, and men of moderate wealth won a majority of seats in most states, displacing the rich who had dominated colonial assemblies. As in Virginia, other states stripped the governor of patronage powers and of most royal prerogatives, such as the power to dissolve the legislature. Until 1780, only New York gave the governor a veto, which could be overridden by a two-thirds vote of both houses.

Most other states lacked Virginia's political consensus, however, and many of them disagreed on constitutional issues. Pennsylvania learned how troubling these questions could become. The radicals who overthrew Crown, proprietor, and assembly in June 1776 rejected the leadership of both the old Quaker and Proprietary parties and brought artisans into power in Philadelphia and ordinary farmers in rural areas. Until 1776 most officeholders had been Quakers and Anglicans. Now, they were Scots-Irish Presbyterians and German Lutherans or Calvinists. A new constitution became a major step in their quest for legitimacy.

In keeping with the most advanced opinion of the day, the radicals assembled a special convention whose only task was to write a constitution. That document established a unicameral assembly and a plural executive of twelve men, one of whom would preside and would thus be called "president." All freemen who paid taxes, and their adult sons living at home, could vote. Elections were annual, voting was by secret ballot, legislative sessions were open to the public, and no representative could serve for more than four years out of any seven. All bills proposed in a legislative session were to be published and distributed throughout the state for public discussion. Only at the next session could they be passed into law, except in emergencies. Pennsylvania also created a "Council of Censors" to meet every seven years to determine whether the constitution had been violated. It could also recommend amendments.

The Pennsylvania constitution never worked as planned, and it generated intense conflict in late 1776 as British armies drew near. In this emergency, the convention that drafted the constitution also began to pass laws, destroying any distinction between itself and the legislature it created. Likewise, the convention and the legislatures that eventually succeeded it rarely delayed the enactment of a bill until the voters had time to discuss it. The war lent a sense of emergency to almost every measure. Finally, the radicals discovered that many Pennsylvania residents regarded the state constitution as illegitimate. The men driven from power in 1776 never consented to it and saw no moral reason why they should accept it. The radicals, calling themselves "Constitutionalists," required everyone to take oaths to uphold the constitution and then disfranchised Quakers, German pacifists, and anyone else who could not in conscience support the war.

These illiberal measures guaranteed that the radicals would hold a majority in the legislature into the 1780s and kept turnout quite low in most elections, though some men (mostly leaders of the old Proprietary party) took the oaths only to become an opposition party. Called "Anti-Constitutionalists" at first (that is, opponents of the 1776 constitution), they soon took the name "Republicans." After the war, as the disfranchised regained the right to vote, Republicans won a solid majority in the legislature. By 1787 they were strong enough to win ratification of the Federal Constitution and then, in 1790, to replace the 1776 state constitution with a new one that created a bicameral legislature and an elective governor with a qualified veto. By then, Massachusetts had brought the constitutional learning process at the state level to its culmination.

Massachusetts Redefines Constitutionalism

Another bitter struggle occurred in Massachusetts, but there the result moved toward a new consensus about what a constitution should be. After four years of intense debate, Massachusetts found a way to lodge sovereignty with the people and not with government, that is, to distinguish a constitution from ordinary acts of legislation.

In response to the Massachusetts Government Act, passed by Parliament in 1774 (see Chapter 6), the colonists had risen and prevented the royal courts from sitting. In the three western counties of Worcester, Hampshire, and Berkshire, they had ousted from office a group of wealthy, intermarried families (called "river gods" in Connecticut Valley towns), most of whom subsequently became loyalists. The courts remained closed until the British withdrew from Boston in March 1776 and the Provincial Congress moved into the city and rees-

tablished itself as the General Court under the royal charter of 1691. The legislature then reapportioned itself to let towns choose representatives in proportion to population. Under the old system, most towns elected a single representative. A few (such as Salem) chose two, and only Boston could elect four. The new system rewarded older, more populous eastern towns at the expense of lightly populated western ones.

When the General Court revived royal practice by appointing its own members as county judges or justices of the peace, the western counties exploded. Their hatred of the river gods extended to eastern gentlemen as well. Denouncing the "antient Mode of Government among us which we so much detest and abhor," they attacked the reapportionment act and refused to reopen the courts in Hampshire and Berkshire Counties. Most of Berkshire's radicals were Baptists in religion and Lockeans in politics. They insisted upon contracts or compacts as the basis of authority in both church and state and continued to use county conventions in place of the courts. In England, a convention was an imperfect legislature that met only to handle an emergency and was then replaced by a legitimate Parliament, as happened during the Glorious Revolution of 1688–1689. But the Berkshire Constitutionalists regarded a "convention" as the purest expression of the will of the people, superior to any legislature. These uneducated farmers demanded a formal constitution for the state.

In the fall of 1776 the General Court asked the towns to authorize it to draft a constitution. By a two-to-one margin the voters agreed, a result that probably reflected a growing *distrust* of the legislature. Six months earlier hardly anyone would have questioned this procedure. The legislature drafted a constitution by stages over the next year and then, more cautious than other states, submitted the result to the towns for ratification. To the astonishment of the lawmakers, the voters rejected the constitution by a margin of five to one. Some towns objected to the lack of a bill of rights, and a few insisted that any constitution should be drafted by a separate convention. Several towns wanted the governor to be directly elected by the people, but most gave no reason for their rejection. Voters who were angry with a particular clause were likely to condemn the whole document.

Admitting defeat, the General Court urged the towns to postpone the question until after the war. Hampshire reopened its courts in April 1778, but Berkshire would not back down. The county demanded a constitutional convention and threatened to secede from the state. Citing the words of John Locke, these farmers insisted that they were now in a "state of nature," subject to no legitimate government. They could either set up on their own or join any neighboring state that had adopted a proper constitution. At a time when Vermont was making good its secession from New York, this ultimatum was no idle threat.

The General Court gave in, and a convention met in Boston in December 1779. John Adams drafted a constitution for it to consider. The convention used his text as a starting point. A final version was not submitted to the voters until after Adams left for a diplomatic post in Europe. This process marked the birth of the American model of constitution-making, the way to make the people the source of authority. A constitution should be drafted by a convention elected for that purpose alone, and the people had to ratify the result.

Since 1776, Adams's thoughts on the separation of powers and bicameralism had matured. Like the Virginia constitution, the Massachusetts constitution began with a bill of rights. Both houses would be elected annually. The House of Representatives would be chosen by the towns, as reapportioned in 1776. Senators were to be elected by counties and apportioned according to property values, not according to population. The governor was to be popularly elected and had a qualified veto (it could be over-ridden by two-thirds of both houses). Property qualifications rose as a citizen's duties increased. Voters had to own at least £50 of real property or £100 of personal property, representatives £100 in land or £200 in other property, senators £300 or £600 respectively, and the governor had to own £1,000 in landed property. He also had to be a Christian. For purposes of ratification only, all free adult males were eligible to vote. In accepting the basic social compact, everyone (that is, all free *men*) ought to have a chance to consent. Voters would be asked to vote on each article separately, not on the document as a whole.

During the spring of 1780 town meetings took up the constitution. A committee dominated by

John Adams, Portrait by John Trumbull (1793)   At the time of this painting, Adams was in his second term as vice president of the United States, an honor he earned through his important contributions to American constitutionalism and through his diplomatic services in France, the Netherlands, and Britain before 1789.

easterners tallied the results and declared that it had received the required two-thirds majority. The committee juggled the figures on two articles, both involving religion, to get this result. Those articles provided for the public support of ministers and required the governor to be a Christian. Most Baptists objected to all taxes for the support of religion, while strict Protestants wanted to exclude Catholics from the governorship. The new constitution promptly went into effect and, though it has often been amended, is still in force, making it the oldest constitution in the world. Starting with New Hampshire in 1784, other states followed the Massachusetts model.

Confederation

The creativity exhibited by the states had no counterpart in the Continental Congress, which met almost continuously in Philadelphia during the war except when the British army forced it to flee elsewhere. Before independence, hardly anyone had given serious thought to how an *American* nation ought to be governed. Dozens of colonists had drafted plans of conciliation with Britain, some quite innovative. But through 1775 only Benjamin Franklin and Silas Deane, a Connecticut delegate, had presented plans for an American union. Franklin's was an updated version of the Albany Plan of 1754 (see Chapter 5). Another proposal appeared in an American newspaper, but none of the three attracted public debate. Colonists energetically discussed the empire and their state governments, but not America.

Congress began serious debate on an American union in the summer of 1776 but then took nearly a year and a half to draft a final text of what became the "Articles of Confederation and perpetual Union." Ever since the First Continental Congress met in 1774 (Chapter 6), Congress had been voting by state. Delegates from large states had suggested representation according to population, but no census existed to give precise population totals, and the small states insisted on being treated as equals. So long as the British hovered nearby, ready to embrace any state that defected, the small states possessed great leverage. Thus, John Dickinson rejected proportional representation in favor of state equality early in the debate on American union. His draft of the Articles of Confederation enumerated the powers of Congress, which did not include levying taxes or regulating trade. During July and August 1776, Congress could not agree on how to apportion requisitions among the states. The northern states insisted that slaves should be counted in deciding how much revenue to requisition from each state. The southern states disagreed. Western lands were another tough issue. States with fixed borders, strongly encouraged by land speculators, pressured states with boundary claims stretching into the Ohio or Mississippi Valleys to surrender those claims to Congress.

In August 1776 Congress postponed the subject for six months. When the debate resumed after Washington's victories at Trenton and Princeton, Thomas Burke of North Carolina introduced a resolution that eventually became part of the Articles of Confederation: "Each state retains its sovereignty, freedom and independence, and every power, jurisdiction, and right, which is not by this confederation expressly delegated to the United States in Congress assembled." The acceptance of Burke's resolution, with only Virginia dissenting, ensured that the Arti-

cles would contain a firm commitment to state sovereignty. Only after Saratoga, however, was Congress able to complete and approve the Articles. In the final version, Congress was given no power over western land claims, and the formula for requisitions excluded slaves from the valuations. (In 1781 Congress changed the formula so that each slave was counted as three-fifths of a person for the purposes of requisition.)

In November 1777 Congress asked the states to ratify the Articles by March 10, 1778, but only Virginia met the deadline. Most states tried to attach conditions, which Congress rejected, but by midsummer ten had ratified. The three holdouts were Delaware, New Jersey, and Maryland—all states without western land claims who feared their giant neighbors. Maryland held out for more than three years, until Virginia agreed to cede its land claims north of the Ohio River to Congress. The Articles finally went into force on March 1, 1781.

By then, the Congress had lost most of its power. Some of its most talented members returned home to help reshape their state governments (Jefferson, Dickinson, Patrick Henry, Samuel Adams), or took army commands (Washington), or accepted diplomatic assignments (Franklin, John Adams, John Jay). The congressional effort to manage everything through committees overwhelmed the delegates and created bottlenecks. In 1776 the states had looked to Congress to confer legitimacy on their new governments, especially in the Middle Colonies, as independence approached (Chapter 6), but as the states adopted their own constitutions, their legitimacy became more obvious than that of Congress.

One problem loomed larger than all others. Congress met its expenses by printing money, using the Spanish dollar as its basic monetary unit. With the French alliance bolstering American credit, this practice worked reasonably well into 1778. The money depreciated but without causing great dissatisfaction. In 1779, however, with the economy deteriorating in what seemed to be an endless war, the value of continental money fell to less than a penny on the dollar. Congress agreed in early 1780 to stop the printing presses and to rely instead on requisitions from the states and on foreign and domestic loans. But it found that, without paper, it could not even pay the army. Britain used that opportunity to attack, this time in the Deep South.

THE CRISIS OF THE REVOLUTION, 1779–1783

Americans expected a quick victory under the French alliance. Instead, the struggle turned into a grim war of attrition, testing which side would first exhaust its resources or lose the will to fight. Loyalists became much more important to the British war effort, both as a source of manpower and as the government's main justification for continuing the war. Most settlers, argued Lord North, were still loyal to Britain. Properly organized, they could turn the contest around. To abandon them would be dishonorable and might lead to a bloodbath. As the British finished their global redeployment, they looked to the Deep South as the likeliest recruiting ground for armed loyalists. The Carolinas, bitterly divided in the 1760s over the Regulator movements and vulnerable to massive slave defections, seemed highly promising.

The Loyalists

Most loyalists were strongly committed to English ideas of liberty. Many of them had objected openly to the Stamp Act and other British measures but doubted that the home government was preparing a general assault on representative government in the colonies. They also thought that an untried American union was a far riskier venture than remaining part of the British empire. For many, the choice of loyalties was quite painful. Some waited until the fighting reached their neighborhood before deciding which side to shoot at or flee from. Loyalists quickly learned a stark truth, that they could not fire at their neighbors and expect to retain their homes except under heavy protection from the British army. The British, in turn, were slow to take advantage of the loyalists. In the early years of the war, British officers regarded the loyalists' very considerable military potential with the same disdain that they bestowed on the patriots. But as the war continued, the loyalists, who stood to lose everything in an American victory, demonstrated that they could be fierce soldiers.

About one-sixth of the white population chose the British side in the war, and nineteen thousand men joined more than forty loyalist military units, mostly after 1778 when Britain grew desperate for soldiers. Unlike most patriots, loyalists served long terms, even for the duration, because they could not go home unless they won. By 1780 the number of loyalists under arms probably exceeded the number of Continentals by two to one. State governments retaliated by banishing prominent loyalists under pain of death and by confiscating their property.

Freedom Fighters: Black Loyalists   When given the choice, most slaves south of New England also sided with Britain. In New England, where slaves sensed

An Offer of Freedom   An American newspaper reported on the efforts of the British to gain the support of slaves by offering them freedom.

Extract of a letter from Monmouth county, June 12.
"Ty, with his party of about 20 blacks and whites, last Friday afternoon took and carried off prisoners, Capt. Barns Smock and Gilbert Vanmater; at the same time spiked up the iron four pounder at Capt. Smock's house, but took no ammunition: Two of the artillery horses, and two of Capt. Smock' horses, were likewise taken off."
The above-mentioned Ty is a Negroe, who bears the title of Colonel, and commands a motly crew at Sandy-Hook.

Encampment of Loyalists at Johnston, Ontario, June 6, 1784 This painting by James Peachey depicts the arrival of loyalist exiles in Upper Canada.

that they could gain freedom by joining the rebels, they volunteered for military service. Elsewhere, although some fought for the Revolution, they realized that their best chance of emancipation lay with the British army. During the war, more than fifty thousand slaves (about 10 percent) fled their owners; of that total, about twenty thousand were eventually evacuated by the British. The decision to flee carried big risks. In South Carolina, hundreds reached the sea islands in an effort to join the British during Clinton's invasion of 1776, only to face their owners' wrath when the British had to withdraw without them. Others approached British units only to be treated as contraband (property) and face possible resale, but most of the slaves who reached British lines won their freedom, even though the British army never considered itself as an instrument of systematic emancipation. When the British withdrew, blacks scattered with them, many to Jamaica, some to Nova Scotia, others to London. In the 1780s the British government even created a colony of former slaves at Sierra Leone on the west coast of Africa.

Refugees: British Canada The struggle for loyalties thus created an enormous stream of refugees, black and white, chiefly at the end of the war. In addition to 20,000 former slaves, some 60,000 to 70,000 settlers left the thirteen states for other parts of the British empire. The American Revolution cre-

ated 30 refugees for every 1,000 people, compared with 5 per 1,000 produced by the French Revolution in the 1790s. About 35,000 found their way to Nova Scotia, the western half of which became the province of New Brunswick in the 1780s. Another 6,000 to 10,000 fled to Quebec, settled upriver from the older French population, and in 1791 became the new province of Upper Canada (later Ontario). A generous land policy, which required an oath of allegiance to George III, attracted thousands of new immigrants to Canada from the United States in the 1780s and 1790s. By the War of 1812, four-fifths of Upper Canada's 100,000 people were American-born. Though only one-fifth of these could be traced to loyalist resettlement, all the settlers supported Britain in that war. In a very real sense the American Revolution laid the foundation of two new nations—the United States and Canada—and competition between them for settlers and loyalties continued long after the fighting ended.

The Indian Struggle for Unity and Survival

Indians also began to play a more active role in the war. For them, the stakes were higher than they were for the settlers. Most of them saw that an American victory threatened their survival as a people on their ancestral lands. Nearly all of them sided with Britain, not out of loyalty or affection, but because they hoped that a British victory would stem the flood of western settlement that was roaring into Kentucky and the Ohio Valley. In the final years of the war, the eastern woodlands Indians achieved an unprecedented level of unity.

When the war began, most Indians tried to remain neutral. British agents were rebuffed when they asked the Iroquois to take up arms against the settlers. The Delawares and Shawnees, defeated in Lord Dunmore's War in 1774 (Chapter 6), also favored neutrality. Only the Cherokees heeded the British call to arms in 1776. Short on ammunition and other British supplies, they took heavy losses in 1776 before making peace and accepting neutrality. The Chickamaugas, a splinter group, continued to resist. In the Deep South, only the Catawbas — by now much reduced in number — were willing to fight on the American side.

Burgoyne's invasion brought the Iroquois into the war in 1777. The Mohawks in the east and the Senecas in the west sided with Britain under the leadership of Joseph Brant, a literate and educated Mohawk. His sister, Mary Brant, emerged as a skillful diplomat in the alliance between the Iroquois and the loyalists. A minority of Oneidas and some Tuscaroras fought with the Americans, thus rupturing the Iroquois League. Most of them were in the process of converting to Christianity under a Congregational missionary, Samuel Kirkland, a patriot.

A minority of Shawnees, led by Cornplanter, and of Delawares, led by White Eyes and Killbuck, also tried to keep on friendly terms with the Americans. They were willing to provide intelligence to American forces and even to serve as wilderness guides, but they refused to fight other Indians and tried to use their influence to preserve peace along the frontier. The Indians at the Christian Moravian missions in the Ohio country took a similar stance. The reluctance of Indians to kill other Indians, already visible during the Seven Years' War between Britain and France, became even more obvious during the Revolution. Loyalists and patriots were far more willing to kill each other.

The growth of racism along the frontier, already conspicuous by Pontiac's War, spread with alarming intensity during the Revolution. It made Indian neutrality all but impossible. Backcountry settlers from Virginia through New York refused to accept the neutrals on their own terms. Indian warriors, especially young men strongly influenced by nativist

Joseph Brant, Portrait by Gilbert Stuart (1786)   Brant, a Mohawk and a Freemason, was one of Britain's ablest commanders of loyalist and Indian forces. After the war he led most of the Six Nations to Canada for resettlement.

prophets (see Chapter 5), increasingly believed that the Great Spirit had created whites, Indians, and blacks as separate peoples who ought to remain apart. This Indian militancy further enraged the settlers. Young white hunters, often disdained by easterners as "near savages," proved their worth as "whites" by killing Indians.

The hatred of Indians grew so vicious that it threatened to undercut the Americans' own goals. In 1777 a Continental officer had Cornplanter murdered, and in 1778 American militia killed White Eyes. Four years later a frontier force massacred a hundred unarmed Moravian mission Indians at Gnadenhutten in the Ohio country. Nearly all of them were women and children, who knelt in prayer as they were murdered one by one. This atrocity brutalized Indians as well as settlers. Until then, most Indians had refrained from the ritual torture of prisoners. After Gnadenhutten they resumed the custom, not as a general practice, but as a punishment for atrocities. When they captured over four hundred Americans later that year, including many

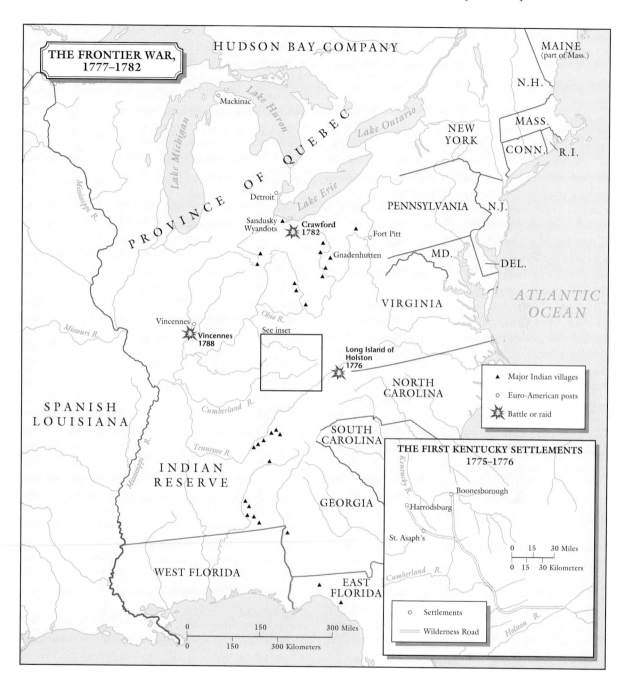

THE FRONTIER WAR, 1777–1782

THE FIRST KENTUCKY SETTLEMENTS 1775–1776

known participants in the massacre, they burned its leaders alive.

Faced with this hatred, Indians united to protect their lands. They won the frontier war north of the Ohio River. The Iroquois ravaged the Wyoming Valley of Pennsylvania in 1778. When an American army devastated Iroquoia in 1779 and committed many atrocities along the way, the Indians fell back on their British supply base at Niagara and continued the struggle. In 1779 nearly all Indians, from the Creeks on the Gulf Coast to the nations of the Great Lakes, exchanged emissaries and planned an all-out war against frontier settlers. George Rogers Clark of Virginia thwarted their offensive with a daring winter raid in which he captured Vincennes and cut off the western nations from British supplies. But the Indians regrouped against the Virginia "Long Knives" and drove them out of the Ohio country by 1782.

Attrition

After 1778, as the struggle became a global war of attrition, much of the British public began to suspect that the war could not be won. Trade was badly disrupted, thousands of ships were lost to privateers, taxes and the national debt soared, military recruits became harder to find, a cross-Channel invasion became a serious threat, and political dissent rose sharply. British determination to continue the war bitterly divided the country. Lord North's hard-pressed government began quietly recruiting Irish Catholics into the army and supported a modest degree of open toleration for English and Scottish Catholics. Popular discontent with the war took several forms, including a growing demand for the reduction of royal patronage and for the reform of Parliament. The new leniency toward Catholics produced a huge surge of anti-Catholic violence which culminated in the Gordon riots, named for Lord George Gordon, an anti-Catholic agitator. For nearly a week in June 1780 angry crowds dominated the streets of London, smashing Catholic chapels attached to foreign embassies, liberating prisoners from city jails, and finally attacking the Bank of England. The army, supported by Lord Mayor John Wilkes, suppressed the rioters, and for a time all demands for reform were discredited. Lord North had one more chance to win the war, this time with much greater support from loyalists and Indians.

Attrition weakened the United States even more seriously. The long war badly damaged the American economy. Indian raids reduced harvests, and military levies kept thousands of men away from productive work. Frequent British incursions into Connecticut and New Jersey wore down the defenders and destroyed a great deal of property. A large raid on Virginia in 1779 carried off or wrecked property worth £2 million. Merchants could not easily export goods to Europe or the West Indies, though some of them made enormous profits through blockade running or privateering raids against British commerce but average household income plunged by more than 40 percent. William Beadle, a Connecticut shopkeeper,

shot himself after slitting the throats of his wife and children rather than leave them all impoverished.

Even American triumphs sometimes came at a high price. Burgoyne's surrender left Americans with the burden of feeding his army for the rest of the war. When a large French fleet called at Boston, the crews devoured an alarming share of available provisions, as did a French army that landed at Newport in July 1780. Taken together, these heavy demands contributed to the collapse of the continental dollar in 1779–1780 and forced Congress and the army to requisition supplies directly from farmers in exchange for certificates geared to an inflation rate of forty to one, well below what it really was. Many farmers, rather than lose money on their crops, simply cut back production.

Continental soldiers—unpaid, ill-clothed, and often poorly fed—grew discontented and mutinous. As they became more professional through frequent drill, they also grew contemptuous of civilians. The winter of 1779–1780, the severest of the century, marked a low point in morale, especially among the main force of Continentals snowed in with Washington at Morristown, New Jersey. Many deserted. In May 1780 two Connecticut regiments of the Continental Line, without food for three days, mutinied and threatened to go home, raising the danger that the whole army might melt away. Their officers were barely able to restore control. On paper, Washington had sixteen thousand men. His real strength was about thirty-six hundred, and he did not have enough horses to move his artillery.

Sensing a unique opportunity in 1780, the British regrouped and attacked in force, concentrating on the southern colonies. For most of that year they seemed close to success. The Revolution entered its most critical phase and almost collapsed. "I have almost ceased to hope," Washington confessed. He longed for a burst of political energy to inspire the American people and end the war. He waited in vain.

The British Offensive in the South

In December 1778 a small British amphibious force had taken Savannah, Georgia, and had held it through 1779 against an American and French counterthrust. The British even managed to restore royal government with an elective assembly in Georgia between 1780 and 1782. By early 1780 the British were ready

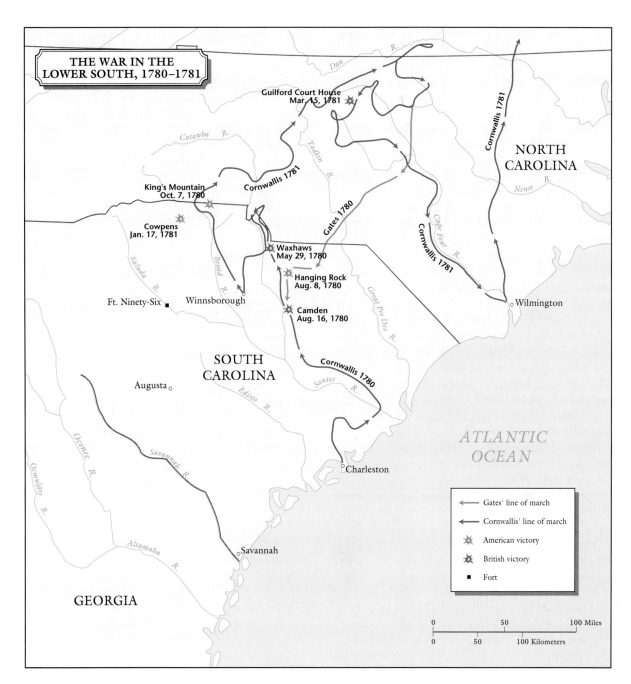

THE WAR IN THE LOWER SOUTH, 1780–1781

Guilford Court House
Mar. 15, 1781

Cornwallis 1781

NORTH CAROLINA

King's Mountain
Oct. 7, 1780

Cornwallis 1781

Cowpens
Jan. 17, 1781

Gates 1780

Cornwallis 1781

Waxhaws
May 29, 1780

Hanging Rock
Aug. 8, 1780

Ft. Ninety-Six   Winnsborough

Camden
Aug. 16, 1780

Wilmington

SOUTH CAROLINA

Augusta

Cornwallis 1780

ATLANTIC OCEAN

Charleston

Gates' line of march
Cornwallis' line of march
American victory
British victory
Fort

Savannah

GEORGIA

0   50   100 Miles
0   50   100 Kilometers

to move from this enclave and launch a general offensive. Their commander, General Clinton, was a cautious man who had been in charge of Britain's war effort in America since 1778 and had exasperated most of his subordinates, especially the loyalists, by remaining on the defensive in New York City. By the time he took command in Georgia in January

1780, he had finally devised a strategy for winning the war, but he revealed it to no one else.

That strategy called for much of the New York garrison to invade South Carolina, take Charleston, and unleash armed loyalists to pacify and police the countryside. Once Charleston had fallen, Clinton would leave part of his regular forces in the Carolinas under Lord Cornwallis to deal with any other army the Americans might put in the field. He himself would take the rest of his regulars back to New York and land on the Jersey coast with a force three times greater than Washington's at Morristown. By dividing his army into two columns, Clinton could break through both passes of the Watchung Mountains leading to Morristown. Washington would either have to hold fast on the defensive and be overwhelmed, or else abandon his artillery for lack of horses and attack one of the invading columns on unfavorable terms. Either way, Clinton reasoned, the Continental Army would be destroyed. If the French landed in Newport, as everyone expected, Clinton would then move against them with nearly his entire New York fleet and garrison. If he succeeded there too, he would have smashed every professional force in North America within a year's time. His only remaining task would be pacification, much of which he could leave to loyalists. He was also negotiating secretly with Benedict Arnold for the surrender of West Point, which would have opened the Hudson River to British ships as far north as Albany. Arnold, who thought that Congress had never really appreciated his heroism, had begun trading intelligence for cash in 1779.

Clinton's invasion of South Carolina began with awesome successes. While the British navy sealed off Charleston from the sea, an army of ten thousand closed off the land approaches to the city and trapped Benjamin Lincoln and five thousand defenders. Their surrender on May 12 gave Britain its largest haul of prisoners in the entire war. Even before their capitulation, Clinton turned loose his angry, well-trained loyalists under Banastre Tarleton and Patrick Ferguson. Tarleton caught the 350 remaining continentals at the Waxhaws near the North Carolina border on May 29 and, in what became infamous as "Tarleton's quarter," cut down even those who had already surrendered.

Britain's pacification policy began with a deliberate brutality designed to terrorize civilians into submission. It cowed most of them at first. But Thomas Sumter, after loyalists burned his plantation, began to fight back. He put together a mounted force that raided British outposts and terrorized loyalists. At Hanging Rock on August 6, Sumter's eight hundred men attacked five hundred loyalists, killing or wounding nearly half of them before Sumter's own men embarked on an orgy of looting and drinking. Not one of the combatants in this action was a British soldier. All were colonists. A vicious partisan war had begun.

Leaving Cornwallis in command of 8,300 men in South Carolina, Clinton sailed north with one-third of his Carolina army, only to learn that his plans for New Jersey had gone awry. During his absence the leading loyalists, convinced that Clinton would never take the initiative in the north, had persuaded Wilhelm, baron von Knyphausen, the temporary commander, to land in New Jersey with six thousand men on the night of June 6–7, 1780, and challenge Washington. Even a force that small posed a grave threat to Washington unless the militia came to his aid. Most loyalists thought the militia would not come forth, given the hard winter they had suffered and the punishment they had taken in numerous raids. Indeed, some militia units had even begun to muster women. To the dismay of the British, however, the militia turned out in force on June 7.

Only then, after an inconclusive engagement, did Knyphausen learn that Clinton was on his way by sea with his own plan of attack. The British pulled back to the coast and waited, but the element of surprise had been lost. When Clinton arrived, he attacked at Springfield on June 23 while loyalists set fire to the village. The battle became America's civil war in miniature, with New Jersey loyalist regiments attacking the New Jersey regiments of the Continental Line, who were assisted by New Jersey militia. The defense was stout enough to persuade Clinton to withdraw to New York. And because Washington's army remained intact, the British ignored the French when they landed at Newport. After June 1780 the British put all their hopes on the southern campaign. Even Arnold's attempt to betray West Point was thwarted in September. Clinton's agent, John André, was caught and hanged, but Arnold escaped to British lines and became a brigadier general in the British army with a generous pension.

Despite Sumter's harassment, Cornwallis's conquest of the Carolinas proceeded rapidly. Congress scraped together about nine hundred tough Maryland and Delaware Continentals, put Horatio Gates in command, and sent them south against Cornwallis. Bolstered by two thousand Virginia and North Carolina militia, Gates rashly offered battle at Camden on August 16 after many of his men had been up all night with diarrhea from eating half-baked bread. The militia, who lacked bayonets, fled in panic at the first British bayonet charge. The Continentals, left exposed, fought bravely but were crushed. Gates rode an astonishing 240 miles away from the scene in three days and, from Hillsborough, North Carolina, informed Congress that he had suffered "total Defeat." Two days after Camden, Tarleton surprised Sumter at his camp at Fishing Creek, killing 150 men and wounding 300.

Between May and August the British had destroyed all of the Continental forces in the Deep South and had mauled Sumter's band of partisans. These victories seemed to have given Georgia and the Carolinas to the British, fulfilling Clinton's boast that Britain's southern army would strip "three stripes . . . from the detestable thirteen." When the French foreign minister heard the news, he quietly asked whether Britain would make peace on the condition that each side keep what it currently possessed. Cornwallis turned the pacification of South Carolina over to his loyalists, many of whom were exiles from other states, and marched confidently into North Carolina to liberate that colony.

The Partisan War

But resistance continued. In one engagement, Tarleton and Sumter fought to a draw. Farther west, the threats of Patrick Ferguson's loyalists merely roused the frontier riflemen, already angered by Britain's alliance with the Indians, to cross the Blue Ridge, unite into a force of perhaps 1,800 men, and challenge Ferguson, who first retreated and then decided to stand at King's Mountain near the North Carolina border on October 7, 1780. Nearly all of the combatants on both sides were Americans. Losing only eighty-eight men, rebel marksmen picked off many defenders, advanced from tree to tree, and finally overwhelmed the loyalists, killing 160 men, including Ferguson, and capturing 860. They shot many prisoners and hanged a dozen, their answer to "Tarleton's quarter." This victory, the first British setback in the Deep South, stung Cornwallis, who halted his drive into North Carolina.

After Camden, Congress sent Nathanael Greene to the Carolinas with a small Continental force in October 1780. When Sumter withdrew from campaigning for several months to nurse a wound, Francis Marion took his place. A much abler leader, Marion operated from remote bases in the swampy coastal lowcountry. Yet Greene's prospects seemed desperate. He was shocked by the ugliness of the partisan war,

by the mutilation of corpses, the killing of prisoners, and the wanton destruction of property. And the condition of his own soldiers appalled him. Yet he and Marion devised a masterful strategy of partisan warfare that wore down the British and regained the Lower South for the Revolution.

In the face of a greatly superior enemy, Greene ignored a standard maxim of war and divided up his meager force of 1,800 Continentals. In smaller bands they would be easier to feed, but Greene's decision involved more than supplies. He sent three hundred men east to bolster Marion, and sent Daniel Morgan and three hundred riflemen west to threaten the British outpost of Ninety-Six. Tarleton urged Cornwallis to turn and crush the one thousand men still with Greene, but Greene had no intention of offering battle to a larger force. Worried that, after King's Mountain, Morgan might raise the entire backcountry against the British, Cornwallis divided his own army. He sent Tarleton with a mixed force of 1,100 British and loyalists after Morgan, who decided to stand with his back to a river at a place called Cowpens, where a loyalist, Hiram Saunders, kept his cattle. Augmented by militia, Morgan had 1,040 men.

Tarleton attacked on January 17, 1781. In another unorthodox move, Morgan sent his militia out front as skirmishers. He ordered them to fire two rounds and then retire to the left and redeploy in his rear as a reserve. Relieved of their fear of a bayonet charge, they obeyed. As they withdrew, the British rushed forward only to meet the Continentals, who also retreated at first, then wheeled and discharged a lethal volley. Morgan sent his cavalry charging into the British left flank, and the militia returned to the fray. Although Tarleton escaped, Morgan annihilated his army. For the first time in the war, an American force had clearly outfought the British army without an advantage of numbers or terrain. Once again, as in the 1776 campaign, the British seemed likely to lose the struggle for hearts and minds.

As Morgan rejoined Greene, Cornwallis staked everything on his ability to find Greene and crush him, precisely what he had failed to do to Washington after Trenton and Princeton four years earlier. But Greene had already outthought him. Anticipating the spring rains, he placed flatboats in his rear at major river crossings and then lured Cornwallis into a march of exhaustion. In a race to the Dan River, Cornwallis burned his baggage in order to travel lightly. Greene escaped with his flatboats across the flooded Yadkin River just ahead of Cornwallis, who had to march to a ford ten miles upstream, cross the river, and then march back while Greene rested. Greene repeated this stratagem all the way to the Dan until he judged that Cornwallis was so weak that the Americans could offer battle at Guilford Court House on March 15, 1781. With his militia, he outnumbered the British 4,400 to 1,900. Even though the British retained possession of the battle-field, they lost one-quarter of their force and the strategic initiative.

Cornwallis retreated to the coast at Wilmington to refit. He then decided to head north into Virginia — the seat of southern resistance, he told his superiors, and the one place where Britain could achieve decisive results. Instead of following him, Greene returned to South Carolina, where he and Marion overran the surviving British outposts one by one. After the British evacuated Ninety-Six on July 1, 1781, they held only Savannah and Charleston in the Deep South. Against heavy odds, Greene had reclaimed the region for the Revolution.

Mutiny and Reform

After the Camden disaster, Continental officers and state politicians demanded reforms to strengthen Congress and win the war. Encouraged by Washington, the state legislatures sent their ablest men to Congress. Maryland, the last state to hold out, finally agreed to complete the American union by ratifying the Articles of Confederation.

Before any reforms could take effect, discontent erupted in the army. Insisting that their three-year enlistments had expired, 1,500 men of the Pennsylvania Line got drunk on New Year's Day, 1781, killed three of their officers, and marched out of their winter quarters at Morristown. General Clinton sent agents from New York to promise the men a pardon and their back pay if they would defect to the British. But the mutineers marched south toward Princeton, not east to New York, and turned Clinton's men over to Pennsylvania authorities, who executed them. Congress, reassured, decided to negotiate with the soldiers. Over half of them accepted discharges, and those who remained in service got furloughs and bonuses for reenlistment. Encouraged by this treatment, two hundred New Jersey soldiers at Pompton also mutinied, but Washington used New England units from West Point to disarm them and

had two of their leaders executed. The army did not disintegrate, but well into 1781 there were still more loyalists serving in the British army than there were Continentals under Washington's direct command.

Civilian violence, such as the "Fort Wilson" riot in Philadelphia, also prompted Congress to change policies. Radical artisans blamed the city's rich merchants for the rampant inflation of 1779 and demanded price controls as a remedy. The merchants blamed paper money. In October, several men were killed when the antagonists exchanged shots near the fortified home of James Wilson, a wealthy lawyer. Spokesmen for the radicals deplored the violence and abandoned the quest for price controls. For city dwellers rich and poor, sound money seemed the only solution to the devastating inflation.

Congress interpreted these disturbances as a call for reform, for devising better ways to conduct national affairs. While armed partisans were making the war itself more radical, politics veered in a conservative direction, toward the creation of European state forms in America.

The states and Congress gave up efforts at price control and allowed the market to set prices and the value of money. Congress stopped issuing paper money, abandoned its cumbersome committee system, and created separate executive departments of foreign affairs, finance, war, and marine. Robert Morris, a wealthy Philadelphia merchant, became the first Secretary of Finance, helped to organize the Bank of North America (America's first), and made certain that the army was well fed and well clothed. Congress paid for supplies with interest-bearing notes and began to requisition revenue from the states. The states, in turn, imposed heavy taxes, but they never collected enough to meet both local and national expenses. Finally, Congress voted to amend the Articles of Confederation by asking the states to approve a 5 percent duty on all imports. Most states quickly ratified the "impost," but Rhode Island rejected it in 1783. Because amendments to the Articles needed unanimous approval by the states, that opposition killed the measure. A new impost of 1783 was defeated by New York in 1786.

The reforms of 1781 just barely kept a smaller army in the field for the rest of the war, but the creation of executive departments had a major unforeseen effect. Congress had been a plural executive, America's answer to the imperial Crown. But once Congress created its own departments, it began to

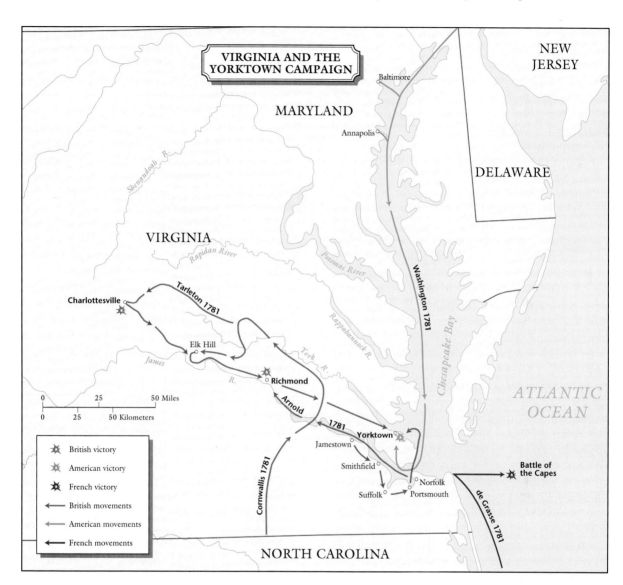

look like a national legislature, and a very feeble one at that, for it still had no power to compel civilians to obey its measures. It began to pass, not just administrative "orders" and "resolves," but also "ordinances," which were intended to be permanent and legally binding. But Congress could not prosecute anyone for noncompliance, which may be why it never passed any "laws."

The Ravaging of Virginia, Yorktown — and Peace

Cornwallis and Washington believed that what happened in Virginia would decide the war. When a large

British force raided the state in October and November 1780, Governor Thomas Jefferson raised enough militia to keep the British bottled up in Portsmouth, while he continued to ship men and supplies to Greene in the Carolinas. Thereafter, the state's ability to raise men and supplies almost collapsed.

In January 1781, Clinton sent Benedict Arnold by sea from New York with 1,600 men, mostly loyalists. They sailed up the James River, took the new capital of Richmond almost without resistance, and destroyed the city. When Jefferson called out the militia, few responded. Virginia had not experienced the partisan struggles that mobilized men on both sides in New Jersey and the Carolinas. The state provided a different kind of test for the central values of the Revolution. Could the voluntaristic ethic prevail in a long war? It very nearly failed. Most Virginia freemen above the age of sixteen had already done service, if only as short-term militia, thousands of them in response to the 1780 raid. They had already done their duty. For them, the crisis of 1781 was someone else's responsibility.

For months, there was no one else. When Cornwallis reached Virginia from Wilmington and took command in April, Arnold departed for New York. But the raids continued into the summer, sweeping as far west as Charlottesville, where Tarleton, who had recruited a new legion since his Cowpens defeat, scattered the Virginia legislature and came within minutes of capturing Jefferson on June 3, the day after his term as governor expired. Many of Jefferson's slaves greeted the British as liberators. Washington did send Lafayette with 1,200 New England and New Jersey Continentals to try to contain the damage.

At last, Washington got the opportunity he had been waiting for. He learned that Cornwallis had made Yorktown his principal base and that a powerful French fleet under François, comte de Grasse, would sail with three thousand soldiers from St. Domingue on August 13 and would remain in Chesapeake Bay for two months. Cooperating closely with the French commander, Jean Baptiste Donatier, comte de Rochambeau, Washington finally sprang the ultimate trap. Rochambeau led his five thousand soldiers from Newport to the outskirts of New York, where they joined Washington's five thousand Continentals. After feinting an attack on the British garrison to freeze Clinton in place, Washington marched the combined French and American armies four hundred miles south to tidewater Virginia, where they linked up with Lafayette's Americans and the other French army brought by de Grasse. After de Grasse's fleet beat off a British relief force at the Battle of the Capes on September 5, Washington cut off all retreat routes and besieged Cornwallis at Yorktown. On October 19, 1781, Cornwallis surrendered his entire army of eight thousand men. Virginia planters hovered nearby to reclaim their thousands of escaped slaves, only to find that many of them had died during the siege.

News of the disaster brought down the British government in March 1782. Lord North resigned, and George III even drafted an abdication message, though he never delivered it. The new ministry, committed to American independence as the price of peace, continued to fight the French in the Caribbean and the Spanish at Gibraltar, but the British evacuated Savannah and Charleston while the negotiations proceeded, concentrating their remaining forces in New York City. Contrary to the French Treaty of 1778 and against Franklin's advice, John Jay and John Adams opened secret peace negotiations with the British. They won British recognition of the Mississippi, though without New Orleans, as the western boundary of the new republic. New Englanders retained the right to fish off Newfoundland. The treaty recognized the validity of prewar debts owed to British merchants, and Congress promised to urge the states to restore confiscated loyalist property. These terms gave American diplomats almost everything they could have desired. At an advanced phase of the negotiations, the Americans told Vergennes, the French foreign minister, what they were doing. He feigned indignation, but the threat of a separate peace gave him the leverage he needed with Spain. Spain dropped its demand that France keep fighting until Britain surrendered Gibraltar. The Treaty of Paris, though signed and ratified months later, ended the war in February 1783.

Western Indians were appalled to learn that, despite their own military successes, the treaty gave their lands to the United States. They knew that they had not been conquered, whatever European diplomats might say. Their war for survival continued with few breaks into 1795.

Congress faced other ominous problems as well. In March 1783 discontented Continental officers hinted that they might stage a coup d'etat unless Congress granted them generous pensions. Washington, confronting them at their encampment at Newburgh, New York, fumbled for his glasses and remarked, "I have grown old in the service of my country, and now find that I am growing blind." Tears filled the eyes of his comrades in arms, and the threat of a coup vanished.

In Philadelphia two months later, unpaid Pennsylvania soldiers marched on the state house where both Congress and the state's executive council sat. Ignoring Congress altogether, they demanded that the Commonwealth of Pennsylvania redress their grievances. Congress decided that it had been insulted and voted to leave the city for Princeton, where it reconvened in Nassau Hall. Its archives and administrative departments remained in Philadelphia.

"I confess I have great apprehensions for the union of the states," wrote Charles Thomson, secretary to Congress since 1774, "& begin to fear that America will experience internal convulsions, and that the fabrick of her liberty will be stained with the blood of her sons." In the opinion of many delegates, only British hostility had created the American Union, and that Union might dissolve with the return of peace. Congress moved from Princeton to Annapolis and eventually settled in New York. Whether the Union could survive remained uncertain.

A REVOLUTIONARY SOCIETY?

Independence transformed American life. In the decade after 1776, religious dissenters disestablished the Church of England in every southern state. Religious liberty and the pluralism it created became not just tolerated but admired. Within American society, the biggest winners were free householders, who gained enormously from the democratization of politics and the opportunity to colonize the Great West. Besides the loyalists, the biggest losers were Indians, who continued their resistance to settler expansion. Many slaves won their freedom, and women struggled to win greater dignity. Both succeeded only when their goals proved compatible with the ambitions of most white householders.

Religious Transformations

Once the colonies proclaimed their independence, the Church of England, with George III as its "supreme head," was vulnerable to attack. Although most Anglican clergymen either supported the Revolution or tried to remain neutral, an aggressive loyalist minority stirred the wrath of patriots. Religious dissenters in the southern colonies successfully deprived the Church of England of its tax support and other privileges, such as the sole right to perform marriages. In 1786 Virginia passed Thomas Jefferson's eloquent Statute for Religious Freedom, which declared that "God hath created the mind free" and that efforts to use coercion in matters of religion "tend only to beget habits of hypocrisy and meanness." In Virginia, church attendance and the support of ministers became purely voluntary activities.

Other states proceeded more cautiously. In New England (apart from Rhode Island) the established

Interior of Touro Synagogue, Newport, Rhode Island It is the best surviving example of Jewish artistic taste in eighteenth-century America.

Congregational churches strongly supported the Revolution and were less vulnerable to attack. Their ministers' salaries continued to be paid out of public taxes, although recognized dissenters, such as Baptists, could insist that their church taxes go to their own clergy. The Congregational Church exercised other public or quasi-public functions, especially on thanksgiving, fast, and election days. Disestablishment did not become complete until 1818 in Connecticut and 1833 in Massachusetts.

Although most states still restricted officeholding to Christians or Protestants, many people were coming to regard the coercion of anyone's conscience as morally wrong. Jews and Catholics both gained from the new atmosphere of tolerance. When Britain recognized the Catholic Church in the Quebec Act of 1774, Americans had shuddered with anxiety. But in 1790, when John Carroll of Maryland became the first Roman Catholic bishop in the United States, hardly anyone protested. Before independence, an Anglican bishop had been an explosive issue in several colonies. But in the 1780s the Church of England reorganized itself as the Protestant Episcopal Church and quietly began to consecrate its own bishops. Both the Episcopalians and the Presbyterians showed their acceptance of republican values by adopting written constitutions for their churches.

The First Emancipation

The Revolution freed tens of thousands of slaves, mostly south of Pennsylvania. But it also gave new vitality to slavery in the region that people were beginning to call "the South." Within a generation, it also brought about the abolition of slavery in the emerging "North." Race was the defining factor in these regional differences. In the South, most blacks remained slaves. In the North, they became free but not equal. The independent householder and his voluntaristic ethic remained almost a white monopoly.

Many slaves actually freed themselves. State governments either tried to prevent emancipation or to catch up with it and regularize it. The British army enabled over half the slaves of Georgia and perhaps a quarter of those in South Carolina to win their freedom. A similar process was under way in Virginia in 1781, only to be cut off at Yorktown. Hundreds of New England slaves won freedom by volunteering for military service. They announced what they were fighting for in the surnames they adopted. Jeffrey Liberty, Cuff Liberty, Dick Freeman, and Jube Freeman served in one Connecticut regiment. After the Massachusetts Bill of Rights proclaimed that all people were "born free and equal," Elizabeth (Bett) Freeman sued her master in 1781 and won her liberty. Thereafter, most of the slaves in Massachusetts and New Hampshire simply walked away from their masters.

Elsewhere, legislative action was necessary. Pennsylvania led the way in 1780 with the modern world's

Gravestone of John Jack of Concord, Massachusetts, 1773   The epitaph on Jack's gravestone was written by Daniel Bliss, a loyalist. It was frequently reprinted by nineteenth-century abolitionists.

first gradual emancipation statute. Instead of freeing current slaves, it declared that all children born to Pennsylvania slaves would become free at age 28, a provision meant to compensate the slaveholders. Slaves would have to pay the cost of their own emancipation, a requirement that prevented them from competing on equal terms with free whites, who usually entered adult life with inherited property. Some masters sold their slaves to southerners before the moment of emancipation, and some whites tried to kidnap free blacks and carry them south. The Pennsylvania Abolition Society fought these abuses and tried to make gradual abolition a reality. By 1800 Philadelphia had the largest community of free blacks in North America, with its own churches and other voluntary societies.

The Pennsylvania pattern was followed in most of the other northern states, with variations in detail. In regions where slaves constituted more than 10 percent of the population, such as southern New York and northeastern New Jersey, slaveholders' resistance to abolition delayed legislation for years. New York yielded in 1799. New Jersey was the last northern state to provide for gradual abolition, in 1804.

In the Upper South, most Methodists and some Baptists came out for abolition in the 1780s, only to retreat over the next two decades. Maryland and Virginia passed laws permitting the manumission of individual slaves. By 1810 over one-fifth of Maryland's slaves had been freed, as had 10,000 of Virginia's 300,000 slaves, including over 300 freed under Washington's will at his death in 1799. But slaves were the cornerstone of the plantation economy and usually their masters' most valuable asset. In the South, abolition would have amounted to a social revolution and the impoverishment of the planter class. Planters resisted emancipation, especially with the rise of cotton as a new cash crop in the 1790s, but they encouraged reforms to humanize the institution and supported the Christianization of their slaves.

In Maryland and Virginia, where the birth rate among slaves was increasing their population beyond what the tobacco economy could absorb, state governments banned the Atlantic slave trade, as had all states outside the Deep South. Georgia and South Carolina, both to make up for their loss of slaves during the war and to meet the demand for cotton after 1790, reopened the Atlantic slave trade. South Carolina alone imported nearly 60,000 Africans between the end of the war and federal prohibition of the African slave trade in 1808.

The Challenge to Patriarchy

Nothing as dramatic as abolition occurred during the Revolution to alter gender relations, though subtle changes did emerge. With many of the men away from home fighting the war, women were left in charge of the household, sometimes with interesting consequences. "I hope you will not consider yourself as commander in chief of your own house," Lucy Knox warned Henry, her soldier husband, in 1777, "but be convinced . . . that there is such a thing as equal command." Though some women acquired new authority, nearly all of them had to work harder to keep their households functioning. The war cut off the supply of European consumer goods. Household manufactures, mostly the work of women, had to fill that gap. At a time when husbands and sons were risking their lives, women seem to have accepted their responsibilities without demanding an expansion of their legal and political rights. But soaring food prices made many women assertive and violent. In food riots from Massachusetts to Virginia through 1779, women often took the lead in trying to make merchants lower prices or stop hoarding grain.

Attitudes toward marriage were also changing. The common-law rule of coverture (see Chapter 4) still denied wives any legal personality, but some of them, citing their own support of the Revolution, persuaded state governments not to impoverish them by confiscating the property of their loyalist husbands. Many writers insisted that good marriages rested on mutual affection, not on property settlements. In wealthy northeastern family portraits, husbands and wives were beginning to appear as equals (see Photo Essay following this chapter). Parents were urged to respect the personalities of their children and to avoid severe discipline. In popular culture, the traditional reverence for the elderly was giving way to a fascination with youth and energy.

Some women took up reform causes. Esther de Berdt Reed organized the Philadelphia Ladies Association in 1780 to relieve the sufferings of Continental soldiers. It was the first women's society in American history to take on a public role.

Other developments were less obvious but still significant. Women did not demand equal political rights at any point in the Revolution, but the New Jersey Constitution of 1776 let women vote if they headed a household (usually as a widow) and paid taxes, a privilege that was revoked in 1807. Especially in the Northeast, more women began to read and most tried to learn to write. Philosophers, clergymen, and even popular writers were beginning to treat women as morally superior to men, a sharp reversal of earlier assumptions and a powerful current within the Scottish Enlightenment (Chapter 4). The notion of the "republican wife" and the "republican mother" began to take hold in this context, giving wives and mothers in literate households an expanded educational role within the family as they tried to encourage diligence in their husbands and patriotism in their sons. In the 1790s the novel emerged as a major cultural form in the United States. Its main audience was female, as were many of the authors. Novels cast women as major characters in the drama of life and warned readers, especially young women, that the world was a cruel place populated by greedy men and seducers. More women went to school in the 1780s than ever before. The first female academies were founded in the 1790s. By the 1830s nearly all native-born women in the Northeast were literate.

Western Expansion, Discontent, and Conflict with Indians

Westward expansion continued during the Revolutionary War. With thirty axmen, Daniel Boone, a North Carolina hunter, hacked out the Wilderness Road from Cumberland Gap to the Kentucky bluegrass country in early 1775. When the first settlers arrived, they challenged the speculative Transylvania Company, which claimed title to the land. The settlers called Kentucky "the best poor-man's country" and claimed it should belong to those who tilled its soil, not to men with paper titles from governments far to the east in North Carolina, Virginia, or London.

Few Indians lived in Kentucky, but it was used as the favorite hunting ground of the Shawnees and other nations. Their frequent raids often prevented the settlers from planting crops. The settlers ate game and put up log cabins against the inside walls of large rectangular stockades, ten feet high and built from oak logs. At each corner, a blockhouse with a protruding second story permitted the defenders to fire along the outside walls. Cabin roofs sloped inward so that settlers could put out fires without facing enemy bullets. Three of these so-called "Kentucky stations" were built—at Boonesborough, St. Asaph, and Harrodsburg—and they managed to withstand Indian attacks until late in the war.

Because of the constant danger, settlement grew slowly at first. In 1779, when George Rogers Clark's victory at Vincennes provided a brief period of security, thousands of settlers moved in. After 1780, however, the Indians renewed their attacks, this time with British allies who could smash the stockades with their artillery. Throughout the Revolution, Kentucky lived up to its old Indian reputation as the "dark and bloody ground." Only a few thousand settlers stuck it out until the war ended, when they were joined by swarms of newcomers. By then, speculators and absentees were claiming the best bluegrass land.

The Federal Census of 1790 listed 74,000 settlers and slaves in Kentucky and about half that many in Tennessee, where the Cherokees had ceded a large

Portrait of Esther de Berdt Reed by Charles Willson Peale

Boonesborough   Boonesborough was the most famous Kentucky station founded during the Revolutionary War.

Both Congress and the states hoped to compel the Indians to pay a large share of the cost of the Revolutionary War without giving them much in return. Many states and the Congress had raised soldiers by promising them land after the war, and now they needed the western lands in order to meet these pledges. Tragically, the few Indian nations that had supported the United States suffered the most. In the 1780s, after Joseph Brant led most of the Iroquois north to Canada, New York confiscated most of the land of the friendly Iroquois who stayed. South Carolina dispossessed the Catawbas of most of their ancestral lands. The states had a harder time seizing the land of hostile Indians, who usually had Spanish or British allies.

Throughout the West, secessionist movements peaked in the late 1780s when neither Congress nor eastern state governments seemed able to solve western problems. Some Tennessee settlers seceded from North Carolina in the 1780s and for a time maintained a separate state called Franklin. Separatist sentiment also ran strong in Kentucky. Even the settlers of western Pennsylvania thought of setting up on their own after Spain closed the Mississippi to American traffic in 1784. James Wilkinson explored the possibility of creating an independent republic west of the Appalachians under Spanish protection. When Congress refused to recognize Vermont's independence from New York, even the radical Green Mountain Boys sounded out British officials about readmission to the empire as a separate province.

Congress did, however, persuade states with colonial charter claims to land north of the Ohio River to cede them to the United States. Virginia's compliance in early 1781 prompted other states to follow suit. Jefferson drafted a congressional resolution in 1784, never implemented, which would have created ten or more new states in this Northwest Territory. Each state would adopt the constitution and laws of any one of the older states and, when its population reached twenty thousand would be admitted to the Union on terms of full equality with the original thirteen. The possibility that the northwestern states, plus Kentucky, Tennessee, and perhaps Vermont, might outvote the old thirteen made Congress hesitate. But in the Land Ordinance of 1785, Congress did authorize the survey of the Northwest Territory and its division into townships six miles square, each composed of 36 "sections" of 640 acres apiece. Surveyed land would be sold at auction starting at a dollar an acre.

tract after their defeat in 1776. These settlers thrived both because few Indians lived there and because British and Spanish raiders found it hard to reach the region. To the south and north of this bulge, settlement was much riskier. After the war, Spain supplied arms and trade goods to Creeks, Cherokees, Choctaws, and Chickasaws willing to resist Georgia's attempt to settle its western lands. North of the Ohio River, where confederated Indians had won their military struggle, the British refused to withdraw their garrisons and traders from Niagara, Mackinac, Detroit, and a few other places, even though, according to the Treaty of Paris, those outposts now lay within the boundaries of the United States. To justify their refusal, the British pointed to the failure of Congress to honor America's obligations to loyalists and British creditors under the treaty. Although small groups of Indians sold large tracts of land to Georgia, Pennsylvania, and New York, as well as the Congress, the Indian nations repudiated these sales and, supported by either Spain or Britain, continued to resist into the 1790s.

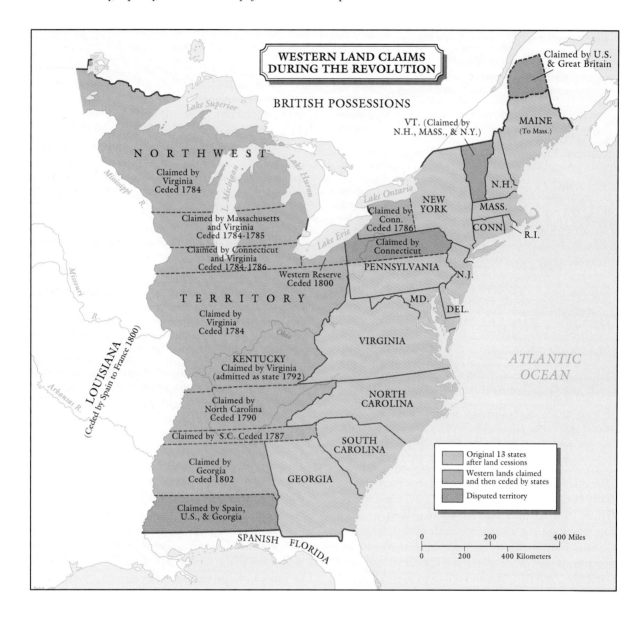

Alternate townships would be sold in sections or as a whole, to satisfy settlers and speculators, respectively.

In July 1787, while the Constitutional Convention deliberated in Philadelphia, Congress (sitting in New York) returned to the problem of governing the Northwest Territory. By then, Massachusetts veterans were organizing the Ohio Company under the Reverend Manassah Cutler to obtain a huge land grant from Congress. Cutler joined forces with William Duer, a New York speculator who was organizing the Scioto Company. Together they pried

from Congress 1.5 million acres for the Ohio Company veterans and an option on 5 million more acres, which the Ohio Company promptly assigned to the Scioto Company. The Ohio Company agreed to pay Congress two installments of $500,000 in depreciated securities. To meet the first payment, Duer's backers lent Cutler's $200,000. Once again speculators, rather than settlers, seemed to be winning the West.

During that same month, Congress passed the Northwest Ordinance of 1787 to provide government for the region. Rejecting Jefferson's goal of ten or more states, the Ordinance authorized the creation of from three to five states, to be admitted to the Union as full equals of the original thirteen. In short, the Ordinance rejected colonialism among white people except as a temporary phase through which a "territory" would pass on its way to statehood. Congress would first appoint a governor and a council to rule until population reached five thousand. At that point, the settlers could elect an assembly that was empowered to pass laws, although the appointed governor (obviously modeled on earlier royal governors) had an absolute veto. When population reached sixty thousand, the settlers could adopt their own constitution and petition Congress for statehood. The Ordinance protected civil liberties, set aside one section of each township for education, and prohibited slavery forever within the region.

Southern delegates all voted for the Ordinance despite its antislavery clause. They probably hoped that Ohio would become what Georgia had been in the 1730s, a society of armed freemen able to protect vulnerable slave states, such as Kentucky, from invasion by hostile forces (see Chapter 4). In the 1780s the Ohio Valley was the republic's most dangerous frontier. Southern delegates also thought that most settlers of the territory would come from Maryland, Virginia, and Kentucky. Even if the settlers could not bring slaves with them, they would have southern loyalties. New Englanders, by contrast, were counting on the Ohio Company to lure their own veterans to the region.

Finally, the antislavery clause may have been part of a larger "Compromise of 1787," involving both the Ordinance and the clauses on slavery in the federal Constitution, especially the one that permitted states to count three-fifths of their slaves for purposes of representation, which was adopted in Philadelphia at the same time. The concession to northerners in the Ordinance was offset by the concession to southerners in Philadelphia. Several Congressmen who were also delegates to the Constitutional Convention were traveling back and forth between Philadelphia and New York at precisely the time these decisions were made. They may have struck a deal.

Congress had finally adopted a coherent western policy. After 1787 only the Indians prevented its implementation. They drove away hundreds of squatters. Federal surveyors risked their lives in Ohio, and

when the first townships were offered for sale in late 1787, there were few buyers. By 1789, however, the Ohio Company had established the town of Marietta, Kentuckians had founded a town that would soon be called Cincinnati, and tiny outposts had been set up at Columbia and Gallipolis. But the settlers in these communities could not take on the Indians without massive help from the new federal government.

A MORE PERFECT UNION

The 1780s were difficult times. The economy did not rebound, debtors and creditors quarreled fiercely, and state politics displayed persistent cleavages. Out of this ferment arose the demand to amend or even replace the Articles of Confederation.

Commerce, Debt, and Shays' Rebellion

British merchants flooded American markets with exports worth £3.7 million in 1784, the highest total since 1771. But Americans could not pay for the goods. Their exports to Britain that year were £750,000, not even half of the £1.9 million they had shipped in 1774, the last year of peace. When Britain invoked the Navigation Acts against the former colonies by closing the British West Indies to American ships (but not to American goods), indirect returns through the once profitable Caribbean trade also faltered. Trade with France closed some of the gap but remained disappointing because the French could not offer the long-term credit that London and Glasgow had provided. The American economy entered a deep depression that lifted only slightly in 1787–1788 before it finally rebounded in the 1790s. Imports from Britain dropped by 40 percent in 1785 and another 30 percent in 1786. Exports improved to almost £900,000 but remained far below prewar levels.

These hardships turned private debts into a huge social problem that the states, buried under their own war debts, could not easily mitigate. Merchants, dunned by their British creditors, sued their customers, many of whom could not even pay their taxes. Farmers, faced with the loss of their crops, livestock, and even their farms, resisted foreclosures and looked to the state governments for relief.

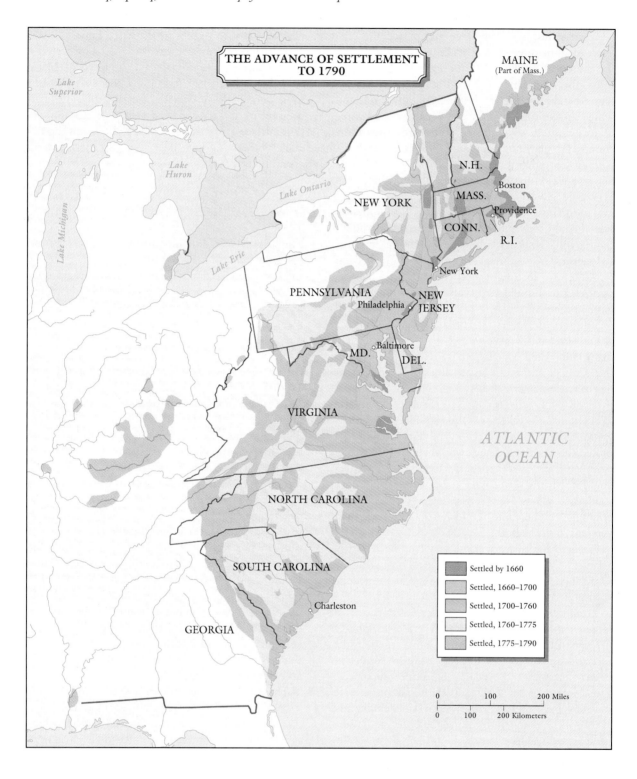

THE ADVANCE OF SETTLEMENT TO 1790

Lake Superior

Lake Huron

Lake Michigan

Lake Ontario

Lake Erie

MAINE
(Part of Mass.)

N.H.

MASS.

Boston

NEW YORK

Providence

CONN.

R.I.

New York

PENNSYLVANIA

NEW JERSEY

Philadelphia

Baltimore

MD.

DEL.

VIRGINIA

ATLANTIC
OCEAN

NORTH CAROLINA

SOUTH CAROLINA

Charleston

GEORGIA

Settled by 1660

Settled, 1660–1700

Settled, 1700–1760

Settled, 1760–1775

Settled, 1775–1790

0   100   200 Miles

0   100   200 Kilometers

The Sons of Coke and Littleton, Returning from a Rich Feast at Concord Court   This engraving from *Bickerstaff's Almanack*, 1787, shows the hatred of the Shaysites for lawyers, here depicted as men feeding upon the distresses of ordinary citizens. Coke and Littleton were famous legal treatises.

About half of the states issued paper money in the 1780s, and many passed stay laws to postpone the date on which a debt would come due. Massachusetts, which remembered its fierce conflicts over paper money before 1750 (see Chapter 4), rejected both options and raised taxes to an unprecedented level. In 1786 many farmers in Hampshire County took matters into their own hands. Large crowds gathered to prevent the courts from conducting business, much as patriots had done against the British in 1774. But Governor James Bowdoin insisted that action that had been appropriate against a tyrannical monarch was not acceptable in a republican government elected by the people. In the winter of 1787 the protestors, loosely organized under a Continental Army veteran, Captain Daniel Shays, tried to storm the federal arsenal at Springfield. An army of volunteers under Benjamin Lincoln marched west, opened fire with artillery, and scattered the Shaysites. Yet, in the May assembly elections, men sympathetic to Shays won enough seats to pass a stay law.

The impotence of Congress in the crisis alarmed Shays' opponents. Congress asked the states for volunteers, but only Virginia responded and then not in time to affect the outcome. In Massachusetts, Shays' Rebellion converted into nationalists many gentlemen and artisans who until then had opposed efforts to strengthen the central government.

Cosmopolitans versus Localists: State and Congressional Politics

The tensions that racked Massachusetts were present elsewhere. Crowds in other states also prevented courts from sitting or even besieged the legislature.

State politics reflected a persistent cleavage between what historians describe as "cosmopolitan" and "localist" coalitions. Merchants, urban artisans, commercial farmers, southern planters, and former Continental Army officers made up the cosmopolitan bloc. They looked to energetic government, both state and continental, to solve the country's problems. They favored aggressive trade policies, sound money, repayment of the public debt, good salaries for executive officials and judges, and leniency to returning loyalists. The "localists" were farmers, rural artisans, and militia veterans who distrusted most of these policies while favoring paper money and debtor relief. They preferred generous salaries for representatives (thus permitting ordinary men to serve), which cosmopolitans resisted.

In most states, localists defeated their opponents most of the time. During and after the war, they destroyed the feudal revival (see Chapter 6) by confiscating the gigantic land claims of the Granville District, the Fairfax estate, the Calvert and Penn proprietaries, and the manorial estates of New York loyalists. (Because their owners were patriots, Rensselaerswyck and Livingston Manor survived, to become the site of agrarian discontent and violence into the 1840s, when they were finally abolished.) Except in Vermont, localists were much less adept at blocking the claims of speculators in western lands, some of whom put together enormous tracts. But cosmopolitans lost so often that many of them despaired of state politics and looked to the central government for relief, provided they could find a way to strengthen it.

But Congress too had to face harsh fiscal and diplomatic problems. Between October 1781 and February 1786, it requisitioned $15.7 million from the states but received only $2.4 million. Its annual income had fallen to $400,000 at a time when interest on its debt approached $2.5 million and when the principal on the foreign debt was about to come due. Requisitions were beginning to seem as hopelessly inefficient as George Grenville had predicted when he proposed the Stamp Act (Chapter 5).

Foreign relations also took an ominous turn. In 1786 Foreign Secretary John Jay negotiated a treaty with Don Diego de Gardoqui, the Spanish minister to the United States. It gave northern merchants new trading privileges with the Spanish colonies, provided Congress accepted Spain's closing of the Mississippi to American traffic for twenty-five years. All five southern states in Congress rejected these terms, thus defeating the treaty which, under the Articles of Confederation, needed nine votes. But seven northern states voted for it. Angry talk of disbanding the Union soon filled Congress. Delegates began negotiating over which state would join what union if the breakup occurred. In February 1787 the controversy became public when a Boston newspaper called for multiple confederations.

By the mid-1780s many cosmopolitans were becoming nationalists who looked for ways to strengthen the Union. Many of them had served long, frustrating years in Congress or the army, unable to carry out vital policies. In 1785 some of them tried to see what could be done outside Congress. To resolve disputes about navigation rights on the Potomac River, George Washington invited Virginia and Maryland delegates to a conference at Mt. Vernon, where they drafted an agreement that proved acceptable to both states and to Congress. James Madison, a former congressman, then persuaded the Virginia legislature to issue a call to all the states to participate in a convention at Annapolis. It would suggest ways to improve American trade.

Four states, including Maryland, ignored the call, and the New Englanders had not yet arrived when, in September 1786, the delegates from the four middle states and Virginia accepted a report drafted by Alexander Hamilton of New York, a distinguished veteran of the Continental Army. It urged all of the states to send delegates to a general convention at Philadelphia in May "to devise such further provisions as shall appear to them necessary to render the constitution of the Foederal Government adequate to the exigencies of the Union." Seven states accepted the invitation before Congress endorsed the convention on February 21, 1787, and five accepted later. Rhode Island refused to participate. Madison used the winter months to study the defects of Greek and European confederacies and to draft a plan for a much stronger American union.

The Philadelphia Convention

With Washington presiding, the delegates began in May 1787 with a plan that resembled the Virginia Constitution of 1776. It proposed almost a sovereign Parliament for the United States. By September the delegates had produced a document much closer to the Massachusetts Constitution of 1780, including a clear separation of powers. In effect, the convention, in four months of secret sessions, repeated the constitutional learning process that had taken four years at the state level between 1776 and 1780.

Governor Edmund Randolph opened the convention with the Virginia, or "large state," plan. Drafted largely by Madison, it proposed a bicameral legislature with representation in both houses apportioned according to population. The legislature would choose the national executive and the national judiciary. It would possess all powers currently lodged in Congress and the power "to legislate in all cases to which the separate States are incompetent." It could "negative all laws passed by the several States, contravening in the opinion of the National

Legislature the articles of Union." Remarkably, the plan did not include the explicit power to tax or regulate trade. Madison apparently believed it wiser to be vague and sweeping, rather than explicit. His plan also required that the proposed constitution be ratified by separate state conventions, not by state legislatures. Within two weeks, the delegates had agreed on three-year terms for members of the lower house and seven-year terms for the upper house, and that the executive should be a single person chosen by the legislature for a single, seven-year term.

By mid-June, small-state delegates were strong enough to strike back. William Paterson introduced the New Jersey Plan, which merely gave the existing Congress the power to levy import duties and a stamp tax (rather like George Grenville's imperial reforms of 1764–1765), to regulate trade, and to use force against states that did not pay their requisitions (as in Lord North's Conciliatory Proposition of 1775). Each state would have one vote. Perhaps only to terrify the small states, Hamilton proposed a government in which both the senate and the executive would serve "on good behavior"—that is, for life! To him, the British constitution was still the best in the world.

At that point, all of the options before the convention seemed counterrevolutionary. Madison's Parliament for America, Paterson's emulation of Grenville and North, and Hamilton's enthusiasm for the British empire all challenged in major ways the principles of 1776. But as the summer progressed, the delegates thought carefully about what the voters would or would not accept and relearned the hard lessons of popular sovereignty that the state constitutions had taught. The result was a federal Constitution that was indeed revolutionary.

The debate grew as hot as the summer weather. The small states warned that their voters would never accept a constitution that let the large states swallow them up. The large states replied that they could not accept a union that did not include proportional representation in both houses. "The Large States dare not dissolve the Confederation," retorted Delaware's Gunning Bedford in the most explosive outburst of the convention. "If they do the small ones will find some foreign ally of more honor and good faith, who will take them by the hand and do them justice." Then Connecticut delegates made it clear that

they would be happy with state equality in one house and proportional representation in the other.

In late July, the delegates accepted this "Connecticut Compromise" and over the next six weeks completed the document. They finally realized that they were devising a government of laws, to be enforced on individuals through a new federal court system, and not propping up a system of congressional resolutions to be carried out (or ignored) by the states. Terms for representatives were reduced to two years and terms for senators to six (with each state legislature choosing two senators). The president would serve four years, could be reelected, and would be chosen by an electoral college. Each state received as many electors as it had congressmen and senators combined, and the states would decide how to choose their electors. Each elector had to vote for two candidates, one of whom had to be from another state. This provision reflected the fear that localist impulses might prevent a majority vote for anyone, although the delegates knew that Washington would become the first president. After him there was no obvious choice.

In other provisions, free and slave states agreed to count only three-fifths of the slaves in apportioning both representation and direct taxes. The enumeration of congressional powers became lengthy and explicit and included taxation, the regulation of foreign and interstate commerce, and the catchall "necessary and proper" clause. Madison's negative on state laws disappeared, replaced by the gentler "supreme law of the land" clause. Over George Mason's last-minute objection, the delegates voted not to include a bill of rights.

With little debate, the Convention approved a revolutionary clause that specified how the Constitution would be ratified. It required special conventions in each state and declared that the Constitution would go into force as soon as any nine states had ratified it, even though the Articles of Confederation required the unanimous approval of all amendments. As the delegates fully realized, they were proposing an illegal—but peaceful—overthrow of the existing legal order. If all the states approved, it would, they hoped, become both peaceful and legal. The Constitution would then rest on popular sovereignty in a way that the Articles never had. The "Federalists," as supporters of the Constitution now called themselves, knew that they would have to use persuasion, not force, to win approval. But they were willing to risk destroying the Union in order to save it.

Ratification

When Federalist delegates returned home, they made a powerful case for the Constitution in newspapers, most of which favored a stronger central government. Most "Antifederalists," as opponents of the Constitution were now called, were "localists" with few interstate contacts and not much access to the press. The Federalists gave them little time to organize. Congress submitted the Constitution to the states on September 28, and the first ratifying conventions met in December. Delaware ratified unanimously on December 7, Pennsylvania by a 46-to-23 vote five days later, and New Jersey unanimously on December 18. After Georgia ratified unanimously on January 2, Connecticut approved by a better than three-to-one margin a week later.

Except in Pennsylvania, these victories all came in small states. Paradoxically, although the Constitution was mostly a large-state document, small states embraced it while large ones hesitated. Small states, once they had been given equality in the senate, saw many advantages in a strong central government. Under the Articles, for example, New York and Pennsylvania had forced New Jersey residents to pay duties on foreign goods imported through Philadelphia and New York City. New Jersey had to tax land to meet both state and congressional expenses, while its citizens paid taxes to the governments of other states. Under the Constitution, all import duties would go to the new federal government, a clear gain for every small state except Rhode Island with its ports of Providence and Newport.

By contrast, Pennsylvania was the only large state with a solid majority for ratification, and even there the Antifederalists were eloquent. They demanded a federal bill of rights and major changes in the structure of the new government. Large states could think of going it alone. Small states could not—except for Rhode Island.

The first hotly contested state was Massachusetts, which set a pattern for struggles in other divided states. Federalists won by a slim margin (187 to 168) in February 1788. They were able to defeat antifederalist demands for *conditional* amendments only by promising to support a bill of rights by constitu-

tional amendment *after* the Constitution had been ratified. In the same month, the Rhode Island legislature voted overwhelmingly not even to summon a ratifying convention. Maryland and South Carolina ratified by lopsided margins in April and May, bringing the total to eight of the nine states required. Then conventions met almost simultaneously in New Hampshire, Virginia, New York, and North Carolina. In each, an initial majority opposed the Constitution.

As resistance stiffened, the ratification controversy became the first great debate on the American Union, on what kind of a nation America would become. By the summer of 1788 Antifederalists were eloquent, sharp, and well organized. They argued that the new government would be too remote from the people to be trusted with the broad powers specified in the Constitution. They warned that in a House of Representatives divided into districts of thirty thousand people (twice the size of Boston), only prominent and wealthy candidates would be elected. The new government would become an aristocracy or an oligarchy that would impose heavy taxes and other burdens on the people. The absence of a bill of rights also worried them.

In the fight for ratification, Alexander Hamilton, James Madison, and John Jay collaborated on a series of eighty-five essays, published first in New York newspapers but widely reprinted elsewhere, in which they defended the Constitution almost clause by clause. Signing themselves "Publius," they later collected the essays and published them as *The Federalist,* the most comprehensive body of political thought produced by the Revolutionary generation. In *Federalist No. Ten,* Madison argued that a large republic would be far more stable than a small one. He challenged two thousand years of accepted wisdom by declaring that small republics were inherently unstable because majority "factions" could easily gain power, trample upon the rights of minorities, and ignore the common good. But in a republic as huge and diverse as the United States, he maintained, factions would seldom be able to forge a majority. "Publius" hoped that the new government would draw on the talents of the wisest and the best-educated citizens. To those who accused him of trying to erect an American aristocracy, he pointed out that the Constitution forbade titles and hereditary rule.

The Great Seal of the United States   "Novus Ordo Seclorum" means "A New Order for the Ages."

Federalists won a narrow majority (57 to 46) in New Hampshire on June 21, and Madison guided Virginia to ratification (89 to 79) five days later, despite the eloquence of Patrick Henry, an Antifederalist. New York approved, by 30 votes to 27, a month later, bringing eleven states into the Union, enough to launch the new government. North Carolina rejected the Constitution in July 1788 but finally ratified in November 1789 after the first Congress had drafted the Bill of Rights and sent it to the states. Rhode Island, after voting seven times against calling a ratifying convention, finally summoned one that ratified the Constitution by a vote of only 34 to 32 in May 1790.

Nothing resembling American federalism had ever been tried before. Sovereignty had been removed from government and bestowed on the people, who then empowered different levels of government through separate constitutions. As the Great Seal of the United States proclaimed, it was a *novus ordo seclorum,* a new order for the ages.

SUGGESTED READING

Major histories of the Revolutionary War include Piers Mackesy, *The War for America, 1775–1783* (1964), which ar-

gues that Britain could have won; Don Higgenbotham, *The War of American Independence: Military Attitudes, Policies, and Practices, 1763–1789* (1971); and Marshall Smelser, *The Winning of Independence* (1972). Charles Royster, *A Revolutionary People at War: The Continental Army and American Character, 1775–1783* (1979) and James Kirby Martin and Mark E. Lender, *A Respectable Army: The Military Origins of the Republic, 1763–1789* (1982) differ sharply on the Continental Army. John Shy, *A People Numerous and Armed: Reflections on the Military Struggle for American Independence,* rev. ed. (1990) contains several provocative essays, especially on the political role of the militia. Howard H. Peckham, ed., *The Toll of Independence: Engagements and Battle Casualties of the American Revolution* (1974) documents the war's high mortality rate. Outstanding state histories include John E. Selby, *The Revolution in Virginia, 1775–1783* (1988) and Richard Buel, *Dear Liberty: Connecticut's Mobilization for the Revolutionary War* (1981).

Strong studies of major campaigns include Ira D. Gruber, *The Howe Brothers and the American Revolution* (1972); Thomas Fleming, *1776: Year of Illusions* (1975); Alfred H. Bill, *The Campaign of Princeton, 1776–1777* (1948); John S. Pancake, *1777: The Year of the Hangman* (1977); Max M. Mintz, *The Generals of Saratoga: John Burgoyne and Horatio Gates* (1990); David G. Martin, *The Philadelphia Campaign, June 1777–July 1778* (1993); Thomas Fleming, *The Forgotten Victory: The Battle for New Jersey* (1975) on Springfield in 1780; John S. Pancake, *This Destructive War: The British Campaign in the Carolinas, 1780–1782* (1985); Russell F. Weigley, *The Partisan War: The South Carolina Campaign of 1780–1782* (1970), which is brief but brilliant; and Thomas Fleming, *Beat the Last Drum: The Siege of Yorktown, 1781* (1963). The essays in Ronald Hoffman, Thad W. Tate, and Peter J. Albert, eds., *An Uncivil War: The Southern Backcountry during the American Revolution* (1985) offer a variety of perspectives on the region most fiercely divided by the Revolution. Diplomacy is well covered in Jonathan R. Dull, *A Diplomatic History of the American Revolution* (1985) and Richard B. Morris, *The Peacemakers: The Great Powers and American Independence* (1965). Lee Kennett, *The French Forces in America, 1780–1783* (1977) is standard.

Most major men of the Revolutionary Era have attracted multiple and often multivolume biographies. Among the more accessible are Peter Shaw, *The Character of John Adams* (1976); James T. Flexner, *The Traitor and the Spy: Benedict Arnold and John André* (1953, or 1975 illustrated ed.); Isabel T. Kelsay, *Joseph Brant, 1743–1807: Man of Two Worlds* (1984); John Mack Faragher, *Daniel Boone: The Life and Legend of an American Pioneer* (1992); Theodore Thayer, *Nathanael Greene: Strategist of the American Revolution* (1960); John C. Miller, *Alexander Hamilton, Portrait in Paradox* (1959); Merrill D. Peterson, *Thomas Jefferson and the New Nation: A Biography* (1970); Ralph Ketcham, *James Madison: A Biography* (1971); Richard K. Mathews, *If Men Were Angels: James Madison and the Heartless Empire of Reason* (1995); Marcus Cunliffe, *George*

Washington: Man and Monument (1958); and Garry Wills, *George Washington and the Enlightenment: Images of Power in Early America* (1984).

Gordon S. Wood, *The Creation of the American Republic, 1776–1787* (1969) has been the most influential study of early American republicanism and constitutionalism. Thomas L. Pangle dissents sharply from Wood in *The Spirit of Modern Republicanism: The Moral Vision of the American Founders and the Philosophy of Locke* (1988). Other important contributions include Willi Paul Adams, *The First American Constitutions: Republican Ideology and the Making of the State Constitutions in the Revolutionary Era* (1980); and H. James Henderson, *Party Politics in the Continental Congress* (1974).

Robert M. Calhoon, *The Loyalists in Revolutionary America* (1973) is comprehensive, while Wallace Brown, *The Good Americans: Loyalists in the American Revolution* (1969) is briefer. Important specialized studies include Paul H. Smith, "The American Loyalists: Notes on Their Organization and Numerical Strength," *William and Mary Quarterly*, 3d ser., 25 (1968), 259–277; Smith, *Loyalists and Redcoats: A Study in British Revolutionary Policy* (1964); Mary Beth Norton, *The British Americans: Loyalist Exiles in England, 1774–1789* (1972); Norton, "The Fate of Some Black Loyalists of the American Revolution," *Journal of Negro History*, 58 (1973), 202–226; Charles Royster, "'The Nature of Treason': Revolutionary Virtue and American Reactions to Benedict Arnold," *William and Mary Quarterly*, 3d ser., 36 (1979), 163–193; Janice Potter, *The Liberty We Seek: Loyalist Ideology in Colonial New York and Massachusetts* (1983); Ann G. Condon, *The Envy of the American States: The Loyalist Dream for New Brunswick* (1984); and Jane Errington, *The Lion, the Eagle, and Upper Canada: A Developing Colonial Ideology* (1987).

Gregory E. Dowd, *A Spirited Resistance: The North American Indian Struggle for Unity, 1745–1815* (1992), and Barbara Graymont, *The Iroquois in the American Revolution* (1972) cover most eastern woodland Indian nations during the Revolution. Stephen Aron, *How the West Was Lost: The Transformation of Kentucky from Daniel Boone to Henry Clay* (1995) is fresh and challenging. E. James Ferguson, *The Power of the Purse: A History of American Public Finance, 1776–1790* (1961) and John K. Alexander, "The Fort Wilson Incident of 1779: A Study of the Revolutionary Crowd," *William and Mary Quarterly*, 3d ser., 31 (1974), 589–612 remain standard on hyperinflation and its consequences. Carl Van Doren, *Mutiny in January: The Story of a Crisis in the Continental Army* (1943) and Richard H. Kohn, "The Inside History of the Newburgh Conspiracy: America and the Coup d'État," *William and Mary Quarterly*, 3d ser., 27 (1970), 187–220 are still the fullest studies of army discontent.

John F. Jameson, *The American Revolution Considered as a Social Movement* (1925) remains provocative. Benjamin Quarles, *The Negro in the American Revolution* (1961); Ira Berlin and Ronald Hoffman, eds., *Slavery and Freedom in the Age of the*

American Revolution (1983); Sylvia R. Frey, *Water from the Rock: Black Resistance in a Revolutionary Age* (1991); Arthur Zilversmit, *The First Emancipation: The Abolition of Slavery in the North* (1967); Gary B. Nash, *Forging Freedom: The Formation of Philadelphia's Black Community, 1720–1840* (1988); and Shane White, *Somewhat More Independent: The End of Slavery in New York City, 1770–1810* (1991) are indispensable studies of slavery and emancipation. Mary Beth Norton, *Liberty's Daughters: The Revolutionary Experience of American Women, 1750–1800* (1979); Linda Kerber, *Women of the Republic: Intellect and Ideology in Revolutionary America* (1980); Rosemarie Zagarrie, "Morals, Manners, and the Republican Mother," *American Quarterly*, 44 (1992), 192–215; Ronald Hoffman and Peter J. Albert, eds., *Women in the Age of the American Revolution* (1989); and David Hackett Fischer, *Growing Old in America* (1978) are comprehensive studies of gender and age relations in the era. More specialized but highly significant studies include Laurel Thatcher Ulrich, *A Midwife's Tale: The Life of Martha Ballard, Based on Her Diary, 1785–1812* (1990); Barbara Clark Smith, "Food Rioters and the American Revolution," *William and Mary Quarterly*, 3d ser., 51 (1994), 3–38; Judith A. Klinghoffer and Lois Elkis, "The Petticoat Electors: Women's Suffrage in New Jersey, 1776–1807," *Journal of the Early Republic*, 12 (1992), 159–193; Cathy N. Davidson, *Revolution and the Word: The Rise of the Novel in America* (1986); and Joel Perlman and Dennis Shirley, "When Did New England Women Acquire Literacy?" *William and Mary Quarterly*, 3d ser., 48 (1991), 50–67.

General histories of the Confederation Era include Merrill Jensen, *The New Nation: A History of the United States during the Articles of Confederation* (1950); Forrest McDonald, *E Pluribus Unum: The Formation of the American Republic* (1965); and Richard B. Morris, *The Forging of the Union, 1781–1789* (1987). Jackson Turner Main, *Political Parties before the Constitution* (1973) is a comprehensive study of state politics. His "Government by the People: The American Revolution and the Democratization of the Legislatures," *William and Mary Quarterly*, 3d ser., 23 (1966), 354–367 is essential reading. Robert J. Taylor, *Western Massachusetts in the Revolution* (1954) and John L. Brooke, "To the Quiet of the People: Revolutionary Settlements and Civil Unrest in Western Massachusetts, 1774–1789," *William and Mary Quarterly*, 3d ser., 46 (1989), 425–462 cover the region from the rise of the Berkshire Constitutionalists through Shays's Rebellion. Peter S. Onuf, *Statehood and Union: A History of the Northwest Ordinance* (1987), and Staughton Lynd, "The Compromise of 1787," *Political Science Quarterly*, 71 (1966), 225–250 offer challenging perspectives on the Northwest Ordinance. Recent studies of the Constitutional Convention include Forrest McDonald, *Novus Ordo Seclorum: The Intellectual Origins of the Constitution* (1985) and Thornton Anderson, *Creating the Constitution: The Convention of 1787 and the First Congress* (1993). Robert A. Rutland, *The Ordeal of the Consti-*

tution: The Antifederalists and the Ratification Struggle of 1787–1788 (1966) is still the fullest history of the ratification struggle, but Saul Cornell, "Aristocracy Assailed: The Ideology of Backcountry Anti-Federalism," *Journal of American History,* 76 (1989–1990), 1148–1172 and Kenneth R. Bowling, "'A Tub to the Whale': The Founding Fathers and the Adop-

tion of the Federal Bill of Rights," *Journal of the Early Republic,* 8 (1988), 223–251 both have telling points to make.

Videos: *Mary Silliman's War* (Heritage Film and Citadel Film, 1993) is a powerful dramatization of how the loyalist–patriot struggle affected the life of a Connecticut woman in 1779.

POWER, PATRIARCHY, AND THE HEROIC: THE REVOLUTION AND THE TRANSFORMATION OF AMERICAN SENSIBILITIES

If we look closely, we can see power relationships expressed in the most ordinary art forms. Before the American Revolution, family portraits reflected conventional patriarchal values. The father was always elevated above his wife and their children. A woman's role as wife was depicted more prominently than her role as mother, and artists tried to make women sexually attractive, often exposing quite a bit of cleavage. The conventions of the time idealized a very light complexion and frowned upon any hint of a suntan because tanning implied working outdoors.

The standards of the day also forbade the exposure of a gentleman's forearms, legs, or neck. Forearms were deeply symbolic. Anyone who exposed them announced that he, or she, performed some kind of manual labor. A lady's sleeves, but not a gentleman's, were often pulled up because she did some routine housework (even if servants took care of most of it), but her hands were always unmarked. For gentlemen, only the classical tradition provided an exception to this rule. Heroic conventions permitted the exposure of the arms and legs of a hero, provided he was displayed in a Greek or Roman costume. Nearly all heroes were depicted as Romans and were assumed to be gentlemen. Pennsylvania artist Charles Willson Peale's 1766 portrait of William Pitt follows this tradition. By contrast, when painters portrayed ruddy-cheeked men who had to earn a living, they typically showed more than a little condescension. Joshua Greenwood's *Sea Captains Carousing in Surinam* (1750s) suggests that even working people with major economic responsibilities will get drunk whenever they can, that is, whenever their occupations do not keep them busy. Gentlemen did not expect heroic deeds from working men in the eighteenth century. In the armies of the day, only officers, motivated by honor, became heroes. Soldiers did their duty out of fear of the lash. Ordinary people might be celebrated as martyrs, as were the victims of the Boston Massacre of 1770, but they were not expected to perform heroic deeds.

North American painters, including several loyalists living in Britain, transformed some of these conventions during the American Revolution. Benjamin West (1738–1820), a Pennsylvanian, moved to London in 1763 and made his reputation with *The Death of General Wolfe* in 1771. West shattered tradition by depicting Brigadier General James Wolfe and his contemporaries in their actual uniforms during the Battle of Quebec, where Wolfe was fatally shot in 1759. This painting so impressed King George III that he created a position for West as historical painter to the royal court. West remained in England for the rest of his career, but during the Revolutionary War he also gave money, quietly, to captured American sailors who had managed to escape from prison.

West had profound influence on fellow American painters—among them John Trumbull of Connecticut, who won great admiration with his *Death of General Montgomery* in the American assault on Quebec on December 31, 1775, and his *The Death of General Warren* at the battle of Bunker Hill. Scenes of death in combat became perhaps the most distinctive subject matter of American painting in the Revolutionary era. The poses of the dying in these paintings are nearly identical, or are mirror images of one another. West, who had spent several years in Italy, modeled Wolfe on Raphael's 1507 painting of Christ being carried to the tomb, and West's students copied this convention.

Even more striking was the democratization of heroism during the war itself—on both sides of the battle lines. When George Washington established the Purple Heart as the Continental Army's first badge of distinction, he made enlisted men eligible to receive it, and the first men so honored were sergeants. John Singleton Copley, a Boston portrait artist and a moderate loyalist who studied with West in London, painted *Brook Watson and the Shark* in 1778. It dramatically displayed how Watson, a Nova Scotia merchant and a loyalist, had lost his leg when a shark attacked him while he was swimming in Havana Harbor in 1749. The shark made three passes before the crew of a small boat drove it off and rescued Watson, then a fourteen-year-old boy. In this riveting painting, a black man holds the traditional central and elevated place of honor. The man trying to harpoon the shark has an exposed leg. No one on the boat is a gentleman. Ordinary men, Copley announced through this painting, can be heroes.

The Revolution also challenged patriarchal values, at least within genteel northeastern families. Family portraits elevated the mother to symbolic equality with the father. In middle-class households by the second quarter of the nineteenth century, the husband was no longer depicted as a colorful peacock but instead as a sober, respectable citizen, usually clad in a dark suit and a white shirt with no hint of a heroic role. The wife's position as mother increasingly triumphed over her sexuality. In a typical portrait, everything but her face and hands was covered, and the dress of the day thoroughly disguised her feminine curves. These families were prouder of their possessions than of their manly or womanly qualities.

But as democratization moved westward, it also revived the patriarchal ideal that was declining in the Northeast. Pioneer men, usually clad in buckskin, led their wives and children to new fertile lands, and artists again gave men greater prominence than other members of their families. William S. Jewett's *The Promised Land—The Grayson Family* (1850) shows a peaceful scene, but Grayson is armed and ready to protect his wife and daughter. The iconography surrounding Daniel Boone soon gave a racist twist to patriarchy in the West. The lithograph of *Daniel Boone Protects his Family* (1874) was copied from a statue by Horatio Greenough (1852), which depicted a typical pioneer family and was meant to illustrate, in Greenough's words, "the superiority of the white man" over other races. Contemporaries quickly decided that Greenough's hero was really Boone. Here the ordinary male performs heroic deeds, while both wife and child cower helplessly. Only the dog is not intimidated. But then, as one commentator remarked, the West was hell for women and horses, but heaven for men and dogs.

Isaac Royall and his Family   This 1741 painting by Robert Feke is typical of family portraits before the Revolution. It celebrates the patriarchal ideal by elevating the husband/father above the rest of the family.

Mr. Pitt, by Charles Willson Peale (1766)   Peale's work illustrates heroic conventions before Benjamin West changed them. Pitt, Britain's great war minister during the conquest of Canada, is displayed as a Roman hero.

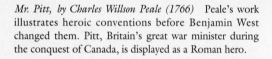

Patrick Lyon at the Forge, by John Neagle (1827)   Only men who performed physical labor exposed their arms in public.

Sea Captains Carousing in Surinam, by John Greenwood (1750s)   Working men, according to Greenwood, got drunk when not busy.

Death of General Wolfe   This 1771 painting by Benjamin West transformed the heroic tradition and began a new genre of historical scenes. John Trumbull's *Death of General Warren at Bunker Hill* (1786 — see Chapter 6) and John Singleton Copley's *The Death of the Earl of Chatham* (1779–1781 — see Chapter 7) both imitated West's painting, as did many others

Brook Watson and the Shark   John Singleton Copley's 1778 painting began the democratization of heroism.

Joseph Moore and His Family by Erastus Salisbury Field (1839)   Field's painting illustrates the decline of the patriarchal ideal in family portraits in the Northeast after the Revolution. The mother here is even more prominent than the father.

Portrait of the Haight Family (1849)   This family retains more eighteenth-century sensibilities than did the Moores but still reflects the transistion to a child-centered household. The father wears a luxurious coat. The classical statuary in the background reflects the owners' refined taste while suggesting that love binds families together. Both parents are absorbed with their children. The oldest daughter, soon to be of marriageable age, has the most elevated position in the portrait. She exposes her arms, neck and part of her shoulders, while her mother conceals everything but her hands and face.

The Promised Land — The Grayson Family, by William S. Jewett (1850)   In the West, the democratization of the hero also encouraged a revival of patriarchal values. The husband/father is again elevated above the rest of the family.

Daniel Boone Protects his Family   This 1874 lithograph, copied from Horatio Greenough's statue of 1852, identified the democratic hero with both patriarchy and Indian killing.

Chapter 8

The Democratic Republic, 1790–1820

This idealized American farm was sketched in 1802. Cattle browse in an outlying pasture; the farmer tills land nearer the house, while his wife (who is engaged in the new activity of reading) and child stay near the house.

In 1782 J. Hector St. John de Crèvecoeur, a French soldier who had settled in rural New York, explained America's agrarian republic through the words of a fictionalized farmer. First of all, he said, the American farmer owns his own land and bases his claim to dignity and citizenship on that fact. He spoke of "the bright idea of property," and went on: "This formerly rude soil has been converted by my father into a pleasant farm, and in return, it has established all our rights; on it is founded our rank, our freedom, our power as citizens, our importance as inhabitants of [a rural neighborhood]. . . ." Second, he said, farm ownership endows the American farmer with the powers and responsibilities of fatherhood. "Often when I plant my low ground," he said, "I place my little boy on a chair which screws to the beam of the plough—its motion and that of the horses please him; he is perfectly happy and begins to chat. As I lean over the handle, various are the thoughts which crowd into my mind. I am now doing for him, I say, what my father did for me; may God enable him to live that he may perform the same operations for the same purposes when I am worn out and old!"

Crèvecoeur's farmer, musing on liberty and property, working the ancestral fields with his male heir strapped to the plough, was a conscious participant in America's agrarian republic. His wife, his African slaves (yes, Crèvecoeur's farmer owned slaves), and his son were not. Postrevolutionary America bestowed power and equal rights upon propertied white men, and powerlessness and dependence upon nearly everyone else. Yet even as they formed their patriarchal republic, increasing numbers of men found it hard to maintain their status as propertied citizens or to pass on that status to their offspring.

By 1815 the agrarian republic, with its promise of widespread proprietorship and well-ordered paternal authority, was in deep peril. A more individualistic, democratic, and insecure order was taking its place.

THE FARMER'S REPUBLIC

From New England through the mid-Atlantic and on into the southern Piedmont and backcountry, few farmers in 1790 thought of farming as a business. Their first concern was to provide a subsistence for their households. Their second was to achieve long-term security and the ability to pass their farm on to their sons. The goal was to create what rural folks called a "competence": the ability to live up to neighborhood standards of material decency while protecting the long-term independence of their household. Most farmers raised a variety of animals and plants, ate most of what they grew, traded much of the rest within their neighborhoods, and sent small surpluses into outside markets.

West Indian and European markets for American meat and grain had been growing steadily since the mid-eighteenth century and had expanded dramatically between 1793 and 1815 when war disrupted farming in Europe. These overseas markets sustained household independence. Farmers continued to provide for their families from their own farms and neighborhoods and risked little by sending surpluses overseas. Thus they profited from world markets without becoming dependent on them.

Households

Production for overseas markets after 1790 did, however, alter relationships within rural households. Farm labor in postrevolutionary America was carefully divided by sex. Men worked in the fields, and production for markets both intensified that labor and made it more exclusively male. In the grain fields, for instance, the long-handled scythe was replacing the sickle as the principal harvest tool. Women could use the sickle efficiently, but the long, heavy scythe was designed to be wielded by men. At the same time, farmers completed the substitution of ploughs for hoes as the principal cultivating tools—not only because ploughs worked better but because rural Americans had developed a prejudice against women working in the fields. By the early nineteenth century visitors to the long-settled farming

Thomas Jefferson, *Notes on the State of Virginia*

Those who labour in the earth are the chosen people of God, if ever he had a chosen people, whose breasts he has made his peculiar deposit for substantial and genuine virtue. It is the focus in which he keeps alive that sacred fire, which otherwise might escape from the face of the earth. Corruption of morals in the mass of cultivators is a phaenomenon of which no age nor nation has furnished an example. It is the mark set on those, who not looking up to heaven, to their own soil and industry, as does the husbandman, for their subsistance, depend for it on the casualties and caprice of customers. Dependance begets subservience and venality, suffocates the germ of virtue, and prepares fit tools for the designs of ambition. This, the natural progress and consequence of the arts, has sometimes perhaps been retarded by accidental circumstances: but, generally speaking, the proportion which the aggregate of the other classes of citizens bears in any state to that of its husbandmen, is the proportion of its unsound to its healthy parts, and is a good-enough barometer whereby to measure its degree of corruption.

areas (with the exception of some mid-Atlantic German communities) seldom saw women in the fields. In his travels through France, Thomas Jefferson spoke harshly of peasant communities where he saw women doing field labor.

At the same time, household responsibilities multiplied and fell more exclusively to women. It was farm women's labor and ingenuity that helped create a more varied and nutritious rural diet in these years. Bread and salted meat were still the staples. The bread was the old mix of Indian corn and coarse wheat ("rye and Injun," the farmers called it), with crust so thick that it was used as a scoop for soups and stews. Though improved brines and pickling techniques augmented the supply of salt meat that could be laid by, farmers' palates doubtless told them that it was the same old salt meat. A variety of other foods were now available, however. By the 1790s, improved winter feeding for cattle and better techniques for making and storing butter and cheese kept dairy products on the tables of the more prosperous farm families throughout the year. Chickens became more common, and farm women began to fence and manure their kitchen gardens, planting them with potatoes, turnips, cabbages, squashes, beans, and other vegetables that could be stored in the root cellars that were becoming standard features of farm houses. By the 1830s a resident of Weymouth, Massachusetts, claimed that "a man who did not have a large garden of potatoes, crooked-necked squashes, and other vegetables . . . was regarded [as] improvident." He might have added poultry and dairy cattle to the list, and he might have noted that all were more likely to result from the labor of women than from the labor of men.

Industrial outwork provided many farmers with another means of protecting their independence by working their wives and children harder. From the 1790s onwards, city merchants provided country workers with raw materials and paid them for finished shoes, furniture, cloth, brooms, and other handmade goods. In Marple, Pennsylvania, a farming town near Philadelphia, fully one-third of households were engaged in weaving, furniture making, and other household industry in the 1790s. As late as the 1830s, when the rise of the factory system had reduced the demand for household manufactures, 33,000 New England women were still weaving palm leaf hats at home.

Most of the outwork was taken on by large, relatively poor families, with the work organized in ways that shored up the authority of fathers. When young Caleb Jackson and his brother began making shoes for a Massachusetts merchant in 1803, the account was carried in their father's name. And when New Hampshire women and girls fashioned hats, the accounts were kept in the name of the husband or father. In general, household industry was part-time work performed only by the dependent women and children of the household. And when it was the family's principal means of support, the work was arranged in ways that supported traditional notions of fatherhood and proprietorship. In eastern Massachusetts in the 1790s, for instance, when thousands of farmers on small plots of worn-out land became household shoemakers, the men cut the leather and shaped the uppers, while the sewing and binding were left to the women. In the town of North Reading, the family of Mayo Greanleaf Patch made shoes throughout the 1790s. Patch was a poor man who drank too much and lived on a small plot of land owned by his father-in-law; the family income came largely from shoemaking. Yet Patch, when asked to name his occupation, described himself as a "yeoman"—a fiction subsidized by the labor of Patch's wife and children.

Neighbors

The struggle to maintain household independence involved most authentic yeomen in elaborate net-works of neighborly cooperation. Few farmers possessed the tools, the labor, and the food they would have needed to be truly independent. They regularly worked for one another, borrowed oxen and plows, and swapped surpluses of one kind of food for another. Women traded ashes, herbs, butter and eggs, vegetables, seedlings, baby chicks, goose feathers, and the products of their spinning wheels and looms. The regular exchange of such goods and services was crucial to the workings of a rural neighborhood. Some cooperative undertakings—house and barn raisings and husking bees, for example—brought the whole neighborhood together, transforming a chore into a pleasant social event. The gossip, drinking, and dancing that took place on such occasions were welcome rewards for neighborly cooperation.

Few neighborhood transactions called for the use of money. Indeed, in 1790 no paper money had yet been issued by the states or the federal government, and the widespread use of Spanish, English, and French coins testified to the shortage of specie. In New England, farmers kept careful accounts of neighborhood debts. In the South and West, farmers used a "changing system" in which they simply remembered what they owed; they regarded the New England practice as a sign of Yankee greed and lack of character. Yet farmers everywhere relied more on barter than on cash. "Instead of money going incessantly backwards and forwards into the same hands," observed a French traveler in Massachusetts in 1790, Americans "supply their needs in the countryside by direct reciprocal exchanges. The tailor and the bootmaker go and do their work at the home of the farmer . . . who most frequently provides the raw material for it and pays for the work in goods. They write down what they give and receive on both sides, and at the end of the year they settle a large variety of exchanges with a very small quantity of coin." Such a system created an elaborate network of neighborhood debt. In Kent, Connecticut, for instance, the average farmer left 20 creditors when he died. The debts were indicators not of exploitation and class division, however, but of a highly structured and absolutely necessary system of neighborly cooperation.

Inheritance

The agrarian republicanism envisioned by men like Jefferson and Crèvecoeur rested on widespread farm

Rural Scene, New Hampshire, c. 1790–1810   This New England river town, surrounded by prosperous, neatly-tended farms, was among the relatively small number of Northeastern communities with easy water access to markets.

ownership and on a rough equality among adult male householders. Even as they were formulating that vision, however, its social base was disintegrating. Overcrowding and the growth of markets caused the price of good farmland to rise sharply throughout the older settlements. Most young men could expect to inherit only a few acres of exhausted land, or to move to wilderness land in the backcountry. Failing those, they would quit farming altogether. Crèvecoeur's baby boy — who in fact ended up living in Boston — was in a more precarious position than his seat on his father's plough might have indicated.

In Revolutionary America, fathers had been judged by their ability to support and govern their households, to serve as good neighbors, and to pass land on to their sons. After the war, fewer farm fathers were able to do that. Those in the old settlements had small farms and large families, which made it impossible for them to provide a competence for all their offspring. Fathers felt that they had failed as fathers. And their sons, with no prospect of an adequate inheritance, were obliged to leave home. Most fathers tried valiantly to provide for all their heirs (generally by leaving land to their sons and personal property to their daughters.) Few left

all their land to one son, and many stated in their wills that the sons to whom they left the land must share barns and cider mills — even the house — on farms that could be subdivided no further. Such provisions fitted a social system that guaranteed the independence of the household head through complex relations with kin and neighbors. But they were also an indication that that system had reached the end of the line.

Outside New England, farm tenancy was on the increase. In parts of Pennsylvania and in other areas as well, farmers often bought farms when they became available in the neighborhood, and rented them to tenants to augment the household income, and then gave them to their sons when they reached adulthood. The sons of poorer farmers often rented a farm in the hope of saving enough money to buy it. Some fathers bought tracts of unimproved land in the backcountry — sometimes on speculation, more often to provide their sons with land they could make into a farm. Others paid to have their sons educated, or arranged an apprenticeship to provide them with an avenue of escape from a declining countryside. As a result, more and more young men left home. The populations of the old farming communities grew older and more female, while the populations of the rising frontier settlements and seaport cities became younger and more male. The young men who stayed home often had nothing to look forward to but a lifetime as tenants or hired hands.

Standards of Living

The rise of markets in the late eighteenth and early nineteenth centuries improved living standards for some families but widened the disparity between rich and poor. Most farm houses in the older rural areas were small, one-story structures. Few farmers, especially in the South and West, bothered to keep their surroundings clean or attractive. They repaired their fences only when they became too dilapidated to function. They rarely planted trees or shrubs, and housewives threw out garbage to feed the chickens and pigs that foraged near the house.

Inside, there were few rooms and many people. Beds stood in every room, and few family members slept alone. Growing up in Bethel, Connecticut, the future show-business entrepreneur P. T. Barnum shared a bed with his brother and an Irish servant; guests shared beds in New England taverns until the 1820s. The hearth remained the source of heat and light in most farm houses. In the period from 1790

to 1810, over half the households in central Massachusetts, an old and relatively prosperous area, owned only one or two candlesticks. One of the great disparities between wealthy families and their less affluent neighbors was that the wealthy families could light their houses at night. Another disparity was in the outward appearance of houses. The wealthier families painted their houses white as a token of pristine republicanism. But their bright houses stood apart from the weathered grey-brown clapboard siding of their neighbors in stark and unrepublican contrast.

Some improvements emerged in personal comfort. Beds in most houses may have been shared, but as time passed more of them had mattresses stuffed with feathers. At mealtimes, only the poorest families continued to eat with their fingers or with spoons from a common bowl. By 1800 individual place settings with knives and forks and china plates, along with chairs instead of benches, had become common in rural America. Although only the wealthiest families had upholstered furniture, ready-made chairs were widely available; the number of chairs per household in Massachusetts, for instance, doubled in the first third of the nineteenth century. Clocks, one of the first items to be mass-produced

The Dining Room of Dr. Whitbridge, a Rhode Island Country Doctor, about 1815   It is a comfortable, neatly furnished room, but there is little decoration, and the doctor must sit near the fire in layered clothing against the morning chill.

in the United States, appeared in the more prosperous rural households: as early as the 1790s, 35 percent of the families in Chester County, Pennsylvania, owned at least one clock.

FROM BACKCOUNTRY TO FRONTIER

The United States was a huge country in 1790, at least on paper. In the treaty that ended the War of Independence in 1783, the British ignored Indian claims and ceded all the land from the Atlantic Ocean to the Mississippi River to the new republic, with the exceptions of Spanish Florida and New Orleans. The states then surrendered their individual claims to the federal government, and in 1790 George Washington became president of a nation that stretched nearly 1,500 miles inland. But most white Americans were still living on a thin strip of settlement along the Atlantic coast and along the few navigable rivers that emptied into the Atlantic. Some were pushing their way into the wilds of Maine and northern Vermont, and in New York they had set up communities as far west as the Mohawk Valley. Pittsburgh was a struggling new settlement, and two outposts had been established on the Ohio River—at Marietta and at what would become Cincinnati. Farther south, farmers had occupied the Piedmont lands up to the eastern slope of the Appalachians and were spilling through the Cumberland Gap into the new lands of Kentucky and Tennessee. But north of the Ohio River the Shawnee, Miami, Delaware, and Potawatomie nations, along with smaller tribes, controlled nearly all the land shown on the Northwest Ordinance's neatly gridded and largely fictitious map. To the south, Indians the whites called the Five Civilized Tribes still occupied much of their ancestral land: the Cherokees in the Carolinas and northern Georgia, the Creeks in Georgia and Alabama, the Choctaws and Chickasaws in Mississippi, and the Seminoles in southern Georgia and Spanish Florida. Taken together, Indian peoples occupied most of the land that treaties and maps showed as the interior of the United States.

The Destruction of the Woodlands Indians

Though many of the woodland tribes were still intact and still living on the ancestral lands in 1790, they were in serious trouble. The members of the old Iroquois Federation had been restricted to reservations in New York and Pennsylvania; many had fled to Canada. The once-powerful Cherokees had been severely punished for fighting for the British during the Revolution and by 1790 had ceded three-fourths of their territory to the Americans. Like the Iroquois, by this time they were nearly surrounded by white settlements.

In the Old Northwest, the Shawnee, Miami, and other tribes, with the help of the British who still occupied seven forts within what was formally the United States—continued to trade furs and to impede white settlement. Skirmishes with settlers, however, brought reprisals, and the Indians faced not only hostile pioneers but the United States Army as well. In the Ohio country, expeditions led by General Josiah Harmar and General Arthur St. Clair failed in 1790 and 1791—the second ending in an Indian victory in which 630 soldiers died. In 1794 President Washington sent a third army, under General "Mad Anthony" Wayne, which defeated the Indians at Fallen Timbers, near present-day Toledo. The Treaty of Greenville forced the Native Americans to cede two-thirds of what are now Ohio and southeastern Indiana. It was at this point that the British decided to abandon their forts in the Old Northwest. Following their victory at Fallen Timbers, whites filtered into what remained of Indian lands. In 1796 President Washington threw up his hands and announced that "I believe scarcely any thing, short of a Chinese Wall, or a line of troops, will restrain Land Jobbers and the encroachment of settlers upon the Indian Territory." Five years later Governor William Henry Harrison of Indiana Territory admitted that frontier whites "consider the murdering of the Indians in the highest degree meritorious."

Relegated to smaller territory but still dependent on the European fur trade, the natives of the Northwest now fell into competition with settlers and other Indians for the diminishing supply of game. The Creeks, Choctaws, and other tribes of the Old Southwest faced the same problem: even when they chased settlers out of their territory, the settlers managed to kill or scare off the deer and other wildlife, thus ruining the old hunting grounds. When the Shawnee sent hunting parties farther west, they were opposed by western Indians. The Choctaws also sent hunters across the Mississippi, where they found new sources of furs, along with the angry warriors of the Osage and other peoples of Louisiana and Arkansas.

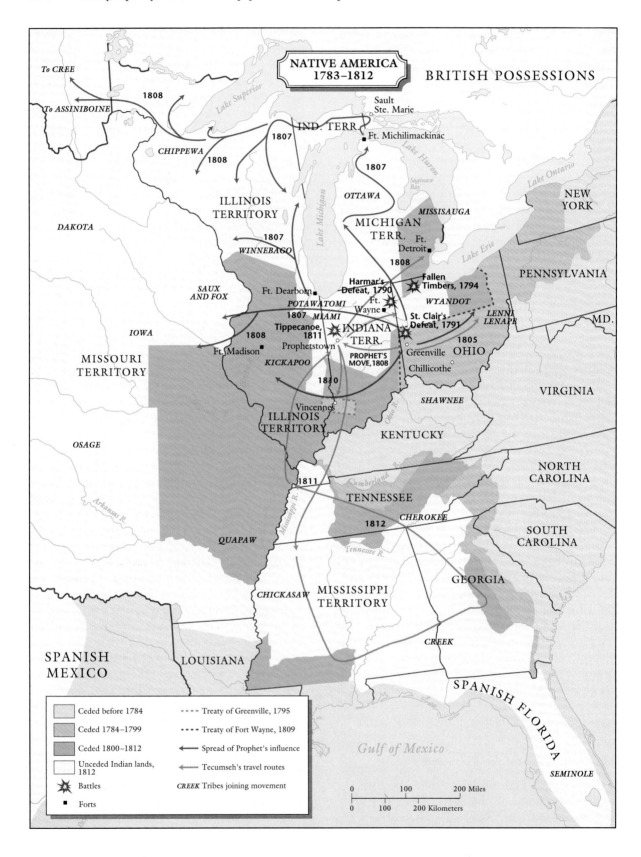

NATIVE AMERICA 1783–1812

BRITISH POSSESSIONS

To CREE

1808

To ASSINIBOINE

CHIPPEWA

1808

1807

Lake Superior

Sault Ste. Marie

IND. TERR.

■ Ft. Michilimackinac

1807

Lake Huron

Saginaw Bay

Lake Ontario

NEW YORK

ILLINOIS TERRITORY

Lake Michigan

OTTAWA

MISSISAUGA

MICHIGAN TERR.

■ Ft. Detroit

Lake Erie

PENNSYLVANIA

DAKOTA

1807

WINNEBAGO

1808

SAUX AND FOX

Ft. Dearborn ■

POTAWATOMI

1807   MIAMI

Harmar's Defeat, 1790

Fallen Timbers, 1794

Ft. Wayne ■

WYANDOT

LENNI LENAPE

MD.

IOWA

Tippecanoe, 1811

1808

Prophetstown

Ft. Madison ■

KICKAPOO

INDIANA TERR.

St. Clair's Defeat, 1791

1805

Greenville

OHIO

MISSOURI TERRITORY

PROPHET'S MOVE, 1808

Chillicothe

VIRGINIA

OSAGE

1810

Vincennes

ILLINOIS TERRITORY

SHAWNEE

KENTUCKY

NORTH CAROLINA

1811

Cumberland R.

TENNESSEE

Arkansas R.

QUAPAW

Mississippi R.

1812

CHEROKEE

Tennessee R.

SOUTH CAROLINA

GEORGIA

CHICKASAW

MISSISSIPPI TERRITORY

SPANISH MEXICO

LOUISIANA

CREEK

SPANISH FLORIDA

Gulf of Mexico

SEMINOLE

☐ Ceded before 1784	- - - - Treaty of Greenville, 1795
▨ Ceded 1784–1799	■ ■ ■ ■ Treaty of Fort Wayne, 1809
▨ Ceded 1800–1812	← Spread of Prophet's influence
☐ Unceded Indian lands, 1812	← Tecumseh's travel routes
✸ Battles	*CREEK* Tribes joining movement
■ Forts	

0   100   200 Miles

0   100   200 Kilometers

The Indians of the interior now realized that the days of the fur trade, on which they depended for survival, were numbered.

Faced with shrinking territories, the disappearance of wildlife, and diminished opportunities to be traditional hunters and warriors, many Indian societies sank into despair. Epidemics of European diseases (smallpox, influenza, measles), attacked peoples who were increasingly sedentary and vulnerable. Old internal frictions grew nastier. In the Old Southwest, full-blooded Indians came into conflict with mixed-blood Indians—who often no longer spoke the native language and who wanted their people to adopt white ways. Murder and clan revenge plagued the tribes, and depression and suicide became more common. The use of alcohol, which had been a scourge on Indian societies for two centuries, increased. Indian males spent more time in their villages and less on the hunt, and by most accounts they drank more and grew more violent.

Out of this cultural wreckage emerged visionary leaders who spoke of a regenerated native society and the expulsion of all whites from the old tribal lands. One of the first was Chief Alexander McGillivray, a mixed-blood Creek who had sided with the British during the Revolution. Between 1783 and 1793, McGillivray tried to unite the Creeks under a national council that could override local chiefs, and to form alliances with other tribes and with Spanish Florida. McGillivray's premature death in 1793 prevented the realization of his vision.

The Cherokees north and east of the Creeks did succeed in making a unified state. Angered by the willingness of the old chiefs to be bribed and flattered into selling land, and by the departure of tribe members to remote locations in the Appalachians or to government land in Arkansas, a group of young chiefs staged a revolt between 1808 and 1810. Previously, being a Cherokee had meant loyalty to one's clan and kin group and adherence to the tribe's ancient customs. Now it meant remaining on the tribe's ancestral land (migration across the Mississippi was regarded as treason) and unquestioning acceptance of the laws, courts, and police controlled by the national council. By 1810 the Cherokee had transformed themselves from a defeated and divided tribe into a nation within a nation.

Among the many prophets who emerged during these years, the one who came closest to military success was Tenskwatawa, a fat, one-eyed, alcoholic

Sequoya   The Cherokee linguist Sequoya displays the eighty-six-symbol alphabet that transformed Cherokee into the first Native American written language.

Shawnee who had failed as a warrior and medicine man. When he went into a deep trance in 1805, the people thought he was dead and prepared his funeral. But he awoke and told them he had visited heaven and hell and had received a prophetic vision. First, all the Indians must stop drinking and fighting among themselves. They must also return to their traditional food, clothing, tools, and hairstyles, and must extinguish all their fires and start new ones without using European tools. All who opposed the new order (including local chiefs, medicine men, shamans, and witches) must be put down by force. When all that had been done, God (a monotheistic, punishing God borrowed from the Christians) would restore the world that Indians had known before the whites came over the mountains.

Tenskwatawa's message soon found its way to the Delawares (who attacked the Christians among their people as witches), and other native peoples of the Northwest. When converts flooded into the prophet's home village, he moved to Prophetstown (Tippecanoe) in what is now Indiana. There with the help of his brother Tecumseh, he created an army estimated by the whites at anywhere between

Tenskwatawa   The Shawnee prophet Tenskwatawa ("The Open Door"), brother of Tecumseh, was painted by George Catlin in 1836—long after the defeat of his prophetic attempt to unify Native America.

650 and 3,000 warriors, and pledged to end further encroachment by whites. Tecumseh, who took control of the movement, announced to the whites that he was the sole chief of all the Indians north of the Ohio River; land cessions by anyone else would be invalid. Tenskwatawa's prophecy and Tecumseh's leadership had united the Indians of the Old Northwest in an unprecedented stand against white encroachment.

Tecumseh's confederacy posed a threat to the United States. A second war with England was looming, and Tecumseh was receiving supplies and encouragement from the British in Canada. He was also planning to visit the southern tribes in an attempt to bring them into his confederacy. The prospect of unified resistance by the western tribes in league with the British jeopardized every settler

west of the Appalachians. In 1811 William Henry Harrison led an army toward Prophetstown. With Tecumseh away, Tenskwatawa ordered an unwise attack on Harrison's army and was beaten at the Battle of Tippecanoe.

Tecumseh's still-formidable confederacy, joined by the traditionalist wing of the southern Creeks, fought alongside the British in the War of 1812 and lost (Chapter 9). With that, the military power of the Indians east of the Mississippi River was destroyed. General Andrew Jackson forced the Creeks (including those who had served as his allies) to cede millions of acres of land in Georgia and Alabama. The other southern tribes, along with the members of Tecumseh's northern confederacy, watched helplessly as new settlers took over their hunting lands. Some of the Indians moved west, and others tried to farm what was left of their old land. All of them had to deal with settlers and government officials who neither feared them nor took their sovereignty seriously. By this time most whites simply assumed that the Indians would have to move on to the barren land west of the Mississippi (see Chapter 12).

The Backcountry, 1790–1815

To easterners, the backcountry whites who had replaced the Indians were no different from the defeated aborigines. Indeed in accommodating themselves to a borderless forest used by both Indians and whites, many settlers—like many Indians—had melded Indian and white ways. To clear the land, backcountry farmers simply girdled the trees and left them to die and fall down by themselves. Then they ploughed the land by navigating between the stumps. Worse, to easterners, the fields were often worked by women. Like the Indians, backcountry whites depended on game for food and animal skins for trade. And like the Indians, they often spent long periods away on hunting trips, leaving the women to tend the fields. The arch-pioneer Daniel Boone, for instance, braided his hair, dressed himself in Indian leggings, and, with only his dogs for company, disappeared for months at a time on "long hunts." When easterners began to "civilize" his neighborhood, Boone moved further west.

Eastern visitors were appalled not only by the poverty, lice, and filth of frontier life but by the drunkenness and violence of the frontiersmen. Americans everywhere drank heavily in the early years of the nineteenth century. But everyone agreed that frontiersmen drank more and were more violent when drunk than men anywhere else. Travel accounts tell of no-holds-barred fights in which frontiersmen gouged the eyes and bit off the noses and ears of their opponents. No account was complete without a reckoning of the number of one-eyed, one-eared men the traveler had met on the frontier. Stories arose of half-legendary heroes like Davy Crockett of Tennessee who wrestled bears and alligators and had a recipe for Indian stew, and Mike Fink, a Pennsylvania boatman who brawled and drank his way along the rivers of the interior until he was shot and killed in a drunken episode that none of the participants could clearly remember. Samuel Holden Parsons, a New Englander serving as a judge in the Northwest Territory, called the frontiersmen "our white savages." The Massachusetts conservative Timothy Pickering branded them "the least worthy subjects of the United States. They are little less savage than the Indians."

After 1789 settlers of the western backcountry made two demands of the new national government: protection from the Indians and a guarantee of the right to navigate the Ohio and Mississippi Rivers. The Indians were pushed back in the 1790s and finished off in the War of 1812, and in 1803 Jefferson's Louisiana Purchase (see Chapter 9), ended the European presence on the rivers. Over these years the pace of settlement quickened. In 1790 only ten thousand settlers were living west of the Appalachians—about one American in forty. By 1800 the number of settlers had risen to nearly a million. By 1820, two million Americans were westerners—one in four.

The new settlers bought land from speculators who had acquired tracts under the Northwest Ordinance in the Northwest, from English, Dutch, and American land companies in western New York, and from land dealers in the Southwest and in northern New England. They built frame houses surrounded by cleared fields, planted marketable crops, and settled into the struggle to make farms out of the wildness and to meet mortgage payments along the way. By 1803 four frontier states had entered the union: Vermont (1791), Kentucky (1792), Tennessee (1796), and Ohio (1803). Louisiana soon followed (1812),

Backwoods Brawl This backwoods brawl was cariacatured in the popular *Crockett Almanac* of 1840. Biting, gouging, and scratching were routine; so was the audience of drunken neighbors.

and with the end of the war in 1815 one frontier state after another gained admission: Indiana (1816), Mississippi (1817), Illinois (1818), Alabama (1818), Maine (1820), and Missouri (1821).

As time passed, the term *backcountry,* which easterners had used to refer to the wilderness and the dangerous misfits who lived in it, fell into disuse. By 1820 the term *frontier* had replaced it. The new settlements were no longer in the backwash of American civilization. They were on its cutting edge.

THE PLANTATION SOUTH, 1790–1820

In 1790 the future of slavery in the Chesapeake (the states of Virginia, Maryland, and Delaware, where the institution first took root in North America) was uncertain. The tobacco market had been precarious since before the Revolution, and it continued to decline after 1790. Tobacco depleted the soil, and by

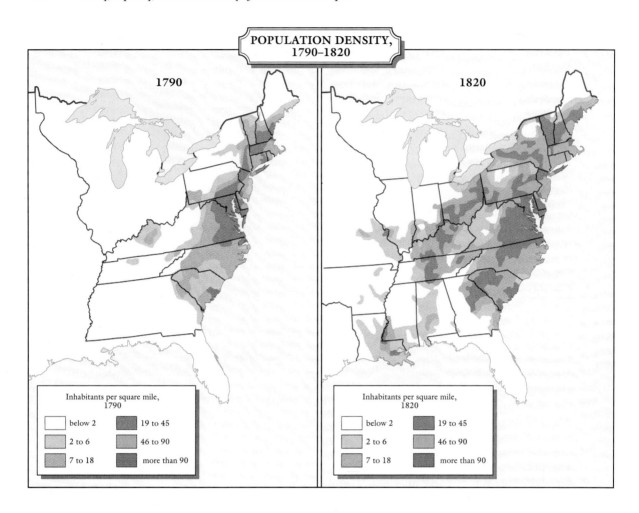

POPULATION DENSITY,
1790–1820

1790

1820

Inhabitants per square mile,
1790

below 2
2 to 6
7 to 18
19 to 45
46 to 90
more than 90

Inhabitants per square mile,
1820

below 2
2 to 6
7 to 18
19 to 45
46 to 90
more than 90

the late eighteenth century tidewater farms and plantations were giving out. As lands west of the Appalachians were opened to settlement, white tenants, laborers, and small farmers left the Chesapeake in droves. Many of them moved to Kentucky, Tennessee, or the western reaches of Virginia. But many others found new homes in nonslave states north of the Ohio River. Faced with declining opportunities within the slave societies of the Chesapeake, thousands of the poorer whites had voted with their feet.

The Recommitment to Slavery

With slave labor less and less necessary, Chesapeake planters continued to switch to grain and livestock — crops that required less labor than tobacco — and tried to think up new uses for slaves. Some planters divided their land into small plots and rented both the plots and their slaves to white tenant farmers.

Others, particularly in Maryland, recruited tenants from the growing ranks of free blacks. Still others hired out their slaves as artisans and urban laborers. None of these solutions, however, could employ the great mass of slaves or repay the planters' huge investment in slave labor.

In this situation many Chesapeake planters (who had, after all, fought a revolution in the name of natural rights) began to manumit their slaves. The farmers of Maryland and Delaware in particular set their slaves free; by the time those states sided with the North in 1861 over half the blacks in Maryland and nine-tenths of those in Delaware were free. Virginia's economic and cultural commitment to the plantation was stronger, but even in the Old Dominion there was a strong movement to manumit slaves. George Washington stated that he wished "to liberate a certain species of property," and manumitted his slaves by will. (The manumissions were to take place at the death of his widow—thus, as one wag declared, surrounding Mrs. Washington with one hundred people who wanted her dead.) Robert Carter, reputedly the largest slaveholder in Virginia, also freed his slaves, as did many others. The free black population of Virginia stood at 2,000 in 1782, when the state passed a law permitting manumission. The number of free blacks rose to 12,766 in 1790, to 20,124 in 1800, and to 30,570 in 1810. In all, the proportion of Virginia blacks who were free increased from 4 percent in 1790 to 7 percent in 1810.

There were, however, limits on the manumission of Virginia slaves. First, few planters could afford to free their slaves without compensation. Second, white Virginians feared the social consequences of black freedom. Thomas Jefferson, for instance, owned 175 slaves when he penned the phrase that "all men are created equal." He lived off their labor, sold them to pay his debts, gave them as gifts, and sometimes sold them away from their families as a punishment. Through it all he insisted that slavery was wrong. He could not imagine emancipation, however, without the colonization of freed slaves far from Virginia. A society of free blacks and whites, Jefferson insisted, would end in disaster: "Deep rooted prejudices entertained by the whites; ten thousand recollections, by the blacks, of the injuries they have sustained; new provocations; the real distinctions which nature has made . . . [will] produce convulsions which will probably never end but in the extermination of the one or the other race." Jefferson went on to a virulently racist argument for black inferiority and to the insistence that "When freed, [blacks are] to be removed beyond the reach of mixture." Near the end of an adult lifetime of condemning slavery but doing nothing to end it, Jefferson cried out that white Virginians held "a wolf by the ears": they could not hold onto slavery forever, and they could never let it go.

Jefferson's dilemma was eased by the rise of cotton cultivation further south. British industrialization created a demand for cotton from the 1790s onward, and planters knew they could sell all the cotton they could grow. But long-staple cotton, the only variety that could be profitably grown, was a delicate plant that thrived only on the Sea Islands off Georgia and South Carolina. The short-staple variety was hardier, but its sticky seeds had to be removed by hand before the cotton could be milled. It took a whole day for an adult slave to clean a single pound of short-staple cotton—an expenditure of labor that took the profit out of cotton. In 1790 the United States produced only 3,000 bales of cotton, nearly all of it on the plantations of the Sea Islands.

In 1793 Eli Whitney, a Connecticut Yankee who had come south to work as a tutor, set his mind to the problem. Within a few days he had made a model of a cotton "gin" (a southern contraction of "engine") that combed the seeds from the fiber with metal pins fitted into rollers. Working with Whitney's machine, a slave could clean fifty pounds of short-staple cotton in a day. At a stroke, cotton became the great American cash crop and plantation agriculture was rejuvenated. Cotton production grew to 73,000 bales in 1800, to 178,000 bales in 1810, and to 334,000 bales in 1820. By 1820, cotton accounted for more than half the value of all agricultural exports.

Short-staple cotton grew well in the hot, humid climate and the long growing season of the Lower South (roughly, the land below the southern borders of Virginia and Kentucky), and it grew almost anywhere: in the rolling Piedmont country east of the Appalachians, in the coastal lowlands, and—especially—in the virgin lands of the Old Southwest. It was also a labor-intensive crop that could be

Cotton Gin   The basis for later large-scale milling operations, Eli Whitney's simple, hand-cranked cotton gin made the production of short-staple cotton profitable and revolutionized southern agriculture.

grown in either small or large quantities; farmers with few or no slaves could make a decent profit, and planters with extensive land and many slaves could make enormous amounts of money. Best of all, the factories of England and, eventually, of the American Northeast, had a seemingly insatiable appetite for southern cotton.

The result was the rejuvenation of plantation slavery and its rapid spread into new regions of the South. Chesapeake planters, who lived too far north to grow cotton, continued to diversify. But the cotton frontier paid high prices for Chesapeake slaves; farmers sold their excess slaves to finance the transition to mixed agriculture. Up until about 1810, most of the slaves who left Virginia had traveled with their masters to Kentucky or Tennessee. Thereafter, most of them left as commodities in the burgeoning interstate slave trade, headed for the new plantations of Georgia, Alabama, and Mississippi.

The movement of slaves out of the Chesapeake was immense. In the 1790s one in twelve Virginia and Maryland slaves was taken south and west. The

figure rose to one in ten between 1800 and 1810, and to one in five between 1810 and 1820. In 1790 planters in Virginia and Maryland had owned 56 percent of all American slaves; by 1860 they owned only 15 percent. The demand for slaves in the new cotton lands provided many Chesapeake planters with a means of disposing of an endangered investment and with cash to pay for their transition to new crops.

The other region that had been a center of slavery during the eighteenth century — coastal South Carolina and Georgia — made a massive recommitment to slave labor in the years after the Revolution. There the principal crop was rice, which, along with other American foodstuffs, was experiencing a sharp rise in international demand. For their secondary crop, most planters in this region were switching from indigo (a source of blue dye) to cotton, creating an increase in the demand for slaves. Thousands of slaves in this region had either run away or been carried off by the British in the Revolution, and planters knew that the African slave trade was sched-

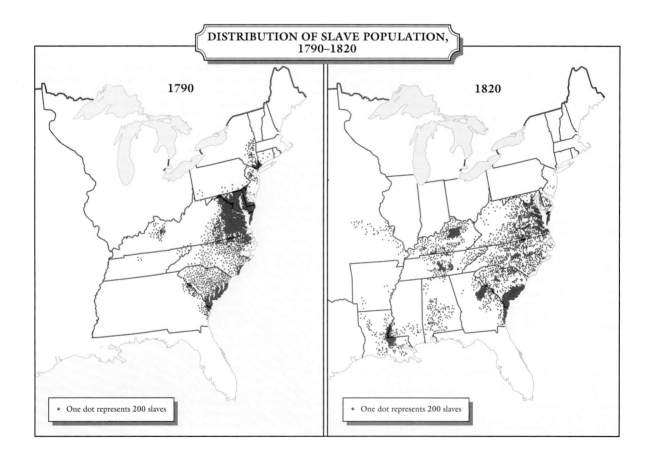

DISTRIBUTION OF SLAVE POPULATION, 1790–1820

1790

1820

• One dot represents 200 slaves

• One dot represents 200 slaves

uled to end in 1808. With slave prices rising and slave-produced crops becoming steadily more profitable, they rushed to import as many African slaves as they could in the time remaining. Between 1788 and 1808, 250,000 slaves were brought directly from Africa to the United States—nearly all of them to Charleston and Savannah. That figure equalled the number of Africans who had been brought to North America during the whole colonial period.

Race, Gender, and Southern Labor

The transition to grain and livestock raising in the Chesapeake and the rise of the cotton belt in the Lower South imposed new kinds of labor upon the slaves. The switch to mixed farming in Maryland and Virginia brought about a shift in the chores assigned to male and female slaves. Wheat cultivation, for example, meant a switch from the hoes used for tobacco to the plow and grain cradle—both of which called for the upper-body strength of adult men. The grain economy also required carts, wagons, mills, and good roads and thus created a need for greater numbers of slave artisans—nearly all of whom were men. Many of these were hired out to

urban employers, and lived as a semifree caste in cities and towns. In the diversifying economy of the Chesapeake, male slaves did the plowing, mowing, sowing, ditching, and carting and performed most of the tasks requiring artisanal skills. All of this work demanded high levels of training and could be performed by someone working either by himself or in a small group with little need for supervision.

Slave women were left with all the lesser tasks. Contrary to legend, few slave women in the Chesapeake worked as domestic servants in the planter's house. A few of them were assigned to such chores as cloth manufacture, sewing, candle molding, and the preparation of salt meat. But most female slaves still did farm work—hoeing, weeding, spreading manure, cleaning stables—that was monotonous, called for little skill, and was closely supervised. This new division of labor was clearly evident during the wheat harvest. On George Washington's farm, for example, male slaves, often working beside temporary white laborers, moved in a broad line as they mowed the grain. Following them came a gang of children and women bent over and moving along on their hands and knees as they bound wheat into shocks. Similarly Thomas Jefferson, who had been

An Overseer Doing His Duty In 1798 the architect and engineer Benjamin Latrobe sketched a white overseer smoking a cigar and supervising slave women as they hoed newly cleared farm land near Fredericksburg, Virginia. A critic of slavery, Latrobe sarcastically entitled the sketch "An overseer doing his duty."

shocked to see French women working in the fields, abandoned his concern for female delicacy when his own slaves were involved. At the grain harvest he instructed his overseers to organize "gangs of half men and half women."

On the rice and cotton plantations of South Carolina and Georgia, planters faced different labor problems. Slaves made up 80 percent of the population in this region, over 90 percent in many parishes. Farms were large, and the two principal crops demanded skilled, intensive labor. The environment encouraged deadly summer diseases and kept white owners and overseers out of the fields. Planters solved these problems by organizing slaves according to the so-called "task system." Each morning the owner or overseer assigned a specific task to each slave; when the task was done, the rest of the day belonged to the slave. Slaves who did not finish their task were punished, and when too many slaves finished early the owners assigned heavier tasks. In the eighteenth century, each slave had been expected to tend three to four acres of rice each day. In the early nineteenth, with the growth of the rice market, the assignment was raised to five acres.

The task system encouraged slaves to work hard without supervision, and they turned the system to their own uses. Often several slaves would work together, until all their tasks were completed. And strong young slaves would sometimes help older and weaker slaves after they had finished their own tasks. Once the day's work was done, the slaves would share their hard-earned leisure out of sight of the owner. A Jamaican visitor remarked that South Carolina and Georgia planters were "very particular in employing a negro, without his consent, after his task is finished, and agreeing with him for the payment which he is to receive." Further west, lowcountry slaves who were moved onto the cotton frontier often imposed the task system on new plantations, sometimes against the resistance of masters.

Slaves under the task system won the right to cultivate land as "private fields"—not the little garden plots common in the Chesapeake but farms of up to five acres on which they grew produce and raised livestock for market. There was a lively trade in slave-produced goods, and by the late 1850s slaves in the lowcountry not only produced and exchanged

Rice Fields of the South   The rice fields of coastal South Carolina, with their complex systems of irrigation, were often created by Africans who had done similar work in West Africa before their enslavement.

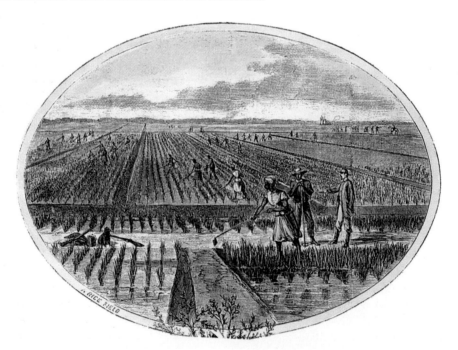

property but passed it on to their children. The owners tolerated such activity because slaves on the task system worked hard, required minimal supervision, and made money for their owners. The rice and cotton planters in South Carolina and Georgia were among the richest men in the country.

THE SEAPORT CITIES, 1790–1815

When the first federal census takers made their rounds in 1790, they found that 94 percent of the population was living on farms and in rural villages. The remaining 6 percent lived in 24 towns with a population of more than 2,500 (a census definition of "urban" that included many communities that were, by modern standards, very small.) Only five communities had a population over 10,000: Boston (18,038), New York (33,131), Philadelphia (42,444), Baltimore (13,503), and Charleston (16,359). All five were seaport cities—testimony to the key role of international commerce in the economy of the early republic.

The Growth of the Seaport Cities

These cities had grown steadily during the eighteenth century, handling imports from Europe and farm exports from America. With the outbreak of war between Britain and France in 1793—a world war that lasted until 1814—the overseas demand for American foodstuffs and for shipping to carry products from the Caribbean islands to Europe further strengthened the seaport cities. Foreign trade during these years was risky and uneven, subject to the tides of war and the strategies of the belligerents. French seizures of American shipping and the resulting undeclared war of 1798–1800, the British ban on America's reexport trade in 1805, Jefferson's nonimportation of 1806 and his trade embargo of 1807, and America's entry into the war in 1812 all disrupted the maritime economy and threw the seaports into periods of economic collapse. But by 1815, it was clear that wartime commerce had transformed the seaports and the institutions of American business. New York City had become the nation's largest city, with a population that had grown from 33,131 in 1790 to 96,373 in 1810. Philadelphia's population had risen to 53,722 by 1810; Boston's to 34,322; and Baltimore's to 46,555. Between 1800

and 1810, for the first time in American history, the growth of the urban population exceeded the growth of the rural population.

Seaport merchants in these years amassed the private fortunes and built the financial infrastructure that would soon take up the task of commercializing and industrializing the northern United States. Old merchants like the Brown brothers of Providence and Elias Hasket Darby of Salem grew richer, and newcomers like the immigrant John Jacob Astor of New York City built huge personal fortunes. To manage those fortunes, new institutions emerged. Docking and warehousing facilities expanded dramatically. Bookkeepers were replaced by accountants familiar with the new double-entry system of accounting, and insurance and banking companies were formed to handle the risks and rewards of wartime commerce.

The bustle of prosperity was evident on the waterfronts and principal streets of the seaport cities. An Englishman who visited the New York City docks during the wartime boom left this description: "The carters were driving in every direction; and the sailors and labourers upon the wharfs, and onboards the vessels, were moving their ponderous burdens from place to place. The merchants and their clerks were busily engaged in their countinghouses, or upon the piers. The Tontine coffee-house was filled with under-writers, brokers, merchants, traders, and politicians. . . . The steps and balcony of the coffee-house were crowded with people bidding, or listening to the several auctioneers, who had elevated themselves upon a hogshead of sugar, a puncheon of rum, or a bale of cotton; and with Stentorian voices were exclaiming, 'Once, twice. Once, twice.' 'Another cent.' 'Thank ye, gentlemen. . . .' The coffee-house slip, and the corners of Wall and Pearl Streets were jammed up with carts, drays, and wheelbarrows; horses and men were huddled promiscuously together, leaving little or no room for passengers to pass. . . . Everything was in motion; all was life, bustle, and activity."

Classes

Away from the waterfront, the main thoroughfares and a few of the side streets were paved with cobblestones and lined with fine shops and townhouses. But in other parts of the cities, visitors learned that the boom was creating unprecedented poverty as

A Scene near the New York City Docks in 1798 or 1799   The large building on the left is the Tontine Coffee House, which housed the Stock Exchange and the principal insurance offices, at the corner of Water and Wall Streets.

well as wealth. There had been poor people and depressed neighborhoods in the eighteenth-century seaports too, but not on the scale that prevailed between 1790 and 1820. A few steps off the handsome avenues were narrow streets crowded with ragged children, browsing dogs, pigs, horses, and cattle, with garbage and waste filling the open sewers. Epidemics had become more frequent and deadly. New York City, for example, experienced six severe epidemics of yellow fever between 1791 and 1822. Each time, the disease entered through the seaport and settled in the slums. Life expectancy in Boston, reputedly the healthiest city in America, was three to five years lower than in the surrounding countryside.

The slums were evidence that money created by commerce was being distributed in undemocratic ways. Per capita wealth in New York rose 60 percent between 1790 and 1825, but the wealthiest 4 percent of the population owned over half of that wealth. The wages of skilled and unskilled labor rose in these years, but the increase in seasonal and temporary employment, together with the recurring interruptions of foreign commerce, cut deeply into

the security and prosperity of ordinary women and men. Added to the old insecurities of sickness, fire, accident, aging, and any number of personal misfortunes, these ate up the gains made by laborers, sailors, and most artisans and their families.

Meanwhile, the status of artisans in the big cities was undergoing change. In 1790, artisans were the self-proclaimed "middling classes" who demanded and usually received the respect of their fellow citizens. When a clerk in Boston refused to attend dancing classes that one of the town's master saddlers had joined, a newspaper scolded him (a mere "stockjobber's lackey") for considering himself the social superior of the saddler and other "reputable mechanics." Artisans constituted about half the male work force of the seaport cities, and their respectability and usefulness, together with the role they had played in the Revolution (see Chapter 6), had earned them an honorable status.

That status rested in large part on their independence. In 1790 most artisan workshops had been household operations with at most one or two apprentices and hired journeymen, who looked for-

Pewterer's Flag   Carried by the New York Society of Pewterers in the parade celebrating ratification of the Constitution in 1788, this flag is a powerful emblem of the artisan republic, extolling partiotism, citizenship, and useful work.

ward to owning their own shops one day. Timothy Dwight, the conservative president of Yale College, observed that there were few of those "amphibious beings" in America who remained journeymen for life. Most master craftsmen lived modestly (on the borderline of poverty in many cases) and aspired only to the ability to support their household in security and decency. They identified their way of life with republican virtue. A doggerel verse dedicated to New York's stonemasons in 1805 reflects their view of themselves:

> I pay my debts
> I steal from no man; would not cut a throat
> To gain admission to a great man's purse
> Or a whore's bed. I'd not betray my friend
> To get his place of fortune; I scorn to flatter
> A blown up fool above me or crush
> The wretch beneath me.

This was a classic statement of the republican honesty and virtue that characterized the self-descriptions of skilled workmen. Thomas Jefferson catered to these sensibilities when he pronounced artisans "the yeomanry of the cities."

As in the countryside, however, the patriarchal base of that republicanism was being eroded. With the growth of the maritime economy, the nature of construction work, shipbuilding, the clothing trades, and other specialized crafts was undergoing change. Artisans were being replaced by cheaper labor, and

undercut by subcontracted "slop work" performed by semiskilled outworkers. Perhaps one in five master craftsmen entered the newly emerging business class. The others took work as laborers or journeymen (the term for wage-earning craftsmen.) By 1815 most young craftsmen could no longer hope to own their own shops. About half of New York City's journeymen that year were over thirty years old; nearly a quarter were over forty. Most of them were married, and about half of them headed a household that included four or more dependents. In short, they had become wage-earners for life. In the seaport cities between 1790 and 1820, the world of artisans like Paul Revere, Benjamin Franklin, and Thomas Paine was passing out of existence and was being replaced by wage labor.

The loss of independence undermined the paternal status of artisan husbands and fathers. As wage earners few could support their family unless the wife and children earned money to augment family income. Working-class women took in boarders and did laundry and found work as domestic servants or as peddlers of fruit, candy, vegetables, cakes, or hot corn. They sent their children out to scavenge in the streets. The descent into wage labor and the reliance on the earnings of women and children were at variance with the republican, patriarchal assumptions of fathers.

THE ASSAULT ON AUTHORITY

In the fifty years following the Declaration of Independence, the patriarchal republic created by the Founding Fathers became a democracy. The decline of authority and deference and the rise of individualistic, democratic social and political forms had many roots—most obviously in rural overcrowding, the movement of young people west and into the towns, and, more happily, in the increasingly democratic implications of American Revolutionary ideology. But most Americans witnessed the initial stirrings of change as a withering of paternal authority in their own households. For some—slaves and many women in particular—the decline of patriarchy could be welcomed. For others (the fathers themselves, disinherited sons, and women who looked to the security of old ways) it was a disaster of unmeasured proportions. But whether they experienced the transformation as a personal rise or fall,

Americans by the early nineteenth century had entered a world where received authority and the experience of the past had lost their power. A new democratic faith emerged, grounded in the experience, intellect, and intuition of ordinary people.

Paternal Power in Decline

The philosopher Ralph Waldo Emerson, who reached adulthood in the 1830s, later mused that he had had the misfortune to be young when age was respected, and to have grown old when youth counted for everything. Arriving in America at about the time Emerson came of age, the French visitor Alexis de Tocqueville observed that paternal power was largely absent in American families. "All that remains of it," he said, "are a few vestiges in the first years of childhood. . . . But as soon as the young American approaches manhood, the ties of filial obedience are relaxed day by day; master of his thoughts, he is soon master of his conduct. . . . At the close of boyhood the man appears and begins to trace out his own path."

From the mid-eighteenth century onward, especially after the Revolution, many young people grew up knowing that their father would be unable to help them, and that they would have to make their own way in the world. The consequent decline of parental power became evident in many ways—perhaps most poignantly in changing patterns of courtship and marriage. In the countryside, young men knew that they would not inherit the family farm, and young women knew that their father would be able to provide only a small dowry. As a result, fathers had less control over marriage choices than they had had when marriage was accompanied by a significant transfer of property. Young people now courted away from parental scrutiny and made choices based on affection and personal attraction rather than on property or parental pressure. In eighteenth-century America, rural marriages had united families; now they united individuals. One sign of the independence of young people (and of their lack of faith in their future) was the high number of pregnancies outside of marriage. In the seventeenth-century North, such things had seldom happened. But in the second half of the eighteenth century and in the first decades of the nineteenth, the number of first births that occurred within eight months of marriage averaged between 25 and 30

percent—with the rates running much higher among poor couples. Apparently fathers who could not provide for their children could not control them either.

The Alcoholic Republic

The erosion of paternal authority was paralleled by a dramatic rise in alcohol consumption. Americans had been drinking alcohol since the time of the first settlements. (The Puritan flagship *Arabella* had carried three times as much beer as water.) But drinking, like everything else that was "normal," took place within a structure of paternal authority. Americans tippled every day in the course of their ordinary activities: at family meals and around the fireside, at work, and at barn-raisings, militia musters, dances, court days (even judges and juries passed the bottle), weddings, funerals, corn-huskings—even at the ordination of ministers. Under such circumstances, drinking—even drunkenness—seldom posed a threat to authority or to the social order.

That old pattern of communal drinking persisted into the nineteenth century. But during the fifty years following the Revolution it gradually gave way to a new pattern. Farmers, particularly those in newly settled areas, regularly produced a surplus of grain that they turned into whiskey. In Washington County in western Pennsylvania, for example, one family in ten operated a distillery in the 1790s. Whiskey was safer than water and milk, which were often tainted, and it was cheaper than coffee or tea. It was also cheaper than imported rum. So Americans embraced whiskey as their national drink and consumed extraordinary quantities of it. Per capita consumption of pure alcohol in all its forms increased from three to four gallons annually between 1790 and 1830. Most of the increase was in the consumption of cheap and potent whiskey. By 1830 per capita consumption of distilled spirits was over five gallons per year—the highest it has ever been, and three times what it is in the United States today. The United States had indeed become, as one historian has said, an "alcoholic republic."

The nation's growing thirst was driven not by conviviality or neighborliness but by a desire to get drunk. Most Americans drank regularly, though there were wide variations. Men drank far more than women, the poor and the rich drank more than the emerging middle class, city dwellers drank more than farmers, westerners drank more than easterners, and southerners drank a bit more than northerners. Throughout the nation, the heaviest drinking took place among the increasing numbers of young men who lived away from their family and outside the old social controls: soldiers and sailors, boatmen and other transport workers, lumberjacks, schoolmasters, journeyman craftsmen, college students. Among such men the controlled tippling of the eighteenth century gave way to the binge and to solitary drinking. By the 1820s American physicians were learning to diagnose delirium tremens—the trembling and the paranoid delusions brought on by withdrawal from physical addiction to alcohol. By that decade, as we shall see (see Chapter 13), social reformers branded alcohol as a threat to individual well-being, to social peace, and to the republic itself.

The Democratization of Print

Of course Americans freed from the comforts and constraints of patriarchal authority did more than fornicate and drink. Many seized more constructive opportunities to think and act for themselves. That tendency was speeded by a rise in literacy and by the emergence of a print culture that catered to popular tastes. The literacy rate in the preindustrial United States was among the highest ever recorded. In 1790 approximately 85 percent of adult men in New England and 60 percent of those in Pennsylvania and the Chesapeake could read and write. The literacy rate was lower among women—about 45 percent in New England—but on the rise. By 1820 all but the poorest white Americans, particularly in the North, could read and write. The rise in literacy was accompanied by an explosive growth in the amount and kinds of reading matter available to the public. At its simplest and most intimate, this took the form of personal letters. Increased mobility separated families and friends and encouraged letter writing. In 1790 there were only 75 post offices in the United States. By 1800 there were 903. The amount of mail increased similarly, and—if what has survived to the present is an indication—the

Interior of an American Inn, 1813   In this democratic, neighborly scene in a country inn in the early republic, men of varying degrees of wealth, status, and inebriety are drinking and talking freely with each other. One man's wife and daughter have invaded this male domain, perhaps to question the time and money spent at the inn.

proportion made up of family correspondence and the proportion of that correspondence written and read by women, all increased dramatically.

Women were also the principal readers of novels, a new form of reading matter that Thomas Jefferson and other authorities denounced as frivolous and aberrant. The first best-selling novel in the United States was *The Power of Sympathy*, a morally ambiguous tale of seduction and betrayal that exposed hypocrisy in male authorities who punished (generally poor and vulnerable) women for their own seductions. Such tales were seen as dangerous not only because they contained questionable subject matter but because girls and women read them silently and in private, without proper surveillance.

The most widely distributed publications, however, were newspapers. In 1790, 90 newspapers were being published in the United States. In 1830 there were 370, and they had grown chattier and more informal. Still, even in New England, only one household in ten or twelve subscribed to a newspaper. The papers were passed from hand to hand, read aloud in groups, and made available at taverns and public houses. Timothy Dwight hated newspapers and associated them with gambling, tavern-haunting, and drinking.

The increase in literacy and in printed matter accelerated the democratizing process. In the eighteenth century, when books and newspapers were scarce, most Americans had experienced the written word only as it was read aloud by fathers, ministers, or teachers. Between 1780 and 1820 private, silent reading of new kinds of texts became common—religious tracts, inexpensive Bibles, personal letters, novels, newspapers, and magazines. No longer were authority figures the sole interpreters of the world for families and neighborhoods. The new print culture encouraged Americans to read and think for themselves, and to interpret information without the mediation of the old authorities.

Citizenship

The transition from republic to democracy—and the relation of that transition to the decline of rural patriarchy—took on formal, institutional shape in a redefinition of republican citizenship. The revolutionary constitutions of most states retained the colonial freehold (property) qualifications for voting. Thomas Jefferson had affirmed these laws, proclaiming the Americans uniquely suited for republican

citizenship because they were "a people of property; almost every man is a freeholder."

In the yeoman societies of the late eighteenth century, freehold qualifications granted the vote to from one-half to three-quarters of adult white men. Many of the disenfranchised were dependent sons who expected to inherit citizenship along with land. Some states dropped the freehold clause and gave the vote to all adult men who paid taxes, but with little effect on the voting population. Both the freehold and taxpaying qualifications tended to grant political rights to adult men who headed households, thus reinforcing classical republican notions that granted full citizenship to independent fathers and not to their dependents. Statesmen often defended the qualifications in those terms. Arthur St. Clair, the territorial governor of Ohio, argued for retention of the Northwest Ordinance's fifty-acre freehold qualification for voting in territorial elections in set-piece republican language: "I do not count independence and wealth always together," he said, "but I pronounce poverty and dependence inseparable." When Nathaniel Macon, a respected old revolutionary from North Carolina, saw that his state would abolish property qualifications in 1802, he suggested that the suffrage be limited to married men. Like St. Clair's, it was an attempt to maintain the old distinction between citizen-householders and disfranchised dependents.

Between 1790 and 1820 republican notions of citizenship grounded in fatherhood and proprietorship gave way to a democratic insistence on equal rights for all white men. In 1790 only Vermont granted the vote to all free men. Kentucky entered the Union in 1792 without property or taxpaying qualifications; Tennessee followed with a freehold qualification, but only for newcomers who had resided in their counties for less than six months. The federal government dropped the fifty-acre freehold qualification in the territories in 1812; of the eight territories that became states between 1796 and 1821 none kept a property qualification, only three maintained a taxpaying qualification, and five explicitly granted the vote to all white men. In the same years, one eastern state after another widened the franchise. By 1840 only Rhode Island retained a propertied electorate—primarily because Yankee farmers in that state wanted to retain power in a society made up more and more of urban, immigrant wage earners. (When Rhode Island finally reformed the franchise in 1843, the new law included a freehold requirement that applied only to the foreign-born.) With that exception, the white men of every state held the vote.

Early nineteenth-century suffrage reform gave political rights to propertyless men, and thus took a long step away from the Founders' republic and toward mass democracy. At the same time, however, reformers explicitly limited the democratic franchise to those who were white and male. New Jersey's revolutionary constitution, for instance, had granted the vote to "persons" who met a freehold qualification. This loophole enfranchised property-holding widows, many of whom exercised their rights. A law of 1807 abolished property restrictions and gave the vote to all white men; the same law closed the loophole that had allowed propertied women to vote. The question of woman's suffrage would not be raised again until women raised it in 1848 (see Chapter 12); it would not be settled until well into the twentieth century.

New restrictions also applied to African Americans. The revolutionary constitutions of Massachusetts, New Hampshire, Vermont, and Maine—northeastern states with tiny black minorities—granted the vote to free blacks. New York and North Carolina laws gave the vote to "all men" who met the qualifications, and propertied African Americans (a tiny but symbolically crucial minority) in many states routinely exercised the vote. Postrevolutionary laws that extended voting rights to all white men often specifically excluded or severely restricted votes for blacks. Free blacks lost the suffrage in New York, New Jersey, Pennsylvania, Connecticut, Maryland, Tennessee, and North Carolina—all states in which they had previously voted. By 1840 fully 93 percent of Northern blacks lived in states that either banned or severely restricted their right to vote. And the restrictions were explicitly about race. A delegate to the New York constitutional convention of 1821, noting the movement of freed slaves into New York City, argued against allowing them to vote: "The whole host of Africans that now deluge our city (already too impertinent to be borne), would be placed upon an equal with the citizens." A Michigan legislator later confirmed the distinction between "Africans" and "citizens" when he insisted that neither blacks nor Indians belonged to the "great North American Family," and thus could never be citizens of the republic.

Thus the "universal" suffrage of which many Americans boasted was far from universal: new laws dissolved the old republican connections between political rights and property, and thus saved the citizenship of thousands who were becoming propertyless tenants and wage earners; the same laws that gave the vote to all white men, however, explicitly barred other Americans from political participation. Faced with the disintegration of Jefferson's republic of proprietors, the wielders of power had chosen to blur the emerging distinctions of social class while they hardened the boundaries of sex and race. It was a formula that the "democracy" of white men would return to over and over again as the nineteenth century wore on.

REPUBLICAN RELIGION

The Founding Fathers had been largely indifferent to organized religion, though a few were pious men. Some, like George Washington, a nominal Episcopalian, attended church out of a sense of obligation. Many of the better-educated, including Thomas Jefferson, subscribed to deism, the belief that God had created the universe but did not intervene in its affairs. Many simply did not bother themselves with thoughts about religion. When asked why the Constitution mentioned neither God nor religion, Alexander Hamilton is reported to have smiled and answered, "We forgot."

The Decline of Established Churches

In state after state, postrevolutionary constitutions withdrew government support from religion, and the First Amendment to the Constitution clearly prescribed the national separation of church and state. Reduced to their own sources of support, the established churches went into decline. The Episcopal Church, which until the Revolution had been the established Church of England in the southern colonies, went into decline. In Virginia, only 40 of the 107 Episcopal parishes supported ministers in the early nineteenth century. Nor did the Episcopal Church travel west with southern settlers. Of the 408 Episcopal congregations in the South in 1850, 315 were in the old seaboard states.

In New England, the old churches fared little better. The Connecticut Congregationalist Ezra Stiles reported in 1780 that 60 parishes in Vermont and an equal number in New Hampshire were without a minister. In Massachusetts Stiles reported that 80 parishes were without a minister. In all, about one-third of New England's Congregational pulpits were vacant in 1780, and the situation was worse to the north and west. In Vermont between 1763 and 1820, the founding of churches followed the incorporation of towns by an average of fifteen years, an indication that frontier settlement in that state proceeded almost entirely without the benefit of organized religion. In 1780 there were 750 Congregational churches in the United States (nearly all of them in New England) and the total was only 1,100 in 1820 — this over a period when the nation's population was rising from 4 to 10 million. Ordinary women and men were leaving the churches that had dominated the religious life of colonial America, sometimes ridiculing the learned clergy as they departed. To Ezra Stiles and other conservatives, it seemed that the republic was plunging into atheism.

The Rise of the Democratic Sects

The collapse of the established churches, the social dislocations of the postrevolutionary years, and the increasingly antiauthoritarian, democratic sensibilities of ordinary Americans provided fertile ground for the growth of new democratic sects. These were the years of camp-meeting revivalism, years in which Methodists and Baptists grew from small, half-organized sects into the great popular denominations they have been ever since. They were also years in which fiercely independent drop-outs from older churches were putting together a loosely organized movement that would become the Disciples of Christ. At the same time, ragged, half-educated preachers were spreading the Universalist and Freewill Baptist messages in upcountry New England, while in western New York young Joseph Smith was experiencing the visions that would lead to Mormonism (see Chapter 11).

The result was, first of all, a vast increase in the variety of choices on the American religious landscape. But within that welter of new churches was a roughly uniform democratic style shared by the fastest-growing sects. First, they renounced the need for an educated, formally authorized clergy. Religion was now a matter of the heart and not the head; crisis conversion (understood in most churches as personal transformation that resulted from direct experience of the Holy Spirit) was a necessary credential for preachers; a college degree was not. The new preachers substituted emotionalism and storytelling for Episcopal ritual and Congregational theo-

logical lectures; stories attracted listeners, and they were harder for the learned clergy to refute. The new churches also held up the Bible as the one source of religious knowledge, thus undercutting all theological knowledge and placing every literate Christian on a level with the best-educated minister. These tendencies often ended in Restorationism — the belief that all theological and institutional changes since the end of biblical times were manmade mistakes, and that religious organizations must restore themselves to the purity and simplicity of the church of the Apostles. In sum, this loose democratic creed rejected learning and tradition and raised up the priesthood of all believers.

Baptists and Methodists were by far the most successful at preaching to the new populist audience. In 1783 there were only 50 Methodist churches in the United States; by 1820 there were 2,700. Over those same years the number of Baptist churches rose from 400 to 2,700. Together, in 1820, these two denominations outnumbered Episcopalians and Congregationalists three to one, almost a reversal of their relative standings forty years earlier. Baptists based much of their appeal in localism and congregational democracy. Methodist success, on the other hand, was due to skillful national organization. Bishop Francis Asbury, the head of the church in its fastest-growing years, built an episcopal bureaucracy that seeded churches throughout the republic, and sent circuit-riding preachers to places that had none. These early Methodist missions were grounded in self-sacrifice to the point of martyrdom. Asbury demanded much of his itinerant preachers, and until 1810 he strongly suggested that they remain celibate. "To marry," he said, "is to locate." Asbury also knew that married circuit riders would leave many widows and orphans behind, for hundreds of them worked themselves to death. Of the men who served as Methodist itinerants before 1819, 60 percent died before the age of forty.

From seaport cities to frontier settlements, few Americans escaped the sound of Methodist preaching in the early nineteenth century. The Methodists were common men who spoke plainly, listened carefully to others, and carried hymnbooks with simple tunes that anyone could sing. They also, particularly in the early years, shared traditional folk beliefs with their humble flocks. Some of the early circuit riders relied heavily on dreams; some could predict the future; many visited heaven and hell and returned with full descriptions. But in the end it was the hopefulness and simplicity of the Methodist message that at-

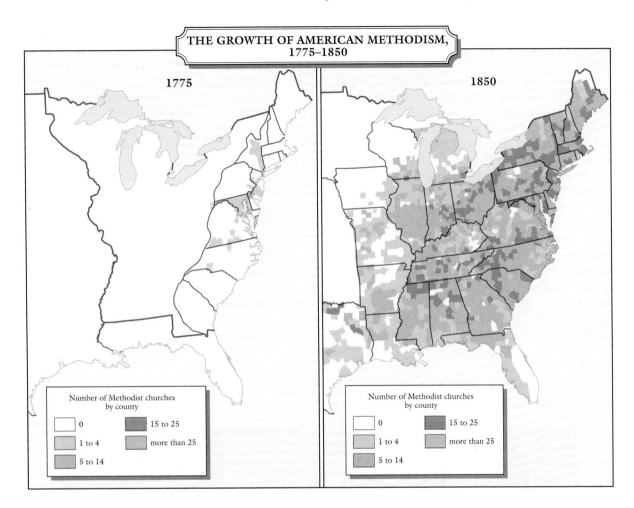

THE GROWTH OF AMERICAN METHODISM,
1775–1850

1775

1850

Number of Methodist churches
by county

0	15 to 25
1 to 4	more than 25
5 to 14	

Number of Methodist churches
by county

0	15 to 25
1 to 4	more than 25
5 to 14	

tracted ordinary Americans. The Methodists rejected the old terrors of Calvinist determinism and taught that while salvation comes only through God, men and women can *decide* to open themselves to divine grace and thus play a decisive role in their own salvation. They also taught that a godly life is a gradual, lifetime growth in grace—thus allowing for repentance for minor, and sometimes even major, lapses of faith and behavior. It was by granting responsibility (one might say sovereignty) to the individual believer that the Methodists established their democratic credentials and drew hundreds of thousands of Americans into their fold.

The Christianization of the White South

It was during these same years that evangelical Protestantism became the dominant religion of the white South. That triumph constituted a powerful assault on the prerevolutionary structure of authority, for the Baptists, Methodists, and evangelical Presbyterians who achieved it saw it as a revolt of poor and middling folk against the cultural dominance of the gentry. The essence of southern evangelicalism was a violent conversion experience followed by a life of piety and a rejection of what evangelicals called "the world." To no small degree, "the world" was the economic, cultural, and political world controlled by the planters. James McGready, who preached in rural North Carolina, openly condemned the gentry: "The world is in all their thoughts day and night. All their talk is of corn and tobacco, of land and stock. The price of merchandise and negroes are inexhaustible themes of conversation. But for them, the name of Jesus has no charms; it is rarely mentioned unless to be profaned." In the 1790s this was dangerous talk, as McGready learned when young rakes rode their horses through one of his outdoor meetings, tipped over the benches, set the altar on fire, and threatened to kill McGready himself.

Southern Baptists, Methodists, and Presbyterians spread their democratic message in the early nineteenth century through the camp meeting. Though its origins stretched back into the eighteenth century, the first full-blown camp meeting took place at Cane Ridge, Kentucky, in 1801. Here the annual "Holy Feast," a three-day communion service of Scotch-Irish Presbyterians, was transformed into an outdoor, interdenominational revival at which hundreds experienced conversion under Presbyterian, Methodist, and Baptist preaching. Estimates of the crowd at Cane Ridge ranged from 10,000 to 20,000 persons, and by all accounts the enthusiasm was nearly unprecedented. Some converts fainted; others succumbed to uncontrolled bodily jerkings, while a few barked like dogs—all of them visibly taken by the Holy Spirit. Such exercises fell upon women and

men, whites and blacks, rich and poor, momentarily erasing southern social distinctions in moments of profound and very public religious ecstasy. A witness to a later camp meeting recounted that "to see a bold and courageous Kentuckian (undaunted by the horrors of war) turn pale and tremble at the reproof of a weak woman, a little boy, or a poor African; to see him sink down in deep remorse, roll and toss, and gnash his teeth, till black in the face, entreat the prayers of those he came to devour . . . who can say the change was not supernatural?"

Southern evangelicalism was a subversive movement from its origins before the Revolution into the early nineteenth century. But despite its critique of worldliness and its antiauthoritarian emphasis, it was at bottom conservative, for it seldom questioned the need for social hierarchy. As the nineteenth century progressed, the Baptists, Methodists, and Presbyterians of the South, though they never stopped railing against greed and pride, learned to live com-

Camp Meeting   Painted in 1839, when camp meetings had become routine, this striking watercolor depicts swooning, crying, and other "exercises" of converts (most of them women) under the sway of revival preachers.

fortably within a system of fixed hierarchy and God-given social roles.

Slavery became the major case in point. For a brief period after the Revolution, evangelicals included slavery on their list of worldly sins. Methodists and Baptists preached to slaves as well as to whites, and Bishop Francis Asbury, principal architect of American Methodism, was familiar with John Wesley's statement that slavery was against "all the laws of Justice, Mercy, and Truth." In 1780 a conference of Methodist preachers ordered circuit riders to free their slaves and advised all Methodists to do the same. In 1784 the Methodists declared that they would excommunicate members who failed to free their slaves within two years. Lay Methodists took the order seriously: on the Delmarva Peninsula (Delaware and the Eastern Shore of Maryland and Virginia), for instance, Methodist converts freed thousands of slaves in the late eighteenth century. Other evangelicals shared their views. As early as 1787, southern Presbyterians prayed for "final abolition," and two years later Baptists condemned slavery as "a violent deprivation of the rights of nature and inconsistent with a republican government."

The period of greatest evangelical growth, however, came during the years in which the South was committing irrevocably to plantation slavery. As increasing numbers of both slaves and slaveowners came within the evangelical fold, the southern churches had to rethink their position on slavery. The Methodists never carried out their threat to excommunicate slaveholders, confessing in 1816 that southerners were so committed to slavery that "little can be done to abolish the practice so contrary to moral justice." Similarly, the Baptists and Presbyterians never translated their antislavery rhetoric into action. By 1820, evangelicals were coming to terms with slavery. Instead of demanding freedom for slaves, they suggested, as the Methodist James O'Kelly put it, that slaveowners remember that slaves were "dear brethren in Christ" who should not be treated cruelly and who should be allowed to attend religious services. By the 1830s, with large numbers of the planter elite converted to the evangelical fold, this was transformed into a full-scale effort to Christianize the institution of slavery (see Chapter 11).

Thus by 1820 few southern evangelicals were speaking out against slavery. Those who held to their antislavery views were concentrated in the upcountry, where few whites owned slaves. Many of these were joining the stream of poor and middling whites who were moving to free states north of the Ohio River. A Kentucky farmer and carpenter named Thomas Lincoln, for instance, belonged to a Baptist congregation that had separated from its parent church over the question of slavery. When he moved his family to a site near Pidgeon Creek, Indiana, Lincoln helped build an antislavery Baptist church and served it as trustee. He also arranged a job as church sexton for his young son Abraham.

The Beginnings of African-American Christianity

In the South Carolina and Georgia lowcountry there were few slave Christians before 1830. But in the slave communities of the Upper South, as well as the burgeoning free and semifree urban black populations of both the North and South, the evangelical revivals of the late eighteenth and early nineteenth centuries appealed powerfully to African Americans who sensed that the bonds of slavery were loosening. By 1820 most blacks outside the Deep South considered themselves Christians.

There were, of course, Christian slaves in the seventeenth and eighteenth centuries, most of whom had been converted by Anglican missions. Blacks had participated in the revivals of the southern Great Awakening, and the number of Christian slaves had increased steadily in the second half of the eighteenth century. But during the years from 1780 to 1820, for the first time, thousands of slaves embraced Christianity and began to turn it into a religion of their own. Slaves attended camp meetings (there was a black preacher, probably from the independent church in Lexington, at the Cane Ridge revival), listened to itinerant preachers, and joined the Baptist and Methodist congregations of the southern revival.

Blacks were drawn to revival religion for many of the same reasons as whites. They found the informal, storytelling evangelical preachers more attractive than the old Anglican missionaries. The revivalists, in turn, welcomed slaves and free blacks to their meetings and sometimes recruited them as preachers. Evangelical, emotional preaching, the falling, jerking, and other camp-meeting "exercises," the revivalists' emphasis on singing and other forms of audience participation, was much more attractive than the cold, high-toned preaching of the Anglicans. So were the humility and suffering of the evangelical whites. Slaves respected Methodist missionaries who entered their cabins and talked with them on their own terms; they listened more closely to men like James McGready than to the slaveholders who rode horses through McGready's meetings. Finally, the slaves gloried in the evangelicals' assault on the slaveholders' culture and in the antislavery sentiments of many white evangelicals. The result was a huge increase in the number of African-American Christians. Methodists, who counted converts more carefully than some others, claimed twenty thousand black members in 1800 — one in three American Methodists.

Neither antislavery beliefs nor openness to black participation, however, persisted long among white evangelicals. Though there were exceptions, most "integrated" congregations in both the North and South were in fact internally segregated, with blacks sitting in the back of the church or upstairs in the gallery, and with only whites serving in positions of authority. Blacks began organizing independent churches. In Philadelphia, the black preachers Richard Allen and Absalom Jones rebelled against segregated seating in St. George's Methodist Church and, in 1794, founded two separate black congregations; by 1800 40 percent of Philadelphia's blacks belonged to one of those two churches. Similar secessions resulted in new churches farther south: in Baltimore, in Wilmington, Delaware, in Richmond, in Norfolk, and in the cluster of villages that had risen to serve the Chesapeake's new mixed economy. Even Charleston boasted an independent Methodist conference made up of four thousand slaves and free blacks in 1815. By 1820 there were roughly seven hundred independent black churches in the United States. Thirty years earlier there had been none at all. The creation of an independent Christian tradition among the majority of blacks who remained plantation slaves took place only after 1830 (see Chapter 11). But the democratic message of the early southern revival, the brief attempt of white and black Christians to live out the implications of that message, and the independent black churches that rose from the failure of that attempt all left a permanent stamp on American Protestantism, black and white.

Black Republicanism: Gabriel's Rebellion

Masters who talked of liberty and natural rights sometimes worried that slaves might imagine that such language could apply to themselves. The Age of the Democratic Revolution took a huge step in that direction in 1789, when the French Revolution — fought in the name of "Liberty, Equality, and Fraternity" — went beyond American notions of restored English liberties and into the heady regions of universal natural rights. Among the first results outside of France was a revolution on the Caribbean island of Saint Dominque. That island's half million slaves fought out a complicated political and military revolt that began with the events in Paris in 1789 and resulted — after the defeats of Spanish, English, and French armies — with the creation of the independent black Republic of Haiti. Slave societies throughout the hemisphere heard tales of terror from refugee French planters and stories of hope from the slaves they brought with them (twelve thousand of these entered South Carolina and Louisiana alone). In 1800 a conservative Virginia white complained that "Liberty and Equality has been infused into the minds of the negroes." A South Carolina Congressman agreed that "this new-fangled French philosophy of liberty and equality" was stirring up the slaves. Even Thomas Jefferson, who applauded the spread of French republicanism, conceded that "the West Indies appears to have given considerable impulse to the minds of the slaves . . . in the United States."

Slaves from the 1790s onward whispered of natural rights and imagined themselves as part of the Democratic Revolution. This covert republic of the slaves sometimes came into the open, most ominously in Richmond in 1800, where a slave blacksmith named Gabriel hatched a well-planned conspiracy to overthrow Virginia's slave regime. Gabriel had been hired out to Richmond employers for most of his adult life; he was shaped less by plantation slavery than by the democratic, loosely interracial underworld of urban artisans. In the late 1790s the repressive acts of the Federalist national government and the angry responses of the Jeffersonian opposition (see Chapter 9), along with the news from Saint Dominque, drove the democratic sensibilities of that world to new heights. Gabriel's plans took shape within that heated ideological environment.

Gabriel, working with his brother and other hired-out slave artisans, planned his revolt with military precision. Working at religious meetings, barbecues, and the grog shops of Richmond, they recruited soldiers among slave artisans, adding plantation slaves only at the last moment. Gabriel planned to march an army of one thousand on Richmond in three columns. The outside columns would set diversionary fires in the warehouse district and prevent the militia from entering the town. The center would seize Capitol Square, including the treasury, the arsenal, and Governor James Monroe.

While his army would be made up of slaves, and while his victory would end slavery in Virginia, Gabriel hoped to make a republican revolution, not a slave revolt. His chosen enemies were the Richmond "merchants" who had controlled his labor. Later, a co-conspirator divulged the plan: the rebels would hold Governor Monroe hostage and split the state treasury among themselves, and "if the white people agreed to their freedom they would then hoist a white flag, and [Gabriel] would dine and drink with the merchants of the city on the day when it would be agreed to." Gabriel expected what

he called "the poor white people" and "the most redoubtable republicans" to join him. He in fact had the shadowy support of two Frenchmen, and there were rumors that other whites were involved— though never at levels that matched the delusions of the conspirators. Gabriel would kill anyone who opposed him, but he would spare Quakers, Methodists, and Frenchmen, for they were "friendly to liberty." Unlike earlier slave insurgents, Gabriel's dreams did not center on violent retribution or a return to or reconstruction of West Africa. He was an American revolutionary, and he dreamed of a truly democratic republic for Virginia. His army would march into Richmond under the banner "Death or Liberty."

Gabriel and his co-conspirators recruited at least 150 soldiers who agreed to gather near Richmond on August 30, 1800. The leaders expected to be joined by 500 to 600 more rebels as they marched

Bethel AME Church   Founded in 1794 by the Reverend Richard Allen and nine other blacks who resented discrimination at the hands of white Methodists, Philadelphia's Bethel African Methodist Episcopal Church became a cornerstone of the city's free black community.

upon the town. But on the appointed day it rained heavily. Rebels could not reach the meeting point, and amid white terror and black betrayals Gabriel and his henchmen were hunted down, tried, and sentenced to death. In all, the state hanged 27 supposed conspirators, while others were sold and transported out of Virginia. The condemned carried their radical republican dreams to their graves. A white Virginian marvelled that rebels on the gallows displayed a "sense of their [natural] rights, [and] a contempt of danger." When asked to explain the revolt, one condemned man replied in terms that could only have disturbed the white republicans of Virginia: "I have nothing more to offer than what General Washington would have had to offer, had he been taken by the British and put to trial by them. I have adventured my life in endeavoring to obtain the liberty of my countrymen, and am a willing sacrifice in their cause."

SUGGESTED READING

James A. Henretta, *The Origins of American Capitalism: Collected Essays* (1991) and Alan Kulikoff, *The Agrarian Origins of American Capitalism* (1992) are theoretically sophisticated surveys of the American economy in these years. Still essential is Douglas C. North, *The Economic Growth of the United States, 1790–1860* (1961).

On rural society after the Revolution, the most thorough regional study is Christopher Clark, *The Roots of Rural Capitalism: Western Massachusetts, 1780–1860* (1990). Laurel Thatcher Ulrich, *A Midwife's Tale: The Life of Martha Ballard, Based on Her Diary, 1785–1812* (1990) is a beautiful and insightful account. Jack Larkin, *The Reshaping of Everyday Life, 1790–1840* is a valuable synthesis of scholarship on material culture, particularly in the Northeast. Also valuable are Winifred Barr Rothenberg, *From Market-Places to Market Economy: The Transformation of Rural Massachusetts, 1750–1850* (1994); Joan M. Jensen, *Loosening the Bonds: Mid-Atlantic Farm Women, 1750–1850* (1986); Toby L. Ditz, *Property and Kinship: Inheritance in Early Connecticut, 1750–1820* (1986); and the essays in Stephen Innes, ed., *Work and Labor in Early America* (1988). Other relevant studies are cited in the Suggested Reading for Chapter 10.

Study of the postrevolutionary frontier begins with the final chapters of Richard White's magesterial *The Middle Ground: Indians, Empires, and Republics in the Great Lakes Region, 1650–1815* (1991). Graceful and thoughtful accounts of Native Americans in these years include R. David Edmunds, *The Shawnee Prophet* (1983); Anthony F. C. Wallace, *The Death*

and Rebirth of the Seneca (1969); William G. McLoughlin, *Cherokee Renaissance in the New Republic* (1986); and Gregory Evans Dowd, *A Spirited Resistance: The North American Indian Struggle for Unity, 1745–1815* (1992). Frontier whites are ably treated in John Mack Faragher, *Daniel Boone: The Life and Legend of an American Pioneer* (1992); Andrew R. L. Cayton, *The Frontier Republic: Ideology and Politics in the Ohio Country, 1780–1825* (1986); Alan Taylor, *Liberty Men and Great Proprietors: The Revolutionary Settlement on the Maine Frontier, 1760–1820* (1990); and Thomas P. Slaughter, *The Whiskey Rebellion: Frontier Epilogue to the American Revolution* (1986).

Economic and demographic change in the plantation South is traced in Robert William Fogel and Stanley L. Engerman, *Time on the Cross: The Economics of American Negro Slavery*, 2 vols. (1974); Robert William Fogel, *Without Consent or Contract: The Rise and Fall of American Slavery* (1989); and Peter A. Coclanis, *The Shadow of a Dream: Economic Life and Death in the South Carolina Lowcountry, 1670–1920* (1989). The essays in Ira Berlin and Ronald Hoffman, eds., *Slavery and Freedom in the Age of the American Revolution* (1983) are essential, as are Barbara Jeane Fields, *Slavery and Freedom on the Middle Ground: Maryland during the Nineteenth Century* (1985); Ira Berlin, *Slaves without Masters: The Free Negro in the Antebellum South* (1974); Robert McColley, *Slavery and Jeffersonian Virginia* (2nd ed., 1973). The limits of southern antislavery in these years are traced in David Brion Davis, *The Problem of Slavery in the Age of Revolution, 1770–1823* (1975), and the relevant essays in Peter S. Onuf, ed., *Jeffersonian Legacies* (1993). Further studies of economic and social life in the South are listed in the Suggested Reading for Chapter 10.

David T. Gilchrist, ed., *The Growth of the Seaport Cities, 1790–1825* (1967) ably treats its subject. Thomas C. Cochran, *Frontiers of Change: Early Industrialization in America* (1981) synthesizes urban economic development. For the social history of cities in these years, see Howard B. Rock, *Artisans of the New Republic: The Tradesmen of New York City in the Age of Jefferson* (1979); Charles G. Steffen, *The Mechanics of Baltimore: Workers and Politics in the Age of Revolution, 1763–1812* (1984); the early chapters of Sean Wilentz, *Chants Democratic: New York City and the Rise of the American Working Class* (1984) and Christine Stansell, *City of Women: Sex and Class in New York, 1789–1860* (1986); Stuart M. Blumin, *The Emergence of the Middle Class: Social Experience in the American City, 1760–1900* (1989); and Elizabeth Blackmar, *Manhattan for Rent, 1785–1850* (1989). For other relevant studies, see the Suggested Reading for Chapter 10.

A stirring introduction to the "democratization of mind" in these years is the concluding section of Gordon S. Wood, *The Radicalism of the American Revolution* (1992). On suffrage, see Chilton Williamson, *American Suffrage from Property to Democracy* (1960); on print culture, see Cathy N. Davidson, *Revolution and the Word: The Rise of the Novel in America* (1986), Davidson, ed., *Reading in America: Literature and Social*

History (1989), and William J. Gilmore, *Reading Becomes a Necessity of Life: Material and Cultural Life in Rural New England, 1780–1835* (1989); on drinking, W. J. Rorabaugh, *The Alcoholic Republic: An American Tradition* (1979).

The study of American religion in the postrevolutionary years begins with two books: Nathan O. Hatch, *The Democratization of American Christianity* (1989) and Jon Butler, *Awash in a Sea of Faith: Christianizing the American People* (1990). More specialized accounts include Paul K. Conkin, *Cane Ridge: America's Pentecost* (1990); John B. Boles, *The Great Revival, 1787–1805* (1972); and Stephen A. Marini, *Radical Sects of Revolutionary America* (1982). Religious developments among slaves and free blacks are treated in Sylvia R. Frey, *Water from the Rock: Black Resistance in a Revolutionary Age* (1991); Albert J. Raboteau, *Slave Religion: The 'Invisible Institution' in the Antebellum South* (1978); and the early essays in Paul E. Johnson, ed., *African-American Christianity: Essays in History* (1994). Douglas R. Egerton, *Gabriel's Rebellion: The Virginia Slave Conspiracies of 1800 & 1802* (1993) is imaginative and thorough. The "republicanization" of slave resistance is described in Eugene D. Genovese, *From Rebellion to Revolution: Afro-American Slave Revolts in the Making of the Modern World* (1979). Other works on early nineteenth century religion are listed in the Suggested Reading for Chapter 11.

Chapter 9

Completing the Revolution

The inauguration of George Washington took place at Federal Hall in New York City in April 1790. The oath of office was administered by Robert R. Livingston, Chancellor of the State of New York, who ended the ceremony by shouting "Long live George Washington, President of the United States." It was a sign of regal things to come.

George Washington left Mount Vernon for the temporary capital in New York City in April 1789. The way was lined with the grateful citizens of the new republic. Militia companies and local dignitaries escorted him from town to town, crowds cheered, church bells marked his progress, and lines of girls in white dresses waved demurely as he passed. At Newark Bay he boarded a flower-bedecked barge and, surrounded by scores of boats, crossed to New York City. There he was welcomed by jubilant citizens as he made his way to the president's house. He arrived on April 23 and was inaugurated seven days later.

ESTABLISHING THE GOVERNMENT

Washington and his closest advisors (they would soon call themselves Federalists) believed that the balance between power and liberty had tipped toward anarchy after the Revolution. They had made the Constitution to counter democratic excesses, and they arrived in New York determined to make a national government strong enough to command respect abroad and to impose order at home. For the most part, they succeeded. But in the process they aroused a determined opposition that swung the balance back toward liberty and limited government. These self-styled Democratic Republicans (led from the beginning by Thomas Jefferson) were as firmly tied to revolutionary ideals of limited government and the yeoman republic as the Federalists were tied to visions of an orderly commercial republic with a powerful national state. The fight between Federalists and Democratic Republicans echoed the revolutionary contest between liberty and power— conducted this time against an ominousbackdrop of international intrigue and war between France (which entered a republican revolution of its own in 1789) and Britain. Only when this Age of Democratic Revolution ended with the defeat of Napoleon in 1815 could the Americans survey the kind of society and government that their Revolution had made.

The "Republican Court"

Reporting for work, President Washington found the new government embroiled in its first controversy — an argument over the dignity that would attach to his office. Vice President John Adams had asked the Senate to create a title of honor for the President. Adams, along with many of the Senators, wanted a resounding title that would reflect the power of the new executive. They rejected "His Excellency" because that was the term used for ambassadors, colonial governors, and other minor officials. Among the other titles they considered were "His Highness," "His Mightiness," "His Elective Highness," "His Most Benign Highness," "His Majesty," and "His Highness, the President of the United States, and Protector of Their Liberties." The Senate debated the question for a full month, then gave up when it became clear that the more democratic House of Representatives disliked titles. They settled on the austere dignity of "Mr. President." A Senator from Pennsylvania expressed relief that the "silly business" was over. Thomas Jefferson, not yet a member of the government, pronounced the whole affair "the most superlatively ridiculous thing I ever heard of."

Jefferson would learn, however, that much was at stake in the argument over titles. The Constitution provided a blueprint for the republic, but it was George Washington's administration that would translate that blueprint into a working state. Members of the government knew that their decisions would set precedents. It mattered very much what citizens called their President, for that was part of the huge constellation of laws, customs, and forms of etiquette that would give the new government either a republican or (as many Antifederalists feared) a courtly tone. Many of those close to Washington wanted to protect presidential power from the localism and democracy that, they felt, had nearly killed the republic in the 1780s. Washington's stately inaugural tour, the high salaries being paid to executive appointees, the endless round of formal balls and presidential dinners, the observance of the English custom of cele-

George Washington near the End of His Presidency in 1796
The artist captured the austere dignity of the first president, and surrounded him with gold, red velvet, a presidential throne, and other emblems of kingly office.

brating the executive's birthday — all were meant to bolster the power and grandeur of the new government, particularly of its executive. When Jefferson became Secretary of State and attended official social functions, he often found himself the only democrat at the dinner table. Aristocratic sentiments prevailed, said Jefferson, "unless there chanced to be some [democrat] from the legislative Houses." Thus the battle over presidential titles was not "silly business." It was a revealing episode in the argument over how questions of power and liberty that Americans had debated since the 1760s would finally be answered.

The First Congress

Leadership of the First Congress fell to James Madison, the Virginia Congressman who had helped author the Constitution. Under his guidance Congress strengthened the new national government at every turn. First it passed a tariff on imports that would be the government's chief source of income. Then it turned to amendments to the Constitution that had been demanded by the state ratifying conventions. Madison proposed nineteen amendments to the House. The ten that survived congressional scrutiny and ratification by the states became the Bill of Rights. They reflected fears raised by a generation of struggle with centralized power. The First Amendment guaranteed the freedom of speech, press, and religion against federal interference. The Second and Third Amendments, prompted by old fears of a standing army, guaranteed the continuation of a militia of armed citizens and stated the specific conditions under which soldiers could be quartered in citizens' households. The Fourth, Fifth, Sixth, Seventh, and Eighth Amendments protected and defined a citizen's rights in court and when under arrest — rights whose violation had been central to the Revolution's list of grievances. The Ninth Amendment stated that the enumeration of specific rights in the first eight amendments did not imply a denial of other rights; the Tenth stated that powers not assigned to the national government by the Constitution remained with the states and the citizenry.

Madison, a committed nationalist, had performed skillfully. Many doubters at the ratifying conventions had called for amendments that would change the government detailed in the Constitution. By channeling their fears into the relatively innocuous area of civil liberties, Madison soothed their mistrust while preserving the government of the Constitution. The Bill of Rights was an important guarantee of individual liberties. But in the context in which it was written and ratified, it was an even more important guarantee of the power of the national government.

To fill out the framework of government outlined in the Constitution, Congress then created the executive departments of War, State, and Treasury and guaranteed that the heads of those departments and their assistants would be appointed solely by the President, thus removing them from congressional control. Congress then created the federal courts that were demanded but not specified in the Constitution. The Judiciary Act of 1789 established a Supreme Court with six members, along with thirteen district courts and three circuit courts of appeal. The act made it possible for certain cases to be appealed from state courts to federal circuitcourts, which would be presided over by traveling Supreme Court Justices, thus dramatizing federal power. As James Madison and other members of the intensely nationalist First Congress surveyed their handiwork, they could congratulate themselves on having strengthened national authority at every opportunity.

Hamiltonian Economics

Washington filled posts in what would become the cabinet with familiar faces. As Secretary of War he chose Henry Knox, an old comrade from the Revolution. The State Department went to his fellow Virginian Thomas Jefferson. He chose Alexander Hamilton of New York, his trusted aide-de-camp from Revolutionary days, to head the Department of the Treasury.

The most single-minded nationalist in the new government, Hamilton was a brilliant economic thinker, an admirer of the British system of centralized government and finance, and a supremely arrogant and ambitious man. More than other cabinet members, and perhaps even more than Washington himself (he later referred to Washington's Presidency as "my administration"), Hamilton directed the making of a national government.

In 1789 Congress asked Secretary of the Treasury Hamilton to report on the public debt. The debt fell into three categories, Hamilton reported. The first was the $11 million owed to foreigners — primarily debts to France incurred during the Revolution. The second and third — roughly $24 million each — were debts owed by the national and state governments to American citizens who had supplied food, arms, and other resources to the revolutionary cause. Congress agreed that both justice and the credibility of the new government dictated that the foreign debts be paid in full. But the domestic debts raised troublesome questions. Those debts consisted of notes issued during the Revolution to soldiers, and to merchants, farmers, and others who had helped the war effort. Over the years, speculators had bought up many of these notes at a fraction of their face value; when word spread that the Constitution would create a government likely to pay its debts, speculators and their agents fanned out across the countryside buying up all the notes they could find. By 1790 the government debt was concentrated in the hands of businessmen and speculators—most of them northeasterners—who had bought notes for from 10 to 30 percent of their original value. Full payment would bring them enormous windfall profits.

The Revolutionary War debts of the individual states were another source of contention. Nationalists, with Hamilton at their head, wanted to assume the debts of the states as part of a national debt—a move that would concentrate the interests of public creditors, the need for taxation, and an expanded civil service in the national government. The state debts had also been bought up by speculators, and they posed another problem as well: many states, including all the southern states with the exception of South Carolina, had paid off most of their notes in the 1780s; the other states still had significant outstanding debts. If the federal government assumed the state debts and paid them off at the face value of the notes, money would flow out of the southern, middle, and western states into the Northeast, whose citizens would hold fully four-fifths of the combined national debt.

That is precisely what Hamilton proposed in his Report on Public Credit, issued in January 1790. He urged Congress to assume the state debts and to combine them with the federal government's foreign and domestic debts into a consolidated national debt. He agreed that the foreign debt should be paid promptly and in full, but he insisted that the domestic debt be a permanent, tax-supported fixture of government. Under his plan, the government would issue securities to its creditors and would pay an annual rate of interest of 4 percent. Hamilton's funding and assumption plans announced to the international community and to actual and potential government creditors that the United States would pay its bills. But Hamilton had domestic plans for the debt as well. A permanent debt would attract the wealthiest financiers in the country as creditors and would render them loyal and dependent on the federal government. It would bring their economic power to the government, and at the same time would require a significant enlargement of the federal civil service, national financial institutions, and increased taxes. The national debt, in short, was at the center of Alexander Hamilton's plans for a powerful national state.

As part of that plan, Hamilton asked Congress to charter a Bank of the United States. The government would store its funds in the bank and would supervise its operations, but the bank would be controlled by directors representing private stockholders. The Bank of the United States would print and back the national currency and would regulate other banks. Hamilton's proposal also made stock in the bank payable in government securities, thus adding to the value of the securities, giving the bank a powerful interest in the fiscal stability of the government, and binding the holders of the securities even closer to the national government. Those who looked closely saw that Hamilton's Bank of the United States was a carbon copy of the Bank of England.

To fund the national debt, Hamilton called for a federal excise tax on wines, coffee, tea, and spirits. The tax on spirits would fall most heavily on the whiskey produced in abundance on the frontier. Its purpose, stated openly by Hamilton, was not only to produce revenue but to establish the government's power to create an internal tax and to collect it in the most remote regions in the republic. The result, as we shall see, was a "Whiskey Rebellion" in the west and an overwhelming display of federal force (see Chapter 9).

Passed in April 1791, the national bank and the federal excise measures completed Hamilton's organization of government finances. Taken separately, the consolidated government debt, the national bank, and the federal excise tax ably solved discrete problems of government finance. Taken together, however, they constituted a full-scale replica of the treasury-driven government of Great Britain.

The Rise of Opposition

In 1789 every branch of government was staffed by supporters of the Constitution. The most radical anti-Federalists took positions in state governments or left politics altogether. Nearly everyone in the national government was committed to making the new government work. In particular, Alexander Hamilton at Treasury and James Madison in the House of Representatives expected to continue the political and personal friendship they had made while writing the Constitution and working to get it ratified. Yet in the debate over the national debt Madison led congressional opposition to Hamilton's proposals. In 1792 Thomas Jefferson joined the opposition, insisting that Hamilton's schemes would dismantle the

Revolution. Within a few short years the consensus of 1789 had degenerated into an angry argument over what sort of government would finally result from the American Revolution. More than twenty-five years later, Jefferson still insisted that the battles of the 1790s had been "contests of principle between the advocates of republican and those of kingly government."

Hamilton presented his national debt proposal to Congress as a solution to specific problems of government finance, not as part of a blueprint for an English-style state. Madison and other southerners opposed it because they did not want northern speculators—many of whom had received information from government insiders—to reap fortunes from notes bought at rock-bottom prices from soldiers, widows, and orphans. Calling Hamilton's plan "public plunder," Madison favored payment plans that discriminated between original holders and speculators—a solution that would ease his ethical scruples and reduce the flow of money out of the South.

At the urging of Jefferson and others, Madison and members of the congressional opposition compromised with Hamilton. In exchange for accepting his proposals on the debt, they won his promise to locate the permanent capital of the United States at a site on the Potomac River. The compromise went to the heart of American revolutionary republicanism. Hamilton intended to tie northeastern commercial interests to the federal government. If New York or Philadelphia became the permanent capital, political and economic power might be concentrated there as it was in Paris and London—court cities in which power, wealth, and every kind of excellence were in league against a plundered and degraded countryside. Benjamin Rush, a Philadelphian, condemned the "government which has begun so soon to ape the corruption of the British Court, conveyed to it through the impure channel of the City of New York." Madison and other agrarians considered Philadelphia just as bad, and supported Hamilton only on condition that the capital be moved south. The compromise would distance the commercial power of the cities from the federal government and would put an end to the "republican court" that had formed around Washington. This radically republican move ensured that the capital of the United States would be, except for purposes of government, a place of no importance.

When Hamilton proposed the Bank of the United States, republicans in Congress immediately noted its similarity to the Bank of England and voiced deep suspicion of Hamilton's economic and governmental plans. It was at this point that Thomas Jefferson joined the opposition, arguing that the Constitution did not grant Congress the right to charter a bank, and that allowing Congress to do so would revive the popular fears of centralized despotism that had nearly defeated ratification of the Constitution. Hamilton responded with the first argument for expanded federal power under the clause in the Constitution empowering Congress "to make all laws which shall be necessary and proper" to the performance of its duties. President Washington and a majority in Congress ultimately sided with Hamilton.

Jefferson's strict constructionism (his insistence that the government had no powers beyond those specified in the Constitution) was tied to fears of the de facto constitution that Hamilton's system was making. Jefferson argued that the federal bank was unconstitutional, that a federal excise tax was certain to arouse public opposition, and that funding the debt would reward speculators and penalize ordinary citizens. But more important, Jefferson argued, Hamilton used government securities and stock in the Bank of the United States to buy the loyalty not only of merchants and speculators but of members of Congress. Thirty Congressmen owned stock in the Bank of the United States, and many others held government securities or had close ties to men who did. Jefferson charged that this "corrupt squadron" of "paper men" in Congress was, in the classic fashion of evil ministers, enabling Hamilton to control Congress from his nonelective seat in the executive branch. "The ultimate object of all this," insisted Jefferson, "is to prepare the way for a change, from the present republican form of government, to that of a monarchy, of which the English constitution is to be the model."

For their part, Hamilton and his supporters (who by now were calling themselves Federalists) insisted that the centralization of power and a strong executive were necessary to the survival of the republic. The alternative was a return to the localism and public disorder of the 1780s and ultimately to the failure of the Revolution. The argument drew its urgency from the understanding of both Hamilton and his detractors that the United States was a small revolutionary republic in a world governed by kings and aristocrats, and that republics had a long history of failure; they all knew that it was still very possible for Americans to lose their Revolution. Until late 1792, however, the argument over Hamilton's centralizing schemes was limited very largely to members of the government. Hamilton and his supporters tried to mobilize the commercial elite on the side of government, while Madison and Jefferson struggled to hold off the perceived monarchical plot until the citizens could be aroused to defend their liberties. Then, as both sides began to mobilize popular support, events in Europe came to dominate the politics of the American republican experiment, to place that experiment in even greater jeopardy, and to increase the violence of American politics to the point at which the republic almost failed.

THE REPUBLIC IN A WORLD AT WAR, 1793–1800

Late in 1792 French revolutionaries rejected monarchy and proclaimed the French Republic. They beheaded Louis XVI in January 1793. Eleven days later the French, already at war with Austria and Prussia, declared war on conservative Britain, thus launching a war between French republicanism and British-led reaction that, with periodic outbreaks of peace, would embroil the Atlantic world until the defeat of France in 1815.

Americans and the French Revolution

Americans could not have escaped involvement even had they wanted to. Treaties signed in 1778 allied the United States with France. Americans had overwhelmingly supported the French Revolution of 1789 and had applauded the progress of French republicanism during its first three years. But gratitude for French help during the American Revolution and American hopes for international republicanism were put to severe tests in 1793, when the French Republic began to execute thousands of aristocrats, priests, and other "counter-revolutionaries," and when the French threatened the sovereignty of nations by declaring a war of all peoples against all monarchies. The argument between Jeffersonian Republicanism and Hamiltonian centralization was no longer a squabble within the United States government. National politics was now caught up and subsumed within the struggle over international republicanism.

As Britain and France went to war in 1793, President Washington declared American neutrality, thereby abrogating obligations made in the 1778 treaties with the French. Washington and most of his advisors realized that the United States was in no condition to fight a war. They also wanted to stay on good terms with Great Britain. Ninety percent of American imports came from Britain, and 90 percent of the federal revenue came from customs duties on those imports. Thus the nation's commerce and the financial health of the government both depended on good relations with Great Britain. Moreover, Federalists genuinely sympathized with the British in the war with France. They regarded the United States as a "perfected" England and viewed Britain as the defender of hierarchial society and ordered liberty against the homicidal anarchy of the French.

Jefferson and his friends saw things differently. They applauded the French for carrying on the republican revolution Americans had begun in 1776, and they had no affection for the "monarchical" politics of the Federalists or for American's continued neocolonial dependence upon British trade. The faction led by Jefferson and Madison wanted to abandon the English mercantile system and trade freely with all nations. They did not care if that course of action hurt commercial interests (most of which supported the Federalists) or impaired the government's ability to centralize power in itself. While they agreed that the United States should stay out of the war, the Jeffersonians sympathized as openly with the French as the Federalists did with the British.

Citizen Genêt

Throughout the war years from 1793 to 1815, both Great Britain and France, by intervening freely in the internal affairs of the United States, made American isolationism impossible.

In April 1793 the French sent Citizen Edmond Genêt as minister to the United States. Genêt's ruling Girondists were the revolutionary faction that had declared the war on all monarchies; they ordered Genêt to enlist American aid with or without the Washington administration's consent. After the President's proclamation of neutrality, Genêt openly commissioned American privateers to harass British shipping and enlisted Americans in intrigues against the Spanish outpost of New Orleans. Genêt then opened France's Caribbean colonies to American shipping, providing American shippers a choice between French free trade and British mercantilism. (Genêt's mission came to an abrupt end in the summer of 1793, when the Girondists fell from power. Learning that he would be guillotined if he returned to France, he accepted the hospitality of Americans, married a daughter of George Clinton, the old anti-Federalist governor of New York, and lived out the rest of his life as an American country gentleman.)

The British responded to Genêt's free-trade declaration with a promise to seize any ship trading with French colonies in the Caribbean. Word of these Orders in Council—almost certainly by design—reached the Royal Navy before American merchant seamen had heard of them, with the result that 250 American ships fell into British hands. The Royal Navy also began searching American ships for English sailors who had deserted or who had switched to safer, better-paying work in the American merchant marine. Inevitably, some American sailors were kidnapped into the British Navy, in a contemptuous and infuriating assault on American sovereignty. Meanwhile the British, operating from Canada and from their still-garrisoned forts in the Northwest, began promising military aid to the Indians north of the Ohio River. Thus while the French ignored the neutrality of the United States, the English engaged in both overt and covert acts of war.

Western Troubles

In the Northwest the situation came to a head in the summer and fall of 1794. The Shawnee and allied tribes, emboldened by two victories over American armies, plotted with the British and talked of driving all settlers out of their territory. At the same time, frontier whites, sometimes with the encouragement of English and Spanish officials, grew increasingly contemptuous of a national government that could neither pacify the Indians nor guarantee their free use of the Mississippi River. President Washington heard that two thousand Kentuckians were armed and ready to attack New Orleans—a move that would have started a war between the United States and Spain. Settlers in Georgia were making unauthorized forays against the Creeks. Worst of all, settlers up and down the frontier refused to pay the Federalists'

excise tax on whiskey, a direct challenge to federal authority. In western Pennsylvania, mobs tarred and feathered excise officers and burned the property of distillers who paid the tax. In July 1794, five hundred militiamen near Pittsburgh marched on the house of General John Neville, one of the most hated of the federal excise collectors. Neville, his family, and a few federal soldiers fought the militiamen, killing two and wounding six before they abandoned the house to be looted and burned. Two weeks later, six thousand "Whiskey Rebels" met at Braddock's Field near Pittsburgh, threatening to attack the town.

Faced with serious international and domestic threats to his new government, Washington did what he could: he defeated the Indians and the Whiskey rebels by force—and thus secured American control of the Northwest—and he capitulated to the British on the high seas. Washington sent General "Mad" Anthony Wayne against the northwestern tribes. Wayne's decisive victory at Fallen Timbers in August 1794—fought almost in the shadow of a British fort—ended the Indian-British challenge in the Northwest for many years (see Chapter 8.)

The Jay Treaty

In September, Washington ordered 12,000 federalized militiamen from eastern Pennsylvania, Maryland, Virginia, and New Jersey to quell the Whiskey Rebellion. The president promised amnesty to rebels who pledged to support the government and prison terms to those who did not. As the army marched west from Carlisle, they found defiant liberty poles but no armed resistance. Arriving at Pittsburgh, the army arrested 20 suspected rebels—none of them leaders—and marched them back to Philadelphia for trial. In the end only two "rebels," both of them feeble-minded, were convicted. President Washington pardoned them and the Whiskey Rebellion was over.

While he sent armies against Indians and frontiersmen, President Washington sent John Jay, Chief Justice of the Supreme Court, to negotiate a treaty with Britain. Armed with news of Wayne's victory, Jay negotiated a promise from the British to remove their troops from American territory in the Northwest. But on every other point of dispute he agreed to British terms. Jay's Treaty made no mention of impressment or other violations of American maritime rights, nor did it refer to the old issue of British payments for slaves carried off during the

Revolution. The Treaty did allow small American ships back into the West Indies, but only on terms that the Senate would reject. In short, Jay's Treaty granted British trade a most-favored-nation basis in exchange for the agreement of the British to abandon their northwestern forts. Given the power of Great Britain, it was the best that Americans could

expect. Washington, obliged to choose between an unpopular treaty and an unwinnable war, passed Jay's Treaty on to the Senate, which in June 1795 ratified it by a bare two-thirds majority.

It was during the fight over Jay's Treaty that dissension within the government was first aired in public. The seaport cities and much of the Northeast reacted favorably to the Treaty. It ruled out war with England and cemented an Anglo-American trade relationship that strengthened both Hamilton's national state and the established commercial interests that supported it. Moreover, there was little enthusiasm for the French Revolution in the Northeast — particularly in New England, with its long history of colonial wars with France. The South, on the other hand, saw Jay's Treaty as a blatant sign of the designs of Britain and the Federalists to subvert republicanism in both France and the United States. The Virginia legislature branded the Treaty unconstitutional, and Republican Congressmen demanded to see all documents relating to Jay's negotiations. Washington responded by telling them that their request could be legitimate only if the House was planning to initiate impeachment proceedings — thus tying approval of the Treaty to his enormous personal prestige.

On March 3, 1796, Washington released the details of a treaty that Thomas Pinckney had negotiated with Spain. In the treaty, Spain recognized American neutrality and set the border between the United States and Spanish Florida on American terms. Most important, Pinckney's Treaty put an end to Spanish claims to territory in the Southwest and gave Americans the unrestricted right to navigate the Mississippi River and to transship produce at the Spanish port of New Orleans. Coupled with the victory at Fallen Timbers, the British promise to abandon their Northwest posts, and Washington's personal popularity, Pinckney's Treaty helped turn the tide in favor of the unpopular Jay's Treaty. With a diminishing number of hotheads willing to oppose Washington, western representatives joined the Northeast and increasing numbers of southerners to ratify Jay's treaty.

Washington's Farewell

George Washington refused to run for reelection in 1796—thus setting a two-term limit that was observed by every president until Franklin Roosevelt (see Chapter 25). Washington could be proud of his accomplishment. He had presided over the creation of a national government. He had secured American control over the western settlements by ending British, Spanish, and Indian military threats and by securing free use of the Mississippi River for western produce. Those policies, together with the fed-

eral invasion of western Pennsylvania, had made it evident that the government could and would control its most distant regions. He had also avoided war with Great Britain — though not without overlooking assaults on American sovereignty. As he was about to leave government he wrote, with substantial help from Hamilton, his Farewell Address. In it he warned against long-term "entangling alliances" with other countries; America, he said, should stay free to operate on its own in international affairs — an ideal that many felt had been betrayed in Jay's Treaty. Washington also warned against internal political divisions. Of course, he did not regard his own Federalists as a "party" — they were simply friends of the government. But he saw the Democratic-Republicans (the name by which Jefferson's allies called themselves) as a self-interested, irresponsible "faction," thus branding them, in the language of classical republicanism, as public enemies. Washington's call for national unity and an end to partisanship was in fact a parting shot at the Republican opposition.

The Election of 1796

Washington's retirement opened the way to the fierce competition for public office that he had feared, and in 1796 Americans experienced their first contested presidential election. The Federalists chose as their candidate John Adams, an upright conservative from Massachusetts who had served as vice president. The Republicans nominated Thomas Jefferson. According to the gentlemanly custom of the day, neither candidate campaigned in person. Jefferson stayed home at Monticello; Adams retired to his farm near Boston. But the friends of the candidates, the newspaper editors who enjoyed their patronage, and even certain European governments ensured that the election would be intensely partisan.

Since it was clear that Adams would carry New England and that Jefferson would carry the South, the election would be decided in Pennsylvania and New York. Some states, most of them in the South, chose presidential electors by direct vote. But in most states, including the crucial mid-Atlantic states, state legislatures selected presidential electors. The election of 1796 would be decided in elections to the legislatures of those states, and in subsequent intriguing within those bodies. John Beckley, clerk of the House of Representatives, devised the Republican strategy in Pennsylvania. He secretly circulated a list of well-known and respected candidates for the state legislature who were committed to Jefferson's election as president. Discovering the Republican slate only when it was too late to construct a similar list, the Federalists lost the elections. In December, Beckley delivered all but one of Pennsylvania's electoral votes to Jefferson. In New York, however, there was no John Beckley. Adams took the state's electoral votes and won the national election. The distribution of electoral votes revealed the bases of Federalist and Republican support: Adams received only two electoral votes south of the Potomac, and Jefferson received only eighteen (all but five of them in Pennsylvania) north of the Potomac.

The voting was over, but the intriguing was not. Alexander Hamilton, who since his retirement from the Treasury in 1795 had directed Federalist affairs from his New York law office, knew that he could not manipulate the independent and almost perversely upright John Adams. So he secretly instructed South Carolina's Federalist electors to withhold their votes from Adams. That would have given the presidency to Adams' running mate, Thomas Pinckney, relegating Adams to the vice presidency. (Prior to the ratification of the Twelfth Amendment in 1804, the candidate with a majority of the electoral votes became president, and the second-place candidate became vice president.) Like some of Hamilton's other schemes, this one backfired. New England electors heard of the plan and angrily withheld their votes from Pinckney. As a result, Adams was elected president and his opponent Thomas Jefferson became vice president. Adams narrowly won the election, but he took office with a justifiable mistrust of many members of his own party, and with the head of the opposition party as his second in command. It was not an auspicious beginning.

Troubles with France, 1796–1800

As Adams entered office an international crisis was already in full swing. France, regarding Jay's Treaty as an Anglo-American alliance, had recalled its envoy in 1796 and had broken off relations with the United States. The French hinted that they intended to overthrow the reactionary government of the United States, but would postpone taking action in the hope that a friendlier Thomas Jefferson would

replace "old man Washington" in 1797. Then, during the crucial elections in Pennsylvania, they stepped up their seizures of American ships trading with Britain, giving the Americans a taste of what would happen if they did not elect a government friendlier to France. When the election went to John Adams, the French gave up on the United States and set about denying Britain its new de facto ally. In 1797 France expelled the American minister and refused to carry on relations with the United States until it addressed French grievances. The French ordered that American ships carrying "so much as a handkerchief" made in England be confiscated without compensation and announced that American seamen serving in the British navy would be summarily hanged if captured.

President Adams wanted to protect American commerce from French depredations. But he knew that the United States might not survive a war with France. He also knew that French grievances (including Jay's Treaty and the abrogation of the French-American treaties of 1778) were legitimate. So he decided to send a mission to France, made up of three respected statesmen: Charles Cotesworth Pinckney of South Carolina, John Marshall of Virginia, and Elbridge Gerry of Massachusetts. But when these prestigious delegates reached Paris, they were left cooling their heels in the outer offices of the Directory—the revolutionary committee of five that had replaced France's beheaded king. At last three French officials (the correspondence identified them only as "X, Y, and Z") discreetly hinted that France would receive them if they paid a bribe of $250,000, arranged for the United States to loan $12 million to the French government, and apologized for unpleasant remarks that John Adams had made about France. The delegates refused, saying "No, not a sixpence," and returned home. There a journalist transformed their remark into "Millions for defense, but not a cent for tribute."

President Adams asked Congress to prepare for war, and the French responded by seizing more American ships. Thus began, in April 1798, an undeclared war between France and the United States in the Caribbean. While the French navy dealt with the British in the North Atlantic, French privateers inflicted costly blows on American shipping. After nearly a year of fighting, with the British providing powder and shot for American guns, the U.S. navy chased the French privateers out of the Caribbean.

The Crisis at Home, 1798–1800

The troubles with France precipitated a crisis at home. The disclosure of the XYZ correspondence, together with the quasi-war in the Caribbean, produced a surge of public hostility toward the French and, to some extent, toward their Republican friends in the United States. Many Federalists, led by Alexander Hamilton, wanted to use the crisis to destroy their political opponents. Without consulting President Adams, the Federalist-dominated Congress passed a number of wartime measures. The first was a federal property tax — graduated, spread equally between sections of the country, and justified by military necessity, but a direct federal tax nonetheless. Congress then passed four laws known as the Alien and Sedition Acts. The first three were directed at immigrants: they extended the naturalization period from five to fourteen years and empowered the President to detain enemy aliens during wartime and to deport those he deemed dangerous to the United States. The fourth law — the Sedition Act — set jail terms and fines for persons who advocated disobedience to federal law or who wrote, printed, or spoke "false, scandalous, and malicious" statements against "the government of the United States, or the President of the United States [note that Vice President Jefferson was not included], with intent to defame . . . or to bring them or either of them, into contempt or disrepute."

President Adams never used the powers granted under the Alien Acts. But the Sedition Act resulted in the prosecution of fourteen Republicans, most of them journalists. William Duane, editor of the *Philadelphia Aurora*, was indicted when he and two Irish friends circulated a petition against the Alien Act on the grounds of a Catholic church. James Callendar, editor of a Jeffersonian newspaper in Richmond, was arrested, while another prominent Republican went to jail for statements made in a private letter. Jedediah Peck, a former Federalist from upstate New York, was arrested when he petitioned Congress to repeal the Alien and Sedition Acts. Matthew Lyon, a scurrilous and uncouth Republican Congressman from Vermont, had brawled with a Federalist representative in the House chamber; he went to jail for his criticisms of President Adams, Federalist militarism, and what he called the "ridiculous pomp" of the national administration.

Republicans, charging that the Alien and Sedition Acts violated the First Amendment, turned to the states for help. Southern states, which had provided only 4 of the 44 congressional votes for the Sedition Act, took the lead. Jefferson provided the Kentucky legislature with draft resolutions, and Madison did the same for the Virginia legislature. These so-called Virginia and Kentucky Resolves restated the constitutional fundamentalism that had guided Republican opposition to the Federalists through the 1790s. Jefferson's Kentucky Resolves reminded Congress that the Alien and Sedition Acts gave the national government powers not mentioned in the Constitution and that the Tenth Amendment reserved such powers to the states. He also argued that the Constitution was a "compact" between sovereign states, and that state legislatures could "nullify" federal laws they deemed unconstitutional — thus anticipating constitutional theories that states-rights southerners would use after 1830.

The Virginia and Kentucky Resolves demonstrated the extremes to which Jefferson and Madison might go. Beyond that, however, they had few immediate effects. Opposition to the Sedition Act ranged from popular attempts to obstruct the law to fist fights in Congress, and Virginia began calling up its militia. But no other states followed the lead of Virginia and Kentucky, and talk of armed opposition to Federalist policies was limited to a few areas in the South.

Federalists took another ominous step by implementing President Adams' request that Congress create a military prepared for war. Adams wanted a stronger navy, both because the undeclared war with France was being fought on the ocean and because he agreed with other Federalists that America's future as a commercial nation required a respectable navy. Hamilton and others (who were becoming known as "High Federalists") preferred a standing army. At the urging of Washington and against his own judgment, Adams had appointed Hamilton Inspector General. As such, Hamilton would be de facto commander of the army. Congress authorized a 20,000-man army and Hamilton proceeded to raise it. Congress also provided for a much larger army to be called up if there was a declaration of war. When he expanded the officer corps in anticipation of such an army, Hamilton excluded Republicans and commissioned only his political friends. High Federalists wanted a standing army to enforce

PROPERTY PROTECTED. a la *Françoise*.

The XYZ Affair   Disclosure of the XYZ affair created a wave of anti-French sentiment in the United States. Here America (depicted, as Liberty was usually depicted, as a young woman) is accosted by the five lascivious, money-hungry members of the Directorate.

the Alien and Sedition Acts and to put down an impending rebellion in the South. Beyond that, there was little need for such a force. The war was being fought at sea, and most Americans believed that the citizen militia could hold off any land invasion until an army was raised. The Republicans, President Adams himself, and many other Federalists now became convinced that Hamilton and his High Federalists were determined to destroy their political opponents, enter into an alliance with Great Britain, and impose Hamilton's statist designs on the nation by force. By 1799 Adams and many of his Federalist friends had come to believe that Hamilton and his supporters were dangerous, antirepublican militarists.

Adams was both fearful and angry. First the Hamiltonians had tried to rob him of the presidency, and then had passed the Alien and Sedition Acts, the direct tax, and plans for a standing army without consulting him. None of this would have been possible had it not been for the crisis with France. Adams, who had resisted calls for a declaration of war, began looking for ways to declare peace. In a move that he knew would split his party and probably cost him reelection in 1800, he opened negotiations with France and stalled the creation of Hamilton's army while the talks took place. At first the Senate refused to send an envoy to France. The

senators relented when Adams threatened to resign and leave the presidency to Vice President Jefferson. In the agreement that followed, the French cancelled the obligations the United States had assumed under the treaties of 1778. But they refused to pay reparations for attacks on American shipping since 1793 — the very point over which many Federalists had wanted to declare war. Peace with France cut the ground from under the more militaristic and repressive Federalists and intensified discord among the Federalists in general. (Hamilton would campaign against Adams in 1800.) It also damaged Adams' chances for reelection.

The Election of 1800

Thomas Jefferson and his Democratic-Republicans approached the election of 1800 better organized and more determined than they had been four years earlier. Moreover, events in the months preceding the election worked in their favor. The Alien and Sedition Acts, the direct tax of 1798, and the Federalist military build-up were never popular. The army suppressed a minor tax rebellion led by Jacob Fries in Pennsylvania; prosecutions under the Sedition Act revealed its partisan origins; and the Federalists showed no sign of repealing the tax or abandoning the Alien and Sedition Acts and the new military even when peace seemed certain. Taken together, these events gave credence to the Republicans' allegation that the Federalists were using the crisis with France to increase their power, destroy their opposition, and overthrow the American republic. The Federalists' actions, charged the Republicans, were not only expensive, repressive, unwise, and unconstitutional; they constituted the classic means by which despots destroyed liberty. The Federalists countered by warning that the election of Jefferson and his radical allies would release the worst horrors of the French Revolution onto the streets of American towns. Each side believed that its defeat in the election would mean the end of the republic.

The Democratic-Republicans were strong in the South and weak in the Northeast; South Carolina was the one southern state in which Adams had significant support. Jefferson knew that in order to achieve a majority in the electoral college he had to win New York, the state that had cost him the 1796 election. Jefferson's running mate, Aaron Burr, arranged a truce in New York between Republican factions led by the Clinton and Livingston families and chose candidates for the state legislature who were likely to win. In New York City, Burr played skillfully on the interests and resentments of craftsmen and granted favors to merchants who worked outside the British trade, which was dominated by Federalist insiders. The strategy succeeded. The Republicans carried New York City and won a slight majority in the legislature; New York's electoral votes belonged to Jefferson. The election was decided in South Carolina, which after a brisk campaign cast its votes for Jefferson. (When it became clear that Jefferson had won, Hamilton suggested changing the law so that New York's electors would be chosen by popular vote; John Jay, the Federalist Governor of New York, rejected the suggestion.)

When the electoral votes were counted, Jefferson and Burr had won with 73 votes each. Adams had 65 votes, and his running mate Charles Cotesworth Pinckney had 64. (In order to distinguish between their presidential and vice-presidential candidates—and thus thwart yet another of Hamilton's attempts to rig the election—the Federalists of Rhode Island had withheld one vote from Pinckney.) Congress, which was still controlled by Federalists, would have to decide whether Jefferson or Burr was to be President of the United States. After 35 ballots, with most of the Federalists supporting Burr, a compromise was reached whereby the Federalists turned in blank ballots and thus avoided voting for the hated Jefferson. (In 1804, the Twelfth Amendment, which requires electors to vote separately for president and vice president, was ratified to prevent a repetition of this situation.)

THE JEFFERSONIANS IN POWER

On the first Tuesday in March 1801 Thomas Jefferson left his rooms at Conrad and McMunn's boarding house in the half-built capital city of Washington and walked up Pennsylvania Avenue. There were military salutes along the way, but Jefferson forbade the pomp and ceremony that had ushered Washington into office. Jefferson, accompanied by a few friends and a company of artillery from the Maryland militia (and not by the professional military of which Hamilton had dreamed) walked up the street and into the unfinished capital building. The central tower and the wing that would house Congress were only half completed. Jefferson joined Vice President Burr, other members of the government, and a few foreign diplomats in the newly finished Senate chamber.

Jefferson took the oath of office from Chief Justice John Marshall, a distant relative and political opponent from Virginia. Then, in a small voice that was almost inaudible to those at a distance, he delivered his inaugural address. Referring to the political discord that had brought him into office, he began with a plea for unity, insisting that "every difference of opinion is not a difference of principle. We have called by different names brethren of the same principle. We are all Republicans, we are all Federalists."

Jefferson did not mean that he and his opponents should forget their ideological differences. He meant only to invite moderate Federalists into a broad Republican coalition in which there was no room for the statist designs of Alexander Hamilton and his High Federalist friends.

Jefferson went on to outline the kind of government a republic should have. Grateful that the Atlantic Ocean separated the United States from "the exterminating havoc" of Europe and that his countrymen were the possessors of "a chosen country,

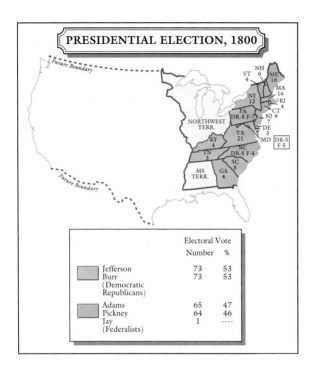

PRESIDENTIAL ELECTION, 1800

	Electoral Vote	
	Number	%
Jefferson	73	53
Burr	73	53
(Democratic Republicans)		
Adams	65	47
Pickney	64	46
Jay	1	----
(Federalists)		

Portrait of Jefferson, by Charles Willson Peale, 1805
A self-consciously plain President Jefferson posed for this portrait near the end of his first term in January 1805. He wears an unadorned fur-collared coat, is surrounded by no emblems of office, and gazes calmly and directly at the viewer.

with room for our descendants to the thousandth and thousandth generation," he declared that Americans were a free people with no need for a national state built on European models. A people blessed with isolation, bountiful resources, and liberty needed only "a wise and frugal Government, which shall restrain men from injuring one another, shall leave them otherwise free to regulate their own pursuits of industry and improvement, and shall not take from the mouth of labor the bread it has earned. This is the sum of good government, and thus is necessary to close the circle of our felicities."

In particular, Jefferson's "wise and frugal" government would respect the powers of the individual states. It would also defend the liberties ensured by the Bill of Rights. It would be made smaller, and it would pay its debts without incurring new ones, thus ending the need for taxation and cutting the ground from beneath the burgeoning Federalist state. It would rely for defense on "a disciplined militia" that would fight invaders while regulars were being trained—thus getting rid of Hamilton's standing army. It would protect republican liberties from enemies at home and from the nations of Europe. And, Jefferson promised, it would ensure "the encouragement of agriculture, and of commerce as its handmaiden." Beyond the fostering of an agrarian republic and the maintenance of limited, frugal government, Jefferson promised very little. Blessed with peace abroad and the defeat of the High Federalists at home, he believed that the United States could at last enter into its experiment with truly republican government.

Cleansing the Government

The simplicity of Jefferson's inauguration set the social tone of his administration. The new President reduced the number and grandeur of formal balls, levees, and dinners. He sent his annual messages to

Congress to be read by a clerk rather than delivering them in person, in the manner of English kings and Federalist presidents. He refused to ride about Washington in a carriage, preferring to carry out his errands on horseback. Abandoning the grand banquets favored by his predecessors, Jefferson entertained senators and congressmen at small dinners — dinners that were served at a round table without formal seating, thus abandoning the fine-tuned hierarchy of the Federalists' old arrangements. Jefferson presided over the meals without wearing a wig, and dressed in old homespun and a pair of worn bedroom slippers. The casualness (slovenliness, said some of his critics) did not extend to what was served, however. The food was prepared by expert chefs and accompanied by fine wines. And it was followed by brilliant conversation perfected by Jefferson while he was a diplomat and a visitor to the salons of Paris. The President's dinners set examples of the unpretentious excellence through which this cultivated country squire hoped to govern the republic that he claimed to have saved from monarchists.

Jefferson's first order of business was to reduce the size and expense of government. The Federalists, despite their elitism and their statist dispositions, had left a surprisingly small federal establishment. Jefferson found only 316 employees who were subject to presidential appointment and removal. Those employees, together with seven hundred clerks and assistants and three thousand post office workers, made up the entire federal civil service. Jefferson reduced the diplomatic corps and replaced officeholders who were incompetent, corrupt, or avowedly antirepublican. But the rate of turnover was only about 50 percent during his first term. The replacements were not the violent revolutionaries that Federalists had warned against but Republican gentlemen who matched or exceeded the social status of the departed Federalists. Jefferson altered the politics of the civil service, but he left its size and shape intact.

Jefferson made more substantial cuts in the military. The Federalists had built a sizable army and navy to prepare for war and, if necessary, to put down opposition at home. Legislation passed in March 1802 reduced the army to two regiments of infantry and one of artillery — a total of 3,350 officers and men, most of whom were assigned to western posts far from the centers of white population. Similar cutbacks were made in the navy. The goal,

"Mad Tom in a Rage" This Federalist cartoon of 1801 portrays Jefferson, with the help of the devil and a bottle of brandy, pulling down the government that Washington and Adams had built.

Jefferson explained, was to rely mainly on the militia for national defense but to maintain a small, well-trained professional army as well. (The same legislation that reduced the army created the military academy at West Point.) At Jefferson's urging, Congress also abolished the direct tax of 1798 and repealed the parts of the Alien and Sedition Acts that had not already run out. Jefferson personally pardoned the ten victims of those acts who were still in jail and repaid with interest the fines that had been levied under them.

Thus with a few deft strokes, Jefferson dismantled the repressive apparatus of the Federalist state. And by reducing government expenditures he reduced the government's debt and the army of civil servants and "paper men" gathered around it. During Jefferson's administration the national debt fell from

$80 million to $57 million, and the government built up a treasury surplus even after paying $15 million in cash for the Louisiana Purchase (see Chapter 9). Though some doubted the wisdom of such stringent economy, no one doubted Jefferson's frugality.

The Jeffersonians and the Courts

Jefferson's demands for a "wise and frugal" government applied to the federal judiciary as well as to other branches. The Constitution had created the Supreme Court but had left the creation of lesser federal courts to Congress. The First Congress had created a system of circuit courts presided over by Justices of the Supreme Court. Only Federalists had served on the Supreme Court under Washington and Adams, and Federalists on the circuit courts had extended federal authority into the hinterland—a fact that their prosecution of Jeffersonians under the Alien and Sedition Acts had made abundantly clear. Thus Jeffersonian Republicans had ample reason to distrust the federal courts. Their distrust was intensified by the Judiciary Act of 1801, which was passed just before Jefferson's inauguration by the lame-duck Federalist Congress. Coupled with President Adams's appointment of the Federalist John Marshall as Chief Justice in January, the Judiciary Act assured long-term Federalist domination of the federal courts. First, it reduced the number of Associate Justices of the Supreme Court from six to five when the next vacancy occurred, thus reducing Jefferson's chances of appointing a new member to the Court. The Judiciary Act also took Supreme Court Justices off circuit and created a new system of circuit courts. This allowed Adams to appoint sixteen new judges, along with a full array of marshals, federal attorneys, clerks, and justices of the peace. He worked until 9 o'clock on his last night in office signing commissions for these new officers. All of them were staunch Federalists.

Republicans disagreed on what to do about the Federalists' packing of the courts. A minority distrusted the whole idea of an independent judiciary and wanted judges elected by popular vote. Jefferson and most in his party wanted the courts shielded from democratic control; at the same time, they deeply resented the uniformly Federalist "midnight judges" created by the Judiciary Act of 1801. Jeffer-

son did replace the new federal marshals and attorneys with Republicans and dismissed some of the federal justices of the peace. But judges were appointed for life and could be removed only through impeachment. The Jeffersonians hit on a simple solution: they would get rid of the new judges by abolishing their jobs. Early in 1802, with some of Jefferson's supporters questioning the constitutionality of what they were doing, Congress repealed the Judiciary Act of 1801 and thus did away with the midnight appointees.

With the federal courts scaled back to their original size, Republicans in Congress, led by the Virginia agrarian John Randolph, went after High Federalists who were still acting as judges. As a first test of removal by impeachment they chose John Pickering, a federal attorney with the circuit court of New Hampshire. Pickering was a highly partisan Federalist. He was also a notorious alcoholic and clearly insane. The Federalists who had appointed him had long considered him an embarrassment. The House drew up articles of impeachment and Pickering was tried by the Senate, which, by a strict party vote, removed him from office.

On the same day, Congress went after bigger game: they voted to impeach Supreme Court Justice Samuel Chase. Chase was a much more prominent public figure than Pickering, and his "crimes" were not alcoholism or insanity but mere partisanship. He hated the Jeffersonians, and he had prosecuted sedition cases with real enthusiasm. He had also delivered anti-Jeffersonian diatribes from the bench, and he had used his position and his formidable legal skills to bully young lawyers with whom he disagreed. In short, Chase was an unpleasant, overbearing, and unashamedly partisan member of the Supreme Court. But his faults did not add up to the "high crimes and misdemeanors" that are the constitutional grounds for impeachment.

Moderate Republicans in the government doubted the wisdom of the Chase impeachment, and their uneasiness grew when Congressman John Randolph took over the prosecution. Randolph led a radical states'-rights faction that violently disapproved, among other things, of the way Jefferson had settled a southern land controversy. A corrupt Georgia legislature had sold huge parcels in Mississippi and Alabama to the Yazoo Land Company, which in turn had sold them to private investors—many of

Samuel Chase   Samuel Chase was a Supreme Court Justice and arch-enemy of those he considered disturbers of the republic — including Jefferson's Democratic Republicans.

publicans in the Senate joined the Federalists in voting to acquit Samuel Chase.

Justice Marshall's Court

Chief Justice John Marshall probably cheered the acquittal of Justice Chase, for it was clear that Marshall was next on the list. Secretary of State under John Adams, Marshall was committed to Federalist ideas of national power, as he demonstrated with his decision in the case of *Marbury* v. *Madison*. William Marbury was one of the justices of the peace whom Jefferson had eliminated in his first few days in office. He sued Jefferson's Secretary of State James Madison for the nondelivery of his commission. Although Marbury never got his job, Marshall used the case to hand down a number of important rulings. The first ruling, which questioned the constitutionality of Jefferson's refusal to deliver Marbury's commission, helped to convince Republican moderates to repeal the Judiciary Act of 1801. The last ruling, delivered in February 1803, laid the basis for the practice of judicial review — that is, the Supreme Court's power to rule on the constitutionality of acts of Congress. In arguing that Congress could not alter the jurisdiction of the Supreme Court, Marshall stated that the Constitution is "fundamental and paramount law" and that it is "emphatically the province and duty of the judicial department to say what law is."

Some Republicans saw Marshall's ruling as an attempt to arrogate power to the Court. But John Marshall was not a sinister man. As Secretary of State under John Adams, he had helped to end the undeclared war with France, and he had expressed doubts about the wisdom and necessity if not the constitutionality of the Alien and Sedition Acts. Of more immediate concern, while he disliked Congress's repeal of the 1801 legislation, he did not doubt the right of Congress to make and unmake laws and he was determined to accept the situation. While the decision in *Marbury* v. *Madison* angered many Republicans, Jefferson and the moderate Republicans noted that Marshall was less interested in the power of the judiciary than in its independence. Ultimately, they decided they trusted Marshall more than they trusted the radicals in their own party. With the acquittal of Justice Chase, Jeffersonian attacks on the federal courts ceased.

them New England speculators. When a new Georgia legislature rescinded the sale and turned the land over to the federal government in 1802, Jefferson agreed to pay off the investors' claims with federal money.

As Randolph led the prosecution of Samuel Chase, he lectured in his annoying, high-pitched voice that Jefferson was double-crossing southern Republicans in an effort to win support in the Northeast. Most of the Republican Senators disagreed, and some of them withdrew their support from the impeachment proceedings in order to isolate and humiliate Randolph and his friends. With Jefferson's approval, many Re-

John Marshall   A Virginian and a distant relative of Thomas Jefferson, John Marshall became Chief Justice of the Supreme Court in the last months of John Adams' administration. He used the Court as a conservative, centralizing force until his death in 1835.

Louisiana

It was Jefferson's good fortune that Europe remained at peace during his first term and stayed out of American affairs. Indeed the one development that posed an international threat to the United States turned into a grand triumph: the purchase of the Louisiana Territory from France in 1803.

By 1801 a half-million Americans lived west of the Appalachians. While Federalists feared the barbarism of the westerners, Republicans saw westward expansion as the best hope for the survival of the republic. Social inequality and the erosion of yeoman independence would almost inevitably take root in the East, but the vast lands west of the mountains would enable the republic to renew itself for many generations to come. To serve that purpose, however, the West needed ready access to markets through the river system that emptied into the Gulf of Mexico at New Orleans. "There is on the globe," wrote President Jefferson, "one single spot, the possessor of which is our natural and habitual enemy. It is New Orleans."

In 1801 Spain owned New Orleans and under Pinckney's Treaty allowed Americans to transship produce from the interior. The year before, however, Spain had secretly ceded the Louisiana Territory (roughly, all the land west of the Mississippi drained by the Missouri and Arkansas rivers) to France. Napoleon Bonaparte had plans for a new French empire in America with the sugar island of Saint Dominque (present-day Haiti and the Dominican Republic) at its center, and with mainland colonies feeding the islands and thus making the empire self-sufficient. Late in 1802, the Spanish, who had retained control of New Orleans, closed the port to American commerce, giving rise to rumors that they would soon transfer the city to France. To forestall such a move, which would threaten the very existence of American settlements west of the Appalachians, President Jefferson sent a delegation to Paris early in 1803 with authorization to buy New Orleans for the United States.

By the time the delegates reached Paris, events had dissolved French plans for a new American empire. The slaves of Saint Dominque had revolted against the French and had defeated their attempts to regain control of the island (see Chapter 8). At the same time, another war between Britain and France seemed imminent. Napoleon—reputedly chanting "Damn sugar, damn coffee, damn colonies"—decided to bail out of America and concentrate his resources in Europe. He astonished Jefferson's del-egation by announcing that France would sell not only New Orleans but the whole Louisiana Territory—which would roughly double the size of the United States—for the bargain price of $15 million.

Jefferson, who had criticized Federalists whenever they violated the letter of the Constitution, faced a dilemma: the Constitution did not give the President the power to buy territory. But the chance to buy Louisiana was too good to pass up. It would assure Americans access to the rivers of the interior, it would eliminate a serious foreign threat on America's western border, and it would give American

The Louisiana Purchase   This panorama of New Orleans celebrated the Louisiana Purchase in 1803. The patriotic caption promised prosperity for the city and (by inference) for the American settlements upriver.

farmers enough land to sustain the agrarian republic for a long time to come. Swallowing his constitutional scruples (and at the same time half-heartedly asking for a constitutional amendment to legalize the purchase), Jefferson told the American delegates to buy Louisiana. Republican senators, who shared few of Jefferson's doubts, quickly ratified the Louisiana treaty over Federalist objections that the purchase would encourage rapid settlement and add to backcountry barbarism and Republican strength. Most Americans agreed that the accidents of French and Haitian history had given the United States a grand opportunity, and Congress's ratification of the Louisiana Purchase met with overwhelming public approval. For his part, Jefferson was certain that the republic had gained the means of renewing itself through time. He had bought, he claimed in his Second Inaugural, a great "empire of liberty."

As Jefferson stood for reelection in 1804, he could look back on an astonishingly successful first term. He had dismantled the government's power to coerce its citizens, and he had begun to wipe out the national debt. The Louisiana Purchase had doubled the size of the republic at remarkably little cost. Moreover, by eliminating France from North America it had strengthened the argument for reducing

the military and the debts and taxes that went with it. Jefferson was more certain than ever that the republic could preserve itself through peaceful expansion. The "wise and frugal" government he had promised in 1801 was becoming a reality.

The combination of international peace, territorial expansion, and inexpensive, unobtrusive government left the Federalists without an issue in the 1804 election. They went through the motions of nominating Charles Pinckney of South Carolina as their presidential candidate and then watched as Jefferson captured the electoral votes of every state but Delaware and Connecticut. As he began his second term in 1805, Jefferson could assume that he had ended the Federalist threat to the republic.

THE REPUBLIC AND THE NAPOLEONIC WARS, 1804–1815

In the spring of 1803, a few weeks after closing the deal for Louisiana, Napoleon Bonaparte declared war on Great Britain. This eleven-year war, like the wars of the 1790s, dominated the national politics of the United States. Most Americans wanted to remain neutral. Few Republicans supported Bonaparte

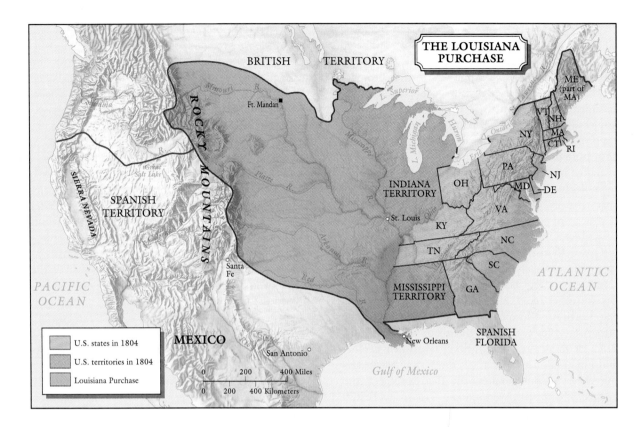

as they had supported the French revolutionaries of 1789, and none but the most rabid Federalists wanted to intervene on the side of Great Britain. But neither France nor Britain would allow Americans to remain neutral.

The Dilemmas of Neutrality

At the beginning, both Britain and France, whose rural economies were disrupted by war, encouraged the Americans to resume their role as neutral carriers and suppliers of food. For a time, Americans made huge profits. Between 1803 and 1807 U.S. exports—mostly foodstuffs and plantation staples—rose from $66.5 million to $102.2 million. Reexports—goods produced in the British, Spanish, and French islands of the Caribbean, picked up by American vessels and then reloaded in American ports onto American ships bound for Europe—rose even faster: from $13.5 million to $58.4 million.

In 1805 France and Great Britain began systematically to interfere with that trade. In 1805 the Royal Navy under Lord Nelson destroyed the French and

Spanish fleets at the Battle of Trafalgar. Later that year Napoleon's armies won a decisive victory over Austria and Russia at the Battle of Austerlitz, and won effective control of Europe. The war reached a stalemate: Napoleon's army occupied Europe, the British navy controlled the seas.

Britain decided to use its naval supremacy to blockade Europe and starve the French into submission. In the Essex Decision of 1805, the British ministry dusted off what was known as the Rule of 1756, which stated that a European country could not use a neutral merchant marine to conduct its wartime trade with its colonies unless that trade was legal during peace. Translated into the realities of 1805, the Essex Decision meant that the Royal Navy could seize American ships engaged in the reexport trade with France. In the spring of 1806 Congress, angered by British seizures of American ships, passed a Non-Importation Act forbidding the importation of British goods that could be bought elsewhere or that could be manufactured in the United States. A month after that Britain blockaded long stretches of the European coast. Napoleon responded with the Berlin Decree, which outlawed all trade with the British Isles. The British answered with an Order in Council that demanded that neutral ships trading with Europe stop first for inspection and licensing in a British port. Napoleon responded with the Milan Decree, which stated that any vessel that obeyed the British decrees or allowed itself to be searched by the Royal Navy was subject to seizure by France. Beginning in 1805 and ending with the Milan Decree in December 1807, the barrage of European decrees and counter-decrees meant that virtually all American commerce with Europe had been outlawed by one or the other of the warring powers.

Given British naval supremacy, French decrees were effective only against American ships that entered ports controlled by France. The Royal Navy, on the other hand, maintained a loose blockade of the North American coast and stopped and searched American ships as they left the major seaports. Hundreds of ships were seized, along with their cargoes and crews. Under British law, the Royal Navy during wartime could impress any British subject into service. The British were certain that many British subjects, including legions of deserters from the Royal Navy, were hiding in the American merchant marine. They were right. The danger, low pay, bad food, and draconian discipline on British warships encouraged many British sailors to jump ship and take jobs on American merchantmen. Many of the British warships that stopped American merchant ships on the high seas were undermanned; the sailors their officers commandeered often included Englishmen who had taken out U.S. citizenship (an act the British did not recognize) and, inevitably, native-born Americans. An estimated 6,000 American citizens were impressed into the Royal Navy between 1803 and 1812.

The kidnapping of American sailors, even more than maritime seizures of American property and other violations of American neutral rights, enraged the citizens of the United States and brought the country close to war in the summer of 1807. In June the American naval frigate *Chesapeake,* which was outfitting in Norfolk, Virginia, signed on four English deserters from the British navy, along with some Americans who had joined the British navy and then deserted. The British warship HMS *Leopard* also was docked at Norfolk, and some of the deserters spotted their old officers and taunted them on the streets. The *Leopard* left port and resumed its patrol of the American coast. Then, on June 21, its officers caught the *Chesapeake* off Hampton Roads and demanded the return of the British deserters. When the captain refused, the British fired on the *Chesapeake,* killing three Americans and wounding eighteen. The British then boarded the *Chesapeake,* seized the four deserters, and later hanged one of them. The *Chesapeake* limped back into port.

The *Chesapeake* affair set off huge anti-British demonstrations in the seaport towns and angry cries for war throughout the country. President Jefferson responded by barring British ships from American ports and American territorial waters, and by ordering state governors to prepare to call up as many as 100,000 militiamen. The United States stood at the brink of full-scale war with the most powerful nation in the world.

Embargo

Jefferson wanted to avoid war. War inevitably brought high taxes, government debt, the repression of dissent, and the creation of a bloated military and civil service—precisely the evils that Jefferson had vowed to eliminate. Worse, war carried the danger of defeat and thus the possible failure of America's republican experiment.

Jefferson had one more card to play: he could suspend trade with Europe altogether and thus keep American ships out of harm's way. For many years, Jefferson had assumed that U.S. farm products and the U.S. market for imported goods had become crucial to the European economies. He could use trade as a means of "peaceable coercion" that would both ensure respect for American neutral rights and keep the country out of war. "Our commerce," he wrote just before taking office, "is so valuable to them, that they will be glad to purchase it, when the only price we ask is to do us justice." Convinced that America's yeoman republic could survive without European luxuries more easily than Europe could survive without American food, Jefferson decided to give "peaceable coercion" a serious test. Late in 1807 he asked Congress to suspend all U.S. trade with foreign countries.

Congress passed the Embargo Act on December 22. By the following spring, however, it was clear that peaceable coercion would not work. The British found other markets and other sources of food. They encouraged the smuggling of American goods into Canada. And American merchantmen who had been at sea when the embargo went into effect stayed away from their home ports and functioned as part of the British merchant marine. A loophole in the Embargo Act allowed U.S. ships to leave port in order to pick up American property stranded in other countries, and an estimated 6,000 ships set sail under that excuse. Hundreds of others, plying the coastal trade, were "blown off course" and found themselves thrust into international commerce. For his part, Napoleon seized American ships in European ports, explaining that, since the Embargo kept all American ships in port, those trading under American flags must be British ships in disguise.

The embargo hurt American commerce badly. In 1807 American exports had stood at $108 million. In 1808 they dropped to $22 million. The economy slowed in every section of the country, but it ground to a halt in the cities of the Northeast. While the ocean-going merchant fleet rotted at anchor, unemployed sailors, dockworkers, and other maritime workers and their families sank to levels of economic despair that had seldom been seen in British North America. Northeastern Federalists branded Jefferson's embargo a "Chinese" solution to the problems of commerce and diplomacy. Commerce, they argued, was the great civilizer: "Her victories are over ferocious passions, savage manners, deep rooted prejudices, blind superstition and delusive theory." Federalists accused Jefferson of plotting an end to commerce and a reversion to rural barbarism, and they often took the lead in trying to subvert the embargo through smuggling and other means. In Connecticut, the Federalist governor flatly refused Jefferson's request to mobilize the militia to enforce the embargo.

The Federalists gained ground in the elections of 1808. James Madison, Jefferson's old ally and chosen successor, won the presidency with 122 electoral votes to 47 for his Federalist opponent, C. C. Pinckney. And although Republicans retained control of both houses of Congress, Federalists made significant gains in Congress and won control of several state legislatures. Federalist opposition to the embargo, and to the supposed southern, agrarian stranglehold on national power that stood behind it, was clearly gaining ground.

The Road to War

When President Madison took office in the spring of 1809 it was clear that the embargo had failed to coerce the British. On the contrary, it had created misery in the seaport cities, choked off the imports that were the source of 90 percent of federal revenue, and revived Federalist opposition to Republican dominance. Early in 1809 Congress passed the Non-Intercourse Act, which retained the ban on trade with Britain and France but reopened trade with other nations. It also gave President Madison the power to reopen trade with either Britain or France once they had agreed to respect American rights. Neither complied, and the Non-Intercourse Act proved nearly as ineffective as the embargo.

In 1810 Congress passed Macon's Bill No. 2, a strange piece of legislation that rescinded the ban on trade with France and Britain but then authorized the President to reimpose the Non-Intercourse Act on either belligerent if the other agreed to end its restrictions on U.S. trade. Napoleon decided to test the Americans. In September 1810 the French foreign minister, the Duc de Cadore, promised, with vague conditions, that France would repeal the Berlin and Milan Decrees. Though the proposal was a clear attempt to lead the United States into conflict with Great Britain, Madison felt he had no

Anti-Embargo Propaganda A Federalist cartoonist heard the Embargo Act denounced as a "terrapin policy," and drew a snapping turtle sizing a tobacco smuggler by the seat of the pants. The man cries out "Oh! this cursed Ograb me"—an anagram of embargo.

choice but to go along with it. He accepted the French promise and proclaimed in November 1810 that the British had three months to follow suit. "It promises us," he said of his proclamation, "at least an extrication from the dilemma, of a mortifying peace, or a war with both the great belligerents."

In the end, Madison's proclamation led to war. The French repealed only those sections of the Berlin and Milan Decrees that applied to the neutral rights of the United States. The British refused to revoke their Orders in Council and told the Americans to withdraw their restrictions on British trade until the French had repealed theirs. The United States would either have to obey British orders (thus making American exports and the American merchant marine a part of the British war effort—a neocolonial situation utterly repugnant to most Americans) or go to war. When Congress reconvened in November 1811, it voted military measures in preparation for war with Great Britain.

The War Congress, 1811–1812

The Republicans controlled both houses of Congress in 1811–1812: 75 percent of the House and 82 percent of the Senate identified themselves as members of President Madison's party. But they were a divided majority. The Federalist minority, which was united against Madison, was joined on many issues by northeastern Republicans who followed the pro-British, Federalist line on international trade, and by Republicans who wanted a more powerful military than other Republicans would allow. Also opposed to Madison were the self-styled Old Republicans of the South, led by John Randolph. Thus it was a deeply divided Congress that met the war crisis.

In this confused situation a group of talented young Congressmen took control. Nearly all of them were Republicans from the South or the West: Richard M. Johnson and Henry Clay of Kentucky, John C. Calhoun and William Lowndes of South Carolina, George M. Troup of Georgia, Peter B. Porter from the Niagara district of New York, and others. Called the "War Hawks," these men were ardent nationalists who were more than willing to declare war on England to protect U.S. rights. Through their organizational, oratorical, and intellectual power, they won control of Congress. Henry Clay, only 34 years old and serving his first term in Con-

gress, was elected Speaker of the House. More vigorous than his predecessors, Clay controlled debate, packed key committees, worked tirelessly behind the scenes, and imposed order on his fellow Congressmen. When John Randolph, one of the most feared members of the House, brought his dog into the House chamber, Speaker Clay pointedly ordered the dog removed. Earlier speakers had not dared give such an order.

In the winter and spring of 1811–1812 the War Hawks led Congress into a declaration of war. In November they voted military preparations, and in April they enacted a 90-day embargo—not to coerce the British but to get American ships safely into port before war began. (As in 1807, the embargo prompted seaport merchants to rush their ships to sea.) On June 1, Madison sent a war message to Congress. This was to be the first war declared under the Constitution, and the President stayed out of congressional territory by not asking explicitly for a

Henry Clay   This protrait of Henry Clay was engraved at about the time the brilliant first-term congressman from Kentucky, as Speaker of the House, helped his fellow War Hawks steer the United States into the War of 1812.

declaration of war. He did, however, present a list of British crimes that could be interpreted in no other way: the enforcement of the Orders in Council, even within the territorial waters of the United States; the impressment of American seamen; the use of spies and provocateurs within the United States; and the wielding of "a malicious influence over the Indians of the Northwest Territory." Madison concluded that war had in fact begun: "We behold . . . on the side of Great Britain a state of war against the United States; and on the side of the United States, a state of peace toward Great Britain."

Congress declared war on June 18. The vote was far from unanimous: 79 to 49 in the House of Representatives, 19 to 13 in the Senate. All 30 Federalists voted against the declaration. So did one in five Republicans, nearly all of them from the Northeast. Thus the war was declared by the Republican party, more particularly by the Republicans of the South and the West. The Northeast, whose commercial rights were supposedly the issue at stake, opposed the declaration.

The War of 1812

War Hawks declared a war to defend the sovereignty and maritime rights of the United States. The war that they planned and fought, however, bore the stamp of southern and western Republicanism. Federalists and many northeastern Republicans expected a naval war. After all, it was on the ocean that the British had committed their atrocities, and some remembered U.S. naval successes against France in the quasi-war of 1798–1800 (see Chapter 9) and predicted similar successes against Great Britain. Yet when Madison asked Congress to prepare for war, the War Hawks led a majority that strengthened the army and left the navy weak. Reasoning that no U.S. naval force could challenge British control of the seas, they prepared instead for a land invasion of British Canada.

The decision to invade Canada led the Federalists, along with many of Randolph's Old Republicans, to accuse Madison and the congressional majority of planning a war of territorial aggression. Some members of Congress did indeed want to annex Canada to the United States. But most saw the decision to invade Canada as a matter of strategy. Lightly garrisoned and with a population of only half a million

(many of them French, and most of the others American emigres whose loyalties were doubtful), Canada seemed the easiest and most logical place in which to damage the British. It was also from bases in Canada that the British armed Tecumseh's formidable Indian confederacy (see Chapter 8). The western Republicans were determined to end that threat once and for all. Finally, Canada was a valuable colony of Great Britain. The American embargoes, coupled with Napoleon's control of Europe, had impaired Britain's ability to supply her plantation colonies in the West Indies, and Canadian farmers had begun to fill the gap. Thus Canada was both valuable and vulnerable, and American policymakers reasoned that they could take it and hold it hostage while demanding that the British back down on other issues. Although Canada was the focus of U.S. military strategy, maritime rights and national honor, along with the British-fed Indian threat west of the Appalachians, were the central issues in 1812. As John C. Calhoun, who was instrumental in taking the nation to war, concluded, "The mad ambition, the lust of power, and commercial avarice of Great Britain have left to neutral nations an alternative only between the base surrender of their rights, and a manly vindication of them."

The American Offensive, 1812–1813

The United States opened its offensive against Canada in 1812, with disastrous results. The plan was to invade Upper Canada (Ontario) from the Northwest, thus cutting off the Shawnee, Potawatomi, and other pro-British tribes from their British support. When General William Hull, Governor of Michigan Territory, took a poorly supplied, badly led army of militiamen and volunteers into Canada from a base in Detroit, he found that the British had outguessed him. The area was crawling with British troops and their Indian allies. With detachments of his army overrun and with his supply lines cut, he retreated to the garrison at Detroit. Under siege, he heard that an Indian force had captured the garrison at Fort Dearborn. British General Isaac Brock, who knew that Hull was afraid of Indians, sent a note into the fort telling him that "the numerous body of Indians who have attached themselves to my troops, will be beyond my controul the moment the contest commences." Without consulting his officers, Hull

American Troops Invade Canada   A Canadian artist depicted the failed American invasion at Queenston Heights in October 1812. British troops on the right are rushing to repel the Americans who have occupied the cliffs at center.

surrendered his army of 2,000 to the smaller British force. Though Hull was later court-martialed for cowardice, the damage had been done: the British and their Indian allies occupied many of the remaining American garrisons in the Northwest and transformed the U.S. invasion of Upper Canada into a British occupation of much of the Northwest.

The invasion of Canada from the East went no better. In October a U.S. force of 6,000 faced 2,000 British and Indians across the Niagara River separating Ontario from western New York. The U.S. regular army crossed the river, surprised the British, and established a toehold at Queenston Heights. While the British were preparing a counterattack, New York militiamen refused to cross the river to reinforce the regular troops. Ohio militiamen had behaved the same way when Hull invaded Canada, and there had been similar problems with the New York militia near Lake Champlain. Throughout the war citizen soldiers proved that Jefferson's confidence in the militia could not be extended to the invasion of other countries. The British regrouped and slaughtered the outnumbered, exhausted U.S. regulars at Queenston Heights.

As winter set in, it was clear that Canada would not fall as easily as the Americans had assumed. Indeed the invasion, which U.S. commanders had thought would knife through an apathetic Canadian population, had the opposite effect: the attacks by the United States turned the rag-tag assortment of American loyalist emigres, discharged British soldiers, and American-born settlers into a self-consciously British Canadian people. Years later, an Englishwoman touring Niagara Falls asked a Canadian ferry boatman if it was true that Canadians had thrown Americans off Queenston Heights to their death on the rocky banks of the Niagara River. "Why yes," he replied, "there was a good many of them; but it was right to show them that there was water between us, and you know it might help to keep the rest of them from coming to trouble us on our own ground."

At the same time, Tecumseh's Indian confederacy, bruised but not broken in the Battle of Tippecanoe (Chapter 8), allied itself with the British. On a trip to the southern tribes Tecumseh found the traditionalist wing of the Creeks—led by prophets who called themselves Red Sticks—willing to join him. The augmented confederacy provided stiff resistance to the United States throughout the war. The Red Sticks chased settlers from much of Tennessee. They then attacked a group of settlers who had taken

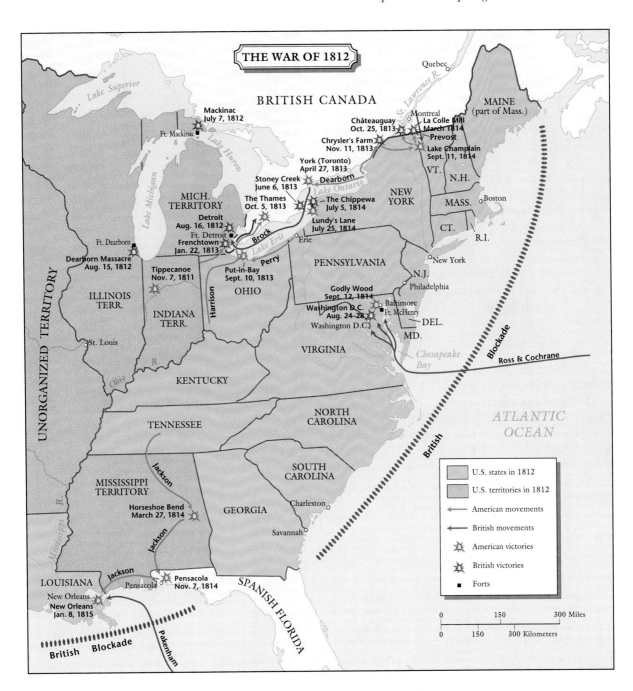

refuge in a stockade surrounding the house of an Alabama trader named George Mims. In what whites called the Massacre at Fort Mims, the Red Sticks (reputedly with the collusion of black slaves within the fort) killed at least 247 men, women, and children. In the Northwest, Tecumseh's warriors, fighting alongside the British, spread terror throughout the white settlements.

A wiser U.S. army returned to Canada in 1813. They raided and burned the Canadian capital at York (Toronto) in April, and then fought inconclusively through the summer. An autumn offensive toward Montreal failed, but the Americans had better luck on Lake Erie. The barrier of Niagara Falls kept Britain's salt-water navy out of the upper Great Lakes, and on Lake Erie the British and Americans engaged in a frenzied shipbuilding contest through the first year of the war. The Americans won. In September 1813 Commodore Oliver Hazard Perry cornered the British fleet at Put-in-Bay and destroyed it. Control of Lake Erie enabled the United States to cut off supplies to the British in the Northwest, and a U.S. army under William Henry Harrison retook the area and continued on into Canada. On October 5 Harrison caught up with a force of British and Indians at the Thames River and beat them badly. In the course of that battle Richard M. Johnson, a War Hawk Congressman acting as commander of the Kentucky militia, killed Tecumseh. Proud militiamen returned to Kentucky with pieces of hair and clothing and even swatches of skin torn from Tecumseh's corpse. Their officers reaped huge political rewards: the Battle of the Thames would eventually produce a President of the United States (Harrison), a Vice President (Johnson), three governors of Kentucky, three lieutenant governors, four United States Senators, and about twenty Congressmen. There is no more telling evidence of how seriously the settlers of the interior had taken Tecumseh.

The following spring General Andrew Jackson's Tennessee militia, aided by Choctaw, Creek, and Cherokee allies, attacked and slaughtered the Red Sticks who had fortified themselves at Horse Shoe Bend in Alabama. With the Battles of the Thames and of Horse Shoe Bend, the military power of the Indian peoples east of the Mississippi River was broken.

Tecumseh   Tecumseh, military and political leader of the Northwestern tribes that sided with the British in 1812, came closer than any other Native American leader to unifying Indian peoples against white territorial expansion.

The British Offensive, 1814

The British defeated Napoleon in April 1814, thus ending the larger war of which the War of 1812 was a part. With both sides thinking about peace, the British decided to concentrate their resources on the American war and in 1814 went on the offensive. The British had already blockaded much of the American coast and had shut down ports from Georgia to Maine. During the summer of 1814 they began to raid the shores of Chesapeake Bay and marched on Washington, D.C. As retribution for the torching of the Canadian capital at York, they chased the army and politicians out of town and then burned down the capitol and the President's mansion. In September the British attacked the much larger city of Baltimore, but they could not blast their way past the determined garrison that com-

manded the harbor from Fort McHenry. This was the battle that inspired Francis Scott Key to write "The Star-Spangled Banner," a doggerel poem that was later set to music and chosen as the national anthem in the 1930s. When a British offensive on Lake Champlain stalled during the autumn, the war reached a stalemate: Britain had prevented the invasion of Canada and had blockaded the American coast, but neither side could take and hold the other's territory.

The British now shifted their attention to the Gulf Coast, particularly to New Orleans, a city that was of vital importance to the trade and communications networks of the trans-Appalachian United States. Peace negotiations had begun in August and the British wanted to capture and hold New Orleans as a bargaining chip. A large British amphibious force sailed up the mouth of the Mississippi and

The Burning of the Capitol   The burning of the Capitol by British troops in 1814 was one of the greatest military embarrassments ever suffered by the United States. This painting was made for an archway in the present-day Capitol in 1974.

camped eight miles south of New Orleans. There they were met by an American army made up of Kentucky and Tennessee militiamen, clerks, work-ingmen, and free blacks from the city, and about a thousand French pirates—all under the command of Andrew Jackson of Tennessee. Throughout late December and early January, unaware that a peace treaty had been signed on December 24, the armies exchanged artillery barrages and the British probed and attacked American lines. Then, on January 8, the British launched a frontal assault. A formation of 6,000 British soldiers marched across open ground toward 4,000 Americans concealed behind breast-works. With the first American volley, it was clear that the British had made a mistake. Veterans of the bloodiest battles of the Napoleonic Wars swore that they had never seen such withering fire; soldiers in the front ranks who were not cut down threw themselves to the ground and surrendered when the shooting stopped. The charge lasted half an hour. At the end, 2,000 British soldiers lay dead or wounded. American casualties numbered only seventy. Fought nearly two weeks after the peace treaty, the Battle of New Orleans had no effect on the outcome of the war or on the peace terms. But it salved the injured

pride of Americans and made a national hero and a political power of Andrew Jackson.

The Hartford Convention

While most of the nation celebrated Jackson's vic-tory, events in Federalist New England went very differently during the closing months of the war. New Englanders had considered themselves the vic-tims of Republican trade policies, and their Con-gressmen had voted overwhelmingly against going to war. The New England states seldom met their quotas of militiamen for the war effort, and some Federalist leaders had openly urged resistance to the war. The British had encouraged that resistance by not extending their naval blockade to the New England coast, and through the first two years of the war New England merchants and farmers had traded freely with the enemy. In 1814, after the Royal Navy had extended its blockade northward and had begun to raid the towns of coastal Maine, some Federalists talked openly about seceding and making a separate peace with Britain. In an attempt to undercut the secessionists, moderate Federalists called a convention at Hartford to air the region's grievances. The Hartford Convention, which met in late December 1814, proposed amendments to the Constitution that point to New England's position as a self-conscious minority within the Union. First, the convention delegates wanted the three-fifths clause, which led to overrepresentation of the South in Congress and the Electoral College (see Chapter 7), stricken from the Constitution; they wanted to deny naturalized citizens—who were strongly Republican—the right to hold office; they wanted to make it more difficult for new states—all of which sided with the Republicans and their southern leadership—to enter the Union; and finally, they wanted to require a two-thirds majority of both houses for a declaration of war—a requirement that would have prevented the War of 1812.

The Federalist leaders of the Hartford Convention, satisfied that they had headed off the secessionists, took their proposals to Washington in mid-January. They arrived to find the capitol celebrating the news of the peace treaty and Jackson's stunning victory at New Orleans. When they aired their sectional complaints and their constitutional proposals, they were branded as negative, selfish, and unpatriotic. Although Federalists continued for a few years to wield power in southern New England, the Hartford debacle ruined any chance of a nationwide Federalist resurgence after the war. Andrew Jackson had stolen control of American history from New England. He would do it again in the years ahead.

The Treaty of Ghent

Britain's defeat of Napoleon had spurred British and American efforts to end a war that neither wanted. In August 1814 they opened peace talks in the Belgian city of Ghent. Perhaps waiting for the results of their 1814 offensive, the British opened with proposals that the Americans were certain to reject. They demanded the right to navigate the Mississippi. Moreover, they wanted territorial concessions and the creation of the permanent, independent Indian buffer state in the Northwest that they had promised their Indian allies. The Americans ignored these proposals and talked instead about impressment and maritime rights. As the autumn wore on and the war reached stalemate, both sides began to compromise. The British knew that the Americans would grant concessions in the interior only if they were thoroughly defeated, an outcome that most British com-

manders thought impossible. For their part, the Americans realized that the British maritime depredations were by-products of the struggle with Napoleonic France. Faced with peace in Europe and a senseless military stalemate in North America, negotiators on both sides began to withdraw their demands. The Treaty of Ghent, signed on Christmas Eve 1814, simply put an end to the war. The border between Canada and the United States remained where it had been in 1812, Indians south of that border—defeated and without allies—were left to the mercy of the United States, and British maritime violations were not mentioned. The makers of the treaty stopped a war that neither side could win, trusting that a period of peace would resolve the problems created by two decades of world war.

Conclusion

In 1816 Thomas Jefferson was in retirement at Monticello, satisfied that he had defended liberty against the Federalists' love of power. The High Federalist attempt to militarize government and to jail their enemies had failed. Their direct taxes were repealed. Their debt and their national bank remained in place, but only under the watchful eyes of true republicans. And their attempt to ally the United States with the antirepublican designs of Great Britain had ended in what many called the "Second War of American Independence."

Yet for all his successes, Jefferson in 1816 saw that he must sacrifice his dreams of agrarianism. Throughout his political life, Jefferson envisioned American yeomen trading farm surpluses for European manufactured goods—a relationship that would ensure rural prosperity, prevent the growth of cities and factories, and thus sustain the landed independence on which republican citizenship rested. Westward expansion, he had believed, would ensure the yeoman republic for generations to come. By 1816 that dream was ended. The British and French had "cover[ed] the earth and sea with robberies and piracies," disrupting America's vital export economy whenever it suited their whims. Arguing as Hamilton had argued in 1790, Jefferson insisted that "we must now place the manufacturer by the side of the agriculturalist." As he wrote, a Republican congress was taking steps that would help transform the yeoman republic into a market society and a boisterous capitalist democracy.

SUGGESTED READING

Stanley Elkins and Eric McKitrick, *The Age of Federalism: The Early American Republic, 1788–1800* (1993) is the best study of politics in the 1790s. James Roger Sharp, *American Politics in the Early Republic: The New Nation in Crisis* (1993) is an extended interpretive essay; John C. Miller, *The Federalist Era, 1789–1801* (1960) remains the best brief account. Stephen G. Kurtz, *The Presidency of John Adams* (1957) is a valuable study of the second Federalist presidency.

Federalist approaches to government and administration are the subjects of Ralph Ketcham, *Presidents above Party: The First American Presidency, 1789–1829* (1984); Leonard D. White, *The Federalists: A Study in Administrative History* (1948); and Carl E. Prince, *The Federalists and the Origins of the U.S. Civil Service* (1977). Specific issues are handled ably in Robert A. Rutland, *The Birth of the Bill of Rights, 1776–1791* (1955); Thomas G. Slaughter, *The Whiskey Rebellion: Frontier Epilogue to the American Revolution* (1986); Richard H. Kohn, *Eagle and Sword: The Federalists and the Creation of the Military Establishment in America, 1783–1802* (1975); James M. Smith, *Freedom's Fetters: The Alien and Sedition Laws and American Civil Liberties,* (rev. ed., 1967). The rise of Jeffersonian opposition is treated in Richard Hostadter, *The Idea of a Party System: The Rise of Legitimate Opposition in the United States, 1780–1840* (1970); Lance Banning, *The Jeffersonian Persuasion: Evolution of a Party Ideology* (1980); and Joyce Appleby, *Capitalism and a New Social Order: The Republican Vision of the 1790s* (1984).

Henry Adams, *History of the United States of America during the Administrations of Thomas Jefferson and of James Madison* (9 vols., 1889–1891; reprint, 2 vols., 1986) is the classic work on national politics from 1801 to 1815. Marshall Smelser, *The Democratic Republic, 1801–1815* (1968) is a solid modern account, while Forrest McDonald, *The Presidency of Thomas Jefferson* (1976) is both critical and thoughtful. Drew R. McCoy, *The Elusive Republic: Political Economy in Jeffersonian America* (1980) is a stimulating essay on Jeffersonian economic policy. See also John R. Nelson, Jr., *Liberty and Property: Political Economy and Policymaking in the New Nation, 1789–1812* (1987). The court controversies are treated in Richard E. Ellis, *The Jeffersonian Crisis: Courts and Politics in the Young Republic* (1971); Mary K. B. Tachau, *Federal Courts in the Early Republic: Kentucky, 1789–1816* (1978); Robert Lowry Clinton, *Marbury vs. Madison and Judicial Review* (1989); R. Kent Newmyer, *The Supreme Court under Marshall and Taney* (1968). Other studies of domestic questions during the Jefferson and Madison administrations include Leonard B. White, *The Jeffersonians: A Study in Administrative History, 1801–1829* (1951); R. M. Johnstone, *Jefferson and the Presidency* (1978); Robert W. Tucker and David C. Hendrickson, *Empire of Liberty: The Statecraft of Thomas Jefferson* (1990). Opposition to the Jeffersonians is treated in Norman K. Risjord, *The Old Republicans: Southern Conservatism in the Age of Jefferson* (1965); Robert E. Shalhope, *John Taylor of Caroline: Pastoral Republican* (1980); Linda K. Kerber, *Federalists in Dissent: Imagery and Ideology in Jeffersonian America* (1970); and James M. Banner, Jr., *To the Hartford Convention: The Federalists and the Origins of Party Politics in Massachusetts, 1789–1815* (1969).

A convenient introduction to foreign policy under the Federalists and Jeffersonians is Bradford Perkins, *The Creation of a Republican Empire, 1776–1860,* volume 1 of *The Cambridge History of American Foreign Relations* (1993). Also helpful is Reginald Horsman, *The Diplomacy of the New Republic, 1776–1815* (1985). More specialized accounts include Harry Ammon, *The Genêt Mission* (1973); Samuel F. Bemis's classic studies of *Jay's Treaty* (2nd ed., 1962) and *Pinckney's Treaty* (2nd ed., 1960); Jerald A. Combs, *The Jay Treaty* (1970); Wiley Sword, *President Washington's Indian War: The Struggle for the Old Northwest, 1790–1795* (1985); Alexander DeConde, *The Quasi-War: Politics and Diplomacy of the Undeclared War with France, 1797–1801* (1966); William Stinchcombe, *The XYZ Affair* (1981); Lawrence Kaplan, *"Entangling Alliances with None": American Foreign Policy in the Age of Jefferson* (1987); Bradford Perkins, *The First Rapprochement: England and the United States, 1795–1805* (1967); Alexander DeConde, *This Affair of Louisiana* (1976). On the diplomatic, political, and military history of the War of 1812, the essential accounts are Bradford Perkins, *Prologue to War: England and the United States, 1805–1812* (1961); Clifford L. Egan, *Neither Peace nor War: Franco-American Relations, 1803–1812* (1983); J. C. A. Stagg, *Mr. Madison's War: Politics, Diplomacy, and Warfare in the Early Republic, 1783–1830* (1983); Donald R. Hickey, *The War of 1812: A Forgotten Conflict* (1989).

National politics under the Federalists and Jeffersonians can be approached through a number of excellent biographies. The multivolume works of Douglas Southall Freeman on Washington, Dumas Malone on Jefferson, and Irving Brant on Madison are definitive. The following are good single-volume studies of individuals: John R. Alden, *George Washington: A Biography* (1984); Marcus Cunliffe, *George Washington: Man and Monument* (1958); Gerald Stourzh, *Alexander Hamilton and the Idea of a Republican Government* (1970); Forrest McDonald, *Alexander Hamilton: A Biography* (1979); Peter Shaw, *The Character of John Adams* (1976); Merrill Peterson, *Thomas Jefferson and the New Nation* (1960); Nobel E. Cunningham, *In Pursuit of Reason: The Life of Thomas Jefferson* (1987); Ralph Ketcham, *James Madison: A Biography* (1971); Drew R. McCoy, *The Last of the Fathers: James Madison and the Republic Legacy* (1989).

Chapter 10

The Market Revolution, 1815–1860

Flour Mills   Springing up on a site that had been wilderness in 1815, Rochester, New York, with its spectacular waterfall, with its water-powered flour mills, and with the Erie Canal running through its center, became a symbol of the progress wrought by the market revolution.

Jeffersonian Democrats had tied their hopes to the yeoman-artisan republic: Americans, they argued, could trade farm and plantation products for European manufactured goods, thus enjoying material comforts without sacrificing the landed independence on which Jefferson's republic rested. But two decades of world war demonstrated the vulnerability of American dependence on the export economy, and by 1816 Jefferson himself advised his countrymen to build enough factories to serve domestic needs.

The Americans went further than that, and after 1815 a market revolution transformed Jefferson's republic into the market-oriented, capitalist society that it has been ever since. Improvements in transportation made that transformation possible. But it was decisions made by thousands of farmers, planters, craftsmen, and merchants that pulled farms and workshops out of old household and neighborhood

relationships and into production for distant markets. By the 1830s and 1840s the northern United States was experiencing a full-blown market revolution: new cities and towns provided financing, retailing, and manufacturing, while commercial farms traded food for what the cities made. The southern economy grew nearly as fast. But southerners continued to produce plantation staples for export, while most southern households remained marginal to the market. Thus the old slaveholder's republic persisted in the southern states. But now it faced a burgeoning capitalist democracy in the North.

GOVERNMENT AND MARKETS

The Fourteenth Congress met in the last days of 1815. Made up overwhelmingly of Jeffersonian Republicans, this Congress would reverse many of the positions taken by Jefferson's old party. It would charter a national bank, enact a protective tariff, and debate whether or not to build a national system of roads and canals at federal expense. As late as 1811, the Republicans viewed such programs as heresy. But by 1815 the Republican majority in Congress had come to accept it as orthodox. The War of 1812 had demonstrated that the United States was unable to coordinate a fiscal and military effort. It had also convinced many Republicans that reliance on foreign trade rendered the United States dependent on Europe. The nation, they said, must abandon Jefferson's export-oriented agrarianism and encourage national independence through subsidies to commerce and manufactures.

The American System

The nationalist Henry Clay retained his power in the postwar Congress, and headed the drive for a neo-Federalist program of protective tariffs, internal improvements, and a national bank. He called his program the "American System," arguing that it would foster national economic growth and a salutary interdependence between geographical sections, thus a happy and healthy republic.

In 1816 Congress chartered a Second Bank of the United States, headquartered in Philadelphia and empowered to establish branches wherever it saw fit. The government agreed to deposit its funds in the Bank, to accept the Bank's notes as payment for government land, taxes, and other transactions, and to buy one-fifth of the Bank's stock. The Bank of the United States was more powerful than the one that had been rejected by a Republican Congress as unconstitutional in 1811. The fiscal horrors of the War of 1812, however, had convinced most representatives that it would be a good idea to move toward a national currency and centralized control of money and credit. The alternative was to allow state banks—which had increased in number from 88 to 208 between 1813 and 1815—to issue unregulated and grossly inflated notes that might throw the anticipated postwar boom into chaos.

With no discussion of the constitutionality of what it was doing, Congress chartered the Bank of the United States as the sole banking institution empowered to do business throughout the country. Notes issued by the Bank would be the first sem-

blance of a national currency (they would soon constitute from one-tenth to one-third of the value of notes in circulation). Moreover, the Bank could regulate the currency by demanding that state bank notes used in transactions with the federal government be redeemable in gold. In 1816 the Bank set up shop in Philadelphia's Carpenter's Hall, and in 1824 moved around the corner to a Greek Revival edifice modeled after the Parthenon—a marble embodiment of the conservatism that directors of the Bank of the United States adopted as their fiscal stance. From that vantage point they would fight a running battle with state banks and local interests in an effort to impose direction on the transition to a market society.

In 1816 Congress drew up the first overtly protective tariff in U.S. history. Shepherded through the House by Clay and his fellow nationalist Calhoun, the Tariff of 1816 raised tariffs an average of 25 percent, extending protection to the nation's infant industries at the expense of foreign trade and American consumers. Again, wartime difficulties had paved the way: since Americans could not depend on imported manufactures, Congress saw the encouragement of domestic manufactures as a patriotic necessity. The tariff was well supported by the Northeast and the West, with enough southern support to ensure its passage by Congress. Tariffs would rise and fall between 1816 and the Civil War, but the principle of protectionism would persist.

Bills to provide federal money for roads, canals, and other "internal improvements" had a harder time winning approval. The British wartime blockade had hampered coastal shipping and had made Americans dependent on the wretched roads of the interior. Many members of the Fourteenth Congress, after spending days of bruising travel on their way to Washington, were determined to give the United States an efficient transportation network. Some urged completion of the National Road linking the Chesapeake with the trans-Appalachian west. Some talked of an inland canal system to link the northern and southern coastal states. Others wanted a federally subsidized turnpike from Maine to Georgia. But consensus was hard to come by. Internal improvements were subject to local ambitions, and they were doubtful constitutionally as well. Congress agreed to complete the National Road, but President Madison and his Republican successor James Monroe both refused to support

The Bank of the United States   The classical Greek facade of the Bank of the United States reinforced its image as a conservative, centralizing — but still republican — financial force.

further internal improvements without a constitutional amendment. In 1822 Monroe even vetoed a bill authorizing repairs on the National Road, stating once again that the Constitution did not empower the federal government to build roads within the sovereign states.

With a national government that was squeamish about internal improvements, state governments took up the cause. As a result, the transportation network that took shape after 1815 reflected the designs of the most ambitious states rather than the nationalizing dreams of men like Henry Clay. New York's Erie Canal was the most spectacular accomplishment, but the canal systems of Pennsylvania and Ohio were almost as impressive. Before 1830 most toll roads were built and owned by corporations chartered by state governments, with the governments providing $5 million of the $30 million that it cost to build the roads. State expenditures on canals and railroads were even greater. Fully $41.2 million of the $58.6 million spent on the canals before 1834 came from state governments. And of the $137 million spend on railroads before 1843, over one-third was put up by the states. Much of the rest came from foreign investors. Private entrepreneurs could not have built the transportation network that brought the market economy into being without the active support of state governments — through direct funding, through bond issues, and through the granting of corporate charters that gave the turnpike, canal, and railroad com-

panies the privileges and immunities that made them attractive to private investors.

Markets and the Law

The Revolution replaced British courts with national and state legal systems based in English common law — systems that made legal action accessible to most white males. Thus many of the disputes generated in the transition to market society ended up in court. The courts removed social conflicts from the public arena and brought them into a peaceful courtroom. There they dealt with the conflicts in language that only lawyers understood and resolved them in ways that tended to promote the entrepreneurial use of private property, the sanctity of contracts, and the right to do business shielded from neighborhood restraints and the tumult of democratic politics.

John Marshall, who presided over the Supreme Court from 1801 to 1835, took the lead. From the beginning he saw the Court as a conservative hedge against the excesses of democratically elected legislatures. His early decisions protected the independence of the courts and their right to review legislation (see Chapter 9). From 1816 onward, his decisions encouraged business and strengthened the national government at the expense of the states. Marshall's most important decisions protected the sanctity of contracts and corporate charters against state legislatures. For example, in *Dartmouth College* v. *Woodward* (1816), Dartmouth was defending a royal charter granted in the 1760s against changes introduced by a Republican legislature that was determined to transform Dartmouth from a privileged bastion of Federalism into a state college. Daniel Webster, who was both a Dartmouth alumnus and the school's highly paid lawyer, finished his argument before the Supreme Court on an emotional note: "It is, sir, as I have said, a small college. And yet there are those who love it—." Reputedly moved to tears, Marshall ruled that Dartmouth's corporate charter could not be altered by a state legislature. Though in this case the Supreme Court was protecting Dartmouth's independence and its chartered privileges, Marshall and Webster knew that the decision also protected the hundreds of turnpike and canal companies, manufacturing corporations, and other ventures that held privileges under corporate charters granted by state governments. Once the charters had been granted, the states could neither regulate the corporations nor cancel their privileges. Thus corporate charters acquired the legal status of contracts, beyond the reach of democratic politics.

Two weeks after deciding the Dartmouth case, Marshall handed down the majority decision in *Mc-Culloch* v. *Maryland*. The Maryland legislature, nurturing old Jeffersonian doubts about the constitutionality of the Bank of the United States, had attempted to tax the Bank's Baltimore branch, and the Bank had challenged the legislature's right to do so. Marshall decided in favor of the Bank. He stated, first, that the Constitution granted the federal government "implied powers" that included chartering the Bank, and he denied Maryland's right to tax the Bank or any other federal agency: "The power to tax," he said, "involves the power to destroy." It was Marshall's most explicit blow against Jeffersonian strict constructionism. Americans, he said, "did not design to make their government dependent on the states." And yet there were many, particularly in Marshall's native South, who remained certain that that was precisely what the founders had intended.

In *Gibbons* v. *Ogden* (1824) the Marshall Court broke a state-granted steamship monopoly in New York. The monopoly, Marshall argued, interfered with federal jurisdiction over interstate commerce. Like the Dartmouth case and *McCulloch* v. *Maryland,* this decision empowered the national government in relation to the states. And like them, it encour-

aged private entrepreneurialism. As much as Congressmen who supported the American System, John Marshall's Supreme Court assumed that a natural and beneficial link existed between federal power and market society.

Meanwhile, the state courts were working quieter but equally profound transformations of American law. In the early republic, state courts had often viewed property not only as a private possession but as part of a neighborhood. Thus when a miller built a dam that flooded upriver farms or impaired the fishery, the courts might make him take those interests into account, often in ways that reduced the business uses of his property. By the 1830s, New England courts were routinely granting the owners of industrial millsites unrestricted water rights, even when the exercise of those rights inflicted damage on their neighbors. As early as 1805, the New York Supreme Court in *Palmer* v. *Mulligan* had asserted that the right to develop property for business purposes was inherent in the ownership of property. A Kentucky court, asked to decide whether a railroad could come into downtown Louisville despite the protests of residents over the noise and the showers of sparks, decided that the public need for transportation outweighed the danger and annoyance to nearby residents. Railroads were necessary, and "private injury and personal damage . . . must be expected." "The onward spirit of the age," concluded the Kentucky court, "must, to a reasonable extent, have its way." In the courts of northern and western states, that "onward spirit" demanded legal protection for the business uses of private property, even when such uses conflicted with old common law restraints.

THE TRANSPORTATION REVOLUTION

After 1815 dramatic improvements in transportation—more and better roads, steamboats, canals, and finally railroads—tied old communities together and penetrated previously isolated neighborhoods. It was these improvements that made the transition to a market society physically possible.

Transportation in 1815

In 1815 the United States was a rural nation stretching from the old settlements on the Atlantic coast to the trans-Appalachian frontier, with transportation facilities that ranged from primitive to nonexistent. Americans despaired of communicating, to say nothing of doing business on a national scale. In 1816 a Senate committee reported that $9 would move a ton of goods across the 3,000-mile expanse of the North Atlantic from Britain to the United States; the same $9 would move the same ton of goods only 30 miles inland. A year later, the cost of transporting wheat from the new settlement of Buffalo to New York City was three times greater than the selling price of wheat in New York. Farming for profit made sense only for farmers near urban markets or with easy river access to the coast.

West of the Appalachians, transportation was almost entirely undeveloped. Until about 1830, most westerners were southern yeomen who settled near tributaries of the Ohio-Mississippi River system—a network of navigable streams that reached the sea at New Orleans. Frontier farmers floated their produce downriver on jerry-built flatboats; at New Orleans it was transshipped to New York and other eastern ports. Most boatmen knocked down their flatboats, sold the lumber and then walked home to Kentucky or Ohio over the dangerous Natchez Trace.

Transporting goods *to* the western settlements was even more difficult. Keelboatmen like the legendary Mike Fink could navigate upstream—using eddies and back currents, sailing when the wind was right, but usually poling their boat against the current. Skilled crews averaged only fifteen miles a day, and the trip from New Orleans to Louisville took three to four months. (The downstream trip took a month.) Looking for better routes, some merchants dragged finished goods across Pennsylvania and into the West at Pittsburgh, but transport costs made these goods prohibitively expensive. Consequently the trans-Appalachian settlements—home to one in five Americans by 1820—remained marginal to the market economy. By 1815 New Orleans was shipping about $5 million of western produce annually—an average of only $15 per farm family in the interior.

Improvements

In 1816 Congress resumed construction of the National Road (first authorized in 1802) that linked the Potomac River with the Ohio River at Wheeling, Virginia. The smooth, crushed-rock thoroughfare reached Wheeling in 1818. At about the same time, Pennsylvania extended the Lancaster Turnpike to make it run from Philadelphia to the Ohio River at Pittsburgh. These ambitious roads into the West, however, had few effects. The National Road made it easier for settlers and a few merchants' wagons to reach the West. But the cost of moving bulky farm produce over the road remained very high. Eastbound traffic on the National Road consisted largely of cattle and pigs, which carried themselves to market. Farmers continued to float their corn, cotton, wheat, salt pork, and whiskey south by river boat and thence to eastern markets.

It was the steamboat that first made commercial agriculture feasible in the West. Tinkerers and mechanics had been experimenting with steam-powered boats for a generation or more when an entrepreneur named Robert Fulton launched the *Clermont* on an upriver trip from New York City to Albany in 1807. Over the next few years Americans developed flat-bottomed steamboats that could navigate rivers even at low water. The first steamboat reached Louisville from New Orleans in 1815. Two years later, with seventeen steamboats already working western rivers, the *Washington* made the New Orleans–Louisville run in twenty-five days, a feat that convinced westerners that two-way river trade was possible. By 1820, sixty-nine steamboats were operating on western rivers. The 60,000 tons of produce that farmers and planters had shipped out of the interior in 1810 grew to 500,000 tons in 1840. By the eve of the Civil War 2,000,000 tons of western produce—most of it southwestern cotton—reached the docks at New Orleans. The steamboat had transformed the interior from an isolated frontier into a busy commercial region that traded farm and plantation products for manufactured goods.

In the East, state governments created rivers where nature had made none. In 1817 Governor DeWitt Clinton talked the New York legislature into building a canal linking the Hudson River with Lake Erie—thus opening a continuous water route between the Northwest and New York City. The Erie Canal was a near-visionary feat of engineering: designed by self-taught engineers and built by gangs of Irish immigrants, local farmboys, and convict laborers, it stretched 364 miles from Albany to Buffalo. Although "Clinton's Ditch" passed through carefully chosen level ground, it required a complex system of eighty-three locks, and it passed over eighteen rivers on stone aqueducts. Construction began in 1819,

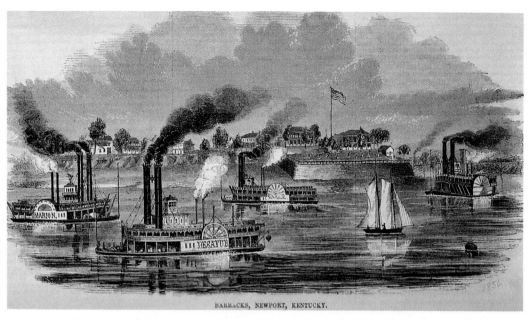

BARRACKS, NEWPORT, KENTUCKY.

Ohio River Traffic near Newport, Kentucky, in the 1850s   Steamboats, traveling with equal ease up and down river, revolutionized the river trade.

and the canal reached Buffalo in 1825. It was clear even before then that the canal would repay New York state's investment of $7.5 million many times over, and that it would transform the territory that it served.

The Erie Canal's first and most powerful effects were on western New York, which had been a raw frontier accessible to the East only over a notoriously bad state road. By 1830 the New York corridor of the Erie Canal, settled largely from hill-country New England, was one of the world's great grain-growing regions, dotted with market towns and new cities like Syracuse, Rochester, and Buffalo.

The Erie Canal was an immense success, and legislators and entrepreneurs in other states joined a canal boom that lasted for twenty years. When construction began on the Erie Canal there were fewer then 100 miles of canal in the United States. By 1840 there were 3,300 miles, nearly all of it in the Northeast and Northwest. Northwestern states, Ohio in particular, built ambitious canal systems that linked isolated areas to the Great Lakes and thus to the Erie Canal. Northeastern states followed suit: a canal between Worcester and Providence linked the farms of central Massachusetts with Narragansett Bay. Another canal linked the coal mines of northeastern

Pennsylvania with the Hudson River at Kingston, New York. In 1835 Pennsylvania completed a canal from Philadelphia to Pittsburgh, though at one point goods were shifted onto an unwieldy railroad that crossed a mountain.

The first American railroads connected burgeoning cities to rivers and canals. The Baltimore and Ohio Railroad, for example, linked Baltimore to the rivers of the West. Although the approximately 3,000 miles of railroads built between the late 1820s and 1840 helped the market positions of some cities, they did not constitute a national or even a regional rail network. A national system was created by the 5,000 miles of track laid in the 1840s and by the flurry of railroad building that gave the United States a rail network of 30,000 miles by 1860—a continuous, integrated system that created massive links between the East and the Northwest and that threatened to put canals out of business. In fact, the New York Central, which paralleled the Erie Canal, rendered that canal obsolete. Other railroads, particularly in the Northwestern states, replaced canal and river transport almost completely, even though water transport remained cheaper. By 1860 few farmers in the North and West lived more than twenty road miles from railroads, canals, and rivers that could

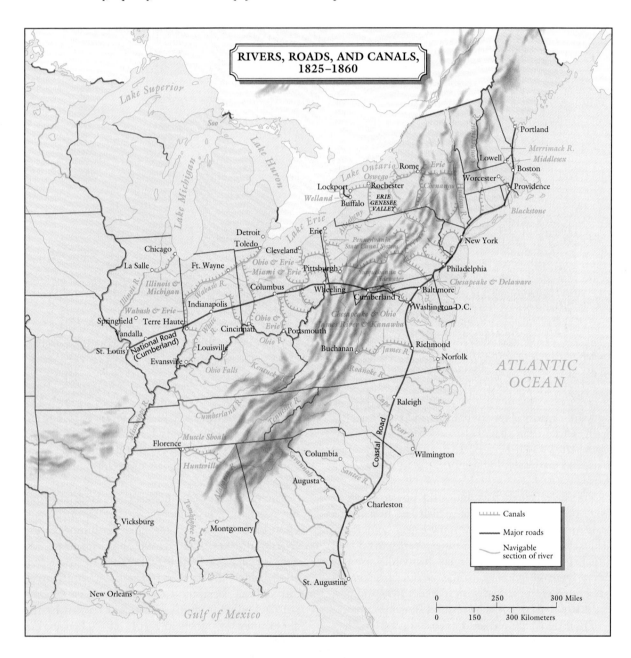

RIVERS, ROADS, AND CANALS,
1825–1860

deliver their produce to regional, national, and international markets.

Time and Money

The transportation revolution brought a dramatic reduction in the time and money it took to move heavy goods. Turnpikes cut the cost of wagon transport in half between 1816 and 1860—from 30 cents per ton mile to 15 cents. In 1816 freight rates on the Ohio-Mississippi system had been 1.3 cents per ton mile for downriver travel and 5.8 cents for upriver travel; steamboats cut both costs to a bit more than a third of a cent. The Erie Canal and the Ohio canals reduced the distance between East and West and carried goods at about a cent per ton mile; the railroads of the 1850s carried freight much faster, though at two to three times the cost. And the longer the

The Erie Canal   The complex of locks on the Erie Canal at Lockport, New York, was among the most admired engineering feats of the 1820s and 1830s. The town itself, filled with boatmen and construction workers, had a reputation for violence.

haul the greater the per-mile savings: overall, the cost of moving goods over long distances dropped 95 percent between 1815 and 1860.

Improvements in speed were nearly as dramatic. The overland route from Cincinnati to New York in 1815 (by keelboat upriver to Pittsburgh, then by wagon the rest of the way) had taken a minimum of fifty-two days. Steamboats traveled from Cincinnati to New Orleans, then passed goods on to coasting ships that finished the trip to New York City in a total of twenty-eight days. By the 1840s, upriver steamboats carried goods to the terminus of the Main Line Canal at Pittsburgh, which delivered them to Philadelphia, which sent them by train to New York City for a total transit time of eighteen to twenty days. At about the same time, the Ohio canal system enabled Cincinnati to send goods north through Ohio, across Lake Erie, over the Erie Canal, and down the Hudson to New York City—an all-water route that reduced costs and made the trip

in eighteen days. By 1852 the Erie Railroad and its connectors could make the Cincinnati–New York City run—though at a higher cost than water routes—in six to eight days. Similar improvements occurred in the densely settled and increasingly urbanized Northeast. By 1840 travel time between the big northeastern cities had been reduced to from one-fourth to one-eleventh of what it had been in 1790, with people, goods, and information traveling at an average of fifteen miles an hour. It was such improvements in speed and economy that made a national market economy possible.

By 1840 improved transportation had made a market revolution. Foreign trade, which had driven American economic growth up to 1815, continued to expand. The value of American exports in 1815 had stood at $52.6 million; imports totaled $113 million. Both rose dramatically in the years of the market revolution: exports (now consisting more of southern cotton than of northern food crops)

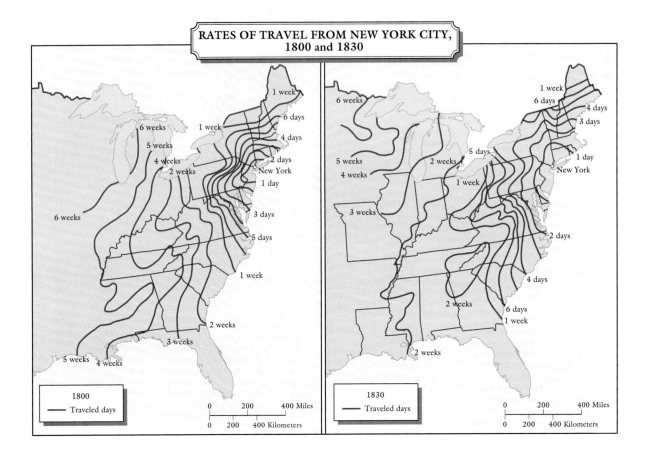

RATES OF TRAVEL FROM NEW YORK CITY, 1800 and 1830

increased sixfold to $333.6 million by 1860; imports (mostly European manufactured goods) tripled to $353.6 million. Yet the increases in foreign trade represented vast reductions in the *proportion* of American market activity that involved other countries. Before 1815 Americans had exported about 15 percent of their total national product; by 1830 exports accounted for only 6 percent of total production. The reason for this shift was that after 1815 the United States developed self-sustaining domestic markets for farm produce and manufactured goods. The great engine of economic growth—particularly in the North and West—was not the old colonial relationship with Europe but a self-sustaining internal market.

Markets and Regions

Henry Clay and other proponents of the American System dreamed of a market-driven economy that would transcend sectionalism and create a unified United States. But until at least 1840 the market revolution produced greater results within regions than between them. The farmers of New England traded food for finished goods from Boston, Lynn, Lowell, and other towns in what was becoming an urban, industrial region. Philadelphia sold its manufactures to and bought its food from the farmers of the Delaware Valley. Although the Erie Canal created a huge potential for interregional trade, until 1839 most of its eastbound tonnage originated in western New York. In the West, market-oriented farmers fed such rapidly growing cities as Rochester, Cleveland, Chicago, and Cincinnati, which in turn supplied the farmers with locally manufactured farm tools, furniture, shoes, and other goods. Farther south, the few plantations that did not produce their own food bought surpluses from farmers in their own region. Thus until about 1840 the market revolution was more a regional than an interregional phenomenon.

In the 1840s and 1850s, however, the new transport networks turned the increasingly industrial Northeast

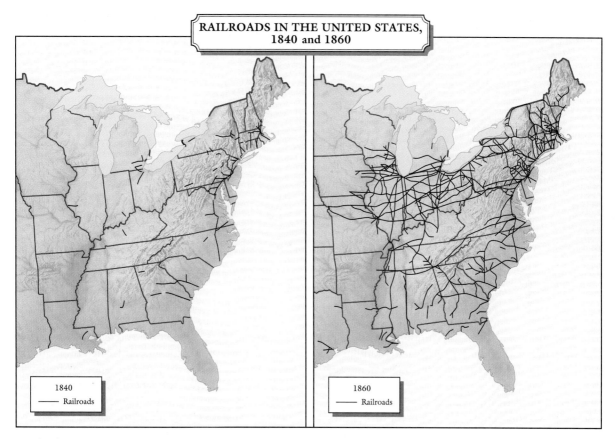

RAILROADS IN THE UNITED STATES, 1840 and 1860

1840
— Railroads

1860
— Railroads

See also the transportation maps in Chapter 15.

and mid-Atlantic and the commercial farms of the Old Northwest into a unified market society. The earliest settlers in the Northwest were southerners who had carried on a limited trade through the river system that led to New Orleans. From the 1840s onward produce left the Northwest less often by the old Ohio River route than by canal and railroad directly to the Northeast. Of the total produce exported from the Old Northwest in 1853, only 29 percent went by way of the river system; 60 percent went by way of the Erie Canal alone. At the same time, canals and roads from New York, Philadelphia, and Baltimore became the favored passageways for commodities *entering* the West. As early as 1835, 55 percent of the West's imported sugar, salt, iron, and coffee entered the region by the Great Lakes, Pennsylvania, or Wheeling routes. By 1853 that figure stood at 71 percent. In those years the Ohio-Mississippi river system carried vastly increased amounts of goods. But that increase, particularly after 1840, added up to a shrinking share of the expanded total. In short, western

farmers and northeastern businessmen and manufacturers were building a national market from which the South was largely excluded.

FROM YEOMAN TO BUSINESSMAN: THE RURAL NORTH AND WEST

In the old communities of the Northeast, the market revolution sent some of the young people off to cities and factory towns and others to the West. Those who remained at home engaged in new forms of agriculture on a transformed rural landscape, while their cousins in the Northwest transformed a wilderness into cash-producing farms.

The Old Settlements

An early nineteenth-century New England farm geared toward family subsistence required only three acres of cultivated land, twelve acres of pasture and

The First Railroad Train on the Hudson and Mohawk Railroad   The earliest locomotives were simply steam engines on wheels;
passenger cars were modeled on horse-drawn carriages.

meadow, another acre for the house, outbuildings, and vegetable garden, and a thirty-acre woodlot to stoke the hearth that cooked the food and heated the house. Visitors to even the oldest towns found farmsteads, tilled fields, and pastures scattered across a heavily wooded landscape. Eighteenth-century overcrowding had encouraged some farmers to turn woodlots into poor farmland. In the nineteenth century, however, millions of trees were stripped from the New England countryside and livestock raising replaced mixed farming. New Englanders who tried to grow grain on their rocky, worn-out soil could not compete with the farmers of western New York and the Old Northwest with their fertile lands and ready access to markets. At the same time, however, the factories and cities of the Northeast provided Yankee farmers with a market for meat and other perishables. Beef became the great New England cash crop. Dairy products were not far behind, and the proximity to city markets encouraged the spread of poultry and egg farms, fruit orchards, and truck gardens. The burgeoning shoe industry bought leather from the farmers, and woolen mills created a demand for wool. In 1840 there were 5.75 times more sheep than people in Vermont.

The rise of livestock specialization reduced the amount of land under cultivation. Early in the century New Englanders still tilled their few acres in the old three-year rotation: corn the first year, rye the second, fallow the third. By the 1820s and 1830s, as farmers raised more livestock and less grain, the land that remained in cultivation was farmed more intensively. Farmers saved manure and ashes for fertilizer, plowed more deeply and systematically, and tended their crops more carefully. These improved techniques, along with cash from the sale of their livestock and the availability of food at stores, encouraged Yankee farmers to allocate less and less land to the growing of food crops. In Concord, Massachusetts—the home town of the agrarian republic—the portion of town land in tillage dropped from 20 percent to 7 percent between 1771 and 1850.

The transition to livestock raising transformed woodlands into open pastures. As farmers leveled the forests, they sold the wood to fuel-hungry cities. In 1829 a cord of wood sold for $1.50 in Maine and for $7 in Boston. Over the next decade manufacturers began marketing cast-iron stoves that heated houses more cheaply and more efficiently than open hearths, and canals brought cheap Pennsylvania anthracite to the Northeast. Farmers who needed pastureland could gain substantial one-time profits from the sale of cut wood. The result was massive deforestation. In 1790, in the central Massachusetts town of Petersham, forest covered 85 percent of the town lands. By 1830 the creation of pastureland through commercial woodcutting had reduced the forested area to 30 percent. By 1850 woods covered only 10 percent of the town, the pasturelands were overgrazed and ruined, and the landscape was dotted

A New England Farm in the 1840s   A woman stands in the doorway with a broom; another woman tends barnyard animals. A man and a boy drive into the farmyard, perhaps from the outlying fields.

with abandoned farms. The pattern was the same throughout New England. At the beginning of European settlement, 95 percent of the region had been covered by forest. By 1850 forest covered only 30 percent of Connecticut, 32 percent of Rhode Island, 40 percent of Massachusetts, 45 percent of Vermont, and 50 percent of New Hampshire.

On that denuded landscape, poor families with many children continued to supplement their income with industrial outwork (see Chapter 8). But the quickening of market activity brought new kinds of dependence. Before the 1820s outworkers had used local raw materials like wool, leather, and flax and had spent only their spare time on such work. Merchants who bought their finished products often complained that they kept their best work for themselves and for exchange with their neighbors. In the 1820s the manufacture of shoes and textiles began to be concentrated in factories, and outworkers who remained were reduced to dependence. Merchants now provided them with raw materials with which to make such items as cloth-covered buttons and palm-leaf hats (imported materials that only merchants could supply), and set the pace of labor and the quality of the finished goods. In the 1830s fully 33,000 New England women were fashioning palm-leaf hats in their homes, far more than the 20,000 who worked in New England's much-publicized

cotton mills. Although outwork still helped poor families to maintain their independence, control of their labor had passed to merchants and other agents of the regional economy.

With the shift to specialized market agriculture, New England farmers became customers for necessities that their forebears had produced themselves or had acquired through barter. They heated their houses with coal dug by Pennsylvania miners. They wore cotton cloth made by the factory women at Lowell. New Hampshire farm girls made straw hats for them, and the craftsmen of Lynn made their shoes. By 1830 or so, many farmers were even buying their food. The Erie Canal and the western grain belt sent flour from Rochester into eastern neighborhoods where grain was no longer grown. Many farmers found it easier to produce specialized crops for market, and to buy butter, cheese, eggs, and vegetables at country stores.

The turning point came in the 1820s. The storekeepers of Northampton, Massachusetts, for instance, had been increasing their stock in trade by about 7 percent per decade since the late eighteenth century. In the 1820s they increased it 45 percent and now carried not only local farm products and sugar, salt, and coffee, but bolts of New England cloth, sacks of western flour, a variety of necessities and little luxuries from the wholesale houses of New York City

A New England Country Store   A Massachusetts country store of the 1830s was a community gathering place, a market for farm produce, and the source of a growing variety of commodities from the outside world.

and Boston, and pattern samples from which to order silverware, dishes, wallpaper, and other household goods. Those goods were better than what could be made at home and were for the most part cheaper. The price of finished cloth, for instance, declined six-fold between 1815 and 1830; as a result, spinning wheels and handlooms disappeared from the farm houses of New England. Farm families preferred pies and bread made from western white flour to the old "Rye and Injun" (see Chapter 8), and gladly turned their woodlands and unproductive grain fields into cash-producing pastures. Coal and cast-iron stoves replaced the family hearth.

Material standards of living rose. But more and more families "felt" poor, and many more were incapable of feeding, clothing, and warming themselves in years when the market failed. By the 1820s and 1830s northeastern farmers depended on markets in ways that their fathers and grandfathers would have considered dangerous not only to family welfare but to the welfare of the republic itself.

The Northwest

One reason the market revolution in the Northeast went as smoothly as it did was that young people

with little hope of inheriting land in the old settlements moved away to towns and cities or to the new farmlands of the Northwest. It was between 1815 and 1840—precisely the years in which northeastern agriculture became a cash-crop business— that migrants from the older areas transformed the Northwest Territory into a working agricultural landscape. In 1789 there had been no American settlers in the whole of the Territory. When the Treaty of Greenville made southern and eastern Ohio safe, settlers poured in. By 1800 the white population of Ohio numbered 45,365. In 1810 the population of Ohio, Indiana, and Illinois numbered 267,562, and settlement skyrocketed after the peace of 1815. By 1830 1,438,379 whites were living in Ohio, Indiana, and Illinois. By 1860 the population of those three states, along with that of the new states of Wisconsin and Michigan, numbered 6,926,884—22 percent of the nation's total population. (With the inclusion of the Old Southwest, nearly half of the population was west of the Appalachians; the geographic center of population was near Chillicothe, Ohio.)

In the Northwest until about 1830 most settlers were yeomen from Kentucky and Tennessee, usually a generation removed from Virginia, the Carolinas, and western Maryland. They moved along the Ohio and up the Muskingum, Miami, Scioto, Wabash, and Illinois Rivers to set up farms in the southern and central counties of Ohio, Indiana, and Illinois. When southerners moved north of the Ohio River into territory that banned slavery, they often did so saying that slavery blocked opportunities for poor whites. The Methodist preacher Peter Cartwright left Kentucky thinking, "I would get entirely clear of the evil of slavery," and "could raise my children to work where work was not thought a degradation." Similar hopes drew thousands of other southern yeomen north of the Ohio.

But even those who rejected slavery seldom rejected southern folkways. Like their kinfolk in Kentucky and Tennessee, the farmers of southern and central Ohio, Indiana, and Illinois remained tied to the river trade and to a mode of agriculture that favored free-ranging livestock over cultivated fields. The typical farmer fenced in a few acres of corn and left the rest of his land in woods to be roamed by southern hogs known as "razorbacks" and "land sharks." As late as 1860, southern-born farmers in the Northwest averaged twenty hogs apiece. These animals were thin and tough (they seldom grew to over 200 pounds), and they could run long distances, leap fences, fend for themselves in the woods, and walk to distant markets. They were notoriously fierce; many more settlers were injured by their own hogs than by wild animals. When it was time to gather the hogs for slaughter, many settlers played it safe and hunted them with guns.

The southern-born pioneers of the Northwest, like their cousins across the Ohio River, depended more on their families and neighbors than on distant markets. Newcomers found that they could neither rent tools from their southern neighbors nor present them with "gifts" during hard times. Southerners insisted on repaying debts in kind and on lending tools rather than renting them—thus engaging outsiders in the elaborate network of "neighboring" through which transplanted southerners made their livings. As late as the 1840s, in the bustling town of Springfield, Illinois, barter was the preferred system of exchange. "In no part of the world," said a Scotsman in southern Illinois, "is *good neighborship* found in greater perfection than in the western territory."

Around 1830 a stream of northeastern migrants entered the Northwest via the Erie Canal and on Great Lakes steamships. They filled the new lands of Wisconsin and Michigan and the northern counties of the older northwestern states. Most of them were New Englanders who had spent a generation in western New York (such settlers accounted for three-fourths of the early population of Michigan). The rest came directly from New England or—from the 1840s onward—from Germany and Scandinavia. Arriving in the Northwest along the market's busiest arteries, they duplicated the intensive, market-oriented farming they had known at home. They penned their cattle and hogs and fattened them up, making them bigger and worth more than those farther south. They planted their land in grain and transformed the region—beginning with western New York's Genesee Country in the 1820s and rolling through the Northwest—into one of the world's great wheat-producing regions. In 1820 the Northwest had exported only 12 percent of its agricultural produce. By 1840 that figure had risen to 27 percent, and it stood even higher among northern-born grain farmers. By 1860 the Northwest, intensively commercialized and tied by canals and railways to eastern markets, was exporting 70 percent of its wheat. In that year it produced 46 percent of the nation's wheat crop, nearly all of it north of the line of southern settlement.

The new settlers were notably receptive to improvements in farming techniques. While there were plenty of southern proponents of "progress" and plenty of "backward" northerners, the line between new and old agricultural ways separated northern grain farmers from corn, hogs, and southern settlers. In breaking new land, for instance, southerners still used the old shovel plow, which dug a shallow furrow and skipped over roots. Northerners preferred newer, more expensive cast-iron plows, which cut cleanly through oak roots four inches thick. By the 1830s the efficient, expensive grain cradle had become the standard harvest tool in northwestern wheat fields. From the 1840s onward, even this advanced hand tool was replaced by mass-produced machinery such as the McCormick reaper. Instead of threshing their grain by driving cattle and horses over it, farmers bought new horse-powered and treadmill threshers and used hand-cranked fanning mills to speed the process of cleaning the grain.

Most agricultural improvements were tailored to grain and dairy farming, and were taken up most avidly by the northern farmers. Others rejected them as expensive and "unnatural." They thought that cast-iron plows poisoned the soil and that fanning mills made a "wind contrary to nater," and thus offended God. John Chapman, an eccentric Yankee

The Testing of the First Reaping Machine Near Steele's Tavern. Va. A.D. 1831.

The McCormick Reaper   The best-known machine in American wheat fields was Cyrus McCormick's mechanical reaper. He tested the first model near his home in Virginia in 1831; by the 1850s his Chicago factory turned out twenty thousand reapers each year for Midwestern farmers.

who earned the nickname "Johnny Appleseed" by planting apple tree cuttings in southern Ohio and Indiana before the settlers arrived, planted only low-yield, common trees; he regarded grafting, which farmers farther north and east were using to improve the quality of their applies, as "against nature." Southerners scoffed at the Yankee fondness for mechanical improvements, the systematic breeding of animals and plants, careful bookkeeping, and farm techniques learned from magazines and books. "I reckon," said one, "I know as much about farming as the printers do."

Conflict between intensive agriculture and older, less market-oriented ways reached comic proportions when the Illinois legislature imposed stiff penalties on farmers who allowed their small, poorly bred bulls to run loose and impregnate cows with questionable sperm, thereby depriving the owners of high-bred bulls of their breeding fees and rendering the systematic breeding of cattle impossible. When the poorer farmers refused to pen their bulls, the law was rescinded. A local historian explained that "there

was a generous feeling in the hearts of the people in favor of an equality of privileges, even among bulls."

Households

The market revolution transformed eighteenth-century households into nineteenth-century homes. For one thing, Americans began to limit the size of their families. White women who married in 1800 had given birth to an average of 6.4 children. Those who married between 1800 and 1849 averaged 4.9 children. The decline was most pronounced in the North, particularly in commercialized areas. Rural birthrates remained at eighteenth-century levels in the southern uplands, in the poorest and most isolated communities of the North, and on the frontier. (As the New Yorker Washington Irving passed through the Northwest in the 1830s, he noted in his journal: "Illinois—famous for children and dogs—in house with nineteen children and thirty-seven dogs.") These communities practiced the old labor-intensive agriculture and relied on the labor of large families. For farmers who used newer techniques or switched to livestock, large families made less sense. Moreover, large broods hampered the ability of future-minded parents to provide for their children, and conflicted with new notions of privacy and domesticity that were taking shape among an emerging rural middle class.

The commercialization of agriculture was closely associated with the emergence of the concept of housework. Before 1815 farm wives had labored in the house, the barnyard, and the garden while their husbands and sons worked in the fields. With the market revolution came a sharper distinction between male work that was part of the cash economy and female work that was not. Even such traditional women's tasks as dairying, vegetable gardening, and poultry raising became men's work once they became cash-producing specialties. (A Pennsylvanian who lived among market-oriented New Englanders in the Northwest was appalled at such tampering with hallowed gender roles and wrote the Yankees off as "a shrewd, selfish, enterprising, cow-milking set of men.")

At the same time, new kinds of women's work emerged within households. Though there were fewer children to care for, the culture began to demand forms of child-rearing that were more intensive, individualized, and mother-centered. Store-bought white flour, butter, and eggs and the new iron stoves eased the burdens of food preparation, but they also created demands for pies, cakes, and other fancy foods that earlier generations had only dreamed of. And while farm women no longer spun and wove their own cloth, the availability of manufactured cloth created the expectation that their families would dress more neatly and with greater variety than they had in the past—at the cost of far more time spent by women on sewing, washing, and ironing. Similar expectations demanded greater personal and domestic cleanliness, and farm women from the 1830s onward spent time planting flower beds, cleaning and maintaining prized furniture, mirrors, rugs, and ceramics, and scrubbing floors and children. The market and housework grew hand in hand: among the first mass-produced commodities in the United States was the household broom.

Housework was tied to new notions of privacy, decency, and domestic comfort. Before 1820 farmers cared little about how their houses looked, often tossing trash and garbage out the door for the pigs and

A Soap Advertisement from the 1850s   The rigors of "Old Washing Day" lead the mother to abuse the children and house pets, while her husband leaves the house. With American Cream Soap, domestic bliss returns: The children and cats are happy, the husband returns, and the wife has time to sew.

chickens that foraged near the house. In the 1820s and 1830s, as farmers began to grow cash crops and adopt middle-class ways, they began to plant shade trees and kept their yards free of trash. They painted their houses and sometimes their fences and outbuildings, arranged their woodpiles into neat stacks, surrounded their houses with flowers and ornamental shrubs, and tried to hide their privies from view. The new sense of refinement and decorum extended into other aspects of country life. The practice of chewing (and spitting) tobacco was gradually banned in churches and meeting halls, and in 1823 the minister in Shrewsbury, Massachusetts, ordered dogs out of the meetinghouse.

Inside, prosperous farm houses took on an air of privacy and comfort. Separate kitchens and iron stoves replaced open hearths. Many families used a set of matched dishes for individual place settings, and the availability of finished cloth permitted the regular use of table cloths, napkins, doilies, curtains, bedspreads, and quilts. Oil lamps replaced home-made candles, and the more prosperous families began to decorate their homes with wallpaper and upholstered furniture. Farm couples moved their beds away from the hearth and (along with the children's beds that had been scattered throughout the house) put them into spaces designated as bedrooms. They took the wash stands and basins, which were coming into more common use, out of the kitchen and put them into the bedroom, thus making sleeping, bathing, and sex more private than they had been in the past. At the center of this new house stood the farm wife, apart from the bustling world of commerce but decorating and caring for the amenities that commerce bought, and demanding that men respect the new domestic world that commerce had made possible.

Neighborhoods

By the 1830s and 1840s the market revolution had transformed the rural landscape of the Northeast. The forests had been reduced, the swamps had been drained, and most of the streams and rivers were interrupted by mill dams. Bears, panthers, and wolves had disappeared, along with the beaver and many of the fish. Now there were extensive pastures where English cattle and sheep browsed on English grasses dotted with English wildflowers like buttercups, daisies, and dandelions. Next to the pastures were neatly cultivated croplands that were regularly fertilized and seldom allowed to lie fallow. And at the center stood brightly painted houses and outbuildings surrounded by flowers and shrubs and vegetable gardens. Many towns, particularly in New England, had planted shade trees along the country roads, completing a rural landscape of straight lines and human cultivation—a landscape that made it easy to think of nature as a commodity to be altered and controlled.

Within that landscape, old practices and old forms of neighborliness fell into disuse. Neighbors continued to exchange goods and labor and to contract debts that might be left unpaid for years. But debts were more likely to be owed to profit-minded storekeepers and creditors, and even debts between neighbors were often paid in cash. Traditionally, storekeepers had allowed farmers to bring in produce and have it credited to a neighbor/creditor's account—a practice that made the storekeeper an agent of neighborhood bartering. In 1830 half of all

the stores in rural New England carried accounts of this sort; by 1850 that figure had dropped to one in four. Storekeepers began to demand cash payment or to charge lower prices to those who paid cash. The farm newspapers that appeared in these years urged farmers to keep careful records of the amount of fertilizer used, labor costs, and per-acre yields and discouraged them from relying on the old system of neighboring. Neighborly rituals like parties, husking bees, barn-raisings—with their drinking and socializing—were scorned as an inefficient and morally suspect waste of time. *The Farmer's Almanac* of 1833 warned New England farmers, "If you love fun, frolic, and waste and slovenliness more than economy and profit, then make a husking."

Thus the efficient farmer after the 1820s concentrated on producing commodities that could be marketed outside the neighborhood, and used his cash income to buy material comforts for his family and to pay debts and provide a cash inheritance for his children. Though much of the old world of household and neighborhood survived, farmers created a subsistence and maintained the independence of their households not through those spheres but through unprecedented levels of dependence on the outside world.

THE INDUSTRIAL REVOLUTION

In the fifty years following 1820 American cities grew faster than ever before or since. The old seaports—New York City in particular—grew rapidly in these years, but the fastest growth was in new cities that served commercial agriculture and in factory towns that produced for a largely rural domestic market. Even in the seaports, growth derived more from commerce with the hinterland than from international trade. Paradoxically, the market revolution in the countryside had produced the beginnings of industry and the greatest period of urban growth in U.S. history.

Factory Towns

Jeffersonians held that the United States must always remain rural. Americans, they insisted, could expand into the rich new agricultural lands of the West, trade their farm surpluses for European finished goods, and thus avoid creating cities with their dependent social classes. Federalists argued that Americans, in order to retain their independence, must produce their own manufactured goods. Neo-Federalists combined those arguments after the War of 1812. Along with other advocates of industrial expansion, they argued that America's abundant water power—particularly the fast-running streams of the Northeast—would enable Americans to build their factories across the countryside instead of creating great industrial cities. Such a decentralized factory system would provide employment for country women and children and thus subsidize the independence of struggling farmers. It was on those premises that the first American factories were built.

The American textile industry originated in industrial espionage. The key to the mass production of cotton and woolen textiles was a water-powered machine that spun yarn and thread. The machine had been invented and patented by the Englishman Richard Arkwright in 1769. The British government, to protect its lead in industrialization, forbade the machinery or the people who worked with it to leave the country. Scores of textile workers, however, defied the law and made their way to North America. One of them was Samuel Slater, who had served an apprenticeship under Jedediah Strutt, a partner of Arkwright who had improved on the original machine. Working from memory while employed by Moses Brown, a Providence merchant, Slater built the first Arkwright spinning mill in America at Pawtucket, Rhode Island, in 1790.

Slater's first mill was a small frame building tucked among the town's houses and craftsmen's shops. Though its capacity was limited to the spinning of cotton yarn, it provided work for children in the mill and for women who wove yarn into cloth in their homes. Thus this first mill satisfied the neo-Federalists' requirements: it did not require the creation of a factory town, and it supplemented the household incomes of farmers and artisans. As his business grew and he advertised for widows with children, however, Slater was greeted by families headed by landless, impoverished men. Slater's use of children from these families prompted "respectable" farmers and craftsmen to pull their children out of Slater's growing complex of mills. More poor families arrived to take their places, and during the first years of the century Pawtucket grew rapidly into a disorderly mill town.

Soon Slater and other mill owners built factory villages in the countryside where they could exert

Samuel Slater's Mill at Pawtucket, Rhode Island   The first mill was small, painted white, and topped with a cupola. Set among craftsmen's workshops and houses, it looked more like a Baptist meeting house than a first step into industrialization.

better control over their operations and their workers. The practice became known as the Rhode Island or "family" system. At Slatersville, Rhode Island, at Oxford, Massachusetts, and at other locations in southern New England, mill owners built whole villages surrounded by company-owned farmland that they rented to the husbands and fathers of their mill workers. The workplace was closely supervised, and drinking and other troublesome practices were forbidden in the villages. Fathers and older sons either worked on rented farms or as laborers at the mills. By the late 1820s Slater and most of the other owners were getting rid of the outworkers and were buying power looms, thus transforming the villages into disciplined, self-contained factory towns that turned raw cotton into finished cloth—but at great cost to old forms of household independence. When President Andrew Jackson visited Pawtucket in 1829, he remarked to Samuel Slater, "I understand you taught us how to spin, so as to rival Great Britain in her manufactures; you set all these thousands of spindles to work, which I have been delighted in viewing, and which have made so many happy, by a lucrative employment." "Yes sir," replied Slater. "I suppose that I gave out the psalm and they have been singing to the tune ever since."

A second act of industrial espionage was committed by a wealthy, cultivated Bostonian named Francis Cabot Lowell. Touring English factory districts in 1811, Lowell asked the plant managers questions and made secret drawings of the machines he saw. He also experienced a genteel distaste for the squalor of the English textile towns. Returning home, Lowell joined with wealthy friends to form the Boston Manufacturing Company—soon known as the Boston Associates. In 1813 they built their first mill at Waltham, Massachusetts, and then expanded into Lowell, Lawrence, and other new towns near Boston during the 1820s. The company built mills that differed from the early Rhode Island mills in two ways: first, they were heavily capitalized and as fully mechanized as possible; they turned raw cotton into finished cloth with little need for skilled workers. Second, the operatives who tended their machines were young, single women recruited from the farms of northern New England—farms that were switching to livestock raising, and thus had little need for the labor of daughters. The company provided carefully supervised boarding houses for them and enforced rules of conduct both on and off the job. The young women worked steadily, never drank, seldom stayed out late, and attended church faithfully. They dressed neatly—often stylishly—and read newspapers and attended lectures. They impressed visitors, particularly those who had seen factory workers in other places, as a dignified and self-respecting work force.

The brick mills and prim boarding houses set within landscaped towns and occupied by sober, well-behaved farm girls signified the Boston Associates' desire to build a profitable textile industry without creating a permanent working class. The women would work for a few years in a carefully controlled environment, send their wages back to their family, and return home to live as country housewives. These young farm women did in fact form an efficient, decorous work force. But the decorum was imposed less by the owners than by the women themselves. In order to protect their own reputations, they punished misbehavior and shunned fellow workers whose behavior was questionable. Nor did they send their wages home or, as was popularly believed, use them to pay for their brothers' college education. Some saved their money to use as dowries that their fathers could not afford. More, however, spent their wages on themselves—particularly on clothes and books.

The owners of the factories expected that the young women's sojourn would reinforce their own paternalistic position and that of the girls' fathers. Instead, it produced a self-respecting sisterhood of independent, wage-earning women. Twice in the 1830s the women of Lowell went out on strike, proclaiming that they were not wage slaves but "the daughters of freemen"; in the 1840s they were among the leaders of a labor movement in the region. After finishing their stint in the mills, a good many Lowell women entered public life as reformers. Most of them married and became housewives, but not on the same terms their mothers had known. One in three married Lowell men and became city dwellers. Those who returned home to rural neighborhoods remained unmarried longer than their sisters who had stayed at home and then married men about their own age who worked at something other than farming. Thus through the 1840s the Boston Associates kept their promise to produce cotton cloth profitably without creating a permanent working class. But they did not succeed in shuttling young women between rural and urban paternalism and back again. Wage labor, the ultimate degradation for agrarian-republican men, opened a road to independence for thousands of young women.

Cities

The market revolution hit American cities—the old seaport cities as well as the new marketing and manufacturing towns—with particular force. Here there was little concern for creating a classless industrial society: vastly wealthy men of finance, a new middle class that bought and sold an ever-growing range of consumer goods, and the impoverished women and men who produced those goods lived together in communities that unabashedly recognized the reality of social class.

The richest men were seaport merchants who had survived and prospered during the world wars that ended in 1815. They carried on as importers and exporters, took control of banks and insurance companies, and made great fortunes in urban real estate. Those in Boston constituted an elite, urbane, and responsible cluster of families known as the Boston Brahmins. The elite of Philadelphia was less unified and perhaps less responsible, that of New York even less. These families continued in international commerce, profiting mainly from cotton exports and from a vastly expanded range of imports.

Below the old mercantile elite (or, in the case of the new cities of the interior, at the top of society) stood a growing middle class of wholesale and retail merchants, master craftsmen who had transformed themselves into manufacturers, and an army of lawyers, salesmen, auctioneers, clerks, bookkeepers, and accountants who took care of the paperwork for a new market society. At the head of this new middle class were the wholesale merchants of the seaports who bought hardware, crockery, and other commodities from importers and then sold them in smaller lots to storekeepers from the interior. The greatest concentration of wholesale firms was on Pearl Street in New York City. Slightly below them were the large processors of farm products, including the meatpackers of Cincinnati and the flourmillers of Rochester, and large merchants and real estate dealers in the new cities of the interior. Another step down were specialized retail merchants who dealt in books, furniture, crockery, or some other consumer goods. In Hartford, Connecticut, for instance, the proportion of retailers who specialized in certain commodities rose from 24 percent to 60 percent between 1792 and 1845. Alongside the merchants stood master craftsmen who had become manufacturers. With their workers busy in backrooms or in household workshops, they now called themselves shoe dealers and merchant tailors. At the bottom of this new commercial world were hordes of clerks, most of them young men who hoped to rise in the world. Indeed many of them—one study puts the figure at between 25 and 38 percent—did move up in society. Both in numbers and in the nature of the work, this white-collar army formed a new class created by the market revolution—particularly by the emergence of a huge consumer market in the countryside.

In the 1820s and 1830s the commercial classes transformed the look and feel of American cities. As retailing and manufacturing became separate activities (even in firms that did both), the merchants, salesmen, and clerks now worked in quiet offices on downtown business streets. The seaport merchants built counting rooms and decorated their warehouses in the "new counting house style." Both in the seaports and the new towns of the interior, impressive brick and glass storefronts appeared on the main streets. Perhaps the most typical monu-

Women in the Mills   Two women weavers from a Massachusetts textile mill proudly display the tools of their trade. This tintype was taken in about 1860, when New England farm women such as these were being replaced by Irish immigrant labor.

ments of the self-conscious new business society were the handsome retail arcades that began going up in the 1820s. Boston's Quincy Market (1825), a two-story arcade on Philadelphia's Chestnut Street (1827), and Rochester's four-story Reynolds Arcade (1828) provided consumers with comfortable, gracious space in which to shop.

While businessmen were developing a new middle-class ethos, and while their families were flocking to the new retail stores to buy emblems of their status, the people who made the consumer goods were growing more numerous and at the same time were disappearing from view. With the exception of textiles and a few other commodities, few goods were made in mechanized factories before the 1850s. Most of the clothes and shoes, brooms, hats, books, furniture, candy, and other goods available in country stores and city shops were made

Charles Oakford's Hat Store in Philadelphia, about 1855   Such specialized retail establishments (unlike the craftsmen's shops that preceded them) hid the process of manufacturing from view.

by hand. City merchants and master craftsmen met the growing demand by hiring more workers. The largest handicrafts—shoemaking, tailoring, and the building trades—were divided into skilled and semiskilled segments and farmed out to subcontractors who could turn a profit only by cutting labor costs. The result was the creation of an urban working class, not only in the big seaports and factory towns but in scores of milling and manufacturing towns throughout the North and the West.

The rise of New York City's ready-made clothing trade provides an example. In 1815 wealthy Americans wore tailor-made clothing; everyone else wore clothes sewn by women at home. In the 1820s the availability of cheap manufactured cloth and an expanding pool of cheap—largely female—labor, along with the creation of the southern and western markets, transformed New York City into the center of a national market in ready-made clothes. The first big market was in "Negro cottons"—graceless, hastily assembled shirts, pants, and sack dresses with which southern planters clothed their slaves. Within a few years New York manufacturers were sending dungarees and hickory shirts to western farmers and supplying shoddy, inexpensive clothing to the growing ranks of urban workers. By the 1830s many New York tailoring houses, including the storied Brooks Brothers, were offering fancier ready-made clothes to members of the new middle class.

High rents and costly real estate, together with the absence of water power, made it impossible to set up large factories in cities. But the nature of the clothing trade and the availability of cheap labor gave rise to a system of subcontracting that transformed needlework into the first "sweated" trade in America. Merchants kept a few skilled male tailors to take care of the custom trade, and to cut cloth into patterned pieces for ready-made clothing. The pieces were sent out, often by way of subcontractors, to needleworkers who sewed them together in their homes. Male tailors continued to do the finishing work on men's suits. But most of the work—on cheap goods destined for the South and West—was done by women who worked long hours for piece rates that ranged from 75 cents to $1.50 per week. In 1860, Brooks Brothers, which concentrated on the high end of the trade, kept 70 workers in its shops and used 2,000 to 3,000 outworkers, most of them women. Along with clothing, women in garrets and tenements manufactured the items with which the middle class decorated itself and its homes: embroidery, doilies, artificial flowers, fringe, tassels, fancy-bound books, and parasols. All provided work for ill-paid legions of female workers. In 1860 25,000 women (about one-fourth of the total work force) worked in manufacturing jobs in New York City, fully two-thirds of them in the clothing trades.

Other trades followed similar patterns. For example, northeastern shoes were made in uniform sizes and sent in barrels all over the country. Like tailoring, shoemaking was divided into skilled operations and time-consuming unskilled tasks. The relatively skilled and highly paid work of cutting and shaping the uppers was performed by men; the drudgery of sewing the pieces together went to low-paid women. In the shops of Lynn, Massachusetts, in the shoemakers' boarding houses in Rochester and other new manufacturing cities of the interior, and in the cellars and garrets of New York City, skilled shoemakers performed the most difficult work for taskmasters who passed the work along to subcontractors who controlled poorly paid, unskilled workers. Skilled craftsmen could earn as much as $2 a day making custom boots and shoes. Men shaping uppers in boarding houses earned a little more than half of that; women binders could work a full week and earn as little as 50 cents. In this as in other trades, wage rates and gendered tasks reflected the old family division of labor, which was based on the assumption that female workers lived with an income-earning husband or father. In fact, increasing numbers of them were young women living alone or older women who had been widowed, divorced, or abandoned—often with small children.

In their offices, counting rooms, and shops, members of the new middle class entertained notions of gentility based on the distinction between manual and nonmanual work. Lowly clerks and wealthy merchants prided themselves on the fact that they worked with their heads and not their hands. They fancied that it was their entrepreneurial and managerial skills that were making the market revolution happen, while manual workers simply performed tasks thought up by the middle class. The old distinction between proprietorship and dependence—a distinction that had placed master craftsmen and independent tradesmen, along with farm-owning yeomen, among the respectable "middling sort"—disappeared. The men and women of an emerging working class struggled to create dignity and a sense of public worth in a society that hid them from view and defined them as "hands."

THE MARKET REVOLUTION IN THE SOUTH

With the end of war in 1815, the cotton belt of the South expanded dramatically. The resumption of international trade, the revival of textile production in Britain and on the continent, and the emergence of factory production in the northeastern United States

encouraged southern planters to extend the short-staple cotton lands of South Carolina and Georgia into a belt that would stretch across the Old Southwest and beyond the Mississippi into Texas and Arkansas. The speed with which that happened startled contemporaries: by 1834 the new southwestern states of Alabama, Mississippi, and Louisiana grew more than half the U.S. cotton crop; by 1859 these states, along with Georgia, produced fully 79 percent of American cotton.

The southwestern plantation belt produced stupendous amounts of cotton. In 1810 the South produced 178,000 bales of ginned cotton—more than 59 times the 3,000 bales it had produced in 1790. By 1820 production stood at 334,000 bales. With the opening of southwestern cotton lands, production jumped to 1,350,000 bales in 1840 and to 4,800,000 on the eve of the Civil War. Over these years cotton accounted for one-half to two-thirds of the value of all U.S. exports. The South produced three-fourths of the world supply of cotton—a commodity that, more than any other, was the raw material of industrialization in Britain and Europe and, increasingly, in the northeastern United States.

Plantation Labor

The plantations of the cotton belt were among the most intensely commercialized farms in the world. Many of them grew nothing but cotton—a practice that produced huge profits in good years but in bad years sent planters into debt and forced them to sell slaves and land. Other plantations grew supplementary cash crops and produced their own food. But nearly all of the plantation owners, from the proudest grandee to the ambitious farmer with a few slaves, organized their labor in ways that maximized production and reinforced the dominance of the white men who owned the farms.

Cotton, which requires a long growing season and a lot of attention, was well suited to slave labor and to the climate of the Deep South. After the land was cleared and ploughed, it was set out in individual plants. Laborers weeded the fields with hoes throughout the hot, humid growing season. In the fall, the cotton ripened unevenly. In a harvest season that lasted up to two months, pickers swept through the fields repeatedly, selecting only the ripe bolls. Plantations that grew their own food cultivated large cornfields and vegetable gardens and kept large

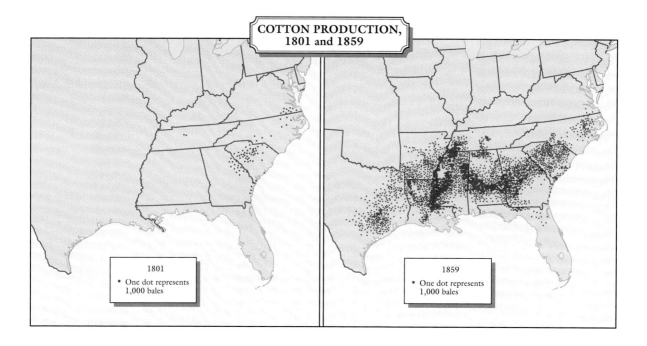

**COTTON PRODUCTION,
1801 and 1859**

1801
• One dot represents
1,000 bales

1859
• One dot represents
1,000 bales

numbers of hogs. To cope with diverse growing seasons and killing times that overlapped with the cotton cycle, planters created complex labor systems.

On a large plantation in Louisiana in the 1850s, Frederick Law Olmstead, a New York landscape architect, watched a parade of slaves going into the fields. First came the hoe gang: "forty of the largest and strongest women I ever saw together: they were all in a single uniform dress of bluish check stuff, and skirts reaching little below the knee; their legs and feet were bare; they carried themselves loftily, each with a hoe sloping over the shoulder and walking with a free powerful swing, like Zouaves on the march." Following the hoe gang came the "cavalry, thirty strong, mostly men, but some women, two of whom rode astride, on the plow mules."

Though this slave force was larger than most, its organization was familiar to every southerner: gangs of women wielded the hoes and men did the plowing, accompanied, especially during the busiest times, by strong women who rode "astride" (and not, like white ladies, side saddle). The division of labor by sex was standard: even at harvest festivals teams of men shucked the corn while women prepared the meal and the after-supper dance. And during the harvest, when every slave was in the fields, men tended to work beside men, women beside women. Most of the house slaves were women, and female

slaves often worked under the direction of the plantation mistress, seeing to the dairy cattle, chickens and geese, and tending vegetable gardens and orchards.

While black women routinely worked in southern fields, white women did so only on the poorest farms and only at the busiest times of the year. Like their northern cousins, they took care of the poultry and cattle and the vegetable gardens—and not the profit-oriented fields. As the larger farms grew into plantations, white women took on the task of supervising the household slaves instead of doing the work themselves. According to northern visitors, this association of labor with slavery encouraged laziness among southern whites and robbed work of the dignity it enjoyed in other parts of the country.

On the whole, the exploitation of slave labor after 1820 became both more systematic and more humane. An estimated 55 percent of southern slaves spent all their time cultivating cotton, and it was brutal work by any standards. The arduous chore of transforming wilderness into cotton land demanded steady work in gangs, as did the yearly cotton cycle itself. Planters paid close attention to labor discipline: they supervised the work more closely than in the past, tried (often unsuccessfully) to substitute gang labor for the task system, and forcibly "corrected" slaves whose work was slow or sloppy. At the same time, however, planters clothed the new discipline

Hauling the Whole Week's Picking   William Henry Brown made this collage of a slave harvest crew near Vicksburg, Mississippi in 1842. The rigors of the harvest put everyone, including small children, into the fields.

within a larger attempt to make North American slavery into a system that was both paternalistic and humane. Food and clothing seems to have improved, and individual cabins for slave families became standard. State laws often forbade the more brutal forms of discipline, and they uniformly demanded that slaves be given Sunday off. More and more, the slaves spent that day listening to Christian missionaries provided by the planters.

The systematic paternalism on nineteenth-century farms and plantations was the result both of planter self-interest and a genuine attempt to exert a kindly, paternal control over slaves that planters uniformly called "our people" or "our family, black and white." The Louisiana planter Bennet H. Barrow insisted that the master must make the slave "as comfortable at home as possible, affording him what is essentially necessary for his happiness—you must provide for him your self and by that means creat[e] in him a habit of perfect dependence on you." We shall see that slaves endured the discipline and accepted the food, clothing, time off, and religious instruction—but used all of them to serve themselves and not the masters (see Chapter 11). But for all that, material standards rose. One rough indicator is physical height. On the eve of the Civil War, southern slaves averaged about an inch shorter than northern whites. But they were fully three inches taller than newly imported Africans, two inches taller than slaves on the Caribbean island of Trinidad, and an inch taller than British Marines. While slaves suffered greater infant mortality than whites, those

who survived infancy lived out "normal" lifespans. The most telling evidence is that while Brazil, Cuba, and other slave societies had to import Africans to make up for the deaths of slaves, the slave population of the United States increased threefold—from 1,191,354 to 3,953,760—between 1810 and 1860. With the import of new Africans banned after 1808 (and with runaways outnumbering new Africans who were smuggled into the country), the increase was due entirely to the fact that—alone among slave populations of the Western Hemisphere—births outnumbered deaths among North American slaves.

Southern Yeomen

Cotton brought economies of scale: planters with big farms and many slaves operated more efficiently and more profitably than farmers with fewer resources. And as the price of slaves and good land rose, fewer and fewer owners shared in the profits of the cotton economy, and wealth became more concentrated. Good farmland with ready access to markets was dominated by large plantations. By 1861 only one in four southern white households owned slaves. The market revolution had commercialized southern agriculture, but a shrinking proportion of the region's white population shared in the benefits. The result was not simply an unequal distribution of wealth, but the creation of a dual economy: plantations at the commercial center and a white yeomanry on the fringes.

There were, of course, small farmers in the plantation counties—most of them on poor, hilly land far from navigable rivers. They tended to be commercial farmers, growing a few bales of cotton with family labor and perhaps a slave or two. Many of them were poor relatives of prosperous plantation owners. They voted the great planters into office, and used their cotton gins and tapped into their marketing networks. Some of them worked as overseers for their wealthy neighbors, sold them food, and served on local slave patrols. Economic disparities between planters and farmers in the plantation belt continued to widen, but the farmers remained tied to the cotton economy and its economic and social imperatives.

Most small farmers, however, lived away from the plantations in what was called the upcountry: to their old stronghold on the eastern slopes of the Appalachians from the Chesapeake through Georgia, the yeomanry added the western slopes of the mountains in Kentucky and Tennessee and the pine-covered hill country of northern Mississippi and Alabama, parts of Texas and Louisiana, and most of the Ozark Plateau in Missouri and Arkansas. All of these lands were too high, cold, isolated, and heavily wooded to support plantation crops. Here the farmers built a yeoman society that shared many of the characteristics of the eighteenth-century countryside, North and South (see Chapter 8). But while northern farmers commercialized, their southern cousins continued in a household- and neighborhood-centered agriculture until the Civil War and beyond. Indeed many southern farmers stayed outside the market almost entirely. The mountaineers of the southern Appalachians sent a trickle of livestock and timber out of their neighborhoods, but the mountains remained largely outside the market until the coming of big-business coal mines in the late nineteenth century. Moreover, farmers in large parts of the upcountry South preferred to raise livestock instead of growing cotton or tobacco. They planted cornfields and let their pigs run loose in the woods and on unfenced private land. In late summer and fall they rounded up the animals and sold them to drovers who conducted cross-country drives and sold the animals to flatland merchants and planters. These hill-country yeomen lived off a market with which they had little firsthand experience. It was a way of life that sustained some of the most fiercely independent neighborhoods in the country.

A larger group of southern yeomen practiced mixed farming for household subsistence and neighborhood exchange, with the surplus sent to market. Most of these farmers owned their own land. Indeed the settlement of new lands in the old backcountry and the southwestern states reversed the eighteenth-century growth of white tenancy (see Chapter 8). Few of these farmers kept slaves. In the counties of upland Georgia, for instance, between seven in ten and nine in ten households were without slaves. These farmers practiced a "subsistence plus" agriculture that was complicated by the nature of southern cash crops. Northern yeomen before 1815 had grown grain and livestock with which they fed their families and traded with neighbors. Whatever was left over they sent to market. But cotton, like tobacco and other southern cash crops, was not a food; it contributed nothing to family subsistence. Most middling and poor farmers played it safe: they put most of their land into subsistence crops and livestock, cultivating only a few acres of cotton. They devoted more acreage to cotton as transportation made markets more accessible—particularly when railroads penetrated piedmont neighborhoods in the 1850s—but few southern yeomen allowed themselves to become wholly dependent on the market. With the income from a few bales of cotton they could pay their debts and taxes and buy coffee, tea, sugar, tobacco, cloth, and shoes. But they continued to enter and leave the market at will, for their own purposes. The market served the interests of southern yeomen. It seldom dominated them.

This way of life discouraged acquisitiveness and ambition. Since few farms were self-sufficient, the yeomen farmers routinely traded labor and goods with each other. In the plantation counties, such cooperation tended to reinforce the power of planters who put some of their resources at the disposal of their poorer neighbors. In the upcountry, cooperation reinforced neighborliness. As one upland Georgian remarked, "Borrowing . . . was neighboring." Debts contracted within the network of kin and neighbors were generally paid in kind or in labor, and creditors often allowed their neighbors' debts to go unpaid for years.

Among southern neighborly restraints on entrepreneurialism, none was more distinctive than the region's attitude toward fences. Northerners never tired of comparing their neatly fenced farms with the dilapidated or absent fences of the South. In the bourgeois North, well-maintained fences were a sign of ambitious, hardworking farmers. The poor fences of the South, on the other hand, were a sign of laziness. Actually, the scarcity of fences in most southern neighborhoods was the result of local custom and state law. Georgia, for instance, required farmers to fence their planted fields but not the rest of their land. In country neighborhoods where families fished and hunted for food, and where livestock roamed freely, fences conflicted with a local economy that required neighborhood use of privately owned land. In this sense, the northerners were right: the lack of fences in the South reflected neighborhood constraints on the private use of private property, and thus on individual acquisitiveness and ambition. Such constraints, however, were necessary to the subsistence of families and neighborhoods as they were organized in the upland South.

A Balance Sheet:
The Plantation and Southern Development

In 1858 James H. Hammond, a slaveholding senator from South Carolina, asked, "What would happen if no cotton was furnished for three years. . . . England would topple headlong and carry the whole civilized world with her save the south. No, you dare not make war on cotton. No power on earth dares to make war on cotton. Cotton is king." Along with other planter-politicians, Hammond argued, as Jefferson had argued in 1807, that farmers at the fringes of the world market economy could coerce the commercial-industrial center. He was wrong. The commitment to cotton and slavery had not only isolated the South politically; it had deepened the South's dependence on the world's financial and industrial centers. The North and West underwent a qualitative market revolution after 1815—a revolution that enriched both, and that transformed the Northeast from a part of the old colonial periphery (the suppliers of food and raw materials) into a part of the core (the suppliers of manufactured goods and financing) of the world market economy. In contrast, the South—by exporting plantation staples in exchange for imported goods, worked itself deeper and deeper into dependence—now as much upon the American Northeast as the old colonial rulers in London.

That does not mean that plantation agriculture was unprofitable. Indeed, James Hammond and his fellow planters were among the richest men in the Western Hemisphere. In 1860 the twelve wealthiest counties in the United States were in the South; the wealthiest of all was Adams County, on the Mississippi River in Mississippi. Southern wealth, however, was concentrated in fewer and fewer hands. The slaves whose labor created the wealth owned nothing. As much as a third of southern white families lived in poverty, and a declining proportion of the others owned slaves. In 1830, 36 percent of southern white households had owned at least one slave. By 1850 the percentage had dropped to 31 percent, by 1860 to 26 percent. And huge disparities existed even among the slaveholding minority; in 1860 only one-fifth of the slaveholders (one in twenty white families) owned 20 or more slaves, thus crossing the generally acknowledged line that separated "farmers" from "planters." At the apex of southern society were men like James Hammond: from 2 to 3 percent of southern white men owned half of all the southern slaves.

The widening gap between planters and yeomen created a dangerous fault line in southern politics (see Chapter 13). In economic terms, the concentration of wealth in the hands of a few planters had profound effects on how the market revolution affected the region. Much of the white population remained marginal to the market economy. A South Carolina yeoman who raised cattle claimed, "I never spent more than ten dollars a year, which was for salt, nails, and the like. Nothing to wear, eat or drink was purchased, as my farm provided all." Whereas in the North the rural demand for credit, banking facilities, farm tools, clothing, and other consumer goods fueled a revolution in commerce, finance, and industry, the South remained a poor market for manufactured goods. The slaves wore cheap cloth made in the Northeast, and the planters furnished themselves and their homes with finery from Europe. In the North the exchange of farm produce for finished goods was creating self-sustaining economic growth by the 1840s. But the South continued to export its plantation staples and to build only those factories, commercial institutions, and cities that served the plantation. A market revolution produced commercial agriculture, a specialized labor force, and technological innovation in the North. In the South it simply produced more slavery.

Not that the South neglected technological innovation and agricultural improvement. Southerners developed Eli Whitney's hand-operated cotton gin into equipment capable of performing complex milling operations; they made many significant improvements in steamboat design as well. They also developed—among many others—a machine with a huge wooden screw powered by horses or mules to press ginned cotton into tight bales for shipping. Jordan Goree, a slave craftsman in Huntsville, Texas, won a reputation for being able to carve whole trees into perfect screws for these machines. Yet there were few such innovations, and they had to do with the processing and shipping of cotton rather than with its production. The truth is that cotton was a labor-intensive crop that discouraged innovation. Moreover, plantation slaves often resisted their enslavement by sabotaging expensive tools and draft animals, scattering manure in haphazard ways, and passively resisting innovations that would have added to their drudgery. So the cotton fields continued to be cultivated by clumsy, mule-drawn plows that barely scratched the soil, by women wielding hoes, and by gangs who harvested the crop by hand.

Southern state governments spent little on internal improvements. A Virginia canal linked the flour mills at Richmond with inland grain fields, and another connected Chesapeake Bay with the National Road. But planters in the cotton belt had ready access to the South's magnificent system of navigable rivers, while upland whites saw little need for expensive, state-supported internal improvements. Nor did the South build cities. In 1800, 82 percent of the southern work force and about 70 percent of the northern work force were employed in agriculture. By 1860 only 40 percent of the northern work force was so employed, but in the South the proportion had risen to 84 percent. The South used its canals and railroads mainly to move plantation staples to towns that transshipped them out of the region. Southern cities were located on the periphery of the region and served as transportation depots for plantation crops. River cities like Louisville, Memphis, and St. Louis were little more than stopping places for steamboats. The great seaports of New Orleans, Charleston, and Baltimore sometimes shipped cotton directly to British and European markets. More often, however, they sent it by coasting vessel to New York City, where it was transshipped to foreign ports.

Thus while the North and the Northwest developed towns and cities throughout their regions, southern cities continued to be few, and to perform the colonial functions of eighteenth-century seaport towns. Southern businessmen turned to New York City for credit, insurance, and coastal and export shipping. And it was from New York that they ordered finished goods for the southern market. *DeBow's Review,* the principal business journal of the South, reported that South Carolina storekeepers who bought goods from Charleston wholesalers

A Cotton Press   Mule-driven presses such as this packed southern cotton into bales for easier transport to market. The cotton was pressed into a frame by a wooden screw carved from a whole tree.

concealed that fact and claimed they had bought them directly from New York City. For it was well known that New York provided better goods at lower prices than any supplier in the South. DeBow himself testified to the superior skill and diversification of the North when, after trying several New Orleans sources, he awarded the contract for his *Review* to a northern printer. That was not surprising in any case, because DeBow received three-fourths of his income from northern advertisers. In all, southerners estimated that 40 cents of very dollar produced by cotton remained in the Northeast.

SUGGESTED READING

Charles G. Sellers, *The Market Revolution: Jacksonian America, 1815–1848* (1991) is a broad synthesis of economic, cultural, and political development. More narrowly economic surveys include Douglas C. North, *The Economic Growth of the United States, 1790–1860* (1961); George Rogers Taylor, *The Transportation Revolution, 1815–1860* (1951); Allan R. Pred, *Urban Growth and the Circulation of Information: The United States System of Cities, 1790–1840* (1973); Harry N. Scheiber, *Ohio Canal Era: A Case Study of Government and the Economy, 1820–1861* (2nd ed., 1987); Ronald E. Shaw, *Erie Water West* (1966); Albert Fishlow, *American Railroads and the Transformation of the Ante-Bellum Economy* (1965); and Erik F. Haites, James Mak, and Gary M. Walton, *Western River Transportation: The Era of Early Internal Development, 1810–1860* (1975). On the role of federal and state courts, see R. Kent Newmeyer, *The Supreme Court under Marshall and Taney* (1968); Francis N. Stites, *John Marshall: Defender of the Constitution* (1981); and, especially, Morton J. Horwitz, *The Transformation of American Law, 1780–1860* (1977).

The market revolution in northern and western agriculture is treated in Christopher Clark, *The Roots of Rural Capitalism: Western Massachusetts, 1780–1860* (1990); Carolyn Merchant, *Ecological Revolutions: Nature, Gender, and Science in New England* (1989); John Mack Faragher, *Sugar Creek: Life on the Illinois Prairie* (1986); Joan M. Jensen, *Loosening the Bonds: Mid-Atlantic Farm Women, 1750–1850* (1986); and Jack Larkin, *The Reshaping of Everyday Life, 1790–1840* (1988).

Still very useful is R. Carlyle Buley, *The Old Northwest: Pioneer Period, 1815–1840* (2 vols., 1950).

Solid studies of early industrial communities include Thomas Dublin, *Women at Work: The Transformation of Work and Community in Lowell, Massachusetts, 1826–1860* (1979); Jonathan Prude, *The Coming of Industrial Order: Town and Factory Life in Rural Massachusetts, 1810–1860* (1983); Anthony F. C. Wallace, *Rockdale: The Growth of an American Village in the Early Industrial Revolution* (1978); Alan Dawley, *Class and Community: The Industrial Revolution in Lynn* (1976); Mary H. Blewett, *Men, Women, and Work: Class, Gender, and Protest in the New England Shoe Industry, 1780–1910* (1990). On the transformation of cities, see Stuart M. Blumin, *The Emergence of the Middle Class: Social Experience in the American City, 1760–1900* (1989); Edward Pessen, *Riches, Class, and Power before the Civil War* (1973); Bruce Laurie, *Working People of Philadelphia, 1800–1850* (1980); Sean Wilentz, *Chants Democratic: New York City & the Rise of the American Working Class, 1788–1850* (1984); and Christine Stansell, *City of Women: Sex and Class in New York, 1789–1860* (1986).

Economic studies of the plantation South begin with Robert William Fogel and Stanley Engerman, *Time on the Cross: The Economics of American Negro Slavery* (2 vols., 1974), and R. W. Fogel, *Without Consent or Contract: The Rise and Fall of American Slavery* (1989). Other useful studies include Orville Vernon Burton, *In My Father's House Are Many Mansions: Family and Community in Edgefield, South Carolina* (1985); Eugene D. Genovese, *The Political Economy of Slavery: Studies in the Economy and Society of the Slave South* (2nd ed., 1989); James Oakes, *The Ruling Race: A History of American Slaveholders* (1982); Gavin Wright, *The Political Economy of the Cotton South: Households, Markets, and Wealth in the Nineteenth Century* (1978); and Elizabeth Fox-Genovese, *Within the Plantation Household: Black and White Women of the Old South* (1988). On the southern yeomanry, see Steven Hahn, *The Roots of Southern Populism: Yeomen Farmers and the Transformation of the Georgia Upcountry, 1850–1890* (1983); J. William Harris, *Plain Folk and Gentry in a Slave Society: White Liberty and Black Slavery in Augusta's Hinterlands* (1985); and Grady McWhiney, *Cracker Culture: Celtic Folkways in the Old South* (1988). Works on the earlier phases of questions covered in this chapter are included in the Suggested Reading for Chapter 8.

Chapter 11

Toward an American Culture

A Middle-Class New England Family at Home, 1837   The room is carpeted and comfortably furnished. Father reads his newspaper while books rest on the table. Mother entertains their only child, and a sentimentalized kitten joins the family. This is the domestic foundation of sentimental culture on display.

Americans after 1815 experienced wave after wave of social change. Territorial expansion, the market revolution, and the spread of plantation slavery uprooted Americans and broke old social patterns. Americans in these years reinvented family life. They created distinctively American forms of popular literature and art, and they found new ways of having fun. They flocked to evangelical revivals — meetings designed to produce religious conversions and led by preachers who were trained to that task — in which they revived and remade American religious life.

The emerging American culture was more or less uniformly republican, capitalist, and Protestant. But different kinds of Americans made different cultures out of the revolutionary inheritance, the market revolution, and revival religion. Southern farmers and their northern cousins thought very differently about fatherhood, motherhood, and the proper way to make a family. Northeastern businessmen and southern planters agreed that economic progress was

indeed progress, but they differed radically on its moral implications. Slaveholders, slaves, factory hands, rich and poor farmers, and middle-class women all heard the same Bible stories and learned different lessons. The result, visible from the 1830s onward, was an American national culture composed largely of subcultures based on region, class, and race.

THE NORTHERN MIDDLE CLASS

"The most valuable class in any community," declared the poet-journalist Walt Whitman in 1858, "is the middle class . . ." At that time, the term *middle class* (and the social group that it described) was no more than thirty or forty years old. The market revolution since 1815 had created new towns and cities and transformed the old ones, and it had turned the rural North into a landscape of family-owned commercial farms. Those who claimed the title "middle class" were largely the new kinds of proprietors made by the market revolution—city and country merchants, master craftsmen who had turned themselves into manufacturers, and the mass of market-oriented farmers.

A disproportionate number of them were New Englanders. New England was the first center of factory production, and southern New England farms were thoroughly commercialized by the 1830s. Yankee migrants dominated the commercial heartland of western New York and the northern regions of the Northwest. Even in the seaport cities (New York's Pearl Street wholesale houses are a prime example) businessmen from New England were often at the center of economic innovation. This Yankee middle class invented cultural forms that became the core of an emerging business civilization. They upheld the autonomous and morally accountable individual against the claims of traditional neighborhoods and traditional families. They devised an intensely private, mother-centered domestic life. Most of all, they adhered to a reformed Yankee Protestantism whose moral imperatives became the foundation of American middle-class culture.

C. G. Finney   The evangelist Charles Grandison Finney, pictured here at the height of his preaching power in the 1830s, was remarkably successful at organizing the new middle-class culture into a millennial crusade.

The Evangelical Base

In November 1830 the evangelist Charles Grandison Finney preached in Rochester, New York, to a church full of middle-class men and women. Most of them were transplanted New Englanders, the heirs of what was left of Yankee Calvinism. In their ministers' weekly sermons, in the formal articles of faith drawn up by their churches, and in the set prayers their children memorized, they reaffirmed the old Puritan beliefs in providence and original sin. The earthly social order (the fixed relations of power and submission between men and women, rich and poor, children and parents, and so on) was necessary because humankind was innately sinful and prone to selfishness and disorder. Christians must obey the rules governing their station in life; attempts to rearrange the social order were both sinful and doomed to failure.

Yet while they reaffirmed those conservative Puritan beliefs in church, the men and women in Finney's audience routinely ignored them in their daily lives. The benefits accruing from the market

revolution were clearly the result of human effort. Just as clearly, they added up to "improvement" and "progress." And as middle-class Christians increasingly envisioned an improved material and social world, the doctrines of human inability and natural depravity, along with faith in divine providence, made less and less sense.

It was to such men and women that Charles Finney preached what became the organizing principle of northern middle-class evangelicalism: "God," he insisted, "has made man a moral free agent." Neither the social order, the troubles of this world, nor the spiritual state of individuals were divinely ordained. People would make themselves and the world better by choosing right over wrong, though they would choose right only after an evangelical conversion experience in which they submitted their rebellious wills to the will of God. It was a religion that valued individual holiness over a permanent and sacred social order. It made the spiritual nature of individuals a matter of prayer, submission, and choice. Thus it gave Christians the means—through the spread of revivals—to bring on the thousand-year reign of Christianity that would precede the Second Coming of Christ. As Charles Finney told his Rochester audience, "If [Christians] were united all over the world the Millennium might be brought about in three months."

Charles Finney's Rochester revival—a six-month marathon of preaching and praying—was no isolated event. Yankee evangelists had been moving toward Finney's formulation since the turn of the century. Like Finney, they borrowed revival techniques from the Methodists (week-long meetings, meetings in which women prayed in public, an "anxious bench" for the most likely converts), but toned them down for their own more "respectable" and affluent audience. But while they used democratic methods and preached a message of individualism and free agency, however, middle-class evangelicals retained the Puritans' Old Testament sense of cosmic history: they enlisted personal holiness and spiritual democracy in a fight to the finish between the forces of good and the forces of evil in this world. In acting out the imperatives of the new evangelicalism, the entrepreneurial families of the East and Northwest constructed an American middle-class culture after 1825. That culture was based, paradoxically, in an intensely private and emotionally loaded family life coupled with an aggressively reformist stance toward the world at large.

Domesticity

The Yankee middle class made crucial distinctions between the home and the world—distinctions that grew from the disintegration of the old patriarchal household economy. Men in cities and towns now went off to work, leaving wives and children to spend the day at home. Even commercializing farmers made a clear distinction between (male) work that was oriented toward markets and (female) work that was tied to the maintenance of the household (see Chapter 10). The new middle-class evangelicalism encouraged this division of domestic labor. The public world of politics and economic exchange, said the preachers, was the proper sphere of men; women, on the other hand, were to exercise new kinds of moral influence within households. As one evangelical put it, "Each has a distinct sphere of duty—the husband to go out into the world—the wife to superintend the household." "Man profits from connection with the world," he went on, "but women never; their constituents [sic] of mind are different. The one is raised and exalted by mingled association. The purity of the other is maintained in silence and seclusion."

The result was a feminization of domestic life. In the old yeoman-artisan republic, the fathers who owned property, headed households, and governed family labor were lawgivers and disciplinarians. They were God's delegated authorities on earth, assigned the task of governing women, children, and other underlings who were mired in original sin. Middle-class evangelicals raised new spiritual possibilities for women and children. Mothers replaced fathers as the principle child-rearers, and they enlisted the doctrines of free agency and individual moral responsibility in that task. Middle-class mothers raised their children with love and reason, not fear. They sought to develop the children's conscience and their capacity to love, to teach them to make good moral choices, and to prepare themselves for conversion and a lifetime of Christian service.

Middle-class mothers were able to do that because they could concentrate their efforts on household duties and because they had fewer children than their mothers or grandmothers had had. In Utica, New York, for example, women who began having children in the 1830s averaged only 3.6 births apiece; those who entered their childbearing years only ten years earlier had averaged 5.1. Housewives also spaced their pregnancies differently. Unlike their forebears, who gave birth to a child about once every two years throughout their childbearing years, Utica's middle-class housewives had their children at five-year intervals, which meant that they could give each child close attention. As a result, households were quieter and less crowded; children learned from their mothers how to govern themselves and seldom experienced the rigors of patriarchal family government. Thus mothers assumed responsibility for making children who would be carriers of the new middle-class culture, and fathers, ministers, and other authorities recognized the importance of that job. Edward Kirk, a minister in Albany, insisted that "the hopes of human society are to be found in the character, in the views, and in the conduct of mothers."

The new ethos of moral free agency was mirrored in the Sunday schools. When Sunday schools first appeared in the 1790s, their purpose was to teach working-class children to read and write by having them copy long passages from the Bible. Their most heavily publicized accomplishments were feats of memory: in 1823 Jane Wilson, a 13-year-old in Rochester, memorized 1,650 verses of scripture; Pawtucket, Rhode Island, claimed a mill girl who could recite the entire New Testament.

After the revivals of the 1820s and 1830s, the emphasis shifted from promoting feats of memory to preparing children's souls for conversion. Middle-class children were now included in the schools, corporal punishment was forbidden, and Sunday school teachers now tried to develop the moral sensibilities of their charges. They had the children read a few Bible verses each week and then led them in a discussion of the moral lessons conveyed by the text. The proudest achievements of the new schools were children who made good moral choices. Thus Sunday schools became training grounds in free agency and moral accountability—a transformation that made sense only in a sentimental world where children could be trusted to make moral choices.

Sentimentality

Improvements in the printing, distribution, and marketing of books led to an outpouring of popular literature, much of it directed at the middle class. There were cookbooks, etiquette books, manuals on housekeeping, sermons, and sentimental novels—many of them written and most of them read by women. The works of popular religious writers such as Lydia Sigourney, Lydia Maria Child, and Timothy Shay Arthur found their way into thousands of middle-class homes. Sarah Josepha Hale, whose *Gody's Ladies Book* was the first mass-circulation magazine for women, acted as an arbiter of taste not only in furniture, clothing, and food but in sentiments and ideas. Upon reviewing the cloying, sentimental literature read in middle-class homes, Nathaniel Hawthorne was not the only "serious" writer to deplore a literary marketplace dominated by "a damned mob of scribbling women."

Hawthorne certainly had economic reason for complaint. Sentimental novels written by women outsold by wide margins his *The Scarlet Letter* and *The House of Seven Gables*, Ralph Waldo Emerson's essays, Henry David Thoreau's *Walden*, Herman Melville's *Moby Dick*, Walt Whitman's *Leaves of Grass*,

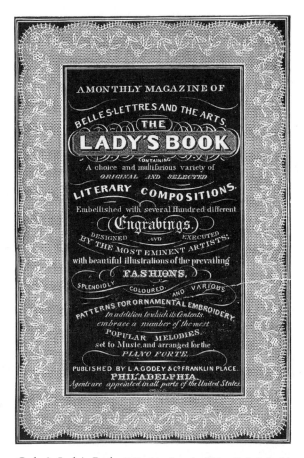

Godey's Lady's Book   Edited by Josepha Hale, *Godey's Lady's Book* provided middle-class women with everything from sentimental fiction and sewing patterns to sheet music and fashion tips.

and other works of the "American Renaissance" of the 1850s. Susan Warner's *The Wide, Wide World* broke all sales records when it appeared in 1850. Harriet Beecher Stowe's *Uncle Tom's Cabin* (1852) broke the records set by Warner. In 1854 Maria Cummin's *The Lamplighter* (the direct target of Hawthorne's lament about scribbling women) took its place as the third of the monster best-sellers of the early 1850s.

These sentimental novels upheld the new middle-class domesticity. They sacralized the middle-class home and the trials and triumphs of Christian women. The action in each takes place indoors, usually in the kitchen or parlor, and the heroines are women (in Stowe's book, docile slave Christians are included) who live under worldly patriarchy but who triumph through submission to God. The stories have to do with spiritual struggle, the renunciation of greed and desire, and mother love. The home is a shrine (and keeping it clean is a sacrament) that is juxtaposed to the marketplace and the world of competition, brutality, and power. Unlike the female characters in British and European novels of the time, the women in these American novels are intelligent, generous persons who grow in strength and independence. (The French visitor Alexis de Tocqueville commented that European women "almost think it a privilege to appear futile, weak, and timid. The women of America never lay claim to rights of that sort.")

In sentimental domestic fiction, women assume the role of evangelical ministers, demonstrating Christian living by precept, example, and moral persuasion. Female moral influence, wielded by women who had given themselves to God, is at war with the male world of politics and the marketplace—areas of power, greed, and moral compromise. While few sentimental writers shared the views of the feminist Margaret Fuller, they would have agreed with her on the place of religion in women's lives. "I wish women to live *first* for God's sake," she wrote. "Then she will not make an imperfect man her God, and thus sink to idolatry."

The most successful sentimental novel was Harriet Beecher Stowe's *Uncle Tom's Cabin*. (See also the discussion in Chapter 14) The book's spectacular popularity stemmed from its indictment of slavery as a system of absolute power at odds with the domestic values held dear by Stowe's audience of evangelical women. The novel reverses the power relations of this world: in it, the home, and particularly the kitchen, is the ultimate locus of good, while law, politics, and the marketplace—the whole realm of men—are moved to the periphery and defined as unfeeling destroyers. Based solidly in revival Christianity, the novel lambastes the rational calculation, greed, and power hunger of the "real world" that was made and governed by white men, and upholds domestic space filled with women, slaves, and children who gain spiritual power through submission to Christ. The two most telling scenes—the deaths of the Christian slave Uncle Tom and the perfect child Eva St. Claire—reenact the crucifixion of Jesus. Uncle Tom prays for his tormentors as he is beaten to death, and little Eva extracts promises of Christian behavior from her deathbed. Both are

powerless, submissive characters who die in order to redeem a fallen humankind. Their deaths are thus Christian triumphs that convert the powerful and hasten the millennial day when the world will be governed by a feminized Christian love and not by male power.

Thus *Uncle Tom's Cabin* and other popular sentimental novels were not, as Hawthorne and his friends believed, frivolous fairy tales into which housewives retreated from the "real" world. They were subversive depictions of a higher spiritual reality that would move the feminine ethos of the Christian home to the center of civilization. As we shall see in Chapter 13, that vision was underneath an organized public assault on irreligion, drunkenness, prostitution, slavery, and other practices and institutions that substituted passion and force for Christian love, an assault that tried to "domesticate" the world and shape it in the image of the middle-class evangelical home.

Fine Arts

Educated Americans of the postrevolutionary generation associated the fine arts with the sensuality, extravagance, and artificiality of European courts and European Catholicism. To them, the fine arts were the products of despotism and had nothing to offer the republicans of America. In making government buildings and monuments, building expensive homes, and painting portraits of wealthy and powerful men, American artists copied the classic simplicity of ancient Greece and Rome—republican styles that had been tested by time and that were free of any hint of sensuality or luxury.

In the 1820s and 1830s, however, educated Americans began to view literature and the arts more favorably. There were a number of reasons for that change. First, American nationalists began to demand an American art that could compete with the arts of the despotic Old World. At the same time, evangelical Christianity and sentimental culture glorified a romantic cult of feeling that was, within its limits, far more receptive to aesthetic experience than Calvinism and the more Spartan forms of republicanism had been. Finally, the more comfortable and educated Americans fell into a relationship with nature that called out for aesthetic expression. From the beginnings of English settlement, Americans had known that their civilization would be made in a contest with wilderness — wilderness that was dark, filled with demons, and implacably hostile to civilization. After 1815, with the Indians finally broken and scattered, with the agricultural frontier penetrating deep into the interior, and with improvements in transportation and communications annihilating distance, educated northeasterners became certain that Americans would win their age-old contest with nature — that civilization would supplant wilderness on the North American continent. The result was a multivoiced conversation about the relations between nature and civilization — a conversation that occupied a large portion of a new American art and literature that rose between 1830 and the Civil War.

Much of the new American art went into objects that were lived in and used. Andrew Jackson Downing and other landscape designers and architects created beautiful country cottages surrounded by gardens — producing a domestic environment that used art as an avenue to the grand lessons of nature. At the same time, cities began to build cemeteries in the surrounding countryside, replacing the old ill-tended graveyards at the center of town. In 1831 several wealthy Boston families put up the money to build Mount Auburn Cemetery, the first graveyard designed to serve as a cultural institution. Mount Auburn was situated on rolling ground, with footpaths following the contours of the land. Much of the natural vegetation was left untouched, and wildflowers were planted to supplement it. The headstones, which had to be approved by a board of directors, were small and dignified. Mount Auburn became a kind of public park in which nature's annual cycle of death and renewal taught chastening and reassuring lessons to the living. Copied in Brooklyn, Rochester, and other northern cities, the rural cemeteries embodied the faith that nature could teach moral lessons, particularly if nature was shaped and made available to humankind through art.

Not surprisingly, the leading artists of this generation were landscape painters. Thomas Cole, in his "Essay on American Scenery" (1835), reminded readers that the most distinctive feature of America was its wilderness: ". . . in civilized Europe the primitive features of scenery have long since been destroyed or modified. . . . And to this cultivated state our western world is fast approaching; but nature is still predominant, and there are those who regret that with the improvements of cultivation the sublimity of the wilderness should pass away; for those scenes of solitude from which the hand of nature has never been lifted, affect the mind with a more deep toned emotion than aught which the hand of man has touched. Amid them the consequent associations are of God the creator — they are his undefiled works, and the mind is cast into contemplation of eternal things."

In what became a manifesto of American intellectual and aesthetic life, Cole had found God in nature (previous generations had been taught to see wilderness as the devil's domain), and thus endowed art that depicted nature with religious purpose. Among educated persons, art was no longer subversive of the Protestant republic; done right, it was a bulwark of good citizenship and true religion. American housewives who planted and tended flower gardens were acting on that premise. So were the landscape architects who designed rural cemeteries and public and private gardens; the philosopher Ralph Waldo Emerson, who told Americans that "every natural process is a version of a moral sentence"; his friend Henry David Thoreau, who lived in the woods and embraced not only nature's beauties but bad weather, wars between insects, and the corpses of horses in an attempt, as he put it, to live "deliberately" in a simple relationship with nature. These and thousands of educated middle- and upper-class northerners after 1830 built a cultural conversation in which Americans defined themselves by talking about American nature — a nature that had become Christianized and benign.

That conversation was strongest among urban northeasterners who benefited from the market revolution and who believed that theirs was an age of progress. Indeed some would argue that the feminization of family life, the rise of sentimentality, and the romantic cult of nature could have appeared only when American civilization had turned the tide in its age-old battle with wilderness. The most sensitive and articulate northeasterners — Emerson, Thoreau, and Thomas Cole among them — warned that the victory might be too complete, and that the United States could become as "unnatural" and "artificial" as an overcultivated Europe. Similarly, ministers and mothers worried that the marketplace could corrupt the "natural" relations of family life, while middle-class women and men cultivated personal "sincerity" as a badge of moral status and a hedge against the artificiality and dishonesty that thrived in an anonymous market society. At every level, middle-class culture was balanced, sometimes uncomfortably, between pride in economic and technological progress and veneration of what was "natural."

The uneasy balance of art and nature can be illustrated with what became the most venerated spot in America: Niagara Falls. Niagara became part of the border between the United States and British Canada in 1783, but few Americans visited the place, and even fewer settled there. The Falls could be reached only by a difficult and expensive voyage up the St. Lawrence and across Lake Ontario or, after 1804, over New York's notoriously bad state road. The Niagara frontier remained an unfriendly border, then one of the principal battlegrounds of the War of 1812. The few Americans who wrote about Niagara Falls before the 1820s had stressed the power, wildness and danger of the place along with its stunning beauty. These reactions aped literary convention that demanded terror as part of the apprehension of the sublime in nature; they also repeated old American fears of wilderness. In 1815 Niagara remained part of an unconquered American wilderness.

Completion of the Erie Canal in 1825 brought civilization to Niagara Falls. Every summer crowds of tourists traveled the easy water route to Buffalo, then took carriages to the Falls, where entrepreneurs had built hotels, paths, and stairways and offered boat rides and guided tours. The Falls were now surrounded by commerce and viewed comfortably from various sites by well-dressed tourists. In early paintings of the Falls, the foreground figure had usually been an Indian hunter or fisherman; now the Indians were replaced by tourist couples, the women carrying parasols. The sublime experience of terror and wonder had disappeared. Tourists read travel accounts before their trip and, once they had arrived, bought guidebooks and took guided tours, aware that they were sharing their experience with thousands of others. Many of the tourists were women, and many men conceded that women possessed the "genuine emotion" that enabled them to experience Niagara Falls correctly. Niagara Falls had become controlled, orderly, and beautiful, a grand sermon in which God revealed His benign plan to humankind. Young Harriet Beecher Stowe visited Niagara in the early 1830s and gushed, "Oh, it is lovelier than it is great; it is like the Mind that made it: great, but so veiled in beauty that we gaze without terror. I felt as if I could have gone over with the waters; it would be so beautiful a death. . . ." Niagara had

Niagara Falls   Frederic Edwin Church, who was among the most renowned of American landscape artists, painted Niagara Falls in 1857. Church's Niagara is immense and powerful, yet somehow ordered, benign, and calming.

become, for Stowe and thousands of others, a part of sentimental culture.

THE PLAIN PEOPLE OF THE NORTH

From the 1830s onward, northern middle-class evangelicals proposed their religious and domestic values as a national culture for the United States. But even in their own region they were surrounded and outnumbered by Americans who rejected their cultural leadership. The plain people of the North were a varied lot: settlers in the lower Northwest who remained culturally southern, hill-country New Englanders, New Yorkers, and Pennsylvanians who had experienced little of what their middle-class cousins called "progress," refugees from the countryside who had taken up urban wage labor, and increasing thousands of Irish and German immigrants. What they shared was a cultural conservatism—often grounded in the traditional, father-centered family—that rejected sentimentalism and reformist religion out of hand.

Religion and the Common Folk

The doctrines of churches favored by the northern plain folk varied as much as the people themselves. They ranged from the voluntaristic "free grace" doctrines of the Methodists to the iron-bound Calvinism of most Baptists, from the fine-tuned hierarchy of the Mormons to the near-anarchy of the Disciples of Christ. They included the most popular faiths (Baptists and Methodists came to contain two-thirds of America's professing Protestants, North and South) to such smaller sects as Hicksite Quakers, Universalists, Adventists, Moravians, and Freewill Baptists. Yet for all their diversity, these churches had important things in common. Most shared an evangelical emphasis on individual experience over churchly authority. Most favored democratic, local control of religious life and distrusted outside organization and religious professionalism—not only the declining colonial establishments but the emerging missionary network created by middle-class evangelicals. And they rejected middle-class optimism and reformism, reaffirming God's providence and humankind's duty to accept an imperfect world even while waging war against it.

The most pervasive strain was a belief in providence—the conviction that human history was part of God's vast and unknowable plan, and that all events were willed or allowed by God. Middle-class evangelicals spoke of providence, too, but they seemed to assume that God's plan was manifest in the progress of market society and middle-class religion. Humbler evangelicals held to the older notion that providence was immediate, mysterious, and unknowable. They believed that the events of everyday life were parts of a vast blueprint that existed only in the mind of God—and not in the vain aspirations of women and men. When making plans, they added the caveat, "The Lord willing," and they learned to accept misfortune with fortitude. They responded to epidemics, bad crop years, aches and pains, illness, and early death by praying for the strength to endure, asking God to "sanctify" their suffering by making it an opportunity for them to grow in faith.

Child's Gravestone This baby girl's gravestone, decorated with a weeping willow, carries an inscription affirming that death has set the child "free from trouble and pain," and ushered her into a better life.

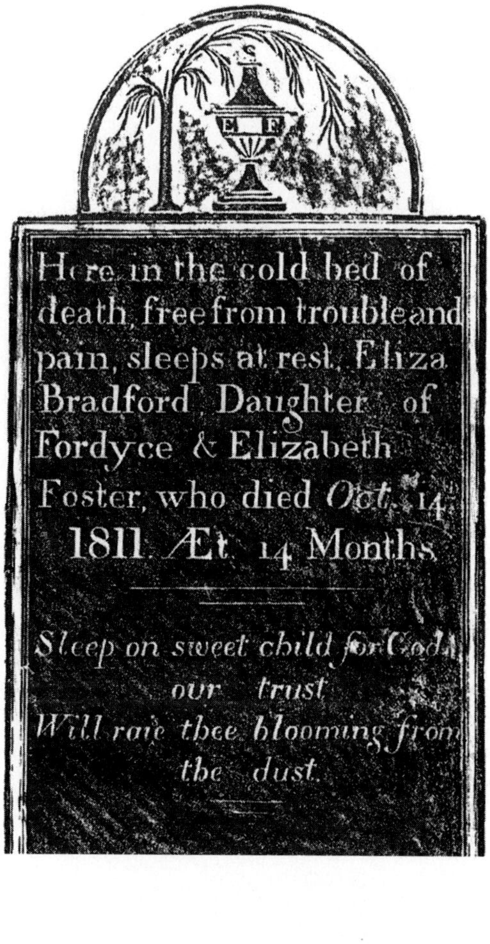

As a minister told the Scots Covenanters of Cambridge, New York, "It is through tribulation that all the saints enter into the kingdom of God." "The tempest sometimes ceases," he went on, "the sky is clear, and the prospect is desirable, but by the by the gathering clouds threaten a new storm; here we must watch, and labor, and fight, expecting rest with Christ in glory, not on the way to it."

The providential world view, the rejection of this world, and the notion that God granted spiritual progress only through affliction came directly into play when a member of a poor Protestant family died. Country Baptists and working-class Methodists mourned their dead, but they were careful not to "murmur" against God. In a world governed by providence, the death of a loved one was a test of faith. Plain folk considered it a privilege to witness a death in the family, for it released the sufferer from the tribulations of this world and sent him or her to a better place. The death of children in particular called for a heroic act of submission to God's will; parents mourned the loss but stopped short of displaying grief that would suggest selfishness and lack of faith. Poor families washed and dressed the dead body themselves and then buried it in a churchyard or on a hilltop plot on the family farm. While the urban middle class preferred formal funerals and carefully tended cemeteries, humbler people regarded death as a lesson in the futility of pursuing worldly goals and in the need to submit to God's will.

Popular Millennialism

The plain Protestants of the North seldom talked about the millennium. Middle-class evangelicals were *postmillennialists*: they believed that Christ's Second Coming would occur at the *end* of a thousand years of social perfection that would be brought about by the missionary conversion of the world. Ordinary Baptists, Methodists, and Disciples of Christ, however, assumed that the millennium would arrive with world-destroying violence, followed by the thousand years of Christ's rule on earth. But most did not dwell on this terrifying *premillennialism*, assuming that God would end the world in His own time. Now and then, however, the ordinary evangelicals of the North predicted the fiery end of the world. Prophets rose and fell, and thousands of people looked for signs of the approaching millennium in thunderstorms, shooting stars, eclipses, economic panics and

depressions, and—especially—in hints that God had placed in the Bible.

An avid student of those hints was William Miller, a rural New York Baptist who, after years of systematic study, concluded that God would destroy the world during the year following March 1843. Miller publicized his predictions throughout the 1830s, and near the end of the decade the Millerites (as his followers were called) gathered together thousands of believers—most of them conservative Baptists, Methodists, and Disciples in hill-country New England and in poor neighborhoods in New York, Ohio, and Michigan. As the end approached, the believers read the Bible, prayed, and attended meeting after meeting. A publicist named Henry Jones reported that a shower of meat and blood had fallen on Jersey City, and newspapers published stories alleging that the Millerites were insane and guilty of sexual license. Some of them, the press reported, were busy sewing "ascension robes" in which they would rise straight to heaven without passing through death.

When the end of the year—March 23, 1844—came and went, most of the believers quietly returned to their churches. A committed remnant, however, kept the faith and by the 1860s founded the Seventh-Day Adventist Church. The Millerite movement was a reminder that hundreds of thousands of northern Protestants continued to believe that the God of the Old Testament governed everything from bee stings to the course of human history, and that one day He would destroy the world in fire and blood.

Family and Society

Baptists, Methodists, Disciples of Christ and the smaller popular sects evangelized primarily among persons who had been bypassed or hurt by the market revolution. Many had been reduced to dependent, wage-earning status. Others had become market farmers or urban storekeepers or master workmen; few had become rich. Their churches taught them that the attractions and temptations of market society were at the center of the world they must reject.

Often their rhetoric turned to criticism of market society, its institutions, and its centers of power. The Quaker schismatic Elias Hicks, a Long Island farmer who fought the worldliness and pride of wealthy

Prophetic Chart   A fixture at Millerite Adventist meetings, prophetic charts such as this displayed the succession of Biblical kingdoms and the prophecies of Daniel and John. Millerites revised their chart when the world failed to end in 1843.

Quakers, listed these among the mistakes of the early nineteenth century: railroads, the Erie Canal, fancy food and other luxuries, banks and the credit system, the city of Philadelphia, and the study of chemistry. The Baptist millenarian William Miller expressed his hatred for banks, insurance companies, stock-jobbing, chartered monopolies, personal greed, and the city of New York. In short, what the evangelical middle-class identified as the march of progress, poorer and more conservative evangelicals often condemned as a descent into worldliness that would almost certainly provoke God's wrath.

Along with doubts about economic change and the middle-class churches that embraced it, members of the popular sects often held to the patriarchal family form in which they had been raised, and with which both the market revolution and middle-class domesticity seemed at war. For hundreds of thousands of northern Protestants, the erosion of domes-

tic patriarchy was a profound cultural loss and not, as it was for the middle-class, an avenue to personal liberation. Their cultural conservatism was apparent in their efforts to sustain the father-centered family of the old rural North, or to revive it in new forms.

For some, religious conversion came at a point of crisis in the traditional family. William Miller, for example, had a strict Calvinist upbringing in a family in which his father, an uncle, and his grandfather were all Baptist ministers. As a young man he rejected his family, set about making money, and became a deist—actions that deeply wounded his parents. When his father died, Miller was stricken with guilt. He moved back to his hometown, took up his family duties, became a leader of the Baptist church, and (after reading a sermon entitled "Parental Duties") began the years of Bible study that resulted in his world-ending prophecies. Alexander Campbell, one of the founders of the Disciples of Christ, dramatized his filial piety when he debated the free-thinking socialist Robert Owen before a large audience in the Methodist meeting house in Cincinnati in 1828. He insisted that his white-haired father (himself a Scots Presbyterian minister) stand in the pulpit above the debaters.

The weakening of the patriarchal family and the attempt to shore it up were central to the life and work of one of the most unique and successful religious leaders of the period: the Mormon Prophet Joseph Smith (see also Chapter 14). Smith's father was a landless Vermont Baptist who moved his wife and nine children to seven rented farms within twenty years. Around 1820, when young Joseph was approaching manhood, the family was struggling to make mortgage payments on a small farm outside Palmyra, New York. That farm—Joseph referred to it as "my father's house"—was a desperate token of the Smith family's commitment to yeoman independence and an endangered rural patriarchy. Despite the efforts of Joseph and his brothers, a merchant cheated the Smith family out of the farm. With that, both generations of the Smiths faced lifetimes as propertyless workers. To make matters worse, Joseph's mother and some of his siblings began to attend an evangelical Presbyterian church in Palmyra—apparently against the father's wishes.

Before the loss of the farm, Joseph had received two visions warning him away from existing churches and telling him to wait for further instructions. In 1827 the Angel Moroni appeared to him and led him to golden plates that translated into *The Book of Mormon.* It told of a light-skinned people, descendants of the Hebrews, who had sailed to North America long before Columbus. They had had an epic, violent history, a covenanted relationship with God, and had been visited and evangelized by Jesus following His crucifixion and resurrection.

Joseph Smith later declared that his discovery of *The Book of Mormon* had "brought salvation to my father's house" by unifying the family. It eventually unified thousands of others under a patriarchal faith based on restored theocratic government, male dominance, and a democracy among fathers. The good priests and secular leaders of *The Book of Mormon* are farmers who labor alongside their neighbors; the villains are self-seeking merchants, lawyers, and bad priests. The account alternates between periods when the people obey God's laws and periods when they do not—each period accompanied by the blessings or punishments of a wrathful God. Smith carried that model of brotherly cooperation and patriarchal authority into the Church of Jesus Christ of Latter-day Saints that he founded in 1830. The new church was ruled, not by professional clergy, but by an elaborate lay hierarchy of adult males. On top sat the father of Joseph Smith, rescued from destitution and shame, who was appointed Patriarch of the Church. Below him were Joseph Smith and his brother Hyrum, who were called First and Second Elders. The hierarchy descended through a succession of male authorities that finally reached the fathers of households. Smith claimed that this hierarchy restored the ancient priesthood that had disappeared over the eighteen centuries of greed and error that he labeled the "Great Apostasy" of the Christian churches. But Americans who knew the history of the market revolution and the Smith family's travails within it might have noted similarities between the restored ancient order and a poor man's visionary retrieval of the social order of the eighteenth-century North.

THE RISE OF POPULAR CULTURE

Of course, not all the northern plain folk spent their time in church. Particularly in cities and towns, they became both producers and consumers of a nonreligious (sometimes irreligious) commercial popular culture.

Blood Sports

Urban working-class neighborhoods were particularly fertile ground for the making of popular amusements. Young working men formed a bachelor subculture that contrasted with the piety and self-restraint of the middle class. They organized volunteer fire companies and militia units that spent more time drinking and fighting rival groups than they did drilling or putting out fires. Gathering at fire houses, saloons, and street corners, they drank, joked, and boasted, and nurtured notions of manliness based on physical prowess and coolness under pressure.

They also engaged in such "blood sports" as cock fighting, ratting, and dog fighting, even though many states had laws forbidding such activities. In 1823 an English tourist in New York City noted that "it is perfectly common for two or three cockfights to regularly take place every week." Such contests grew increasingly popular during the 1850s and were often staged by saloonkeepers doubling as sports impresarios. One of the best known was Kit Burns of New York City, who ran Sportsman Hall. Actually this was a saloon frequented by prizefighters, criminals, and their hangers-on. Behind the saloon was a space—reached through a narrow doorway that could be defended against the police—with animal pits and a small amphitheater that seated 250 but that regularly held 400 yelling spectators.

Although most of the spectators were working men, a few members of the old aristocracy who rejected middle-class ways also attended these events. In 1861, 250 spectators paid as much as $3 each to witness a fight between roosters belonging to the prize fighter John Morrissey and Mr. Genet, president of the New York City board of aldermen. A newspaper estimated that $50,000 had been bet on the event. Frederick Van Wyck, scion of a wealthy old New York family, remembered an evening he had spent at Tommy Norris' livery stable, where he witnessed a fight between billy goats, a rat baiting, a cockfight, and a boxing match between bare-breasted women. "Certainly for a lad of 17, such as I," he recalled, "a night with Tommy Norris and his attraction was quite a night."

Prize fighting emerged from the same subterranean culture that sustained cockfights and other blood sports. This sport, which was imported from Britain, called for an enclosed ring, clear rules, cornermen, a referee, and a paying audience. The early fighters were Irish or English immigrants, as were many of the promoters and spectators. Boxing's popularity rose during the 1840s and 1850s, a time of increasing immigration and violence in poor city neighborhoods. Many of the fighters had close ties with ethnic-based saloons, militia units, fire companies, and street gangs, such as New York's (Irish) Dead Rabbits and (native) Bowery B'hoys, and many labored at occupations with a peculiarly ethnic base. Some of the best American-born fighters were New York City butchers—a licensed, privileged trade from which cheap immigrant labor was systematically excluded. Butchers usually finished work by 10:00 A.M. They could spend the rest of the day idling at a fire house or a bar and were often prominent figures in neighborhood gangs. A prize fight between an American-born butcher and an Irish day laborer would attract a spirited audience that understood its class and ethnic meaning.

Prize fighting was a way of rewarding courage and skill and, sometimes, of settling scores through contests that were fair and limited to two combatants. Nonetheless, the fights were brutal. Boxers fought with bare knuckles, and a bout ended only when one of the fighters was unable to go on. In an infamous match in 1842, for instance, the English-

man Christopher Lilly knocked down his Irish opponent Thomas McCoy 80 times; the fight ended with round 119, when McCoy died in his corner.

Although boxing was closely associated with ethnic rivalries, the contestants often exhibited a respect for one another that crossed ethnic lines. For example, the native-born Tom Hyer, who had defeated Irish "Yankee" Sullivan in one of the great early fights, later bailed Sullivan out of jail. And when in 1859 Bill Harrington, a retired native-born boxer, disappeared and left a widow and children, his old opponent Irish John Morrisey arranged a sparring match and sent the proceeds to Harrington's widow.

An American Theater

In the eighteenth and early nineteenth centuries, the only theaters were in the large seaport cities. Those who attended were members of the urban elite, and nearly all the plays, managers, and actors were English. After 1815, however, improvements in transportation and communication, along with the rapid growth of cities, created a much broader audience. Theaters and theater companies sprang up not only in New York and Philadelphia but also in Cincinnati, Saint Louis,

The Match between James "Yankee" Sullivan and Tom Hyer, February, 1849   Sullivan was an Irish immigrant, Hyer was native-born; both were active in New York street gangs. Hyer defeated Sullivan in sixteen rounds.

San Francisco, Rochester, and dozens of other new towns west of the Appalachians. All catered to mostly male, working-class audiences. Before 1830 these theatergoers occupied the cheap balcony seats (with the exception of the second balcony, which was reserved for prostitutes), while wealthier and more genteel patrons sat near the stage. Those sitting in the balcony joined in the performance: they ate and drank, talked, and shouted encouragement and threats to the actors. The genteel New Yorker Washington Irving lamented the "discharge of apples, nuts, and gingerbread" flying out of the balconies "on the heads of honest folks" in the orchestra.

As time passed, however, rowdyism turned into violence. The less genteel members of theater audiences protested the elegant speech, gentlemanly bearing, and understated acting of the English actors, which happened to match the speech, manners, and bearing of the American urban elite. Thus the protests were directed not only at the English actors but also at the ladies and gentlemen in the orchestra who were seen as symbols of English culture that did not belong in a democratic republic.

The first theater riot occurred in 1817 when the English actor Charles Incledon refused a New York audience's demand that he stop what he was doing and sing "Black-Eyed Susan." Such assaults grew more common during the 1820s. By the 1830s there were separate theaters and separate kinds of performances for rich and poor. But violence continued. It culminated in the rivalry between the American actor Edwin Forrest and the English actor William Charles Macready. Macready was a trained Shakespearean actor, and his restrained style and attention to the subtleties of the text had won him acclaim both in Britain and in the United States. Forrest, on the other hand, played to the cheap seats. With his bombast and histrionics he transformed Shakespeare's tragedies into melodramas. Forrest and Macready carried out a well-publicized feud that led to a mob attack on Macready in 1849. Led by E. Z. C. Judson (who, under the pen name Ned Buntline, wrote scores of dime novels), the mob descended on Macready's performance at the exclusive Astor Place Opera House. The militia was waiting for them, and in the ensuing riot and gunfight twenty persons lost their lives.

Playhouses that catered to working-class audiences continued to feature Shakespearean tragedies (*Richard III*, played broadly and with a lot of swordplay, was the favorite), but they now shared the stage with works written in the American vernacular. The stage "Yankee," rustic but shrewd, appeared at this time and so did Mose the Bowery B'hoy, a New York volunteer fireman who performed feats of derring-do. Both frequently appeared in the company of well-dressed characters with English accents; the Yankee outsmarted them, Mose beat them up.

Minstrelsy

The most popular form of theater was the blackface minstrel show. Though these shows conveyed blatant racism, they were the preferred entertainment of working men in northern cities (few women attended the shows) from 1840 to 1880. The first minstrel show was presented in 1831 when a white showman named Thomas Rice blacked his face and "jumped Jim Crow," imitating a shuffle-dance he had seen on the Cincinnati docks. Within a few years a formula for these shows had emerged that every theatergoer knew by heart.

The minstrel shows lasted an hour and a half and were presented in three sections. The first consisted of songs and dances performed in a walkaround, in which the audience was encouraged to clap and sing along. This was followed by a longer middle section in which the company sat in a row with a character named Tambo at one end and a character named Bones at the other (named for the tambourine and bones, the instruments they played), with an interlocutor in the middle. The Tambo character, often called Uncle Ned, was a simpleminded plantation slave dressed in plain clothing; the Bones character, usually called Zip Coon, was a dandified, oversexed free black dressed in top hat and tails. The interlocutor was the straight man— fashionably dressed, slightly pretentious, with an English accent. This middle section consisted of a conversation among the three which included pointed political satire, skits ridiculing the wealthy and the educated, and sexual jokes that bordered on pornography. The third section featured songs, dances, and jokes—most of them familiar enough so that the audience could sing along and laugh at the right places.

The minstrel shows introduced African-American song and dance—in toned-down, Europeanized

The Astor Place Riot   The rivalry between the English actor William Charles Macready and the American actor Edwin Forrest culminated in the bloody Astor Place Riot in New York City in May, 1849.

form—to audiences who would not have permitted black performers onto the stage. They also reinforced racial stereotypes that were near the center of American popular culture. Finally, they dealt broadly with aspects of social and political life that other performers avoided.

Minstrel shows and other theatrical entertainments were among the urban products that the new transportation network carried to rural America. The Grecian Dog Apollo, for example, after arriving in New York from London in 1827, played cards, solved problems in arithmetic "with the celerity of an experienced clerk," and answered questions on astronomy and geography. Apollo then traveled the Erie Canal circuit, playing at a theater in Rochester and at an outdoor festival at Niagara Falls before returning to Peale's Museum in New York for the 1828 season. Actors traveled well-established circuits, calling on local amateurs for their supporting casts. Minstrel companies traveled the river system of the interior and played to enthusiastic audiences wherever the river boats tied up. Mark Twain recalled them fondly: "I remember the first Negro musical show I ever saw. It must have been in the early forties. It was a new institution. In our village of Hannibal [Missouri] . . . it burst upon us as a glad and stunning surprise." Among Americans who had been taught to distrust cities by cultural leaders ranging from Thomas Jefferson to Emerson and Thoreau to the evangelical preachers in their own neighborhoods, minstrel shows and other urban entertainments gave rural folk a sense of the variety and excitement of city life.

Novels and the Penny Press

Among the many commodities the market revolution made available, few were more ubiquitous than newspapers and inexpensive books. Improvements in printing and paper-making enabled entrepreneurs to sell daily newspapers for a penny. Cheap "story papers" became available in the 1830s, "yellow-backed" fiction in the 1840s, and dime novels from the 1850s onward. Though these offerings were distributed throughout the North and the West, they found their first and largest audience among city workers.

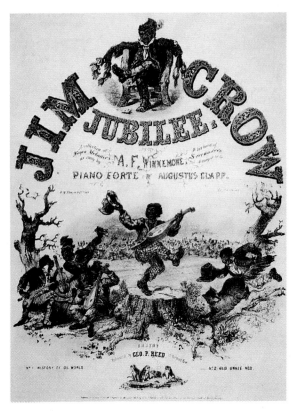

The Virginia Minstrels   In the 1840s, the Virginia Minstrels, white entertainers in grotesque black masquerade, claimed in their advertisements to be "able delineators of the sports and pastimes of the Sable Race of the South. . . ."

Mass-audience newspapers carried political news and local advertisements, but they were heavily spiced with sensationalism. The *Philadelphia Gazette* in late summer of 1829, for instance, treated its eager readers to the following: "Female Child with Two Heads," "Bats," "Another Shark," "Horrid Murder," "More Stabbing," "Steam Boat Robbery," "Fishes Travelling on Land," "Poisoning by Milk," "Dreadful Steam Boat Disaster," "Picking Pockets," "Raffling for Babies," "Combat with a Bear," "Lake Serpent," "Atrocious Murder," "Frauds on the Revenue," and much, much more. Henry David Thoreau commented on the "startling and monstrous events as fill the family papers," while his friend Ralph Waldo Emerson reported that Americans were "reading all day murders & railroad accidents." While such sensational stories are most remarkable for their variety, they did portray a haunted, often demonic nature that regularly produced monstrosities and ruined the

works of humankind, and a *human* nature that, despite appearances, was often deceptive and depraved.

Working-class readers discovered a similarly untrustworthy world in cheap fiction. George Lippard's *Quaker City* (1845) sold 60,000 copies in its first year and 30,000 in each of the next five years, making it the best-selling American book before the sentimental blockbusters of the 1850s. Lippard's book was a fictional "exposé" of the hypocrisy, lust, and cruelty of Philadelphia's outwardly genteel and Christian elite. Lippard and other adventure writers (whose works accounted for 60 percent of all American fiction titles published between 1831 and 1860) indulged in a pornography of violence that included cannibalism, blood drinking, and murder by every imaginable means. They also dealt with sex in unprecedentedly explicit ways. The yellow-back novels of the 1840s introduced readers not only to seduction and rape but to transvestitism, child pornography, necrophilia, miscegenation, group sex, homosexuality, and—perhaps most shocking of all—women with criminal minds and insatiable sexual appetites. The scenes of gore and sexual depravity were presented voyeuristically—as self-righteous exposés of the perversions of the rich and powerful and stories of the Founders' Republic trampled upon by a vicious elite that pretended virtue but lived only for its appetites.

Popular fictions—like most popular plays, Edwin Forrest's Shakespeare, and much of what went on in blood sports, the prize ring, and the penny press—were melodramatic contests between good and evil. Evil was described in terms reminiscent of original sin: it was the background of all human action, and heroes met a demonic and chaotic world with courage and guile without hoping to change it. Indeed, melodramatic heroes frequently acknowledged evil in themselves while claiming moral superiority over the hypocrites and frauds who governed the world. A murderer in Ned Buntline's *G'hals of New York* (1850) remarks, "There isn't no *real* witue [virtue] and honesty nowhere, 'cept among the perfessional *dis*honest." (By contrast, in middle-class sentimental novels, the universe is benign; good can be nurtured, and evil can be defeated and transformed. Harriet Beecher Stowe's slavedriver Simon Legree—the best-known villain in American literature—is evil not because of a natural disposition toward evil but because he had been deprived of a mother's love during childhood.)

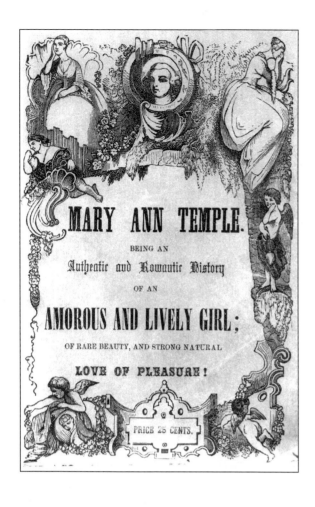

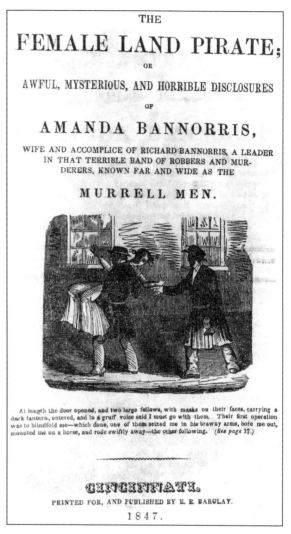

Yellow-Back Novels   Here are two pulp fiction hits of the 1840s: an erotic novel about the "amorous and lively" Mary Ann Temple and a crime story about robberies and murders of a "Female Land Pirate"—not the kinds of women encountered in middle-class sentimental fiction.

FAMILY, CHURCH, AND NEIGHBORHOOD: THE WHITE SOUTH

The antebellum white Southerners remained localistic and culturally conservative. Farm and plantation labor and the routines of family life were still conducted within the household, and prospects for most whites remained rooted in inherited land and family help. While the new northern middle class nourished a cosmopolitan culture and a domestic sentimentalism that subverted traditional authority, southerners—planters and yeomen alike— distrusted outsiders and defended rural neighborhood grounded in the authority of fathers and the integrity of families.

Southern Families

Most southern whites regarded themselves less as individuals than as representatives of families that extended through time from the distant past to unborn generations. Southern boys often received the family names of heroes as first names: Jefferson Davis, or Thomas Jefferson (later, General "Stonewall")

Jackson. More often, however, they took the name of a related family—Peyton Randolph, Preston Brooks, Langdon Cheves—and carried them as proud and often burdensome badges of who they were. Children learned early on that their first duty was to their family's reputation. When young Benjamin Tillman of South Carolina was away at school, his sister wrote "Don't relax in your efforts to gain a good education. . . . I want you to be an ornament to your family." Two years later, another sister wrote, "Do, Bud, study hard and make good use of your time. . . . I want you to do something for the Tillman name."

In the white South, reputation and the defense of family honor were everything. Boys and girls were taught to act as though everyone were watching them, ready to note any hint of inadequacy. A boy with a reputation for cowardice, for ineptness at riding or fighting, or for failure to control his emotions or hold his liquor, was an embarrassment to his family. Membership in the South's democracy of white men depended less upon wealth than upon the maintenance of personal and family integrity. An "unsullied reputation," insisted Albert Gallatin Brown of Mississippi, placed a man "on a social level with all his fellows." As John Horry Dent, an Alabama slaveholder and bad amateur poet put it,

Honor and shame from all conditions rise;
Act well your part and their [sic] the honor lies.

Among southern white men, wealth generally counted for less than maintaining one's personal and family honor and thus winning membership in the democracy of honorable males.

The code of honor, while it forged ties of equality and respect among white men, made rigid distinctions between men and women and whites and blacks. Women and girls who misbehaved—with transgressions ranging from simple gossip to poor housekeeping to adultery—damaged not only their own reputation but also the honor of fathers, brothers, or husbands who could not control them. Such a charge could mean social death in a rural community made up of patriarchal households and watchful neighbors. In 1813 Bolling Hall of Alabama advised his daughter, "If you learn to restrain every thought, action, and word by virtue and religion, you will become an ornament." A "good man" or a "good woman" was someone who upheld the family by acting within a prescribed social role ("Act well your part. . . ."), and not, as the children of the northern middle class were being taught, by acting as an autonomous, self-governing individual.

The southern code of honor blunted attacks upon social hierarchy and inherited status. When sentimental northerners attacked slavery because it denied the freedom of the individual, one southerner responded in a way that was meant to end the argument: "Do you say that the slave is held to involuntary service? So is the wife," whose "relation to her husband, in the great majority of cases, is made for her and not by her." Few white southerners would have questioned the good sense of that response. Southern life was not about freedom, individual fulfillment, or social progress; it was about honoring the obligations to which one was born.

Southern Entertainments

Southerners of all classes and races were leisure-loving people. But the rural character of the South threw them upon their own resources rather than on commercial entertainments. They drank, told stories, engaged in wrestling and boxing matches, and danced. For evangelicals who withdrew from such entertainments, church socials and camp meetings filled the gap, while rural southerners both in and out of the churches engaged in corn-huskings, birthday celebrations, berry-picking expeditions, and so forth. Books were not as readily available as they were in the North. The big publishing houses produced many titles aimed at northern and western readers and at such specialized constituencies as commercial farmers or middle-class housewives. The southern literary market, however, was too small to justify such special attention. Most southern families owned a Bible, and wealthier families often read histories, religious and political tracts, and English (seldom American) literature—with Shakespeare leading the way and Sir Walter Scott's tales of medieval chivalry not far behind. (Such stories exercised a strong fascination on some southerners; in the last years before the Civil War, jousting tournaments were held in which southern gentlemen clad in armor fought from horseback with lances and broadswords.) Hunting and fishing were passionate pursuits among southern men. Fox and deer hunts provided the gentry with an opportunity to display

Colonel and Mrs. Whiteside   Colonel and Mrs. James A. Whiteside, at home at their mansion on the heights above Chattanooga, are properly comfortable and genteel. Their infant son wears the traditional small child's dress, and the slaves who serve them are rendered grotesquely small.

their skill with horses and guns, while the hunts of poorer whites and slaves both provided sport and enhanced their threatened roles as providers. Though state laws forbade slaves to own guns or dogs, thousands of slaveowners found it wise to overlook the laws and to allow slaves a favorite recreation.

The commercial entertainments in the South were concentrated in the larger towns and along the major rivers. Showboats brought theatrical troupes, minstrel shows, animal acts, and other entertainment to the river towns. The gentry's love of horses and competition made New Orleans the horse racing capital of the country; New Orleans was also the only southern city where one could watch a professional prize fight. Various violent contests appealed to New Orleans audiences. In 1819 a New Orleans impresario advertised this program: a bull vs. six "of the strongest dogs in the country"; six bulldogs vs. a Canadian bear; a "beautiful Tiger" vs. a black bear; twelve dogs vs. a "strong and furious Opeloussas Bull." The advertisement further promised that "If

the tiger is not vanquished in his fight with the Bear, he will be sent alone against the last Bull; and if the latter conquers all his enemies, several pieces of fireworks will be placed on his back, which will produce a very entertaining amusement." The impresario then stated that the premises had been inspected by the Mayor of New Orleans, and that children would be admitted at half price. Though such events were outlawed in later years, they continued to be held on the sly. In 1852, five thousand spectators gathered outside New Orleans to watch a grizzly bear and a bull fight to the death.

From Camp Meeting to Community

The camp-meeting revivals of the early nineteenth century had transformed the South into an evangelical Bible Belt (see Chapter 8). By 1860, 88 percent of southern church members were Methodist, Baptist, Presbyterian, or Disciples of Christ. Revival religion had spread from the frontier and upcountry yeomanry into both the slave cabins and the plantation mansions. Some evangelicals had risen into the slaveholding class, and many of the old families had been converted. As a result, the deist or indifferently Anglican gentry of the eighteenth century became outnumbered by earnest Baptist and Methodist planters who considered themselves the fathers of an inclusive southern Christian community.

Southern revivals continued throughout the antebellum years, but they were no longer the inclusive, ecstatic camp meetings of the past. They were often limited to a single denomination—usually Methodist—and were held on permanent camp grounds maintained by the churches. Conducted with more decorum than in the past, they were routine community events: women began baking a week ahead of time, and looked forward to visiting with neighbors and relatives as much as they did to getting right with God.

The goal of camp meetings was still to induce spiritual crisis and conversion, and sinners still wept and fell on their way to being saved. But such manifestations as the barking exercise and the jerks (see Chapter 8) disappeared. Unfriendly observers after the 1820s could find nothing worse than breaches of decorum among the women. In 1828 an Englishwoman attended a meeting near Cincinnati at which nearly one hundred women came forward to fall at the feet of Christ until "they were soon all lying on the ground in an indescribable confusion of heads and legs." The southern humorist George W. Harris described a camp meeting at which his comic character Sut Lovingood put lizards up the preacher's pant leg. A fat woman fainted in the confusion, rolled down a hill, "tangled her laig an' garters in the top of a huckilberry bush, wif her head in the branch and jis' lay still."

The churches that grew out of southern revivals reinforced localistic neighborhoods and the patriarchal family. Some southern communities began when a whole congregation moved onto new land; others were settled by the chain migration of brothers and cousins, and subsequent revivals spread through family networks. Rural isolation limited most households to their own company during the week, but on Sundays church meetings united the neighborhood's cluster of extended families into a community of believers. In most neighborhoods, social connections seldom extended beyond that. The word "church" referred ultimately to the worldwide community of Christians, and the war between the "church" and the "world" referred to a cosmic history that would end in millennial fire. But in the day-to-day understandings of southern evangelicals, the church was the local congregation and the world was local sins and local sinners—many of whom were related to members of the church. Churches disciplined members for such worldly practices as drinking, gambling, dancing, swearing, fornication, and adultery, and even for giving the *impression* of sinful behavior. Mount Olive Baptist Church in North Carolina, for example, expelled Mary Bivens because she was "too thick with young men."

Southern evangelicalism began, like religious conservatism in the North, with the sovereignty of God, a conviction of human sinfulness, and an acceptance of disappointment and pain as part of God's grand and unknowable design. "Oh man," lamented one slaveholder, "when will thou meekly submit to God without a murmur. . . . His will be done should be your constant prayer." Southern church people continued to interpret misfortune as divine punishment. When yellow fever was killing a thousand people every week in New Orleans in 1853, the Episcopal Bishop (and soon to be Confederate general) Leonidas Polk asked God to "turn us from the ravages of the pestilence, wherewith for our iniquities, thou are visiting us."

The same view held at home. When the young son of a planter family died, the mother was certain that God had killed the child because the parents had loved him more than God: "*But God took* him for he saw he was our idol." A grieving South Carolinian received this consolation from a relative: "Hope you are quite reconciled to the loss of your darling babe. As it was the will of God to take him, we must obey, and He will be angry at us if we go past moderate grief." Francis Pickens, another South Carolinian, wrote after losing his wife and child, "I had almost forgot there was a God, and now I stand the scattered . . . and blasted monument of his just wrath." It was a far cry from the middle-class North's garden cemeteries and the romantic, redemptive deaths of children in sentimental fiction.

Southern cultural conservatism was rooted in religion, in the family, and in a system of fixed social roles. Southern preachers assumed that patriarchal social relations were crucial to Christian living within an irredeemably imperfect and often brutal world. Southerners revered the patriarch and slaveholder

Abraham more than any other figure in the Bible, and John C. Calhoun proclaimed "Hebrew Theocracy" the best government ever experienced by humankind. The father must—like Abraham—govern and protect his household, the mother must assist the father, and the women, children, and slaves must faithfully act out the duties of their stations. That meant a Christian strove to be a good mother, a good father, a good slave; by the same token, a Christian never questioned his or her God-given social role.

Proslavery Christianity

In Revolutionary and early national America, white southerners had been the most radical of republicans. Jeffersonian planter-politicians led the fights for equal rights and the absolute separation of church and state, and southern evangelicals were the early republic's staunchest opponents of slavery. By 1830, however, the South was an increasingly conscious minority within a democratic and capitalist nation. The northern middle classes proclaimed a link between material and moral progress, identifying both with individual autonomy and universal rights. A radical northern minority was agitating for the immediate abolition of slavery.

Southerners met this challenge with an "intellectual blockade" against outside publications and ideas and with a moral and religious defense of slavery. The Bible provided plenty of ammunition. Proslavery clergymen constantly stated that the Chosen People of the Old Testament had been patriarchs and slaveholders, and that Jesus had lived in a society that sanctioned slavery and never criticized the institution. Some ministers claimed that blacks were the descendants of Ham and thus deserved enslavement. The most common religious argument, however, was that slavery had given millions of heathen Africans the priceless opportunity to become Christians and to live in a Christian society. Thornton Stringfellow, a Virginia Baptist minister, insisted that "their condition . . . is now better than that of any equal number of laborers on earth, and is daily improving."

Like their northern counterparts, southern clergymen applauded the material improvements of the age. But they insisted that *moral* improvement occurred only when people embraced the timeless truths of the Bible. The South Carolinian William F. Hutson put it simply: "In religion and morals, we doubt all improvements, not known to certain fishermen who lived eighteen hundred years ago." Northern notions of progress through individual liberation, equal rights, and universal Christian love were wrong-headed and dangerous. The Presbyterian John Adger asserted that relations of dominance and submission (and not "barbarism and personal savage independence") were utterly necessary to both social and individual fulfillment, and that the distribution of rights and responsibilities were unequal and God-given. "The rights of the father are natural, but they belong only to the fathers. Rights of property are natural, but they belong only to those who have property"—and such natural rights were coupled with the awesome duties of fatherhood and proprietorship. In the end, southern proslavery intellectuals rejected Jefferson's "self-evident" equality of man; Edmund Ruffin, for instance, branded that passage of the Declaration of Independence as "indefensible" as well as "false and foolish."

THE PRIVATE LIVES OF SLAVES

In law, in the census, and in the minds of planters, slaves were members of a plantation household over which the owner exercised absolute authority not only as owner but also as paternal protector and lawgiver. Yet both slaveholders and slaves knew that slaves could not be treated like farm animals or little children. Wise slaveholders learned that the success of a plantation depended less on terror and draconian discipline (though whippings—and worse—were common) than on the accommodations by which slaves traded labor and obedience for some measure of privilege and autonomy within the bounds of slavery. After achieving privileges, the slaves called them their own: holidays, garden plots, friendships and social gatherings both on and off the plantation, hunting and fishing rights, and so on. Together, these privileges provided some of the ground on which they made their own lives within slavery.

The Slave Family

The most precious privilege was the right to make and maintain families. As early as the Revolutionary era, most Chesapeake slaves lived in units consisting of mother, father, and small children. On Charles

Five Generations of a Slave Family on a South Carolina Sea Island Plantation, 1862   Complex family ties such as these were among the most hard-won and vulnerable cultural accomplishments of enslaved blacks.

Carrol's Maryland farms in 1773, for example, 325 of the 400 slaves lived in such families. At Thomas Jefferson's Monticello, most slave marriages were for life, and small children almost always lived with both parents. The most common exceptions to this practice were fathers who had married away from their own plantations and who visited "broad wives" and children during their off hours. In Louisiana between 1810 and 1864, half the slaves lived in families headed by both parents; another one-fourth lived in single-parent families. Owners encouraged stable marriages because they made farms more peaceful and productive and because they flattered the owners' own religious and paternalistic sensibilities. For their part, slaves demanded families as part of the price of their labor.

Yet slave families were highly vulnerable. Many slaveholders assumed that they had the right to coerce sex from female slaves; some kept slaves as concubines, and a few even moved them into the main house. They tended, however, to keep these liaisons within bounds. While the slave community—in contrast to the whites—seldom punished sex before marriage, it took adultery seriously. Slaveholders knew that violations of married slave women could be enormously disruptive and strongly discouraged

them. A far more serious threat to slave marriages was the death, bankruptcy, or departure of the slaveholders. Between one-fifth and one-third of slave marriages were broken by such events.

Slaveholders who encouraged slave marriages—even perhaps solemnizing them with a religious ceremony—knew that marriage implied a form of self-ownership that conflicted with the slaves' status as property. Some conducted ceremonies in which couples "married" by jumping over a broomstick; others had the preacher omit the phrases "let no man put asunder" and "till death do you part" from the ceremony. Slaves knew that such ceremonies had no legal force. A Virginia slave remarked, "We slaves knowed that them words wasn't bindin'. Don't mean nothin' lessen you say, 'What God has jined, caint no man pull asunder.' But dey never would say dat. Jus' say 'Now you married.'" A black South Carolina preacher routinely ended the ceremony with "Till death or buckra [whites] part you."

Slaves modified their sense of family and kinship to accommodate such uncertainties. Because separation from father or mother was common, children spread their affection among their adult relatives, treating grandparents, aunts, and uncles almost as though they were parents. In fact, slaves often re-

Plantation Burial   Slave funerals retained strong West African as well as Christian accents. The ceremony was often held at night, and mourners were careful to placate the spirits of the dead, who remained temporarily in this world and could torment their enemies.

ferred to all their adult relatives as "parents." They also called nonrelatives "brother," "sister," "aunt," and "uncle," thus extending a sense of kinship to the slave community at large. Slaves chose as surnames for themselves the names of former owners, Anglicized versions of African names, or names that simply sounded good. They rarely chose the name of their current owner, however. Families tended to use the same given names over and over, naming boys after their father or grandfather—perhaps to preserve the memory of fathers who might be taken away. They seldom named girls after their mother, however. Unlike Southern whites, slaves never married a first cousin—even though many members of their community were close relatives. The origins and functions of some of these customs are unknown. We know only that slaves practiced them consistently, usually without the knowledge of the slaveholders.

White Missions, Slave Christians

By the 1820s southern evangelicalism had long since abandoned its hostility toward slavery, and slaveholders commonly attended camp meetings and revivals. These prosperous converts faced conflicting

duties. Their churches taught them that slaves had immortal souls and that they were as responsible for the spiritual welfare of their slaves as they were for the spiritual welfare of their own children. One preacher remarked that it was difficult "to treat them as property, and at the same time render to them that which is just and equal as immortal and accountable beings, and as heirs of the grace of life, equally with ourselves." A planter on his deathbed told his children that humane treatment and religious instruction for slaves was the duty of slaveowners; if these were neglected, "we will have to answer for the loss of their souls." After Nat Turner's bloody revolt in 1831, missions to the slaves took on new urgency: if the churches were to help create a family-centered, Christian society in the South, it would have to include the slaves. The result after 1830 was a concerted attempt to Christianize the slaves.

Charles Colcock Jones, a Presbyterian minister from Georgia, spent much of his career writing manuals on how to preach to slaves. He taught that there was no necessary connection between social position and spiritual worth—that there were good and bad slaveholders and good and bad slaves. But he also taught, preaching from the Epistles of Paul

("Servants, obey your masters"), that slaves must accept their master's authority as God's, and that obedience was their prime religious virtue. Jones warned white preachers never to become personally involved with their slave listeners—to pay no attention to their quarrels, their complaints about their master or about their fellow slaves, or about working conditions on the plantation. "We separate entirely their *religious* from their *civil* condition," he said, "and contend that one may be attended to without interfering with the other." The catechism Jones prepared for slaves included the question, "What did God make you for?" The answer was, "To make a crop."

The evangelical mission to the slaves was not as self-serving as it may seem. For to accept one's worldly station, to be obedient and dutiful within that station, and to seek salvation outside of this world were precisely what the planters demanded of themselves and their own family. An important goal of plantation missions was of course to create safe and profitable plantations. Yet that goal was to be achieved by Christianizing both slaveholders and slaves—a lesson that some slaveholders learned when they were expelled from their churches for mistreating their slaves.

The white attempt to Christianize slavery, however, depended on the acceptance of slavery by the slaves. But the biblical notion that slavery could be punishment for sin, and the doctrine of divinely ordained social orders, never took root among the slaves. Hannah Scott, a slave in Arkansas, remarked on what she heard a white preacher say: "But all he say is 'bedience to de white folks, and we hears 'nough of dat without him telling us." One slave asked a white preacher, "Is us slaves gonna be free in heaven?" The preacher quickly changed the subject. As one maid boldly told her mistress, *"God never made us to be slaves for white people."*

Although the slaves ignored much of what the missionaries taught, they embraced evangelical Christianity and transformed it into an independent African-American faith. Some slaveowners encouraged them by building "praise houses" on their plantations and by permitting religious meetings. Others tried to resist the trend, but with little success. After 1830 most of the southern states outlawed black preachers, but the laws could not be enforced. James Henry Hammond, a rich South Carolina planter, tried for twenty years to stop his slaves from holding religious meetings, but at night they would slip off

to secret gatherings in the woods. Sometimes slaves met in a cabin—preaching, praying, and singing in a whisper. At their meetings they rehearsed a faith that was at variance with the faith of the slaveholders. Reverend Anderson Edwards, a slave preacher from Texas, recalled that he "had to preach what Massa told me. And he say tell them niggers iffen they obeys the Massa they goes to heaven, but I knowed there's something better for them, but daren't tell them 'cept on the sly. That I done lots. I tells 'em iffen they keeps prayin' the Lord will set 'em free."

One way in which slave religion differed from what was preached to them by whites was in the practice of conjuring, folk magic, root medicine, and other occult knowledge—most of it passed down from West Africa. Such practices provided help in areas in which Christianity was useless. They could cure illnesses, make people fall in love, ensure a good day's fishing, or bring harm to one's enemies. Sometimes African magic was in competition with plantation Christianity. Just as often, however, slaves combined the two. For instance, slaves sometimes determined the guilt or innocence of a person accused of stealing by hanging a Bible by a thread, then watching the way it turned. The form was West African; the Bible was not. The slave root doctor George White boasted that he could "cure most anything," but added that "you got to talk wid God an' ask him to help out." "Maum Addie," a slave in coastal South Carolina, dealt with the malevolent African spirits called plat-eyes with a combination of African potions, the Christian God, and a stout stick: "So I totes mah powder en sulphur en I carries mah stick in mah han en puts mah truss in Gawd."

While Christianity could not cure sick babies or identify thieves, it gave slaves something more important: a sense of themselves as a historical people with a role to play in God's cosmic drama. In slave Christianity, Moses the liberator (and not the slaveholders' Abraham) stood beside Jesus. Indeed the slaves' appropriation of the book of Exodus denied the smug assumption of the whites that they were God's chosen people who had escaped the bondage of despotic Europe to enter the promised land of America. To the slaves, America was Egypt, they were the chosen people, and the slaveholders were Pharaoh. Thomas Wentworth Higginson, a Boston abolitionist who went south during the Civil War to lead a Union regiment of freed South Carolina slaves, wrote that his men knew the Old Testament books of Moses and the New Testament book of Revelation. "All that lies between," he said, "even the life of Jesus, they hardly cared to read or to hear." He found their minds "a vast bewildered chaos of Jewish history and biography; and most of the events of the past, down to the period of the American Revolution, they instinctively attribute to Moses." The slaves' religious songs, which became known as spirituals, told of God's people, their travails, and their ultimate deliverance. In songs and sermons the figures of Jesus and Moses were often blurred, and it was not always clear whether deliverance—accompanied by divine retribution—would take place in this world or the next. But deliverance always meant an end to slavery, with the possibility that it might bring a reversal of relations between slaves and masters. "The idea of a revolution in the conditions of the whites and blacks," said the escaped slave Charles Ball, "is the corner-stone of the religion of the latter."

Religion and Revolt

In comparison with slaves in Cuba, Jamaica, Brazil, and other New World plantation societies, North American slaves seldom went into organized, armed revolt. The environment of the United States was unfriendly to such events. American plantations were relatively small and dispersed, and the southern white population was large, vigilant, and very well armed. Whites also enjoyed—until the cataclysm of the Civil War—internal political stability. There were thus few situations in which slaves could hope to win their freedom by violent means. Thousands of slaves demonstrated their hatred of the system by running away. Others fought slaveowners or overseers, sabotaged equipment and animals, stole from planters, and found other ways to oppose slavery. But most knew that open revolt was suicide.

Christianity convinced slaves that history was headed toward an apocalypse that would result in divine justice and their own deliverance, and thus held out the possibility of revolt. But slave preachers seldom indulged in prophecy and almost never told their congregations to become actively engaged in God's divine plan, for they knew that open resistance was hopeless. Slave Christians believed that God hated slavery and would end it, but that their role was to have faith in God, to take care of one another, to preserve their identity as a people, and to

await deliverance. Only occasionally did slaves take retribution and deliverance into their own hands.

The most ambitious conspiracy was hatched by Denmark Vesey, a free black of Charleston, South Carolina. Vesey was a leading member of an African Methodist congregation that had seceded from the white Methodists and had been independent from 1817 to 1821. At its height, the church had 6,000 members—most of them slaves. Vesey and some of the other members read widely in political tracts, including the antislavery arguments in the Missouri debates (see Chapter 12) and in the Bible. They talked about their delivery out of Egypt, with all white men, women, and children being cut off. They identified Charleston as Jericho and planned its destruction in 1822: a few dozen Charleston blacks would take the state armory, then arm rural slaves who would rise up to help them. They would kill the whites, take control of the city, and then commandeer ships in the harbor and make their getaway—presumably to black-controlled Haiti. Word of the conspiracy spread secretly into the countryside, largely through the efforts of Gullah Jack, who was both a Methodist and an African conjurer. Jack recruited African-born slaves as soldiers, provided them with charms as protection against whites, and used his spiritual powers to terrify others into keeping silent.

In the end, the Vesey plot was betrayed by slaves. As one coerced confession followed another, white authorities hanged Vesey, Gullah Jack, and 34 other accused conspirators—22 of them in one day. But frightened whites knew that most of the conspirators (estimates ranged from 600 to 9,000) remained at large and unidentified.

In August 1831, in a revolt in Southampton County, Virginia, some 60 slaves shot and hacked to death 55 white men, women, and children. Their leader was Nat Turner, a Baptist lay preacher. Turner was neither a conjurer like Gullah Jack (indeed, he violently opposed plantation conjurers) nor a republican revolutionary like Denmark Vesey or the Richmond slave Gabriel (see Chapter 8). He was, he told his captors, an Old Testament prophet and an instrument of God's wrath. As a child, he had prayed and fasted often, and the spirit—the same spirit that had spoken to the prophets of the Bible—had spoken directly to him. When he was a young man, he had run away in order to escape a cruel overseer. But when God said that He had not chosen him

Nat Turner   This contemporary woodcut depicts scenes from Nat Turner's Rebellion. Fifty-five whites, most of them women and children, were shot and hacked to death in this bloodiest of all North American slave revolts.

merely to have him run away, Nat had returned. He justified his return by quoting one of the slaveowners' favorite verses of scripture: "He who knoweth his master's will and doeth it not, shall be beaten with many stripes." But Turner made it clear that his Master was God, not a slaveowner.

Around 1830, Turner received visions of the final battle in Revelation, recast as a fight between white and black spirits. He saw Christ crucified against the night sky, and the next morning he saw Christ's blood in a cornfield. Convinced by a solar eclipse in February 1831 that the time had come, Turner began telling other slaves about his visions, recruited his force, and launched his bloody and hopeless revolt.

The Vesey and Turner revolts, along with scores of more limited conspiracies, deeply troubled southern whites. Slaveholders were committed to a paternalism that was increasingly tied to the South's attempt to make slavery both domestic and Christian. For their part, slaves recognized that they could receive decent treatment and pockets of autonomy in return for outward docility. Vesey and Turner opened wide cracks in that mutual charade. During the Turner revolt, slaves whose masters had been murdered joined the rebels without a second thought. A plantation mistress who survived by hiding in a closet listened to the murders of her husband and children, then heard her house servants arguing over posses-

sion of her clothes. A Charleston grandee named Elias Horry, upon finding that his coachman was among the Vesey conspirators, asked him, "What were your intentions?" The formerly docile slave replied that he had intended "to kill you, rip open your belly, and throw your guts in your face."

Such stories sent a chill through the white South — a suspicion that despite the appearance of peace, they were surrounded by people who would kill them in an instant. While northerners patronized plays and cheap fiction that dramatized the trickery and horror beneath placid appearances, the nightmares of slaveholding paternalists were both more savage and closer to home.

Coda

These years of cultural creation were the years in which Jefferson's agrarian republic became Andrew Jackson's noisy and deeply divided mass democracy. Politicians, who were both consumers and producers of the new popular culture, tapped skillfully into the national patchwork of aspiration, fear, and resentment. John Quincy Adams, Henry Clay, and other National Republicans and Whigs concocted visions of smooth-running, government-sponsored national transportation and monetary systems that echoed the beliefs in material progress and cosmic order that had become cultural axioms for the more prosperous and cosmopolitan Americans. Against them stood Andrew Jackson, casting himself as a melodramatic hero who trusted providence, popular democracy, and his own iron will to rescue the old republic from the trickery and deceit of his outwardly respectable foes.

SUGGESTED READING

Stuart M. Blumin, *The Emergence of the Middle Class: Social Experience in the American City, 1760–1900* (1989) is a thorough study of work and material life among the urban middle class. Studies that treat religion, family, and sentimental culture include Paul E. Johnson, *A Shopkeeper's Millennium: Society and Revivals in Rochester, New York, 1815–1837* (1978); Mary P. Ryan, *Cradle of the Middle Class: The Family in Oneida County, New York, 1790–1865* (1981); Carroll Smith-Rosenberg, *Disorderly Conduct: Visions of Gender in Victorian America* (1985); Karen Halttunen, *Confidence Men and Painted Women: A Study of Middle-Class Culture in America, 1830–1870* (1982); and Jane Tompkins, *Sensational Designs: The Cultural Work of American Fiction, 1790–1860* (1985). On art and artists, see Neil Harris, *The Artist in American Society: The Formative Years, 1790–1860* (1966); Barbara Novak, *Nature and Culture: American Landscape and Painting, 1825–1875* (1980); Angela Miller, *The Empire of the Eye: Landscape Representation and American Cultural Politics, 1825–1875* (1993); and Elizabeth McKinsey, *Niagara Falls: Icon of the American Sublime* (1985).

Lewis O. Saum, *The Popular Mood of Pre–Civil War America* (1980) is a valuable study of the unsentimental culture of antebellum plain folk. The most thorough treatments of popular evangelicalism are the works of Jon Butler and Nathan Hatch listed in the Suggested Reading for Chapter 8. See also Curtis D. Johnson, *Redeeming America: Evangelicals and the Road to Civil War* (1993); Michael Barkun, *Crucible of the Millennium: The Burned-Over District of New York in the 1840s* (1986); David L. Rowe, *Thunder and Trumpets: Millerites and Dissenting Religion in Upstate New York, 1800–1850* (1985); Paul E. Johnson and Sean Wilentz, *The Kingdom of Matthias: A Story of Sex and Salvation in 19th-Century America* (1994); and John L. Brooke, *The Refiner's Fire: The Making of Mormon Cosmology, 1644–1844* (1994).

Studies of popular literature and entertainments in these years include Elliott J. Gorn, *The Manly Art: Bare-Knuckle Prize Fighting in America* (1986); Melvin L. Adelman, *A Sporting Time: New York City and the Rise of Modern Athletics* (1986); Alexander P. Saxton, *The Rise and Fall of the White Republic: Class Politics and Mass Culture in Nineteenth-Century America* (1990); Eric Lott, *Love & Theft: Blackface Minstrelsy and the American Working Class* (1993); Michael Denning, *Mechanic Accents: Dime Novels and Working-Class Culture in America* (1987); David S. Reynolds, *Beneath the American Renaissance: The Subversive Imagination in the Age of Emerson and Melville* (1988). New directions in literary criticism in these years can be sampled in Sacvan Bercovitch and Myra Jehlen, eds., *Ideology and Classic American Literature* (1986).

Peter Kolchin's *American Slavery, 1619–1877* (1993) is a brilliant synthesis of recent scholarship on the Old South. On the family culture of southern whites, see Bertram Wyatt-Brown, *Southern Honor: Ethics & Behavior in the Old South* (1982); Elizabeth Fox-Genovese, *Within the Plantation Household: Black and White Women in the Old South* (1988); and Carol Bleser, ed., *In Joy and in Sorrow: Women, Family, and Marriage in the Victorian South, 1830–1900* (1991). Eugene D. Genovese, *The Slaveholders' Dilemma: Freedom and Progress in Southern Conservative Thought, 1820–1860* (1992) demonstrates the pervasive paternalism of southern social thought. Donald G. Matthews, *Religion in the Old South* (1977) is a valuable introduction to its subject. Other studies of southern religion are listed in the Suggested Reading to Chapter 8.

A now classic overview of slave culture is Eugene D. Genovese, *Roll, Jordan, Roll: The World the Slaves Made* (1974). Also essential are Lawrence W. Levine, *Black Culture and Black Consciousness: Afro-American Folk Thought from Slavery to Freedom* (1977), and Charles Joyner, *Down by the Riverside: A South Carolina Slave Community* (1984). Study of the slave family begins with Herbert G. Gutman, *The Black Family in Slavery and Freedom, 1750–1925* (1976), which can now be supplemented with Ann Patton Malone, *Sweet Chariot: Slave Family and Household Structure in Nineteenth-Century Louisiana* (1992). John Michael Vlach, *Back of the Big House: The Architecture of Plantation Slavery* (1993) is a valuable cultural study. Slave religion is treated in Mechal Sobel, *Travelin' On: The Slave Journey to an Afro-Baptist Faith* (1979) and Margaret Washington Creel, *"A Peculiar People": Slave Religion and Community-Culture among the Gullahs* (1988). Other essential studies on these and related topics are cited in the Suggested Reading for Chapters 8 and 10.

Chapter 12

Jacksonian Democracy

Andrew Jackson struck a romantic military pose for this portrait painted in 1820. Posing as democracy incarnate and as an extravagantly melodramatic hero, Jackson imposed himself upon his times as few Americans have done.

PROLOGUE: 1819

Jacksonian Democracy was rooted in two events that occurred in 1819. First, the angry debate that surrounded Missouri's admission as a slave state revealed the centrality and vulnerability of slavery within the Union. Second, a severe financial collapse led many Americans to wonder whether the market revolution was compatible with the Jeffersonian republic. By 1820 politicians were determined to reconstruct the limited-government, states'-rights coalition that had elected Thomas Jefferson. By 1828 they had formed the Democratic Party, with Andrew Jackson at its head.

The West, 1803–1840s

When Jefferson bought the Louisiana Territory in 1803, he knew that he was giving future generations of Americans a huge "Empire for Liberty." About the new land, however, he knew almost nothing.

Only a few French trappers and traders had traveled the plains between the Mississippi and the Rocky Mountains, and no white person had seen the territory drained by the Columbia River. In 1804 Jefferson sent an expedition under Meriweather Lewis, his private secretary, and William Clark, brother of the Indian fighter George Rogers Clark, to explore the land he had bought. To prepare for the expedition, Lewis studied astronomy, zoology, and botany; Clark was already an accomplished mapmaker. The two kept meticulous journals of one of the epic adventures in American history.

In May 1804 Lewis and Clark and forty-one companions boarded a keelboat and two large canoes at the village of St. Louis. That spring and summer they poled and paddled 1,600 miles up the Missouri River, passing through rolling plains dotted by the farm villages of the Pawnee, Oto, Missouri, Crow, Omaha, Hidatsa, and Mandan peoples. The villages of the lower Missouri had been cut off from the western buffalo herds and reduced to dependence by

A Birds-Eye-View by George Catlin The Mandan village at the Big Bend of the Missouri River hosted the Lewis and Clark party in 1804–1805. The village was painted by George Catlin in 1832. Within a few years, the Mandans were extinct, victims of smallpox and the Sioux.

mounted Sioux warriors who had begun to establish their hegemony over the northern plains.

Lewis and Clark traveled through Sioux territory and stopped for the winter at the prosperous, heavily fortified Mandan villages at the big bend of the Missouri River in Dakota country. In the spring they hired Toussaint Charbonneau, a French fur trader, to guide them to the Pacific. Though Charbonneau turned out to be useless, his wife, a teenaged Shoshone girl named Sacajawea, was an indispensable guide, interpreter, and diplomat. With her help, Lewis and Clark navigated the upper Missouri, crossed the Rockies to the Snake River, and followed that stream to the Columbia River. They reached the Pacific in November 1805 and spent the winter at what is now Astoria, Oregon. Retracing their steps the following spring and summer, they reached St. Louis in September 1806. They brought with them many volumes of drawings and notes, along with assurances that the Louisiana Purchase had been worth many, many times its price.

Early White Settlements in Louisiana Territory As time passed, Americans began to settle the southern portions of the Louisiana Purchase. Louisiana itself,

strategically crucial and already the site of sugar plantations and the town of New Orleans, entered the Union in 1812. Settlers were also filtering into northern Louisiana and the Arkansas and Missouri territories. Farther north and west, the Sioux extended their control over the northern reaches of the land that Jefferson had bought.

The Expansion of the Sioux The Sioux were aided in their conquest by the spread of smallpox. The disease moved up the Missouri River periodically from the 1790s onward; by the 1830s, epidemics were ravaging the sedentary peoples of the Missouri. The Mandans, who had been so hospitable to Lewis and Clark, got the worst of it: they were completely wiped out. The Sioux and their Cheyenne allies, who lived in small bands and were constantly on the move, fared better. Their horse-raiding parties now grew into armies of mounted invaders numbering as many as 2,000, and they extended their hunting lands south into what is now southern Nebraska and as far west as the Yellowstone River. In the 1840s white settlers began crossing the southern plains, while white politicians entered into a fateful debate on whether these lands would become the site of northern farms or southern plantations. At the same time, the newly victorious Sioux never doubted that the northern plains would be theirs forever.

The Missouri Crisis

Early in 1819 slave-holding Missouri applied for admission to the Union as the first new state to be carved out of the Louisiana Purchase. New York Congressman James Tallmadge, Jr., quickly proposed two amendments to the Missouri statehood bill. The first would bar additional slaves from being brought into Missouri (16 percent of Missouri's people were already slaves). The second would emancipate Missouri slaves born after admission when they reached their twenty-fifth birthday. Put simply, the Tallmadge Amendments would admit Missouri only if Missouri agreed to become a free state.

The Politics of Slavery   The congressional debates on the Missouri question had nothing to do with humanitarian objections to slavery and everything to do with political power. Rufus King of New York, an old Federalist who led the northerners in the Senate, insisted that he opposed the admission of a new slave state "solely in its bearing and effects upon great political interests, and upon the just and equal rights of the freemen of the nation." Northerners had long chafed at the added representation in Congress and in the electoral college that the three-fifths rule granted to the slave states (see Chapter 7). The rule had, in fact, added significantly to southern power: in 1790 the South, with 40 percent of the white population, controlled 47 percent of the votes in Congress—enough to decide close votes both in Congress and in presidential elections. Federalists pointed out that of the twelve additional electoral votes the three-fifths rule gave to the South, ten had gone to Thomas Jefferson in 1800 and had given him the election. Without the bogus votes provided by slavery, they argued, Virginia's stranglehold on the presidency would have been broken with Washington's departure in 1796.

Deadlock   In 1819 the North held a majority in the House of Representatives. The South, thanks to the recent admissions of Alabama and southern-oriented Illinois, controlled a bare majority in the Senate. Voting on the Tallmadge Amendments was starkly sec-

tional: northern congressmen voted 86 to 10 for the first amendment, 80 to 14 for the second; southerners rejected both, 66 to 1 and 64 to 2. In the Senate, a unanimous South defeated the Tallmadge Amendments with the help of the two Illinois senators and three northerners. Deadlocked between a Senate in favor of admitting Missouri as a slave state and a House dead set against it, the Congress broke off one of the angriest sessions in its history and went home.

Compromise   The new Congress that convened in the winter of 1819–1820 passed the legislative package that became known as the Missouri Compromise. Massachusetts offered its northern counties as the new free state of Maine, thus neutralizing fears that the South would gain votes in the Senate with the admission of Missouri. Senator Jesse Thomas of Illinois then proposed the so-called Thomas Proviso: if the North would admit Missouri as a slave state, the South would agree to outlaw slavery in territories north of the 36° 30' north latitude—a line extending from the southern border of Missouri to Spanish (within a year, Mexican) territory. That line would open Arkansas Territory (present-day Arkansas and Oklahoma) to slavery and would close to slavery the remainder of the Louisiana Territory, land that subsequently became all or part of nine states.

Congress admitted Maine with little debate. But the admission of Missouri under the terms of the Thomas Proviso met northern opposition. A joint Senate-House committee finally decided to separate the two bills. With half of the southern representatives and nearly all of the northerners supporting it, the Thomas Proviso passed. Congress then took up the admission of Missouri. With the votes of a solid South and fourteen compromise-minded northerners, Missouri entered the Union as a slave state. President Monroe applauded the "patriotic devotion" of the northern representatives "who preferr'd the sacrifice of themselves at home to" endangering the Union. His words were prophetic: nearly all of the fourteen were voted out of office when they faced angry northern voters in the next election.

The Missouri crisis brought the South's commitment to slavery and the North's resentment of southern political power into collision, revealing an uncompromisable gulf between slave and free states. While northerners vowed to relinquish no more territory to slavery, southerners talked openly of disunion and civil war. A Georgia politician announced that the Missouri debates had lit a fire that "seas of blood can only extinguish." John Quincy Adams saw the debates as an omen: northerners would unanimously oppose the extension of slavery whenever the question came to a vote. Adams confided to his diary:

> Here was a new party ready formed, . . . terrible to the whole Union, but portentiously terrible to the South — threatening in its progress the emancipation of all their slaves, threatening in its immediate effect that Southern domination which has swayed the Union for the last twenty years. . . .

Viewing the crisis from Monticello, the aging Thomas Jefferson was distraught:

> A geographical line, coinciding with a marked principle, moral and political, once conceived and held up to the angry passions of men, will never be obliterated; every new irritation will mark it deeper and deeper. . . . This momentous question, like a fire-bell in the night, awakened and filled me with terror. I considered it at once the knell of the Union.

The Panic of 1819

Politicians debated the Missouri question against a darkening backdrop of economic depression — a downturn that would shape political alignments as much as the slavery question. The origins of the Panic of 1819 were international and numerous: European agriculture was recovering from the Napoleonic Wars, thereby reducing the demand for American foodstuffs; war and revolution in the New World had cut off the supply of precious metals (the base of the international money supply) from the mines of Mexico and Peru; debt-ridden European governments hoarded the available specie; and American bankers and businessmen met the situation by expanding credit and issuing banknotes that were mere dreams of real money. Coming in the first years of the market revolution, this speculative boom was encouraged by American bankers who had little experience with corporate charters, promissory notes, bills of exchange, or stocks and bonds.

Collapse and Depression: Failure of the Market Economy One of the reasons Congress had chartered the Second Bank of the United States in 1816 (see

Chapter 10) was to impose order on this situation. But the Bank itself under the presidency of the genial Republican politician William Jones, became part of the problem: the western branch offices in Cincinnati and Lexington became embroiled in the speculative boom, and insiders at the Baltimore branch hatched criminal schemes to enrich themselves. With matters spinning out of control, Jones resigned early in 1819. The new president, Langdon Cheves of South Carolina, curtailed credit and demanded that state bank notes received by the Bank of the United States be redeemed in specie (precious metals). By doing so, Cheves rescued the Bank from the paper economy created by state-chartered banks, but at huge expense: when the state banks were forced to redeem their notes in specie, they demanded payment from their own borrowers, and the national money and credit system collapsed.

The depression that followed the Panic of 1819 was the first failure of the market economy. There had been local ups and downs since the 1790s, but this collapse was nationwide. Employers who could not meet their debts went out of business, and hundreds of thousands of wage workers lost their jobs. In Philadelphia, unemployment reached 75 percent; 1,800 workers in that city were imprisoned for debt. A tent city of the unemployed sprang up on the outskirts of Baltimore. Other cities and towns were hit as hard, and the situation was no better in the countryside. Thomas Jefferson reported that farms in his neighborhood were selling for what had earlier been a year's rent, while a single session of the county court at Nashville handled over 500 suits for debt.

Faced with a disastrous downturn that none could control and that few understood, many Americans turned their resentment on the banks, particularly on the Bank of the United States. John Jacob Astor, a New York merchant and possibly the richest man in America, admitted that "there has been too much Speculation and too much assumption of Power on the Part of the Bank Directors which has caused [sic] the institution to become unpopular. . . ." William Gouge, who would become the Jacksonian Democrats' favorite economist, put it more bluntly: when the Bank demanded that state bank notes be redeemed in specie, he said, "the Bank was saved and the people were ruined." By the end of 1819 the Bank of the United States had won the name that it would carry to its death in the 1830s: the Monster.

REPUBLICAN REVIVAL

The crises of 1819–1820 prompted demands for a return to Jeffersonian principles. President James Monroe's happily proclaimed "Era of Good Feelings" — a new era of partyless politics created by the collapse of Federalism — was, according to worried Republicans, a disaster. Without opposition, Jefferson's dominant Republican Party had lost its way. The nationalist Congress of 1816 had enacted much of the Federalist program under the name of Republicanism; the result, said the old Republicans, was an aggressive government that helped bring on the Panic of 1819. At the same time, the collapse of Republican Party discipline in Congress had allowed the Missouri question to degenerate into a sectional free-for-all. By 1820 many Republicans were calling for a Jeffersonian revival that would limit government power and guarantee southern rights within the Union.

Martin Van Buren Leads the Way

The busiest and the most astute of those Republicans was Martin Van Buren, leader of New York's Bucktail Republican faction, who took his seat in the Senate in 1821. An immensely talented man with no influential family connections (his father was a Hudson Valley tavernkeeper) and little formal education, Van Buren had built his political career out of a commitment to Jeffersonian principles, personal charm, and party discipline. Arriving in Washington in the aftermath of the Missouri debates and the Panic of 1819, he hoped to apply his political expertise to what he perceived as a dangerous turning point in national politics.

Van Buren's New York experience, along with his reading of national politics, told him that disciplined political parties were necessary democratic tools. The Founding Fathers — including Jefferson — had denounced parties, claiming that republics rested on civic virtue, not competition. Van Buren, on the other hand, claimed that the Era of Good Feelings had turned public attention away from politics, allowing privileged insiders — many of them unreconstructed Federalists — to create a big national state and to reorganize politics along sectional lines. Van Buren insisted that competition and party divisions were inevitable and good, but that they must be made to serve the republic.

> We must always have party distinctions, and the old ones are the best. . . . If the old ones are suppressed, geographical differences founded on local instincts or what is worse, prejudices between free & slave holding states will inevitably take their place.

Working with likeminded politicians, Van Buren reconstructed the coalition of northern and southern agrarians that had elected Thomas Jefferson. The result was the Democratic party and, ultimately, a national two-party system that persisted until the eve of the Civil War.

The Election of 1824

With the approach of the 1824 presidential election, Van Buren and his friends supported William H. Crawford, Monroe's Secretary of War and a staunch Georgia Republican. The Van Burenites controlled the Republican congressional caucus, the body that traditionally chose the party's presidential candidates. The public distrusted the caucus as undemocratic, for it represented the only party in government and thus could dictate the choice of a president. But Van Buren continued to regard it as a necessary tool of party discipline. With most congressmen fearing their constituents, only a minority showed up for the caucus vote. They dutifully nominated Crawford.

The Candidates   With Republican party unity broken, the list of sectional candidates grew. John Quincy Adams was the son of a Federalist president, successful Secretary of State under Monroe, and one of the northeastern Federalist converts to Republicanism who, according to people like Van Buren and Crawford, had blunted the republican thrust of Jefferson's old party. He entered the contest as New England's favorite son. Henry Clay of Kentucky, a nationalist who claimed as his own the American System of protective tariffs, centralized banking, and government-sponsored internal improvements, expected to carry the West. John C. Calhoun of South Carolina announced his candidacy; but when he saw the swarm of candidates, he dropped out and put himself forth as the sole candidate for vice president.

The wild card was Andrew Jackson of Tennessee, who in 1824 was known only as a military hero — scourge of the southern Indians and victor over the British at New Orleans (see Chapter 9). He was also a frontier nabob with a reputation for violence: he had killed a rival in a duel, had engaged in a shoot-

Henry Clay   Clay, posed here with emblems of commerce, agriculture, and manufacturing, was the most consistent and eloquent spokesman for the American System. His supposed participation in the "Corrupt Bargain" of 1825 severely hurt his chances of becoming president.

out in a Nashville tavern, and had reputedly stolen his wife from her estranged husband. According to Jackson's detractors, such impetuosity marked his public life as well. As commander of U.S. military forces in the South in 1818, Jackson had led an unauthorized invasion of Spanish Florida, claiming that it was a hide-out for Seminole warriors who raided into the United States and a sanctuary for runaway Georgia slaves. During the action he had occupied Spanish forts, summarily executed Seminoles, and hanged two British subjects. Secretary of State John Quincy Adams had belatedly approved the raid, knowing that the show of American force would encourage the Spanish to sell Florida to the

United States. Secretary of War Crawford, on the other hand, as an "economy" measure, had reduced the number of major generals in the U.S. Army from two to one, thus eliminating Jackson's job. After being appointed governor of newly acquired Florida in 1821, Jackson retired from public life later that year. In 1824 eastern politicians knew Jackson only as a "military chieftain," "the Napoleon of the woods," a frontier hothead, and, possibly, a robber-bridegroom.

The Vote   Jackson may have been all those things. But what the easterners did not take into account in the election of 1824 was his immense popularity, particularly in the new states of the South and the West. In the sixteen states that chose presidential electors by popular vote (six states still left the choice to their legislatures), Jackson polled 152,901 votes to Adams's 114,023 and Clay's 47,217. Crawford, who suffered a crippling stroke during the campaign, won 46,979 votes. Jackson's support was more nearly national than that of his opponents. Adams carried only his native New England and a portion of New York. Clay's meager support was limited to the Northwest, and Crawford's to the Southeast and to the portions of New York that Van Buren was able to deliver. Jackson carried 84 percent of the votes of his own Southwest, and won victories in Pennsylvania, New Jersey, North Carolina, Indiana, and Illinois, while running a close second in several other states.

The Decision   Jackson assumed that he had won the election: he had received 42 percent of the popular vote to his nearest rival's 33 percent, and he was clearly the nation's choice. But his 99 electoral votes were 32 shy of the plurality demanded by the Constitution. And so, acting under the Twelfth Amendment, the House of Representatives would select a president from among the top three candidates. As the candidate with the fewest electoral votes, Henry Clay was eliminated. But he remained Speaker of the House, and he had enough support to throw the election to either Jackson or Adams. Years later, Jackson told a dinner guest that Clay had offered to support him in exchange for Clay's appointment as Secretary of State—an office that traditionally led to the presidency. When Jackson turned him down, according to Jacksonian legend, Clay went to Adams and made the same offer. Adams accepted what

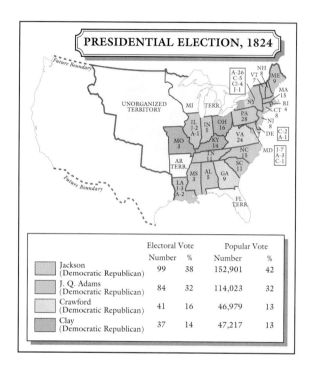

PRESIDENTIAL ELECTION, 1824

	Electoral Vote		Popular Vote	
	Number	%	Number	%
Jackson (Democratic Republican)	99	38	152,901	42
J. Q. Adams (Democratic Republican)	84	32	114,023	32
Crawford (Democratic Republican)	41	16	46,979	13
Clay (Democratic Republican)	37	14	47,217	13

became known as the "Corrupt Bargain" in January 1825. A month later, the House of Representatives voted: Clay's supporters, joined by several old Federalists, switched to Adams, giving him a one-vote victory. Soon after becoming president, Adams appointed Henry Clay as his Secretary of State.

The Reaction: Jackson Attacks Political Corruption
Reaction to the alleged "Corrupt Bargain" between John Quincy Adams and Henry Clay dominated the Adams administration and gave rise to a rhetoric of intrigue and betrayal that nourished a rising democratic movement. Before the vote took place in the House of Representatives, Andrew Jackson remarked, "Rumors say that deep intrigue is on foot," and predicted that there would be "bargain & sale" of the presidency. After the election, Jackson declared that the "gamester" Henry Clay has subverted the democratic will to his own purposes, and that "the rights of the people have been bartered for promises of office." "So you see," Jackson said, "The *Judas* of the West has closed the contract and will receive the thirty pieces of silver. His end will be the same." Others in Washington were equally appalled. Robert Y. Hayne of South Carolina denounced the "monstrous union between Clay & Adams," while Louis

McLane of Delaware declared the coalition of Clay and Adams utterly "unnatural & preposterous." (Eventually, Clay challenged Virginia Senator John Randolph, one of his nastiest critics, to a duel. Clay's shot passed harmlessly through Randolph's flowing coat, and Randolph fired a gentlemanly shot into the air. But the charge of corruption would follow Clay for the rest of his political life.)

Andrew Jackson regarded the intrigues that robbed him of the presidency in 1825 as the culmination of a long train of corruption that the nation had suffered over the last ten years. Although in the campaign he had made only vague policy statements, he had firm ideas of what had gone wrong with the republic. In 1821, after having been "betrayed" by members of Monroe's cabinet over his raid into Florida, Jackson had retired to his plantation near Nashville, had pondered the state of the nation, and had filled page after page with what he called "memorandums." (This was the kind of gaffe that appalled his educated eastern opponents and pleased nearly everyone else.)

A frontier planter with a deep distrust of banks, Jackson claimed that the Panic of 1819 had been brought on by self-serving miscreants in the Bank of the United States. He insisted that the national debt was another source of corruption; it must be paid off and never allowed to recur. The federal government under James Monroe was filled with swindlers, and in the name of a vague nationalism they were taking power for themselves and scheming against the liberties of the people. The politicians had been bought off, said Jackson, and had attempted—through "King Caucus"—to select a president by backstairs deals rather than by popular election. Finally, in 1825, they had stolen the presidency outright.

Like hundreds of thousands of other Americans, Jackson sensed that something had gone wrong with the republic—that selfishness and intrigue had corrupted the government. In the language of revolutionary republicanism, which Jackson had learned as a boy in the Carolina backwoods and would speak throughout his life, a corrupt power once again threatened to snuff out liberty.

In his "memorandums," Jackson set against the designs of that power the classic republican safeguard: a virtuous citizenry. But unlike most of his revolutionary forebears, he believed that government should be subject to the will of popular majorities. An aroused public, he said, was the republic's best

The Election of 1824   Cartoonist David Claypoole Johnston portrayed the election of 1824 as a footrace. At left, Adams and Crawford run neck and neck while Jackson has the outside track. At right, Clay has dropped out, but a supporter is helping him to make plans.

hope: "My fervent prayers are that our republican government may be perpetual, and the people alone by their virtue, and independent exercise of their free suffrage can make it perpetual."

More completely than any of his rivals, Jackson had captured the rhetoric of the revolutionary republic. And, with his fixation on secrecy, corruption, and intrigues, he transformed both that rhetoric and his own biography into popular melodrama. Finally, with a political alchemy that his rivals never understood, Jackson submerged old notions of republican citizenship into a firm faith in majoritarian democracy: individuals might become selfish and corrupt, he believed, but a democratic majority was, by its very nature, opposed to corruption and governmental excess. Thus the republic was safe only when governed by the will of the majority. The "Corrupt Bargain" of 1825 had made that clear: either the people or political schemers would rule.

ADAMS VERSUS JACKSON

While Jackson plotted revenge, John Quincy Adams assumed the duties of the presidency. He was well

prepared. The son of a Federalist president, he had been an extraordinarily successful Secretary of State under Monroe, guiding American diplomacy in the postwar world.

Nationalism in an International Arena

In the Rush-Bagot Treaty of 1817 and the British-American Convention of 1818 Adams helped pacify the Great Lakes, restore American fishing rights off of Canada, and draw the United States–Canadian boundary west to the Rocky Mountains — actions that transformed the Canadian-American frontier from a battleground into the peaceful border that it has been ever since. He pacified the southern border as well. In 1819, following Jackson's raid into Florida, the Adams-Onís Treaty procured Florida for the United States and defined the United States–Spanish border west of the Mississippi in ways that gave the Americans claims to the Pacific Coast in the Northwest.

Trickier problems had arisen when Spanish colonies in the Americas declared their independence. Spain could not prevent this, and the powers of Europe, victorious over Napoleon and determined to roll back the republican revolution, talked openly of helping the Spanish or of annexing South American territory for themselves. Both the Americans and the British opposed such a move, and the British proposed a joint statement outlawing the interference of any outside power (including themselves) in Latin America. Adams had thought it better for the United States to make its own policy than to "come in as cock-boat in the wake of the British man-of-war." In 1823 he wrote what became the Monroe Doctrine. Propounded at the same time that the United States recognized the new Latin American republics, it declared American opposition to any European attempt at colonization in the New World without (as the British had wanted) denying the right of the United States to annex new territory. Though the international community knew that the British navy, and not the Monroe Doctrine, kept the European powers out of the Americas, Adams had announced that the United States was determined to become the preeminent power in the Western Hemisphere.

Nationalism at Home

As president, Adams tried to translate his fervent nationalism into domestic policy. But while the brilliant, genteel Adams had dealt smoothly with European diplomats, as president of a democratic republic he went out of his way to isolate himself and to offend popular democracy. In his first annual message to Congress, Adams outlined an ambitious program for national development under the auspices of the federal government: roads, canals, a national university, a national astronomical observatory ("lighthouses of the skies"), and other costly initiatives.

> The spirit of improvement is abroad upon the earth, . . . While foreign nations less blessed with . . . freedom . . . than ourselves are advancing with gigantic strides in the career of public improvement, were we to slumber in indolence or fold up our arms and proclaim to the world that we are palsied by the will of our constituents, would it not . . . doom ourselves to perpetual inferiority?

Congressmen could not believe their ears as they listened to Adams's extravagant proposals. Here was a president who had received only one in three votes and who had entered office accused of intrigues against the democratic will. And yet at the first op-

portunity he was telling Congress to pass an ambitious program and not to be "palsied" by the will of the electorate. Even members of Congress who favored Adams's program (and there were many of them) were afraid to vote for it.

Adding to his reputation as an enemy of democracy whenever opportunity presented itself, Adams heaped popular suspicions not only on himself but on his program. Hostile politicians and journalists never tired of joking about Adams's "lighthouses to the skies." More lasting, however, was the connection they drew between federal public works projects and high taxes, intrusive government, the denial of democratic majorities, and expanded opportunities for corruption, secret deals, and special favors. Congress never acted on the president's proposals, and the Adams administration emerged as little more than a long prelude to the election of 1828.

The Election of 1828

As early as 1825, it was clear that the election of 1828 would pit Adams against Andrew Jackson. To the consternation of his chief supporters, Adams did nothing to prepare for the contest. He refused to remove even his noisiest enemies from appointive office, and he built no political organization for what promised to be a stiff contest for reelection. The opposition was much more active. Van Buren and like-minded Republicans (with their candidate Crawford hopelessly incapacitated) switched their allegiance to Jackson. They wanted Jackson elected, however, not only as a popular hero but as head of a disciplined and committed Democratic Party that would continue the states'-rights, limited-government positions of the old Jeffersonian Republicans.

The new Democratic Party linked popular democracy with the defense of southern slavery. Van Buren began preparations for 1828 with a visit to John C. Calhoun of South Carolina. Calhoun was moving along the road from postwar nationalism to states'-rights conservatism; he also wanted to stay on as vice president and thus keep his presidential hopes alive. After convincing Calhoun to support Jackson and to endorse limited government, Van Buren wrote to Thomas Ritchie, editor of the *Richmond Enquirer* and leader of Virginia's Republicans, who could deliver Crawford's southern supporters to Jackson. In his letter, Van Buren proposed to revive the alliance of "the planters of the South and the plain Republicans of the North" that had won Jefferson the presidency. Reminding Ritchie of how one-party government had allowed the Missouri question to get out of hand, Van Buren insisted that "if the old [party loyalties] are suppressed, prejudices between free and slave holding states will inevitably take their place." Thus a new Democratic Party, committed to an agrarian program of states' rights and minimal government and dependent on the votes of both slaveholding and nonslaveholding states (beginning, much like Jefferson's old party, with Van Buren's New York and Ritchie's Virginia), would ensure democracy, the continuation of slavery, and the preservation of the Union. The alternative, Van Buren firmly believed, was an expensive and invasive national state (Adams's "lighthouses to the skies"), the isolation of the slaveholding South, and thus mortal danger to the republic.

The new Jacksonian Democratic Party needed publicists as well as political leaders, and Van Buren's growing coalition put together an impressive network of party newspapers. Party leaders financed Duff Green's *United States Telegraph* in Washington, D.C. They also brought Thomas Ritchie's *Richmond Enquirer* and the *Albany Argus,* mouthpiece for the Van Buren party in New York, into the Jackson camp, along with Isaac Hill's New Hampshire *Patriot,* James Gordon Bennet's New York *Enquirer,* Nathaniel Greene's Boston *Statesman,* and the *Argus of Western America,* edited by Amos Kendall and Francis Preston Blair of Kentucky. These editors put the new skills of popular entertainment and manipulation at the disposal of the Democratic Party.

The presidential campaign of 1828 was an exercise in slander rather than a debate on public issues. Adhering to custom, neither Adams nor Jackson campaigned directly. But their henchmen viciously personalized the campaign. Jacksonians hammered away at the "Corrupt Bargain" of 1825 and at the dishonesty and weakness that Adams had supposedly displayed in that affair. The Adams forces attacked Jackson's character. They reminded voters of his duels and tavern brawls and circulated a "coffin handbill" describing Jackson's execution of militiamen during the Creek War. One of Henry Clay's newspaper friends circulated the rumor that Jackson was a bastard and that his mother was a prostitute. But the most egregious slander of the campaign centered on Andrew Jackson's marriage. In 1790

Rachel Donelson Jackson as a Mature Plantation Mistress
Andrew Jackson supposedly wore this miniature portrait of his beloved Rachel over his heart after her death in 1828.

Jackson had married Rachel Donelson, probably aware that she was estranged but not formally divorced from a man named Robards. Branding the marriage an "abduction," the Adams team screamed that Jackson had "torn from a husband the wife of his bosom," and had lived with her in a state of "open and notorious lewdness." They branded Rachel Jackson (now a deeply pious plantation housewife) an "American Jezebel," a "profligate woman," and a "convicted adulteress" whose ungoverned passions made her unfit to be first lady of a "Christian nation."

The Adams strategy backfired. Many voters agreed that only a man who strictly obeyed the law was fit to be president, and that Jackson's "passionate" and "lawless" nature disqualified him. Many others, however, criticized Adams for permitting Jackson's private life to become a public issue. Some claimed that Adams's rigid legalism left no room for privacy or for local notions of justice. Whatever the legality of their marriage, Andrew and Rachel Jackson had lived as models of marital fidelity and romantic love for nearly forty years; their neighbors had long ago forgiven whatever transgressions they may have committed. Thus on the one hand, Jackson's supporters accused the Adams campaign of a gross violation of privacy and honor. On the other, they defended Jackson's marriage — and his duels, brawls, executions, and unauthorized military ventures — as a triumph of what was right and just over what was narrowly legal. The attempt to brand Jackson as a lawless man, in fact, enhanced his image as a melodramatic hero who battled shrewd, unscrupulous, legalistic enemies by drawing on his natural nobility and force of will.

The campaign caught the public imagination. Voter turnout was double what it had been in 1824, totaling 56.3 percent. Jackson won the election with 56 percent of the popular vote (a landslide that would not be matched until the twentieth century) and with a margin of 178 to 83 in electoral votes. Adams carried New England, Delaware, and most of Maryland and took 16 of New York's 36 electoral votes. Jackson carried every other state. It was a clear triumph of democracy over genteel statesmanship, of limited government over expansive nationalism, and of the South and the West over New England. Just as clearly, it was a victory of popular melodrama over old forms of cultural gentility.

A People's Inauguration

Newspapers estimated that from 15,000 to 20,000 citizens (Duff Green's *Telegraph* claimed 30,000) came to Washington to witness Jackson's inauguration on March 4, 1829. They were "like the inundation of the northern barbarians into Rome," remarked Senator Daniel Webster; many had traveled as much as 500 miles, and *"they really seem to think that the country is rescued from some dreadful danger."* As members of the Washington establishment watched uneasily, the crowd filled the open spaces and the streets near the east portico of the Capitol Building, where Jackson was to deliver his inaugural address.

Jackson arrived at the Capitol in deep mourning. In December his wife Rachel had gone to Nashville to shop and had stopped to rest in a newspaper office. There, for the first time, she read the accusations

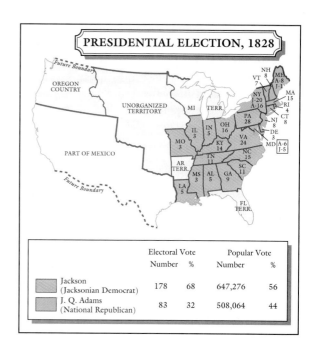

PRESIDENTIAL ELECTION, 1828

		Electoral Vote		Popular Vote	
		Number	%	Number	%
	Jackson (Jacksonian Democrat)	178	68	647,276	56
	J. Q. Adams (National Republican)	83	32	508,064	44

that had been made against her. She fainted on the spot. Though she had been in poor health, no one would ever convince Jackson that her death in January had not been caused by his political enemies. As he arrived to assume the presidency, he wore a black suit and black tie, a black armband, and a black hat band that trailed down his neck in what was called a weeper.

Jackson's inaugural address was vague. He promised "proper respect" for states' rights and a "spirit of equity, caution, and compromise" on the question of the tariff, which was beginning to cause sectional controversy. He promised to reform the civil service by replacing "unfaithful or incompetent" officers, and he vowed to retire the national debt through "a strict and faithful economy." Beyond that, he said very little, though he took every opportunity to flatter the popular majority. He had been elected "by the choice of a free people" (and not, as he did not have to say, by King Caucus or Corrupt Bargains), and he pledged "the zealous dedication of my humble abilities to their service and their good." He finished — as he often finished an important statement — by reminding Americans that a benign providence looked over them. He then looked up to a roar of applause.

The new president traveled slowly from the Capitol to the White House, with the throng following and growing noisier along the way. The crowd followed him into the White House, where refreshments had been laid out. Soon Jackson's well-wishers were ranging through the mansion, mud-dying the carpets, tipping things over, breaking dishes, and standing in dirty boots on upholstered chairs. Jackson had to retreat to avoid being crushed. The White House staff lured much of the crowd outside by moving the punch bowls and liquor to the lawn. A wealthy Washington matron who had admired the well-behaved crowd at the inaugural address exclaimed, "What a scene did we witness! *The Majesty of the People* had disappeared, and a rabble, a mob, of boys, negros, women, children, scrambling, fighting, romping. What a pity, what a pity." Another guest pronounced the occasion a "Saturnalia . . . of mud and filth." A Democratic newspaper reported more favorably: "General Jackson is *their own* President . . .

he was greeted by them with an enthusiasm which bespoke him the Hero of a popular triumph."

A People's Government

Jackson had begun to assemble his administration months before he took office. Martin Van Buren, who had mobilized much of the support Jackson gained between 1824 and 1828, was the new Secretary of State — positioned to succeed Jackson as president. Van Buren quit his newly won post as governor of New York and came to Washington, where he became Jackson's most valued adviser. Other appointments were less promising. John M. Berrien, a Georgia politician of dubious ability, took on the duties of Attorney General. John Branch, an undistinguished senator from North Carolina and an old Jackson supporter, became Secretary of the Navy. As head of the Post Office — the largest government department — Jackson choose William T. Barry of

The President's Levee   Robert Cruikshank drew Jackson's inaugural levee with men and women of all classes, children, dogs, and bucking horses celebrating the Old General's victory. Cruikshank subtitled his lighograph *All Creation Going to the White House.*

Kentucky, a poor administrator who would botch the job. John Henry Eaton, Jackson's old military comrade, campaign biographer, and surrogate son, was named Secretary of War. Eaton was of questionable competence, and his recent marriage, as we shall see, was a source of Washington gossip. A critic looked at Jackson's cabinet and pronounced it—with the exception of Van Buren—"the Millennium of the Minnows."

Others were more concerned about what Jackson would do to the civil service than about whom he named to his cabinet. During the campaign, Jackson had vowed to fire corrupt officeholders—a term he applied to grafters, incompetents, long-term officeholders who considered their jobs personal property, and those who supported John Quincy Adams. Early in the administration, opponents complained that Jackson was replacing able, educated, patriotic public servants with some very dubious appointments. They soon had convincing evidence: Samuel Swarthout, whom Jackson had appointed Collector of the Port of New York (an office that handled $15 million dollars in tariff revenue annually), stole $1.2 million and took off for Europe.

Actually, much of the furor over Jackson's "spoils system" was overwrought and misdirected. All he wanted to do, Jackson claimed, was to institute "rotation in office" and to get rid of officeholders who expected to hold lifetime appointments. Arguing that most government jobs could be performed by any honest, reasonably intelligent citizen, Jackson proposed ending the long tenures that, he said, turned the civil service into "support of the few at the expense of the many." Jackson removed about one in ten executive appointees during his eight years in office, and his replacements (at least at the level of ambassadors, federal judges and attorneys, and cabinet members) were as wealthy and well-educated as their predecessors. They were, however, most decidedly *political* appointees. Acting out of his own need for personal loyalty and on the advice of Van Buren and other architects of the Democratic Party, Jackson filled vacancies—down to postmasters in the smallest towns—with Democrats who had worked for his election.

Jackson sought Van Buren's advice on appointments. Van Buren knew the political value of dispensing government jobs; indeed it was one of his henchmen who coined the phrase "To the victor belongs the spoils." In resorting to patronage to build the party, however, Jackson gave his opponents an important issue. Revolutionary republicans feared a government of lackeys dependent on a powerful executive, and congressional opponents argued that Jackson was using appointments to "convert the entire body of those in office into corrupt and supple instruments of power. . . ." "A standing army," railed Henry Clay in the Senate, "has been, in all free countries, a just object of jealousy and suspicion. But is not a corps of one hundred thousand dependents upon government, actuated by one spirit, obeying one will, and aiming at one end, more dangerous than a standing army . . . ?" It became an anti-Jacksonian axiom that Jackson had made the federal civil service an arm of the Democratic Party.

JACKSONIAN DEMOCRACY AND THE SOUTH

In the 1828 election, though Jackson ran strongly in every region but New England, the base of his support was in the South, where he won eight of every ten votes. Southerners had grown wary of an activist government in which they were in the minority. They looked to Jackson not only as a military hero but as a Tennessee planter who talked about getting back to republican fundamentals. But while southerners expected Jackson to look after southern interests, there was disagreement within the administration on how those interests should be protected. Some sided with Vice President Calhoun, who believed that any state had the right to veto federal legislation and even in extreme cases to secede from the Union. Others agreed with Secretary of State Van Buren that the Union was inviolable, and that the South's best safeguard was in a political party committed to states' rights within the Union. The differences were fought out in the contest between Calhoun and Van Buren for the right to succeed Jackson as president, a contest that shaped every major issue of Jackson's first term.

Indian Removal

When Jackson entered office, a final crisis between frontier whites and the native peoples of the eastern woodlands was under way. By the 1820s few Native Americans were left east of the Appalachians. The Iroquois of New York were penned into tiny reservations, and the tribes of the Old Northwest were broken and scattered. But in the Old Southwest 60,000 Cherokees, Creeks, Choctaws, Chickasaws, and Seminoles were still living on their ancestral lands, with tenure guaranteed by federal treaties that (at least implicitly) recognized them as sovereign peoples. Congress had appropriated funds for schools, tools, seeds, and training to help these "Civilized Tribes" make the transition to farming. Most government officials assumed that the tribes would eventually trade their old lands and use their farming skills on new land west of the Mississippi.

Southwestern whites resented federal Indian policy as an affront to both white democracy and states' rights. The poorer farmers coveted the Indians' land, and states'-rights southerners denied that the federal government had the authority to make treaties or to recognize sovereign peoples within their states. Resistance centered in Georgia, where Governor George Troup brought native lands under the state's jurisdiction and then turned them over to poor whites by way of lotteries—thus tying states' rights to white hunger for Indian land. At one point, Troup sent state surveyors onto Creek territory before federal purchase from the Indians was complete, telling President Adams that if he resisted state authority he would be considered a "public enemy." The Cherokees in Georgia pressed the issue in 1827 by declaring themselves a republic with its own constitution, government, courts, and police. But almost at the same time, a gold discovery on their land made it even more attractive to whites. The Georgia legislature promptly declared Cherokee law null and void, extended Georgia's authority into Cherokee country, and began surveying the lands for sale. Hinting at the old connection between state sovereignty and the protection of slavery, Governor Troup warned that the federal "jurisdiction claimed over one portion of our population may very soon be asserted

Trail of Tears In 1838 the Army marched eighteen thousand Cherokee men, women, and children, along with their animals and whatever they could carry, out of their home territory and into Oklahoma. Four thousand—most of them old or very young—died on the march.

over *another*." Alabama and Mississippi quickly followed Georgia's lead by extending state authority over Indian lands and denying federal jurisdiction.

President Jackson agreed that the federal government lacked the authority to recognize native sovereignty within a state and declared that he could not protect the Cherokees and the other Civilized Tribes from state governments. Instead, he offered to remove them to federal land west of the Mississippi, where they would be under the authority of the benevolent federal government. Congress made that offer official in the Indian Removal Act of 1830.

The Cherokees, with the help of New England missionaries, had taken their claims of sovereignty to court in the late 1820s. In 1830 John Marshall's Supreme Court ruled in *Cherokee Nation* v. *Georgia* that the Cherokees could not sue Georgia because they were not a sovereign people but "domestic dependent nations," thus dependents of the federal government, and not of the state of Georgia, though somehow "nations" as well. The Court's decision in *Worcester* v. *Georgia* (1832) declared that Georgia's extension of state law over Cherokee land was unconstitutional. President Jackson ignored the decision, however, reportedly telling a Congressman, "John Marshall has made his decision: *now let him enforce it!*" In the end, Jackson sat back as the southwestern states encroached on the Civilized Tribes. In 1838 his successor, Martin Van Buren, sent the army to march the eighteen thousand remaining Cherokee to Oklahoma. Along this "Trail of Tears," four thousand of them died of exposure, disease, starvation, and white depredation.

Indian removal had profound political consequences. It violated Supreme Court decisions and thus strengthened Jackson's reputation as an enemy of the rule of law and a friend of local, "democratic" solutions; at the same time, it reaffirmed the link between racism and white democracy in the South and announced Jackson's commitment to state sovereignty and limited federal authority.

Nullification

In 1828 the Democratic Congress, acting under the direction of Van Buren and his congressional sidekick Silas Wright, set about writing a tariff that would win votes for Jackson in the upcoming presidential election. Assured of support in the South, the creators of the tariff bill fished for votes in the Mid-

dle Atlantic states and in the Old Northwest by including protective levies on raw wool, flax, molasses, hemp, and distilled spirits. The result was a patchwork tariff that pleased northern and western farmers but that worried the South and violated Jackson's own ideas of what a "judicious" tariff should be. Protective tariffs hurt the South by diminishing exports of cotton and other staples and by raising the price of manufactured goods. More ominous, they demonstrated the power of other sections to write laws that helped them and hurt the outnumbered South—a power, as southerners constantly reminded themselves, that might some day be used to destroy southern institutions. Calling the new bill a "Tariff of Abominations," the legislature of one southern state after another denounced it as (this was Virginia's formulation) "unconstitutional, unwise, unjust, unequal, and oppressive."

South Carolina, guided by Vice President Calhoun, took the lead in opposing the Tariff of 1828. During the War of 1812 and the ensuing Era of Good Feelings, Calhoun's South Carolina—confident of its future and deeply engaged in international markets for its rice and cotton—had favored the economic nationalism of the American System. But the Missouri debates had sent Carolinians looking for ways to safeguard slavery. And then the Denmark Vesey Conspiracy of 1822 (see Chapter 11) had stirred fears among the outnumbered whites of coastal South Carolina; their fears grew more intense when federal courts shot down a state law forbidding black merchant seamen from moving about freely while their ships were docked at Charleston. Carolinians were disturbed too by persistent talk of gradual emancipation—at a time when their own commitment to slavery was growing stronger. Finally, southerners noted that in the congressional logrolling that made the Tariff of 1828, many western representatives had abandoned their old Jeffersonian alliance with the South to trade favors with the Northeast. With the growth in the Northeast of urban markets for western produce, the American System's promise of interdependence among regions was beginning to work—but in ways that excluded the export-oriented South. The Tariff of 1828 was the last straw: it benefited the city and commercial food producers at the expense of the plantation, and it demonstrated that the South could do nothing to block the passage of such laws.

As early as 1827 Calhoun had embraced the principle that the states had the right to nullify federal laws. In 1828, in his anonymously published essay *Exposition and Protest,* he argued that the Constitution was a compact between sovereign states, and that the states (not the federal courts) could decide the constitutionality of federal laws. A state convention (like the conventions that had ratified the Constitution) could nullify any federal law within state borders. "Constitutional government and the government of a majority," Calhoun argued, "are utterly incompatible." *Exposition and Protest* echoed the Virginia and Kentucky Resolves of 1798–1799 and anticipated the secessionist arguments of 1861: the Union was a voluntary compact between sovereign states, states were the ultimate judges of the validity of federal law, and states could break the compact if they wished.

Nullification was the strongest card held by the southern extremists, and they avoided playing it. They knew that President Jackson was a states'-rights slaveholder who disliked the Tariff of 1828, and they assumed that Vice President Calhoun would succeed to the presidency in time and would protect southern interests. They were wrong on both counts. Jackson favored states' rights, but only within a perpetual and inviolable Union. His Indian policy, which had emboldened some southerners, was simply an acknowledgement of state jurisdiction over institutions within state boundaries. A tariff, on the other hand, was ultimately a matter of foreign policy, clearly within the jurisdiction of the federal government. To allow a state to veto a tariff would be to deny the legal existence of the United States.

Jackson aired his views at a program celebrating Jefferson's birthday on April 13, 1830. Calhoun's southern friends dominated the speechmaking, and Jackson listened quietly as speaker after speaker defended the extreme states' rights position. After the formal speeches were over, the President rose to propose an after-dinner toast. It was a powerful denunciation of what he had just heard: "Our Federal Union," he said in measured tones, *"It must be preserved."* Isaac Hill, a New Hampshire Democrat and a supporter of Van Buren, reported that "an order to arrest Calhoun where he sat would not have come with more blinding, staggering force." Dumb-struck, the southerners looked to Calhoun, who as vice president was to propose the second toast. Obviously shaken by Jackson's unqualified defense of the Union,

Calhoun offered this toast: "The Union. Next to our liberties the most dear." They were strong words, but they had little meaning after Jackson's affirmation of the Union. A few days later, a South Carolina congressman on his way home asked the president if he had any message for him to take back. "Yes, I have," replied Jackson. "Please give my compliments to my friends in your State, and say to them, that if a single drop of blood shall be shed there in opposition to the laws of the United States, I will hang the first man I can lay my hand on engaged in such treasonable conduct, upon the first tree I can reach."

Having reaffirmed the Union and rejected nullification, Jackson asked Congress to reduce the tariff rates in the hope that he could isolate the nullifiers from southerners who simply hated the tariff. The resulting Tariff of 1832 lowered the rates on many items but still affirmed the principle of protectionism. That, along with the Boston abolitionist William Lloyd Garrison's declaration of war on slavery in 1831, followed by Nat Turner's bloody slave uprising in Virginia that same year (see Chapter 11), led the whites of South Carolina and Georgia to intensify their distrust of outside authority and their insistence on the right to govern their own neighborhoods. South Carolina, now with Calhoun's open leadership and support, called a state convention that nullified the Tariffs of 1828 and 1832.

In Washington, President Jackson raged that nullification (not to mention the right of secession that followed logically from it) was illegal. Insisting that "Disunion . . . is *treason,*" he asked Congress for a Force Bill empowering him to personally lead a federal army into South Carolina. At the same time, however, he supported the rapid reduction of tariffs. When Democratic attempts at reduction bogged down, Henry Clay, now back in the Senate, took on the tricky legislative task of rescuing his beloved protective tariff while quieting southern fears. The result was the Compromise Tariff of 1833, which by lowering tariffs over the course of several years, gave southern planters the relief they demanded while maintaining moderate protectionism and allowing northern manufacturers time to adjust to the lower rates. Congress also passed the Force Bill. Jackson signed both into law on March 2, 1833.

With that, the nullification crisis came to a quiet end. No other southern state had joined South Carolina in nullifying the tariff, though some states had made vague pledges of support in the event that Jackson led his army to Charleston. The Compromise Tariff of 1833 isolated the South Carolina nullifiers. Deprived of their issue and most of their support, they declared victory and disbanded their convention—but not before nullifying the Force Bill. Jackson chose to overlook that last defiant gesture, and the crisis passed.

The "Petticoat Wars"

The spoils system, Indian removal, nullification, and other heated questions of Jackson's first term were fought out against a backdrop of gossip, intrigue, and angry division within the inner circles of Jackson's government. The talk centered on Peggy O'Neal Timberlake, a Washington tavernkeeper's daughter who, in January 1829, had married John Henry Eaton, Jackson's old friend and soon to be his Secretary of War. Timberlake's husband, a navy purser, had recently committed suicide, and it was rumored that her affair with Eaton was the cause. Eaton was middle-aged; his bride was twenty-nine, pretty, flirtatious, and, according to Washington gossip, "frivolous, wayward, [and] passionate." Knowing that his marriage might cause trouble for the new administration, Eaton had asked for and received Jackson's blessings—and, by strong implication, his protection.

The marriage of John and Peggy Eaton came at a turning point in the history of Washington society. Until the 1820s most officeholders had left their families at home. They took lodgings at taverns and boarding houses and lived in a bachelor world of shirtsleeves, tobacco, card-playing, and occasional liaisons with local women. In the 1820s the boarding-house world was giving way to high society. Cabinet members, senators, congressmen, and other officials moved into Washington houses, and their wives presided over the round of dinner parties through which much of the government's business was done. As in other wealthy families, political wives imposed new forms of gentility and politeness upon these affairs, and they assumed the responsibility of drawing up the guest lists. Many of them determined to exclude Peggy Eaton from polite society.

The exclusion of Peggy Eaton split the Jackson administration in half. Jackson himself was committed to protect her. He had met his own beloved Rachel while boarding at her father's Nashville

tavern, and their grand romance (as well as the gossip that surrounded it) was a striking parallel to the affair of John and Peggy Eaton. That, coupled with Jackson's honor-bound agreement to the Eaton marriage, ensured that he would protect the Eatons to the bitter end. Always suspicious of intrigues, Jackson labeled the "dark and sly insinuations" about Peggy Eaton part of a "conspiracy" against his presidency. Motivated by chivalry, personal loyalty, grief and rage over Rachel's death, and angry disbelief that political intrigue could sully the private life of a valued friend, Jackson insisted to his cabinet that Peggy Eaton was "as chaste as a virgin!" Jackson noted that the rumors were being spread not only by politicians' wives but by prominent clergymen (most prominently, Ezra Styles Ely of Philadelphia, who had recently called for an evangelical "Christian Party in politics") and blamed the conspiracy on "females with clergymen at their head."

In fact, Mrs. Eaton's tormentors included most of the cabinet members as well as Jackson's own White House "family." Widowed and without children, Jackson had invited his nephew and private secretary, Andrew Jackson Donelson, along with his wife and her sister, to live in the White House. Donelson's wife, serving as official hostess, resolutely shunned Peggy Eaton. Jackson, who valued domestic harmony and personal loyalty, assumed that schemers had invaded and subverted his own household. Before long, his suspicions centered on Vice President Calhoun, whose wife, Floride Bonneau Calhoun, a haughty and powerful Washington matron, was a leader of the assault on Peggy Eaton. Only Secretary of State Van Buren, a widower and an eminently decent man, included the Eatons in official functions. Sensing that Jackson was losing his patience with Calhoun, Van Buren's friends, soon after the Jefferson birthday banquet in the spring of 1830, showed Jackson a letter from William H. Crawford revealing that while serving in Monroe's cabinet Calhoun, contrary to his protestations, had favored censuring Jackson for his unauthorized invasion of Florida in 1818. An open break with Calhoun became inevitable.

Jackson resolved the Peggy Eaton controversy, as he would resolve nullification, in ways that favored Van Buren in his contest with Calhoun. He sent Donelson, his wife, and his sister-in-law back to Tennessee and invited his friend W. B. Lewis and his daughter to take their place. But he pointedly made Peggy Eaton the official hostess at the White House. In the spring of 1831 Van Buren gave Jackson a free hand to reconstruct his tangled administration. He offered to resign his cabinet post and engineered the resignations of nearly all other members of the cabinet—thus allowing Jackson to remake his administration without firing anyone. Many of those who left were southern supporters of Calhoun. Jackson replaced them with a mixed cabinet that included political allies of Van Buren. It was also at this time that President Jackson began to consult with an informal "Kitchen Cabinet" that included journalists Amos Kendall and Francis Preston Blair, along with Van Buren and a few others. The Peggy Eaton controversy and the resulting shakeup in the administration were contributing mightily to the success of Van Buren's southern strategy.

Van Buren's victory over Calhoun came to a quick conclusion. As part of his cabinet reorganization, Jackson appointed Van Buren minister to Great Britain—an important post that would remove him from the heat of Washington politics. Vice President Calhoun, sitting as president of the Senate, rigged the confirmation so that he cast the deciding vote against Van Buren's appointment—a petty act that turned out to be his last exercise of national power. Jackson replaced Calhoun with Van Buren as the vice-presidential candidate in 1832 and let it be known that he wanted Van Buren to succeed him as president.

Petitions, the Gag Rule, and the Southern Mails

Van Buren and other architects of the Democratic Party promised to protect slavery with a disciplined national coalition committed to states' rights within an inviolable Union. The rise of a northern antislavery movement (see Chapter 13) posed a direct challenge to that formulation. Middle-class evangelicals, who were emerging as the reformist core of the northern Whig Party, had learned early on that Jacksonian Democrats wanted to keep moral issues out of politics. In 1828 and 1829, when they petitioned the government to stop movement of the mail on Sundays, Jackson had turned them down. They then petitioned the government for humane treatment of the Civilized Tribes, whose conversion to Christianity had been accomplished largely by New England

The Rats leaving a Falling House.

An Opposition Cartoon on the Cabinet Shuffle of 1831 The cabinet rats run from the falling house of government, while a bewildered Jackson retains Van Buren by standing on his tail.

missionaries; again, the Jackson administration had refused. The evangelicals suspected Jackson of immorality and they were appalled by his defense of Peggy Eaton and his attack on gentlewomen and preachers. Most of all, reformist evangelicals disliked the Democrats' rigid party discipline, which in each case had kept questions of morality from shaping politics.

In the early 1830s a radical minority of evangelicals formed societies committed to the immediate abolition of slavery, and they devised ways of making the national government confront the slavery question. In 1835 abolitionists launched a "postal campaign," flooding the mail—both North and South—

with antislavery tracts that southerners and most northerners considered "incendiary." From 1836 onward, they bombarded Congress with petitions — most of them for the abolition of slavery and the slave trade in the District of Columbia (where Congress had undisputed jurisdiction), others against the interstate slave trade, slavery in the federal territories, and the admission of new slave states.

Some Jacksonians, including Jackson himself, wanted to put a stop to the postal campaign with a federal censorship law. Calhoun and other southerners, however, argued that the states had the right to censor mail crossing their borders. Knowing that state censorship of the mail was unconstitutional and that federal censorship of the mail would be a political disaster, Amos Kendall, a Van Burenite who had become Postmaster General in the cabinet shuffle, proposed an informal solution. Without changing the law, he would simply look the other way as local postmasters violated postal regulations and removed abolitionist materials from the mail. Almost all such materials were published in New York City and mailed from there. The New York postmaster, a loyal appointee, proceeded to sift them out of the mail and thus cut off the postal campaign at its source. The few tracts that made it to the South were destroyed by local postmasters. Calhoun and his supporters continued to demand that the states be given the power to deal with the mailings, but the Democrats had no intention of relinquishing federal control over the federal mail. They made it clear, however, that no abolitionist literature would reach the South so long as Democrats controlled the U.S. Post Office.

The Democrats dealt in a similar manner with antislavery petitions to Congress. Southern extremists demanded that Congress disavow its power to legislate on slavery in the District of Columbia, but Van Buren, who was getting ready to run for president, declared that Congress did indeed have that power but should never use it. In dealing with the petitions, Congress simply voted at each session from 1836 to 1844 to table them without reading them — thus acknowledging that they had been received but sidestepping any debate on them. This procedure, which became known as the "Gage Rule," was passed by southern Whigs and southern Democrats with the help of most (usually 80 percent or more) of the northern Democrats. Increasingly, abolitionists sent their petitions to ex-President John Quincy Adams, who had returned to Washington as a Whig congressman from Massachusetts. Like other northern Whigs, Adams openly opposed both slavery and the gag rule in Congress. Northern Whigs began calling him "Old Man Eloquent," while Calhoun dubbed him "a mischievous, bad old man." But most southerners saw what the Democrats wanted them to see: that their surest guarantee of safety within the Union was a disciplined Democratic Party determined to avoid sectional arguments.

Thus the Jacksonians answered the question that had arisen with the Missouri debates: how to protect the slaveholding South within the federal Union. Calhoun and other southern radicals found the answer in nullification and other forms of state sovereignty. Jackson and the Democratic coalition, on the other hand, insisted that the Union was inviolable, and that any attempt to dissolve it would be met with force. But a Democratic Party uniting northern and southern agrarians into a states'-rights, limited-government majority could guarantee southern rights within the Union. This answer to the southern question stayed in place until the breakup of the Democratic Party on the eve of the Civil War.

JACKSONIAN DEMOCRACY AND THE MARKET REVOLUTION

Jacksonian Democrats cherished the simplicity, honesty, and naturalness of Jefferson's agrarian republic. They assumed power at the height of the market revolution. Jacksonian Democrats spent much of the 1830s and 1840s trying to reconcile the market and the republic. Like the Jeffersonians before them, Jacksonian Democrats welcomed commerce so long as it served the independence and rough equality of white men on which republican citizenship rested. But paper currency and the dependence on credit that came with the market revolution posed problems. The so-called "paper economy" separated wealth from "real work" and encouraged an unrepublican spirit of luxury and greed. Worst of all, the new paper economy required government-granted privileges that the Jacksonians, still speaking the language of revolutionary republicanism, branded "corruption." For the same reasons, the protective tariffs and government-sponsored roads and canals of the

American System were antirepublican and unacceptable. It was the goal of the Jackson presidency to curtail government involvement in the economy, to end special privilege, and thus to rescue the republic from the "Money Power."

The Bank War

To Jackson and other agrarian republicans, the most dangerously privileged institution in the country was the Bank of the United States, which had been chartered by Congress in 1816 (see Chapter 10). Because the government deposited its revenue in the Bank, the federal treasury was at the disposal of the private credit system. At the same time, the government deposits gave the Bank enormous power over other banks. Speculators used notes issued by state banks to purchase government land, and the notes ended up in the Bank's vaults. The Bank then presented them to the state bank that had issued them, demanding face value in gold or silver. That demand discouraged state banks from issuing notes that they could not honor, and, thus, functioned as a safeguard to the money supply and a brake on inflation. In this way, the Bank of the United States performed the rudimentary functions of a central bank. The amounts of gold and silver coins (specie) minted by the federal government were far too small to meet the demands of a market economy. By issuing bank notes of its own and by controlling the notes of other banks the Bank hoped to provide a uniform and stable paper currency.

Most members of the business community valued the services performed by the Bank of the United States. But millions of Americans resented and distrusted the national bank, citing its role in the Panic of 1819 as evidence of the dangers posed by privileged, powerful institutions. President Jackson agreed with them. A southwestern agrarian who had lost money in an early speculation, he was leery of paper money, banks, and the credit system. He insisted that both the Bank and paper money were unconstitutional, and that the only safe, natural, republican currency was gold and silver. Above all, Jackson saw the Bank of the United States as a government-sponsored concentration of power that threatened the republic.

The Bank's charter ran through 1836. But Senators Henry Clay and Daniel Webster encouraged Nicholas Biddle, the Bank's brilliant, aristocratic president, to apply for recharter in 1832. Clay planned to oppose Jackson in the presidential election later that year, and he knew that Jackson hated the Bank. He and his friends hoped to provoke the hot-tempered and supposedly erratic Jackson into a response that could be used against him in the election.

Biddle applied to Congress for a recharter of the Bank of the United States in January 1832. The bill made its way through committees and came to a vote in July. The Senate voted for recharter 28 to 20; the House approved 107 to 85. Legislators from the Northeast and Middle Atlantic voted in favor; the Southeast voted against, the Southwest and the Northwest were divided. The bill went on to the president, who understood that the early request for recharter was a political ploy. On July 4, Van Buren visited the White House and found Jackson sick in bed; Jackson took Van Buren's hand and said, "The bank, Mr. Van Buren, is trying to kill me, *but I will kill it!*" Jackson vetoed the bill.

Jackson's Bank Veto Message, sent to Congress on July 10, was a manifesto of Jacksonian Democracy. Written by Amos Kendall, Francis Preston Blair, and Roger B. Taney—republican fundamentalists who both hated the Bank and understood the popular culture that shared their hatred—the message combined Jeffersonian verities with appeals to the public's prejudice. Jackson declared that the Bank was "unauthorized by the Constitution, subversive of the rights of the states, and dangerous to the liberties of the people." Its charter, Jackson complained, bestowed special privilege on the Bank and its stockholders—almost all of whom were northeastern businessmen or, worse, British investors. Having made most of its loans to southerners and westerners, the Bank was a huge monster that sucked resources out of the agrarian South and West and poured them into the pockets of wealthy, well-connected northeastern gentlemen and their English friends. The granting of special privilege to such people (or to any others) threatened the system of equal rights that was essential in a republic. Jackson granted that differences in talents and resources inevitably created social distinctions. But he stood firm against "any prostitution of our Government to the advancement of the few at the expense of the many. . . ." He concluded with a call to the civic virtue and the conservative, God-centered Protestantism in which he and most of his agrarian constituency had been raised: "Let us firmly rely on that kind Providence which I am sure watches with peculiar care over the destinies of our Republic, and on the intelligence and wisdom of our countrymen. Through *His* abundant goodness and *their* patriotic devotion our liberty and Union will be preserved."

Henry Clay, Nicholas Biddle, and other anti-Jacksonians had expected the veto. And the Bank Veto Message was a long, rambling attack that, in their opinion, demonstrated Jackson's unfitness for office. "It has all the fury of a chained panther biting the bars of its cage," said Biddle, concluding that "it really is a manifesto of anarchy." So certain were they that the public shared their views that Clay's supporters distributed Jackson's Message as *anti*-Jackson propaganda during the 1832 campaign. They were wrong: a majority of the voters shared Jackson's attachment to a society of virtuous, independent producers and to republican government in its pristine form; they also agreed that the republic was in danger of subversion by parasites who grew rich by manipulating credit, prices, paper money, and government-bestowed privileges. Jackson portrayed himself as both the protector of the old republic and a melodramatic hero contending with illegitimate, aristocratic, privileged, secretive powers. With the Bank and Jackson's veto as the principal issues, Jackson won reelection by a landslide in 1832.

"King Andrew I"

Jackson began his second term determined to kill the Bank of the United States before Congress could reverse his veto. The Bank would be able to operate under its old charter until 1836. But Jackson was determined to speed its death by withdrawing government deposits as they were needed and by depositing new government revenues in carefully selected state banks—soon to be called "Pet Banks" by the opposition. By law, the decision to remove the deposits had to be made by the Secretary of the Treasury, and Treasury Secretary Louis McLane, along with most of the cabinet, doubted the wisdom if not the legality of withdrawing them. So Jackson transferred McLane to the vacant post of Secretary of State and named William J. Duane as Treasury Secretary. Duane, too, refused to withdraw the deposits. Jackson fired him and appointed Roger B. Taney, the Attorney General and a close adviser who had helped write the Bank Veto Message. A loyal

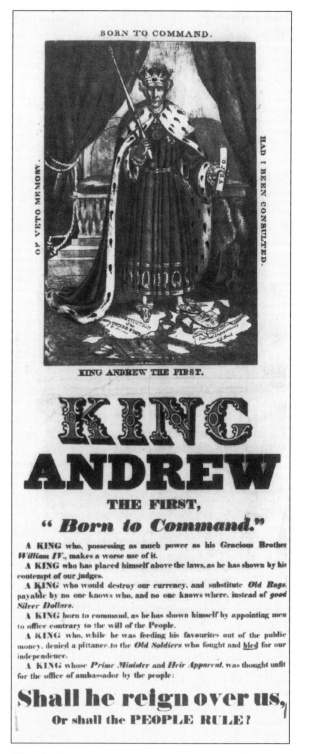

King Andrew   In this widely distributed opposition cartoon, King Andrew, with a scepter in one hand and a vetoed bill in the other, tramples on internal improvements, the Bank of the United States, and the Constitution.

Democrat who hated banks as much as Jackson did, Taney withdrew the deposits. In 1835, when the old Federalist John Marshall died, Jackson rewarded Taney by making him Chief Justice of the Supreme Court—a post from which he continued to serve the Democratic Party.

It was over deposit removal and over related questions of presidential power that the opposition to the Jacksonian Democrats coalesced into the Whig Party in 1834. The name of the party signified opposition to what the members of the party called "executive usurpation." Jackson, they argued, had transformed himself from the limited executive described in the Constitution into "King Andrew I." Jackson was indeed changing the presidency. Pointing out that he was the only government official elected by the whole country, he posed as the protector of the people's liberties against special privilege and partial legislation. Earlier presidents had exercised the veto only nine times, usually on unimportant bills and always on the grounds that the proposed legislation was unconstitutional. Jackson used the veto often, in effect making himself a participant in the legislative process. In May 1830, for instance, Jackson vetoed an attempt by Congress to buy stock in a turnpike to run from the terminus of the National Road at Louisville to Maysville, Kentucky. Jackson argued that since the road would be entirely in Kentucky it was "partial" legislation that would take money from the people to benefit just one locality. He also questioned whether such federal subsidies were constitutional. Most important, however, Jackson was determined to reduce federal expenditures in order to retire the national debt. In short, he had simply decided to veto any legislation with which he disagreed. His use of the veto, which Jackson repeated often throughout his presidency, transformed the president into a powerful legislator, ensuring that Congress would take the possibility of a presidential veto into account when writing legislation. Subsequent presidents have followed his lead.

Jackson also transformed the cabinet. Prior to 1829, members of the cabinet, because their appointments were ratified by the Senate, had enjoyed job security and an independent base of power. Jackson changed all that. The uproar over Peggy Eaton and the search for an amenable Treasury Secretary had created a flurry of resignations, firings, and hirings that established the president's right to demand loyalty from cabinet members and to ap-

point and remove them at will. Again, subsequent presidents have assumed that they have the right to maintain a disciplined, loyal administration.

The question of "executive usurpation" came to a head in 1834. Withdrawal of the government deposits from the Bank of the United States, together with Jackson's high-handed treatment of his Treasury Secretaries, caused uneasiness even among his supporters. His enemies took extreme measures. Nicholas Biddle, announcing that he must clean up the affairs of the Bank before closing its doors, demanded that all its loans be repaid—a demand that undermined the credit system and produced a sharp financial panic. There is no doubt that one reason for Biddle's action was to punish Andrew Jackson. While Congress received a well-orchestrated petition campaign to restore the deposits, Henry Clay led an effort in the Senate to censure the president—which it did in March 1834. Daniel Webster, the Bank's best friend in government, and Clay, who had watched as Jackson denied one component after another of his American System (see Chapter 10) led the old National Republican coalition (the name that anti-Jacksonians had assumed since 1824) into the new Whig Party. They were joined by southerners (including Calhoun) who resented Jackson's treatment of the South Carolina nullifiers and Biddle's bank, and who distrusted his assurances on slavery. But it was Jackson's war on the Bank that did the most to separate parties. His withdrawal of the deposits chased lukewarm supporters into the opposition, while Democrats who closed ranks behind him could point to an increasingly sharp division between the money power and the old republic. James K. Polk of Tennessee, who led the Democrats in the House of Representatives, in referring to Biddle's panic of 1834, declared that "the question is in fact whether we shall have the Republic without the Bank or the Bank without the Republic."

One of the reasons Jackson had removed the deposits was that he anticipated a federal surplus revenue that, if handed over to Biddle's Bank, would have made it stronger than ever. The Tariffs of 1828 and 1832 produced substantial government revenue, and Jackson's frugal administration spent very little of it. Even the Compromise Tariff of 1833 left rates temporarily high. And the brisk sale of public lands was adding to the surplus. In 1833, for the only time in history, the United States paid off its national debt. Without Jackson's removal of the deposits, a

SHIN-PLASTER CARICATURE OF GENERAL JACKSON'S WAR ON THE UNITED STATES BANK, AND ITS CONSEQUENCES, 1837.

A Mock Bank Note Decrying the Democrats' Destruction of the Bank of the United States   A gang of officeholders pull Van Buren into perdition over the prostrate bodies of honest citizens. At left, Jackson, dressed as an old woman, looks on.

huge sum of federal money would have gone into the Bank and would have found its way to the hated paper economy.

Early in his administration, Jackson had favored distributing surplus revenue to the states to be used for internal improvements. But he came to distrust even that minimal federal intervention in the economy, fearing that redistribution would encourage Congress to keep land prices and tariff rates high. Whigs, who by now despaired of ever creating a federally subsidized, coordinated transportation system, picked up the idea of redistribution. With some help from the Democrats, they passed the Deposit Act of 1836, which increased the number of banks receiving federal deposits (thus taking power away from Jackson's "Pet Banks") and distributed any federal surplus to the states to be spent on roads, canals, and schools. Jackson, who distrusted state-chartered banks as much as he distrusted the Bank of the United States, feared that the new deposit banks would use their power to issue mountains of new bank notes. He demanded a provision limiting their right to print bank notes. With that provision, he reluctantly signed the Deposit Act.

Jackson and many members of his administration were deeply concerned—for both fiscal reasons and moral reasons—about the inflationary boom that accompanied the rapid growth of commerce, credit, roads, canals, new farms, and the other manifestations of the market revolution in the 1830s. After insisting that his hard-money, anti-inflationary provision be added to the Deposit Act, Jackson issued a Specie Circular in 1836, which provided that speculators could buy large parcels of public land only with silver and gold coins while settlers could continue to buy farm-sized plots with bank notes. Henceforth, speculators would have to bring wagonloads of coins from eastern banks to frontier land offices. With this provision, Jackson hoped to curtail speculation and to reverse the flow of specie out of the South and West and into the Northeast. The Specie Circular was Jackson's final assault on the paper economy. It repeated familiar themes: it favored hard currency over paper, settlers over speculators, and the South and West over the Northeast.

THE SECOND AMERICAN PARTY SYSTEM

In his farewell address in 1837 Jackson spoke once again of the incompatibility between the republic and the money power. He warned against a revival of the Bank of the United States and against all banks, paper money, the spirit of speculation, and every aspect of the "paper system." That system encouraged greed and luxury, which were at odds with republican virtue, he said. Worse, it thrived on special privilege, creating a world in which insiders meeting in "secret conclaves" could buy and sell elections. The solution, as always, was an arcadian society of small producers, a vigilant democratic electorate, and a chaste republican government that granted no special privileges.

"Martin Van Ruin"

Sitting beside Jackson as he delivered his farewell address was his chosen successor, Martin Van Buren. In the election of 1836 the Whigs had acknowledged that Henry Clay, the leader of their party, could not win a national election. So they ran three sectional candidates—Daniel Webster in the Northeast, the old Indian fighter William Henry Harrison in the West, and Hugh Lawson White of Tennessee, a turncoat Jacksonian, in the South. With this ploy the Whigs hoped to deprive Van Buren of a majority and throw the election into the Whig-controlled House of Representatives.

The strategy failed. Van Buren had engineered a national Democratic Party that could avert the dangers of sectionalism, and he questioned the patriotism of the Whigs and their sectional candidates, asserting that "true republicans can never lend their aid and influence in creating geographical parties." That, along with his association with Jackson's popular presidency, won him the election. Van Buren carried fifteen of the twenty-six states and received 170 electoral votes as against 124 for his combined opposition. His popular plurality, however, was only 50.2 percent.

The Times   This Whig cartoon from the 1840 campaign blames the Panic of 1837 on the Democrats. The factories are closed, the bank has suspended specie payments, and sailors and craftsmen are out of work. But the sheriff, the prison, the pawnbroker, and the liquor store are doing a booming business.

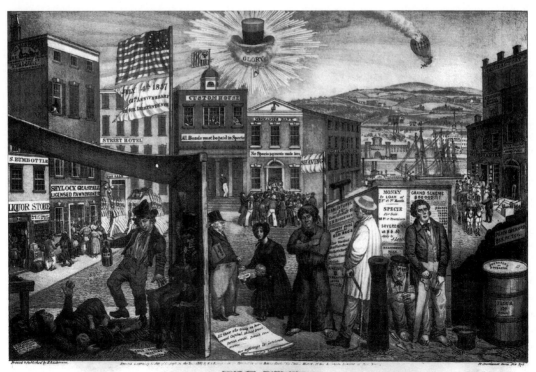

Van Buren had barely taken office when the inflationary boom of the mid-1830s collapsed. Economic historians ascribe the Panic of 1837 and the ensuing depression largely to events outside the country. The Bank of England, concerned over the flow of British gold to American speculators, cut off credit to firms that did business in the United States. As a result, British demand for American cotton fell sharply, and the price of cotton dropped by half. With much of the speculative boom tied to cotton grown in the Southwest, the collapse of the economy was inevitable. The first business failures came in March 1837, just as Van Buren took office. By May, New York banks, unable to accommodate people who were demanding hard coin for their notes, suspended specie payments. Other banks followed suit, and soon banks all over the country—including Nicholas Biddle's newly renamed Bank of the United States of Pennsylvania—went out of business. Although few American communities escaped the economic downturn, it was the commercial and export sectors of the economy that suffered most. In the seaport cities, one firm after another closed its doors, and about one third of the work force was unemployed. Wages for those who kept their jobs declined by some 30 to 50 percent. It was the deepest, most widespread, and longest economic depression Americans had ever faced.

Whigs blamed the depression on Jackson's hard-money policies—particularly his destruction of the Bank of the United States and his Specie Circular. With economic distress the main issue, Whigs scored huge gains in the elections of 1838, even winning control of Van Buren's New York with a campaign that castigated the president as "Martin Van Ruin." Democrats blamed the crash on speculation, luxury, and Whig paper money. While Whigs demanded a new national bank, Van Buren proposed the complete divorce of government from the banking system through what was known as the "Sub-treasury," or "Independent Treasury." Under this plan, the federal government would simply hold and dispense its money without depositing it in banks; it would also require that tariffs and land purchases be paid in gold and silver coins or in notes from specie-paying banks, a provision that allowed government to regulate state bank notes without resorting to a central bank. Van Buren asked Congress to set up the Independent Treasury in 1837, and Congress spent the

rest of his time in office arguing about it. The Independent Treasury Bill was finally passed in 1840, completing the Jacksonian separation of bank and state.

The Election of 1840

Whigs were confident that they could blame Van Buren for the country's economic troubles and take the presidency away from him in the election of 1840. Trying to offend as few voters as possible, they passed over their best-known leaders, Senators Henry Clay and Daniel Webster, and nominated William Henry Harrison of Ohio as their presidential candidate. Harrison was the hero of the Battle of Tippecanoe (see Chapter 8), and a westerner whose Virginia origins made him palatable in the South. He was also a proven vote-getter: as the Whigs' "western" candidate in 1836 he had carried seven states scattered through the Northwest, the Middle Atlantic, New England, and the Upper South. Best of all, he was a military hero who had expressed few opinions on national issues and who had no political record to defend. As his running mate, the Whigs chose John Tyler, a states'-rights Virginian who had

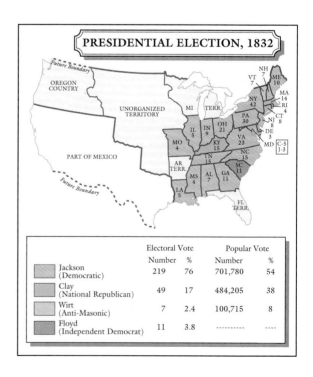

PRESIDENTIAL ELECTION, 1832

	Electoral Vote		Popular Vote	
	Number	%	Number	%
Jackson (Democratic)	219	76	701,780	54
Clay (National Republican)	49	17	484,205	38
Wirt (Anti-Masonic)	7	2.4	100,715	8
Floyd (Independent Democrat)	11	3.8	----------	----

joined the Whigs out of hatred for Jackson. To promote this baldly pragmatic ticket, the Whigs came up with a catchy slogan: "Tippecanoe and Tyler Too." Philip Hone, a wealthy New York City Whig, admitted that the slogan (and the ticket) had "rhyme, but no reason in it."

Early in the campaign a Democratic journalist, commenting on Harrison's political inexperience and alleged unfitness for the presidency, wrote, "Give [Harrison] a barrel of hard cider, and settle a pension of two thousand a year on him, and my word for it, he will sit out the remainder of his days in his log cabin. . . ." Whigs who had been trying to shake their elitist image seized on the statement and launched what was known as the "Log Cabin Campaign." The log cabin, the cider barrel, and Harrison's folksiness and heroism constituted the entire Whig campaign, while Van Buren was pictured as living in luxury at the public's expense. The Whigs conjured up an image of a nattily dressed President "Van Ruin" sitting on silk chairs and dining on gold and silver dishes while farmers and workingmen struggled to make ends meet. Whig doggerel contrasted Harrison the hero with Van Buren the professional politician:

An 1840 Campaign Flag for William Henry Harrison
Whigs celebrated Harrison's military heroism and his (spurious) ties to the pioneer life of log cabins and hard cider.

The knapsack pillow'd Harry's head
The hard ground eas'd his toils;
While Martin on his downy bed
Could dream of naught but spoils.

Democrats howled that Whigs were peddling lies and refusing to discuss issues. But they knew they had been beaten at their own game. Harrison won only a narrow majority of the popular vote, but a landslide of 234 to 60 votes in the electoral college.

Two Parties

The election of 1840 signalled the completion of the second party system—the most fully national alignment of parties in U.S. history. Andrew Jackson had won in 1828 with Jefferson's old southern and western agrarian constituency; in 1832 he had carried his old voters and had won added support in the Middle Atlantic states and in northern New England. In 1836, Whigs capitalized on southern resentment of Jackson's defeat of Calhoun and nullification and on southern mistrust of the New Yorker Van Buren to break the Democratic hold on the South. Whigs came out of their old northeastern strongholds to carry Ohio, Illinois, Kentucky, Georgia, South Carolina, and even Jackson's Tennessee. Jackson had won eight in ten southern votes; Van Buren carried barely half but won majorities in old anti-Jackson neighborhoods in New England. The election of 1840 completed the transition: Harrison and Van Buren contested the election in nearly every state; perhaps most significantly, they received nearly equal levels of support in the slave and free states. Van Buren's dream of a national party system was realized. Ironically, the final pieces fell into place in an election that cost him the presidency.

The election of 1840 also witnessed the high-water mark of voter turnout. Whig and Democratic organizations focused on presidential elections, and prospective voters met a quadrennial avalanche of oratory, door-to-door canvassing, torchlight parades, and party propaganda. And as the contests became national, there was no state in the Union that Demcrats or Whigs could take for granted. (In 1828 winning candidates carried individual states by an average of 36 percent; by 1840 that figure had dropped to 11 percent.) Both Whigs and Democrats maintained organizations and contested elections in nearly every

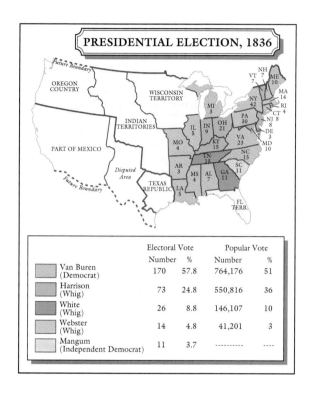

PRESIDENTIAL ELECTION, 1836

	Electoral Vote		Popular Vote	
	Number	%	Number	%
Van Buren (Democrat)	170	57.8	764,176	51
Harrison (Whig)	73	24.8	550,816	36
White (Whig)	26	8.8	146,107	10
Webster (Whig)	14	4.8	41,201	3
Mangum (Independent Democrat)	11	3.7	----------	----

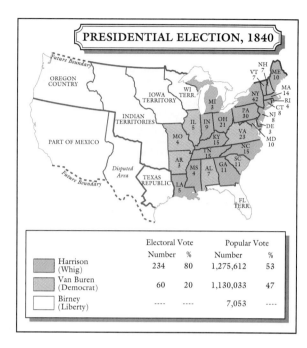

PRESIDENTIAL ELECTION, 1840

	Electoral Vote		Popular Vote	
	Number	%	Number	%
Harrison (Whig)	234	80	1,275,612	53
Van Buren (Democrat)	60	20	1,130,033	47
Birney (Liberty)	----	----	7,053	----

neighborhood in the country, and the result was increased popular interest in politics. In 1824 about one in four adult white men had voted in the presidential election. Jackson's vengeful campaign of 1828 lifted the turnout to 56.3 percent, and it stayed at about that level in 1832 and 1836. The campaign of 1840 brought out 78 percent of the eligible voters, and the turnout remained at that high level throughout the 1840s and 1850s. By 1840 American politics took place within a stable, national system of two parties—both of which depended on support in every section of the country. As Van Buren had predicted, it was a system that focused on questions of economics and state-making and that avoided any discussion of sectional questions. It worked that way until it disintegrated on the eve of the Civil War.

SUGGESTED READING

Arthur M. Schlesinger, Jr., *The Age of Jackson* (1945) is a now-classic overview of politics from the 1820s to the 1840s. Charles Sellers, *The Market Revolution: Jacksonian America,*

1815–1846 (1991) synthesizes social, economic, and cultural history, while Harry L. Watson, *Liberty and Power: The Politics of Jacksonian America* (1990) is an excellent account of politics. Aging but still valuable (and friendlier to the Whigs) is Glyndon G. Van Deusen, *The Jacksonian Era, 1828–1848* (1959). This period has been particularly well served by biographers. See especially Robert V. Remini, *Andrew Jackson and the Course of American Freedom, 1822–1833* (1981) and *Andrew Jackson and the Course of American Democracy, 1833–1845* (1984); Merrill D. Peterson, *The Great Triumvirate: Webster, Clay, and Calhoun* (1987); John Niven, *Martin Van Buren: The Romantic Age of American Politics* (1983); John Niven, *John C. Calhoun and the Price of Union* (1988); Irving H. Bartlett, *Daniel Webster* (1978); Robert V. Remini, *Henry Clay: Statesman for the Union* (1991); Samuel Flagg Bemis, *John Quincy Adams and the Foundations of American Foreign Policy* (1949); and Bemis, *John Quincy Adams and the Union* (1956).

On presidential elections in these years, the best start is the essays in Arthur M. Schlesinger, Jr., and Fred J. Israels, eds., *History of American Presidential Elections, 1789–1968* (3 vols., 1971). George Dangerfield, *The Era of Good Feelings* (1953) and Glover Moore, *The Missouri Controversy, 1819–1821* (1953) are the standard treatments of their subjects. On Jacksonian administrative policies and the spoils system, see Leonard D. White, *The Jacksonians: A Study in Administrative History, 1829–1861* (1954); Sidney H. Aronson, *Status and Kinship in the Higher Civil Service* (1964); and Matthew A.

Crenson, *The Federal Machine: Beginnings of Bureaucracy in Jacksonian America* (1975).

William W. Freehling, *The Road to Disunion: Secessionists at Bay, 1776–1854* (1990) provides an interpretive overview of the South and slavery in national politics. On nullification, see Freehling, *Prelude to Civil War: The Nullification Controversy in South Carolina, 1816–1836* (1965); Richard E. Ellis, *The Union at Risk: Jacksonian Democracy, States' Rights and the Nullification Crisis* (1987); Merrill D. Peterson, *Olive Branch and Sword: The Compromise of 1833* (1982). Michael Paul Rogin, *Fathers and Children: Andrew Jackson and the Subjugation of the American Indian* (1975) is an imaginative essay, though students should also consult the works in Native American history cited in the Suggested Reading for Chapter 8. The best account of Congress's dealings with the abolitionists is in Leonard L. Richards, *The Life and Times of Congressman John Quincy Adams* (1986).

Study of the bank war still begins and ends with Bray Hammond, *Banks and Politics in America from the Revolution to the Civil War* (1957). Students should also consult Peter Temin, *The Jacksonian Economy* (1969) and Robert V. Remini, *Andrew Jackson and the Bank War* (1967).

On party development, see Richard Hofstadter, *The Idea of a Party System: The Rise of Legitimate Opposition in the United States, 1780–1840* (1969); Richard P. McCormick, *The Second American Party System: Party Formation in the Jacksonian Era* (1966); McCormick, *The Presidential Game: The Origins of American Presidential Politics* (1982); Joel H. Silbey, *The Partisan Imperative: The Dynamics of American Politics before the Civil War* (1985); and Silbey, *The American Political Nation, 1838–1893* (1991).

Chapter 13

Society, Culture, and Politics, 1820–1840

The crusade against alcohol, often tied to the Whig and Republican Parties, was central to political culture and political debate from the 1830s onward. From the beginning, it was grounded in middle-class notions of family life.

Jacksonian Democrats reduced the role of the federal government during the 1830s and 1840s. But government remained a very real presence in the lives of Americans. Important policy questions fell to the states, where Whigs and Democrats fought out such matters as support for internal improvements, the creation of public school systems, the care of the insane, and the prohibition of alcohol. The Whigs argued for government support of economic growth and social progress; the Democrats wanted to keep government small and inexpensive.

CONSTITUENCIES

From the 1830s onward, Whigs and Democrats formed a thoroughly national two-party system. Citizens remained loyal to their parties in selecting officeholders ranging from local coroners and school board members to state legislators and presidents of the United States. Thus, the stupendous diversity of American society was reduced to two political choices. The fact that only white men were citizens narrowed diversity, but even with that limitation, the Whig and Democratic Parties were coalitions of ill-matched regional, economic, ethnic, and religious groups. They were united by distinct Whig and Democratic political cultures — consistent attitudes toward government and politics that were embedded in religion, family, and economic life. For all their patchwork diversity, the Democratic and Whig Parties appealed to coherent constituencies and proposed coherent programs in every corner of the republic.

The North and West

In the North and West, Whigs found their most loyal support at the centers of the market revolution and

The County Election The Whig artist–politician George Caleb Bingham said this election-day scene was "illustrative of the manners of a free people and free institutions." It was a wry comment: many of the figures are Missouri Democratic politicians who had, Bingham thought, cheated him in a contested election to the state legislature.

the Finneyite revival. The broad band of Yankee commercial farms stretching across southern New England, western New York, and the Old Northwest was the northern Whig heartland. Whigs also enjoyed support in northern cities and towns. The wealthiest men in cities were Whigs; more than eight in ten among the merchant elite of Boston and New York supported them. The new urban commercial classes created in the market revolution also supported the Whigs. Factory owners were solidly Whig, and native-born factory workers often joined them—in part because Whigs promised opportunities to rise in the world, in part because Whigs protected their jobs by encouraging domestic markets for what they made, and, increasingly, because Whigs pandered to their fears of immigrant labor. For similar reasons, many skilled urban artisans supported the Whigs, as did smaller numbers of dockworkers, day laborers, and others among the unskilled.

Northern Whiggery was grounded in the market revolution, but the Whig political agenda ranged far beyond economic life. The strongholds of Whiggery and the market were also the strongholds of the Finneyite revival. Among the urban middle class and

in the more prosperous rural neighborhoods, the inheritors of Puritan theocracy translated individual spiritual transformations of the late 1820s and early 1830s revivals into an avowedly Christian Whig politic. Northern and western Whigs demanded that government actively encourage the transition to market society. At the same time, they called for moral legislation on such issues as Sabbath observance, temperance, and Bible-based public schools. Marching under the banner of activist government, economic development, and moral progress, Whigs set the political agenda in most northern states.

They met a determined Democratic opposition. Campaigning as defenders of the Jeffersonian republic, autonomous neighborhoods, and private conscience, Democrats found supporters among cultural traditionalists who had gained little from the expansion of national markets and who had no use for the moral agenda of the Whigs. The "Butternuts" (so named for the yellow vegetable dye with which they colored their homespun clothing) of the southern, river-oriented counties of the Northwest joined the Democratic Party. Farmers in the Allegheny Mountains of southern New York and northen Pennsylvania, in the declining countryside of the Hudson

River Valley, and in the poor and isolated hill towns of northern and western New England also supported the Democrats.

In cities and towns, Democrats made up substantial minorities among businessmen, master craftsmen, and professionals, but most urban Democrats were wage earners. Perhaps the most overwhelmingly Democratic group in the country were immigrant Irish Catholics, who were filling the lower ranks of the urban work force. Indeed, their presence in the Democratic Party pushed increasing numbers of native Protestant workers into the Whig ranks—a division that appeared in New York City in the early 1830s, in most cities and towns by the 1840s, and that pervaded the North and West in the 1850s.

When confronted with opposition to evangelical legislation, Whigs labelled the Democratic Party the party of atheism and immorality. Democrats responded that they opposed theocracy, not religion. True, most freethinkers, atheists, and persons who simply did not care about religion supported the Democratic Party. So did immigrant Catholics, who rightfully feared the militant Protestantism of the Whigs. But Democrats won the support of hundreds of thousands of evangelical Protestants as well. A majority of Methodists, Baptists, Disciples of Christ, Old School Presbyterians, and members of Reformed churches put their faith in providence and individual piety, and deeply distrusted what they called "church and state" Whiggery and the mixing of politics and religion. "I am myself a candidate," said a Methodist Democrat in 1840, "but it is for *eternal life*. I aspire to a throne, but I must have one which will not perish." Evangelical Democrats were joined by sectarian Christians who looked to the Democrats for protection: Freewill Baptists, Universalists, Lutherans, Scots Covenanters, many Quakers, Mormons, and others. These Democratic church-goers rejected Whig moral legislation as anti-republican and as Yankee cultural imperialism. George Washington Bethune, a Dutch Reformed minister and a New York Democrat, put the Democratic creed succinctly: "Religion is not to be advanced by civil power."

The South

Throughout the 1830s and 1840s, Southern states divided their votes equally between Whigs and Democrats. But most southern localities were solidly Democratic or Whig. In the 1844 elections, for instance, the counties of Virginia and Alabama supported their favored candidates by margins of 23 and 27 percent, respectively—landslide margins by the standards of two-party politics. (The comparable figure for New York counties was 9 percent.) Much more than in the North, southern differences in party preference were tied to differences in economic life.

Isolationist southern neighborhoods strongly tended to support the Democrats. Thus Democrats ran strongest in yeoman neighborhoods with few slaves and relatively little market activity—upcountry communities that valued household independence and the society of neighbors and that deeply resented intrusions from the outside. The more cosmopolitan southern communities tended to support the Whigs. In general, this meant that Whigs were strongest in plantation counties, where they commanded the votes not only of wealthy planters but of smaller farmers, and of lawyers, storekeepers, and craftsmen in county-seat towns. Upland, nonplantation neighborhoods in which Whigs ran well (eastern Tennessee, western North Carolina, and parts of Virginia are examples) were places where Whigs promised state-sponsored internal improvements that would link ambitious but isolated farmers to outside markets. On the other hand, some plantation districts with easy access to markets, such as the South Carolina low country, opposed expensive Whig projects that would benefit other areas.

Many other southern exceptions to the link between commerce and the Whig Party were grounded in the prestige and power of local leaders. Southern statesmen who broke with the Jacksonians in the 1830s—Calhoun in South Carolina, Hugh Lawson White in Tennessee, and others—took personal and regional followings with them. Political campaigners also had to contend with southerners such as George Reynolds of Pickens County, Alabama. Reynolds was a half-literate yeoman who fathered 17 children and had 234 direct descendants living in his neighborhood, and he delivered them as a bloc to politicians who pleased him. But despite the vagaries of southern kinship and community, Whigs knew that their core constituency in the South was in communities that were or wanted to be linked to commercial society.

In sharp contrast with the North and West, southern political divisions had little to do with religion.

The South was thoroughly evangelized by 1830, but southern Baptists, Methodists, and Presbyterians considered religion a private matter. The southern evangelical churches had begun as marginal movements that opposed the Anglican establishment; they continued to distrust ties between church and state. While they enforced morality within their own households and congregations, southern evangelicals seldom asked state legislatures to pass moral legislation. In extreme cases, southern premillennialists rejected politics altogether, insisting that Jesus would soon return to take the reins of government. (One political canvasser faced with that argument responded, "I will bet one hundred dollars he can't carry Kentucky.") Southern evangelicals who embraced the world of the market assumed, along with their northern Whig counterparts, that the new economy encouraged a Christian, civilized life. Other southern churchgoers responded to the Jacksonians' denunciations of greed and the spirit of speculation. Thus, while many southern communities were bitterly divided over religion, the divisions did not shape party politics.

The social, religious, cultural, and economic bases of party divisions formed coherent Whig and Democratic political cultures. Whig voters in the North and South were persons who either were or hoped to become beneficiaries of the market revolution and who wanted government to subsidize economic development. In the North, they also demanded that government help shape market society into a prosperous, orderly, and homogeneous Christian republic. Democrats, North and South, demanded a minimal government that kept taxes low and that left citizens, their families, and their neighborhoods alone.

THE POLITICS OF ECONOMIC DEVELOPMENT

Both the Whigs and the Democrats accepted the transition to market society, but they wanted to direct it into different channels. Whigs wanted to use government and the market to make an economically and morally progressive — albeit hierarchical — republic. Democrats viewed both government and the new institutions of market society with suspicion and vowed to allow neither to subvert the equal rights and rough equality of condition that were, in their view, the preconditions of republican

citizenship. In language that echoed their Jeffersonian forbears, Jacksonian Democrats demanded that the market remain subservient to the republic.

Government and Its Limits

"The government," remarked a New York City Whig in 1848, "is not merely a machine for making wars and punishing felons, but is bound to do all that is within its power to promote the welfare of the People — its legitimate scope is not merely negative, representative, defensive, but also affirmative, creative, constructive, beneficent. . . ." *The American Review,* a Whig periodical, agreed: "Forms of government are instituted for the protection and fostering of virtue, and are valuable only as they accomplish this. . . ."

The Whigs insisted that economic development, moral progress, and social harmony were linked and that government should foster them. Market society, they argued, opened up opportunities for individual Americans. So long as people developed the work habits and moral discipline that fitted them for success, they would be rewarded. To poor farmers and city workers who felt that the market revolution undermined their independence, Whigs promised social mobility within a new system of interdependence — but only to deserving individuals. According to the *New York Herald* in 1836, "The mechanic who attends quietly to his business — is industrious and attentive — belongs to no club — never visits the porter-house — is always at work or with his family — such a man gradually rises in society and becomes an honor to himself, his friends, and to human nature." The editor continued, "On the contrary, look at the Trade Unionist — the pot-house agitator — the stirrer-up of sedition — the clamorer for higher wages — After a short time, he ends his career in the Pen or State Prison." Whigs believed that the United States exhibited a harmony of class interests and an equality of opportunity that every virtuous person would recognize and that only resentful, mean-spirited, unworthy people would doubt. Pointing to self-made Whigs such as Daniel Webster and Abraham Lincoln, they demanded activist government that nurtured the economic, cultural, and moral opportunities provided by market society.

Democrats seldom praised or condemned market society *per se.* Instead, they argued for the primacy of citizenship: neither government nor the market, they said, should be allowed to subvert the civil and legal equality among independent men on which the republic rested. Often sharing a view of human nature that was (in contrast to the Whigs' more optimistic views) a grim combination of classical republicanism and gothic romance, Democrats saw government not as a tool of progress but as a dangerous—though regrettably necessary—concentration of power in the hands of imperfect, self-interested men. The only safe course was to limit its power. In 1837, *The United States Magazine and Democratic Review* declared, "The best government is that which governs least," and went on to denounce the "natural imperfection, both in wisdom and judgment and purity of purpose, of all human legislation, exposed constantly to the pressure of partial interest; interests which, at the same time that they are essentially selfish and tyrannical, are ever vigilant, persevering, and subtle in all the arts of deception and corruption."

Democrats argued that the Whig belief in benign government and social harmony was absurd. Corporate charters, privileged banks, and subsidies to turnpike, canal, and railroad companies, they said, benefited privileged insiders and transformed republican government into an engine of inequality. Granting such privileges, warned one Democrat, was sure "to break up that social equality which is the legitimate foundation of our institutions, and the destruction of which would render our boasted freedom a mere phantom." George Bancroft, a radical Democrat from Massachusetts, concurred: "A republican people," he said, "should be in an equality in their social and political condition"; "pure democracy," he went on, "inculcates equal rights—equal laws—equal means of education—and *equal means* of wealth also. . . ." By contrast, the government favored by the Whigs would enrich a favored few. Bancroft and other Democrats demanded limited government that was deaf to the demands of special interests.

Banks

Following Andrew Jackson's destruction of the Bank of the United States (see Chapter 12), regulation of banking, credit, and currency fell to the state governments. The proper role of banks emerged as a central political issue in nearly every state, particularly after the widespread bank failures following the

crash of 1837. Whigs defended banks as agents of economic progress, arguing that they provided credit for roads and canals, loans to businessmen and commercial farmers, and the bank notes that served as the chief medium of exchange. Democrats, on the other hand, branded banks as agents of inequality dominated by insiders who controlled artificial concentrations of money, who enjoyed chartered privileges, and who issued bank notes and expanded or contracted credit to their own advantage. In short, they regarded banks as government-protected institutions that enabled a privileged few to make themselves rich at the public's expense.

The economic boom of the 1830s and the destruction of the national bank created a dramatic expansion in the number of state-chartered banks—from 329 in 1830 to 788 in 1837. Systems varied from state to state. South Carolina, Georgia, Tennessee, Kentucky, and Arkansas had state-owned banks. Many new banks in the Old Northwest were also partially state-owned. Such banks often operated as public-service institutions. Georgia's Central Bank, for example, served farmers who could not qualify for private loans, as did other state-owned banks in the South. The charter of the Agricultural Bank of Mississippi (1833) stipulated that at least half of the bank's capital be in long-term loans (farm mortgages) rather than in short-term loans to merchants.

Beginning in the 1820s many states had introduced uniform banking laws to replace the unique charters previously granted to individual banks. The new laws tried to stabilize currency and credit. In New York, a Safety-Fund Law (1829) required banks to pool a fraction of their resources to protect both bankers and small noteholders in the case of bank failures. The result was a self-regulating and conservative community of state banks. Laws in other states required that banks maintain a high ratio of specie (precious metals) to notes in circulation. Such laws, however, were often evaded. Michigan's bank inspectors, for instance, complained that the same cache of silver and gold was taken from bank to bank one step ahead of them. At one bank, an inspector encountered a bank teller who had ten metal boxes behind his counter. The teller opened one of the boxes and showed that it was full of federal silver dollars. The wary inspector picked up another one and found that it was full of nails covered with a thin layer of silver dollars. All the other boxes were

A Three Dollar Bill   This three-dollar bill was no joke. It was one of the small private bank notes that Democrats wanted to take out of circulation.

the same, except for one that was filled with broken glass. Many Americans greeted such stories with a knowing wink until the Panic of 1837, when they presented state bank notes for redemption in specie and were turned down.

"Hard Money" Democrats (those who wanted to get rid of paper money altogether) regarded banks as centers of trickery and privilege and proposed that they be abolished. Banks, they claimed, with their manipulation of credit and currency, encouraged speculation, luxury, inequality, and the separation of wealth from real work. Jackson himself branded banks "a perfect humbug." An Alabama Democrat declared that banking was "in conflict with justice, equity, morality and religion" and that there was "nothing evil that it does not aid—nothing good that it is not averse to." Senator Bedford Brown of North Carolina doubted "whether banking institutions were at all compatible with the existence of a truly republican government," while Richard Swinton of Iowa dismissed banks as "a set of swindling machines." Samuel Medary of Ohio cast banks as the villains of Democratic melodrama. Banks possess, Medary wrote, "every inducement to attract the confidence of the unwary and seduce into their grasp the most watchful and shrewd, by the convenience and safety they hold out to the public through a thousand pretenses of being the exclusive friends and engines of trade and commerce."

In state legislatures, Whigs defended what had become a roughly standard system of private banks chartered by state governments. They had the right to circulate bank notes and had limited liability to protect directors and stockholders from debts incurred by their bank. Many Democrats proposed abolishing all banks. Others proposed reforms. They demanded a high ratio of specie reserves to bank notes as a guard against inflationary paper money. They proposed eliminating the issuance of bank notes in small denominations, thus ensuring that day-to-day business would be conducted in hard coin, and protecting wage earners and small farmers from speculative ups and downs. Democrats also wanted to hold bank directors and stockholders responsible for corporate debts and bankruptcies; some proposed banning corporate charters altogether.

By these and other means, Democrats in the states protected currency and credit from the government favoritism, dishonesty, and elitism that, they argued, enriched Whig insiders and impoverished honest Democrats. Whigs responded that corporate privileges and immunities and an abundant, elastic currency were keys to economic development, and they fought Democrats every step of the way.

Internal Improvements

The Democrats blocked federally funded roads and canals. In response, the states launched the transportation revolution themselves, either by taking direct action or by chartering private corporations to do the work (see Chapter 10). State legislatures everywhere debated the wisdom of direct state action, of corporate privileges, of subsidies to canals and railroads, and of the accumulation of government debt. Whigs, predictably, favored direct action by state governments. Democrats were lukewarm toward the whole idea of internal improvements, convinced that debt, favoritism, and corruption would inevitably result from government involvement in the economy.

Whigs assumed a connection between market society and moral progress, and they argued for internal improvements in those terms. William Seward, the Whig governor of New York, supported transportation projects because they broke down neighborhood isolation and hastened the emergence of a market society with "all the consequent advantages of morality, piety, and knowledge." The historian Henry Adams, who grew up in a wealthy Whig household in Boston, later recalled that he had learned from his father that there was a strong connection between good roads and good morals. In the minds of Whig legislators, a vote for internal improvements was a vote for moral progress and for individual opportunity within a prosperous and happily interdependent market society.

Democratic legislators, though with less enthusiasm, supported at least some internal improvements. But they opposed "partial" legislation that would benefit part of the state at the expense of the rest, and they opposed projects that would lead to higher taxes and put state governments into debt—arguments that they made with increased force after the crash of 1837 bankrupted states that had overextended themselves in the canal boom of the 1830s. The Democrats made the same argument in every state: beneath Whig plans for extensive improvements lay schemes to create special privilege, inequality, debt, and corruption—all at the expense of a hoodwinked people.

THE POLITICS OF SOCIAL REFORM

In the North, it was the churchgoing middle class that provided the Whig Party with a political culture, a reform-oriented social agenda, and most of its electoral support. Whig evangelicals believed that with God's help they could improve the world by improving the individuals within it, and they enlisted the Whig Party in that campaign. On issues ranging from prostitution to temperance, to public education, and to state-supported insane asylums and penitentiaries, Whigs used government to improve individual morality and discipline. Democrats, on the other hand, argued that attempts to dictate morality through legislation were both antirepublican and wrong. It was on questions of social reform that Democrats and Whigs, particularly in the North, often differed most angrily.

Public Schools

During the second quarter of the nineteenth century, local and state governments built systems of tax-supported public schools, known as "common" schools. Before that time, most children learned reading, writing, and arithmetic at home, in poorly staffed town schools, in private schools, or in charity schools run by churches or other benevolent organizations. Despite the lack of any "system" of education, most children learned to read and write. That was, however, more likely among boys than among girls, among whites than among blacks, and among northeasterners than among westerners or southerners.

By the 1830s Whigs and Democrats agreed that providing common schools was a proper function of government. And Democrats often agreed with Whigs that schools could equalize opportunity. The Massachusetts Democrat Robert Rantoul, for example, believed that rich and poor children should "be brought equally and together up to the starting point at the public expense; after that we must shift for ourselves." More radical Democrats, however, wanted public schooling that would erase snobbery. A newspaper declared in 1828 that "the children of the rich and the poor shall receive a national education, calculated to make republicans and banish aristocrats." Marcus Morton, Democratic governor of Massachusetts, agreed that it was the job of the common schools to democratize children "before the pride of family or wealth, or other adventitious distinction has taken a deep root in the young heart."

The reformers who created the most advanced, expensive, and centralized state school systems were Whigs: Horace Mann of Massachusetts, Henry Barnard of Connecticut, Calvin Stowe (husband of Harriet Beecher) of Ohio, and others. These reformers talked more about character-building and Whig

Protestant culture than about the three Rs, convinced that it was the schools' first duty to train youngsters to respect authority, property, hard work, and social order. They wanted schools that would downplay class divisions, but they were interested less in democratizing wealthy children than in civilizing the poor. Calvin H. Wiley, the Whig superintendent of schools in North Carolina, promised that proper schools would make Americans "homogeneous . . . intelligent, eminently republican, sober, calculating, moral and conservative." A Whig newspaper in Ohio declared in 1836 that character-building schools were essential in a democracy: "Other nations have hereditary sovereigns, and one of the most important duties of their governments is to take care of the education of the heir to their throne; these children all about your streets . . . are your future sovereigns." Governor William Seward, a New York Whig, insisted that "education tends to produce equality, not by levelling all to the condition of the base, but by elevating all to the association of the wise and good."

The schools taught a basic Whig axiom: that social questions could be reduced to questions of individual character. A textbook entitled *The Thinker, A Moral Reader* (1855) told children to "remember that all the ignorance, degradation, and misery in the world, is the result of indolence and vice." To teach that lesson, the schools had children read from the King James Bible and recite prayers acceptable to all the Protestant sects. Such texts reaffirmed a common Protestant morality while avoiding divisive doctrinal matters. Until the arrival of significant numbers of Catholic immigrants in the 1840s and 1850s, few parents complained about Protestant religious instruction in the public schools.

Political differences centered less on curriculum than on organization. Whigs wanted state-level centralization and proposed state superintendents and state boards of education, normal schools (state teachers' colleges), text chosen at the state level and used throughout the state, and uniform school terms. They also (often with the help of economy-minded Democrats) recruited young women as teachers. In addition to fostering Protestant morality in the schools, these women were a source of cheap labor: salaries for female teachers in the northern states were from 40 to 60 percent lower than the salaries of their male coworkers. Largely as a result, the percentage of women among Massachusetts teachers rose from 56 percent in 1834 to 78 percent in 1860.

The Eureka Schoolhouse in Springfield, Vermont   Mandated by state law and supported by local taxes, such one-room schools taught generations of American children the three Rs.

Democrats objected to the Whigs' insistence on centralization as elitist, intrusive, and expensive. They preferred to give power to individual school districts, thus enabling local school committees to tailor the curriculum, the length of the school year, and the choice of teachers and texts to local needs. Centralization, they argued, would create a metropolitan educational culture that served the purposes of the rich but ignored the preferences of farmers and working people. It was standard Democratic social policy: inexpensive government and local control. Henry Barnard, Connecticut's superintendent of schools, called his Democratic opponents "ignorant demagogues" and "a set of blockheads." Horace Mann denounced them as "political madmen." As early as 1826 Thaddeus Stevens, who would become a prominent Pennsylvania Whig, argued that voters must "learn to dread ignorance more than taxation."

The argument between Whig centralism and Democratic parsimony dominated the debate over public education until the children of Irish and German immigrants began to enter schools by the thousands in the mid-1840s. Most immigrant families were poor and relied on their children to work and supplement the family income. Consequently, the children's attendance at school was irregular at best. Moreover, most immigrants were Catholics. The Irish regarded Protestant prayers and the King James Bible as heresies and as hated tools of British oppression. Some of the textbooks were worse. Olney's *Practical System of Modern Geography,* a standard textbook, declared that "the Irish in general are quick of apprehension, active, brave and hospitable; but passionate, ignorant, vain, and superstitious." A nun in Connecticut complained that Irish children in the public schools "see their parents looked upon as an inferior race."

Many Catholic parents simply refused to send their children to school. Others demanded changes in textbooks, the elimination of the King James Bible (perhaps to be replaced by the Douay Bible), tax-supported Catholic schools, or at least tax relief for parents who sent their children to parish schools. Whigs, joined by many native-born Democrats, saw Catholic complaints as popish assaults on the Protestantism that they insisted was at the heart of American republicanism.

Many school districts, particularly in the rural areas to which many Scandinavian and German immigrants found their way, created foreign-language schools and provided bilingual instruction. In other places, state support for church-run charity schools persisted. Catholic as well as Protestant schools received such support in New York City until 1825, in Lowell, Massachusetts, Hartford and Middletown, Connecticut, and Milwaukee, Wisconsin, at various times from the 1830s through the 1860s; New Jersey extended state support to Catholic as well as other church schools until 1866. But in Northeastern cities, where immigrant Catholics often formed militant local majorities, such demands led to violence and to organized nativist (anti-immigrant) politics. In 1844 the Native American Party, with the endorsement of the Whigs, won the New York City elections. That same year in Philadelphia, riots that pitted avowedly Whig Protestants against Catholic immigrants, ostensibly over the issue of Bible reading in schools, killed thirteen people. Such conflicts would severely damage the northern Democratic coalition in the 1850s (see Chapter 14).

Prisons

From the 1820s onward, state governments built institutions to house orphans, the dependent poor, the insane, and criminals. The market revolution increased the numbers of such persons and made them more visible, more anonymous, and more separated from family and community resources. Eighteenth-century Americans (and many nineteenth-century Americans as well) had assumed that poverty, crime, insanity, and other social ills were among God's ways of punishing sin and testing the human capacity for both suffering and charity. By the 1820s, however, reformers were arguing that deviance was the result of childhood deprivation. "Normal" people, they suggested, learned discipline and respect for work, property, laws, and other people from their parents. Deviants were the products of brutal, often drunken households devoid of parental love and discipline. The cure was to place them in a controlled setting, teach them work and discipline, and turn them into useful citizens.

In state legislatures, Whigs favored putting deviants in institutions for rehabilitation. Democrats, though they agreed that the states should care for criminals and dependents, regarded attempts at rehabilitation as wrong-headed and expensive; they favored institutions that isolated the insane, warehoused the dependent poor, and punished criminals. Most state systems were a compromise between the two positions.

Pennsylvania built prisons at Pittsburgh (1826) and Philadelphia (1829) that put solitary prisoners into cells to contemplate their misdeeds and to plot a new life. The results of such solitary confinement included a few reformations and numerous attempts at suicide. Only New Jersey imitated the Pennsylvania system. Far more common were institutions based on the model developed in New York at Auburn (1819) and Sing Sing (1825). In the "Auburn System," prisoners slept in solitary cells and marched in military formation to meals and workshops, where they were forbidden to speak to one another at any time. The rule of silence, it was believed, encouraged both discipline and contemplation. The French writer Alexis de Tocqueville, visiting a New York prison in 1830, remarked that "the silence within these vast walls . . . is that of death. . . . There were a thousand living beings, and yet it was a vast desert solitude."

The Auburn System was designed both to reform criminals and to reduce expenses, for the prisons sold workshop products to the outside. Between these two goals Whigs favored rehabilitation. Democrats favored profit-making workshops, and thus lower operating costs and lower taxes. Robert Wiltse, named by the Democrats to run Sing Sing prison in the 1830s, used harsh punishments (including flogging and starving), sparse meals, and forced labor in order to punish criminals and make the prison pay for itself. In 1839 William H. Seward, the newly elected Whig governor of New York, fired Wiltse and appointed administrators who substituted privileges and rewards for punishment and emphasized rehabilitation over profit making. They provided religious instruction, improved food and working conditions, and they cut back on the use of flogging. When Democrats took back the statehouse in the 1842 elections, they discovered that the Whigs' brief experiment in kindness had produced a $50,000 deficit, so they swiftly reinstated the old regime.

Asylums

The leading advocate of humane treatment of the insane was Dorothea Dix, a Boston humanitarian who was shocked by the incarceration and abuse of the insane in common jails. She traveled throughout the country urging citizens to pressure their state

Auburn Prison Inmates at New York's Auburn State Prison were forbidden to speak, and were marched in military formation between workshops, dining halls, and their cells.

Prisoners at the State Prison at Auburn.

legislatures into building insane asylums committed to what reformers called "moral treatment." The asylums were to be clean and pleasant places, preferably outside the cities, and the inmates were to be treated humanely. Attendants were not to beat inmates or tie them up, though they could use cold showers as a form of discipline. Dix and other reformers wanted the asylums to be safe, nurturing environments in which the insane could be made well.

By 1860 the legislatures of twenty-eight of the thirty-three states had established state insane asylums. Whig legislators, with little support from Democrats, approved appropriations for the more expensive and humane moral treatment facilities. Occasionally, however, Dorothea Dix won Democratic support as well. In North Carolina, she befriended the wife of a powerful Democratic legislator as the woman lay on her deathbed; the dying woman convinced her husband to support the building of an asylum. His impassioned speech won the approval of the lower house for a state asylum to be named Dix Hills. In the North Carolina senate, however, the proposal was supported by 91 percent of the Whigs and by only 14 percent of the Democrats—a partisan division that was repeated in state after state.

The South and Social Reform

On most economic issues, the legislatures of the southern states divided along the same lines as northern legislatures: Whigs wanted government participation in the economy, Democrats did not. On social questions, however, southern Whigs and Democrats responded in distinctly southern ways. The South was a rural, culturally conservative region of patriarchal households in which every attempt at government intervention was seen as a threat to independence. Most southern voters, Whigs as well as Democrats, perceived attempts at "social improvement" as expensive and wrong-headed.

The southern states enacted compulsory school attendance laws and drew up blueprints for state school systems. But since the white South was culturally homogeneous, it had little need for schools to enforce a common culture. Moreover, the South had less money and less faith in government. Consequently southern schools tended to be locally controlled, infused with southern evangelical culture, and had a limited curriculum and a short school

year. In 1860 northern children attended school for an average of more than fifty days a year; white children in the South attended school for an average of ten days annually.

By 1860 every slave state except Florida (which had a tiny population) and the Carolinas operated prisons modeled on the Auburn System. Here, however, prisons stressed punishment and profits over rehabilitation. Though some southerners favored northern-style reforms, they knew that southern voters would reject them. Popular votes in Alabama in 1834 and in North Carolina in 1846 brought in resounding defeats for proposals to reform the penitentiaries in those states. While northern evangelicals preached that criminals could be rescued, southern preachers demanded Old Testament vengeance, arguing that hanging, whipping, and branding were sanctioned by the Bible, inexpensive, and more effective than mere incarceration. Other southerners, defending the code of honor, charged that victims and their relatives would be denied vengeance if criminals were tucked away in prisons. Some southern prisons leased prison labor (and sometimes whole prisons) to private entrepreneurs, while dreams of reforming southern criminals were forgotten.

The South did participate in temperance—the all-consuming reform that will be discussed in the next section. By the 1820s Baptists and Methodists had made deep inroads into southern society. Southern ministers preached against duelling, fighting, dancing, gambling, and drinking, while churchgoing women discouraged their husbands, sons, and suitors from drinking. Many southern men either stopped drinking altogether or sharply reduced their consumption. Accordingly, the South contributed its share to the national drop in alcohol consumption. During the 1840s the Washington Temperance Society and other voluntary temperance groups won a solid footing in southern towns. But the religious and temperance organizations of the South were based on individual decisions to abstain. Prohibition, which became dominant in the North, got nowhere in the South. In the 1850s, when one northern legislature after another passed statewide prohibition, the one slave state to follow was tiny, northern-oriented Delaware.

At bottom, southern resistance to social reform stemmed from a conservative, Bible-based acceptance of suffering and human imperfection and a commit-

the big state and the Whig cultural agenda was at the center of party formation in the North. The most persistent issue around which that argument was conducted was the question of alcohol, so much so that in many places the temperance question defined the differences between Democrats and Whigs.

The Whipping Post and Pillory at New Castle, Delaware Delaware was a slave state that continued to inflict public, corporal punishment on lawbreakers. Many of the witnesses to this whipping are small children, who are supposedly learning a lesson.

Ardent Spirits

Drinking had been a part of social life since the beginning of English settlement. But the withering of authority and the disruptions of the market revolution led to increased consumption, increased public drunkenness, and a perceived increase in the violence and social problems caused by alcohol (see Chapter 8). Beginning in the 1790s physicians and a few clergymen attacked not only habitual drunkenness but also alcohol itself. And for a short time after 1812, Federalist politicians and Congregational clergymen formed "moral societies" in New England that discouraged strong drink. Their imperious tone and their association with the old seats of authority, however, doomed them to failure.

The temperance crusade began in earnest in 1826, when northeastern evangelicals founded the American Society for the Promotion of Temperance (soon renamed the American Temperance Society). The movement's manifesto was Lyman Beecher's *Six Sermons on the Nature, Occasions, Signs, Evils, and Remedy of Intemperance* (1826). Addressing the churchgoing middle class, Beecher declared alcohol an addictive drug and warned that even moderate drinkers risked becoming hopeless drunkards. Thus temperance, like other evangelical reforms, was presented as a contest between self-control and slavery to one's appetites. By encouraging total abstinence, reformers hoped to halt the creation of new drunkards while the old ones died out. But while Beecher pinned his hopes on self-discipline, he wanted middle-class abstainers to spread reform through both example and coercion. As middle-class evangelicals eliminated alcohol from their own lives, they would cease to offer it to their guests, buy or sell it, or provide it to their employees, and they would encourage their friends to do the same.

In the atmosphere surrounding the middle-class revivals of the 1820s and 1830s, Beecher's crusade gathered strength. Charles Grandison Finney, in his revival at Rochester, made total abstinence a

ment to the power and independence of white men who headed families. Any proposal that sounded like social tinkering or the invasion of paternal rights was doomed to failure. To make matters worse, many reforms—public schools, Sunday schools, prohibitionism, humane asylums—were seen as the work of well-funded and well-organized missionaries from the Northeast who wanted to fashion society in their own self-righteous image. The southern distrust of reform was powerfully reinforced after 1830, when northern reformers began to call for abolition of slavery and equality of the sexes—reforms that were unthinkable to most white southerners.

EXCURSUS:
THE POLITICS OF ALCOHOL

The fight between evangelical Whigs who demanded that government regulate public (and often private) morality and Democrats who feared both

STEP 1.
A glass
with
a Friend.

STEP 2.
A glass to
keep the
cold out.

STEP 3.
A glass too
much.

STEP 4.
Drunk
and
riotous.

STEP 5.
The summit attained
Jolly companions
A confirmed drunkard.

STEP 6.
Poverty
and
Disease.

STEP 7.
Forsaken
by
Friends.

STEP 8.
Desperation
and
crime.

STEP 9.
Death
by
suicide.

The Drunkard's Progress   This popular print describes *The Drunkard's Progress* from social drinking to alcoholism, isolation, crime, and death by suicide. His desolate wife and daughter and his burning house are at bottom.

condition of conversion. Many other ministers and churches followed suit, and by the middle 1830s members of the middle class had largely disengaged themselves from alcohol and from the people who drank it. Following a temperance lecture by Finney's co-worker Theodore Dwight Weld, Elijah and Albert Smith, Rochester grocers, rolled their stock of whiskey out on the sidewalk, smashed the barrels, and let the liquor spill into the street. Other merchants threw their liquor into the Erie Canal or sold it off at cost. Hundreds of evangelical businessmen pledged that they would refuse to rent to merchants who sold liquor, sell grain to distillers, or enter a store that sold alcohol. Many of them made abstinence a condition of employment, placing ads that carried the line "None But Temperate Men Need Apply." Abstinence and opposition to the use of distilled spirits (people continued to argue about wine and beer) had become a badge of middle-class respectability.

Among themselves, the reformers achieved considerable success. By 1835 the American Temperance Society claimed 1.5 million members and estimated that 2 million Americans had renounced ardent spir-

its (whiskey, rum, and other distilled liquors); 250,000 had formally pledged to completely abstain from alcohol. The Society further estimated that 4,000 distilleries had gone out of business, and that many of the survivors had cut back their production. Many politicians no longer bought drinks to win voters to their cause. The Kentucky Whig Henry Clay, once known for keeping late hours, began to serve only cold water when he entertained at dinner. And in 1833, members of Congress formed the American Congressional Temperance Society. The regular army put an end to the age-old liquor ration in 1832, and increasing numbers of militia officers stopped supplying their men with whiskey. The annual consumption of alcohol, which had reached an all-time high in the 1820s, dropped by more than half in the 1830s (from 3.9 gallons of pure alcohol per adult in 1830 to 1.8 gallons in 1840).

In the middle 1830s Whigs made temperance a political issue. Realizing that voluntary abstinence would not put an end to drunkenness, Whig evangelicals drafted coercive, prohibitionist legislation. First, they attacked the licenses granting grocery stores and taverns the right to sell liquor by the drink and to permit it to be consumed on the premises. The licenses were important sources of revenue for local governments. They also gave local authorities the power to cancel the licenses of troublesome establishments. Militant temperance advocates, usually in association with local Whigs, demanded that the authorities use that power to outlaw all public drinking places. In communities throughout the North, the licensing issue, always freighted with angry divisions over religion and social class, became the issue around which local parties organized. The question first reached the state level in Massachusetts when in 1838 a Whig legislature passed a "Fifteen-Gallon Law," which decreed that merchants could sell ardent spirits only in quantities of fifteen gallons or more—thus outlawing every public drinking place in the state. In 1839 Massachusetts voters sent enough Democrats to the legislature to rescind the law.

The Whig attempt to cancel tavern licenses proved unenforceable, as proprietors simply operated without licenses or found ways to get around the laws. While the Massachusetts Fifteen-Gallon Law was in effect, one Boston tavernkeeper painted stripes on a pig and charged patrons an admission fee of six cents (the price of a drink) to view the "exhibition." He then provided customers—who paid over and over to see the pig—with a "complimentary" glass of whiskey.

Leading Democrats agreed with Whigs that Americans drank too much. But while Whigs insisted that regulating morality was a proper function of government, Democrats warned that government intrusion into areas of private choice would violate republican liberties. The Boston reformer Theodore Parker, a Whig, conceded that prohibition was "an invasion of private rights," but he insisted that it was "an invasion . . . for the sake of preserving the rights of all." Democrats argued that prohibition posed a greater threat to the republic than drink itself. The Democrats of Rochester, New York, responding to the license issue, declared:

> Anything which savours of restraint in what men deem their natural rights is sure to meet with opposition, and men convinced of error by force will most likely continue all their lives unconvinced in their reason. Whatever shall be done to stay the tide of intemperance, and roll back its destroying wave, must be done by *suasive* appeals to the reason, the interest, or the pride of men; but not by force.

In many communities, alcohol was the defining difference between Democrats and Whigs. In 1834, for instance, a Whig campaign worker ventured into a poor neighborhood in Rochester and asked a woman

Striped Pig   This cartoon, filled with the individual sin and misery and the social destruction caused by alcohol, portrays the Massachusetts tavernkeeper's famous striped pig as an instrument of the devil.

Death on the Striped Pig, or an illustration of the present attitude of that noted animal as he appears in New England.
Respectfully dedicated to the real friends of the Temperance reform by their obedient serv't and fellow labourer— Chas Jewett
Published by WHIPPLE & DAMRELL, No. 9 Cornhill, Boston.

how her husband planned to vote. "Why, he has always been Jackson," she said, "and I don't think he's joined the Cold Water."

The Democratization of Temperance

Democratic voters held ambiguous attitudes toward temperance. Many of them continued to drink, while many others voluntarily abstained or cut down. Yet almost without exception they resented the coercive tactics of the Whigs and supported their party's pledge to protect them from evangelical meddling in their private lives. In 1830, when Lyman Beecher's Hanover Street Church in Boston caught fire, the volunteer fire companies (which doubled as working-class drinking clubs) arrived, noted that it was the hated Beecher's church, and made no effort to put out the fire. Unbeknownst to the Reverend Beecher, the church had rented basement space to a merchant who used it to store barrels of rum. The crowd that gathered to watch the church burn to the ground cheered as the barrels exploded one by one.

Many Democrats, despite their opposition to prohibition, spoke out against drunkenness. John Commerford, a New York City trade unionist, argued that the main cause of poverty, ignorance, and associated evils was low wages, but that among the other causes "there is none more prominently conspicuous than that of alcohol." Many craft unions denied membership to heavy drinkers, and hundreds of thousands of rural and urban Democrats quietly stopped drinking. (The sharp drop in alcohol consumption in the 1830s can be explained in no other way.) Then, in the late 1830s, former antiprohibitionists launched a temperance movement of their own.

One evening in 1840—in the depths of a devastating economic depression—six craftsmen were drinking at Chase's Tavern in Baltimore. More or less as a joke, they sent one of their number to a nearby temperance lecture; he came back a teetotaler and converted the others. They then drew up a total abstinence pledge and promised to devote themselves to the reform of other drinkers. Within months, from this beginning a national movement had emerged, called the Washington Temperance Society. With a core membership of men who had

opposed temperance in the 1830s, the Washingtonians differed from older temperance societies in several ways. First, they identified themselves as members of the laboring classes. Second, they were avowedly nonreligious: though many of them were churchgoers (usually Methodist or Baptist), many were not, and the Washingtonians avoided religious controversy by avoiding religion. Third, the Washingtonians—at least those who called themselves "True Washingtonians"—rejected recourse to politics and legislation and concentrated instead on the conversion of drinkers through compassion and persuasion. Finally, they welcomed "hopeless" drunkards—who accounted for about 10 percent of the membership—and hailed them as heroes when they sobered up.

Though Whig reformers welcomed the Washingtonians at first, they soon had second thoughts. The nonreligious character of the movement was disturbing to those who saw temperance as an arm of evangelical reform. Previous advocates of temperance had assumed that sobriety would be accompanied by evangelical decorum. Instead, the meetings, picnics, and parades held by the Washingtonians were continuous with a popular culture that Whig evangelicals opposed. While the temperance regulars read pamphlets and listened to lectures by clergymen, lawyers, and doctors, the Washingtonians enjoyed raucous sing-alongs, comedy routines, barnyard imitations, dramatic skits, and even full-dress minstrel shows geared to temperance themes. Meetings were organized around experience speeches offered by reformed drunkards. Speaking extemporaneously, they omitted none of the horrors of an alcoholic life—attempts at suicide, friendships betrayed, fathers and mothers desolated, wives beaten and abandoned, children dead of starvation. Though Washingtonians had given up alcohol, their melodramatic tales, street parades, song books, and minstrel shows—even when presented with a Methodist or Baptist accent—were continuous with popular culture. It was temperance, but it was not what Lyman Beecher and the Whigs had had in mind.

Nowhere did the Washingtonians differ more sharply from the temperance regulars than in their visions of the reformed life. The Whig reformers tied abstinence to individual ambition and middle-class domesticity, expecting men who quit drinking to withdraw from the male world in which drinking

Sons of Temperance Membership Certificate The Sons of Temperance was one of the temperance lodges that grew out of Washingtonianism in the 1840s. The lodge promised its working- and lower-middle class members a masculinized domestic happiness, friendship, and funeral benefits in exchange for sobriety and heavy dues.

was common and retreat into the comfort of the newly feminized middle-class family. Washingtonianism, on the other hand, translated traditional male sociability into sober forms. Moreover they called former drinkers back to the responsibilities of traditional fatherhood. Their experience stories began with the hurt drunkards had caused their wives and children and ended with their transformation into dependable providers and authoritative fathers. While the Whig temperance regulars tried to extend the ethos of individual ambition and the new middle-class domesticity into society at large, Washingtonians sought to rescue the self-respect and moral authority of working-class fathers.

The Washington Temperance Society collapsed toward the end of the 1840s. Yet its legacy survived. Among former drinkers in the North, it had introduced a new sense of domestic responsibility and a healthy fear of drunkenness. Consumption of pure alcohol dropped from 1.8 to 1.0 gallons annually in the 1840s. Along the way, the Washingtonians and related groups created a self-consciously respectable native Protestant working class in American cities.

It was into neighborhoods stirred by working-class revivals and temperance agitation that millions of Irish and German immigrants arrived in the 1840s and 1850s. The newcomers had their own time-honored relations to alcohol. The Germans introduced lager beer to the United States, thus providing a wholesome alternative for Americans who wished to give up spirits without joining the teetotalers. The Germans also built old-country beer halls in American cities, complete with sausage counters, oompah bands, group singing, and other family attractions. For their part, the Irish reaffirmed their love of whiskey—a love that was forged in colonial oppression, and in a culture that accepted trouble with resignation, and legitimized levels of male drunkenness and violence that Americans—particularly the temperance forces—found appalling. (Differences in immigrant drinking were given architectural expression. German beer halls provided seating arrangements for whole families. Irish bars, on the other hand, provided a bar but no tables or chairs. If a drinker had to sit down, they reasoned, it was time for him to go home.)

In the 1850s native resentment of Catholic immigrants drove thousands of Baptist and Methodist "respectables" out of the Democratic coalition and into nativist Whig majorities that—beginning with Maine in 1851—established legal prohibition throughout New England, in the middle states, and in the Old Northwest. These were often the Democrats who became part of the North's Republican majority on the eve of the Civil War (see Chapter 15).

THE POLITICS OF RACE

Most whites in antebellum America believed in "natural" differences based on sex and race. God, they said, had given women and men and whites and blacks different mental, emotional, and physical capacities. And, as humankind (women and non-whites more than others) was innately sinful and prone to disorder, God ordained a fixed social hierarchy in which white men exercised power over others. Slaves and free blacks accepted their subordinate status only as a fact of life, not as something that was natural and just. Some women also questioned patriarchy. But before 1830 hierarchy based on sex and race was seldom questioned in public, particularly by persons who were in a position to change it.

In the antebellum years, southerners and most northerners stiffened their defence of white paternalism. But northern Whig evangelicals were beginning to envision a world based in Christian love and individual worth, not inherited status. They transformed marriage from rank domination into a sentimental partnership—unequal, but a partnership nonetheless. They also questioned the more virulent forms of racism. From among the Whig evangelicals emerged a radical minority that envisioned a world without power. While conservative Christians insisted that relations based on dominance and submission were the lot of a sinful humankind, reformers argued that such relations interposed human power, too often in the form of brute force, between God and the individual spirit. They called for a world that substituted spiritual freedom and Christian love for every form of worldly domination. The result was a community of uncompromising radical reformers who attacked slavery and patriarchy as national sins.

Free Blacks

Prior to the American Revolution there had been sizeable pockets of slavery in the northern states. But revolutionary idealism, coupled with the growing belief that slavery was inefficient, led one northern state after another to abolish it. Vermont, where there were almost no slaves, outlawed slavery in its revolutionary constitution. By 1804 every northern state had taken some action, usually by passing laws that called for gradual emancipation. The first of such laws, and the model for others, was passed in Pennsylvania in 1780. This law freed slaves born after 1780 when they reached their twenty-eighth birthday. Slaves born before 1780 would remain slaves, and slave children would remain slaves through their

prime working years. Some northern slaveowners, in violation of the laws, sold young slaves into the South as their freedom dates approached. Still, the emancipation laws worked: by 1830 only a handful of aging blacks remained slaves in the North.

The rising population of northern free blacks gravitated to the cities. Most of those who had been slaves in cities stayed there. They were joined by thousands of free blacks who decided to abandon the declining northeastern countryside and move to the city. In many cities—Philadelphia and New York City in particular—they met a stream of free blacks and fugitive slaves from the Upper South, where the bonds of slavery were growing tighter, and where free blacks feared reenslavement. Thus despite the flood of white immigrants from Europe and the American countryside, African Americans constituted a sizeable minority in the rapidly expanding cities. New York City's black population, 10.5 percent in 1800, was still 8.8 percent in 1820; Philadelphia, the haven of thousands of southern refugees, was 10.3 percent African American in 1800 and 11.9 percent in 1820.

Blacks in the seaport cities tended to take stable, low-paying jobs. A few became successful (occasionally wealthy) entrepreneurs, while some others practiced skilled trades. Many of the others took jobs as waiters or porters in hotels, as barbers, and as butlers, maids, cooks, washerwomen, and coachmen for wealthy families. Others worked as dockworkers, laborers, and sailors. Still others became dealers in used clothing, or draymen with their own carts and horses, or food vendors in the streets and in basement shops (oysters in particular were a black monopoly).

From the 1820s onward, however, the growing numbers of white wage-workers began to edge blacks out of their jobs by underselling them, by pressuring employers to discriminate, and by outright violence. As a result, African Americans were almost completely eliminated from the skilled trades, and many unskilled and semiskilled blacks lost their jobs on the docks, in warehouses, and in the merchant marine. In 1834 a Philadelphian reported that "colored persons, when engaged in their usual occupations, were repeatedly assailed and maltreated, usually on the [waterfront]. Parties of white men have *insisted* that no blacks shall be employed in certain departments of labor." And as their old jobs dis-

A Black Oyster Seller in Philadelphia, 1814   In early nineteenth century New York and Philadelphia, African-Americans monopolized the public sale of oysters and clams.

appeared, blacks were systematically excluded from the new jobs that were opening up in factories. By the 1830s black workers in Philadelphia were noting "the difficulty of getting places for our sons as apprentices . . . owing to the prejudices with which we have to contend." In 1838 (during a depression that hit blacks first and hardest) an African-American newspaper complained that blacks "have ceased to be hackney coachmen and draymen, and they are now almost displaced as stevedores. They are rapidly losing their places as barbers and servants. Ten families employ white servants now, where one did twenty years ago."

The depression was followed by waves of desperately poor Irish immigrants. By accepting low wages, and by rioting, intimidation, gunplay, and even murder, the Irish displaced most of the remaining blacks from their toehold in the economic life of the northeastern cities. An observer of the Phil-

adelphia docks remarked in 1849 that "when a few years ago we saw none but Blacks, we now see none but Irish."

Meanwhile, official discrimination against blacks was on the rise. Political democratization for white men was accompanied by the disfranchisement of blacks (see Chapter 8). Cities either excluded black children from public schools or set up segregated schools. In 1845, when Massachusetts passed a law declaring that all children had the right to attend neighborhood schools, the Boston School Committee blithely ruled that the law did not apply to blacks. Blacks were also excluded from white churches or sat in segregated pews; even the Quakers sat blacks and whites separately.

African Americans responded by building institutions of their own. At one end were black-owned gambling houses, saloons, brothels, and dance halls—the only racially integrated institutions to be found in most cities. At the other end were black churches, schools, social clubs, and lodges. The first independent black church was the African Church of Philadelphia, founded in 1790; the African Methodist Episcopal Church, a national denomination still in existence, was founded in Philadelphia in 1816. Schools and relief societies, usually associated with churches, grew quickly. Black Masonic lodges attracted hundreds of members. Many of the churches and social organizations were given names that proudly called up the blacks' African origins. In Philadelphia, for instance, there were African Methodists, Abyssinian Baptists, the Daughters of Ethiopia, the African Dorcas Society, and the African Female Anti-Slavery Society—to name only a few. It was from this matrix of black businesses and institutions that black abolitionists—David Walker in Boston, Fredrick Douglass in New Bedford and Rochester, the itinerant Sojourner Truth, and many others—would emerge to demand abolition of slavery and equal rights for black citizens.

Democratic Racism

Neither the Whigs nor the Democrats encouraged the aspirations of slaves or free blacks. But it was the Democrats, from their beginnings in the 1820s, who incorporated racism into their political agenda. Minstrel shows, for example, often reflected the Democratic line on current events, and Democratic cartoonists often featured bug-eyed, woolly-haired caricatures of blacks. By the time of the Civil War, Democrats mobilized voters almost solely with threats of "amalgamation" and "Negro rule."

Democrats also contributed to the rising tide of antiblack violence. There were plenty of Whig racists, but Democrats seem to have predominated when mobs moved into black neighborhoods, sometimes burning out whole areas. Indeed many Democrats lumped together evangelical reformers, genteel Whigs, and blacks as a unified threat to the white republic. In July 1834 a New York City mob sacked the house of the abolitionist Lewis Tappan, moved on to Charles Finney's Chatham Street Chapel, where abolitionists were said to be meeting, and finished the evening by attacking a British actor at the Bowery theater. The manager saved his theater by waving two American flags and ordering an American actor to perform popular minstrel routines for the mob. In Jackson, Michigan, in 1839, after the local Sunday schools announced an outdoor meeting featuring temperance and antislavery speakers, anti-evangelical rowdies removed the benches from the meeting ground the night before and burned them in the town square. They then dug up the corpse of a black man who had been buried a few days earlier and propped him up in the pulpit of the Presbyterian church, where he greeted the Sunday school the next morning.

The first major American race riot broke out in Philadelphia in 1834 between working-class whites and blacks at a street carnival. While blacks seem to have won the first round, the whites refused to accept defeat. Over the next few nights, they wrecked a black-owned tavern, broke into black households to terrorize families and steal their property, attacked whites who lived with, socialized with, or operated businesses catering to blacks, wrecked the African Presbyterian Church, and destroyed a black church on Wharton Street by sawing through its timbers and pulling it down. Sporadic racial violence wracked the city throughout the 1830s and 1840s, reaching its height in 1849. That summer a firehouse gang of Irish immigrants calling themselves "The Killers" attacked a black-owned tavern and gambling hall called the California House. The black patrons had anticipated the attack and had armed themselves, and in the melee five Killers were shot. For two months, tempers simmered. Finally the Killers set a fire at the California House that spread to nearby

houses. Then they fought off neighborhood blacks, rival firemen, and the police. The riot ended only when the city sent in four companies of militia.

Meanwhile, educated whites had begun to think in racist terms. Among most scientists, biological determinism replaced historical and environmental explanations of racial differences; many argued that whites and blacks were separate species. Democrats welcomed that "discovery." John Van Evrie, a New York doctor and Democratic pamphleteer, declared that "it is a palpable and unavoidable fact that Negroes are a different species," and that the story of Adam and Eve referred only to the origin of *white* people. In 1850 the *Democratic Review* confided, "Few or none now seriously adhere to the theory of the unity of the races. The whole state of the science at this moment seems to indicate that there are several distinct races of men on the earth, with entirely different capacities, physical and mental."

As whites came to perceive racial differences as God-given and immutable, they changed the nature of those differences as well. In the eighteenth and early nineteenth centuries, whites had stereotyped blacks as ignorant and prone to drunkenness and thievery, but they had maintained a parallel stereotype of blacks as loyal and self-sacrificing servants. From the 1820s onward, racists continued to regard blacks as incompetent, but they found it harder to distinguish mere carelessness from dishonesty. Now they saw all blacks as treacherous, shrewd, and secretive; they only *pretended* to feel loyalty to white families and affection for the white children they took care of, while awaiting the chance to steal from them or poison them. The writer Herman Melville, a lifelong Democrat who shared little of his compatriots' racism but who helped to codify their fascination with duplicity and deceit, dramatized these fears in *Benito Cereno*, a novel about slaves who commandeered a sailing ship and its captain and crew, then (with knives secretly at the throats of their captives) acted out a servile charade for unsuspecting visitors who came on board.

Above all, Democratic ideologues pronounced blacks unfit to be citizens of the white man's republic. Whigs often supported various forms of black suffrage; Democrats uniformly opposed it. The insistence that blacks were incapable of citizenship reinforced an equally natural white male political capacity. The exclusion of blacks (by Democrats whose own political competence was often doubted by wealthier and

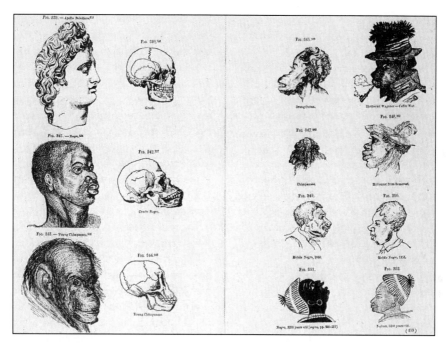

Skull Measurements   This illustration is from *Types of Mankind: or Ethnological Researches* (1845), a scientific text that portrayed white men as Greek gods and black men as apes.

better-educated Whigs) protected the republic while extending citizenship to all white men. The most vicious racist assaults were often carried out beneath symbols of the revolutionary republic. Antiblack mobs in Baltimore, Cincinnati, and Toledo called themselves Minute Men and Sons of Liberty. Philadelphia blacks who gathered to hear the Declaration of Independence read on the Fourth of July were attacked for "defiling the government." The antiabolitionist mob that sacked Lewis Tappan's house rescued a portrait of George Washington and carried it as a banner during their later attacks on Finneyite evangelicals and English actors.

Antislavery

Before 1830 only a few whites had thought of slavery as a moral question. Quakers, at their annual meeting in 1758, had condemned both the slave trade and slavery, and Methodists and some Baptists had done the same late in the century. Washington, Jefferson, and other Chesapeake gentlemen doubted the wisdom if not the morality of holding slaves; New England Federalists had condemned slavery in the course of condemning Jeffersonian masters. But

there were too few Quakers to make a difference, and the movement to free slaves in the Upper South and the antislavery sentiments of southern evangelicals both died out early in the nineteenth century. Southerners and most northerners—when they bothered to think about it at all—tended to accept slavery as the result of human (read *black*) depravity and God's unknowable plan.

Organized opposition to slavery before 1831 was pretty much limited to the American Colonization Society, founded in 1816. Led by wealthy, generally conservative northern churchmen and a contingent of Chesapeake gentlemen, the Society proposed the voluntary, gradual, and compensated emancipation of slaves and the "repatriation" of free blacks to West Africa. Though the Society transported a few thousand blacks to Liberia, it never posed a serious threat to slavery. Southerners, who owned 2 million slaves by 1830, opposed emancipation whether compensated or not, and few free blacks were interested in moving to Africa. The Society's campaign to deport them so disturbed many free blacks that they substituted "Colored" for "African" in naming their institutions. One black churchman explained that references to Africa provided "an available excuse for a powerful enemy, the American Colonization Society, to use. . . as a weapon of our own make, to expel ourselves from our beloved country."

But while few white Americans actively opposed slavery before 1830, the writing was on the wall. Emancipation in the North, though it came about quietly, constituted an implicit condemnation of slavery in the South. So did events outside the United States. Toussaint L'Ouverture's successful slave revolution in Haiti in 1804 threatened slavery everywhere (see Chapter 8). The British, whose navy could enforce their dictates on the seas, outlawed the Atlantic slave trade in 1808. Mexico, Peru, Chile, Gran Colombia (present-day Colombia, Venezuela, Equador, and Panama) and other new republics carved out of the Spanish empire emancipated their slaves. The most powerful blow came in 1830 when the British Parliament emancipated the slaves of Jamaica, Bermuda, and other Caribbean islands ruled by Britain.

It was at this time — the late 1820s and early 1830s — that religious revivals created a reform-minded evangelical culture in the northern United States. Radical abolitionism dates from 1831, when William Lloyd Garrison published the first issue of *The Liberator*. Already a veteran reformer, Garrison condemned slavery as a national sin and demanded immediate emancipation — or at least an immediate start toward emancipation. "I am in earnest," he declared in his first editorial. "I will not equivocate — I will not excuse — I will not retreat a single inch — AND I WILL BE HEARD."

In 1833 Garrison and like-minded abolitionists formed the American Anti-Slavery Society. Some of them — Wendell Phillips, Thomas Wentworth Higginson, Theodore Parker — were Unitarians who opposed slavery as an affront to both humanity and rationality; others — most notably the poet John Greenleaf Whittier — were Quakers who were happy to join the movement. But abolitionists found their greatest support in southern New England, western New York, northern Ohio, and among the new middle classes of the northeastern cities — ground that Yankee settlement, the market revolution, and Finneyite revivals had turned into the heartland of the northern Whig Party.

Opposition to slavery was a logical extension of middle-class evangelicalism. Charles Finney, Lyman Beecher, and other Whig evangelicals retained a Puritan inheritance that demanded that God's people legislate the behavior of others. But the new evangelicalism was grounded in the morally accountable individual, and not in coercive institutions. Whig evangelicals posed a contest between Christian love and moral free agency on the one hand and every kind of passion, brutality, and force on the other. They often promised that their reforms would liberate the individual spirit from "slavery" to alcohol, lust, or ignorance — thus phrasing moral legislation as liberation, not coercion. It was not long before some discovered that slavery itself, an institution that obliterated moral choice and encouraged the worst human passions, was America's great national sin.

The American Anti-Slavery Society demanded immediate emancipation of slaves and full civil and legal rights for blacks. Assuming that God had created blacks and whites as members of one human family, abolitionists opposed the scientific racism spouted by Democrats. Moderates and latecomers to abolitionism spoke of inherent racial characteristics but tended to view blacks in benign (if condescending) ways. Harriet Beecher Stowe, for instance, portrayed blacks as simple, innocent, loving people who possessed a capacity for sentiment and emotionalism that most whites had lost. In 1852, Horace Mann told an audience of blacks in Ohio that "in intellect, the blacks are inferior to the whites, while in sentiment and affections, the whites are inferior to the blacks." Radical abolitionists, however, remained committed environmentalists. Lydia Maria Child of New York City declared, "In the United States, colored persons have scarcely any chance to rise. But if colored persons are well treated, and have the same inducements to industry as others, they [will] work as well and behave as well."

Antislavery, unlike other reforms, was a radical attack on one of the nation's central institutions, and the movement attracted a minority even among middle-class evangelicals. Indeed, both Lyman Beecher and Charles Finney opposed the abolitionists in the 1830s, arguing that emancipation would come about sooner or later as a result of the religious conversion of slaveowners; antislavery agitation and the denunciation of slaveholders, they argued, would divide Christians, slow the revival movement, and thus actually delay emancipation. Finney warned his abolitionist friend Theodore Dwight Weld that the logical end of antislavery was civil war.

Savoring its role as a beleaguered minority, the American Anti-Slavery Society staged a series of

Anti-Slavery Declaration   This abolitionist manifesto of 1833 calls for the end of slavery, both as a realization of God's will and as an act completing the American Revolution.

campaigns to force government and the public at large to confront the question of slavery. In 1835 the society launched a "Postal Campaign," flooding the nation's postal system with abolitionist tracts that southerners and most northerners regarded as "incendiary." From 1836 onward, they petitioned Congress to abolish slavery and the slave trade in the District of Columbia and to deny the slaveholding Republic of Texas admission to the Union. These tactics forced President Andrew Jackson to permit southern postal workers to censor the mails; they also forced Democrats and southern Whigs to abridge the right of petition to avoid discussion of slavery in Congress (see Chapter 12).

In these ways, a radical minority forced politicians to demonstrate the complicity of the party system

(and the Democrats in particular) in the institution of slavery, brought the slavery question to public attention, and tied it to questions of civil liberties in the North and political power in the South. They were a dangerous minority indeed.

THE POLITICS OF GENDER AND SEX

Whigs valued a reformed masculinity that was lived out in the sentimentalized homes of the northern business classes or in the Christian gentility of the Whig plantation and farm. Jacksonian voters, on the other hand, often defended domestic patriarchy. While most were unimaginative paternalists, Democrats often made heroes of men whose flamboyant, rakish lives directly challenged Whig domesticity. Whigs denounced Andrew Jackson for stealing Rachel Donelson from her lawful husband; Democrats often admired him for the same reason. Jackson's handling of the Peggy Eaton affair displayed a similar disregard for domesticity. Richard M. Johnson of Kentucky, who was vice president under Van Buren, openly kept a mulatto mistress and had two daughters by her; with his pistols always at hand, he accompanied her openly around the capitol. "Prince" John Van Buren, the president's son and himself a prominent New York Democrat, met a "dark-eyed, well-formed Italian lady" who called herself Amerigo Vespucci and claimed to be a direct descendant of the man for whom America was named. She became young Van Buren's "fancy lady," remaining with him until he lost her in a high-stakes card game.

Whigs made Democratic contempt for sentimental domesticity a political issue. William Crane, a Michigan Whig, claimed that Democrats "despised no man for his sins. . . ," and went on to say that "brothel-haunters flocked to this party, because here in all political circles, and political movements, they were treated as nobility." Much of the Whig cultural agenda (and much of Democratic hatred of that agenda) was rooted in contests between Whig and Democratic masculine styles.

Appetites

Many of the reforms urged by Whig evangelicals had to do with domestic and personal life rather than with politics. Their hopes for the perfection of the world hinged more on the character of individuals than on the role of institutions. Calvinism had taught that since human beings were innately selfish and subject to animal appetites, they must submit to godly authority. Evangelicals, on the other hand, defined original sin as a *tendency* to selfishness and sin that could be fought off—with God's help—through prayer and personal discipline. They hoped to perfect the world by filling it with godly, self-governing individuals.

It was not an easy task, for opportunities to indulge in vanity, luxury, and sensuality were on the rise. Charles Finney, for instance, preached long and hard against vanity. "A self-indulgent Christian," he said, "is a contradiction. You might as well write on your clothes 'NO TRUTH IN RELIGION,'" he told fashionably dressed women, for their dress proclaimed "GIVE ME DRESS, GIVE ME FASHION, GIVE ME FLATTERY, AND I AM HAPPY." Finney also worried about the effect of money, leisure time, and cheap novels on middle-class homes. He could not, he said, "believe that a person who has ever known the love of God can relish a secular novel" or open his or her home to "Byron, Scott, Shakespeare, and a host of triflers and blasphemers of God." Evangelicals also disdained luxury in home furnishings; they discouraged the use of silks and velvets and questioned the propriety of decorating the home with mahogany, mirrors, brass furnishings, and upholstered chairs and sofas.

Members of the evangelical middle class tried to define levels of material comfort that would separate them from the indulgences of those above and below them. They made similar attempts in the areas of food and sex. Sylvester Graham (now remembered for the cracker that bears his name) gave up the ministry in 1830 to become a full-time temperance lecturer. Before long, he was lecturing on the danger of excess in diet and sex. He claimed that the consumption of red meat, spiced foods, and alcohol produced bodily excitement that resulted in weakness and disease. Sex—including fornication, fantasizing, masturbation, and bestiality—affected the body in even more destructive ways, and the two appetites reinforced each other. (Graham admitted that marital sex, though it was physiologically no different from other forms of sex, was preferable, for it was the least exciting.)

Acting on Graham's concerns, reformers established a system of Grahamite boarding houses in which young men who were living away from home were provided with diets that helped them control their other appetites. Oberlin College, when it was founded by evangelicals in 1832, banned "tea and coffee, highly seasoned meats, rich pastries, and all unholsome [sic] and expensive foods." Among others who heeded Graham's advice were such future feminists as Lucy Stone, Susan B. Anthony, and Amelia Bloomer. Reformers who did not actually adopt Graham's system shared his concern over the twin evils of rich food and sexual excess. John R. McDowall, a divinity student who headed a mission to New York City prostitutes, admitted, "Having eaten until I am full, lust gets the control of me." John Humphrey Noyes (another divinity student who turned to reform) set up a community in Oneida, New York, that indulged in plural marriage but at the same time urged sexual self-control; he also believed that in a perfect Christian world there would be no meat-eating.

Moral Reform

Although most middle-class households did not embrace Grahamism, simple food and sexual control became badges of class status. The assumption was that it was men who had the greatest difficulty taming their appetites. The old image—beginning with Eve and including Delilah and Jezebel and other dangerous women of the Old Testament—of woman as seductress persisted in the more traditionalist churches and in the pulp fiction from which middle-class mothers tried to protect their sons (see Chapter 11). Whig evangelicals had made the discovery that women were naturally free of desire and that only men were subject to the animal passions. "What terrible temptations lie in the way of your sex," wrote Harriet Beecher Stowe to her husband. "Tho I did love you with an almost insane love before I married you, I never knew yet or felt the pulsation which showed me that I could be tempted in that way. I loved you as I now love God." The middle-class ideal combined female purity and male self-control. For the most part it was a private reform, contained within the home. Sometimes, however, evangelical domesticity produced moral crusades to impose that ethos on the world at large. Many of these crusades were led by women.

In 1828 a band of Sunday school teachers—most of them women—initiated an informal mission to prostitutes that grew into the New York Magdalen

Society. Taking a novel approach to an age-old question, the Society argued that prostitution was created by brutal fathers and husbands who abandoned their young daughters or wives, by dandies who seduced them and turned them into prostitutes, and by lustful men who bought their services. Prostitution, in other words, was not the result of the innate sinfulness of prostitutes; it was the result of the brutality and lust of men. The solution was to remove young prostitutes from their environment, pray with them, and convert them to middle-class morality.

The Magdalen Society's *First Annual Report* (1831) inveighed against male lust and printed shocking life histories of prostitutes. Some men read it as pornography; others used it as a guidebook to the seamier side of New York City. The wealthy male evangelicals who had bankrolled the Society withdrew their support, and the Society fell apart. Thereupon many of the women reformers set up the Female Moral Reform Society with a House of Industry in which prostitutes were taught morality and household skills to prepare them for new lives as domestic servants in pious middle-class homes. This too failed, largely because few prostitutes were interested in domestic service or evangelical religion. That fact became distressingly clear when in 1836 the Society was obliged to close the House of Industry after the inmates had taken it over during the caretaker's absence.

The Female Moral Reform Society was more successful with members of its own class. Its newspaper, *The Advocate of Moral Reform,* circulated throughout the evangelical North, eventually reaching 555 auxiliary societies with 20,000 readers. Now, evangelical women fought prostitution by publishing the names of customers. They campaigned against pornography, obscenity, lewdness, and seduction and accepted the responsibility of rearing their sons to be pure, even when it meant dragging them out of brothels. Occasionally they prosecuted men who took advantage of servant girls. They also publicized the names of adulterers, and they had seducers brought into court. In the process, women reformers fought the sexual double standard and assumed the power to define what was respectable and what was not.

Women's Rights

From the late 1820s onward, middle-class women in the North assumed roles that would have been unthinkable to their mothers and grandmothers. Evangelical domesticity made loving mothers (and not stern fathers) the principal rearers of children. Housewives saw themselves as missionaries to their families, responsible for the choices their children and husband made between salvation or sin. It was in that role that women became arbiters of fashion, diet, and sexual behavior. That same role motivated them to join the temperance movement and moral reform societies, where they became public reformers while posing as mothers protecting their sons from rum sellers and seducers. Such experiences gave them a sense of spiritual empowerment that led some to question their own subordinate status within a system of gendered social roles. Lydia Maria Child, a writer of sentimental fiction and manuals on household economy as well as a leading abolitionist and moral reformer, proclaimed, "Those who urged women to become missionaries and form tract societies . . . have changed the household utensil to a living, energetic being, and they have no spell to turn it into a broom again."

It was through the antislavery movement that many women became advocates of women's rights. Abolitionists, following the perfectionist implications of Whig evangelicalism to their logical ends, called for absolute human equality and a near anarchist rejection of impersonal institutions and prescribed social roles. It became clear to some female abolitionists that the critique of slavery (a root and branch denunciation of patriarchy and prescribed hierarchy) applied as well to inequality based on sex.

Radical female abolitionists reached the conclusion that they were human beings first and females second. In 1837 Sarah Grimke announced, "The Lord Jesus defines the duties of his followers in his Sermon on the Mount . . . without any reference to sex or condition . . . never even referring to the distinction now so strenuously insisted upon between masculine and feminine virtues. . . . Men and women are CREATED EQUAL! They are both moral and accountable beings and whatever is right for a man to do is right for woman." A woman's rights convention put it just as bluntly in 1851: "We deny the right of any portion of the species to decide for another portion . . . what is and what is not their 'proper sphere'; that the proper sphere for all human beings is the largest and highest to which they are able to attain."

Beginning around 1840, women lobbied state legislatures and won significant changes in the laws

Seneca Falls Commemorative Stamp The first Women's Rights Convention was held at Seneca Falls, New York, in 1848. At left and right are Elizabeth Cady Stanton and Lucretia Mott, abolitionist women who organized and directed the Seneca Falls Convention. At center is Carrie Chapman Catt, who carried on the fight until national women's suffrage was enacted in 1920.

governing women's rights to property, to the wages of their own labor, and to custody of children in cases of divorce. Fourteen states passed such legislation, culminating in New York's Married Women's Property Act in 1860.

Women's progress in achieving political rights, however, came more slowly. The first Women's Rights Convention, held at Seneca Falls, New York, in 1848, began with a Declaration of Sentiments and Resolutions, based on the Declaration of Independence, that denounced "the repeated injuries and usurpations on the part of man towards woman."

The central issue was the right to vote, for citizenship was central to the "democratic" pattern that granted formal equality to white men regardless of class and excluded Americans who were not white and male. Thus female participation in politics was a direct challenge to a male-ordained women's place. A distraught New York legislator agreed: "It is well known that the object of these unsexed women is to overthrow the most sacred of our institutions. . . . Are we to put the stamp of truth upon the libel here set forth, that men and women, in the matrimonial relation, are to be equal?" Later, the feminist Elizabeth Cady Stanton recalled such reactions. "Political rights," she said, "involving in their last results equality everywhere, roused all the antagonism of a dominant power, against the self-assertion of a class hitherto subservient."

SUGGESTED READING

There are a number of careful studies of constituencies and issues at the state and local levels during the Jacksonian Era. Students should consult Lee Benson, *The Concept of Jacksonian Democracy: New York as a Test Case* (1961); John L. Hammond, *The Politics of Benevolence: Revival Religion and American Voting Behavior* (1979); Ronald P. Formisano, *The Transformation of Political Culture: Massachusetts Parties, 1790s–1840s* (1983); Formisano, *The Birth of Mass Political Parties: Michigan, 1827–1861* (1971); John L. Brooke, *The Heart of the Commonwealth: Society and Political Culture in Worcester County, Massachusetts, 1713–1861* (1989); Amy Bridges, *A City in the Republic: Antebellum New York and the Origins of Machine Politics* (1984); Harry L. Watson, *Jacksonian Politics and Community Conflict: The Emergence of the Second American Party System in Cumberland County, North Carolina* (1981); Lacy K. Ford, Jr., *Origins of Southern Radicalism: The South Carolina Upcountry, 1800–1860* (1988); and David W. Crofts, *Old Southampton: Politics and Society in a Virginia County, 1834–1869* (1992). Richard J. Carwardine, *Evangelicals and Politics in Antebellum America* (1993) is a good study of relations between religion and politics in these years.

On party ideologies and political culture, see John Ashworth, *'Agrarians & Aristocrats': Party Political Ideology in the United States, 1837–1846* (1983); Daniel Walker Howe, *The Political Culture of the American Whigs* (1979); Anne Norton, *Alternative Americas: A Reading of Antebellum Political Culture* (1986); and Jean H. Baker, *Affairs of Party: The Political Culture of Northern Democrats in the Mid-Nineteenth Century* (1983). Aging but still very valuable are John William Ward, *Andrew Jackson: Symbol for an Age* (1953), and Marvin Meyers, *The Jacksonian Persuasion: Politics and Belief* (1957).

Party debates on banking and internal improvements are discussed in James Roger Sharp, *The Jacksonians versus the Banks: Politics in the States after the Panic of 1837* (1970); Harry N. Scheiber, *Ohio Canal Era: A Case Study of Government and the Economy, 1820–1861* (2nd ed., 1987); L. Ray Gunn, *The Decline of Authority: Public Economic Policy and Political Development in New York, 1800–1860* (1988); and Oscar Handlin's now-classic *Commonwealth: A Study of the Role of Government in the American Economy: Massachusetts, 1774–1861* (rev. ed., 1969). Political controversies surrounding schools are the subject of Carl F. Kaestle, *Pillars of the Republic: Common Schools and American Society, 1780–1860* (1983), and Kaestle, *The Evolution of an Urban School System: New York City, 1750–1850* (1973). An influential study of prisons and asylums is David J. Rothman, *The Discovery of the Asylum: Social Order and Disorder in the New Republic* (1971). It should be supplemented with W. David Lewis, *From Newgate to Dannemora: The Rise of the Penitentiary in New York, 1796–1848* (1965), and Edward L. Ayers, *Vengeance and Justice: Crime and Punishment in the 19th-Century South* (1984). Drinking and temperance are the subjects of W. J. Rorabaugh, *The Alcoholic Republic: An American Tradition* (1979); and Ian Tyrrell, *Sobering Up: From Temperance to Prohibition in Ante-Bellum America, 1800–1860* (1979). The best discussion of Washingtonianism is in Teresa Anne Murphy, *Ten Hours' Labor: Religion, Reform, and Gender in Early New England* (1992).

The standard study of northern free blacks is Leon F. Litwack, *North of Slavery: The Negro in the Free States, 1790–1860* (1960). It can now be supplemented by Gary B. Nash, *Forging Freedom: The Formation of Philadelphia's Black Community, 1720–1840* (1988). James Brewer Stewart, *Holy Warriors: The Abolitionist and American Slavery* (1976), is a graceful overview of the crusade against slavery. Students should also consult Robert H. Abzug, *Cosmos Crumbling: American Reform and the Religious Imagination* (1994); Thomas Bender, ed., *The Antislavery Debate: Capitalism and Abolition-ism as a Problem in Historical Interpretation* (1992); and Lewis Perry, *Radical Aboli-tionism: Anarchy and the Government of God in Antislavery Thought* (1973).

On the origins of the women's rights movement, students should consult Ellen Carol DuBois, *Feminism and Suffrage: The Emergence of an Independent Women's Movement in America, 1848–1869* (1978); Jean Fagan Yellin, *Women & Sisters: The Antislavery Feminists in American Culture* (1989); and Lori D. Ginzberg, *Women and the Work of Benevolence: Morality, Politics, and Class in the 19th-Century United States* (1990).

Chapter 14

Manifest Destiny:
An Empire for Liberty—
or Slavery?

The patriotic impulses of the United States
have been awakened to fresh and greatly augmented vigor and enthusiasm.
The minds of men have been awakened to a clear conviction of the destiny
of this great nation of freemen. No longer bounded by those limits which nature
had in the eye of those of little faith in the last generation, assigned to the
dominion of republicanism on this continent, the pioneers of Anglo-Saxon
civilization and Anglo-Saxon free institutions, now seek distant territories,
stretching even to the shores of the Pacific; and the arms of the republic,
it is clear to all men of sober discernment, must soon embrace the whole
hemisphere, from the icy wilderness of the North to the most prolific regions
of the smiling and prolific South.

New York Herald, September 25, 1845

GROWTH AS THE AMERICAN WAY

By 1850, older Americans had seen the area of the United States quadruple in their own lifetime. The Louisiana Purchase of 1803 had doubled the nation's territory; from 1845 to 1848, the annexation of Texas, the settlement of the Oregon boundary dispute with Britain, and the acquisition of California and the Southwest from Mexico had nearly doubled it again. And during those 47 years the American population had quadrupled too. If those rates of growth had continued after 1850, the United States at the end of the twentieth century would contain 1.8 *billion* people and would occupy every square foot of land on the globe. If the sevenfold increase in the gross national product that Americans enjoyed from 1800 to 1850 had persisted, the United States economy today would be larger than that of the whole world.

Many Americans in 1850 took this prodigious growth for granted. They considered it evidence of God's beneficence to this virtuous republic, this haven for the oppressed from Old World tyranny, this land where all (white) men stood equal before the law. During the 1840s a group of expansionists affiliated with the Democratic party began to call themselves the "Young America" movement. They proclaimed that it was the "Manifest Destiny" of the United States to grow from sea to sea, from the Arctic Circle to the tropics. It is "our manifest destiny to overspread and to possess the whole of the continent which Providence has given us for the development of the great experiment of liberty," wrote John L. O'Sullivan, editor of the *Democratic Review,* in 1845. "Yes, more, more, more! . . . till our national destiny is fulfilled and . . . the whole boundless continent is ours."

Not all Americans thought this unbridled expansion was a good thing. For the earliest Americans,

Manifest Destiny   This painting portrays the self-serving symbolism of America's westward expansion in the mid-nineteenth century. White pioneers on foot, on horseback, and in oxen-drawn wagons cross the plains, driving the Indians and buffalo before them while a farmer breaks the sod on the farming frontier. A stagecoach and puffing locomotives follow an ethereal Columbia in flowing raiment bearing a schoolbook and stringing telegraph wire across the continent.

whose ancestors had arrived on the continent thousands of years before the Europeans, it was a story of defeat and contraction rather than of conquest and growth. By 1850 the white man's diseases and guns had reduced the Indian population north of the Rio Grande to fewer than half a million, a fraction of the number who had lived there two or three centuries earlier. The relentless westward march of white settlements had pushed all but a few thousand Indians beyond the Mississippi. In the 1840s the U.S. government decided to create a "permanent Indian frontier" at about the 95th meridian (roughly the western borders of Iowa, Missouri, and Arkansas). But white emigrants were already violating that frontier on the overland trails to the Pacific, and settlers were pressing against the borders of Indian territory. In little more than a decade the idea of "one big reservation" in the West would give way to the policy of forcing Indians onto small reservations. The government "negotiated" with Indian chiefs for vast cessions of land in return for annuity payments that were soon spent on the white man's firewater and other purchases from shrewd or corrupt traders. Required to learn the white man's ways or perish,

many Indians perished—of disease, malnutrition, and alcohol, and in futile efforts to break out of the reservations and regain their land. In California alone, the Indian population fell from an estimated 150,000 in 1845 to 35,000 by 1860.

If the manifest destiny of white Americans spelled doom for red Americans, it also presaged a crisis in the history of black Americans. By 1846 the Empire for Liberty that Thomas Jefferson had envisioned for the Louisiana Purchase seemed to have become an empire for slavery. Territorial acquisitions since 1803 had brought into the republic the slave states of Louisiana, Missouri, Arkansas, Florida, Texas, and parts of Alabama and Mississippi, while only Iowa, admitted in 1846, had joined the ranks of the free states.

The division between slavery and freedom in the rest of the Louisiana Purchase had supposedly been settled by the Compromise of 1820, but for a quarter of a century thereafter, the issue frequently disturbed public tranquillity. So long as the controversy focused on the morality of slavery where it already existed, however, the two-party system, in which both major parties did their best to evade the issue, managed to contain its explosive potential. But, when the issue became the expansion of slavery into new territories, evasion and containment no longer sufficed. The issue first arose with the annexation of Texas, which helped provoke war with Mexico in 1846—a war that many antislavery northerners considered an ugly effort to expand slavery.

The Westering Impulse

For Americans of European descent, the future was to be found in the West. "Westward the course of empire takes its way," Bishop George Berkeley had written of the New World in the 1720s. "Eastward I go only by force," said Henry David Thoreau more than a century later, "but westward I go free. Mankind progresses from East to West." In the 1840s Horace Greeley urged, "Go West, young man." And to the West they went in unprecedented numbers, driven in part by the depression of 1837–1843 that prompted thousands to search for cheap land and better opportunity. "The West is our object, there is no other hope left for us," declared one farmer as he and his family set out on the Oregon trail. "There is nothing like a new country for poor folks."

An earlier wave of migration had populated the region between the Appalachians and the Missouri River, bringing a new state into the Union on an average of every three years. During those years, reports from explorers, fur traders, missionaries, and sailors filtered back from California and the Pacific Northwest telling of the bounteous resources and benign climate of those wondrous regions. Richard Henry Dana's story of his *Two Years before the Mast* in the cowhide and tallow trade between California and Boston, published in 1840, alerted thousands of Americans to this new Eden on the Pacific. Guidebooks rolled off the presses describing the boundless prospects that awaited settlers who would turn "those wild forests, trackless plains, untrodden valleys" into "one grand scene of continuous improvements, universal enterprise, and unparalleled commerce. . . . Those fertile valleys shall groan under the immense weight of their abundant products."

Of course, another people of partial European descent already lived in portions of the region west of the 98th meridian. The frontier of New Spain had pushed north of the Rio Grande early in the seventeenth century. By the time Mexico won its independence from Spain in 1821, some eighty thousand Mexicans lived in this region. Three-fourths of them

Missouri Is Free!—An Advertisement of Missouri Farmland for Sale by the Hannibal and St. Joseph Railroad   Railroads received land grants from state governments and later the federal government to help them raise capital for construction. The railroads in turn sold the land to farmers to promote settlement along their lines. The land was not "free," of course, nor was Missouri a "free" state before the abolition of slavery there in 1865.

had settled in the Rio Grande valley of New Mexico and most of the rest in California. Centuries earlier the Spaniards had introduced horses, cattle, and sheep to the New World (Chapter 1). These animals became the economic mainstay of Hispanic society along New Spain's northern frontier. Later, Anglo-Americans would adopt Hispanic ranching methods to invade and subdue the lands of the arid western plains. That the ranching economy of the nineteenth-century American West was built on Hispanic foundations is evidenced by the Spanish origins of words to describe the tools of the trade and the very land itself: bronco, mustang, lasso, rodeo, stampede, canyon, arroyo, mesa.

Colonial society on New Spain's northern frontier had centered on the missions and the presidios. Intended to Christianize Indians, the missions also became an instrument to exploit their labor, while

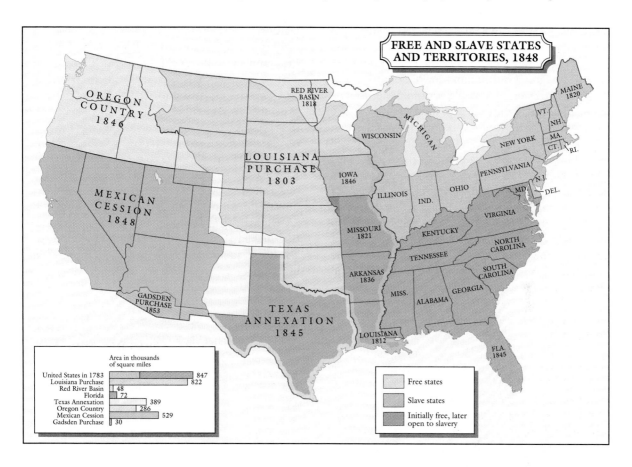

FREE AND SLAVE STATES AND TERRITORIES, 1848

OREGON COUNTRY 1846

RED RIVER BASIN 1818

MICHIGAN

MAINE 1820

VT.

NH.

WISCONSIN

NEW YORK

MA.

CT.

RI.

LOUISIANA PURCHASE 1803

IOWA 1846

PENNSYLVANIA

N.J.

MEXICAN CESSION 1848

ILLINOIS

IND.

OHIO

MD.

DEL.

MISSOURI 1821

KENTUCKY

VIRGINIA

GADSDEN PURCHASE 1853

ARKANSAS 1836

TENNESSEE

NORTH CAROLINA

SOUTH CAROLINA

TEXAS ANNEXATION 1845

MISS.

ALABAMA

GEORGIA

LOUISIANA 1812

FLA. 1845

Area in thousands of square miles

United States in 1783	847
Louisiana Purchase	822
Red River Basin	48
Florida	72
Texas Annexation	389
Oregon Country	286
Mexican Cession	529
Gadsden Purchase	30

Free states

Slave states

Initially free, later open to slavery

the presidios (military posts) protected the settlers from hostile Indians—and foreign nationals hoping to gain a foothold in Spanish territory. By the late eighteenth century, the mission system had fallen into decline and a decade and a half after Mexican independence in 1821, it collapsed entirely. The presidios, underfunded and understaffed, also declined after Mexican independence, so that more and more the defense of Mexico's far northern provinces fell to the residents themselves. But by the 1830s, many New Mexico and California residents were more interested in bringing American traders in than in keeping American settlers out. A flourishing trade over the Santa Fe Trail from Independence, Missouri, to Santa Fe brought American manufactured goods to New Mexico (and points south) in exchange for Mexican horses, mules, beaver pelts, and silver. New England ships carried American goods all the way around the horn of South America to San Francisco and other California ports in exchange for tallow and hides produced by *californio*

ranchers. This trade linked the economies of New Mexico and California more closely to the United States than to the Mexican heartland. Santa Fe was six hundred miles closer to Independence than to Mexico City. The trickle of Americans into California and New Mexico in the 1820s presaged the flood that would engulf these regions two decades later.

In 1842 and 1843, "Oregon fever" swept the Mississippi Valley. Thousands of farm families sold their land, packed their worldly goods in covered wagons along with supplies for five or six months on the trail, hitched up their oxen, and headed out from Independence or St. Joseph, Missouri, for the trek of almost two thousand miles to the river valleys of Oregon or California. On the way, they passed through regions claimed by three nations—the United States, Mexico, and Britain—and they settled on land owned by Mexico (California) or claimed jointly by the United States and Britain (Oregon, which then stretched north to the border of Russian Alaska). But no matter who claimed the land, it was occupied mostly by Indians, who viewed this latest intrusion with wary eyes. Few of the emigrants thought about settling down along the way, for this vast reach of arid plains, forbidding mountains, and burning deserts was then known as "the Great American Desert." White men considered it suitable only for Indians and the disappearing breed of mountain men who had roamed the region trapping beaver and trading with Indians for the once plentiful and valuable pelts that were no longer either plentiful or valuable.

During the next quarter century, half a million men, women, and children crossed half a continent in one of the great sagas of American history. The original migration of farm families to Oregon and California was followed in 1846 by the Mormon exodus to a new Zion in the basin of the Great Salt Lake and in 1849 by the gold rush to California. The story of all these migrants was one of triumph and tragedy, survival and death, courage and despair, success and failure. Most of them made it to their destination; some died on the way—victims of disease, exposure, starvation, suicide, or homicide by Indians or by fellow emigrants. Of those who arrived safely, a few struck it rich, most carved out a modest though hard living, and some drifted on, still looking for the pot of gold that had thus far eluded them. Together, they generated pressures that helped bring a vast new empire—more than a million square miles—into the United States by 1848.

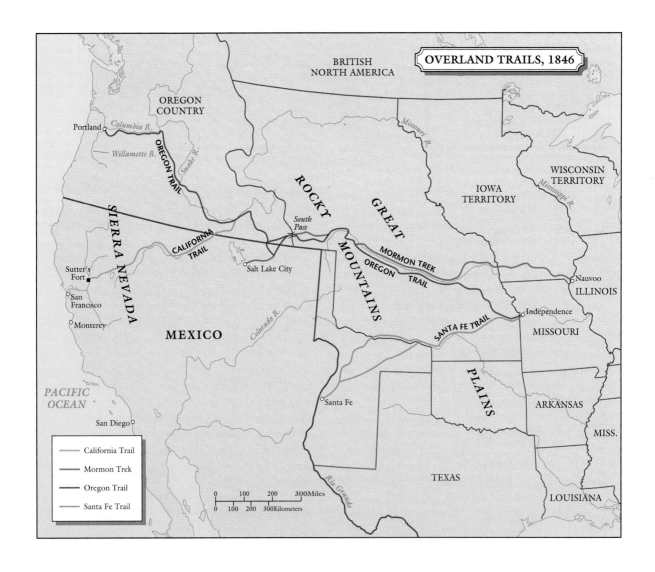

Migration was mostly a male enterprise. The California gold rush was overwhelmingly so. Adult men outnumbered women on the Oregon Trail and on the California Trail before the gold rush by more than two to one, and in the gold rush by more than ten to one. The quest for new land, a new start, a chance to make a big strike, represented primarily masculine ideals. Women, on the other hand, felt themselves more rooted in family, home, and community, less willing to pull up stakes to march into the wilderness. Yet for men too, the family was the linchpin of society. Even on the rough mining frontier of the West, men sought to replicate as soon as possible the home and community they had left behind. "We want families," wrote a Californian in 1858, "because their homes and hearth stones everywhere, are the only true and reliable basis of any nation." Except during the gold rush, and the figures for the absolute numbers of men and women notwithstanding, family groups predominated on the overland trails. Half of the emigrants were mothers and children, and some of the single men had relatives among the travelers.

Many of the women were reluctant migrants. Though middle-class urban families had made some small beginnings toward equal partnership in marriage, men still ruled the family on the midwestern farms from which most of the migrants came. Men made the decision to go; women obeyed. Diaries kept by women on the trail testify to their unhappiness:

> What had possessed my husband, anyway, that he should have thought of bringing us away out through this God-forsaken country? . . . Oh, how I wish we never had started for the Golden Land. . . . I would make a brave effort to be cheerful and patient until the camp work was done. Then . . . I would throw myself down on the tears, wishing myself back home with my friends and chiding myself for consenting to take this wild goose chase.

For many families it did turn out to be a wild goose chase. But for those who stayed the course and settled in the far West, it was a success story, made so in great measure by the women. They turned houses into homes, settlements into communities.

Emigrants Making Camp in the Snow   This drawing portrays the harsh conditions and dangers faced by many pioneers who crossed plains and mountains. Women often had to do a man's work as well as to cook and take care of children. One can only hope that this family did not suffer the fate of the Donner party, trapped by an early snowfall in the Sierra Nevada Mountains in October 1846. Nearly half of the eighty-seven people in the Donner party died during the subsequent winter.

Joseph Mustering the Nauvoo Legion   This painting depicts a self-defense force organized by Mormons in Nauvoo, Illinois, in the early 1840s. Beleaguered by Gentiles, the Mormons decided to emigrate to Mexican territory in the West after Joseph Smith was murdered in 1844.

Because there were proportionately fewer women than there were back East, they may have been more highly prized. But it would be a mistake to think that the frontier broke down the separate spheres of men and women or elevated women to something like equal status with men. On the contrary, woman's sphere in the West was still the home and the family, the bearing and the nurturing of children, the management of the household economy. Man's sphere remained the world of public events and economic production.

Patriarchal rule was strongest among those migrants with the most nearly equal sex ratio—the Mormons. One of several religious sects that emerged from the social ferment of the "burned-over district" in western New York, the Church of Jesus Christ of Latter-Day Saints survived despite—perhaps even because of—persecution that had harried its members from New York to Ohio to Missouri to Illinois. At a town they named Nauvoo, Illinois, the Mormons built a thriving community of 15,000 souls, based on collective economic effort and theocratic discipline imposed by founder and prophet,

Joseph Smith. But the people of Illinois proved no more hospitable to the Mormons than the sect's previous Gentile neighbors had been. Smith did not make things any easier. His insistence that God spoke through him, his autocratic suppression of dissent, and his assertion that the Saints were the only true Christians and would inherit the earth did not sit well with Gentiles, who also feared the Nauvoo Legion, a private army commanded by Smith. When a dissident faction of Mormons published Smith's latest revelation, which sanctioned polygamy, he ordered their printing press destroyed. The county sheriff arrested him, and in June 1844 a mob broke into the jail and killed him.

Smith's martyrdom prompted yet another exodus, this time as far away from Gentiles as possible. Under the leadership of Smith's successor, Brigham Young, the Mormons began the long trek westward that would eventually lead them to the Great Salt Lake basin in what was then Mexican territory but would soon become part of the territory ceded to the United States in the wake of the Mexican War. A man of iron will and administrative genius, Young organized the migration down to the last detail. Arriving with the advance guard of Mormon pioneers at a pass overlooking the Great Basin on July 24, 1847, Young, ill with tick fever, struggled from his wagon and stared at the barren desert and mountains surrounding the lake. "This is the right place," he declared. Few Gentiles were likely to covet this region, and the Saints could build their Zion here undisturbed.

They built a flourishing community, making the desert bloom with grain and vegetables irrigated by water that was ingeniously diverted from mountain streams. Organizing the economy and the civil society as he had organized the exodus, Young reigned as leader of the church, and from 1850 to 1857 as governor of the newly created Utah Territory. But Zion did not remain undisturbed. Relations with the Gentiles back in Washington and with those sent out as territorial officials were never smooth, especially after Young's proclamation in 1852 authorizing polygamy. (Though Young himself married a total of fifty-five women, most Mormon men could afford to support no more than one wife and her children; about one-sixth of Mormon marriages were polygamous.) When conflict between the Mormons and the U.S. Army broke out in 1857, Young surrendered his civil authority and made an uneasy peace with the government. The Kingdom of the Saints continued to prosper and grow, however, attaining a population of forty thousand in Utah by 1860.

The Annexation of Texas

As the Mormons were starting west, a crisis between Mexico and the United States was coming to a boil. The trouble had its roots two decades earlier with the settlement of Americans in the Mexican state of Coahuila–Texas. Having first welcomed these Anglo farmers and planters, by 1830 the government in Mexico City had become alarmed. The Americans retained their language, culture, and allegiance to the United States. They also brought in slaves, in defiance of a recent Mexican law abolishing slavery. Despite Mexican efforts to ban any further immigration, by 1835 there were thirty thousand Americans in Texas, outnumbering Mexicans six to one.

American settlers, concentrated in east Texas, initially had very little contact with Mexican *tejanos,* whose settlements were further south and west, but political events in Mexico City in 1835 had reper-

cussions on the northern frontier. A new conservative national government seemed intent on consolidating its authority over the northern territories, including Coahuila–Texas. In response, the Anglo-American settlers and the Mexican *tejanos* forged a political alliance to protest against any further loss of autonomy in their province. When the Mexican government responded militarily, many Texans—both Anglo and Mexican—were radicalized; the seeds of revolution had been sown. Fighting flared fitfully for a year. Then, in March 1836, delegates from across Texas met in convention, at a village appropriately called Washington, and declared Texas an independent republic, adopting a Constitution based on the U.S. model.

The American Revolution had lasted seven years; it took the Texans less than seven months to win and consolidate their independence. Mexican President Antonio López de Santa Anna personally led the Mexican army that captured the Alamo (a former mission converted to a fort) in San Antonio on March 6, 1836, killing all 187 of its defenders, including the legendary Americans Davy Crockett and Jim Bowie. Rallying to the cry "Remember the Alamo!" Texans swarmed to the revolutionary army commanded by Sam Houston. When the Mexican army slaughtered another force of more 300 men after they had surrendered at Goliad on March 19, the Texans were further inflamed. A month later, Houston's army, aided by volunteers from southern states, routed a larger Mexican force on the San Jacinto River (near present-day Houston) and captured Santa Anna himself. Under duress, he signed a treaty granting Texas independence. The Mexican Congress later repudiated the treaty but could not muster enough strength to reestablish its authority north of the Nueces River. The *tejanos,* increasingly marginalized by the Anglo-Americans, now became "foreigners in their native land," as one of their leaders noted. In the succeeding years, conflicts over land titles, slavery, language, and religion would exacerbate ethnic tensions. The victorious Texans, for their part, elected Sam Houston president of their new republic and petitioned for annexation to the United States.

President Andrew Jackson, wary of provoking war with Mexico or quarrels with antislavery northerners who charged that the annexation of Texas was a plot to expand slavery, rebuffed the annexationists. So did his successor, Martin Van Buren. Though

The Fall of the Alamo   Originally a Spanish mission in San Antonio, the Alamo became a fort after 1793. From February 23 to March 6, 1836, fewer than two hundred Anglo Texans held off attacks by several thousand Mexicans, but were finally overpowered and killed to the last man—five of them after surrendering.

disappointed, the Texans turned their energies to building their republic and even talked of extending it all the way to the Pacific by taking more Mexican territory. The British government encouraged the Texans, in the hope that they would stand as a buffer against further U.S. expansion and would free the British textile industry from dependence on the American South for cotton. Abolitionists in England even cherished the notion that Britain might persuade the Texans to abolish slavery. Texas leaders made friendly responses to some of the British overtures, probably in the hope of provoking American annexationists to take action. They did.

Soon after Vice President John Tyler became president on the death of William Henry Harrison in 1841, he broke with the Whig Party that had elected him. A states'-rights Virginian, Tyler opposed the Whig program for a national bank, higher tariffs, and federal aid for roads and waterways. Seeking to create a new coalition to reelect him in 1844, Tyler reorganized his administration to attract southern support. He also seized on the annexation of Texas as "the only matter that will take sufficient hold of the feelings of the South to rally it on a southern candidate."

Tyler named John C. Calhoun, of South Carolina, as secretary of state to negotiate a treaty of annexation. The southern press ran scare stories about a British plot to use Texas as a beachhead for an assault on slavery, and annexation became a popular issue in the South. Calhoun concluded a treaty with the eager Texans. But then he made a mistake: he released to the press a letter he had written to the British minister to the United States, informing him that, together with other reasons, Americans wanted to annex Texas in order to protect slavery, an institution "essential to the peace, safety, and prosperity" of the United States. This seemed to confirm abolitionist charges that annexation was a proslavery plot. Northern senators of both parties—and even some southern Whigs who wanted to punish the renegade Tyler—provided more than enough votes to defeat the treaty in June 1844.

By then, Texas had become the main issue in the forthcoming presidential election. Whig candidate Henry Clay had come out against annexation, as had the leading contender for the Democratic nomination, former president Martin Van Buren. Van Buren's stand ran counter to the rising tide of Manifest Destiny sentiment within the Democratic Party. It also angered southern Democrats, who were determined to have Texas. Through eight ballots at the Democratic national convention they blocked Van Buren's nomination; on the ninth, the southerners broke the stalemate by nominating one of their own, James K. Polk of Tennessee. The first "dark horse" candidate (not having been a contender before the convention), Polk was a staunch Jacksonian who had served as Speaker of the House of Representatives during Jackson's presidency. Southerners exulted in their victory. "We have triumphed," wrote one of Calhoun's lieutenants. "Polk is nearer to *us* than any public man who was named. He is a large Slave holder and [is for] Texas — States rights *out & out.*" Polk's nomination undercut President Tyler's forlorn hope of being reelected on the Texas issue, so he bowed out of the race.

Polk ran on a platform that called not only for the annexation of Texas but also for the acquisition of all of Oregon up to 54°40′ (the Alaskan border). That demand was aimed at voters in the western free states, who felt that bringing Oregon into the Union would balance the expansion of slavery into Texas with the expansion of free territory in the Northwest. Polk was more than comfortable with this platform. In fact, he wanted not only Texas and Oregon, but California and New Mexico as well.

"Texas fever" swept the South during the campaign. So powerful was the issue that Clay began to waver, stating that he would support annexation if it could be done without starting a war with Mexico. This concession won him few southern votes but angered northern antislavery Whigs. Many of them voted for James G. Birney, candidate of the Liberty Party, which opposed any more slave territory. In fact, Birney's vote was nine times greater than it had been in 1840. He probably took enough Whig votes from Clay in New York to give Polk victory there and in the electoral college.

Although the election was extremely close (Polk won only a plurality of 49.5 percent of the popular vote), Democrats regarded it as a mandate for annexation. Eager to leave office in triumph, lame-duck President Tyler submitted a joint resolution of annexation to Congress, which required only a simple majority in both houses, instead of the two-thirds majority in the Senate that a treaty would have required. Congress passed the resolution on the eve of Polk's inauguration in March 1845. Texas thus bypassed the territorial stage and came in as the fifteenth slave

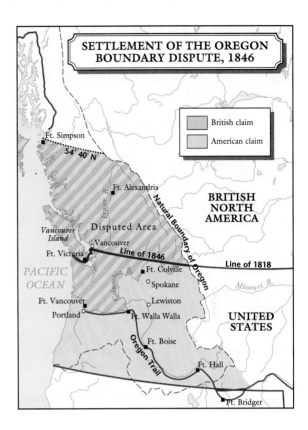

state in December 1845. Backed now by the United States, Texans claimed a southern and western border beyond the Nueces River all the way to the Rio Grande, which nearly tripled the area that Mexico had formerly defined as Texas. Mexico responded by breaking off diplomatic relations with the United States. The stage was set for five years of bitter controversy that included a shooting war with Mexico and political warfare in the United States over the issue of slavery expansion. When the dust settled, James K. Polk had presided over the acquisition of more territory by the United States than had any other president. But he left a legacy that would flare into civil war a dozen years later.

"Our title to the country of the Oregon is 'clear and unquestionable,'" said Polk in his inaugural address. "Already our people are preparing to perfect that title by occupying it with their wives and children." The problem was to get Britain to recognize the title. Both countries had jointly "occupied" Oregon since 1818, overseeing the fur trade carried on by British and American companies. Chanting the slogan "Fifty-four forty or fight!" many Americans in 1845 demanded all of Oregon, as pledged in the Democratic platform. But Polk proved unwilling to fight for 54°40'. So far, Americans had settled only in the region south of the Columbia River, at roughly the forty-sixth parallel. In June 1846, Polk accepted a compromise treaty that split the Oregon country between the United States and Britain at the forty-ninth parallel. Several Democratic senators from the Old Northwest (states north of the Ohio River and west of Pennsylvania) accused Polk of betrayal and voted against the treaty. They had supported Texas to the Rio Grande, and they had expected Polk to support Oregon to 54°40'. A sectional breach had opened in the Democratic Party that would soon grow wider.

THE MEXICAN WAR

Having finessed a war with Britain, Polk provoked one with Mexico in order to get California and New Mexico. In 1845 he sent a special envoy to Mexico City with an offer to buy California and New Mexico for $30 million. To help Mexico make the right response, he ordered federal troops to the disputed border area between Mexico and Texas, dispatched a naval squadron to patrol the gulf coast of Mexico, and instructed the American consul at Monterey (the Mexican capital of California) to stir up annexation sentiment among settlers there. These strong-arm tactics provoked a political revolt in Mexico City that brought a militant anti-American regime to power vowing to spurn all offers of gringo gold and to recover the "stolen province" of Texas.

Polk responded in January 1846 by ordering four thousand soldiers under General Zachary Taylor to advance all the way to the Rio Grande. Recognizing that he could achieve his goals only through armed conflict, Polk waited for news from Texas that would justify a declaration of war, but none came. His patience having run out, on May 9, 1846, he began to draft a message to Congress asking for a declaration of war on general grounds of Mexican defiance. That evening, word finally arrived that two weeks earlier Mexican troops had crossed the Rio Grande and had attacked an American patrol, killing eleven soldiers. Polk had what he had been waiting for. He quickly revised his message and sent it to Congress on May 11. Most Whigs opposed war with Mexico.

American Forces in Saltillo, Mexico   This posed photograph of General John E. Wool and his staff of Zacharay Taylor's army on its march southward from Monterrey through Saltillo in November, 1846, is the earliest known photograph of an American military force. Photography had recently been invented, and such pictures as this one were extremely rare before the 1850s.

But not wanting to be branded unpatriotic, all but a handful of them, in the end, voted for the final declaration of war, which passed the House by 174 to 14 and the Senate by 40 to 2. Despite their continuing opposition to what they called "Mr. Polk's War," most Whigs voted supplies for the army. Having witnessed the demise of the Federalist Party after it had opposed the war in 1812, one Whig congressman said sarcastically that from then on he had decided to vote for "war, pestilence, and famine."

The United States went to war with a tiny regular army of fewer than eight thousand men, supplemented by sixty thousand volunteers who flocked to the colors in state regiments, and an efficient navy that quickly established domination of the sea lanes. Mexican soldiers outnumbered American in most of the battles. But the Americans had higher morale, better leadership, better weapons (especially artillery), a more determined, stable government, and a far richer, stronger economy. The U.S. forces won every battle—and the war—in a fashion that humiliated the proud Mexicans and left a legacy of national hostility and border violence. Especially remarkable, in retrospect, was the prominent role played by junior American officers trained at West Point, for whom the Mexican War was a rehearsal for a larger conflict fifteen years later: Robert E. Lee, Ulysses S. Grant, Pierre G. T. Beauregard, George B. McClellan, Braxton Bragg, George H. Thomas, Thomas J. Jackson, George G. Meade, Jefferson Davis, and others, whose names would become household words during the Civil War.

The Mexican War proceeded through three phases, all of which grew out of the American purpose to seize control of Mexican territory and to force the Mexicans to make peace on American terms. The first phase was carried out by Zachary Taylor's 4,000 regulars on the Rio Grande. In two small battles, at Palo Alto and Resaca de la Palma, they routed numerically superior Mexican forces on May 8 and 9, even before Congress had declared war. Those victories made "Old Rough and Ready" Taylor a hero, a reputation he rode to the presidency two years later. Reinforced by several thousand volunteers, Taylor pursued the retreating Mexicans a hundred miles south of the Rio Grande to the heavily fortified city of Monterrey. The city was taken after four days of fighting in September 1846. Mexican resistance in the area had crumbled, and Taylor's force settled down as an army of occupation.

Meanwhile, the second phase of American strategy had gone forward in New Mexico and California. In June 1846 General Stephen Watts Kearny led an army of 1,500 tough frontiersmen west from Fort Leavenworth toward Santa Fe. Kearny bluffed and intimidated the New Mexico governor, who fled southward without ever ordering the local three thousand-man militia into action. Kearny's army occupied Santa Fe on August 18 without firing a shot. With closer economic ties to the United States than to their own country, which taxed them well but governed them poorly, many New Mexicans seemed willing to accept American rule.

After receiving reinforcements, Kearny left a small occupation force and divided the rest of his troops into two contingents, one of which he sent under Colonel Alexander Doniphan into the Mexican province of Chihuahua. In the most extraordinary campaign of the war, these eight hundred unwashed, untamed Missourians marched three thousand miles, foraging supplies along the way, fought and beat two much larger enemy forces, and finally linked up with Zachary Taylor's army at Monterrey in the spring of 1847.

Kearny led the other contingent across deserts and mountains to California. Events there had antic-

ipated his arrival. In June 1846 a group of American settlers backed by Captain John C. Frémont, a renowned western explorer with the Army topographical corps, captured Sonoma and raised the flag of an independent California, displaying the silhouette of a grizzly bear. Marked by exploits both courageous and comic, this "bear-flag revolt" paved the way for the conquest of California by the *americanos.* The U.S. Pacific fleet seized California's ports and the capital at Monterrey; sailors from the fleet and volunteer soldiers under Frémont subdued Mexican resistance; Kearny's weary and battered force arrived in December 1846, barely in time to help with the mopping up.

New Mexico and California had fallen into American hands, Mexican armies had experienced nothing but defeat, but the Mexican government refused to admit that the war was over. Indeed, a political maneuver by President Polk to secure a more tractable government in Mexico had backfired. In one of Mexico's many palace revolts, Santa Anna had been overthrown and forced into exile in Cuba in 1844. A shadowy intermediary convinced Polk in July 1846 that if Santa Anna returned to power, he would make peace on American terms in return for $30 million. Polk instructed the navy to pass Santa Anna through its blockade of Mexican ports. The wily Mexican general then rode in triumph to Mexico City, where yet another new government named him supreme commander of the army and president of the republic. Breathing fire, Santa Anna spoke no more of peace. Instead, he raised new levies and marched north early in 1847 to attack Taylor's army near Monterrey.

Taylor, sixty-two years old, was still rough but not as ready to withstand a counteroffensive as he had been a few weeks earlier. After capturing Monterrey in September 1846, he had let the defeated Mexican army go and had granted an eight-week armistice in the hope that it would allow time for peace negotiations. Angry at Taylor's presumption in making such a decision and suspicious of the general's political ambitions, Polk canceled the armistice. He was now convinced that Taylor was not the man to command a campaign against Mexico City, the third phase of the war. He turned instead to General-in-Chief Winfield Scott, who thus far had fought the war from his desk in Washington. A large, punctilious man, like Taylor a veteran of the War of 1812, Scott had acquired the nickname "Old Fuss and Feathers"

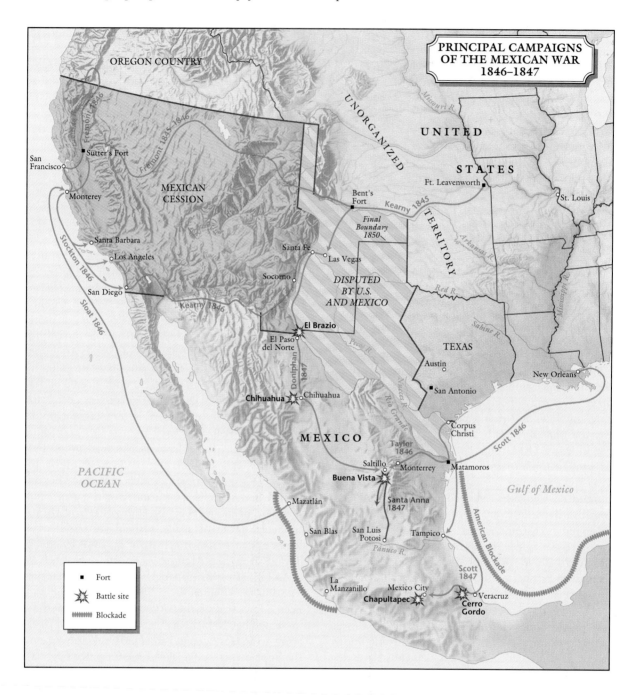

PRINCIPAL CAMPAIGNS OF THE MEXICAN WAR 1846–1847

for a military professionalism that contrasted with the homespun manner of "Rough and Ready" Zach Taylor. Scott decided to lead an invasion of Mexico's heartland from a beachhead at Veracruz and in January 1847 ordered the transfer of more than half of Taylor's troops to his own expeditionary force.

Left with fewer than five thousand men, most of them untried volunteers, Taylor complained bitterly

of political intrigue and military favoritism. Nevertheless, he marched out to meet Santa Anna's army of eighteen thousand. In a two-day battle on February 22–23 at Buena Vista, Taylor's little force bent but never broke. They inflicted twice as many casualties as they suffered in a fierce struggle highlighted by the brilliant counterattack of a Mississippi regiment commanded by Jefferson Davis. The bloodied

Mexican army retreated toward the capital. When news of the victory reached the East, Taylor's popularity soared to new heights. If Polk had wanted to quash a political rival by taking away most of his troops—as Taylor believed—he had achieved just the opposite.

But the war was actually won by Scott. With a combined army–navy force, he took the coastal fortress at Veracruz in March 1847. Then over the next five months, his army, which never totaled more than fourteen thousand men (with considerable turnover because of expiring one-year enlistments), marched and fought its way over mountains and plains two hundred sixty miles to Mexico City. It was a bold action. The risks were high. When Scott's forces reached the fortifications of Mexico City, held by three times their numbers, the Duke of Wellington, who was following the campaign closely, predicted, "Scott is lost—he cannot capture the city and he cannot fall back upon his base." But capture it he did, on September 14, after fierce hand-to-hand combat in the battles of Contreras, Churubusco, Molino del Rey, and Chapultepec. It was a brilliant success—even though it owed much to wrangling among Mexican leaders that forced Santa Anna to spend almost as much time facing down his internal enemies as fighting the Americans.

Anti-War Sentiment

The string of military victories prevented significant anti-war sentiment in the United States from winning even wider support. The war was enthusiastically supported in the South and the West and among Democrats. But the Whigs and many of the people in the Northeast, especially in New England, considered it "a wicked and disgraceful war." Democrats and Whigs had different notions of "progress." Democrats believed in expanding American institutions over *space*—in particular, the space occupied by Mexicans and Indians. Whigs, on the other hand, believed in improving American institutions over *time*. "Opposed to the instinct of boundless acquisition stands that of Internal Improvement," said Horace Greeley. "A nation cannot simultaneously devote its energies to the absorption of others' territories and the improvement of its own."

Antislavery people dubiously raised their eyebrows when they heard Manifest Destiny rhetoric about "extending the blessings of American liberty" to those benighted regions. They suspected that the

real reason was the desire to extend slavery. Hosea Biglow, the rustic Yankee philosopher invented by the abolitionist poet James Russell Lowel, observed:

> They jest want this Californy
> So's to lug new slave-states in
> To abuse ye an' to scorn ye,
> And to plunder ye like sin.

The Wilmot Proviso

The slavery issue overshadowed all others in the debate over the Mexican War. President Polk could not understand what the fuss was about. "There is no probability," he wrote in his diary, "that any territory will ever be acquired from Mexico in which slavery would ever exist." But other Americans were not so sure. Many southerners hoped that slavery would spread into the fertile lowlands of Mexican territory. Many northerners feared that it might. Their fear was strengthened by an editorial in a Charleston newspaper: "California is peculiarly adapted for slave labor. The right to have [slave] property protected there is not a mere abstraction." The issue came to a head early in the war. On August 8, 1846, Pennsylvania Democratic Congressman David Wilmot offered an amendment to an army appropriations bill: ". . . that, as an express and fundamental condition of the acquisition of any territory from the Republic of Mexico . . . neither slavery nor involuntary servitude shall ever exist in any part of said territory."

This famous "Wilmot Proviso" framed the national debate over slavery for the next fifteen years. The House passed the amendment. Nearly all northern Democrats joined all northern Whigs in the majority, while southern Democrats and southern Whigs voted almost unanimously against it. (In the Senate, greater southern strength defeated the proviso.) This outcome marked an ominous wrenching of the party division between Whigs and Democrats into a *sectional* division. It was a sign that the two-party system might not be able to contain the convulsive question of slavery expansion.

Several factors underlay the split of northern Democrats from their own president on this issue. Ever since southern Democrats had blocked Van Buren's nomination in 1844, resentment had been growing in the party's northern wing. Polk's acceptance of 49° latitude for Oregon's northern boundary exacerbated this feeling. "Our rights to Oregon have been shamefully compromised," fumed an Ohio Democrat. "The administration is Southern,

Slave Auction in St. Louis   The public buying and selling of human beings in cities like St. Louis made a mockery of American boasts of liberty and gave a powerful impetus to the drive to prohibit the expansion of slavery into the territories acquired from Mexico. This painting hints at the ugliest dimension of the slave trade, the sale of mothers and children apart from fathers and sometimes apart from each other.

Southern, Southern! . . . Since the South have fixed boundaries for free territory, let the North fix boundaries for slave territories." The reduced rates of the Walker tariff in 1846 (sponsored by Robert J. Walker of Mississippi, Polk's secretary of the treasury) annoyed Democrats from Pennsylvania's industrial districts. And Polk angered Democrats from the Old Northwest by vetoing a rivers and harbors bill that would have provided federal aid for transportation improvements in their districts. The Wilmot Proviso was in part the product of these pent-up frustrations over what more and more northerners—abolitionists, Whigs, and Democrats alike—were calling "the slave power." "The time has come," said a Democratic congressman in 1846, "when the Northern Democracy should make a stand. Every thing has taken a Southern shape and been controlled by Southern caprice for years. . . . We must satisfy the Northern people . . . that we are not to extend the institution of slavery as a result of this war."

Although the House passed the Wilmot Proviso several times, the Senate never concurred. Neverthe-

less, the issue of slavery hung like the sword of Damocles over Polk's efforts to negotiate peace with Mexico. Polk also came under pressure from expansionist Democrats who, excited by military victory, wanted more Mexican territory, perhaps even "all Mexico." Polk had sent a diplomat, Nicholas Trist, with Scott's army to negotiate the terms of Mexican surrender. Authorized to pay Mexico $15 million for California, New Mexico, and a Texas border on the Rio Grande, Trist worked out such a treaty with the new Mexican government that had overthrown Santa Anna after his loss of Mexico City. In the meantime, though, Polk had succumbed to the "all Mexico" clamor. He ordered Trist back to Washington, intending to replace him with someone who would exact greater concessions from Mexico. Trist ignored the recall, signed the treaty of Guadalupe Hidalgo on February 2, 1848, and sent it to Washington. Although angered by Trist's defiance, Polk nonetheless decided to end the controversy by submitting the treaty to the Senate, which approved it on March 10 by a vote of 38 to 14. Half the opposition came from Democrats who wanted more Mexican territory and half from Whigs who wanted none. As it was, the treaty sheared off half of Mexico and increased the size of the United States by one-fourth.

THE ELECTION OF 1848

The treaty did nothing to settle the question of slavery in the new territory, however. Mexico had abolished the institution two decades earlier; would the United States reintroduce it? Many Americans looked to the election of 1848 to decide the matter. Four positions on the issue emerged, each identified with a candidate for the presidential nomination.

The Wilmot Proviso represented the position of those determined to bar slavery from all territories. The Liberty Party, which held its national convention early, endorsed the proviso and nominated Senator John P. Hale of New Hampshire for president.

Southern Democrat John C. Calhoun formulated the "southern rights" position. Directly challenging the Wilmot Proviso, Calhoun introduced resolutions in the Senate in February 1847 affirming the right of slaveowners to take their human property into any territory. The Constitution protected the right of property, Calhoun pointed out; Congress could no more prevent a settler from taking his slaves to California than it could prevent him from taking his horses there.

Although most southerners agreed with Calhoun, the Democratic party sought a middle ground between the antislavery position and the proslavery position. The Polk administration endorsed the idea of extending the old Missouri Compromise line of 36°30' to the Pacific. This would have excluded slavery from present-day Washington, Oregon, Idaho, Utah, Nevada, and the northern half of California, but would have allowed it in present-day New Mexico, Arizona, and southern California. Secretary of State James Buchanan, also a candidate for the Democratic presidential nomination (Polk did not seek renomination), embraced this position, as did a number of moderate Whigs from both North and South.

Another compromise position became known as "popular sovereignty." Identified in 1848 with Senator Lewis Cass of Michigan, yet another contender for the Democratic nomination, this concept proposed to let the settlers of each territory decide for themselves whether to permit slavery. This solution contained a crucial ambiguity, which was both its strength and its weakness: it did not specify *at what stage* the settlers of a territory could decide on slavery. Most northern Democrats assumed that a territorial legislature would make that decision as soon as it was organized. Most southerners assumed that it would not be made until the settlers had drawn up a state constitution. That would normally happen only after several years as a territory, during which time slavery might well have taken deep enough root to be implanted in the state constitution. So long as neither assumption was tested, each faction could support popular sovereignty — but at the cost of friction when they tried to put it into practice.

The Democratic convention nominated Cass for president, thereby seeming to endorse popular sovereignty. Significantly, however, in an attempt to prevent the party from splitting into northern and southern wings, the platform made no mention of the matter. The attempt was not entirely successful: two Alabama delegates walked out when the convention refused to endorse Calhoun's "southern rights" position, and an antislavery faction from New York walked out when it failed to win a credentials fight.

The Whig convention tried to avoid a similar schism by adopting no platform at all. But it was a forlorn hope; the slavery issue would not die down. In the eyes of many antislavery delegates who styled themselves "Conscience Whigs," the party made itself ridiculous by nominating Zachary Taylor for president. (In an extension of the irony, General Winfield Scott was also a prominent Whig and an aspirant for nomination.) Desperate for victory, the Whigs chose a hero from a war that most of them had opposed to run against the party that took credit for winning that war. But the fact that Taylor was also a large slaveholder who owned several plantations in Louisiana and Mississippi was too much for the Conscience Whigs. They bolted from the party and formed a coalition with the Liberty Party and antislavery Democrats. It became a new antislavery third party.

This "Free Soil" party met in convention in August 1848. The meeting resembled a religious camp meeting more than a political gathering. Speakers proclaimed slavery "a great moral, social, and political evil — a relic of barbarism which must necessarily be swept away in the progress of Christian civilization." The convention did not say how that would be done, but it did adopt a platform calling for "no more Slave States and no more Slave Territories." The Free Soil party nominated former President Martin Van Buren, with Charles Francis Adams, the son and grandson of presidents, as his running mate.

The campaign was marked by the futile efforts of both major parties to bury the slavery issue. Free Soil pressure compelled both northern Democrats and Whigs to take a stand against slavery in the territories. Whigs pointed to their earlier support of the Wilmot Proviso, while Democrats said popular sovereignty would keep the territories free. In the South, though, the two parties presented other faces. There, the Democrats pointed with pride to their expansionist record that had brought to the nation hundreds of thousands of square miles of territory — territory into which slavery might expand, if the settlers wanted it. But Taylor proved to be the strongest candidate in the South, because he was a southerner and a slaveholder. "Will the people of [the South] vote for a Southern President or a Northern one?" asked southern newspapers. "We prefer Old Zack with his sugar and cotton plantations and four hundred negroes to all their compromises."

Taylor carried eight of the fifteen slave states and increased the Whig vote in the South by 10 percent over 1844, while the Democratic vote declined by 4 percent. Though he did less well in the North, he carried New York and enough other states to win the election. The Free Soilers won no electoral votes but polled 14 percent of the popular vote in the North. They also elected nine congressmen along with two senators who would be heard from in the future: Salmon P. Chase of Ohio, architect of the Free Soil coalition in 1848, and Charles Sumner of Massachusetts, leader of the Conscience Whigs.

THE COMPROMISE OF 1850

Though small in numbers as yet, the Free Soilers would exert enough pressure in the coming years to determine much of the national political agenda. The first item on that agenda was organization of the territories acquired from Mexico. About the time Nicholas Trist was putting the finishing touches on a treaty to make California part of the United States, workers building a sawmill on the American River near Sacramento discovered flecks of gold in the riverbed. The news gradually leaked out, reaching the East in August 1848, where a public surfeited with tall tales out of the West greeted it with skepticism. But in December, Polk's final message to Congress confirmed the "extraordinary" discoveries of gold. Two days later, a tea caddy containing 320 ounces of pure gold from California arrived in Washington. Now all doubts disappeared. By the spring of 1849 a hundred thousand gold-seekers were poised to take off by foot on the overland trail, or by ship — either around Cape Horn or to the isthmus of Central America, where after a relatively shorter land crossing, they could board another ship to take them up the Pacific Coast to the new boom town of San Francisco. Eighty thousand actually made it that first year (five thousand succumbed to a cholera epidemic). Some of them struck it rich; most kept hoping to; more kept coming by the scores of thousands every year.

The political organization of California could not be postponed. The mining camps needed law and order; the settlers needed courts, land and water laws, mail service, and other amenities of established government. In New Mexico, the sixty thousand former Mexican citizens, now Americans, also needed a governmental structure for their new allegiance. And the growing Mormon community at Salt Lake could not be ignored either.

But the slavery question paralyzed Congress. In December 1848 lame-duck President Polk recommended extension of the Missouri Compromise 36°30′ line to the Pacific. The Whig-controlled House defied him, reaffirmed the Wilmot Proviso, drafted a bill to organize California as a free territory, and debated abolishing the slave trade and even slavery itself in the District of Columbia. Fistfights flared in Congress; southerners declared that they would secede if any of those measures became law; the Democratic Senate quashed all the bills. A southern caucus asked Calhoun to draft an "address" setting forth its position. He eagerly complied, producing in January 1849 a document that breathed fire against "unconstitutional" northern efforts to keep slavery out of the territories. Calhoun reminded southerners that their "property, prosperity, equality, liberty, and safety" were at stake and prophesied secession if the South did not get its way.

But Calhoun's firebomb fizzled. Only two-fifths of the southern congressmen and senators signed it. The Whigs wanted nothing to do with it. They

California Gold Rush   Seekers of gold in the foothills of California's Sierra Nevada came from all over the world, including China. This photograph shows American and Chinese miners near Auburn, California, a year or two after the initial gold rush of 1849.

looked forward to good times in the Taylor administration and opposed rocking the boat. "We do not expect an administration which we have brought into power [to] do any act or permit any act to be done [against] our safety," said Robert Toombs of Georgia, a leading Whig congressman. "We feel *secure* under General Taylor," added his fellow Georgian Alexander H. Stephens.

They were in for a rude shock. Taylor viewed matters as a nationalist, not as a southerner. New York's antislavery Senator William H. Seward became one of his principal advisers. A novice in politics, Taylor was willing to be guided by Seward. As a military man, he was attracted to the idea of vanquishing the territorial problem by outflanking it. He proposed to admit California and New Mexico (the latter comprising present-day New Mexico, Arizona, Nevada, Utah, and part of Colorado) immediately as *states,* skipping the territorial stage.

From the South came cries of outrage. Immediate admission would bring in two more free states, for slavery had not existed under Mexican law and most

of the forty-niners were Free Soil in sentiment. Indeed, with the administration's support, Californians held a convention in October 1849, drew up a constitution excluding slavery, and applied to Congress for admission as a state. Taylor's end run would tip the existing balance of fifteen slave and fifteen free states in favor of the North, probably forever. The South would lose its *de facto* veto in the Senate. "For the first time," said freshman Senator Jefferson Davis of Mississippi, "we are about permanently to destroy the balance of power between the sections." This was a "plan of concealing the Wilmot Proviso under a so-called state constitution." Davis insisted that slave labor was suitable to mining and that slavery should be permitted in California. Southerners vowed never to "consent to be thus degraded and enslaved" by such a "monstrous trick and injustice" as admission of California as a free state.

California and New Mexico became the focal points of a cluster of slavery issues that faced the new Congress in 1849–1850. An earlier Supreme Court decision (*Prigg* v. *Pennsylvania,* 1842) had relieved state officials of any obligation to enforce the return of fugitive slaves who had escaped into free states, declaring that this was a federal responsibility. Southerners therefore demanded a strong national fugitive slave law (in utter disregard of their oft-stated commitment to states' rights). Antislavery northerners, on the other hand, were calling for an end to the disgraceful buying and selling of slaves in the national capital. And in the Southwest, a shooting war threatened to break out between Texas and New Mexico. Having won the Rio Grande as their southern border with Mexico, Texans insisted that the river must also mark their western border with New Mexico. (That would have given Texas more than half of the present state of New Mexico.) This dispute also involved slavery, for the terms of Texas's annexation authorized the state to split into as many as five states, and the territory it carved out of New Mexico would create the potential for still another slave state.

These problems produced a crisis and an opportunity. The crisis lay in the southern threat to break up the Union. From Mississippi had gone forth a call for a convention of southern states at Nashville in June 1850 "to devise and adopt some mode of resistance to northern aggression." Few doubted that the mode would be secession unless Congress met southern demands at least halfway. But Congress got off to an unpromising start. Sectional disputes prevented either major party from commanding a majority in electing a Speaker of the House. Through three weeks and sixty-two ballots, the contest went on while tempers shortened. Northerners and southerners shouted insults at each other, fistfights broke out, and a Mississippian drew a revolver during one heated debate. Southern warnings of secession became a litany: "If, by your legislation, you seek to drive us from the territories of California and New Mexico," thundered Toombs of Georgia, *"I am for disunion."* On the sixty-third ballot, the exhausted legislators finally elected Howell Cobb of Georgia as Speaker by a plurality rather than a majority.

As he had in 1820 and 1833, Henry Clay hoped to turn the crisis into an opportunity — to once again settle a sectional crisis by accommodation. Seventy-two years old, a veteran of thirty years in Congress, three times an unsuccessful candidate for president, Clay was the most respected and still the most magnetic figure in the Senate. A nationalist

from the border state of Kentucky, he hoped to unite North and South in a compromise and avert disunion. On January 29, 1850, he presented eight proposals to the Senate and supported them with an eloquent speech, the first of many to be heard in that body during what turned out to be the most famous congressional debate in U.S. history. Clay grouped his first six proposals in three pairs, each pair offering one concession to the North and one to the South. The first pair would admit California as a free state but would organize the rest of the Mexican cession without restrictions against slavery. The second would settle the Texas boundary dispute in favor of New Mexico but would compensate Texas to enable the state to pay off bonds it had sold when it was an independent republic. (Many holders of the Texas bonds were southerners.) The third pair of proposals would abolish the slave trade in the District of Columbia but would guarantee the continued existence of slavery there unless both Maryland and Virginia consented to abolition. If this package of six proposals seemed to tilt slightly toward the North, Clay redressed the balance with his final two proposals. One affirmed that Congress had no jurisdiction over the interstate slave trade; the other called for a strong national fugitive slave law.

The final shape of the Compromise of 1850 closely resembled Clay's package. But a long, grueling process of bargaining was required to achieve it. The public face of this process was marked by set speeches in the Senate. The most notable were those of John C. Calhoun, Daniel Webster, and William H. Seward. Calhoun and Webster (along with Clay) represented the grand Senate triumvirate of the previous generation; Seward was the rising star of a new generation, whose speech on the Compromise catapulted him into renown. Each senator spoke for one of the three principal viewpoints on the issues.

Calhoun went first, on March 4. Suffering from consumption (he would die within a month), Calhoun sat shrouded in flannel as a colleague read his speech to a rapt audience. Calhoun's words of gloom seemed almost to come from the grave. Unless northerners returned fugitive slaves in good faith, he warned, unless they consented to the expansion of slavery into the territories and accepted a constitutional amendment "which will restore to the South, in substance, the power she possessed of protecting herself before the equilibrium between the two sections was destroyed," southern states could not "remain in the Union consistently with their honor and safety."

Webster's famous "seventh of March" speech three days later was both a reply to Calhoun and an appeal to the North for compromise. In words memorized by generations of schoolchildren, Webster announced his theme: "I wish to speak to-day, not as a Massachusetts man, nor as a Northern man, but as an American. I speak to-day for the preservation of the Union. Hear me for my cause." Secession could no more take place "without convulsion," he told the South, than "the heavenly bodies [could] rush from their spheres . . . without causing the wreck of the universe!" But while Webster had himself voted for the Wilmot Proviso, he now urged Yankees to forgo "taunt or reproach" of the South by insisting on the proviso. Nature would exclude slavery from New Mexico. "I would not take pains uselessly to reaffirm an ordinance of nature, nor to re-enact the will of God." Believing that God helped those who helped themselves, many of Webster's former antislavery admirers repudiated his leadership—especially since he also endorsed a fugitive slave law.

On March 11 Seward expressed the antislavery position in what came to be known as his "higher law" speech. Both slavery and compromise were "radically wrong and essentially vicious," he said. In reply to Calhoun's arguments for the constitutional protection of slavery in the territories, he invoked "a higher law than the Constitution," the law of God in whose sight all persons were equal. Instead of legislating the expansion of slavery or the return of fugitive slaves, the country should be considering how to bring slavery peacefully to an end, for "you cannot roll back the tide of social progress."

While these speeches were being delivered, committee members worked ceaselessly behind the scenes to fashion compromise legislation. They were aided by lobbyists for Texas bondholders and for business interests that wanted an end to this distracting crisis. But, in reaching for a compromise, Clay chose what turned out to be the wrong tactic. He lumped most of his proposals together in a single bill, hoping that supporters of any given part of the compromise would vote for the whole in order to get the part they liked. Instead, most senators and representatives voted against the package in order to defeat the parts they disliked. President Taylor derisively labeled Clay's compromise an "Omnibus Bill"

and continued to insist on the immediate admission of California (and New Mexico, when it was ready) with no *quid pro quo* for the South. Exhausted and discouraged, Clay fled Washington's summer heat for Newport's cool breezes, leaving a young senator from Illinois, Stephen A. Douglas, to lead the forces of compromise.

Another rising star of the new generation, Douglas reversed Clay's tactics. Starting with a core of supporters made up of Democrats from the Old Northwest and Whigs from the Upper South, he built a majority for each part of the Compromise by submitting it separately and then adding its supporters to his core: northerners for a free California, southerners for a fugitive slave law, and so on. This effort benefited from Taylor's sudden death of gastroenteritis on July 9 after consuming large quantities of iced milk and cherries on a hot Fourth of July. The new president, Millard Fillmore, was a conservative Whig from New York who gave his support to the Compromise. One after another, in August and September, the separate measures became law: the admission of California as a free state; the organization of the rest of the Mexican cession into the two territories of New Mexico and Utah without restrictions against slavery; the settlement of the Texas–New Mexico border dispute in favor of New Mexico and the compensation of Texas with ten million dollars; the abolition of the slave trade in the District of Columbia and the guarantee of slavery there; and the passage of a new fugitive slave law. When it was all over, most Americans breathed a sigh of relief, the Nashville convention adjourned tamely, and President Fillmore christened the Compromise of 1850 "a final settlement" of all sectional problems. Calhounites in the South and antislavery activists in the North branded the Compromise a betrayal of principle. But, for the time being, they seemed to be in a minority.

The consequences of the Compromise turned out to be different from what many anticipated. California came in as the sixteenth free state, to be sure, but its senators during the 1850s turned out to be conservative Democrats who voted with the South on most issues. Court decisions in California even allowed slaveowners to keep their slaves while "sojourning" in the state. The territorial legislatures of Utah and New Mexico legalized slavery, but few slaves were brought there. And the fugitive slave law, one of the least-debated parts of the Compromise, generated more trouble and controversy than all the other parts of this "final settlement" combined.

The Fugitive Slave Issue

Whenever the federal government seemed to be threatening slavery, the South favored states' rights. But whenever it seemed to be protecting slavery, the South supported a strong national government. The Fugitive Slave Act of 1850 gave the federal government more power than any other law yet passed by Congress.

The Constitution required that a slave who escaped into a free state must be returned to his or her owner. But it did not specify how that should be done. Under a 1793 law, slaveowners could take their recaptured property before any state or federal court to prove ownership. This procedure worked well enough so long as officials in free states were willing to cooperate. But as the antislavery movement gained momentum in the 1830s, some officials proved uncooperative. And professional slave-catchers sometimes went too far—kidnapping free blacks, forging false affidavits to "prove" they were slaves, and selling them south into bondage. Several northern states responded by passing anti-kidnapping laws giving alleged fugitives the right to testify in their own behalf and the right of trial by jury. The laws also prescribed criminal penalties for kidnapping. In *Prigg* v. *Pennsylvania* (1842) the U.S. Supreme Court declared Pennsylvania's anti-kidnapping law unconstitutional. But the Court also ruled that enforcement of the Constitution's fugitive slave clause was entirely a federal responsibility, thereby absolving the states of any need to cooperate in enforcing it. Nine northern states thereupon passed personal liberty laws prohibiting the use of state facilities (courts, jails, police or sheriffs, and so on) in the recapture of fugitives.

Fugitive slaves dramatized the poignancy and cruelties of bondage more vividly than anything else. A man or a woman risking all for freedom was not an abstract issue but a real human being whose plight invited sympathy and help. Consequently, many northerners who did not necessarily oppose slavery in the South and did not particularly care for black people in the North nonetheless felt outrage at the idea of fugitives being seized in a land of freedom and returned to slavery. The "underground railroad" that helped spirit slaves out of bondage took on leg-

Kidnapping Again! This is a typical poster printed by abolitionist opponents of the Fugitive Slave Law. It was intended to rally the citizens of Boston against the recapture and reenslavement of Anthony Burns, a fugitive slave from Virginia seized in Boston in May 1854.

endary status. Stories of secret chambers where fugitives were hidden, dramatic trips in the dark of the moon between "stations" on the underground, and clever or heroic measures to foil pursuing bloodhounds exaggerated the legend beyond reality.

Probably fewer than one thousand of a total three million slaves actually escaped to freedom each year. That was hardly a serious threat to slavery. But to southerners the return of those fugitives, like the question of the legality of slavery in California or New Mexico, was a matter of *honor* and *rights*. "Although the loss of property is felt," said Senator James Mason of Virginia, sponsor of the Fugitive Slave Act, "the loss of honor is felt still more." The fugitive slave law, said another southern politician, was "the only measure of the Compromise [of 1850] calculated to secure the rights of the South." Southerners therefore regarded obedience to the law as a test of the North's good faith in carrying out the Compromise. President Millard Fillmore vowed to prove that good faith by strictly enforcing the law.

The provisions of that law were extraordinary. It created a federal commissioner who could issue warrants for arrests of fugitives and before whom a slaveholder would bring a captured fugitive to prove ownership. All the slaveholder needed for proof was an affidavit from a slave-state court or the testimony of white witnesses. The fugitive had no right to testify in his or her own behalf. The commissioner received a fee of $10 if he found the owner's claim valid, but only $5 if he let the fugitive go. (The difference was supposedly justified by the larger amount of paperwork required to return the fugitive to slavery.) The federal treasury would pay all costs of enforcement. The commissioner could call on federal marshals to apprehend fugitives, and the marshals in turn could deputize any citizen to help. A citizen who refused could be fined up to $1,000, and anyone who harbored a fugitive or obstructed his or her capture would be subject to imprisonment. Northern senators had tried in vain to weaken some of these provisions and to amend the law to give alleged fugitives the rights to testify, to *habeas corpus*, and to a jury trial.

Abolitionists, both black and white, denounced the law as draconian, immoral, and unconstitutional. They vowed to resist it. Opportunities soon came, as slaveowners sent agents north to recapture fugitives, some of whom had escaped years earlier (the act set no statute of limitations). In February 1851 slave-catchers arrested a black man living with his family in Indiana and returned him to an owner who said he had run away nineteen years before. A Maryland man tried to claim ownership of a Philadelphia woman who he said had escaped twenty-two years earlier; he also wanted her six children, all born in Philadelphia. In this case, the commissioner disallowed his claim to both mother and children. But the impression that the law was rigged in favor of the claimants is borne out by statistics. In the first fifteen months of its operation, 84 fugitives were returned to slavery and only 5 were released. (For the entire decade of the 1850s the ratio was 332 to 11.)

Unable to protect their freedom through legal means, many blacks, with the support of white allies, resorted to flight and resistance. Thousands of northern blacks fled to Canada—three thousand in the last three months of 1850 alone—sometimes under the very nose of slave catchers. Two years earlier, a near-white slave woman named Ellen Craft had escaped from Georgia by cutting her hair short and posing as an ailing white gentleman traveling north for medical treatment. She was accompanied by her husband, posing as a servant. They traveled on above-ground railroads, stayed at the best hotels, and reached Boston safely. There they lived openly, joining the church of Theodore Parker, a prominent abolitionist and Unitarian clergyman who headed

the Boston Vigilance Committee, an organization founded to resist the new fugitive slave law. As soon as the law was passed, the Crafts' furious owner sent agents to Boston. But they found themselves less than welcome. Armed Vigilance Committee members protected the Crafts while Bostonians harassed the agents on the streets and warned them to take the next train south. They did. President Fillmore censured the Bostonians and even offered to put the army at the disposal of the Crafts' owner. By then, however, the couple were on a ship headed for England. By way of a parting shot, Theodore Parker sent a letter to Fillmore: "I would rather lie all my life in jail, and starve there, than refuse to protect one of these parishioners of mine. . . . You cannot think that I am bound to stand by and see my own church carried off to slavery and do nothing."

Boston was a hard place to enforce the fugitive slave law. In February 1851 slave catchers arrested a fugitive who had taken the name Shadrach when he escaped from Virginia a year earlier. They rushed him to the federal courthouse, where a few deputy marshals held him, pending a hearing. But a group of black men broke into the courtroom, overpowered the deputies, and spirited Shadrach out of the country to Canada. This was too much for the Fillmore administration. In April 1851 another fugitive, Thomas Sims, was arrested in Boston, and the president sent 250 soldiers to help 300 armed deputies enforce the law and return Sims to slavery.

Continued rescues and escapes kept matters at fever pitch for the rest of the decade. In the fall of 1851 a Maryland slaveowner and his son accompanied federal marshals to Christiana, Pennsylvania, a Quaker village, where two of the man's slaves had taken refuge. The hunters ran into a fusillade of gunfire from a house where a dozen black men were protecting the fugitives. When the shooting stopped, the slaveowner was dead and his son was seriously wounded. Three of the blacks fled to Canada. This time Fillmore sent in the marines. They helped marshals arrest thirty black men and half a dozen whites, who were indicted for treason. But the government's case fell apart, and the U.S. attorney dropped charges after a jury acquitted the first defendant, a Quaker.

Another white man who aided slaves was not so lucky. Sherman Booth was an abolitionist editor in Wisconsin who led a raid in 1854 to free a fugitive from custody. Convicted in a federal court, Booth appealed for a writ of *habeas corpus* from the Wisconsin

Return of Thomas Sims and Anthony Burns   This symbolic woodcut depicts soldiers and marines returning two of the most famous fugitives to slavery while Bostonians vent their frustration and rage. Although the incidents were real, the Sims and Burns cases
occurred three years apart, in 1851 and 1854.

Supreme Court. The court freed him and declared
the Fugitive Slave Law unconstitutional. That assertion of states' rights prompted the southern majority
on the Supreme Court to overrule the Wisconsin
court, assert the supremacy of federal law, and order
Booth back to prison, where he remained until 1861.

Two of the most famous fugitive slave cases of the
1850s ended in deeper tragedy. In the spring of 1854
federal marshals in Boston arrested a Virginia fugitive, Anthony Burns. His case became a cause célèbre
as angry abolitionists poured into Boston to save
him. Some of them tried to attack the federal courthouse, where a deputy was killed in an exchange of
gunfire. But the new president, Franklin Pierce, was
determined not to back down. "Incur any expense,"
he wired the district attorney in Boston, "to enforce
the law." After every legal move to free Burns had
failed, Pierce sent a U.S. revenue cutter to carry
Burns back to Virginia. While thousands of angry
Yankees lined the streets under American flags hanging upside down to signify the loss of liberty in the
cradle of the Revolution, soldiers of the Army, Ma-

rine Corps, and Artillery marched this lone black
man back into bondage.

Two years later Margaret Garner escaped from
Kentucky to Ohio with her husband and four children. When a posse of marshals and deputies caught
up with them, Margaret seized a kitchen knife and
tried to kill her children and herself rather than return to slavery. She managed to cut her three-year-
old daughter's throat before she was overpowered.
After complicated legal maneuvers, including an attempt by Ohio to retain jurisdiction to try Garner
for murder, the federal commissioner remanded the
fugitives to their Kentucky owner. He promptly sold
them down the river to Arkansas, and, in a steamboat accident along the way, one of Margaret Garner's sons drowned in the Mississippi.

Such events had a profound impact on public
emotions. Most northerners were not abolitionists,
and few of them regarded black people as equals. But
millions of them moved closer to an antislavery —
or perhaps it would be more accurate to say anti-
southern — position in response to the shock of see-

ing armed slave-catchers on their streets. "When it was all over," agreed two theretofore conservative Whigs in Boston after the Anthony Burns affair, "I put my face in my hands and wept. I could do nothing less. . . . We went to bed one night old fashioned, conservative, compromise Union Whigs and waked up stark mad Abolitionists." Several northern states passed new personal liberty laws after 1854 in defiance of the South. Although those laws did not make it impossible to recover fugitives, they made it so difficult, expensive, and time-consuming that many slaveowners gave up trying. The failure of the North to honor the Fugitive Slave Law, part of the Compromise of 1850, was one of the South's bitter grievances in the 1850s. Several southern states cited it as one of their reasons for seceding in 1861.

Uncle Tom's Cabin

A novel inspired by the plight of fugitive slaves further intensified public sentiment. Harriet Beecher Stowe, author of *Uncle Tom's Cabin,* was the daughter of Lyman Beecher, the most famous clergyman-theologian of his generation, and the sister of Henry Ward Beecher, the foremost preacher of the next generation. Writing this book made her more famous than either of them. Having grown up in the doctrinal air of New England Calvinist notions of sin, guilt, and atonement, Harriet lived for eighteen years in Cincinnati, where she got to know fugitive slaves who had escaped across the Ohio River. During the 1840s, in spare moments that she carved out from the duties of bearing and nurturing seven children, Stowe wrote numerous short stories. Outraged by the Fugitive Slave Law in 1850, she responded to her sister-in-law's suggestion: "Hattie, if I could use a pen as you can, I would write something that will make this nation feel what an accursed thing slavery is."

In 1851, writing by candlelight after putting the children to bed, Stowe turned out a chapter a week for nine months for serial publication in an antislavery newspaper. When the installments were published as a book in the spring of 1852, *Uncle Tom's Cabin* became a runaway best-seller. Within a year it

Uncle Tom's Cabin on the Stage   Within weeks of its publication as a book, *Uncle Tom's Cabin* was adapted for the stage. Scores of different productions have appeared since 1852, some of them grotesque caricatures, others faithful to the spirit of the novel. It is still being presented in theaters today, testimony to the universality of its themes of oppression and courage.

had sold 300,000 copies (the equivalent of more than 3 million today) in the United States alone, even more in Britain, and it was eventually translated into twenty languages. Contrived in plot, didactic in style, steeped in sentiment, *Uncle Tom's Cabin* is nevertheless a powerful novel with unforgettable characters. Uncle Tom himself is not the fawning, servile Sambo of later caricature, but a Christlike figure who bears the sins of white people and carries the salvation of black people on his shoulders. The novel's central theme is the tragedy of the breakup of families by slavery—the theme most likely to pluck at the heartstrings of middle-class Americans of that generation. Few eyes remained dry as they read about Eliza fleeing across the ice-choked Ohio River to save her son from the slave trader, or about Tom grieving for the wife and children he had left behind in Kentucky when he was sold.

Though banned in some parts of the South, *Uncle Tom's Cabin* found a wide but hostile readership there. A measure of the defensiveness of southerners toward the book is the tone of the reviews that appeared in southern journals. The editor of the South's leading literary periodical instructed the reviewer: "I would have the review as hot as hellfire, blasting and searing the reputation of [this] vile wretch in petticoats." Proslavery authors rushed into print with more than a dozen novels challenging Stowe's themes, but all of them together made nothing like the impact of *Uncle Tom's Cabin*. The book helped shape a whole generation's view of slavery. When Abraham Lincoln met Harriet Beecher Stowe a decade after its publication, he reportedly remarked, "So you're the little woman who wrote the book that made this great war."

FILIBUSTERING

If the prospects for slavery in New Mexico appeared unpromising, southerners could contemplate a closer region where slavery already existed—Cuba. Enjoying an economic boom based on slave-grown sugar, this Spanish colony only ninety miles from American shores had nearly 400,000 slaves in 1850—more than any American state except Virginia. President Polk, his appetite for territory not yet sated by the acquisition of Texas, Oregon, and half of Mexico, offered Spain $100 million for Cuba in 1848. The Spanish foreign minister spurned the offer, stat-

ing that he would rather see the island sunk in the sea than sold.

If money did not work, revolution might. Cuban planters, restive under Spanish rule, intrigued with American expansionists in the hope of fomenting an uprising on the island. Their leader was Narciso Lopez, a Venezuelan-born Cuban soldier-of-fortune. In 1849 Lopez recruited several hundred American adventurers for the first "filibustering" expedition against Cuba (from the Spanish *filibustero*, a freebooter or pirate). When President Taylor ordered the navy to prevent Lopez's ships from leaving New York, Lopez shifted his operations to the friendlier environs of New Orleans, where he raised a new force of filibusters, many of them Mexican War veterans. Port officials in New Orleans looked the other way when the expedition sailed in May 1850, but Spanish troops drove the filibusters into the sea after they had established a beachhead in Cuba.

Undaunted, Lopez escaped and returned to a hero's welcome in the South, where he raised men and money for a third try in 1851. This time, William Crittenden of Kentucky, nephew of the U.S. attorney general, commanded the 420 Americans in the expedition. But the invasion ended in fiasco and tragedy. Spanish soldiers suppressed a local uprising timed to coincide with the invasion and then defeated the filibusters, killing 200 and capturing the rest. Lopez was garroted in the public square of Havana. Then 50 American prisoners, including Crittenden, were lined up and executed by firing squad.

These events dampened southern enthusiasm for Cuba, but only for a time. "Cuba must be ours," declared Jefferson Davis, in order to "increase the number of slaveholding constituencies." A southern pamphleteer explained that "the Pearl of the West Indies, with her thirteen or fifteen representatives in Congress, would be a powerful auxiliary to the South." In 1852 the Democrats nominated Franklin Pierce of New Hampshire for president. Though a Yankee, Pierce had a reputation as a "doughface"—a northern man with southern principles. And, indeed, southern Democrats were delighted with his nomination. Pierce was "as reliable as Calhoun himself," wrote one, while another said that "a nomination so favorable to the South had not been anticipated." Especially gratifying was Pierce's support for annexing Cuba, which he made one of the top priorities of his new administration after winning a landslide victory over a demoralized Whig Party weakened by schism between its northern and southern wings.

Pierce covertly encouraged a new filibustering expedition to Cuba. This one was to be led by former Governor John Quitman of Mississippi. While Quitman was recruiting thousands of volunteers, southerners in Congress introduced a resolution to suspend the neutrality law that prohibited American interference in the internal affairs of other countries. But, at the last moment, Pierce backed off, fearful of political damage in the North if his administration became openly identified with filibustering. The Quitman expedition never sailed.

Pierce tried again to buy Cuba, instructing the American minister in Madrid to offer Spain $130 million. The minister was Pierre Soulé, a flamboyant Louisianian who managed to alienate most Spaniards by his clumsy intriguing. Soulé's crowning act came in October 1854 at a meeting with the American ministers to Britain and France in Ostend, Belgium. He persuaded them to sign what came to be known as the Ostend Manifesto. "Cuba is as necessary to the North American republic as any of its present . . . family of states," declared this document. If Spain persisted in refusing to sell, then "by every law, human and divine, we shall be justified in wresting it from Spain."

This "manifesto of the brigands," as antislavery Americans called it, caused an international uproar. Reeling from a domestic backlash against the Kansas–Nebraska Act that cost the Democrats control of the House (Chapter 15), the administration repudiated the Ostend Manifesto and recalled Soulé. Nevertheless, acquisition of Cuba remained an objective of the Democratic Party. The issue played a role in the 1860 presidential election and in the secession controversy of 1860–1861. Meanwhile, the focus of American filibustering shifted 750 miles south of Havana to Nicaragua. There, the most remarkable of the *filibusteros,* William Walker, had proclaimed himself president and had restored the institution of slavery.

A native of Tennessee and a brilliant, restless man, Walker had earned a medical degree from the University of Pennsylvania and had studied and practiced law in New Orleans, where he also edited a newspaper before joining the 1849 rush to California. Weighing less than 120 pounds, Walker seemed an unlikely fighter or leader of men. But he fought three duels, and his luminous eyes, which seemed to transfix his fellows, won him the sobriquet "gray-eyed man of destiny."

Walker found his true calling in filibustering. At the time, numerous raids were taking place back and forth across the border with Mexico, some of them staged to seize more of that country for the United States. In 1853 Walker led a ragged "army" of footloose forty-niners into Baja California and Sonora and declared the region an independent republic. Exhaustion and desertion depleted his troops, however, and the Mexicans drove the survivors back to California. A jury in San Francisco took only eight minutes to acquit Walker of violating the neutrality law.

This encouraged him to try again, with another goal. American influence was already apparent in Nicaragua, a land bridge in the transit of passengers and freight between California and the eastern United States. Many southerners eyed the potential of this tropical region for growing cotton, sugar, coffee, and other crops. The chronic instability of the Nicaraguan government offered a tempting target. In 1854 Walker signed a contract with rebel leaders in the civil war of the moment. The following spring, he led an advance guard of filibusters to Nicaragua and proclaimed himself commander in chief of the rebel forces. At the head of two thousand American soldiers, he gained control of the country and named himself president in 1856. The Pierce administration extended diplomatic recognition to Walker's regime.

But things soon turned sour. The other Central American republics formed an alliance to invade Nicaragua and overthrow Walker. To win greater support from the southern states, Walker issued a decree in September 1856 reinstituting slavery in Nicaragua (which had been abolished in 1824). A convention of southern economic promoters meeting in Savannah praised Walker's efforts "to introduce civilization in the States of Central America, and to develop these rich and productive regions by slave labor." Boatloads of new recruits arrived in Nicaragua from New Orleans. But in the spring of 1857 they succumbed to disease and to the Central American armies.

Walker escaped to New Orleans, where he was welcomed as a hero. He had no trouble recruiting men for another attempt, but the navy stopped him in November 1857. Southern congressmen condemned the naval commander and encouraged Walker to try again. He did, in December 1858, after a New Orleans jury refused to convict him of violating the neutrality law. On this third expedition, Walker's ship struck a reef and sank. Undaunted, he tried yet again. He wrote a book to raise funds for another invasion of Nicaragua, urging "the hearts of Southern youth to answer the call of honor. . . . The true field for the expansion of slavery is in tropical America." A few more southern youths answered the call, but they were stopped in Honduras. There, on September 12, 1860, the gray-eyed man met his destiny before a firing squad.

Long before this, however, the focus of the slavery-expansion controversy had shifted to Kansas, where for several years a small civil war raged as a prelude to the larger one that erupted in 1861.

SUGGESTED READING

For the West and the rise of Manifest Destiny, the best introductions are Malcolm J. Rohrbough, *The Trans-Appalachian Frontier: People, Societies, and Institutions 1775–1850* (1978) and Ray Allen Billington, *The Far Western Frontier, 1830–1860* (1956). Two books by Frederick Merk, *Manifest Destiny and Mission in American History* (1963) and *The Monroe Doctrine and American Expansion 1843–1849* (1967), explore the expansionism of the 1840s, while Norman A. Graebner, *Empire on the Pacific: A Study of American Continental Expansionism* (1955) traces its results.

Westward migration on the overland trails is chronicled and analyzed in John D. Unruh, Jr., *The Plains Across: The Overland Emigrants and the Trans-Mississippi West, 1840–1860* (1979), John Mack Faragher, *Women and Men on the Overland Trail* (1978), and Julie Roy Jeffries, *Frontier Women: The Trans-Mississippi West, 1840–1860* (1979). Migration to Oregon is treated in Malcolm Clark, *Eden Seekers: The Settlement of Oregon, 1812–1862* (1981), while the California gold rush and its consequences are described by Rodman Paul, *California Gold: The Beginning of Mining in the Far West* (1947) and Donald D. Jackson, *Gold Dust* (1980). For the harrowing story of the Donner Party, see George R. Stewart, *Ordeal by Hunger: The Story of the Donner Party* (1960).

For the Mormon migration and the creation of their Zion in Utah, see Wallace Stegner, *The Gathering of Zion: The Story of the Mormon Trail* (1964); Leonard J. Arrington, *Brigham Young: American Moses* (1985); and Leonard J. Arrington and Davis Bitton, *The Mormon Experience: A History of the Latter-Day Saints* (1979).

A fine introduction to the impact of American expansion westward on the Indian residents of this region is Philip Weeks, *Farewell, My Nation: The American Indian and the United States, 1820–1890* (1990). Other important studies include Ronald M. Satz, *American Indian Policy in the Jacksonian Era*

(1975); Robert A. Trennert, Jr., *Alternatives to Extinction: Federal Indian Policy and the Beginnings of the Reservation System, 1846–1851* (1975); and Robert M. Utley, *The Indian Frontier of the American West, 1846–1890* (1984).

For Texas and the northern frontier of Mexico that became part of the United States in 1848, see David J. Weber, *The Mexican Frontier, 1821–1846: The American Southwest under Mexico* (1982). American settlement in Texas and its annexation by the United States are described in Frederick Merk, *Slavery and the Annexation of Texas* (1972); Marshall De Bruhl, *Sword of San Jacinto: A Life of Sam Houston* (1993); and John Hoyt Williams, *Sam Houston* (1993). The impact of settlement of these regions by Anglo-Americans and the absorption of the region into the United States are analyzed by Leonard Pitts, *The Decline of the Californios: A Social History of the Spanish-Speaking Californians, 1846–1890* (1970) and Arnoldo De León, *The Tejano Community, 1836–1900* (1982).

A good study of the relationship between American expansion and the coming of the war with Mexico is David Pletcher, *The Diplomacy of Annexation: Texas, Oregon, and the Mexican War* (1973). Mexican viewpoints are described in Gene M. Brack, *Mexico Views Manifest Destiny: An Essay on the Origins of the Mexican War* (1975). Glen M. Price, *Origins of the War with Mexico: The Polk-Stockton Intrigue* (1967), charges Polk with deliberately provoking Mexico to war, while Charles G. Sellers, *James K. Polk, Continentalist 1843–1846* (1966), is more sympathetic to the American president. The most detailed study of the Mexican War is still Justin H. Smith, *The War with Mexico,* 2 vols. (1919). Modern studies include Seymour V. Connor and Odie B. Faulk, *North America Divided: The Mexican War, 1846–1848* (1971); K. Jack Bauer, *The Mexican War* (1974); and John S. D. Eisenhower, *So Far from God: The U.S. War with Mexico 1846–1848* (1989). John H. Schroeder, *Mr. Polk's War: American Opposition and Dissent, 1846–1848* (1973), documents antislavery and Whig opposition, while Robert W. Johannsen, *To the Halls of the Montezumas: The Mexican War in the American Imagination* (1985), focuses on the popularity of the war among Democrats and expansionists.

There is a huge literature on the sectional conflict provoked by the issue of slavery's expansion into the territory acquired from Mexico. For an introduction, consult David M. Potter, *The Impending Crisis 1848–1861* (1976) and Allan Nevins, *Ordeal of the Union,* 2 vols. (1947). The best single study of antislavery politics in this era is Richard H. Sewell, *Ballots for Freedom: Antislavery Politics in the United States 1837–1860* (1976). For northern Democrats and the Wilmot Proviso, see Chaplain Morrison, *Democratic Politics and Sectionalism: The Wilmot Proviso Controversy* (1967). The divisive impact of the slavery issue on Whigs is treated in Kinley J. Brauer, *Cotton versus Conscience: Massachusetts Whig Politics and Southwestern Expansion 1843–1848* (1967). The Free Soil Party and the 1848 presidential election are treated in Joseph Rayback, *Free Soil: The Election of 1848* (1970) and Frederick

J. Blue, *The Free Soilers: Third Party Politics 1848–1854* (1973). For the South and the sectional controversy over slavery's expansion, see William J. Cooper, Jr., *The South and the Politics of Slavery, 1828–1856* (1978); William W. Freehling, *The Road to Disunion: Secessionists at Bay, 1776–1854* (1990); John Barnwell, *Love of Order: South Carolina's First Secession Crisis* (1982); and a study of nine southern nationalists, Eric H. Walther, *The Fire-Eaters* (1992).

The fullest study of the Compromise of 1850 is Holman Hamilton, *Prologue to Conflict: The Crisis and Compromise of 1850* (1964). The careers of the three great senators who played such an important part in the compromise debate are portrayed in Merrill Peterson, *The Great Triumvirate: Webster, Clay, and Calhoun* (1987). For these and other key figures, see the following biographies: Robert F. Dalzell, *Daniel Webster and the Trial of American Nationalism 1843–1852* (1972); Robert V. Remini, *Henry Clay: Statesman for the Union* (1991); John Niven, *John C. Calhoun and the Price of Union* (1988); Robert W. Johannsen, *Stephen A. Douglas* (1973); Glyndon G. Van Deusen, *William Henry Seward* (1967); and K. Jack Bauer, *Zachary Taylor: Soldier, Planter, Statesman of the Old Southwest* (1985). The failed efforts of fire-eaters to capitalize on resentment of events that surrounded the compromise are treated in Thelma Jennings, *The Nashville Convention: Southern Movement for Unity 1848–1850* (1980), while the destructive impact of these events on the southern Whigs is narrated in Arthur C. Cole, *The Whig Party in the South* (1913).

The basic study of the passage and enforcement of the Fugitive Slave Act is Stanley W. Campbell, *The Slave Catchers* (1970). See also Paul Finkelman, *An Imperfect Union: Slavery, Federalism, and Comity* (1980). For northern personal liberty laws, see Thomas D. Morris, *Free Men All: The Personal Liberty Laws of the North 1780–1861* (1974). A scholarly study of the underground railroad is Larry Gara, *Liberty Line: The Legend of the Underground Railroad* (1961). For the hostility of many northern states toward blacks—fugitive or otherwise—see Eugene Berwanger, *The Frontier against Slavery: Western Anti-Negro Prejudice and the Slavery Extension Controversy* (1971). The powerful impact of Harriet Beecher Stowe's novel is measured by Thomas F. Gossett, *Uncle Tom's Cabin and American Literature* (1985).

The best accounts of southern expansionism and filibustering in the 1850s are Robert E. May, *The Southern Dream of a Caribbean Empire 1854–1861* (1971) and Charles H. Brown, *Agents of Manifest Destiny: The Lives and Times of the Filibusterers* (1979). For licit as well as illicit attempts to obtain Cuba, see Basil Rauch, *American Interest in Cuba 1848–1855* (1948). The remarkable career of William Walker is chronicled in William O. Scroggs, *Filibusters and Financiers: The Story of William Walker and His Associates* (1916) and Albert Z. Carr, *The World and William Walker* (1963).

Chapter 15

❧

The Gathering Tempest,
1853–1860

This drawing by an antislavery Northerner shows proslavery Congressman Preston Brooks of South Carolina beating Senator Charles Sumner of Massachusetts with a heavy cane on the floor of the Senate on May 22, 1856. It portrays the inability of the South to respond to the power of Northern arguments, symbolized by the pen in Sumner's right hand and a speech in his left hand, except with the unthinking power of the club. Note other southern senators in the background smiling on the scene or preventing northern senators from coming to Sumner's aid. The caning of Sumner was the worst of several instances of North–South violence or threatened violence on the floor of Congress in the 1850s, presaging the violence on the battlefields of the 1860s.

❧

The wounds caused by the 1850 battle over slavery in the territories had barely healed when they were reopened. This time the strife was over the question of slavery in the Louisiana Purchase territory—though that question had presumably been settled thirty-four years earlier by the Missouri Compromise, which had admitted Missouri as a slave state but had banned slavery from the rest of the Purchase north of 36°30′.

KANSAS AND THE RISE OF THE REPUBLICAN PARTY

By 1853 land-hungry settlers had pushed up the Missouri River to its confluence with the Kansas and Platte rivers, and entrepreneurs were talking about a railroad across the continent to San Fran-

cisco. But settlement of the country west of Missouri and land surveys for a railroad through this region would require that it be organized as a territory. Accordingly, in 1853 the House passed a bill creating the Nebraska Territory, embracing the area north of Indian Territory (present-day Oklahoma) up to the Canadian border. But the House bill ran into trouble in the Senate. Under the Missouri Compromise, slavery would be excluded from the new territory, and it would eventually come into the Union as one or more free states. Having lost California, however, the proslavery forces were determined to salvage something from Nebraska. Missourians were particularly adamant, because a free Nebraska would leave them surrounded on three sides by free soil. "This species of property" (slaves), explained a St. Louis newspaper, "would become insecure, if not valueless in Missouri." Senator David

R. Atchison of Missouri vowed to see Nebraska "sink in hell" before having it become free soil.

As president pro tem of the Senate, Atchison wielded great influence. And because Pierce's vice-president had died, Atchison was next in line for the presidency. A profane, gregarious man, he had inherited Calhoun's mantle as leader of the southern rights faction. In the 1853–1854 session of Congress, he kept raising the asking price for southern support of a bill to organize the Nebraska Territory.

The sponsor of the Senate bill was Stephen A. Douglas, chairman of the Senate Committee on Territories. Though only five feet four inches tall, Douglas was confident that he was big enough for the job. He had earned the nickname "Little Giant" for his parliamentary skill, which he had demonstrated most dramatically in helping to get the Compromise of 1850 through Congress. In Douglas's opinion, the application of popular sovereignty to the slavery question in New Mexico and Utah had been the centerpiece of the Compromise. So the initial draft of his Nebraska bill merely repeated the language used for those territories, specifying that when any portion of the Nebraska Territory came in as a state, it could do so "with or without slavery, as its constitution may provide."

This was not good enough for Atchison and his southern colleagues. After talking with them, Douglas announced that because of a "clerical error," a provision calling for the *territorial legislature* to decide on slavery had been omitted from the draft. But Atchison raised the price once again, insisting on an explicit repeal of the Missouri Compromise. Sighing that this "will raise a hell of a storm," Douglas agreed. He further agreed to divide the area in question into two territories: Kansas west of Missouri, and Nebraska west of Iowa and Minnesota. To many northerners this looked suspiciously like a scheme to mark Kansas out for slavery and Nebraska for freedom. Douglas then joined Jefferson Davis, Atchison, and other southern senators on a visit to the White House, where they twisted President Pierce's arm to give the revised Kansas–Nebraska bill the administration's support and to make its approval "a test of [Democratic] party orthodoxy."

The bill did indeed raise a hell of a storm. Contemporaries and historians have speculated endlessly on Douglas's motives. Some thought he wanted to win southern support for the presidential nomination in 1856. Perhaps, but he risked losing northern

Stephen A. Douglas   The Little Giant began his meteoric rise to leadership of the Democratic Party with his successful effort to have the Compromise of 1850 enacted by Congress. Having forestalled sectional schism in 1850, he drove a wedge more deeply than ever between North and South with the Kansas–Nebraska bill of 1854. Six years later, Douglas became a victim of sectional schism when the Democratic Party split into northern and southern factions and thereby ruined his chance of winning the presidency.

support. Others point out that Douglas's real estate holdings in Illinois would have risen in value if a transcontinental railroad were to traverse the Nebraska Territory, and that southern opposition could block this route. But the most likely reason was Douglas's passionate belief in Manifest Destiny, in filling up the continent with American settlers and institutions. "The tide of immigration and civilization must be permitted to roll onward," he proclaimed. For this, he was willing to pay the South's price for support of his Kansas–Nebraska bill. And despite his earlier "weather forecast," he clearly

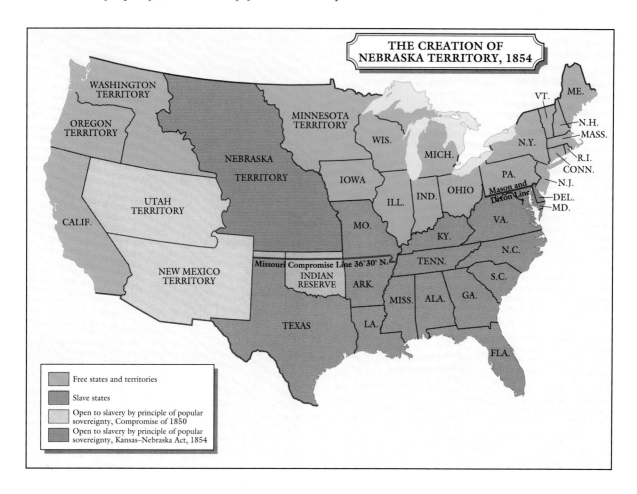

THE CREATION OF
NEBRASKA TERRITORY, 1854

Legend:
- Free states and territories
- Slave states
- Open to slavery by principle of popular sovereignty, Compromise of 1850
- Open to slavery by principle of popular sovereignty, Kansas–Nebraska Act, 1854

underestimated the fury of the storm that erupted. He failed to recognize the depth of northern opposition to the "slave power" and to the expansion of slavery. Douglas himself did not have firm moral convictions about slavery. He said that he cared not whether the settlers voted slavery up or down; the important thing was to give them a chance to vote.

But millions of Americans did care. They regarded the expansion of slavery as a national question, too important to be left to territorial voters. One of them was an old acquaintance of Douglas's, a fellow Illinoisan, Abraham Lincoln. An antislavery Whig who had served several terms in the Illinois legislature and one term in Congress, Lincoln was propelled back into politics by the shock of the Kansas–Nebraska bill. He acknowledged the constitutional right to hold slavery property in the states where it already existed. But he believed slavery was wrong in principle, "an unqualified evil to the negro, the white

man, and to the state. . . . There can be no moral right in connection with one man's making a slave of another." Lincoln admitted he did not know how to bring this deeply entrenched institution to an end. He understood that race prejudice was a powerful obstacle to emancipation. Still, the country must face up to the problem. It must stop any further expansion of slavery as the first step on the long road to its "ultimate extinction."

Lincoln excoriated Douglas's "care not" attitude toward whether slavery was voted up or down. "I can not but hate" this "*declared* indifference, but as I must think, covert *real* zeal for the spread of" slavery. The assertion that slavery would never be imported into Kansas anyway, because of the region's unsuitable climate, Lincoln branded as a "LULLABY argument." The climate of eastern Kansas was similar to that of the Missouri River Valley in Missouri, where slaves were busily raising hemp and tobacco.

Missouri slaveholders were already poised to take their slaves into the Kansas River Valley. "Climate will not . . . keep slavery out of these territories," said Lincoln. "Nothing in *nature* will." The founding fathers had looked forward to the day when slavery would no longer exist in republican America. Instead, the United States had become the world's largest slaveholding society, and Douglas's bill would permit slavery to expand even further. "The spirit of seventy-six and the spirit of Nebraska, are utter antagonisms," said Lincoln.

> Little by little . . . we have been giving up the old for the new faith. Near eighty years ago we began by declaring that all men are created equal; but now from that beginning we have run down to the other declaration, that for some men to enslave others is a "sacred right of self-government." These principles cannot stand together. . . . The monstrous injustice of slavery . . . deprives our republican example of its just influence in the world— enables the enemies of free institutions, with plausibility, to taunt us as hypocrites. . . . Let us re-adopt the Declaration of Independence, and with it, the practices, and policy, which harmonize with it. . . . If we do this, we shall not only have saved the Union; but we shall have so saved it, as to make, and to keep it, forever worthy of the saving.

With this eloquent declaration, Lincoln gave voice to the feelings that fostered an uprising against the Kansas–Nebraska bill. Abolitionists, Free Soilers, northern Whigs, and even a good many northern Democrats held impassioned meetings to form "anti-Nebraska" coalitions. But they could not stop passage of the bill. It cleared the Senate easily, supported by a solid South and fifteen of the twenty northern Democrats. In the House, where all the northern Democrats would have to face the voters in the fall elections, the Pierce administration and the Democratic leadership were still able to wield the whip of patronage and party pressure and force half of them to vote for the bill. It passed by a vote of 113 to 100.

These proceedings completed the destruction of the Whigs as a national party. Southern Whigs had been disappearing ever since Zachary Taylor had "betrayed" them on the issue of a free California. After the presidential election of 1852, there were few Whigs left in the cotton South. In that year, the Whig Party nominated General Winfield Scott for president. Though a Virginian, Scott, like Taylor, took a national rather than a southern view. He was the candidate of the northern Whigs in the national convention, which nominated him on the fifty-third ballot after a bitter contest between the northern and southern wings of the party. A mass exodus of southern Whigs into the Democratic party enabled Franklin Pierce to carry all but two slave states in the election. The unanimous vote of northern Whigs in Congress against the Kansas–Nebraska bill was the final straw. The Whig Party never recovered its influence in the South.

It seemed to be on its last legs in the North as well. Antislavery Whig leaders like Seward and Lincoln hoped to channel the flood of anti-Nebraska sentiment through the Whig Party. But that was like trying to contain Niagara Falls. Free Soilers and antislavery Democrats who provided much of the energy for the new movement spurned the Whig label. Political coalitions arose spontaneously in the North under various names: Anti-Nebraska; Fusion; People's; Independent. But the name that caught on was one that evoked memories of America's first fight for freedom in 1776: Republican. The first use of this name seems to have been at an anti-Nebraska rally in a Congregational church at Ripon, Wisconsin, in May 1854. It soon became the label under which most of the congressional candidates fielded by anti-Nebraska coalitions ran their campaigns.

The elections of 1854 were disastrous for northern Democrats. One-fourth of Democratic voters deserted the party. Having won the legislatures of all but two northern states in 1852, the Democrats won only two in 1854. They also lost control of the U.S. House of Representatives when sixty-six of ninety-one incumbent free-state Democratic congressmen (including thirty-seven of the forty-four who had voted for the Kansas–Nebraska bill) went down to defeat. Combined with the increase in the number of Democratic congressmen from the South, where the party had picked up the pieces of the shattered Whig organization, this rout brought the party more than ever under southern domination.

But who would pick up the pieces of old parties in the North? The new Republican Party hoped to, but it suffered a shock in urban areas of the Northeast. Hostility to immigrants created a tidal wave of nativism that threatened to swamp the anti-Nebraska movement. "Nearly everybody appears to have gone deranged on Nativism," reported a Pennsylvania Democrat, while a Whig in upstate New York warned that his district was "very badly infected with Knownothingism." Described as a "tornado," a

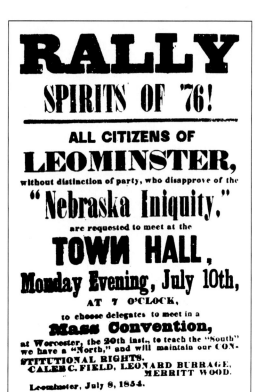

Birth of the Republican Party   The Kansas–Nebraska Act galvanized antislavery northerners of all parties into new "anti-Nebraska" organizations opposed to the repeal of the Missouri Compromise's ban on slavery in Louisiana Purchase territories north of 36°30′. Appealing to the "spirit of '76," these organizations coalesced into the Republican Party, which held its first convention at Pittsburgh on Washington's birthday in 1856 to organize a national party in preparation for the presidential nominating convention later that year.

"hurricane," a "freak of political insanity," the "Know Nothings" won landslide victories in Massachusetts and Delaware, polled an estimated 40 percent of the vote in Pennsylvania, and did well elsewhere in the Northeast and border states. Who were these mysterious Know Nothings? What did they stand for? What part did they play in the political upheaval of 1854?

IMMIGRATION AND NATIVISM

White Americans are quite literally a nation of immigrants—and their descendants. But, during the early nineteenth century, immigration was less pronounced than in most other periods of U.S. history. The volume of immigration (expressed as the number of immigrants during a decade in proportion to the whole population at its beginning) was little more than 1 percent in the 1820s, increasing to 4 percent in the 1830s. Three-quarters of the newcomers were Protestants, mainly from Britain. Most

of them were skilled workers, farmers, or members of white-collar occupations.

In the 1840s a combination of factors caused a sudden quadrupling in the volume of immigration and a change in its ethnic and occupational makeup. The pressure of expanding population on limited land in Germany and the successive failures of the potato crop in Ireland impelled millions of German and Irish peasants to emigrate. A majority came to the United States, where recovery from the depression of the early 1840s brought an economic boom with its insatiable demand for labor. During the decade after 1845, three million immigrants entered the United States—15 percent of the total American population in 1845, the highest proportional volume of immigration in American history. Many of them, especially the Irish, joined the unskilled and semiskilled labor force in the rapidly growing eastern cities and in the construction of railroads that proliferated to all points of the compass.

Most of them were also Roman Catholics. Anti-Catholicism had roots centuries deep in Anglo-

"Know Nothing"   This idealized portrait of a native-born, clean-featured American "citizen" symbolized the opposition to foreign-born voters, especially Irish Catholics, whom the Know Nothings feared as threats to Protestant American values and institutions.

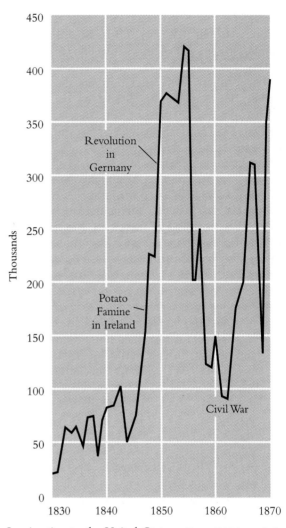

Immigration to the United States   (From *Division and the Stresses of Reunion 1845–1876*, by David M. Potter. Copyright © 1973 Scott, Foresman and Company. Reprinted by permission.)

American Protestant culture. Bloody Mary, Guy Fawkes Day, and the Glorious Revolution of 1688 were deeply seared in the folk memory; John Foxe's *Book of Martyrs* could be found alongside the King James Bible in many Protestant homes (Chapter 2). Fear of the pope and of the Roman church as autocratic and anti-republican was never far from the surface of American political culture, and a scurrilous anti-Catholic literature circulated during the 1830s. Several ethnic riots between Protestant and Catholic workers over the years culminated in pitched battles and numerous deaths in Philadelphia in 1844. Short-lived nativist political parties that sprang up in several eastern cities in the early 1840s called for curbing the political rights of immigrants. Some of the "nativists" were actually immigrants from Britain and Northern Ireland who brought their anti-Catholicism with them.

Nativism appeared to subside with the revival of prosperity after 1844. But the decline proved temporary, as the vast increase of immigration proved too much for the country to absorb. Not only were most of the new immigrants Catholics; many of them also spoke a foreign language and had alien cultural values. The temperance crusade had sharply curtailed drinking among native-born Protestants but had made little impact on the Irish and Germans, much of whose social and political life revolved around taverns and beer parlors (see Chapter 13). Old Americans perceived newer Americans as responsible for an increase of crime and poverty in the cities. Cincinnati's overall crime rate tripled between 1846 and 1853; its murder rate increased sevenfold. Boston's expenditures for poor relief tripled during the same period.

The political power of immigrants also grew. In Boston, for example, the number of foreign-born voters (mostly Irish) increased by 200 percent from 1850 to 1855 while the number of native-born voters grew by only 14 percent. Most of the immigrants became Democrats, because that party welcomed or at least tolerated them while many Whigs did not. Foreign-born voters leaned toward the proslavery wing of the Democratic Party, even though seven-eighths of them settled in free states. Mostly working-class and poor, they rubbed shoulders against the small northern black population; Irish-American mobs sometimes attacked black neighborhoods and rioted against black workers. They supported the Democratic Party as the best means of keeping blacks in slavery and out of the North. These attitudes sparked hostility toward immigrants among many antislavery people, some of whom equated slavery with Catholicism as a backward, despotic, repressive institution.

The Roman Catholic hierarchy did little to allay that hostility. Pope Pius IX (1846–1878) led the Church into a period of reaction against secular liberalism. The Church sided with the counterrevolutionary forces that crushed the European uprisings of 1848, which sought greater political and social democracy. In the United States the leading Catholic prelate, Archbishop John Hughes of New York, taking his cue from the pope, attacked abolitionists, free soilers, and various Protestant reform movements as akin to the "Red Republicanism" of Europe. In 1850, in a widely publicized address titled "The Decline of Protestantism and Its Causes," Hughes noted proudly that Catholic church membership in the United States had grown three times faster than Protestant membership over the previous decade, and he predicted an eventual Catholic majority. "Protestantism is effete, powerless, dying out. . . and conscious that its last moment is come when it is fairly set, face to face, with Catholic truth."

Two of the hottest issues in state and local politics during the early 1850s were temperance and schools. The temperance crusaders had grown confident and aggressive enough to go into politics. The drunkenness and rowdiness they associated with Irish immigrants became one of their particular targets. Beginning with Maine in 1851, twelve states enacted prohibition laws in the next four years. Though enforcement was spotty and several of the laws were soon weakened by the courts or repealed by legislatures, the controversies that surrounded them exacerbated ethnic tensions.

So did battles over public schools versus parochial schools. Catholics resented the Protestant domination of public education and the reading of the King James Bible in schools. Archbishop Hughes flayed the public schools as purveyors of "Socialism, Red Republicanism, Universalism, Infidelity, Deism, Atheism, and Pantheism." The Church began to build parochial schools for the faithful, and in 1852 the first Plenary Council of American bishops decided to seek tax support for these schools or tax relief for Catholic parents who sent their children to them. This effort set off heated election contests in numerous northern cities and states. "Free school" tickets generally won by promising to defend public schools against the "bold effort" of this "despotic faith" to "uproot the tree of Liberty" and "substitute the mitre for our liberty cap."

The Rise of the "Know Nothings"

In many states matters came to a head in 1854—which happened to be the year when immigration reached a peak not to be equaled for two decades. It was in this context that the "Know Nothings" (their formal name was the American Party) burst onto the political scene. This party was the result of the merger in 1852 of two secret fraternal societies that limited their membership to native-born Protestants: the Order of the Star-Spangled Banner and the Order of United Americans. Recruiting mainly young men in skilled blue-collar and lower white-collar occupations, the merged Order had a membership of one million or more by 1854. The Order instructed its members to vote for certain candidates or parties at election time. They generally supported temperance and opposed tax support for parochial schools. They wanted public office restricted to native-born men and sought to lengthen the naturalization period before immigrants could become citizens and voters from five to twenty-one years. Members were pledged to secrecy about the Order; if asked, they were to reply "I know nothing."

This was the tornado that swept through the Northeast in the 1854 elections, doing to the Whig

Know Nothings on Election Day   In Baltimore, nativist political clubs called "Blood Tubs" and "Plug Uglies" patrolled the streets at election time to intimidate foreign-born voters. An election riot in 1854 left seventeen dead in Baltimore; similar riots in St. Louis and Louisville also resulted in many deaths. This cartoon satirizes Baltimore's Know Nothing street gangs.

Party there what the slavery issue had done to it in the South. Although the American Party drew voters from both major parties, it cut more heavily into the Whig constituency. As a cultural force, nativism had found a more congenial home in the Whig Party than in the Democratic Party. Two years before, in the 1852 presidential election, the Whigs had tried to capitalize on William H. Seward's rapport with Catholics in New York and on General Scott's friendship with Catholics (his daughters were educated in a convent) by appealing to the Irish vote. This clumsy effort backfired, as the Irish voted solidly Democratic and many disgusted Whigs stayed home. In the temperance elections of these years, the Whigs also came up short. Fearful of alienating Wet voters, the Whig Party straddled the fence and thus alienated

the Drys in their ranks. So when the American Party raised its banner in 1854, many northern Whigs who had not already gone over to the Republicans flocked to the Know Nothings.

When the dust of the 1854 elections settled, it was clear that those who opposed the Democrats would control the next House of Representatives. But who would control the opposition—antislavery Republicans or nativist Americans? In truth, some northern voters and the congressmen they elected adhered to both political faiths. A Know-Nothing convention in Massachusetts resolved that "there can exist no real hostility to Roman Catholicism which does not also abhor slavery." In New England, several Know-Nothing leaders were actually Republicans in disguise who had jumped on the nativist bandwagon with the intention of steering it in an antislavery direction.

But many Republicans warned against flirting with religious bigotry. "How can any one who abhors the oppression of negroes, be in favor of degrading classes of white people?" asked Abraham Lincoln in a letter to a friend.

> As a nation, we began by declaring that *"all men are created equal."* We now practically read it "all men are created equal, *except negroes."* When the Know-Nothings get control, it will read "all men are created equal, except negroes, *and foreigners, and catholics."* When it comes to this I should prefer emigrating to some country where they make no pretense of loving liberty — to Russia, for instance, where despotism can be taken pure, and without the base alloy of hypocrisy.

Other Republicans echoed Lincoln. Since "we are against Black Slavery, because the slaves are deprived of human rights," they declared, "we are also against . . . [this] system of Northern Slavery to be created by disfranchising the Irish and Germans." Many Republicans also considered nativism a red herring that distracted people's attention from the true danger confronting the country. "Neither the Pope nor the foreigners ever can govern the country or endanger its liberties," wrote the managing editor of the *New York Tribune,* "but the slavebreeders and slavetraders *do* govern it."

The Decline of Nativism

In 1855 Republican leaders maneuvered skillfully to divert the energies of northern Know Nothings from the crusade against the pope to a crusade against the slave power. Two developments helped them. The first was turmoil in Kansas, which convinced many northerners that the slave power was indeed a greater threat to republican liberties than the pope was. The second was a significant shift southward in the center of nativist gravity. The American Party continued to do well in off-year elections in New England during 1855, but it also won elections in Maryland, Kentucky, and Tennessee and polled at least 45 percent of the votes in five other southern states. Violence in several southern cities with large immigrant populations preceded or accompanied these elections. Riots left ten dead in St. Louis, seventeen in Baltimore, and twenty-two in Louisville, evidencing a significant streak of nativism in the South. But the success of the American Party

there probably owed a great deal to the search by former Whigs for a new political home outside the Democratic Party. Areas of American Party strength in seven or eight southern states more or less coincided with areas of former Whig strength.

These developments had important implications for political nativism at the national level. Southern Know Nothings were proslavery while many of their Yankee counterparts were antislavery. Just as the national Whig Party had foundered on the slavery issue, so did the American Party in 1855–1856. At the party's first national council, in June 1855, most of the northern delegates walked out when southerners and northern conservatives joined forces to pass a resolution endorsing the Kansas–Nebraska Act. A similar scene occurred at an American Party convention in 1856. By that time, most northern members of the party had, in effect, become Republicans. At the convening in December 1855 of the House of Representatives that had been elected in 1854, a protracted fight for the speakership again took place. The Republican candidate was Nathaniel P. Banks of Massachusetts, a former Know Nothing who now considered himself a Republican. Banks finally won on the 133rd ballot with the support of about thirty Know Nothings who thereby declared themselves Republicans. This marriage was consummated in the summer of 1856 when the "North Americans" endorsed the Republican candidate for president.

By that time, nativism had faded. The volume of immigration had suddenly dropped by more than half in 1855 and stayed low for the next several years. Ethnic tensions eased, and cultural issues like temperance and schools also seemed to recede. Although the Republican Party took on some of the cultural baggage of nativism when it absorbed many northern Know Nothings, party leaders shoved the baggage into dark corners. The real conflict turned out to be not the struggle between native and immigrant, or between Protestant and Catholic, but between North and South over the extension of slavery. That was the conflict that led to civil war — and the war seemed already to have begun in the territory of Kansas.

BLEEDING KANSAS

When it became clear that southerners had the votes to pass the Kansas–Nebraska Act, William H.

Seward stood up in the Senate and told his southern colleagues: "Since there is no escaping your challenge, I accept it in behalf of the cause of freedom. We will engage in competition for the virgin soil of Kansas, and God give victory to the side which is stronger in numbers as it is in right." Senator David Atchison of Missouri was ready for the expected influx of Free-Soil settlers to the new Kansas Territory. "We are playing for a mighty stake," he wrote. "If we win we carry slavery to the Pacific Ocean; if we fail we lose Missouri, Arkansas, Texas and all the territories; the game must be played boldly."

Atchison did play boldly. At first, because of their closer proximity, Missouri settlers in Kansas posted the stronger numbers. But as the year 1854 progressed, settlers from the North came pouring in and the scramble for the best lands in Kansas intensified. Alarmed by the growing numbers of northern settlers, bands of Missourians, labeled "border ruffians" by the Republican press, rode into Kansas prepared to vote as many times as necessary to install a proslavery government. In the fall of 1854 they cast at least 1,700 illegal ballots and sent a proslavery territorial delegate to Congress. When the time came for the election of a territorial legislature the following spring, even greater efforts were needed, for numerous Free-Soil settlers had taken up claims during the winter. But Atchison was equal to the task. He returned home from the Senate to lead a contingent of border ruffians to Kansas for the election. "There are eleven hundred coming over from Platte County to vote," he told his followers, "and if that ain't enough, we can send five thousand—enough to kill every God-damned abolitionist in the Territory."

His count was accurate. Five thousand was about the number who came—4,968 to be precise, as determined by a congressional investigation—and voted illegally to elect a proslavery territorial legislature. The territorial governor appointed by President Pierce wrung his hands in despair and pleaded with Pierce to nullify the election. But Pierce listened to Atchison and fired the governor. Meanwhile, the new territorial legislature legalized slavery and adopted a slave code that authorized severe penalties for anyone who opposed it, including death for helping a slave to escape. The legislature also declared valid all the ballots that had been cast in the election that had created it.

The "free state" party, outraged by these proceedings, had no intention of obeying laws enacted by this "bogus legislature." By the fall of 1855 they constituted a majority of bona fide settlers in Kansas. So they called a convention, adopted a free-state constitution, and elected their own legislature and governor. By January 1856, on the eve of a presidential election, two territorial governments in Kansas stood with their hands at each others' throat.

Kansas now became the leading issue in national politics. The Democratic Senate and the president recognized the proslavery legislature meeting in the town of Lecompton, while the Republican House recognized the antislavery legislature in the town of Lawrence. Southerners saw the struggle as crucial to their future. "The admission of Kansas into the Union as a slave state is now a point of honor," wrote Congressman Preston Brooks of South Carolina. "The fate of the South is to be decided with the Kansas issue. If Kansas becomes a hireling [i.e., free] State, slave property will decline to half its present value in Missouri." On the other side, Charles Sumner of Massachusetts gave a well-publicized speech in the Senate on May 19–20 entitled "The Crime against Kansas." "Murderous robbers from Missouri," charged Sumner, "from the drunken spew and vomit of an uneasy civilization" had committed the "rape of a virgin territory, compelling it to the hateful embrace of slavery." Among the southern senators whom Sumner singled out for special condemnation and ridicule was Andrew Butler of South Carolina, a cousin of Congressman Brooks. Butler was a "Don Quixote," said Sumner, "who had chosen a mistress to whom he has made his vows . . . the harlot, Slavery."

Sumner's speech incensed southerners, none more than Preston Brooks, who decided to avenge his cousin. He knew that Sumner would never accept a challenge to a duel. Anyway, dueling was for gentlemen, and even horsewhipping was too good for this Yankee blackguard. Two days after the speech, Brooks walked into the Senate chamber, where he found Sumner seated at his desk. Explaining that Sumner had insulted his cousin, Brooks began beating him with a heavy cane. His legs trapped beneath the desk bolted to the floor, Sumner wrenched it loose as he stood up to try to defend himself, whereupon Brooks clubbed him so ferociously that Sumner slumped forward bloody and unconscious.

News of the incident sent a thrill of pride through the South and a rush of rage through the North. Charleston newspapers praised Brooks for "standing

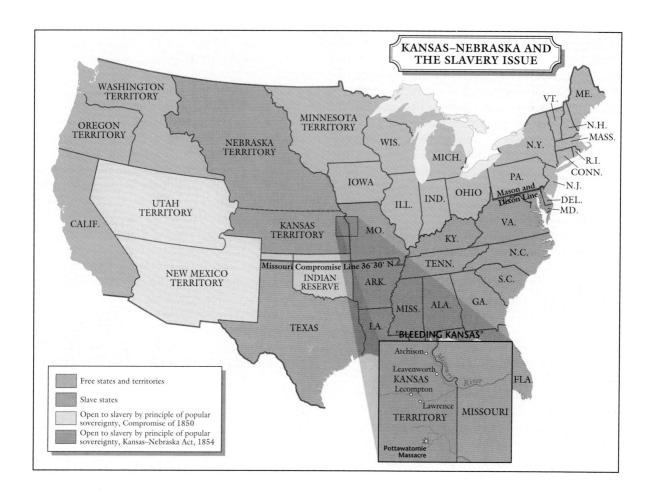

KANSAS–NEBRASKA AND
THE SLAVERY ISSUE

Free states and territories

Slave states

Open to slavery by principle of popular
sovereignty, Compromise of 1850

Open to slavery by principle of popular
sovereignty, Kansas–Nebraska Act, 1854

"BLEEDING KANSAS"

forth so nobly in defense of . . . the honor of South Carolinians." Brooks resigned from Congress after censure by the House and was unanimously re-elected. From all over the South came gifts of new canes, some inscribed with such mottoes as "Hit Him Again" and "Use Knock-Down Arguments." But, in the North, the Republican Party gained thousands of voters as a result of the affair. It seemed to prove their contentions about "the barbarism of slavery." "Has it come to this," asked the poet William Cullen Bryant, who edited the *New York Evening Post,* "that we must speak with bated breath in the presence of our Southern masters? . . . Are we to be chastised as they chastise their slaves?" A veteran New York politician reported that he had "never before seen anything at all like the present state of deep, determined, & desperate feelings of hatred, & hostility to the further extension of slavery, & its political power."

Republicans were soon able to add "Bleeding Kansas" to "Bleeding Sumner" in their repertory of winning issues. Even as Sumner was delivering his speech in Washington, an "army" of proslavery Missourians, complete with artillery, marched on the free-state capital of Lawrence, Kansas. On May 21 they shelled and sacked the town, burning several buildings. A rival force of free-state men arrived too late to intercept them. One of the free-state "captains" was John Brown, an abolitionist zealot who looked and acted like an Old Testament prophet. He had settled in Kansas with six of his sons and considered himself anointed by the Lord to avenge the sins of slaveholders. When he learned of the murder of several free-state settlers and the sack of Lawrence, he "went crazy — *crazy,*" according to one of his followers. We must "fight fire with fire," Brown declared. "Something must be done to show these barbarians that we, too, have rights." Leading four of his sons and three other men to a proslavery settlement at Pottawatomie Creek on the night of May 24–25, 1856, Brown dragged five men from their cabins and split open their heads with broadswords.

Here was the Old Testament doctrine of an eye for an eye. Brown's murderous act set off a veritable civil war in Kansas. One of Brown's sons was among the estimated two hundred men killed in the bushwhackings and raids. Not until President Pierce sent a tough new territorial governor and 1,300 federal troops to Kansas in September 1856 did the violence subside—just in time to save the Democrats from possible defeat in the presidential election.

THE ELECTION OF 1856

By 1856 the Republicans had become the largest party in the North. With the old Free Soilers as their radical core, they had recruited about three-fourths of the former Whigs and one-fifth of the Dem-ocrats. But they were also the first truly sectional party in American history, for they had little prospect of carrying a single county in the slave states. At their first national convention, the Republicans wrote a platform that focused mainly on that "relic of barbarism," slavery. The platform also incorporated the old Whig program of federal aid to internal improvements, including a railroad to California. For its presidential nominee, the party steered away from its most prominent leaders, who were identified with the old parties, and turned instead to John C. Frémont. This "Pathfinder of the West" had won a dashing image as a result of his deeds as an explorer and his role in the acquisition of California. With little political experience, he had few political enemies. But his antislavery credentials were satisfactory.

The Democrats chose as their candidate James Buchanan, a veteran of thirty years in various public offices. He had been out of the country as minister to Britain during the Kansas–Nebraska controversy and so was not tainted with its unpopularity in the North, as were Pierce and Douglas, the other aspirants for nomination. The Democratic platform endorsed popular sovereignty and condemned the Republicans as a "sectional party" that incited "treason and armed resistance in the Territories."

This would be a three-party election, for the American Party was still in the field, despite the ex-

John C. Frémont   This portrait of Frémont is based on a photograph from the 1850s. The strong features and the eyes focused on a distant object are meant to emphasize Frémont's reputation as an explorer and a topographical engineer in the West with his gaze fixed firmly on America's future.

odus of most of its northern members to the Republicans. Having become mainly a way station for former southern Whigs, the party nominated ex-Whig Millard Fillmore. The three-party campaign sifted out into a pair of two-party contests: Democrats *vs.* Americans in the South; Democrats *vs.* Republicans in the North. Fillmore, despite a good showing of 44 percent of the popular vote in the South, carried only the single slave state of Maryland. Considering Buchanan colorless but safe, the rest of the South gave him three-fourths of the electoral votes he needed for victory.

The real excitement in this election showed itself in the North. For many Republicans the campaign was a moral cause, an evangelical crusade against the sin of slavery. Republican "Wide Awake" clubs marched in torchlight parades chanting "Free

COUNTIES CARRIED BY CANDIDATES IN THE 1856 PRESIDENTIAL ELECTION

Frémont (Republican)
Buchanan (Democrat)
Fillmore (American)
No returns, unsettled, etc.

Soil, Free Speech, Free Men, Frémont!" A veteran politician in Indiana marveled: "Men, Women & Children all seemed to be out, with a kind of fervor I have never witnessed before in six Pres. Elections in which I have taken an active part." The turnout of eligible voters in the North was a remarkable 83 percent. One awestruck journalist, anticipating a Republican victory, wrote that "the process now going on in the United States is a *Revolution.*"

Not quite. Though the Republicans swept New England and the upper parts of New York state and the Old Northwest, both settled by New Englanders, where evangelical and antislavery reform movements had taken hold, the contest in the lower North was

close. Buchanan needed only to carry Pennsylvania and either Indiana or Illinois to win the presidency, and the campaign focused on those states. The immigrant and working-class voters of the eastern cities and the rural voters of the lower Midwest, descendants of upland southerners who had settled there, were anti-black and anti-abolitionist in sentiment. They were ripe for Democratic propaganda that accused Republicans of favoring racial equality. "Black Republicans," declared an Ohio Democratic newspaper, intended to "turn loose . . . millions of negroes, to elbow you in the workshops, and compete with you in fields of honest labor." A Democrat in Pennsylvania told voters that "the one aim" of the Repub-

Table 15-1

Popular and Electoral Votes in the 1856 Presidential Election

Candidate	Free States		Slave States		Total	
	Popular	*Electoral*	*Popular*	*Electoral*	*Popular*	*Electoral*
Buchanan (Democrat)	1,227,000	62	607,000	112	1,833,000	174
Frémont (Republican)	1,338,000	114	0	0	1,338,000	114
Fillmore (American)	396,000	0	476,000	8	872,000	8

licans was "to elevate the African race in this country to complete equality of political and economic condition with the white man." Indiana Democrats organized parades, with young girls in white dresses carrying banners inscribed "Fathers, save us from nigger husbands."

The Republicans in these areas denied that they favored racial equality. They insisted that the main reason for keeping slavery out of the territories was to enable white farmers and workers to make a living there without competition from black labor. They pointed out that the constitution written by the free-state faction in Kansas barred free blacks as well as slaves from coming in. But their denials were in vain. Support for the Republican Party by prominent black leaders, including Frederick Douglass, convinced hundreds of thousands of voters that the "Black Republicans" were racial egalitarians. For the next two decades, that sentiment would be one of the most potent weapons in the Democratic arsenal.

In 1856, though, the charge that a Republican victory would destroy the Union was even more effective. Buchanan himself set the tone in his instructions to Democratic Party leaders: "The Black Republicans must be . . . boldly assailed as disunionists, and the charge must be re-iterated again and again." It was. And southerners helped the cause by threatening to secede if Frémont won. We "should not pause," said Senator James Mason of Virginia, "but proceed at once to 'immediate, absolute, and eternal separation.'" Fears of disruption caused many conservative ex-Whigs in the North to support Buchanan over Frémont or Fillmore (who had no chance of winning). Buchanan carried Pennsylvania, New Jersey, Indiana, Illinois, and California and won the presidency.

But southerners did not intend to let Buchanan forget that he owed his election mainly to the South. "Mr. Buchanan and the Northern Democracy are dependent on the South," wrote a Virginian after the election. "If we can succeed in Kansas . . . and add a little more slave territory, we may yet live free men under the Stars and Stripes."

The Dred Scott Case

The South took the offensive at the very outset of the Buchanan administration. Its instrument was the Supreme Court, which had a majority of five justices from slave states led by Chief Justice Roger B. Taney of Maryland. Those justices saw the Dred Scott case as an opportunity to settle once and for all the question of slavery in the territories.

Dred Scott was a slave whose owner, an army surgeon, had kept him at military posts in Illinois and in Wisconsin Territory for several years before taking him back to Missouri. After the owner's death, Scott sued for his freedom on the grounds of his prolonged stay in Wisconsin Territory, where slavery had been outlawed by the Missouri Compromise. The case worked its way up from Missouri courts through a federal circuit court to the Supreme Court. There it began to attract attention as a test case of Congress's power to prohibit slavery in the territories.

The southern Supreme Court justices decided to declare that the Missouri Compromise ban on slavery in the territories was unconstitutional. But to avoid the appearance of a purely sectional decision, they sought the concurrence of at least one northern Democratic justice. They found their man in Robert Grier of Pennsylvania, and President-elect

Buchanan played an improper role by pressing his fellow Pennsylvanian to go along with the southern majority. Having obtained Justice Grier's concurrence, Chief Justice Taney issued the court's ruling stating that Congress did not have the power to keep slavery out of a territory, because slaves were property and the Constitution protects the right of property. For good measure, Taney also wrote that the circuit court should not have accepted the Scott case in the first place, since black men, having "no rights which a white man was bound to respect," were not citizens of the United States and therefore had no standing in its courts. Five other justices wrote concurring opinions. The two non-Democratic northern justices (both former Whigs, one of them now a Republican) dissented vigorously from both parts of the Court's decision. They stated that blacks were legal citizens in several northern states and were therefore citizens of the United States. And to buttress their opinion that Congress could prohibit slavery in the territories, they cited the provision of the Constitution giving Congress power to make "all needful rules and regulations" for the territories.

Modern scholars agree with the dissenters. But in 1857 Taney had a majority and his ruling became law. Modern scholars have also demonstrated that Taney was motivated by his passionate commitment "to southern life and values" and by his determination to stop "northern aggression" by cutting the ground from under the hated Republicans. His ruling that their program to exclude slavery from the territories was unconstitutional was designed to do just that. Southerners certainly expressed their gratitude to Taney and their delight over his decision. "Southern opinion upon the subject of Southern slavery . . . is now the supreme law of the land," they gloated. The ruling "crushes the life out of that miserable . . . Black Republican organization."

But the Republicans refused to be crushed. They denounced Taney's "jesuitical decision" as based on "gross perversion" of the Constitution. The *New York Tribune* sneered that the Dred Scott decision was "entitled to just as much moral weight as would be the judgment of a majority of those congregated in any Washington bar-room." Several Republican state legislatures resolved that the ruling was "not binding in law and conscience." They probably did not mean to advocate civil disobedience. But they did look forward to the election of a Republican presi-

dent who could "reconstitute" the Court and secure a reversal of the decision. "The remedy," said the *Chicago Tribune,* "is the ballot box. . . . Let the next President be Republican, and 1860 will mark an era kindred with that of 1776."

The Lecompton Constitution

Instead of settling the slavery controversy, the Dred Scott decision intensified it. Meanwhile, the proslavery forces, having won legalization of slavery in the territories, moved to ensure that it would remain legal when Kansas became a state. That required deft maneuvering, because legitimate antislavery settlers outnumbered proslavery settlers by more than two to one. In 1857 the proslavery legislature (elected by the fraudulent votes of border ruffians two years earlier) called for a constitutional convention at Lecompton to prepare Kansas for statehood. But because the election for delegates was rigged, Free-Soil voters refused to participate in it. One-fifth of the registered voters thereupon elected convention delegates, who met at Lecompton and wrote a state constitution that made slavery legal.

Then a nagging problem turned up. Buchanan had promised that the Lecompton constitution would be presented to the voters in a fair referendum. Congress would surely refuse to grant Kansas statehood without such a referendum. The problem was how to get the proslavery constitution approved given the antislavery majority of voters. The convention came up with an ingenious solution. Instead of a referendum on the whole constitution, it would allow the voters to choose between a constitution "with slavery" and one "with no slavery." But there was a catch. The constitution "with no slavery" guaranteed slaveowners' "inviolable" right of property in the two hundred slaves already in Kansas and their progeny. And it did nothing to prevent future smuggling of slaves across the 200-mile border with Missouri. Once in Kansas, they too would become "inviolable" property.

Free-state voters branded the referendum a farce and boycotted it. One-quarter of the eligible voters went to the polls in December 1857 and approved the constitution "with slavery." Meanwhile, in a fair election policed by federal troops, the antislavery party won control of the new territorial legislature and promptly submitted both constitutions to a referendum that was boycotted by proslavery voters. This time, 70 percent of the eligible voters went to the polls and overwhelmingly rejected both constitutions.

Which referendum would the federal government recognize? That question engrossed the 1857–1858 session of Congress and proved even more divisive than the Kansas–Nebraska debate four years earlier. President Buchanan faced a dilemma. The Lecompton constitution was a test case for popular sovereignty, and Buchanan had promised a fair referendum. But southerners, who dominated both the Democratic Party and the administration (the vice president and four of the seven cabinet members were from slave states), threatened secession if Kansas was not admitted to statehood under the Lecompton constitution "with slavery." "If Kansas is *driven out of the Union for being a Slave State,*" thundered Senator James Hammond of South Carolina, "can any Slave State remain in it with honor?" Buchanan caved in. He explained to a shocked northern Democrat that if he did not accept the Lecompton constitution, southern states would "secede from the Union or take up arms against us." So he sent the Lecompton constitution to Congress with a message recommending statehood. Kansas, said the president, "is at this moment as much a slave state as Georgia or South Carolina."

What would Stephen Douglas do? He was the real leader of the Democratic Party, or at least of its northern portion. But if he endorsed the Lecompton constitution, he would undoubtedly be defeated in his bid for reelection to the Senate in 1858. And he regarded the Lecompton constitution as a travesty of popular sovereignty. So he broke with the administration on the issue. He could not vote to "force this constitution down the throats of the people of Kansas," he told the Senate, "in opposition to their wishes and in violation of our pledges."

The fight in Congress was long and bitter. The South and the administration had the votes they needed in the Senate and won handily there. But the Democratic majority in the House was so small that the defection of even a few northern Democrats would defeat the Lecompton constitution. The House debate, at one point, got out of hand, and a wild fistfight erupted between Republicans and southern Democrats. "There were some fifty middle-aged and elderly gentlemen pitching into each other like so many Tipperary savages," wrote a bemused reporter, "most of them incapable, from want of wind and muscle, from doing each other any serious harm." It might have been a different matter if any of these combatants had been armed; and indeed after this affray, some congressmen began carrying arms.

When the vote was finally taken, two dozen northern Democrats defected, providing enough votes to defeat Lecompton. Both sides then accepted a compromise proposal to resubmit the constitution to Kansas voters, who decisively rejected it. This meant that while Kansas would not come in as a slave state, neither would it come in as a free state for some time yet. Nevertheless, the Lecompton debate had split the Democratic Party, leaving a legacy of undying enmity between southerners and Douglas, whom they had considered one of their most reliable northern allies. But they now pronounced him "a *Dead Cock* in the Pit . . . at the head of the Black Column . . . stained with the dishonor of treachery without a parallel." The election of a Republican president in 1860 was now all but assured.

THE ECONOMY IN THE 1850s

After recovery from a depression in the mid-1840s, the American economy enjoyed a dozen years of unprecedented growth and prosperity. Railroads were the leading sector of growth: the number of miles in operation quintupled during those years. Railroad construction provided employment for a large number of immigrants and spurred growth in industries that produced rails, rolling stock, and other railroad equipment. Most of the railroad construction took place in the Old Northwest, linking the region more closely to the Northeast through the consolidation of several trunk lines, and continuing the reorientation of transportation networks from a north-south river pattern to an east-west canal and rail pattern. By the mid-1850s the tonnage of freight carried on the east-west rail and water routes was more than double the north-south river tonnage. This binding more closely of the western and eastern states reinforced the effect of slavery in creating a self-conscious "North" and "South."

Although the Old Northwest remained predominantly agricultural, the rapid expansion of railroads there laid the basis for its industrialization. During the 1850s the growth rate of industrial output in the

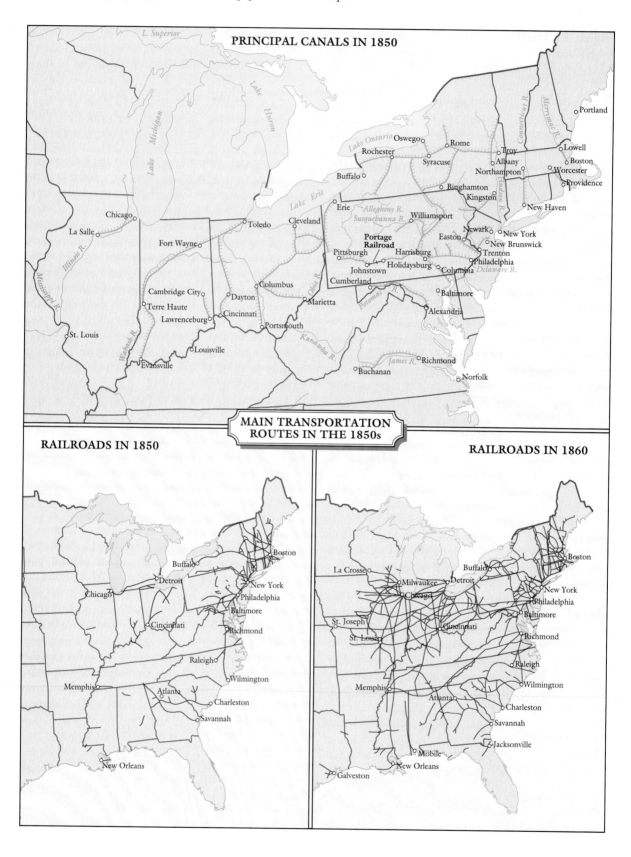

PRINCIPAL CANALS IN 1850

MAIN TRANSPORTATION
ROUTES IN THE 1850s

RAILROADS IN 1850

RAILROADS IN 1860

free states west of Pennsylvania was twice as great as the rate in the Northeast and three times as great as the rate in the South. The rate of urbanization was three and four times greater in the Northwest than in the Northeast and South, respectively. Chicago became the terminus for fifteen rail lines in the 1850s, during which its population grew by 375 percent. In 1847 two companies that contributed to the rapid growth of agriculture during this era built their plants in Illinois: the McCormick reaper works at Chicago and the John Deere steel-plow works at Moline.

According to almost every statistical index available from that period, the rate of economic expansion considerably outstripped even the prodigious rate of population increase. While the number of Americans grew by 44 percent during these twelve years (1844–1856), the value of both exports and imports increased by 200 percent, the tonnage of coal mined by 270 percent, the amount of banking capital, industrial capital, and industrial output by approximately 100 percent, the value of farmland by 100 percent, and the amount of cotton, wheat, and corn harvested by about 70 percent. These advances meant a significant increase of *per capita* production

and income—though the increase of income was greater among upper-class groups than among those at the lower end of the scale. The poor were getting richer, but the rich were getting richer at a greater rate, and the distance between rich and poor was widening—a phenomenon that has characterized all capitalist economies during stages of rapid industrial growth.

By the later 1850s the United States had forged ahead of most other countries to become the second-leading industrial producer in the world, behind only Britain. But the country was still in the early stages of industrial development, with the processing of agricultural products and raw materials still playing the dominant role. By 1860, the four leading industries, measured by value added in manufacturing, were cotton textiles, lumber products, boots and shoes, and flour milling. Iron and machinery, industries typical of a more mature manufacturing economy, ranked sixth and seventh.

The United States had pioneered in one crucial feature of modern industry: the mass production of interchangeable parts. This was a revolutionary concept that had begun with the manufacture of firearms earlier in the century and had spread to many

Chicago in the 1850s   By this decade, Chicago was one of the country's fastest-growing cities. A transportation hub on the Great Lakes, Chicago was a creation of the railroads that radiated outward in every direction, making the city a distribution center for Midwestern agricultural products as well as a burgeoning industrial giant.

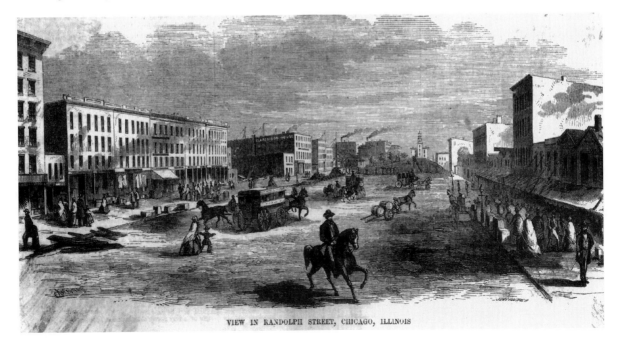

VIEW IN RANDOLPH STREET, CHICAGO, ILLINOIS

products by the 1850s. High wages and a shortage of the skilled craftsmen who had traditionally fashioned guns, furniture, locks, watches, and other products had compelled American entrepreneurs to seek alternative methods. The "Yankee ingenuity" that was already world-famous came up with an answer: special-purpose machine tools that would cut and shape an endless number of parts that could be fitted together with other similarly produced parts to make whole guns, locks, clocks, and sewing machines in mass quantities. These products were less elegant and less durable than products made by skilled craftsmen. But they were also less expensive and thus more widely available to the "middling classes" of a society that professed to be more democratic than Europe in its consumer economy as well as in its politics.

Such American-made products were the hit of the first world's fair, the Crystal Palace Exhibition, at London in 1851. British manufacturers were so impressed by Yankee techniques, which they dubbed "the American system of manufactures," that they sent two commissions to the United States to study them. "The labouring classes are comparatively few," reported one commission in 1854, "and to this very want . . . may be attributed the extraordinary ingenuity displayed in many of these labour-saving machines, whose automatic action so completely supplies the place of the more abundant hand labour of the older manufacturing countries." The British firearms industry imported American experts to help set up the Enfield Armoury in London to manufacture the new British army rifle. And they invited Samuel Colt of Connecticut, inventor of the famous six-shooting revolver, to set up a factory in England stocked with machinery from Connecticut. In testimony before a parliamentary committee in 1854, Colt summed up the American system of manufactures in a single sentence: "There is nothing that cannot be produced by machinery." Although the British had a half-century head start over Americans in the industrial revolution, Colt's testimony expressed a philosophy that would enable the United States to surpass Britain as the leading industrial nation by 1880.

The British industrial commissions also cited the American educational system as an important reason for the country's technological proficiency. "Educated up to a far higher standard than those of a much superior grade in the Old World," reported the 1854 commission, "every [American] workman seems to be continually devising some new thing to

Colt Arms Plant in Hartford, Connecticut   Samuel Colt's factory for manufacturing firearms was a showpiece for the American system of manufactures in the 1850s. All of the processes for production of the famous Colt revolver were housed under one roof, with power-driven machinery cutting the metal and shaping the interchangeable parts. Hand filing was necessary, however, for a perfect fit of the parts because the tolerances of machine tools were not yet as finely calibrated as they later became.

assist him in his work, and there is a strong desire . . . to be 'posted up' in every new improvement." By contrast, the British workman, trained by long apprenticeship "in the trade," rather than in school, lacked "the ductility of mind and the readiness of apprehension for a new thing" and was therefore "unwilling to change the methods he has been used to."

Whether this British commission was right in its belief that American schooling encouraged the "adaptative versatility" of Yankee workers, it was certainly true that public education and literacy were more widespread in the United States than in Europe. Almost 95 percent of adults in the free states were literate in 1860, compared with 65 percent in England and 55 percent in France. The standardization and expansion of public school systems that had begun earlier in New England had spread to the mid-Atlantic states and into the Old Northwest by the 1850s. Nearly all children received a few years of schooling, and most completed at least six or seven years. This improvement in education coincided with the feminization of the teaching profession, which opened up new career opportunities for young women. The no-tion that "woman's sphere" was in the home, raising and nurturing children, ironically projected that sphere outside the home into the schoolroom when schools took over part of the responsibility of socializing and educating children. By the 1850s nearly three-quarters of the public school teachers in New England were women (who worked for lower salaries than male teachers), a trend that was spreading to the mid-Atlantic states and the Old Northwest as well.

The Southern Economy

The feminization of teaching had not yet reached the South. Nor had the idea of universal public education taken deep root in the slave states. In contrast to the North, where only 6 percent of the population could not read and write, nearly 20 percent of the free population and 90 percent of the slaves in the South were illiterate. This was one of several differences between North and South that antislavery people pointed to as evidence of the backward, repressive, and pernicious nature of a slave society in a free-enterprise capitalist democracy.

The Country School   This famous painting by Winslow Homer portrays the typical one-room rural schoolhouse in which millions of American children learned the three Rs in the nineteenth century. By the 1850s, elementary schoolteaching was a profession increasingly dominated by women, an important change from earlier generations.

Still, the South shared in the economy's rapid growth following recovery from the depression of 1837–1843. Cotton prices and production both doubled between 1845 and 1855. Similar increases in price and output emerged in two of the South's other cash crops, tobacco and sugar. The price of slaves, a significant index of prosperity in the southern economy, also doubled during this decade. Southern crops provided three-fifths of all U.S. exports, with cotton alone supplying more than half.

But a growing number of southerners deplored the fact that the "colonial" economy of the South was so dependent on the export of agricultural products and the import of manufactured goods. The ships that carried southern cotton were owned by northern or British firms; the financial and commercial services that facilitated the marketing of southern crops were provided mostly by Yankees or Englishmen. In the years of rising sectional tensions around 1850, many southerners began calling for economic independence from the North. How could they obtain their "rights," they asked, if they were "financially more enslaved than our negroes?" Yankees "abuse and denounce slavery and slaveholders," declared a southern newspaper in 1851, yet "we purchase all our luxuries and necessaries from the North. . . . Our slaves are clothed with Northern manufactured goods and work with Northern hoes, ploughs, and other implements. . . . The slaveholder dresses in Northern goods. . . . In Northern vessels his products are carried to market . . . and on Northern-made paper, with a Northern pen, with Northern ink, he resolves and re-resolves in regard to his rights."

We must "throw off this humiliating dependence," declared James D. B. De Bow, the young champion of economic diversification in the South. In 1846 De Bow had founded in New Orleans a periodical that came to be known as *De Bow's Review.* Proclaiming on its cover that "Commerce is King," the *Review* set out to make this slogan a southern reality. De Bow took the lead in organizing annual "commercial conventions" that met in various southern cities during the 1850s. In its early years, this movement encouraged southerners to invest in shipping lines, railroads, textile mills ("bring the spindles to the cotton"), and other enterprises. "Give us factories, machine shops, work shops," declared southern proponents of King Commerce, "and we shall be able ere long to assert our rights."

Economic diversification in the South did make headway during the 1850s. The slave states quadrupled their railroad mileage, increased the amount of capital invested in manufacturing by 77 percent, and boosted their output of cotton textiles by 44 percent. But like Alice in Wonderland, the faster the South ran, the farther behind it seemed to fall—for northern industry was growing even faster. The slave states' share of the nation's manufacturing capacity actually dropped from 18 to 16 percent during the decade. In 1860 the North had five times more industrial output per capita than the South, and it had three times the railroad capital and mileage per capita and per thousand square miles. Southerners had a larger percentage of their capital invested in land and slaves in 1860 than they had had ten years earlier. Some 80 percent of the South's labor force worked in agriculture—the same as sixty years earlier. By contrast, while farming remained the largest single occupation in the North, at 40 percent, the northern economy developed a strong manufacturing and commercial sector whose combined labor force almost equaled that of agriculture by 1860.

A good many southerners preferred to keep it that way. "That the North does our trading and manufacturing mostly is true," wrote an Alabama planter in 1858. "We are willing that they should. Ours is an agricultural people, and God grant that we may continue so. It is the freest, happiest, most independent, and with us, the most powerful condition on earth." By the later 1850s the drive for economic diversification in the South had begun to lose steam. King Cotton reasserted its primacy over King Commerce as cotton output *and* prices continued to rise, suffusing the South in a glow of prosperity. "Our Cotton is the most wonderful talisman on earth," declared a planter. "By its power we are transmuting whatever we choose into whatever we want." In a speech that became famous, James Hammond of South Carolina told his fellow senators in 1858 that "the slaveholding South is now the controlling power of the world. Cotton, rice, tobacco, and naval stores command the world. . . . No power on earth dares to make war on cotton. Cotton *is* king."

Even the commercial conventions in the South seem to have embraced this gospel. In 1854 they merged with a parallel series of planters' conventions, and thereafter the delegates heard as much about cotton as they did about commerce. By the

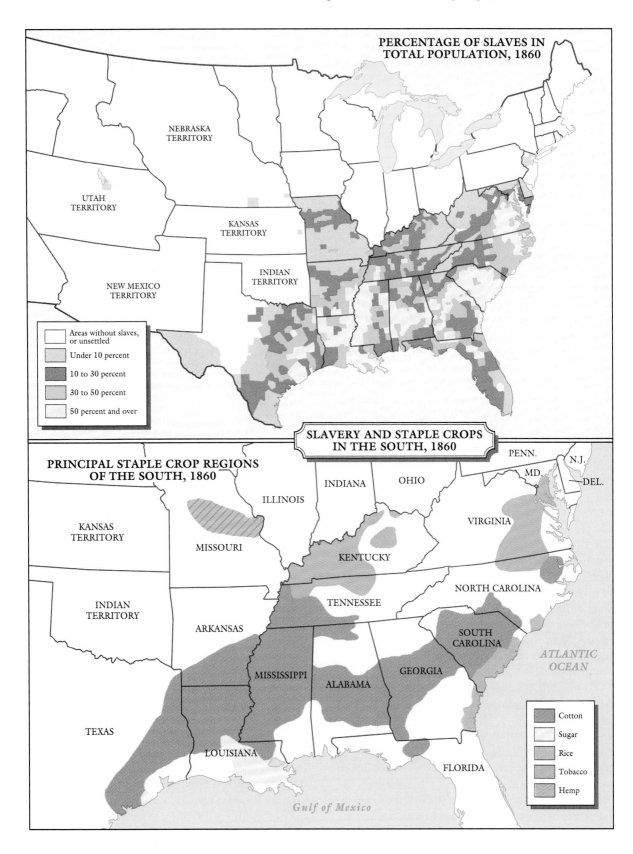

PERCENTAGE OF SLAVES IN
TOTAL POPULATION, 1860

Areas without slaves,
or unsettled

Under 10 percent

10 to 30 percent

30 to 50 percent

50 percent and over

SLAVERY AND STAPLE CROPS
IN THE SOUTH, 1860

PRINCIPAL STAPLE CROP REGIONS
OF THE SOUTH, 1860

Cotton

Sugar

Rice

Tobacco

Hemp

later 1850s, one of the main goals of these conventions was to reopen the African slave trade, prohibited by law since 1808. But many southerners rejected that goal, partly on moral grounds and partly on economic grounds. Older slave states like Virginia, which profited from the sale of slaves to the booming cotton frontier of the Deep South, objected to any goal that would lower the price of their largest export. The conventions also lobbied for the annexation of Cuba, which would bring a productive agricultural economy and 400,000 more slaves into the United States.

As part of their reaffirmation of agrarian values, southerners amplified a major theme of the proslavery argument: black slaves in the South enjoyed a higher standard of living than white "wage slaves" in northern factories. Black slaves never suffered from unemployment or wage cuts; they received free medical care; they were taken care of in old age. Nowhere did one see in the South, said defenders of slavery, such "scenes of beggary, squalid poverty, and wretchedness" as one could find in any northern city.

This argument reached its fullest development in the writings of George Fitzhugh, a Virginia farmer-lawyer whose newspaper articles were gathered into two books published in 1854 and 1857, *Sociology for the South* and *Cannibals All*. Free-labor capitalism, said Fitzhugh, was a war of each against all, a competition in which the strong exploited and starved the weak. Slavery, by contrast, was a paternal institution that guaranteed protection of the workers. "Capital exercises a more perfect compulsion over free laborers than human masters over slaves," wrote Fitzhugh, "for free laborers must at all times work or starve, and slaves are supported whether they work or not. . . . What a glorious thing is slavery, when want, misfortune, old age, debility, and sickness overtake [the slave]." Therefore, "we slaveholders say you [in the North] must recur to domestic slavery . . . the natural and normal condition of the laboring man, white or black."

These ideas reached the floor of the U.S. Senate in James Hammond's "King Cotton" speech of March 4, 1858. "Your whole hireling class of manual laborers and 'operatives,' as you call them, are essentially slaves," Hammond maintained. "In all social systems there must be a class to do the menial duties, to perform the drudgery of life. . . . It constitutes the very mud-sill of society. . . . Fortunately for the South, she found a race adapted to the purpose. . . . We use them for our purpose, and call them slaves. . . . The difference between us is that our slaves are hired for life and well compensated. . . . Yours are hired by the day, not cared for, and scantily compensated."

Labor Conditions in the North

How true was this portrait of poverty and starvation among northern workers? Some northern labor leaders did complain that the "slavery" of the wage system gave "bosses" control over the hours, conditions, and compensation of labor. But the use of this wage-slavery theme in labor rhetoric declined during the prosperous years of the 1850s. And there is no evidence that a northern workingman ever offered to change places with a southern slave. Average per capita income was about 40 percent higher in the North than in the South. Although that average masked large disparities between rich and poor—indeed, between the middle class and the poor—those disparities were no greater, and probably less, in the North than in the South.

To be sure, substantial numbers of recent immigrants, day laborers, and young single women in large northern cities lived on the edge of poverty—or slipped over the edge. Many women seamstresses, shoe binders, milliners, and the like, who worked sixty or seventy hours a week in the outwork system common to several consumer-products industries, earned less than a living wage. Some of them resorted to prostitution in order to survive. The widespread adoption of the newly invented sewing machine in the 1850s did nothing to make life easier for seamstresses; it only lowered their per-unit piece-work wages and forced them to turn out more shirts and trousers than before. Many urban working-class families could not have survived on the wages of an unskilled or semiskilled father. The mother had to take in laundry, boarders, or outwork, and one or more children had to work. Much employment was seasonal or intermittent, leaving workers without wages for long periods of time, especially during the winter. The poverty, overcrowding, and disease in the tenement districts of a few large cities—especially New York City—seemed to lend substance to proslavery claims that slaves were better off.

But they were not—even apart from the psychological contrast between being free and being a slave. New York City's poverty, though highly concentrated and visible, was exceptional. In the North, only one-fourth of the people lived in cities or towns of over 2,500 people. Wages and opportunities

Southern Portraits of Slavery and Free Labor These proslavery illustrations compare happy, well-fed slaves picking cotton with ill-kempt, malnourished poor families crowded into northern slums. Whatever such propaganda did for the consciences of slaveholders, it influenced few in the North.

for workers were greater in the North than anywhere else in the world, including the South. That was why four million immigrants came to the United States from 1845 to 1860 and why seven-eighths of them settled in free states. It was also why twice as many white residents of slave states migrated to free states than vice versa. And it was one reason why northern farmers and workers wanted to keep slaves *and* free blacks out of the territories, where their cheaper labor would undercut white labor.

The Panic of 1857

For several months in the winter of 1857–1858, however, the proslavery picture of misery and discontent among northern workers seemed to ring true. A financial panic in the fall of 1857 brought on what turned out to be a short-lived but intense depression. Causes of the panic stemmed partly from the international economy and partly from domestic overexpansion. When the Crimean War in Europe (1854–1856) cut off Russian grain from the European market, U.S. exports mushroomed to meet the deficiency. Then they slumped in 1857 after the war ended. The sharp rise in interest rates in Britain and France, caused by the war, then spread to U.S. financial markets in 1857 and dried up sources of credit. Meanwhile, the economic boom of the preceding years had caused the American economy to overheat: land prices had soared; railroads had built beyond the capacity of earnings to service their debts; banks had made too many risky loans.

This speculative house of cards came crashing down in September 1857. The failure of one banking house sent a wave of panic through the financial community. Banks suspended specie payments, businesses failed, railroads went bankrupt, construction halted, factories shut down. Hundreds of thousands of workers were laid off, and others went on part-time schedules or took wage cuts as the cold winter months came on. The specter of class conflict such as had occurred during the European revolutions of 1848 haunted the public. Unemployed workers in several northern cities marched in parades carrying banners demanding work or bread. A mob broke into the shops of flour merchants in New York City. On November 10 a crowd gathered in Wall Street and threatened to break into the U.S. customs house and subtreasury vaults, where $20 million was stored. Soldiers and marines had to be called out to disperse the mob.

But the country got through the winter with little violence. No one was killed in the demonstrations — in contrast to the dozens who were killed in ethnic riots a few years earlier and the hundreds killed in the guerrilla war in Kansas. Class conflict turned out to be the least threatening of the various discords that endangered society in the 1850s. Charity and public works helped tide the poor over the winter, and the Panic inspired a vigorous religious revival. Spontaneous prayer meetings arose in many northern cities, bringing together bankers and seamstresses, brokers and streetsweepers. They asked God's forgiveness for the greed and materialism that, in a self-flagellating mood, they believed had caused the Panic.

Perhaps God heeded their prayers. In any event, the depression did not last long. By early 1858 banks had resumed specie payments; the stock market rebounded in the spring; factories reopened; railroad construction resumed; and by the spring of 1859 recovery was complete. The depression had run its course in just eighteen months, compared with the six years (1837–1843) the previous depression had lasted. The modest labor-union activities of the 1850s revived after the depression, as workers in some industries went on strike to bring wages back to pre-Panic levels. In February 1860 the shoemakers of Lynn, Massachusetts, began a strike that became the largest in U.S. history up to that time, eventually involving 20,000 workers in the New England shoe industry. Nevertheless, in spite of the organization of several national unions of skilled workers during the 1850s, less than 1 percent of the labor force was unionized in 1860.

The Panic of 1857 probably intensified sectional hostility more than it did class conflict. The South largely escaped the depression. Its export-driven economy seemed insulated from domestic downturns. After a brief dip, cotton and tobacco prices returned to their high pre-Panic levels and production continued to increase: the cotton crop set new records in 1858 and again in 1859. Southern boasts about the superiority of the region's economic and labor systems took on added bravado. "Who can doubt, that has looked at recent events, that cotton is supreme?" asked Senator James Hammond in March 1858. "When thousands of the strongest commercial houses in the world were coming down," he told

The Panic on Wall Street   This cartoon satirizes the consternation among New York investors and financiers when banks and businesses crashed in the autumn of 1857. Notice the smirk on the faces of two men in the foreground, who undoubtedly stood to benefit from foreclosures on defaulted property. The Panic was no laughing matter, for it led to a short but sharp recession in 1857 and 1858.

Yankees, "when you came to a dead lock, and revolutions were threatened, what brought you up? . . . We have poured in upon you one million six hundred thousand bales of cotton. . . . We have sold it for $65,000,000, and saved you."

Northerners were not grateful for their rescue. In fact, many of them actually blamed the South for causing the depression or for blocking measures to ease its effects in the North. Southern congressmen had provided most of the votes for a new tariff in 1857 that brought duties to their lowest levels in forty years. Some northern Republicans of Whig origin blamed the tariff for causing the Panic and wanted to revise certain duties upward to help hard-hit industries, especially Pennsylvania iron, which were being undercut by cheaper imports. They directed their arguments for tariff revision to workers as much as to manufacturers. "We demand that American laborers shall be protected against the pauper labor of Europe," they declared. Tariff revision would "give employment to thousands of mechanics, artisans, laborers, who have languished for months in unwilling idleness." In each session of Congress from 1858 through 1860, however, a combination of southerners and about half of the northern Democrats blocked Republican efforts to raise tariffs. In the words of one bitter Pennsylvania Republican, this was proof that Congress remained "shamelessly prostituted, in a base subserviency to the Slave Power." Republicans made important gains in the Pennsylvania congressional elections of 1858, setting the stage for a strong bid in a state that they had to carry if they were to win the presidency in 1860.

Three other measures that had been before Congress for several years acquired additional significance after the Panic of 1857. Republicans supported each of them as a means to promote economic health and to aid farmers and workers. But southerners perceived all of them as aimed at helping *northern* farmers and workers and used their power to defeat them. One was a homestead act to grant 160 acres of public land to each farmer who settled and worked the land. Believing that this bill "would prove a most efficient ally for Abolition by encouraging and stimulating the settlement of free farms with Yankees," southern senators defeated it after the House had passed it in 1859. The following year both houses passed it, but Buchanan vetoed it and southern senators blocked an effort to pass it over his veto. A similar fate befell bills for land grants to a transcontinental railroad and for building agricultural and mechanical colleges to educate farmers and workers. In the Old Northwest, where these measures were popular, Republican prospects for 1860 were enhanced by southern and Democratic opposition to them.

THE FREE LABOR IDEOLOGY

By the later 1850s the Republican antislavery argument had become a finely honed philosophy that historians have labeled a "free labor ideology." It held that all work in a free society was honorable, but that slavery degraded the calling of manual labor by equating it with bondage. Slaves worked unwillingly, inefficiently, by compulsion; free men were stimulated to work hard and efficiently by the desire to get ahead, to earn higher wages, to acquire a business of their own. Social mobility was central to the free labor ideology. Free workers who practiced the virtues of industry, thrift, self-discipline, and sobriety could move up the ladder of success. "I am not ashamed to confess," Abraham Lincoln told a working-class audience in 1860, "that twenty-five years ago I was a hired laborer, mauling rails, at work on a flat-boat — just what might happen to any poor man's son!" But in the free states, said Lincoln, a man knows that "he can better his condition. . . . There is no such thing as a freeman being fatally fixed for life, in the condition of a hired laborer. . . . The man who labored for another last year, this year labors for himself, and next year will hire others to labor for him. . . . The *free* labor system opens the way for all — gives hope to all, and energy, and progress, and improvement of condition to all."

Lincoln drew too rosy a picture of northern *reality,* for large numbers of wage laborers in the North

had little hope of advancing beyond that status. Still, he expressed a *belief* that was widely shared in the antebellum North. "There is not a working boy of average ability in the New England states, at least," observed a visiting British industrialist in 1854, "who has not an idea of some mechanical invention or improvement in manufactures, by which, in good time, he hopes to better his condition, or rise to fortune and social distinction." A Cincinnati newspaper commented in 1860 that "of all the multitude of young men engaged in various employments in this city, there is not one who does not desire, and even confidently expect, to become rich." Americans could point to numerous examples of men who had achieved dramatic upward mobility. Lincoln pointed to himself. Belief in this "American dream" was most strongly held by Protestant farmers, skilled workers, and white-collar workers who had some real hope of getting ahead. These men tended to support the Republican Party and its goal of excluding slavery from the territories.

For slavery was the antithesis of upward mobility. Bondsmen were "fatally fixed in that condition for life," as Lincoln noted. Slaves could not hope to move up the ladder of success, nor could free men who lived in a society where they had to compete with slave labor. "Slavery withers and blights all it touches," insisted the Republicans. "It is a curse upon the poor, free, laboring white men." Wherever slavery goes, "there is in substance no middle class. Great wealth or hopeless poverty is the settled condition." In the United States, social mobility often depended on geographic mobility. The main reason so many families moved into new territories was to acquire land, get a new start, move up, get ahead. But if slavery goes into the territories, "the free labor of all the states will not," declared a Republican editor. "If the free labor of the states goes there, the slave labor of the southern states will not, and in a few years the country will teem with an active and energetic population."

Southerners contended that free labor was prone to unrest and strikes. Of course it was, said Lincoln in a speech to a New England audience during the shoemakers' strike of 1860. *"I am glad to see that a system prevails in New England under which laborers CAN strike when they want to* (Cheers). . . . I *like* the system which lets a man quit when he wants to, and wish it might prevail everywhere (Tremendous applause)." Strikes were one of the ways in which free workers could try to improve their prospects. "I want every man," said Lincoln, "to have the chance—and I believe a black man is entitled to it—in which he can better his condition." That was why Republicans were determined to contain the expansion of slavery, for if the South got its way in the territories "free labor that *can* strike will give way to slave labor that *cannot!*"

From the South came a maverick voice that echoed the Republicans. Hinton Rowan Helper considered himself a spokesman for the non-slaveholding whites of the South. Living in upcountry North Carolina, a region of small farms and few slaves, he had brooded for years over slavery's retarding influence on southern development. In 1857 he poured out his bitterness in a book entitled *The Impending Crisis of the South.* Using selective statistics from the 1850 census, he pictured a South mired in economic backwardness, widespread illiteracy, poverty for the masses, and great wealth for the elite. He contrasted this dismal situation with the bustling, prosperous northern economy and its near-universal literacy, neat farms, and progressive institutions. What was the cause of this startling contrast? "Slavery lies at the root of all the shame, poverty, ignorance, tyranny, and imbecility of the South," he wrote. Slavery monopolized the best land, degraded all labor to the level of bond labor, denied schools to the poor, and impoverished all but "the lords of the lash" who "are not only absolute masters of the blacks [but] of all non-slaveholding whites, whose freedom is merely nominal, and whose unparalleled illiteracy and degradation is purposely and fiendishly perpetrated." The remedy? Non-slaveholding whites must organize and use their votes to overthrow "this entire system of oligarchical despotism. . . . Now is the time for them to assert their rights and liberties . . . [and] strike for Freedom in the South."

No southern publisher dared touch this book. So Helper lugged his bulky manuscript to New York City, where a printer brought it out in the summer of 1857. *The Impending Crisis* was virtually banned in the South, and few southern whites read it. But the book made a huge impact in the North. Republicans welcomed it as confirmation of all they had been saying about the evils of slavery and the virtues of free labor. The Republican Party subsidized an abridged edition and distributed thousands of copies as campaign documents. During the late 1850s, a war of books (Helper's *Impending Crisis* vs. Fitzhugh's *Cannibals All*) exacerbated sectional tensions. Fitzhugh's book circulated freely in the North, whereas

A Southern Yeoman Farmer's Home   This modest log cabin on the edge of a small clearing, with the farmer's wife drawing water from a well in the foreground, was typical of non-slaveholders' farms in the southern backcountry. Often stigmatized as "poor whites," many of these families were in fact comfortable by the standards of the day. They did not feel the sense of oppression by the planter class that Hinton Rowan Helper believed they should feel.

the sale or possession of Helper's book was a criminal offense in many parts of the South. The New England Antislavery Society even invited Fitzhugh to New Haven to debate the abolitionist Wendell Phillips. Fitzhugh expressed surprise at his courteous reception in the North, aware that Phillips and other abolitionists could not set foot in the South without peril to their life. Northern spokesmen did not hesitate to point the moral: A free society could tolerate free speech and a free press, while a slave society could not.

Southern Non-Slaveholders

How accurate was Helper's portrayal of southern poor whites degraded by slavery and ready to revolt against it? The touchy response of many southern leaders, and the alarm they expressed about potential Republican efforts to win the support of non-slaveholders, suggested that the planters felt uneasy about that question. After all, slaveholding families constituted less than one-third of the white population in slave states, and the proportion was declining as the price of slaves continued to rise. One reason for the campaign to reopen the African slave trade was a desire to lower slave prices so that more white farmers could afford a slave or two, thereby binding themselves to the system. Open hostility to the planters' domination of society and politics was evident in the mountainous and upcountry regions of the South. These would become areas of Unionist sentiment during the Civil War and of Republican strength after it.

But Helper and the Republicans surely exaggerated the disaffection of most non-slaveholders in the South. Three bonds held them to the system: kinship, economic interest, and race. In the Piedmont and the low country regions of the South, nearly half of the whites belonged to slaveholding families. Many of the rest were cousins or nephews or in-laws of slaveholders in the South's extensive and tightly knit kinship network. Moreover, many young, ambitious non-slaveholders hoped to buy slaves eventually. Some of them *rented* slaves. And because slaves could be made to do the menial, unskilled labor in the South—the "mudsill" tasks, in Senator Hammond's language, or "nigger work" in common parlance—white workers monopolized the more skilled, higher-paying jobs.

Most important, even if they did not own slaves, white people owned the most important asset of all—a white skin. White supremacy was an article of faith in the South (and in most of the North, for that matter). Race was a more important social distinction than class. The southern legal system, politics, and social ideology were based on the concept labeled by historians as "*herrenvolk* democracy" (the equality of all who belonged to the "master race"). Subordination was the Negro's fate, and slavery was the best means of subordination. Emancipation would loose a flood of free blacks on society and would undermine the foundations of white supremacy. Thus, many of the "poor whites" in the South and immigrant workers or poorer farmers in the North supported slavery. And some antislavery spokesmen, including Hinton Rowan Helper and several leading Republicans, urged that emancipation be accompanied by the colonization of the freed slaves abroad.

The *herrenvolk* theme permeated proslavery rhetoric. "With us," said John C. Calhoun in 1848, "the two great divisions of society are not the rich and the poor, but white and black; and all the former,

the poor as well as the rich, belong to the upper class, and are respected and treated as equals." True freedom as Americans understood it required equality of rights and status (though not of wealth or income). Slavery ensured that freedom for all whites by putting a floor under them, a mudsill of black slaves that kept whites from falling into the mud of inequality. "Break down slavery," said a Virginia congressman, "and you would with the same blow destroy the great Democratic principle of equality among men." From the tense period following Bacon's rebellion in 1767 down to the Civil War, the existence of black slavery united all classes of whites in their equality of whiteness. As the *Richmond Enquirer* put it in 1856, "freedom is not possible without slavery."

THE LINCOLN–DOUGLAS DEBATES

Abraham Lincoln believed the opposite. For him, slavery and freedom were incompatible; the one must die that the other might live. This became the central theme of a memorable series of debates between Lincoln and Douglas in 1858, which turned out to be a dress rehearsal for the presidential election of 1860.

The debates were arranged after Lincoln was nominated to oppose Douglas's reelection to the Senate. State legislatures elected U.S. senators at that time, so the campaign was technically for the election of the Illinois legislature. But the real issue was the senatorship, and Douglas's prominence gave the contest national significance. Lincoln launched his bid with what became his most notable speech until he went to Gettysburg five years later. " 'A house divided against itself cannot stand,' " he said, quoting the words of Jesus recorded in the Gospel of Mark. "I believe this government cannot endure, permanently half *slave* and half *free*. . . . It will become *all* one thing, or *all* the other." Under the Dred Scott decision, which Douglas had endorsed, slavery was legal in all the territories. And what, asked Lincoln, would prevent the Supreme Court, using the same reasoning that had led it to interpret the Constitution as protecting property in slaves, from legalizing slavery in free states? (A case based on this question was then before the New York courts.) The advocates of slavery, charged Lincoln, were trying to "push it forward, till it shall become lawful in *all* the States."

The Lincoln–Douglas Debates   This painting puts Lincoln in the center of the picture because the artist, with hindsight, knew that Lincoln had gone on to become the country's greatest president during its greatest crisis; while Douglas, sitting to Lincoln's right, fell by the wayside and died in June 1861. Note several women in the crowd; though women could not then vote, many of them avidly followed political events.

But Republicans intended to keep slavery out of the territories, thus stopping its growth and placing it "where the public mind shall rest in the belief that it is in the course of ultimate extinction."

The seven open-air debates between Douglas and Lincoln focused almost entirely on the issue of slavery. Why could the country not continue to exist half slave and half free as it had for seventy years? Douglas asked. Lincoln's talk about the "ultimate extinction" of slavery would provoke the South to secession. Douglas professed himself no friend of slavery — he did not want it in Illinois — but if people in the southern states or in the territories wanted it, they had the right to have it. Douglas did not want black people — either slave *or* free — in Illinois. But Lincoln's policy would not only free the slaves but would grant them equality. "Are you in favor of conferring upon the negro the rights and privileges of citizenship?" Douglas called out to supporters in the crowd. "No, no!" they shouted back.

> Do you desire to strike out of our State Constitution that clause which keeps slaves and free negroes out of the State . . . in order that when Missouri abolishes slavery she can send one hundred thousand emancipated slaves into Illinois, to become citizens and voters on an equality with

yourselves? ("Never," "no.") . . . If you desire to allow them to come into the State and settle with the white man, if you desire to vote . . . then support Mr. Lincoln and the Black Republican party, who are in favor of the citizenship of the negro. ("Never, never.")

Douglas's demagoguery put Lincoln on the defensive. He responded with cautious denials that he favored "social and political equality" of the races. The "ultimate extinction" of slavery might take a century. It would require the voluntary cooperation of the South and would perhaps be contingent on the emigration of some freed slaves from the country. But come what may, freedom must prevail. Americans must reaffirm the principles of the founding fathers. A black person was

> entitled to all the natural rights enumerated in the Declaration of Independence, the right to life, liberty and the pursuit of happiness. (Loud cheers.) I hold that he is as much entitled to these as the white man. I agree with Judge Douglas he is not my equal in many respects. . . . But in the right to eat the bread, without leave of anybody else, which his own hand earns, *he is my equal and the equal of Judge Douglas, and the equal of every living man.* (Great applause.)

Lincoln deplored Douglas's "care not" attitude whether slavery was voted up or down. He *"looks to no end of the institution of slavery,"* said Lincoln. Indeed, by endorsing the Dred Scott decision he looks to its *"perpetuity and nationalization."* Douglas was thus "eradicating the light of reason and liberty in this American people." That was the real issue in the election, insisted Lincoln.

> That is the issue that will continue in this country when these poor tongues of Judge Douglas and myself shall be silent. It is the eternal struggle between these two principles—right and wrong—throughout the world. . . . The one is the common right of humanity and the other the divine right of kings. . . . No matter in what shape it comes, whether from a king who seeks to bestride the people of his own nation and live by the fruit of their labor, or from one race of men as an apology for enslaving another race, it is the same tyrannical principle.

The popular vote for Republican and Democratic state legislators in Illinois was virtually even in 1858. But because apportionment favored the Democrats, they won a majority of seats and reelected Douglas. But Lincoln was the ultimate victor, for his performance in the debates lifted him from political obscurity, while Douglas further alienated southern Democrats. In the debate at Freeport, Lincoln had asked Douglas how he reconciled his support for the Dred Scott decision with his policy of popular sovereignty, which supposedly gave residents of a territory the power to vote slavery down. Douglas replied that even though the Court had legalized slavery in the territories, the enforcement of that right would depend on the people who lived there. This was a popular answer in the North. But it gave added impetus to southern demands for congressional passage of a federal slave code in territories like Kansas, where the Free-Soil majority had by 1859 made slavery virtually null. In the next two sessions of Congress after the 1858 elections, southern Democrats, led by Jefferson Davis, tried to pass a federal slave code for all territories. Douglas and northern Democrats joined with Republicans to defeat it. Consequently, southern hostility toward Douglas mounted as the presidential election of 1860 approached.

The 1859–1860 session of Congress was particularly contentious. Once again a fight over the speakership of the House set the tone. Republicans had made important gains in the 1858 elections and had won a plurality of House seats. But without a majority they could not elect a Speaker without the support of a few border-state representatives from the American Party. The problem was that the Republican candidate for Speaker was John Sherman, who, along with sixty-seven other congressmen, had signed an endorsement of Hinton Rowan Helper's *The Impending Crisis of the South* (without, Sherman later admitted, having read it). This was a red flag to southerners, even to ex-Whigs from the border states, who refused to vote for Sherman. Through forty-three ballots and two months, the House remained deadlocked. Tensions escalated, and members came armed to the floor. One observer commented that "the only persons who do not have a revolver and knife are those who have two revolvers."

As usual, southerners threatened to secede if a Black Republican became Speaker. Several of them wanted a shootout on the floor of Congress. We "are willing to fight the question out," wrote one, "and to settle it right there." The governor of South Carolina told one of his state's congressmen: "If . . . you upon consultation decide to make the issue of force in Washington, write or telegraph me, and I will have a regiment in or near Washington in the shortest possible time." To avert a crisis, Sherman withdrew his candidacy and the House finally elected a conservative ex-Whig as Speaker on the forty-fourth ballot.

JOHN BROWN AT HARPERS FERRY

Southern tempers were frayed even at the start of this session of Congress because of what had happened at Harpers Ferry, Virginia, the October before. After his exploits in Kansas, John Brown had disappeared from public view. But he had not been idle. Like the Old Testament warriors he admired and resembled, Brown intended to carry his war against slavery into Babylon—the South. His favorite New Testament passage was Hebrews 9:22: "Without shedding of blood there is no remission of sin." Brown worked up a plan to capture the federal arsenal at Harpers Ferry, arm slaves with the muskets he seized there, and move southward along the Appalachian Mountains attracting more slaves to his army along the way until the "whole accursed system of bondage" collapsed.

Brown recruited five black men and seventeen whites, including three of his sons, for this reckless scheme. He also had the secret support of a half-dozen Massachusetts and New York abolitionists who had helped him raise funds. On the night of October 16, 1859, Brown led his men across the Po-

John Brown   This modern mural of John Brown is full of symbolism. Holding an open Bible, Brown bestrides the earth like an Old Testament prophet while dead Union and Confederate soldiers lie at his feet. Other soldiers clash behind him, slaves struggle to break free, and God's wrath at a sinful nation sends a destructive tornado to earth in the background.

tomac and occupied the sleeping town of Harpers Ferry without resistance. Few slaves flocked to his banner, but the next day state militia units poured into town and drove Brown's band into the fire-engine house. At dawn on October 18 a company of U.S. marines commanded by Colonel Robert E. Lee and Lieutenant J. E. B. Stuart stormed the engine house and captured the surviving members of Brown's party. Four townsmen, one marine, and ten of Brown's men (including two of his sons) were killed; not a single slave was liberated.

John Brown's raid lasted thirty-six hours; its repercussions resounded for years. Brown and six of his followers were promptly tried by the state of Virginia, convicted, and hanged. But this scarcely ended matters. The raid sent a wave of revulsion and alarm through the South. Though no slaves had risen in revolt, it revived the fears of slave insurrection that were never far beneath the surface of southern consciousness. Exaggerated reports of Brown's network of abolitionist supporters seemed to confirm southern suspicions that a widespread northern conspiracy was afoot, determined to destroy their society. Although Republican leaders denied any connection with Brown and disavowed his actions, few

southerners were in a mood to believe them. Had not Lincoln talked of the "extinction" of slavery? And had not William H. Seward, who was expected to be the next Republican presidential nominee, given a campaign speech in 1858 in which he predicted an "irrepressible conflict" between the free and slave societies?

Many northerners, impressed by Brown's dignified bearing and eloquence during his trial, considered him a martyr to freedom. "I see a book kissed, which I suppose to be the Bible," Brown said in his final statement to the court,

> which teaches me that all things whatsoever I would that men should do to me, I should do even so to them. It teaches me, further, to remember them that are in bonds as bound with them. I endeavored to act up to that instruction. . . . Now, if it is deemed necessary that I should forfeit my life for the furtherance of the ends of justice, and mingle my blood further with the blood of my children and with the blood of millions in this slave country whose rights are disregarded by wicked, cruel, and unjust enactments, I say, let it be done.

On the day of Brown's execution, bells tolled in hundreds of northern towns, guns fired salutes, ministers preached sermons of commemoration. "The death of no man in America has ever produced so profound a sensation," commented one northerner. "I have seen nothing like it," said another. John Brown's *act* was wrong, said a leading Massachusetts Republican, but "John Brown himself is right." Ralph Waldo Emerson declared that Brown had made "the gallows as glorious as the cross."

This outpouring of northern sympathy for Brown shocked and enraged southerners and weakened the already frayed threads of the Union. "The Harper's Ferry invasion has advanced the cause of disunion more than any event that has happened since the formation of the government," observed a Richmond newspaper. "I have always been a fervid Union man," wrote a North Carolinian, but "the endorsement of the Harper's Ferry outrage . . . has shaken my fidelity. . . . I am willing to take the chances of every possible evil that may arise from disunion, sooner than submit any longer to Northern insolence."

Something approaching a reign of terror now descended on the South. Every Yankee seemed to be another John Brown; every slave who acted suspiciously seemed to be an insurrectionist. Hundreds of northerners were run out of the South in 1860, some wearing a coat of tar and feathers. Several "incendiaries," both white and black, were lynched. "Defend yourselves!" Senator Robert Toombs cried out to the southern people. "The enemy is at your door . . . meet him at the doorsill, and drive him from the temple of liberty, or pull down its pillars and involve him in a common ruin."

It was in this mood that the South prepared for the most fateful presidential election in U.S. history.

SUGGESTED READING

For general studies of the mounting sectional conflict during the 1850s, see David M. Potter, *The Impending Crisis 1848–1861* (1976); Allan Nevins, *Ordeal of the Union,* 2 vols. (1947) and *The Emergence of Lincoln,* 2 vols. (1950); Avery Craven, *The Coming of the Civil War,* 2nd ed. (1957); Michael F. Holt, *The Political Crisis of the 1850s* (1978); and James M. McPherson, *Battle Cry of Freedom: The Civil War Era* (1988).

The Kansas–Nebraska Act and the ensuing conflict in Kansas are treated in Gerald W. Wolff, *The Kansas–Nebraska Bill: Party, Section, and the Coming of the Civil War* (1977); James A. Rawley, *Race and Politics: "Bleeding Kansas" and the Coming of the Civil War* (1969); and Alice Nichols, *Bleeding Kansas* (1954). Biographies of key figures in this controversy include Robert W. Johannsen, *Stephen A. Douglas* (1973) and

Larry Gara, *The Presidency of Franklin Pierce* (1991).

The foregoing books contain a great deal of material about the relationship between the Kansas conflict and the origins of the Republican Party. For the crosscutting issue of nativism and the Know Nothings, see especially William E. Gienapp, *The Origins of the Republican Party, 1852–1856* (1987) and Tyler Anbinder, *Nativism and Politics: The Know Nothing Party in the Northern United States* (1992). Other important studies of immigration and the nativist response include Oscar Handlin, *Boston's Immigrants* (1941); Robert Ernst, *Immigrant Life in New York City, 1825–1863* (1949); Jay P. Dolan, *The Immigrant Church: New York's Irish and German Catholics 1815–1865* (1975); and Dale T. Knobel, *Paddy and the Republic: Ethnicity and Nationality in Antebellum America* (1985). The best general narrative of nativism is still Ray Allen Billington, *The Protestant Crusade 1800–1861* (1938). See also Ira M. Leonard and Robert D. Parmet, *American Nativism, 1830–1860* (1971).

Three of the numerous state studies of the political transformation in northern states are Mark L. Berger, *The Revolution in the New York Party Systems, 1840–1860* (1973); Steven E. Maizlish, *The Triumph of Sectionalism: The Transformation of Ohio Politics, 1844–1856* (1983); and Dale Baum, *The Civil War Party System: The Case of Massachusetts, 1848–1876* (1984). The Kansas–Nebraska Act brought Abraham Lincoln back into the political arena; for a fine study of Lincoln's role in the rise of the Republican Party, see Don E. Fehrenbacher, *Prelude to Greatness: Lincoln in the 1850's* (1962). A somewhat different interpretation is provided by Robert W. Johannsen, *Lincoln, the South, and Slavery* (1991). Two other valuable biographical studies are David Donald, *Charles Sumner and the Coming of the Civil War* (1960) and Frederick Blue, *Salmon P. Chase: A Life in Politics* (1987).

The Southern response to these events in the North is chronicled in Avery Craven, *The Growth of Southern Nationalism 1848–1861* (1953); John McCardell, *The Idea of a Southern Nation* (1979); William L. Barney, *The Road to Secession: A New Perspective on the Old South* (1972); and William J. Cooper, Jr., *The South and the Politics of Slavery 1828–1856* (1978). The widening North–South fissure in the Democratic Party is treated in Philip S. Klein, *President James Buchanan* (1962); Elbert B. Smith, *The Presidency of James Buchanan* (1975); and Roy F. Nichols, *The Disruption of American Democracy* (1948). The year 1857 witnessed a convergence of many of these events; for a stimulating book that pulls together the threads of that year of crisis, see Kenneth M. Stampp, *America in 1877: A Nation on the Brink* (1990). Another account of an important issue during this period is Mark W. Summers, *The Plundering Generation: Corruption and the Crisis of the Union, 1849–1861* (1987).

For economic developments during this era, a still valuable classic is George Rogers Taylor, *The Transportation Revolution, 1815–1860* (1951). Agriculture is treated in Paul W. Gates, *The Farmer's Age: Agriculture, 1815–1860* (1960). Important studies of railroads include Albert Fishlow, *American Railroads and the Transformation of the Antebellum Economy* (1965) and John F. Stover, *Iron Road to the West: American Railroads in the 1850s* (1978). For the "American System of Manufactures," see Nathan Rosenberg, ed., *The American System of Manufactures* (1969); David A. Hounshell, *From the American System to Mass Production, 1800–1932* (1983); and Donald R. Hoke, *Ingenious Yankees: The Rise of the American System of Manufactures in the Private Sector* (1990). For the relationship of education to social and economic change, see Frederick M. Binder, *The Age of the Common School 1830–1865* (1974); Lee Soltow and Edward Stevens, *The Rise of Literacy and the Common School in the United States* (1981); Carl F. Kaestle, *Pillars of the Republic: Common Schooling and American Society, 1780–1860* (1983); and Carl F. Kaestle and Maris A. Vinovskis, *Education and Social Change in Nineteenth-Century Massachusetts* (1980).

For the southern economy in these years, see Gavin Wright, *The Political Economy of the Cotton South* (1978) and Fred Bateman and Thomas Weiss, *A Deplorable Scarcity: The Failure of Industrialization in the Slave Economy* (1981). Herbert Wender, *Southern Commercial Conventions 1837–1859* (1930) chronicles the efforts of southerners to promote economic diversification. Other important studies include Harold D. Woodman, *King Cotton and His Retainers: Financing and Marketing the Cotton Crop of the South* (1968) and Laurence Shore, *Southern Capitalists: The Ideological Leadership of an Elite, 1832–1885* (1986). The Panic of 1857 and its sectional and political consequences are treated in James L. Huston, *The Panic of 1857 and the Coming of the Civil War* (1987).

The best study of the Republican free-labor ideology is Eric Foner, *Free Soil, Free Labor, Free Men: The Ideology of the Republican Party before the Civil War* (1970). Howard Floan, *The South in Northern Eyes 1831–1861* (1953) summarizes various northern images of the South. Still the fullest account of the southern defense of slavery and its way of life is William S. Jenkins, *Pro-Slavery Thought in the Old South* (1935), which should be supplemented by Drew Gilpin Faust, ed., *The Ideology of Slavery: Proslavery Thought in the Antebellum South* (1981).

The numerous studies of white social structure and nonslaveholders in the South include Frank L. Owsley, *Plain Folk of the Old South* (1949); Bruce Collins, *White Society in the Antebellum South* (1985); Steven Hahn, *The Roots of Southern Populism: Yeoman Farmers and the Transformation of the Georgia Upcountry, 1850–1890* (1983); Paul D. Escott, *Many Excellent People: Power and Privilege in North Carolina, 1850–1900* (1985); J. William Harris, *Plain Folk and Gentry in a Slave Society: White Liberty and Black Slavery in Augusta's Hinterlands* (1985); and Bill Cecil-Fronsman, *Common Whites: Class and Culture in Antebellum North Carolina* (1992).

The best single study of the Dred Scott case is Don E. Fehrenbacher, *The Dred Scott Case: Its Significance in American Law and Politics* (1978), which was published in an abridged version with the title *Slavery, Law, and Politics: The Dred Scott Case in Historical Perspective* (1981). There are several editions of the Lincoln–Douglas debates; the fullest is Paul M. Angle, ed., *Created Equal? The Complete Lincoln–Douglas Debates of 1858* (1958). For analyses of the debates, see Harry F. Jaffa, *Crisis of the House Divided* (1959) and David Zarefsky, *Lincoln, Douglas and Slavery in the Crucible of Public Debate* (1990). See also Damon Wells, *Stephen Douglas: The Last Years, 1857–1861* (1971) and William E. Baringer, *Lincoln's Rise to Power* (1937). For John Brown's raid on Harpers Ferry, see Stephen B. Oates, *To Purge This Land with Blood: A Biography of John Brown* (1970); Jeffrey S. Rossback, *Ambivalent Conspirators: John Brown, the Secret Six, and a Theory of Slave Violence* (1982); and Benjamin Quarles, *Allies for Freedom: Blacks and John Brown* (1974).

Chapter 16

Secession and Civil War, 1860–1862

T he new Constitution [of the Confederate States] has put at rest forever all the agitating questions relating to our peculiar institution — African slavery as it exists among us — the proper status of the negro in our form of civilization. This was the immediate cause of the late rupture and present revolution. [Thomas] Jefferson, in his forecast, had anticipated this, as the 'rock upon which the old Union would split.' He was right . . . But whether he fully comprehended the great truth upon which that rock stood and stands, may be doubted. The prevailing ideas entertained by him and most of the leading statesmen at the time of the formation of the old Constitution were, that the enslavement of the African was in violation of the laws of nature; that it was wrong in principle, socially, morally, and politically. It was an evil they knew not well how to deal with; but the general opinion of the men of that day was, that, somehow or other, in the order of Providence, the institution would be evanescent and pass away . . . Those ideas, however, were fundamentally wrong. . . . Our new Government is founded upon exactly the opposite ideas; its foundations are laid, its cornerstone rests, upon the great truth that the negro is not equal to the white man; that slavery, subordination to the superior race, is his natural and moral condition. This, our new Government, is the first, in the history of the world, based upon this great physical, philosophical, and moral truth.

From a speech by Alexander H. Stephens, Vice President of the Confederate States of America, March 21, 1861

As the year 1860 began, the Democratic party was one of the few national institutions left in the country. The Methodists and the Baptists had split into northern and southern churches in the 1840s over the issue of slavery; several voluntary associations had done the same; the Whig Party and the nativist American Party had been shattered by sectional antagonism in the mid-1850s. Finally, even the Democratic Party, at its national convention in Charleston, South Carolina, in April 1860, split into northern and southern camps, foreshadowing the split of the country before the year was out.

THE ELECTION OF 1860

A hotbed of southern rights radicalism, Charleston turned out to be the worst possible place for a national convention. Northern delegates felt like unwanted outsiders. Sectional confrontations took place inside the convention hall and on the streets. Since 1836 the Democratic Party had required a two-thirds majority of delegates for a presidential nomination, a rule that gave southerners veto power if they voted together. Although Stephen A. Douglas had the backing of a simple majority of the delegates, southern Democrats were determined to deny him the nomination. His opposition to the Lecompton constitution in Kansas and to a federal slave code for the territories had convinced proslavery southerners that they would be unable to control a Douglas administration.

The first test came in the debate on the platform. Southern delegates insisted on a plank favoring a federal slave code for the territories. Douglas could not run on a platform that contained such a plank; and if the party adopted it, Democrats were sure to lose every northern state. By a slim majority, the convention rejected the plank and reaffirmed the 1856 platform endorsing popular sovereignty. By prearrangement, fifty southern delegates, led by William L. Yancey of Alabama, thereupon walked

out of the convention. Even after they left, Douglas still could not muster a two-thirds majority, nor could any other candidate. After fifty-seven futile ballots, the convention adjourned to meet in Baltimore six weeks later to try again.

But the party was so badly shattered that it could not be put back together. That pleased some proslavery radicals, who were convinced that the South would never be secure in a nation dominated by a northern majority. The election of a "Black Republican" president, they felt, would provide the shock necessary to mobilize a southern majority for secession. Two of the most prominent secessionists were Yancey and Edmund Ruffin, who had been talking about a plan to split the party since 1858. In that year, they founded the League of United Southerners to "fire the Southern heart . . . and at the proper moment, by one organized, concerted action, we can precipitate the Cotton States into a revolution." Having walked out of the first Democratic convention, the eloquent Yancey inspired a huge crowd in Charleston's moonlit courthouse square to give

The Political Quadrille   This cartoon depicts the four presidential candidates in 1860. Clockwise from the upper left are John C. Breckinridge, Southern Rights Democrat; Abraham Lincoln, Republican; John Bell, Constitutional Union; and Stephen A. Douglas, Democrat. All are dancing to the tune played by Dred Scott, symbolizing the importance of the slavery issue in this campaign. Each candidate's partner represents a political liability: for example, Breckinridge's partner is the disunionist William L. Yancey wearing a devil's horns, while Lincoln's partner is a black woman who supposedly gives color to Democratic accusations that Republicans believed in miscegenation.

three cheers "for an Independent Southern Republic" with his concluding words: "Perhaps even now, the pen of the historian is nibbed to write the story of a new revolution."

The convention in Baltimore reprised the first act at Charleston. This time, an even larger number of southern delegates walked out. They formed their own Southern Rights Democratic party and nominated John C. Breckinridge of Kentucky (the incumbent vice president) for president on a slave-code platform. When regular Democrats glumly nominated Douglas, the stage was set for what would become a four-party election. A coalition of former southern Whigs, who could not bring themselves to vote Democratic, and northern Whigs, who considered the Republican Party too radical, formed the Constitutional Union Party, which nominated John Bell of Tennessee for president. Bell had no chance of winning; the party's purpose was to exercise a conservative influence on a campaign that threatened to polarize the country.

From the moment the Democratic Party broke apart, it became clear that 1860 could be the year when the dynamic young Republican Party elected its first president. The Republicans could expect no electoral votes from the fifteen slave states. But in 1856 they had won all but five northern states, and they needed only two or three of those five to win the presidency. The crucial states were Pennsylvania, Illinois, and Indiana, states in which Republicans had been gaining strength since 1856. But despite the Democrats' break-up, Douglas might still carry them and throw the presidential election into the House (which had last occurred in 1824), where anything might happen. Thus the Republicans had to carry at least two of the swing states to win.

As the Republican delegates poured into Chicago for their convention in a huge building nicknamed "the Wigwam" because of its shape, their leading presidential prospect was William H. Seward of New York. An experienced politician who had served as governor and senator, Seward was by all odds the most prominent Republican. But in his long career he had made a number of enemies. His anti-nativist policies had alienated some former members of the American Party, whose support would be needed to carry Pennsylvania. His "Higher Law" speech against the Compromise of 1850 and his "Irrepressible Conflict" speech in 1858, predicting the ultimate overthrow of slavery, had given him a reputation for

radicalism that might drive away voters in the vital swing states of the lower North.

Several of the delegates, uneasy about that reputation, staged a stop-Seward movement. The candidate who then came to the fore was Abraham Lincoln. Though he too had opposed nativism, he had done so less noisily than Seward. His "House Divided" speech had made essentially the same point as Seward's "Irrepressible Conflict" speech, but his reputation was still that of a more moderate man. He was from one of the lower-North states where the election would be close, and his rise from a poor farm boy and rail-splitter to successful lawyer and political leader fitted perfectly the free-labor theme of social mobility extolled by the Republican Party. By picking up second-choice votes from states that switched from their favorite sons, Lincoln overtook Seward and won the nomination on the third ballot. Seward accepted the outcome gracefully, and the Republicans headed into the campaign as a united, confident party.

Their confidence stemmed in part from their platform, which appealed to many groups in the North. Its main plank pledged exclusion of slavery from the territories. Other planks called for a higher tariff (especially popular in Pennsylvania), a homestead act (popular in the Northwest), and federal aid for construction of a transcontinental railroad and for improvement of river navigation. This was a program designed for a future in which the house divided would become a free-labor society modeled on northern capitalism. Its blend of idealism and materialism proved especially attractive to young people; a large majority of first-time voters in the North, who had come of age since 1856, voted Republican in 1860. Thousands of them joined "Wide-Awake" clubs and marched in huge torchlight parades through the cities of the North.

Militant enthusiasm in the North was matched by fear and rage in the South. Few southerners could see any difference between Lincoln and Seward—or for that matter between Lincoln and William Lloyd Garrison. They were all "Black Republicans" and "Abolitionists." Had not Lincoln branded slavery a moral, social, and political evil? Had he not said that the Declaration of Independence applied to blacks as well as whites? Had he not expressed a hope that excluding slavery from the territories would put it on the road to ultimate extinction? To southerners, the Republican pledge not to interfere with slavery in the states was meaningless.

Wide-Awake Parade in New York, October 5, 1860   The Wide-Awakes were an organization of young Republicans who roused political enthusiasm by marching in huge torchlight parades during the political campaign of 1860. A year later, many of these same men would march down the same streets in army uniforms carrying rifles instead of torches on their way to the front.

A Republican victory in the presidential election would put an end to the South's political control of its destiny. From 1789 to 1860, southerners (all of them slaveholders) had been president of the United States two-thirds of the time. Two-thirds of the Speakers of the House and presidents pro tem of the Senate had been southerners. Southern justices had been a majority on the Supreme Court since 1791. Lincoln's election would mark an irreversible turning away from this southern ascendancy. Even southern moderates warned that the South could not remain in the Union if Lincoln won. "This Government and Black Republicanism cannot live together," said one of them. "At no period of the world's history have four thousand millions of property [i.e., the slaveowners] debated whether it ought to submit to the rule of an enemy." And what about the three-quarters of southern whites who did not belong to slaveholding families? Lincoln's election, warned an Alabama secessionist, would show that "the North [means] to free the negroes and force amalgamation between them and the children of the poor men of the South." If Georgia remained in a Union "ruled by Lincoln and his crew," a secessionist in that state told non-slaveholders, "in TEN years or less our CHILDREN will be the *slaves* of negroes."

Most of the southern whites voted for Breckinridge, who carried eleven slave states. Bell won the more conservative upper-South states of Virginia, Kentucky, and Tennessee. Missouri went to Douglas—the only state he carried, though he came in second in the popular vote. While Lincoln received less than 40 percent of the popular vote, he won every free state and swept the presidency by a substantial margin in the electoral college (three of New Jersey's seven electoral votes went to Douglas).

THE LOWER SOUTH SECEDES

Lincoln's victory provided the shock that southern fire-eaters had been hoping for. The tension that had been building up for years suddenly exploded like a string of firecrackers, as seven states seceded one after another. South Carolina was the first to go. Its legislature ordered an election of delegates to a convention to consider withdrawing from the United States. According to the theory of secession, when each state ratified the Constitution and joined the Union in 1787–1788 or later, it authorized the national government to act as its agent in the exercise of certain functions of sovereignty, but the states had

Table 16-1

Voting in the 1860 Election

	All States		Free States (18)		Slave States (15)	
	Popular Votes	*Electoral Votes*	*Popular Votes*	*Electoral Votes*	*Popular Votes*	*Electoral Votes*
Lincoln	1,864,735	180	1,838,347	180	26,388	0
Opposition to Lincoln	2,821,157	123	1,572,637	3	1,248,520	120
"Fusion" Tickets	595,846	—	580,426	—	15,420	—
Douglas	979,425	12	815,857	3	163,568	9
Breckinridge	669,472	72	99,381	0	570,091	72
Bell	576,414	39	76,973	0	499,441	39

never given away their fundamental underlying sovereignty itself. Any state, then, by the act of its own convention, could withdraw from its "compact" with the other states and reassert its individual sovereignty. That is what the South Carolina convention did, on December 20, 1860, by a vote of 169 to 0.

The outcome was closer in other lower-South states. Unconditional unionism was rare, but many conservatives and former Whigs, including Alexander H. Stephens of Georgia, shrank from the drastic step of secession. In each of the next six states to secede, some delegates tried to delay matters with vague proposals for "cooperation" among all southern states, or even with proposals to wait until after Lincoln's inauguration on March 4, 1861, to see what course he would pursue. But those minority factions were overridden by those who favored immediate secession. One after another the conventions followed the example of South Carolina and voted to take their states out of the Union: Mississippi on January 9, 1861, Florida on the 10th, Alabama on the 11th, Georgia on the 19th, Louisiana on the 26th, and Texas on February 1. In those six states as a whole, 20 percent of the delegates voted against secession. But most of these, including Stephens, "went with their states" after the final votes had been tallied. Delegates from the seven seceding states met in Montgomery, Alabama, in February to create a new nation to be called the Confederate States of America.

Most northerners considered secession unconstitutional and treasonable. Even President Buchanan, previously pro-southern in his policies, denied the right of secession. In his final annual message to Congress, on December 3, 1860, he had insisted that the Union was not "a mere voluntary association of States, to be dissolved at pleasure by any one of the contracting parties." Americans had adopted the Constitution in 1789 to form "a more perfect Union" than the one existing under the Articles of Confederation, which had stated that "the Union shall be perpetual." If secession was consummated, Buchanan warned, it would create a disastrous precedent that would make the United States government

> a rope of sand. . . . Our thirty-three States may resolve themselves into as many petty, jarring, and hostile republics. . . . By such a dread catastrophe the hopes of the friends of freedom throughout the world would be destroyed. . . . Our example for more than eighty years would not only be lost, but it would be quoted as proof that man is unfit for self-government.

European monarchists and conservatives were already expressing smug satisfaction at "the great smashup" of the republic in North America. They predicted that other disaffected minorities would also secede and that the United States would ultimately collapse into anarchy and revolution. That was precisely what northern and even some upper-South Unionists feared. "The doctrine of secession is anarchy," declared a Cincinnati newspaper. "If any minority have the right to break up the Government at pleasure, because they have not had their way, there is an end of all government." Lincoln denied that the states had ever possessed independent

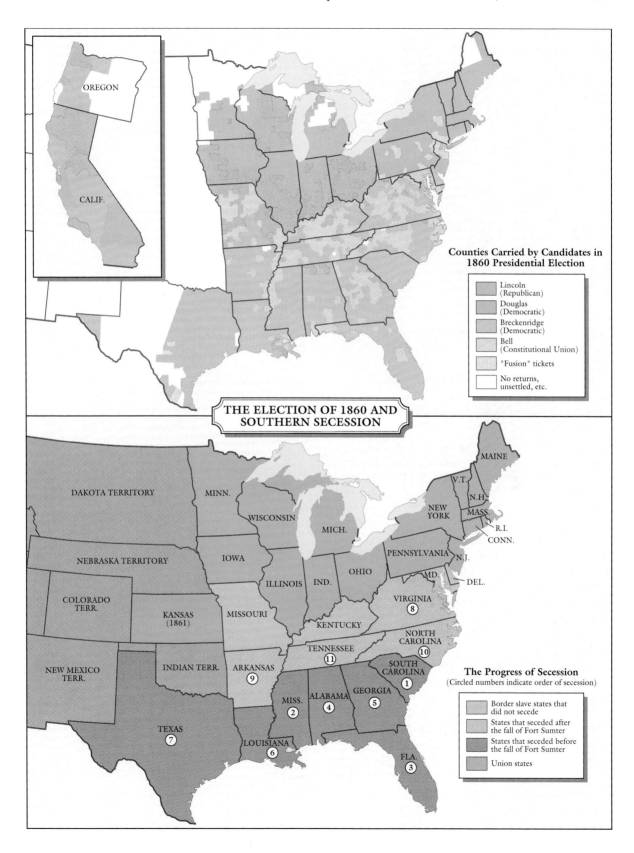

OREGON

CALIF.

Counties Carried by Candidates in 1860 Presidential Election

	Lincoln (Republican)
	Douglas (Democratic)
	Breckenridge (Democratic)
	Bell (Constitutional Union)
	"Fusion" tickets
	No returns, unsettled, etc.

THE ELECTION OF 1860 AND SOUTHERN SECESSION

DAKOTA TERRITORY

MINN.

WISCONSIN

MICH.

MAINE

V.T.

N.H.

NEW YORK

MASS.

R.I.

CONN.

NEBRASKA TERRITORY

IOWA

ILLINOIS

IND.

OHIO

PENNSYLVANIA

N.J.

MD.

DEL.

COLORADO TERR.

KANSAS (1861)

MISSOURI

KENTUCKY

VIRGINIA ⑧

NEW MEXICO TERR.

INDIAN TERR.

ARKANSAS ⑨

TENNESSEE ⑪

NORTH CAROLINA ⑩

SOUTH CAROLINA ①

TEXAS ⑦

MISS. ②

ALABAMA ④

GEORGIA ⑤

LOUISIANA ⑥

FLA. ③

The Progress of Secession
(Circled numbers indicate order of secession)

	Border slave states that did not secede
	States that seceded after the fall of Fort Sumter
	States that seceded before the fall of Fort Sumter
	Union states

Banner of the South Carolina Secession Convention   With a palmetto tree as a centerpiece and a snake reminiscent of the American Revolution's "Don't Tread on Me" slogan, the South Carolina secession convention in 1860 looked forward to a grand new southern republic composed of all fifteen slave states and built on the ruins of the old Union. Note the large South Carolina keystone of the arch and the stones of free states lying cracked and broken on the ground.

withdrew their allegiance from George III and set up for themselves . . . Secessionists?"

Northerners could scarcely deny the right of revolution: they too were heirs of 1776. But "the right of revolution, is never a legal right," said Lincoln. "At most, it is but a moral right, when exercised for a morally justifiable cause. When exercised without such a cause revolution is no right, but simply a wicked exercise of physical power." The South, in Lincoln's view, had no morally justifiable cause. In fact, the event that had precipitated secession was his own election by a constitutional majority. For southerners to cast themselves in the mold of 1776 was "a libel upon the whole character and conduct" of the founding fathers, said the antislavery poet and journalist William Cullen Bryant. They rebelled "to establish the rights of man . . . and principles of universal liberty," while southerners in 1861 were rebelling to protect "a domestic despotism. . . . Their motto is not liberty, but slavery."

Compromise Proposals

Bryant conveniently overlooked the fact that slavery had existed in most parts of the republic founded by the revolutionaries of 1776. In any event, most northerners agreed with Lincoln that secession was a "wicked exercise of physical power." The question was what to do about it. All kinds of compromise proposals came before Congress when it met in December 1860. To sort them out, the Senate and the House each set up a special committee. The Senate committee came up with a package of compromises sponsored by Senator John J. Crittenden of Kentucky. Crittenden's proposal would have required the North, in particular the Republicans, to make all the concessions. The Crittenden Compromise consisted of a series of proposed constitutional amendments: to guarantee slavery in the states perpetually against federal interference; to prohibit Congress from abolishing slavery in the District of Columbia or on any federal property (forts, arsenals, naval bases, and so on); to deny Congress the power to interfere with the interstate slave trade; to compensate slaveholders who were prevented from recovering fugitive slaves who had escaped to the North; and, most important, to protect slavery south of latitude 36°30′ in all territories "now held *or hereafter acquired*."

Given the appetite of the South for more slave territory in the Caribbean and Central America, that

sovereignty before becoming part of the United States. Rather, they had been colonies or territories that never would have become part of the *United* States had they not accepted unconditional sovereignty of the national government. No government, said Lincoln, "ever had provision in its organic law for its own termination. . . . No State, upon its own mere motion, can lawfully get out of the Union. . . . They can only do so against law, and by revolution."

In that case, answered many southerners, we invoke the right of revolution to justify secession. After all, the United States itself was born of revolution. The secessionists maintained that they were merely following the example of their forefathers in declaring independence from a government that threatened their rights and liberties. An Alabaman asked rhetorically: Were not "the men of 1776, who

italicized phrase, in the view of most Republicans, might turn the United States into "a great slave-breeding and slavetrading empire." But even though endorsement of the territorial clause in the Critten-den Compromise would require Republicans to re-pudiate the platform on which they had just won the election, some conservatives in the party were willing to accept it in the interest of peace and con-ciliation. Their votes, together with those of De-mocrats and upper-South Unionists whose states had not seceded, might have gotten the compromise through Congress—though it is doubtful that the approval of three-quarters of the states required for ratification would have been forthcoming. In any case, from Springfield, Illinois, where President-elect Lincoln was preparing for his inaugural trip to Washington, came word to key Republican senators and congressmen to stand firm against compromise on the territorial issue. "Entertain no proposition for a compromise in regard to the *extension* of slavery," wrote Lincoln.

> Filibustering for all South of us, and making slave states would follow . . . to put us again on the high-road to a slave empire. . . . We have just carried an election on principles fairly stated to the people. Now we are told in advance, the government shall be broken up, unless we surrender to those we have beaten. . . . If we surrender, it is the end of us. They will repeat the experiment upon us *ad libitum*. A year will not pass, till we shall have to take Cuba as a condition upon which they will stay in the Union.

Lincoln's advice was decisive. The Republicans voted against the Crittenden Compromise, which therefore failed in Congress. Most Republicans, though, went along with a proposal by Virginia for a "peace conven-tion" of all the states to be held in Washington in Feb-ruary 1861. Although the seven seceded states did not send delegates, the possibility that the convention might accomplish something encouraged Unionists in the eight other slave states either to reject secession or to adopt a wait-and-see attitude. In the end, the peace convention came up with nothing better than a modi-fied version of the Crittenden Compromise, which suffered the same fate as the original.

Nothing that happened in Washington would have made any difference to the seven states that had seceded. No compromise could bring them back. "We spit upon every plan to compromise," said one secessionist. No power could "stem the wild torrent of passion that is carrying everything before it," wrote former U.S. Senator Judah P. Benjamin of

Louisiana. Secession "is a revolution" that "can no more be checked by human effort . . . than a prairie fire by a gardener's watering pot."

ESTABLISHMENT OF THE CONFEDERACY

While the peace convention deliberated in Washing-ton, attention in the seceded states focused on a convention in Montgomery, Alabama, that drew up a constitution and established a government for the new Confederate States of America. For the most part, the Confederate Constitution was a verbatim copy of the U.S. Constitution. But it contained clauses that guaranteed slavery in both the states and the territories, strengthened the principle of state sovereignty, and prohibited Congress from enacting a protective (as distinguished from a revenue) tariff or granting government aid to internal improve-ments. It limited the president to a single six-year term and gave him a line-item veto over appropria-tions. The convention delegates constituted them-selves a provisional Congress for the new nation until regular elections could be held in November 1861. For provisional president and vice president, the convention turned away from radical secession-ists like Yancey and elected Jefferson Davis, a moder-ate secessionist, and Alexander Stephens, who had originally opposed Georgia's secession but ulti-mately had supported it.

Davis and Stephens were two of the ablest men in the South, with twenty-five years of service in the U.S. Congress between them. A West Point graduate, Davis had commanded a regiment in the Mexican War and had been secretary of war in the Pierce ad-ministration—a useful fund of experience if civil war became a reality. But perhaps the main reason they were elected was to present an image of mod-eration and respectability to the eight upper-South states still in the Union. The Confederacy needed those states—at least some of them—if it was to be a viable nation, especially if war came. Without the upper South, the Confederate states would have less than one-fifth of the population (and barely one-tenth of the free population) and only one-twenti-eth of the industrial capacity of the Union states.

Confederate leaders appealed to the upper South to join them because of the "common origin, pursuits, tastes, manners and customs" that "bind together in one brotherhood the . . . slaveholding states." The principal bond was slavery. If Lincoln's election threatened the future of that institution in the cotton states, the threat was even greater in the states of the upper South now that secession had left them a smaller minority within the Union. In a speech at Savannah on March 21 aimed in part at the upper South, Vice President Alexander Stephens defined slavery as the "cornerstone" of the Confederacy. The northern threat to slavery, he stated bluntly, was *"the immediate cause of the late rupture and revolution."* Disputes about slavery had kept the old Union in constant controversy and had menaced the stability of southern society. The creation of the Confederacy made slavery secure. "Our new Government," said Stephens, "is founded upon . . . the great truth that the negro is not equal to the white man; that slavery, subordination to the superior race, is his natural and moral condition. This, our new Government, is the first, in the history of the world, based on this great physical, philosophical, and moral truth."

Residents of the upper South were indeed concerned about preserving slavery. But the issue was less salient there than in the cotton South. Slaves constituted 47 percent of the population in the seven Confederate states but only 24 percent in the upper South; 37 percent of the white families in Confederate states owned slaves compared with 20 percent of the families in the eight slave states still in the Union. A strong heritage of Unionism competed with the commitment to slavery in the upper South. Virginia, the "mother of presidents," had contributed more men to the pantheon of founding fathers than any other state. Tennessee took pride in being the state of Andrew Jackson, famous for his stern warning to John C. Calhoun: "Our Federal Union—It must be preserved." Kentucky was the home of Henry Clay, the "Great Pacificator" who had put together compromises to save the Union on three occasions. These states would not leave the Union without greater cause. The incoming administration hoped to avoid giving them that cause.

THE FORT SUMTER ISSUE

As each state seceded, it seized the virtually undefended federal forts, arsenals, customs houses, mints, and other federal property within its borders. But

still in federal hands were two remote forts in the Florida keys, another on an island off Pensacola, and Fort Moultrie in the Charleston harbor. Moultrie quickly became a bone of contention. In December 1860 the self-proclaimed republic of South Carolina demanded its evacuation by the eighty-four-man garrison of the United States Army. An obsolete fortification, Moultrie was vulnerable to attack by the South Carolina militia that swarmed into the area. On the day after Christmas 1860, Major Robert Anderson, commander at Moultrie, moved his men to Fort Sumter, an uncompleted but immensely strong bastion on an artificial island in the channel leading into Charleston Bay. A Kentuckian married to a Georgian, Anderson deplored the possibility of war. Sympathetic to the South but loyal to the United States, he hoped that moving the garrison to Sumter would ease tensions by reducing the possibility of an attack. Instead, it lit a fuse that eventually set off the war.

South Carolina sent a delegation to President Buchanan to negotiate the withdrawal of the federal troops, which Carolinians considered the army of a foreign power. Buchanan, previously pliable, surprised them by saying no. He even tried to reinforce the garrison. On January 9 the unarmed merchant ship *Star of the West,* carrying two hundred soldiers for Sumter, tried to enter the bay but was driven away by South Carolina artillery. Loath to start a war, Major Anderson did not return the fire with Sumter's guns. Matters then settled into an uneasy truce. The Confederate government organized itself, sent General Pierre G. T. Beauregard to take command of the troops ringing Charleston Bay with their cannons pointed at Fort Sumter, and waited to see what the incoming Lincoln administration would do.

When Abraham Lincoln took the oath of office as the sixteenth—and, some speculated, the last—president of the *United* States, he knew that his inaugural address would be the most important inaugural address in American history. On his words would hang the issues of union or disunion, peace or war. His goal was to keep the upper South in the Union while cooling passions in the lower South, hoping that, in time, its old loyalty to the Union would reassert itself. In his inaugural address, he demonstrated both firmness and forbearance: firmness in purpose to preserve the Union, forbearance in the means of doing so. He repeated his pledge not "to interfere with the institution of slavery where it exists." He assured the Confederate states that "the government will not assail *you*." His first draft had also included the phrase, "unless you *first* assail it," but William H. Seward, whom Lincoln had appointed secretary of state, persuaded him to drop the phrase as too provocative. Lincoln's first draft had also stated his intention to use "all the powers at my disposal" to "reclaim the public property and places which have fallen." But he deleted that as too war-like and said only that he would "hold, occupy, and possess the property, and places belonging to the government," without defining exactly what he meant or how he would do it. In his eloquent peroration, Lincoln appealed to southerners as Americans who shared with other Americans four score and five years of national history. "We are not enemies, but friends," he said.

> Though passion may have strained, it must not break, our bonds of affection. The mystic chords of memory, stretching from every battlefield and patriot grave to every living heart and hearthstone all over this broad land, will yet swell the chorus of the Union when again touched, as surely they will be, by the better angels of our nature.

Lincoln hoped to buy time with his inaugural address—time to demonstrate his peaceful intentions and to enable southern Unionists (whose numbers Republicans vastly overestimated) to regain the upper hand. But the day after his inauguration, Lincoln learned that time was running out. A dispatch from Major Anderson informed him that provisions for the soldiers at Fort Sumter would soon be exhausted. The garrison would have to be either resupplied or evacuated. Any attempt to send in supplies by force would undoubtedly provoke a response from Confederate guns at Charleston. And by putting the onus of starting a war on Lincoln's shoulders, such an action would undoubtedly divide the North and unite the South, driving at least four more states into the Confederacy. Thus, most of the members of Lincoln's cabinet, along with General-in-Chief Winfield Scott of the army, advised Lincoln to withdraw the troops from Sumter. But that would bestow great moral victory on the Confederacy. It would confer legitimacy on its government and would probably lead to diplomatic recognition by foreign powers. Having pledged to "hold, occupy, and possess" national property, could Lincoln afford to abandon that policy during his first month in office? If he did, he would go down in history as the president who consented to the dissolution of the United States.

The pressures from all sides caused Lincoln many sleepless nights; one morning he rose from bed and keeled over in a dead faint. But he finally hit upon a solution that evidenced the mastery that would mark his presidency. He decided to send in unarmed ships with supplies but to hold troops and warships outside the harbor with authorization to go into action only if the Confederates used force to stop the supply ships. And he would notify Confederate officials in advance of his intention. This was a stroke of genius. It shifted the decision for war or peace to Jefferson Davis. In effect, Lincoln flipped a coin and said to Davis: "Heads I win; tails you lose." If Confederate troops fired on the supply ships, the South would stand convicted of starting a war by attacking "a mission of humanity" bringing "food for hungry men." If Davis allowed the supplies to go in peacefully, the U.S. flag would continue to fly over Fort Sumter. The Confederacy would lose face at home and abroad, and southern Unionists would take courage.

Davis did not hesitate. He ordered General Beauregard to compel Sumter's surrender before the supply ships got there. At 4:30 A.M. on April 12, 1861, Confederate guns set off the Civil War by firing on Fort Sumter. After a thirty-three-hour bombardment in which the rebels fired four thousand rounds and the skeleton gun crews in the garrison replied with a thousand—with no one killed on either side—the burning fort lowered the U.S. flag in surrender.

CHOOSING SIDES

News of the attack triggered an outburst of anger and war fever in the North. "The town is in a wild state of excitement," wrote a Philadelphia diarist. "The American flag is to be seen everywhere. . . . Men are enlisting as fast as possible." A Harvard professor born during George Washington's presidency was astounded by the public response. "The heather is on fire," he wrote. "I never knew what a popular excitement can be." A New York woman wrote that the "time before Sumter" seemed like another century. "It seems as if we were never alive till now; never had a country till now."

South Carolina Confederate Soldiers Firing on Fort Sumter   This lantern slide shows South Carolinians wearing red cockades on their hats as a symbol of the state's defiance of the United States. They are firing from Fort Moultrie, abandoned by U.S. troops when they had moved to Fort Sumter the previous December.

Because the tiny United States Army, most of whose 16,000 soldiers were stationed at remote frontier posts, was inadequate to quell the "insurrection," Lincoln called on the states for 75,000 militia. The free states filled their quotas immediately. More than twice as many men volunteered than Lincoln had called for. Recognizing that the ninety days' service to which the militia were limited by law would be too short a time, Lincoln, on May 3, issued a call for three-year volunteers. Before the war was over, more than two million men would serve in the Union army and navy.

The eight slave states that were still in the Union rejected Lincoln's call for troops. Four of them — Virginia, Arkansas, Tennessee, and North Carolina — soon seceded and joined the Confederacy "for the defense of our rights and those of our Southern brothers," as the governor of Tennessee explained.

Forced by the outbreak of actual war to choose between the Union and the Confederacy, most residents of those four states chose the Confederacy. As a former Unionist in North Carolina remarked, "The division must be made on the line of slavery. The South must go with the South. . . . Blood is thicker than Water." Few found the choice harder to make than Robert E. Lee of Virginia. One of the most promising officers in the United States Army, Lee did not believe that southern states had a legal right to secede. General-in-Chief Winfield Scott wanted Lee to become field commander of the Union army. Instead, Lee resigned sadly from the army after the Virginia convention passed an ordinance of secession on April 17. "I must side either with or against my section," Lee told a northern friend. "I cannot raise my hand against my birthplace, my home, my children." Along with three sons and a nephew, Lee joined the

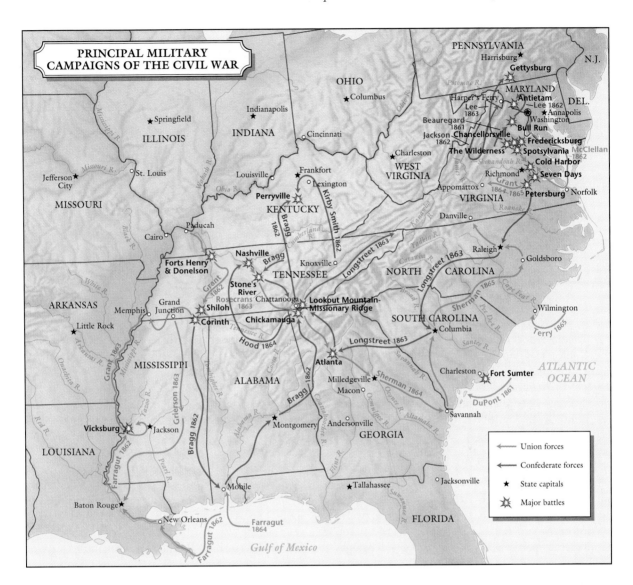

Confederate army. "I foresee that the country will have to pass through a terrible ordeal," he wrote, "a necessary expiation perhaps for our national sins."

Most southern whites embraced war against the Yankees with less foreboding and with a great deal more enthusiasm. When news of Sumter's surrender reached Richmond, a huge crowd poured into the state capitol square and ran up the Confederate flag. "Everyone is in favor of secession" and "perfectly frantic with delight," wrote a participant. "I never in all my life witnessed such excitement." The London *Times* correspondent described crowds in North Carolina with "flushed faces, wild eyes, screaming mouths, hurrahing for 'Jeff Davis' and 'the Southern

Confederacy.'" No one in those cheering crowds could know that before the war ended at least 260,000 Confederate soldiers would lose their lives (along with 365,000 Union soldiers) and that the slave South they fought to defend would be utterly destroyed.

The Border States

The slave states that bordered free states were sharply divided by the outbreak of war. Delaware remained firmly in the Union. Maryland's governor was a Unionist, but many members of the legislature were

Table 16-2

Slavery and Secession

The higher the proportion of slaves and slaveholders in the population of a southern state, the greater the intensity of secessionist sentiment.

Order of Secession	Percentage of Population Who Were Slaves	Percentage of White Population in Slaveholding Families
Seven States that Seceded December 1860–February 1861 (South Carolina, Mississippi, Florida, Alabama, Georgia, Louisiana, Texas)	47%	38%
Four States that Seceded after the Firing on Fort Sumter (Virginia, Arkansas, Tennessee, North Carolina)	32%	24%
Four Border Slave States Remaining in Union (Maryland, Delaware, Kentucky, Missouri)	14%	15%

not. The governors of Kentucky and Missouri favored the Confederacy, but a majority of their constituents were Unionists. Leaders in all three states talked vaguely of "neutrality," but they were to be denied that luxury—Maryland and Missouri immediately, and Kentucky in September 1861 when first Confederate and then Union troops crossed its borders and confronted each other along a 300-mile line.

The first blood was shed in Maryland on April 19 when a mob attacked part of a Massachusetts regiment traveling through Baltimore on its way to Washington. The soldiers fired back, leaving twelve Baltimoreans and four soldiers dead on the street. Confederate partisans in the state burned bridges and tore down telegraph wires, cutting Washington off from the North for nearly a week until additional troops from Massachusetts and New York reopened communications and seized key points in Maryland. The troops also arrested many Confederate sympathizers, including the mayor and police chief of Baltimore, a judge, and two dozen state legislators. To prevent Washington from becoming surrounded by enemy territory, federal forces turned Maryland into an occupied state. Although thousands of Marylanders slipped into Virginia to join the Confederate army, a substantial majority of Maryland residents remained loyal to the Union.

The same was true of Missouri, even though that state was wracked by guerrilla warfare and several pitched battles throughout the entire four years of war. Aggressive action by the Union commander there, Nathaniel Lyon, provoked a showdown be-

tween Unionist and pro-Confederate militia that turned into a full-scale riot in St. Louis on May 10–11, 1861, in which thirty-six people were killed. Lyon then led his troops in a summer campaign that drove the Confederate militia, along with the governor and pro-southern legislators, into Arkansas, where they formed a Missouri Confederate government in exile. Reinforced by Arkansas regiments, these rebel Missourians invaded their home state, and on August 10 defeated Lyon (who was killed) in the bloody battle of Wilson's Creek in the southwest corner of Missouri. The victorious Confederates marched northward all the way to the Missouri River, capturing a Union garrison at Lexington forty miles east of Kansas City on September 20. By then, Union forces made up of regiments from Iowa, Illinois, and Kansas as well as Missouri had regrouped and once again drove the ragged Missouri Confederates back into Arkansas by the end of 1861.

From then until the war's end, military power enabled Unionists to maintain political control of Missouri. But continued guerrilla attacks by Confederate "bushwhackers" and counterinsurgency tactics by Unionist "jayhawkers" turned large areas of the state into a no-man's land of hit-and-run raids, arson, ambush, and murder. During these years, the famous postwar outlaws Jesse and Frank James and Cole and Jim Younger rode with the notorious rebel guerrilla chieftains William Quantrill and "Bloody Bill" Anderson. More than any other state, Missouri suffered from a civil war within the Civil War, and its bitter legacy persisted for generations.

In elections held during the summer and fall of 1861, Unionists gained firm control of the Kentucky and Maryland legislatures. Kentucky Confederates, like those of Missouri, formed a state government in exile. When the Confederate Congress admitted both Kentucky and Missouri to full representation, the Confederate flag acquired its thirteen stars. Nevertheless, two-thirds of the white population in the four border slave states favored the Union—though some of that support was undoubtedly induced by the presence of Union troops.

The war itself produced a fifth Union border state: West Virginia. Most of the delegates from the portion of Virginia west of the Shenandoah Valley had voted against secession. A region of mountains, small farms, and few slaves, its economy was linked more closely to nearby Ohio and Pennsylvania than to the South. Western Virginia's largest city, Wheeling, was 330 miles from Richmond but only 60 miles from Pittsburgh. Delegates who had opposed Virginia's secession from the Union returned home determined to carry out the western region's secession from Virginia. With the help of Union troops, who crossed the Ohio River and won a few small battles against Confederate forces in the region during the summer of 1861, they accomplished their goal. Through a complicated process of conventions and referendums—carried out in the midst of continuing raids and skirmishes—they created in 1862 the new state of West Virginia, which entered the Union in 1863.

To the south and west of Missouri, civil war raged along a different "border"—between southern states and territories—for control of the resources of that vast region. In the Indian Territory (present-day Oklahoma), the native Americans, who had been resettled there from Eastern states in the generation before the war, chose sides and carried on bloody guerrilla warfare with each other that rivaled the bushwhacking in Missouri in its ferocity. The more prosperous Indians of the five "civilized tribes" (Cherokees, Creeks, Seminoles, Chickasaws, and Choctaws), many of them of mixed blood and some of them slaveholders, tended to side with the Confederacy. Some tribes signed treaties of alliance with the Confederate government. Aided by white and black Union regiments operating out of Kansas and Missouri, the pro-Union Indians gradually gained control of most of the Indian Territory.

In the meantime, Confederates had made their boldest bid to fulfill antebellum Southern ambitions to win the Southwest. A small army composed mostly of Texans pushed up the Rio Grande valley into New Mexico in 1861. The following February they launched a deeper strike to capture Santa Fe. With luck, they might be able to push even farther westward and northward to gain the mineral wealth of California and Colorado gold mines, whose millions were already helping to finance the Union war effort and could do wonders for Confederate finances. A good many Southerners lived in these Western territories and in California. At first the Confederate drive up the Rio Grande went well. The Texans won a victory over the Unionist New Mexico militia and a handful of regulars at the battle of Valverde, a hundred miles south of Albuquerque, on February 21, 1862. They continued up the valley, occupied Albuquerque and Santa Fe, and pushed on toward Fort Union near Santa Fe. But Colorado miners who had organized themselves into Union regiments and had carried out the greatest march of the war, over the rugged Rockies in winter, met the Texans in the battle of Glorieta Pass on March 26-28. The battle was a draw tactically, but a unit of Coloradans destroyed the Confederate wagon train, forcing the Southerners into a disastrous retreat all the way back to Texas. Of the 3,700 who had started out to win the West for the Confederacy, only 2,000 made it back. The Confederates had shot their bolt in this region; the West and Southwest remained safe for the Union.

THE BALANCE SHEET OF WAR

If one counts three-quarters of the border-state population (including free blacks) as pro-Union, the total number of people in Union states in 1861 was 22.5 million, compared with 9 million in the Confederate states. The North's advantage was even greater in military manpower, since the Confederate total included 3.7 million slaves compared with 300,000 slaves in Union areas. At first, neither side expected to recruit blacks as soldiers. Eventually, the Union did enlist 180,000 black soldiers (and 10,000 black sailors); the Confederacy held out against that drastic step until the war was virtually over. Altogether, about 2.1 million men fought for the Union and 850,000 for the Confederacy. That was close to half of the northern male population of military age (18 to 40) and three-quarters of the comparable Confederate white population. Since the labor force of the South consisted mainly of slaves, the Confederacy was able to enlist a larger proportion of its white population.

In the economic resources needed to wage war, northern superiority was even greater. The Union states possessed nine-tenths of the country's industrial capacity and registered shipping, four-fifths of its bank capital, three-fourths of its railroad mileage and rolling stock, and three-fourths of its taxable wealth.

These statistics gave pause to some southerners. In a long war that mobilized the total resources of both sides, northern advantages might prove decisive. But in 1861, few anticipated how long and intense the war would be. Both sides expected a short and victorious conflict. Confederates seemed especially confident, partly because of their vaunted sense of martial superiority over the "blue-bellied" Yankee nation of shopkeepers. Many southerners really did believe that one southerner could lick three Yankees. "Let brave men advance with flint-locks and old-fashioned bayonets, on the popinjays of Northern cities," said ex-Governor Henry Wise of Virginia, now a Confederate general, and "the Yankees would break and run."

Although this turned out to be a grievous miscalculation, southerners did have some reason to believe that their martial qualities were superior. A higher proportion of southerners than northerners had attended West Point and other military schools, had fought in the Mexican War, or had served as officers in the regular army. Volunteer military companies were more prevalent in the antebellum South than in the North. As a rural people, southerners were proficient in hunting, riding, and other outdoor skills useful in military operations. Moreover, the South had begun to prepare for war earlier than the North. As each state seceded, it mobilized a militia and volunteer military companies. On March 6, 1861, the Confederate Congress had authorized an army of 100,000 men. By the time Lincoln called for 75,000 militia after the fall of Fort Sumter, the Confederacy already had 60,000 men under arms. Not until the summer of 1861 would the North's greater manpower begin to make itself felt in the form of a larger army.

Even when fully mobilized, the North's superior resources did not guarantee success. Its military task was much more difficult than that of the South. The Confederacy had come into being in firm control of 750,000 square miles — a vast territory larger than all of western Europe and twice as large as the thirteen colonies in 1776. To win the war, Union forces would have to invade, conquer, and occupy much of that territory, cripple its people's ability to sustain a war of independence, and destroy their armies. Britain had been unable to accomplish a similar task in the war for independence, despite the fact that it enjoyed a far greater superiority of resources over the United States in 1776 than the Union enjoyed over the Confederacy in 1861. (Nor would the United States be able to accomplish a similar task against North Vietnam and the Vietcong in the 1960s and 1970s.) Victory does not always ride with the heaviest battalions.

To "win" the war, the Confederacy did not need to invade or conquer the Union or even to destroy its armies; it needed only to stand on the defensive and prevent the North from destroying Southern armies — to hold out long enough to discourage the northerners and convince them that the cost of victory was too high. Most Confederates were confident in 1861 that they were more than equal to the task. Most European military experts agreed. The military analyst of the London *Times* wrote:

> It is one thing to drive the rebels from the south bank of the Potomac, or even to occupy Richmond, but another to reduce and hold in permanent subjection a tract of country nearly as large as Russia in Europe. . . . No war of independence ever terminated unsuccessfully except where the disparity of force was far greater than it is in this case. . . . Just as England during the revolution had to give up conquering the colonies so the North will have to give up conquering the South.

The important factor of morale also seemed to favor the Confederacy. To be sure, northerners fought for powerful symbols: Nation, Flag, Constitution. "We are fighting to maintain the best government on earth" was a common phrase in the letters and diaries of northern soldiers. It is a "grate struggle for Union, Constitution, and law," wrote a New Jersey soldier. A Chicago newspaper declared that the South had "outraged the Constitution, set at defiance all law, and trampled under foot that flag which has been the glorious and consecrated symbol of American Liberty."

But Confederates, too, fought for Nation, Flag, Constitution, and Liberty — of whites. In addition, they fought to defend their land, homes, and families against invading "Yankee vandals" who many southern whites quite literally believed were coming to "free the negroes and force amalgamation between them and the children of the poor men of the South." An army fighting in defense of its homeland generally has the edge in morale. "We shall have the enormous advantage of fighting on our own territory and for our very existence," wrote a Confederate leader. "All the world over, are not one million of men defending themselves at home against invasion stronger in a mere military point of view, than five millions [invading] a foreign country?"

Organization of Union and Confederate Armies   Normal commanding officer of each unit appears in capital letters. Numbers below each unit indicate full quota of men; numbers in parentheses indicate typical size of combat units by second year of war. (By the last two years of the war, brigades often contained five or six regiments; divisions sometimes contained four brigades; and corps sometimes contained four divisions.) Arrows indicate attachment of artillery and cavalry to infantry units; broken arrows indicate occasional attachments to these units. Cavalry often operated independently of infantry units.

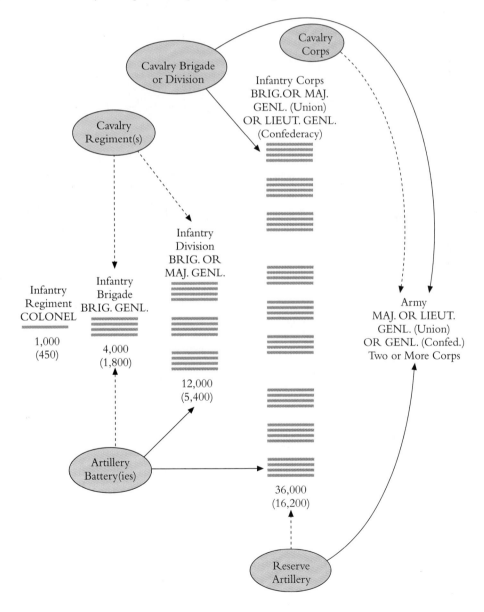

Mobilizing for War

More than four-fifths of the soldiers on both sides were volunteers; in the first two years of the war, nearly all of them were. The Confederacy passed a conscription law in April 1862, and the Union followed suit in March 1863. But even afterward, most recruits continued to be volunteers. In both North and South, patriotic rallies with martial music and speeches motivated the men of a county or town or city neighborhood to enlist in a company (100 men) organized by leading citizens in that locality. The recruits elected their own company officers (a captain and two lieutenants), who received their commissions from the state governor. A regiment consisted of ten infantry companies, and each regiment was commanded by a colonel, with a lieutenant colonel and a major as second and third in command—all of them appointed by the governor. Cavalry regiments were organized in a similar manner. Field artillery units were known as "batteries," a grouping of four or six cannon with their caissons and limber chests (two-wheeled, horse-drawn vehicles) to carry ammunition; the full complement of a six-gun battery was 155 men and 72 horses.

Volunteer units received a state designation and number in the order of their completion, for example, the 2nd Massachusetts Volunteer Infantry, the 5th Virginia Cavalry, the 10th Ohio Light Battery, and so on. In most regiments the men in each company all came from the same town or locality. Some Union regiments were composed mostly of men of a particular ethnic group: Irish, German, or Scandinavian. By the end of the war, the Union army had raised about two thousand infantry and cavalry regiments and seven hundred batteries; the Confederates had organized just under half as many. The proportions in both armies were 75 to 80 percent infantry, 15 to 20 percent cavalry (some cavalry units were converted to infantry and vice versa), and 6 percent artillery. As the war went on, the original 1,000-man complement of a regiment was whittled down by disease, casualties, desertions, and detachments, so that the average combat strength of a regiment after several months was 500 men or less. The states generally preferred to organize new regiments rather than keep the old ones up to full strength.

These were citizen soldiers, not professionals. They carried peacetime notions of democracy and discipline with them into the army. That is why, in

Union Recruiting Poster Nearly one-quarter of Union soldiers in the Civil War were foreign-born. Most of them had come to the United States as children during the years of heavy immigration in the 1840s and 1850s. They enlisted for the same motives of patriotism and adventure that actuated native-born Americans. This recruiting poster appeals to these motives in several languages.

the tradition of the citizen militia, the men elected their company officers and sometimes their field officers (colonel, lieutenant colonel, and major) as well. Professional military men deplored the egalitarianism and slack discipline that resulted. Political influence often counted for more than military training in the election and appointment of officers. In many Union regiments, there was scarcely a handful of officers or men with military experience. These civilians in uniform were extremely awkward and unmilitary at first, and some regiments suffered battlefield disasters because of inadequate training, discipline, and leadership. Yet this was the price that a democratic society with a tiny professional army had to pay to mobilize large armies almost overnight to meet a crisis. In time, these raw recruits became battle-hardened veterans commanded by experienced officers who had survived the weeding-out process of combat or of examination boards or who had been promoted from the ranks.

As the two sides organized their field armies, both grouped four or more regiments into brigades, and three or more brigades into divisions. By 1862, they began grouping two or more divisions into corps, and two or more corps into armies. Each of these larger units was commanded by a general appointed by the president. Most of the higher-ranking generals on both sides were West Point graduates, but others were appointed because they represented an important political, regional, or (in the North) ethnic constituency whose support Lincoln or Davis wished to solidify. Some of these "political" generals, like elected regimental officers, turned out to be incompetent. But as the war went on, they too either learned their trade or were weeded out. Some outstanding generals emerged from civilian life and were promoted up the ranks during the war. In both the Union and the Confederate armies, the best officers (including generals) *led* their men by example as much as by precept; they commanded from the front, not the rear. Combat casualties were higher among officers than among privates, and highest of all among generals, who were killed in action at a rate 50 percent higher than enlisted men.

The Richmond Grays This photograph depicts a typical southern volunteer military unit that joined the Confederate army in 1861. Note the determined and confident appearance of these young men. By 1865, one-third of them would be dead and several others maimed for life.

Weapons and Tactics

While artillery made the most noise in Civil War battles, the infantry rifle was the most lethal weapon. Muskets and rifles caused 80 to 90 percent of the combat casualties. From 1862 on, most of these weapons were "rifled"—that is, they had spiral grooves cut in the barrel to impart a spin to the bullet. This innovation was only a decade old, dating to the perfection in the 1850s of the "minie ball" (named after French army Captain Claude Minié, its principal inventor), a cone-shaped lead bullet whose base expanded upon firing to "take" the rifling of the barrel. This made it possible to load and fire a muzzle-loading rifle as rapidly (two or three times

per minute) as the old smoothbore musket. Moreover, the rifle had greater accuracy and at least four times the effective range (400 yards or more) of the smoothbore.

Civil War infantry tactics adjusted only gradually to the greater lethal range and accuracy of the new rifle, however, for the prescribed massed formations had emerged from experience with the smoothbore musket. Close-order assaults against defenders equipped with rifles resulted in enormous casualties from 1862 on. The defensive power of the rifle became even greater when troops began digging into trenches from 1863 on. Massed frontal assaults became almost suicidal. Soldiers and their officers learned the hard way to adopt skirmishing tactics,

Union Army Wagon-Train in Virginia, 1863   By 1863, the productive power of northern farms and factories had made the Union army the best-fed and best-equipped army in history to that time. This supply wagon-train testifies to the logistical efficiency of Union forces.

taking advantage of cover and working around the enemy flank rather than attacking frontally.

Logistics

Wars are fought not only by men and weapons but by the logistical apparatus that supports and supplies them. The Civil War is often called the world's first "modern" war because of the role played by railroads, steam-powered ships, and the telegraph—which did not exist in earlier wars fought on a similar scale (those of the French Revolution and Napoleon). Railroads and steamboats transported supplies and soldiers with unprecedented speed and efficiency; the telegraph provided instantaneous communication between army headquarters and field commanders.

Yet these modern forms of transport and communications were extremely vulnerable. Cavalry raiders and guerrillas could cut telegraph wires, burn railroad bridges, and tear up the tracks. Confederate cavalry became particularly skillful at sundering the supply lines of invading Union armies and thereby neutralizing forces several times larger than their own. The more deeply the Union armies penetrated into the South, the greater the number of men they had to detach to guard bridges, depots, and supply dumps.

And once the campaigning armies had moved away from their railhead or wharfside supply base, they were as dependent on animal-powered transport as earlier armies had been. Depending on terrain, road conditions, length of supply line, and proportion of artillery and cavalry, Union armies required one horse or mule for every two or three men. Thus a large invading Union army of 100,000 men (the approximate number in Virginia from 1862 to 1865 and in Georgia in 1864) would need about 40,000 draft animals. Confederate armies, operating mostly in friendly territory closer to their bases, needed fewer. The poorly drained dirt roads typical of much of the South, compounded by the red-clay soil in many areas of operation, especially Virginia, turned roads into a morass of mud in wet weather—which was frequent.

These logistical problems did much to offset the industrial supremacy of the North, particularly during the first year of the war when bottlenecks, shortages, and inefficiency marked the logistical effort on both sides. By 1862, though, the northern economy had fully geared up for war and was churning out guns and butter on a scale that made the Union army the best-supplied army in history up to that time.

Confederate officials accomplished impressive feats of improvisation in creating war industries, especially munitions and gunpowder, but the southern industrial base was too slender to sustain adequate production. Particularly troublesome for the Confederacy was its lack of capacity to replace rails and rolling stock for its railroads. Although southern agriculture was producing plenty of food, the railroads deteriorated to the point where they could not get the food to soldiers or civilians. As the war went into its third and fourth years, the northern economy grew stronger and the southern economy grew weaker until, in the winter of 1864–1865, it collapsed.

Financing the War

One of the greatest defects of the Confederate economy was finance. Of the three methods of paying for a war—taxation, loans, and treasury notes (paper money)—treasury notes are the most inflationary, for they pump new money into the economy. By contrast, taxation and loans (war bonds) soak up money and thus counteract inflation. Though Confederate treasury officials were quite aware of this, the Confederate Congress, wary of dampening patriotic ardor, was slow to raise taxes. And because most southern capital was tied up in land and slaves, the amount available for buying war bonds was very limited.

So, expecting a short war, the Confederate Congress in 1861 authorized a limited issue of treasury notes, to be redeemable in specie (gold or silver) within two years after the end of the war. The first modest issue was followed by successive issues at an ever-accelerating pace, because the notes declined in value from the outset. The rate of decline increased during periods of Confederate military reverses, when people wondered whether the government would survive. At the end of 1861 the Confederacy was experiencing an inflation rate of 12 percent; by early 1863 it took eight dollars to buy what one dollar had bought two years earlier; just before the war's end the Confederate dollar was worth one U.S. cent.

In 1863 the Confederate Congress tried to stem runaway inflation by passing a comprehensive law that taxed income, consumer purchases, and business transactions and included a "tax in kind" on agricultural products, allowing tax officials to seize 10 percent of a farmer's crops. This tax was extremely unpopular among farmers, many of whom hid their crops and livestock or refused to plant, thereby worsening the Confederacy's food shortages. The tax legislation was too little and too late to remedy the South's fiscal chaos. The Confederate government raised less than 5 percent of its revenue by taxes and less than 40 percent by loans, leaving 60 percent to be created by the printing press. That turned out to be a recipe for disaster.

In contrast, the Union government raised 66 percent of its revenue by selling war bonds, 21 percent by taxes, and only 13 percent by printing treasury notes. The Legal Tender Act authorizing these notes—the famous "greenbacks," the origin of modern paper money in the United States—was passed at a crucial time in February 1862. Congress had enacted new taxes in 1861—including the first income tax in American history—and had authorized the sale of war bonds. But by early 1862 these measures had not yet raised enough revenue to pay for the rapid military buildup. So, to avert a crisis, Congress created the greenbacks. Instead of promising to redeem them in specie at some future date, as the South had done, Congress made them "legal tender"—that is, it required everyone to accept them as real money at face value. The timing was fortunate, because Union armies won a series of important victories in the first half of 1862, and the greenbacks floated out on a wave of public confidence. The northern economy suffered some inflation during the war—about 80 percent over four years—but that was mild compared with the 9,000 percent inflation in the Confederacy. The greater strength and diversity of the northern economy, together with wiser fiscal legislation, accounted for the contrast.

The Union Congress passed an additional wartime law that rationalized and modernized the American monetary system: the National Banking Act of 1863. Before the war, the principal form of money in the United States had been notes issued by state-chartered banks. After Andrew Jackson's destruction of the Second Bank of the United States (Chapter 12)—which had imposed some degree of restraint and order on the state banks—the number and variety of bank notes had skyrocketed until in 1860 seven thousand different kinds of state bank notes were circulating. Some were virtually worthless; others circulated at a discount from face value. The National Banking Act of 1863 resulted from the desire of Whiggish Republicans to resurrect the centralized banking system Jackson had destroyed and to create a more stable bank-note currency, and from the need to finance the war. The act authorized the chartering of national banks, which could issue bank notes up to 90 percent of the value of the U.S. bonds they held. This provision created a market for the bonds and, in combination with the greenbacks, replaced the glut of state bank notes with a more uniform national currency. To further the cause, Congress in 1865 imposed a tax of 10 percent on state bank notes, thereby taxing them out of existence. National bank notes were an important form of money for the next half-century. They had two defects, however: since the number of notes that could be issued was tied to each bank's holdings of U.S. bonds, the volume of currency available was dependent on the amount of federal debt rather than on the economic needs of the country; and the bank notes themselves tended to be concentrated in the Northeast, where most of the large national banks were located, leaving the South and West short. The creation of the Federal Reserve System in 1913 (Chapter 21) largely remedied these defects. But it was Civil War legislation that established the principle of a uniform national currency issued and regulated by the federal government.

NAVIES, THE BLOCKADE, AND FOREIGN RELATIONS

To sustain its war effort, the Confederacy needed to import large quantities of material from abroad, particularly from Britain. To shut off these imports, and the exports of cotton used to pay for them, Lincoln, on April 19, 1861, proclaimed a blockade of Confederate ports. At first, the blockade was more a policy than a reality, for the navy had only a few ships on hand to enforce it. The task was formidable; the Confederate coastline stretched for 3,500 miles, with two dozen major ports and another 150 bays and coves where cargo could be landed. The United States Navy, which since the 1840s had been converting from sail to steam, recalled its ships from distant seas, took old sailing vessels out of mothballs, and bought or chartered merchant ships and armed them in an attempt to create a blockade fleet overnight. Eventually the navy placed several hundred warships on blockade duty. But in 1861 the blockade was so thin that nine out of ten vessels slipped through it on their way to or from Confederate ports.

The Confederacy, however, inadvertently contributed to the blockade's success when in 1861 it adopted a foreign policy that has been called "King Cotton diplomacy." Cotton was vital to the British economy because textiles were at the heart of British industry — and three-fourths of Britain's supply of raw cotton came from the South. If that supply was cut off, southerners reasoned, British factories would shut down, unemployed workers would starve, and Britain would face the prospect of revolution. Rather than risk such a consequence, southerners believed that Britain (and other powers) would recognize the Confederacy's independence and then use the powerful British navy to break the blockade.

Southerners were so firmly convinced of King Cotton's paramount importance to the British economy that they kept the 1861 cotton crop at home rather than try to export it through the blockade, hoping thereby to compel the British to intervene. But the strategy backfired. Bumper crops in 1859 and 1860 had piled up a surplus of raw cotton in British warehouses and delayed until 1862 the "cotton famine" on which southerners had counted. In the end, the South's 1861 voluntary embargo of cotton cost them dearly. The Confederacy missed its chance, while the blockade was still weak, to ship out its cotton and store it abroad, where it could be used as collateral for loans to purchase munitions and other war matériel.

Moreover, the Confederacy's King Cotton diplomacy contradicted its own foreign-policy objectives: to persuade the British and French governments to refuse to recognize the legality of the blockade. Under international law, a blockade must be "physically effective" to be respected by neutral nations. Confederate diplomats claimed that the Union effort was a mere "paper blockade," yet the dearth of cotton reaching European ports as a result of the South's embargo suggested to British and French diplomats that the blockade was at least partly effective. And indeed, by 1862 it was. Slow sailing ships with large cargo capacity rarely tried to run the blockade, and the sleek, fast, steam-powered "blockade runners" that became increasingly prominent had a smaller cargo capacity and charged high rates because of the growing risk of capture or sinking by the Union navy. Although most of these runners got through, by 1862 the blockade had reduced the Confederacy's seaborne commerce enough to

Confederate Blockade Runners in the Harbor at Hamilton, Bermuda   Confederate armies were heavily dependent on supplies brought in from abroad on blockade runners, paid for by cotton smuggled out through the Union naval cordon by these same blockade runners. The sleek, narrow-beamed ships with raked masts and smokestacks (which could be telescoped to deck level) pictured in this painting were designed for speed and deception to elude the blockade — a feat successfully accomplished on four-fifths of their voyages during the war.

convince the British government to recognize it as legitimate. The blockade was also squeezing the southern economy. After lifting its cotton embargo in 1862, the Confederacy found it increasingly difficult to export enough cotton through the blockade to meet the spiraling cost of the imports it needed.

Confederate foreign policy also failed to win diplomatic recognition by other nations. That recognition would have conferred international legitimacy on the Confederacy and might even have led to treaties of alliance or of foreign aid, as French recognition of the new United States had in 1778. In 1861–1862 the French Emperor Napoleon III expressed sympathy for the Confederacy, as did influential groups in the British Parliament and the British public. But Prime Minister Lord Palmerston and Foreign Minister John Russell were cautious. They did not want to recognize the Confederacy prematurely, while it was engaged in a war it might

lose, especially if recognition might jeopardize relations with the United States. The Union foreign-policy team of Secretary of State Seward and Minister to England Charles Francis Adams did a superb job in their dealings with the British. Seward issued blunt warnings against recognizing the Confederacy; Adams softened them with the velvet glove of diplomacy. Other nations followed Britain's lead; by 1862 it had become clear that Britain would withhold recognition until the Confederacy had virtually won its independence — but, of course, such recognition came too late to help the Confederacy win.

The Trent Affair

If anything illustrated the frustrations of Confederate diplomacy, it was the "*Trent* Affair" — which came tantalizingly close to rupturing British–American relations to Confederate advantage, but did not. In

October 1861 southern envoys James Mason and John Slidell slipped through the blockade at Charleston on the first leg of a voyage to Europe, where Mason hoped to represent the Confederacy in London and Slidell in Paris. On November 8, Captain Charles Wilkes of the *U.S.S. San Jacinto* stopped the British mail steamer *Trent*, with Mason and Slidell on board, on the high seas near Cuba. Wilkes arrested the two southerners, took them to Boston, and became an instant hero in the North. But when the news reached England, the government and the public were outraged by Wilkes's "high-handed" action. Although the Royal Navy had done similar things during the centuries when Britannia ruled the waves, John Bull (England) would not take this behavior from his brash American cousin Jonathan (the United States). The British government demanded an apology and the release of Mason and Slidell. The popular press on both sides of the Atlantic stirred up war fever. The British navy sent reinforcements to its North American squadron. But good sense soon prevailed on both sides. The Palmerston government softened its demands. And with a philosophy of "One war at a time," the Lincoln administration released Mason and Slidell the day after Christmas 1861, declaring that Captain Wilkes had acted "without instructions." The British accepted this statement in lieu of an apology, and a warm glow of good will enveloped Britain and the United States.

The Confederate Navy

Lacking the capacity to build a naval force at home, the Confederacy hoped to use British shipyards for the purpose. Through a loophole in the British neutrality law, two fast commerce raiders built in Liverpool made their way into Confederate hands in 1862. Named the *Florida* and the *Alabama*, they roamed the seas for the next two years, capturing or sinking Union merchant ships and whalers. The *Alabama* was the most feared raider. Commanded by the leading Confederate sea dog, Raphael Semmes, she sank sixty-two merchant vessels plus a Union warship before another warship, the *U.S.S. Kearsarge* (whose Captain, John A. Winslow, had once been Semmes's messmate in the old navy), sank the *Alabama* off Cherbourg, France, on June 19, 1864. Altogether, Confederate privateers and commerce raiders destroyed or captured 257 Union merchant vessels and drove at least 700 others to foreign reg-

istry. The U.S. merchant marine never recovered. But this Confederate achievement, though spectacular, made only a tiny dent in the Union war effort, especially when compared with the 1,500 blockade runners captured or destroyed by the Union navy, not to mention the thousands of others that decided not even to try to beat the blockade.

The *Monitor* and the *Virginia*

Because of inadequate shipbuilding facilities, the Confederate navy was never able to challenge Union seapower where it counted most—along the coasts and rivers of the South. But it was not for lack of trying. Though plagued by shortages on every hand, the Confederate Navy Department demonstrated great skill at innovation. Southern engineers developed "torpedoes" (mines) that sank or damaged forty-three Union warships in southern bays and rivers. Even more innovative (though less successful) was the building of ironclad "rams" to sink the blockade ships. The idea of iron armor for warships was not new; the British and French navies had prototype ironclads in 1861. But the Confederacy built the first one to see action. It was the *C.S.S. Virginia*, commonly called (even by southerners) the *Merrimac* because it was rebuilt from the steam frigate *U.S.S. Merrimack*, which had been burned to the waterline by the Union navy at Norfolk when the Confederates seized the naval base there in April 1861. Ready for its trial-by-combat on March 8, 1862, the *Virginia* steamed out to attack the blockade squadron at Hampton Roads. She sank one frigate with her iron ram and another with the firepower of her eleven guns. Other Union ships ran aground trying to escape, to be finished off (Confederates expected) the next day. Union shot and shells bounced off the *Virginia's* armor plate. It was the worst day the United States Navy would have until December 7, 1941.

Panic seized Washington and the whole northeastern seaboard. But almost in Hollywood fashion, the Union's own ironclad sailed into Hampton Roads in the nick of time and saved the rest of the fleet. This was the *U.S.S. Monitor*, which had been completed just days earlier at the Brooklyn navy yard. Much smaller than the *Virginia*, with two eleven-inch guns in a revolving turret (an innovation) set on a deck almost flush with the water, the *Monitor* looked like a "tin can on a shingle." It was a formidable warship, though. It presented a small target and was capable of

The Monitor *and* Merrimac   The black and white photograph shows the crew of the Union ironclad *Monitor* standing in front of its revolving two-gun turret. In action, the sun canopy above the turret would be taken down and all sailors would be at their stations inside the turret or the hull, as shown in the color painting of the famed battle, on March 9, 1862, between the *Monitor* and the Confederate *Virginia* (informally called the *Merrimac* because it had been converted from the captured U.S. frigate *Merrimack*). There is no photograph of the *Virginia*, which was blown up by its crew two months later when the Confederates retreated toward Richmond because its draft was too deep to go up the James River.

concentrating considerable firepower in a given direction with its revolving turret. Next day, the *Monitor* fought the *Virginia* in history's first battle between ironclads. It was a draw, but the *Virginia* limped home to Norfolk never again to menace the Union fleet. Although the Confederacy built other ironclad rams, some never saw action and none achieved the initial success of the *Virginia*. By the war's end, the Union navy had built or started fifty-eight ships of the *Monitor* class (some of them double-turreted), launching a

new age in naval history that ended the classic "heart of oak" era of warships.

CAMPAIGNS AND BATTLES, 1861–1862

Wars can be won only by hard fighting—at least wars waged with the depth of passion and ideological conviction of the American Civil War. This was a truth that some leaders on both sides overlooked.

Harvest of Death   This photograph of a Confederate soldier killed in action in Virginia speaks more eloquently than words of the grim reality of war.

One of them was Winfield Scott, General-in-Chief of the United States Army, a veteran of the War of 1812 and commander of the army that captured Mexico City in 1847. Scott, a Virginian who had remained loyal to the Union, evolved a military strategy based on his conviction that there were a great many southerners eager to be won back to the Union. The main elements of his strategy were a naval blockade and a combined Army–Navy expedition to take control of the Mississippi, thus sealing off the Confederacy on all sides and enabling the Union to "bring them to terms with less bloodshed than by any other plan." The northern press ridiculed Scott's strategy as "the Anaconda Plan," after the South American snake that squeezes its prey to death.

The Battle of Bull Run

Most northerners believed that the South could be overcome only by victory in battle. Virginia emerged as the most likely battleground, especially after the Confederate government moved its capital to Rich-

mond in May 1861. "Forward to Richmond," clamored northern newspapers. And forward toward Richmond moved a Union army of 35,000 men in July, despite Scott's misgivings and those of the army's field commander, Irvin McDowell, who did not believe his raw, ninety-day militia were ready to fight a real battle. They got no farther than Bull Run, a sluggish stream twenty-five miles southwest of Washington, where a Confederate army commanded by Beauregard had been deployed to defend a key rail junction at Manassas.

Another small Confederate army in the Shenandoah Valley under General Joseph E. Johnston had given a Union force the slip and had traveled to Manassas by rail to reinforce Beauregard. On July 21 the attacking Federals forded Bull Run and hit the rebels on the left flank, driving them back. By early afternoon, the Federals seemed to be on the verge of victory. But a Virginia brigade commanded by Thomas J. Jackson stood "like a stone wall," earning Jackson the nickname he carried ever after. By midafternoon Confederate reinforcements — including one brigade just off the train from the Shenandoah Valley — had grouped for a screaming counterattack (the famed "rebel yell" was first heard here). They drove the exhausted and disorganized Yankees back across Bull Run in a retreat that turned into a rout.

Although the Battle of Manassas (or Bull Run, as northerners called it) was small by later Civil War standards, it made a profound impression on both sides. Of the 18,000 soldiers actually engaged on each side, Union casualties (killed, wounded, and captured) were about 2,800 and Confederate casualties 2,000. The victory exhilarated Confederates and confirmed their belief in their martial superiority over the Yankees. It also gave the Confederate forces a morale advantage over Union forces in the Virginia theater that persisted for two years. And yet, Manassas bred overconfidence in the Confederacy. Some southerners thought the war was won. Northerners, by contrast, were jolted out of their expectations of a short war. A new mood of reality and grim determination gripped the North. Congress authorized the enlistment of up to a million three-year volunteers. Hundreds of thousands flocked to recruiting offices in the next few months. Lincoln called General George B. McClellan to Washington to organize the new troops into the Army of the Potomac.

An energetic, talented officer only thirty-four years old, small of stature but great with an aura of

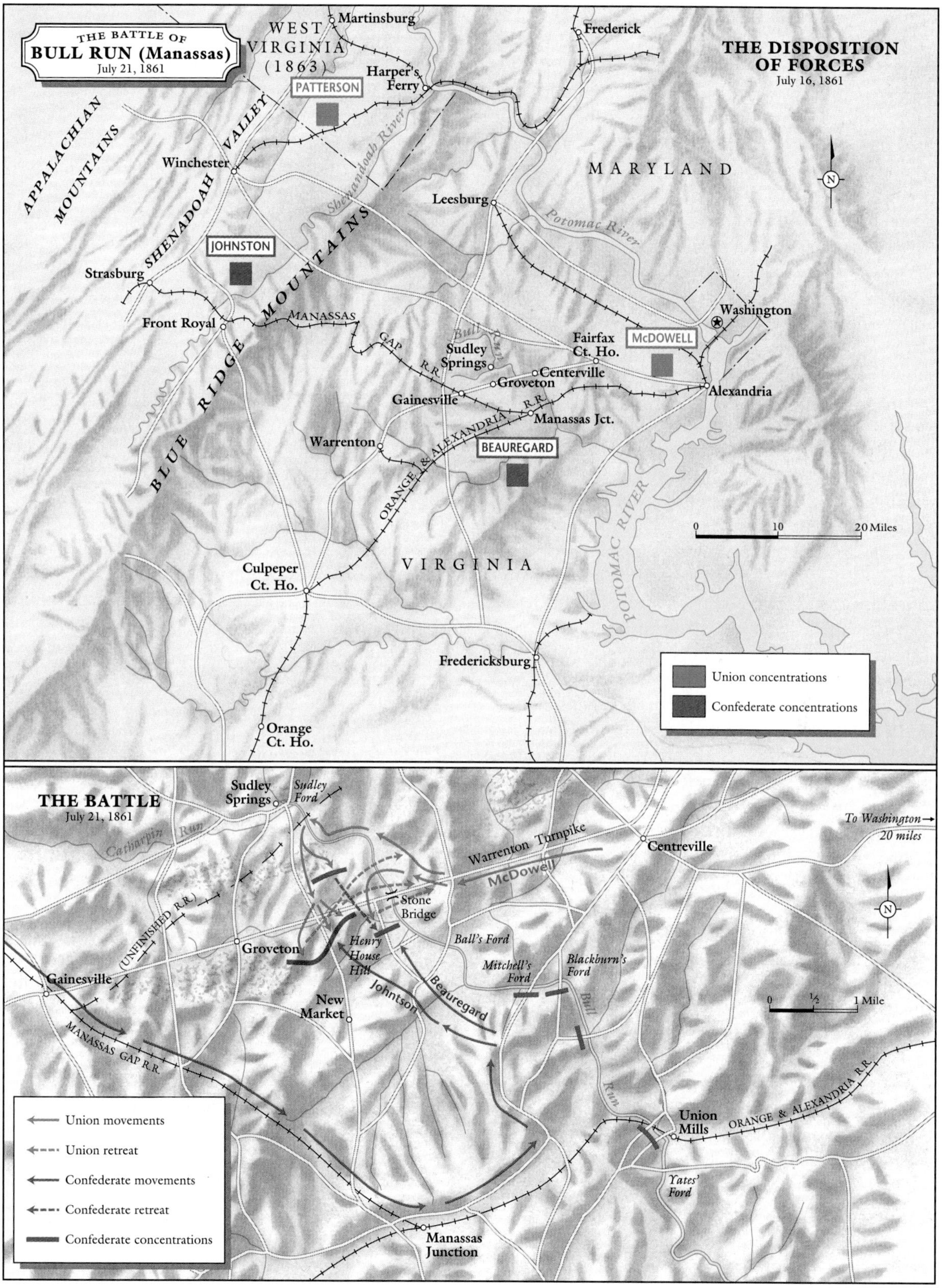

THE BATTLE OF
BULL RUN (Manassas)
July 21, 1861

WEST VIRGINIA (1863)

THE DISPOSITION OF FORCES
July 16, 1861

Martinsburg

Frederick

PATTERSON

Harper's Ferry

MARYLAND

APPALACHIAN MOUNTAINS

Winchester

SHENANDOAH VALLEY

Shenandoah River

Leesburg

Potomac River

JOHNSTON

BLUE RIDGE MOUNTAINS

Strasburg

Front Royal

MANASSAS GAP R.R.

Bull Run

Washington

Fairfax Ct. Ho.

McDOWELL

Sudley Springs

Centerville

Groveton

Gainesville

Alexandria

Warrenton

ORANGE & ALEXANDRIA R.R.

Manassas Jct.

BEAUREGARD

POTOMAC RIVER

0   10   20 Miles

Culpeper Ct. Ho.

VIRGINIA

Fredericksburg

Orange Ct. Ho.

Union concentrations
Confederate concentrations

THE BATTLE
July 21, 1861

Sudley Springs

Sudley Ford

Catharpin Run

Warrenton Turnpike

Centreville

To Washington →
20 miles

McDowell

Stone Bridge

(UNFINISHED R.R.)

Groveton

Ball's Ford

Henry House Hill

Mitchell's Ford

Blackburn's Ford

Gainesville

New Market

Johntson

Beauregard

Bull Run

MANASSAS GAP R.R.

Union Mills

ORANGE & ALEXANDRIA R.R.

0   ½   1 Mile

Yates' Ford

Manassas Junction

← Union movements
←---- Union retreat
← Confederate movements
←---- Confederate retreat
▬▬ Confederate concentrations

destiny, McClellan soon won the nickname "The Young Napoleon." He had commanded the Union army that won control of West Virginia, and he took firm control in Washington during the summer and fall of 1861. He organized and trained the Army of the Potomac into a large, well-disciplined, and well-equipped fighting force. He was just what the North needed after its dispiriting defeat at Bull Run. When Scott stepped down as general-in-chief on November 1, McClellan took his place.

But as winter approached and McClellan did nothing to advance against the smaller Confederate army whose outposts stood only a few miles from Washington, his failings as a commander began to show themselves. He was a perfectionist in a profession where nothing could ever be perfect. His army was perpetually *almost* ready to move. McClellan was afraid to take risks; he never learned the military lesson that no victory can be won without risking defeat. He consistently overestimated the strength of enemy forces facing him (sometimes by multiples of two or three) and used these faulty estimates as a reason for inaction until he could increase his own force. When criticism of McClellan began to appear in the press, from within the administration and among Republicans in Congress (he was a Democrat), he grew defensive and accused his critics of political motives. Having built a fine fighting machine, he was afraid to start it up for fear it might break. The caution and defensive-mindedness that McClellan instilled in the Army of the Potomac's officer corps persisted for more than a year after Lincoln removed him from command in November 1862.

Naval Operations

Because of McClellan, no significant action occurred in the Virginia theater after the Battle of Bull Run until the spring of 1862. Meanwhile, the Union navy won a series of victories over Confederate coastal forts at Hatteras Inlet on the North Carolina coast, Port Royal Sound in South Carolina, and at other points along the Atlantic and Gulf coasts. These successes provided the navy with new bases from which to expand and tighten the blockade. They also provided small Union armies with takeoff points for operations along the southern coast. In February and March 1862, an expeditionary force under General Ambrose Burnside won

a string of victories and occupied several crucial ports on the North Carolina sounds. Another Union force captured Fort Pulaski at the mouth of the Savannah River, cutting off that important Confederate port from the sea.

One of the Union navy's most impressive achievements was the capture in April 1862 of New Orleans, the Confederacy's largest city and principal port. Most of the Confederate troops defending southern Louisiana had been called up the Mississippi to confront a Union invasion of Tennessee, leaving only some militia, an assortment of steamboats converted into gunboats, and two strong forts flanking the river seventy miles below New Orleans to defend the city. That was not enough to stop Union naval commander David G. Farragut, a native of Tennessee who had remained loyal to the U.S. Navy in which he had served for half a century. In a daring action on April 24, 1862, Farragut led his fleet upriver past the forts, scattering the Confederate fleet and fending off fire rafts. He lost four ships, but the rest got through and compelled the surrender of New Orleans with nine-inch naval guns trained on its streets. Fifteen thousand Union soldiers marched in and occupied the city and its hinterland.

Fort Henry and Fort Donelson

These victories demonstrated the importance of seapower even in a civil war. Even more important in their strategic consequences were significant northern victories won by the combined efforts of the army and fleets of river gunboats on the Tennessee and Cumberland rivers, which flow through Tennessee and Kentucky and empty into the Ohio River just before it joins the Mississippi. The unlikely hero of these victories was Ulysses S. Grant, who had failed in several civilian occupations after resigning from the peacetime army in 1854. Rejoining the army when war broke out, he had demonstrated a quiet efficiency and a determined will that won him promotion from Illinois colonel to brigadier general and the command of a small but growing force based at Cairo, Illinois, in the fall of 1861. When Confederate units entered Kentucky in September, Grant moved quickly to occupy the mouths of the Cumberland and Tennessee rivers. Unlike McClellan, who had known nothing but success in his career and was afraid to jeopardize that record, Grant's experience of failure made him willing to take risks, having little to lose. He demonstrated that willingness dramatically in the early months of 1862.

Military strategists on both sides understood the importance of these navigable rivers as highways of invasion into the South's heartland. The Confederacy had built forts at strategic points along the rivers and had begun to convert a few steamboats into gunboats and rams to back up the forts. The Union also converted steamboats into "timberclad" gunboats—so-called because they were armored just enough to protect the engine and the paddle wheels but not enough to impair speed and shallow draft for river operations. The Union also built a new class of ironclad gunboats designed for river warfare. Carrying thirteen guns, these flat-bottomed, wide-beamed vessels drew only six feet of water. Their hulls and paddle-wheels were protected by a

sloping casemate sheathed in iron armor up to $2\frac{1}{2}$ inches thick.

When the first of these strange-looking but formidable craft were ready, in February 1862, Grant struck. His objectives were Forts Henry and Donelson on the Tennessee and Cumberland rivers just south of the Kentucky–Tennessee border. The gunboats knocked out Fort Henry on February 6 without the help of Grant's 15,000 troops. Fort Donelson proved a tougher nut to crack. Its guns repulsed a gunboat attack on February 14. Next day the 17,000-man Confederate army, in an attempt to break out of the fort, attacked Grant's besieging army, which had been reinforced to 27,000 men. With the calm decisiveness that became his trademark, Grant repaired a breach in his lines caused by the Confederate attack and directed a counterattack that penned the defenders back up in their fort. Cut off from support by either land or river, the Confederate commander asked

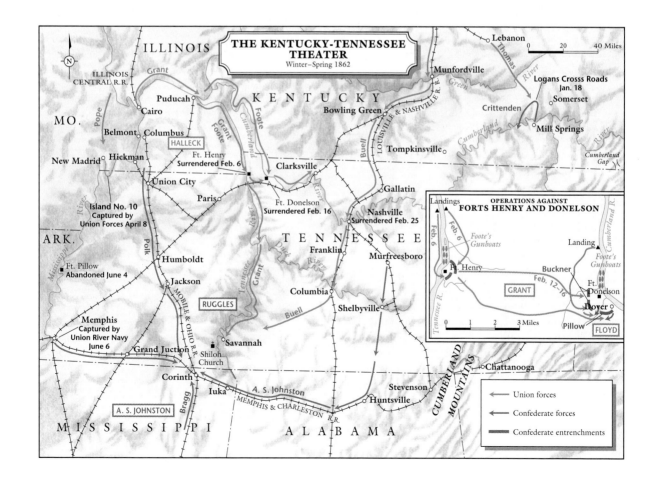

The Hornet's Nest at Shiloh   In the bloody fighting on April 6 at the Battle of Shiloh, portions of three Union divisions held out along a sunken farm road for several hours. Virtually surrounded by Confederate attackers, the 2,200 Union survivors surrendered in midafternoon. This was a costly Confederate success, for General Albert Sidney Johnston was mortally wounded while directing the attack. The volume of fire from Union defenders was so great that the Confederates called the enemy position the "hornet's nest" because of the angry whizzing bullets coming from it. The stubborn Union fighting at the hornet's nest bought Grant time to establish a defensive line from which he launched a successful counterattack the next day.

for surrender terms on February 16. Grant's reply made him instantly famous when it was published in the North: "No terms except an immediate and unconditional surrender can be accepted. I propose to move immediately upon your works." With no choice, the 13,000 surviving Confederates surrendered (some had escaped), giving Grant the most striking victory in the war thus far.

The strategic consequences of these victories were far-reaching. Union gunboats now ranged all the way up the Tennessee River to northern Alabama, enabling a Union division to occupy the region, and up the Cumberland to Nashville, which became the first Confederate state capital to surrender to Union forces, on February 25. Confederate military units pulled out of Kentucky and most of Tennessee and reassembled at the rail junction of

Corinth in northern Mississippi. Jubilation spread through the North and despair through the South. But by the end of March 1862 the Confederate commander in the western theater, Albert Sidney Johnston (not to be confused with Joseph E. Johnston in Virginia), had built up an army of 40,000 men at Corinth. His plan was to attack Grant's force of 35,000, which had established a base twenty miles away at Pittsburg Landing on the Tennessee River just north of the Mississippi–Tennessee border.

The Battle of Shiloh

On April 6 the Confederates attacked at dawn near a church called Shiloh, which gave its name to the battle. They caught Grant by surprise and drove the

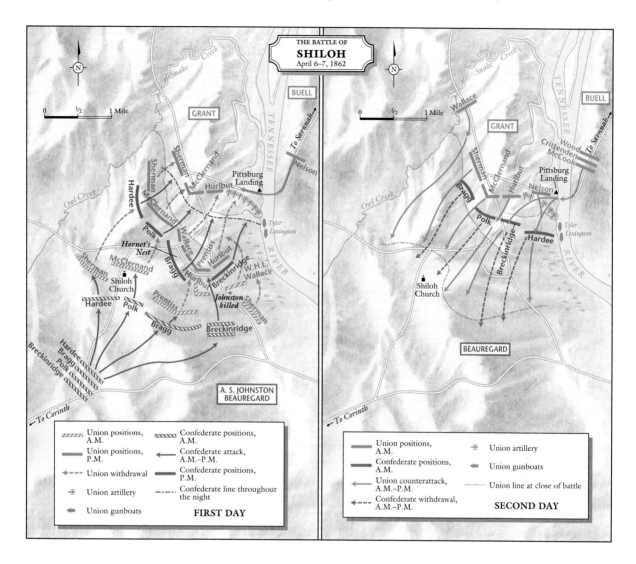

THE BATTLE OF
SHILOH
April 6–7, 1862

⬚ Union positions, A.M.	⬚ Confederate positions, A.M.	
▬ Union positions, P.M.	⬅ Confederate attack, A.M.–P.M.	
⬅--- Union withdrawal	▬ Confederate positions, P.M.	
⚒ Union artillery	--- Confederate line throughout the night	
◼ Union gunboats	**FIRST DAY**	

▬ Union positions, A.M.	⚒ Union artillery	
▬ Confederate positions, A.M.	◼ Union gunboats	
⬅ Union counterattack, A.M.–P.M.	--- Union line at close of battle	
⬅--- Confederate withdrawal, A.M.–P.M.	**SECOND DAY**	

unprepared Yankees toward the river. After a day's fighting of unprecedented intensity, with total casualties of 15,000, Grant's men brought the Confederate onslaught to a halt at dusk. One of the Confederate casualties was Johnston, who bled to death when a bullet severed an artery in his leg—the highest-ranking general on either side to be killed in the war. Pierre G. T. Beauregard, who had been transferred from Virginia to the West, took command after Johnston's death.

Some of Grant's subordinates advised retreat during the dismal night of April 6–7, but Grant would have none of it. Reinforced overnight by fresh troops from a Union army commanded by General Don Carlos Buell, which had been on its way to link up with Grant, the Union counterattacked next morning (April 7) and, after 9,000 more casualties to the two sides, drove the Confederates back to Corinth. Though Grant had snatched victory from the jaws of defeat, his reputation nevertheless suffered a decline for a time because of the heavy Union casualties (13,000) and the suspicion that he had been caught napping the first day.

Union triumphs in the western theater continued during that 1862 springtime of northern hope. The combined armies of Grant and Buell, under the overall command of the top-ranking Union general in the West, Henry W. Halleck, drove the Confederates out of Corinth at the end of May. Meanwhile, the Union gunboat fleet fought its way

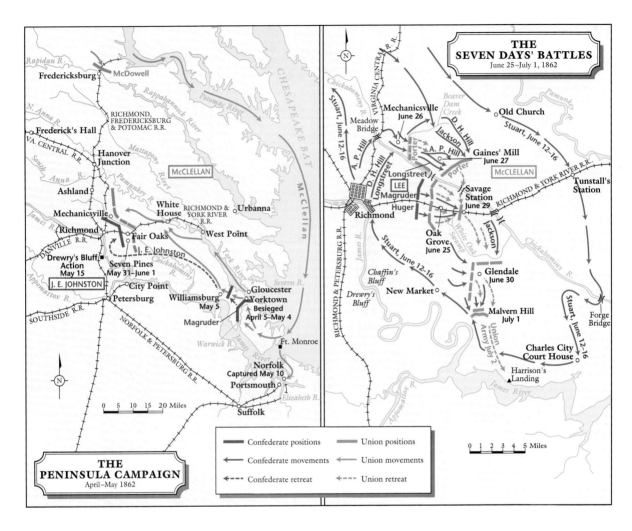

**THE
SEVEN DAYS' BATTLES**
June 25–July 1, 1862

**THE
PENINSULA CAMPAIGN**
April–May 1862

Confederate positions	Union positions
Confederate movements	Union movements
Confederate retreat	Union retreat

down the Mississippi to Vicksburg, virtually wiping out the Confederate fleet in a spectacular battle at Memphis on June 6. At Vicksburg the Union gunboats from the north connected with part of Farragut's fleet that had come up from New Orleans, taking Baton Rouge and Natchez along the way. The heavily fortified Confederate bastion at Vicksburg proved too strong for the firepower of the Union naval fleet to subdue. But the dramatic succession of Union triumphs in the West from February to June—including a decisive victory at the battle of Pea Ridge in northwest Arkansas on March 7–8—convinced the North that the war was nearly won. "Every blow tells fearfully against the rebellion," boasted the leading northern newspaper, the *New York Tribune,* on May 23, 1862. "The rebels themselves are panic-stricken, or despondent.

It now requires no very far reaching prophet to predict the end of this struggle."

The Virginia Theater

The *Tribune's* confidence stemmed from the situation in Virginia as well as from the situation in the West. But even as the editorial writer wrote these words, affairs in Virginia were about to take a sharp turn in favor of the Confederacy. Within three months the Union, so near a knockout victory that spring, would be back on the defensive.

In the western theater the broad rivers had facilitated the Union's invasion of the South. But in Virginia a half-dozen small rivers flowing west to east lay athwart the line of operations between Washington and Richmond and provided the Confederates with natural lines of defense. So McClellan, still in command of the Army of the Potomac, persuaded a reluctant Lincoln to approve a plan to transport the army down Chesapeake Bay to the tip of the Virginia peninsula, formed by the tidal portions of the York and James rivers. That would shorten the route to Richmond and would give the Union army a seaborne supply line secure from harassment by Confederate cavalry and guerrillas.

This was a good plan — in theory. And the logistical achievement of transporting 110,000 men and all their equipment, animals, and supplies by sea to the jump-off point near Yorktown was impressive. But then McClellan's failings began to surface. A small Confederate blocking force at Yorktown held him for the entire month of April, as he cautiously dragged up siege guns to blast a way through defenses that his large army could have punched through in days on foot. McClellan slowly followed the retreating Confederate force up the peninsula to a new defensive line only a few miles east of Richmond, all the while bickering with Lincoln and Secretary of War Edwin M. Stanton over the reinforcements they were withholding to protect Washington against a possible strike by "Stonewall" Jackson's small army in the Shenandoah Valley.

Jackson's month-long campaign in the Shenandoah (May 8–June 9), generally considered one of the most brilliant of the war, demonstrated what could be accomplished through deception, daring, and mobility. With only 17,000 men, Jackson moved by forced marches so swift that his infantry earned the nickname "Jackson's foot cavalry." Darting here and there through the Valley, they marched 350 miles in the course of one month; won four battles against three separate Union armies, whose combined numbers were more than twice their own (but which Jackson's force always outnumbered at the point of contact); and compelled Lincoln to divert to the Valley some of the reinforcements McClellan wanted for his offensive on the Peninsula.

Even without those reinforcements, McClellan's army substantially outnumbered the Confederate force defending Richmond, commanded by Joseph E. Johnston. As usual, though, McClellan overestimated Johnston's strength at double what it was and acted accordingly. Even so, by the last week of May, McClellan's army was within six miles of Richmond. A botched Confederate counterattack

on May 31–June 1 (the Battle of Seven Pines) produced no result except 6,000 Confederate and 5,000 Union casualties. But one of those casualties was Joseph Johnston, who had been wounded in the shoulder. Jefferson Davis named Robert E. Lee to replace him.

The Seven Days' Battles

That appointment marked a major turning point in the campaign. Lee had done little so far to earn a wartime reputation, having failed in his only field command to dislodge Union forces from control of West Virginia. But his qualities as a commander immediately manifested themselves when he took over what he renamed "The Army of Northern Virginia." Those qualities were boldness, a willingness to take great risks, an almost uncanny ability to read the enemy commander's mind, and a charisma that won the devotion of his men. While McClellan continued to dawdle and to feud with Lincoln over reinforcements, Lee sent his dashing cavalry commander Jeb Stuart to lead a reconnaissance around the Union army to discover its weak points, then brought Jackson's army in from the Shenandoah Valley, and with the combined forces launched a June 26 attack on McClellan's right flank in what became known as the Seven Days' battles — the heaviest fighting of the war thus far. Constantly attacking, Lee's army of 88,000 drove McClellan's 100,000 away from Richmond and forced them to retreat to a new fortified base on the James River. The offensive cost the Confederates 20,000 casualties (compared with 16,000 for the Union) and turned Richmond into one vast hospital. But it reversed the momentum of the war.

CONFEDERATE COUNTEROFFENSIVES

Northern sentiments plunged from the height of euphoria in May to the depths of despair in July. "The feeling of despondency here is very great," wrote a New Yorker, while a southerner exulted that "Lee has turned the tide, and I shall not be surprised if we have a long career of successes." The tide turned in the western theater as well. Union conquests there in the spring had brought 50,000 square miles of Confederate territory under Union control.

But to occupy and administer this vast area many thousands of soldiers had to be drawn from combat forces. These depleted forces dangled deep in enemy territory, at the end of long supply lines, and were vulnerable to cavalry raids. Confederate horsemen were quick to take advantage of the opportunity. During the summer and fall of 1862 the cavalry commands of Tennesseean Nathan Bedford Forrest and Kentuckian John Hunt Morgan staged repeated raids in which they burned bridges, blew up tunnels, tore up tracks, and captured supply depots and the Union garrisons trying to defend them. By August the once-formidable Union war machine in the West seemed to have broken down.

The Confederate cavalry raids paved the way for infantry counteroffensives. The Confederate army that had been driven out of Corinth in May was now divided into two parts. After recapturing some territory, Earl Van Dorn's Army of West Tennessee got a bloody nose when it tried and failed to retake Corinth on October 3–4. At the end of August, Braxton Bragg's Army of Tennessee launched from Chattanooga a drive northward through east Tennessee and Kentucky. It had almost reached the Ohio River in September but was turned back at the Battle of Perryville on October 8 and forced to retreat to central Tennessee. Even after these defeats, the Confederate forces in the western theater were in better shape than they had been four months earlier.

The Second Battle of Bull Run

Most attention, though, focused on Virginia. Lincoln reorganized the Union corps near Washington, which were not part of McClellan's Army of the Potomac, into the Army of Virginia under General John Pope, who had won minor successes as commander of a small army in Missouri and Tennessee. In August, Lincoln ordered the withdrawal of the Army of the Potomac from the peninsula to reinforce Pope for a drive southward from Washington. Lee quickly seized the opportunity provided by the separation of the two Union armies confronting him, by the ill will between McClellan and Pope and their subordinates, and by the bickering among various factions in Washington. To attack Pope before McClellan could reinforce him, Lee shifted most of his army to northern Virginia, sent Jackson's "foot cavalry" on a deep raid to the Union's rear to destroy its supply base at

Manassas Junction, and then brought his army back together to inflict a second humiliating defeat on a Union army near Bull Run on August 29–30. The demoralized Union forces retreated into the Washington defenses, where Lincoln reluctantly gave McClellan command of the two armies and told him to reorganize them into one.

Lee, despite the exhaustion of his troops and his lack of supplies, decided to keep up the pressure by invading Maryland. On September 4, his weary troops splashed across the Potomac at a ford forty miles upriver from Washington. Momentous possibilities accompanied this move, which took place at the same time Braxton Bragg was invading Kentucky. Maryland might be won for the Confederacy. Another victory by Lee might influence the northern congressional elections in November and help Democrats who opposed Lincoln's war policies gain control of Congress and paralyze the northern war effort—perhaps even force the Lincoln administration to negotiate peace with the Confederacy. The invasion of Maryland, coming on top of other Confederate successes, might even persuade Britain and France to recognize the Confederacy and intervene to end the war—especially since the long-expected cotton famine had finally materialized. In September 1862 the British and French governments were indeed considering recognition and were awaiting the outcome of Lee's invasion to decide whether to proceed. Great issues rode with the armies as Lee crossed the Potomac and McClellan cautiously moved north to meet him.

SUGGESTED READING

The most comprehensive one-volume study of the Civil War years is James M. McPherson, *Battle Cry of Freedom: The Civil War Era* (1988). The same ground is covered in greater detail by Allan Nevins, *The War for the Union,* 4 vols. (1959–1971). For single-volume accounts of the Confederacy and the Union that emphasize the home fronts, see Emory M. Thomas, *The Confederate Nation, 1861–1865* (1979); George C. Rable, *The Confederate Republic* (1994); and Phillip Shaw Paludan, *"A People's Contest": The Union and Civil War, 1861–1865* (1988). The important roles of women in many facets of the war effort are described by Mary Elizabeth Massey, *Bonnet Brigades* (1966); Agatha Young, *Women and the Crisis: Women of the North in the Civil War* (1959); and

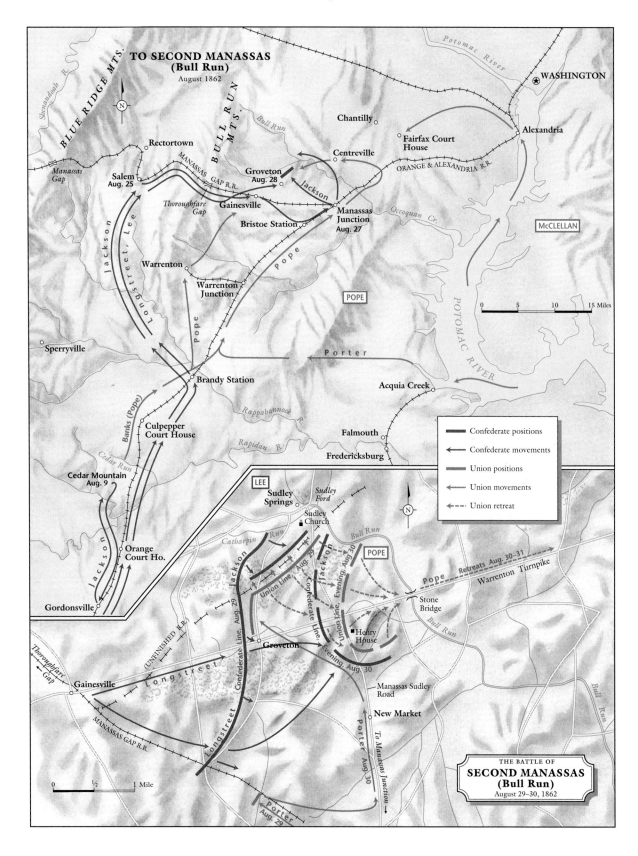

**TO SECOND MANASSAS
(Bull Run)**
August 1862

	Confederate positions
←	Confederate movements
	Union positions
←	Union movements
←--	Union retreat

**THE BATTLE OF
SECOND MANASSAS
(Bull Run)**
August 29–30, 1862

George C. Rable, *Civil Wars: Women and the Crisis of Southern Nationalism* (1989). Two multivolume classics that concentrate mainly on military campaigns and battles are Bruce Catton, *The Centennial History of the Civil War,* vol. 1: *The Coming Fury* (1961); vol. 2: *Terrible Swift Sword* (1963); and vol. 3: *Never Call Retreat* (1965); and Shelby Foote, *The Civil War: A Narrative,* 3 vols. (1958–1974). Social history is the main focus of two collections of essays: Maris A. Vinovskis, ed., *Toward a Social History of the American Civil War* (1990) and Catherine Clinton and Nina Silber, eds., *Divided Houses: Gender and the Civil War* (1992).

For penetrating studies of the officers and men in three of the Civil War's most famous armies, see Bruce Catton's three volumes on the Army of the Potomac: *Mr. Lincoln's Army* (1951); *Glory Road* (1952); and *A Stillness at Appomattox* (1953); Douglass Southall Freeman's study of officers in the Army of Northern Virginia, *Lee's Lieutenants: A Study in Command,* 3 vols. (1942–1944); and Thomas L. Connelly's two works on the Army of Tennessee, *Army of the Heartland* (1967) and *Autumn of Glory* (1971), plus Larry J. Daniel, *Soldiering in the Army of Tennessee: A Portrait of Life in the Confederate Army* (1991). The classic studies of Civil War soldiers by Bell Irvin Wiley are *The Life of Johnny Reb* (1943) and *The Life of Billy Yank* (1952). For additional insights into the character and experience of soldiers, see Reid Mitchell, *Civil War Soldiers* (1988); Reid Mitchell, *The Vacant Chair: The Northern Soldier Leaves Home* (1993); and James M. McPherson, *What They Fought For, 1861–1865* (1994).

Biographies of leading Civil War figures are of great value for understanding the period. For Abraham Lincoln, see especially Benjamin P. Thomas, *Abraham Lincoln* (1952); Stephen B. Oates, *With Malice Toward None: The Life of Abraham Lincoln* (1977); Mark E. Neely, Jr., *The Last Best Hope of Earth: Abraham Lincoln and the Promise of America* (1993); James G. Randall, *Lincoln the President,* 4 vols. (1945–1955; vol. 4 completed by Richard N. Current); and James M. McPherson, *Abraham Lincoln and the Second American Revolution* (1991). For Jefferson Davis, the best one-volume biography is William C. Davis, *Jefferson Davis: The Man and His Hour* (1991). See also Hudson Strode, *Jefferson Davis,* 3 vols. (1955–1964). The classic biography of Robert E. Lee is Douglass Southall Freeman, *R. E. Lee: A Biography,* 3 vols. (1934–1935), which has been condensed into a one-volume abridgment by Richard Harwell, *Lee* (1961). For revisionist interpretations of Lee, see Thomas L. Connelly, *The Marble Man: Robert E. Lee and His Image in American Society* (1977) and Alan T. Nolan, *Lee Considered: General Robert E. Lee and Civil War History* (1991). Biographies of two other leading Confederate generals are Grady McWhiney, *Braxton Bragg and Confederate Defeat* (1969); Judith Lee Hallock, *Braxton Bragg and Confederate Defeat* (1991); and Craig L. Symonds, *Joseph E. Johnston: A Civil War Biography* (1992). On the Union side, the standard one-volume biography of Ulysses S. Grant is William S. McFeely, *Grant: A Biography* (1981). For a

fuller account of Grant during the war, see Bruce Catton, *Grant Moves South* (1960); Bruce Catton, *Grant Takes Command* (1969); and Brooks D. Simpson, *Let Us Have Peace: Ulysses S. Grant and the Politics of War and Reconstruction, 1861–1868* (1991). There are many biographies of William T. Sherman; two of the most valuable are Basil H. Liddell Hart, *Sherman: Soldier, Realist, American* (1929), and John F. Marszalek, *Sherman: A Soldier's Passion for Order* (1993). For George B. McClellan, the best biography is Stephen W. Sears, *George B. McClellan: The Young Napoleon* (1988).

The election of 1860 and the crisis of secession have been the subject of numerous studies: Emerson D. Fite, *The Presidential Campaign of 1860* (1911); Reinhard H. Luthin, *The First Lincoln Campaign* (1944); Ollinger Crenshaw, *The Slave States in the Presidential Election of 1860* (1945); William E. Baringer, *Lincoln's Rise to Power* (1937); Dwight L. Dumond, *The Secession Movement 1860–1861* (1931); Ralph Wooster, *The Secession Conventions of the South* (1962); Donald E. Reynolds, *Editors Make War: Southern Newspapers in the Secession Crisis* (1970); Steven A. Channing, *A Crisis of Fear: Secession in South Carolina* (1970); William L. Barney, *The Secessionist Impulse: Alabama and Mississippi in 1860* (1974); Michael P. Johnson, *Toward a Patriarchal Republic: The Secession of Georgia* (1977); Daniel W. Crofts, *Reluctant Confederates: Upper South Unionists in the Secession Crisis* (1989); David M. Potter, *Lincoln and His Party in the Secession Crisis* (1942; new ed. 1962); and Kenneth M. Stampp, *And the War Came: The North and the Secession Crisis, 1860–1861* (1950). The best account of the standoff at Fort Sumter that led to war is Richard N. Current, *Lincoln and the First Shot* (1963).

The bitter experiences of the border states in the war are chronicled by William E. Parrish, *Turbulent Partnership: Missouri and the Union 1861–1865* (1963); Jean H. Baker, *The Politics of Continuity: Maryland Political Parties from 1858 to 1870* (1973); William H. Townsend, *Lincoln and the Bluegrass: Slavery and Civil War in Kentucky* (1955); and Lowell Harrison, *The Civil War and Kentucky* (1975). For guerrilla warfare along the border, particularly in Missouri, the best studies are Jay Monaghan, *Civil War on the Western Border 1854–1865* (1955) and Michael Fellman, *Inside War: The Guerrilla Conflict in Missouri during the Civil War* (1989). For the creation of West Virginia, see Richard O. Curry, *A House Divided: A Study of Statehood Politics and the Copperhead Movement in West Virginia* (1964).

The problem of Confederate war finance is treated by Richard C. Todd, *Confederate Finance* (1954) and Douglas B. Ball, *Financial Failure and Confederate Defeat* (1990). For Union war finance, see Bray Hammond, *Sovereignty and an Empty Purse: Banks and Politics in the Civil War Era* (1970).

There is a large literature on Civil War navies and the blockade. Perhaps the best place to begin is William M. Fowler, Jr., *Under Two Flags: The American Navy in the Civil War* (1990). The fullest account of naval warfare is Virgil C. Jones, *The Civil War at Sea,* 3 vols. (1960–1962). For the river war, see H. Allen Gosnell, *Guns on the Western Waters: The Story of River Gunboats in the Civil War* (1949); John D. Milligan, *Gunboats down the Mississippi* (1965); and James M. Merrill, *Battle Flags South: The Story of the Civil War Navies on Western Waters* (1970). For the blockade and blockade running, see Robert Carse, *Blockade: The Civil War at Sea* (1958) and Stephen R. Wise, *Lifeline of the Confederacy: Blockade Running during the Civil War* (1988). The story of Confederate commerce raiding is told in George W. Dalzell, *The Flight from the Flag* (1943) and Edward C. Boykin, *Ghost Ship of the Confederacy: The Story of the "Alabama" and Her Captain* (1957).

Foreign policy complications caused by Confederate shipbuilding in Britain are treated in Frank J. Merli, *Great Britain and the Confederate Navy* (1970). The most concise account of Civil War diplomacy is David P. Crook, *The North, the South,*

and the Powers 1861–1865* (1974), an abridged version of which was published with the title *Diplomacy during the Civil War* (1975). The classic study of Confederate diplomacy is Frank L. Owsley, *King Cotton Diplomacy* (1931; rev. ed. 1959). British–American and British–Confederate relations have received exhaustive attention; the fullest studies are Ephraim D. Adams, *Great Britain and the American Civil War,* 2 vols. (1925); Brian Jenkins, *Britain and the War for the Union,* 2 vols. (1974–1980); and Howard Jones, *The Union in Peril: The Crisis over British Intervention in the Civil War* (1992). For the *Trent* Affair, consult Gordon H. Warren, *Fountains of Discontent: The "Trent" Affair and the Freedom of the Seas* (1981). For relations between France and the two warring parties, see Lynn M. Case and Warren F. Spencer, *The United States and France: Civil War Diplomacy* (1970).

Chapter 17

A New Birth of Freedom, 1862–1865

The Almighty has His own purposes. "Woe unto the world because of offences! For it must needs be that offences come; but woe to that man by whom the offence cometh!" If we shall suppose that American Slavery is one of those offences which, in the providence of God, must needs come, but which, having continued through His appointed time, He now wills to remove, and that He gives to both North and South, this terrible war, as the woe due to those by whom the offence came, shall we discern therein any departure from those divine attributes which the believers in the Living God always ascribe to Him? Fondly do we hope — fervently do we pray — that this mighty scourge of war may speedily pass away. Yet, if God wills that it continue, until all the wealth piled by the bond-man's two hundred and fifty years of unrequited toil shall be sunk, and until every drop of blood drawn with the lash, shall be paid by another drawn with the sword, as was said three thousand years ago, so still it must be said "the judgments of the Lord, are true and righteous altogether."

From Abraham Lincoln's Second Inaugural Address,
March 4, 1865

One of the great issues awaiting resolution as the armies moved into Maryland in September 1862 was emancipation of the slaves. The war had taken on new dimensions since the hope for a quick Union victory had collapsed that summer. It had become a "total war," requiring the mobilization or the destruction of every resource that might bring victory or inflict defeat. To abolish slavery would strike at a vital Confederate resource (slave labor) and mobilize that resource for the Union along with the moral power of fighting for freedom. Slaves had already made clear their choice for liberty and Union by escaping to Union lines by the tens of thousands. Lincoln had made up his mind to issue an emancipation proclamation and was waiting for a Union victory to give it credibility and potency.

SLAVERY AND THE WAR

At first, the leaders of both the Union and the Confederacy tried to keep the issue of slavery out of the war. Although white southerners generally were committed to slavery, two-thirds of the white families in the Confederacy owned no slaves. For southern leaders to proclaim that the defense of slavery was the aim of the war might prompt non-slaveholders to ask why they were risking their lives to protect their rich neighbors' property. Even more important, it might jeopardize Confederate efforts to win recognition and support from Britain. So the Confederates proclaimed not slavery, but liberty as their war aim — the same liberty their ancestors had fought for in 1776. The unspoken corollary of that aim was the liberty of whites to own blacks.

In the North, the issue of slavery—or, more accurately, of emancipation—was deeply divisive. Lincoln had been elected on a platform pledged to contain the expansion of slavery as the first step toward placing it in the "course of ultimate extinction." But that pledge had provoked most of the southern states to quit the Union. For the administration to take action against slavery in 1861 would be to risk the break-up of the fragile coalition Lincoln had stitched together to fight the war: Republicans, Democrats, and border-state Unionists. Spokesmen for the latter two groups served notice that, though they supported a war *for* the Union, they would not support a war *against* slavery. In July 1861, with Lincoln's endorsement, Congress passed a resolution affirming that northern war aims included no intention "of overthrowing or interfering with the rights or established institutions of the States"—in plain words, slavery—but intended only "to defend and maintain the supremacy of the Constitution and to preserve the Union."

But many antislavery supporters did not see it that way. They insisted that a rebellion sustained *by* slavery in defense *of* slavery could be suppressed only by striking *against* slavery. As the black leader Frederick Douglass stated, "To fight against slaveholders, without fighting against slavery, is but a half-hearted business, and paralyzes the hands engaged in it. . . . War for the destruction of liberty must be met with war for the destruction of slavery." A good many Union soldiers, some who had held no previous antislavery convictions, began to grumble about protecting the property of traitors in arms against the United States.

Wars tend to develop a logic and momentum of their own that go beyond the original purposes of the participants. That is especially true of wars as vast as the American Civil War. When northerners discovered at Bull Run in July 1861 that they were not going to win an easy victory, many of them began to take a harder look at slavery. Both sides were mobilizing all their resources for a long-term military effort, and one of the most important Confederate resources was slavery. Slaves constituted the principal labor force in the South. They raised most of the food and fiber, built most of the military fortifications, worked on the railroads and in mines and munitions factories. Southern newspapers boasted that

slavery was "a tower of strength to the Confederacy" because it enabled the South "to place in the field a force so much larger in proportion to her white population than the North." Precisely, responded abolitionists. So why not convert this Confederate asset to a Union advantage by confiscating slaves as enemy property and using them to help the northern war effort? As the war ground on into 1862 and as casualties mounted, this argument began to make sense to many Yankees.

The "Contrabands"

The slaves themselves entered this debate in a dramatic fashion. As Union armies penetrated the South, a growing number of slaves voted with their feet for freedom. By twos and threes, by families, eventually by scores, they escaped from their masters and came over to the Union lines. By creating a situation in which Union officers would either have to return them to slavery or accept them, these escaped slaves took the first step toward making it a war for freedom—and they turned the theory of confiscation of Confederate property into a reality.

For while some commanders returned escaped slaves to their masters or prevented them from entering Union camps, most increasingly did not. Their rationale was first expressed by General Benjamin Butler. In May 1861 three slaves who had been working for the Confederate army escaped to Butler's lines near Fortress Monroe at the mouth of the James River in Virginia. Butler refused to return them, on the grounds that they were "contraband of war." The phrase caught on. For the rest of the war, slaves who came within Union lines were known as contrabands. On August 6, 1861, Congress legitimized this concept by passing a confiscation act that authorized the seizure of all property, including slaves, that was being used for military purposes by the Confederates. The following March, Congress forbade the return of slaves who entered Union lines—even those belonging to owners loyal to the Union.

The Border States

This problem of slavery in the loyal border states preoccupied Lincoln. On August 30, 1861, John C. Frémont, whose political influence had won him a commission as major general and command of

A Ride for Liberty   This splendid painting of a slave family escaping to Union lines during the Civil War dramatizes the experiences of thousands of slaves who thereby became "contrabands" and gained their freedom. Most of them came on foot, but this enterprising family stole a horse as well as themselves from their master.

Union forces in Missouri, issued an order freeing the slaves of all Confederate sympathizers in Missouri. This caused such a backlash among border-state Unionists who feared it was a prelude to a general abolition edict that Lincoln felt compelled to revoke Frémont's order, lest it "alarm our Southern Union friends, and turn them against us."

In the spring of 1862, Lincoln tried persuasion instead of force in the border states. At his urging, Congress passed a resolution offering federal compensation to states that voluntarily abolished slavery. Three times, from March to July 1862, Lincoln summoned border-state congressmen to the White House to discuss the matter. He told them that the Confederate hope that their states might join the rebellion was helping to keep the war alive. Accept the proposal for compensated emancipation, he pleaded, and that hope would die. The pressure for a bold antislavery policy was growing stronger, he warned them in May. Another Union general had issued an emancipation order; Lincoln had suspended it, but "you cannot," Lincoln told the border-state congressmen, "be blind to the signs of the times."

But they did seem to be blind. They complained that they were being coerced, bickered about the amount of compensation, and wrung their hands over the prospects of economic ruin and race war, even if emancipation were to take place gradually over a thirty-year period, as Lincoln had suggested. At a final meeting, on July 12, Lincoln, in effect, gave them an ultimatum: accept compensated emancipation or face the consequences. "The incidents of the war cannot be avoided," he said. Thousands of slaves had already run away to Union camps in the border states. "If the war continue long . . . the institution in your states will be extinguished by mere friction and abrasion . . . and you will have nothing valuable in lieu of it." But again they failed to see the light and by a vote of 20 to 9, they rejected the proposal for compensated emancipation.

The Decision for Emancipation

That very evening, Lincoln made up his mind to issue an emancipation proclamation in his capacity as commander in chief with power to order the seizure of enemy property used to wage war against the United States. Several factors, in addition to the recalcitrance of the border states, impelled Lincoln to this fateful decision. One was a growing demand from his own party for bolder action: Congress had just passed a second confiscation act calling for seizure of the property of active Confederates. Another was rising sentiment in the army to take off the "kid gloves" when dealing with "traitors." "The iron gauntlet," wrote one Union officer in Tennessee, "must be used more than the silken glove to crush this serpent." From General Henry W. Halleck, who had been summoned to Washington as general-in-chief, went orders to General Grant in northern Mississippi instructing him on the treatment of rebel sympathizers inside Union lines: "Handle that class without gloves, and take their property for public use." Grant himself had written several months earlier that if the Confederacy "cannot be whipped in any other way than through a war against slavery, let it come to that." Finally, Lincoln's decision reflected his sentiments about the "unqualified evil" and "monstrous injustice" of slavery.

It was the military situation, however, rather than his moral convictions, that would determine the timing and scope of Lincoln's emancipation policy. Northern hopes that the war would soon be ended had risen after the victories of early 1862 but had then plummeted amid the reverses of that summer. Lincoln had been obliged to make an agonizing reappraisal of war measures.

Three courses of action seemed possible. One, favored by the so-called Peace Democrats, urged an armistice and peace negotiations to patch together some kind of Union, but that would have been tantamount to conceding Confederate victory. Republicans therefore reviled the Peace Democrats as traitorous "Copperheads," after the poisonous snake. A second alternative was to keep on fighting—in the hope that with a few more Union victories, the rebels would lay down their arms and the Union could be restored. But such a policy would leave slavery intact. General McClellan was one of the most prominent advocates for this course of action. He wrote Lincoln an unsolicited letter of advice on July 7, 1862, warning him that "neither confiscation of property . . . [n]or forcible abolition of slavery should be contemplated for a moment." Yet that was precisely what Lincoln was contemplating. This was the third alternative: total war to mobilize all the resources of the North and to destroy all the resources of the South, including slavery—a war not to restore the old Union but to build a new one on the ashes of the old.

After his meeting with the border-state representatives convinced him there could be no compromise, Lincoln made his decision. The next day, July 13, he privately informed two members of the Cabinet, and a week later formally notified the whole Cabinet of his intention to issue an emancipation proclamation. It was "a military necessity, absolutely essential to the preservation of the Union," said Lincoln, according to Secretary of the Navy Gideon Welles's later transcription of the president's words. "We must free the slaves or be ourselves subdued. The slaves [are] undeniably an element of strength to those who [have] their service, and we must decide whether that element should be with us or against us. . . . We wanted the army to strike more vigorous blows. The Administration must set an example, and strike at the heart of the rebellion."

The Cabinet agreed, except for Postmaster-General Montgomery Blair, a resident of Maryland and a former Democrat, who warned that the border states and the Democrats would rebel against the proclamation and perhaps cost the administration the fall congressional elections as well as vital support for the war. Lincoln might have agreed—two months earlier. But now he believed that the strength gained from an emancipation policy—from the slaves themselves, from the dynamic Republican segment of northern opinion, and in the eyes of foreign nations—would more than compensate for the hostility of Democrats and border-state Unionists. But Lincoln did accept the advice of Secretary of State Seward to delay the proclamation "until you can give it to the country supported by military success." Otherwise, Seward argued, it might be viewed "as the last measure of an exhausted government, a cry for help . . . our last *shriek,* on the retreat." So Lincoln slipped his proclamation into a desk drawer and waited for a military victory. It would prove to be a long wait.

Meanwhile, the Union government put into effect other measures to step up the war effort. Lincoln issued a call for 300,000 new three-year volunteers for the army. In July, Congress passed a militia act giving the president greater powers to mobilize the state militias into federal service and to draft men into the militia if the states failed to do so. This was not yet a national draft law, such as the Confederacy had enacted in April at a low point in its military fortunes. But it was a step in that direction. In August, Lincoln called up 300,000 militia for nine months of service, in addition to the 300,000 three-year volunteers. (These calls eventually yielded 421,000 three-year volunteers and 88,000 nine-month militia.) The Peace Democrats railed against these measures and provoked anti-draft riots in some localities. The government responded by arresting rioters and anti-war activists under the president's suspension of the writ of *habeas corpus*.[1]

Democrats denounced these "arbitrary arrests" as unconstitutional violations of civil liberties—and added this issue to others on which they hoped to gain control of the next House of Representatives in the fall elections. With the decline in northern morale following the defeat at Second Bull Run and the early success of the Confederate invasion of Kentucky, prospects for a Democratic triumph seemed bright. One more military victory by Lee's Army of Northern Virginia might crack the northern will to continue the fighting. It would certainly bring diplomatic recognition of the Confederacy by Britain and France. Lee's legions began crossing the Potomac into Maryland on September 4, 1862.

Antietam and the Emancipation Proclamation

The Confederate invasion ran into difficulties from the start. The people of western Maryland, the most Unionist part of the state, responded impassively to Lee's proclamation that he had come "to aid you in throwing off this foreign yoke" of Yankee rule. Lee split his army into five parts. Three of them, under the overall command of Stonewall Jackson, occupied the heights surrounding the Union garrison at Harpers Ferry which lay athwart the Confederate supply route from the Shenandoah Valley. The other

two remained on watch in the South Mountain passes west of Frederick. Then, on September 13, Union commander George B. McClellan had an extraordinary stroke of luck. In a field near Frederick, two of his soldiers found a copy of Lee's orders for these deployments. Wrapped around three cigars, they had apparently been dropped by a careless southern officer when the Confederate army passed through Frederick four days earlier. With this new information, McClellan planned to pounce on the separated segments of Lee's army before they could reunite. "Here is a paper," he exulted, "with which if I cannot whip 'Bobbie Lee,' I will be willing to go home."

But McClellan moved so cautiously that he lost much of his advantage. Union troops overwhelmed the Confederate defenders of the South Mountain passes on September 14. But they advanced too slowly to save the garrison at Harpers Ferry, which surrendered 12,000 men to Jackson on September 15. Lee then managed to reunite most of his army near the village of Sharpsburg by September 17, when McClellan finally crossed Antietam Creek to attack. Even so, the Union army outnumbered the Confederates by almost two to one (75,000 to 40,000 men), but McClellan, as usual, believed that the enemy outnumbered *him*. Thus he missed several opportunities to inflict a truly crippling defeat on the Confederacy. The one-day battle of Antietam (called Sharpsburg by the Confederates) nevertheless proved to be the single bloodiest day in American history, with more than 23,000 casualties (killed, wounded, and captured) in the two armies.

Attacking from right to left on a four-mile front, McClellan's Army of the Potomac achieved potential breakthroughs at a sunken road northeast of Sharpsburg (known ever after as Bloody Lane) and in the rolling fields southeast of town. But fearing counterattacks from those phantom reserves that he was sure Lee possessed, McClellan held back 20,000 of his troops as a reserve and failed to follow through. Thus the battle ended in a draw. The battered Confederates still clung to their precarious line, with the Potomac at their back, at the end of a day in which more than 6,000 men on both sides were killed or mortally wounded—almost as many Americans as were killed or mortally wounded in combat during the entire seven years of the Revolutionary War. Even though he received reinforcements the next day and Lee received none, McClellan did not renew the attack. Nor did he follow up vigorously when

---

[1] The writ of *habeas corpus* is an order issued by a judge to law enforcement officers requiring them to bring an arrested person before the court to be charged with a crime so that the accused can have a fair trial. The Constitution of the United States, however, permits the suspension of this writ "in cases of rebellion or invasion," so that the government can arrest enemy agents, saboteurs, or any individual who might hinder the defense of the country, and hold such individuals without trial. Lincoln had suspended the writ, but political opponents charged him with doing so in order to curb the freedom of speech of anti-war opponents and political critics who were guilty of nothing more than speaking out against the war. This issue of "arbitrary arrests" became a controversial matter in both the Union and Confederacy (where the writ was similarly suspended during part of the war).

the Confederates finally retreated across the Potomac on the night of September 18.

Lincoln was not happy with this equivocal Union victory. But it was a victory, nevertheless, with important consequences. Britain and France decided to withhold diplomatic recognition of the Confederacy. Northern Democrats failed to gain control of the House in the fall elections. And most significant of all, on September 22, two long months after he had placed it in his desk drawer, Lincoln seized upon the occasion of a Union victory to issue his preliminary emancipation proclamation. This did not come as a total surprise to the public, for the president had already hinted that something of the sort might be in the offing. A month earlier, after Horace Greeley had written a strong editorial in the *New York Tribune* calling for action against slavery, Lincoln had responded with a public letter to Greeley (much as a

president today might use a televised news conference). "My paramount object in this struggle," wrote Lincoln, "*is* to save the Union." If "I could save the Union without freeing *any* slave I would do it, and if I could save it by freeing *all* the slaves I would do it; and if I could save it by freeing some and leaving others alone I would also do that." Knowing that the issue of Union united northerners, while the prospect of emancipation still divided them, Lincoln had crafted these phrases carefully to maximize public support for his anticipated proclamation. He portrayed emancipation not as an end in itself—despite his personal convictions to that effect—but only as an instrument, a *means* toward the end of saving the Union.

Lincoln's proclamation of September 22 did not go into effect immediately. Rather, it stipulated that if any state, or part of a state, was still in rebellion on

January 1, 1863, the president would proclaim the slaves therein "forever free." Confederate leaders scorned this warning as an act of desperation, and by January 1 no southern state had returned to the Union. After hosting a New Year's Day reception at the White House, Lincoln went to his office and signed the final Proclamation as an "act of justice" as well as "a fit and necessary war measure for suppressing said rebellion."

It was only a first step toward the legal abolition of slavery, but the Emancipation Proclamation set in motion the events that would bring about a new birth of freedom. The Proclamation exempted the border states, plus Tennessee and those portions of Louisiana and Virginia that were already under Union occupation, since these areas were deemed not to be in rebellion, and Lincoln's constitutional authority for the Proclamation derived from his power as commander in chief to confiscate *enemy* property. Although, practically speaking, the Proclamation could do nothing to liberate slaves in areas under Confederate control, it essentially made the northern soldiers an army of liberation—however reluctant many of them were to risk their lives for that purpose. The North was now fighting for free-

dom as well as for Union. If the North won the war, slavery would die. But in the winter and spring of 1862–1863 victory was far from assured.

A WINTER OF NORTHERN DISCONTENT

Although Lee's retreat from Maryland and Braxton Bragg's retreat from Kentucky suggested that the Confederate tide might be ebbing, the tide soon turned. The Union could never win the war simply by turning back Confederate invasions. Northern armies would have to invade the South, defeat its armies, and destroy its ability to resist the United States government. The three main Union armies, two of them under new commanders, made sluggish attempts in November 1862 to do just that.

Displeased by McClellan's "slows" after Antietam, Lincoln replaced him on November 7 with General Ambrose E. Burnside. An imposing man whose muttonchop whiskers gave the anagram "sideburns" to the language, Burnside proposed to cross the Rappahannock River at Fredericksburg for a move on Richmond before bad weather forced both sides

The Emancipation Proclamation   This famous contemporary painting by Francis Carpenter portrays Lincoln and his cabinet discussing the Emancipation Proclamation, which lies on the desk before Lincoln. The other members of the cabinet, from left to right, are Secretary of War Edwin M. Stanton, Secretary of the Treasury Salmon P. Chase, Secretary of the Navy Gideon Welles, Secretary of the Interior Caleb B. Smith, Secretary of State William H. Seward (seated facing Lincoln), Postmaster-General Montgomery Blair, and Attorney-General Edward Bates.

into winter quarters. Though Lee put his men into a strong defensive position on the heights behind Fredericksburg, Burnside nevertheless attacked on December 13. He was repulsed with heavy casualties that shook the morale of both the army and the public. When Lincoln heard the news, he said: "If there is a worse place than hell, I am in it."

News from the western theater did little to dispel the gloom in Washington. The Confederates had fortified the city of Vicksburg on bluffs commanding the Mississippi River. This precaution enabled them to maintain control of an important stretch of the river and to preserve transportation links between the states to the east and west. To sever those links was the goal of Ulysses S. Grant, who, in November 1862, launched a two-pronged drive against Vicksburg. With 40,000 men, he marched fifty miles southward from Memphis by land, while his principal subordinate William T. Sherman came down the river with 32,000 men accompanied by a gunboat fleet for an amphibious assault on the heights north of Vicksburg. But raids by the Confederate cavalry frustrated Grant's progress by destroying the railroads and supply depots in his rear, forcing him to retreat to Memphis. Meanwhile, Sherman attacked the Confederates at Chickasaw Bluffs on December 29, with no more success than Burnside had enjoyed at Fredericksburg.

The only bit of cheer for the North came in central Tennessee at the turn of the year. In that theater, Lincoln had removed General Don Carlos Buell from command of the Army of the Cumberland for the same reason he had removed McClellan—lack of vigor and aggressiveness. Buell's successor was William S. Rosecrans, who had proved himself a fighter in subordinate commands. On the Confederate side, Jefferson Davis stuck with Braxton Bragg as commander of the Army of Tennessee, despite dissension from some subordinate commanders within his ranks.

On the day after Christmas 1862, Rosecrans moved from his base at Nashville to attack Bragg's force thirty miles to the south at Murfreesboro. The ensuing three-day battle (called Stones River by the Union and Murfreesboro by the Confederacy) resulted in Confederate success on the first day (December 31) but defeat on the last. Both armies suffered devastating casualties, equal to a third of their strength, leaving them crippled for months. The Confederate retreat to a new base forty miles farther

south enabled the North to call Stones River a victory. Lincoln expressed his gratitude to Rosecrans: "I can never forget, whilst I remember anything, that you gave us a hard-earned victory which, had there been a defeat instead, the nation could scarcely have lived over."

The nation scarcely lived over the winter of 1862–1863 as it was. Morale declined, and desertions rose so sharply in the Army of the Potomac that Lincoln was compelled to replace Burnside with Joseph Hooker, a controversial general whose nickname "Fighting Joe" at least seemed to promise a vigorous offensive. Hooker did lift morale in the Army of the Potomac. But elsewhere things went from bad to worse.

Renewing the campaign against Vicksburg, Grant bogged down in the endless swamps and rivers which protected that Confederate bastion on three sides. Only on the east, away from the river, was there high ground suitable for an assault on Vicksburg's defenses. Grant's problem was to get his army across the Mississippi to that high ground, along with supplies and transportation to support an assault. For three months, he floundered in the Mississippi–Yazoo bottomlands, while disease and exposure took a fearful toll of his troops. False rumors of excessive drinking that had dogged Grant for years broke out anew, but Lincoln resisted pressures to remove him from command. "What I want," Lincoln said, "is generals who will fight battles and win victories. Grant has done this, and I propose to stand by him." It was at this time that Lincoln reportedly said he would like to know Grant's brand of whiskey so he could send some to his other generals.

Lincoln's own reputation reached a low point during this northern winter of discontent. A visitor to Washington in February 1863 found that "the lack of respect for the President in all parties is unconcealed. . . . If a Republican convention were to be held tomorrow, he would not get the vote of a State." In this depressed climate, the "Copperhead" faction of the Democratic party found a ready audience for its message that the war was a failure and should be abandoned. Having won control of the Illinois and Indiana legislatures the preceding fall, Democrats in those states called for an armistice and a peace conference. They also demanded retraction of the "wicked, inhuman, and unholy" Emancipation Proclamation and threatened to withdraw

Illinois and Indiana troops from the war. The Republican governors of the two states blocked that action.

But in Ohio, the foremost Peace Democrat, Congressman Clement L. Vallandigham, was planning to run for governor. What had this wicked war accomplished, Vallandigham asked northern audiences during the winter and spring of 1863. "Let the dead at Fredericksburg and Vicksburg answer." The Confederacy could never be conquered; the only trophies of the war were "debt, defeat, sepulchres." The solution was to "stop the fighting. Make an armistice. Withdraw your army from the seceded states." Above all, give up the unconstitutional effort to abolish slavery. "I see more of barbarism and sin," said Vallandigham, "a thousand times more, in the continuance of this war and the enslavement of the white race by debt and taxes" than in the continuation of slavery. "In considering the terms of settlement, we should look only to the welfare, peace, and safety of the white race, without reference to the effect that settlement may have on the African."

Vallandigham and other Copperhead spokesmen had a powerful effect on northern morale. Alarmed by a wave of desertions, the army commander in Ohio had Vallandigham arrested in May 1863. A military court convicted him of treason for aiding and abetting the enemy by uttering disloyal sentiments. The court's action raised serious questions of civil liberties. Was the conviction a violation of Vallandigham's First Amendment right of free speech? Could a military court try a civilian under martial law in a state like Ohio where civil courts were functioning? (In a similar case after the war, the U.S. Supreme Court ruled that wartime trials of civilians in military courts are unconstitutional.)

Lincoln was embarrassed by the swift arrest and trial of Vallandigham, which he learned about from the newspapers. To keep Vallandigham from becoming a martyr, Lincoln commuted his sentence from imprisonment to banishment—to the Confederacy! On May 15, Union cavalry escorted Vallandigham under a flag of truce to Confederate lines in Tennessee, where the southerners reluctantly accepted this uninvited guest. He soon escaped to Canada on a blockade runner, making his way to Windsor, Ontario, across the border from Detroit. There, from exile, Vallandigham conducted his campaign for governor of Ohio—an election he lost in October 1863, after the military fortunes of the Union had improved.

ECONOMIC PROBLEMS IN THE SOUTH

Discouragement and defeatism in the North were a malaise of the spirit caused by military defeat. By contrast, southerners were buoyed by their military success but were suffering from food shortages and hyperinflation. The tightening Union blockade, the weaknesses and imbalances of the Confederate economy, the escape of slaves to Union lines, and enemy occupation of some of the South's prime agricultural areas made it increasingly difficult for the southern economy to produce both guns and butter. Despite the conversion of hundreds of thousands of acres from cotton to food production, the deterioration of southern railroads and the priority given to army shipments made food scarce in some areas. A drought in the summer of 1862 made matters worse. Prices rose much faster than wages. The price of salt—necessary to preserve meat in that pre-refrigeration age—shot out of sight. Even the middle class suffered, especially in Richmond, whose population had more than doubled since the war's beginning. "The shadow of the gaunt form of famine is upon us," wrote a war department clerk in March 1863. "I have lost twenty pounds, and my wife and

Wartime Inflation in the Confederacy and Union

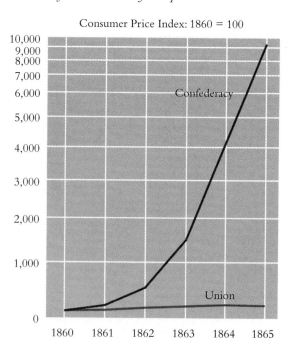

Consumer Price Index: 1860 = 100

children are emaciated." The rats in his kitchen were so hungry that they nibbled bread crumbs from his daughter's hand "as tame as kittens. Perhaps we shall have to eat them!"

Things were even worse for the poor—especially for the wives and children of non-slaveholding farmers and workers who were away in the army. By the spring of 1863, food supplies were virtually gone. "A crowd of we Poor women went to Greenesborogh yesterday for something to eat as we had not a mouthful of meet nor bread in my house," wrote a North Carolina farm woman to the governor in April 1863. "What did they do but put us in gail in plase of giveing us aney thing to eat. . . . I have 6 little children and my husband in the armey and what am I to do?"

Some women took matters into their own hands. Denouncing "speculators" who allegedly hoarded goods to drive up prices, they marched in a body to stores, asked the price of bacon or cornmeal or salt, denounced such "extortion," took what they wanted without paying, and marched away. Bread riots broke out in several places. On April 2, 1863, a mob of over a thousand women and boys looted several shops in Richmond before the militia, under the personal command of Jefferson Davis, forced them to disperse. The Confederate government subsequently released some emergency food stocks to civilians, and state and county governments provided aid to the families of soldiers. Better crops in 1863 helped to alleviate the worst shortages, but serious problems persisted.

THE WARTIME DRAFT AND CLASS TENSIONS

In both South and North, the draft intensified social unrest and turned it in the direction of class conflict. The burst of patriotic enthusiasm that had prompted a million men to join the colors in North and South during 1861 had waned by the spring of 1862. That April, the Confederacy enacted a draft that made all white men (with certain occupational exemptions) aged 18 to 35 liable to conscription. A drafted man could hire a substitute, but the price of substitutes soon rose beyond the means of the average southern farmer or worker, giving rise to the bitter cry that it was "a rich man's war and a poor man's fight."

The cry grew louder in October 1862 when the Confederate Congress raised the draft age to 45 and added a clause exempting one white man from the draft on every plantation with twenty or more slaves. The purpose of this "overseer exemption" was to ensure discipline over the slaves in order to keep up production and prevent slave uprisings. It had been prompted by the complaints of planters' wives, who had been left alone to manage the slaves after the departure of husbands, sons, and overseers for the army. But the so-called Twenty Negro Law was regarded as blatant discrimination by non-slaveholding farm families whose men also were at the front. And raising the age limit to 45 also took away many fathers of children who were too young to work the farm. The law provoked widespread draft-dodging and desertions.

The Richmond Bread Riot Illustrating the economic problems of the Confederacy and the suffering of poor civilians in overcrowded cities, the bread riot in Richmond involved a thousand women and boys who broke into shops to take food and other goods on April 2, 1863. The rioters were white, though a few black children may have gotten into the act, as portrayed by the artist of this woodcut.

Similar discontent greeted the enactment of a conscription law in the North. In the summer of 1863, some 30,000 Union soldiers who had enlisted in 1861 for two years rather than the normal three would be leaving the army, along with 80,000 of the nine-month militia called into service the preceding autumn. To meet the looming shortfall of men, Congress decreed in March that all male citizens aged 20 to 45 must enroll for the draft. Not all of them would necessarily be called (by administrative policy, married men over 35 were, in effect, exempted), but all would be liable.

The law was intended more to encourage volunteers to come forward than it was to draft men directly into the army. In each of the president's four calls for troops under this law, the War Department set a quota for every congressional district and gave it fifty days to meet its quota with volunteers before resorting to a draft lottery. Some districts avoided having to draft anyone by offering large bounties to volunteers to fill the quotas. By this time, the reservoir of men who had enlisted for patriotic reasons had been pretty well exhausted. The bounty system produced glaring abuses, including "bounty jumpers" who enlisted and then deserted as soon as they got their money—often to enlist again under another name somewhere else.

The drafting process itself also was open to abuse. Like the Confederate law, the Union law permitted the hiring of substitutes. But to keep the price of hiring a substitute from skyrocketing as it had in the Confederacy, the law allowed a drafted man the alternative of paying a "commutation fee" of $300 that exempted him from the current draft call (but not necessarily from the next one). That provision raised the cry of "rich man's war, poor man's fight" in the North as well. Indeed, this sense of class resentment was more dangerous in the North than in the South, because it was nurtured by the Democratic party and intensified by racism. Democrats in Congress opposed conscription, just as they opposed emancipation. Democratic newspapers told white workers, especially the large Irish-American population, that the draft would force them to fight a war to free the slaves, who would then come north to take their jobs and perhaps try to marry their daughters. This volatile issue helped spark widespread violence when the northern draft got under way in the summer of 1863. The worst riot occurred in New York City on July 13–16, where huge mobs consisting mostly of Irish-Americans demolished draft offices, lynched several blacks, and destroyed huge areas of the city in four days of looting and burning.

Draft riots in the North and bread riots in the South exposed alarming class fissures that were deepened by the strains of full-scale war. Although inflation was much less serious in the North than in the South, northern wages lagged behind price increases. Labor unions sprang up in several industries and struck for higher wages. In some areas, such as the anthracite coalfields of eastern Pennsylvania, labor organizations dominated by Irish Americans combined resistance to the draft and opposition to emancipation with violent strikes against industries owned by Protestant Republicans. Troops sent in to enforce the draft sometimes suppressed the strikes as well. These class, ethnic, and racial hostilities provided a volatile mixture in several northern communities.

But in some important respects, the grievance that it was a rich man's war and a poor man's fight was more apparent than real in both North and South. The principal forms of taxation at local, state, and national levels to sustain the war were property, excise, and income taxes that bore proportionately more heavily on the wealthy than on the poor. In the South, the property of the rich—including plantations and slaves—suffered greater damage and confiscation than did the property of non-slaveholders. The war liberated four million slaves, the poorest class in America. Both the Union and Confederate armies were made up of men from all strata of society in proportion to their percentage of the population. If anything, among those who volunteered in 1861–1862, the planter class was overrepresented in the Confederate army and the northern middle class in the Union army, for those more-privileged groups believed they had more at stake in the war and joined up in larger numbers during the early months of enthusiasm. It was those volunteers—especially the officers, most of whom came from the middle and upper classes—who suffered the highest percentage of combat casualties.

Nor did conscription itself fall much more heavily on the poor than on the rich. Those who escaped the draft by decamping to the woods, the territories, or Canada came mostly from the poor. The Confederacy abolished substitution in December 1863 and made men who had previously sent substitutes liable to the draft. In the North, several city councils, po-

The New York City Draft Riot   The worst urban violence in American history occurred in New York City on July 13 to 16, 1863, when thousands of men and women, mostly poor Irish-Americans, attacked draft offices, homes, businesses, and individuals. Black residents of the city were among the mob's victims because they symbolized labor competition to Irish-Americans, who did not want to be drafted to fight a war to free the slaves. This illustration shows the burning of the Colored Orphan Asylum, a home for black orphans. More than one hundred people were killed in the riot, most of them rioters shot down by police and soldiers.

litical machines, and businesses contributed funds to pay the commutation fees of drafted men who were too poor to pay out of their own pockets. In the end, it was neither a rich man's war nor a poor man's fight. It was an American war.

BLUEPRINT FOR MODERN AMERICA

The 37th Congress of the United States (1861–1863) — the Congress that enacted conscription, passed measures for confiscation and emancipation, and created the greenbacks and the national banking system (see Chapter 16) — also enacted three laws, that together with this war legislation, provided what one historian has called "a blueprint for modern

America": the Homestead Act; the Morrill Land-Grant College Act; and the Pacific Railroad Act. For several years before the war, Republicans and some northern Democrats had tried to pass these laws to provide social benefits and to promote economic growth through the disposal of public lands, only to see them defeated by southern opposition or by President Buchanan's veto. The secession of southern states, ironically, enabled Congress to pass all three in 1862.

The Homestead Act granted a farmer 160 acres of land virtually free after he had lived on the land for five years and had made improvements on it. The Morrill Land-Grant College Act gave each state thousands of acres to fund the establishment of colleges for the teaching of "agricultural and mechanical arts." The Pacific Railroad Act granted land and loans to railroad companies to spur the building of a transcontinental railroad from Omaha to Sacramento. Under these laws, the U.S. government ultimately granted 80 million acres to homesteaders, 25 million acres to states for land-grant colleges, and 120 million acres to several transcontinental railroads. Although waste and corruption and exploitation of the original Indian owners of this land attended the administration of these laws, they helped farmers to settle some of the most fertile land in the world, studded the land with state colleges, and spanned it with steel rails in a manner that altered the landscape of the western half of the country.

WOMEN AND THE WAR

The war advanced many other changes that transformed the social landscape, particularly with respect to women. In factories and on farms in both North and South, women took the place of the men who had gone off to war. Explosions in Confederate ordnance plants and arsenals killed at least one hundred women, who were as surely war casualties as men who were killed in battle. The war accelerated the entry of women into the teaching profession, a trend that had already begun in the Northeast and now spread to other parts of the country. It also brought significant numbers of women into the civil service. During the 1850s a few women had worked briefly in the U.S. Patent Office (including Clara Barton, who became a famous wartime nurse and founded the American Red Cross). The huge expansion of

Union Army Hospital   This painting of a wartime hospital in Washington, D.C., accurately portrays the prominence of women nurses in Civil War medicine.

government bureaucracies after 1861 and the departure of male clerks to the army provided openings that were filled partly by women—openings that proved to be permanent. The example was not lost on the private sector, which began hiring women as clerks, bookkeepers, "typewriters" (the machine itself was invented in the 1870s), and telephone operators (the telephone was another postwar invention).

But it was in medicine that women made the most visible impact. The outbreak of war prompted the organization of soldiers' aid societies, hospital societies, and other voluntary associations to provide homefront support for the soldiers, with women playing a leading role. Their most important function was to help—and sometimes to prod—the medical branches of the Union and Confederate armies to provide more efficient, humane care for sick and wounded soldiers. Dr. Elizabeth Blackwell, the first American woman to earn an M.D. (1849), organized a meeting of three thousand women in New York City on April 29, 1861. They put together the Women's Central Association for Relief, which became the nucleus for the most powerful voluntary association of the war, the United States Sanitary Commission.

Eventually embracing seven thousand local auxiliaries, the Sanitary Commission was an essential ad-

junct of the Union army's medical bureau. Most of its local volunteers were women. So were most of the nurses it provided to army hospitals. Nursing was not a new profession for women. But it had not been a respectable wartime profession, being classed only slightly above prostitution. The fame won by Florence Nightingale of Britain in the Crimean War a half-dozen years earlier had begun to change that perception. And the flocking of thousands of middle- and even upper-class women volunteers to Union and Confederate army hospitals did a great deal to transform nursing from a menial occupation to a respected profession.

The nurses had to overcome the deep-grained suspicions of old-school army surgeons. They also had to overcome the opposition of husbands and fathers who shared the cultural sentiment that the foul-smelling, visually shocking, embarrassingly physical atmosphere of an army hospital was no place for a respectable woman. But many thousands of women did it, winning grudging and then enthusiastic admiration. One Confederate surgeon praised women nurses as far superior to the convalescent soldiers who had formerly done that job, "rough country crackers" who did not "know castor oil from a gun rod nor laudanum from a hole in the ground." In the North, the treasurer of the Sanitary Commission, who at first had disliked the idea of his wife working as a nurse, was astonished and con-verted by her performance as a volunteer for the Sanitary Commission during the summer of 1862. "The little woman has come out amazingly strong during these past two months," he wrote. "Have never given her credit for a tithe of the enterprise, pluck, discretion, and force of character that she has shown."

The war also gave an impetus to the fledgling women's rights movement. It was no coincidence that Elizabeth Cady Stanton and Susan B. Anthony founded the National Woman Suffrage Association in 1869, only a few short years after the war had ended. Although it did not win final victory for half a century—after women had contributed their ser-vices in another great war—this movement could not have achieved the momentum that made it a force in American life without the work of women in the Civil War.

THE CONFEDERACY AT HIGH TIDE

The Army of Northern Virginia and the Army of the Potomac spent the winter of 1862–1863 on opposite banks of the Rappahannock River. With the coming of spring, Union commander Joe Hooker resumed the offensive with hopes of redeeming the December disaster at Fredericksburg. On April 30, instead of charging straight across the river, Hooker crossed his men several miles upriver and came in on Lee's rear. But Lee, instead of retreating, quickly faced most of

Women Spies and Soldiers   In addition to working in war industries and serving as army nurses, some women pursued traditionally male wartime careers as spies and soldiers. One of the most famous Confederate spies was Rose O'Neal Greenhow, a Washington widow and socialite who fed information to officials in Richmond. Federal officers arrested her in August 1861 and deported her to Richmond in the spring of 1862. She was photographed with her daughter in the Old Capitol prison in Washington, D.C., while await-ing trial. In October 1864 she drowned in a lifeboat off Wilmington, North Carolina, after a blockade runner carrying her back from a European mission was run aground by a Union warship.

The second photograph shows a Union soldier who enlisted in the 95th Illinois Infantry under the name of Albert Cashier and fought through the war. Not until a farm accident in 1911 revealed Albert Cashier to be a woman, whose real name was Jennie Hodgers, was her secret disclosed. Most of the other estimated four hundred women, who evaded the superficial physical exams and passed as men to enlist in the Union and Confederate armies, were more quickly discovered and discharged—six of them after they had babies while in the army. A few, however, served long enough to be killed in action.

his troops about and confronted the enemy in dense woods, known locally as the Wilderness, near the crossroads hostelry of Chancellorsville. Nonplussed, Hooker lost both his nerve and the initiative.

The Battle of Chancellorsville

Even though the Union army outnumbered the Confederate forces by almost two to one, Lee boldly went over to the offensive in the riskiest operation of his career. It paid off. On May 2, Stonewall Jackson led 28,000 men on a stealthy march through the woods to attack the Union right flank late in the afternoon. Owing to the laxness of the Union commanders, the surprise was complete. Jackson's assault crumpled the Union flank as the sun dipped below the horizon. Jackson then rode out to scout the terrain for a renewal of the attack by moonlight and was wounded on his return by jittery Confederates who mistook him and his staff for Union cavalry. Nevertheless, Lee resumed the attack next day. In three more days of fighting that brought 12,800

Confederate and 16,800 Union casualties (the largest number for a single battle in the war so far), Lee drove the Union troops back across the Rappahannock. It was a brilliant victory.

In the North, the gloom grew deeper. "My God!" exclaimed Lincoln when he heard the news of Chancellorsville. "What will the country say?" Copperhead opposition to the war intensified. Southern sympathizers in Britain renewed efforts for diplomatic recognition of the Confederacy. Southern elation was tempered by grief at the death on May 10 of Stonewall Jackson, who had contracted pneumonia after amputation of his arm. Nevertheless, Lee decided to parlay his tactical victory at Chancellorsville into a strategic offensive by again invading the North. A victory on Union soil would convince northerners and foreigners alike that the Confederacy was invincible. As his army began to move north in June 1863, Lee was confident of success. "There never were such men in an army before," he wrote of his troops. "They will go anywhere and do anything if properly led."

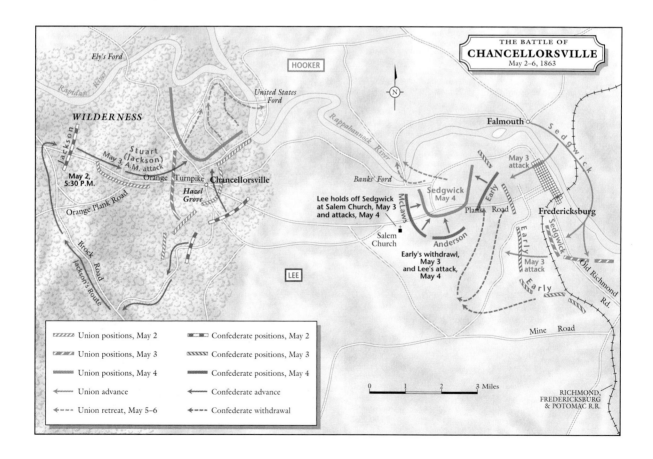

The Gettysburg Campaign

At first, all went well. The Confederates brushed aside or captured Union forces in the northern Shenandoah Valley and in Pennsylvania. Stuart's cavalry threw a scare into Washington by raiding behind Union lines into Maryland and Pennsylvania. But that very success led to trouble. With Stuart's cavalry separated from the rest of the army, Lee was deprived of the vital intelligence that the cavalry garnered as the eyes of the army. By June 28 several detachments of Lee's forces were scattered about Pennsylvania, far from their base and vulnerable to being cut off by the Union army.

At this point, Lee learned that the Army of the Potomac was moving toward him, now under the command of George Gordon Meade, a seasoned officer whom Lee respected. Lee immediately ordered his own army to reassemble in the vicinity of Gettysburg, an agricultural and college town at the hub of a dozen roads leading in from all directions. There, on the morning of July 1, the vanguard of the two armies met in a clash that grew into the greatest battle in American history.

As the fighting spread west and north of town, couriers pounded up the roads on lathered horses to summon reinforcements to both sides. The Confederates got more men into the battle and broke the Union lines late that afternoon, driving the survivors to a defensive position on Cemetery Hill south of town. General Richard Ewell, Jackson's successor as commander of the Confederate 2nd Corps, judging this position too strong to take with his own troops, chose not to press the attack as the sun went down on what promised to be another Confederate victory.

But when the sun rose next morning, the reinforced Union army was holding a superb defensive position from Culp's Hill and Cemetery Hill south to Little Round Top. Lee's principal subordinate, 1st Corps commander James Longstreet, advised against attack, urging instead a maneuver to the south, toward Washington, to force the Federals to attack the Confederates in a strong defensive position. But Lee's blood was up. He believed his army invincible. After its victory on July 1, a move to the south might look like a retreat. Pointing to the Union lines, he said: "The enemy is there, and I am going to attack him there."

The Battle of Gettysburg   This is one of many paintings of Pickett's assault on the Union center on Cemetery Ridge at the climactic moment of the battle on July 3, 1863. The painting depicts "the high tide of the Confederacy" as Virginia and North Carolina troops pierce the Union line only to be shot down or captured—a fate suffered by half of the 13,000 Confederate soldiers who participated in Pickett's charge.

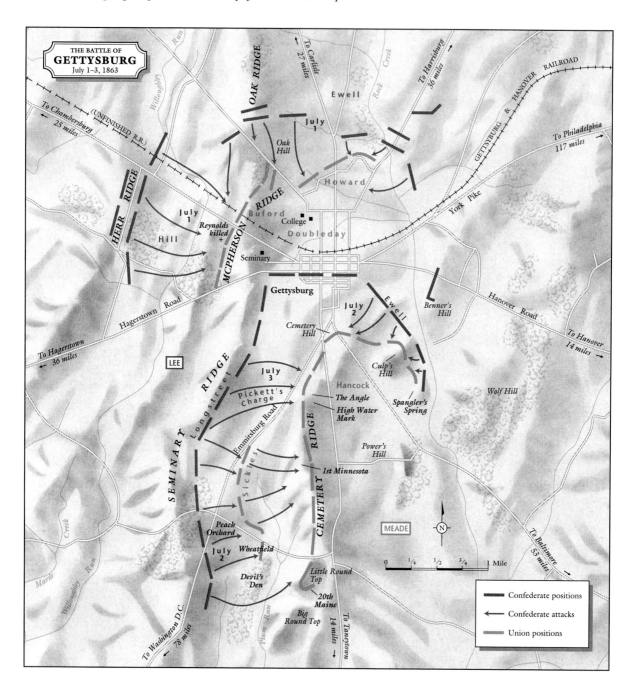

THE BATTLE OF
GETTYSBURG
July 1–3, 1863

Longstreet reluctantly led the attack on the Union left. Once committed, his men fought with fury. But the Union troops fought back with equal fury. As the afternoon passed, peaceful areas with names like Peach Orchard, Wheat Field, Devil's Den, and Little Round Top were turned into killing fields. By the end of the day, Confederate forces had made small gains at great cost, but the main Union line had held firm.

Lee was not yet ready to yield the offensive. In fact, he regarded this second day of battle as a Confederate victory. Having attacked both Union flanks, he thought the center might be weak, so on July 3 he ordered a frontal attack on Cemetery Ridge,

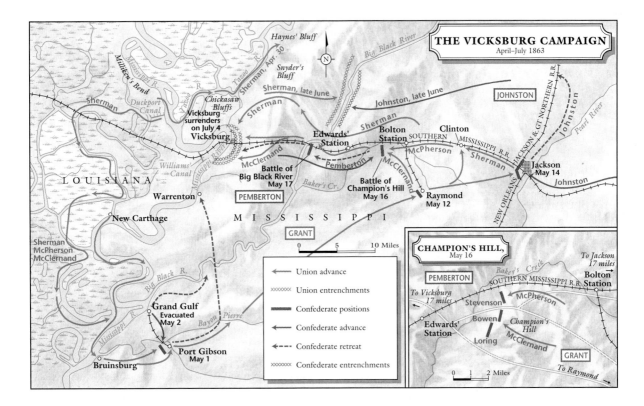

spearheaded by a fresh division under George Pickett. After a two-hour artillery barrage, Pickett's 5,000 men joined by 8,000 additional troops moved forward on that sultry summer afternoon in a picture-book assault that forms our most enduring image of the Civil War. "Pickett's Charge" was shot to pieces; scarcely half of the men returned unwounded to their own lines. It was the final act in an awesome three-day drama that left some 50,000 men killed, wounded, or captured: 23,000 Federals and 25,000 to 28,000 Confederates.

THE TIDE TURNS

Lee limped back to Virginia pursued by the Union troops. Lincoln was unhappy with Meade for not cutting off the Confederate retreat and perhaps crushing the crippled Army of Northern Virginia. Nevertheless, Gettysburg was a great northern victory, perhaps the greatest of the war. And it came at the same time as other important Union successes in Mississippi, Louisiana, and Tennessee.

The Vicksburg Campaign

In mid-April, General Grant had begun a move that would put Vicksburg in a vise. The Union ironclad fleet ran downriver past the big guns at Vicksburg with little damage. Grant's troops marched down the Mississippi's west bank and were ferried across the river forty miles south of Vicksburg. There they kept the Confederate defenders off balance by striking east toward Jackson, the state capital, instead of marching straight north to Vicksburg. Grant's purpose was to scatter the Confederate forces in central Mississippi and to wreck the rail network so that his rear would not be vulnerable when he ultimately turned toward Vicksburg. It was a brilliant strategy, flawlessly executed. During the first three weeks of May, Grant's troops marched 180 miles, won five battles, and penned up 32,000 Confederate troops and 3,000 civilians, who remained stuck at Vicksburg, caught between the Union army on land and the Union gunboats on the river.

But the Confederate army was still full of fight. It threw back Union assaults against the Vicksburg trenches on May 19 and 22. Grant then settled down for a siege. By late June he had built up his army to 70,000 men to ward off a Confederate army of 30,000, which was scraped together by Joseph Johnston to try to rescue Vicksburg. Running out of supplies, the Vicksburg garrison surrendered on July 4—the same day Lee began his weary retreat from Gettysburg. Grant then turned east and drove off Johnston's force. On July 9, the Confederate garrison at Port Hudson, 200 river miles south of Vicksburg, surrendered to a besieging Union army. Northern forces now controlled the entire length of the Mississippi River. "The Father of Waters again goes unvexed to the sea," said Lincoln. The Confederacy had been torn in two. And Lincoln knew who deserved the credit. "Grant is my man," he said, "and I am his the rest of the war."

Chickamauga and Chattanooga

Northerners had scarcely finished celebrating the twin victories of Gettysburg and Vicksburg when they learned of an important—and almost bloodless—triumph in Tennessee. After the battle of Stones River

at the end of 1862, the Union Army of the Cumberland and the Confederate Army of Tennessee had shadowboxed for nearly six months as they recovered from the trauma of the battle. On June 24, Union commander William S. Rosecrans finally launched an offensive to dislodge the Confederates from their defenses in the Cumberland foothills of east-central Tennessee. He used his cavalry and a mounted infantry brigade armed with new repeating rifles to get around the Confederate flanks while his infantry threatened the Confederate front. In the first week of July, the Confederates retreated all the way to Chattanooga.

After a pause for resupply, Rosecrans's army advanced again in August, this time in tandem with a smaller Union army in eastern Tennessee commanded by Ambrose Burnside, who had come to this theater after being removed from command in Virginia. Again the outnumbered Confederates fell back, evacuating Knoxville on September 2 and Chattanooga on September 9. This action severed the South's only direct east-west rail link. Having sliced the Confederacy in half with the capture of Vicksburg and Port Hudson, Union forces now

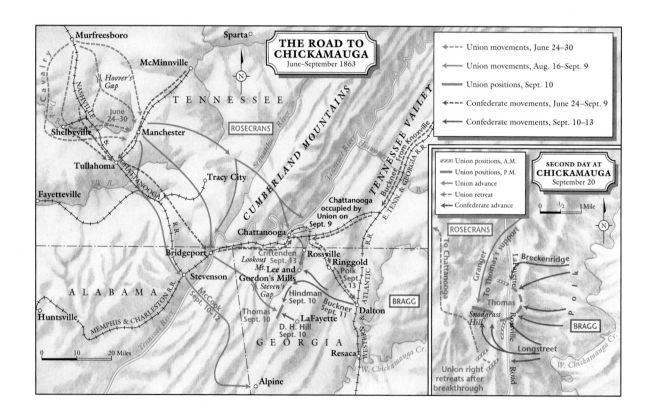

stood poised in Chattanooga for a campaign into Georgia that threatened to slice it into three parts. It was one of the low points of the war for the Confederacy—a stunning reversal of the situation only four months earlier, after Chancellorsville, when the Union cause had appeared hopeless.

But Confederate General Braxton Bragg reached into his bag of tricks and sent fake deserters into Union lines with tales of a Confederate retreat toward Atlanta. He then laid a trap for Rosecrans's troops as they advanced through the mountain passes south of Chattanooga. To help him spring it, Jefferson Davis approved the detachment of Longstreet with two divisions from the Army of Northern Virginia to reinforce Bragg. On September 19, the Confederates turned and counterattacked Rosecrans's now outnumbered army in the valley of Chickamauga Creek.

The Indian word *chickamauga* means "river of death." And a river of death it was. Over the next two days, in ferocious fighting that produced more casualties (36,000) than any other single battle save Gettysburg, the Confederates finally scored a victory. On September 20, after a confusion of orders left a division-size gap in the Union line, Longstreet drove his divisions through, sending part of the Union army reeling back to Chattanooga. Only a firm stand by corps commander George H. Thomas—a Virginian who had remained loyal to the Union—prevented a complete Union rout. For this feat, Thomas earned the nickname "Rock of Chickamauga." Lincoln subsequently appointed Thomas commander of the Army of the Cumberland to replace Rosecrans, who was, in Lincoln's words, "confused and stunned like a duck hit on the head" after Chickamauga.

Lincoln also sent two army corps from Virginia under Joe Hooker and two from Vicksburg under William T. Sherman to reinforce Thomas, whose troops in Chattanooga were under virtual siege by Bragg's forces, which held most of the surrounding heights. More important, Lincoln ordered Grant to Chattanooga to take overall command of the beefed-up Union forces there. When Grant arrived in late October, the tide began to turn back in the Union's favor. He welded the various northern units into a new army and opened a new supply line into Chattanooga. On November 24, Hooker's troops drove Confederate besiegers off massive Lookout Mountain. Next day, an assault on Bragg's main line at

Missionary Ridge east of Chattanooga won a smashing success against seemingly greater odds than Pickett had faced at Gettysburg. The Union troops that had been routed at Chickamauga two months earlier redeemed themselves by driving the Confederates off Missionary Ridge and twenty miles south into Georgia.

These battles at Chattanooga had important consequences. They climaxed a string of Union victories in the second half of 1863, which made that year one of "calamity . . . defeat . . . utter ruin," in the words of a Confederate official. The southern diarist Mary Boykin Chesnut found "gloom and unspoken despondency hang[ing] like a pall everywhere." Jefferson Davis removed the discredited Bragg from command of the Army of Tennessee and reluctantly replaced him with Joseph E. Johnston, in whom Davis had little confidence. Lincoln summoned Grant to Washington and appointed him general-in-chief of all Union armies in March 1864, signifying a relentless fight to the finish.

BLACK MEN IN BLUE

The events of the latter half of 1863 also confirmed emancipation as a Union war aim. Northerners had not greeted the Emancipation Proclamation with great enthusiasm. Democrats and border-state Unionists continued to denounce it, and many Union soldiers resented the idea that they would now be risking their lives for black freedom. The Democratic party had hoped to capitalize on this opposition, and on Union military failures, to win important off-year elections—especially for governor of Pennsylvania and governor of Ohio (where Vallandigham was the nominee despite his exile in Canada). Northern military victories knocked one prop out from under the Democratic platform, and the performance of black soldiers fighting for the Union and for their own freedom knocked out another.

The enlistment of black soldiers was a logical corollary of emancipation. Free Negroes in the North had tried to enlist in 1861, but they were rejected. "This is a government of white men," thundered a Democratic congressman, "made by white men for white men, to be administered, protected, defended, and maintained by white men." Proposals to recruit black soldiers, Democrats said, were part of a Republican plot to establish "the equality of the black and white races." In a way, that charge was correct. One consequence of black men fighting for the Union would be to advance the black race a long way toward equal rights. This was a prime purpose of the abolitionists and black leaders who kept up pressure for the acceptance of black soldiers. "Once let the black man get upon his person the brass letters, U.S.," said Frederick Douglass, "let him get an eagle on his button, and a musket on his shoulder and bullets in his pocket, and there is no power on earth which can deny that he has earned the right to citizenship."

But it was pragmatism more than principle that pushed the North toward black recruitment. One purpose of emancipation was to deprive the Confederacy of black labor and to use that labor for the Union cause. Putting some of those former laborers in uniform was a compelling idea, especially as white enlistments lagged and the North had to enact conscription in 1863. Some Union commanders in occupied portions of Louisiana, South Carolina, and Missouri began to organize black regiments in 1862. The Emancipation Proclamation legitimized this policy with its proposal to enroll able-bodied male contrabands in new regiments. These black regiments would serve as labor battalions, supply troops, and garrison forces rather than as frontline combat troops. They would be paid less than white soldiers, and their officers would be white. In other words, black men in blue would be second-class soldiers, just as free blacks in the North were second-class citizens.

Black Soldiers in Combat

But continuing pressure from abolitionists, as well as military necessity, eroded discrimination somewhat. Congress enacted equal pay in 1864. Officers worked for better treatment of their men. Above all, the regiments themselves lobbied for the right to *fight* as combat soldiers. Even some previously hostile white soldiers came around to the notion that black men might just as well stop enemy bullets as white men.

Black Union Artillerymen   This photograph shows the crew of a gun in Battery A of the 2nd U.S. Colored Artillery, an outfit of freed slaves who served in the Tennessee theater and participated in the battle of Nashville on December 15 and 16, 1864. They were among the 190,000 black soldiers and sailors who fought for the Union.

In May and June 1863, black regiments in Louisiana fought well in an assault on Port Hudson and in defense of a Union outpost at Milliken's Bend, near Vicksburg. "The bravery of the blacks in the battle of Milliken's Bend completely revolutionized the sentiment of the army with regard to the employment of negro troops," wrote the assistant secretary of war, who had been on the spot with Grant's army. "I heard prominent officers who formerly in private had sneered at the idea of the negroes fighting express themselves after that as heartily in favor of it."

Even more significant was the action of the 54th Massachusetts Infantry, the first black regiment raised in the North. Its officers, headed by Colonel Robert Gould Shaw, came from prominent New England antislavery families. Two sons of Frederick Douglass were in the regiment—one of them as sergeant major. Shaw worked hard to win the right for the regiment to fight. And on July 18, 1863, he succeeded: the 54th was assigned "the post of honor" to lead an assault on Fort Wagner, part of the network of Confederate defenses protecting Charleston. Though the attack failed, the 54th fought courageously, suffering 50 percent casualties, including Colonel Shaw, who was killed by a bullet through his heart. This battle "made Fort Wagner such a name to the colored race as Bunker Hill had been for ninety years to the white Yankees," declared the *New York Tribune*.

The battle took place just after the occurrence of draft riots in New York where white mobs had lynched blacks—including the nephew of a sergeant in the 54th, who was himself killed in the attack on Fort Wagner. Abolitionist and Republican commentators drew the moral: black men who fought for the Union deserved more respect than white men who rioted against it. Lincoln made this point eloquently in a widely published letter to a political meeting in August 1863. "Some of the commanders of our armies in the field who have given us our most important successes [he meant Grant], believe the emancipation policy, and the use of colored troops, constitute the heaviest blow yet dealt to the rebellion," wrote the president. When final victory was achieved, "there will be some black men who can remember that, with silent tongue, and clenched teeth, and steady eye, and well-poised bayonet, they have helped mankind on to this great consummation; while, I fear, there will be some white ones, unable to forget that, with malignant heart, and deceitful speech, they have strove to hinder it."

Emancipation Confirmed

Lincoln's letter set the tone for Republican campaigns in state elections that fall. The party swept them all, including Ohio, where they buried Vallandigham under a 100,000-vote margin swelled by the soldier vote, which went 94 percent for his opponent. In effect, the elections were a powerful endorsement of the administration's emancipation policy. If the Emancipation Proclamation had been submitted to a referendum a year earlier, observed a newspaper editor in November 1863, "the voice of a majority would have been against it. And yet not a year has passed before it is approved by an overwhelming majority."

But emancipation would not be assured of survival until it had been christened by the Constitution. On April 8, 1864, the Senate passed the Thirteenth Amendment to abolish slavery, but Democrats in the House blocked the required two-thirds majority there. Not until after Lincoln's reelection in 1864 would the House finally pass the Amendment, which became part of the Constitution on December 6, 1865. In the end, though, the fate of slavery depended on the outcome of the war. And despite Confederate defeats in 1863, that outcome was by no means certain. Some of the heaviest fighting lay ahead.

THE CONFEDERACY'S WINTER OF DISCONTENT

Many southerners succumbed to defeatism in the winter of 1863–1864. "I have never actually despaired of the cause," wrote a Confederate War Department official in November, but "steadfastness is yielding to a sense of hopelessness." Desertions from Confederate armies increased just as they had from Union armies the winter before. Inflation galloped out of control. A Richmond diarist recorded this incident in October 1863: A merchant told a poor woman that the price of a barrel of flour was $70. "'My God!' exclaimed she, 'how can I pay such prices? I have seven children; what shall I do?' 'I don't know, madam,' said he, coolly, 'unless you eat your children.'"

The Davis administration, like the Lincoln administration a year earlier, had to face congressional elections during a time of public discontent, for the Confederate Constitution mandated such elections in odd-numbered years. Political parties had ceased to exist in the Confederacy after Democrats and former Whigs had tacitly declared a truce in 1861 to form a united front for the war effort. Many congressmen had been elected without opposition in 1861. By 1863, however, significant hostility to Davis had emerged. Though it was not channeled through any organized party, it took on partisan trappings, as an inchoate anti-Davis faction surfaced in the Confederate Congress and in the election campaign of 1863.

Ominously, some anti-administration candidates ran on a quasi-peace platform (analogous to that of the Copperheads in the North) that called for an armistice and peace negotiations to end the killing. Left unresolved were the terms of such negotiations—reunion or independence. But any peace overture from a position of weakness was tantamount to conceding defeat. The peace movement was especially strong in North Carolina, where for a time it appeared that the next governor would be elected on a peace platform (in the end, the "peace candidate" was defeated). Still, anti-administration candidates made significant gains in the 1863 Confederate elections, though they fell about fifteen seats short of a majority in the House and two seats short in the Senate.

OUT OF THE WILDERNESS

Shortages, inflation, political discontent, military defeat, high casualties, and the loss of thousands of slaves (some of them now in arms against the Confederacy) bent but did not break the southern spirit. A religious revival within the Confederate armies helped to sustain morale. As the spring of 1864 came on, a renewed determination infused both home front and battle front. The Confederate armies were no longer powerful enough to invade the North or to try to win the war with a knockout blow, as they had attempted to do in 1862 and 1863. But they were still strong enough to fight a war of attrition, as the patriots had done in the War of 1775–1783 against Britain (Chapter 7). If they could hold out long enough and inflict enough casualties on the Union armies, they might weaken the northern will to continue fighting. And if they could just hold out until the Union presidential election in November, northern voters might reject Lincoln and elect a Peace Democrat. "If we can break up the enemy's arrangements early and throw

him back," wrote General Longstreet, "he will not be able to recover his position or his morale until the Presidential election is over, and then we shall have a new President to deal with."

Northerners were vulnerable to this strategy of psychological attrition. Military success in 1863 had created a mood of confidence, and people expected a quick, decisive victory in 1864. The mood was fed by Grant's appointment as general-in-chief. When Grant decided to remain in Virginia with the Army of the Potomac and to leave Sherman in command of the Union forces in northern Georgia, northerners expected these two heavyweights to floor the Confederacy with a one-two punch. Lincoln was alarmed by this euphoria. "The people are too sanguine," he told a reporter. "They expect too much at once." Disappointment might trigger despair.

And that is what almost happened. Grant started the military campaign of 1864 with a strategic plan elegant in its simplicity. While smaller Union armies in peripheral theaters carried out auxiliary campaigns, the two principal armies in Virginia and Georgia would attack the main Confederate forces under Lee and Johnston. Convinced that in years past Union armies in various theaters had "acted independently and without concert, like a balky team, no two ever pulling together," Grant ordered simultaneous offensives on all fronts, to prevent the Confederates from shifting reinforcements from one theater to another.

Grant's offensives began the first week of May. The heaviest fighting occurred in Virginia. When the Army of the Potomac crossed the Rapidan River, Lee decided to attack it in the flank while it was still in the Wilderness, a thick scrub forest where Union superiority in numbers and artillery would count for little (and where Lee had defeated Joe Hooker a year earlier in the battle of Chancellorsville). Lee's action brought on two days (May 5–6) of the most confused, frenzied fighting the war had yet seen. Hundreds of wounded men burned to death in brush fires set off by exploding shells or muzzle flashes. The battle surged back and forth, with the Confederates inflicting 18,000 casualties and suffering 12,000 themselves. Having apparently halted Grant's offensive, they claimed a victory.

Spotsylvania and Cold Harbor

But Grant did not admit defeat. Nor did he retreat, as other Union commanders in Virginia had done.

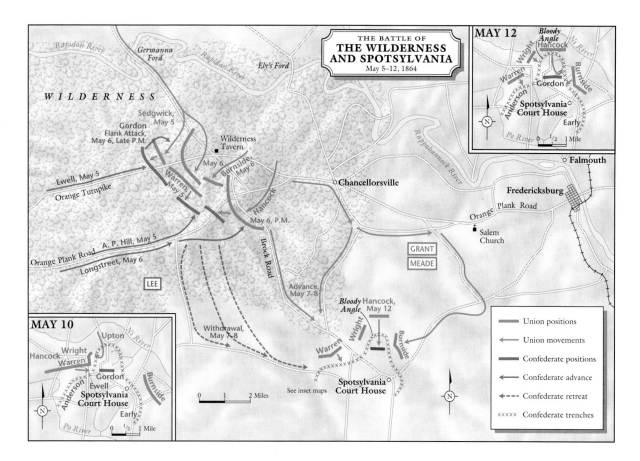

Instead, he moved to his left toward Spotsylvania Courthouse, a key crossroads ten miles closer to Richmond. Skillfully, Lee pulled back to cover the road junction and entrenched. Repeated Union assaults during the next twelve days (May 8–19) left another 18,000 northerners and 12,000 southerners killed, wounded, or captured. The Confederates fought from an elaborate network of trenches and log breastworks they had constructed virtually overnight. Civil War soldiers had learned the advantages of entrenchment, which gave the defense an enormous advantage and made frontal assaults almost suicidal. By the time the war was over, Virginia—and northern Georgia—would look as if giant moles had burrowed their way across the countryside.

Having achieved no better than stalemate around Spotsylvania, Grant again moved south around Lee's right flank in an effort to force the outnumbered Confederates into an open fight. But Lee, anticipating Grant's moves, confronted him from behind for-

midable defenses at the North Anna River, Totopotomoy Creek, and near the crossroads inn of Cold Harbor, only ten miles northeast of Richmond. Believing the Confederates must be exhausted and demoralized by their repeated retreats, Grant decided to attack at Cold Harbor on June 3—a costly mistake, as it turned out. Lee's troops were ragged and hungry but far from demoralized. Fighting from their trenches, they greeted the Union assault with withering fire, inflicting 7,000 casualties in less than an hour. (By coincidence, this was the same number of casualties suffered in the same length of time by the men in Pickett's Charge at Gettysburg exactly eleven months before.) "I regret this assault more than any other one I have ordered," said Grant.

Stalemate in Virginia

Now, for the fifth time, Grant shifted to the left in an attempt to get around Lee's flank. This time he moved all the way across the James River to strike at

Trench Warfare in 1864–1865   During the grueling campaigns of 1864 and 1865, the opposing armies entrenched wherever they paused. By the end of the war, hundreds of square miles in Virginia and Georgia looked like this, especially along a thirty-five mile line from a point east of Richmond to one southwest of Petersburg, where the armies confronted each other for more than nine months. Note not only the elaborate trench networks but also the absence of trees, cut down to provide firewood and to create open fields of fire for rifles and cannons.

Petersburg, an industrial city twenty miles south of Richmond, where several rail lines came together. If Petersburg fell, Grant knew, the Confederates could not hold Richmond. But once more Lee's troops raced southward on the inside track and blocked Grant's troops. Four days of Union assaults (June 15–18) against the trenches at Petersburg produced another 11,000 northern casualties but no breakthrough.

Union losses during the six weeks' campaign thus far had been so high—some 65,000 killed, wounded, and captured, compared with 37,000 Confederate casualties—that the Army of the Potomac had lost its fighting power. Grant reluctantly settled down for a siege along the Petersburg-Richmond front that would last more than nine grueling months.

Meanwhile, other Union operations in Virginia had achieved little success. General Benjamin Butler bungled an attack up the James River against Richmond and was stopped by a scraped-together army under General P. G. T. Beauregard, who made a dramatic reappearance in Virginia after two years of relative obscurity as commander of Charleston's de-

fenses. A Union thrust up the Shenandoah Valley was blocked at Lynchburg in June by Jubal Early, commanding Stonewall Jackson's old corps, which Lee had detached from the Cold Harbor trenches. Early then led a raid down the Valley, across the Potomac, all the way to the outskirts of Washington on July 11–12 before being driven back to Virginia. Union cavalry raids commanded by Philip Sheridan, whom Grant had brought east to command the Army of the Potomac's horsemen, inflicted considerable damage on Confederate resources in Virginia—including the mortal wounding of Jeb Stuart in the battle of Yellow Tavern on May 11—but they did not strike a crippling blow. In the North, frustration set in over failure to win the quick, decisive victory the public had expected when the campaign began.

THE ATLANTA CAMPAIGN

In Georgia, Sherman's army seemed to have accomplished more at less cost than Grant had in Virginia. But there too, Union efforts had bogged down in apparent stalemate by August. The strategy and tactics of both Sherman and Johnston in Georgia contrasted with those of Grant and Lee in Virginia. Grant constantly forced Lee back by flanking moves to the Union left, but only after bloody battles. Sherman forced Johnston south toward Atlanta by constantly flanking him to the Union right, generally without bloody battles. By the end of June, Sherman had advanced eighty miles at the cost of 17,000 casualties to Johnston's 14,000—only one-third of the combined losses of Grant and Lee in Virginia.

The Davis administration grew alarmed by Johnston's apparent willingness to yield territory without a fight. Sherman again flanked the Confederate defenses (after a failed attack) at Kennesaw Mountain in the first week of July. He crossed the Chattahoochee River and drove Johnston back to Peach-

tree Creek less than five miles from Atlanta, a major rail and manufacturing center. Fearing that Johnston would abandon the city, Davis, on July 17, replaced him with John Bell Hood.

A fighting general from Lee's army who had come south with Longstreet the September before for the battle of Chickamauga (where he lost a leg), Hood immediately prepared to counterattack against the Yankees closing in on Atlanta. He did so three times, in the battles of Peachtree Creek (July 20), Atlanta (July 22), and Ezra Church (July 28). Each time, the Confederates reeled back in defeat, suffering a total of 15,000 casualties to Sherman's 6,000. At last, Hood retreated into the formidable earthworks ringing Atlanta and launched no more attacks. But his army did manage to keep Sherman's cavalry and infantry from taking the two railroads

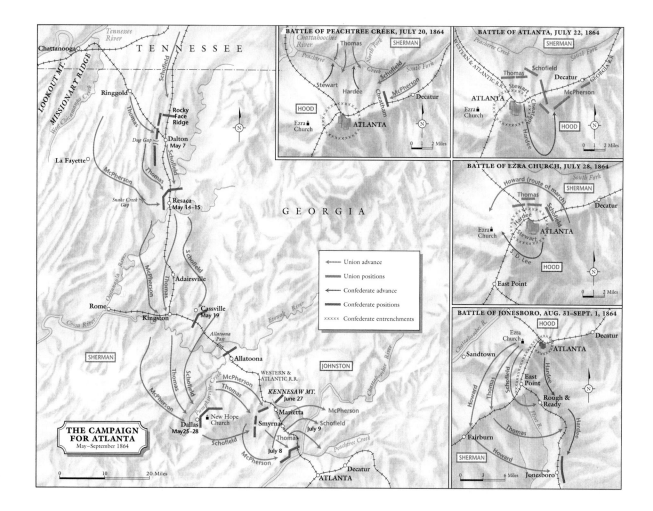

leading into Atlanta from the south. Like Grant at Petersburg, Sherman seemed to settle down for a siege.

PEACE, POLITICS, AND PRISONERS OF WAR

By August, the Confederate strategy of attrition—to hold out until the Union presidential election and to exhaust the northern will to continue fighting—seemed to be working. Union casualties on all fronts during the preceding three months totaled a staggering 110,000—double the number for any comparable period of the war. "Who shall revive the withered hopes that bloomed at the opening of Grant's campaign?" asked the leading Democratic newspaper, the *New York World*. "STOP THE WAR!" shouted Democratic headlines. "All are tired of this damnable tragedy. If nothing else would impress upon people the absolute necessity of stopping this war, its utter failure to accomplish any results would be sufficient."

Even Republicans joined the chorus of despair. "Our bleeding, bankrupt, almost dying country longs for peace," wrote editor Horace Greeley of the *New York Tribune*. Greeley became involved in abortive "peace negotiations" spawned by Confederate agents in Canada intent on stirring up anti-war sentiment in the United States. Those agents managed to convince Greeley that they carried peace overtures from Jefferson Davis, but Lincoln, aware that Davis's condition for peace was Confederate independence, was skeptical. Still, given the mood of the North in midsummer 1864, Lincoln could not reject any opportunity, however dubious, to stop the bloodshed. He deputized Greeley to meet with the Confederate agents in Niagara Falls on the Canadian side of the border. At almost the same time (mid-July), two other northerners met under a flag of truce with Jefferson Davis and Confederate Secretary of State Judah P. Benjamin in Richmond. Lincoln had carefully instructed them—and Greeley—that his conditions for peace were "restoration of the Union and abandonment of slavery."

Of course, Davis would no more accept those terms than Lincoln would accept his. Their war aims were irreconcilable. Although neither of the peace contacts came to anything, the Confederates managed to gain a propaganda victory by claiming that Lincoln's terms, especially emancipation, had been the only obstacle to peace. Northern Democrats, picking up on this theme, ignored the southern refusal to accept reunion as a condition of peace and focused on the slavery issue as the sole stumbling block. "Tens of thousands of white men must yet bite the dust to allay the negro mania of the President," ran a typical Democratic editorial. By August, even staunch Republicans like national party chairman Henry Raymond and his associate Thurlow Weed were convinced that "the desire for peace" and the impression that Lincoln "is fighting not for the Union but for the abolition of slavery" made his reelection "an impossibility." Lincoln thought so too. "I am going to be beaten," he told a friend in August, "and unless some great change takes place, *badly* beaten."

Lincoln was subjected to enormous pressure to drop emancipation as a condition of peace so the onus could be shifted to Jefferson Davis's insistence on Confederate independence. But Lincoln refused to yield. He would rather lose the election than go back on the promise he had made in the Emancipation Proclamation. "No human power can subdue this rebellion without using the Emancipation lever as I have done," he told weak-kneed Republicans. Some 130,000 black soldiers and sailors were fighting for the Union. They would not do so if they thought the North intended to

> betray them. . . . If they stake their lives for us they must be prompted by the strongest motive . . . the promise of freedom. And the promise being made, must be kept. . . . There have been men who proposed to me to return to slavery the[se] black warriors. . . . I should be damned in time & eternity for so doing. The world shall know that I will keep my faith to friends and enemies, come what will.

At the end of August, the Democrats nominated none other than George B. McClellan for president. Although McClellan believed in war for Union (but not abolition), the platform on which he ran declared that "after four years of failure to restore the Union by the experiment of war . . . [we] demand that immediate efforts be made for a cessation of hostilities." Southerners were jubilant. Democratic victory on that platform, said the *Charleston Mercury*, "must lead to peace and our independence" if "for the next two months *we hold our own and prevent military success by our foes.*"

The Prisoner-Exchange Controversy

The Democratic platform also condemned the Lincoln administration's "shameful disregard" of prisoners of war in Confederate prison camps. This raised another contentious matter. By midsummer 1864 the plight of Union and Confederate captives in prisoner-of-war camps had become one of the most bitter issues of the war. Because of the upcoming presidential election, and also because conditions were generally worse in southern prisons—most notoriously at Andersonville, Georgia—it was a political issue mainly in the North.

In 1862 the Union and Confederate armed forces had signed a cartel for the exchange of prisoners captured in battle. The arrangement had worked reasonably well for a year, making large prison camps unnecessary. But when the Union army began to organize regiments of former slaves, the Confederate government announced that it would refuse to treat them as legitimate soldiers. If captured, they and their white officers would be put to death for the crime of fomenting slave insurrections. In practice, however, the Confederate government did not enforce this policy, for Lincoln threatened retaliation on Confederate prisoners of war if it did so. But Confederate troops sometimes murdered black soldiers and their officers as they tried to surrender—most notably at Fort Pillow, a Union garrison on the Mississippi north of Memphis, where cavalry commanded by Nathan Bedford Forrest slaughtered scores of black (and some white) prisoners on April 12, 1864.

In most cases, though, Confederate officers returned captured black soldiers to slavery or put them to hard labor on southern fortifications. Expressing outrage at this treatment of soldiers wearing the United States uniform, the Lincoln administration in 1863 suspended the exchange of prisoners until the Confederacy agreed to treat white and black prisoners alike. The Confederacy refused. The South would "die in the last ditch," said the Confederate exchange agent, before "giving up the right to send slaves back to slavery as property recaptured."

There matters stood as the heavy fighting of 1864 poured scores of thousands of captured soldiers into hastily contrived prison compounds that quickly became death camps. Prisoners were subjected to overcrowding, poor sanitation, contaminated water, scanty rations, inadequate medical facilities, and the exposure of northern prisoners to the heat of a deep-South summer and southern prisoners to the cold of a northern winter. The suffering of northern prisoners was especially acute, because the deterioration of the southern economy made it hard to feed and clothe even Confederate soldiers and civilians, let alone Yankee prisoners. Nearly 16 percent of all Union soldiers held in southern prison camps died, compared with 12 percent of Confederate soldiers in northern camps. Andersonville was the most notorious hellhole. A stockade camp of twenty-six acres with neither huts nor tents, designed to accommodate 15,000 prisoners, it held 33,000 in August 1864. They died at the rate of more than one hundred a day. Altogether, 13,000 northern soldiers died at Andersonville. For a generation or more after the war, many northerners saw the graves of those soldiers as a symbol of southern barbarism; as sectional passions cooled, the graves came to be seen as a symbol of the barbarism of war.

The suffering of Union prisoners brought heavy pressure on the Lincoln administration to renew exchanges, but the Confederates would not budge on the question of exchanging black soldiers. After a series of battles on the Richmond-Petersburg front in September 1864, General Lee proposed an informal

Burial of Union POWs at Andersonville   Every day in the summer of 1864 at least one hundred Union prisoners of war died of disease, malnutrition, or exposure at Andersonville Prison in Georgia. This scene of burial in long trenches became so commonplace as to dull the sense of horror.

exchange of prisoners. Grant agreed, on condition that black soldiers captured in the fighting be included "the same as white soldiers." Lee replied that "negroes belonging to our citizens are not considered subjects of exchange and were not included in my proposition." No exchange, then, responded Grant. The Union government was "bound to secure to all persons received into her armies the rights due to soldiers." Lincoln backed this policy; just as he would not recede from emancipation as a condition of peace, he would not sacrifice the principle of equal treatment of black prisoners, even though local Republican leaders warned that many northerners "will work and vote against the President, because they think sympathy with a few negroes, also captured, is the cause of a refusal" to exchange prisoners.

The Issue of Black Soldiers in the Confederate Army

During the winter of 1864–1865 the Confederate government quietly abandoned its refusal to exchange black prisoners, and exchanges resumed. One reason for this reversal was a Confederate decision to recruit slaves to fight for the South. Two years earlier, Jefferson Davis had denounced the North's arming of freed slaves as "the most execrable measure recorded in the history of guilty man." But by February 1865, southern armies were desperate for manpower, and slaves constituted the only remaining reserve. Supported by the powerful influence of Robert E. Lee, the Davis administration pressed the Confederate Congress to enact a bill for recruitment of black soldiers. The assumption that any slaves who fought for the South would have to be granted freedom as a reward generated bitter opposition to the measure. "What did we go to war for, if not to protect our property?" asked a Virginia senator. By three votes in the House and one in the Senate, the Confederate Congress finally passed the bill on March 13, 1865. Before any southern black regiments could be organized, however, the war was over.

THE REELECTION OF LINCOLN

Despite Republicans' fears, events on the battlefield, rather than political controversies, had the strongest impact on northern voters in 1864. In effect, the election became a referendum on whether to continue fighting for unconditional victory. And suddenly, within days after the Democratic national convention had declared the war a failure, the military situation changed dramatically.

The Capture of Atlanta

After a month of apparent stalemate on the Atlanta front, Sherman's army again made a large movement by the right flank to attack the last rail link into Atlanta from the south. At the battle of Jonesboro on August 31–September 1, Sherman's men captured the railroad. Confederate commander John Bell Hood abandoned Atlanta to save his army. On September 2, jubilant Union troops marched into Atlanta, whose symbolic as well as substantive value to the Confederacy was by now second only to Richmond's. Sherman sent a jaunty telegram to Washington: "Atlanta is ours, and fairly won."

This news had an enormous impact on the election. "VICTORY!" blazoned Republican headlines. "IS THE WAR A FAILURE? OLD ABE'S REPLY TO THE DEMOCRATIC CONVENTION." A New York Republican wrote that the capture of Atlanta, "coming at this political crisis, is the greatest event of the war." The *Richmond Examiner* glumly concurred. The fall of Atlanta, it declared, "came in the very nick of time" to "save the party of Lincoln from irretrievable ruin. It will obscure the prospect of peace, late so bright. It will also diffuse gloom over the South."

The Shenandoah Valley

If Atlanta was not enough to brighten the prospects for Lincoln's reelection, events in Virginia's Shenandoah Valley were. After Jubal Early's raid through the Valley all the way to Washington in July, Grant had put Philip Sheridan in charge of a reinforced Army of the Shenandoah, telling him to "go after Early and follow him to the death." Sheridan was just the man for the job. He infused the same spirit into the three infantry corps of the Army of the Shenandoah that he had previously imbued in his cavalry. On September 19 they attacked Early's force near Winchester and after a day-long battle sent the Confederates flying to the south. Sheridan pursued them, attacking again on September 22 at Fisher's Hill twenty miles south of Winchester. Once more the

Confederate line collapsed, and Early's routed army fled sixty more miles to the south.

Early's retreat enabled Sheridan to carry out the second part of his assignment in the Shenandoah Valley, which had twice served as a Confederate route of invasion and whose farms helped feed Confederate armies. Sheridan now set about destroying the Valley's crops and mills so thoroughly that "crows flying over it for the balance of the season will have to carry their provender with them." In October, Sheridan wired the War Department that by the time he was through, "the Valley, from Winchester up to Staunton, ninety-two miles, will have little in it for man or beast."

But Jubal Early was not yet willing to give up. Reinforced by a division from Lee, on October 19 he launched a dawn attack across Cedar Creek, a dozen miles south of Winchester. He caught the Yankees by surprise and drove them back in disorder. At the time of the attack, Sheridan was on his way back from Washington, where he had gone to confer on future strategy. Galloping from Winchester to the battlefield on a ride that later became celebrated in poetry and legend, he arrived in early afternoon. By sundown, his extraordinary charisma and tactical leadership had turned the battle from a Union defeat into another Confederate rout. The battle of Cedar Creek ended Confederate power in the Valley.

The victories won by Sherman and Sheridan ensured Lincoln's reelection on November 8 by a majority of 212 to 21 in the Electoral College. Soldiers played a notable role in the balloting. Every northern state except three whose legislatures were controlled by Democrats had passed laws allowing absentee voting by soldiers at the front. Despite the lingering affection of some soldiers for their old commander McClellan, 78 percent of the army vote went to Lincoln—compared with 54 percent of the civilian vote. The men who were doing the fighting had sent a clear message that they meant to finish the job.

THE END OF THE CONFEDERACY

Many southerners got the message. But not Jefferson Davis. The Confederacy remained "as erect and defiant as ever," he told his Congress in November 1864. "Nothing has changed in the purpose of its Govern-

ment, in the indomitable valor of its troops, or in the unquenchable spirit of its people." It was this last-ditch resistance that William T. Sherman set out to break in his famous march from Atlanta to the sea.

Sherman had long pondered the nature of the war. He had concluded, "We are not only fighting hostile armies, but a hostile people." Defeat of the Confederate armies was not enough to win the war; the railroads, factories, and farms that supported those armies must also be destroyed. The will of the civilians who sustained the war must be crushed. Sherman expressed more bluntly than anyone else the meaning of total war and was ahead of his time in his understanding of psychological warfare. "We cannot change the hearts of those people of the South," he said, "but we can make war so terrible and make them so sick of war that generations would pass away before they would again appeal to it."

From Atlanta to the Sea

In Tennessee and Mississippi, Sherman's troops had burned everything of military value that was within their reach—and much else besides. Now Sherman proposed to do the same in Georgia. He urged Grant to let him cut loose from his base and march through the heart of Georgia, living off the land and destroying all resources not needed by his army—the same policy Sheridan was carrying out in the Shenandoah Valley. Grant and Lincoln were reluctant to authorize such a risky move, especially with Hood's army of 40,000 men still intact and hovering in northern Alabama ready to move into Tennessee if Sherman were to march off in the opposite direction. But Sherman assured them that he would send George Thomas to take command of a force of 60,000 men in Tennessee who would be more than a match for Hood. With another 60,000, Sherman could "move through Georgia, smashing things to the sea. . . . I can make the march, and make Georgia howl!"

Lincoln and Grant finally consented. On November 16, Sherman's avengers marched out of Atlanta after burning a third of the city, including some nonmilitary property. Sherman and his men cared little; in their opinion, the rebels had sown the wind and deserved to reap the whirlwind. Southward they marched 280 miles to Savannah, wrecking everything in their path that could by any stretch of the imagination be considered of military value.

Sherman's Soldiers Tearing up the Railroad in Atlanta   One of the objectives of Sherman's march from Atlanta to the sea was to wreck the railroads so they could not transport supplies to Confederate armies. The soldiers did a thorough job. They tore up the rails and ties, made a bonfire of the ties, heated the rails in the fire, and then wrapped them around trees, creating "Sherman neckties."

The Battles of Franklin and Nashville

They encountered little resistance. Instead of chasing Sherman, Hood had invaded Tennessee with the hope of recovering that state for the Confederacy. But this campaign turned into a disaster that virtually destroyed Hood's army. On November 30, the Confederates attacked part of the Union force at Franklin, a town on the Harpeth River twenty miles south of Nashville. It was a slaughter that claimed no fewer than 12 Confederate generals and 54 regimental commanders as casualties. But instead of retreating, Hood moved on to Nashville, where on December 15–16 Thomas launched an attack that almost wiped out the Army of Tennessee. Its remnants retreated to Mississippi, where Hood resigned in January 1865. Of the 50,000 infantrymen in the army when Hood had taken command the previous July, fewer than 15,000 were left.

Fort Fisher and Sherman's March through the Carolinas

News of Hood's defeat produced, in the words of a southern diarist, "the darkest and most dismal day" of the Confederacy's short history. But worse was yet to come. Lee's army in Virginia drew its dwindling supplies overland from the Carolinas and through the port of Wilmington, North Carolina, the only city still accessible to blockade runners. That was because the mouth of the Cape Fear River below Wilmington was guarded by massive Fort Fisher, whose big guns kept blockade ships at bay and protected the runners. The Union navy had long wanted to attack Fort Fisher and shut this back door to Richmond. But the diversion of ships and troops to the long, futile campaign against Charleston had delayed the effort. In January 1865, though, the largest armada of the war, 58 ships with 627 guns, pounded Fort Fisher

HOOD'S TENNESSEE CAMPAIGN
Oct.–Nov. 1864

← Confederate advance
▬ Confederate positions
▬ Union positions
←--- Union retreat

NASHVILLE
Dec. 15–16, 1864

▬ Confederate defenses, Dec. 15   ▬ Union positions
← Confederate retreat, Dec. 15   ×××××× Union entrenchments
▨ Confederate defenses, Dec. 16   ← Union assault
←--- Confederate retreat, Dec. 16

for two days, disabling most of its big guns. Army troops and marines landed and stormed the fort, capturing it on January 15. That ended the blockade running, and Sherman soon put an end to supplies from the Carolinas as well.

At the end of January, Sherman's soldiers headed north from Savannah, eager to take revenge on South Carolina, which to their mind had started the war. They made even less distinction between civilian and military property in South Carolina than they had in Georgia, and left even less of Columbia standing than they had of Atlanta. Seemingly invincible, Sherman's army pushed into North Carolina and brushed aside the force that Joseph E. Johnston had assembled to stop them. The trail of devastation left in their wake appalled Confederates. "All is gloom, despondency, and inactivity," wrote a South Carolina physician. "Our army is demoralized and

the people panic stricken. To fight longer seems to be madness."

But the war would not end until the Confederate armies had surrendered, as Lincoln made clear in his second inaugural address on March 4, 1865. In the best known words from that address, he urged a binding up of the nation's wounds "with malice toward none" and "charity for all." But even more significant, given that the conflict still raged, were these words:

American Slavery is one of those offences which, in the providence of God . . . He now wills to remove [through] this terrible war, as the woe due to those by whom the offence came. . . . Fondly do we hope—fervently do we pray—that this mighty scourge of war may speedily pass away. Yet if God wills that it continue, until all the wealth piled by the bondman's two hundred and fifty years of unrequited toil shall be sunk, and until every drop of blood drawn with the lash, shall be paid by another drawn with

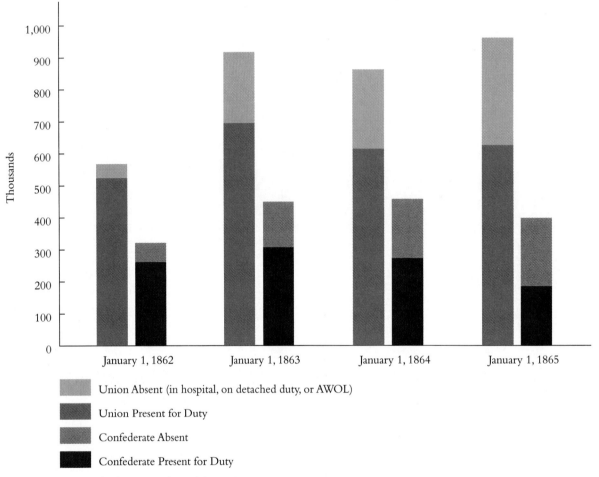

Union Absent (in hospital, on detached duty, or AWOL)

Union Present for Duty

Confederate Absent

Confederate Present for Duty

Comparative Strength of Union and Confederate Armies

the sword, as was said three thousand years ago, so still it must be said "the judgments of the Lord, are true and righteous altogether."

The Road to Appomattox

Ulysses S. Grant did not intend the war to last that long. He knew that the Army of Northern Virginia — the only entity that now kept the Confederacy alive — was on the verge of disintegration. Scores of its soldiers were deserting every day. On April 1, Sheridan's cavalry (which had returned from the Shenandoah Valley) and an infantry corps smashed the right flank of Lee's line at Five Forks and cut off the last railroad into Petersburg. Next day, Grant attacked all along the line and forced Lee to abandon both Petersburg and Richmond. As the Confederate government fled its capital, its army set fire to all the military stores it could not carry. The fires spread

and destroyed more of Richmond than the northern troops had destroyed of Atlanta or Columbia.

Lee's starving men limped westward, hoping to turn south and join the remnants of Johnston's army in North Carolina. But Sheridan's cavalry raced ahead and cut them off at Appomattox, ninety miles from Petersburg, on April 8. When the weary Confederates tried a breakout attack the next morning, their first probe revealed solid ranks of Union infantry arrayed behind the cavalry. It was the end. "There is nothing left for me to do," said Lee, "but to go and see General Grant, and I would rather die a thousand deaths." Lee met with Grant at the house of Wilmer McLean, who in 1861 had lived near Manassas where a shell had crashed through his kitchen roof during the first battle of Bull Run. McLean had moved to the remote village of Appomattox to escape the war, only to have its final drama

The Surrender at Appomattox   This is one of many paintings of Grant and Lee agreeing to the surrender terms of Lee's army in Wilmer McLean's parlor at Appomattox Court House. Unfortunately, no photographer was present to record the scene, but many eyewitnesses provided descriptions to guide artists. Lee was accompanied by a lone aide; Grant was accompanied by nearly a dozen of his generals and staff officers. Standing immediately to the left of the seated Grant is George G. Meade, commander of the Army of the Potomac, and standing to Meade's left is Philip Sheridan, commander of the army's cavalry.

played out in his parlor. There, the son of an Ohio tanner dictated surrender terms to a scion of one of Virginia's First Families.

The terms were generous. Thirty thousand captured Confederates were allowed to go home on condition that they promise never again to take up arms against the United States. These terms became the model for the surrender of the other Confederate armies over the next few weeks. Appomattox ended the war. After completing the surrender formalities on April 9, Grant introduced Lee to his staff, which included Colonel Ely Parker, a Seneca Indian. As Lee shook hands with Parker, he stared for a moment at Parker's dark features and said: "I

am glad to see one real American here." Parker replied solemnly: "We are all Americans." And indeed they now were.

THE ASSASSINATION OF LINCOLN

Wild celebrations broke out in the North at news of the fall of Richmond followed soon by news of Appomattox. But almost overnight, the celebrations turned to mourning. On the evening of April 14, the careworn Abraham Lincoln sought to relax by attending a comedy at Ford's Theatre. In the middle of the play, John Wilkes Booth broke into Lincoln's box and shot the president fatally in the head. An aspiring young actor, overshadowed by the greater fame of his father and older brother Edwin, Booth was a native of Maryland, a Confederate supporter, and a frustrated, unstable egotist who hated Lincoln for what he had done to Booth's beloved South. As he jumped from Lincoln's box to the stage and

Abraham Lincoln in 1865   This is the last photograph of Lincoln, taken on April 10, 1865, four days before his assassination. Four years of war had left their mark on the 56-year-old president; note the lines of strain, fatigue, and sadness in his face.

Table 17-1

Casualties in Civil War Armies and Navies

Confederate records are incomplete; the Confederate data listed here are therefore estimates. The actual Confederate totals were probably higher.

	Killed and Mortally Wounded in Combat	Died of Disease	Died in Prison	Miscellaneous Deaths(Accidents, Drownings,Cause not Stated, etc.)	Total Deaths	Wounded, not Mortally	Total Casualties
Union	111,904	197,388	30,192	24,881	364,345	277,401	641,766
Confederate (Estimated)	94,000	140,000	26,000	No Estimates	260,000	195,000	455,000
Both Armies (Estimated)	205,904	337,388	56,192	24, 881	624,365	472,401	1,096,766

escaped out a back door, he shouted Virginia's state motto at the stunned audience: "Sic semper tyrannis" (thus always to tyrants).

Thus, the tragedy of the American Civil War, begun by the secessionist Edmund Ruffin, who pulled the lanyard on the first cannon fired at Fort Sumter on April 12, 1861, ended with an assassin's bullet fired by another southern partisan on April 14, 1865. At the cost of nearly 625,000 lives, the United States was preserved as one nation, indivisible, and slavery was abolished. But in 1865 the shape of that nation and of its new birth of freedom was yet to be determined.

SUGGESTED READING

For works that cover the whole period of the Civil War, including the years encompassed by this chapter, see the books cited in the first three paragraphs of the "Suggested Reading" for Chapter 16. In addition, for analyses of military strategy and leadership that focus mainly on the period 1862–1865, consult T. Harry Williams, *Lincoln and His Generals* (1952); Archer Jones, *Civil War Command and Strategy* (1992); Joseph T. Glatthaar, *Partners in Command: The Relationships between Leaders in the Civil War* (1993); and Steven E. Woodworth, *Jefferson Davis and His Generals* (1990). Richard M. McMurry, *Two Great Rebel Armies* (1989), analyzes the reasons for the success of the Army of Northern Virginia and the relative failure of the Army of Tennessee, while Michael C. Adams, *Our Masters the Rebels: A Speculation on Union Military Defeat in the East, 1861–1865* (1978), reissued under the title *Fighting for Defeat* (1992), offers an interpretation of the Army of the Potomac's problems. Charles W. Royster, *The Destruc-*

tive War: William Tecumseh Sherman, Stonewall Jackson, and the Americans (1991), provides a provocative analysis of the escalating destructiveness of the war. Five studies canvass various explanations for Union victory: David Donald, ed., *Why the North Won the Civil War* (1960); Herman Hattaway and Archer Jones, *How the North Won: A Military History of the Civil War* (1983); Richard E. Beringer, Herman Hattaway, Archer Jones, and William N. Still, Jr., *Why the South Lost the Civil War* (1986), an abridged version of which was published with the title *The Elements of Confederate Defeat* (1988); Grady McWhiney and Perry D. Jamieson, *Attack and Die: Civil War Military Tactics and the Southern Heritage* (1982); and Gabor S. Boritt, ed., *Why the Confederacy Lost* (1992). See also Drew Gilpin Faust, *The Creation of Confederate Nationalism* (1988).

On the issues of slavery and emancipation in the war, the best place to begin is Ira Berlin, Barbara J. Fields, Steven F. Miller, Joseph P. Reidy, and Leslie S. Rowland, *Slaves No More: Three Essays on Emancipation and the Civil War* (1992). An older but still useful study is Bell I. Wiley, *Southern Negroes 1861–1865* (1938). A superb study for one Confederate state is Clarence L. Mohr, *On the Threshold of Freedom: Masters and Slaves in Civil War Georgia* (1986), while a classic account of the experience of emancipation on the South Carolina sea islands is Willie Lee Rose, *Rehearsal for Reconstruction: The Port Royal Experiment* (1964). Two books on Maryland provide the best studies of slavery and emancipation in a border state: Charles L. Wagandt, *The Mighty Revolution: Negro Emancipation in Maryland 1862–1864* (1964) and Barbara Jeane Fields, *Slavery and Freedom on the Middle Ground: Maryland during the Nineteenth Century* (1985). See also Victor B. Howard, *Black Liberation in Kentucky: Emancipation and Freedom, 1862–1884* (1983). For the hopes and realities of freedom as experienced by the slaves, see Leon F. Litwack, *Been in the Storm So Long: The Aftermath of Slavery* (1979). A fine study of the Emancipation Proclamation is John Hope Franklin, *The Emancipation*

Proclamation (1963).Two books by James M. McPherson ana-lyze the role of Northern abolitionists and black leaders in the achievement of emancipation: *The Struggle for Equality: Abolitionists and the Negro in the Civil War and Reconstruction* (1964) and *The Negro's Civil War* (1965, new ed. 1991). The impact of the loss of slavery on the slaveholding class is chron-icled by James L. Roark, *Masters Without Slaves: Southern Planters in the Civil War and Reconstruction* (1977).

For black soldiers in the Union army, the best studies are Dudley T. Cornish, *The Sable Arm: Negro Troops in the Union Army* (1956) and Joseph T. Glatthaar, *Forged in Battle:The Civil War Alliance of Black Soldiers and White Officers* (1990).A classic account by a white officer of a black regiment is Thomas Wentworth Higginson, *Army Life in a Black Regiment* (1869; reprinted 1961). For the Confederate debate about arming and freeing slaves, see Robert Durden, *The Gray and the Black: The Confederate Debate on Emancipation* (1972).

Anti-black and anti-emancipation sentiments in the North are the focus of V. Jacque Voegeli, *Free but Not Equal:The Mid-west and the Negro during the Civil War* (1967) and Forrest G. Wood, *Black Scare:The Racist Response to Emancipation and Re-construction* (1968). Hostility to emancipation was at the core of Copperheadism in the North, a phenomenon provocatively interpreted in three books by Frank L. Klement: *The Copper-heads in the Middle West* (1960); *The Limits of Dissent: Clement L.Vallandigham and the Civil War* (1970); and *Dark Lanterns: Se-cret Political Societies, Conspiracies, and Treason Trials in the Civil War* (1984). See also Wood Gray, *The Hidden Civil War: The Story of the Copperheads* (1942). For the Northern Democrats, one should also consult Joel Silbey, *A Respectable Minority:The Democratic Party in the Civil War Era* (1977).

Three studies of the Lincoln administration's record on civil liberties and related constitutional issues are important: Mark E. Neely, Jr., *The Fate of Liberty: Abraham Lincoln and Civil Liberties* (1990); Dean Sprague, *Freedom under Lincoln* (1965); and James G. Randall, *Constitutional Problems Under Lincoln* (rev. ed., 1951). Other studies of constitutional issues during the war include Harold M. Hyman, *A More Perfect Union:The Impact of the Civil War and Reconstruction on the Con-stitution* (1973) and Phillip S. Paludan, *A Covenant with Death: The Constitution, Law, and Equality in the Civil War Era* (1975). William B. Hesseltine, *Lincoln and the War Governors* (1948) is a valuable study of federal-state relations in the crucible of war.

Still a useful book on the Confederate economy is Charles W. Ramsdell, *Behind the Lines in the Southern Confederacy* (1944), while for the Union, the same can be said of Emer-son D. Fite, *Social and Economic Conditions in the North during the Civil War* (1910). Railroads in North and South are treated in George E. Turner, *Victory Rode the Rails* (1953); Thomas Weber, *The Northern Railroads in the Civil War* (1952); and Robert C. Black, *The Railroads of the Confederacy* (1952). Robert V. Bruce, *Lincoln and the Tools of War* (1956) is a fasci-nating study of northern technology in the war, while Ed-ward Hagerman, *The American Civil War and the Origins of Modern Warfare* (1988) is the fullest study of logistics.

Class conflict and political dissent in the Confederacy are discussed in Paul D. Escott, *After Secession: Jefferson Davis and the Failure of Confederate Nationalism* (1978); Bell I.Wiley, *The Plain People of the Confederacy* (1943); Fred Arthur Bailey, *Class and Tennessee's Confederate Generation* (1987); Wayne K. Dur-rill, *War of Another Kind: A Southern Community in the Great Rebellion* (1990); and Frank L. Owsley, *State Rights in the Con-federacy* (1966).The most dramatic manifestation of class con-flict in the North was the New York draft riot. Two impor-tant studies of it are Adrian Cook, *The Armies of the Streets: The New York City Draft Riots of 1863* (1974) and Iver Bern-stein, *The New York City Draft Riots:Their Significance for Ameri-can Society and Politics in the Age of the Civil War* (1990). For the conflict in the Pennsylvania coal fields, see Grace Pal-ladino, *Another Civil War: Labor, Capital, and the State in the An-thracite Regions of Pennsylvania* (1990).

Controversies about conscription lay at the root of much wartime class conflict. For studies of the draft in South and North, see Albert B. Moore, *Conscription and Conflict in the Confederacy* (1924); Eugene C. Murdock, *One Million Men:The Civil War Draft in the North* (1971); and James W. Geary, *We Need Men:The Union Draft in the Civil War* (1991). The mod-ernizing legislation of the Union Congress that drafted a "blueprint for modern America" is analyzed by Leonard P. Curry, *Blueprint for Modern America: Non-Military Legislation of the First Civil War Congress* (1968). For a provocative interpre-tation of the Confederacy's attempted crash program of mod-ernization and industrialization, see Emory M. Thomas, *The Confederacy as a Revolutionary Experience* (1971; new ed. 1991).

For Civil War medicine, in addition to the books about women in the war cited in the first paragraph of Suggested Reading for Chapter 16, see Paul E. Steiner, *Disease in the Civil War* (1968); George W. Adams, *Doctors in Blue:The Medical His-tory of the Union Army in the Civil War* (1952); and Horace H. Cunningham, *Doctors in Gray: The Confederate Medical Service* (1958). The basic history of the U.S. Sanitary Commission is William Q. Maxwell, *Lincoln's Fifth Wheel:The Political History of the United States Sanitary Commission* (1956).A stimulating inter-pretation of the Sanitary Commission in the context of wartime transformations in northern attitudes toward other so-cial and cultural issues is George M. Fredrickson, *The Inner Civil War: Northern Intellectuals and the Crisis of the Union* (1965).

The complex relationships between peace negotiations and the Union presidential election of 1864 are discussed in Edward C. Kirkland, *The Peacemakers of 1864* (1927);William F. Zornow, *Lincoln and the Party Divided* (1954); David E. Long, *The Jewel of Liberty:Abraham Lincoln's Re-Election and the End of Slavery* (1994); and Larry E. Nelson, *Bullets, Ballots, and Rhetoric: Confederate Policy for the United States Presidential Con-test of 1864* (1980).The best analysis of Lincoln's assassination and of the many unsubstantiated conspiracy theories to ex-plain it is William Hanchett, *The Lincoln Murder Conspiracies* (1983). See also William A. Tidwell, James O. Hall, and David Winfred Gaddy, *Come Retribution:The Confederate Secret Service and the Assassination of Lincoln* (1988).

Chapter 18

Reconstruction, 1863–1877

During the Civil War, Winslow Homer traveled with the Union Army in Virginia as an artist for *Harper's Weekly*. In the 1870s Homer returned to Virginia, where he painted the new world of freedom that had turned the world of slavery upside down. Black and white meet on even terms in this post-war painting. The black women are respectful but not obsequious; their former mistress is respectful but not domineering. The quiet subtlety of this painting conveys volumes of meaning.

Reconstruction as a period of American history is usually taken to be the twelve years after the Civil War (1865–1877). Actually, it began while the war was still in progress. Indeed, the North's principal war aim was to "reconstruct" the Union. But controversies soon arose over what the Union should be after it had been reconstructed. Should it be the old Union of 1861? The abolition of slavery ensured that it would not be that. But what rights would the freed slaves and their former masters have in the reconstructed Union?

WARTIME RECONSTRUCTION

Lincoln pondered these questions long and hard. At first he feared that southern whites would never extend equal rights to the freed slaves. After all, even most northern states denied full civil equality to the few black people within their borders. In 1862–1863, Lincoln encouraged freedpeople to emigrate

to all-black countries like Haiti, where they would have a chance to get ahead without having to face the racism of whites. But black leaders, abolitionists, and many Republicans objected to that policy, on the grounds that it would punish the victims of racial prejudice rather than its perpetrators. Black people were Americans. Why should they not have the rights of American citizens instead of being urged to leave the country?

Lincoln eventually was converted to the logic and justice of that view. But in beginning the process of reconstruction, Lincoln first reached out to southern *whites* whose allegiance to the Confederacy was lukewarm and who might be enticed to renew their allegiance to the United States. On December 8, 1863, Lincoln issued his Proclamation of Amnesty and Reconstruction, the document that was to frame the debate over the terms of reconstruction for the rest of the war and well into the postwar years.

The Proclamation of Amnesty offered presidential pardon to all southern whites (with the exception of

Confederate government officials and high-ranking military officers) who took an oath of allegiance to the United States and accepted the abolition of slavery. Furthermore, in any state where the number of white males twenty-one or older who took this oath equaled 10 percent of the number of voters in 1860, that nucleus could reestablish a state government to which Lincoln promised presidential recognition. Since the war was still raging, this policy could be carried out only where Union troops controlled substantial portions of a Confederate state: Louisiana, Arkansas, and Tennessee in early 1864. Nevertheless, Lincoln hoped that once the process had begun in those areas, it might snowball as Union military victories convinced more and more Confederates that their cause was hopeless. As matters turned out, those military victories were long delayed, and reconstruction in most parts of the South did not begin until 1865.

Another problem that slowed the process was a growing opposition within Lincoln's own party. Many Republicans believed that the amnesty policy favored former Confederates at the expense of freedmen. White men who had fought *against* the Union, they said, should not be rewarded with a restoration of their political rights while black men who had fought *for* the Union were denied those rights. In the Proclamation of Reconstruction, Lincoln had stated that "any provision which may be adopted by [a reconstructed] State government in relation to the freed people of such State, which shall recognize and declare their permanent freedom, provide for their education, and which may yet be consistent, as a temporary arrangement, with their present condition as a laboring, landless, and homeless class, will not be objected to by the national Executive." This seemed to mean that white landowners and former slaveholders, even if they had been Confederates, could adopt labor regulations and other measures to control former slaves, so long as they recognized their freedom and made minimal provision for their education.

These were radical advances over slavery, but for many Republicans they were not radical enough. Led by Thaddeus Stevens in the House and Charles Sumner in the Senate, and backed by black leaders and abolitionists like Frederick Douglass and Wendell Phillips, the radical Republicans wanted to go much further. If the freedpeople were landless, they said, provide them with land by confiscating the plantations of leading Confederates as punishment for treason. Radical Republicans also distrusted oaths of allegiance sworn by ex-Confederates. Rather than simply restoring the old ruling class to power, asked Charles Sumner, why not give freed slaves the vote, to provide a genuinely loyal nucleus for the restoration of the southern states to the Union?

These radical positions did not command a majority of Congress in 1864. Yet the experience of Louisiana, the first state to reorganize under Lincoln's more moderate policy, convinced even nonradical Republicans to block that policy. With the protection of Union soldiers in the occupied portion of Louisiana (New Orleans and several parishes in the southern half of the state), enough white men took the oath of allegiance to satisfy Lincoln's conditions. They adopted a new state constitution and formed a government that abolished slavery and provided a school system for blacks. But despite Lincoln's private appeal to the new government to grant literate blacks and black Union soldiers the right to vote, the reconstructed Louisiana legislature chose not to do so. It also authorized planters to enforce restrictive labor policies on black plantation workers that seemed, to abolitionists, only a slight improvement over slavery itself. Louisiana's actions alienated a majority of congressional Republicans, who refused to admit representatives and senators from the "reconstructed" state of Louisiana — or from Arkansas and Tennessee, which had also reorganized under Lincoln's plan. Congress also refused to count the electoral votes of these three states in the presidential election of 1864.

At the same time, though, Congress failed to enact a reconstruction policy of its own. This was not for lack of trying. In fact, both houses passed the Wade-Davis reconstruction bill (named for Senator Benjamin Wade of Ohio and Representative Henry Winter Davis of Maryland) in July 1864. That bill did not enfranchise blacks (such a radical policy still did not command a Republican majority). But it did impose such stringent loyalty requirements on southern whites that few of them could take the required oath. Lincoln therefore killed the bill with a pocket veto (whereby a bill passed at the end of a congressional session fails to become law if it is not signed by the president).

Lincoln's action infuriated many Republicans. Wade and Davis published a blistering "manifesto" denouncing the president. This bitter squabble

Lincoln's Funeral Procession in Chicago, May 1, 1865   After a public funeral in Washington, D.C., on April 19, Lincoln's remains were transported by special train to New York City and then west to their final resting place in Springfield, Illinois, where Lincoln was buried on May 4, 1865. The funeral train stopped in major cities, where grieving citizens paid their last respects. An estimated seven million people lined the tracks along the train's thousand-mile journey, which reversed the route Lincoln had taken from Springfield to Washington, D.C., in February 1861.

threatened for a time to destroy Lincoln's chances of being reelected. But Union military success in the fall of 1864, combined with sober second thoughts about the consequences of a Democratic electoral victory, reunited the Republicans behind Lincoln. The collapse of Confederate military resistance the following spring set the stage for compromise between President and Congress on a policy for the post-war South. Two days after Appomattox, Lincoln promised that he would soon announce such a policy, which probably would have included voting rights for some blacks and stronger measures to protect their civil rights. But three days later, Lincoln was assassinated.

ANDREW JOHNSON AND RECONSTRUCTION

In 1864 Republicans had adopted the name "Union Party" to attract the votes of War Democrats and border-state Unionists who could not bring themselves to vote "Republican." For the same reason, they also nominated Andrew Johnson of Tennessee as Lincoln's running mate.

Of "poor white" heritage, Johnson had learned the tailoring trade and had clawed his way up in the rough-and-tumble politics of East Tennessee. This was a region of small farms and few slaves that had little love for the planters of central and western

Tennessee who controlled the state. Neither did Andrew Johnson, who denounced the planters as "stuck-up aristocrats" who had no sympathy with the southern yeomen for whom Johnson became a self-appointed spokesman. In 1861 most of his East Tennessee constituents were Unionists, and Johnson, though a Democrat, was the only senator from a Confederate state who refused to support the Confederacy. For this, the Republicans rewarded him with the vice-presidential nomination, hoping that his presence on the ticket would attract the votes of pro-war Democrats and upper-South Unionists.

Booth's bullet therefore elevated to the presidency a man who still thought of himself as primarily a Democrat and a southerner. The trouble this might cause in a party that was mostly Republican and northern was not immediately apparent, however. In fact, Johnson's enmity toward the "stuck-up aristocrats" whom he blamed for leading the South into secession prompted him to utter dire threats against "traitors." "Treason is a crime and must be made odious," he said soon after becoming president. "Traitors must be impoverished. . . . They must not only be punished, but their social power must be destroyed."

Radical Republicans liked the sound of this. It seemed to promise the type of reconstruction they favored—one that would deny political power to ex-Confederates and would enfranchise blacks. They envisioned a coalition between these new black voters and the small minority of southern whites who had never supported the Confederacy that would become the basis for a new order in the South. These men could be expected to vote Republican, the party of Union and emancipation. Republican governments in southern states would guarantee freedom and would pass laws to provide civil rights and economic opportunity for freed slaves. Not incidentally, they would also strengthen the Republican Party nationally.

Johnson's Policy

From a combination of pragmatic, partisan, and idealistic motives, therefore, radical Republicans in the spring of 1865 prepared to implement a progressive reconstruction policy. But Andrew Johnson unexpectedly refused to cooperate. Instead of calling Congress into special session (the next regular session would not begin until the following December), he moved ahead on his own without consulting Republicans in the Congress. On May 29, Johnson issued two proclamations. The first provided for a blanket amnesty for all but the highest-ranking Confederate officials and military officers, plus those ex-Confederates with taxable property worth $20,000 or more—the "stuck-up aristocrats." The second named a provisional governor for North Carolina and directed him to call an election of delegates to frame a new state constitution. Only white men who had received amnesty and taken an oath of allegiance could vote. Similar proclamations soon followed for other former Confederate states. Johnson's policy was clear. He would exclude both blacks and upper-class whites from the reconstruction process. The backbone of the new South would be yeomen whites, those who, like himself, had remained steadfastly loyal to the Union, along with those who now proclaimed themselves loyal.

Many Republicans supported Johnson's policy at first. But the radicals were dismayed. They feared that restricting the vote to whites would open the door to the oppression of the newly freed slaves and to the restoration of the old power structure in the South, minus only slavery. They began to sense that Johnson (who had owned slaves) was as dedicated to white supremacy as any Confederate. "White men alone must govern the South," he told a Democratic senator. After a tense confrontation with a group of black men led by Frederick Douglass, who had visited the White House to urge black suffrage, Johnson told his private secretary: "Those d——d sons of b——s thought they had me in a trap! I know that d——d Douglass; he's just like any nigger, and he would sooner cut a white man's throat than not."

Moderate Republicans believed that black men should participate to some degree in the reconstruction process, but they were not prepared to break with the president in 1865. They regarded his policy as a beginning—an "experiment" that would be modified and expanded as time went on. "Loyal negroes must not be put down, while disloyal white men are put up," wrote a moderate Republican. "But I am quite willing to see what will come of Mr. Johnson's experiment." If the new southern state constitutions did not enfranchise at least literate blacks and those who had fought in the Union army, said another moderate, "the President then will be at liberty to pursue a sterner policy."

Southern Defiance

As it happened, none of the state conventions enfranchised a single black. Some of them even balked at ratifying the Thirteenth Amendment (which abolished slavery) and at repudiating the Confederate debt. The rhetoric of some southerners began to take on a renewed anti-Yankee tone of defiance that sounded like 1861 all over again. Reports from Unionists and army officers in the South told of neo-Confederate violence against blacks and their white sympathizers. Johnson seemed to encourage such activities by his own rhetoric, which sounded increasingly like that of a southern Democrat, and by his allowance of the organization of white militia units in the South. "What can be hatched from such an egg," asked a Republican newspaper, "but another rebellion?"

Then there was the matter of presidential pardons. After talking fiercely about punishing traitors, and after excluding several classes of them from his amnesty proclamation, Johnson began to issue special pardons to many ex-Confederates — 13,500 by September 1865 — restoring to them all property and political rights. Moreover, under the new state constitutions established by Johnson's policy, southern voters were electing hundreds of ex-Confederates to state offices. Even more alarming to northerners, who thought they had won the war, was the election to the Congress of no fewer than nine ex-Confederate congressmen, seven Confederate state officials, four generals, four colonels, and the former Confederate Vice President Alexander H. Stephens. To apprehensive Republicans, it appeared that the rebels, unable to capture Washington in war, were about to do so in peace.

Somehow the aristocrats and traitors Johnson had denounced in April had taken over the reconstruction process — with Johnson's apparent blessing. What had happened? Flattery of the presidential ego was part of the answer. In applying for pardons, thousands of prominent ex-Confederates or their tearful female relatives had confessed the error of their ways and had appealed for presidential mercy. Reveling in his power over these once-haughty aristocrats who had disdained him as a humble tailor, Johnson waxed eloquent on his "love, respect, and confidence" toward southern whites, for whom he now felt "forbearing and forgiving."

More important, perhaps, was the praise and support Johnson received from leading northern Democrats at a time when more and more Republicans were beginning to criticize him publicly. Though the Republicans had placed him on their presidential ticket in 1864, Johnson was after all a Democrat. That party's leaders enticed Johnson with visions of his reelection as a Democrat in 1868 if he could manage to reconstruct the South in a manner that would preserve a Democratic majority there.

The Black Codes

That was just what the Republicans feared. And their concern that white-supremacy state governments would reduce the freedpeople to a condition close to slavery was confirmed by the enactment of "Black Codes" by some of those governments in the fall of 1865. One of the first tasks of the legislatures of the reconstructed states was to define the rights of four million former slaves who were now free. The option of treating them exactly like white citizens was scarcely considered. Instead, the states created a category of second-class citizenship that excluded black people from juries and the ballot box, did not permit them to testify against whites in court, banned interracial marriage, and punished blacks more severely than whites for certain crimes. Some states defined any unemployed black person as a vagrant and hired him out to a planter; forbade blacks to lease land; and provided for the apprenticing to whites of black youths who did not have adequate parental support.

These Black Codes — especially those of South Carolina and Mississippi, which were the most discriminatory — aroused anger among northern Republicans, who saw them as a brazen attempt to reinstate a quasi-slavery. "We tell the white men of Mississippi," declared the *Chicago Tribune,* "that the men of the North will convert the State of Mississippi into a frog pond before they will allow such laws to disgrace one foot of the soil in which the bones of our soldiers sleep and over which the flag of freedom waves." And, in fact, the Union army's occupation forces did suspend the implementation of Black Codes that discriminated on racial grounds. Meanwhile, Congress wrestled with civil rights legislation to define the status of the nation's newest citizens.

LAND AND LABOR IN THE POSTWAR SOUTH

The Black Codes, though clumsy and discriminatory, were designed to address a genuine problem.

Black Codes   Thomas Nast of *Harper's Weekly* was one of the best political cartoonists in American history. The right-hand panel of this satirical cartoon portrays southern states' treatment of the freed slaves, including the Black Codes, as a continuation of slavery, represented by a slave auction in the left-hand panel. The cartoon dates from 1866; note the heading "?Slavery is Dead?" The cartoon provided a boost to congressional enactment of a civil rights bill over President Johnson's veto in 1866.

The end of the war had left southern black–white relations in a state of limbo, and capital–labor relations in a state of chaos. Slavery was gone (though its formal legal demise would not come until final ratification of the Thirteenth Amendment in December 1865). The southern economy was in a shambles. Burned-out plantations, fields growing up in weeds, and railroads without tracks, bridges, or rolling stock marked the trail of war. Nearly half of the livestock in the Confederacy and most other tangible assets except the land itself had been destroyed. Many people, white as well as black, literally did not know where their next meal was coming from. Law and order broke down in many areas because of the sudden collapse of authority. The war had ended early enough in the spring to allow the planting of at least some food crops. But who would plant and cultivate them? A quarter of the southern

white farmers had been killed in the war; the slaves were slaves no more. "We have nothing left to begin anew with," lamented a South Carolina planter. "I never did a day's work in my life, and I don't know how to begin."

But life went on. Soldiers' widows and their children plowed and planted. Slaveless planters and their wives calloused their hands for the first time. Confederate veterans drifted home and went to work. Former slaveowners asked their former chattels to work the land for wages or shares of the crop. Many freedpeople did so. But others refused, because for them to leave the old place was an essential part of freedom. In slavery times, the only way to become free was to run away, and the impulse to leave the scene of bondage persisted. "You ain't, none o' you, gwinter feel rale free," said a black preacher to his congregation, "till you shakes de dus' ob de Ole

Plantashun offen yore feet an' goes ter a new place whey you kin live out o' sight o' de gret house."

Thus the roads were alive with freedpeople on the move in the summer of 1865. Many of them signed on to work at farms just a few miles from their old homes. Others moved into town. Some looked for relatives who had been sold away during slavery or from whom they had been separated during the war. Some wandered aimlessly. Crime increased as people, both blacks and whites, stole food to survive—and as whites organized vigilante groups to discipline blacks and force them to work.

The Freedmen's Bureau

Into this vacuum stepped the United States Army and the Freedmen's Bureau. Tens of thousands of troops remained in the South as an occupation force that put the ex-Confederate states under martial law until civil government could be restored. The Freedmen's Bureau (its official title was Bureau of Refugees, Freedmen, and Abandoned Lands), created by Congress in March 1865, became the principal agency for overseeing relations between former slaves and owners. Staffed by army officers, the Bureau established posts throughout the South to supervise free-labor wage contracts between landowners and freedpeople, and to enforce them in Bureau courts. The Freedmen's Bureau also issued food rations to 150,000 people daily during 1865, one-third of them to whites.

Because it was a northern agency that intervened between whites and blacks to enforce a degree of justice and equity in southern labor and race relations, the Freedmen's Bureau was viewed with hostility by whites. But without it, the postwar chaos and devastation in the South would have been much greater—as some whites privately admitted. Bureau agents used their influence with black people to encourage them to sign free-labor contracts and return to work.

In negotiating labor contracts, the Bureau tried to establish minimum wages. Because there was so little money in the South, however, many contracts called for share wages—that is, payment of workers in shares of the crop when it was harvested. At first, landowners worked their laborers in large groups (called gangs) under direct supervision. But many black workers resented this as reminiscent of slavery. Thus, a new system gradually evolved, called share-

Sharecroppers Working in the Fields   After the war, former planters tried to employ their former slaves in gang labor to grow cotton and tobacco, with the only difference from slavery being the grudging payment of wages. Freedpeople resisted this system as too reminiscent of slavery. They compelled landowners to rent them plots of land on which black families struggled to raise corn and cotton or tobacco, paying a share of the crop as rent—hence "sharecropping." This posed photograph was intended to depict the family labor of sharecroppers; in reality, most black farmers had a mule to pull their plow.

cropping, whereby a black family worked a piece of land in return for a share of the crop they produced.

Land for the Landless

Freedpeople, of course, would have preferred to farm their own land rather than to work for shares. "What's de use of being free if you don't own land enough to be buried in?" asked one black sharecropper. "Might juss as well stay slave all yo' days." Some black farmers did manage to save up enough money to buy a small plot of land. Demobilized black soldiers purchased land with their bounty payments, sometimes pooling their money to buy an entire plantation on which several black families settled. Northern philanthropists helped some freedmen to buy land. But for most ex-slaves the purchase of land was impossible. Few of them had money, and even if they did, whites often refused to sell or prevented others from selling because it would mean losing a source of cheap labor and encouraging notions of black independence.

Several northern radicals proposed legislation to confiscate ex-Confederate land and redistribute it to freedpeople. But those proposals got nowhere. And the most promising effort to put thousands of slaves on land of their own also failed. In January 1865, after his march through Georgia, General William T. Sherman had issued a military order setting aside thousands of acres of abandoned plantation land (the owners had fled) in the Georgia and South Carolina lowcountry for settlement by freed slaves on forty acres per family. The army even turned over some of its surplus mules to black farmers. The expectation of "forty acres and a mule" excited freedpeople in 1865. But President Johnson's Amnesty Proclamation and his wholesale issuance of pardons restored most of this property to pardoned ex-Confederates. The same thing happened to white-owned land elsewhere in the South. Placed under the temporary care of the Freedmen's Bureau for subsequent possi-ble distribution to freedpeople, by 1866 nearly all of this land had been restored to its former owners by order of President Johnson.

Education

Abolitionists were more successful in helping freed-people to get an education than in helping them to acquire land. During the war, freedmen's aid societies and missionary societies founded by abolition-ists had sent teachers to Union-occupied areas of the South to set up schools for freed slaves, 90 percent of whom were illiterate. After the war, this effort was expanded with the aid of the Freedmen's Bureau. Two thousand northern teachers, three-quarters of them women, fanned out into every part of the South. There they trained the black teachers who would staff first the mission schools and later the public schools established by Reconstruction state governments. After 1870 the missionary soci-eties concentrated more heavily on making higher education available to African Americans. Most of the black colleges in the South were founded and supported by their efforts. This education crusade,

A Black School during Reconstruction   Southern states forbade the teaching of slaves to read and write. Thus, about 90 percent of the freedpeople were illiterate in 1865. One of their top priorities was education. At first, most of the teachers in the freedmen's schools established by northern missionary societies were northern white women. But as black teachers were trained, they took over the ele-mentary schools, such as this one photographed in the 1870s.

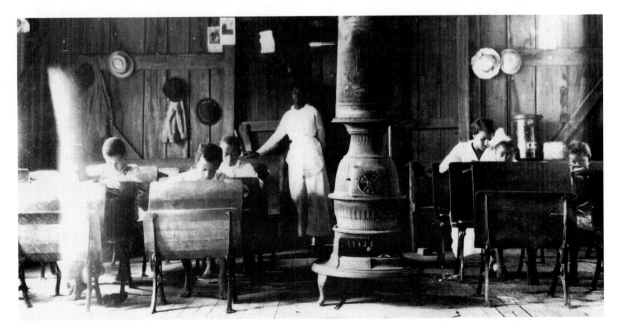

which the black leader W. E. B. Du Bois described as "the most wonderful peace-battle of the nineteenth century," reduced the southern black illiteracy rate to 70 percent by 1880 and to 48 percent by 1900.

THE ADVENT OF CONGRESSIONAL RECONSTRUCTION

The issues of land, labor, and education—as well as the civil and political rights of freedpeople—would be shaped by the terms of political reconstruction. By the time Congress met in December 1865, the Republican majority was determined to take control of the process by which former Confederate states would be restored to full representation. Congress refused to admit the representatives and senators elected by southern states under Johnson's reconstruction policy and set up a special committee to formulate new terms. The committee held hearings at which southern Unionists, freedpeople, and army officers testified to abuse and terrorism in the South. Their testimony convinced Republicans of the need for stronger federal intervention to define and protect the civil rights of freedpeople. Many radicals wanted to go further and grant the ballot to black men, so that they could join with southern white Unionists and northern settlers in the South to form a southern Republican Party.

Most Republicans realized that northern voters would not support such a radical policy, however. Racism was still strong in the North, where most states denied the right to vote to the few blacks living within their borders. Moderate Republicans feared that Democrats would exploit northern racism in the congressional elections of 1866 if Congress made black suffrage a cornerstone of Reconstruction. So the special committee decided to draft a constitutional amendment that would encourage southern states to enfranchise blacks but would not require them to do so.

Schism between President and Congress

Meanwhile, Congress passed two laws to protect the economic and civil rights of freedpeople. The first extended the life of the Freedmen's Bureau and expanded its powers. The second defined freedpeople as citizens with equal legal rights and gave federal courts appellate jurisdiction to enforce those rights. Senator Lyman Trumbull of Illinois, chairman of the Senate Judiciary Committee that drafted these bills and a former close associate of Lincoln, consulted Andrew Johnson about them and thought he had the president's support. But to Trumbull's dismay, and to the dismay of other moderates who were trying to heal the widening breach between the president and Congress, Johnson vetoed both measures. And he followed this action with an intemperate speech to Democratic supporters on Washington's birthday (February 22), in which he denounced Republican leaders as traitors who did not want to restore the Union except on terms that would degrade white southerners. Democratic newspapers applauded the president for vetoing bills that would "compound our race with niggers, gypsies, and baboons."

The Fourteenth Amendment

Johnson had thrown down the gauntlet to congressional Republicans. They did not hesitate to take it up. With more than a two-thirds majority in both houses, they passed the Freedmen's Bureau and Civil Rights bills over the president's vetoes. Then on April 30, the special committee submitted to Congress its proposed Fourteenth Amendment to the Constitution. After lengthy debate, the amendment received the required two-thirds majority in Congress on June 13 and went to the states for ratification. Section 1 defined all native-born or naturalized persons, including blacks, as American citizens and prohibited the states from abridging the "privileges and immunities" of citizens, from depriving "any person of life, liberty, or property without due process of law," and from denying to any person "the equal protection of the laws." Section 2 gave states the option of either enfranchising black males or losing a proportionate number of congressional seats and electoral votes. Section 3 disqualified from holding federal or state office a significant number of ex-Confederates. Section 4 guaranteed the national debt and repudiated the Confederate debt. Section 5 empowered Congress to enforce the Fourteenth Amendment by "appropriate legislation."

It would take an additional two years before the amendment was ratified by the states, but the Fourteenth Amendment has had far-reaching consequences. Section 1 has become the most important provision in the Constitution for defining and enforcing civil rights. Unlike the first ten amendments (the Bill of Rights), which imposed limitations on the powers of the federal government, the Fourteenth Amendment vastly expanded federal powers to prevent state violations of civil rights. It also greatly enlarged the rights of blacks and reduced the political power of ex-Confederates. That is why President Johnson and the Democratic Party, with their states' rights, proslavery southern heritage, opposed it.

The 1866 Elections

Republicans entered the campaign for the 1866 congressional elections with the Fourteenth Amendment as their platform. They made clear that any southern state that ratified the Amendment would be declared "reconstructed" and that its representatives and senators would be seated in Congress. Tennessee ratified the amendment and its representatives and senators were promptly seated. But Johnson counseled other southern legislatures to reject the amendment, and they did so. Johnson then prepared for an all-out campaign to gain a friendly northern majority in the congressional elections.

He created a "National Union Party" made up of a few conservative Republicans who disagreed with their party, some border-state Unionists who supported the president, and Democrats. The inclusion of Democrats doomed the effort from the start. Northern Democrats still carried a Copperhead taint from the war, and most northern voters did not trust them. The National Union Party was further damaged by race riots in Memphis and New Orleans, where white mobs including former Confederate soldiers killed eighty blacks, among them several former Union soldiers. The riots lent credence to Republican arguments that national power was necessary to protect "the fruits of victory" in the South. Perhaps the biggest liability of the National Union Party was Andrew Johnson himself. In a whistle-stop tour through northern states, he traded insults with hecklers and embarrassed his supporters by comparing himself to Christ and his Republican adversaries to Judas.

Republicans swept the election. They would have a three-to-one majority in the next Congress. Having rejected the reconstruction terms embodied in the Fourteenth Amendment, the southern Democrats could blame nobody but themselves for the

more stringent terms that now appeared inevitable. "They would not cooperate in rebuilding what they destroyed," wrote an exasperated moderate Republican who now professed himself a radical, so "we must remove the rubbish and rebuild from the bottom. Whether they are willing or not, we must compel obedience to the Union and demand protection for its humblest citizen."

THE RECONSTRUCTION ACTS OF 1867

In March 1867 the new Congress enacted over Johnson's vetoes two laws prescribing new procedures for the full restoration of the former Confederate states (except Tennessee, already readmitted) to the Union. These laws represented a complex compromise between radicals and moderates that had been hammered out in a confusing sequence of committee drafts, caucus decisions, all-night debates on the floor, and frayed tempers. The Reconstruction acts of 1867 divided the ten southern states into five military districts, directed army officers to register voters for the election of delegates to new constitutional conventions, and enfranchised males twenty-one and older (including blacks) to vote in those elections. But it also disfranchised (for these elections only) those ex-Confederates who were disqualified for office-holding under the not-yet-ratified Fourteenth Amendment—fewer than 10 percent of all white voters. When a state had adopted a new constitution that granted equal civil and political rights regardless of race and had ratified the Fourteenth Amendment, it would be declared reconstructed and its newly elected congressmen would be seated.

These measures embodied a true revolution—"the maddest, most infamous revolution in history," in the opinion of one white South Carolinian. Just a few years earlier, he and his fellow southerners had been masters of four million slaves and leaders of an independent Confederate nation. Now they were shorn of political power, with their former slaves not only freed but also politically empowered. To be sure, radical Republicans who warned that the revolution was incomplete so long as the old master class retained economic and social power, turned out in the end to be right. But in 1867 it seemed that the emancipation and enfranchisement of black Americans was, as a sympathetic French journalist described

NEW YORK, SATURDAY, MAY 26, 1866.

Burning of a Freedmen's School   Because freedpeople's education symbolized black progress, whites who resented and resisted this progress sometimes attacked and burned freedmen's schools, as in this dramatic illustration of the burning of a school by a white mob during antiblack riots in Memphis in May 1866.

it, "one of the most radical revolutions known in history."

Like most revolutions, the reconstruction process did not go smoothly. Many southern Democrats breathed defiance and refused to cooperate. The presence of the army minimized anti-black violence. But thousands of whites who were eligible to vote refused to do so, hoping that their nonparticipation would delay the process long enough for northern voters to come to their senses and elect Democrats to Congress to reverse this "mad revolution."

Blacks and their white Unionist and northern allies organized Union leagues to inform and mobilize the new black voters into the Republican Party. Democrats contemptuously branded southern white Republicans as "scalawags" and northern settlers as "carpetbaggers." By September 1867, 735,000 black voters and only 635,000 white voters had been registered in the ten states, a virtual reversal of the 56 percent white majority in those states. And at least one-third of the registered white voters were Republicans. It was clear, therefore, that Republicans would control the upcoming constitutional conventions.

President Johnson put every roadblock he could in the way of the reconstruction process. He removed several Republican generals from command of southern military districts and appointed Democrats in their stead. He had his attorney general issue a ruling that interpreted the Reconstruction acts narrowly, contrary to the intent of Congress, and thereby forcing a special session of Congress to pass a supplementary act in July 1867. And he encouraged southern whites to engage in obstructive tactics to delay the registration of voters and the election of convention delegates.

Never had a president and Congress been so bitterly at odds. Johnson's purpose was to slow the process until 1868 in the hope that northern voters would repudiate Reconstruction in the presidential election that year, when Johnson planned to run as the Democratic candidate. Off-year state elections in the fall of 1867 encouraged that hope. Republicans suffered setbacks in several northern states, especially in those states where they endorsed referendum measures to enfranchise black men. "I almost pity the radicals," chortled one of President Johnson's aides after the 1867 elections. "After giving ten states to the negroes, to keep the Democrats from getting them, they will have lost the rest. . . . Any party with an abolition head and a nigger tail will soon find itself with nothing left but the head and the tail."

THE IMPEACHMENT OF ANDREW JOHNSON

Johnson struck even more boldly against Reconstruction after the 1867 elections, despite warnings that he was risking impeachment. "What does Johnson mean to do?" exasperated Republicans asked one another. "Does he mean to have another rebellion on the question of Executive powers & duties? . . . I am afraid his doings will make us all favor impeachment." In February 1868, Johnson took a fateful step. He removed from office Secretary of War Edwin M. Stanton, who had administered the War Department in support of the congressional reconstruction policy. This was the final straw. It appeared to violate the Tenure of Office Act, passed the year before over Johnson's veto, which required Senate consent for such removals. By a vote of 126 to 47 along party lines, the House impeached Johnson on February 24. The official reason for impeachment was that he had violated the Tenure of Office Act (which Johnson considered unconstitutional). But the real reason was Johnson's stubborn defiance of the will of three-quarters of Congress on the most important issue before the country—reconstruction.

Under the United States Constitution, impeachment by the House does not remove an official from office. It is more like a grand jury indictment that

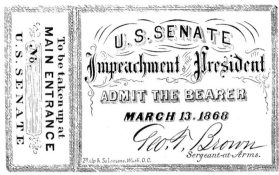

FAC-SIMILE OF TICKET OF ADMISSION TO THE IMPEACHMENT TRIAL.

Ticket to Impeachment Proceedings   Interest in the impeachment trial of President Andrew Johnson was so great that tickets had to be printed for admission to limited seating in the Senate chamber. Such tickets became the most sought-after items in Washington during the trial.

must be tried by a petty jury—in this case, the Senate, which sat as a court to try Johnson on the impeachment charges brought by the House. If convicted by a two-thirds majority of the Senate, he would be removed from office and the president pro tem of the Senate, Benjamin Wade, would become president.

Tension filled the Senate chambers as the impeachment trial began on March 4. The trial proved to be long and complicated, which worked in Johnson's favor by allowing passions to cool. The Constitution specifies the grounds on which a president can be impeached and removed: "Treason, Bribery, or other high Crimes and Misdemeanors." The issue was whether Johnson was guilty of any of these acts. His able defense counsel, who included the former attorney general, a former Supreme Court justice, and a future secretary of state, exposed technical ambiguities in the Tenure of Office Act that raised doubts about whether Johnson had actually violated it. Several moderate Republicans feared that the precedent of impeachment might upset the delicate balance of powers between Executive, Congress, and the Judiciary that was an essential element of the Constitution. They also disliked Benjamin Wade and considered him too radical. Behind the scenes, Johnson strengthened his case by promising to appoint the respected General John M. Schofield as secretary of war and to stop obstructing the Reconstruction acts. In the end, seven Republican senators voted for acquittal on May 16, and the final tally fell one vote short of the necessary two-thirds majority.

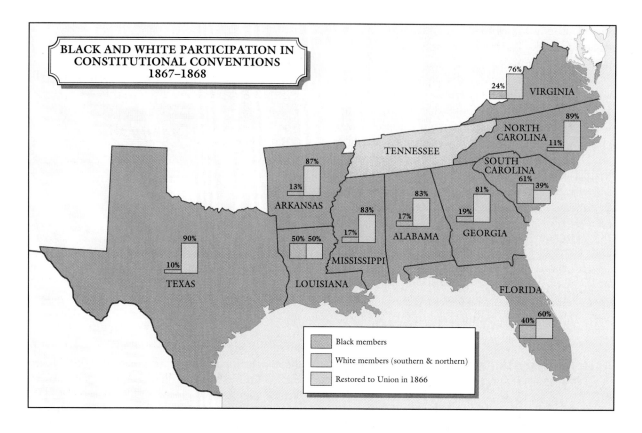

THE COMPLETION OF FORMAL RECONSTRUCTION

The end of the impeachment trial cleared the poisonous air in Washington and Johnson quietly served out his term. Constitutional conventions met in the South during the winter and spring of 1867–1868. Hostile whites described them as "Bones and Banjoes Conventions" and the Republican delegates as "ragamuffins and jailbirds." In sober fact, however, the delegates were earnest advocates of a new order and the constitutions they wrote were among the most progressive in the nation. Three-quarters of the delegates to the ten conventions were Republicans. About 25 percent of those Republicans were northern whites who had relocated to the South after the war; 45 percent were native southern whites who braved the social ostracism of the white majority to cast their lot with the despised Republicans; and 30 percent were blacks. Only in the South Carolina convention were blacks in the majority.

The new state constitutions enacted universal male suffrage, putting them ahead of most northern states on that score. Some of the constitutions disfranchised certain classes of ex-Confederates for several years, but by 1872 all such disqualifications had been removed. The constitutions mandated state-wide public schools for both races for the first time in the South. Most states permitted segregated schools, but schools of any kind for blacks represented a great step forward. Most of the constitutions increased the state's responsibility for social welfare beyond anything previously known in the South.

Violence in some parts of the South marred the voting on ratification of these state constitutions. A night-riding white terrorist organization with the ominous name of Ku Klux Klan (originally founded as a fraternal society in 1866) made its first appearance during the elections. Nevertheless, voters in seven states ratified their constitutions and elected new legislatures that ratified the Fourteenth Amendment in the spring of 1868. That Amendment became part of the United States Constitution the fol-

struction. It prohibited states from denying the right to vote on grounds of race, color, or previous condition of servitude. Its purpose was not only to prevent any future revocation of black suffrage by the reconstructed states, but also to extend equal suffrage to the border states and to the North itself. With final ratification of the Fifteenth Amendment in 1870, the Constitution became truly color-blind for the first time in U.S. history. But the challenge of enforcing the Amendment lay ahead.

The Election of 1868

Just as the presidential election of 1864 was a referendum on Lincoln's war policies, so the election of 1868 was a referendum on the reconstruction policy of the Republicans. Who the Republican nominee would be was a foregone conclusion: General Ulysses S. Grant. Though he had no political experience, Grant commanded greater authority and prestige than anyone else in the country. As general-in-chief of the army, he had become opposed to Johnson's reconstruction policy in 1866 and had broken openly with the president in January 1868. That spring, Grant allowed himself to be persuaded that he must run for the presidency to preserve in peace the victory for Union and liberty he had won in war.

The Democrats turned away from Andrew Johnson, who carried too many political liabilities. They nominated Horatio Seymour, the wartime governor of New York, bestowing on him the dubious privilege of running against Grant. Hoping to put together a majority consisting of the South plus New York and two or three other northern states, the Democrats adopted a militant platform denouncing the Reconstruction acts as "a flagrant usurpation of power . . . unconstitutional, revolutionary, and void." The platform also demanded "the abolition of the Freedmen's Bureau, and all political instrumentalities designed to secure negro supremacy."

The vice-presidential candidate, Frank Blair of Missouri, became the point man for the Democrats. In a public letter that set the tone for the campaign, he proclaimed, "There is but one way to restore the Government and the Constitution, and that is for the President-elect to declare these [Reconstruction] acts null and void, compel the army to undo its usurpations at the South, disperse the carpet-bag State Governments, [and] allow the white people to reorganize their own governments."

Two Members of the Ku Klux Klan   Founded in Pulaski, Tennessee, in 1866 as a social organization similar to a college fraternity, the Klan evolved into a terrorist group whose purpose was intimidation of southern Republicans. The Klan, in which former Confederate soldiers played a prominent part, was responsible for the beating and murder of hundreds of blacks and whites alike from 1868 to 1871.

lowing summer, and the newly elected representatives and senators from those seven states, nearly all of them Republicans, took their seats in the House and Senate.

The Fifteenth Amendment

The remaining three southern states completed the reconstruction process in 1869 and 1870. Congress required them to ratify the Fifteenth as well as the Fourteenth Amendment. The Fifteenth Amendment crowned the constitutional achievements of Recon-

The only way to achieve this bold counterrevolutionary goal was to terrorize and thus suppress Republican voters in the South. This the Ku Klux Klan tried its best to do. Federal troops had only limited success in preventing the violence because martial law had been lifted in the states where civilian governments had been restored. In Louisiana, Georgia, Arkansas, and Tennessee, the Klan or Klan-like groups committed dozens of murders and intimidated thousands of black voters. The violence helped the Democratic cause in the South but probably hurt it in the North, where many voters perceived the Klan as an organization of neo-Confederate paramilitary guerrillas. And indeed they were, for many Klansmen were former soldiers, and such famous Confederate generals as Nathan Bedford Forrest and John B. Gordon held high positions in the Klan.

Seymour did well in the South, carrying five former slave states and coming close in others despite the solid Republican vote of the newly enfranchised blacks. But Grant won the same percentage of northern votes as Lincoln had in 1864 and swept the electoral vote 214 to 80. Seymour actually won a slight majority of the white voters nationally, so without black enfranchisement, Grant would have had a minority of the popular vote.

THE GRANT ADMINISTRATION

A great military commander, Grant is usually branded a failure as president. That indictment is partly correct. Grant's inexperience and errors of judgment betrayed him into several unwise appointments of

The Inauguration of Ulysses S. Grant   Throngs of onlookers witnessed the inaugural ceremonies at the east front of the Capitol building on March 4, 1869. With the slogan "Let us have peace," Grant took office amid high hopes that he could achieve the reconstruction of the Union as effectively in peace as he had saved it in war. But the problems of peace proved more intractable than those of war.

officials who were later found guilty of corruption, and his two administrations (1869–1877) were plagued by scandals: his private secretary became involved in the infamous "Whiskey Ring," a network of collusion among distillers and revenue agents that deprived the government of millions of tax dollars; his secretary of war was impeached for selling appointments to army posts and Indian reservations; and his attorney general and secretary of the interior resigned under suspicion of malfeasance in 1875.

Honest himself, Grant was too trusting of subordinates. He appointed many former members of his military family, as well as several of his wife's relatives to offices for which they were scarcely qualified. But not all of the scandals were Grant's fault. This was an era notorious for corruption at all levels of government. The Tammany Hall "Ring" of "Boss" William Marcy Tweed in New York City may have stolen more money from taxpayers than all the federal agencies combined, and the New York legislature was famous for the buying and selling of votes. It was said of the Pennsylvania legislature that the only thing the Standard Oil Company could not do with it was to refine it. In Washington, one of the most widely publicized scandals, the Credit Mobilier affair, concerned Congress rather than the Grant administration. Several congressmen had accepted stock in the Credit Mobilier, a construction company for the Union Pacific Railroad, which received loans and land grants from the government in return for ensuring lax congressional supervision, thereby permitting financial manipulations by the company.

What accounted for this explosion of corruption in the postwar decade, which one historian has called "The Era of Good Stealings"? The expansion of government contracts and the bureaucracy during the war had created new opportunities for the unscrupulous. Then came a relaxation of tensions and standards following the intense sacrifices of the war years. Rapid postwar economic growth, led by an extraordinary rush of railroad construction, encouraged greed and get-rich-quick schemes of the kind satirized by Mark Twain and Charles Dudley Warner in their 1873 novel *The Gilded Age,* which gave its name to the era.

Civil Service Reform

But some of the increase in corruption during the Gilded Age (Chapter 19) was more apparent than real. A civil service reform movement arose with the purpose of purifying the government bureaucracy and making it more efficient. Reformers focused a harsh light into the dark corners of corruption hitherto unilluminated because of the nation's preoccupation with sectional conflict, war, and reconstruction. Thus, the actual extent of corruption may have been exaggerated by the publicity that reformers gave it. And in reality, during the Grant administration several government agencies made real progress in eliminating abuses that had flourished in earlier administrations.

The chief target of civil service reform was the "spoils system," which had been entrenched in the government since Andrew Jackson's administration. With the slogan "To the victor belongs the spoils," the victorious party in an election rewarded party workers with appointments as postmasters, customs collectors, and the like. The hope of getting appointed to a government post was the glue that kept the faithful together when the party was out of power. An assessment of 2 or 3 percent on the beneficiaries' government salaries kept party coffers filled when in power. The spoils system politicized the bureaucracy and staffed it with unqualified personnel who spent more time working for the party than for the government. It also plagued every incoming president (and other elected officials) with the "swarm of office seekers" that loom so large in contemporary accounts (including those of the humorist Orpheus C. Kerr, whose *nom de plume* was pronounced "Office Seeker").

Civil service reformers wanted to separate the bureaucracy from politics by instituting competitive examinations for the appointment of civil servants. This movement gathered steam during the 1870s and finally achieved success with the passage in 1883 of the Pendleton Act, which established the modern structure of the civil service. When Grant became president, he seemed to share the sentiments of civil service reformers; several of his cabinet officers inaugurated examinations for certain kinds of appointments and promotions in their departments. Grant also named a civil service commission headed by George William Curtis, a leading reformer and editor of *Harper's Weekly.* But many congressmen, senators, and other politicians strenuously resisted civil service reform. Patronage was the grease of the political machines that kept them in office and all too often enriched them and their political chums. They managed to subvert reform, sometimes using Grant as an unwitting ally and thus turning many reformers against the president.

Foreign Policy Issues

A foreign policy fiasco added to Grant's woes. The irregular procedures by which his private secretary had negotiated a treaty to annex Santo Domingo (now the Dominican Republic) alienated leading Republican senators, who defeated ratification of the treaty. Grant's political naiveté blinded him to the unsavory aspects of this affair. And his political inexperience led him to act like a general who needed only give orders rather than as a president who must cultivate supporters. The fallout from the Santo Domingo affair widened the fissure in the Republican party between "spoilsmen" and "reformers."

But the Grant administration had some solid foreign policy achievements to its credit. Hamilton Fish, the able secretary of state, negotiated the Treaty of Washington in 1871 to settle the vexing "Alabama Claims." These were damage claims against Britain for the destruction of American shipping by the *C.S.S. Alabama* and other Confederate commerce raiders built in British shipyards. The issue had poisoned Anglo-American relations for years. The Treaty of Washington established an international tribunal to arbitrate the U.S. claims, thus creating a precedent for the peaceful settlement of disputes. It resulted in the award of $15.5 million in damages to U.S. shipowners and a British expression of regret that defused Anglo-American tensions.

The events leading to the Treaty of Washington also resolved another long-festering issue in Anglo-American relations: the status of Canada. The seven separate British North American colonies were especially vulnerable to U.S. desires for annexation. In fact, the bitterness of many northerners toward Britain for the wartime depredations of the *Alabama* and other commerce raiders had produced demands for the British cession of Canadian colonies to the United States as fair payment for these damages. Such demands tended to strengthen the loyalty of many Canadians to Britain as a counterweight to the aggressive Americans. In 1867 Parliament passed the British North America Act, which united most of the Canadian colonies into a new and largely self-governing Dominion of Canada.

Pro-British Canadian nationalism was further strengthened by the actions of the Irish-American Fenian Brotherhood. A secret society organized during the Civil War, the Fenians believed that an invasion of Canada would strike a blow for the independence of Ireland. Three times from 1866 to 1871, small "armies" of Fenians, composed mainly of Irish-American veterans of the Union army, crossed the border into Canada, only to be driven back after comic-opera skirmishes. The Fenian raids intensified Canadian anti-Americanism and complicated the negotiations leading to the Washington Treaty. But the successful conclusion of the Treaty cooled Canadian–American tensions. It also led to the resolution of disputes over American commercial fishing in Canadian waters. U.S. troops prevented further Fenian raids. American demands for annexation of Canada faded away. These events gave birth to the modern nation of Canada, whose 3,500-mile border with the United States has remained the longest unfortified frontier in the world.

Financial Issues

Another problem facing the Grant administration was the resolution of questions left by the financing of the war. The issuance of treasury "greenback" notes in 1862 (see Chapter 16) had created a dual currency — gold and greenbacks — with the value of the greenback dollar in relation to gold rising and falling with the military fortunes of the Union. After the war the Treasury's policy was to bring the greenback dollar to par with gold by reducing the amount of greenbacks in circulation. That policy caused deflation (a fall in prices), which hurt farmers by reducing the prices they received for their crops more than it reduced their fixed costs. Deflation also hurt debtors by requiring them to pay their debts with dollars worth more than when they borrowed the money. To complicate matters further, national banknotes backed by the banks' holding of government bonds continued to circulate as money. Because national banks were concentrated in the Northeast, the South and West suffered from downward pressures on prices they received for their crops because of scarcity in money supply. Western farmers were particularly vociferous in their protests against this situation, which introduced a new sectional conflict into politics — not North against South, but East against West.

Because parity between greenbacks and gold was not reached until 1879, a controversy arose in the postwar years over whether Union war bonds should be paid off in greenbacks or in gold. Congress resolved this issue in 1869 by passing the Public Credit Act, which required payment in gold. Because little silver had been coined into money for years, Congress enacted in 1873 a law that ended the coinage of silver dollars, thus putting the United States on the road to joining the international gold standard. In 1874 Grant vetoed a bill sponsored by anti-deflation western congressmen to increase the number of greenbacks in circulation, setting the stage for enactment in 1875 of the important Specie Resumption Act. When the provisions of this act went fully into effect on January 1, 1879, the U.S. dollar reached par with the gold dollar on the international market. Grant played a more important role in bringing about these steps toward "sound money" than he is usually given credit for.

But the benefits of his achievement were sharply debated then and remain controversial today. On the one hand, they strengthened the dollar, placed government credit on a firm footing, and helped create a financial structure for the remarkable economic growth that tripled the gross national product during the last quarter of the nineteenth century. On the other hand, the restraints on money supply hurt

the rural economy in the South and West; they hurt debtors who found that deflation enlarged their debts by increasing the value of greenbacks; and they probably worsened the two major depressions of the era (1873–1878 and 1893–1897) by constraining credit. Monetary policy and fiscal policy were the most pressing and divisive political issues of the 1880s and 1890s, as we shall see in the next chapter.

RECONSTRUCTION IN THE SOUTH

During Grant's two administrations, however, the "Southern Question" was the most controversial and intractable issue. A phrase in Grant's acceptance of the presidential nomination in 1868 had struck a responsive chord in the North: "Let us have peace." Four years of war followed by three years of political warfare over the terms of Reconstruction had left the country weary. With the ratification of the Fifteenth Amendment, many people breathed a sigh of relief at this apparent resolution of "the last great point that remained to be settled of the issues of the war." It was time to deal with other matters that had been long neglected. Ever since the annexation of Texas a quarter-century earlier, the nation had known scarcely a moment's respite from sectional strife. "Let us have done with Reconstruction," pleaded the *New York Tribune* in 1870. "LET US HAVE PEACE."

But there was no peace. Reconstruction was not over; it had hardly begun. State governments elected by black and white voters were in place in the South. But Democratic violence in protest to Reconstruction and the instability of the Republican coalition that sustained those governments portended trouble.

Blacks in Office

Since the Republican Party had no antebellum roots in the South, most southern whites perceived it as a symbol of conquest and humiliation. In the North, the Republican Party represented the most prosperous, educated, and influential elements of the population; but in the South, most of its adherents were poor, illiterate, and propertyless.

About 80 percent of southern Republican voters were black. While most black leaders were educated and many had been free before the war, the mass of

Index of Wholesale Commodity Prices   This graph illustrates the pace of deflation in post-Civil War prices.

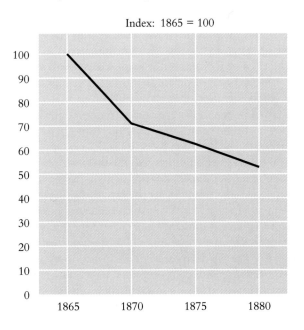

Index: 1865 = 100

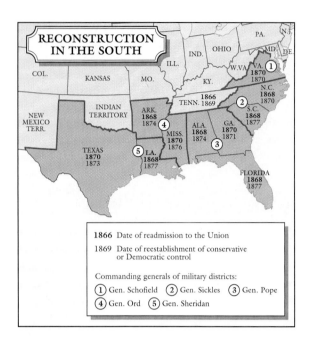

RECONSTRUCTION
IN THE SOUTH

1866   Date of readmission to the Union

1869   Date of reestablishment of conservative
       or Democratic control

Commanding generals of military districts:

① Gen. Schofield   ② Gen. Sickles   ③ Gen. Pope
④ Gen. Ord   ⑤ Gen. Sheridan

fraternal organizations proliferated during Reconstruction and provided a forum that tutored African-Americans in their rights and responsibilities.

Linked to the myth of black incompetence was the legend of the "Africanization" of southern governments during Reconstruction. The theme of "Negro rule," by which the "barbarous African" exercised "unbridled power" in ten southern states, was a staple of Democratic propaganda. It was enshrined in folk memory and in generations of textbooks. In fact, blacks held only 15 to 20 percent of public offices, even at the height of Reconstruction in the early 1870s. There were no black governors (though the black lieutenant governor of Louisiana acted as governor for a month) and only one black state supreme court justice. Nowhere except in South Carolina did blacks hold office in numbers anywhere near their proportion of the population; in that state, they constituted 52 percent of all state and federal elective officials from 1868 to 1876.

black voters were illiterate ex-slaves. Neither the leaders nor their constituents, however, were as ignorant or as venal as stereotypes have portrayed them. Of fourteen black representatives and two black senators elected in the South from 1868 to 1876, all but three had attended secondary school and four had attended college. Several of the blacks elected to state offices were among the best-educated men of their day. Jonathan Gibbs, secretary of state in Florida from 1868 to 1872 and state superintendent of education from 1872 to 1874, was a graduate of Dartmouth College and Princeton Theological Seminary. Francis L. Cardozo, secretary of state in South Carolina for four years and treasurer for another four, had been educated at the University of Glasgow and at theological schools in Edinburgh and London.

It is true that some lower-level black officeholders, as well as their constituents, could not read or write. But the fault for that lay not with them but with the slave regime that had denied them education. Illiteracy did not preclude an understanding of political issues for them any more than it did for Irish-American voters in the North, many of whom also were illiterate. Southern blacks thirsted for education; it was their party that established public school systems in the South. Participation in the Union League and the experience of voting were themselves a form of education. Black churches and

"Carpetbaggers"

Next to "Negro rule," carpetbagger corruption and scalawag rascality have been the prevailing myths of Reconstruction. "Carpetbaggers" did hold a disproportionate number of high political offices in southern state governments during Reconstruction. More than half of the Republican governors and nearly half of the congressmen and senators were northerners. A few of them did resemble the proverbial adventurer who came south with nothing but a carpetbag in which to stow the loot plundered from a helpless people. But most of them were Union army officers who stayed on in the South after the war as Freedmen's Bureau agents, teachers in black schools, investors in economic enterprises, pioneers of a new political order — or simply because they liked the climate.

Like others who migrated to the West as a frontier of opportunity, those who settled in the postwar South hoped to rebuild its society in the image of the free-labor North. Many were college graduates at a time when less than 2 percent of Americans had attended college. Most brought not empty carpetbags but considerable capital, which they invested in what they hoped would become a new South. They also invested human capital — themselves — in a drive to modernize the region's social structure and democratize its politics. But they underestimated the hostility of southern whites, most of whom regarded them as agents of an alien culture and leaders of an enemy army — as indeed they had been — in a war that for many southerners was not yet over.

"Scalawags"

Most of the native-born whites who joined the southern Republican Party came from the upcountry Unionist areas of western North Carolina and Virginia, eastern Tennessee, and elsewhere. Others were former Whigs who saw an opportunity to rebuild the southern economy in partnership with equally Whiggish northern Republicans. Republicans, said a North Carolina "scalawag," were the "party of progress, of education, of development. . . . Yankees and Yankee notions are just what we want in this country. We want their capital to build factories and work shops, and railroads."

But Yankees and Yankee notions were just what most southern whites did not want. Democrats recognized that the southern Republican Party they abhorred was a fragile coalition of blacks and whites, Yankees and southerners, hill-country yeomen and low-country entrepreneurs, illiterates and college graduates. They also recognized that the party was weakest along the seams where these disparate elements joined — especially the racial seam. Democrats attacked that weakness with every weapon at their command, from social ostracism of white Republicans to economic intimidation of black employees and sharecroppers. But the most potent Democratic weapon was violence.

The Ku Klux Klan

The generic name for the secret groups that terrorized the southern countryside was the Ku Klux Klan. But some went by other names (the Knights of the White Camelia in Louisiana, for example). By whatever name, their activities rose to a crescendo in 1870–1871. Part of the Klan's purpose was social control of the black population. Sharecroppers who tried to extract better terms from landowners, or black people who were considered too "uppity," were likely to receive a midnight whipping, or worse, from white-sheeted Klansmen. Scores of black schools, perceived as a particular threat to white supremacy, went up in flames, and some of their teachers were run out of town or murdered.

But the Klan's main purpose was political: to destroy the Republican Party by terrorizing its voters and, if necessary, by murdering its leaders. No one knows the number of politically motivated killings that took place in the South during the years of Reconstruction. It was certainly in the hundreds, probably in the thousands. Nearly all of the victims were Republicans; most of them were black. In one notorious incident, the "Colfax Massacre" in Louisiana (April 18, 1873), a clash between black militia and armed whites left three whites and nearly a hundred blacks dead. Half of the blacks were killed in cold blood after they had surrendered.

In some places, most notably Tennessee and Arkansas, militias formed by Republicans to protect themselves suppressed and disarmed many Klansmen. But in most areas the militias were outgunned and outmaneuvered by Confederate veterans who had joined the Klan. Some Republican governors were reluctant to use black militia against white guerrillas for fear of sparking a racial bloodbath — as happened at Colfax.

The answer seemed to be federal troops. In 1870 and 1871 Congress enacted three laws intended to enforce the Fourteenth and Fifteenth Amendments with federal marshals and troops if necessary. These laws made interference with voting rights a federal offense and defined as a felony any attempt by one or more persons to deprive another person of civil or political rights. The third law, passed on April 20, 1871, and popularly called the Ku Klux Klan Act, gave the president power to suspend the writ of habeas corpus and send in federal troops to suppress armed resistance to federal law.

Armed with these laws, the Grant administration moved against the Klan. But because Grant was sensitive to charges of "military despotism," he used his powers with restraint. He suspended the writ of habeas corpus only in nine South Carolina counties. Nevertheless, there and elsewhere federal marshals backed by troops arrested thousands of suspected Klansmen. Federal grand juries handed down more than three thousand indictments, and several hundred defendants pleaded guilty in return for suspended sentences. To clear clogged court dockets so that the worst offenders could be tried quickly, the Justice Department dropped charges against nearly two thousand others. About six hundred Klansmen were convicted; most of them received fines or light jail sentences, but sixty-five went to a federal penitentiary for terms of up to five years.

The Granger Collection, New York

"Let Us Clasp Hands over the Bloody Chasm"   The cartoonist Thomas Nast hammered away at Horace Greeley's presidential candidacy week after week in the pages of *Harper's Weekly*. Here he portrays Greeley shaking hands with a southern white man who has just murdered the men lying at his feet, while in the background more neo-Confederate Democrats attack black Republicans. Nast's cartoons helped bury Greeley under Grant's reelection landslide.

THE ELECTION OF 1872

These measures broke the back of the Klan in time for the 1872 presidential election. In that election year, a group of dissident Republicans had emerged to challenge Grant's reelection. They were disillusioned with his record on civil service reform and convinced that conciliation of southern whites rather than continued military intervention to prop up Republican governments was the only way to achieve peace in the South. Calling themselves Liberal Republicans, these dissidents nominated for president Horace Greeley, the famous editor of the *New York Tribune*. Under the slogan "Anything to beat Grant," the Democratic Party also endorsed Greeley's nomination, though he had long been their antagonist. On a platform denouncing "bayonet rule" in the South, Greeley urged his fellow northerners to put the issues of the Civil War behind them and to "clasp hands across the bloody chasm which has too long divided" North and South.

This phrase would come back to haunt Greeley. Most northern voters were still not prepared to trust Democrats or southern whites. Powerful anti-Greeley cartoons by political cartoonist Thomas Nast showed Greeley shaking hands "across the bloody chasm" with a rebel who had shot a Union soldier. Another showed him shaking the hand of a Klansman dripping with the blood of a murdered black Republican. Nast's most famous cartoon portrayed Greeley as a pirate captain bringing his craft alongside the ship of state, while Confederate leaders, armed to the teeth, hid below waiting to board it.

Grant swamped Greeley on election day. Republicans carried every northern state and ten of the sixteen southern and border states. Blacks in the South enjoyed more freedom in voting than they would enjoy again for a century. But this apparent triumph of Republicanism and Reconstruction would soon unravel.

THE PANIC OF 1873

The U.S. economy had grown at an unprecedented pace since recovering in 1867 from a mild postwar recession. As many miles of new railroad track (35,000 miles) were laid down in eight years as in the preceding thirty-five. The first transcontinental railroad had been completed on May 10, 1869, when a golden spike was driven at Promontory Point, Utah Territory, to link the Union Pacific and the Central Pacific. But it was the building of a second transcontinental line, the Northern Pacific, that precipitated a Wall Street panic in 1873 and plunged the economy into a five-year depression.

The hero of Civil War finance, Jay Cooke, became the goat of the Panic of 1873. Cooke's banking firm, fresh from its triumphant marketing of Union war bonds, had taken over the Northern Pacific in 1869. Despite government land grants and loans, the railroad had not yet laid a mile of track. Cooke pyramided every conceivable kind of equity and loan financing to attain the money to begin laying rails west from Duluth. Other investment firms did the same as a fever of speculative financing for a variety of enterprises gripped the country. In September 1873 the pyramid of paper collapsed. Cooke's firm was the first to go bankrupt. Like dominoes, hundreds of banks and businesses also collapsed. Eighteen thousand failed in two years. Unemployment had risen to 14 percent by 1876 and hard times set in.

Anti-Railroad Sentiments

Having brought prosperity to many parts of the country, railroads now became a favorite object of blame for the depression, especially in rural areas. A drop in war-inflated crop prices caused distress among farmers. Prices for corn and wheat declined by half between 1867 and 1872, while railroad freight rates declined only slightly. Railroads lent credence to farmers' charges of monopoly exploitation by keeping rates higher in areas of no competition (most farmers lived in areas served by only one line) than in regions with competition. Grain elevators, many of which were owned by railroad companies, came under attack for cheating farmers by rigging the classification of their grain.

Farmers responded by organizing cooperatives to sell their crops and buy needed supplies. The umbrella organization for many of these cooperatives was the Patrons of Husbandry, or the Grange, founded in 1867. But farmers could not build their own railroads. So they went into politics, organized "antimonopoly" parties, and elected state legislators who enacted "Granger laws" in several states. These laws established railroad commissions that fixed maximum freight rates and warehouse charges. Railroads challenged the laws in court. Eight challenges made their way to the U.S. Supreme Court, which in *Munn* v. *Illinois* (1877) ruled that states could regulate businesses clothed with a "public interest"—railroads and other common carriers, millers, innkeepers, and the like. It was a landmark decision.

The Strikes of 1877

Railroads also became a focal point of labor strife. Although the real wages of most workers rose after the war (that is, their actual wages remained about the same while inflated wartime prices declined), the continuing mechanization of many trades eroded craft skills and worker independence. The depression that set in after 1873 brought wage reductions, unemployment, and the crippling of many labor unions founded during the preceding decade. Numerous strikes broke out, with considerable violence, especially in the anthracite coal mines of eastern Pennsylvania. The most ominous violence occurred in the great railroad strikes of 1877.

Citing declining revenues, several railroads cut wages by as much as 35 percent between 1874 and 1877 (during that same period, the price index fell only 8 percent). When the Baltimore and Ohio Railroad announced its third 10 percent wage cut on July 16, 1877, workers struck and prevented B&O trains from running. The strike spread rapidly to other lines. Traffic from St. Louis to the East Coast came to a halt. Ten states called out their militia. Strikers and militia fired on each other, and workers set fire to rolling stock and roundhouses. By the time federal troops brought things under control in the first week of August, at least one hundred strikers, militiamen, and bystanders had been killed, hundreds more had been injured, and uncounted millions of dollars of property had gone up in smoke. It was the worst labor violence in U.S. history to that time; the specter of class conflict frightened many Americans and gave rise to a desperate view of the future.

The Railroad Strikes of 1877   This illustration shows striking workers on the Baltimore and Ohio Railroad forcing the engineer and fireman from a freight train at Martinsburg, West Virginia, on July 17, 1877.

THE RETREAT FROM RECONSTRUCTION

It is an axiom of American politics that the voters will punish the party in power in times of economic depression. That axiom held true in the 1870s. Labor violence, debates over fiscal and monetary policy, and, above all, the depression weakened the Republican Party. Democrats made large gains in the congressional elections of 1874, winning a majority in the House for the first time in eighteen years.

Public opinion also began to turn against Republican policies in the South. The campaign by Liberal Republicans and Democrats against "bayonet rule" and "carpetbag corruption" had left most northern voters unmoved in 1872. But those charges found a growing audience in subsequent years. Intra-party battles among Republicans in southern states enabled Democrats to regain control of several state governments. Well-publicized corruption scandals, especially in Louisiana, also discredited Republican leaders. Although corruption was probably no worse in south-

ern states than in many parts of the North, the postwar poverty of the South made waste and extravagance seem worse and gave the drive for reform an extra impetus. White Democrats scored propaganda points by claiming that corruption proved the incompetence of "Negro-carpetbag" regimes and the unfitness of blacks to participate in political life.

Northerners grew increasingly weary of what seemed the endless turmoil of southern politics. Most of them had never had a very strong commitment to racial equality, and they were growing more and more willing to let white supremacy regain sway in the South. "The truth is," confessed a northern Republican, "our people are tired out with this worn out cry of 'Southern outrages'!!! Hard times & heavy taxes make them wish the 'nigger,' 'everlasting nigger,' were in hell or Africa."

By 1875 only four southern states remained under Republican control: South Carolina, Florida, Mississippi, and Louisiana. In those states, white Democrats had revived paramilitary organizations under various names: White Leagues (Louisiana);

Rifle Clubs (Mississippi); and Red Shirts (South Carolina). Unlike the Klan, these groups operated openly. In Louisiana, they fought pitched battles with Republican militias in which scores were killed. When the Grant administration sent large numbers of federal troops to Louisiana, people in both North and South cried out against military rule. The protests grew even louder when soldiers marched onto the floor of the Louisiana legislature in January 1875 and expelled several Democratic legislators after a contested election. Was this America? asked Republican Senator Carl Schurz in a widely publicized speech. "If this can be done in Louisiana, how long will it be before it can be done in Massachusetts and Ohio? How long before a soldier may stalk into the national House of Representatives, and, pointing to the Speaker's mace, say 'Take away that bauble!'"

The Mississippi Election of 1875

The backlash against the Grant administration had an effect on the Mississippi state election of 1875. Democrats there devised a campaign strategy called the Mississippi Plan, which combined features of campaigns that had "redeemed" other southern states from Republican rule. The first step was to "persuade" the 10 to 15 percent of white voters who still called themselves Republicans to switch to the Democratic Party. Only a handful of "carpetbaggers" could resist the economic pressures, social ostracism, and threats that made it "too damned hot for [us] to stay out," wrote one white Republican who changed parties. "No white man can live in the South in the future and act with any other than the Democratic Party unless he is willing and prepared to live a life of social isolation and remain in political oblivion."

The second step in the Mississippi Plan was to intimidate black voters, for even with all whites voting Democratic, the party could still be defeated by the 55 percent black majority. Economic coercion against black sharecroppers and workers kept some of them away from the polls. But violence was the most effective method. Democratic "rifle clubs" showed up at Republican rallies, provoked riots, and shot down dozens of blacks in the ensuing melees. Governor Adelbert Ames—a native of Maine, a Union general who had won a congressional medal of honor in the war, and one of the ablest of south-

ern Republicans—called for federal troops to control the violence. Grant intended to comply, but Ohio Republicans warned him that if he sent troops to Mississippi, the Democrats would exploit the issue of bayonet rule to carry Ohio in that year's state elections. Grant yielded—in effect giving up Mississippi for Ohio. The U.S. attorney general replied to Ames's request for troops: "The whole public are tired out with these annual autumnal outbreaks in the South, and the great majority are now ready to condemn any interference on the part of the government. . . . Preserve the peace by the forces in your own state, and let the country see that the citizens of Mississippi, who are . . . largely Republican, have the courage to *fight* for their rights."

Governor Ames did try to organize a loyal state militia. But that proved difficult—and in any case, he was reluctant to use a black militia for fear of provoking a race war worse than anything yet experienced in Reconstruction. "No matter if they are going to carry the State," said Ames with weary resignation, "let them carry it, and let us be at peace and have no more killing." The Mississippi Plan worked like a charm. In five of the state's counties with large black majorities, the Republicans polled twelve, seven, four, two, and zero votes, respectively. What had been a Republican majority of thirty thousand in the previous election became a Democratic majority of thirty thousand in the election of 1875.

The Supreme Court and Reconstruction

Even if Grant had been willing to continue intervening in southern state elections, Congress and the courts would have constricted such efforts. The new Democratic majority in the House threatened to cut any appropriations for the Justice Department and the army intended for use in the South. And in 1876 the Supreme Court handed down two decisions that declared parts of the 1870–1871 laws for enforcement of the Fourteenth and Fifteenth Amendments unconstitutional. In *U.S.* v. *Cruikshank* and *U.S.* v. *Reese,* the Court ruled on cases from Louisiana and Kentucky. Both cases grew out of provisions in the 1870–1871 laws authorizing federal officials to prosecute *individuals* (not states) for violations of the civil and voting rights of blacks. But, the Court pointed out, the Fourteenth and Fifteenth Amendments apply to actions by *states:* "No State shall . . . deprive any person of life, liberty, or property . . . nor

"OF COURSE HE WANTS TO VOTE THE DEMOCRATIC TICKET!"

DEMOCRATIC "REFORMER." "You're as free as air, ain't you? Say you are, or I'll blow yer black head off!"

How the Mississippi Plan Worked   This cartoon shows how black counties could report large Democratic majorities in the Mississippi state election of 1875. The black voter holds a Democratic ticket while one of the men, holding a revolver to his head, described in the caption as a "Democratic reformer," tells him: "You're as free as air, ain't you? Say you are, or I'll blow your black head off!"

deny to any person . . . equal protection of the laws": the right to vote "shall not be denied . . . by any State." Therefore, those portions of the 1870–1871 laws that empowered the federal government to prosecute individuals were unconstitutional, said the Supreme Court: "The power of Congress . . . to legislate for the enforcement of such a guarantee [of equal rights] does not extend to the passage of laws for suppression of ordinary crime within the States. . . . That duty was originally assumed by the States; and it still remains there."

The Court did not say what could be done when states were controlled by white-supremacy Democrats who had no intention of enforcing equal rights. In the mid-twentieth century, the Supreme Court reversed itself and interpreted the Fourteenth and Fifteenth Amendments much more broadly.

Meanwhile, in another ruling, *Civil Rights Cases* (1883), the Court declared unconstitutional a civil rights law passed by Congress in 1875. That law, enacted on the eve of the Democratic takeover of the House elected in 1874, was a crowning achievement of Reconstruction. A sort of memorial to the longtime champion of civil rights, Senator Charles Sumner, who had died in 1874, it banned racial discrimination in all forms of public transportation and public accommodations. If enforced, it would have effected a sweeping transformation of race relations—in the North as well as in the South. (The law did not apply to schools, however.) But even some of the congressmen who voted for the bill doubted its constitutionality, and the Justice Department had made little effort to enforce it. Several cases made their way to the Supreme Court, which in 1883 ruled the law unconstitutional—again on grounds that the privileges and immunities and equal protection clauses of the Fourteenth Amendment applied only to states, not to individuals. Several states—all in the North—passed their own civil rights laws in the 1870s and 1880s, which applied to schools as well as to public accommodations. But less than 10 percent of the black population resided in those states. The mass of African Americans lived a segregated existence.

THE ELECTION OF 1876 AND THE COMPROMISE OF 1877

In 1876 the Republican state governments that still survived in the South fell victim to the passion for "reform." The mounting revelations of corruption and "rings" at all levels of government—the Tweed Ring in New York City, the Canal Ring in New York State, the Whiskey Ring in Washington, and various smaller "rings" in the South—ensured that reform would be the leading issue in the presidential election. In this centennial year of the birth of the United States, marked by a great exposition in Philadelphia, Americans wanted to put their best foot forward. Both major parties gave their presidential nominations to governors who had earned reform reputations in their states: Democrat Samuel J. Tilden of New York and Republican Rutherford B. Hayes of Ohio.

Democrats entered the campaign as favorites for the first time in two decades. It seemed likely that they would be able to put together an electoral majority from a "solid South" plus New York and two or three other northern states. To ensure a solid South, they looked to the lessons of the Mississippi Plan. In 1876 a new word came into use to describe Democratic techniques of intimidation: "bulldozing." To bulldoze black voters meant to trample them down or keep them away from the polls. In South Carolina and Louisiana, the Red Shirts and the White Leagues mobilized for an all-out bulldozing effort.

The most notorious incident, the "Hamburg Massacre," occurred in the village of Hamburg, South Carolina, where a battle between a black militia unit and two hundred Red Shirts resulted in the capture of several militiamen, five of whom were shot "while attempting to escape." This time Grant did send in federal troops. He pronounced the Hamburg Massacre "cruel, blood-thirsty, wanton, unprovoked . . . a

repetition of the course that has been pursued in other Southern States" governed "by officials chosen through fraud and violence such as would scarcely be accredited to savages."

The federal government also put several thousand deputy marshals and election supervisors on duty in the South. Though they kept an uneasy peace at the polls, they could do little to prevent assaults, threats, and economic coercion in backcountry districts, which reduced the potential Republican tally in the former Confederate states by at least a quarter of a million votes.

Disputed Results

When the results were in, Tilden had carried four northern states, including New York with its thirty-five electoral votes, and all the former slave states except—apparently—Louisiana, South Carolina, and Florida. From those three states came disputed returns. Since Tilden needed only one of them to win the presidency, while Hayes needed all three, and since on the face of the returns Tilden seemed to have carried Louisiana and Florida, it appeared initially that he had won the presidency. But frauds and irregularities reported from several bulldozed districts in the three states clouded the issue. For example, a Louisiana parish that had recorded 1,688 Republican votes in 1874 reported only one in 1876. There were many other similar discrepancies. The official returns ultimately sent to Washington gave all three states—and therefore the presidency—to Hayes. But the Democrats refused to recognize the results—and they controlled the House.

The country now faced a serious constitutional crisis. Armed Democrats threatened to march on Washington. Many people feared another civil war. The Constitution offered no clear guidance on how to deal with the matter. It required the concurrence of both houses of Congress in order to count the electoral votes of the states, but with a Democratic House and a Republican Senate such concurrence was not forthcoming. To break the deadlock, Congress created a special electoral commission consisting of five representatives, five senators, and five Supreme Court justices split evenly between the two parties, with one member, a Supreme Court justice, supposedly an independent—but in fact a Republican.

The commission faced a conundrum. Tilden had won a national majority of 252,000 popular votes,

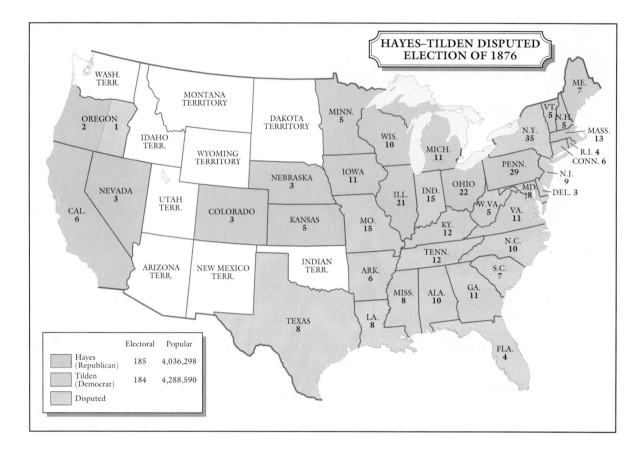

HAYES–TILDEN DISPUTED
ELECTION OF 1876

	Electoral	Popular
Hayes (Republican)	185	4,036,298
Tilden (Democrat)	184	4,288,590
Disputed		

and the raw returns gave him a majority of the three disputed states. But an estimated 250,000 southern Republicans had been bulldozed away from the polls. In a genuinely fair and free election, the Republicans might have carried Mississippi and North Carolina, as well as the three disputed states whose Republican election boards had reported an official Republican majority. While the commission agonized, Democrats and Republicans in Louisiana and South Carolina each inaugurated their own separate governors and legislatures (Republicans in Florida gave up the fight at the state level). Only Federal troops in the capitals at New Orleans and Columbia protected the Republican governments in those states.

In February 1877, three months after voters had gone to the polls, the electoral commission issued its rulings. By a partisan vote of eight to seven — with the "independent" justice voting with the Republicans — it awarded all the disputed states to Hayes. The Democrats cried foul and began a fili-

buster in the House to delay the final electoral count beyond the inauguration date of March 4, so as to throw the election to the House of Representatives, an eventuality that threatened to bring total anarchy. But, behind the scenes, a compromise began to take shape. Both northern Republicans and southern Democrats of Whig heritage had similar interests in liquidating the sectional rancor and in getting on with the business of economic recovery and development. Among these neo-Whigs were Hayes and his advisers. To wean southern Whiggish Democrats away from a House filibuster, Hayes promised his support as president for federal appropriations to rebuild war-destroyed levees on the lower Mississippi and federal aid for a southern transcontinental railroad. Hayes's lieutenants also hinted at the appointment of a southerner as postmaster general, who would have a considerable amount of patronage at his disposal.

But, most important, southerners wanted to know what Hayes would do about Louisiana and South

The End of Reconstruction

Such promises were easier to make than to keep, as future years would reveal. In any case, the Democratic filibuster collapsed and Hayes was inaugurated on March 4. He soon fulfilled his part of the Compromise of 1877: ex-Confederate Democrat David Key of Tennessee became postmaster general; the South received more federal money in 1878 for internal improvements than ever before; and federal troops left the capitals of Louisiana and South Carolina. The last two Republican state governments collapsed. The old abolitionist and radical Republican warhorses denounced Hayes's actions as a sellout of southern blacks, a policy "of weakness, of subserviency, of surrender," in the words of the venerable crusader William Lloyd Garrison, a policy that sustained "might against right . . . the rich and powerful against the poor and unprotected."

But such voices of protest could scarcely be heard above the sighs of relief that the electoral crisis was over. Most Americans—including even most Republicans—wanted no more military intervention in state affairs. "I have no sort of faith in a local government which can only be propped up by foreign bayonets," wrote the editor of the *New York Tribune* in April 1877. "If negro suffrage means that as a permanency then negro suffrage is a failure."

The withdrawal of federal troops in 1877 constituted both a symbolic and a substantive end of the twelve-year postwar era known as Reconstruction. Reconstruction had achieved the two great objectives inherited from the Civil War: to reincorporate the former Confederate states into the Union, and to accomplish a transition from slavery to free labor in the South. But that transition was marred by the economic inequity of sharecropping and the social injustice of white supremacy. And the third goal of Reconstruction, enforcement of the equal civil and political rights promised in the Fourteenth and Fifteenth Amendments, was betrayed by the Compromise of 1877. In subsequent decades the freed slaves and their descendants suffered repression into segregated second-class citizenship. Not until another war hero-turned-president sent troops into Little Rock, eighty years after they had been withdrawn from New Orleans and Columbia, did the federal government launch a second Reconstruction to fulfill the promises of the first.

The Granger Collection, New York

Reading Election Bulletin by Gaslight   The early returns seemed to have elected Democrat Samuel J. Tilden as president. But the results in three southern states that were still controlled by Republicans—South Carolina, Florida, and Louisiana—were in dispute, leading to uncertainty, anxiety, and arguments. If all three states went for the Republican Rutherford B. Hayes, he would be elected. If any one of them went for Tilden, he would become the next president.

Carolina. Would he keep troops there to uphold the Republican state governments that had been repudiated by white voters? Or would he withdraw the troops and allow the Democrats who already governed those states in fact to do so in law as well? Hayes signaled his intention to end "bayonet rule," which he had for some time considered a bankrupt policy. He wished to substitute conciliation for coercion. He believed that the good will and influence of southern moderates would offer better protection for black rights than federal troops could provide. In return for his commitment to withdraw the troops, Hayes asked for—and received—promises of fair treatment of freedpeople and respect for their constitutional rights.

SUGGESTED READING

The most comprehensive and incisive general history of Reconstruction is Eric Foner, *Reconstruction: America's Unfinished Revolution 1863–1877* (1988). For a skillful abridgement of this book, see Eric Foner, *A Short History of Reconstruction* (1990). A more concise survey of this era can be found in James M. McPherson, *Ordeal by Fire: The Civil War and Reconstruction,* 2nd ed. (1992), Part 3. Still valuable are Kenneth M. Stampp, *The Era of Reconstruction, 1865–1877* (1965) and John Hope Franklin, *Reconstruction: After the Civil War* (1961). The essays in Eric Anderson and Alfred A. Moss, Jr., eds., *The Facts of Reconstruction: Essays in Honor of John Hope Franklin* (1991), offer important insights. The constitutional issues involved in the era are analyzed by Harold M. Hyman, *A More Perfect Union: The Impact of the Civil War and Reconstruction on the Constitution* (1973).

For the evolution of federal reconstruction policies during the war and early postwar years, see three books by Herman Belz: *Reconstructing the Union: Theory and Policy during the Civil War* (1969); *A New Birth of Freedom: The Republican Party and Freedmen's Rights* (1976); and *Emancipation and Equal Rights: Politics and Constitutionalism in the Civil War Era* (1978). Also valuable is David Donald, *The Politics of Reconstruction 1864–1867* (1967). Important for their insights on Lincoln and the reconstruction question are Peyton McCrary, *Abraham Lincoln and Reconstruction: The Louisiana Experiment* (1978) and LaWanda Cox, *Lincoln and Black Freedom: A Study in Presidential Leadership* (1981). A superb study of the South Carolina Sea Islands as a laboratory of Reconstruction is Willie Lee Rose, *Rehearsal for Reconstruction: The Port Royal Experiment* (1964).

For the vexed issues of Andrew Johnson, Congress, and Reconstruction from 1865 to 1868, the following are essential: Eric L. McKitrick, *Andrew Johnson and Reconstruction* (1960); LaWanda Cox and John H. Cox, *Politics, Principle, and Prejudice 1865–1866* (1963); William R. Brock, *An American Crisis: Congress and Reconstruction 1865–1867* (1963); Michael Les Benedict, *A Compromise of Principle: Congressional Republicans and Reconstruction* (1974); Hans L. Trefousse, *The Radical Republicans: Lincoln's Vanguard for Racial Justice* (1969); Hans L. Trefousse, *Andrew Johnson: A Biography* (1989); and David Warren Bowen, *Andrew Johnson and the Negro* (1989). The two best studies of Johnson's impeachment are Michael Les Benedict, *The Impeachment and Trial of Andrew Johnson* (1973) and Hans L. Trefousse, *Impeachment of a President: Andrew Johnson, the Blacks, and Reconstruction* (1975).

For the political and judicial dimensions of the Fourteenth and Fifteenth Amendments and their enforcement, see Joseph B. James, *The Framing of the Fourteenth Amendment* (1956); Joseph B. James, *The Ratification of the Fourteenth Amendment* (1984); Michael Kent Curtis, *No State Shall Abridge: The Fourteenth Amendment and the Bill of Rights* (1986); William E. Nelson, *The Fourteenth Amendment: From Political Principle to Judicial Doctrine* (1988); William Gillette, *The Right to Vote: Politics and Passage of the Fifteenth Amendment* (1965); and Robert J. Kaczorowski, *The Politics of Judicial Interpretation: The Federal Courts, Department of Justice and Civil Rights, 1866–1876* (1985).

For the social and political scene in the South during Reconstruction, a good introduction is Howard N. Rabinowitz, *The First New South, 1865–1920* (1991). Dan T. Carter, *When the War Was Over: the Failure of Self-Reconstruction in the South, 1865–1867* (1985) and Michael Perman, *Reunion without Compromise: The South and Reconstruction, 1865–1868* (1973) portray the early postwar years, while Michael Perman, *The Road to Redemption: Southern Politics, 1868–1879* (1984) is a provocative interpretation. Otto H. Olsen, ed., *Reconstruction and Redemption in the South* (1980), contains essays on the Reconstruction process in a half-dozen states. For the role of the Ku Klux Klan and other white paramilitary organizations, see Allen W. Trelease, *White Terror: The Ku Klux Klan Conspiracy and Southern Reconstruction* (1974) and George C. Rable, *But There Was No Peace: The Role of Violence in the Politics of Reconstruction* (1984). For a fresh and intelligent look at the "carpetbaggers," see Richard Nelson Current, *Those Terrible Carpetbaggers: A Reinterpretation* (1988). Economic issues are the subject of Mark W. Summers, *Railroads, Reconstruction, and the Gospel of Prosperity: Aid under the Radical Republicans, 1865–1877* (1984) and Terry L. Seip, *The South Returns to Congress: Men, Economic Measures, and Intersectional Relationships, 1868–1879* (1983).

Two classics that portray sympathetically the activities of freedpeople in Reconstruction are W. E. Burghardt Du Bois, *Black Reconstruction* (1935) and Leon F. Litwack, *Been in the Storm So Long: The Aftermath of Slavery* (1979). A challenging brief interpretation is provided by Eric Foner, *Nothing But Freedom: Emancipation and Its Legacy* (1983). Howard N. Rabinowitz, *Race Relations in the Urban South, 1865–1890* (1978) and Howard N. Rabinowitz, ed., *Southern Black Leaders of the Reconstruction Era* (1982), add important dimensions to the subject. There are many good studies of black social and political life in various states during Reconstruction; two of the best deal with the state in which African Americans played the most active part: Joel Williamson, *After Slavery: The Negro in South Carolina during Reconstruction 1861–1877* (1965) and Thomas Holt, *Black over White: Negro Political Leadership in South Carolina during Reconstruction* (1977).

For the evolution of sharecropping and other aspects of freedpeople's economic status, see Roger L. Ransom and Richard Sutch, *One Kind of Freedom: The Economic Consequences of Emancipation* (1977) and William Cohen, *At Freedom's Edge: Black Mobility and the Southern White Quest for Racial Control, 1861–1915* (1991). Two sound studies of the Freedmen's Bureau are George R. Bentley, *A History of the Freedmen's Bureau* (1955) and Donald G. Nieman, *To Set the Law in Motion: The Freedmen's Bureau and the Legal Rights of Blacks 1865–1868* (1979). For the education of freedpeople, see especially William Preston Vaughan, *Schools for All: The Blacks & Public Education in the South 1865–1877* (1974); Joe M. Richardson, *Christian Reconstruction, The American Missionary Association and Southern Blacks, 1861–1890* (1986); and James M. McPherson, *The Abolitionist Legacy: From Reconstruction to the NAACP* (1975).

The national political scene in the 1870s and the retreat from Reconstruction are the subject of William Gillette, *Retreat from Reconstruction: A Political History 1867–1878* (1979). The issues of corruption and civil service reform receive ex-haustive treatment in Mark Wahlgren Summers, *The Era of Good Stealings* (1993). The classic analysis of the disputed election of 1876 and the Compromise of 1877 is C. Vann Woodward, *Reunion and Reaction: The Compromise of 1877 and the End of Reconstruction* (rev. ed., 1956); for challenges to aspects of Woodward's thesis, see Keith I. Polakoff, *The Politics of Inertia: The Election of 1876 and the End of Reconstruction* (1973) and Michael Les Benedict, "Southern Democrats in the Crisis of 1876–1877: A Reconsideration of *Reunion and Reaction*," *Journal of Southern History* 46 (1980): 489–524.

THE AMBIVALENT RELATIONSHIP OF LIBERTY AND POWER

From the Revolution to the Civil War, most Americans viewed the power wielded by a strong government as a grave threat to liberty. "There is a tendency in all governments to an augmentation of power at the expense of liberty," wrote James Madison in 1788. To curb this tendency, Madison and other framers of the Constitution devised a series of checks and balances—dividing power among three branches of the national government, between two houses of Congress, and among the state and federal governments—as an "essential precaution in favor of liberty." But for many Americans even this precaution did not go far enough to protect individual liberties. They insisted on a bill of rights which, in the first ten amendments to the Constitution, imposed a straitjacket of "thou shalt nots" on the federal government.

The Civil War transformed this negative relationship between power and liberty—at least for a time. The crux of this transformation was slavery, an institution embedded in the framework of American liberty from the beginning. One of the liberties for which Confederates fought was the liberty to own slaves. But as Abraham Lincoln put it in 1864, this liberty for white people meant oppression of black people. "We all declare for liberty," said Lincoln, "but in using the same *word* we do not all mean the same *thing*. With some the word liberty may mean for each man to do as he pleases with himself, and the product of his labor; while with others the same word may mean for some men to do as they please with other men, and the product of other men's labor." Lincoln left no doubt of the version of liberty he meant to enforce—the abolition of chattel slavery. That required *power*. As commander in chief, Lincoln wielded more power over internal affairs than anyone else in American history. It took every ounce of that power to accomplish the "new birth of freedom" that Lincoln invoked at Gettysburg.

This new birth radically changed the course of American constitutional development. In place of the "shall nots" of the first ten amendments to the Constitution, six of the next seven amendments, adopted after the Civil War, strengthened the national government at the expense of states and individuals, and contained the phrase "Congress *shall have the power* to enforce this article" (italics added). The Thirteenth, Fourteenth, and Fifteenth Amendments expanded national power to ensure the abolition of slavery and to guarantee equal rights for freed people. Republicans in Congress believed that liberty could not be sustained without such an expansion of power. "We must lay the heavy hand of military authority upon these rebel communities," said Congressman (and future President) James Garfield in 1867, and "plant liberty on the ruins of slavery."

During the post-Civil War decade, Congress passed civil rights laws and enforcement legislation to accomplish this purpose. Federal marshals and troops patrolled the polls to protect black voters, arrested thousands of Klansmen and other violators of black civil rights, and even occupied state capitals to prevent Democratic paramilitary groups from overthrowing legitimately elected Republican state governments. But by 1875 many northerners had grown tired of or alarmed by this continued use of military power to intervene repeatedly in the internal affairs of states. The Supreme Court stripped the federal government of much of its authority to enforce certain provisions of the Fourteenth and Fifteenth Amendments. Traditional fears of military power as a threat to individual liberties came to the fore again.

This process can best be viewed through the eyes of Carl Schurz. A radical emigré from the failed revolution of 1848 in Germany, Schurz had risen to prominence as a Republican political leader of German-Americans. As a senator from Missouri during Reconstruction, Schurz had done as much as anyone to forge expanded national power to protect liberty. In a speech advocating legislation to enforce the Fifteenth Amendment in 1870, Schurz scorned the Democrats' incessant harping on "what they euphoniously called local self-government and . . . State sovereignty. . . . In the name of liberty they asserted the right of one man, under State law, to deprive another man of his freedom," and now "they will tell you that they are no longer true freemen in their States because . . . they can no longer deprive other men of their rights." But "the great Constitutional revolution" wrought by the Civil War, said Schurz, brought "the vindication of individual rights by the National power. The revolution found the rights of the individual at the mercy of the States . . . and placed them under the shield of National protection."

By 1875, however, Schurz was singing the tune of individual and states' rights against national power that he had scorned five years earlier. And others also changed their tune. When federal troops marched into the Louisiana legislature in 1875 to expel several Democratic members whose election had been challenged by Republican opponents, many northern Republicans joined the swelling chorus of concern that "bayonet rule" was undermining traditional liberties. Carl Schurz gave voice to this concern in a Senate speech. The "insidious advance of irresponsible power" had drawn sustenance from the argument that it was "by Federal bayonets only that the colored man may be safe," said Schurz. He conceded that "brute force" might make "every colored man perfectly safe, not only in the exercise of his franchise but in everything else. . . . You might have made the National Government so strong that, right or wrong, nobody could resist

it." That is "an effective method to keep peace and order," acknowledged Schurz. "It is employed with singular success in Russia." But "what has in the meantime become of the liberties and rights of all of us?" If military expulsion of legislators could be done in a southern state, how long before it might happen in the North? "How long before a soldier may stalk into the National House of Representatives, and, pointing to the Speaker's mace, say, 'Take away that bauble'?"

Americans have never fully resolved the tension between power and liberty. The national government withdrew the last troops from southern state capitals in 1877. Most white Americans hailed this action as a triumph of individual liberties over oppressive power. But for black people it signaled a cessation of efforts to protect their rights. Not until the 1950s, when President Dwight Eisenhower sent federal troops to Little Rock to enforce desegregation at Central High School, did the national government again wield military power to protect black rights. And it took twelve thousand soldiers to enforce the right of one black man, James Meredith, to attend the University of Mississippi in 1962.

Troubling questions about the relationship of power and liberty remain. What role should military force play in civil affairs? Over the century and more since the railroad strikes of 1877, federal troops and state militia have repeatedly intervened against strikers. The Chicago police brutally attacked demonstrators at the Democratic National Convention in 1968. National guardsmen killed four antiwar student demonstrators at Kent State University in 1970. Responsible use of power can protect liberty, but it is not easy to draw the line between responsible and irresponsible use of power. Nor is it always clear when the use of force to protect the rights or liberty of one person or group shades into the denial of rights or liberty to another group (for example, strikers). The ambivalent relationship of power and liberty has been a vexing problem through American history. The problem is not likely to go away.

Victory Parade by Union Troops in Washington, D.C. On May 23–24, 1865, two hundred thousand soldiers of the victorious Union army marched down Pennsylvania Avenue in a celebratory "Grand Review." This display of the armed might of the republic demonstrated the power that had given the United States "a new birth of freedom."

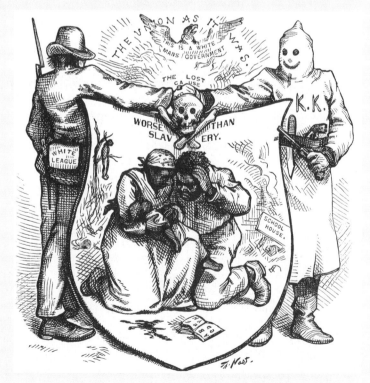

"Worse Than Slavery" This cartoon by Thomas Nast in 1875 depicts members of the two principal anti-Reconstruction paramilitary groups in the South, the White League and the Ku Klux Klan. Armed to the teeth, they shake hands above a defenseless black family whose rights they seek to overturn by violence. Only the power of the national government, the cartoon suggests, can overcome the unholy alliance and ensure the liberty of freed slaves.

The Freedmen's Bureau Created in 1865, the Freedmen's Bureau stood between freed slaves and their former masters in the postwar South, charged with the task of protecting freedpeople from injustice and repression. Staffed by officers of the Union army, the Bureau symbolized the military power of the government in its efforts to keep peace in the South.

"The Problem We All Live With" Eighty years after the withdrawal of federal troops from enforcement of Reconstruction in southern states in 1877, they returned to enforce school desegregation against resistance by southern whites. This 1960 painting by Norman Rockwell shows a lonely, scared black girl being escorted by U. S. marshals to a newly desegregated school in New Orleans while an unseen mob screams obscenities and threats.

Company E of the 4th U.S. Colored Troops Recruited in the District of Columbia in 1863, this regiment saw a great deal of action in the Virginia theater in 1864 and suffered heavy casualties fighting for their own freedom and that of four million other slaves. Here was an outstanding example of black people exerting power in behalf of their own liberty.

Federal Marshals and Troops with James Meredith at the University of Mississippi   In 1962 a federal court ordered the admission of James Meredith to the University of Mississippi. Massive riots by whites against this action prompted President John F. Kennedy to order 12,000 soldiers into Oxford, Mississippi, where they remained for months to enforce Meredith's right to attend the university.

Confrontation between Police and Anti-War Demonstrators   Chicago police clubbed and arrested activists protesting American involvement in the Vietnam War outside the halls of the Democratic National Convention in 1968. Here was a use of state power to infringe First Amendment liberties.

George Wallace Confronts Federal Marshals over Desegregation   In 1964, Governor George Wallace of Alabama vowed to "stand in the schoolhouse door" to prevent school desegregation. Here he makes a symbolic gesture for the cameras, standing at the entrance of a University of Alabama building to defy the court-ordered admission of two black students. After the cameras departed, the students registered under the protection of National Guard troops.

Truckload of Miners under Arrest during 1930 Strike   The Great Depression of the 1930s provoked many confrontations and much violence between labor and management. Police or National Guard troops often intervened to arrest strikers who defied court orders against picketing or preventing access to company property.

National Guard Troops Prepare for Street Duty in Los Angeles in 1992   When riots erupted in Los Angeles to protest the acquittal of police officers accused of beating Rodney King, a black man, the governor sent in the Guard to help suppress the rioters and protect property.

National Guard Troops Fire on Students at Kent State University, 1970   Soldiers of the Ohio National Guard confronted students demonstrating against the incursion of American troops into Cambodia during the Vietnam War in May 1970. Shortly after this photograph was taken, the jittery Guardsmen opened fire, killing four students.

Appendix

The Declaration of Independence

THE UNANIMOUS DECLARATION OF
THE THIRTEEN UNITED STATES OF AMERICA,

When in the Course of human events it becomes necessary for one people to dissolve the political bands which have connected them with another, and to assume among the Powers of the earth, the separate and equal station to which the Laws of Nature and of Nature's God entitle them, a decent respect to the opinions of mankind requires that they should declare the causes which impel them to the separation.

We hold these truths to be self-evident, that all men are created equal, that they are endowed by their Creator with certain unalienable Rights, that among these are Life, Liberty and the pursuit of Happiness. That to secure these rights, Governments are instituted among Men, deriving their just Powers from the consent of the governed. That whenever any Form of Government becomes destructive of these ends, it is the Right of the People to alter or to abolish it, and to institute new Government, laying its foundation on such principles and organizing its Powers in such form, as to them shall seem most likely to effect their Safety and Happiness. Prudence, indeed, will dictate that Governments long established should not be changed for light and transient causes; and accordingly all experience hath shewn, that mankind are more disposed to suffer, while evils are sufferable, than to right themselves by abolishing the forms to which they are accustomed. But when a long train of abuses and usurpations, pursuing invariably the same Object evinces a design to reduce them under absolute Despotism, it is their right, it is their duty, to throw off such Government, and to provide new Guards for their future security. Such has been the patient sufferance of these Colonies; and such is now the necessity which constrains them to alter their former Systems of Government. The history of the present King of Great Britain is a history of repeated injuries and usurpations, all having in direct object the establishment of an absolute Tyranny over these States. To prove this, let Facts be submitted to a candid world.

He has refused his Assent to Laws, the most wholesome and necessary for the public good.

He has forbidden his Governors to pass Laws of immediate and pressing importance, unless suspended in their operation till his Assent should be obtained; and when so suspended, he has utterly neglected to attend to them.

He has refused to pass other Laws for the accommodation of large districts of people, unless those people would relinquish the right of Representation in the Legislature, a right inestimable to them and formidable to tyrants only.

He has called together legislative bodies at places unusual, uncomfortable, and distant from the depository of their Public Records, for the sole Purpose of fatiguing them into compliance with his measures.

He has dissolved Representative Houses repeatedly, for opposing with manly firmness his invasions on the rights of the People.

He has refused for a long time, after such dissolutions, to cause others to be elected; whereby the Legislative Powers, incapable of Annihilation, have returned to the People at large for their exercise; the State remaining in the mean time exposed to all the dangers of invasion from without, and convulsions within.

He has endeavoured to prevent the Population of these States; for that purpose obstructing the Laws for Naturalization of Foreigners; refusing to pass others to encourage their migrations hither, and raising the conditions of new Appropriations of Lands.

He has obstructed the Administration of Justice, by refusing his Assent to Laws for establishing Judiciary Powers.

Text is reprinted from the facsimile of the engrossed copy in the National Archives. The original spelling, capitalization, and punctuation have been retained. Paragraphing has been added.

He has made Judges dependent on his Will alone, for the tenure of their offices, and the amount and payment of their salaries.

He has erected a multitude of New Offices, and sent hither swarms of Officers to harass our People, and eat out their substance.

He has kept among us, in times of peace, Standing Armies without the Consent of our legislatures.

He has affected to render the Military independent of and superior to the Civil Power.

He has combined with others to subject us to a jurisdiction foreign to our constitution, and unacknowledged by our laws; giving his Assent to their Acts of pretended Legislation:

For Quartering large bodies of armed troops among us:

For protecting them, by a mock Trial, from Punishment for any Murders which they should commit on the Inhabitants of these States:

For cutting off our Trade with all parts of the world:

For imposing Taxes on us without our Consent:

For depriving us in many cases, of the benefits of Trial by Jury:

For transporting us beyond Seas to be tried for pretended offences:

For abolishing the free System of English Laws in a neighbouring Province, establishing therein an Arbitrary government, and enlarging its Boundaries so as to render it at once an example and fit instrument for introducing the same absolute rule into these Colonies:

For taking away our Charters, abolishing our most valuable Laws, and altering fundamentally the Forms of our Governments:

For suspending our own Legislatures, and declaring themselves invested with Power to legislate for us in all cases whatsoever.

He has abdicated Government here, by declaring us out of his Protection, and waging War against us.

He has plundered our seas, ravaged our Coasts, burnt our towns, and destroyed the lives of our people.

He is at this time transporting large Armies of foreign Mercenaries to compleat the works of death, desolation and tyranny, already begun with circumstances of Cruelty and perfidy scarcely paralleled in the most barbarous ages, and totally unworthy the Head of a civilized nation.

He has constrained our fellow Citizens taken Captive on the high Seas to bear Arms against their Country, to become the executioners of their friends and Brethren, or to fall themselves by their Hands.

He has excited domestic insurrections amongst us, and has endeavoured to bring on the inhabitants of our frontiers, the merciless Indian Savages, whose known rule of warfare, is an undistinguished destruction of all ages, sexes and conditions.

In every stage of these Oppressions We have Petitioned for Redress in the most humble terms: Our repeated Petitions have been answered only by repeated injury. A Prince, whose character is thus marked by every act which may define a Tyrant, is unfit to be the ruler of a free People.

Nor have We been wanting in attentions to our British brethren. We have warned them from time to time of attempts by their legislature to extend an unwarrantable jurisdiction over us. We have reminded them of the circumstances of our emigration and settlement here. We have appealed to their native justice and magnanimity, and we have conjured them by the ties of our common kindred to disavow thee usurpations, which, would inevitably interrupt our connections and correspondence. They too have been deaf to the voice of justice and of consanguinity. We must, therefore, acquiesce in the necessity, which denounces our Separation, and hold them, as we hold the rest of mankind, Enemies in War, in Peace Friends.

WE, THEREFORE, the Representatives of the UNITED STATES OF AMERICA, in General Congress, Assembled, appealing to the Supreme Judge of the world for the rectitude of our intentions, do, in the Name, and by Authority of the good People of these Colonies, solemnly publish and declare, That these United Colonies are, and of Right ought to be FREE AND INDEPENDENT STATES; that they are Absolved from all Allegiance to the British Crown, and that all political connection between them and the State of Great Britain, is and ought to be totally dissolved; and that, as Free and Independent States, they have full Power to levy War, conclude Peace, contract Alliances, establish Commerce, and to do all other Acts and Things which Independent States may of right do. And for the support of this Declaration, with a firm reliance on the protection of divine Providence, we mutually pledge to each other our Lives, our Fortunes and our sacred Honor.

The Constitution of the United States of America

We the People of the United States, in Order to form a more perfect Union, establish Justice, insure domestic Tranquility, provide for the common defence, promote the general Welfare, and secure the Blessings of Liberty to ourselves and our Posterity, do ordain and establish this Constitution for the United States of America.

Article. I.

Section. 1. All legislative Powers herein granted shall be vested in a Congress of the United States, which shall consist of a Senate and House of Representatives.
Section. 2. The House of Representatives shall be composed of Members chosen every second Year by the People of the several States, and the Electors in each State shall have the Qualifications requisite for Electors of the most numerous Branch of the State Legislature.

No Person shall be a Representative who shall not have attained to the Age of twenty five Years, and been seven Years a Citizen of the United States, and who shall not, when elected, be an Inhabitant of that State in which he shall be chosen.

Representatives and direct Taxes[1] shall be apportioned among the several States which may be included within this Union, according to their respective Numbers, which shall be determined by adding to the whole Number of free Persons, including those bound to Service for a Term of Years, and excluding Indians not taxed, three fifths of all other Persons.[2] The actual Enumeration shall be made within three Years after the first Meeting of the Congress of the United States, and within every subsequent Term of ten Years, in such Manner as they shall by Law direct. The Number of Representatives shall not exceed one for every thirty Thousand, but each State shall have at Least one Representative; and until such enumeration shall be made, the State

of New Hampshire shall be entitled to chuse three; Massachusetts eight; Rhode Island and Providence Plantations one; Connecticut five; New York six; New Jersey four; Pennsylvania eight; Delaware one; Maryland six; Virginia ten; North Carolina five; South Carolina five; and Georgia three.

When vacancies happen in the Representation from any State, the Executive Authority thereof shall issue Writs of Election to fill such Vacancies.

The House of Representatives shall chuse their Speaker and other Officers; and shall have the sole Power of Impeachment.
Section. 3. The Senate of the United States shall be composed of two Senators from each State, chosen by the Legislature thereof, for six Years; and each Senator shall have one Vote.[3]

Immediately after they shall be assembled in Consequence of the first Election, they shall be divided as equally as may be into three Classes. The Seats of the Senators of the first Class shall be vacated at the Expiration of the second Year, of the second Class at the Expiration of the fourth Year, and of the third Class at the Expiration of the sixth Year, so that one third may be chosen every second Year; and if Vacancies happen by Resignation, or otherwise, during the Recess of the Legislature of any State, the Executive thereof may make temporary Appointments until the next Meeting of the Legislature, which shall then fill such Vacancies.[4]

No Person shall be a Senator who shall not have attained to the Age of thirty Years, and been nine Years a Citizen of the United States, and who shall not, when elected, be an Inhabitant of that State for which he shall be chosen.

The Vice President of the United States shall be President of the Senate, but shall have no Vote, unless they be equally divided.

The Senate shall chuse their other Officers, and also a President pro tempore, in the Absence of the Vice President, or when he shall exercise the Office of President of the United States.

Text is from the engrossed copy in the National Archives. Original spelling, capitalization, and punctuation have been retained.

[1]Modified by the Sixteenth Amendment.

[2]Replaced by the Fourteenth Amendment.

[3]Superseded by the Seventeenth Amendment.

[4]Modified by the Seventeenth Amendment.

The Senate shall have the sole Power to try all Impeachments. When sitting for that Purpose, they shall be on Oath or Affirmation. When the President of the United States is tried, the Chief Justice shall preside: And no Person shall be convicted without the Concurrence of two thirds of the Members present.

Judgment in Cases of Impeachment shall not extend further than to removal from Office, and disqualification to hold and enjoy any Office of honor, Trust or Profit under the United States: but the Party convicted shall nevertheless be liable and subject to Indictment, Trial, Judgment and Punishment, according to Law.

Section. 4. The Times, Places and Manner of holding Elections for Senators and Representatives, shall be prescribed in each State by the Legislature thereof, but the Congress may at any time by Law make or alter such Regulation, except as to the Places of chusing Senators.

The Congress shall assemble at least once in every Year, and such Meeting shall be on the first Monday in December, unless they shall by Law appoint a different Day.[5]

Section. 5. Each House shall be the Judge of the Elections, Returns and Qualifications of its own Members, and a Majority of each shall constitute a Quorum to do Business; but a smaller Number may adjourn from day to day, and may be authorized to compel the Attendance of absent Members, in such Manner, and under such Penalties as each House may provide.

Each House may determine the Rules of its Proceedings, punish its Members for disorderly Behaviour, and, with the Concurrence of two thirds, expel a Member.

Each House shall keep a Journal of its Proceedings, and from time to time publish the same, excepting such Parts as may in their Judgment require Secrecy; and the Yeas and Nays of the Members of either House on any question shall, at the Desire of one fifth of those Present, be entered on the Journal.

Neither House, during the Session of Congress, shall, without the Consent of the other, adjourn for more than three days, nor to any other Place than that in which the two Houses shall be sitting.

Section. 6. The Senators and Representatives shall receive a Compensation for their Services, to be as-

certained by Law, and paid out of the Treasury of the United States. They shall in all Cases, except Treason, Felony and Breach of the Peace, be privileged from Arrest during their Attendance at the Session of their respective Houses, and in going to and returning from the same; and for any Speech or Debate in either House, they shall not be questioned in any other Place.

No Senator or Representative shall, during the Time for which he was elected, be appointed to any civil Office under the Authority of the United States, which shall have been created, or the Emoluments whereof shall have been encreased during such time; and no Person holding any Office under the United States, shall be a Member of either House during his Continuance in Office.

Section. 7. All Bills for raising Revenue shall originate in the House of Representatives; but the Senate may propose or concur with Amendments as on other Bills.

Every Bill which shall have passed the House of Representatives and the Senate shall, before it become a Law, be presented to the President of the United States; If he approve he shall sign it, but if not he shall return it, with his Objections to that House in which it shall have originated, who shall enter the Objections at large on their Journal, and proceed to reconsider it. If after such Reconsideration two thirds of that House shall agree to pass the Bill, it shall be sent, together with the Objections, to the other House, by which it shall likewise be reconsidered, and if approved by two thirds of that House, it shall become a Law. But in all such Cases the Votes of both Houses shall be determined by yeas and Nays, and the Names of the Persons voting for and against the Bill shall be entered on the Journal of each House respectively. If any Bill shall not be returned by the President within ten Days (Sundays excepted) after it shall have been presented to him, the Same shall be a Law, in like Manner as if he had signed it, unless the Congress by their Adjournment prevent its Return, in which Case it shall not be a Law.

Every Order, Resolution, or Vote to which the Concurrence of the Senate and House of Representatives may be necessary (except on a question of Adjournment) shall be presented to the President of the United States; and before the Same shall take Effect, shall be approved by him, or being disapproved by him shall be repassed by two thirds of the Senate

---

[5]Superseded by the Twentieth Amendment.

and House of Representatives, according to the Rules and Limitations prescribed in the Case of a Bill.

Section. 8. The Congress shall have power To lay and collect Taxes, Duties, Imposts and Excises, to pay the Debts and provide for the common Defence and general Welfare of the United States; but all Duties, Imposts and Excises shall be uniform throughout the United States;

To borrow Money on the credit of the United States;

To regulate Commerce with foreign Nations, and among the several States, and with the Indian Tribes;

To establish an uniform Rule of Naturalization, and uniform Laws on the subject of Bankruptcies throughout the United States;

To coin Money, regulate the Value thereof, and of foreign Coin, and fix the Standard of Weights and Measures;

To provide for the Punishment of counterfeiting the Securities and current Coin of the United States;

To establish Post Offices and post Roads;

To promote the Progress of Science and useful Arts, by securing for limited Times to Authors and Inventors the exclusive Right to their respective Writings and Discoveries;

To constitute Tribunals inferior to the supreme Court;

To define and punish Piracies and Felonies committed on the high Seas, and Offences against the Law of Nations;

To declare War, grant Letters of Marque and Reprisal, and make Rules concerning Captures on Land and Water;

To raise and support Armies, but no Appropriation of Money to that Use shall be for a longer Term than two Years;

To provide and maintain a Navy;

To make Rules for the Government and Regulation of the land and naval Forces;

To provide for calling forth the Militia to execute the Laws of the Union, suppress Insurrections and repel Invasions;

To provide for organizing, arming, and disciplining, the Militia, and for governing such Part of them as may be employed in the Service of the United States, reserving to the States respectively, the Appointment of the Officers, and the Authority of training the Militia according to the discipline prescribed by Congress;

To exercise exclusive Legislation in all Cases whatsoever, over such District (not exceeding ten Miles square) as may, by Cession of particular States, and the Acceptance of Congress, become the Seat of the Government of the United States, and to exercise like Authority over all Places purchased by the Consent of the Legislature of the State in which the Same shall be, for the Erection of Forts, Magazines, Arsenals, dock-Yards, and other needful Buildings; — And

To make all Laws which shall be necessary and proper for carrying into Execution the foregoing Powers, and all other Powers vested by this Constitution in the Government of the United States, or in any Department or Officer thereof.

Section. 9. The Migration or Importation of such Persons as any of the States now existing shall think proper to admit, shall not be prohibited by the Congress prior to the Year one thousand eight hundred and eight, but a Tax or duty may be imposed on such Importation, not exceeding ten dollars for each Person.

The Privilege of the Writ of Habeas Corpus shall not be suspended, unless when in Cases of Rebellion or Invasion the public Safety may require it.

No Bill of Attainder or ex post facto Law shall be passed.

No Capitation, or other direct, Tax shall be laid, unless in Proportion to the Census or Enumeration herein before directed to be taken.

No Tax or Duty shall be laid on Articles exported from any State.

No Preference shall be given by any Regulation of Commerce or Revenue to the Ports of one State over those of another: nor shall Vessels bound to, or from, one State, be obliged to enter, clear, or pay Duties in another.

No Money shall be drawn from the Treasury, but in Consequence of Appropriations made by Law, and a regular Statement and Account of the Receipts and Expenditures of all public Money shall be published from time to time.

No Title of Nobility shall be granted by the United States: And no Person holding any Office of Profit or Trust under them, shall, without the Consent of the Congress, accept of any present, Emolument, Office, or Title, of any kind whatever, from any King, Prince, or foreign State.

Section. 10. No State shall enter into any Treaty, Alliance, or Confederation; grant Letters of Marque and Reprisal; coin Money; emit Bills of Credit; make any Thing but gold and silver Coin a Tender in Payment of Debts; pass any Bill of Attainder, ex post facto Law, or Law impairing the Obligation of Contracts, or grant any Title of Nobility.

No State shall, without the Consent of the Congress, lay any Imposts or Duties on Imports or Exports, except what may be absolutely necessary for executing its inspection Laws: and the net Produce of all Duties and Imposts, laid by any State on Imports or Exports, shall be for the Use of the Treasury of the United States; and all such Laws shall be subject to the Revision and Controul of the Congress.

No State shall, without the Consent of Congress, lay any Duty of Tonnage, keep Troops, or Ships of War in time of Peace, enter into any Agreement or Compact with another State, or with a foreign Power, or engage in War, unless actually invaded, or in such imminent Danger as will not admit of delay.

Article. II.

Section. 1. The executive Power shall be vested in a President of the United States of America. He shall hold his Office during the Term of four Years, and, together with the Vice President, chosen for the same Term, be elected, as follows:

Each State shall appoint, in such Manner as the Legislature thereof may direct, a Number of Electors, equal to the whole Number of Senators and Representatives to which the State may be entitled in the Congress: but no Senator or Representative, or Person holding an Office of Trust or Profit under the United States, shall be appointed an Elector.

The Electors shall meet in their respective States, and vote by Ballot for two Persons, of whom one at least shall not be an Inhabitant of the same State with themselves. And they shall make a List of all the Persons voted for, and of the Number of Votes for each; which List they shall sign and certify, and transmit sealed to the Seat of the Government of the United States, directed to the President of the Senate. The President of the Senate shall, in the Presence of the Senate and House of Representatives, open all the Certificates, and the Votes shall then be counted. The Person having the greatest Number of Votes shall be the President, if such Number be a Majority of the whole Number of Electors appointed; and if there be more than one who have such Majority, and have an equal Number of Votes,

then the House of Representatives shall immediately chuse by Ballot one of them for President; and if no Person have a Majority, then from the five highest on the List the said House shall in like Manner chuse the President. But in chusing the President, the Votes shall be taken by States, the Representation from each State having one Vote; A quorum for this Purpose shall consist of a Member or Members from two thirds of the States, and a Majority of all the States shall be necessary to a Choice. In every Case, after the Choice of the President, the Person having the greatest Number of Votes of the Electors shall be the Vice President. But if there should remain two or more who have equal Votes, the Senate shall chuse from them by Ballot the Vice President.[6]

The Congress may determine the Time of chusing the Electors, and the Day on which they shall give their Votes; which Day shall be the same throughout the United States.

No Person except a natural born Citizen, or a Citizen of the United States, at the time of the Adoption of this Constitution, shall be eligible to the Office of President; neither shall any Person be eligible to that Office who shall not have attained to the Age of thirty five Years, and been fourteen Years a Resident within the United States.

In Case of the Removal of the President from Office, or of his Death, Resignation, or Inability to discharge the Powers and Duties of the said Office, the Same shall devolve on the Vice President, and the Congress may by Law provide for the Case of Removal, Death, Resignation or Inability, both of the President and Vice President, declaring what Officer shall then act as President, and such Officer shall act accordingly, until the Disability be removed, or a President shall be elected.[7]

The President shall, at stated Times, receive for his Services, a Compensation, which shall neither be encreased nor diminished during the Period for which he shall have been elected, and he shall not receive within that Period any other Emolument from the United States, or any of them.

Before he enter on the Execution of his Office, he shall take the following Oath or Affirmation:— "I do solemnly swear (or affirm) that I will faithfully execute the Office of President of the United States,

---

[6]Superseded by the Twelfth Amendment.

[7]Modified by the Twenty-fifth Amendment.

and will to the best of my Ability, preserve, protect and defend the Constitution of the United States."

Section. 2. The President shall be Commander in Chief of the Army and Navy of the United States, and of the Militia of the several States, when called into the actual Service of the United States; he may require the Opinion, in writing, of the principal Officer in each of the executive Departments, upon any Subject relating to the Duties of their respective Offices, and he shall have Power to grant Reprieves and Pardons for Offences against the United States, except in Cases of Impeachment.

He shall have Power, by and with the Advice and Consent of the Senate, to make Treaties, provided two thirds of the Senators present concur; and he shall nominate, and by and with the Advice and Consent of the Senate, shall appoint Ambassadors, other public Ministers and Consuls, Judges of the supreme Court, and all other Officers of the United States, whose Appointments are not herein otherwise provided for, and which shall be established by Law; but the Congress may by Law vest the Appointment of such inferior Officers, as they think proper, in the President alone, in the Courts of Law, or in the Heads of Departments.

The President shall have Power to fill up all Vacancies that may happen during the Recess of the Senate, by granting Commissions which shall expire at the End of their next Session.

Section. 3. He shall from time to time give the Congress Information of the State of the Union, and recommend to their Consideration such Measures as he shall judge necessary and expedient; he may, on extraordinary Occasions, convene both Houses, or either of them, and in Case of Disagreement between them, with Respect to the Time of Adjournment, he may adjourn them to such Time as he shall think proper; he shall receive Ambassadors and other public Ministers; he shall take Care that the Laws be faithfully executed, and shall Commission all the Officers of the United States.

Section. 4. The President, Vice President and all civil Officers of the United States, shall be removed from Office on Impeachment for, and Conviction of, Treason, Bribery, or other high Crimes and Misdemeanors.

Article. III.

Section. 1. The judicial Power of the United States, shall be vested in one supreme Court, and in such inferior Courts as the Congress may from time to time ordain and establish. The Judges, both of the supreme and inferior Courts, shall hold their Offices during good Behaviour, and shall, at stated Times, receive for their Services, a Compensation, which shall not be diminished during their Continuance in Office.

Section. 2. The judicial Power shall extend to all Cases, in Law and Equity, arising under this Constitution, the Laws of the United States, and Treaties made, or which shall be made, under their Authority; — to all Cases affecting Ambassadors, other public Ministers and Consuls; — to all Cases of admiralty and maritime Jurisdiction; — to Controversies to which the United States shall be a Party; — to Controversies between two or more States; — between a State and Citizens of another State;[8] — between Citizens of different States, — between Citizens of the same State claiming Lands under Grants of different States, and between a State, or the Citizens thereof, and foreign States, Citizens or Subjects.

In all Cases affecting Ambassadors, other public Ministers and Consuls, and those in which a State shall be Party, the supreme Court shall have original Jurisdiction. In all the other Cases before mentioned, the supreme Court shall have appellate Jurisdiction, both as to Law and Fact, with such Exceptions, and under such Regulations as the Congress shall make.

The Trial of all Crimes, except in Cases of Impeachment, shall be by Jury; and such Trial shall be held in the State where the said Crimes shall have been committed; but when not committed within any State, the Trial shall be at such Place or Places as the Congress may by Law have directed.

Section. 3. Treason against the United States, shall consist only in levying War against them, or in adhering to their Enemies, giving them Aid and Comfort. No Person shall be convicted of Treason unless on the Testimony of two Witnesses to the same overt Act, or on Confession in open Court.

The Congress shall have Power to declare the Punishment of Treason, but no Attainder of Treason shall work Corruption of Blood, or Forfeiture except during the Life of the Person attainted.

Article. IV.

Section. 1. Full Faith and Credit shall be given in each State to the public Acts, Records, and judicial

---

[8]Modified by the Eleventh Amendment.

Proceedings of every other State. And the Congress may by general Laws prescribe the Manner in which such Acts, Records and Proceedings shall be proved, and the Effect thereof.

Section. 2. The Citizens of each State shall be entitled to all Privileges and Immunities of Citizens in the several States.

A Person charged in any State with Treason, Felony, or other Crime, who shall flee from Justice, and be found in another State, shall on Demand of the executive Authority of the State from which he fled, be delivered up, to be removed to the State having Jurisdiction of the Crime.

No Person held to Service or Labour in one State, under the Laws thereof, escaping into another, shall, in Consequence of any Law or Regulation therein, be discharged from such Service or Labour, but shall be delivered up on Claim of the Party to whom such Service or Labour may be due.

Section. 3. New States may be admitted by the Congress into this Union; but no new State shall be formed or erected within the Jurisdiction of any other State, nor any State be formed by the Junction of two or more States, or Parts of States, without the Consent of the Legislatures of the States concerned as well as of the Congress.

The Congress shall have Power to dispose of and make all needful Rules and Regulations respecting the Territory or other Property belonging to the United States; and nothing in this Constitution shall be so construed as to Prejudice any Claims of the United States, or of any particular State.

Section. 4. The United States shall guarantee to every State in this Union a Republican Form of Government, and shall protect each of them against Invasion; and on Application of the Legislature, or of the Executive (when the Legislature cannot be convened) against domestic Violence.

Article. V.

The Congress, whenever two thirds of both Houses shall deem it necessary, shall propose Amendments to this Constitution, or, on the Application of the Legislatures of two thirds of the several States, shall call a Convention for proposing Amendments, which, in either Case, shall be valid to all Intents and Purposes, as Part of this Constitution, when ratified by the Legislatures of three fourths of the several States, or by Conventions in three fourths thereof, as the one or the other Mode of Ratification may be pro-

posed by the Congress; Provided that no Amendment which may be made prior to the Year One thousand eight hundred and eight shall in any Manner affect the first and fourth Clauses in the Ninth Section of the first Article; and that no State, without its Consent, shall be deprived of its equal Suffrage in the Senate.

Article. VI.

All Debts contracted and Engagements entered into, before the Adoption of this Constitution, shall be as valid against the United States under this Constitution, as under the Confederation.

This Constitution, and the Laws of the United States which shall be made in Pursuance thereof; and all Treaties made, or which shall be made, under the Authority of the United States, shall be the supreme Law of the Land; and the Judges in every State shall be bound thereby, any Thing in the Constitution or Laws of any State to the Contrary notwithstanding.

The Senators and Representatives before mentioned, and the Members of the several State Legislatures, and all executive and judicial Officers, both of the United States and of the several States, shall be bound by Oath or Affirmation, to support this Constitution; but no religious Test shall ever be required as a Qualification to any Office or public Trust under the United States.

Article. VII.

The Ratification of the Conventions of nine States, shall be sufficient for the Establishment of this Constitution between the States so ratifying the Same.

done in Convention by the Unanimous Consent of the States present the Seventeenth Day of September in the Year of our Lord one thousand seven hundred and Eighty seven and of the Independence of the United States of America the Twelfth. **In witness** whereof We have hereunto subscribed our Names,

Articles in Addition to, and Amendment of, the Constitution of the United States of America, Proposed by Congress, and Ratified by the Legislatures of the Several States, Pursuant to the Fifth Article of the Original Constitution.

Amendment I[9]

Congress shall make no law respecting an establishment of religion, or prohibiting the free exercise thereof; or abridging the freedom of speech, or of the press; or the right of the people peaceably to assemble, and to petition the Government for a redress of grievances.

Amendment II

A well regulated Militia, being necessary to the security of a free State, the right of the people to keep and bear Arms shall not be infringed.

Amendment III

No Soldier shall, in time of peace, be quartered in any house, without the consent of the Owner, nor in time of war, but in a manner to be prescribed by law.

Amendment IV

The right of the people to be secure in their persons, houses, papers, and effects, against unreasonable searches and seizures, shall not be violated, and no Warrants shall issue, but upon probable cause, supported by Oath or affirmation, and particularly describing the place to be searched, and the persons or things to be seized.

Amendment V

No person shall be held to answer for a capital or otherwise infamous crime, unless on a presentment or indictment of a Grand Jury, except in cases arising in the land or naval forces, or in the Militia, when in actual service in time of War or public danger; nor shall any person be subject for the same offence to be twice put in jeopardy of life or limb; nor shall be compelled in any criminal case to be a witness against himself, nor be deprived of life, liberty, or property, without due process of law; nor shall private property be taken for public use, without just compensation.

Amendment VI

In all criminal prosecutions, the accused shall enjoy the right to a speedy and public trial, by an impartial jury of the State and district wherein the crime shall have been committed, which district shall have been previously ascertained by law, and to be informed of the nature and cause of the accusation; to be confronted with the witnesses against him; to have compulsory process for obtaining witnesses in his favor, and to have the Assistance of Counsel for his defence.

Amendment VII

In suits at common law, where the value in controversy shall exceed twenty dollars, the right of trial by jury shall be preserved, and no fact tried by a jury, shall be otherwise reexamined in any Court of the United States, than according to the rules of the common law.

Amendment VIII

Excessive bail shall not be required, nor excessive fines imposed, nor cruel and unusual punishments inflicted.

Amendment IX

The enumeration in the Constitution, of certain rights, shall not be construed to deny or disparage others retained by the people.

Amendment X

The powers not delegated to the United States by the Constitution; nor prohibited by it to the States, are reserved to the States respectively, or to the people.

Amendment XI[10]

The Judicial power of the United States shall not be construed to extend to any suit in law or equity, commenced or prosecuted against one of the United States by Citizens of another State, or by Citizens or Subjects of any Foreign State.

Amendment XII[11]

The Electors shall meet in their respective States and vote by ballot for President and Vice-President, one of whom, at least, shall not be an inhabitant

---

[9]The first ten amendments were passed by Congress September 25, 1789. They were ratified by three-fourths of the states December 15, 1791.

[10]Passed March 4, 1794. Ratified January 23, 1795.

[11]Passed December 9, 1803. Ratified June 15, 1804.

of the same State with themselves; they shall name in their ballots the person voted for as President, and in distinct ballots the person voted for as Vice-President, and they shall make distinct lists of all persons voted for as President, and of all persons voted for as Vice-President, and of the number of votes for each, which lists they shall sign and certify, and transmit sealed to the seat of the government of the United States, directed to the President of the Senate; — The President of the Senate shall, in the presence of the Senate and House of Representatives, open all the certificates and the votes shall then be counted; — The person having the greatest number of votes for President, shall be the President, if such number be a majority of the whole number of Electors appointed; and if no person have such majority, then from the persons having the highest numbers not exceeding three on the list of those voted for as President, the House of Representatives shall choose immediately, by ballot, the President. But in choosing the President, the votes shall be taken by states, the representation from each state having one vote; a quorum for this purpose shall consist of a member or members from two-thirds of the states, and a majority of all the states shall be necessary to a choice. And if the House of Representatives shall not choose a President whenever the right of choice shall devolve upon them, before the fourth day of March next following, then the Vice-President shall act as President, as in the case of the death or other constitutional disability of the President. — The person having the greatest number of votes as Vice-President, shall be the Vice-President, if such number be a majority of the whole number of Electors appointed, and if no person have a majority, then from the two highest numbers on the list, the Senate shall choose the Vice-President; a quorum for the purpose shall consist of two-thirds of the whole number of Senators, and a majority of the whole number shall be necessary to a choice. But no person constitutionally ineligible to the office of President shall be eligible to that of Vice-President of the United States.

Amendment XIII[12]

SECTION 1. Neither slavery nor involuntary servitude, except as a punishment for crime whereof the party shall have been duly convicted, shall exist within the United States, or any place subject to their jurisdiction.

SECTION 2. Congress shall have power to enforce this article by appropriate legislation.

Amendment XIV[13]

SECTION 1. All persons born or naturalized in the United States, and subject to the jurisdiction thereof, are citizens of the United States and of the State wherein they reside. No State shall make or enforce any law which shall abridge the privileges or immunities of citizens of the United States; nor shall any State deprive any person of life, liberty, or property, without due process of law; nor deny to any person within its jurisdiction the equal protection of the laws.

SECTION 2. Representatives shall be apportioned among the several States according to their respective numbers, counting the whole number of persons in each State, excluding Indians not taxed. But when the right to vote at any election for the choice of electors for President and Vice-President of the United States, Representatives in Congress, the Executive and Judicial officers of a State, or the members of the Legislature thereof, is denied to any of the male inhabitants of such State, being twenty-one years of age, and citizens of the United States, or in any way abridged, except for participation in rebellion, or other crime, the basis of representation therein shall be reduced in the proportion which the number of such male citizens shall bear to the whole number of male citizens twenty-one years of age in such State.

SECTION 3. No person shall be a Senator or Representative in Congress, or elector of President and Vice-President, or hold any office, civil or military, under the United States, or under any State, who, having previously taken an oath, as a member of Congress, or as an officer of the United States, or as a member of any State legislature, or as an executive or judicial officer of any State, to support the Constitution of the United States, shall have engaged in insurrection or rebellion against the same, or given aid or comfort to the enemies thereof. But Congress may by a vote of two-thirds of each House, remove such disability.

---

[12]Passed January 31, 1865. Ratified December 6, 1865.

[13]Passed June 13, 1866. Ratified July 9, 1868.

SECTION **4.** The validity of the public debt of the United States, authorized by law, including debts incurred for payment of pensions and bounties for services in suppressing insurrection or rebellion, shall not be questioned. But neither the United States nor any State shall assume or pay any debt or obligation incurred in aid of insurrection or rebellion against the United States, or any claim for the loss or emancipation of any slave; but all such debts, obligations, and claims shall be held illegal and void.

SECTION *5.* The Congress shall have the power to enforce, by appropriate legislation, the provisions of this article.

Amendment XV[14]

SECTION **1.** The right of citizens of the United States to vote shall not be denied or abridged by the United States or by any State on account of race, color, or previous conditions of servitude—

SECTION **2.** The Congress shall have power to enforce this article by appropriate legislation.

Amendment XVI

The Congress shall have power to lay and collect taxes on incomes, from whatever source derived, without apportionment among the several States, and without regard to any census or enumeration.

Amendment XVII[15]

The Senate of the United States shall be composed of two Senators from each State, elected by the people thereof, for six years; and each Senator shall have one vote. The electors in each State shall have the qualifications requisite for electors of the most numerous branch of the State legislatures.

When vacancies happen in the representation of any State in the Senate, the executive authority of such State shall issue writs of election to fill such vacancies: *Provided,* That the legislature of any State may empower the executive thereof to make temporary appointments until the people fill the vacancies by election as the legislature may direct.

This amendment shall not be so construed as to affect the election or term of any Senator chosen before it becomes valid as part of the Constitution.

Amendment XVIII[16]

SECTION **1.** After one year from the ratification of this article the manufacture, sale, or transportation of intoxicating liquors within, the importation thereof into, or the exportation thereof from the United States and all territory subject to the jurisdiction thereof for beverage purposes is hereby prohibited.

SECTION **2.** The Congress and the several States shall have concurrent power to enforce this article by appropriate legislation.

SECTION **3.** This article shall be inoperative unless it shall have been ratified as an amendment to the Constitution by the legislatures of the several States, as provided in the Constitution, within seven years from the date of the submission hereof to the States by the Congress.

Amendment XIX[17]

The right of citizens of the United States to vote shall not be denied or abridged by the United States or by any State on account of sex.

Congress shall have power to enforce this article by appropriate legislation.

Amendment XX[18]

SECTION **1.** The terms of the President and Vice-President shall end at noon on the 20th day of January, and the terms of Senators and Representatives at noon on the 3d day of January, of the years in which such terms would have ended if this article had not been ratified; and the terms of their successors shall then begin.

SECTION **2.** The Congress shall assemble at least once in every year, and such meeting shall begin at noon on the 3d day of January, unless they shall by law appoint a different day.

SECTION **3.** If, at the time fixed for the beginning of the term of the President, the President elect shall

---

[14]Passed February 26, 1869. Ratified February 2, 1870.

[15]Passed May 13, 1912. Ratified April 8, 1913.

[16]Passed December 18, 1917. Ratified January 16, 1919.

[17]Passed June 4, 1919. Ratified August 18, 1920.

[18]Passed March 2, 1932. Ratified January 23, 1933.

have died, the Vice-President elect shall become President. If a President shall not have been chosen before the time fixed for the beginning of his term, or if the President elect shall have failed to qualify, then the Vice-President elect shall act as President until a President shall have qualified; and the Congress may by law provide for the case wherein neither a President elect nor a Vice-President elect shall have qualified, declaring who shall then act as President, or the manner in which one who is to act shall be selected, and such person shall act accordingly until a President or Vice-President shall have qualified.

SECTION 4. The Congress may by law provide for the case of the death of any of the persons from whom the House of Representatives may choose a President whenever the right of choice shall have devolved upon them, and for the case of the death of any of the persons from whom the Senate may choose a Vice-President whenever the right of choice shall have devolved upon them.

SECTION 5. Sections 1 and 2 shall take effect on the 15th day of October following the ratification of this article.

SECTION 6. This article shall be inoperative unless it shall have been ratified as an amendment to the Constitution by the legislatures of three-fourths of the several States within seven years from the date of its submission.

Amendment XXI[19]

SECTION 1. The eighteenth article of amendment to the Constitution of the United States is hereby repealed.

SECTION 2. The transportation or importation into any State, Territory, or possession of the United States for delivery or use therein of intoxicating liquors, in violation of the laws thereof, is hereby prohibited.

SECTION 3. This article shall be inoperative unless it shall have been ratified as an amendment to the Constitution by conventions in the several States, as provided in the Constitution, within seven years from the date of the submission hereof to the States by the Congress.

Amendment XXII[20]

No person shall be elected to the office of the President more than twice, and no person who has held the office of President, or acted as President, for more than two years of a term to which some other person was elected President shall be elected to the office of the President more than once.

But this Article shall not apply to any person holding the office of President when this Article was proposed by the Congress, and shall not prevent any person who may be holding the office of President, or acting as President, during the term within which this Article becomes operative from holding the office of President or acting as President during the remainder of such term.

Amendment XXIII[21]

SECTION 1. The District constituting the seat of Government of the United States shall appoint in such manner as the Congress may direct:

A number of electors of President and Vice President equal to the whole number of Senators and Representatives in Congress to which the District would be entitled if it were a State, but in no event more than the least populous State; they shall be in addition to those appointed by the States, but they shall be considered, for the purposes of the election of President and Vice President, to be electors appointed by the State; and they shall meet in the District and perform such duties as provided by the twelfth article of amendment.

SECTION 2. The Congress shall have power to enforce this article by appropriate legislation.

Amendment XXIV[22]

SECTION 1. The right of citizens of the United States to vote in any primary or other election for President or Vice President, or for Senator or Representative in Congress, shall not be denied or abridged by the United States or any State by reason of failure to pay any poll tax or other tax.

SECTION 2. The Congress shall have power to enforce this article by appropriate legislation.

---

[19]Passed February 20, 1933. Ratified December 5, 1933.

[20]Passed March 12, 1947. Ratified March 1, 1951.

[21]Passed June 16, 1960. Ratified April 3, 1961.

[22]Passed August 27, 1962. Ratified January 23, 1964.

Amendment XXV[23]

SECTION 1. In case of the removal of the President from office or of his death or resignation, the Vice President shall become President.

SECTION 2. Whenever there is a vacancy in the office of the Vice President, the President shall nominate a Vice President who shall take office upon confirmation by a majority vote of both Houses of Congress.

SECTION 3. Whenever the President transmits to the President pro tempore of the Senate and the Speaker of the House of Representatives his written declaration that he is unable to discharge the powers and duties of his office, and until he transmits them a written declaration to the contrary, such powers and duties shall be discharged by the Vice President as Acting President.

SECTION 4. Whenever the Vice President and a majority of either the principal officers of the executive department or of such other body as Congress may by law provide, transmit to the President pro tempore of the Senate and the Speaker of the House of Representatives their written declaration that the President is unable to discharge the powers and duties of his office, the Vice President shall immediately assume the powers and duties of the office of Acting President

Thereafter, when the President transmits to the President pro tempore of the Senate and the Speaker of the House of Representatives his written declaration that no inability exists, he shall resume the powers and duties of his office unless the Vice President and a majority of either the principal officers of the executive department or of such other body as Congress may by law provide, transmit within four days to the President pro tempore of the Senate and the Speaker of the House of Representatives their written declaration that the President is unable to discharge the powers and duties of his office. Thereupon Congress shall decide the issue, assembling within forty-eight hours for that purpose if not in session. If the Congress, within twenty-one days after receipt of the latter written declaration, or, if Congress is not in session, within twenty-one days after Congress is required to assemble, determines by two-thirds vote of both Houses that the President is unable to discharge the powers and duties of his office, the Vice President shall continue to discharge the same as Acting President; otherwise, the President shall resume the powers and duties of his office.

Amendment XXVI[24]

SECTION 1. The right of citizens of the United States, who are eighteen years of age or older, to vote shall not be denied or abridged by the United States or by any State on account of age.

SECTION 2. The Congress shall have power to enforce this article by appropriate legislation.

Amendment XXVII[25]

No law, varying the compensation for the service of the Senators and Representatives, shall take effect, until an election of Representatives shall have intervened.

---

[23]Passed July 6, 1965. Ratified February 11, 1967.

[24]Passed March 23, 1971. Ratified July 5, 1971.

[25]Passed September 25,1989. Ratified May 7, 1992

Admission of States

Order of admission	State	Date of admission	Order of admission	State	Date of admission
1	Delaware	December 7, 1787	26	Michigan	January 26, 1837
2	Pennsylvania	December 12, 1787	27	Florida	March 3, 1845
3	New Jersey	December 18, 1787	28	Texas	December 29, 1845
4	Georgia	January 2, 1788	29	Iowa	December 28, 1846
5	Connecticut	January 9, 1788	30	Wisconsin	May 29, 1848
6	Massachusetts	February 6, 1788	31	California	September 9, 1850
7	Maryland	April 28, 1788	32	Minnesota	May 11, 1858
8	South Carolina	May 23, 1788	33	Oregon	February 14, 1859
9	New Hampshire	June 21, 1788	34	Kansas	January 29, 1861
10	Virginia	June 25, 1788	35	West Virginia	June 20, 1863
11	New York	July 26, 1788	36	Nevada	October 31, 1864
12	North Carolina	November 21, 1789	37	Nebraska	March 1, 1867
13	Rhode Island	May 29, 1790	38	Colorado	August 1, 1876
14	Vermont	March 4, 1791	39	North Dakota	November 2, 1889
15	Kentucky	June 1, 1792	40	South Dakota	November 2, 1889
16	Tennessee	June 1, 1796	41	Montana	November 8, 1889
17	Ohio	March 1, 1803	42	Washington	November 11, 1889
18	Louisiana	April 30, 1812	43	Idaho	July 3, 1890
19	Indiana	December 11, 1816	44	Wyoming	July 10, 1890
20	Mississippi	December 10, 1817	45	Utah	January 4, 1896
21	Illinois	December 3, 1818	46	Oklahoma	November 16, 1907
22	Alabama	December 14, 1819	47	New Mexico	January 6, 1912
23	Maine	March 15, 1820	48	Arizona	February 14, 1912
24	Missouri	August 10, 1821	49	Alaska	January 3, 1959
25	Arkansas	June 15, 1836	50	Hawaii	August 21, 1959

Population of the United States (1790–1996)

Year	Total population (in thousands)	Number per square mile of land area (continental United States	Year	Total population (in thousands)	Number per square mile of land area (continental United States)
1790	3,929	4.5	1829	12,565	
1791	4,056		1830	12,901	7.4
1792	4,194		1831	13,321	
1793	4,332		1832	13,742	
1794	4,469		1833	14,162	
1795	4,607		1834	14,582	
1796	4,745		1835	15,003	
1797	4,883		1836	15,423	
1798	5,021		1837	15,843	
1799	5,159		1838	16,264	
1800	5,297	6.1	1839	16,684	
1801	5,486		1840	17,120	9.8
1802	5,679		1841	17,733	
1803	5,872		1842	18,345	
1804	5,065		1843	18,957	
1805	6,258		1844	19,569	
1806	6,451		1845	20,182	
1807	6,644		1846	20,794	
1808	6,838		1847	21,406	
1809	7,031		1848	22,018	
1810	7,224	4.3	1849	22,631	
1811	7,460		1850	23,261	7.9
1812	7,700		1851	24,086	
1813	7,939		1852	24,911	
1814	8,179		1853	25,736	
1815	8,419		1854	26,561	
1816	8,659		1855	27,386	
1817	8,899		1856	28,212	
1818	9,139		1857	29,037	
1819	9,379		1858	29,862	
1820	9,618	5.6	1859	30,687	
1821	9,939		1860	31,513	10.6
1822	10,268		1861	32,351	
1823	10,596		1862	33,188	
1824	10,924		1863	34,026	
1825	11,252		1864	34,863	
1826	11,580		1865	35,701	
1827	11,909		1866	36,538	
1828	12,237		1867	37,376	

Figures are from *Historical Statistics of the United States, Colonial Times to 1957* (1961), pp. 7, 8; *Statistical Abstract of the United States: 1974*, p. 5, Census Bureau for 1974 and 1975; and *Statistical Abstract of the United States: 1988*, p. 7.

Year	Total population (in thousands)	Number per square mile of land area (continental United States)	Year	Total population (in thousands)[1]	Number per square mile of land area (continental United States)
1868	38,213		1907	87,000	
1869	39,051		1908	88,709	
1870	39,905	13.4	1909	90,492	
1871	40,938		1910	92,407	31.0
1872	41,972		1911	93,868	
1873	43,006		1912	95,331	
1874	44,040		1913	97,227	
1875	45,073		1914	99,118	
1876	46,107		1915	100,549	
1877	47,141		1916	101,966	
1878	48,174		1917	103,414	
1879	49,208		1918	104,550	
1880	50,262	16.9	1919	105,063	
1881	51,542		1920	106,466	35.6
1882	52,821		1921	108,541	
1883	54,100		1922	110,055	
1884	55,379		1923	111,950	
1885	56,658		1924	114,113	
1886	57,938		1925	115,832	
1887	59,217		1926	117,399	
1888	60,496		1927	119,038	
1889	61,775		1928	120,501	
1890	63,056	21.2	1929	121,700	
1891	64,361		1930	122,775	41.2
1892	65,666		1931	124,040	
1893	66,970		1932	124,840	
1894	68,275		1933	125,579	
1895	69,580		1934	126,374	
1896	70,885		1935	127,250	
1897	72,189		1936	128,053	
1898	73,494		1937	128,825	
1899	74,799		1938	129,825	
1900	76,094	25.6	1939	130,880	
1901	77,585		1940	131,669	44.2
1902	79,160		1941	133,894	
1903	80,632		1942	135,361	
1904	82,165		1943	137,250	
1905	83,820		1944	138,916	
1906	85,437		1945	140,468	

[1]Figures after 1940 represent total population including armed forces abroad, except in official census years.

(continued)

Population of the United States (continued) (1790–1996)

Year	Total population (in thousands)[1]	Number per square mile of land area (continental United States)	Year	Total population (in thousands)[1]	Number per square mile of land area (continental United States)
1946	141,936		1972	208,842	
1947	144,698		1973	210,396	
1948	147,208		1974	211,894	
1949	149,767		1975	213,631	
1950	150,697	50.7	1976	215,152	
1951	154,878		1977	216,880	
1952	157,553		1978	218,717	
1953	160,184		1979	220,584	
1954	163,026		1980	226,546	64.0
1955	165,931		1981	230,138	
1956	168,903		1982	232,520	
1957	171,984		1983	234,799	
1958	174,882		1984	237,001	
1959	177,830		1985	239,283	
1960	178,464	60.1	1986	241,596	
1961	183,672		1987	234,773	
1962	186,504		1988	245,051	
1963	189,197		1989	247,350	
1964	191,833		1990	250,122	
1965	194,237		1991	254,521	
1966	196,485		1992	245,908	
1967	198,629		1993	257,908	
1968	200,619		1994	261,875	
1969	202,599		1995	263,434	
1970	203,875	57.5[2]	1996	266,096	
1971	207,045				

[1]Figures after 1940 represent total population including armed forces abroad, except in official census years.

[2]Figure includes Alaska and Hawaii.

Presidential Elections
(1789–1832)

Year	Number of states	Candidates[1]	Parties	Popular vote	Electoral vote	Percentage of popular vote[2]
1789	11	**George Washington**	No party designations		69	
		John Adams			34	
		Minor Candidates			35	
1792	15	**George Washington**	No party designations		132	
		John Adams			77	
		George Clinton			50	
		Minor Candidates			5	
1796	16	**John Adams**	Federalist		71	
		Thomas Jefferson	Democratic-Republican		68	
		Thomas Pinckney	Federalist		59	
		Aaron Burr	Democratic-Republican		30	
		Minor Candidates			48	
1800	16	**Thomas Jefferson**	Democratic-Republican		73	
		Aaron Burr	Democratic-Republican		73	
		John Adams	Federalist		65	
		Charles C. Pinckney	Federalist		64	
		John Jay	Federalist		1	
1804	17	**Thomas Jefferson**	Democratic-Republican		162	
		Charles C. Pinckney	Federalist		14	
1808	17	**James Madison**	Democratic-Republican		122	
		Charles C. Pinckney	Federalist		47	
		George Clinton	Democratic-Republican		6	
1812	18	**James Madison**	Democratic-Republican		128	
		DeWitt Clinton	Federalist		89	
1816	19	**James Monroe**	Democratic-Republican		183	
		Rufus King	Federalist		34	
1820	24	**James Monroe**	Democratic-Republican		231	
		John Quincy Adams	Independent Republican		1	
1824	24	**John Quincy Adams**	Democratic-Republican	108,740	84	30.5
		Andrew Jackson	Democratic-Republican	153,544	99	43.1
		William H. Crawford	Democratic-Republican	46,618	41	13.1
		Henry Clay	Democratic-Republican	47,136	37	13.2
1828	24	**Andrew Jackson**	Democratic	647,286	178	56.0
		John Quincy Adams	National Republican	508,064	83	44.0
1832	24	**Andrew Jackson**	Democratic	687,502	219	55.0
		Henry Clay	National Republican	530,189	49	42.4
		William Wirt	Anti-Masonic	33,108	7	
		John Floyd	National Republican		11	2.6

[1]Before the passage of the Twelfth Amendment in 1804, the Electoral College voted for two presidential candidates; the runner-up became vice president. Figures are from *Historical Statistics of the United States, Colonial Times to 1957* (1961), pp. 682–83; and the U.S. Department of Justice.

[2]Candidates receiving less than 1 percent of the popular vote have been omitted. For that reason the percentage of popular vote given for any election year may not total 100 percent.

Presidential Elections (1836–1888)

Year	Number of states	Candidates	Parties	Popular vote	Electoral vote	Percentage of popular vote[1]
1836	26	**Martin Van Buren**	Democratic	765,483	170	50.9
		William H. Harrison	Whig		73	
		Hugh L. White	Whig		26	
		Daniel Webster	Whig	739,795	14	
		W. P. Mangum	Whig		11	
1840	26	**William H. Harrison**	Whig	1,274,624	234	53.1
		Martin Van Buren	Democratic	1,127,781	60	46.9
1844	26	**James K. Polk**	Democratic	1,338,464	170	49.6
		Henry Clay	Whig	1,300,097	105	48.1
		James G. Birney	Liberty	62,300		2.3
1848	30	**Zachary Taylor**	Whig	1,360,967	163	47.4
		Lewis Cass	Democratic	1,222,342	127	42.5
		Martin Van Buren	Free Soil	291,263		10.1
1852	31	**Franklin Pierce**	Democratic	1,601,117	254	50.9
		Winfield Scott	Whig	1,385,453	42	44.1
		John P. Hale	Free Soil	155,825		5.0
1856	31	**James Buchanan**	Democratic	1,832,955	174	45.3
		John C. Frémont	Republican	1,339,932	114	33.1
		Millard Fillmore	American	871,731	8	21.6
1860	33	**Abraham Lincoln**	Republican	1,865,593	180	39.8
		Stephen A. Douglas	Democratic	1,382,713	12	29.5
		John C. Breckinridge	Democratic	848,356	72	18.1
		John Bell	Constitutional Union	592,906	39	12.6
1864	36	**Abraham Lincoln**	Republican	2,206,938	212	55.0
		George B. McClellan	Democratic	1,803,787	21	45.0
1868	37	**Ulysses S. Grant**	Republican	3,013,421	214	52.7
		Horatio Seymour	Democratic	2,706,829	80	47.3
1872	37	**Ulysses S. Grant**	Republican	3,596,745	286	55.6
		Horace Greeley	Democratic	2,843,446	[2]	43.9
1876	38	**Rutherford B. Hayes**	Republican	4,036,572	185	48.0
		Samuel J. Tilden	Democratic	4,284,020	184	51.0
1880	38	**James A. Garfield**	Republican	4,453,295	214	48.5
		Winfield S. Hancock	Democratic	4,414,082	155	48.1
		James B. Weaver	Greenback-Labor	308,578		3.4
1884	38	**Grover Cleveland**	Democratic	4,879,507	219	48.5
		James G. Blaine	Republican	4,850,293	182	48.2
		Benjamin F. Butler	Greenback-Labor	175,370		1.8
		John P. St. John	Prohibition	150,369		1.5
1888	38	**Benjamin Harrison**	Republican	5,477,129	233	47.9
		Grover Cleveland	Democratic	5,537,857	168	48.6
		Clinton B. Fisk	Prohibition	249,506		2.2
		Anson J. Streeter	Union Labor	146,935		1.3

[1]Candidates receiving less than 1 percent of the popular vote have been omitted. For that reason the percentage of popular vote given for any election year may not total 100 percent.

[2]Greeley died shortly after the election; the electors supporting him then divided their votes among minor candidates.

Presidential Elections
(1896–1932)

Year	Number of states	Candidates	Parties	Popular vote	Electoral vote	Percentage of popular vote[1]
1892	44	**Grover Cleveland**	Democratic	5,555,426	277	46.1
		Benjamin Harrison	Republican	5,182,690	145	43.0
		James B. Weaver	People's	1,029,846	22	8.5
		John Bidwell	Prohibition	264,133		2.2
1896	45	**William McKinley**	Republican	7,102,246	271	51.1
		William J. Bryan	Democratic	6,492,559	176	47.7
1900	45	**William McKinley**	Republican	7,218,491	292	51.7
		William J. Bryan	Democratic; Populist	6,356,734	155	45.5
		John C. Wooley	Prohibition	208,914		1.5
1904	45	**Theodore Roosevelt**	Republican	7,628,461	336	57.4
		Alton B. Parker	Democratic	5,084,223	140	37.6
		Eugene V. Debs	Socialist	402,283		3.0
		Silas C. Swallow	Prohibition	258,536		1.9
1908	46	**William H. Taft**	Republican	7,675,320	321	51.6
		William J. Bryan	Democratic	6,412,294	162	43.1
		Eugene V. Debs	Socialist	420,793		2.8
		Eugene W. Chafin	Prohibition	253,840		1.7
1912	48	**Woodrow Wilson**	Democratic	6,296,547	435	41.9
		Theodore Roosevelt	Progressive	4,118,571	88	27.4
		William H. Taft	Republican	3,486,720	8	23.2
		Eugene V. Debs	Socialist	900,672		6.0
		Eugene W. Chafin	Prohibition	206,275		1.4
1916	48	**Woodrow Wilson**	Democratic	9,127,695	277	49.4
		Charles E. Hughes	Republican	8,533,507	254	46.2
		A. L. Benson	Socialist	585,113		3.2
		J. Frank Hanly	Prohibition	220,506		1.2
1920	48	**Warren G. Harding**	Republican	16,143,407	404	60.4
		James N. Cox	Democratic	9,130,328	127	34.2
		Eugene V. Debs	Socialist	919,799		3.4
		P. P. Christensen	Farmer-Labor	265,411		1.0
1924	48	**Calvin Coolidge**	Republican	15,718,211	382	54.0
		John W. Davis	Democratic	8,385,283	136	28.8
		Robert M. La Follette	Progressive	4,831,289	13	16.6
1928	48	**Herbert C. Hoover**	Republican	21,391,993	444	58.2
		Alfred E. Smith	Democratic	15,016,169	87	40.9
1932	48	**Franklin D. Roosevelt**	Democratic	22,809,638	472	57.4
		Herbert C. Hoover	Republican	15,758,901	59	39.7
		Norman Thomas	Socialist	881,951		2.2

[1]Candidates receiving less than 1 percent of the popular vote have been omitted. For that reason the percentage of popular vote given for any election year may not total 100 percent.

Presidential Elections
(1936 – 1992)

Year	Number of states	Candidates	Parties	Popular vote	Electoral vote	Percentage of popular vote[1]
1936	48	**Franklin D. Roosevelt**	Democratic	27,752,869	523	60.8
		Alfred M. Landon	Republican	16,674,665	8	36.5
		William Lemke	Union	882,479		1.9
1940	48	**Franklin D. Roosevelt**	Democratic	27,307,819	449	54.8
		Wendell L. Willkie	Republican	22,321,018	82	44.8
1944	48	**Franklin D. Roosevelt**	Democratic	25,606,585	432	53.5
		Thomas E. Dewey	Republican	22,014,745	99	46.0
1948	48	**Harry S Truman**	Democratic	24,105,812	303	49.5
		Thomas E. Dewey	Republican	21,970,065	189	45.1
		J. Strom Thurmond	States' Rights	1,169,063	39	2.4
		Henry A. Wallace	Progressive	1,157,172		2.4
1952	48	**Dwight D. Eisenhower**	Republican	33,936,234	442	55.1
		Adlai E. Stevenson	Democratic	27,314,992	89	44.4
1956	48	**Dwight D. Eisenhower**	Republican	35,590,472	457	57.6
		Adlai E. Stevenson	Democratic	26,022,752	73	42.1
1960	50	**John F. Kennedy**	Democratic	34,227,096	303	49.9
		Richard M. Nixon	Republican	34,108,546	219	49.6
1964	50	**Lyndon B. Johnson**	Democratic	43,126,506	486	61.1
		Barry M. Goldwater	Republican	27,176,799	52	38.5
1968	50	**Richard M. Nixon**	Republican	31,785,480	301	43.4
		Hubert H. Humphrey	Democratic	31,275,165	191	42.7
		George C. Wallace	American Independent	9,906,473	46	13.5
1972	50	**Richard M. Nixon**	Republican	47,169,911	520	60.7
		George S. McGovern	Democratic	29,170,383	17	37.5
1976	50	**Jimmy Carter**	Democratic	40,827,394	297	50.0
		Gerald R. Ford	Republican	39,145,977	240	47.9
1980	50	**Ronald W. Reagan**	Republican	43,899,248	489	50.8
		Jimmy Carter	Democratic	35,481,435	49	41.0
		John B. Anderson	Independent	5,719,437		6.6
		Ed Clark	Libertarian	920,859		1.0
1984	50	**Ronald W. Reagan**	Republican	54,281,858	525	59.2
		Walter F. Mondale	Democratic	37,457,215	13	40.8
1988	50	**George H. Bush**	Republican	47,917,341	426	54
		Michael Dukakis	Democratic	41,013,030	112	46
1992	50	**William Clinton**	Democratic	44,908,254	370	43.0
		George H. Bush	Republican	39,102,343	168	37.4
		Ross Perot	Independent	19,741,065		18.9

[1]Candidates receiving less than 1 percent of the popular vote have been omitted. For that reason the percentage of popular vote given for any election year may not total 100 percent.

Presidents, Vice Presidents, and Cabinet Members

President	Vice President	Secretary of State	Secretary of Treasury	Secretary of War	Secretary of Navy	Postmaster General	Attorney General
George Washington 1789–1797	John Adams 1789–1797	Thomas Jefferson 1789–1794 Edmund Randolph 1794–1795 Timothy Pickering 1795–1797	Alexander Hamilton 1789–1795 Oliver Wolcott 1795–1797	Henry Knox 1789–1795 Timothy Pickering 1795–1796 James McHenry 1796–1797		Samuel Osgood 1789–1791 Timothy Pickering 1791–1795 Joseph Habersham 1795–1797	Edmund Randolph 1789–1794 William Bradford 1794–1795 Charles Lee 1795–1797
John Adams 1797–1801	Thomas Jefferson 1797–1801	Timothy Pickering 1797–1800 John Marshall 1800–1801	Oliver Wolcott 1797–1801 Samuel Dexter 1801	James McHenry 1797–1800 Samuel Dexter 1800–1801	Benjamin Stoddert 1798–1801	Joseph Habersham 1797–1801	Charles Lee 1797–1801
Thomas Jefferson 1801–1809	Aaron Burr 1801–1805 George Clinton 1805–1809	James Madison 1801–1809	Samuel Dexter 1801 Albert Gallatin 1801–1809	Henry Dearborn 1801–1809	Benjamin Stoddert 1801 Robert Smith 1801–1809	Joseph Habersham 1801 Gideon Granger 1801–1809	Levi Lincoln 1801–1805 John Breckinridge 1805–1807 Caesar Rodney 1807–1809
James Madison 1809–1817	George Clinton 1809–1813 Elbridge Gerry 1813–1817	Robert Smith 1809–1811 James Monroe 1811–1817	Albert Gallatin 1809–1814 George Campbell 1814 Alexander Dallas 1814–1816 William Crawford 1816–1817	William Eustis 1809–1813 John Armstrong 1813–1814 James Monroe 1814–1815 William Crawford 1815–1817	Paul Hamilton 1809–1813 William Jones 1813–1814 Benjamin Crowninshield 1814–1817	Gideon Granger 1809–1814 Return Meigs 1814–1817	Caesar Rodney 1809–1811 William Pinkney 1811–1814 Richard Rush 1814–1817
James Monroe 1817–1825	Daniel D. Tompkins 1817–1825	John Quincy Adams 1817–1825	William Crawford 1817–1825	George Graham 1817 John C. Calhoun 1817–1825	Benjamin Crowninshield 1817–1818 Smith Thompson 1818–1823 Samuel Southard 1823–1825	Return Meigs 1817–1823 John McLean 1823–1825	Richard Rush 1817 William Wirt 1817–1825
John Quincy Adams 1825–1829	John C. Calhoun 1825–1829	Henry Clay 1825–1829	Richard Rush 1825–1829	James Barbour 1825–1828 Peter B. Porter 1828–1829	Samuel Southard 1825–1829	John McLean 1825–1829	William Wirt 1825–1829

(continued)

Presidents, Vice Presidents, and Cabinet Members (continued)

President	Vice President	Secretary of State	Secretary of Treasury	Secretary of War	Secretary of Navy	Postmaster General
Andrew Jackson 1829–1837	John C. Calhoun 1829–1833 Martin Van Buren 1833–1837	Martin Van Buren 1829–1831 Edward Livingston 1831–1833 Louis McLane 1833–1834 John Forsyth 1834–1837	Samuel Ingham 1829–1831 Louis McLane 1831–1833 William Duane 1833 Roger B. Taney 1833–1834 Levi Woodbury 1834–1837	John H. Eaton 1829–1831 Lewis Cass 1831–1837 Benjamin Butler 1837	John Branch 1829–1831 Levi Woodbury 1831–1837 Mahlon Dickerson 1834–1837	William Barry 1829–1831 Amos Kendall 1831–1834
Martin Van Buren 1837–1841	Richard M. Johnson 1837–1841	John Forsyth 1837–1841	Levi Woodbury 1837–1841	Joel R. Poinsett 1837–1841	Mahlon Dickerson 1837–1841 James K. Paulding 1838–1841	Amos Kendall 1837–1838 John M. Niles 1840–1841
William H. Harrison 1841	John Tyler 1841	Daniel Webster 1841	Thomas Ewing 1841	John Bell 1841	George E. Badger 1841	Francis Granger 1841
John Tyler 1841–1845		Daniel Webster 1841–1843 Hugh S. Legaré 1843 Abel P. Upshur 1843–1844 John C. Calhoun 1844–1845	Thomas Ewing 1841 Walter Forward 1841–1843 John C. Spencer 1843–1844 George M. Bibb 1844–1845	John Bell 1841 John C. Spencer 1841–1843 James M. Porter 1843–1844 William Wilkins 1844–1845	George E. Badger 1841 Abel P. Upshur 1841–1843 David Henshaw 1843–1844 Thomas Gilmer 1844	Francis Granger 1841 Charles A. Wickliffe 1841–1843 1843–1844 1844 John Y. Mason 1844–1845
James K. Polk 1845–1849	George M. Dallas 1845–1849	James Buchanan 1845–1849	Robert J. Walker 1845–1849	William L. Marcy 1845–1849	George Bancroft 1845–1849	Cave Johnson 1845–1846 John Y. Mason 1846–1849
Zachary Taylor 1849–1850	Millard Fillmore 1849–1850	John M. Clayton 1849–1850	William M. Meredith 1849–1850	George W. Crawford 1849–1850	William B. Preston 1849–1850	Jacob Collamer 1849–1850
Millard Fillmore 1850–1853		Daniel Webster 1850–1852 Edward Everett 1852–1853	Thomas Corwin 1850–1853	Charles M. Conrad 1850–1853	William A. Graham 1850–1853 John P. Kennedy 1852–1853	Nathan K. Hall 1850–1852 Sam D. Hubbard 1852–1853
Franklin Pierce 1853–1857	William R. King 1853–1857	William L. Marcy 1853–1857	James Guthrie 1853–1857	Jefferson Davis 1853–1857	James C. Dobbin 1853–1857	James Campbell 1853–1857

Attorney General	Secretary of Interior
John M. Berrien 1829–1831	
Roger B. Taney 1831–1833	
Benjamin Butler 1833–1837	
Benjamin Butler 1837–1838	
Felix Grundy 1838–1840	
Henry D. Gilpin 1840–1841	
John J. Crittenden 1841	
John J. Crittenden 1841	
Hugh S. Legaré 1841–1843	
John Nelson 1843–1845	
John Y. Mason 1845–1846	
Nathan Clifford 1846–1848	
Isaac Toucey 1848–1849	
Reverdy Johnson 1849–1850	Thomas Ewing 1849–1850
John J. Crittenden 1850–1853	Thomas McKennan 1850
	A. H. H. Stuart 1850–1853
Caleb Cushing 1853–1857	Robert McClelland 1853–1857

(continued)

Presidents, Vice Presidents, and Cabinet Members (continued)

President	Vice President	Secretary of State	Secretary of Treasury	Secretary of War	Secretary of Navy	Postmaster General
James Buchanan 1857–1861	John C. Breckinridge 1857–1861	Lewis Cass 1857–1860 Jeremiah S. Black 1860–1861	Howell Cobb 1857–1860 Philip F. Thomas 1860–1861 John A. Dix 1861	John B. Floyd 1857–1861 Joseph Holt 1861	Isaac Toucey 1857–1861	Aaron V. Brown 1857–1859 Joseph Holt 1859–1861 Horatio King 1861
Abraham Lincoln 1861–1865	Hannibal Hamlin 1861–1865 Andrew Johnson 1865	William H. Seward 1861–1865	Salmon P. Chase 1861–1864 William P. Fessenden 1864–1865 Hugh McCulloch 1865	Simon Cameron 1861–1862 Edwin M. Stanton 1862–1865	Gideon Welles 1861–1865	Horatio King 1861 Montgomery Blair 1861–1864 William Dennison 1864–1865
Andrew Johnson 1865–1869		William H. Seward 1865–1869	Hugh McCulloch 1865–1869	Edwin M. Stanton 1865–1867 Ulysses S. Grant 1867–1868 John M. Schofield 1868–1869	Gideon Welles 1865–1869	William Dennison 1865–1866 Alexander Randall 1866–1869 William M. Evarts 1868–1869
Ulysses S. Grant 1869–1877	Schuyler Colfax 1869–1873 Henry Wilson 1873–1877	Elihu B. Washburne 1869 Hamilton Fish 1869–1877	George S. Boutwell 1869–1873 William A. Richardson 1873–1874 Benjamin H. Bristow 1874–1876 Lot M. Morrill 1876–1877	John A. Rawlins 1869 William T. Sherman 1869 William W. Belknap 1869–1876 Alphonso Taft 1876 James D. Cameron 1876–1877	Adolph E. Borie 1869 George M. Robeson 1869–1877	John A. J. Creswell 1869–1874 James W. Marshall 1874 Marshall Jewell 1874–1876 James N. Tyner 1876–1877
Rutherford B. Hayes 1877–1881	William A. Wheeler 1877–1881	William M. Evarts 1877–1881	John Sherman 1877–1881	George W. McCrary 1877–1879 Alexander Ramsey 1879–1881	R. W. Thompson 1877–1881 Nathan Goff, Jr. 1881	David M. Key 1877–1880 Horace Maynard 1880–1881
James A. Garfield 1881	Chester A. Arthur 1881	James G. Blaine 1881	William Windom 1881 1881	Robert T. Lincoln 1881 1881	William H. Hunt 1881	Thomas L. James 1881
Chester A. Arthur 1881–1885		F. T. Frelinghuysen 1881–1885	Charles J. Folger 1881–1884 Walter Q. Gresham 1884 Hugh McCulloch 1884–1885	Robert T. Lincoln 1881–1885	William E. Chandler 1881–1885	Thomas L. James 1881 Timothy O. Howe 1881–1883 Walter Q. Gresham 1883–1884 Frank Hatton 1884–1885

Attorney General	Secretary of Interior
Jeremiah S. Black 1857–1860	Jacob Thompson 1857–1861
Edwin M. Stanton 1860–1861	
Edward Bates 1861–1864	Caleb B. Smith 1861–1863
James Speed 1864–1865	John P. Usher 1863–1865
James Speed 1865–1866	John P. Usher 1865
Henry Stanbery 1866–1868	James Harlan 1865–1866
O. H. Browning 1866–1869	
Ebenezer R. Hoar 1869–1870	Jacob D. Cox 1869–1870
Amos T. Akerman 1870–1871	Columbus Delano 1870–1875
G. H. Williams 1871–1875	Zachariah Chandler 1875–1877
Edwards Pierrepont 1875–1876	
Alphonso Taft 1876–1877	
Charles Devens 1877–1881	Carl Schurz 1877–1881
Wayne MacVeagh	S. J. Kirkwood
B. H. Brewster 1881–1885	Henry M. Teller 1881–1885

(continued)

Presidents, Vice Presidents, and Cabinet Members (continued)

President	Vice President	Secretary of State	Secretary of Treasury	Secretary of War	Secretary of Navy	Postmaster General
Grover Cleveland 1885–1889	T. A. Hendricks 1885	Thomas F. Bayard 1885–1889	Daniel Manning 1885–1887 Charles S. Fairchild 1887–1889	William C. Endicott 1885–1889	William C. Whitney 1885–1889	William F. Vilas 1885–1888 Don M. Dickinson 1888–1889
Benjamin Harrison 1889–1893	Levi P. Morton 1889–1893	James G. Blaine 1889–1892 John W. Foster 1892–1893	William Windom 1889–1891 Charles Foster 1892–1893	Redfield Procter 1889–1891 Stephen B. Elkins 1891–1893	Benjamin F. Tracy 1889–1893	John Wanamaker 1889–1893
Grover Cleveland 1893–1897	Adlai E. Stevenson 1893–1897	Walter Q. Gresham 1893–1895 Richard Olney 1895–1897	John G. Carlisle 1893–1897	Daniel S. Lamont 1893–1897	Hilary A. Herbert 1893–1897	Wilson S. Bissel 1893–1895 William L. Wilson
William McKinley 1897–1901	Garret A. Hobart 1897–1899 Theodore Roosevelt 1901	John Sherman 1897–1898 William R. Day 1898 John Hay 1898–1901	Lyman J. Gage 1897–1901	Russell A. Alger 1897–1899 Elihu Root 1899–1901	John D. Long 1897–1901	James A. Gary 1897–1898 Charles E. Smith 1898–1901
Theodore Roosevelt 1901–1909	Charles Fairbanks 1905–1909	John Hay 1901–1905 Elihu Root 1905–1909 Robert Bacon 1909	Lyman J. Gage 1901–1902 Leslie M. Shaw 1902–1907 George B. Cortelyou 1907–1909	Elihu Root 1901–1904 William H. Taft 1904–1908 Luke E. Wright 1908–1909	John D. Long 1901–1902 William H. Moody 1902–1904 Paul Morton 1904–1905 Charles J. Bonaparte 1905–1906 Victor H. Metcalf 1906–1908 T. H. Newberry 1908–1909	Charles E. Smith 1901–1902 Henry C. Payne 1902–1904 Robert J. Wynne 1904–1905 George B. Cortelyou 1905—1907 George von L. Meyer 1907–1909
William H. Taft 1909–1913	James S. Sherman 1909–1913	Philander C. Knox 1909–1913	Franklin MacVeagh 1909–1913	Jacob M. Dickinson 1909–1911 Henry L. Stimson 1911–1913	George von L. Meyer 1909–1913	Frank H. Hitchcock 1909–1913
Woodrow Wilson 1913–1921	Thomas R. Marshall 1913–1921	William J. Bryan 1913–1915 Robert Lansing 1915–1920 Bainbridge Colby 1920–1921	William G. McAdoo 1913–1918 Carter Glass 1918–1920 David F. Houston 1920–1921	Lindley M. Garrison 1913–1916 Newton D. Baker 1916–1921	Josephus Daniels 1913–1921	Albert S. Burleson 1913–1921

Attorney General	Secretary of Interior	Secretary of Agriculture	Secretary of Commerce and Labor	
A. H. Garland 1885–1889	L. Q. C. Lamar 1885–1888 William F. Vilas 1888–1889	Norman J. Colman 1889		
W. H. H. Miller 1889–1893	John W. Noble 1889–1893	Jeremiah M. Rusk 1889–1893		
Richard Olney 1893–1895 Judson Harmon 1895–1897	Hoke Smith 1893–1896 David R. Francis 1895–1897	J. Sterling Morton 1893–1897 1896–1897		
Joseph McKenna 1897–1898 John W. Griggs 1898–1901 Philander C. Knox 1901	Cornelius N. Bliss 1897–1898 E. A. Hitchcock 1898–1901	James Wilson 1897–1901		
Philander C. Knox 1901–1904 William H. Moody 1904–1906 Charles J. Bonaparte 1906–1909	E. A. Hitchcock 1901–1907 James R. Garfield 1907–1909	James Wilson 1901–1909	George B. Cortelyou 1903–1904 Victor H. Metcalf 1904–1906 Oscar S. Straus 1906–1909	
G. W. Wickersham 1909–1913	R. A. Ballinger 1909–1911 Walter L. Fisher 1911–1913	James Wilson 1909–1913	Charles Nagel 1909–1913	

			Secretary of Commerce	Secretary of Labor
J. C. McReynolds 1913–1914 T. W. Gregory 1914–1919 A. Mitchell Palmer 1919–1921	Franklin K. Lane 1913–1920 John B. Payne 1920–1921	David F. Houston 1913–1920 E. T. Meredith 1920–1921	W. C. Redfield 1913–1919 J. W. Alexander 1919–1921	William B. Wilson 1913–1921

(continued)

Presidents, Vice Presidents, and Cabinet Members (continued)

President	Vice President	Secretary of State	Secretary of Treasury	Secretary of War	Secretary of Navy	Postmaster General
Warren G. Harding 1921–1923	Calvin Coolidge 1921–1923	Charles E. Hughes 1921–1923	Andrew W. Mellon 1921–1923	John W. Weeks 1921–1923	Edwin Denby 1921–1923	Will H. Hays 1921–1922 Hubert Work 1922–1923 Harry S. New 1923
Calvin Coolidge 1923–1929	Charles G. Dawes 1925–1929	Charles E. Hughes 1923–1925 Frank B. Kellogg 1925–1929	Andrew W. Mellon 1923–1929	John W. Weeks 1923–1925 Dwight F. Davis 1925–1929	Edwin Denby 1923–1924 Curtis D. Wilbur 1924–1929	Harry S. New 1923–1929
Herbert C. Hoover 1929–1933	Charles Curtis 1929–1933	Henry L. Stimson 1929–1933	Andrew W. Mellon 1929–1932 Ogden L. Mills 1932–1933	James W. Good 1929 Patrick J. Hurley 1929–1933	Charles F. Adams 1929–1933	Walter F. Brown 1929–1933
Franklin Delano Roosevelt 1933–1945	John Nance Garner 1933–1941 Henry A. Wallace 1941–1945 Harry S Truman 1945	Cordell Hull 1933–1944 E. R. Stettinius, Jr. 1944–1945	William H. Woodin 1933–1934 Henry Morgenthau, Jr. 1934–1945	George H. Dern 1933–1936 Harry H. Woodring 1936–1940 Henry L. Stimson 1940–1945	Claude A. Swanson 1933–1940 Charles Edison 1940 Frank Knox 1940–1944 James V. Forrestal 1944–1945	James A. Farley 1933–1940 Frank C. Walker 1940–1945
Harry S Truman 1945–1953	Alben W. Barkley 1949–1953	James F. Byrnes 1945–1947 George C. Marshall 1947–1949 Dean G. Acheson 1949–1953	Fred M. Vinson 1945–1946 John W. Snyder 1946–1953	Robert P. Patterson 1945–1947 Kenneth C. Royall 1947	James V. Forrestal 1945–1947	R. E. Hannegan 1945–1947 Jesse M. Donaldson 1947–1953
				Secretary of Defense James V. Forrestal 1947–1949 Louis A. Johnson 1949–1950 George C. Marshall 1950–1951 Robert A. Lovett 1951–1953		
Dwight D. Eisenhower 1953–1961	Richard M. Nixon 1953–1961	John Foster Dulles 1953–1959 Christian A. Herter 1957–1961	George M. Humphrey 1953–1957 Robert B. Anderson 1957–1961	Charles E. Wilson 1953–1957 Neil H. McElroy 1957–1961 Thomas S. Gates 1959–1961		A. E. Summerfield 1953–1961

Attorney General	Secretary of Interior	Secretary of Agriculture	Secretary of Commerce	Secretary of Labor	Secretary of Health, Education and Welfare
H. M. Daugherty 1921–1923	Albert B. Fall 1921–1923 Hubert Work 1923	Henry C. Wallace 1921–1923	Herbert C. Hoover 1921–1923	James J. Davis 1921–1923	
H. M. Daugherty 1923–1924 Harlan F. Stone 1924–1925 John G. Sargent 1925–1929	Hubert Work 1923–1928 Roy O. West 1928–1929	Henry C. Wallace 1923–1924 Howard M. Gore 1924–1925 W. J. Jardine 1925–1929	Herbert C. Hoover 1923–1928 William F. Whiting 1928–1929	James J. Davis 1923–1929	
J. D. Mitchell 1929–1933	Ray L. Wilbur 1929–1933	Arthur M. Hyde 1929–1933 Roy D. Chapin 1932–1933	Robert P. Lamont 1929–1932 William N. Doak 1930–1933	James J. Davis 1929–1930	
H. S. Cummings 1933–1939 Frank Murphy 1939–1940 Robert Jackson 1940–1941 Francis Biddel 1941–1945	Harold L. Ickes 1933–1945	Henry A. Wallace 1933–1940 Claude R. Wickard 1940–1945	Daniel C. Roper 1933–1939 Harry L. Hopkins 1939–1940 Jesse Jones 1940–1945 Henry A. Wallace 1945	Frances Perkins 1933–1945	
Tom C. Clark 1945–1949 J. H. McGrath 1949–1952 James P. McGranery 1952–1953	Harol L. Ickes 1945–1946 Julius A. Krug 1946–1949 Oscar L. Chapman 1949–1953	C. P. Anderson 1945–1948 C. F. Brannan 1948–1953	W. A. Harriman 1946–1948 Charles Sawyer 1948–1953	L. B. Schwellenbach 1945–1948 Maurice J. Tobin 1948–1953	
H. Brownell, Jr. 1953–1957 William P. Rogers 1957–1961	Douglas McKay 1953–1956 Fred Seaton 1956–1961	Ezra T. Benson 1953–1961	Sinclair Weeks 1953–1958 Lewis L. Strauss 1958–1961	Martin P. Durkin 1953 James P. Mitchell 1953–1961	Oveta Culp Hobby 1953–1955 Marion B. Folsom 1955–1958 Arthur S. Flemming 1958–1961

(continued)

Presidents, Vice Presidents, and Cabinet Members (continued)

President	Vice President	Secretary of State	Secretary of Treasury	Secretary of Defense	Postmaster General[1]	Attorney General
John F. Kennedy 1961–1963	Lyndon B. Johnson 1961–1963	Dean Rusk 1961–1963	C. Douglas Dillon 1961–1963	Robert S. McNamara 1961–1963	J. Edward Day 1961–1963 John A. Gronouski 1961–1963	Robert F. Kennedy 1961–1963
Lyndon B. Johnson 1963–1969	Hubert H. Humphrey 1965–1969	Dean Rusk 1963–1969	C. Douglas Dillon 1963–1965 Henry H. Fowler 1965–1968 Joseph W. Barr 1968–1969	Robert S. McNamara 1963–1968 Clark M. Clifford 1968–1969	John A. Gronouski 1963–1965 Lawrence F. O'Brien 1965–1968 W. Marvin Watson 1968–1969	Robert F. Kennedy 1963–1965 N. deB. Katzenbach 1965–1967 Ramsey Clark 1967–1969
Richard M. Nixon 1969–1974	Spiro T. Agnew 1969–1973 Gerald R. Ford 1973–1974	William P. Rogers 1969–1973 Henry A. Kissinger 1973–1974	David M. Kennedy 1969–1970 John B. Connally 1970–1972 George P. Schultz 1972–1974 William E. Simon 1974	Melvin R. Laird 1969–1973 Elliot L. Richardson 1973 James R. Schlesinger 1973–1974	Winton M. Blount 1969–1971	John M. Mitchell 1969–1972 Richard G. Kleindienst 1972–1973 Elliot L. Richardson 1973 William B. Saxbe 1974
Gerald R. Ford 1974–1977	Nelson A. Rockefeller 1974–1977	Henry A. Kissinger 1974–1977	William E. Simon 1974–1977	James R. Schlesinger 1974–1975 Donald H. Rumsfeld 1975–1977		William B. Saxbe 1974–1975 Edward H. Levi 1975–1977

[1]On July 1, 1971, the Post Office became an independent agency. After that date, the Postmaster General was no longer a member of the Cabinet.

Secretary of Interior	Secretary of Agriculture	Secretary of Commerce	Secretary of Labor	Secretary of Health, Education and Welfare	Secretary of Housing and Urban Development	Secretary of Transportation
Stewart L. Udall 1961–1963	Orville L. Freeman 1961–1963	Luther H. Hodges 1961–1963	Arthur J. Goldberg 1961–1963 W. Willard Wirtz 1962–1963	A. H. Ribicoff 1961–1963 Anthony J. Celebrezze 1962–1963		
Stewart L. Udall 1963–1969	Orville L. Freeman 1963–1969	Luther H. Hodges 1963–1965 John T. Connor 1965–1967 Alexander B. Trowbridge 1967–1968 C. R. Smith 1968–1969	W. Willard Wirtz 1963–1969	Anthony J. Celebrezze 1963–1965 John W. Gardner 1965–1968 Wilbur J. Cohen 1968–1969	Robert C. Weaver 1966–1968 Robert C. Wood 1968–1969	Alan S. Boyd 1966–1969
Walter J. Hickel 1969–1971 Rogers C. B. Morton 1971–1974	Clifford M. Hardin 1969–1971 Earl L. Butz 1971–1974	Maurice H. Stans 1969–1972 Peter G. Peterson 1972 Frederick B. Dent 1972–1974	George P. Shultz 1969–1970 James D. Hodgson 1970–1973 Peter J. Brennan 1973–1974	Robert H. Finch 1969–1970 Elliot L. Richardson 1970–1973 Caspar W. Weinberger 1973–1974	George W. Romney 1969–1973 James T. Lynn 1973–1974	John A. Volpe 1969–1973 Claude S. Brinegar 1973–1974
Rogers C. B. Morton 1974–1975 Stanley K. Hathaway 1975 Thomas D. Kleppe 1975–1977	Earl L. Butz 1974–1976	Frederick B. Dent 1974–1975 Rogers C. B. Morton 1975 Elliot L. Richardson 1975–1977	Peter J. Brennan 1974–1975 John T. Dunlop 1975–1976 W. J. Usery 1976–1977	Caspar W. Weinberger 1974–1975 Forrest D. Matthews 1975–1977	James T. Lynn 1974–1975 Carla A. Hills 1975–1977	Claude S. Brinegar 1974–1975 William T. Coleman 1975–1977

Presidents, Vice Presidents, and Cabinet Members (continued)

President	Vice President	Secretary of State	Secretary of Treasury	Secretary of Defense	Attorney General	Secretary of Interior	Secretary of Agriculture
Jimmy Carter 1977–1981	Walter F. Mondale 1977–1981	Cyrus R. Vance 1977–1980 Edmund S. Muskie 1980–1981	W. Michael Blumenthal 1977–1979 G. William Miller 1979–1981	Harold Brown 1977–1981	Griffin Bell 1977–1979 Benjamin R. Civiletti 1979–1981	Cecil D. Andrus 1977–1981	Robert Bergland 1977–1981
Ronald W. Reagan 1981–1989	George H. Bush 1981–1989	Alexander M. Haig, Jr. 1981–1982 George P. Shultz 1982–1989	Donald T. Regan 1981–1985 James A. Baker 1985–1988 Nicholas F. Brady 1988–1989	Caspar W. Weinberger 1981–1987 Frank C. Carlucci 1987–1989	William French Smith 1981–1985 Edwin Meese 1985–1988 Richard Thornburgh 1988–1989	James G. Watt 1981–1983 William P. Clark 1983–1985 Donald P. Hodel 1985–1989	John R. Block 1981–1986 Richard E. Lyng 1986–1989
George H. Bush 1989–1992	J. Danforth Quayle 1989–1992	James A. Baker 1989–1992 Lawrence S. Eagleburger 1992	Nicholas F. Brady 1989–1992	Richard Cheney 1989–1992	Richard Thornburgh 1989–1990 William Barr 1990–1992	Manuel Lujan 1989–1992	Clayton Yeutter 1989–1990 Edward Madigan 1990–1992
William Clinton 1993–	Albert Gore 1993–	Warren M. Christopher 1993–	Lloyd Bentsen 1993–1994 Robert E. Rubin 1994–	Les Aspin 1993–1994 William J. Perry 1994–	Janet Reno 1993–	Bruce Babbitt 1993–	Mike Espy 1993–1994 Dan Glickman 1994–

Secretary of Commerce	Secretary of Labor	Secretary of Health, Education and Welfare	Secretary of Housing and Urban Development	Secretary of Transportation	Secretary of Energy	Secretary of Veterans' Affairs
Juanita Kreps 1977–1981	F. Ray Marshall 1977–1981	Joseph Califano 1977–1979 Patricia Roberts Harris 1979–1980	Patricia Roberts Harris 1977–1979 Moon Landrieu 1979–1981	Brock Adams 1977–1979 Neil E. Goldschmidt 1979–1981	James R. Schlesinger 1977–1979 Charles W. Duncan, Jr. 1979–1981	

		Secretary of Health and Human Services	Secretary of Education			
		Patricia Roberts Harris 1980–1981	Shirley M. Hufstedler 1980–1981			
Malcolm Baldridge 1981–1987 C. William Verity, Jr. 1987–1989	Raymond J. Donovan 1981–1985 William E. Brock 1985–1987 Ann Dore McLaughlin 1987–1989	Richard S. Schweiker 1981–1983 Margaret M. Heckler 1983–1985 Otis R. Bowen 1985–1989	Terrell H. Bell 1981–1985 William J. Bennett 1985–1988 Lauro Fred Cavazos 1988–1989	Samuel R. Pierce, Jr. 1981–1989	Drew Lewis 1981–1983 Elizabeth H. Dole 1983–1987 James H. Burnley 1987–1989	James B. Edwards 1981–1982 Donald P. Hodel 1982–1985 John S. Harrington 1985–1989	
Robert Mosbacher 1989–1991 Barbara Franklin 1991–1992	Elizabeth Dole 1989–19 Lynn Martin 1992	Louis Sullivan 1989–1992	Lamar Alexander 1990–1992	Jack Kemp 1989–1992	Samuel Skinner 1989–1990 Andrew Card 1990–1992	James Watkins 1989–1992	Edward J. Derwinski 1989–1992
Ronald H. Brown 1993–	Robert B. Reich 1993–	Donna E. Shalala 1993–	Richard W. Riley 1993–	Henry G. Cisneros 1993–	Frederico F. Peña 1993–	Hazel O'Leary 1993–	Jesse Brown 1993–

Justices of the U.S. Supreme Court

Chief Justices appear in bold type

	Term of Service	Years of Service	Appointed By
John Jay	1789 – 1795	5	Washington
John Rutledge	1789 – 1791	1	Washington
William Cushing	1789 – 1810	20	Washington
James Wilson	1789 – 1798	8	Washington
John Blair	1789 – 1796	6	Washington
Robert H. Harrison	1789 – 1790	—	Washington
James Iredell	1790 – 1799	9	Washington
Thomas Johnson	1791 – 1793	1	Washington
William Paterson	1793 – 1806	13	Washington
John Rutledge[1]	1795	—	Washington
Samuel Chase	1796 – 1811	15	Washington
Oliver Ellsworth	1796 – 1800	4	Washington
Bushrod Washington	1798 – 1829	31	J. Adams
Alfred Moore	1799 – 1804	4	J. Adams
John Marshall	1801 – 1835	34	J. Adams
William Johnson	1804 – 1834	30	Jefferson
H. Brockholst Livingston	1806 – 1823	16	Jefferson
Thomas Todd	1807 – 1826	18	Jefferson
Joseph Story	1811 – 1845	33	Madison
Gabriel Duval	1811 – 1835	24	Madison
Smith Thompson	1823 – 1843	20	Monroe
Robert Trimble	1826 – 1828	2	J. Q. Adams
John McLean	1829 – 1861	32	Jackson
Henry Baldwin	1830 – 1844	14	Jackson
James M. Wayne	1835 – 1867	32	Jackson
Roger B. Taney	1836 – 1864	28	Jackson
Philip P. Barbour	1836 – 1841	4	Jackson
John Catron	1837 – 1865	28	Van Buren
John McKinley	1837 – 1852	15	Van Buren
Peter V. Daniel	1841 – 1860	19	Van Buren
Samuel Nelson	1845 – 1872	27	Tyler
Levi Woodbury	1845 – 1851	5	Polk
Robert C. Grier	1846 – 1870	23	Polk
Benjamin R. Curtis	1851 – 1857	6	Fillmore
John A. Campbell	1853 – 1861	8	Pierce
Nathan Clifford	1858 – 1881	23	Buchanan
Noah H. Swayne	1862 – 1881	18	Lincoln
Samuel F. Miller	1862 – 1890	28	Lincoln
David Davis	1862 – 1877	14	Lincoln
Stephen J. Field	1863 – 1897	34	Lincoln
Salmon P. Chase	1864 – 1873	8	Lincoln
William Strong	1870 – 1880	10	Grant
Joseph P. Bradley	1870 – 1892	22	Grant
Ward Hunt	1873 – 1882	9	Grant

[1]Acting Chief Justice; Senate refused to confirm appointment.

Chief Justices appear in bold type

	Term of Service	Years of Service	Appointed By
Morrison R. Waite	1874 – 1888	14	Grant
John M. Harlan	1877 – 1911	34	Hayes
William B. Woods	1880 – 1887	7	Hayes
Stanley Matthews	1881 – 1889	7	Garfield
Horace Gray	1882 – 1902	20	Arthur
Samuel Blatchford	1882 – 1893	11	Arthur
Lucius Q. C. Lamar	1888 – 1893	5	Cleveland
Melville W. Fuller	1888 – 1910	21	Cleveland
David J. Brewer	1890 – 1910	20	B. Harrison
Henry B. Brown	1890 – 1906	16	B. Harrison
George Shiras, Jr.	1892 – 1903	10	B. Harrison
Howell E. Jackson	1893 – 1895	2	B. Harrison
Edward D. White	1894 – 1910	16	Cleveland
Rufus W. Peckham	1895 – 1909	14	Cleveland
Joseph McKenna	1898 – 1925	26	McKinley
Oliver W. Holmes, Jr.	1902 – 1932	30	T. Roosevelt
William R. Day	1903 – 1922	19	T. Roosevelt
William H. Moody	1906 – 1910	3	T. Roosevelt
Horace H. Lurton	1910 – 1914	4	Taft
Charles E. Hughes	1910 – 1916	5	Taft
Willis Van Devanter	1911 – 1937	26	Taft
Joseph R. Lamar	1911 – 1916	5	Taft
Edward D. White	1910 – 1921	11	Taft
Mahlon Pitney	1912 – 1922	10	Taft
James C. McReynolds	1914 – 1941	26	Wilson
Louis D. Brandeis	1916 – 1939	22	Wilson
John H. Clarke	1916 – 1922	6	Wilson
William H. Taft	1921 – 1930	8	Harding
George Sutherland	1922 – 1938	15	Harding
Pierce Butler	1922 – 1939	16	Harding
Edward T. Sanford	1923 – 1930	7	Harding
Harlan F. Stone	1925 – 1941	16	Coolidge
Charles E. Hughes	1930 – 1941	11	Hoover
Owen J. Roberts	1930 – 1945	15	Hoover
Benjamin N. Cardozo	1932 – 1938	6	Hoover
Hugo L. Black	1937 – 1971	34	F. Roosevelt
Stanley F. Reed	1938 – 1957	19	F. Roosevelt
Felix Frankfurter	1939 – 1962	23	F. Roosevelt
William O. Douglas	1939 – 1975	36	F. Roosevelt
Frank Murphy	1940 – 1949	9	F. Roosevelt
Harlan F. Stone	1941 – 1946	5	F. Roosevelt
James F. Byrnes	1941 – 1942	1	F. Roosevelt
Robert H. Jackson	1941 – 1954	13	F. Roosevelt
Wiley B. Rutledge	1943 – 1949	6	F. Roosevelt

(continued)

Justices of the U.S. Supreme Court *(continued)*

Chief Justices appear in bold type

	Term of Service	Years of Service	Appointed By
Harold H. Burton	1945 – 1958	13	Truman
Fred M. Vinson	1946 – 1953	7	Truman
Tom C. Clark	1949 – 1967	18	Truman
Sherman Minton	1949 – 1956	7	Truman
Earl Warren	1953 – 1969	16	Eisenhower
John Marshall Harlan	1955 – 1971	16	Eisenhower
William J. Brennan, Jr.	1956 – 1990	34	Eisenhower
Charles E. Whittaker	1957 – 1962	5	Eisenhower
Potter Stewart	1958 – 1981	23	Eisenhower
Byron R. White	1962 – 1993	31	Kennedy
Arthur J. Goldberg	1962 – 1965	3	Kennedy
Abe Fortas	1965 – 1969	4	Johnson
Thurgood Marshall	1967 – 1994	24	Johnson
Warren E. Burger	1969 – 1986	18	Nixon
Harry A. Blackmun	1970 – 1994	24	Nixon
Lewis F. Powell, Jr.	1971 – 1987	15	Nixon
William H. Rehnquist[2]	1971 –	—	Nixon
John P. Stevens III	1975 –	—	Ford
Sandra Day O'Connor	1981 –	—	Reagan
Antonin Scalia	1986 –	—	Reagan
Anthony M. Kennedy	1988 –	—	Reagan
David Souter	1990 –	—	Bush
Clarence Thomas	1991 –	—	Bush
Ruth Bader Ginsburg	1993 –	—	Clinton
Stephen G. Breyer	1994 –	—	Clinton

[2]Chief Justice from 1986 on (Reagan administration).

PHOTO CREDITS

front endsheet
NASA

Chapter 1
p. 2 Folding Screen: The Encounter of Cortes and Mocte-zuma. Collection Banco Nacional de Mexico, Mexico City. **p. 3** © John Maier, Jr/JB Pictures. **p. 7** By permission of The British Library **p. 8** National Museum, Copenhagen. Niels Elswing, photographer. **p. 11** Istanbul University. **p. 12** Jon Adkins © National Geographic Society. **p. 14 (top)** Werner Forman/Art Resource, NY. **p. 14 (bottom)** From Dapper (1686: 320-1). **p. 15** © British Museum. **p. 20** New York Public Library **p. 23 (top left)** Ancient Art and Architecture Collection. **p. 23 (top right)** © Robert Frerck/Tony Stone Worldwide. **p. 24** Boltin Picture Library. **p. 25** Boltin Picture Library. **p. 25** Werner Forman/Art Resource, NY. **p. 27 (top)** Boltin Picture Library. **p. 27 (bottom)** Peabody Museum, Harvard University. Photograph by Hillel Burger. **p. 28 (bottom)** Ancient Art and Architecture. **p. 31** Readers Digest, *Mysteries of the Ancient Americas,* art by Lloyd Kenneth Townsend. **p. 33 (top)** From *Prehistory of North America,* by Jesse D. Jennings (After Judd, 1964). Copyright 1968, McGraw-Hill. Used with permission of McGraw-Hill Book Company. **p. 33 (bottom)** © David Muench 1994. **p. 34** *Moctezuma's Mexico,* by David Carrasco and Eduardo Mato Moctezuma, (c) 1992 University Press of Colorado. Photographs by Salvador Guil'liem Arroyo. **p. 36 (top)** Fray Bernardinode Sahagun, *General History of the Things of New Spain.* **p. 36 (bottom)** New York Public Library. Astor, Lenox and Tilden Foundations, Rare Book Division. **p. 39** © Mexico, Cat. #140 — San Felipe de Jesus. SEDUE, Catedral Metoropolitana, Mexico City. **p. 41** © Jerry Jacka.

Chapter 2
p. 45 Theodore DeBry. **p. 50** New York Public Library. Astor, Lenox and Tilden Foundations, Rare Book Division. **p. 53** Ancient Art and Architecture. **p. 44** © Wendell Metzen/Bruce Coleman Inc. **p. 55** Historical Society of Pennsylvania. **p. 62 (left)** William C. Clements Library, University of Michigan, Ann Arbor. **p. 62 (right)** The Bettmann Archive. **p. 74** New York Public Library. Astor, Lenox and Tilden Foundations, Rare Book Division. **p. 69** North Wind Picture Archives.

Chapter 3
p. 82 E. T. Archives. **p. 85** Copyright British Museum. **p. 94** Engraving by A. Allard. **p. 114** *Dixton Harvesters,* c. 1725 by English Schools, (18th century) Cheltenham Art Gallery and Museums, Gloucestershire/Bridgeman Art Library, London. **p. 113** North Wind Picture Archives. **p. 96** The Bettmann Archives. **p. 101** Patrick M. Malone, *The Skulking Way of War,* Madison Books © 1991. **p. 105** Courtesy of Historic St. Mary's City Commission. **p. 106** *The Virginia Journals of Benjamin Henry Latrobe* (2 vols., New Haven, 1977) I, 181 – 82, 247, plate 21. **p. 107** North Wind Picture Archives. **p. 110** North Wind Picture Archives.

Chapter 4
p. 116 The New-England Courant. **p. 118** Archives Nationales. **p. 122** The Metropolitan Museum of Art, Purchase, The Sylmaris Collection, Gift of George Coe Graves, by ex-change, 1940. (40.127) Photograph by Richard Cheek. **p. 123** Courtesy of The Harvard University Portrait Collection. Bequest of Dr. John Collins Warren, 1856. **p. 126** Courtesy Massachusetts Historical Society. **p. 127** *The Illustrated London News.* **p. 129** after John Barbot, from *Churchill's Voyages.* **p. 130** Colonial Williamsburg Foundation. **p. 137** Courtesy of the University of Georgia Library, Athens, GA. **p. 141** The Bettmann Archive. **p. 120** The Bettmann Archive.

Chapter 5
p. 144 Courtesy Massachusetts Historical Society. **p. 146** Colonial Williamsburg Foundation. **p. 148** National Portrait Gallery, Smithsonian Institution/Art Resource, NY. **p. 150** New Jersey State Museum Collection. **p. 151** Peabody Museum, Harvard University. Photograph by Hillel Burger. **p. 154** Photo by Owen Fitzgerald. **p. 155** Collection of The New York Historical Society. **p. 157** North Wind Picture Archives. **p. 160** Courtesy Derby Museums and Art Gallery. **p. 167** William Hogarth.

Chapter 6
p. 174 Chicago Historical Society. **p. 176** New York Public Library. **p. 179** Courtesy of the John Carter Brown Library at Brown University. **p. 180** Courtesy of the John Carter Brown Library at Brown University. **p. 183** The Granger Collection, New York. **p. 185** The Granger Collection, New York. **p. 186** The Historical Society of Pennsylvania. **p. 194** Library, University of Massachusetts, Amherst. **p. 195** Courtesy of the John Carter Brown Library at Brown University. **p. 196** The Bettmann Archive. **p. 200** The Granger Collection, New York. **p. 201** Yale University Art Gallery. Trumbull Collection. **p. 203** Courtesy of the John Carter Brown Library at Brown University.

Chapter 7
p. 243 Bettman Archive. **p. 210** Gift of the Owners of the Old Boston Museum. Courtesy, Museum of Fine Arts, Boston. **p. 211** Lewis Walpole Library, Yale University. **p. 212** North Wind Picture Archives. **p. 213** Tate Gallery, London/Art Resource, NY. **p. 215** © Alon Reininger/Woodfin Camp. **p. 210** Courtesy, American Antiquarian Society. **p. 221** National Archives of Canada/C-002001. **p. 222** New York State Historical Association, Coopers-town. **p. 231** © J. Gilbert Harrington. **p. 234** Henry Hope Reed III. **p. 239** Courtesy, American Antiquarian Society. **p. 218** National Portrait Gallery, Smithsonian Institution/Art Resource, NY.

Photo Essay
p. 248 (top) Harvard Law Art Collection. Oil on canvas, 56³⁄₁₆ × 77¾. Gift of Dr. George Stevens Jones, Mar. 31, 1879. **p. 248 (middle)** Colonial Williamsburg Foundation. **p. 248 (bottom)** Henry H. and Zoe Oliver Sherman Fund. Courtesy, Museum of Fine Arts, Boston. **p. 249 (top)** The Saint Louis Art Museum, Purchase. **p. 249 (bottom)** Clements Library, University of Michigan, Ann Arbor. **p. 250 (top)** Copley, John Singleton, *Watson and the Shark,* Fedinand Lammot Belin Fund, © 1994 National Gallery of Art, Washington, 1778, oil on canvas. **p. 250 (bottom)** Gift of Maxim Karolik for the M. and M. Karolik collection of American Paintings, 1815 – 1865. Courtesy, Museum of Fine Arts, Boston. **p. 251 (top)** Nicolino Calyo The Richard K. Haight Family, ca. 1848. Museum of the City of New York. Gift of Elizabeth Cushing Iselin. **p. 251 (middle)** Berry-Hill Galleries, New York. **p. 251 (bottom)** Missouri Historical Society.

Chapter 8

p. 252 Courtesy, American Antiquarian Society. **p. 255** Overmantel from the Gardiner Gilman House, Exeter, New Hampshire. Artist Unknown. Oil on panel, c. 1800. 1972.47. Acquisition in Memory of Harry D. M. Grier, Trustee, Amon Carter Museum, 1968–1972. Amon Carter Museum, Fort Worth, Texas. **p. 256** Old Dartmouth Historical Society/ New Bedford Whaling Museum. **p. 259** The Granger Collection, New York. **p. 260** The Granger Collection, New York. **p. 261** The Crockett Almanac, 1840. **p. 263** National Museum of American History, The Smithsonian Institution. **p. 265** Collection of the Maryland Historical Society, Baltimore. **p. 266** The Granger Collection, New York. **p. 268** Collection of The New York Historical Society. **p. 269** Collection of The New York Historical Society. **p. 271** John Lewis Krimmel, American, 1786–1821 *Village Tavern,* 1813–14, oil on canvas, 16⅞ × 22½ in. (42.8 × 56.9 cm) The Toledo Museum of Art, Toledo, Ohio; Purchased with funds from the Florence Scott Libbey Bequest in Memory of her Father, Maurice A. Scott. **p. 276** Old Dartmouth Historical Society/New Bedford Whaling Museum. **p. 279** Historical Commission, Morther Bethel AME Church, Philadelphia, PA.

Chapter 9

p. 282 Engraving by Amos Doolittle. **p. 283** National Portrait Gallery, Smithsonian Institution/Art Resource, NY. **p. 296** The Granger Collection, New York. **p. 293** Courtesy of the Lilly Library, Indiana University, Bloomington, Indiana. **p. 295** The Bettmann Archive. **p. 298** National Portrait Gallery, Smithsonian Institution/Art Resource, NY. **p. 299** Architect of the Capitol. **p. 300** *A View of New Orleans Taken from the Plantation of Marigny, November, 1803* by Boqueto de Woiserie, Chicago Historical Society. **p. 303** North Wind Picture Archives. **p. 304** North Wind Picture Archives. **p. 306** Courtesy of the Royal Ontario Museum, Toronto, Canada. **p. 308** The Field Museum, Neg. #A93581c. **p. 309** Allyn Cox, 1974, Architect of the Capitol.

Chapter 10

p. 312 Collection of The New York Historical Society. **p. 314** The Library Company of Philadelphia. **p. 317** The Bettmann Archive. **p. 319** The Bettmann Archive. **p. 322** Collection of the Albany Institute of History and Art. **p. 324** Old Sturbridge Village, Photo by: Thomas Neill, #25.K74if.1994.2.1. **p. 323** *New England Farmstead,* 1849. by Samuel Gerry 1813–1891. Old Sturbridge Village, photo by Henry E. Peach. #20.1.106-B23486. **p. 326** Chicago Historical Society. **p. 327** The Bettmann Archive. **p. 329** The Granger Collection, New York. **p. 331** Museum of American Textile History. **p. 332** The Library Company of Philadelphia. **p. 335** The Historic New Orleans Collection, Accension #1975.931 & 2. **p. 338** The Historic New Orleans Collection, Accension # 1977.13734311.

Chapter 11

p. 340 Abby Aldrich Rockerfeller Folk Art Center, Williamsbury, VA. **p. 341** Oberlin College Archives, Oberlin, Ohio. **p. 343** The Granger Collection. **p. 346** Frederic Edwin Church *Niagara, 1857.* oil on canvas, 42½ × 90½ in. (107.95 × 229.87 cm) In the Collection of the Corcoran Gallery of Art, Museum Purchase, Gallery Fund. **p. 349** Courtesy American Antiquarian Society. **p. 351** The Bettmann Archive. **p. 353** The Granger Collection, New York. **p. 354** The Granger Collection, New York. **p. 355 (left & right)** Courtesy, American Antiquarian Society. **p. 357** Hunter Museum of American Art, Chattanooga, Tennessee, Gift of Mr. and Mrs. Thomas B. Whiteside. **p. 360** The Historic New Orleans Collection, accession # 1960.46. **p. 361** Reproduced from the collection of the Library of Congress, B811 152.

Chapter 12

p. 366 National Portrait Gallery, Smithsonian Institution/ Art Resource, NY. **p. 367** National Museum of American Art, Washington DC/Art Resource, NY. **p. 373** Collection of The New York Historical Society. **p. 375** The Hermitage: Home of President Andrew Jackson, Nashville, TN. **p. 377** White House Collection. **p. 379** Woolaroc Museum. B. **p. 383** The Historical Society of Pennsylvania. **p. 386** Collection of The New York Historical Society. **p. 388** North Wind Picture Archives. **p. 389** Collection of The New York Historical Society. **p. 391** Mattatuck Museum, Waterbury, CT. **p. 371** Architect of the Capitol.

Chapter 13

p. 394 Courtesy American Antiquarian Society. **p. 395** The Saint Louis Art Museum, Purchase. **p. 399** Public domain. **p. 401** North Wind Picture Archives. **p. 403** The Granger Collection, New York. **p. 409** The Bettmann Archive. **p. 407** © 1995 All Rights Reserved. The Rhode Island Historical Society. **p. 406** Currier and Ives, 1846. **p. 405** North Wind Picture Archives. **p. 411** The Metropolitan Museum of Art, Rogers Fund, 1942. (42.95.18). **p. 413** from J. C. Nott and George R. Gliddon, *Types of Mankind; or, Ethnological Researches* (1845). **p. 415** Reproduced from the Collections of The Library of Congress, #LC-USz62-40758. **p. 418** Courtesy of the American Philatelist Society.

Chapter 14

p. 421 Reproduced from the Collections of the Library of Congress, #LC-USZC4-668. **p. 422** The Bettmann Archive. **p. 425** North Wind Picture Archives. **p. 426** *Joseph Mustering the Nauvoo Legion,* C.C.A. Christensen. © Courtesy Museum of Art, Brigham Young University. All Rights reserved. Photographer: David W. Hawkinson. **p. 428** Reproduced from the Collections of the Library of Congress. **p. 430** Yale Collection of Western Americana, Beinecke Rare Book and Manuscript Library. **p. 434** Missouri Historical Society. MHS art acc# 1939.3.1. **p. 437** California State Library. **p. 440** Courtesy of The Trustees of Boston Public Library. **p. 442** North Wind Picture Archives. **p. 443** © Martha Swope Associates/Carol Rosegg.

Chapter 15

p. 448 Prints Division, The New York Public Library. Astor, Lenox and Tilden Foundations. **p. 449** Reproduced from the Collections of the Library of Congress. **p. 452 (left)** The Bettmann Archive. **p. 452 (right)** The Bettmann Archive. **p. 453** Reproduced from the Collections of the Library of Congress. **p. 455** Maryland Historical Society, Baltimore. **p. 459** The Bettmann Archive. **p. 465** The Bettmann Archive. **p. 466** Reproduced from the Collections of the Library of Congress. **p. 467** The Bettmann Archive. **p. 471 (top)** The Bettmann Archive. **p. 471 (bottom)** The Bettmann Archive. **p. 473** The Bettmann

Archive. **p. 475** North Wind Picture Archives. **p. 477** Courtesy of the Illinois State Historical Library. **p. 479** Kansas State Historical Society.

Chapter 16

p. 483 Reproduced from the Collections of the Library of Congress. **p. 485** From the Ralph E. Becker Collection of Political Americana, The Smithsonian Institution. **p. 489** Courtesy of The South Carolina Historical Society. **p. 492** The Bettmann Archive. **p. 498** Collection of The New York Historical Society. **p. 499** Cook Collection, Valentine Museum, Richmond, Virginia. **p. 500** Photo by Timothy O'Sullivan, Chicago Historical Society, ICHi-08091. **p. 503** The West Point Museum Collections, United States Military Academy, West Point, New York. **p. 505 (top)** National Archives. **p. 505 (bottom)** The Bettmann Archive. **p. 506** Reproduced for the Collections of the Library of Congress. **p. 509** Thomas C. Lindsay, Hornet's Nest, Cincinnati Historical Society.

Chapter 17

p. 520 Eastman Johnson 1924–1906 *A Ride for Liberty—The Fugitive Slave* circa 1862. The Brooklyn Museum 40.59.A, Gift of Miss Gwendolyn O. L. Conkling. **p. 529** New York Historical Society. **p. 530** Architect of the Capitol. **p. 527** Virginia State Library and Archives. **p. 531 (left)** Reproduced from the Collections of the Library of Congress. **p. 531 (right)** Courtesy of the Illinois State Historical Library. **p. 533** National Park Service, Harpers Ferry Center. **p. 538** Chicago Historical Society. **p. 542** Brown Brothers. **p. 545** Reproduced from the Collections of the Library of Congress. **p. 548** Reproduced from the Collections of the Library of Congress. **p. 551 (top)** The Bettmann Archive. **p. 551 (bottom)** Reproduced from the Collections of the Library of Congress. **p. 554** Winslow Homer, *A Visit from the Old Mistress,* 1876, oil on canvas, 18″ × 24⅛″. National Museum of American Art, Smithsonian Institution. Gift of William T. Evans. **p. 556** Courtesy Chicago Historical Society.

Chapter 18

p. 559 Reproduced from the Collections of the Library of Congress. **p. 560** The Bettmann Archive. **p. 561** Reproduced from the Collections of the Library of Congress. **p. 564** Public domain. **p. 565** North Wind Picture Archives. **p. 567** The Bettmann Archive. **p. 568** The Bettmann Archive. **p. 574** The Granger Collection, New York. **p. 576** The Bettmann Archive. **p. 578** The Bettmann Archive. **p. 581** The Granger Collection, New York.

Photo Essay

p. 586 (top) North Wind Picture Archives. **p. 586 (bottom)** Reproduced from the Collections of the Library of Congress. **p. 587 (top)** Reproduced from the Collections of the Library of Congress. **p. 587 (middle)** Printed by permission of the Norman Rockwell Family Trust. Copyright © 1964 the Norman Rockwell Family Trust. **p. 587 (bottom)** Reproduced from the Collections of the Library of Congress. **p. 588 (top)** AP/Wide World Photos. **p. 588 (middle)** UPI/Bettmann. **p. 588 (bottom)** UPI/Bettmann. **p. 589 (top)** UPI/ Bettmann. **p. 589 (middle)** UPI/ Bettmann. **p. 589 (bottom)** © Michael Newman/ Photo Edit.

Chapter 19

p. 592 Wyoming State Museum. **p. 594** Smithsonian Institution, Bureau of American Ethnology. **p. 596** Sophia Smith Collection, Smith College. **p. 600** Nebraska State Historical Society. **p. 602** Erwin E. Smith Collection of the Library of Congress on deposit at the Amon Carter Museum, Fort Worth. **p. 605** The Bettmann Archive. **p. 609** North Wind Picture Archives. **p. 610** The Granger Collection, New York. **p. 613** North Wind Picture Archives. **p. 614** The Bettmann Archive. **p. 615** Kansas State Historical Society. **p. 617** The Bettmann Archive. **p. 622** The Granger Collection, New York.

Chapter 20

p. 626 Keystone-Mast Collection, California Museum of Photography, University of California, Riverside. **p. 628 (left)** The Bettmann Archive. **p. 628 (right)** The Bettmann Archive. **p. 631** The Bettmann Archive. **p. 633** Brown Brothers. **p. 637** The Bettmann Archive. **p. 641 (top)** The Bettmann Archive. **p. 641 (bottom)** Reproduced from the Collections of the Library of Congress. **p. 642** Victor Joseph Gatto *Triangle Fire,* March 25, 1911. Oil on canvas, 19 × 28 inches. Museum of the City of New York, 54.75, Gift of Mrs. Henry L. Moses. **p. 645** Brown Brothers. **p. 646** The Bettmann Archive. **p. 649** The Bettmann Archive. **p. 653** The Bettmann Archive. **p. 654** Brown Brothers.

Chapter 21

p. 660 Culver Pictures. **p. 662** Courtesy of The Frank Lloyd Wright Archives, Taliesin. **p. 664** The Bettmann Archive. **p. 667** Brown Brothers. **p. 673** The Bettmann Archive. **p. 675** The Bettmann Archive **p. 677** The Bettmann Archive. **p. 679** Reproduced from the Collections of the Library of Congress. **p. 685** North Wind Picture Archives.

Chapter 22

p. 694 William H. Walker. *Life,* 1899. **p. 697** Smithsonian Institution Photo No. 85-14366. **p. 699** The Granger Collection, New York. **p. 700** Chicago Historical Society. **p. 702** Grant Hamilton. *Judge,* 1898. **p. 703 (top)** Official U.S. Navy Photograph. **p. 703 (bottom)** National Archives 111-RB-2839. **p. 705** UPI/Bettmann. **p. 709** Reproduced from the Collections of the Library of Congress. **p. 711** The Granger Collection, New York. **p. 714** Panama Canal Company. **p. 716** North Wind Picture Archives. **p. 719** Brown Brothers.

Chapter 23

p. 722 WWI Pictorial Collection/Hoover Institution Archives. **p. 725** Imperial War Museum, London. **p. 726** *The New York Times.* **p. 727** Records of the Women's International League for Peace and Freedom, U.S. Section, Swarthmore College Peace Collection. **p. 733** © The Phillips Collection, Washington, D.C. photo Edward Owen./Francine Seders Gallery Ltd., Seattle, Washington. **p. 734** Brown Brothers. **p. 738** The Bettmann Archive. **p. 739** National Archives #45-WP-115. **p. 741** Imperial War Museum, London. **p. 743** National Archives, #165-WW-164B-1. **p. 744** New York Times, 1919. **p. 745** UPI/Bettmann Newsphotos. **p. 750** Historical Society of Western Pennsylvania. **p. 752** © 1995 Estate of Ben

Shahn/VAGA, New York. Collection of Whitney Museum of American Art. **p. 753** Schomburg Center for Research in Black Culture, New York Public Library, NY.

Photo Essay
p. 758 (top right) Bernhard Gillam, *Judge.* **p. 758 (bottom right)** Reproduced from the Collections of the Library of Congress. **p. 758 (center)** Department of Archives and Manuscript, The Catholic University of America, Washington, DC. **p. 758 (bottom left)** Reproduced from the Collections of the Library of Congress. **p. 759 (top)** UPI/Bettmann. **p. 759 (center)** I.T.U. NEWS, Volume 4#10/April 1940. **p. 759 (bottom)** UPI/Bettmann. **p. 760 (top left)** *For Full Employment After the War, Register-Vote,* 1944. Ben Shahn (Poster for the CIO Political Action Committee.) Offset lithograph, 30″ × 39⅝″. Collection of the Museum of Modern Art, New York. Gift of the CIO Political Action Committee. Estate of Ben Shahn/VAGA, New York. **p. 760 (top)** UPI/Bettmann. **p. 760 (middle)** © FPG International 1995. **p. 760 (bottom)** Archives of Labor and Urban Affairs, Wayne State University. **p. 761 (top left)** AP/Wide World Photos. **p. 761 (top right)** UPI/Bettmann. **p. 761 (bottom)** Reuters/Bettmann.

Chapter 24
p. 762 The Michael Barson Collection/Past Perfect. **p. 763** UPI/Bettmann. **p. 768** The Bettmann Archive. **p. 769** Brown Brothers. **p. 770** Brown Brothers. **p. 771** UPI/Bettmann. **p. 777** The Bettmann Archive. **p. 778** The Bettmann Archive. **p. 779** The Bettmann Archive. **p. 782** Brown Brothers. **p. 785** UPI/Bettmann. **p. 789** The Bettmann Archive. **p. 791** Chicano Studies Research Library, University of California, Los Angeles.

Chapter 25
p. 796 Ben Shahn mural at Jersey Homesteads, Hights-town, New Jersey, 1936. WPA. **p. 797** The Bettmann Archive. **p. 801** The Bettmann Archive. **p. 803** AP/Wide World Photos. **p. 804** Brown Brothers. **p. 808 (top)** Russell Lee, FSA #11693-ML. **p. 808 (bottom)** Kansas State Historical Society. **p. 809** UPI/Bettmann. **p. 810** UPI/ Bettmann. **p. 812** UPI/Bettmann. **p. 813** Ben Shahn mural at Jersey Homesteads, Hightstown, New Jersey, 1936. WPA. **p. 816** © UPI/Bettmann. **p. 819** The Granger Collection. **p. 823 (left)** Brown Brothers. **p. 823 (right)** Springer/Bettmann Film Archive. **p. 824 (right)** Michael Barson Collection/ Past Perfect. **p. 824 (left)** The Rhode Island Historical Society. **p.825** UPI/Bettmann. **p. 826** UPI/Bettmann. **p. 827** Courtesy of SouthWest Organizing Project. **p. 829** Navajo Nation Museum, Window Rock, AZ.

Chapter 26
p. 836 Hoover Institute Archives, Stanford University. U5-6031. **p. 841** UPI/Bettmann. **p. 851** National Archives #127-N-69559-A. **p. 853** UPI/Bettmann. **p. 855 (top)** UPI/Bettmann. **p. 855 (bottom)** UPI/Bettmann. **p. 856** UPI/Bettmann. **p. 859** AP/Wide World Photos. **p. 860** Reproduced from the Collection of the Library of Congress. **p. 862** National Archives Photo # 44-PA-189. **p. 863** AP/Wide World Photos. **p. 874** AP/Wide World Photos.

Chapter 27
p. 877 Michael Barson Collection/Past Perfect. **p. 880** AP/Wide World Photos. **p. 882** AP/Wide World Photos.

p. 884 The Bettmann Archive. **p. 887** UPI/Bettmann. **p. 889** UPI/Bettmann. **p. 890** UPI/Bettmann. **p. 892** UPI/Bettmann. **p. 893** © Elliott Erwitt/Magnum Photos Inc. **p. 894** UPI/Bettmann. **p. 881** Reuters/Bettmann Newsphotos. **p. 903** © Al Hirschfeld. Drawing reproduced by special arrangement with Hirschfeld's exclusive representative, The Margo Feiden Galleries, New York.

Photo Essay
p. 910 (top) © Jose Carrillo/PhotoEdit. **p. 910 (bottom right)** Photofest. **p. 911 (top)** Shomburg Center for Research in Black Culture, New York Public Library, NY. **p. 911 (bottom)** Lewis Hine. **p. 912 (top)** © Jean-Claude Coutausse/Contact Press Images 1990. **p. 912 (middle)** © Paul Conklin/PhotoEdit. **p. 912 (bottom)** UPI/Bettmann. **p. 913 (top)** © 1995 Annette Palaez/Contact Press Images. **p. 913 (middle)** © Gary A. Conner/PhotoEdit. **p. 913 (bottom right)** Express-News Collection, The Institute of Texan Cultures. **p. 913 (bottom left)** © Mark Richards/PhotoEdit.

Chapter 28
p. 916 UPI/Bettmann. **p. 918** UPI/Bettmann. **p. 923** © Joe Munroe/Photo Researchers. **p. 927** The Bettmann Archive. **p. 929** UPI/Bettmann. **p. 931** UPI/Bettmann. **p. 934** UPI/Bettmann. **p. 937** UPI/Bettmann. **p. 938** Standard Oil Company, photo by Rosskam. **p. 940** Hy Peskin/Life Magazine (c) Time Warner Inc. **p. 941** UPI/Bettmann. **p. 944** AP/Wide World Photos. **p. 945** © Danny Lyon/Magnum Photos, Inc.

Chapter 29
p. 948 AP/Wide World Photos. **p. 949** George Tames/ NYT Pictures. **p. 957** UPI/Bettmann. **p. 958** © Fred Ward/Black Star. **p. 961** UPI/Bettmann. **p. 962** UPI/ Bettmann. **p. 963** UPI/Bettmann. **p. 969** UPI/Bettmann. **p. 970** UPI/Bettmann. **p. 971** UPI/Bettmann. **p. 972** UPI/Bettmann.

Chapter 30
p. 960 Courtesy Pagliaro/Kuhlman Advertising. Photograph by Marc Simon. **p. 993** © Elena Rooraid/PhotoEdit. **p. 1005** (c) Felicia Martinez/PhotoEdit. **p. 982** © Paul Conklin/PhotoEdit. **p. 1008** AP/Wide World Photos. **p. 986** Maps courtesy of California Highway Department. **p. 987** Reuters/Bettmann. **p. 989** UPI/Bettmann. **p. 995** UPI/Bettmann. **p. 997** Reuters/Bettmann. **p. 999** AP/ Wide World. **p. 1000** AP/Wide World. **p. 1003** AP/Wide World Photos. **p. 1006** © Jeff Topping/Gamma Liaison. **p. 1007** © Robert Brenner/PhotoEdit. **p. 1009** Reuters/ Bettmann.

Chapter 31
p. 1014 © 1994 Markstein, *Milwaukee Journal.* **p. 1015** AP/Wide World Photos. **p. 1018** UPI/Bettmann. **p. 1021** © 1980 Time Inc., Reprinted by permission. **p. 1022** Courtesy: Jimmy Carter Library. **p. 1026** © Jeff Lowenthal/Woodfin Camp. **p. 1029** AP/Wide World Photos. **p. 1032** © John Ficara 1986/Woodfin Camp. **p. 1036** © John Ficara 1988/Woodfin Camp. **p. 1038** © Sylvie Kreiss/Gamma Liaison. **p. 1044** © 1992, Newsweek, Inc. All rights reserved. Reprinted by permission. **p. 1046** AP/Wide World Photos. **p. 1042** AP/Wide World.

Index